Building the Irish Courthouse and Prison

Building the Irish Courthouse and Prison

A political history, 1750–1850

RICHARD J. BUTLER

CORK UNIVERSITY PRESS

First published in 2020 by
Cork University Press
Boole Library
University College Cork
Cork
T12 ND89
Ireland

Library of Congress Control Number: 2019955492
Distribution in the USA: Longleaf Services, Chapel Hill, NC, USA

ISBN 978-178205-369-9

Book design and typesetting, Anú Design, Tara
Printed in Malta by Gutenberg Press Ltd.

Contents

List of Illustrations vii

Acknowledgements xxiii

Introduction xxvii

Part I: The Assize Courthouse

1. The Spoils of War: Upheaval and rebellion at home and abroad, 1786–1817 3

2. Judging the Neighbours: Grand juries, rivalry, and the peak years of courthouse building, 1817–31 47

3. Against the Tide: Grand-jury reform, economic opportunism, and the last of Ireland's new assize courthouses, 1831–55 91

Part II: The County Gaol

4. Architecture before Reform: Grand juries and the problem of implementing social reform, 1770–1810 135

5. Reform Revisited: Central government, philanthropic societies, and disruptions to grand-jury patronage, 1810–21 187

6. The New Regime: 235
James Palmer, Benjamin Woodward, and grand-jury responses to the renewed call for penal reform, 1821–38

7. A Separate Agenda: 287
Conformity, consolidation, the Famine, and its aftermath, 1838–55

Reflections 337
Identities, Actors, Towns

Notes 349

Appendix A: Buildings Histories 381

Appendix B: Criminal Indictments by County, 1786–1855 527

Appendix C: Grand-Jury Presentments for Courthouse- and Prison-Building Work, 1822–55 539

Appendix D: Central-Government Loans for the Building of Courthouses and Prisons, 1801–55 555

Bibliography 567

List of Illustrations

Title page Nenagh courthouse. Photograph by author, 2017.

Part I: The Assize Courthouse

Chapter 1: The Spoils of War, 1786–1817

1.1 Lifford courthouse, Co. Donegal. Photograph by author, 2014.
1.2 Lifford courthouse, Co. Donegal. Photograph by author, 2014.
1.3 Lifford gaol, Co. Donegal, *c.* 1900. Donegal County Archives.
1.4 Ordnance Survey town map for Lifford, Co. Donegal, *c.* 1850. Trinity College Dublin.
1.5 Ordnance Survey six-inch maps for Lifford and Strabane, Co. Tyrone, 1833–4. Trinity College Dublin.
1.6 Map showing new assize courthouses built in Ireland between 1746 and 1798.
1.7 Tholsel, Kilkenny, *c.* 1900. National Library of Ireland (Eblana Photographic Collection).
1.8 Tholsel, Drogheda, *c.* 1900. National Library of Ireland (Lawrence Collection).
1.9 Carrickfergus courthouse, Co. Antrim. Photograph by author, 2014.
1.10 Longford courthouse, *c.* 1900. National Library of Ireland (Lawrence Collection).
1.11 Roscommon courthouse, unexecuted scheme, elevation. Oliver Crawford, *c.* 1762. National Library of Ireland, MS 10,770(1)–(3).
1.12 Roscommon courthouse, as built, elevation. George Ensor, *c.* 1762. National Library of Ireland, MS 10,770(1)–(3).
1.13 Roscommon courthouse, unexecuted scheme, ground- and first-floor plans. Oliver Crawford, *c.* 1762. National Library of Ireland, MS 10,770(1)–(3).
1.14 Roscommon courthouse, as built, ground-floor plan. George Ensor, *c.* 1762. National Library of Ireland, MS 10,770(1)–(3).
1.15 Roscommon gaol, *c.* 1900. National Library of Ireland (Lawrence Collection).
1.16 Roscommon courthouse. Photograph by author, 2012.
1.17 The Four Courts, Dublin, *c.* 1900. National Library of Ireland (Lawrence Collection).
1.18 The Custom House, Dublin. Photograph by author, 2011.
1.19 Curraghmore, Co. Waterford, *c.* 1900. National Library of Ireland (Lawrence Collection).
1.20 Nottingham Shire Hall, elevation. James Gandon. From *Vitruvius Britannicus* (1771). Reproduced courtesy of Cambridge University Library.
1.21 Plan of Nottingham Shire Hall. James Gandon. From *Vitruvius Britannicus* (1771). Reproduced courtesy of Cambridge University Library.

1.22 Unexecuted plan for Nottingham Shire Hall (later adapted for Waterford city and county courthouse), by Gandon. From *Vitruvius Britannicus* (1771). Reproduced courtesy of Cambridge University Library.
1.23 Vestibule of Waterford city and county courthouse. Irish Architectural Archive.
1.24 Elevation drawing of Waterford city and county courthouse, reconstructed by Conor Rochford, from Rolf Loeber, et al., *Art and Architecture of Ireland: Volume IV: Architecture 1600–2000*, p. 17.
1.25 Ballybricken Green, *c.* 1900. National Library of Ireland (Poole Collection).
1.26 Dublin Green Street courthouse. Photograph by author, 2014.
1.27 Map showing new assize courthouses built in Ireland between 1798 and 1817.
1.28 Clonmel courthouse, *c.* 1900. National Library of Ireland (Lawrence Collection).
1.29 Courtroom, Clonmel courthouse, *c.* 1985. From Rowan, *Morrison*, p. 71.
1.30 Athy courthouse and markethouse, *c.* 1900. National Library of Ireland (Lawrence Collection).
1.31 Limerick county courthouse. Photograph by author, 2013.
1.32 Maryborough (Portlaoise) courthouse. Photograph by author, 2014.
1.33 Philipstown (Daingean) courthouse, *c.* 1900. Historical Picture Archive (Ireland).
1.34 Galway county courthouse and gaol, *c.* 1820. From Hardiman, *Galway*, p. 311.
1.35 Lion, unicorn, and British crown, formerly part of Galway county courthouse. Photograph by author, 2017.
1.36 Ordnance Survey six-inch map for Wexford, Co. Wexford, surveyed January 1840. Trinity College Dublin.
1.37 Wexford courthouse and quays, *c.* 1900. National Library of Ireland (Lawrence Collection).
1.38 Ordnance Survey six-inch map for Armagh, Co. Armagh, surveyed June 1835. Trinity College Dublin.
1.39 James Black, 'City of Armagh', 1810 (detail). Armagh County Museum (accession no. ARMCM. 156.1958).
1.40 Armagh courthouse, first scheme, unexecuted. Francis Johnston, 1805. Irish Architectural Archive, RIAI Murray Collection, Acc. 92/46.4.
1.41 Armagh courthouse, first scheme, unexecuted. Francis Johnston, 1805. Irish Architectural Archive, RIAI Murray Collection, Acc. 92/46.6.
1.42 Armagh courthouse, fourth and final scheme. Francis Johnston, 1808. Irish Architectural Archive, RIAI Murray Collection, Acc. 92/46.18.
1.43 Derry courthouse, plan, by John Bowden, 1813. Public Record Office of Northern Ireland (PRONI), LA/5/8/JA/2.
1.44 Ordnance Survey six-inch map for Derry, Co. Londonderry, surveyed June 1830. Trinity College Dublin.
1.45 Derry courthouse, *c.* 1900. National Library of Ireland (Lawrence Collection).
1.46 Derry courthouse, detail showing coat of arms and date. Photograph by author, 2014.
1.47 Dundalk courthouse, plan, *c.* 1813. Reproduced courtesy of the Old Dundalk

Society and Louth County Council.
1.48 Transverse section of Dundalk courthouse, *c.* 1813. Reproduced courtesy of the Old Dundalk Society and Louth County Council.
1.49 Dundalk courthouse. Photograph by author, 2012.
1.50 Dundalk courthouse and market square, *c.* 1900. National Library of Ireland (Lawrence Collection).

Chapter 2: Judging the Neighbours, 1817–31

2.1 Map showing new assize courthouses built in Ireland between 1817 and 1832.
2.2 Graph showing the number of assize courthouses that were under construction (new or large alterations only) in Ireland between 1770 and 1870.
2.3 Map showing loans made to grand juries for new assize courthouses, 1817–47.
2.4 Kilmainham courthouse, front elevation, unexecuted. Henry, Mullins & McMahon, 1817. Irish Architectural Archive, Guinness Collection, Acc.96/68.5.1.3.
2.5 Kilmainham courthouse, side elevation, unexecuted. Henry, Mullins & McMahon, 1817. Irish Architectural Archive, Guinness Collection, Acc.96/68.5.1.4.
2.6 Kilmainham courthouse, ground-floor plan, unexecuted. Henry, Mullins & McMahon, 1817. Irish Architectural Archive, Guinness Collection, Acc.96/68.5.1.1.
2.7 Kilmainham courthouse, ground-floor plan, as built. William Farrell, *c.* 1817. Harvard University, Houghton Library, William Farrell album, MS Typ 788 (copies in Irish Architectural Archive).
2.8 Kilmainham courthouse, front elevation, as built. William Farrell, *c.* 1817. Harvard University, Houghton Library, William Farrell album, MS Typ 788 (copies in Irish Architectural Archive).
2.9 Kilmainham courthouse, *c.* 1900. National Library of Ireland (Mason Collection).
2.10 Design for a courthouse, front elevation. William Farrell, *c.* 1817. Harvard University, Houghton Library, William Farrell album, MS Typ 788 (copies in Irish Architectural Archive).
2.11 Design for a courthouse, ground-floor plan. William Farrell, *c.* 1817. Harvard University, Houghton Library, William Farrell album, MS Typ 788 (copies in Irish Architectural Archive).
2.12 Cavan courthouse. Photograph by author, 2014.
2.13 Carrick-on-Shannon courthouse. Photograph by author, 2012.
2.14 Castlebar courthouse, *c.* 1900. National Library of Ireland (Lawrence Collection).
2.15 Ordnance Survey six-inch map for Roscommon, Co. Roscommon, surveyed January 1837. Trinity College Dublin.
2.16 Galway town tholsel, by James Hardiman, *c.* 1820. Galway County Council Archives, GS01–2.
2.17 Ordnance Survey six-inch map for Galway, Co. Galway, surveyed January 1838. Trinity College Dublin.

2.18 Galway town courthouse, *c.* 1900. National Library of Ireland (Lawrence Collection).
2.19 Monaghan courthouse. Photograph by author, 2014.
2.20 Monaghan markethouse. Photograph by author, 2014.
2.21 Map showing the seven assize circuits in early nineteenth-century Ireland.
2.22 Bagenalstown courthouse. Photograph by author, 2013.
2.23 Tralee courthouse, ground-floor plan. From Rowan, *Morrison*, p. 169.
2.24 Sir Patrick Dun's Hospital, Dublin, ground-floor plan of unfinished building, 1809. From Rowan, *Morrison*, p. 80.
2.25 Gloucester Shire Hall. Photograph by author, 2019.
2.26 Tralee courthouse, *c.* 1900. National Library of Ireland (Lawrence Collection).
2.27 Carlow courthouse. Alamy Stock Photograph, 2007.
2.28 Carlow Roman Catholic cathedral. Photograph by author, 2012.
2.29 Map of Carlow town, detail. From Matthew McDermott, 'The Morrisons', *RIAI Yearbook* (1977), pp. 81–91, at p. 85.
2.30 Oak Park, Carlow, entrance gateway and carriage turn. Photograph by author, 2014.
2.31 Carlow courthouse, ground-floor plan, early unexecuted design, *c.* 1827. Carlow County Library.
2.32 Carlow courthouse, interior of a courtroom, *c.* 1985. Irish Architectural Archive.
2.33 Carlow courthouse, front-elevation drawing. From McDermott, 'The Morrisons', p. 88.
2.34 Carlow courthouse. Photograph by author, 2012.
2.35 Carlow courthouse, showing metal palisade railings. National Library of Ireland (Lawrence Collection).
2.36 Cork courthouse, *c.* 1900. Cork City Libraries (Hodges and Pike Collection).
2.37 Ordnance Survey twenty-five-inch map for Great George's Street, Cork, surveyed June 1899. Trinity College Dublin.

Chapter 3: Against the Tide, 1831–55

3.1 Map showing new assize courthouses built in Ireland between 1832 and 1855.
3.2 The Four Courts, Dublin, Nisi Prius (civil bills) courtroom extension. Photograph by author, 2014.
3.3 Ordnance Survey six-inch map for Tullamore, King's County (Co. Offaly), surveyed January 1838. Trinity College Dublin.
3.4 Tullamore courthouse and gaol. Photograph by author, 2013.
3.5 Tullamore courthouse, front elevation, unexecuted. William Murray, December 1832. Irish Architectural Archive, RIAI Murray Collection, Acc.92/46.1191.
3.6 Tullamore courthouse, ground-floor plan, unexecuted. William Murray, December 1832. Irish Architectural Archive, RIAI Murray Collection, Acc.92/46.1188.
3.7 Tullamore courthouse, section drawing, unexecuted. William Murray, December 1832. Irish Architectural Archive, RIAI Murray Collection, Acc.92/46.1192.

3.8 Tullamore courthouse, side elevation, unexecuted. William Murray, December 1832. Irish Architectural Archive, RIAI Murray Collection, Acc.92/46.1185.
3.9 Tullamore courthouse, ground floor plan. John B. Keane, 1833. Irish Architectural Archive, Lismore Castle Collection, Acc.97/107.3.
3.10 Tullamore courthouse, *c.* 1900. Courtesy of Mr Michael Byrne, Tullamore.
3.11 Tullamore courthouse, front-elevation drawing, unexecuted. John B. Keane, *c.* 1833. Courtesy of Mr Michael Byrne, Tullamore.
3.12 Plan view of the proposed 'Beaujolois' square, Tullamore, *c.* 1835. Irish Architectural Archive.
3.13 Perspective view of the proposed 'Beaujolois' square, Tullamore, *c.* 1835. Irish Architectural Archive.
3.14 Thurles courthouse, Co. Tipperary. Photograph by author, 2013.
3.15 Ordnance Survey twenty-five-inch map for Nenagh, Co. Tipperary, surveyed June 1902. Trinity College Dublin.
3.16 Nenagh courthouse and Peter Street, *c.* 1900. Tipperary Studies, Tipperary County Council Library Service (Thurles, Co. Tipperary).
3.17 Nenagh courthouse, plan. Ordnance Survey five-feet town map, 1879. Trinity College Dublin.
3.18 Nenagh courthouse. Photograph by author, 2017.
3.19 Waterford county and city courthouse. Photograph by author, 2013.
3.20 Waterford county and city courthouse, plan. From Craig, *Architecture of Ireland*, p. 275. Reproduced courtesy of Mr Michael Craig.
3.21 Ordnance Survey twenty-five-inch map for Waterford, Co. Waterford, surveyed June 1905. Trinity College Dublin.
3.22 Ordnance Survey six-inch map for Limerick, Co. Limerick, surveyed January 1840. Trinity College Dublin.
3.23 Limerick city courthouse, front elevation of proposed entrance, unexecuted. Henry Hill, June 1834. The Allen family, Shanagarry, Co. Cork (copies in Irish Architectural Archive).
3.24 Limerick city courthouse, river elevation, unexecuted. Henry Hill, June 1834. The Allen family, Shanagarry, Co. Cork (copies in Irish Architectural Archive).
3.25 Design for a public building, front elevation, unexecuted. Henry Hill, probably 1830s. The Allen family, Shanagarry, Co. Cork (copies in Irish Architectural Archive).
3.26 Limerick city courthouse, ground-floor plan, unexecuted. Henry Hill, June 1834. The Allen family, Shanagarry, Co. Cork (copies in Irish Architectural Archive).
3.27 Limerick city courthouse, first-floor plan, unexecuted. Henry Hill, June 1834. The Allen family, Shanagarry, Co. Cork (copies in Irish Architectural Archive).
3.28 Limerick city courthouse and city gaol, *c.* 1950. Sean Curtin and the 'Limerick: A stroll down memory lane' project.
3.29 William Turner de Londe, 'The Market Square, Ennis' (1805), oil on canvas, 75.6 cm x 106 cm. The Merrion Hotel, Dublin.

3.30 Ennis courthouse, *c.* 1900. National Library of Ireland (Lawrence Collection).
3.31 Ordnance Survey twenty-five-inch map for Ennis, Co. Clare, surveyed June 1894. Trinity College Dublin.
3.32 The O'Connell Monument, Ennis. Photograph by author, 2017.
3.33 Ordnance Survey six-inch map of Belfast, showing Crumlin Road gaol, surveyed 1858. Ordnance Survey of Northern Ireland (licence no. 14/09/2852).
3.34 Sketch of Belfast by J.H. Connop, 1863, from his *Belfast, Part II*, plate 4. Reproduced courtesy of the Linen Hall Library, Belfast.
3.35 Antrim assize courthouse, Belfast, front-elevation drawing, unexecuted. Charles Lanyon, 1847. Public Record Office of Northern Ireland (PRONI), LA/1/8/JA/119/2.
3.36 Antrim courthouse, Crumlin Road, Belfast. Photograph by author, 2012.
3.37 Sligo courthouse. Photograph by author, 2012.

Part II: The County Gaol

Chapter 4: Architecture before Reform, 1770–1810

4.1 A map showing new county gaols, or large additions made to existing gaols, in Ireland between 1780 and 1810.
4.2 Samuel McSkimmin, Carrickfergus old courthouse and gaol, *c.* 1811, from McSkimmin, *Carrickfergus*, p. 151.
4.3 Nathaniel Grogan, 'North Gate Bridge', Cork, *c.* 1796. Crawford Art Gallery, Cork (cat. no. 873-P).
4.4 John Fitzgerald (after Nathaniel Grogan), 'The South Gate and Bridge, Cork, 1797', *c.* 1850. Crawford Art Gallery, Cork (cat. no. 568-P).
4.5 'A Plan for a County Gaol', by John Howard, from *The State of the Prisons* (1777).
4.6 Newgate Gaol, London. George Dance the younger, 1769. From Howard, *The State of the Prisons* (1777).
4.7 Ordnance Survey five-feet town map for Green Street, Dublin, surveyed 1847. Trinity College Dublin.
4.8 Newgate gaol, Dublin, ground-floor plan. Drawn by Francis Johnston, December 1808, from *Report from the Commissioners Appointed to Inquire into … the State Prisons and Other Gaols in Ireland*, H.C. 1809 (265), vii.
4.9 Newgate gaol, Dublin, principal (east) elevation. From Robert Pool and John Cash, *Views of the Most Remarkable Public Buildings … in the City of Dublin* (Dublin, 1780).
4.10 Newgate gaol, Dublin, principal (east) elevation, from a photograph taken before the gaol's demolition in 1893. Historical Picture Archive (Ireland).
4.11 The River Boyne, Trim, Co. Meath. Photograph by author, 2014.

4.12 Graph showing the number of gaols that were under construction in Ireland between 1770 and 1870.
4.13 Sir Jeremiah Fitzpatrick (*c.* 1740–1810). Mezzotint by William Barnard, after Samuel Drummond, 1801. National Portrait Gallery, London (NPG reference D36947).
4.14 William Ashford, 'A View of Dublin from Chapelizod', 1795–8 (detail). National Gallery of Ireland.
4.15 Kilmainham gaol, ground-floor plan. Drawn by Francis Johnston, December 1808, from *Report from the Commissioners Appointed to Inquire into … the State Prisons and Other Gaols in Ireland*, H.C. 1809 (265) vii.
4.16 Kilmainham courthouse and gaol, from the north-east, *c.* 1835. From *Dublin Penny Journal*, vol. 4, no. 184, 9 January 1836, p. 221.
4.17 Kilmainham gaol, tympanum over the main door. Photograph by author, 2014.
4.18 Downpatrick gaol. Photograph by author, 2014.
4.19 Fisherton Anger (Wiltshire) county gaol, near Salisbury. Thomas Hopper, 1820. Wiltshire and Swindon Archives (WSA), A1/509/3.
4.20 Roscommon gaol. Photograph by author, 2012.
4.21 Maryborough (Portlaoise) gaol, ground-floor plan. Richard Harman, *c.* 1789. Tullynally Castle, Co. Westmeath (copies in Irish Architectural Archive).
4.22 Maryborough (Portlaoise) gaol, elevation of entrance gateway. Richard Harman, *c.* 1789. Tullynally Castle, Co. Westmeath (copies in Irish Architectural Archive).
4.23 Maryborough (Portlaoise) gaol. Photograph by author, 2014.
4.24 Ordnance Survey six-inch map for Maryborough (Portlaoise), Queen's County (Co. Laois), surveyed January 1839. Trinity College Dublin.
4.25 Richard Castle's gateway at Leinster House, Dublin. From Henry F. Berry, *A History of the Royal Dublin Society* (London, 1915).
4.26 Mullingar gaol, site plan, *c.* 1788. Irish Architectural Archive, Guinness Collection, Acc. 96/68.5/5/1–2.
4.27 Mullingar gaol, *c.* 1900. Westmeath County Library, Westmeath Photographic Collection, M/1 (41).
4.28 Ordnance Survey six-inch map for Naas, Co. Kildare, surveyed January 1837. Trinity College Dublin.
4.29 John Longford, 'A Map of [the Old Gaol] at Naas … and Adjoining Concerns', 1824. National Library of Ireland, MS 21 F 35, no. 44.
4.30 Naas old gaol, *c.* 1900. From Stan Hickey and Liam Kenny (eds), *Nás na Ríogh from Poorhouse Road to the Fairy Flax: An illustrated history of Naas* (1990). Naas Local History Group.
4.31 Liverpool borough gaol. Detail from *Ackermann's Panoramic View of Liverpool*, 1847.
4.32 Design for a penitentiary panopticon. Jeremy Bentham, Samuel Bentham, and Willey Reveley, 1791. From John Bowring (ed.), *The Works of Jeremy Bentham*, 11

vols (Edinburgh: William Tait, 1838–43), vol. 4, p. 35.

4.33 Design for a panopticon house of industry. Samuel Bentham and Samuel Bunce, 1797. From John Bowring (ed.), *The Works of Jeremy Bentham*, 11 vols (Edinburgh: William Tait, 1838–43), vol. 4, p. 35.

4.34 Ordnance Survey six-inch map for Derry, Co. Londonderry, surveyed June 1830. Trinity College Dublin.

4.35 Derry gaol, *c.* 1900. National Library of Ireland (Lawrence Collection).

4.36 Lifford gaol, Co. Donegal, *c.* 1900. Donegal County Archives.

4.37 Sligo gaol, elevation and partial plan, unexecuted. Bernard Mullins, *c.* 1801. Irish Architectural Archive, ICEI Collection, Acc. 2005/095.

4.38 Ordnance Survey six-inch map for Kilkenny, Co. Kilkenny, surveyed January 1839. Trinity College Dublin.

4.39 Northleach bridewell, Gloucestershire, ground-floor plan. William Blackburn, 1785. Gloucestershire Archives, D2593/2/38

4.40 Blakes' Castle, Galway. Photograph by author, 2017.

4.41 Ordnance Survey six-inch map for Galway, Co. Galway, surveyed January 1838. Trinity College Dublin.

4.42 General plan of Galway county and town gaols. Samuel Roberts, May 1866. Galway County Council Archives, GS11-02-6.

4.43 Millbank penitentiary, London, ground-floor plan. William Williams and Thomas Hardwick, 1812–18. From George Holford, *An Account of the General Penitentiary at Millbank* (London: Rivington, 1828), p. 66.

4.44 Galway county gaol, *c.* 1940. From Curtin, *Women of Galway Jail*, p. 40.

4.45 Galway town gaol, *c.* 1940. From Curtin, *Women of Galway Jail*, p. 90.

4.46 A detail from William Beauford, 'A Map of the City and Suburbs of Cork', 1801. Cork City Libraries.

4.47 Ordnance Survey six-inch map for Cork, Co. Cork, surveyed January 1841. Trinity College Dublin.

4.48 Cork county gaol, *c.* 1950. Image in public domain (photographer unknown).

Chapter 5: Reform Revisited, 1810–21

5.1 Design for a general penitentiary, ground-floor plan, unexecuted. Francis Johnston, August 1810. Irish Architectural Archive, RIAI Murray Collection, Acc. 92/46.424.

5.2 Design for a general penitentiary, elevation, unexecuted. Francis Johnston, August 1810. Irish Architectural Archive, RIAI Murray Collection, Acc. 92/46.426.

5.3 A map showing new county gaols, or large additions made to existing gaols, in Ireland between 1810 and 1821.

5.4 Graph showing the number of gaols that were under construction in Ireland between 1770 and 1870.

5.5 A map showing central-government loans to Irish grand juries for gaol building between 1810 and 1821.
5.6 Richmond penitentiary, Grangegorman, Dublin. Photograph by author, 2014.
5.7 Richmond general penitentiary, ground-floor plan, unexecuted. Francis Johnston, January 1811. Irish Architectural Archive, RIAI Murray Collection, Acc. 92/46.428.
5.8 Richmond general penitentiary, elevation, unexecuted. Francis Johnston, January 1811. Irish Architectural Archive, RIAI Murray Collection, Acc. 92/46.430.
5.9 Richmond general penitentiary, elevation. Francis Johnston, 1812. Irish Architectural Archive, RIAI Murray Collection, Acc. 92/46.431.
5.10 Richmond bridewell, South Circular Road, Dublin, woodcut perspective drawing, 1866. From *Harper's Weekly* (New York), vol. 10, no. 484, 7 April 1866.
5.11 Richmond bridewell, 'Cease To Do Evil' doorway, elevation and section, *c.* 1813. Irish Architectural Archive, RIAI Murray Collection, Acc.92/46.331.
5.12 Richmond bridewell, 'Cease To Do Evil' doorway. Photograph by author, 2013.
5.13 Ordnance Survey five-feet town map for Richmond bridewell, South Circular Road, Dublin, 1847. Trinity College Dublin.
5.14 Ordnance Survey six-inch map for Grangegorman district, Dublin, surveyed January 1837. Trinity College Dublin.
5.15 The former Richmond Lunatic Asylum, Grangegorman district, Dublin. Photograph by author, 2013.
5.16 George Byfield and John Orridge, Bury St Edmunds county gaol, 1802–3. From John Orridge, *Description of the Gaol at Bury Saint Edmunds* (London, 1819). Reproduced courtesy of the Royal Institute of British Architects Collection.
5.17 Richard Ingleman, Devizes house of correction, 1808–17. Wiltshire and Swindon Archives (WSA), A1/509/4.
5.18 Ordnance Survey six-inch map for Cavan, Co. Cavan, surveyed January 1835. Trinity College Dublin.
5.19 Farnham Street and Cavan gaol, May 1922. From A.F. McEntee, *Memories of … Journalism in Cavan* (1991), pp. 56–7. Reproduced courtesy of *The Anglo-Celt*.
5.20 Cavan gaol, ground-floor plan. Richard Elsam, 1810. From Peter Nicholson, *A Theoretical and Practical Treatise on the Five Orders of Architecture* (London, 1853), plate 64. Reproduced courtesy of the Royal Institute of British Architects Collection.
5.21 Cavan gaol, elevation. Henry, Mullins & McMahon, n.d. (after an original by Richard Elsam, 1810). Irish Architectural Archive, ICEI Collection, Acc.2005/095.
5.22 Cavan gaol, entrance gateway, 1938. Irish Architectural Archive.
5.23 Tralee gaol, ground-floor plan, 1870. From *Forty-eighth Report … on … the Prisons of Ireland, 1869*, H.C. 1870 (C. 173), xxxvii, p. 344.
5.24 Tralee gaol. Photograph by author, 2013.
5.25 Ordnance Survey six-inch map for Enniskillen, Co. Fermanagh, surveyed June 1834. Trinity College Dublin.
5.26 Lough Cutra Castle, near Gort, Co. Galway. Photograph by author, 2013.

5.27 A surviving portion of the former Limerick city gaol. Photograph by author, 2014.

5.28 Drogheda gaol. Photograph by author, 2013.

5.29 Ordnance Survey six-inch map for Roscommon, Co. Roscommon, surveyed January 1837. Trinity College Dublin.

5.30 Roscommon gaol, *c.* 1930. From Rowan, *Morrison*, p. 148.

5.31 Monaghan gaol, ground-floor plan, 1870. From *Forty-ninth Report … on … the Prisons of Ireland, 1870*, H.C. 1871 (C. 359), xxx, p. 247.

5.32 Fisherton Anger (Wiltshire) county gaol, near Salisbury, elevation, unexecuted. Richard Ingleman, 1817. Wiltshire and Swindon Archives (WSA), A1/509/2.

5.33 Fisherton Anger (Wiltshire) county gaol, near Salisbury, ground-floor plan, unexecuted. Richard Ingleman, 1817. Wiltshire and Swindon Archives (WSA), A1/509/2.

5.34 Sligo gaol, 1955. National Library of Ireland (Morgan Aerial Photographic Collection).

5.35 Ordnance Survey six-inch map for Sligo, Co. Sligo, surveyed January 1837. Trinity College Dublin.

5.36 A map showing the counties that replied to a request from the AIPPD in 1819 for information about their gaols and bridewells. Compiled from *First Report of the AIPPD*, p. 10.

5.37 Smithfield penitentiary, Dublin, 1968. Dublin City Libraries.

5.38 Ordnance Survey six-inch map for Castlebar, Co. Mayo, surveyed January 1838. Trinity College Dublin.

5.39 Waterford city house of correction, elevation and ground-floor plan. James Elmes, 23 September 1820. National Archives of Ireland, CSORP 1820/432/6. Reproduced courtesy of the Director of the National Archives of Ireland.

5.40 Yorkshire West Riding (Wakefield) pauper lunatic asylum, ground-floor plan. James Bevans, 15 March 1815. From *Report … on Provisions for Better Regulation of Madhouses in England*, H.C. 1814–15 (295), iv, plate 5.

5.41 Cork city gaol, ground-floor plan, 1870. From *Forty-eighth Report … on … the Prisons of Ireland, 1869*, H.C. 1870 (C. 173), xxxvii, p. 307.

5.42 Cork city gaol. Photograph by author, 2017.

5.43 Cork county gaol, *c.* 1950. From David Lee, *James Pain, Architect* (Limerick: Limerick Civic Trust, 2005), p. 77.

5.44 Cork county gaol, ground-floor plan, 1870. From *Forty-eighth Report … on … the Prisons of Ireland, 1869*, H.C. 1870 (C. 173), xxxvii, p. 284.

5.45 Cork county gaol, 1831. From G.N. Wright, *Ireland Illustrated, from Original Drawings* (London: Fisher, Son & Jackson, 1831), pp. 66–7.

5.46 Cork county gaol, portico, screen and bridge. Photograph by author, 2013.

5.47 Limerick county gaol. From Patrick Fitzgerald and John James McGregor, *The History, Topography, and Antiquities of the County and City of Limerick*, 2 vols (Dublin: McKern, 1827), vol. 2, p. 578.

5.48 Ordnance Survey six-inch map for Limerick, Co. Limerick, surveyed January

1840. Trinity College Dublin.
5.49 Derry gaol, *c.* 1960. Irish Architectural Archive.
5.50 Derry gaol, ground-floor plan, 1870. From *Forty-ninth Report … on … the Prisons of Ireland, 1870*, H.C. 1871 (C. 359), xxx, p. 169.
5.51 Derry gaol, turret. Photograph by author, 2014.

Chapter 6: The New Regime, 1821–38

6.1 Portrait of James Palmer, 1826. Private collection.
6.2 Graph showing the number of gaols that were under construction in Ireland between 1770 and 1870.
6.3 A map showing new county gaols, or large additions made to existing gaols, in Ireland between 1821 and 1838.
6.4 A map showing central-government loans to Irish grand juries for gaol building between 1821 and 1838.
6.5 The polygonal and radial plans. From Holford, *An Account of Millbank Penitentiary*, p. 372.
6.6 Radial-plan gaols of different sizes, by George Thomas Bullar. From SIPD, *Remarks on the Form and Construction of Prisons* (London: Arch, 1826), pp. 50–7. Reproduced courtesy of Cambridge University Library.
6.7 Plan of various buildings at Chester Castle, 1810. From Daniel and Samuel Lysons, *Magna Britannia, Being a Concise Topographical Account of the Several Counties of Great Britain … Volume the Second, Containing Cambridgeshire, and the County Palatine of Chester*, 6 vols (London: Cadell & Davies, 1810), vol. 2, p. 570. Reproduced courtesy of the University of Leicester.
6.8 Lancaster Shire Hall and gaols. From Christopher Clark, *An Historical and Descriptive Account of the Town of Lancaster*, 2nd edn (Lancaster: Clark, 1811), p. 16.
6.9 Ordnance Survey six-inch map for Omagh, Co. Tyrone, surveyed June 1833. Trinity College Dublin.
6.10 Carrick-on-Shannon gaol, Co. Leitrim. Photograph by author, 2012.
6.11 Ordnance Survey five-feet town map for Carrick-on-Shannon, Co. Leitrim, *c.* 1850. Trinity College Dublin.
6.12 Central inspection building, Omagh gaol, *c.* 1970. Irish Architectural Archive.
6.13 Lifford gaol, Co. Donegal, *c.* 1900. Donegal County Archives.
6.14 Lifford gaol, Co. Donegal, under demolition, *c.* 1907. Donegal County Archives.
6.15 Mullingar courthouse. Photograph by author, 2013.
6.16 Central inspection building, Mullingar gaol. Photograph by author, 2017.
6.17 Map of Mullingar gaol, *c.* 1910. Westmeath County Library.
6.18 Entrance gateway, Mullingar gaol, *c.* 1900. Westmeath County Library, Westmeath Photographic Collection, M/1 (33).
6.19 Longford gaol, ground-floor plan, 1870. From *Forty-ninth Report … on … the*

Prisons of Ireland, 1870, H.C. 1871 (C. 359), xxx, p. 184.

6.20 Ordnance Survey six-inch map for Athy, Co. Kildare, surveyed January 1837. Trinity College Dublin.

6.21 Athy gaol, Co. Kildare. Photograph by author, 2014.

6.22 Naas gaol, Co. Kildare, *c.* 1950. From *The Leinster Leader*, 16 March 1985.

6.23 Ordnance Survey six-inch map for Naas, Co. Kildare, surveyed January 1837. Trinity College Dublin.

6.24 Downpatrick gaol, ground-floor plan, 1870. From *Forty-ninth Report … on … the Prisons of Ireland, 1870*, H.C. 1871 (C. 359), xxx, p. 134.

6.25 Downpatrick gaol, Co. Down, *c.* 1900. National Library of Ireland (Lawrence collection).

6.26 Entrance gateway, Downpatrick gaol. Photograph by author, 2014.

6.27 Trim gaol, Co. Meath, 1959. Courtesy of Noel French, Trim, Co. Meath.

6.28 A graph showing the number of 'outrages' in Co. Meath between 1815 and 1843 (where available). Compiled from Mooney, 'Agrarian Violence in Meath, 1790–1828', and ibid., 'Agrarian Violence in Meath, 1828–1835'.

6.29 Entrance gateway, Trim gaol, Co. Meath. Photograph by author, 2014.

6.30 Terrace wall and steps, Trim gaol, Co. Meath. Photograph by author, 2014.

6.31 Terrace wall and steps, Trim gaol, Co. Meath, 1981. Irish Architectural Archive (photograph by Geoff White).

6.32 A graph showing the number of criminal indictments in Munster between 1785 and 1855 (where available). Compiled from Appendix B.

6.33 'General Outline of a Plan of Prison', unexecuted. David Henry, 1826. From *Journal of the House of Commons*, vol. 81, 21 March 1826, Plate B.

6.34 Cavan gaol, ground-floor plan, 1870. From *Forty-ninth Report … on … the Prisons of Ireland, 1870*, H.C. 1871 (C. 359), xxx, p. 108.

6.35 Tullamore gaol, ground-floor plan, unexecuted. William Murray, 1820. Irish Architectural Archive, RIAI Murray Collection, Acc.92/46.1194.

6.36 Tullamore gaol, elevation drawing of central building and cell block, n.d. [*c.* 1826]. National Library of Ireland, AD 2644.

6.37 Tullamore gaol, King's County (Co. Offaly), 1978. Irish Architectural Archive.

6.38 Tullamore gaol, King's County (Co. Offaly), *c.* 1930s. Offaly County Library.

6.39 Maryborough (Portlaoise) gaol, ground-floor plan, 1870. From *Forty-eighth Report … on … the Prisons of Ireland, 1869*, H.C. 1870 (C. 173), xxxvii, p. 431.

6.40 Central inspection building, Carlow gaol. Photograph by author, 2014.

6.41 Table showing the condition of Irish county gaols in 1831 compared with 1822.

6.42 Westminster new bridewell, Tothill Fields, London, ground-floor plan. Robert Abraham, 1829–32. London Metropolitan Archives, COLLAGE, the London Picture Archive, ref. 28610.

6.43 Galway town gaol, ground-floor plan. Frederick Darley, Jnr, 1830. Galway County Council Archives, GS11-02-1.

6.44 Galway town gaol, *c.* 1940. From Curtin, *Women of Galway Jail* (2001), p. 37.
6.45 Castlebar gaol, Co. Mayo, ground-floor plan, 1870. From *Forty-ninth Report … on … the Prisons of Ireland, 1870*, H.C. 1871 (C. 359), xxx, p. 218.
6.46 Castlebar gaol, *c.* 1900 (by Thomas J. Wynne). Mayo County Library.
6.47 Castlebar gaol, inspection building and two radial cell blocks, *c.* 1900 (by Thomas J. Wynne). Mayo County Library.
6.48 Ordnance Survey five-feet town map for Clonmel gaol, Clonmel, Co. Tipperary, 1874. Trinity College Dublin.
6.49 Richmond bridewell, Dublin, ground-floor plan, 1870. From *Forty-ninth Report … on … the Prisons of Ireland, 1870*, H.C. 1871 (C. 359), xxx, p. 558.

Chapter 7: A Separate Agenda, 1838–55

7.1 Graph showing the number of gaols that were under construction in Ireland between 1770 and 1870.
7.2 A map showing new county gaols, or large additions made to existing gaols, in Ireland between 1838 and 1855.
7.3 Cherry Hill penitentiary, Philadelphia, Pennsylvania, perspective view. The Library Company of Philadelphia.
7.4 Pentonville, London, sections of a cell. From *Report of the Surveyor-general of Prisons on the Construction, Ventilation and Details of Pentonville Prison, 1844*, H.C. 1844 (594), xxviii.
7.5 Pentonville, London, ground-floor plan. From *Report of the Surveyor-general of Prisons on the Construction, Ventilation and Details of Pentonville Prison, 1844*, H.C. 1844 (594), xxviii.
7.6 Pentonville, London, perspective view. From *Report of the Surveyor-general of Prisons on the Construction, Ventilation and Details of Pentonville Prison, 1844*, H.C. 1844 (594), xxviii.
7.7 Wicklow gaol. Photograph by author, 2013.
7.8 Wicklow gaol, separate-system cell block. Photograph by author, 2013.
7.9 Wicklow gaol, interior view. Photograph by author, 2013.
7.10 Pentonville, London, interior view. From *Report of the Surveyor-general of Prisons on the Construction, Ventilation and Details of Pentonville Prison*, H.C. 1844 (594), xxviii.
7.11 A graph showing the number of criminal indictments in Co. Fermanagh between 1787 and 1855 (where available). Compiled from Appendix B.
7.12 Enniskillen gaol, ground-floor plan, 1870. From *Forty-ninth Report … on … the Prisons of Ireland, 1870*, H.C. 1871 (C. 359), xxx, p. 146.
7.13 Enniskillen gaol, separate-system block and infirmary. Photograph by author, 2014.
7.14 A graph showing the number of criminal indictments in Co. Wexford between 1800 and 1855 (where available). Compiled from Appendix B.

7.15 Wexford gaol, ground-floor plan, 1870. From *Forty-eighth Report … on … the Prisons of Ireland, 1869*, H.C. 1870 (C. 173), xxxvii, p. 489.
7.16 Wexford gaol. Photograph by author, 2014.
7.17 'Design for Enlarging Kilmainham Gaol', consisting of a new cell block on the separate system for female prisoners. Park Neville, 22 March 1844. Irish Architectural Archive, McCurdy and Mitchell Collection, Acc. 82/49/71/1.
7.18 Mullingar gaol, ground-floor plan, 1870. From *Forty-ninth Report … on … the Prisons of Ireland, 1870*, H.C. 1871 (C. 359), xxx, p. 299.
7.19 Carlow gaol, ground-floor plan, 1870. From *Forty-eighth Report … on … the Prisons of Ireland, 1869*, H.C. 1870 (C. 173), xxxvii, p. 263.
7.20 Carlow gaol. Photograph by author, 2012.
7.21 A graph showing the number of criminal indictments in Cos. Antrim, Down, and Tipperary, between 1786 and 1855 (where available). Compiled from Appendix B.
7.22 Ordnance Survey six-inch map for Nenagh, Co. Tipperary, surveyed January 1840. Trinity College Dublin.
7.23 Belfast (Crumlin Road) gaol, ground-floor plan, 1870. From *Forty-ninth Report … on … the Prisons of Ireland, 1870*, H.C. 1871 (C. 359), xxx, p. 77.
7.24 The cost of building certain prisons, per cell, in England and in Ireland, between *c.* 1800 and 1863. Compiled from Evans, *Fabrication of Virtue*, p. 348, and Appendix A.
7.25 Belfast (Crumlin Road) gaol. Photograph by author, 2013.
7.26 Nenagh gaol, ground-floor plan, 1870. From *Forty-eighth Report … on … the Prisons of Ireland, 1869*, H.C. 1870 (C. 173), xxxvii, p. 442.
7.27 Nenagh gaol, governor's residence. Photograph by author, 2017.
7.28 Nenagh gaol, cell block. Photograph by author, 2017.
7.29 Nenagh gaol, entrance gateway. Photograph by author, 2017.
7.30 A graph showing the number of prisoner deaths in county gaols in Munster between 1845 and 1852, and the expenditure on prisons during this time. Compiled from the annual reports of the Irish prison inspectors.
7.31 Ordnance Survey five-feet town map for Arbour Hill military prison, Dublin, 1847. Trinity College Dublin.
7.32 Spike Island, Co. Cork, Fort Westmorland, barracks buildings. Photograph by author, 2017.
7.33 Mountjoy (male) convict prison, Dublin, ground-floor plan. Unsigned [Office of Public Works], 5 August 1924. National Archives of Ireland, OPW 5HC/4/412. Reproduced courtesy of the Director of the National Archives of Ireland.
7.34 Mountjoy (female) convict prison, Dublin, second-floor plan. James Higgins Owen, 12 May 1855. National Archives of Ireland, OPW 5HC/4/412. Reproduced courtesy of the Director of the National Archives of Ireland.
7.35 St Michan's Park, Green Street, Dublin. Photograph by author, 2014.

7.36 A graph showing the number of criminal indictments in Co. Armagh and Co. Louth between 1787 and 1855 (where available). Compiled from Appendix B.

7.37 'Plan for an Addition to the Gaol of Armagh', ground-floor plan, unexecuted. William Murray, 11 February 1837. Irish Architectural Archive, RIAI Murray Collection, Acc. 92/46.20.

7.38 'Plan for Armagh Gaol with Proposed Additions', ground-floor plan, unexecuted. William Murray, 22 September 1837. Irish Architectural Archive, RIAI Murray Collection, Acc. 92/46.22.

7.39 Three elevation drawings for the main façade of Armagh gaol, showing the present appearance of the gaol, and two schemes for remodelling the gaol, unexecuted. William Murray, 22 September 1837. Irish Architectural Archive, RIAI Murray Collection, Acc. 92/46.25–7.

7.40 Armagh gaol, separate-system cell block, second-floor plan. William Murray, January 1846. Irish Architectural Archive, RIAI Murray Collection, Acc. 92/46.48.

7.41 Armagh gaol, female separate-system cell block. Photograph by author 2017.

7.42 Armagh gaol. Photograph by author, 2014.

7.43 Dundalk gaol, ground-floor plan. John Neville, 1853. From *Civil Engineer and Architect's Journal*, vol. 16, no. 229, April 1853, p. 121.

7.44 Dundalk gaol, perspective drawing. John Neville, 1853. From *Civil Engineer and Architect's Journal*, vol. 16, no. 229, April 1853, p. 121.

7.45 Dundalk gaol, *c.* 1900. National Library of Ireland (Lawrence Collection).

7.46 Kilmainham gaol, Dublin, ground-floor plan, 1870. From *Forty-ninth Report … on … the Prisons of Ireland, 1870*, H.C. 1871 (C. 359), xxx, p. 545.

7.47 Kilmainham gaol, Dublin, separate-system block. National Library of Ireland (Mason Collection).

7.48 Kilmainham gaol, Dublin, boundary wall. Photograph by author, 2014.

7.49 Naas gaol, Co. Kildare, ground-floor plan, 1870. From *Forty-eighth Report … on … the Prisons of Ireland, 1869*, H.C. 1870 (C. 173), xxxvii, p. 361.

7.50 Kilkenny county and city gaol, ground-floor plan, 1870. From *Forty-eighth Report … on … the Prisons of Ireland, 1869*, H.C. 1870 (C. 173), xxxvii, p. 374.

7.51 Kilkenny county and city gaol, entrance gateway, *c.* 1948. Photograph by Billy Brett, reproduced in Walsh, 'Hard Labour', p. 232.

7.52 A graph showing the number of criminal indictments in Waterford county and city between 1800 and 1855 (where available). Compiled from Appendix B.

7.53 Waterford county and city gaol, ground-floor plan, 1870. From *Forty-eighth Report … on … the Prisons of Ireland, 1869*, H.C. 1870 (C. 173), xxxvii, p. 474.

7.54 Waterford county and city gaol, from the air, *c.* 1933. Waterford Museum of Treasures.

7.55 Waterford county and city gaol, entrance gateway, probably during demolition, *c.* 1950. Waterford Museum of Treasures.

Acknowledgements

This book began as a doctoral thesis and I owe a great debt to my supervisors, Frank Salmon at the University of Cambridge, and James S. Donnelly, Jr., at the University of Wisconsin-Madison, for their encouragement, advice, insight, and detailed help. It would not have been possible without them, but any errors in this work are solely my responsibility. At every stage, historians, architects, archivists, graduate students, and other interested persons have volunteered their advice or gone out of the way to help me. It is difficult to attempt to thank them all by name, and unavoidably I will neglect to acknowledge some debts I feel that I owe, but I would like to thank (in no particular order): Edward McParland, Christine Casey, Roger Stalley, Frank Keohane, Ian d'Alton, Ciara Breathnach, Ciaran O'Neill, Olwen Purdue, Andrew Tierney, Robert Tombs, Eugenio Biagini, Marc Caball, Kathleen James-Chakraborty, Myles Campbell, the late David Watkin, the late Gavin Stamp, Deborah Howard, Sarah Goldsmith, Alex Marr, Jon Parry, Karen Latimer, Anthony Malcomson, Bruce Campbell, Virginia Crossman, Judith Hill, Michael Byrne, Damian Murphy, Emily Mann, Simon Bradley, and Eugene Hynes.

To write this history of Ireland's courthouses and prisons, I have been fortunate in being able to visit and study them in person. Over many years I have travelled extensively throughout the island of Ireland, visiting over 300 towns in total, and putting up over 8,000 miles of driving. I am grateful for the grants that I received from the Kettle's Yard Travel Fund (Cambridge History of Art Department), St John's College, Cambridge, the Mary Euphrasia Mosley Research Grant (University of Cambridge), the Society of Architectural Historians of Great Britain, the Gates Cambridge Trust, and the Paul Mellon Centre for Studies in British Art. The inclusion of so many colour illustrations was made possible because of a generous donation from Brian Fenwick-Smith, to whom I am extremely grateful. I would also like to thank the Aurelius Charitable Trust for a donation towards the printing costs.

In different corners of Ireland, friends and family welcomed me after long and tiring days of driving and studying buildings and towns and made me feel instantly at home: Lorna and Liz Farrelly; Martina and Dermot Hanna; Fintan

Lyons; Edward and Primrose Wilson; Peter, Daryl, Lydia, Anne, and Willie Butler; Mary Ruth and Pat Tobin; and John and Patricia DuLong. Many kind people invited me into their homes, gave me private tours of important historic buildings, offered me lunch and tea, and went out of their way to make my travels a success. Thanks in particular to the guard who gave me a tour of Derry's courthouse and its troubled past, the police officers in Ballymoney who brought me around the town's old bridewell, the priest in Millstreet who took me onto the roof of his church, the staff at Lough Cutra Castle who also led me onto the roof of their spectacular mansion, the shopkeeper in Milltown who let me wander around the town's old bridewell, and the farmer who fixed my car in Connemara.

Both archivists and private families in Ireland and abroad have been unfailing in their assistance and enthusiasm. I am particularly indebted to Michael Byrne, the Hill family, and the DuLong family, for letting me study and reproduce material in their private collections. I am also grateful to many local historians, librarians, and archivists, for all their help, and feel that their hard work in protecting our heritage and history is often not properly recognised. In particular, I would like to thank Tom Daly, Hazel Vickery, Sean Barden, Deirdre Condron, Jonathan Smyth, Peter Beirne, Declan Barron, Niamh Brennan, Bernadette Walsh, Colm McQuinn, James Durney, Mario Corrigan, Anne Fitzsimons, Mary Conefrey, Ivor Hamrock, Mario Corrigan, Brian McGee, Patria McWalter, Sinéad Holland, Martin Morris, Lorraine McCann, Diarmaid Bracken, Tom French, Noel French, Catríona Lennon, Mary Guinan-Darmody, John Kelly, Jayne Sutcliffe, Joanne Rothwell, Donnchadh Ó Ceallacháin, Gráinne Doran, Gretta Connell, Paula O'Dornan, Theresa Loftus, David Tilsley, Caitlin Browne, Michael Lynch, Charles Noble, Colum O'Riordan, and all the staff at the Irish Architectural Archive, and the kind staff at the British Library, the National Archives in London and Dublin, the National Library of Ireland, the Cambridge University Library, and Trinity College Dublin. I am also grateful to the peer reviewers and editorial staff at Cork University Press for their detailed and constructive comments.

Many of the illustrations in this book are reproduced courtesy of archives and institutions to which I would like to express my gratitude. They are: Armagh County Museum; Cambridge University Library; Carlow County Library; Cork City Libraries; the Crawford Art Gallery, Cork; Donegal County Archives; Dublin City Libraries; Galway County Archives; Gloucestershire Archives; Historic Liverpool; the Historical Picture Archive (Ireland); the Irish Architectural Archive; the Library Company of Philadelphia; the Linen Hall

Library, Belfast; the London Metropolitan Archives; Mayo County Library; the Merrion Hotel, Dublin; the Ordnance Survey of Northern Ireland; the National Archives of Ireland; the National Gallery of Ireland; the National Portrait Gallery (London); the National Library of Ireland; Offaly County Library; Louth County Archives; the Public Record Office of Northern Ireland; the Royal Institute of British Architects; Tipperary County Library; Trinity College Dublin; the Waterford Museum of Treasures; Westmeath County Library; and Wiltshire and Swindon Archives.

My college, St John's, helped me in innumerable ways during my many years in Cambridge, including full scholarships, prizes, and opportunities for travel. I am especially grateful to the late Master, Christopher Dobson; his wife Mary Dobson; Pat Boyde; Robin Glasscock; Mark Nicholls; and Helen Watson. My doctoral work in Cambridge was kindly funded by the Gates Cambridge Trust, and my year of research and writing at the University of Wisconsin-Madison by the Irish Fulbright Commission. Most of all, I owe a great debt to my family and friends who have supported me, read drafts of this work when it was a thesis, and allowed me to travel so widely. In particular, I would like to thank Aaron Helfand, Otto Saumarez-Smith, Bridget Hembree, Max Bryant, Hannah Malone, Andrew McKay, Benen Harrington, Peter Murray, John Rogers, Frank Callanan, Conrad Koziol, Evan Miles, Diego Bravo, Liz Farrelly, Peter Hession, Diana Leca, Amiya Bhatia, Tom James, Chris Wagner, Andrew Gruen, Tadhg Barrett and Claire Berezowitz, Kathleen and John Salinas, my brothers Daryl and Gary, sister Lydia, and parents Michael and Etna. Most of all, I am grateful to Tamela Maciel for sharing the adventure with me, and for her love and encouragement at every turn on the way.

R. J. B.
Leicester, 23 October 2019

Introduction

Irish cities and towns were transformed by a wave of new public buildings, planned streets, and new housing between roughly 1750 and 1850. The scale of architectural development was unprecedented as the Irish urban streetscape gained new churches and schools, military barracks, and many other buildings. At the same time urban centres were linked by new networks of canals, roads, and – in later years – railways.[1] Of all this architectural development, four types of public buildings stand out from the rest: courthouses, prisons, what were termed 'lunatic asylums', and workhouses. Almost all were built before the catastrophe of the Great Famine – and a majority survive in some form even today.[2] This book offers an architectural and a political history of the most impressive duo of these – the closely linked building of major courthouses and prisons by local government at this time. By the 1860s, the construction of these expensive showpiece buildings had reached what may be termed a conclusion of sorts, after a century of innovation, reform, and political struggle. This book attempts to explain how and why they were erected, who paid for them, how designs evolved, and how plans and sites were chosen. Assize courthouses are considered in the first three chapters, and county gaols in the last four. While there were many obvious connections between the two types of buildings, they are considered separately here to highlight key moments of change in their respective development and the role played by different officials and charitable groups. Together with some reflections at the end of the book, these chapters offer an insight into how Irish local government operated in the Georgian and Victorian eras, and how these new public buildings affected the morphology, appearance, and economy of the county towns in which they were erected.

Ireland's new courthouses and prisons were built in an era marked by extremes of economic prosperity and human catastrophe, peace, domestic rebellions, and international war. In the middle of the period considered, the failure of the great Irish rebellion of 1798 hastened the formation of a full political union between Great Britain and Ireland – the Act of Union of 1800. At the same time, the Napoleonic wars raged across Europe and French forces both attempted and succeeded in landing forces in Ireland in 1796–8; the wars continued until 1815.

The expansion of Irish towns reflected the buoyancy of the late eighteenth-century economy and especially the rich provisions trade of the war years; it also mirrored a rapidly expanding population, scientific improvement in agriculture, and important (though relatively limited) industrial development. Yet endemic agrarian unrest regularly filled courtrooms and prisons with mostly men awaiting trial and punishment; Whiteboys, Rightboys, revolutionaries, Rockites and others kept judges and gaol wardens busy throughout the century covered in this book. Never, of course, were gaols busier than during the Great Irish Famine, and, as discussed in the final chapter, this disaster pushed the nation's prison system into a crisis as profound as that of the newly built workhouses and Poor Law unions. Throughout the period between 1750 and 1850, Irish local government – the grand-jury system – had a surprising degree of financial and political independence and this was reflected in the new courthouses and prisons that these elites built in provincial cities and towns. This book attempts to combine politics and architecture to better understand these networks of large, costly, and impressive new buildings.

In charting this course of political reform, the book contributes to Irish architectural history by analysing many newly identified drawings, previously unpublished private correspondence, and detailed government reports and inquiries. It suggests and clarifies the dates of construction and the identity of the architect responsible for some of Ireland's greatest public buildings – not least the county gaols in Trim and Wexford. By integrating the many drawings, photographs, letters, and grand-jury records found in an exhaustive search through Irish county libraries and archives, as well as sources in national archives and around the world, the book allows for a more complete history than previously available of the building of Ireland's courthouses and prisons. It also explores, for the first time, an important Irish charity from the 1810s and 1820s – the Association for the Improvement of Prisons and of Prison Discipline in Ireland (AIPPD) – whose reports and correspondence have been traced in various archives around the world, including material held privately by descendants of the prison inspector James Palmer now in the United States.

This book focuses on the political and administrative aspects of courthouse- and prison-building, in order, arguably, to best explain how and why they came to exist. Two analytic threads run through the work: government reform, and crime and punishment. There were sustained efforts through the period between 1750 and 1850 to reform the county-based grand-jury system, the backbone of Irish local government. Courthouses and prisons were almost uniformly built, funded, and managed by these bodies. From the Act of Union onwards, central government in Westminster and Dublin redoubled efforts to reform the structure of these bodies and how they funded new public architecture. This book attempts to explain how and why this mattered and analyse its impact on the building of assize courthouses and county gaols. Understanding the nature of local government is essential to understanding its architectural legacy. The judicial and administrative worlds in Ireland shared a great deal: assize courthouses were situated in each of the county towns and heard the most serious criminal cases, as well as more complex civil cases, and were presided over by travelling assize judges within certain 'circuits'. Assizes were held twice in the year – in the spring and summer – and were resplendent affairs with much ceremony, public interest, and press coverage.[3] As Terence Dunne has recently commented, the assizes marked a 'staged performance of power, a symbolic display meant to impress and overawe'.[4] The assizes also demanded that a grand jury be sworn in, to indict accused persons and send them forward for trial, and also to approve of 'presentments' (in effect taxes to be levied off the county or a particular barony within it) to pay for roads, services, and public buildings. Though these grand juries formed the essential core of Irish local government at this time, they were temporary bodies dissolved at the end of each assizes. Their composition varied somewhat but almost always included the principal landholders – and therefore taxpayers – in each county.[5] As K. Theodore Hoppen has remarked, the governing of Ireland in these years was 'subcontracted to a collection of local Protestant notables'.[6]

As a body, grand juries held much greater power than their namesakes in contemporary Britain or elsewhere.[7] In the late eighteenth and early nineteenth centuries, they began to take on more responsibility for infirmaries, prisons, and other public institutions. As the complexity and scale of their work increased, they began to employ some permanent staff to manage their affairs, such as treasurers, county surveyors, and clerks.[8] However, the ever-changing composition of grand juries did little for the accountability of public funds, and the very nature of the system resulted in what would now be termed a lack of 'institutional memory'. This is not to suggest that grand juries were collections of strangers. The twenty-three men (and they were all men) who gathered twice each year shared a great deal in terms of social class, political inclination, and kinship.[9] A place at the grand-jury table signified membership of the elite strata of county society. In addition to this, jurors did not have to face the trials of democratic election and were instead simply appointed by the high sheriff of each county. It is not unreasonable, then, to see the grand juries of this time as oligarchic organisations where 'corruption' (as it would be termed today) and scandal could too easily go unchecked. In the building of roads and the maintenance of public institutions, leading politicians such as Daniel O'Connell regularly accused grand jurors of 'jobbery' – the awarding of public contracts to friends or close family members, leading, all too often, to substandard or incomplete work and the need for further public expenditure.[10] Concerns over corrupt local government practices coloured Westminster and Dublin Castle's view of plans for new courthouses and prisons in Irish cities and towns. In Maurice Craig's often-quoted words, Ireland's assize courthouses were the 'last, and perhaps [the] finest contribution in the sphere of public buildings' from 'the old oligarchical system' of local government.[11] Corruption in the late eighteenth and early nineteenth centuries, of course, must be seen in the context of how local government worked – in Britain and in Ireland – and how normal and everyday such actions were before later nineteenth-century reforms.[12]

The courthouses and prisons that grand juries built and managed, then, must be seen as more than simply the visible instruments of the state's system of justice. Courthouses in particular were also the nuclei of local administration, and places where many elegant grand-jury rooms and the offices for clerks and treasurers were located. Grand jurors held balls and social events there, especially around the time of the assizes, and, through their boards of superintendence, paid regular visits to county prisons.[13] These buildings must then be seen to have a social as well as a judicial presence in the urban landscape. On one hand, they signify the authority and power of the national and the imperial government in the traditional areas of justice and punishment; on the other, they must be seen as the visible presence of the political, economic, and cultural authority of key local elites.[14] Assize courthouses, for example, could be sites for high political drama, as at Ennis in July 1828 when O'Connell was returned as MP for the county, much to the displeasure of the Protestant interests in Clare (who in effect formed its grand jury) and the Tory government in Westminster.[15] The Clare grand-jury records for the time show that the courthouse was 'damaged' during disturbances that followed and 'several repairs' were later required – not least replacing broken glass.[16] The condition of prisons, too, tended to reflect either positively or negatively on the grand jurors of a particular county, and when government officials and assize judges attempted to convince local elites to improve or rebuild their prisons, the strategy adopted was often simply to shame or embarrass jurors by highlighting their supposed public respectability, civic responsibility, or humanitarianism. In this way the character of local government was intimately tied to the perceived self-respect and pride of individual grand jurors.

The history of Ireland's grand juries and their building of courthouses and prisons opens up important questions about Ireland's quasi-colonial status, particularly after the Act of Union.[17] Major public buildings – particularly those serving the state's judicial structures – are often held up as emblematic of imperial or colonial authority. In Ireland – as in other parts of the British Empire and further afield – courthouses and prisons became stages for the acting out of political and revolutionary resistance, and in Ireland many were targeted during the Irish Revolution of the early twentieth century.[18] However, this study makes a major contribution to post-colonial studies by teasing apart the different strata of political and financial agency behind these grand buildings.[19] By focusing on the county grand juries, this book suggests more provincial and local meanings beyond the theatre of quasi-colonial resistance: competition between local elites, consumption and appropriation of fashionable architectural styles, and the influence of humanitarian and charitable societies. It shows how the power dynamic between metropolis and periphery was often contested and was expressed in both directions at different times. It also brings into focus the role played by 'experts' – such as prison inspectors – in local and national decisions and how they formed a governmentality that was based on the state's concepts of rationality, science, and progress.[20]

Grand jurors are here considered as 'consumers' of architecture, following recent theoretical work by Christine Casey, Conor Lucey, Kathleen James-Chakraborty, Andrew Tierney, and others.[21] We may strike a divide between the study of the 'production' and the 'consumption' of architecture. The former – concerned with artistic agency, style, innovation, and influence – has arguably been the mainstay of traditional architectural history. Indeed, many foundational and influential studies on the Irish courthouse and prison take this approach, not least Edward McParland's doctoral thesis (1975) and Maurice Craig's *The Architecture of Ireland* (1982) – both of which form an essential background to this book.[22] However, the patrons of these buildings – the grand juries – have rarely been brought into central focus and analysed as the patrons or 'consumers' of architecture.[23] This book makes a novel contribution to the rich recent literature on material culture and consumption studies within Irish studies, most apparent within early modern studies.[24] As Toby Barnard has commented, 'knowledge of the approved architectural idioms differentiated the cultivated few from the uncouth many. Buildings everywhere contained a powerful moral charge.'[25] Architecture was itself a material culture to be bought and sold, competed for, acquired, and dispersed.

In the context of local government reform and in attempting to answer both how and why these buildings came to exist, the 'consumer' approach is especially rewarding. In some of their patronage decisions, this book shows how grand jurors committed their counties to a profligate indulgence in architectural splendour – far more elaborate than the condition of the local economy might otherwise have supported. The difference was almost always made up by generous loans from central government. Paradoxically, attempts to limit what was seen as unnecessary spending also came from the same source. From the perspective of grand jurors, Dublin and Westminster often gave with one hand and took with the other. While Westminster politicians might query the need to demolish a twenty-year-old courthouse and spend £20,000 on a more elaborate replacement, they also offered generous public-works loans that grand juries were all-too-keen to spend on such projects. Throughout the period between 1750 and 1850 there are countless examples of what might be termed 'extravagant' grand-jury expenditure. In the 1780s, the penal reformer John Howard visited Ireland during the first great rebuilding of county gaols; grand jurors, he argued, were too often led astray by architects who proposed 'pompous fronts', which he thought appeared 'like palaces to the lower class of people'.[26] Forty years later, during a period when many new courthouses were being built, the *Freeman's Journal* condemned the imposition of what they saw as significant unwarranted taxation because of 'the caprice of grand juries': 'it has frequently happened that grand juries have decided that new courthouses … were requisite, and the old … sessions' houses should be pulled down, which, if altered or enlarged, would have perfectly answered the purpose … at great expense and taxation to the people'.[27] In this context, the efforts of central-government reformers to check or limit the expenditure of the grand juries, particularly from the 1810s onwards, can be seen as attempts, however limited or ineffective, to restrict grand-jury consumption. Conversely, central government's promise of large loans and grants for public works, to help alleviate distress during recessions and famines, acted in the opposite manner, and fuelled architectural patronage and consumption. Grand jury expenditure was thus a leaky valve that could at different times be either opened or shut.

The relationship between central and local government was by no means simple. However much key figures such as Robert Peel, Irish chief secretary in the 1810s, deplored the corruption and inefficiencies of the grand juries, central government inevitably depended on these bodies to implement social reforms (such as, for example, improving the condition of prisoners), administer justice in the lower courts, and generally to maintain law and order and the hegemonic power of the British state.[28] This leads naturally to a discussion of the other key analytic used throughout the book: statistics for crime and unrest. At the outset it must be stressed that crime is considered here by county and not as a national average, as this gives a much better insight into the mentality of key grand jurors when considering plans for new buildings in their local area. Crime, and the managing of courthouses and prisons, were fundamentally county – and not national – affairs for these grand jurors. This book tests the hypothesis that the building of new courthouses and prisons was intrinsically linked to increases in local crime rates. We may naturally suppose the connection to be strong – as an increase in crime inevitably led to busy courtrooms and overcrowded prison cells – but did it lead to new and larger courthouses, or additional prison cells? Or were there other factors that were more important in pushing grand jurors into action? As the surviving records for grand-jury debates and deliberations are so scarce, in seeking to answer this question we must consider all the possible influences that will have acted upon them, such as the availability of central-government loans as outlined above, but also the state of crime within their county.[29] In using crime figures, statistics for *criminal indictments* are used extensively as a barometer of unrest in a given county at any time. Indictments reflect the number of persons charged with offences (and so to appear in court) and then held in county prisons (adding to the local prisoner population). They are a particularly useful figure – more so than either reported crimes or convictions – as they more accurately reflect the physical pressures on the court and prison systems. Conviction figures, by comparison, are more valuable when considering issues of transportation or capital punishment (both subjects beyond the scope of this work). Reported crimes, though also a useful measure of unrest, often led to no arrests being made or trials in court, and so did not impact in a physical sense upon a county's courts or prisons. Indictment figures also have the advantage of being consistently available for much of the period under study, and they are tabulated for further study in Appendix B.[30] Of course, these statistics are no more reliable than any others from this time period and their applicability has been a source of debate among social historians.[31]

The first half of this book offers a history of the building of assize courthouses, the largest and most distinguished courthouses in each county, in terms of grand-jury politics and local government reform.[32] The international study of the history of the courthouse, and the placing of its design within broader social, cultural, and legal shifts is a relatively recent pursuit, and the literature on the subject is still quite limited.[33] From at least the late seventeenth century, borough governments in England funded the construction of splendid new courthouses in their towns in attempts to reap the financial dividends from staging assizes and other court sittings.[34] Martha McNamara has shown similar dynamics in county courthouse building in Massachusetts from the eighteenth century onwards, and Judith Resnik and Denny Curtis, in their international survey, suggest courthouse building tracked 'political hopes or confidence intersecting with economic capacity'.[35] And in a pioneering recent study, Katie Barclay has analysed the early nineteenth-century Irish courtroom in terms of gender and power relations with a particular focus on emotion, identity, masculinity, and performativity.[36] She has concluded that 'courtrooms not only signalled the ideal order of legal proceedings, but society itself. The use of court space reinforced the law's embodiment of wider social and gender hierarchies; the gallery suggestive of a burgeoning democracy that would lead to change.'[37]

Barclay and others link the increasing sophistication of courthouse plans and the segregation of courtroom spaces to the professionalisation of lawyers, judges, and clerks, and the re-creation of wider class divisions and expressions of social and moral propriety within judicial settings, especially in limiting interactions between the public, defendants, and legal professionals.[38] McNamara credits the growing political power of lawyers in Massachusetts with reshaping court rituals in the commonwealth, and the creation of 'a judicial landscape' that they could monopolise and use to highlight their own importance.[39] For Linda Mulcahy, changing perceptions towards the actual and moral dangers of defendants and the public led to strict divisions within courtrooms, and also segregated entranceways and corridors. She questions in particular the design and location of the defendant's dock, and how it can preclude fair hearings to accused persons.[40] Patrick Polden in turn emphasises the many benefits legal reform brought to the emerging middle classes in his study of the post-1846 county courts for debt recovery in England, and how this contributed to polite support for the building and operation of increasingly expensive and complex courthouses.[41]

McNamara's focus on the power of legal professionals has been questioned by other scholars. Their direct influence over decisions to build or rebuild courthouses is unclear, and, as one reviewer noted, in the commonwealth of Virginia at least, lawyers also became more powerful at this time but the control of courthouse architecture remained firmly and exclusively with the local landed and mercantile elite, a group often suspicious of the aspirational legal profession.[42] While McNamara points to an insightful correlation, her analysis downplays the role of judges and local government officials in actually instigating courthouse-building projects and choosing designs.[43] In the case of one Irish courthouse, as outlined in Chapter 2, the decision to rebuild lay instead with an assize judge embarrassed by undignified and inadequate facilities, and a cabal of local landlords left feeling out-done by the splendour and sophistication of new courthouses in neighbouring counties. Lawyers and clerks, though slowly professionalising in Ireland as in other Western societies, had less impact than grand jurors and judges, this book argues, on the design of Irish courthouses in the early nineteenth century.[44] This was because the unusual and antiquated structure of Irish local government meant that spending powers remained almost exclusively with county grand juries. Ireland's slowly emerging and, to a certain extent, politically circumscribed middle class had even less control over county taxation than in Britain, and until the 1830s there was little cess-payers could do to stop the rebuilding plans of grand juries. As such this study focuses on grand jurors as patrons and consumers of architecture.

More 'private' meanings and uses of courthouses have been emphasised in work on the subject. C.E.B. Brett and Christine Casey both argue that many new courthouses in Ireland were vanity projects for the most influential grand jurors.[45] In eighteenth-century England, Graham has documented many shire halls and assembly rooms built to stage assemblies, balls, and concerts, as well as court sittings. At Newark, the private or social rooms in the Town Hall occupied almost as much space as those with a judicial function. This other use of courthouses – pleasure palaces for polite society – became less pronounced in the nineteenth century as distinct architectural typologies developed, and legal reform led to increasingly professionalised courtroom settings.[46] The tardiness of comparable local-government reforms in Ireland meant that the assize courthouse continued to serve this social function – akin to a club for local elites with reading and coffee rooms – well into the second half of the nineteenth century.[47] In many new British courthouses, an increasing population and swelling urban crime rate could justify, in purely practical terms, the need for more courtroom space. The same was less true in Ireland, where we find that a sample of counties, faced with broadly similar fluctuations in crime levels, react in different ways and only certain grand juries moved to upgrade their facilities. Furthermore, courthouses – and prisons – often formed the axial terminations of new streets and suburbs, particularly in the early nineteenth century. Grand jurors used new public architecture to embellish and enlarge their county towns as part of town development or 'improvement' schemes: the new courthouses in Tullamore and Nenagh, for example, represented agendas local and private as much as national or imperial.[48]

These themes are taken up in detail in the first three chapters, which open with an overview of the Irish assize courthouse between the mid-eighteenth century and around 1817, a period marked out by a rapidly expanding population, the need to rebuild after the devastation of the 1798 rebellion, the political effects of the Act of Union, the economic boom and high staple prices of the long Napoleonic wars, and aborted attempts to introduce more accountability to grand-jury expenditure and limit corruption and jobbery. In these years, the design and layout of an assize courthouse emerged as a distinct architectural typology, and certain designs became models throughout the country. Much of this chapter focuses on the political actions of grand juries in the northern counties of Derry, Armagh, and Louth, who repeatedly lobbied central government for more freedom to spend vast sums of county money on new and architecturally distinguished courthouses in these years. Their chief achievement was the Irish Court Houses Act of 1813, which removed legal obstacles that had plagued grand juries for more than a decade. By plotting the dates of construction and the commissioned architect for each county, this chapter builds up a picture of how important inter-county rivalry and competition was at this time. Certain counties found themselves surrounded by others who now boasted fine new courthouses, and even though they experienced no sudden increase in crime or unrest into the early 1800s that might necessitate new larger buildings, it is argued that these counties were determined not to be left behind their neighbours in this new competitive spirit.

The second chapter concerns the period from 1817 to 1831, the peak years of assize courthouse building in Irish history. With attempts to reform grand juries and enfranchise Catholic landholders warded off by a Tory government in 1816–17, grand juries had a uniquely extended period of lax accountability and broad political power – their short and glorious twilight – when they retained full control over building courthouses and other large public buildings. The availability of central-government loans and grants from 1817 onwards, ostensibly to provide employment in the post-war slump, added fuel to the grand juries' level of patronage. The inter-county rivalry was only heightened by the comments of travelling assize judges, who by the nature of their labours could quickly compare the courthouses in which they worked, and make pointed comments that pushed grand juries into action. This intense outburst of building activity came to a sudden halt in a series of political and administrative defeats at the end of the decade. After around 1831, central government successfully limited the spending powers of grand juries, and this had a drastic effect on their ability to patronise new public architecture.

Chapter 3 concerns courthouse building from around 1831, when far-reaching reforms were beginning to take effect, through to around 1855. Catholic emancipation in 1829, a strengthened Board of Works from 1831 that took over some powers previously exercised by grand juries, and reform in the structure and taxing powers of grand juries in 1833 made it much more difficult to commit to building new courthouses. In addition, with so many newly built courthouses around the country there was less need to spend money. Among the most striking trends of the 1830s were the extent to which the holding of assizes was associated with economic development in a town or city, and the way in which local elites competed for the right to stage these meetings.[49] It is argued that these trends were in part a response to the economic malaise of the decade and the absence of private capitalist development, especially in southern counties. In Tipperary, Waterford, Offaly, and Antrim, intra-county disputes broke out that, in general, overshadowed the impact of upward trends in crime figures. But in certain cases, such as Tipperary, sustained agrarian unrest proved a useful negotiating tool for the various factions of the grand jury. This chapter focuses on the effects that new assize courthouses had, especially in the towns of Tullamore and Nenagh. Furthermore, an unbuilt scheme for Limerick city is analysed for the first time, and it is suggested that had it been proposed in the more exuberant years of the 1820s, it might have been built, but by the mid-1830s it was seen as too ambitious and a much more modest building was instead put up.

The second half of the book, chapters 4 to 7, complement the earlier chapters on courthouses by focusing on the coeval building of county gaols, the largest and most expensive prisons in each county. The impacts of British and Irish penal-reform debates, as well as proposed and enacted grand-jury reforms, are central to the narrative.[50] There is an enormous body of literature on the history of prisons, penal reform, and issues of crime and punishment more broadly. The most useful analysis of prison architecture, at least in northern European terms, is undoubtedly Robin Evans' brilliant and incisive *The Fabrication of Virtue* (1982).[51] It is complemented by Norman Johnston's work on global prison architecture, and Margaret Heather Tomlinson's unpublished doctoral thesis on later Victorian prisons in Britain.[52] Writings on penal history tend to follow one of two distinct approaches: first, empirical administrative histories that analyse the role played by governments in reforming prisons; and second, more theoretical approaches that, following Weber, Foucault, and others, focus on questions of power.[53] British and Irish historians more associated with the first school include R.B. McDowell, Ursula Henriques, Oliver MacDonagh, Simon Devereaux, and Joanna Innes.[54] Those closer to the second include Evans, V.A.C. Gatrell, Miles Ogborn, Patrick Carroll-Burke, and James J. Willis.[55] In both English and Irish contexts, there are also some very helpful regional studies that show how national ideas filtered through local concerns.[56] This book attempts to place Irish penal reform within the context of contemporary British and American ideas, and while inevitably influenced by the social turn pioneered by Foucault and others, is primarily concerned with studying how and why government reform impacted on the design and building of prisons. It also complements Mary Rogan's work on Irish prison history and policy from around 1920 to the present day.[57]

Chapter 4 considers the history of the Irish county gaol between the mid-eighteenth century and around 1810. During this period the first national inspector of prisons, Sir Jeremiah Fitzpatrick, was appointed by central government to oversee the implementation of a raft of new prison-reform legislation. Almost every county gaol was rebuilt during this time, but often with little reference to contemporary debates in both Ireland and Britain about what would constitute an effective design. Key reformers such as John Howard, William Eden, and John Parnell set new standards for the Irish grand juries in penal issues, and several new gaols were praised as architectural successes in their own time. By the end of the period, however, it is argued that it was apparent to a younger generation of reformers, including Fitzpatrick's successor, the Rev. Forster Archer, that further curtailment of the historic rights of grand juries would be necessary if prison conditions were to be substantially improved, and a parliamentary inquiry in 1809 paved the way for an important reforming act – the Irish Prisons Act of 1810. It is argued that we should not overstate the connection between the high levels of crime and unrest of late eighteenth-century Ireland and the agenda for designing and building new 'reformed' gaols.

The next chapter focuses on the history of the county gaol between 1810 and 1821, a period defined at its opening by a new act of parliament and at its close by the appointment of James Palmer and Benjamin Woodward as the new central-government prison inspectors in 1821. The 1810 act set out in detail the minimum standards for the architecture of a county gaol and demanded that all designs must be approved by central government before building work commenced. It allowed, for the first time, central government to make loans to help grand jurors to improve or rebuild their gaols. After this act the pace of building returned to its previous peak in the 1780s – the era of Howard and Fitzpatrick. It is argued that this second building boom owed more to the 1810 act than to any significant or sustained local increase in crime. Nevertheless, after the Napoleonic wars ended in 1815, unemployment, unrest, and crime added some pressure for the building of larger gaols. Despite the significant new powers that central government wielded, its agents were ill-prepared for their new role as examiners of gaol designs and it took many years for sufficient in-house expertise to accumulate.

In the meantime, many new gaols were approved only to be condemned as inadequate by the new regime under Palmer and Woodward after 1821. Central government often struggled to convince grand jurors of the necessity of engaging in large-scale rebuilding, even with the promise of cheap financing. On the other hand, in certain cases local plans became too ambitious and costly, and central government found itself attempting to rein in the enthusiasm that it had itself fostered. A competitive dynamic in gaol building emerged between grand juries, in a manner similar to the building of new courthouses at this time. Architecturally, the new gaols were to be magnificent as well as practical, ornate as well as secure. By the end of the 1810s, however, the architect's professional independence was coming under further pressure from the new professional and voluntary 'experts': Palmer and Woodward as central-government inspectors, reformers such as Thomas Spring Rice, and philanthropic groups such as the Association for the Improvement of Prisons and of Prison Discipline in Ireland (AIPPD), founded in 1818. With the exact shape and structure of the ideal 'model' prison increasingly prescribed, and with the need for government to approve gaol plans clearly defined, the architect had less involvement in the mechanics of gaol design; his trade was taken over by a resurgent penal-reform movement. In this new environment, the grand jurors had less influence over gaol building than ever before.

Chapter 6 looks at the development of Irish prison architecture between 1821 and 1838, when almost every grand jury again rebuilt their county gaols with the help of extensive central-government loans, and the reorganised and much more professional new prison inspectors. The book shows how the AIPPD, the evangelical humanitarianism of Charles Grant (Irish chief secretary between 1818 and 1822), and the work of the new inspectors paved the way for a new dynamic between central government and the grand juries. It is demonstrated that the state of crime, on a county-by-county basis, was a less important factor in pushing grand jurors to commit to rebuilding their county gaols than the increasingly coherent efforts of central government and voluntary groups to instigate reform. There is an analysis of the effect of contemporary debates on penal reform in Britain, such as the competing views over what constituted the best physical arrangement of a prison building. The effect that philanthropic societies had in improving the condition of female prisoners is briefly explored, as well as the impact of reforms to grand juries in the years between 1829 and 1836, as discussed in relation to courthouse-building in Chapter 3. The analysis concludes with a survey of Irish gaols in the late 1830s and introduces the growing fashion for the 'separate system' of confinement that was formally adopted as the preferred design for gaols in 1840.

Finally, Chapter 7 considers the history of the county gaol up to around 1860. After the perceived failure of the gaols built under the tutelage of the AIPPD and the new central-government inspectors, and a substantial increase in crime levels in the 1820s and early 1830s, new ideas emerged about what could be the design of a better 'model' prison. Borrowing from experimental 'silent-system' and 'separate-system' confinement as practised in the United States of America, and developments in Britain, Irish penal reformers now called for another vast rebuilding programme that would allow prisoners to be kept in individual cells, with little or no contact with the outside world or other inmates. Isolation was seen as a solution to the perennial problem of 'moral contagion' among prisoners, and the logical conclusion of classification. In Ireland, the central-government inspectors concluded that the separate system was the most advantageous type of confinement and, following its formal adoption in an 1840 act of parliament, they set about attempting to convince grand jurors to make extensive alterations to their relatively new gaols in order to implement this system. They were met, understandably, with little enthusiasm. Over the next twenty years, nonetheless, many gaols were slowly adapted, in a piece-meal fashion, to the separate system.

Architecturally, this meant larger cells that were better heated and ventilated. The few completely new gaols built at this time became 'models' for the new system, including the vast prisons at Belfast (Crumlin Road gaol) and Dublin (Mountjoy convict prison), each based upon the British 'model' prison at Pentonville, London. At this time, a series of professional scandals and the singular catastrophe of the Famine years put huge pressure on the prison system. Its foremost advocates, the inspectors, despaired at the unprecedented suffering and crime throughout the country. After the Famine, with a greatly reduced prison population and falling crime rates, the process of converting gaols to the separate system continued, and was largely complete by the mid-1860s. Throughout this period, an increasingly professionalised class of prison reformers, including engineers, statisticians, chaplains, and administrators, left little space for either architectural inventiveness (except in the decorative aspects of façades), or grand-jury individuality; instead, central government extended much more power over gaol building and management. This chapter concludes with a very brief summary of the few gaols that were built in the late 1850s and early 1860s, and how the prison system continued to evolve after this time, culminating in the complete central-government takeover of the prison system in an act introduced in 1877.

This book ends with some reflections on the colonial legacy of these buildings, the roles of different patrons and the changing status of the architect. It brings together discussions throughout the book on the impact this great era of building had on the shape and appearance of Irish provincial cities and towns. It also poses some questions for further research. For example, my focus here is for the most part on the largest and most impressive types of courthouses and prisons in Ireland: the assize courthouse and the county prison. Needless to say, there were many other types of courthouses and prisons throughout the country, not least the vast network of smaller buildings – quarter-session and petty-session courthouses – cheaper, smaller, generally less ornate structures that were found in almost every provincial city and town. Similarly, county gaols were complemented by over one hundred bridewells, corporation prisons, and all manner of small lock-ups. The history of all of these buildings was also greatly affected by grand-jury reform, the state of crime and unrest in a given county, and the availability of central-government loans. They are in the background here not because their story is unimportant but simply because there is not enough space to consider them in the depth that they deserve. A great deal of research remains to be carried out into their history – how and why they were built, and whether their narrative complements or contradicts that suggested for assize courthouses and gaols in this book.[58]

The main body of this book is followed by four substantial appendices that are referenced throughout the seven chapters. Appendix A is a detailed 'buildings history' of every known Irish assize courthouse and county gaol and includes details of the later history of these buildings and remarks on their condition today. Appendices B, C, and D are compiled from parliamentary papers and show respectively figures for criminal indictments, grand-jury presentments for courthouses and prisons, and central-government loans. It is hoped that these will be useful to future scholars who approach the subject or other public-works programmes of the period.

PART 1

The Assize Courthouse

Market house
Crown Court
Civil Bill Court
Store Room
Constabulary Barrack
Military Barrack
Hospital

Chapter 1

The Spoils of War:

Upheaval and rebellion at home and abroad, 1786-1817

The architectural development of the assize courthouse as a distinct type of building in the Irish urban landscape went hand-in-hand with the new opportunities presented by a prolonged period of economic expansion. For most of this period, grand juries – who exercised sole responsibility for the planning and building of assize courthouses – proceeded to improve their county towns with new public buildings unhindered by legal or financial restrictions. This was an environment in which an enterprising architect who promised a more spatially complex or aesthetically distinguished building could introduce new standards for others to follow, as James Gandon did in Waterford in the 1780s (to be discussed shortly). As the assize courthouse moved further and further from its markethouse or 'tholsel' origins (words used interchangeably in Ireland) and became typologically unique and recognisable, so too did grand juries become more receptive to paying for buildings whose architectural sophistication outstripped the ambitions of their predecessors. In some cases, a crisis precipitated building work – and none more so than the destruction caused by the great rebellion of 1798 – but less dramatic forces were as important: an increasingly prosperous and litigious society, and rivalry between neighbouring grand juries. In this early period there was remarkably little involvement from central government in the matter of courthouse building, except of course for the *non plus ultra* of all Irish courthouses, the Four Courts in Dublin, built from the 1770s through to the early 1800s, which was managed and funded entirely by Dublin Castle.[1] This construction site by the River Liffey – a hive of activity at the end of the eighteenth century – brought with it an exacting new standard for public architecture by which grand juries were later judged. As discussed below, in the final years of the long European wars around 1810, new political and economic liberties encouraged some grand juries to compete as best they could with the example set by the Four Courts. This chapter focuses more on architectural and stylistic developments than subsequent chapters – not least because of the relative scarcity of surviving written records for grand juries in the eighteenth century.

Courthouses grew out of markethouses. Though grand juries were permitted to make presentments for building or repairing courthouses as early as 1705, many continued to use small, architecturally undistinguished markethouse buildings until well into the middle of the eighteenth century.[2] Clare Graham has shown that there was a similar lack of interest in architectural expression in many English towns at the same period.[3] It is therefore not surprising that one of the first Irish laws to specifically mention courthouses, in 1768, simply confirmed the long-understood right of grand juries to make presentments for the renting of buildings to hold their sessions.[4] There was no statement of what a grand jury should do if its members decided that a new building was required, and in these cases the legal mechanism was simply to apply standard contract law between an architect (often termed a contractor or an overseer) and one or more members of the grand jury.

The earliest surviving assize courthouse – as distinct from a markethouse – is at Lifford, County Donegal (Fig. 1.1). Planned from 1743, it was built

Fig. 1.1 Lifford courthouse, the earliest surviving assize courthouse, built 1746–54. The building established not only an architectural precedent but also dictated the town's future shape. (*Photograph by author, 2014.*)

between 1746 and 1754 by the local architect Michael Priestley, of whom we know little.[5] The window and door surrounds have details likely taken from the then-fashionable English architect James Gibbs (1682–1754), though a crenelated Gothic parapet, since removed, hints at more provincial sources.[6] The building of this courthouse was a matter of pride for the grand jurors of the time, who took to commemorating themselves and their architect in a plaque and in a framed coat of arms crowning the main entranceway, itself remarkably architecturally literate and modish for such an early date (Fig. 1.2). Like so many assize courthouses that were to follow Lifford's example in the eighteenth century, there was a county gaol in the basement – a grim and unhealthy dungeon used until a new gaol (Fig. 1.3) was built in *c.* 1793 (see Chapter 4).[7] Apart from the embellished doorway, there were few revolutions in design at Lifford, certainly when compared with what would come forty years later in Waterford under a different architect. The interior was little more than two large rectangular rooms, but that was enough in the 1750s to stage the informal and brief assizes. The achievement of the Donegal grand jury was in giving the main façade, facing the market square later known as the Diamond (Fig. 1.4), an appearance different from the typical markethouse that had preceded it, and thereby establishing the Irish roots for this new type of building. Furthermore, by deciding to project the main façade into the square,

Fig. 1.2. Lifford courthouse. As well as naming the architect, the plaque above the doorway lists five members of the Donegal grand jury in 1746. (*Photograph by author, 2014.*)

the architect or his grand-jury patrons chose not to face the River Foyle behind, a choice that influenced all subsequent development in the town.

Although Lifford was an unusually minor county town (population in 1841: 752 persons), by the early nineteenth century it hosted not only a courthouse and county gaol but also an infirmary and a lunatic asylum – the essential quartet of public buildings for any county town.[8] The economic dividends from constructing and maintaining these public institutions were vital to the

Fig. 1.3. Lifford gaol, *c.* 1900. Until this gaol was built in the 1790s (see Chapter 4), Donegal's prisoners were kept in the basement of the courthouse. The courthouse once boasted a Gothic parapet similar to the gaol. (*Reproduced courtesy of Donegal County Archives.*)

town's prospects, even if the nearby and much larger town of Strabane, County Tyrone, benefited more with its better shops, accommodation, and transport links. The proximity of Strabane is at least part of the reason why Lifford courthouse survives so remarkably unaltered to this day, when many other grand juries built and rebuilt courthouses often within a single generation. In Donegal, as in many other similarly sized counties, we find, roughly speaking, a doubling of the average criminal-indictment rate between the first years of the nineteenth century and the decade before the Famine.[9] This phenomenon pushed some grand juries at the time to build larger courthouses, as much to project an architectural expression of the law as to house the larger crowds that attended the trials. Yet in Donegal nothing of substance happened.[10] This was likely because there was little economic dividend for the Donegal grand jurors in committing to architectural expenditure in a town so close to the county boundary (Fig. 1.5). The town of Lifford, therefore, suffered because of its location. Henry David Inglis, visiting in 1834, thought it 'the very least

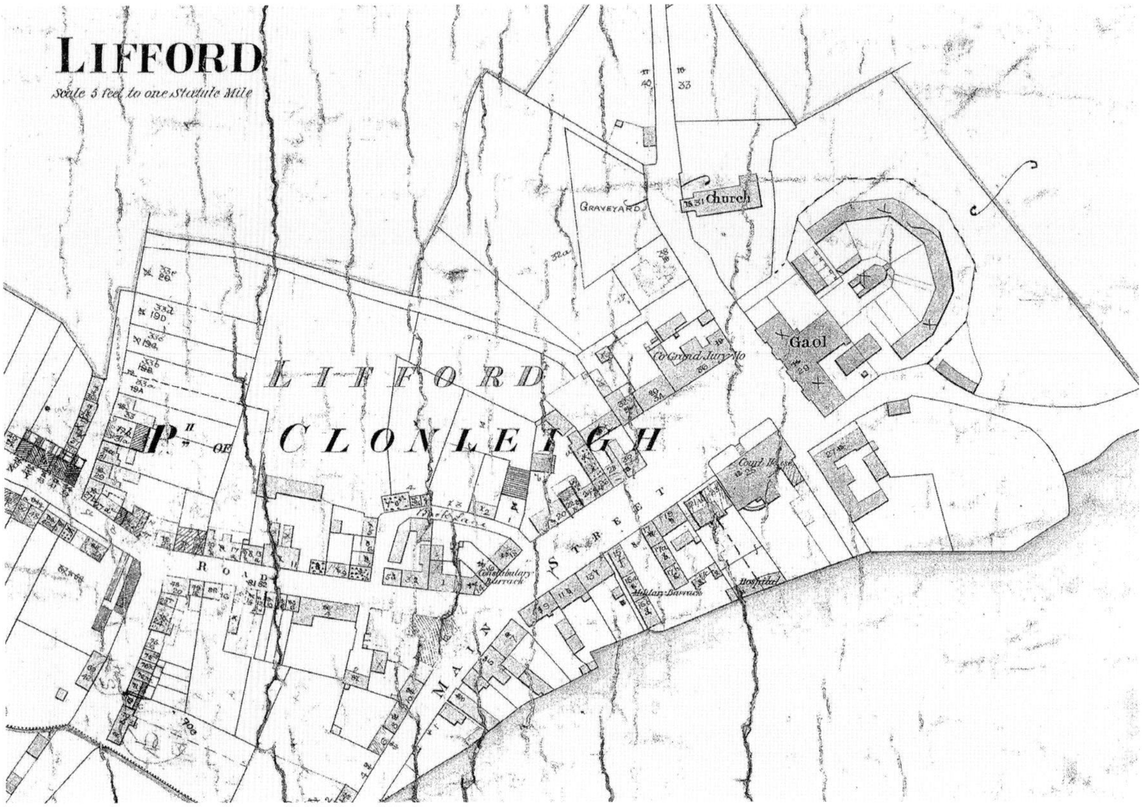

of all county towns' and remarked that 'although the assizes are held … the neighbouring town of Strabane … reaps all the benefit'.[11] And in 1850 the nationalist Charles Gavan Duffy passed through Lifford and considered it a

> withered town …, dead as Herculaneum or Pompeii …. There was an enormous gaol, the stately courthouse, a palace for the police, lodgings for my lords the judges, the messrooms for their worships the grand jury: but not a human creature on the streets, not a pulse of industry – nothing but the grim silent castles of authority and the miserable cabins of the poor.[12]

Fig. 1.4. Lifford Ordnance Survey town map, showing the Diamond, *c.* 1850. By this time the central square had grand-jury rooms, a nearby Protestant church, the county gaol, a lunatic asylum, and the assize courthouse. Together they gave an economic purpose to the town. (*Reproduced courtesy of the Board of Trinity College Dublin.*)

Clearly the geography of a town – as well as the staging of the assizes – could bring either prosperity or stagnation. As discussed in Chapter 3, there were other provincial towns that prospered when they gained assize status later in the nineteenth century.

Fig. 1.5. Lifford and Strabane, separated by the River Foyle. Much of the economic rewards of Donegal's public buildings flowed east to neighbouring County Tyrone. This limited the willingness of the Donegal grand jury to commit resources to rebuilding their courthouse. Ordnance Survey six-inch maps, 1833–4. (*Reproduced courtesy of the Board of Trinity College Dublin.*)

There is no clear trend for which counties decided to build new courthouses in these early years (Fig. 1.6). What is evident is that central government was almost entirely absent in these local decisions – such interference, mostly to limit spending, would only come in the early nineteenth century. Several grand juries sought local acts of parliament in the 1770s and 1780s to give their new courthouse projects some legal standing, but others proceeded without them.[13] The new public architecture of these years must of course be seen in the context of economic prosperity and population growth, of new towns, new streets, and urban renewal.[14] Yet the lack of a clear trend is apparent in a town such as Tullamore – re-planned after a fire in 1785 – which only became the assize town for King's County (Offaly) in the 1830s, and until then continued to use a small old courthouse (as discussed in Chapter 3).[15] There was no unambiguous link in these years between town improvement and the building of new assize courthouses. Where building did occur in the 1760s and 1770s, it tended to be in the historic cities and towns that had independent county status – the wealthier eastern towns of Kilkenny, Drogheda, and Carrickfergus (Figs 1.7–1.9). These maintained their own grand juries, entirely separate from the counties that surrounded them. Carrickfergus thus had two courthouses – one for the town and the other for the county of Antrim, and when the county built a new courthouse in the 1770s, along the lines of Lifford but less ornate, the town took over the old county building.[16] In Kilkenny the town took the initiative first, building a combined markethouse and courthouse in the 1760s in the manner typical of an English markethouse of the time (for example, at Blandford in Dorset), and the county followed later in the century.[17]

Beyond the markethouse

By the 1760s, with the exception of the new courthouse at Lifford, the architectural link between the markethouse and the courthouse had not yet been fully broken, and courthouses continued to serve a multitude of functions – not least private meetings for the grand jurors, occasional banquets, and

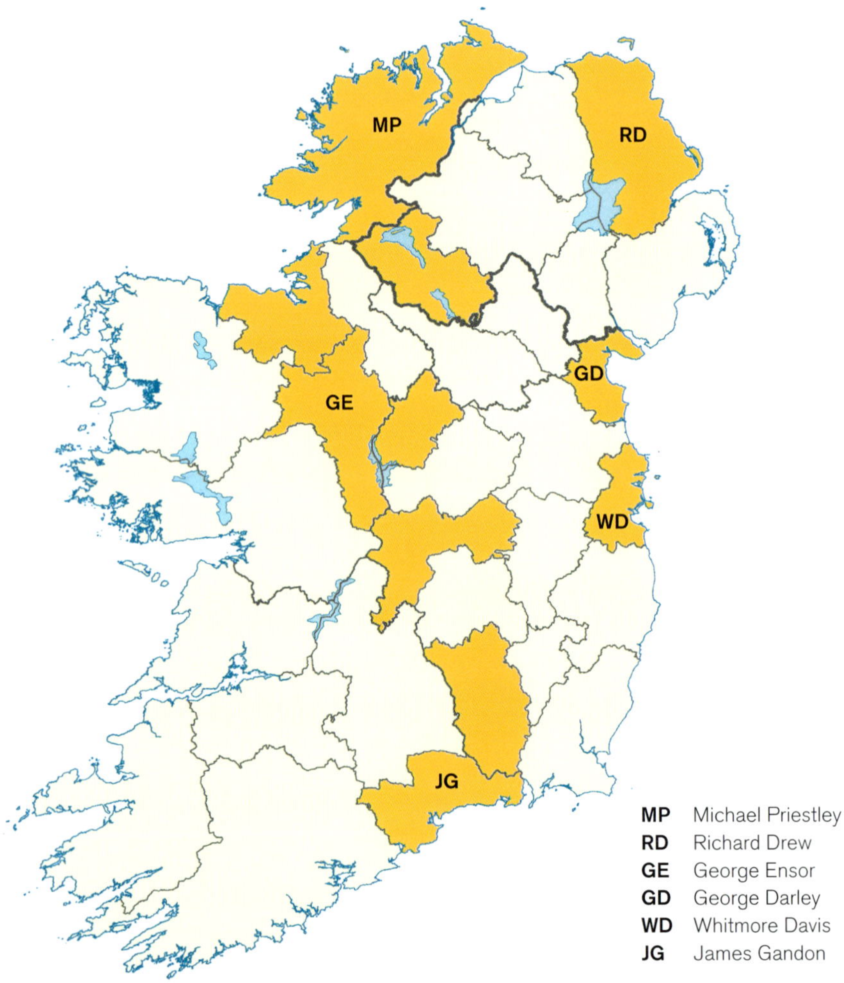

Fig. 1.6. A tentative map of new assize courthouses built from 1746 to 1798, with the architect responsible, where known. A larger number of counties would be highlighted if it were possible to accurately identify significant alterations to existing buildings. From Appendix A.

Fig. 1.7. Kilkenny's tholsel, *c.* 1900. A typical mixed-use markethouse and courthouse from the mid-eighteenth century. Traders were sheltered by the arcade, which so dramatically projects into the street, while court sittings were held upstairs. (*Reproduced courtesy of the National Library of Ireland.*)

Fig. 1.8. Drogheda's tholsel, *c.* 1900. The grand jury of the town of Drogheda held jurisdiction over one of the smallest administrative counties in Ireland. Their combined markethouse and courthouse was located at the crossing of the town's principal streets. (*Reproduced courtesy of the National Library of Ireland.*)

Fig. 1.9. Carrickfergus courthouse. This county courthouse should not be confused with the *town* of Carrickfergus' courthouse, which was located nearby (since demolished). The county courthouse was built at the termination of the town's main street and continued to be used by grand jurors until a shift caused by the gravitational pull of Belfast in the mid-nineteenth century. (*Photograph by author, 2014.*)

Fig. 1.10. Longford courthouse, *c.* 1900. Instead of projecting into the town's main street, the courthouse shows its importance as the chief county building by being set back from nearby buildings. The town's magnate – Lord Longford – was instrumental in its construction. The top storey is a Victorian addition. (*Reproduced courtesy of the National Library of Ireland.*)

space for trading – in addition to hosting court sittings. The next major advance came with events in Roscommon in the 1760s, where we are fortunate to have surviving drawings that show not only the winning design but also an unexecuted alternative. Regionally, the commission appears to have set off a new competitive spirit among the grand juries of nearby counties, and in a relatively short period afterwards both Longford (Fig. 1.10) and Sligo replaced their old courthouses.[18] But Roscommon is without doubt the most important and shows an evolution in architectural typology. The unexecuted design, probably by the little-known architect Oliver Crawford (Figs 1.11, 1.13), is essentially an arcaded markethouse like Kilkenny, with plenty of shelter at ground level for the trading and housing of goods, and with a *piano nobile* meeting room above. Despite its old-fashioned plan, it received support from some members of the grand jury.[19] In this design, the courtroom occupies only a very small portion of the overall building, with the entire ground floor given over to a colonnaded marketplace with flanking store rooms; on the *piano nobile* the courtroom occupies the central three bays of the seven-bay façade. From the main elevation, the judicial function is undoubtedly concealed. Very different is the design by George Ensor, ultimately successful in the competition (Figs 1.12, 1.14). As Edward McParland has remarked, 'accommodation for the market [is] reduced so that the judicial nature of the building is emphasized'.[20] Ensor provided for two courtrooms instead of one, and placed a much smaller market space to the rear of the building; this arrangement led to some inconvenient passages that were criticised by one grand juror at the time (such as for the petty jurors, who had a circuitous route into the crown court) but the grand jurors were provided with a generous meeting room.[21] The main façade was less like a markethouse than any courthouse then built except perhaps Lifford, with two large astylar doors in the Burlington tradition crowned by thermal windows (referred to at the time as 'Egyptian windows') that lit the courtrooms, and with the central focus emphasised by a Serliana window motif.[22] It provided no arcaded shelter for the traders or their goods, and its symmetrical doorways at either end suggested a building with a more complicated internal division of spaces than a single large market space. The courthouse, as at Lifford, faced onto a market square framed by the old county gaol (Fig. 1.15) – an aspect less apparent today owing to substantial later alterations to both buildings (Fig. 1.16). Typical of the feverish building work of the early nineteenth century (see Chapter 2), this courthouse served the county only until about 1824, when another new building was erected nearby.[23]

Fig. 1.11. (top) Roscommon courthouse, unexecuted scheme, elevation, *c.* 1762. Oliver Crawford proposed a recognisable markethouse composition, but the grand jury was willing to be more experimental. Almost the entirety of this building would have been given over to market functions. (*Reproduced courtesy of the National Library of Ireland.*)

Fig. 1.12. (centre) Roscommon courthouse, as built, elevation, *c.* 1762. George Ensor's design sought to end the traditional association of markethouses and courthouses, and his façade expresses this distinction. Both doorways gave direct access to courtrooms. (*Reproduced courtesy of the National Library of Ireland.*)

Fig. 1.13. (bottom) Roscommon courthouse, unexecuted scheme, ground- and first-floor plans, *c.* 1762. Crawford gave over the entire ground floor to market functions – storerooms and a large colonnaded trading area. Upstairs there was just one courtroom. (*Reproduced courtesy of the National Library of Ireland.*)

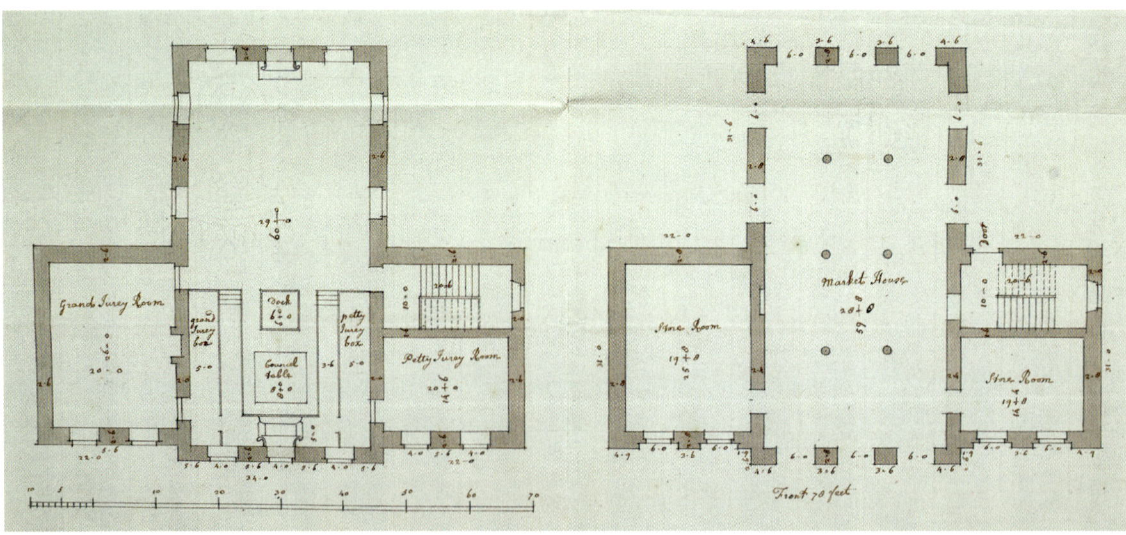

Fig. 1.14. Roscommon courthouse, as built, ground-floor plan, *c.* 1762. Ensor provided for two courtrooms and more space, on the first floor, for the grand jury. The trading area was in turn dramatically reduced in size and importance and was accessible only from the rear. (*Reproduced courtesy of the National Library of Ireland.*)

Fig. 1.15. Roscommon gaol and marketplace, *c.* 1900. Ensor's courthouse looked out onto the county gaol and a cattle market as in this late nineteenth-century view. In the 1820s both courthouse and gaol were relocated elsewhere in the town (see Chapter 2). (*Reproduced courtesy of the National Library of Ireland.*)

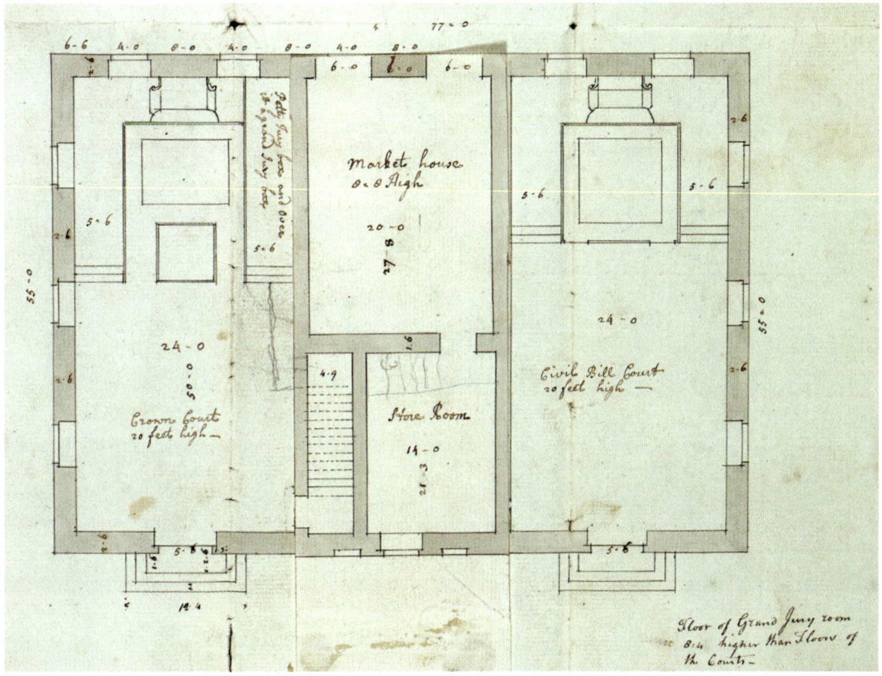

Fig. 1.16. Roscommon courthouse, after many nineteenth-century alterations. Though terminating the principal street of the town, the entrance to the courtrooms was at the opposite side to the view shown. A corner of the crenelated gaol appears in the background. The portico and tower date from the building's later use as a chapel and a bank. (*Photograph by author, 2012.*)

Gandon's courthouse at Waterford

Ensor's design provides us with a benchmark with which to judge the next major advance, that of James Gandon's courthouse at Waterford in the 1780s. By then work had begun on the Four Courts (Fig. 1.17) under the architect Thomas Cooley, but the final design of this celebrated building is closely associated with Gandon, who took control of the project upon Cooley's death in 1784.[24] Gandon had trained with William Chambers in London and brought to Ireland a new style of fashionable neo-classical architecture, heavily indebted to French as well as English sources.[25] The Four Courts is perhaps his most important building, but in terms of courthouse design in Ireland, it was his long-since vanished courthouse in Waterford that had much greater influence. This was because, as types of buildings, the Four Courts and the standard assize courthouse were fundamentally very different. The Four Courts dealt primarily with the most important national cases and appeals and did not have the same social functions as a provincial courthouse. No provincial grand jury could have afforded such an expensive building, and there was no prospect that it could have surpassed the splendour of Gandon's design (or its location). Provincial assize courthouses, by comparison, provided a crown and a civil bills courtroom, and at least one social room for the local grand jury to meet. Thus, to understand the history of the assize courthouse, we must look beyond the Four Courts and explore Gandon's involvement in designing a new joint courthouse and gaol for the city and county grand juries in Waterford. Indeed, his Waterford commission began *before* he took command of works at the Four Courts.[26] The connection between the two projects had been made by the wealthy Dublin patron John Beresford, who brought Gandon to Dublin in 1781 to design a new Custom House (Fig. 1.18). Beresford's brother, George de la Poer Beresford, 2nd Earl of Tyrone, was impressed by Gandon's skills and asked him to come to Waterford and prepare plans for a new courthouse for both grand juries.

The Waterford project in the 1780s represented the first time that two grand juries had joined forces in building a single courthouse and was also the first time that an architect had systematically designed a courthouse with no residual market function (the gaol is discussed in Chapter 4). As McParland has noted, the 'commercial implications' of the markethouse were finally removed, and the transition that Ensor had begun at Roscommon was thus brought to completion.[27] Beresford was an important patron of neo-classical architecture and had employed James Wyatt at his mansion at Curraghmore (Fig. 1.19) in the late 1770s.[28] He lured Gandon out of the political fray of the capital to Waterford but gaining the approval of both grand juries was a more difficult task. Relations between them and Gandon made the project testing for all

Fig. 1.17. The Four Courts, Dublin, built by Thomas Cooley and James Gandon from the 1770s. It was not completed until after the Act of Union. Though easily the most splendid of all Irish courthouses, it had little impact on the design of smaller assize courthouses in the provincial towns. Photograph of *c.* 1900 before it was partially destroyed and rebuilt. (*Reproduced courtesy of the National Library of Ireland.*)

Fig. 1.18. Custom House, Dublin. The building of this new commercial hub for the city brought a talented architect, James Gandon, to Dublin in the 1780s. Through family connections, it also brought him to Waterford where he designed one of the most influential Irish assize courthouses. (*Photograph by author, 2011.*)

Fig. 1.19. Curraghmore, County Waterford, *c.* 1900. Home of the Beresfords, who patronised leading neo-classical architects from Britain such as James Wyatt. As members of the Waterford grand juries, the family also oversaw the erection of a neo-classical courthouse by James Gandon. (*Reproduced courtesy of the National Library of Ireland.*)

involved. They assumed, Gandon later recalled, that he was 'a contractor, or as they termed me, "a projector and undertaker"'.[29] The differences with the grand jurors were later resolved and the courthouse was erected between 1784 and 1786.[30]

Gandon's design for Waterford influenced almost every subsequent courthouse in Ireland, right through to the 1850s. Inspired by Sanderson Miller's work at Warwick Shire Hall in 1754–8, he produced two schemes for the new county hall (effectively assize courthouse) at Nottingham, published in *Vitruvius Britannicus* in 1771 (Fig. 1.20).[31] The less innovative of these schemes had, in the end, been built (Fig. 1.21), but at Waterford Gandon rescued his more adventurous unexecuted design and put it to work. The plan (Fig. 1.22) was remarkably simple – a large vestibule (Fig. 1.23) that led through open colonnades into two parallel courtrooms for crown cases and civil bills. Perhaps it was the simplicity of this arrangement, which provided a large social space for mingling and meetings, and which reduced the transfer of noise between the respective courtrooms, that so appealed to other grand juries in later years. Gandon embellished the interior of the vestibule with string-courses, recessed arches, and niches, giving the whole composition a characteristic statement of his restrained and distinctive neo-classical style. The façade (Fig. 1.24), of granite, with its central triumphal-arch motif and low wings, somewhat resembled a scaled-down Four Courts and hid the county gaol behind from direct view.[32] For the site the grand jury selected a former barracks, at the crest of a small hill south of the historic centre of the city, at the termination of a broad street known as Mayor's Walk and a large market space, Ballybricken Green (Fig. 1.25).[33] Over the next sixty years architects and grand jurors from all around Ireland made pilgrimages to Waterford to learn from the design and improve it further. One foreign traveller in 1835 thought it simply 'a handsome and large establishment'.[34]

Fig. 1.20. Nottingham Shire Hall, elevation, by Gandon. From *Vitruvius Britannicus* (1771). Though Nottingham's courthouse still stands, its sister (or perhaps brother, as Gandon swapped the Ionic for the Doric) in Waterford is long since demolished. (*Reproduced courtesy of Cambridge University Library.*)

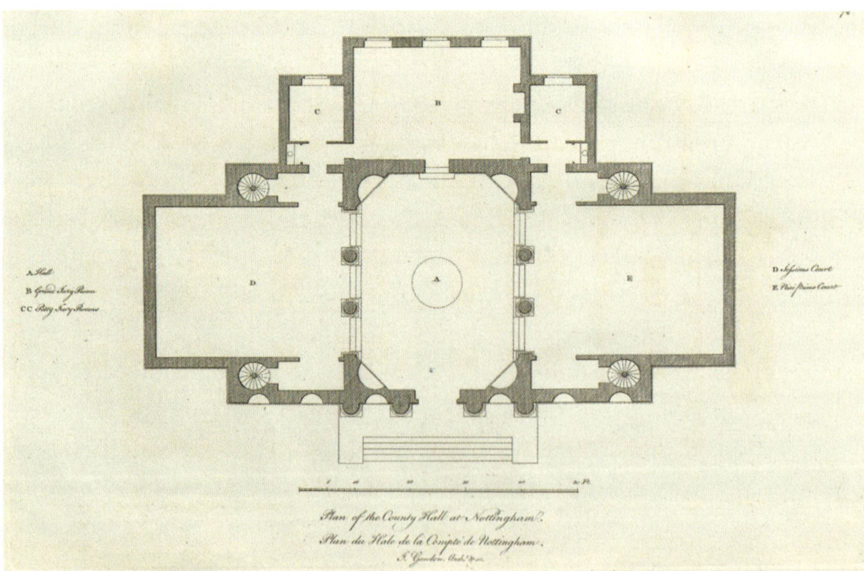

Fig. 1.21. Plan of Nottingham Shire Hall, by Gandon. From *Vitruvius Britannicus* (1771). Both courtrooms opened onto each other axially, screened by colonnades. Some Irish courthouses later followed this arrangement, but more popular was the alternative scheme illustrated by Gandon in the same volume, and which he used in Waterford. (*Reproduced courtesy of Cambridge University Library.*)

Fig. 1.22. Unexecuted plan for Nottingham Shire Hall (later adapted for Waterford city and county courthouse), by Gandon. From *Vitruvius Britannicus* (1771). Depicted as an alternative to the design at Nottingham, this plan is what Gandon deployed at Waterford (with some minor alterations), where a large vestibule gave access to both courtrooms, separated by a series of meeting rooms and stairs to the grand jury's quarters. (*Reproduced courtesy of Cambridge University Library.*)

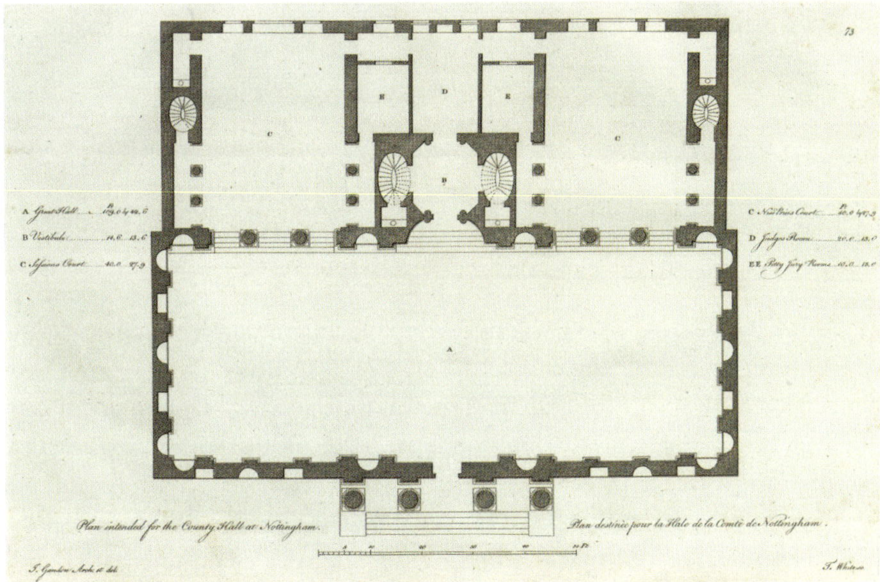

Fig. 1.23. Vestibule of Waterford city and county courthouse, perspective drawing. Gandon provided a new level of architectural sophistication and dignity for the holding of assize courts, using fashionable neo-classical motifs of the time. (*Reproduced courtesy of the Irish Architectural Archive.*)

Before considering the effects of the 1798 rebellion and legislative reforms to grand juries towards the end of the eighteenth century, we turn to a new courthouse in the centre of Dublin. This was for the city of Dublin grand jury at Green Street (Fig. 1.26), within walking distance of the Four Courts, which was built to replace a dangerously unstable seventeenth-century tholsel.[35] Like so many other new courthouses of the time, it was situated adjacent to the city gaol (Newgate, see Chapter 4), allowing easy transfer of prisoners back and forth. Although designed to be used by both city and county grand juries,[36] in practice the county had little need for it, and in plan the courthouse is less interesting than Waterford as it provides only a single courtroom. Yet if the west portion of the courthouse indeed dates from the period of the original building,

Fig. 1.24. Waterford city and county courthouse, elevation drawing reconstructed by Conor Rochford, from a copper plate in the National Library of Ireland's prints and drawings collection. Reminiscent of the tripartite division of the Four Courts, but completed much earlier, Gandon's colonnaded screen hid the county gaol behind. The central block is like his earlier Nottingham design. (*Reproduced courtesy of Conor Rochford and the Royal Irish Academy.*)

Fig. 1.25. Ballybricken Green, Waterford, *c.* 1900, onto which Gandon's courthouse looked. (*Reproduced courtesy of the National Library of Ireland.*)

Fig. 1.26. Dublin Green Street courthouse, from the east. To the left was once Newgate gaol, the city of Dublin's prison, and to the right the sheriff's prison and city marshalsea. (*Photograph by author, 2014.*)

as is currently believed, the porticoed entrance block, mostly of rubble stone, is likely the earliest instance of a completely separate private entrance for grand-jury members, something that became much more common in the nineteenth century, and a clear indicator of the centrality of grand juries in the design and construction of large courthouses. The east façade (Fig. 1.26) may also be a first of kinds – the first time that a temple front appears in an Irish courthouse.

Christine Casey has noted that the 1780s and 1790s were a period of great expansion in the Irish legal system, with new quarter-sessions courts established, and new powers given to grand juries to cover the building of new courthouses.[37] It was also a time of unrest, sporadic threats of rebellion, and the outbreak of war with revolutionary France from 1793 onwards.[38] The reforms to grand juries need to be seen in this broader context. They aimed to make old-style 'corruption' more difficult. One law, enacted in 1796, constituted the first real attempt to limit their spending power. Sworn affidavits were to be produced for planned expenditure for the first time, and though grand juries were allowed to appoint overseers to carry out agreed public works, they were not allowed to pay them more than one shilling in the pound (a commission of five per cent).[39] This provision caused headaches for the more scrupulous grand jurors of the early nineteenth century, keen to follow the letter of the law. Others were less concerned and continued as before. Indeed, this first attempt to reform the building work of grand juries achieved very little in practice, except perhaps to show that central government could in fact encroach on the hitherto autonomous governance of these local bodies. The stage was set for the major showdowns that would follow in the 1810s and 1830s (as discussed in later chapters). In the 1790s, however, other events took precedence. The French invasion scare of 1796 and the large-scale rebellion of 1798 pushed such issues as grand-jury reform onto the back burner for several years, and when they resurfaced, they were debated not in Dublin but at Westminster.[40]

Rebellion and reaction

The sustained economic boom that resulted from the Napoleonic wars provided the dividends that were needed for such extensive courthouse construction, but the destruction of 1798 created a much more urgent need to rebuild, not simply for practical reasons but also as a statement of power and control. The Act of Union also opened up space for a new generation of architects to establish themselves as the most influential of the older generation – Gandon – briefly took refuge from the unrest in England.[41] For the landed elite, many of whom earned new peerages for their 'patriotic' actions against the United Irishmen revolutionaries, the years after 1798 were a chance to consolidate their positions with estate improvements, the planning of towns, and the erection of splendid country houses, increasingly in a symbolically defensive Gothic style that was growing in popularity throughout Europe.[42] Collectively, these members of the landed elite funded new public buildings through their grand juries, and nowhere was this more obvious than in the construction of courthouses. Fifteen were built anew between the rebellion of 1798 and 1817 (Fig. 1.27), and Richard Morrison – an architect who was closely associated with Gandon, and who built many country houses – was responsible for at least half of them. The list of counties that funded new courthouses stretches from Cork to Derry and from Galway to Wexford. Morrison's commercial success can be attributed to two main factors: first, his father's many connections in architectural circles (in, for example, his employment by the Earl of Kingston in re-planning Mitchelstown, County Cork). And second, the convenient design, inspired by Gandon, that he used in most of his schemes. Despite this, Morrison's success was more quantitative than qualitative, and the three most splendid and expensive of the new courthouses of these years went to rival figures, as discussed below: Francis Johnston, John Bowden, and Edward Parke.[43]

Fig. 1.27. New assize courthouses built in Ireland, 1798–1817, with architect responsible, where known. Few counties escaped the frenzied rebuilding and competitive inter-county spirit of the war years, except those which had only recently completed new buildings.

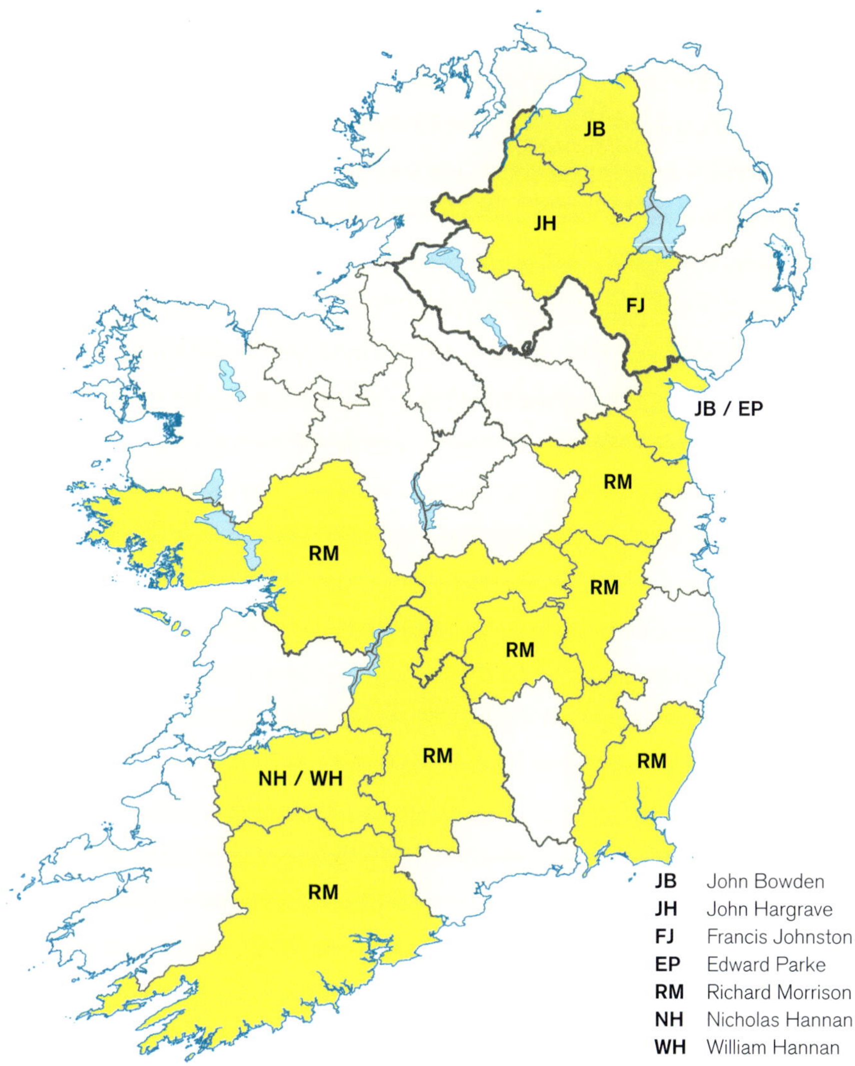

The great Irish rebellion of 1798 had a major effect on the nation's assize courthouses. Many were burned or occupied by the rebels as towns were captured and recaptured. The damage was especially acute in south-east Leinster in the counties of Wicklow, Wexford, Kildare, and Carlow, and in towns such as Naas, Athy, and Wexford, which were severely damaged in the fighting.[44] The unusually low levels of recorded criminal indictments in Irish assize courthouses in 1798 shows not so much the state of the country as the breakdown of the established legal and bureaucratic systems.[45] Travel writing in the immediate aftermath provides a sense of the destruction: John Carr thought Castlecomer in County Kilkenny in late 1805 'still retained many visible

Clockwise from top left: **Fig. 1.28.** Clonmel courthouse, *c.* 1900. One of Richard Morrison's first assize courthouses, this restrained Palladian composition was somewhat old-fashioned by the time it was built in 1800. It replaced a tholsel built in 1674–5 known as the Main Guard. During the agrarian violence of the early nineteenth century few assize courthouses witnessed more trials than this building, but pressure was relieved in the 1830s with the division of Tipperary into two ridings and the construction of a new courthouse and gaol in the North Riding town of Nenagh (discussed in Chapter 3). (*Reproduced courtesy of the National Library of Ireland.*) **Fig. 1.29.** Courtroom of Clonmel courthouse, *c.* 1985. As at Philipstown, the courtrooms were double-height and provided galleries for the public and grand juries. (*Reproduced courtesy of the Irish Architectural Archive.*) **Fig. 1.30.** Athy courthouse and markethouse, *c.* 1900. This building has a rich and extended history, but it is likely that the relief panels showing the scales of justice date from early nineteenth-century work carried out by Richard Morrison. Much later, an additional storey was built, and the cupola was taken down. To the right, in a Tudor style, is the corn exchange of the 1850s, which later became a courthouse. (*Reproduced courtesy of the National Library of Ireland.*)

Fig. 1.31. Limerick county courthouse. When completed in 1814, the county gaol was still situated nearby. In later years, this old gaol was used by the city, which added its own courthouse to the site, reinforcing the administrative character of this part of the city (see Chapter 3). (*Photograph by author, 2013.*)

Fig. 1.32. Maryborough (Portlaoise) courthouse. Another of Richard Morrison's courthouses, it has survived better than most, and shows his restraint in using neo-classical motifs. (*Photograph by author, 2014.*)

marks of its melancholy fate during the rebellion of 1798, when it was nearly reduced to ashes', and in Naas, he observed, 'roofless and half-demolished houses display the gloomy effect of that civil war'.[46] Johann Friedrich Hering, a German soldier serving in Ireland in 1806–7, remarked that he saw, 'here and there, houses that had been destroyed in the rebellion' near Kinnegad in County Westmeath.[47] As late as 1809 a tourist noted that in Arklow, County Wicklow, 'a few old cabins at each end of the town' were little more than 'shapeless ruins'. The same writer could not help seeing the 'whitening skulls

Fig. 1.33. Philipstown (Daingean) courthouse, King's County (Offaly), *c.* 1900. The large arched windows to the side, like a clerestory, hint at the exaggerated height of the courtrooms. The building's dominant presence in the diminutive county town of Philipstown was probably a political statement by the local magnates, the Ponsonbys, of their intention to resist moves from nearby Tullamore to relocate the assizes. The building has since been significantly altered. (*Reproduced courtesy of the Historical Picture Archive (Ireland).*)

which surmount the castle or the court-house, proclaim[ing] the punishment which rebellion calls for'.[48] At the same time the impact of 1798 must not be overstated – far more courthouses survived than were destroyed, for example, and the continued economic prosperity caused by high agricultural prices during the European wars led in many cases to rapid reconstruction.

In the years immediately after the rebellion new assize courthouses were built at Cork, Carlow, Philipstown, Clonmel, Wexford, Naas, Athy, Portlaoise, Limerick, and Galway (Figs 1.28–1.31).[49] Not all were direct responses to the destruction that preceded them: in Maryborough (Fig. 1.32) the threefold increase in criminal indictments between the 1780s and the 1800s was surely sufficient reason to rebuild and expand.[50] In Philipstown (Fig. 1.33) the site was provided by the local magnates, the Ponsonbys, who were keen to ensure that the Charleville family in nearby Tullamore did not succeed in relocating the assizes, with their valuable economic dividends, away from their town.[51] In Galway (Figs 1.34–1.35) all building work revolved around the much more expensive new gaol built at the same time (see Chapter 4).[52] But in Naas, Athy, Carlow, and Wexford, it is clear that the rebellion was the deciding factor, and nowhere was construction more politically fraught than by the banks of the Slaney in Wexford, where the site of the old courthouse – the Bullring – had been requisitioned by rebels during 1798 to manufacture arms, and the long wooden bridge that connected the town with a spit of land to the east had witnessed large-scale slaughter by both sides and became a politically charged site of remembrance and memory afterwards.[53] Travel writers, too, commented on the bridge and its significance – saying that 'the famous bridge of Wexford, the scene of so many murders during the rebellion of 1798, is constructed entirely of wood .... On the draw-bridge, at the end near the town, was the place chosen by the rebels for their executions, which must have been a most conspicuous place.'[54] It was this exact location (Fig. 1.36) – where the bridge met the town – that the Wexford grand jurors picked as the site for their new assize courthouse, on land partly lent by the local merchant and member of the famous Redmond dynasty, John Redmond, whose brother Walter regularly served on the county grand jury and had fought on the British side in 1798.[55] Richard Morrison's design for the building formed an axial conclusion to the bridge, overlooking all the traffic that would use it and serving as a kind of ceremonial gate for entrants to the town. Morrison was also probably involved in rebuilding parts of the nearby quays in these years.[56] The courthouse (since demolished) is known only from several old photographs (Fig. 1.37) taken in the late nineteenth century. They suggest that the façade was similar to Morrison's design for Maryborough and Naas courthouses with pedimented wings and an unpedimented central Doric portico. The plan likely followed his other schemes from these years, essentially Gandon's Waterford with only

Fig. 1.34. Galway county courthouse and county gaol behind, *c.* 1820. A new administrative quarter in Galway was created in the early nineteenth century, with new gaols and courthouses for both the county and town. Here Richard Morrison's county courthouse, with its many similarities to the central block of Gandon's Waterford design, is shown linked with the county gaol behind it by a bridge specially built for the purpose. The dignity of the courthouse is stressed by the metal bollards, a feature (now lost) of many assize courthouses. From Hardiman, *Galway*, p. 311.

minor alterations.[57] In this most politically contentious and dramatic of sites, the Wexford grand jury commissioned two portrait medallions that were inserted into the two roundels above the central portico. They showed George III, the then monarch, and William III, the hero of extreme Protestant groups, and both remained as reminders of the rebellion and the sectarian inclinations

Fig. 1.35. Lion, unicorn, and British crown, formerly part of Galway county courthouse. Removed after independence, these vigorously amateurish sculptures were saved and relocated to a garden at the rear of University College Galway (now NUI Galway). (*Photograph by author, 2017.*)

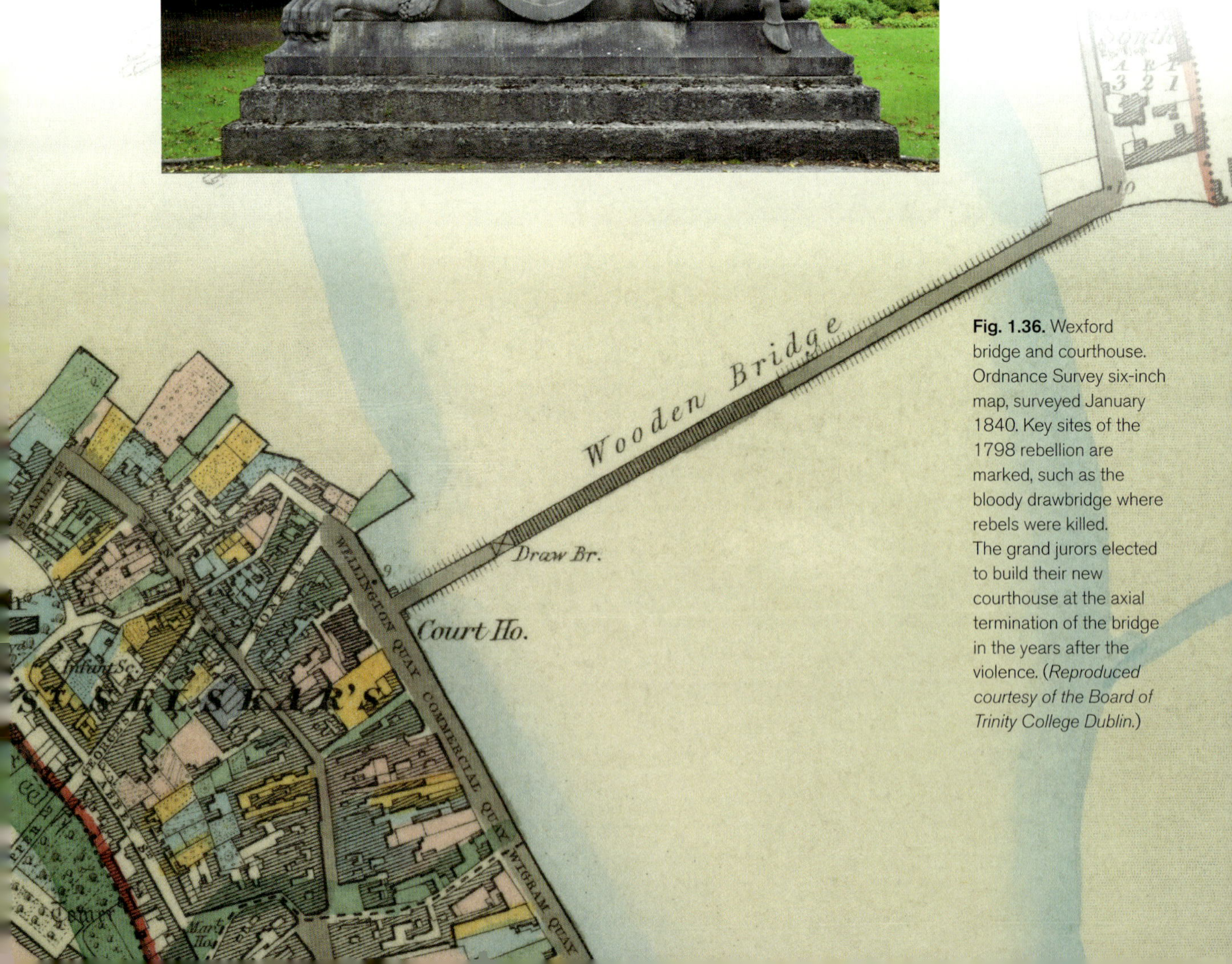

Fig. 1.36. Wexford bridge and courthouse. Ordnance Survey six-inch map, surveyed January 1840. Key sites of the 1798 rebellion are marked, such as the bloody drawbridge where rebels were killed. The grand jurors elected to build their new courthouse at the axial termination of the bridge in the years after the violence. (*Reproduced courtesy of the Board of Trinity College Dublin.*)

of the grand jury until renovations (and changing political balances) caused them to be painted over in the 1860s.[58] For George Cornwallis, sent to Ireland to pacify the country after the 1798 rebellion, the political character of local Protestant elites was all too plain to see: he thought they were 'blinded by their passions and prejudices'.[59] This sectarianism manifested itself in the appearance of a central vista – the bridging point – in the town.

Fig. 1.37. Wexford courthouse and quays, *c.* 1900. One of the roundels is visible above the entrance colonnade, but by the time of this photograph the portrait of William of Orange had vanished. The courthouse was destroyed during the revolutionary period of 1916–23. (*Reproduced courtesy of the National Library of Ireland.*)

Establishing a sounder foundation

In the early nineteenth century, assize courthouses were constructed and reconstructed at an ever-increasing pace. A useful straw in the wind is the Disused Public Buildings (Ireland) Act of 1808, which allowed grand juries to dispose of old courthouses, infirmaries, and gaols surplus to requirements.[60] This was clearly a measure prompted at least in part by the prosperity and opportunities of the time. Yet for all the confidence of the war years, the assize courthouses so far discussed were built under the somewhat ambiguous legal environment of the aforementioned 1796 act. In the years between 1807 and 1813 these difficulties were finally brought into the open and eventually resolved. The centre of architectural and political activity then shifted from the southern counties to a contiguous belt of four northern counties (Louth, Armagh, Tyrone, and Derry), where the desires of certain grand juries clashed with both the existing law and the first real attempts on the part of central government to instigate local government reform and to check the power of these local bodies.

The eighteenth-century Irish parliament in Dublin had provided a particularly useful screen for keeping problems with the Irish administration from the watchful eye of Westminster politicians. After 1800 many of these issues came into plain view, and the imperial parliament took an increased interest in Irish matters. As Gearóid Ó Tuathaigh has commented, Irish matters came to occupy Westminster when 'the drive for efficiency in the machinery of government, which had emerged in late eighteenth-century England, was applied to the Irish administration'.[61] The short-lived Grenville ministry of 1806–7, representing the first time that the Whigs had held power since the fall of the Portland ministry in 1783, marked the beginning of Irish grand-jury reform in the nineteenth century. Grenville's ministry fell in late March 1807 on the issue of Roman Catholic emancipation. Some Irish Whigs such as Sir John Newport (Chancellor of the Exchequer for Ireland in 1806–7), Maurice Fitzgerald, and William Parnell were determined to introduce a bill to reform grand-jury law but were caught off-guard by the early demise of the government. They went ahead and introduced their bill anyway, from the opposition benches, on 20 April 1807.[62] Fitzgerald called attention to the cess tax imposed by the grand juries: an 'enormous sum of half a million', mostly for roads and public buildings. He claimed that the poor bore a disproportionate share of the burden of this tax, as many landlords were absentees and cared little for their Irish estates. He argued that what was needed was 'some new regulations with respect to presentments and the proper accounting for the money'. Hoping that grand juries would consider the proposed measures at the ensuing summer assizes, he promised to return the following year with a more extensive bill.[63]

Yet no revised bill was introduced. Instead, a royal commission was proposed to consider the state of Irish gaols and the condition of prisoners kept incarcerated in them since 1798. The short debate that followed demonstrated the reactionary, defensive position that many Irish grand juries would adopt when faced with the prospect of reform. Richard Sheridan, MP, highlighted several high-profile scandals in gaol construction (see Chapter 4), including the aborted plan to build a new gaol for Cork city in a low-lying and swampy site. Not only were many gaols 'insecure', but the Cork site was 'calculated to produce fevers and agues'. He blamed grand-jury corruption: 'jobbing and avarice had no bounds'. Nevertheless, as will be discussed in Chapter 4, grand juries were staunchly defended by the not entirely disinterested Charles Vereker – MP for Limerick city, a significant landholder in County Galway, and who frequently formed part of the Limerick grand jury.[64] The critics of the grand-jury system in parliament – Sheridan and others – were bolstered by the publication, for the first time, of detailed accounts, running to more than four hundred pages, of all the presentments made during the previous year. This level of scrutiny was deemed so helpful that it became a permanent annual reporting mechanism the following year, in the Highways (Ireland) Act, but it appears that many grand juries were lazy about forwarding their accounts to Westminster.[65] If reforms were to happen, it was clear that they would be resisted at every juncture. The Highways Act – the proud achievement of Edward Synge Cooper, an MP for Sligo – attempted to standardise the lucrative presentments, often mired in allegations of corruption, that grand juries made biannually for road-building.[66] In May 1809 and again in February 1810, Newport and Fitzgerald returned with their promised reform bill that included measures for further regulating the presentment system and for making grand juries' administrative business more transparent, but neither succeeded in passing the Tory-controlled Commons.[67]

While some Irish Whigs repeatedly attempted to introduce reform acts, prominent Irish Tories such as Sir George Hill (in Derry) and John Foster (in Louth) started their own offensive: to clear up the mess caused by the contracting procedures established in the 1796 act (as previously discussed) and to give grand juries more power and freedom to build courthouses (after 1810 prisons were covered by separate legislation).[68] It is not too much of a generalisation to view these forces as working in opposite directions: if at this stage Whigs sought to curtail grand-jury power, Tories focused on removing bottlenecks that held back their ambitions. As the Tories were in power, they were the eventual victors in this game of tug-of-war. Hill and Foster's first attempt was a bill introduced in May 1811, which passed the Commons with relatively little trouble but failed in the Lords (for reasons that remain unclear).[69] A second effort in February 1812 ended with the same impasse.[70] Both men became impatient, as their respective grand juries were hoping to begin building new assize courthouses in their county towns, and they argued that the imperfections of the 1796 act prevented them from doing so. In Dundalk the plans to replace the old courthouse dated to at least 1802, in Derry to 1807.[71] Though the government had seen off Whig attempts to curb grand-jury power, Hill and Foster needed a strong British supporter if they were to

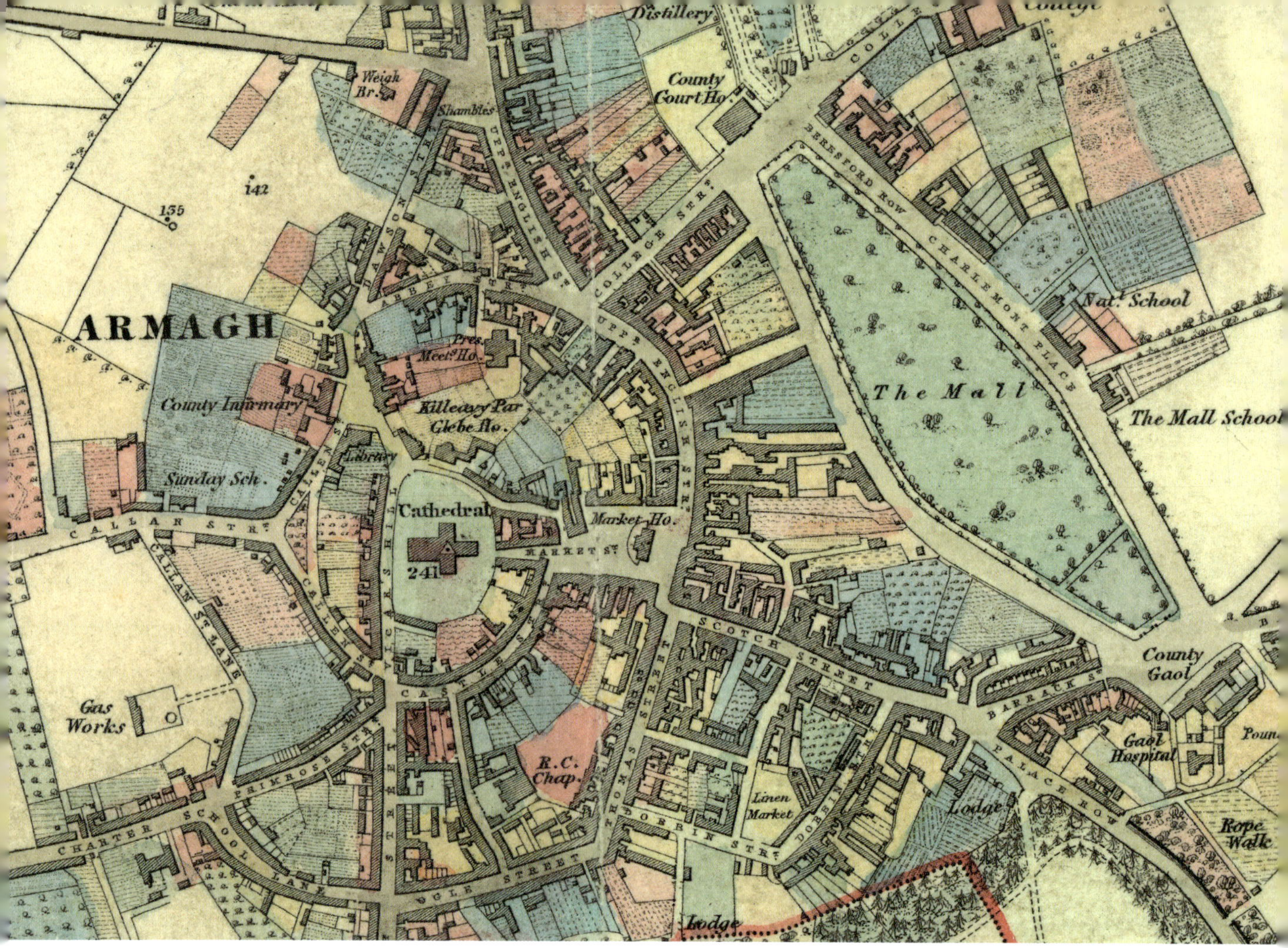

have any chance of success. The situation in April 1812 was not very hopeful, and an envious Leslie Foster (Foster's nephew) privately thought that many other grand juries were acting illegally in building their new courthouses.[72] Later in 1812 both men were rescued from their troubles by a new advocate for their cause, the young Irish chief secretary, Robert Peel, who helped in drafting what became the Court Houses Act of 1813.

Fig. 1.38. Armagh city centre, showing the Mall, courthouse, and gaol. Ordnance Survey six-inch map, surveyed June 1835. Francis Johnston's new courthouse of 1805–8 replaced a much less dignified building in the medieval core of the city. Wartime economic prosperity made possible the project. (*Reproduced courtesy of the Board of Trinity College Dublin.*)

Growing ambitions

Before analysing this act, we should consider why Hill and Foster felt so impatient around 1812. Grand juries had built many new assize courthouses in the southern half of the country, some very splendid and costly buildings. But it is likely that what was happening in County Armagh in these years was a more direct influence. While the Derry and Louth grand jurors waited

Fig. 1.39. James Black, 'City of Armagh', 1810 (detail). Black's painting shows Johnston's recently completed courthouse at the north-west corner of The Mall, with the county gaol dominating the foreground (for the later reconstruction of this gaol, see Chapter 7). (*Reproduced courtesy of Armagh County Museum.*)

for a legal solution, their colleagues in Armagh oversaw the erection of a new courthouse at the northern head of a recently laid out and generously proportioned green known as the Mall (Figs 1.38 and 1.39).[73] A local architect, Francis Johnston, who had risen meteorically in the Dublin artistic world and went on to design the General Post Office, was given the commission.[74] Four different designs for Armagh have survived from 1805 to 1808 and show by their increasing sophistication and architectural literacy a willingness on the part of the grand jury to fund an ever more costly building. Whereas the first scheme had proposed an awkward physical (and acoustic) arrangement of the crown and civil bills courtrooms – with both effectively opening onto each other, and the back of one acting as a corridor for the other (Fig. 1.40) – the final version borrowed heavily from Gandon's Nottingham design in providing a vestibule separating both courts and gave access via a double staircase to a spacious grand-jury room on the first floor (Fig. 1.42). Whereas the façade of the first scheme had little sophistication (Fig. 1.41), the final design projected a full tetrastyle Greek Doric portico, with a Roman Pantheon dome above.[75] The grand jury's repeated instruction to Johnston to further embellish his design is indicative of the economic prosperity of the time, and of the importance they placed on obtaining a dignified new home for their meetings. Yet in the final

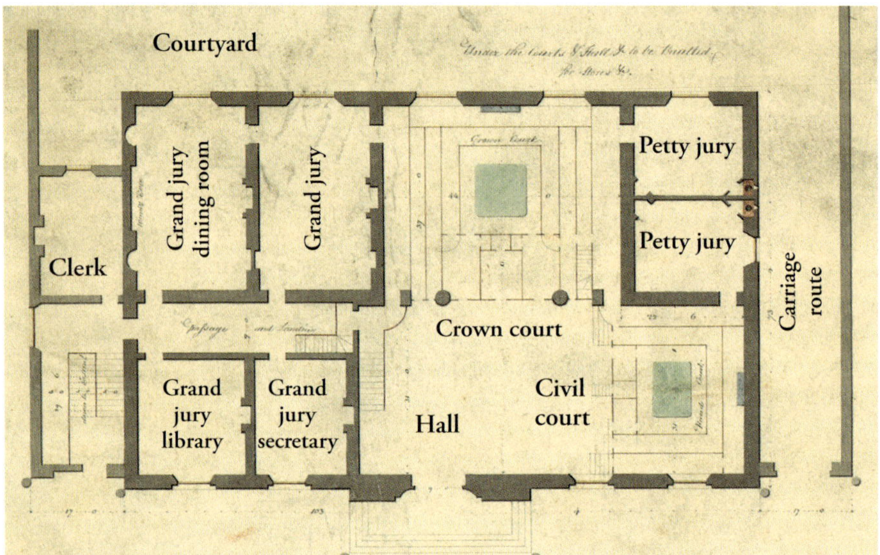

Fig. 1.40. Armagh courthouse, first scheme, unexecuted. Francis Johnston, 1805. Both courtrooms opened onto each other, an arrangement perhaps inspired by Gandon's Nottingham design. Despite the ample space given to the grand jury, the inconveniences of the design led the grand jury to call for modifications. (*Reproduced courtesy of the Irish Architectural Archive.*)

Fig. 1.41. Armagh courthouse, first scheme, unexecuted. Francis Johnston, 1805. At this early stage there was to be no portico in front of the building, but in more elaborate later designs this was added. (*Reproduced courtesy of the Irish Architectural Archive.*)

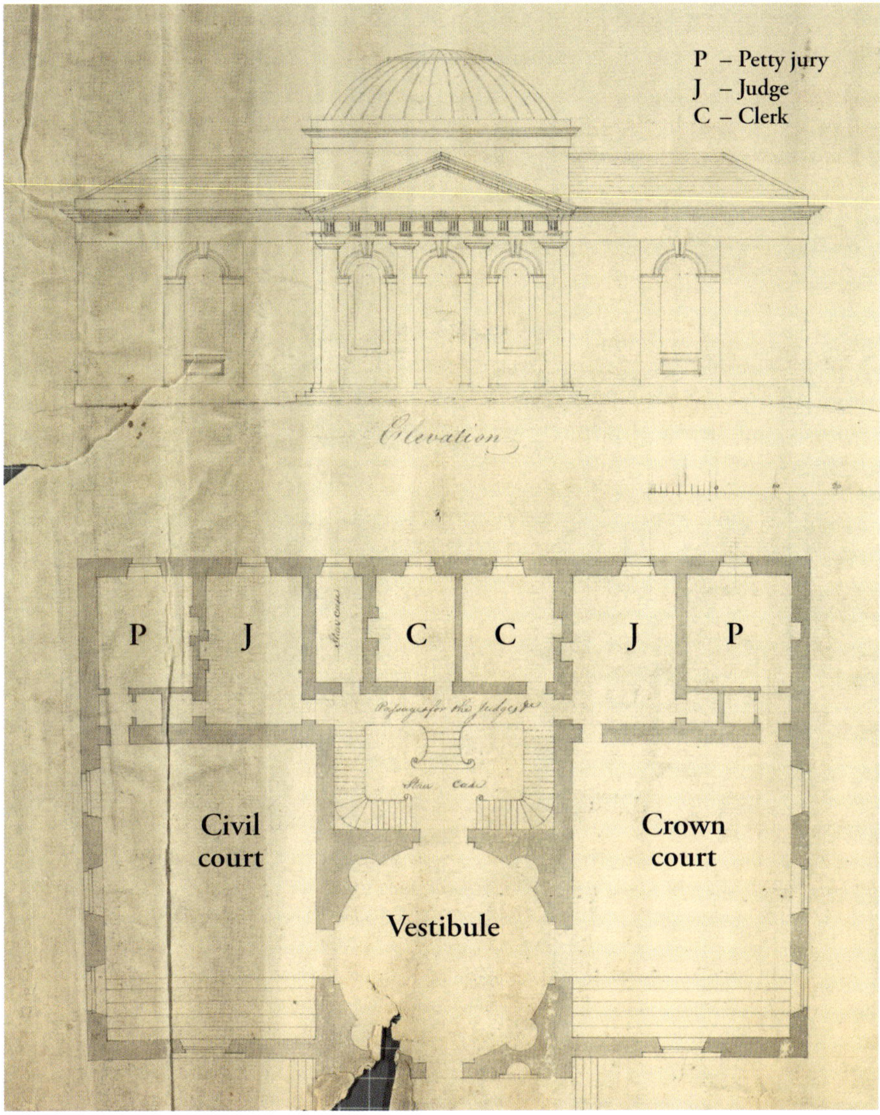

Fig. 1.42. Armagh courthouse, fourth and final scheme, plan and elevation. Francis Johnston, 1808. Despite the poor quality of this surviving drawing, it is possible to discern the double staircase that provided access to the grand jury's rooms. The courthouse as built has minor differences to this drawing, especially in the arrangement of the vestibule. (*Reproduced courtesy of the Irish Architectural Archive.*)

iteration their pretensions may not have matched the depths of their wallets, and to Johnston's great annoyance in later life, the dimensions of the portico's limestone columns were reduced without his approval; he commented that this had been done 'for the greater convenience of getting the stones of which they are composed', and added ruefully, 'they have ruined the portico'. As McParland has shown, at this time Johnston was too busy in Dublin to properly supervise the project, and a contractor likely made the substitution.[76] This imperfection should not detract from the fact that by the time the new courthouse was opened in about 1810, it was easily the most elaborate in the north of Ireland and stood in stark contrast to plainer buildings in neighbouring Dundalk, Carrickfergus, and Derry.

Meanwhile, Hill and Foster watched for their opportunity. After their second attempt had failed in the Lords in early April 1812, Hill moved quickly to avoid another year's delay. The Derry grand jury presented a petition that abandoned the idea of a general public act and instead asked for a local act that would concern only their proposed new courthouse. They thought it less likely that the Lords would reject a bill of this kind. The petitioners made clear their impatience and disappointment at the failure of the general bill, saying that another year's delay would 'be attended with very great inconvenience'.[77] Their wish was granted, and Hill and Foster drafted the Derry bill, which naturally borrowed heavily from their earlier failed attempts.[78] Their instinct to push for a local bill was rewarded, as the Lords passed it quickly with no amendments, and the bill received the royal assent in June 1812.[79] This local act has escaped the attention of other historians of the Irish courthouse, but it was in fact a critical

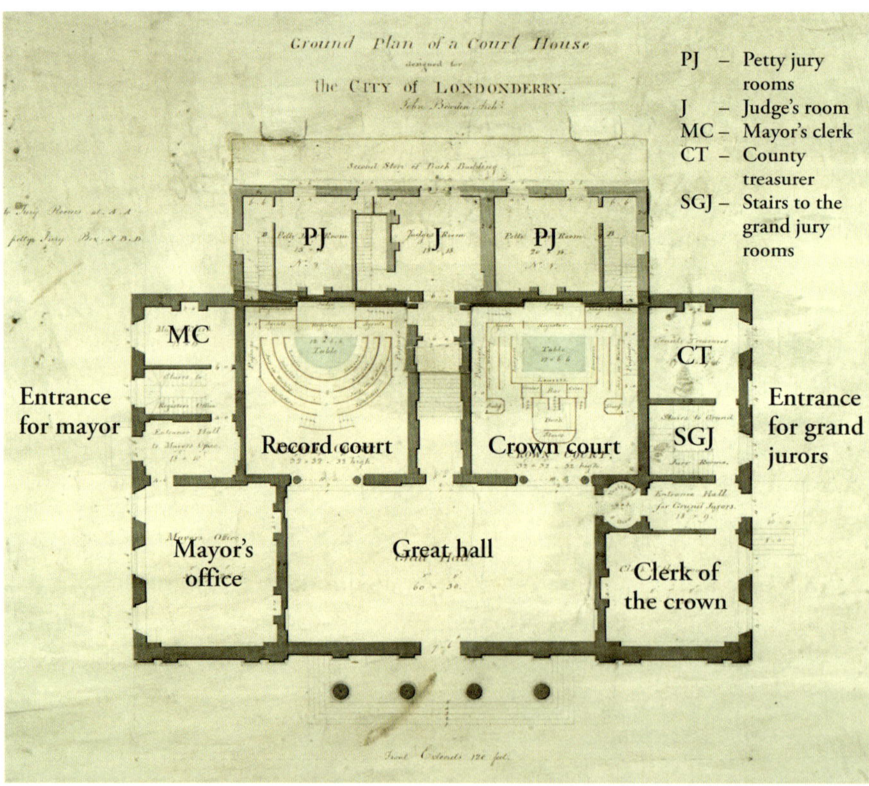

Fig. 1.43. Derry courthouse, plan, 1813. Bowden clearly derived his arrangement from Gandon's Waterford courthouse, but surrounded the principal rooms with a host of private and functional spaces. (*Reproduced courtesy of the Deputy Keeper of the Records, Public Record Office of Northern Ireland.*)

episode in the negotiations between Foster and Peel in drafting the general act that followed in 1813.[80] It not only demonstrates the extent to which grand juries would go to advance courthouse building (and town improvement more generally) during the wartime boom years, but also adds another angle to the torturous saga of the new courthouse at Dundalk, which dragged on for more than twenty years. Specifically, the existence of the Derry act undermines the argument that Foster and the Louth grand jurors made an unpleasant 'discovery' in Dundalk in April 1812 that there were legal problems with their proposed building contract.[81] In fact, Hill and Foster had been working to solve this exact problem since at least May 1811, if not for years before then. The concept of a legal discovery in 1812 implies that the grand jurors were passive in the process of commissioning their new courthouse; in reality, they were intimately involved with all the challenges that the project presented.

Now on sound legal footing, the Derry grand jurors proceeded to arrange a contract with John Bowden for the erection of their new assize courthouse, and it was built between 1813 and 1817.[82] Bowden had trained with Richard Morrison, and though for much of his life he lived in Dublin, many of his early buildings are in the north of the country.[83] With Derry's new assize courthouse came a new level of grand-jury conspicuous consumption: Samuel Lewis states that the final cost, including the purchase of the site and furniture, was almost £30,500.[84] If correct, this sum represents more than four times what was spent on courthouses only a generation earlier. And Derry was exceptional in more than just its financial outlay; this was only one of two instances in the nineteenth century when a grand jury obtained a special act of parliament for the building of a courthouse (the other is discussed in Chapter 3). Following local lobbying, Derry also maintained the unique right to keep paying its new courthouse keeper a generous salary of £50 per year, well above the national limit of just £15.[85] The Derry grand jury was thus generous on many levels. Less exceptional was the plan of the building itself and its location. Still very much based on Gandon's Waterford design with the two courts placed behind a large hall (Fig. 1.43), Bowden added more offices and meeting rooms for judges, barristers, and the grand jury. This proliferation of private rooms was repeated in many other courthouses of these decades. The site (Fig. 1.44) chosen by the grand jury was a tight and cramped one on the main street, obscuring the façade, with its Erechtheum Ionic order, from a clear axial view (Figs 1.45, 1.46).[86] Travel writers of the time stressed the problems with the site; even before construction began John Curwen thought that it would have been

Fig. 1.44. Derry city centre, showing courthouse and gaol. Ordnance Survey six-inch map, surveyed June 1830. The large polygonal addition to the gaol was built in the decade after the new courthouse by architects who had acted as contractors for the earlier project. (*Reproduced courtesy of the Board of Trinity College Dublin.*)

Fig. 1.45. Derry courthouse, *c.* 1900 (and largely as it appears today). Despite the grandeur of the building, the grand jury's choice of site was inferior to those of many neighbouring counties at this time. In the background the tower of the cathedral. (*Reproduced courtesy of the National Library of Ireland.*)

better to leave the site open and allow the cathedral behind to communicate properly with the road.[87] It is not clear why the grand jurors did not choose a more dignified location, such as establishing a square near the county gaol in which to celebrate their hard-won battle for a new courthouse, but a factor that must have played some part was Hill's ownership of a portion of the site, for which he received substantial remuneration.[88]

Fig. 1.46. Derry courthouse, detail showing the coat of arms and the date '1813'. C.E.B. Brett notes that the courthouse 'is signed by John Bowden on the back of this coat of arms – a signature visible only from the gutters of the roof' – see *Court Houses and Market Houses*, p. 90. (*Photograph by author, 2014.*)

The Court Houses Act of 1813

While Derry's local act was progressing through parliament, there was another attempt by Cooper (and for a change, some Tory MPs as well) to bring in a bill to further reform the power of grand juries. Like earlier Whig efforts, it was unsuccessful, not because of opposition from the Commons but on account of the multiplicity of changes requested by the Lords.[89] In August 1812 Peel came to Ireland as chief secretary and by early 1813 his desire for administrative efficiency and reform matched Hill and Foster's need for legislative clarity. Though Cooper introduced his grand-jury reform bill one last time in February 1813, a second reading was repeatedly deferred through the spring; its last appearance was in late May.[90] At the same time, Leslie Foster had been writing to Peel – a friend – to inform him of the problems faced by the Louth and Derry grand juries. 'On the whole,' he commented, 'a new act of parliament seems very necessary.' Peel responded quickly and introduced the Court Houses Bill on 1 June, and by mid-July it was on the statute book.[91] The act allowed grand juries to enter into full and binding contracts with overseers and to advance money to them. Overseers could themselves arrange sub-contracts with architects and craftsmen, and most importantly, the inconvenient 1796 measure limiting commissions to five per cent was abolished.[92] This act is hugely important in the history of the Irish assize courthouse and of grand-jury reform, for it constituted a uniquely explicit instance of central government coming to the aid of the Irish grand juries and granting them extra powers to build large and showpiece public buildings – something unthinkable in the more fraught politics of subsequent decades. It was every bit as important for courthouse building in Ireland as was the Prisons Act of 1810 for Irish prisons, which will be analysed in chapters 4 and 5.

The first beneficiary of the new act was of course Dundalk. Plans had been afoot to replace the old courthouse, built in about 1740, since the turn of the century. Richard Morrison, king of courthouse building in these years, submitted proposals in 1804 and again in 1812, but neither was adopted.[93] For many architects the proposed Dundalk courthouse was a thankless exercise and a testing one too. The grand jury had several members who were keen amateur architects, and they made sure that their views were often heard. One of these was Foster's nephew and Peel's friend John Leslie Foster, and another was Blayney Balfour, who had commissioned a Greek Revival house from Johnston.[94] Even after a contract was concluded with Edward Parke, John Bowden, and the contractor William Moore in April 1813, further changes were made to the design. These are likely to have led to the disagreement with Moore that prompted his dismissal in 1818 and the subsequently ruinous legal action against the grand jury.[95] Claiming £12,000 on top of the £14,525 that had already been advanced to him, he won his case and was awarded £3,500 with costs. The whole embarrassing affair was settled only with a special act of parliament in 1821 that rescued the individual grand jurors, such as Foster, who had paid out Moore's claim. His original contract had been for £16,190, so we can deduce that the total sum expended by the Louth grand jury on their new courthouse was nearly £20,000 – an astronomical sum, even for the war years, for Ireland's smallest county. The expense could not be justified in terms of any meaningful increase in crime in the county: average criminal indictments remained largely unchanged in the twenty years prior to the commencement of building work.[96]

'New fangled theoretic speculations'

Dundalk courthouse, in its architectural embellishment, stands at odds with the modest residence of its chief supporter, John Foster. It gave the Louth grand jurors an opportunity to engage with a level of architectural material culture that they could never aspire to possess on their own estates. Foster had built a small private Greek Doric temple in the 1780s, but his townhouse at Collon is an essay in Georgian modesty, and all the more striking considering Foster's former role as speaker of the Irish House of Commons.[97] He edged close to financial ruin at many stages in his long life, despite a potentially remunerative political position. For him and his nephew, the noted expert on the Greek style of architecture, the corporate funds of the grand jury allowed them to partake in an exercise of elite architectural consumption and urban improvement that rivalled the most distinguished Greek buildings in Britain and on the continent.[98] As has been remarked by Casey and others, one of the most striking documents to survive from the Dundalk courthouse project is the full contract of April 1813 specifying that architectural features of the new building were not to be taken from 'the rules, patterns, and proportions used and directed in the common books of architecture and of ordinary use

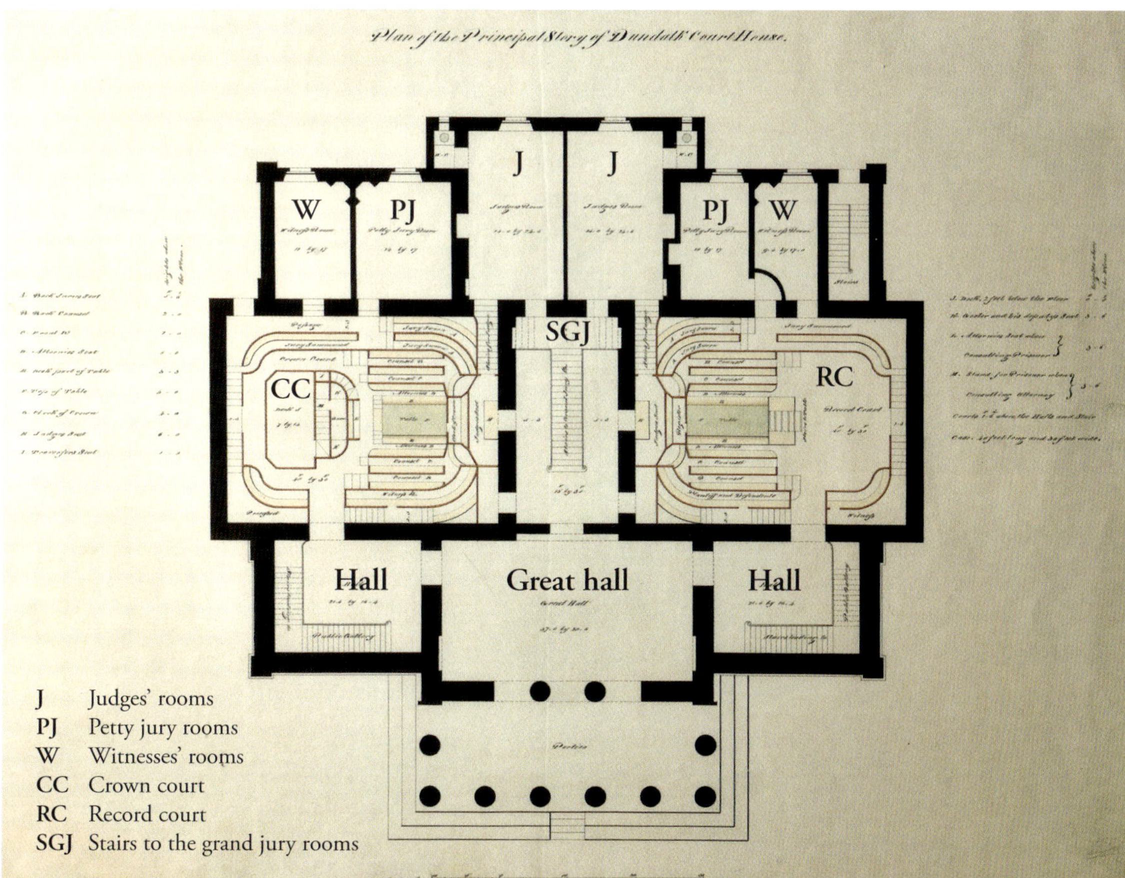

Fig. 1.47. Plan of Dundalk courthouse, *c.* 1813. Parke and Bowden followed Gandon in the arrangement of the courtrooms but drew from fashionable Greek Revival motifs in their great portico. (*Reproduced courtesy of the Old Dundalk Society and Louth County Council.*)

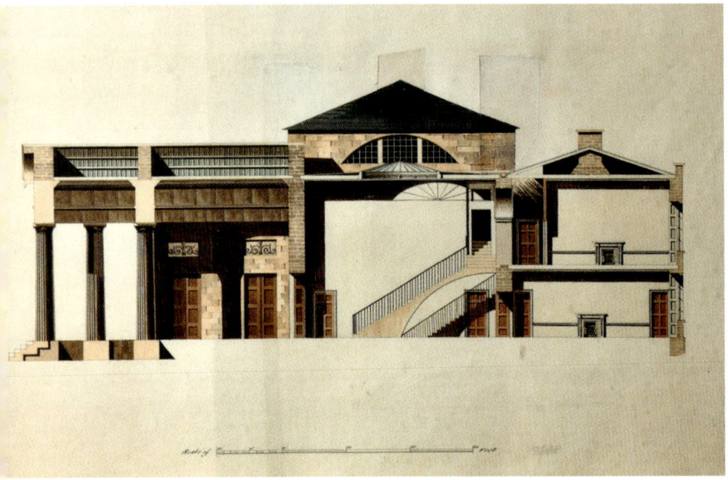

and application in this country', but instead adopted from 'the true forms and proportions expressed as and for such [architectural] members and decorations respectively in a work entitled "Stewart's Antiquities of Athens"'.[99] In an era when the language of neo-classical architecture was increasingly accessible to the rising middle classes, and when so many grand juries were rebuilding their assize courthouses, it was obviously important to mark the showpiece building at Dundalk as unique and superior to those of its neighbours, and as worth the enormous investment of the county's cess-payers. One grand juror, John Jocelyn, complained to Foster in 1819 that perfectly satisfactory old courthouses were being 'wantonly demolished' for 'new fangled theoretic speculations' – but his was a minority view.[100] The majority were immensely proud of their new public building, even if the experience had been a testing and extraordinarily costly one.

Architecturally, Dundalk courthouse follows Gandon in its plan (Fig. 1.47), but with the minor variation that the two courtrooms no longer open directly onto a common vestibule but have separate halls; this granted more privacy to the proceedings. The courtrooms themselves are separated by a top-lit grand staircase (Fig. 1.48) giving access to the grand jury and judges' meeting rooms behind. From outside, the entrance is one of the most dramatic of all Irish courthouses and displays a rigorous adherence to Greek sources. One approaches through a hexastyle Doric portico (Fig. 1.49) and a series of internal Doric screens (one of which was added long after the original contract had been signed) that give access to the courtrooms and the grand-jury staircase.[101] With the adjacent county gaol soon rebuilt (see Chapter 5), the combination

Fig. 1.48. (left) Transverse section of Dundalk courthouse, *c.* 1813. This scheme differs slightly from the plan drawing above in Fig. 1.47, but the key aspects of the design are the same. A central staircase separates the courtrooms and gives access to meeting rooms to the rear. Large thermal windows light both courtrooms. (*Reproduced courtesy of the Old Dundalk Society and Louth County Council.*)

Fig. 1.49. (right) Dundalk courthouse, principal elevation. The Louth grand jurors were clear in their desire for an architecturally 'correct' Greek Revival portico. (*Photograph by author, 2012.*)

of two such large buildings in the centre of the town (Fig. 1.50) was as bold a statement as any yet made of the authority and power of local magistrates and elites, acting collectively through the agency of the grand jury. One traveller in 1823 thought the courthouse a model of architectural beauty, commenting that the portico was 'uncommonly beautiful and striking'.[102] Behind its heavy and monumental appearance on the town's principal square lay not so much a naked show of judicial power in a time of unrest, but a highly developed sense of competition between neighbouring grand juries, an extended struggle between different strata of government over the political and financial freedoms of grand juries, and an ambition that wartime prosperity alone could accommodate.

Fig. 1.50. Dundalk courthouse and market square, *c.* 1900. The county gaol was situated to the rear of the courthouse. (*Reproduced courtesy of the National Library of Ireland.*)

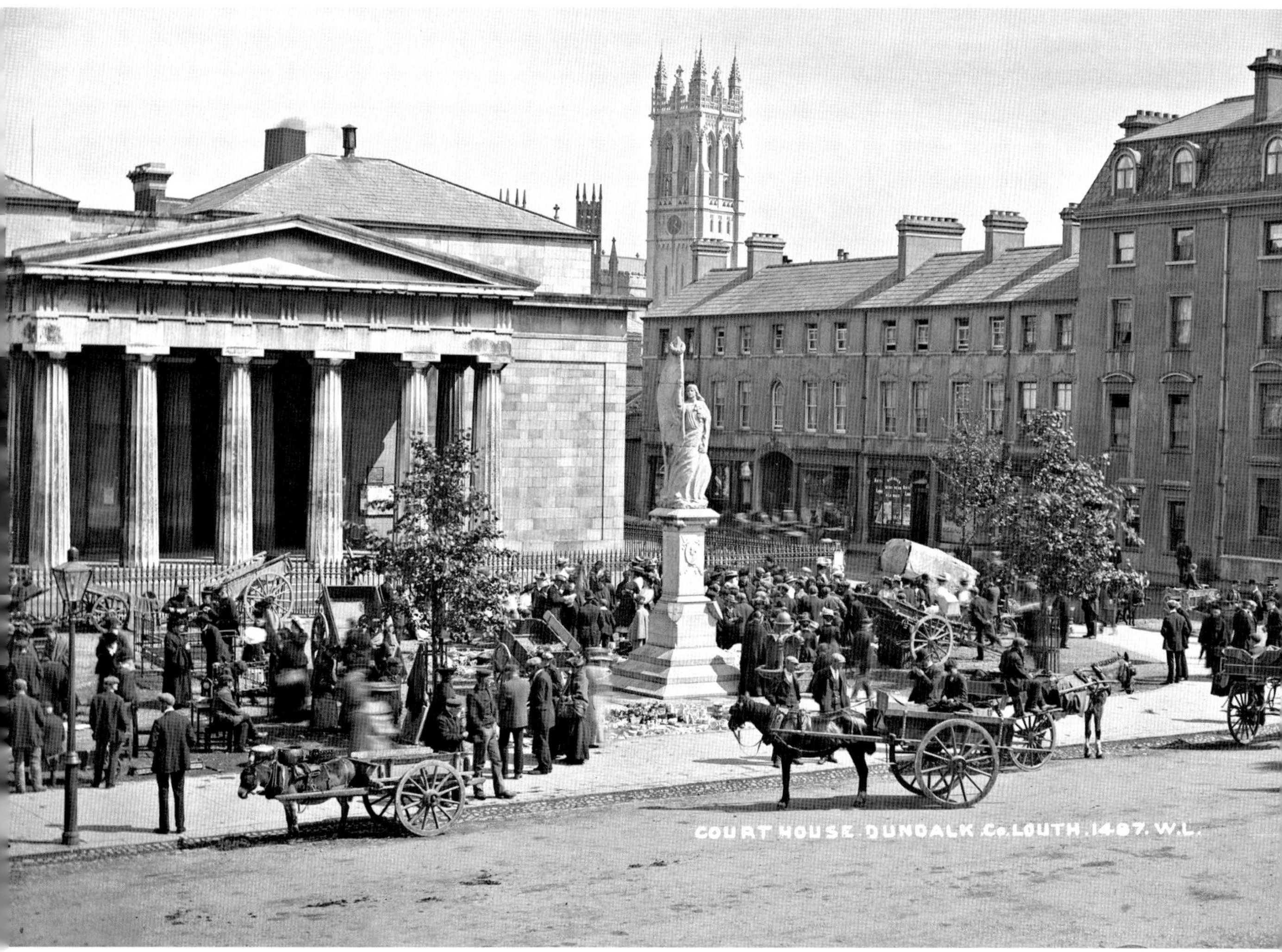

Fever Hospital
Beggars Br.
Chapel
Court.
County Gaol
Hospital
Franciscan Nunnery
Tread Mill
Solitary Cell
Town Gaol
Presentation Convent
Corridor
CRIMEA

Chapter 2

Judging the Neighbours:

Grand juries, rivalry, and the peak years of courthouse building, 1817–31

The late 1810s through to the early 1830s form a distinct period in the history of the Irish courthouse and mark a zenith of building activity not seen before or since. In these years, the grandest of Ireland's provincial courthouses were designed by renowned architects such as William Vitruvius Morrison, John B. Keane, and the Pain brothers, James and George Richard. The boom had its origins in reforms within local government – the grand-jury system – and a new system of loans from central government for 'public works' projects in the post-Napoleonic wars economic recession. It was also closely tied to intense competition and rivalry between neighbouring grand juries. There was, in short, a rush to build – the fruits of which still adorn many Irish county towns.

As set out in the previous chapter, the grand juries of counties Louth and Derry clarified their fundraising and commissioning powers for building new courthouses in the early 1810s. This was an essential background to what came after 1817. They had, in 1812–13, successfully outmanoeuvred the commissioning restrictions of an old 1796 Irish act with new legislation that allowed them to build assize courthouses in their county towns of Derry and Dundalk.[1] It must have appeared to observers of the time that grand juries had more freedom than ever before to commit to such expensive architectural projects, but by 1815 and the end of the Napoleonic wars, grand-jury reform had once more emerged as an issue at Westminster. The old problems – corruption, jobbery, inefficiency – had not gone away. A select committee proposed that 'county surveyors' should be employed by each grand jury, whose role would be to oversee and manage all public-works projects.[2] Robert Peel, as Irish chief secretary, helped to draft the reform act that followed in 1817.[3] His colleague William Vesey Fitzgerald thought that the measure would do 'more good [in] Ireland than [any other act] since the Union'.[4] In spite of objections from prominent grand jurors, who had been involved in lobbying government for the aforementioned courthouse legislation in 1812–13 – such as Sir George Hill in Derry – Peel's act took effect in July 1817. The act stated that county surveyors were to be appointed before the end of the year and that grand juries could make presentments for new courthouses only at their summer meeting. Both measures sought to curb wasteful spending and the potential for 'corruption'. As Hoppen argues, many British politicians saw Irish administration as distinctly, perhaps even uniquely, corrupt (however much that involved turning a blind eye to jobbery at home), and that Irish elites were in large measure responsible for their country's many problems.[5] The proposal to install county surveyors was, in turn, vigorously attacked by Irish elites: Hill denounced the measure, saying that Irish society was 'greatly indebted' to the work of grand juries such as the one he was a member of. His comments show how grand juries in general felt betrayed by central government: the bill 'marks the most offensive distrust of the resident gentry, it transfers almost the whole of their powers to a new-created officer … without whose permission a footpath cannot be mended … and whose acts the grand juries henceforth will be merely empowered to record'.[6]

However, the act quickly became an embarrassing failure for Vesey Fitzgerald and Peel: by January 1818 they had to introduce another bill to repeal its provisions. The problem had simply been a lack of suitable recruits for the poorly remunerated county surveyor positions.[7] Hill had warned of this in his speech the year before while the bill was being debated, and other dissenting voices now emerged to rub salt into the government's wounds. Frederick Flood, MP for Wexford, and one of the grand jurors who had commissioned the overtly 'Orange' new courthouse in that town in the previous decade (see Chapter 1), said that 'grand juries were far better judges of what concerned the interests of their own counties than itinerant surveyors', and he described himself as 'sorry to hear such imputations [of corruption] thrown out against my countrymen'.[8] Peel's amending act that summer was quite a climb-down: gone in particular were the much-maligned surveyors – seen as unwanted intrusions by the grand jurors – and also set aside was the inconvenient ban on their making presentments for new courthouses at their spring assizes. After almost two decades of increasingly intrusive oversight, the grand juries had in this instance dodged a bullet, and the threat of new regulations and oversight receded, if only for a few years.[9]

Yet by this time there were other problems on the horizon, not least the cessation of the Napoleonic wars, which led to a sudden collapse in staple prices and a prolonged period of economic depression throughout the United Kingdom, especially in Ireland.[10] In 1817 poor crop yields aggravated the situation, and the Tory government introduced the Public Works Loan Act, providing £1,750,000 to help alleviate unemployment; of this £250,000 was allocated to Ireland.[11] Further emergency legislation – specific to Ireland – in the years that followed made it easier for grand juries to obtain loans, for any kind of public work, with relatively little oversight or scrutiny.[12] In the House of Lords the prime minister, Lord Liverpool, made it clear that though he found the general principle of these measures 'objectionable', the severity of poverty and unemployment in Ireland created 'special circumstances'.[13] As this chapter shows, such an amount of relatively easily obtained money completely overwhelmed any attempt at grand-jury reform in the 1820s and opened new opportunities for the construction and reconstruction of many large assize courthouses (Figs 2.1, 2.2). Such heavy financial outlays on new buildings, which were amplified by inter-county jealousy and rivalry, could not have been justified by the economic realities of the time, but were instead an artificial boost provided by a rush of central-government loans. The comparison with Britain is instructive: many hundreds of large courthouses were also built in Britain at this time, but relatively few benefited from government loans. In Ireland from 1817 to 1832 eight new assize courthouses (and nineteen smaller courthouses) were funded by these loans.[14] In Britain, obviously a much larger country, there were only *two* loans issued over the same period for *any* kind of courthouse – at the Old Bailey in London and at Presteigne in Wales. If we extend the analysis to 1847, only four more assize courthouses were funded by these means in Britain – at Inverness, Worcester, Pembroke, and Bristol – compared with seventeen in Ireland (and many dozens more smaller courthouses).[15] Thus the funding of courthouses in Ireland and Britain followed different trajectories after 1817: in Britain many of the government loans went to collieries and canal companies. In Ireland the money was spent – perhaps unsurprisingly in a poorer country

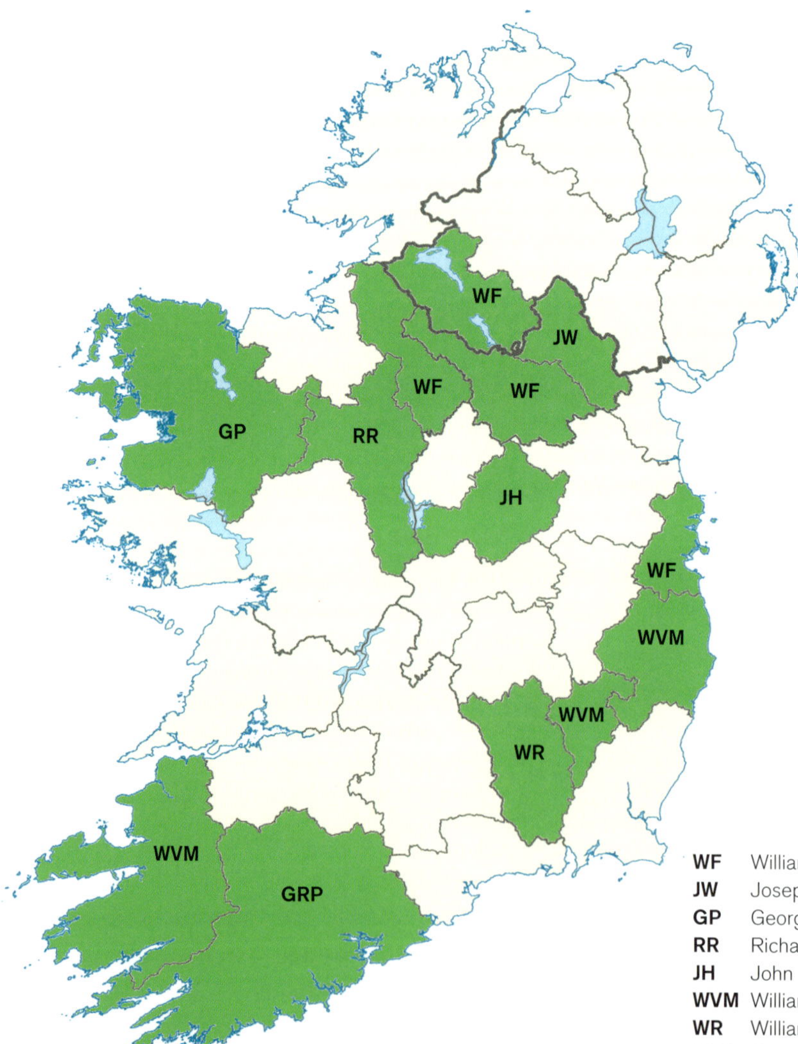

Fig. 2.1. New assize courthouses built in Ireland, 1817–32, with architect responsible, where known. This period was the most dynamic and rich in the history of the Irish courthouse, as public-works loans from central government fuelled a boom in building activity.

Fig. 2.2. A graph showing the number of assize courthouses that were under construction (meaning either building anew or subject to large alterations) in any one year in Ireland between 1770 and 1870. This data naturally comes with many caveats, not least the incomplete survival of documentary sources for many courthouse-building projects. Nevertheless, it is revealing that the only times when the figure exceeds six in any one year are in the early 1800s (after the 1798 rebellion), around 1820 (when public-works loans were first made available) and in the late 1820s–30s (which can be seen as the peak period for the building of the largest and most impressive of new assize courthouses). Contrastingly, the building activity in the years after around 1855 – after the Famine – is made up almost entirely of more modest alterations to existing buildings. Compiled from Appendix A.

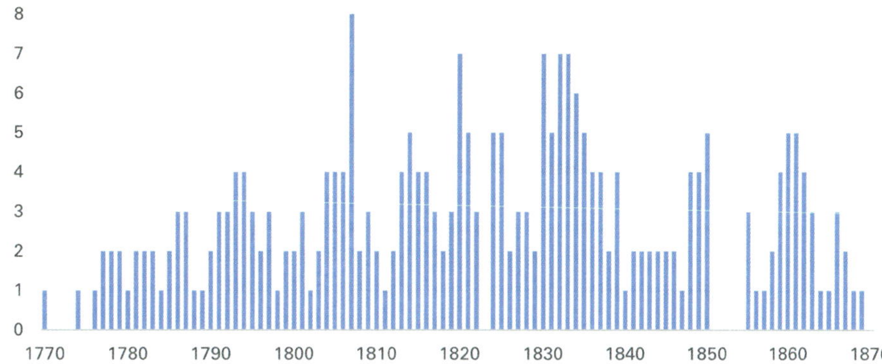

with less industry – on roads, harbours, and public buildings. This allowed the spirit of ambitious wartime assize-courthouse building – such as had occurred at Armagh, Dundalk, and Derry – to continue into the 1820s, and without the same scrutiny from landed and middle-class cess-payers who were becoming more powerful in other parts of the United Kingdom. In all nearly £71,000 was loaned to grand juries in Ireland for new assize courthouses between 1817 and 1847, an average of about £5,000 for each of the counties that applied. The loans were generally charged at five per cent interest and were repayable over the course of twenty years. Geographically the loans were concentrated in the southern half of the country, with the largest amounts gained by Kerry, Waterford, King's County (Offaly), and Dublin (Fig. 2.3).[16]

There was also a political dimension to what happened in 1817 that needs to be explored. Since 1813 the campaign for Catholic emancipation had been reignited, and many (if not all) grand juries opposed the measure.[17] The issue came to a head in May 1817 with a vote in the House of Commons when the granting of emancipation was only narrowly defeated. The government victory, in the eyes of many contemporary observers, could be attributed to Peel and his spirited contributions to the Commons debate. However unfairly, some in the tabloid press thereafter branded him 'Orange' Peel. In this polarised atmosphere, he found himself in an uneasy political alliance with the grand juries, the flawed institution that he had attempted to reform.[18] As Robert Saunders has recently remarked, the 'alliance between Peel and the politics of Protestant defense would always be uneasy'.[19] The failure of the Catholic emancipation vote was an unexpected boost in an era when many Protestants were defeatist and fatalist and convinced that the measure would eventually be granted.[20] Ten days after the vote, Peel wrote to the lord lieutenant commenting that he hoped the grand juries – which he singled out – and the Orange press would not now be

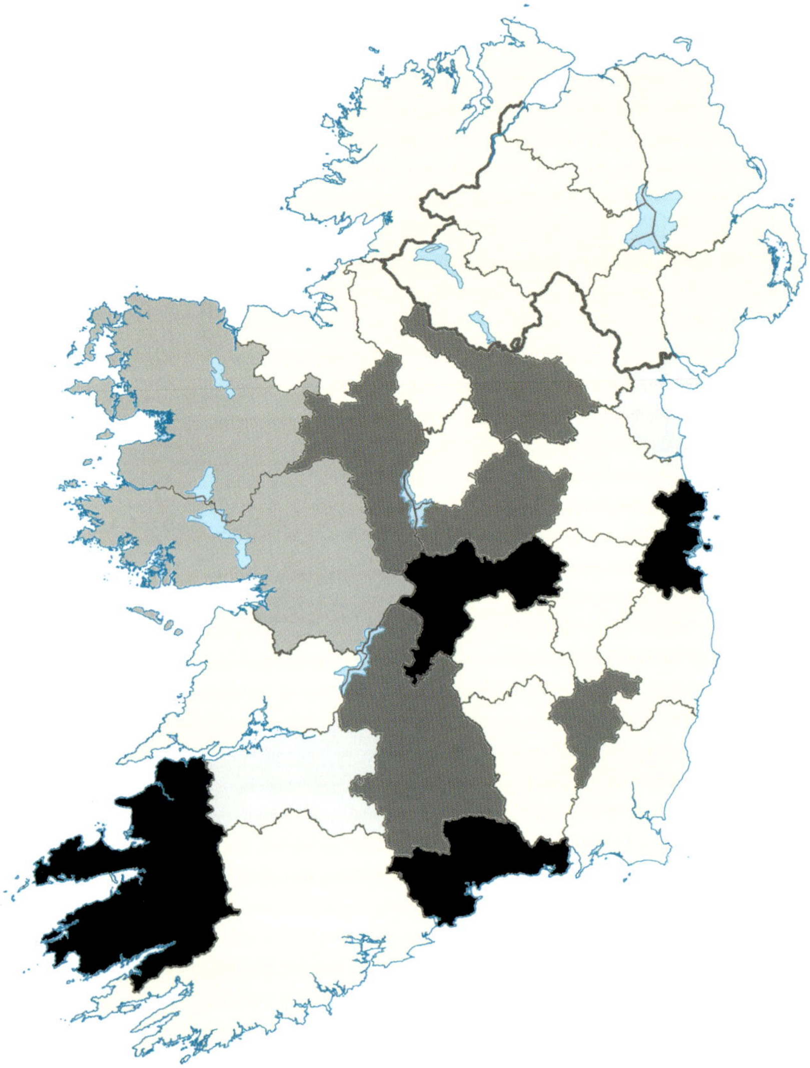

Fig. 2.3. Public-works loans to grand juries for new assize courthouses, 1817–47. Cavan was the only county in Ulster to apply for such a loan. Weightings are by percentage of the total sum: light grey (1–3%), grey (3–6%), dark grey (6–10%), and black (above 10%). King's County (Offaly) received the greatest sum (£9,350) and Louth the least (£1,200). Compiled from Appendix D.

too triumphalist. He urged the 'utmost vigilance and circumspection' in how the vote was reported, as he was conscious always of 'the impolicy of adding irritation to [the] disappointment' of the Catholic side.[21] But in this he was too optimistic: the Dublin city grand jury had already voted to publicly thank him for his role in defeating the bill, roguishly lauding 'the glorious majority' of the House of Commons. All the main Irish newspapers carried their praise for Peel's involvement in upholding what they termed the 'Protestant constitution in church & state'.[22] For the city of Dublin, like many other grand juries, the years around 1820 were an encouraging time of lax regulation, easy money, and now an unexpected political victory. The 1817 decision, then, of the neighbouring grand jury of County Dublin to build a new assize courthouse at Kilmainham must be seen in the light of all these events.

An unbuilt scheme for Kilmainham

A set of unexecuted drawings for a new courthouse at Kilmainham, prepared by the Dublin firm Henry, Mullins & McMahon (hereafter HMM), who were at the time working on the new courthouse in Derry, are dated 5 October 1817. They must have been ordered by the Dublin county grand jurors when they met for their Michaelmas assizes in 1817 when they approved a large presentment to build a new courthouse. These developments occurred at the same time as the aforementioned political drama was playing out at Westminster.[23] To be situated adjacent to the county gaol, the building sketched in the HMM design would have featured an impressive two-storey façade of five bays with two engaged temple-fronts of paired Ionic columns over a rusticated base (Fig. 2.4). To the side was a novel and important development for the time – a completely separate

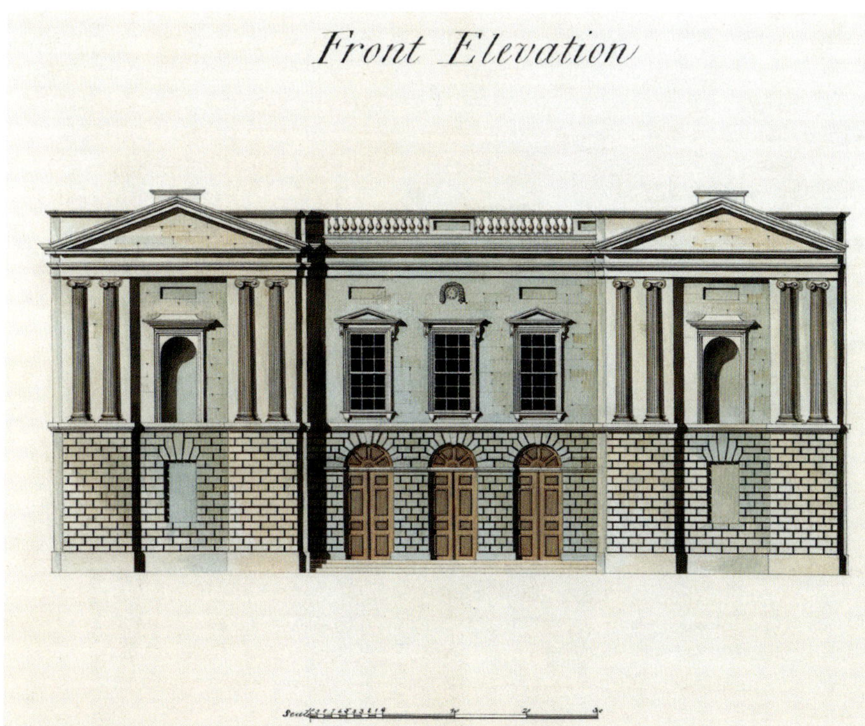

Fig. 2.4. Kilmainham courthouse, front elevation, unexecuted. Henry, Mullins & McMahon, 1817. The formal symmetry concealed the disproportionate amount of space given over to the grand jurors for their meetings and social events, and the comparatively small and asymmetrically placed courtroom. (*Reproduced courtesy of the Irish Architectural Archive.*)

grand-jury entrance (the first to survive that is explicitly marked as such), framed by a giant Ionic order in antis in the Gandon tradition (Fig. 2.5).[24] This private entrance was a clear mark of status and importance for the grand jurors and in the case of Kilmainham would have led via an imperial staircase to their grand-jury room (Fig. 2.6). Overall, the grand jury would have occupied more rooms (and thus more space), if one includes the central hall, than the courtroom and the judges' quarters combined. The design was also unusual in providing only one courtroom instead of the normal two (crown and civil). Nonetheless, the design allowed grand jurors to gain access to the courtroom via a private gallery space that communicated with their meeting room, allowing them to look down from on high at proceedings and accused persons in the dock below.

Remarkably ambitious and indeed revolutionary for its time, the design came to nothing. The reason for its rejection is not entirely clear from surviving minute books and presentments, but the fire at Kilmainham Gaol in December 1817 (see chapters 5 and 6), which destroyed almost half the building, must have seriously weakened the grand jury's financial position (the rebuilding cost almost £2,000).[25] The plans for the new courthouse were scaled back, and in December 1818 the grand jury became the first in Ireland to obtain a government loan under the new scheme (borrowing a total of £8,615 at five per cent).[26] Around

Fig. 2.5. Kilmainham courthouse, side elevation, unexecuted. Henry, Mullins & McMahon, 1817. The private entrance for the grand jury, specifically marked as such. (*Reproduced courtesy of the Irish Architectural Archive.*)

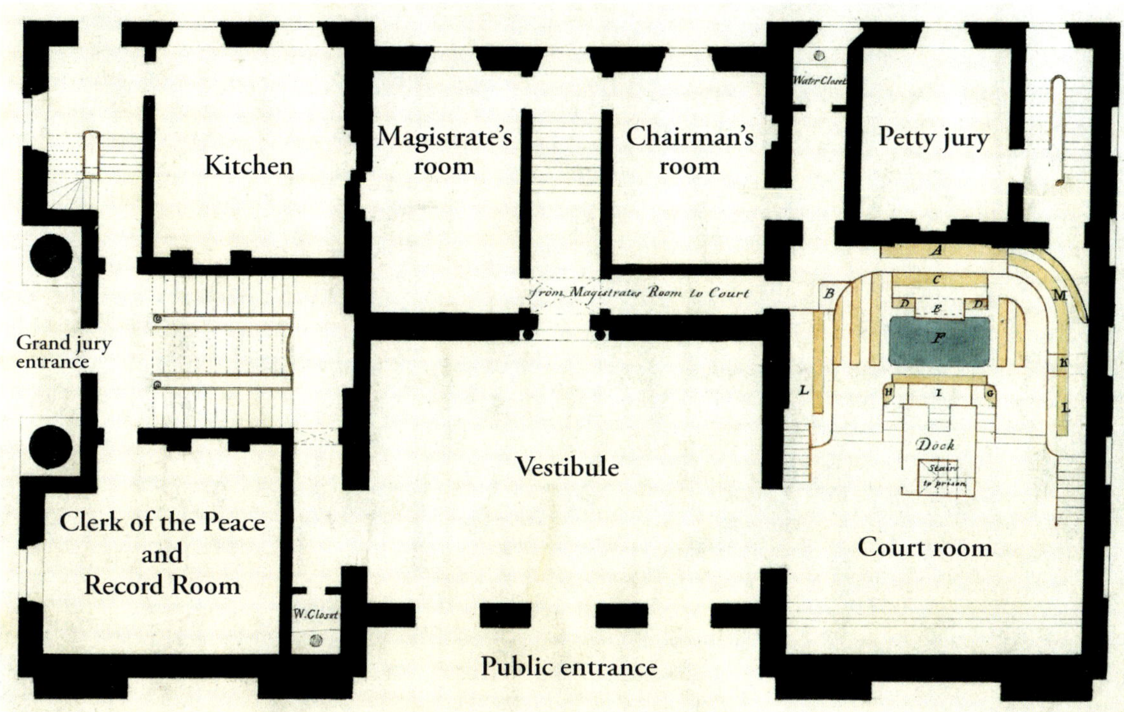

Fig. 2.6. Kilmainham courthouse, ground-floor plan, unexecuted. Henry, Mullins & McMahon, 1817. The imperial staircase to the left, for the grand jury's use, would have led to a suite of large rooms on the first floor for business and social meetings. (*Reproduced courtesy of the Irish Architectural Archive.*)

1818–19 the prominent Dublin architect Henry Aaron Baker was associated with the project; he may have submitted a competing design or been employed to modify and reduce the HMM design. It is also possible that a more modest courthouse might have been a stipulation of the granting of a loan. Whatever the exact sequence of events, the Dublin grand jurors undoubtedly benefited from this large source of relatively cheap funding. They even obtained an extra loan to allow them to purchase land for the new courthouse, something that had little to do with the stated aim of the government's scheme – to provide employment for the poor – and that was not allowed to happen again.[27]

The final executed design was by William Farrell, who is likely to have worked with Francis Johnston at the Board of Works in these years, and the new Dublin county courthouse opened in October 1820.[28] Though he kept certain features of the earlier scheme, such as the provision of a single courtroom and the separate grand-jury entrance to the east, he restored the primary importance of the judicial function of the building by bringing the courtroom into the centre of the plan (Fig. 2.7) and by raising it to nearly three storeys in height, lit by a succession of clerestory windows and by a large thermal window to the rear.[29] To make space for this large courtroom, the adjacent entrance hall projects forward, lending a central focus to the principal elevation whereas the earlier HMM scheme had put emphasis on the pedimented edges. The grand jury still maintained its gallery above the courtroom, but its private function room was reduced in scale and importance. The result was a more even balance between the judicial and social functions of the courthouse. Externally (Figs 2.8, 2.9), much of the architectural detailing of the earlier scheme was jettisoned, such as all the attached Ionic columns. This is partly offset by the central projecting bay that, with its pediment and ceremonial lion, shield, and unicorn (the British crown having since been removed), made up for the plainness of much of the façade. Following his Dublin success Farrell became one of the most sought-after courthouse architects of the 1820s and went on to build in the north-western counties of Cavan, Leitrim, and Fermanagh (Figs 2.10–2.13).

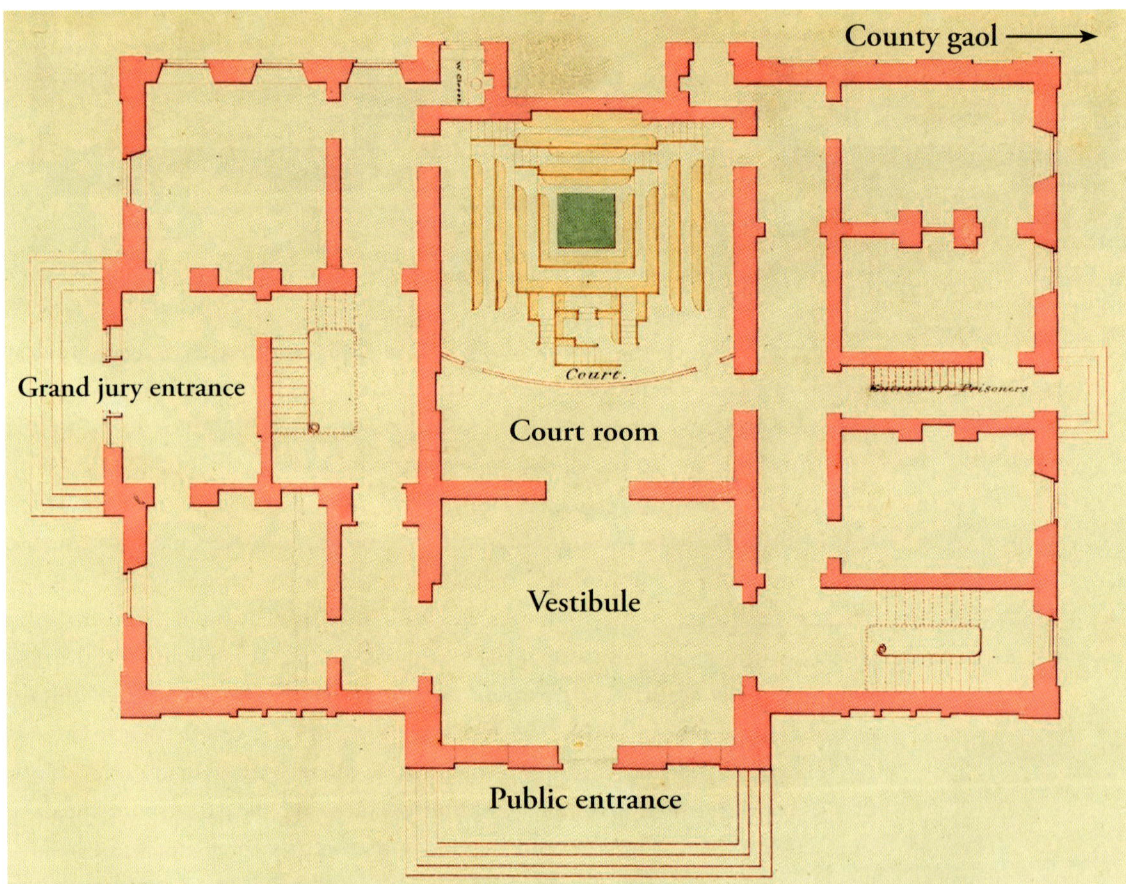

Fig. 2.7. Kilmainham courthouse, ground-floor plan, as built. William Farrell, *c.* 1817. Farrell's executed design brought the courtroom back into central focus, but kept the earlier concept of a separate grand-jury entrance, and large meeting rooms for that body. (*Reproduced courtesy of the Houghton Library, Harvard University.*)

Fig. 2.8. (top) Kilmainham courthouse, front elevation, as built. William Farrell, *c.* 1817. Similar in footprint to the unexecuted Henry, Mullins & McMahon design, but with significantly less architectural detailing and ornamentation, Farrell's scheme was likely a compromise for a grand jury that experienced unexpected financial shocks even as cheap government loans began to open new opportunities. (*Reproduced courtesy of the Houghton Library, Harvard University.*)

Fig. 2.9. (centre) Kilmainham courthouse, with the county gaol behind. The courtroom was accessible via the front public entrance, as visible in this *c.* 1900 photograph, as well as by the private side entrance for the grand jurors and visiting dignitaries. To the right, the county gaol. (*Reproduced courtesy of the National Library of Ireland.*)

Fig. 2.10. (right) Design for a courthouse, front elevation. William Farrell, *c.* 1817. As built in Carrick-on-Shannon (*c.* 1823) and Cavan (1824–5). Farrell's heavy, Schinkel-esque composition brought a new level of architectural sophistication to the judicial-political quarter of two provincial towns in the rural north-west. (*Reproduced courtesy of the Houghton Library, Harvard University.*)

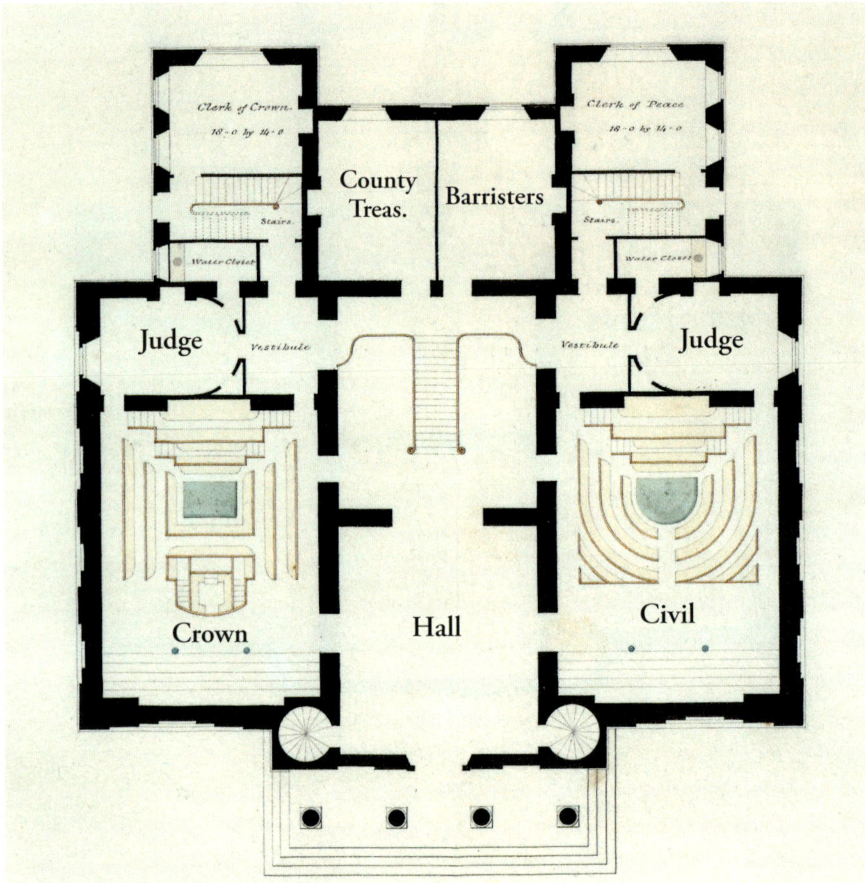

Fig. 2.11. Design for a courthouse, ground-floor plan. William Farrell, *c.* 1817. As built in Carrick-on-Shannon and Cavan. The axial layout of the two courtrooms stretched back to Gandon's design for Nottingham and to a series of courthouses by Morrison, Johnston, and others from the previous decade. The impressive central staircase led to the grand jury's private rooms. (*Reproduced courtesy of the Houghton Library, Harvard University.*)

Fig. 2.12. Cavan courthouse, situated on a new wide street that the proprietor of the town had earmarked for such a building. A generous loan from Dublin Castle smoothed the building process and perhaps permitted the use of such a crisp and long-lasting local Drumellis limestone. (*Photograph by author, 2014.*)

Fig. 2.13. Carrick-on-Shannon courthouse. Now greatly disfigured by an insensitive canopy, which replaced a portico that was taken down in *c.* 1980. Built without any government loans, yet clearly emulating Cavan, the Leitrim grand jury settled for an inferior building stone. (*Photograph by author, 2012.*)

New courthouses in the west

The scale of building activity in the early 1820s rivalled the reconstruction after the 1798 rebellion. A series of contiguous counties – almost all of Connacht, along with parts of south Ulster and north Leinster – rebuilt their assize courthouses at the same time. Most benefited from central-government loans. In October 1822, the Mayo grand jurors received £2,407 to 'improve' their courthouse at Castlebar. They commissioned George Papworth to build what was, in fact, an entirely new building similar to Morrison's most popular design, but with the addition of a striking cast-iron fluted Doric portico that opened onto the town's main square (Fig. 2.14).[30] In neighbouring Roscommon the contractor of the county's recently built gaol (see Chapter 5) provided a new courthouse to replace one less than fifty years old (see Chapter 1), and £5,752 from Westminster went a long way towards making it possible. Planned from at least 1820, it was built in the years 1824–7 (Fig. 2.15) but does not exist today owing to a devastating fire in 1882.[31] Samuel Lewis, in 1837, noted its 'handsome and spacious' interiors, its Doric portico, and, with echoes of Kilmainham, the 'superb room for the grand jury'.[32] The Galway town grand jury was similarly enthusiastic about building a new courthouse at this time. Not to be outdone by the surrounding county (see Chapter 1), some town grand jurors had their old and admittedly rather fragile tholsel (Fig. 2.16) demolished before its replacement was even commenced, ensuring that the project would have to go ahead.[33] One contributor to the *Galway Advertiser* protested at the recklessness of the grand jurors, and there were claims of jobbery and waste: 'it is a notorious fact', claimed this critic, 'that our court house was taken down against the consent of the majority of the town'.[34] A local engineer, Alexander Hay, provided the drawings for its replacement. As the last piece in the jigsaw of large new public architecture in the Nun's Island–Newtownsmith area of the city – a kind of judicial-political quarter that we find in many Irish towns – the new town courthouse was a scaled-down copy of the adjacent county courthouse (Fig. 2.17).[35] A sizeable loan from the government aided the perpetually strained finances of the town grand jurors, and to complete the symmetry, they obtained a second loan in the summer of 1825 to add a matching fluted Doric portico to their new building (Fig. 2.18), a feature we see in all the 'new money' assize courthouses built in the west in these years.[36]

Fig. 2.14. Castlebar courthouse, *c.* 1900. Built by George Papworth in the early 1820s, it was extensively altered in the late 1850s. The central Doric portico was one of the first in Ireland to have been built of cast iron. When it was complete, there were clustered around this little green: two army barracks, two hospitals, the county gaol, and a Protestant church – all the perquisites of a county town. (*Reproduced courtesy of the National Library of Ireland.*)

Fig. 2.15. Roscommon town, showing the old and new gaols (the old to the top right, the new bottom left), and the old and new courthouses (the old marked 'R.C. Chapel', the new to the bottom left). Ordnance Survey six-inch map, surveyed January 1837. With their new gaol complete by 1819, the grand jurors moved to replace their 1760s courthouse (see Chapter 1) with a new building to the designs of Richard Richards. It was built in the years 1824–7 with the help of large government loans and formed a new square with the adjacent gaol, and a new centre of administration for the county. (*Reproduced courtesy of the Board of Trinity College Dublin.*)

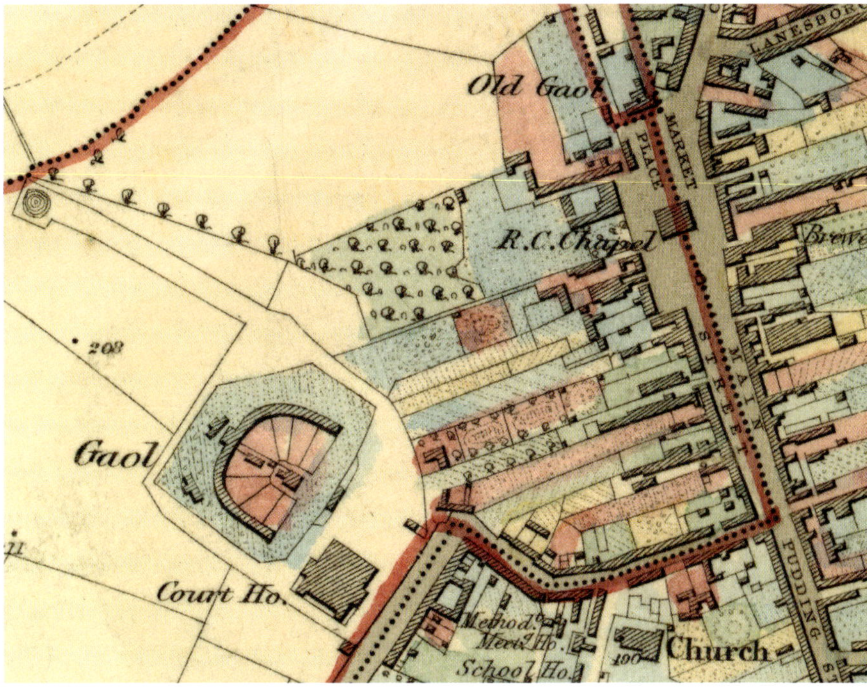

Fig. 2.16. Galway town tholsel, drawn by James Hardiman, *c.* 1820. Dilapidated and unstable by the 1820s, some members of the town grand jury had it pulled down before its replacement was even begun. (*Reproduced courtesy of Galway County Council Archives.*)

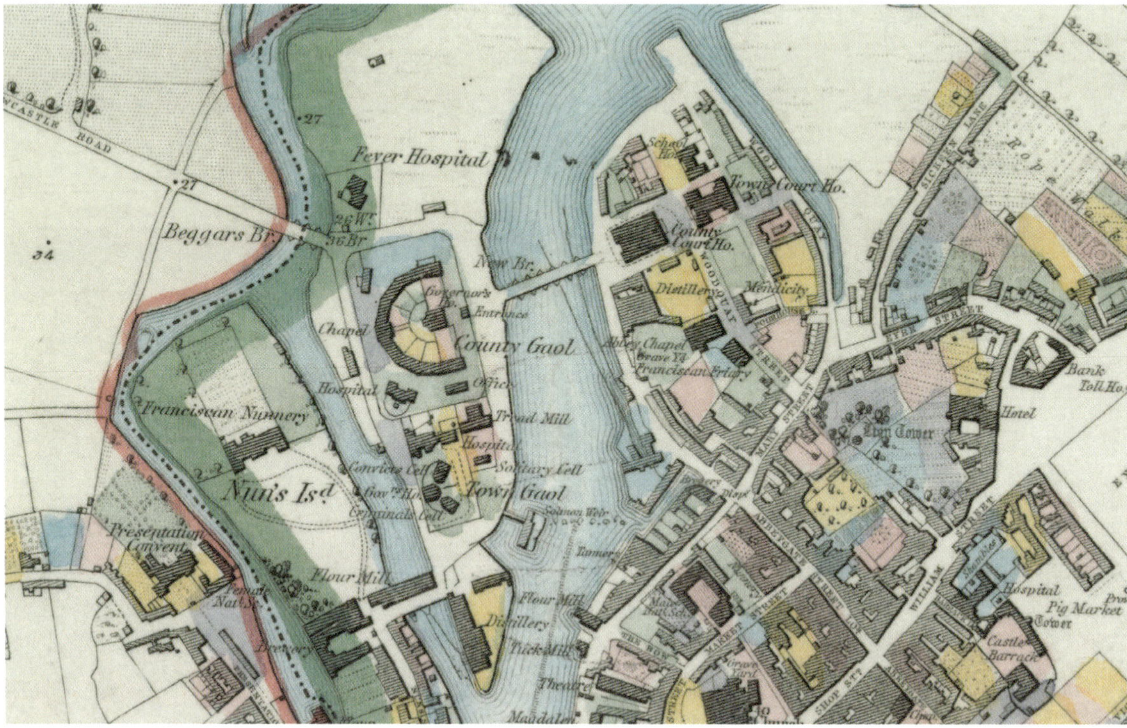

The building of new courthouses, as outlined in the Introduction, is often linked to a state's claim for power and authority, especially in regions marked by unrest or rebellion. The above section has focused mostly on economic and political factors, but we must ask if there were any discernible increases in the crime rates in the counties where new courthouses were planned and later built in these years. A full analysis is hampered by a gap in the publishing of indictment figures in the crucial years around 1820, and the questionable reliability of some surviving figures. For County Dublin the statistics are even more incomplete around the years when the new courthouse at Kilmainham was planned. However, those that survive show that criminal indictments in Dublin County were significantly higher in the early years of the century than in the period immediately before the new courthouse there was started. The picture was different in Roscommon, Cavan, Leitrim, and Fermanagh, where criminal indictments ranged from one-third to one-half higher (on average) in the 1810s than in the 1800s. In the case of Cavan, however, the new courthouse there had been signalled as early as 1807, when indictments were relatively lower, and was conceived as part of a new wide street planned by the local landlord.[37]

Fig. 2.17. Galway town, showing the Nun's Island–Newtownsmith quarter, divided by the River Corrib and its many harbours, races, and channels. Ordnance Survey six-inch map, surveyed January 1838. The opening of the new town courthouse opposite the county's building in the mid-1820s completed the twenty-year process of forming a new judicial-political district, with a bridge linking the two courthouses with their respective gaols. *(Reproduced courtesy of the Board of Trinity College Dublin.)*

Fig. 2.18. Galway town courthouse, with the bollards and chain of the county courthouse visible in the foreground, *c.* 1900. The town courthouse's architect, Alexander Hay, emulated both the fluted Doric order and the ceremonial heraldic animals and crown of Morrison's design from the previous decade. (*Reproduced courtesy of the National Library of Ireland.*)

Thus, the barometer of crime levels in any given county often played second fiddle to the larger agenda of urban 'improvement' in these years, even in cases where habeas corpus was regularly suspended. In Mayo indictment figures were relatively flat, and the great increase in crime and unrest happened only – ironically – in the years after the new courthouse had opened. In Galway town the figures fluctuated greatly, but rarely rose above three indictments a week, and were less than two a week in the year when the new courthouse was begun.[38] Even the dilapidated old tholsel could have accommodated this low level of judicial activity. It appears then, from a brief analysis of crime and unrest in these years, that competition and jealousy between grand juries, the architectural pretensions of key grand jurors (as in Dundalk in the previous decade), and (most crucially) the availability of large and generous loans were more important factors than the rise in crime or unrest in initiating the process of building a new assize courthouse. This is also true for the great crescendo of building activity that followed in the second half of the decade.

Architecture, sectarianism, and grand juries: the new courthouse at Monaghan

The second half of the 1820s witnessed the planning and commencement of the single greatest period of assize courthouse building in Irish history. Many of the characteristic elements of the time – such as inter-county rivalry and

Fig. 2.19. Monaghan courthouse, by Joseph Welland. Its planning exposed deep political divisions within the county grand jury in the years immediately prior to Catholic emancipation. (*Photograph by author, 2014.*)

grand juries' vociferous desire to appropriate the latest in fashionable neo-classical architecture – had deep roots that stretched back to the beginning of the century if not before. The help of generous government loans – coupled with a fall in average building labourers' wages – added to the sense of largesse.[39] The architect William Vitruvius Morrison, gifted and inventive, and son of the prolific courthouse architect Richard Morrison, stands out for his involvement in all of the most important new courthouses of this time. Before analysing three of these – the new courthouses at Tralee, Carlow, and Cork – we must consider the courthouse at Monaghan to understand the context for what would soon follow. The new courthouse there (Fig. 2.19) was built between 1827 and 1830 to the designs of Joseph Welland, a pupil of Bowden, who had erected courthouses in the north in the previous decade at Derry and Dundalk.[40] William Deane Butler had also prepared a design, in 1826, but Welland's was judged the winner in a grand-jury competition, and by July 1827 his design had been formally approved.[41] The grand jury did not seek any government loans, despite being eligible for them; instead, and unusually, they funded the £10,000 project purely from their county cess. Welland's design was primarily Greek in inspiration, and heavy in its details, with a weighty engaged Doric portico providing the central emphasis. The frieze and pediment above were plain, except for the coat of arms, atypically placed in the pediment and not crowning it (and unusually for such sculpture, it is still intact). On the ground floor, channelled rustication (a Palladian device somewhat at odds with the Greek portico) continues behind the engaged columns and piers and onto the flanking arched carriageways, giving the design a Piranesian sense of fortification.[42] It has a strong presence in the centre of the town, located where the old gaol had stood, and adjacent to another old establishment bastion: the Church of Ireland church.

We should question what pushed the Monaghan grand jurors into this action. There was certainly a significant increase in criminal indictments, with the ten-year average rising by half between 1805–15 and 1815–25. However, as before, it seems likely that a more important factor was that Monaghan was the only county in its region not to have rebuilt its assize courthouse by the mid-1820s.[43] The project is of particular interest on account of the divisions that appeared within the grand jury once the decision was made to build – a dispute that originated in the broader political battle for Catholic emancipation and which pitted the majority of the grand jury against one of the largest landholders in the town, Henry Westenra, 3rd Baron Rossmore, and MP for the county. An election in the summer of 1826 had seen rioting and violence in Monaghan, mostly between supporters of the 'Orange' Protestant candidate Charles Leslie, then foreman of the grand jury, and the supporters of the 'Catholic' party, headed by Westenra. He was a Protestant landlord who sympathised with the Catholic cause and this stance lost him much support among his more hard-line Protestant grand-jury colleagues. That summer, following an altercation in the grand-jury room of the old courthouse, a duel was staged between Westenra and a supporter of Leslie. Both men suffered minor injuries.[44] When the grand jury next met for the spring assizes in 1827, the atmosphere was understandably tense and boisterous; Westenra was not in attendance, presumably owing to his parliamentary duties, but the grand jury made clear its support for Leslie with a petition sent to parliament, signed by nineteen of the twenty-three jurors, that protested against 'any further concession' to the Catholics, whose clergy they branded as a 'bigoted priesthood' presiding 'over a population of some millions [with] ambitions of attaining political ascendancy'.[45] On the first evening of the Monaghan assizes, the *Freeman's Journal* reported, there were toasts to the king, the Duke of Wellington, the health of the ill prime minister, and Peel, 'the uncompromising advocate of Protestant principles'. The greatest cheering, described as 'immense' and 'loud and long continued', and nine separate toasts, came for William III and for 'Colonel Leslie and the Protestant interest of the county of Monaghan'. The grand-jury majority and its supporters toasted a host of minor officials and even the MP for neighbouring County Cavan but conspicuous by his absence was Westenra, the magnate of the town where they were gathered, who was not mentioned at all.[46]

At the assizes the grand jurors endorsed Welland's design for the new courthouse, and had copies sent to Dublin Castle for 'approval'. But it was quickly made clear to them that Dublin Castle had no power to interfere with their decision, nor with their application for a public-works loan should they consider applying for one. Such a degree of central-government involvement would come only after the Board of Works was reshaped in late 1831.[47] Nevertheless, Westenra now intervened and wrote in quick succession a series of letters to the lord lieutenant, pointing out serious flaws (as he saw them) with the design, and asking for the viceroy's approval (which Westenra also understood as necessary) to be delayed. 'I object,' he said, 'because a plan as economical and much more perfect, has been rejected, the beauty and magnificence of whose elevation would do credit to the town [and] would do credit to the Irish architect and to Ireland at large'; Welland's design, he claimed, would cost £1,000 more than the one recently rejected.[48] This plan was by William Vitruvius Morrison, who was then working with his father in designing additions and alterations to the Westenra family estate at Rossmore Park.[49] Yet Westenra's support for his architect was also backed up with his belief that Morrison's proposed courthouse had clear practical advantages for judges, jurors, and the public. Later in the summer, Westenra again wrote to Dublin, and while he acknowledged that Welland had

Fig. 2.20. Monaghan markethouse (1792), with the pediment displaying the coat of arms of the Westenra family, the proprietors of the town and one of the more influential political families in the county. (*Photograph by author, 2014.*)

won the premium fairly, he pointed out that the grand jury of County Kerry had adopted Morrison's 'far preferable' plan at less cost, and that other counties were now about to follow their lead. In Cork, he claimed, the design

> has been so much approved of … that a very great anxiety prevails there, (as I have been this day informed) to substitute the Kerry plan in the place of a courthouse they built 12 years ago at an expense of nearly £20,000 – and such a measure is to be proposed at these assizes …. The advantages of the Kerry plan are so obvious and great.[50]

Though McParland refers to Westenra as 'a member of the Monaghan grand jury', it is clear from the tone of his correspondence that he was very much an outsider in his own county, even though he was the local MP; his attempts to alter the legitimate majority decision of the grand jury seem unusually desperate and personally motivated.[51] Westenra was a marginalised figure on the Monaghan grand jury following the dispute over Catholic emancipation, and the majority of 'Orange' members, led by Leslie, were very unlikely to heed his architectural objections. A year later, they proceeded to arrange a contract with Welland to build the new courthouse, ending any possibility that Westenra's desires might be granted. It seems likely that Westenra's steadfast opposition only emboldened their resolve to push on, not to be seen to publicly support, in politics or in architecture, a sympathiser of Catholic emancipation. Welland's previous work at Derry, with its militantly Protestant grand jury, coupled with Westenra's desire to follow the southern (more Catholic majority) counties of Kerry and Cork probably further cemented opinion in the grand-jury room. Though the Westenra family coat of arms adorns the markethouse in the town (Fig. 2.20), and his family held the coveted position of lord lieutenant of the county for much of the 1830s and 1840s, the events of 1826–7 ensured that he would have to make do with Leslie's choice of courthouse.[52] Local landlords were almost always keen and vocal supporters of new buildings in their towns; in Monaghan this was much less the case. Yet the influx of money that the construction site brought, and the sense that the town was being 'improved', may have provided Westenra with some compensation for his political losses.

The flow of information

In Monaghan, politics and religion played a larger role in decision-making by the grand jury than the state of crime and unrest in the county. The case study also brings up some revealing underlying themes that need to be further explored. First, the demonstratively 'Orange' character of the grand jury, and the growing division and infighting within it over the issue of Catholic emancipation, were not at all untypical. In fact, the Monaghan jurors are emblematic of the fractured and weakening position of the Protestant party nationally in the years leading to Catholic emancipation in 1829. Second, Westenra's detailed knowledge of local affairs in counties Kerry and Cork – 'a very great anxiety', as he was able to state – hints at the feverishly competitive spirit among the small political elite of the time. Likewise, it shows the willingness of grand juries to spend vast sums of public money in replacing relatively new courthouses, if only because an architect's inventive design was particularly appealing and capable of generating such acclaim. It is hardly surprising that these peak years of building coincided with hostile opinion pieces in the newspapers, and commentary from travel writers, centred on the waste and excess of the grand juries. The *Freeman's Journal* opined in April 1828 that

> general and competent inspectors should … be selected, and general plans approved by the best engineers …. An additional expense would thereby be avoided, and the caprice of grand juries obviated – for it has frequently happened that grand juries have decided that new courthouses and sessions' houses were requisite, and the old court and sessions' houses should be pulled down, which, if altered or enlarged, would have perfectly answered the purpose …. All this at great expense and taxation to the people.[53]

In a decade marked by the absence of any serious grand-jury reform, James Bicheno, visiting in 1829, thought that 'the Irish gentry have been spoilt by indulgence. The Government has always been ready to help them on every emergency, and they have never been taught to rely upon themselves. Incredible sums have been expended.'[54] The chorus of voices, then, calling for reform was reaching a crescendo at the same time as some of the most impressive and costly assize courthouses were taking shape.

Furthermore, Westenra's knowledge of the plans for new courthouses in Kerry and Cork is interesting and needs to be further explored. We should ask what were the mechanics by which such information was transmitted and disseminated in a country where, as Ian d'Alton has argued, Protestant landowning society was 'extremely localized and inbred'.[55] Without these channels of communication, the inter-county competitive rivalry that we see operating between grand juries could simply not have existed. At the most basic level there were kinship and friendship ties linking geographically dispersed grand juries. Most MPs also served some time on grand juries, and these men would have often met during the parliamentary seasons in Dublin before 1800 and afterwards at Westminster. Newspapers played a critical role, with many assize courthouses having 'newsrooms' – spaces where the local elite could gather to read the news and where information could be circulated. Jonathan Binns noted the 'excellent newsroom' at Cavan courthouse in 1835.[56] The newspapers published in great detail the proceedings of assizes throughout the country and publicised their dates of meeting well in advance.[57] The government also issued an increasing number of widely distributed publications from the 1820s onwards, such as the annual reports of the new prison inspectors, printed and distributed to grand juries from 1823, and quoted at length in the national and local press. The impact of these reports will be considered in more detail in chapters 5, 6 and 7.

But it was the well-publicised commentary of travelling assize judges that is likely to have had the greatest effect. Ireland was divided into seven 'circuits', with judges travelling with full ceremony among them twice every year (Fig. 2.21). They were formally received at the county border by the high sheriff and escorted to the assize town, where they would swear in the grand jury, comment on the state of crime and the condition of public buildings in the county and

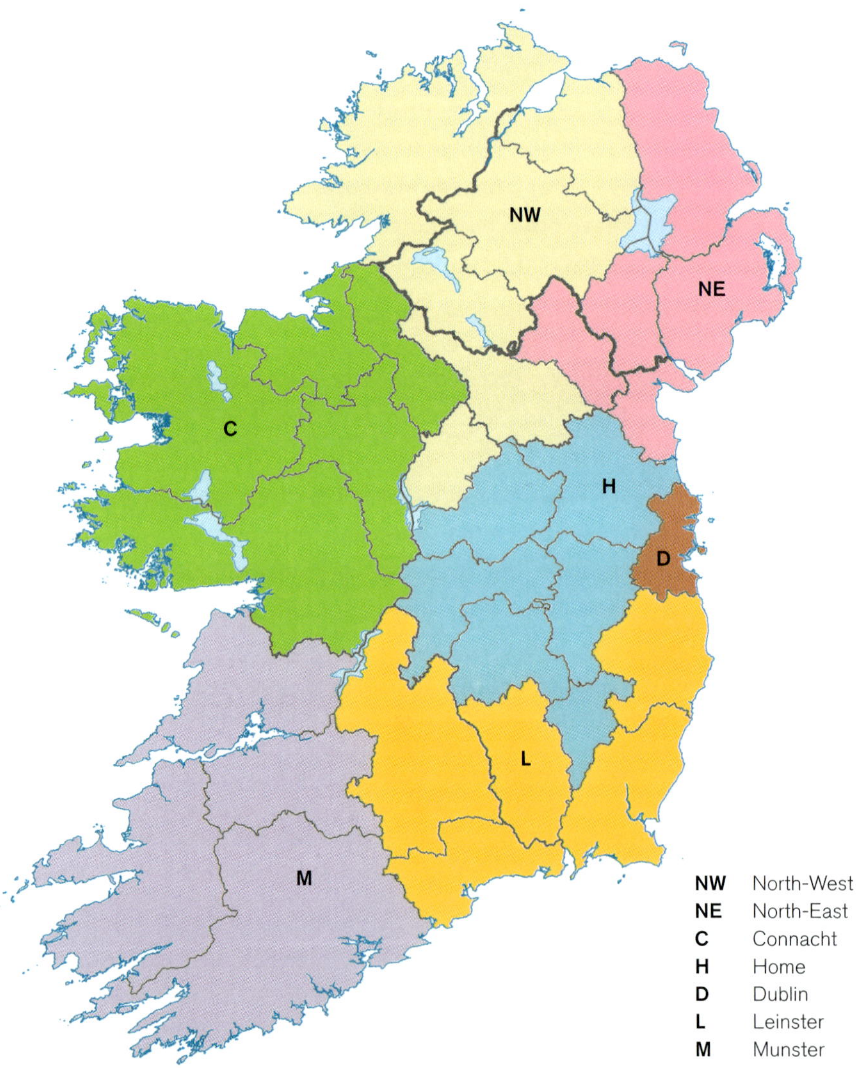

Fig. 2.21. The seven assize circuits in Ireland in the early nineteenth century. Judges used commitments by one grand jury to build new courthouses or gaols as a means of jolting nearby counties into action.

proceed to hear criminal cases and approve presentments. It is surely more than a coincidence that some of these circuits – for example, the Connacht and the North-West circuits – were also regions where clusters of new assize courthouses were built within very short periods of time. The Fermanagh grand jurors, for instance, must have felt somewhat self-conscious in the early 1820s when welcoming the assize judge to their old courthouse so soon after he had spent a week working in neighbouring Cavan's impressive new building. Though it was only from about 1823 that newspapers such as the *Freeman's Journal* and *Finn's Leinster Journal* took an interest in and published judges' comments, they had already been an integral part of the assizes for many years. From the 1820s, however, judges could fortify their opinions with regular reference to the new prison inspectors' reports. By offering critical comments about public buildings that judges knew would be published in the national press, these officials could greatly ratchet up the competitive pressure on the grand juries to maintain the latest, most fashionable, and best-planned courthouses. For a case study, let us take Carlow and the comments of assize judges there in the years leading to the county's decision to rebuild its courthouse.

Protestant politics and assize judges: the planning of Carlow's courthouse

For many years after 1800 the assize judge who travelled the home circuit (counties Carlow, Kildare, Queen's County (now Laois), King's County (now Offaly), Westmeath, and Meath) was the infamous, theatrical, and divisive figure of John Toler, Lord Norbury.[58] Following the 1798 rebellion, Norbury had led many of the heavy-handed prosecutions by the government with, as his biographer has commented, a 'ferocity which was unusual even by the standards of the time'.[59] In the more peaceful years of the 1820s, he enjoyed his visits to Carlow, where the crime rate was very low. At the summer assizes in 1822, for example, only eighteen persons were indicted.[60] Two years later, in 1824, there was not a single 'capital crime' on the books, a circumstance that was all the more impressive because the neighbouring counties of Kilkenny, Queen's, and Kildare had all been placed under the Insurrection Act. The conservative *Carlow Morning Post* suggested that the tranquillity arose from just and fair magistrates, allegedly uncorrupted by any 'Orange' political faction that could inflame tensions.[61] This would appear to have been quite an exaggeration. Norbury arrived in the county on 29 July 1824 and swore in the grand jury at the old courthouse at

Dreighton Hall. Colonel Henry Bruen, a local landlord and magnate of the town, was appointed foreman. Addressing the grand jurors, Norbury observed that 'although you have the heaviest crops, you have the lightest calendar you ever had', adding that they had much to be proud of, and that 'they were doing the best they could for the country – while the brawlers were heaping calumnies on Ireland'. Jovial and in good spirits, he briefly mentioned the county's schools, private charities, and prisons. The *Freeman's Journal* recorded that he had ended by saying that 'he would not detain them longer, for he knew that there were charming works going on in the country, and that they wish "to make hay while the sun shines." (Laughter.)'.[62] The next spring Norbury was back in Carlow and again cheerful, as he congratulated the county on the fact that there were fewer prisoners for trial than members of the grand jury present (twenty-three). Alluding to a recently published propaganda pamphlet, *The Ghost of the Catholic Association of Ireland*, which chronicled O'Connell's struggle to achieve Catholic emancipation, and to the recent suppression of the Catholic Association, Norbury concluded his address by poking fun at the Catholic movement:

> We will administer justice according to law, for we are bound to do it .... We are not menaced by any law ... but are menaced by the GHOST of that body that is just extinguished. – (Laughter.) You will not be extinguished nor intimidated by the *Ghost.* (Loud laughter.) I would not take the Ghost's word for it for £1000 (continued laughter). Gentlemen, go to your room, and do your business.[63]

The warm reception for Norbury's anti-Catholic comments by the local Protestant elite gives us an insight into the political colours of the Carlow grand jury at the time. Two years later, the *Freeman's Journal* carried a piece from the *Kilkenny Independent* in which it named those Carlow gentry whom it believed had signed an anti-Catholic 'Orange' petition: the petition included the names of most of the grand jurors of the time, except for Bruen and a few others.[64] Further sectarian divisions were aired in reports in 1831 that the Carlow grand jury had, at the summer assizes that year, drunk toasts to 'the *brave yeomanry* of Newtownbarry' (a 1798 battle site, now Bunclody, County Wexford), to 'Our feet on the necks of Papists in cold blood', to 'The Pope in the pillory in hell', and to the colourful image of 'the devil pelting priests at him', and finally and rather predictably, to 'the glorious, pious, and immortal memory of King William the Third'. The *Carlow Morning Post* expressed its hope that local magistrates found to have signed this petition would be removed from their positions by the government, but the foreman for that particular grand jury was quick to deny that these toasts had ever happened, saying that he had left the feast at an early hour along with several other members of the grand jury, and that he had no recollection that these inflammatory toasts had occurred. About events later in the night, of course, he could not comment.[65]

It is hardly surprising, then, that figures such as Norbury, stoking the flames of sectarian division, were attacked by O'Connell, who sent a petition to parliament in May 1826 calling for his removal from the bench owing to his diminished faculties, and noting that he was 'so deaf that it requires a great exertion of the human voice to make him hear anything; and he is also affected very frequently with a species of lethargic stupor resembling sleep'.[66] Yet in March of that year Norbury was back in Carlow and commented, 'I am always rejoiced when I come to this part of Ireland, which enjoys so much happiness and tranquillity, at a time when other parts of the country are overwhelmed with criminal excesses.' He heaped praise on the grand jurors, referring to them as a 'valuable resident gentry ... of high intellectual qualifications [and] the proud aristocracy of Ireland'.[67] Norbury was finally convinced to retire in the following year with the offer of an earldom, and at the spring assizes in 1827 he was replaced by Charles Kendal Bushe (1767–1843), the lord chief justice and a former defence barrister.[68] In all his recorded comments at Carlow, Norbury never made any mention of the condition of the old courthouse. Bushe would prove quite the opposite.

The difference in tone – where theatre, performance, and representation were so important – of Bushe's first address to the Carlow grand jury is remarkable. Though he expressed his happiness at the continued low level of crime, he drew attention to the 'very imperfect jail' of the county (something that apparently had not concerned Norbury), which he made clear was the grand jurors' responsibility to improve (see Chapter 6). His role, he said, was to ensure that they followed the recommendations of the prison inspectors, and he specifically referred to his power to *force* them to act if they prevaricated, though he added that this step would hopefully not be necessary. He asked them to 'reflect' on the findings of the report and, using other counties as part of his carrot-and-stick approach, he pointed out to the Carlow grand jurors that their colleagues in Meath had recently presented a very large sum for a new gaol. He then proceeded to criticise the condition of the courthouse:

> [I] could not but express [my] astonishment at the state of the county court-house. Upon looking round [I] could see no accommodation

for the public, for the bar, for juries or for the judge. There was no evidence of cleanliness in its condition, nor of taste in its structure. It was altogether unsuitable for all or any of the purposes to which a court-house should be devoted; and if the gentlemen of the grand jury meant to be frugal of expenditure in its improvement, their parsimony was anything but economy. The court-house was, in a word, everything that was odious and was a reproach to the county.[69]

In all his recorded addresses in Carlow, Norbury had never made comments so stinging and direct in their language. Bushe for his part made no anti-Catholic jibes, and the grand jurors must have had little to laugh about and could only have reflected on his particularly acidic criticisms of their main public buildings. In response, they immediately presented £7,000 for additions to the gaol and £5,000 for a new courthouse when they next met.[70] Bushe's words clearly had had the effect he desired. It is likely that these grand jurors were also spurred into action that year by the recent completion of the architecturally distinguished new quarter-sessions courthouse in nearby Bagenalstown (Fig. 2.22), which had been paid for by the local landlord, and which featured a full Ionic portico of Carlow granite – a majestic folly in a small town.[71] The contrast between Carlow's assize courthouse and this new building turned upside-down the general tendency for assize courthouses to be the most ornate and architecturally embellished courthouse in any given county. At the same time, the neighbouring counties of Kilkenny and Wicklow also refurbished and extended their assize courthouses. Bushe's comments reinforced what must have been apparent to many grand jurors: their old courthouse was now decidedly shabby and outmoded and needed replacement. Rivalry appears to have existed, then, not just between counties but also within them.

Bushe continued to visit Carlow for the assizes in 1827 and 1828, and throughout this period the calendar of trials remained light.[72] There was, then, no correlation between the county's crime rate and the decision of the grand jury to build a new assize courthouse at this time. Clearly other factors, as previously discussed, played a larger role. At the summer assizes in 1828 Bushe sharply addressed the grand jurors and their foreman Bruen, making it clear that he was impatient at the time being taken to begin work on the county's public buildings. Once again he 'called their attention to the condition of the courthouse and to the jail .... [I have] repeatedly besought and entreated [your] especial attention to the cases in question – and to the supply of the public wants.'[73]

Fig. 2.22. Bagenalstown quarter-sessions courthouse. Built about 1826, the majestic splendour of this wayside courthouse threw the dilapidated condition of the county's main building into sharp focus only a year before the grand jurors were strongly encouraged to replace it. (*Photograph by author, 2013.*)

Raising the bar

Like Westenra in Monaghan, by 1828 the Carlow grand jury had learned of a new courthouse design proposed for Tralee by William Vitruvius Morrison. In Kerry the competition lay mostly with the grand jurors of neighbouring Cork, who since 1824 had rebuilt seven of their quarter-sessions courthouses and bridewells to a standard design by the fashionable Munster-based architects James and George Richard Pain, renowned for their association with John Nash, the king's architect in London. The Cork programme was without doubt the most ambitious of its time and set high standards throughout the region. The Pains had also won county-gaol commissions in Limerick and Cork and had built Mitchelstown Castle, the most ostentatious and expensive Gothic-revival country house in Ireland, for the Earl of Kingston. Despite years of negative comments from the prison inspectors about the condition of the bridewells in County Kerry, it was 1827 before the grand jurors there decided to act. They commissioned the Pains to build seven new bridewells throughout the county as well as to extend their county gaol, and at the same time committed to building a new courthouse in Tralee.[74] After years of delays all the building work came at once. As in Cork, the Kerry grand jurors used the crutch of public-works loans to help them to complete such an ambitious plan. The Pains' near monopoly on courthouse architecture in the south-west, however, was broken when the Kerry grand jury settled on the young Morrison, who had returned to Ireland after some years in Italy, France, and England in the mid-1820s, with a new design for a courthouse inspired by Irish, English, and French sources that would revolutionise and in time dominate the courthouse-building market in Ireland.[75]

The unexecuted design that Morrison had submitted for Monaghan was likely very similar in its novel plan and elegant elevation to his built schemes for Tralee and Carlow. His major innovation was to refashion the courtroom as a semi-circular space with surrounding corridors (Fig. 2.23), providing ample space for the public to circulate, and using the central space between the two courtrooms to provide more space for judges, and petty juries, as well as access to function rooms for the grand jury. Here Morrison was probably inspired by the semi-circular lecture theatre that his father had built for Sir Patrick Dun's Hospital in Dublin, built 1803–16 (Fig. 2.24), by the rational and geometrical planning of French Beaux-Arts architects of the late eighteenth century such as J.-N.-L. Durand, and also, and perhaps most recently, by Robert Smirke's Gloucester Shire Hall, built 1814–16 (Fig. 2.25), the merits of which would have been known to many members of the Irish elite owing to Gloucester's being a regular stopping-off point on the route between Ireland and Westminster.[76] In his elevation, Morrison allowed the shape of the courtrooms to dictate the exterior appearance of the building, bulging out on either side of the central portico. He also placed his courthouse on a high and expansive podium (Fig. 2.26) – the new courthouse at Dundalk was criticised by the architect Charles Robert Cockerell on his visit to

Ireland in 1823 for lacking a proper podium.[77] Undoubtedly, the excitement in Monaghan, Cork, Kerry, and Carlow caused by his proposed design confirms that it was seen at the time as the latest, most fashionable, and most advanced plan for an Irish courthouse, and one that ambitious grand jurors, especially those hurt by criticisms (such as those of Carlow) or sensing that they were falling behind their neighbours (like those of Kerry), were keen to emulate.

The old courthouse at Tralee was a small and undistinguished building on the Market Square, described in 1830, using a common trope of the time, as

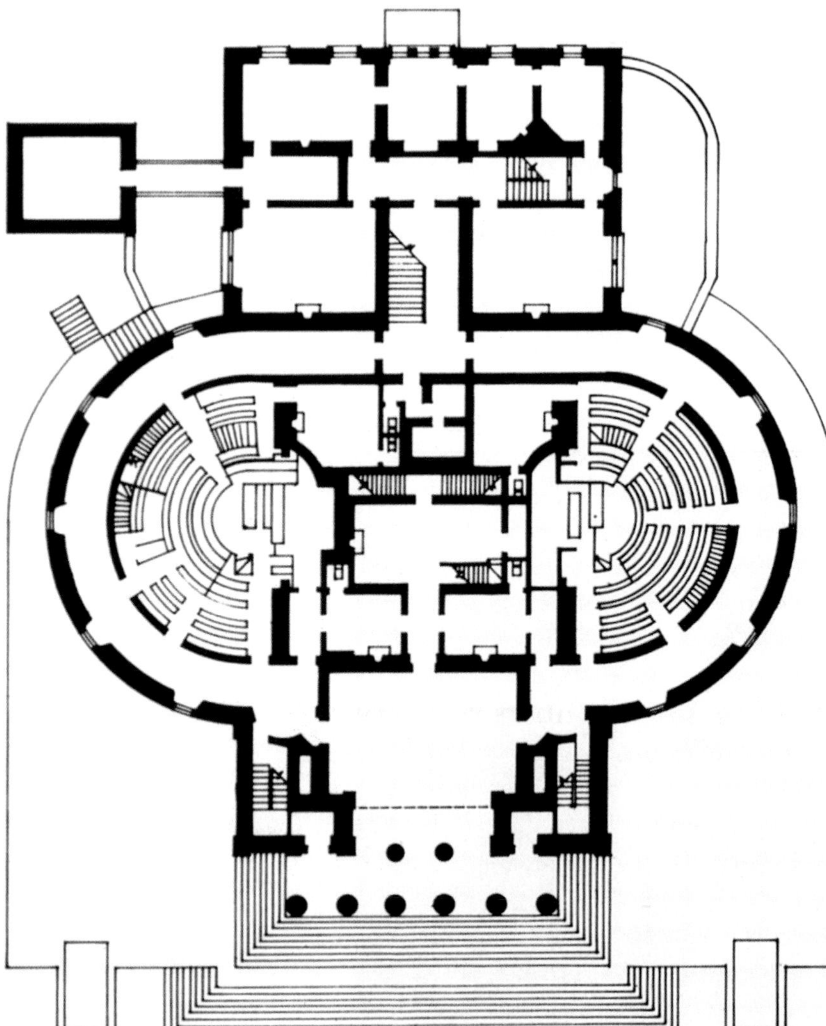

Fig. 2.23. Tralee courthouse, ground-floor plan. William Vitruvius Morrison, built 1830–3. Morrison's semi-circular courtrooms and clever arrangement of meeting rooms was a revolutionary moment in the history of the Irish courthouse and was widely emulated in the following decades. From Rowan, *Architecture of Richard Morrison & William Vitruvius Morrison* (1989). (*Reproduced courtesy of the Irish Architectural Archive.*)

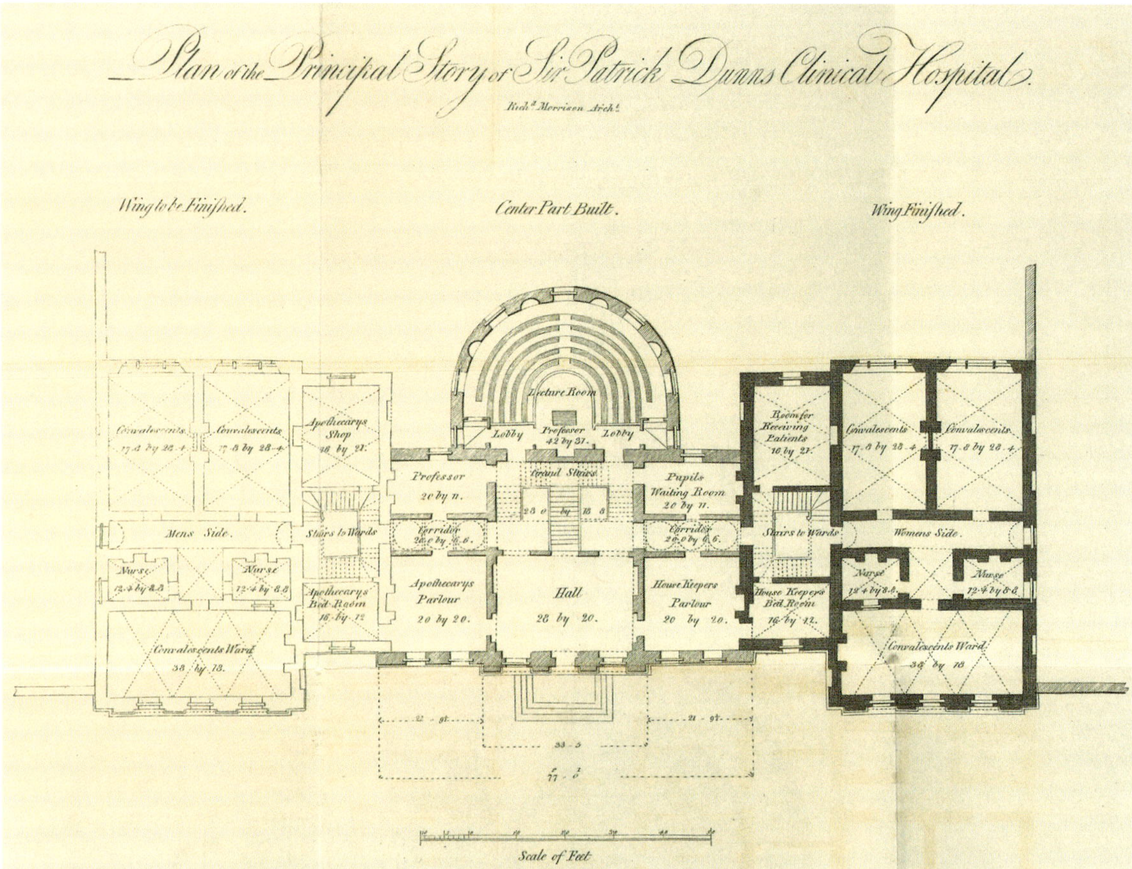

Fig. 2.24. (above) Sir Patrick Dun's Hospital, Dublin, ground-floor plan of unfinished building, 1809. Richard Morrison, 1803–16. The semi-circular lecture theatre (dem.), probably derived from Gondoin's École de Chirurgie in Paris (1780), may have inspired the younger Morrison's courtroom design. From Rowan, *Architecture of Richard Morrison & William Vitruvius Morrison* (1989). (*Reproduced courtesy of the Irish Architectural Archive.*)

Fig. 2.25. (opposite bottom) Gloucester Shire Hall. Robert Smirke, 1814–16. The polygonal courtroom was later emulated by Morrison and others in Ireland. (*Photograph by author, 2019.*)

Fig. 2.26. (above) Tralee courthouse, c. 1900. Set on a high podium, the two great semi-circular courtrooms dictated the exterior appearance of the building. Grand jurors as far apart as Carlow, Monaghan, and Cork were envious of Morrison's elegant new design for Kerry's principal courthouse. (*Reproduced courtesy of the National Library of Ireland.*)

'unsafe' and 'inconvenient'. Following a first presentment at the spring assizes of 1827, overseers were appointed in 1828 and a loan application was sent to the government but owing to a technicality the loan was initially refused. The promoters noted that, as in Carlow, the need for a replacement 'has invariably been pressed upon [us] by every judge of assize'. A second application for £7,000 was in turn refused because insufficient securities had been offered (normally the desired security was a mortgage over some part of the county cess).[78] Clearly impatient by March 1830, the grand jurors made another attempt and this time they were successful and were granted by government £9,350, and an additional sum for building new bridewells in smaller towns.[79] Work began almost immediately and was complete by August 1833. The *Western Herald* commented in 1833 that 'our new County Court House … rises in architectural beauty and splendid decoration'.[80] Soon after, Henry David Inglis visited and found a great number of unemployed persons, who had initially come to the town to seek work in building the new courthouse but whose labour was no longer required.[81]

Morrison exhibited his Tralee design at the Royal Academy in 1828, but by this time its fame, as noted earlier, had spread as far as Monaghan and Cork.[82] The new courthouse comprised two semi-circular courtrooms grouped behind a hexastyle Ionic portico, all placed on a high podium. On the inside the curved wings provided for complex and interesting spaces such as a colonnaded public circulation corridor behind the main benches of the courtrooms, all lit from on high by thermal windows. As McParland has commented regarding the façade, the curved wings look like Martello towers translated into a Greek idiom, with heavy pedimented windows (now filled in) breaking up the monotony of the curves.[83] The site, on a narrow street where the old county gaol had stood, was less than ideal for such a large building.[84] Around this time a new street – Denny Street – was planned and laid out to the south of the town centre; while this might have provided an ideal location for the new courthouse, the grand jury's ownership of the old gaol site must have been both financially and logistically quite convenient.[85] Here again courthouse building intersected with – but also remained independent of – urban improvement more generally. Whatever the criticisms of the site, the overall composition of the new courthouse, with its powerful yet restrained use of the Greek style, expresses more vividly than any courthouse in Ireland built since Dundalk the judicial purposes of the building. This is further emphasised by the lack of decorative sculpture – a final break from the Gandon tradition established at Waterford. Tralee set a very high bar for other grand juries to adapt or copy from the 1820s onwards.

Reverberations at Carlow

The Tralee plan made waves in Carlow (Fig. 2.27) as it had done in Monaghan and Cork. Such was the rush to make a presentment in the wake of Bushe's critical remarks that the first plan was so hastily conceived that it ended in lawsuits and unhappy building contractors in 1828 before any work had even begun. The grand jurors had to admit that, owing to these problems, and the issue of paying compensation to the occupier of the proposed site, the new building could not now be finished before 1831, and in their correspondence with William Gregory in Dublin Castle they expressed a palpable sense of missing out in these feverish years of building. Their language is instructive, when they claimed to be 'the only [county] in Ireland, or at most with the exception of one or two more, that has not within a few years built a new courthouse or repaired the old one on the new & improv'd plan'.[86]

The location of the new courthouse was a matter of controversy. The first contract with Williams & Cockburn of Dublin was abandoned in May 1828 because of a change of mind on the part of the commissioners over the site. By moving from a more central location to the 'Y' junction created by the

Fig. 2.27. Carlow courthouse, portico. The feverish building years of the early nineteenth century, fuelled by wartime prosperity and later large government loans, culminated in the construction of Ireland's grandest and most sublime assize courthouse in one of its smallest counties. (*Photograph taken in 2007.*)

Dublin and Athy roads at the northern edge of the town, the contractors felt that more excavation would be required to set down firm foundations (there had previously been a quarry on the site), and that the exposed surroundings would mean that they would need to employ watchmen both day and night for security.[87] Since the voiding of this contract delayed the entire project by at least two years and left the grand jurors with legal problems that they claimed they were 'totally at a loss' to resolve, we may question why they changed their minds over the site so late in the planning process.[88] It has been suggested in recent years by Mary Teehan that the Catholic bishop of Kildare and Leighlin, James Doyle – a prominent campaigner for Catholic emancipation – wished to build his new cathedral in Carlow on the site where the courthouse was eventually built, and that the grand jurors objected to this and instead took the site for their own use. If this is true, the disagreements must have been settled by March 1828, when Doyle laid the foundation stone for his new cathedral (Fig. 2.28) on an inferior and cramped site in the centre of the town.[89] In view of the presence of 'Orange' elements within the grand jury, as previously mentioned, there may be some truth to this version of events. An alternative theory, as suggested by a rather light-hearted article in the local paper, *The Nationalist and Leinster Times*, in 1888, is that Henry Bruen, the local MP and landlord, forced the change of site (Fig. 2.29) because one of the two roads emanating from the junction led directly to his house, Oak Park. The grand jury, the author claimed,

> demurred to placing the courthouse on a quarry hole at the junction of [two roads] leading to … Colonel Bruen's demesne, as he wished. He could only get time to defer a decision to the next assizes, when he produced a private act of parliament that he managed to smuggle through in the meantime, for building the courthouse over a deep pool [so] as to require some tiers of vaults to raise the building to the intended height, and the confined damp in which caused dry rot, so that most of the woodwork had to be renewed in a few years.[90]

Yet no such act of parliament appears to exist and as such the origins of this rumour are unclear. These reminiscences, in the heated political atmosphere of the 1880s, may have more to do with land politics in the town than architectural patronage, and as a record published nearly forty years after the events in question, the value of this explanation may lie more with the strong association that it suggests between Bruen and the building project. It is telling that when the courthouse was only newly built, an Irish travel writer visiting Carlow credited Bruen with having played a key role in the new courthouse.[91] Furthermore, in the 1830s Bruen employed Morrison to carry out works at his country house, including a triumphal arch with a

Fig. 2.28. Cathedral of the Assumption of the Blessed Virgin Mary, Carlow. Thomas Cobden, 1828–34. (*Photograph by author, 2012.*)

Fig. 2.29. Carlow town, showing the location of the new courthouse at the 'Y' junction of the Dublin and Athy roads. From Matthew McDermott, 'The Morrisons', *RIAI Yearbook* (1977). (*Reproduced courtesy of the RIAI.*)

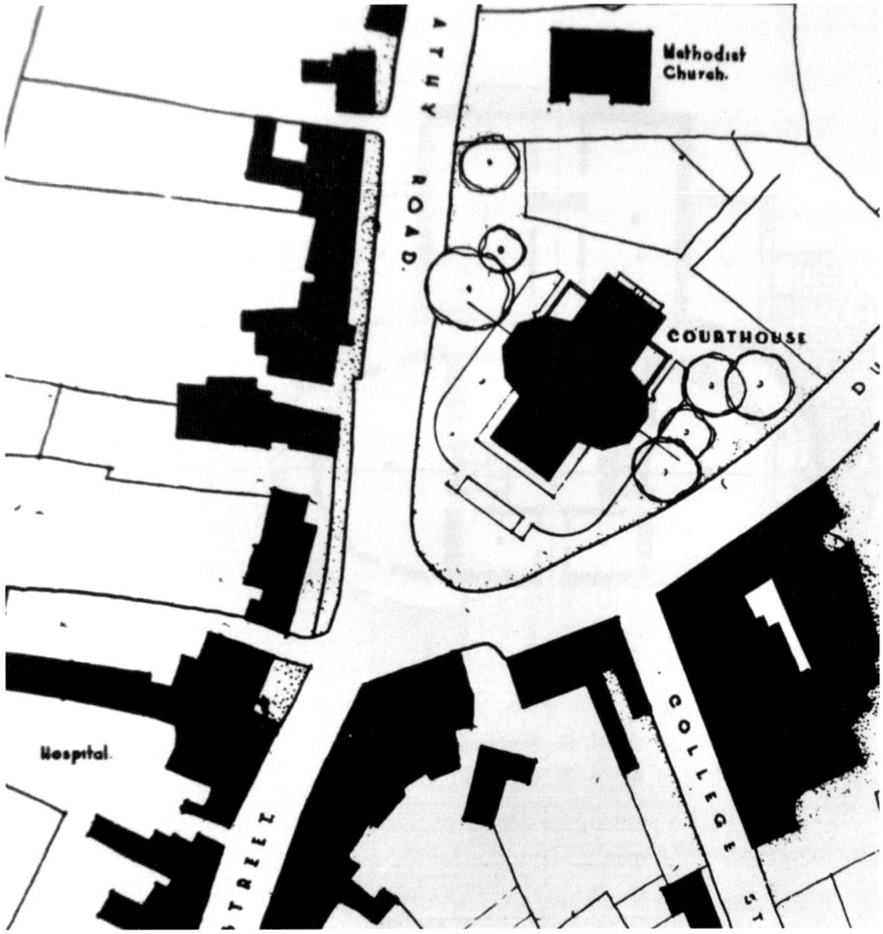

curved turning space for carriages (Fig. 2.30), situated on the road between the new courthouse and his home – a beautiful architectural feature with an Ionic order facing the town, and a Doric one facing his house.[92] For Bruen, then, the building work at Carlow from the late 1820s was likely a part of his broader 'improvement' work on his town and country estate.

The new courthouse at Carlow opened in July 1834 when 'a great number of the gentry of the town and county' gathered to see the grand jury sworn in.[93] It is an architectural achievement of national importance, and one that deserves better protection today. Morrison built on the success of Tralee by reshaping the wings as half-decagons instead of semi-circles (Figs 2.31, 2.32), thereby obviating the rather awkward join between the plain and curved walls that was left unresolved at Tralee. As the government loan for £5,000 was

Fig. 2.30. Oak Park, Carlow, entrance gateway and carriage turn. William Vitruvius Morrison, 1832. While Morrison was building a new courthouse for the county, one of the leading grand jurors, Henry Bruen, procured designs for additions to his country house, including this triumphal arch gateway, through which Bruen passed on his travels to the courthouse. (*Photograph by author, 2014.*)

approved only in August 1832, there was plenty of time for Morrison (and the Board of Works architect after 1831, Jacob Owen) to alter various aspects of the plan.[94] The portico developed from what was originally a tetrastyle design (Fig. 2.31), like Tralee, into the far more impressive octastyle Ilissus-style Ionic one, with, as McParland has noted, a full temple front (Figs 2.33, 2.34) where the 'pronaos is sheltered by having each of its side walls returned for one bay towards the centre, rather than ending in antae'.[95] Not only are the decagonal wings and generous octastyle portico important developments on the Tralee model, but the use of an excellent local granite throughout gives the façade a crisp and monumental elegance that distinguishes it from all other Irish courthouses. In choosing such an open site, the grand jurors ensured that their new courthouse would command a strong presence in the urban fabric of the town, and they used the extra space of this open site to encircle the building with a heavy metal palisade of fasces (Fig. 2.35), following a design very similar to that used in Tullamore's new gaol a few years earlier. An eagle-eyed travel writer visiting Carlow in 1845 specifically noted these fasces as missing from the new courthouse that she had recently seen at Tralee.[96] Stung by the chief justice's criticisms and conscious that neighbouring counties had bettered them in the race to obtain the most luxurious public architecture, the Carlow grand jurors under Bruen responded with force and determination and showed other counties that they were not bystanders in the inter-county competition of these

Fig. 2.31. Carlow courthouse, ground-floor plan, early unexecuted design. William Vitruvius Morrison, *c.* 1827. Clearly adapting his Tralee building, but with polygonal rather than semi-circular courtrooms, its architect transformed the simple tetrastyle portico into a more memorable, full octastyle-temple arrangement. (*Reproduced courtesy of Carlow County Library.*)

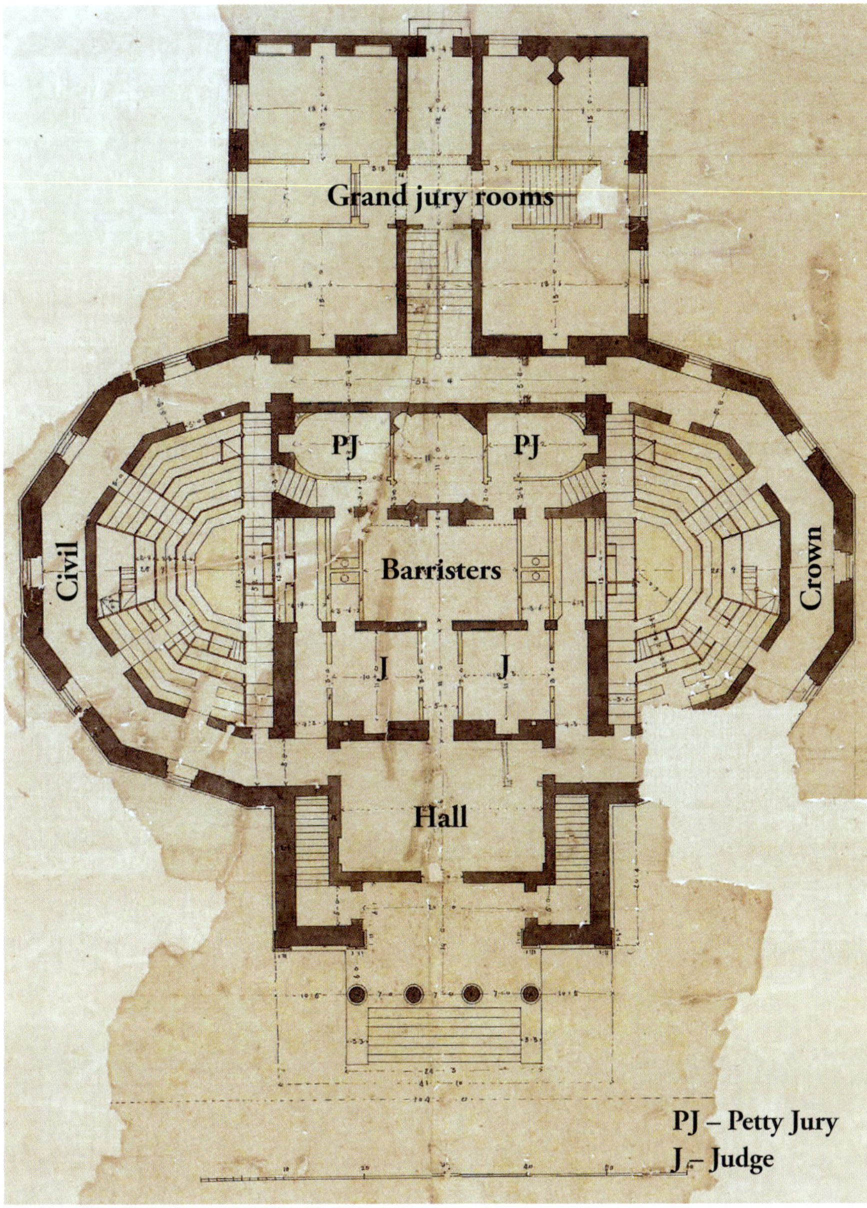

years. Their new courthouse was also a clear political statement in a county riven with sectarian and political divisions.[97] Perhaps because of all these forces, Carlow courthouse is the supreme Irish provincial courthouse of the first half of the nineteenth century, and arguably the greatest building in a county marked by its architectural riches.

Fig. 2.32. Carlow courthouse, interior of a courtroom, *c.* 1985. Above the judge's chair a large thermal window lit the multi-layered seating of the elegant six-sided space. Galleries provided space for journalists and the public. (*Reproduced courtesy of the Irish Architectural Archive.*)

Fig. 2.33. Carlow courthouse, front-elevation drawing. The lower central portion of the building allowed light to enter the courtrooms through large thermal windows, a deceit hidden from normal view by the high podium on which the building is placed. From Matthew McDermott, 'The Morrisons', *RIAI Yearbook* (1977). (*Reproduced courtesy of the RIAI.*)

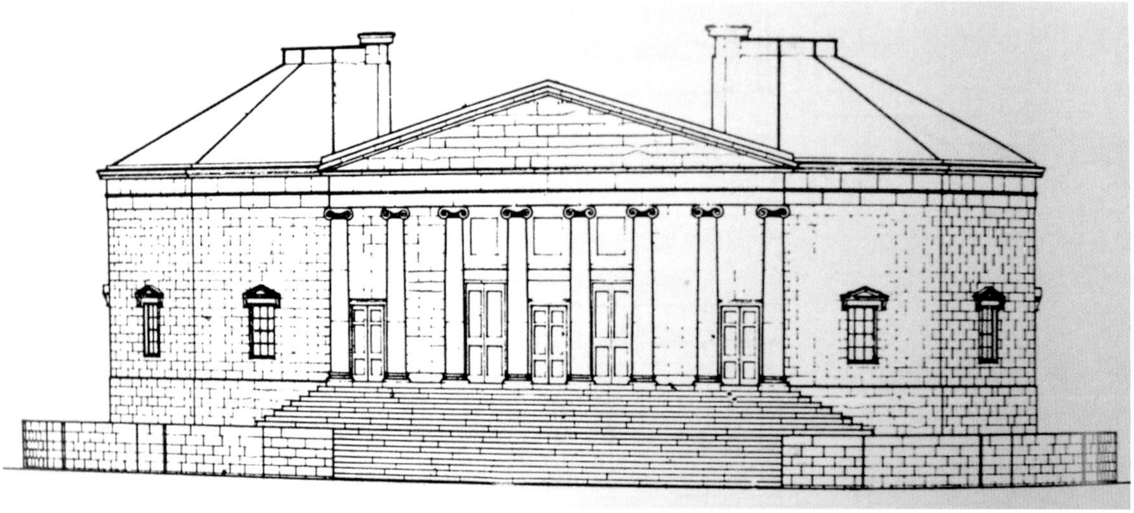

Fig. 2.34. (left) Carlow courthouse. By the time the courthouse was complete in 1834, the political and economic circumstances that had permitted it to be built had been undermined by Catholic emancipation and by a more proactive and reforming central government. (*Photograph by author, 2012.*)

Fig. 2.35. (right) Carlow courthouse, surrounded by metal palisade railings with fasces and axes, a feature of many courthouses and gaols of the early nineteenth century. Lydia Jane Fisher visited Tralee courthouse in 1845 and commented that this was 'a handsome building, [but I] regretted that the paling was not like that which surrounds the court-house at Carlow, which is formed of iron bars, tied in bundles, and made in imitation of the fasces of the Roman lictors – very pretty and very appropriate'. (*Reproduced courtesy of the National Library of Ireland.*)

Cork coda

The last assize courthouse in Ireland to be planned before the granting of Catholic emancipation in 1829 was for the county and city of Cork (Fig. 2.36). The building, which has a complicated design history (both the Pain and Deane families were associated with it at various points), has been the subject of two recent excellent accounts, by Patrick Holohan and Louise Harrington (as part of an investigation into the work of the Cork Wide Streets Commissioners).[98] It is therefore considered here in less detail than the Monaghan, Tralee, and Carlow courthouses. As Westenra's correspondence shows, the Cork County grand jury had been planning to replace their relatively recently built assize courthouse as early as July 1827. Fire damage to their courthouse in February 1827, and the poor condition of the city courthouse, no doubt pushed both grand juries into rebuilding.[99] Following Waterford and Kilkenny in previous decades, the county and city grand juries came together to build a single courthouse (not without some strife); they sent a memorial to Dublin Castle in 1827 requesting the site of the city's old custom house on Nelson Place for the new combined building.[100] But a new street (Great George's Street, now Washington Street) to the west of the city, planned and built by the Cork Wide Streets Commissioners around this time, provided an ideal location (Fig. 2.37) for the new building, and a large site was provided by them at around its halfway point.[101] A competition was held in 1830 and yielded sixteen entries from both Ireland and England, including those of William Vitruvius Morrison, Thomas and Kearns Deane, James and George Richard Pain, and John B. Keane. In the end the Pains won out, beating Morrison (who was placed third) with a design that was effectively taken straight from his innovations at Tralee and Carlow, except that the semi-circular courtrooms were hidden by a rectangular outer wall.[102] As Craig has remarked, this (in general) set a precedent in Irish assize courthouse design, with

the post-Cork designs having their courtrooms 'embedded in the plan' rather than 'expressed externally'.[103]

Completed in 1835 without the help of any public-works loans at a cost of some £22,000, the building was a great improvement on the two existing courthouses and the appropriate finale to the county's extensive courthouse and bridewell rebuilding programme of the 1820s.[104] It features a full Corinthian octastyle portico with a statue of Justice on top of the pediment that is otherwise plain except for the inscription 'WILLIAM IV KING'. For all the virtues of its location in the centre of the city and in forming a dignified entrance from the west, the site is far inferior to Carlow's, with the side façades tightly packed into the fabric of the surrounding streets. To the south many old buildings survived the ambitious rebuilding plans of the Wide Streets Commissioners, and an idea floated in the 1830s to create a large square to front the courthouse came to nothing, with some late nineteenth-century offices now facing the courthouse.[105] In spite of these problems, the Pains' courthouse can be seen as the culmination of a distinct architectural period marked by Morrison's introduction of a new design in about 1826–7, through to Westenra's excitement and anxiety in Monaghan in 1827, and to the design's full realisation at Tralee, Carlow, and finally Cork.

Fig. 2.36. Cork assize courthouse, *c.* 1900. James and George Richard Pain, planned from 1827 and built 1830–5. The centrepiece of the newly carved-out Great George's Street, this joint courthouse for the city and county grand juries borrowed from Morrison's plans for Tralee and Carlow but concealed its semi-circular courtrooms with a rectilinear façade. As in Galway, it was the final jigsaw piece in the decades-long process of rebuilding the county's courthouses, gaols, and bridewells. The dome likely dates to the rebuilding of the courthouse in the 1890s following a fire (see Appendix A). (*Reproduced courtesy of Cork City Libraries.*)

By the time this new courthouse was complete, the political atmosphere had changed dramatically following Wellington and Peel's granting of Catholic emancipation in 1829 and the reforming measures of Whig governments in the early 1830s. A useful straw in the wind was provided by a toast proposed at the Cork Mansion House in 1830, at which it was suggested that the usual call of 'Protestant ascendancy in church and state' be amended to 'the memory of Protestant ascendancy', a rueful reference to the 'glorious memory' of William III that O'Connell himself had satirised in a speech several months beforehand.[106] The Cork courthouse, then, is not only the last of a set of four great buildings from the second half of the 1820s, but it is also the last of a great fifteen years of frenzied architectural activity, driven mostly by inter-county competition and a desire to appropriate the most fashionable public architecture in a period of comparatively lax grand-jury regulation and abundant capital. Those few courthouses planned and built after 1832 are distinctly different in how and why they came to exist.

Fig. 2.37. Great George's Street running east–west through Cork city centre, with the city and county courthouse in the centre. Ordnance Survey twenty-five-inch map, surveyed June 1899. (*Reproduced courtesy of the Board of Trinity College Dublin.*)

COURT HOUSE
Court of Probate
Protestant Hall
St. Catherine's Abbey (Site of)
Lodge
Gas Works
Fountain
Fountain
Cannon
Band Stand
Cannon

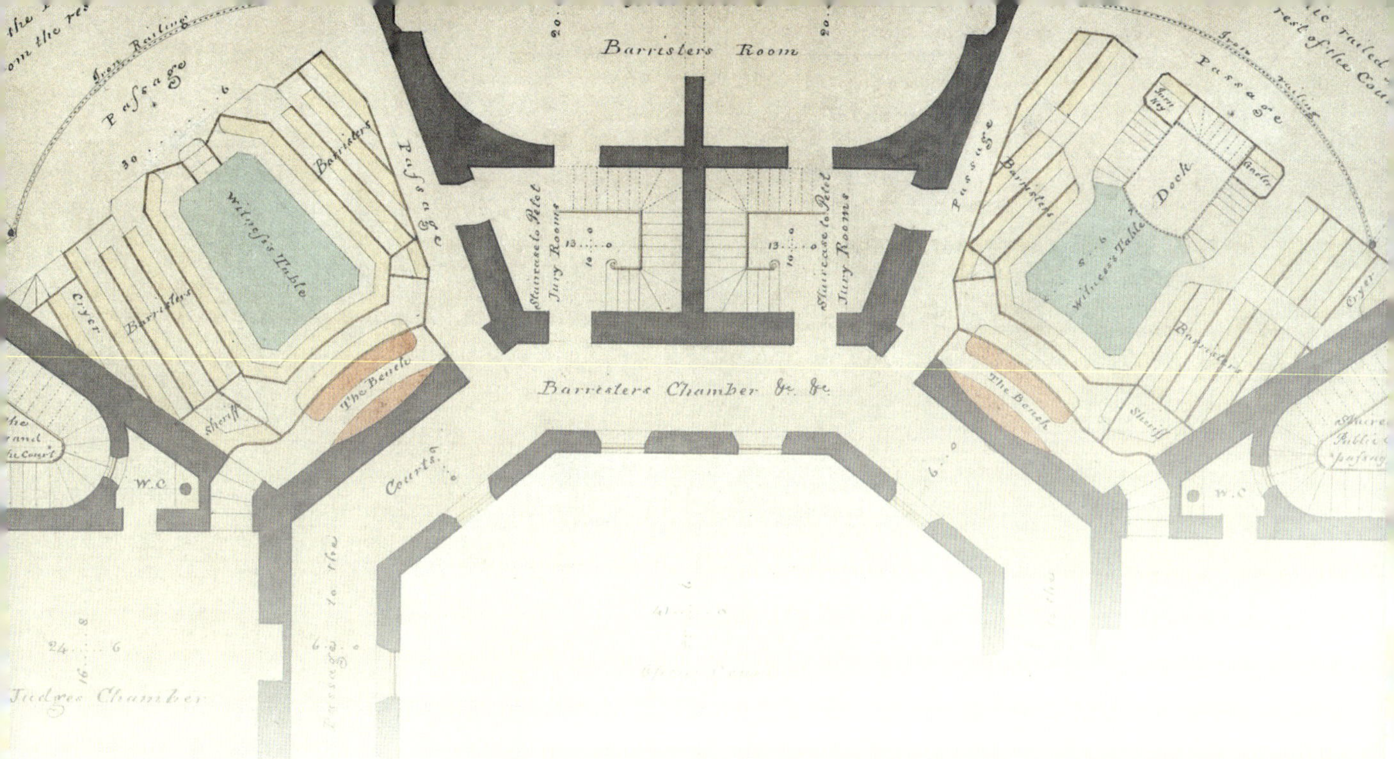

Chapter 3

Against the Tide:

Grand-jury reform, economic opportunism, and the last of Ireland's new assize courthouses, 1831-55

During the 1830s Irish grand juries were reduced by a series of reform acts to a mere shadow of their former selves, losing almost all their freedom and power to be so creative and free-spending as they had been in the decade before. The introduction of the new Poor Law in 1838 with its alternative form of local government managed through Boards of Guardians and Poor Law unions only furthered this sense of retrenchment and decline. Following the granting of Catholic emancipation there were hopes among official circles that

Ireland would prosper – economically and socially – in the 1830s, but these were quickly dashed as economic stagnation, the 'Tithe War', and ballooning crime rates made for a turbulent and politically contentious decade. And in terms of architecture, two of the leading innovative figures of the 1820s – George Richard Pain and William Vitruvius Morrison – spent much of the 1830s in poor health; both died young in 1838.[1] A new generation of architects who had trained with them – John B. Keane, Henry Whitestone, and Henry Hill – came to dominate the field of courthouse design. Yet the reforms introduced by Westminster fundamentally changed the economic basis for this market in

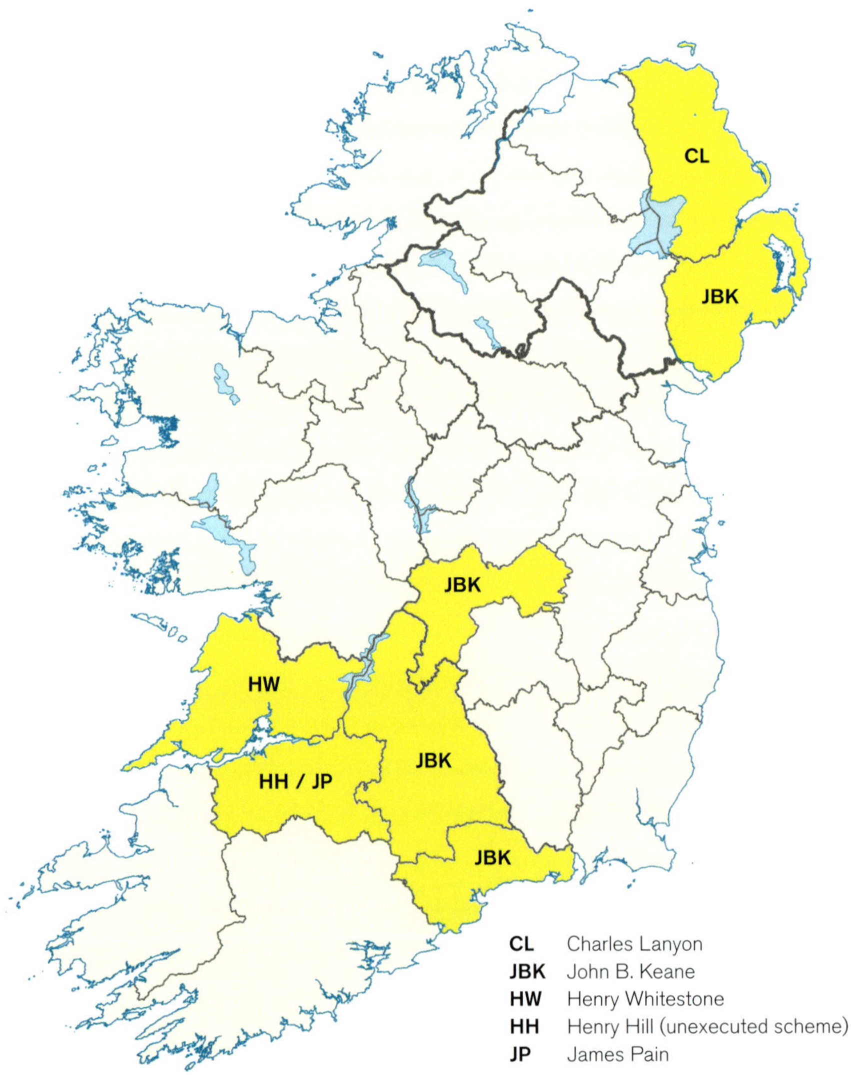

Fig. 3.1. New assize courthouses built in Ireland, 1832–55. The contrast with the preceding fifteen years is self-evident. One man – John B. Keane – was the lead architect in four of the seven projects. In County Down he carried out renovations and extensions rather than an entirely new building.

public architecture, and after 1832 it became increasingly difficult for grand jurors to commit to the kind of large-scale rebuilding work that had defined their great fifteen years between 1817 and 1832, when fourteen new buildings or substantial additions had been funded (see Chapter 2). In the entire period between 1832 and 1855 there were only seven new assize courthouses built (Fig. 3.1), and each of these was in some way a 'one-off' for various local political or economic reasons. They are clustered in north Munster, the south midlands, and north-east Ulster.

With the fall of the Tory government in November 1830 the issue of grand-jury reform returned to the political agenda and found sustained support from the new Whig ministry under Earl Grey. Among Irish civic society there were widespread expectations of reform – evident in the enormous increase in these years in the number of petitions sent to parliament highlighting problems with grand juries stemming from perceived corruption, unjust taxation, and other defects. The inhabitants of Navan, for example, wished in 1831 to have grand jurors elected by ballot, two from each barony, instead of having the jurors appointed by the high sheriff of the county.[2] Irish Whig veterans of the reform movement in the 1810s – such as John Newport – spoke about the grand-jury system in a Commons debate on the findings of a committee that had investigated the condition of the Irish poor. With copious statistical references, he drew attention to the heavy taxation imposed by these bodies. Even moderates and occasional defenders of this old system of local government – such as Thomas Wyse, MP for Tipperary – had to admit that the tide had now turned; though jurors were individually 'honourable men', he observed, the system under which they operated meant that they often could not act 'virtuously'.[3] An extensive reform bill that proposed to give baronies more power over presentments and to make grand juries more accountable was introduced in October 1831, but it did not proceed past its first reading.[4] In the meantime an indirect but highly important reform was brought about through the 1831 Public Works Act, which reshaped the old Board of Works and gave it a new loan fund of £500,000.[5] With many new powers, a better administrative structure, and a strengthened department of in-house architects, this wing of central government became much more powerful in the 1830s. One of its first actions, apart from suggesting changes to W.V. Morrison's design for Carlow courthouse (see Chapter 2), was to have its architect Jacob Owen design a new civil bills courtroom (Fig. 3.2) to be built adjacent to Gandon's Four Courts; this was erected between 1835 and 1839 and forms a seamless connection with the original building. It was a confident start for the newly reformed organisation.[6]

Fig. 3.2. The Four Courts, Dublin, Nisi Prius (civil bills) courtroom extension by Jacob Owen, 1835–9. Owen was employed by the Board of Works, and after this body was reformed in 1831 it became responsible for building or overseeing an increasing number of public buildings throughout Ireland. (*Photograph by author, 2014.*)

In parliament, petitions calling for grand-jury reform continued to pour in during 1832, but it was 1833 before the Grand Jury (Ireland) Act reached the statute book. This has been described by one scholar as a 'drastic limitation on the powers of [a] hitherto all-powerful body'.[7] Many of the ideas that had failed in the reform effort of 1817–18 now returned, including most notably county surveyors who were given power over almost all public works in their county. Grand juries were now obliged to hold 'special sessions' in each barony of their county where presentments would first be vetted before going on to the assizes. This measure gave cess-payers some say in the level of proposed expenditure.[8] Finally, grand juries were no longer allowed to enter into contracts without a public tendering process. The Grand Jury Act emerged from several years of discussions and debate and included some recommendations from earlier Commons inquiries and input from Irish experts such as Robert Peel.[9] The act should also be seen in the context of a broader shift towards 'assimilationist' Irish policy from Westminster in the early nineteenth century.[10] Other reform acts in these years further limited the freedom and authority of grand juries. The Civil Bill Courts Act of 1836, for example, gave Dublin Castle the power to force grand juries to build smaller quarter-sessions courthouses; another act in the same year put a limit on the sum that could be spent on these buildings, and required county surveyors – instead of costly professional architects – to oversee these projects. Though grand juries were still allowed to commission designs from architects, they could now pay them a maximum of £50.[11] In 1839 another reforming measure allowed the Board of Works to purchase sites for new smaller courthouses as well as to actually build them and then charge the total cost to the relevant grand jury.[12] This system emulated the powers that central government had carved out for itself in the building of provincial lunatic asylums in the late 1810s. By 1832, then, there was a marked change in the tone of relations between central and local government and a host of new checks on jurors' desires to engage in the large-scale commission of new public architecture.

The battle for economic dividends in Tullamore

Some of the most defining and contentious events of grand-jury activity in the 1830s were disputes within counties over where their assizes should be held. The wish to reap the economic benefits that the assizes brought was even more heightened at a time of economic stagnation and de-industrialisation throughout much of the south of Ireland.[13] Coupled with these circumstances was a shortage of private capital that made government expenditure via loans increasingly attractive. This dynamic was briefly touched upon in Chapter 1 with reference to the towns of Lifford and Strabane. In some counties these public disputes formed part of long-running battles; in others sudden surges in agrarian unrest and crime played a key part. Perhaps the uniting factor throughout was the understandable economic opportunism of some grand jurors and their determination to promote their home towns.

The dispute in King's County (now Offaly) between the parties in Philipstown (now Daingean) and Tullamore has already been mentioned briefly in terms of how it likely affected the decision to rebuild the courthouse at Philipstown around 1807.[14] Undeterred by this move, Charles Bury, Lord Tullamore, continued to pursue the interests of his town, and in 1821 he secured plans for a new county gaol at the edge of Tullamore (as discussed in Chapter 6). Though Bury's supporters on the King's County grand jury wished to have the tacit support of Dublin Castle for the location of their proposed gaol, it was made clear to them that 'the subject seems to be more for the consideration of the county'. Such a degree of central-government intervention in prison building had not yet arrived.[15] At the spring assizes in 1821 the commissioners for the new gaol commented that 'however desirable' it might be to also move the assizes to Tullamore, the courthouse at Philipstown had been 'lately erected at very considerable expense', and the issue would have to be considered separately at a later date.[16] The foundation stone of the new gaol was laid with local celebrations in 1826; it opened in 1830. Around this time Bury returned to the issue and won a vote at the summer assizes of 1829 to appoint commissioners for overseeing a new courthouse, but the issue remained very divisive among the jurors. Later that year, Bury wrote to the chief secretary, Lord Francis Leveson-Gower, expressing his desire to adopt 'all the latest improvements' in courthouse design by visiting Gloucester and Exeter (Robert Smirke had built a new courthouse at Gloucester between 1814 and 1816 and Philip Stowey and Thomas Jones had built another at Exeter in 1774); Bury asked the government to authorise a public-works loan for the county.[17] At the same time the Ponsonby family in Philipstown launched their own offensive with a letter to Leveson-Gower objecting to a transfer of the assizes and identifying a host of problems with the new gaol at Tullamore.[18] Leveson-Gower was reluctantly caught in the middle of this dispute. For Bury, the issue was clearer, and in correspondence with his mother, he set out his plans in unguarded language:

> It is absolutely necessary for me to go over to Ireland, and fight in person … Ponsonby's relatives …. I think it is a duty I owe, our property the county and myself to spare no personal exertion to secure the success of a measure of such serious importance which I consented to undertake …. The interests of the county supported by all the resident military and gentry must succeed against the jobbery of an absentee landlord and family, however powerful.[19]

Bury's order of priorities here is revealing: property then county. When he attempted to pass a presentment amounting to £11,350 for a new courthouse at the spring assizes in 1830, following the appointment of commissioners in 1829, it was unsurprisingly 'traversed' (opposed) by the Ponsonby family, and so the issue remained deadlocked.[20] Later that year, Bury became more optimistic. Writing again to his mother, he commented, 'I don't like tamely to submit to defeat; it would be a great benefit to the county, to Tullamore and the property, and the greater [the] difficulty, the more honour if we [are] ultimately successful.' Leveson-Gower, whom Bury uncharitably regarded as a 'drowsy, pompous, poetical humbug of a secretary', had since been replaced by Henry Hardinge, 'a clear sighted man of business', and Bury was now confident that he would gain the 'entire and cordial support of government to remove the assizes to Tullamore'. He acknowledged, however, that this was

> the first attempt to alter an assize town in Ireland, and it is next to impossible to discover in whom the authority and right is vested. [Hardinge] is most anxious, as we are also, to avoid the necessity of an act of parliament …. Though the opposition will be strong in parliament, I doubt the government being beaten on a local bill, supported by the county members and persons connected by property with the county.[21]

Bury believed that the assizes would bring £500 in profit to the town each time they were held.[22] If the new courthouse cost £10,000, then this sum could be charged off the county at large and not just off the town; the payback period for Bury would be reduced to a few years at most. With such an intense focus on the potential economic gains, there appears to have been very little concern for the state of crime in the county. The incidence of crime there had remained remarkably steady in terms of ten-year averages throughout the 1810s, 1820s and 1830s.[23] Money was a more central factor. The benefit to the town of Tullamore was noted by George Calladine, an English solider who visited in 1821 and again in 1836, and who thought that in the meantime it 'had altered for the better, having some new streets and a fine courthouse and county jail built since I lay here before, the assizes being changed from Philipstown, which was as much the other way, the barracks being empty and half the houses in the town unoccupied and nearly falling down'.[24]

Bury's belief that the change would require only a local act of parliament proved overly optimistic; in 1832 he was forced to introduce a general public act that attracted more unwelcome attention in parliament. With the support of the Parsons family of nearby Parsonstown (Birr), Bury proposed that the assizes should be relocated.[25] His bill was closely modelled on one that was introduced in the same month to move the Norfolk assizes from Thetford to Norwich, and both bills were in fact discussed on the same day at Westminster.[26] Ponsonby was hostile, as expected, but so too was the Trinity College academic Philip Crampton, who can perhaps be seen as a neutral observer in the dispute (or as neutral as anyone could be in early nineteenth-century Irish politics). Crampton was convinced that a 'sufficient' case had not been made for the change, and noted that the

> building of a new court-house would entail a very heavy expense on the county, and these were not times in which such burthens could be

borne. It would appear that the new jail had been built with the view of affording an argument for the removal of the assizes.[27]

Despite these objections, the bill passed upon a division in a relatively empty house (fifty votes to thirty-eight) and received the royal assent on 4 July 1832.[28] Bury had won the final battle in a fifty-year war. An architectural competition was staged later that year, with the entrants advised that the site for the new courthouse would be on land granted free of charge by Bury's father and

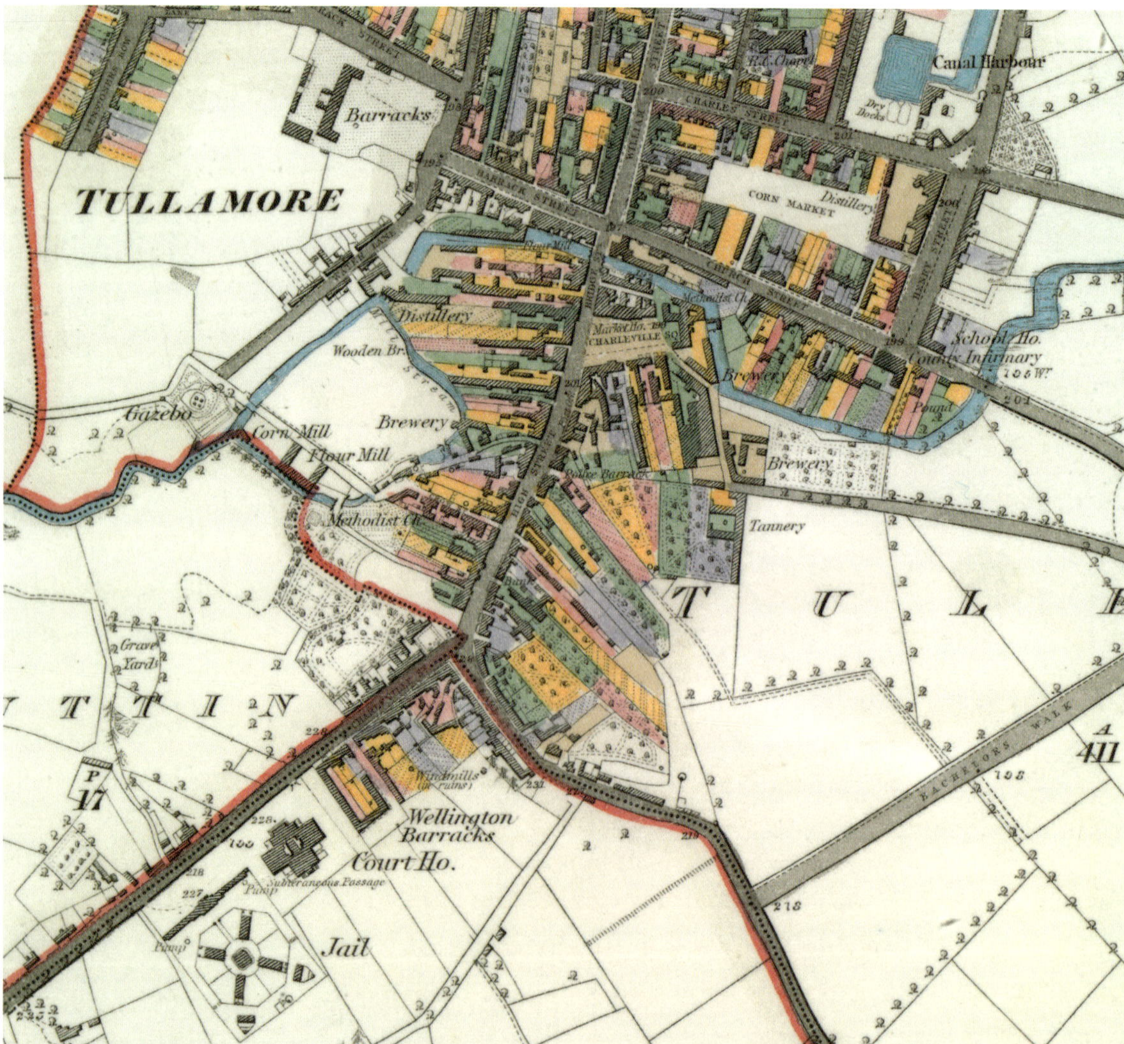

Fig. 3.3. (opposite page) Tullamore, showing the Wellington Barracks, courthouse, and gaol at the southern edge of the town on the road that led to Lord Tullamore's seat at Charleville Forest. Ordnance Survey six-inch map, surveyed January 1838. The line-up of new public buildings impressed visitors, as presumably the leading family had hoped. In later years the town's railway station was built nearby. (*Reproduced courtesy of the Board of Trinity College Dublin.*)

adjacent to the new gaol, on the road that led from the town to their country seat at Charleville Forest (Fig. 3.3).[29]

The English artist Theresa West, visiting several years later and finding that this line-up of public buildings made for a dramatic entrance to the town, commented that the road was 'rendered striking by the gaol and court-house [Fig. 3.4], two excessively handsome buildings in their several ways; the latter Grecian; they stand off the road, on high ground'.[30] The overseers of the competition had suggested that potential architects might follow 'the plan of Gloucester (and Kerry [added later in pen]) courthouse', both seen as 'good models'.[31] By this time Morrison's Tralee courthouse was well under construction and was widely known throughout Ireland. Bury was also the MP for Carlow, and he would have been aware of what the grand jurors there were building and of events in Monaghan through fellow MP Henry Westenra. The specific mention of Kerry's design, then, should not come as a surprise. Of the many entries submitted to the competition, only two have survived – by William Murray, who had trained with Francis Johnston, and by John B. Keane, who had trained with Morrison. Though Morrison himself submitted two designs – one Greek and the other Gothic – neither were successful, and his drawings have not survived. One of the most curious entries came from Bury himself, who prepared a 'Saxon' design in hopes that it would blend well with his Gothic Revival gaol; its provenance is also unknown.[32]

Fig. 3.4. Tullamore courthouse, by John B. Keane, with the Gothic former county gaol, by John Killaly, in the distance. Lord Tullamore feared that the opposing architectural styles would clash, and sketched a courthouse design more sympathetic to the gaol, but this was not built. The courthouse and gaol brought prosperity to the town and were the culmination of a fifty-year dispute between local elites. (*Photograph by author, 2013.*)

The façade of Murray's unexecuted scheme, prepared in December 1832, has been criticised by one historian as dull, too heavy, and overly influenced by the Italianate movement. Its architectural language, however, is in fact derived from Greece and France as well as Italy, and it has several noteworthy features.[33] The principal façade (Fig. 3.5), of nine bays over two storeys, was Palladian in composition but the columns, paired at the ends and forming a tetrastyle portico in the centre, were Greek and free-standing – both significant departures from the standard Palladian form – and their severity contrasted with the Italianate balustrade above and the French haunched-segmental windows and channelled rustication below.[34] Murray's detailing was problematic throughout, especially in the two blind windows on the ground floor (necessitated by the poor arrangement of rooms behind) and in the unusual decision to reduce the importance of the central portico by inserting diminished arched windows where pedimented ones, flanking on both sides, would have worked better. Behind this palazzo-like façade, which tends to conceal the judicial nature of the building and instead suggests a municipal or domestic function, Murray hid the tricks of his plan (Fig. 3.6). Here the principle of having semi-circular (or rather curved) courtrooms was maintained, following Morrison in Kerry and specifically mentioned by the competition's overseers, but the arrangement of the two rooms, at either corner of the rear of the building, bulging out like squashed balloons, was a poorly conceived one. His other variation on the Morrison plan – providing circulation space in a curved corridor that surrounds

Fig. 3.5. Tullamore courthouse, front elevation, unexecuted. William Murray, December 1832. Lord Tullamore worried that 'the ignorant, the vicious, and the radicals in these Reform times' would say that he had 'squandered and frittered' public money 'to indulge his taste regardless of the misery of [sic] the poor endured in paying the tax for it'. This scheme was excessively palatial for the straitened years of the early 1830s. (*Reproduced courtesy of the Irish Architectural Archive.*)

the court – was not possible in this layout. Instead Murray proposed a simple balcony for the public at the rear of each courtroom and reused the concept of a circulation space in the half-octagon of corridors in the centre of the building, enveloping an unroofed courtyard. With the help of some creatively placed staircases Murray was able to provide space for judges, grand and petty juries, barristers and clerks, and even basement rooms for witnesses. Indeed, surviving section drawings show that judges and grand jurors were amply provided for in the design, echoing Kilmainham some years earlier, with first-floor rooms that collectively would have been much larger than the two courtrooms (Fig. 3.7). To the side there would have been separate entrances for the judges and the public, with commensurate levels of architectural detailing (Fig. 3.8). The crown court would have been placed nearer the gaol, allowing for the transportation of accused persons via an underground passage shown in Murray's basement plan.

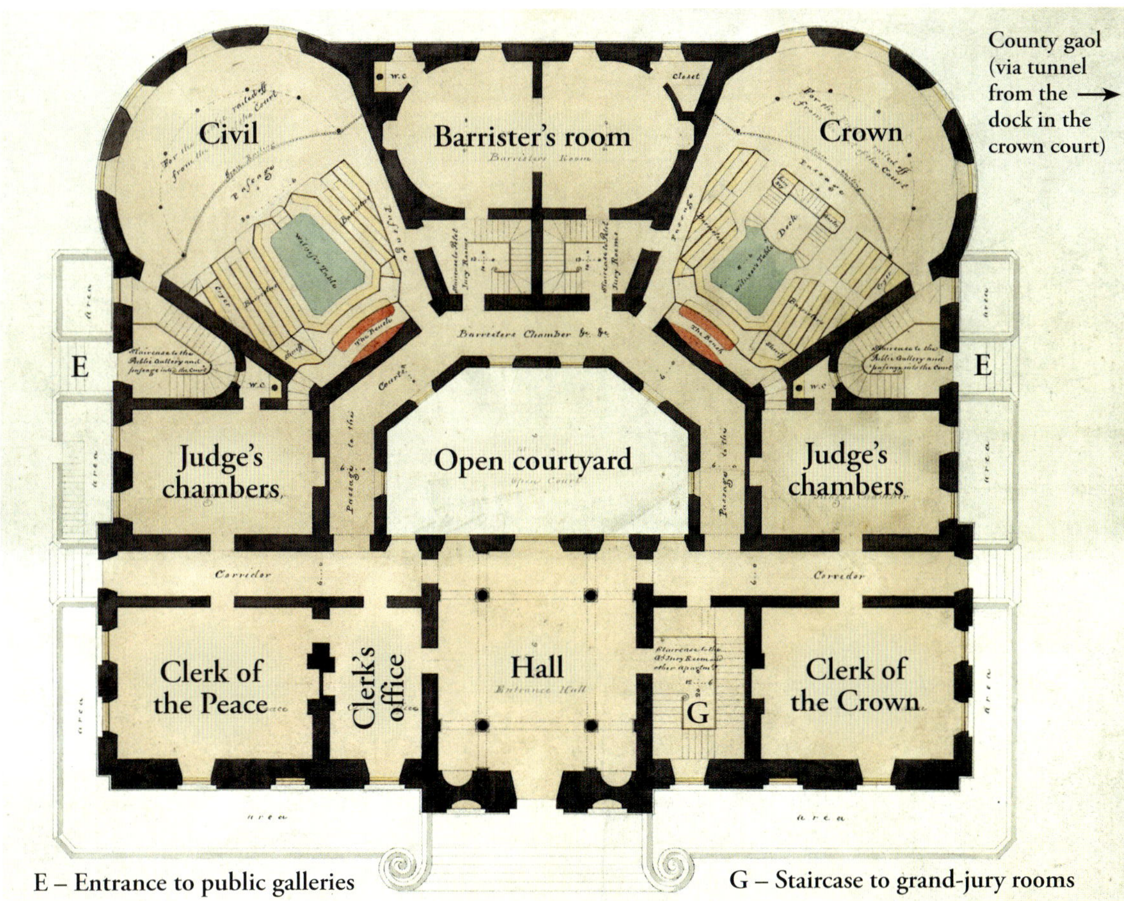

Fig. 3.6. Tullamore courthouse, ground-floor plan, unexecuted. William Murray, December 1832. His arrangement of the courtrooms was derived somewhat haphazardly from Morrison's designs for Tralee and Carlow, and some of the front windows were blind. In its defence, the design would have granted copious numbers of private rooms for the grand jurors on the first floor. (*Reproduced courtesy of the Irish Architectural Archive.*)

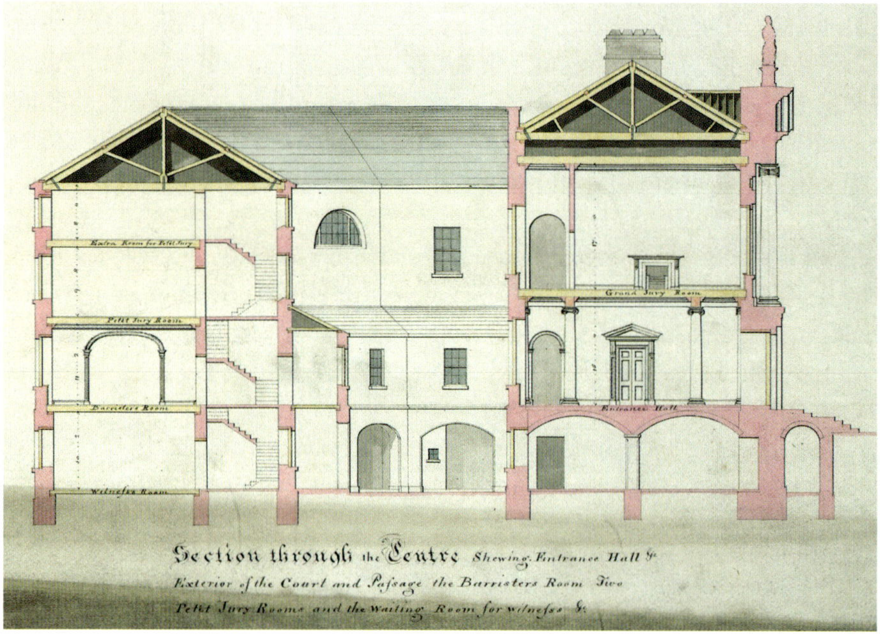

Fig. 3.7. Tullamore courthouse, section drawing, unexecuted. William Murray, December 1832. Above a colonnaded entrance hall Murray placed a suite of large grand-jury rooms. The thermal window that lit the courtrooms is another clear derivation from Morrison. Surviving section drawings for Irish courthouses are rather rare – this is an exception, albeit for an unexecuted project. (*Reproduced courtesy of the Irish Architectural Archive.*)

Fig. 3.8. Tullamore courthouse, side elevation, unexecuted. William Murray, December 1832. The curved courtrooms appear to protrude from the building to the rear, while the public (left) and judge's (right) entrances are treated with commensurate levels of architectural detailing. (*Reproduced courtesy of the Irish Architectural Archive.*)

The awkward elements of the plan – in particular – may well have been enough to doom the scheme, but it is clear that Bury's concern was more with finding a suitable elevation than with a perfect plan. In a letter to his mother in January 1833 he stated:

> We have selected a capital plan of courthouse as far as internal accommodation and convenience, but with Grecian elevation, which I fear will clash with the [Gothic] gaol, but I couldn't get them to

> give a decent Saxon, Norman, rustic, or Elizabethan plan, and the democratic party runs so high that out of all the plans, all Grecian, we chose the plainest exterior, fearing a traverse at the assizes.

Keen to get 'the most accommodation at the least cost', the plan adopted, he argued,

> accomplished that object, and if an Elizabethan elevation had cost the same, the ignorant, the vicious, and the radicals in these Reform times, [would] say [Lord Tullamore] spent public money in ornamenting his town and squandered and frittered it away in pinnacles, carvings, to indulge in his taste regardless of the misery the poor endured in paying the tax for it .... The present plan ... is bold and simple.[35]

Murray's ostentatious proposal – a palace in a manner more identifiable with eighteenth-century precedents in Britain and America or with the Victorian town halls of the industrial north of England – was clearly too ornate for a poor county in the politically and economically troubled years of the 1830s. The perceived simplicity and cheapness of the Greek style made it appealing to many British and Irish architects, and here it provided Bury with a method of deflecting criticism of superfluous spending in a changed political environment where grand juries were under much greater scrutiny.[36] The Greek style, especially as practised by the victor in the competition, John B. Keane, was *de rigueur* austere and sparse in ornamentation. This had little to do with economy in the financial meaning of the word but arose simply from the nature and form of the ancient buildings themselves. All the same, Bury saw additional financial and political reasons for adopting this style for his new courthouse.

Keane's design (Fig. 3.9), with the 'plainest exterior' of all the entrants, was approved at the spring assizes in 1833, and a loan followed later that year. Assizes were held in the building for the first time in the summer of 1835.[37] Keane triumphed over his master Morrison with a design that was essentially a combination of Morrison's own Tralee design with an elevation derived from Pain's courthouse then being erected in Cork city. He provided for two semi-circular courtrooms with a surrounding corridor that connected them with the great entrance hall, the host of rooms in the centre, and offices to the rear. Instead of letting the shape of the courtrooms dictate the exterior façade, as at Tralee and Carlow, Keane squared the curved rooms, using the little and awkward triangular spaces gained in each corner as rooms for witnesses and police (a late adjustment, it would appear, as discussed below). The principal façade is broad, symmetrical, and dominated by a hexastyle Ionic portico with a blank attic behind the pediment, and a lion, shield, crown and unicorn (since removed) (Fig. 3.10). The flanking walls are sparsely articulated, probably as a result of Bury's intention to silence any opposition to the scale of the building, with only shallow pilasters, pedimented windows (on the ground floor), and a full entablature running the length of the façade.

Fig. 3.9. Tullamore courthouse, ground-floor plan. John B. Keane, 1833. The architect's debt to Morrison is evident in his symmetrical semi-circular courtrooms and generous grand-jury accommodation to the rear. (*Reproduced courtesy of the Irish Architectural Archive.*)

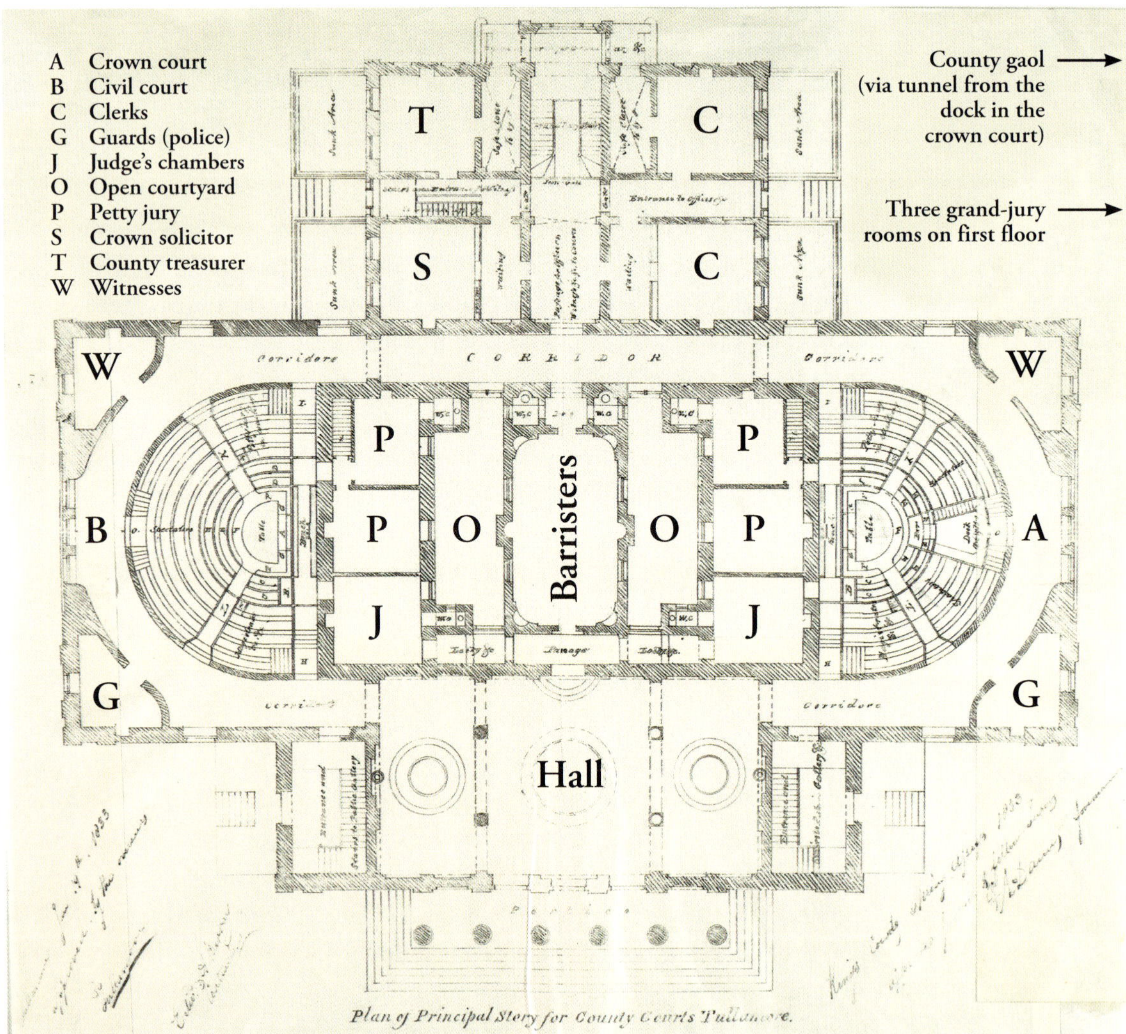

Fig. 3.10. Tullamore courthouse, from the south-west, *c.* 1900. Lord Tullamore believed that the sparsely ornamented façade would help to deflect criticisms from cess-payers. This photograph was taken before the courthouse was burned during the revolutionary period and later rebuilt. (*Reproduced courtesy of Mr Michael Byrne.*)

It appears that Keane had originally intended the façade of his courthouse to be more explicitly based on Morrison's Tralee design than it was as built. An elevation drawing labelled 'County Courts for Tullamore', signed by Keane (Fig. 3.11) and now in the possession of Michael Byrne of Tullamore, shows a slightly different design in one key respect that has escaped the attention of scholars. The truncated appearance of the arched windows at both ends of the drawing clearly indicates that this design was to have had semi-circular wings as at Tralee.[38] Furthermore, the drawing shows three pairs of windows on either side, whereas as built, there is only one pair as well as two pilasters (one of which is at the corner). Therefore, the elevation drawing is not the building we see in Tullamore but instead a variant of it. This discrepancy also accounts for the problematic use of rustication in the central block of the courthouse as built; in the unexecuted elevation drawing Keane shows this rustication carrying onto the curved wings, binding the composition together, but in the final design the rustication is incomplete, an effect particularly obvious in the paired pilasters that cut into the rusticated stonework at either side of the central portico. Keane had clearly intended an appearance of impregnable continuous rustication that we find in such buildings as George Dance's Newgate Gaol, but this did not appear in the façade as built. It is unclear if directives from the grand jurors led to this last-minute adjustment, and if so, what their motives may have been.

Philipstown – bereft of its gaol and assizes – went into near-terminal decline after this time. For Tullamore it was a great victory and the building stood as a monument to the Burys' triumph over the Ponsonby family and to their success in introducing an act of parliament and securing funding for such an impressive courthouse in the turbulent and economically dismal atmosphere of the 1830s. With the courthouse nearing completion, Bury contemplated a new large square (Fig. 3.12) with landscaped features and attractive detached houses on three sides facing the new courthouse from across the road. He hoped to call this estate 'The Beaujolois' after his wife's maiden name. The architectural detailing on these houses (Fig. 3.13), with pointed arches, towers, turrets, and picturesque asymmetrical Gothic detailing, suggests that they were aimed at a middle-class clientele; the scheme was remarkably ambitious for its time. It would also have provided a proper setting for such a large and grand courthouse. The scheme, however, did not proceed beyond the drawing board.[39]

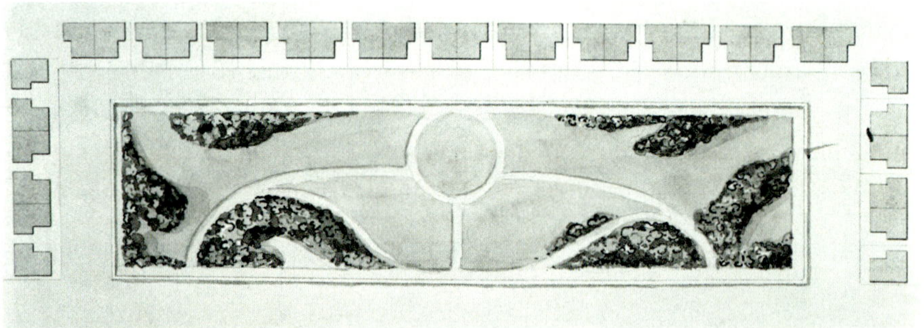

Fig. 3.11. (top to bottom) Tullamore courthouse, front-elevation drawing, unexecuted. John B. Keane, *c.* 1833. In this scheme the courtrooms would have dictated the semi-circular form of the wings, but for unknown reasons this design was later altered to make it more like G.R. Pain's plan for Cork (see Chapter 2). (*Reproduced courtesy of Mr Michael Byrne.*)

Fig. 3.12. An undated sketch, thought to be from about 1835, for a proposed three-sided square of new middle-class houses to face Tullamore's new courthouse. Its author noted that it was to be named 'The Beaujolois' after Lord Tullamore's wife's maiden name. (*Reproduced courtesy of the Irish Architectural Archive.*)

Fig. 3.13. Perspective sketch of 'The Beaujolois', undated but thought to be from about 1835. The picturesque and highly ornamented nature of these houses suggests they were intended for the newly respectable middle-class citizens of a town that had grown dramatically on the back of its new courthouse and gaol. The scheme was not proceeded with. (*Reproduced courtesy of the Irish Architectural Archive.*)

The division of County Tipperary and the new assize courthouse at Nenagh

While still working at Tullamore, Keane became involved in the erection of another assize courthouse in neighbouring Tipperary. After this county was partitioned in 1836, the town of Nenagh staged the assizes for the north riding, with Clonmel, and Richard Morrison's courthouse of the early 1800s, serving the south riding only. Though at the time the partition was presented in terms of a response to the acute agrarian unrest of Ireland's most troubled county and to the great inconvenience of grand jurors from the distant north of the county having to travel to Clonmel in the extreme south for assizes and other meetings, the crucial dynamic underlying the debate was – as in King's County – the economic question of who would reap the benefits from new courthouses and gaols. The division of County Tipperary has been chronicled at length by Donal A. Murphy in his excellent *The Two Tipperarys* (1994). Here the focus is on how the division related to ongoing shifts in grand-jury reform and how this impacted the building of the new courthouse at Nenagh.

Since at least 1828 many landlords in the northern half of Tipperary and especially in the towns of Nenagh, Roscrea, Thurles, and Templemore had been calling for the county to be divided into two ridings, with the historic division of Yorkshire into three ridings as their model. Before railway travel a journey from any of these towns to Clonmel was a long and arduous one and the assizes there were often hectic and rushed affairs on account of the county's extremely high level of crime. The average criminal indictment rate between 1815 and 1825 was 650; between 1825 and 1835 it stood at 900, a per capita rate at least four times the national average.[40] The courthouse at Clonmel, like the gaol, was overcrowded and unworkable. In 1833, Keane submitted to the Tipperary grand jurors a design for a new courthouse and gaol at Nenagh but nothing could be built before the town received its assize status, and this would mean overcoming the objections of a majority of the grand jurors, who were from the more prosperous and heavily populated south of the county. They had no interest in seeing their county split.[41] The situation in King's County was markedly different: there Bury had secured the support of a majority of the grand jurors over a minority party headed by Ponsonby and had won an act of parliament that related to his affairs only. In Tipperary the division into two ridings could happen only if the democratic wishes of a majority of the grand jurors were overruled by central government. The break came in 1835 with the Assizes (Ireland) Act, which was closely modelled on an English act of two years previously. This measure gave the lord lieutenant, in consultation with the Irish privy council, the power to divide a county into any number of ridings and to decide which town(s) in each should hold the assizes.[42] A last-minute and crucial amendment in the Lords added the provision that central government would be able to exercise this power only if 'a memorial shall have been presented … by a majority of the grand jury of the assizes of such county praying that such change or division may be made'.[43] This was a clever move to block the separatist aspirations of the north Tipperary jurors, for the authors of the bill had on their minds a separate dispute in County Waterford and did not wish to see their measure hijacked by the north Tipperary party. The bill had been introduced by Michael O'Loghlen, the O'Connellite MP for Dungarvan and solicitor general for Ireland. He was hoping to move the assizes in Waterford from Gandon's courthouse in Waterford city to his own town of Dungarvan.[44] The disputes in Waterford in the 1830s will be discussed shortly, but in relation to Tipperary it is worth noting that while O'Loghlen might have hoped to garner the support of a majority of his local grand jurors, it would be next to impossible for the north Tipperary jurors to do the same as they made up only, on average, one-third of that grand jury.[45] For them, the 1835 Act achieved little.

The only way in which the northern jurors could overcome this obstacle was to overrule the democratic voting structure of the grand jury. They did this through lobbying central government in 1835 and 1836.[46] The timing was perfect

Fig. 3.14. Thurles courthouse, County Tipperary. Key elites in the town hoped that their courthouse, probably built in the 1810s or 1820s by Richard Morrison or his son William Vitruvius, could be expanded at relatively little cost to host the new assizes for the north riding of County Tipperary. (*Photograph by author, 2013.*)

as their pressure came in the same year as other reforming acts took away much of the traditional power that grand juries had over building smaller courthouses and gave it to the newly reinvigorated Board of Works. From the perspective of the *ancien régime* grand juries, 1836 may be regarded as their *annus horribilis*. Central-government voices argued, however, that these interventions were necessary only because grand juries were failing to fulfil their old responsibilities fairly. The result for the north Tipperary party was the addition of two clauses to the lengthy Grand Jury Act of 1836 that restated the powers claimed by central government in the 1835 Assizes Act but now removed the need for a majority vote by grand jurors. This was a strong centralising measure for the government, giving it power to divide any county into two ridings and to appoint its assize town.[47] The power of the grand juries had been fatally undermined, and their majority decision now meant little.

Soon after the decision to split Tipperary was announced by government, the towns of Nenagh and Thurles both sent petitions to the Irish privy council seeking preferential treatment. Events in Tullamore proved that there were significant economic benefits to be won. When the privy council met in June 1837, the Thurles representative John Hatchell framed his argument in terms of economics: there was no proper courthouse or gaol in Nenagh, he claimed, and new ones would cost £25,000, exclusive of any sites that would need to be purchased. Thurles already had a courthouse (Fig. 3.14) and a bridewell, he added, plus the offer from a local landlord of free land; only £7,000 would be needed to expand the existing buildings. It would thus be unfair to lumber the county with high taxes to pay for wholly new buildings at Nenagh when so much already existed in Thurles.[48] Hatchell's figures, however, were quickly dismantled by Justice Louis Perrin (1782–1864), a known critic of grand juries. While cross-examining the expert put forward by the Thurles delegation – the county surveyor for east Cork, Patrick Leahy – Perrin maintained that Leahy simply 'did not understand the building of gaols or courthouses'. Far greater weight was given to the evidence of one of the prison inspectors – James Palmer – who asserted that the gaol in Clonmel was in very poor condition and needed many additions, and that the small bridewell at Thurles would need £14,000 to make it conform to government regulations. John B. Keane, despite his personal interest in the project, also gave evidence and claimed that a new courthouse and gaol at Nenagh would probably cost around £15,000. The conclusion was that both future assize towns would need £10,000 or more to upgrade their public buildings. The privy council decided in favour of Nenagh.[49] Following further negotiations between the newly reformed grand juries of the north and south ridings it was finally agreed in December 1838 that the north riding grand jurors would foot the entire bill for the new buildings required in Nenagh, but that in return they would be exempted from paying for the necessary additions to the gaol at Clonmel and for its ongoing running costs.[50]

The economic benefits of being the assize town soon became very evident at Nenagh. In March 1838 the *Clonmel Advertiser* announced that it would cease publication and recreate itself as the *Nenagh Guardian and Tipperary North Riding Advertiser* on account of the transfer of the assizes.[51] Later that year, the editor of the *Nenagh Guardian* commented that 'we hope to see Nenagh a well-lit, well-paved, well-cleansed town', and at the staging of the first assizes the editor called for a 'diffusion of wealth, the spread of employment and [an] increase of comfort and happiness' among the citizens of Nenagh.[52] This first assizes was presumably held in the old small courthouse on Pound Street that had formerly held quarter- and petty-sessions, and had the town's small bridewell in the basement.[53] John B. Keane's early involvement in the plans for new buildings in Nenagh was rewarded when he was given the contract for both the new courthouse and the gaol, now estimated to cost £7,000 and £18,000 respectively.[54] A loan of £6,000 from the Board of Works was secured in September 1839, construction started in 1840, and the first assizes were held in the new building in the spring of 1844.[55] A seemingly unusual clause in the 1841 Court Houses (Ireland) Act that gave grand juries the temporary power to cancel existing rental agreements for old and unneeded courthouses was presumably designed to facilitate the north riding grand jurors in their move from Pound Street to their new and far more impressive courthouse.[56]

The new courthouse had a major impact on the urban development of Nenagh. The ambition of the north riding jurors was reflected in the superlative location granted for the new building (Figs 3.15, 3.16). As well as better paving, lighting, a local newspaper, and the influx of county and state funds, Nenagh also got two new streets, one of which – Peter Street, named after the local magnate Peter Holmes – was laid out to frame Keane's new courthouse.[57] As early as May 1840 the *Nenagh Guardian* carried an advertisement for development along the street:

> To capitalists [there is] over 3,000 feet of [the] finest building ground admitting the deepest gardens at the rear, in the large spacious street recently opened, offering incalculable advantages to those desirous of

> laying out their money in a town where not a foot of eligible building ground is to be had, not a private house to be let.[58]

Proudly capping this speculative urban development would be the new courthouse – a monument to the new-found wealth of the town – and behind to the right would be an even larger building – the new gaol – that brought employment and services to the town all year round and not just at the assizes (see Chapter 7). The plan for the courthouse was very similar to Keane's design at Tullamore (Fig. 3.17) but the elevation was simpler (described by Maurice Craig as 'somewhat crude in execution'), with a tetrastyle Ionic portico (Fig. 3.18) in a beige sandstone, later substantially rebuilt, flanked by plain wings of dark grey limestone, punctuated by paired pilasters and arched windows only, and with shallow rustication on the ground floor.[59] The hipped roofs of these wings gave the façade the appearance of having three adjacent pediments

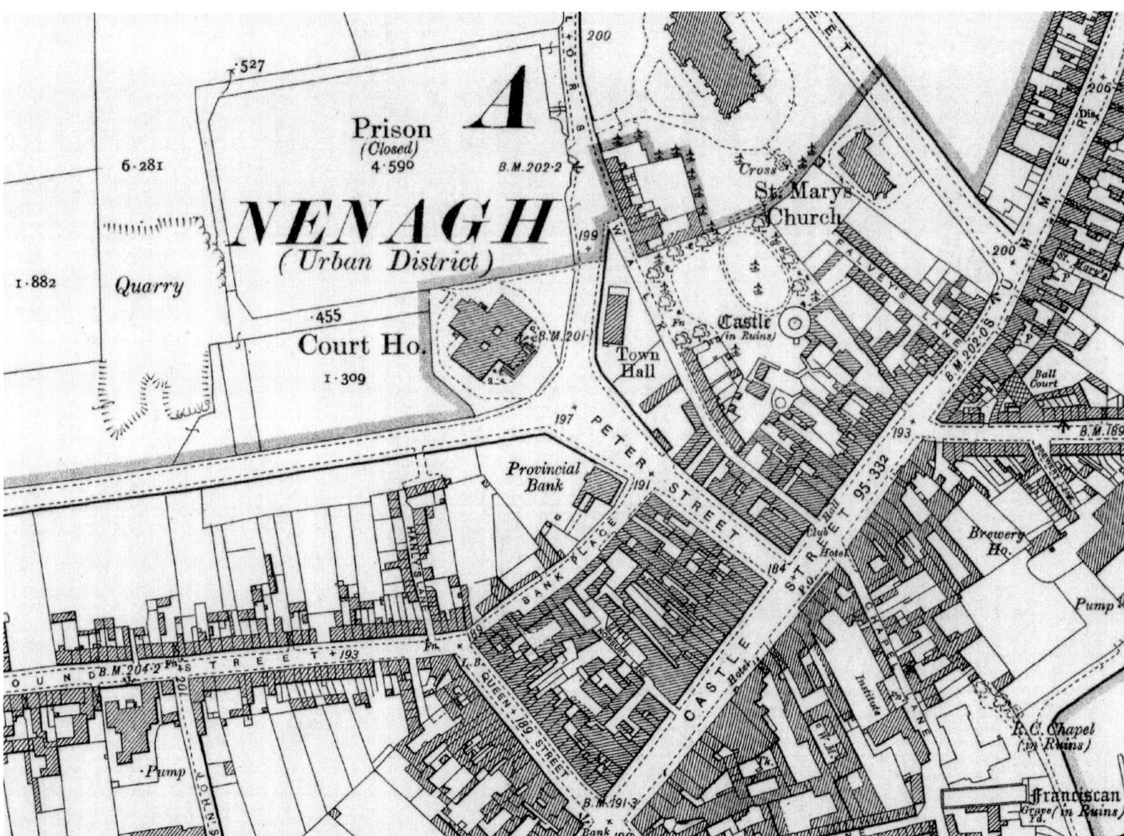

Fig. 3.15. Nenagh town, showing the new quarter of the town laid out around the courthouse and gaol (shown as closed by this time). Ordnance Survey twenty-five-inch map, surveyed June 1902. Peter Street became the preferred location for well-to-do businesses and middle-class townhouses. (*Reproduced courtesy of the Board of Trinity College Dublin.*)

from a distance – an unusual feature that may not have been intended from the outset. Considering that the relatively poor north riding had in these years spent £25,000 or more on new public buildings, the economic return would not be realised for some time, and it is understandable that the new courthouse was a somewhat reduced version of what had been built at Tullamore. Yet its siting was one of the best of all Irish courthouses.

Fig. 3.16. Nenagh courthouse and Peter Street, c. 1900. John B. Keane gave his building an advantageous site on a newly planned street, terminating it axially with its tetrastyle portico. (*Reproduced courtesy of Tipperary Studies, Tipperary County Council Library Service.*)

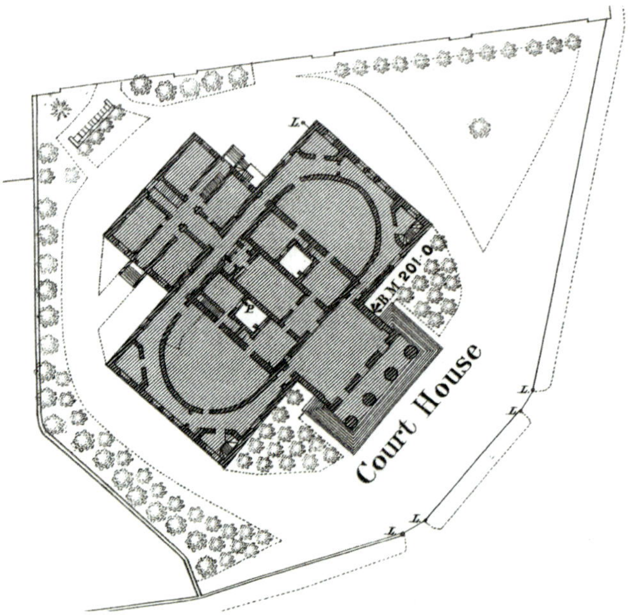

Fig. 3.17. Nenagh courthouse, plan. Ordnance Survey five-feet town map, 1879. Keane copied the arrangement that he used at Tullamore. (*Reproduced courtesy of the Board of Trinity College Dublin.*)

Fig. 3.18. Nenagh courthouse, from the south-east. Keane mixed local limestones and sandstones in the design of the main façade. The portico was substantially rebuilt in the 1890s, and the central sculpture of Justice is a much more recent and rather underwhelming addition. (*Photograph by author, 2017.*)

'When temples of justice are as numerous as churches': grand-jury politics in Waterford

Both Tullamore and Nenagh's new courthouses were 'one-off' projects in terms of how and why they came to exist; neither replaced any substantial existing building. In Waterford, on the other hand, there were efforts at the same time to abandon one of the most influential of all Irish courthouses, designed by Gandon, for a new building in the much smaller town of Dungarvan as part of efforts led by representatives from that town to move the county's assizes.[60] Such a shift was always unlikely for two main reasons: first, a move from a big city to a small town did not make practical sense. Second, the existing building was in any event shared between the county and city grand juries, and to withdraw from this shared arrangement without a justifiable reason would inevitably be questioned at Westminster. From the perspective of Dungarvan the assizes could bring an economic boom to a town that the Duke of Devonshire had been rebuilding and improving since 1807, and it was claimed in a debate surrounding the Assizes Act in 1835 that 'no person' there 'dared to oppose' the relocation plans and also that O'Loghlen was elected the MP only because he had promised to use his influence in government to benefit the town. (How unusual that was – or is – is another matter.)[61]

The initial public reaction to the 1835 Assizes Act was remarkably positive, with the Clonmel liberal paper the *Tipperary Free Press* commenting that

> it will tend materially to give an impetus to industry in several towns in Ireland. Public buildings, such as gaols, court-houses, &c., shall be raised at once under its provisions, and this, added to the influx of visitors during the assizes in those towns …, must tend to alter their condition considerably for the better.[62]

As a general statement, this was perfectly true, but the newspapers in Waterford soon realised the implications for their own county, and even before the act had received the royal assent, the *Waterford Mirror* published an anonymous letter claiming that the act would

> prove that there ought to be a court-house in every village and every townland. Our county will then present a novel scene, unlike whatever before existed, when temples of justice are as numerous as churches and chapels.[63]

Sensing that the bill would soon become law, the Dungarvan promoters and their leader Sir Richard Keane called for a meeting of the county grand jury. He specifically mentioned the Tullamore precedent and won the support of fourteen of the twenty-two jurors for a move to Dungarvan. The majority penned a petition to the lord lieutenant but it was not the only one that arrived on his desk, as over two thousand landholders in the county sent an opposing one at the same time. The privy council met on several occasions in late 1836 to consider the dispute and – as would later happen in relation to Tipperary – the Dungarvan party called witnesses to testify, such as the architect Keane and the prison inspectors Benjamin Woodward and James Palmer. The key issues were – just as in Tipperary – the state of the county gaol, what it would take to expand and upgrade it, and how much this would cost the county's cess-payers. At this juncture, the privy council delayed making a final decision.[64]

At the Waterford spring assizes in 1837 the grand jurors asked Woodward what should be done with their defective county gaol. His response was to say, 'I do not think that anything but building a new gaol … would do.' This played into the hands of the Dungarvan supporters, as a new gaol opened the possibility of a new site and following this meeting a second petition was sent to Dublin Castle. When the privy council again considered the issue in May 1837, Palmer was unequivocal in his condemnation of the gaol. It was 'the worst county gaol in Ireland', he declared, prefiguring Thackeray's comment a few years later that the adjacent courthouse was 'as beggarly and ruinous as the rest of the neighbourhood'.[65] On cross-examination Keane insisted that £25,000 would be needed for a new gaol and courthouse at Dungarvan. Faced with two equally expensive options, the privy council decided that it could not recommend a change of location. Despite some further grand-jury efforts in 1837, this marked the end of the Dungarvan campaign.[66] The issue of what to do with the county gaol still remained, of course, and further caustic reports from the prison inspectors throughout the late 1830s and early 1840s eventually pushed the county grand jurors into action (as discussed in Chapter 7). With the courthouse, things were a little simpler. As in the late eighteenth century (see Chapter 1), the county and city grand juries came together and signed an agreement in October 1844 to build an entirely new shared courthouse in the city.[67] Similar to the tactical move by the Ponsonby family to rebuild Philipstown courthouse around 1807, the new joint courthouse in Waterford was an effective way of neutralising any further threat from the Dungarvan party; afterwards there could be no further suggestion of moving the assizes. Architecture acted as a bulwark against political pressure.

The Clonmel architect William Tinsley made a design for the new courthouse that he exhibited at the Royal Hibernian Academy, but the commission went to Keane, perhaps surprisingly in view of his appearance as a witness for the Dungarvan party at the privy-council hearings.[68] As the most accomplished courthouse builder of his time, and with the new buildings at Tullamore and Nenagh recently finished, Keane had a strong track record that must have reassured the county and city grand juries.[69] Both bodies applied for emergency Famine-related public works funding in May 1846 in order to allow them to proceed with their new courthouse, and construction was reported to be underway in 1848. The new courthouse opened around 1850.[70] Like its contemporary at Ennis, the courthouse is built on a green-field site at the edge of the city in a landscaped park. It was very similar in plan and elevation to Keane's design for Tullamore; its central feature was, as in other Keane designs, a broad hexastyle Greek Ionic portico that is approached from an oblique angle off the main road (Figs 3.19–3.21). Though it was built during the Famine and benefited from the public-works funding of these years, the courthouse owes more to the preceding decade of political infighting by the Waterford county grand jurors and should be seen as marking the end of that turbulent period rather than being solely a 'Famine' project. Soon after it opened, Gandon's old courthouse was demolished – though, for a brief time, prisoners attended mass in his half-ruined vestibule and courtrooms – and the county and city gaol was later rebuilt on the site (see Chapter 7).

Fig. 3.19. Waterford county and city courthouse, from the south. It was built around 1848–50 and is so similar in plan, elevation, and detailing to his other courthouses that it has been attributed to John B. Keane. When it opened, the grand juries abandoned James Gandon's seminal 1784 building in the centre of the city for this more salubrious site in the southern suburbs. (*Photograph by author, 2013 (before recent refurbishment).*)

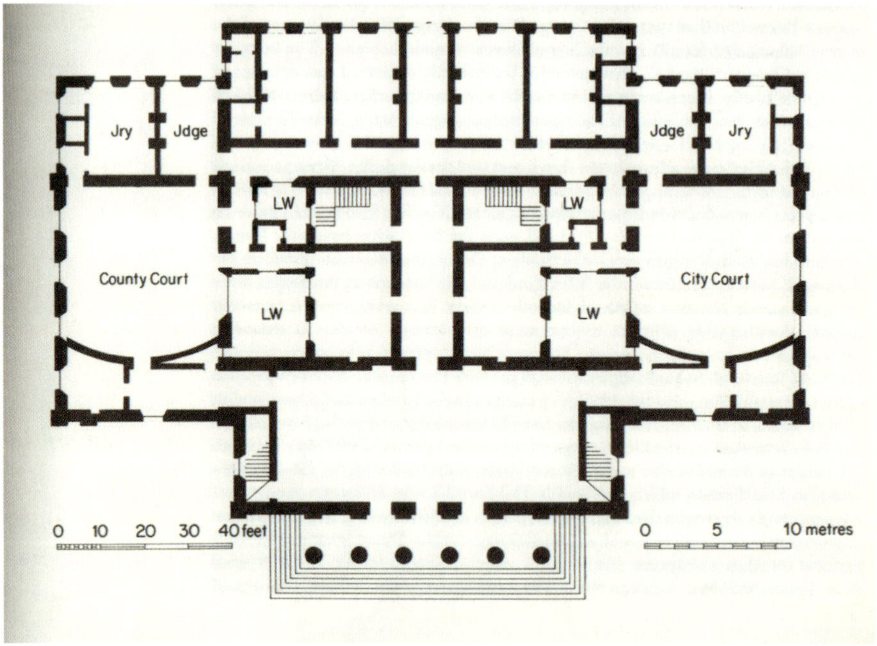

Fig. 3.20. Waterford county and city courthouse, plan. The layout was broadly similar to Keane's other courthouses at Tullamore and Nenagh, but the courtrooms were turned by ninety degrees. In this drawing 'LW' represents a light well, i.e. a small open courtyard (see Fig. 3.21 opposite). From Craig, *The Architecture of Ireland* (1982), p. 275. (*Reproduced courtesy of Mr Michael Craig.*)

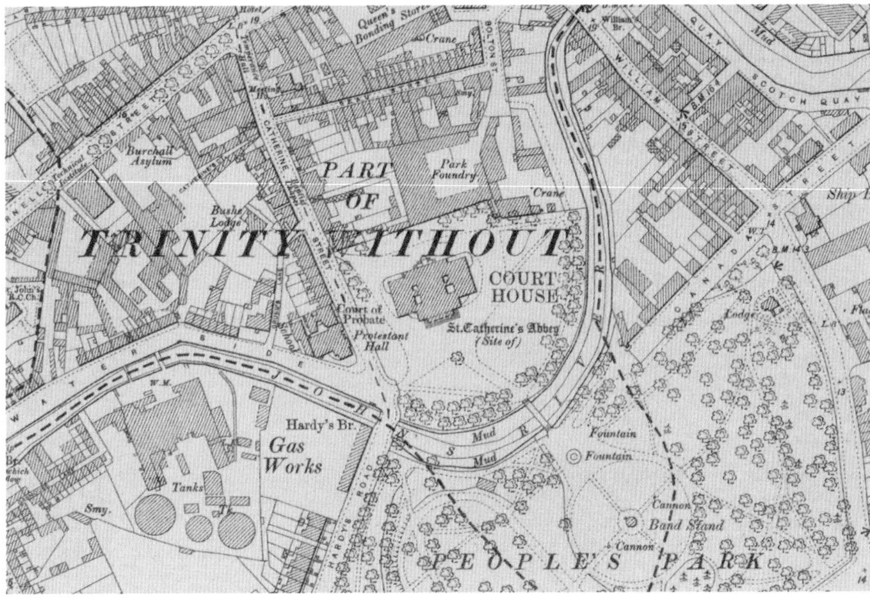

Fig. 3.21. Waterford city showing part of the southern suburbs, including the new county and city courthouse in its landscaped setting. Ordnance Survey twenty-five-inch map, surveyed June 1905. The grand jurors abandoned Gandon's city-centre courthouse of 1784 for more spacious surroundings and later rebuilt a combined gaol on its site. (*Reproduced courtesy of the Board of Trinity College Dublin.*)

An unbuilt scheme in Limerick city

By the mid-1830s, most counties had rebuilt their county courthouse – or at least tried to do so. The Limerick city grand jurors were an exception to this rule. While their colleagues on the Limerick county grand jurors had built a new courthouse between 1807 and 1809, they continued to use a nearby building dating from the 1760s that had itself replaced an earlier tholsel.[71] Why in the mid-1830s the city thought it necessary to replace its perfectly practical building with a new courthouse is unclear. Because the relevant presentment books have not survived this is perhaps an impossible question to answer, but it was certainly not on account of any measured increase in crime – indeed a spike in crime had occurred a full decade earlier in 1819–21 during high unemployment, a banking collapse, and large-scale protest.[72] By the mid-1830s the newspapers regularly note the praise from assize judges for the relatively peaceful and settled state of the city. Whatever the exact sequence of events, the young architect Henry Hill submitted a scheme to the grand jurors at their request in 1834 for a new courthouse that had all the bravado and confidence of the glory years in Tralee and Carlow.[73] If such a building had been proposed in the late 1820s, it might well have succeeded, but the fact that Hill's scheme was never realised says much for the new and more constrained world in which grand juries operated after the reforms of the 1830s. Hill was a Cork-based architect who had likely worked with George Richard Pain, the architect of Cork's new courthouse (see Chapter 2). Hill undertook a short tour – mostly visiting ecclesiastical ruins – through the south of Ireland in 1831.[74] His design for the Limerick city grand jurors, dated June 1834, is one of his earliest known works, done when he was only in his late twenties, and this makes its architectural refinement all the more extraordinary.[75]

Hill envisaged that the new courthouse could be built on an extremely difficult site wedged between the existing county courthouse and the city gaol (Fig. 3.22). Substantial land reclamation from the River Shannon behind, with appropriate embankments, would have been necessary. From the square formed by the existing courthouse and gaol, the new building would have made a very minimal presence (Fig. 3.23) – a screen of two arches, one blank, the other leading to a tight passageway that would have granted access to the courthouse. Above this open arch would have been the only indicator of what lay behind – the words 'CITY COURT' inscribed above the entablature and a royal coat of arms above. The main façade (Fig. 3.24) of the building would have been revealed on approach from the river side, which Hill presumably intended to make accessible with further reclamation to the rear of the existing county courthouse. The river façade – with an elaborate tetrastyle Greek Ionic portico

Fig. 3.22. Limerick north city centre, showing clustered together on Merchant's Quay and Quay Lane, in clockwise order, the county courthouse, the city gaol, the Protestant cathedral, and the old city courthouse. Ordnance Survey six-inch map, surveyed January 1840. Hill's proposed new city courthouse would have been built between the county courthouse and the city gaol, near the word 'Gaol' on this map. Significant land reclamation from the River Shannon would have been required. (*Reproduced courtesy of the Board of Trinity College Dublin.*)

in the centre (following John Bowden's design for Derry courthouse perhaps), wings with three-light windows ending in paired pilasters (in the manner of William Wilkins), and diastyle un-pedimented porticos around the corners – was clearly intended to impress those looking across the broad expanse of the Shannon from nearly bridges, ships, and the far shore. It would have been the first large Irish courthouse since Gandon's Four Courts to have taken advantage of a river vista. Hill's enthusiasm for this porticoed composition is clear from his reuse of it in another undated sketch in his collection of drawings, marked as a design for a 'Public Building' (Fig. 3.25).[76] He clearly intended this river entrance to be more than simply decorative, for in the design the doorway gave access to the grand-jury staircase and meeting room, recalling the unexecuted Kilmainham design of 1817 (see Chapter 2). The awkwardness of having one of the two diastyle side porticos cramped up against the side wall of the county courthouse did not keep Hill from wishing the main façade to be symmetrical.

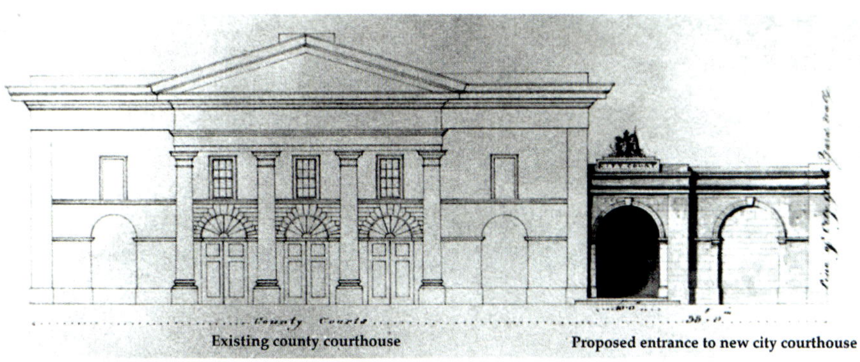

Fig. 3.23. (top) Limerick city courthouse, front elevation of proposed entrance, unexecuted. Henry Hill, June 1834. The new building would have had a minimal presence in a small square already crowded with public buildings. (*Reproduced courtesy of the Allen family.*)

Fig. 3.24. (bottom) Limerick city courthouse, river elevation, unexecuted. Henry Hill, June 1834. Behind its modest square entrance Hill proposed a rich architectural façade overlooking the river. This porticoed entrance was specifically intended for the grand jurors and would have given access to their rooms on the first floor. (*Reproduced courtesy of the Allen family.*)

Fig. 3.25. Design for a public building, front elevation, unexecuted. Henry Hill, probably 1830s. Though little more than a *capriccio* from the young architect, this design was remarkably similar to his Limerick city plan in its columnar arrangement and composition and shows Hill's confidence in his own architectural skills. The figure of Justice is replaced by a rich sculpted attic panel. (*Reproduced courtesy of the Allen family.*)

Behind this rigidly symmetrical and rectilinear façade – so modest in its contribution to the square, yet so confident and full-bodied in its approach to the river – Hill concealed his indebtedness to Morrison's Tralee and Carlow design: his courtroom would have been arranged in a semi-circular fashion with a colonnaded public gallery surrounding it (Figs 3.26, 3.27), two-storeys in height. But where Morrison had placed two courtrooms facing back-to-back, Hill used part of the space gained by the city needing only a single courtroom to provide a single-storey suite of rooms for the judge and petty jury. Evidently keen to reuse the general outline of the two-chamber Morrison plan, but needing only half of it, Hill was unsure of what to do with the surplus space, and so the second curved corridor simply takes visitors around a selection of yards, with no windows at all on the inside. Determined to square-off the façade, as Pain had done in Cork, and presumably in this case because of the existing rectilinear buildings on both sides, Hill proposed that the four awkwardly shaped corner spaces could be used as yards (at Tullamore Keane had found better uses for these spaces). For all its drawbacks, the design had several advantages. First, it provided easy communication with the city gaol nearby, and theoretically too with the county courthouse. Second, it would have given the Limerick city grand jurors the 'obvious and great' advantages (in Henry Westenra's words) of the plan that was adopted in Tralee and Carlow. Thirdly, there were some attractive details, such as separating part of the public gallery for use only by the grand jurors (following Kilmainham again) and providing a very easy communication between this space and the grand-jury staircase nearby. Finally, the river façade would undoubtedly have been one of the most important and beautiful additions to the city's waterfront for many generations.

Nothing came of Hill's design. The old courthouse continued to serve the city grand jurors and in 1840 played host to a series of trials for leaders of food riots in the city.[77] Some years later, in 1843, James Pain – elder brother of George Richard Pain – drew up plans for a new courthouse for the city that necessitated the destruction of a portion of the existing city gaol. Though the prison inspectors protested at the loss of cells in what was then a crowded gaol and won the support of the gaol's Board of Superintendence, the grand jurors pushed ahead and in 1845 sold their old courthouse to the Christian Brothers for the purpose of establishing a school. A loan of £1,250 was obtained for a new courthouse – the last public-works loan issued for an assize court in the period under study.[78] Such a paltry amount could never have built Hill's design, but it was enough for the city's modest new courthouse. James Pain's design for this building (demolished around 1988) was little more than a shadow of Hill's plan – a dull un-pedimented five-bay façade over two storeys (Fig. 3.28).

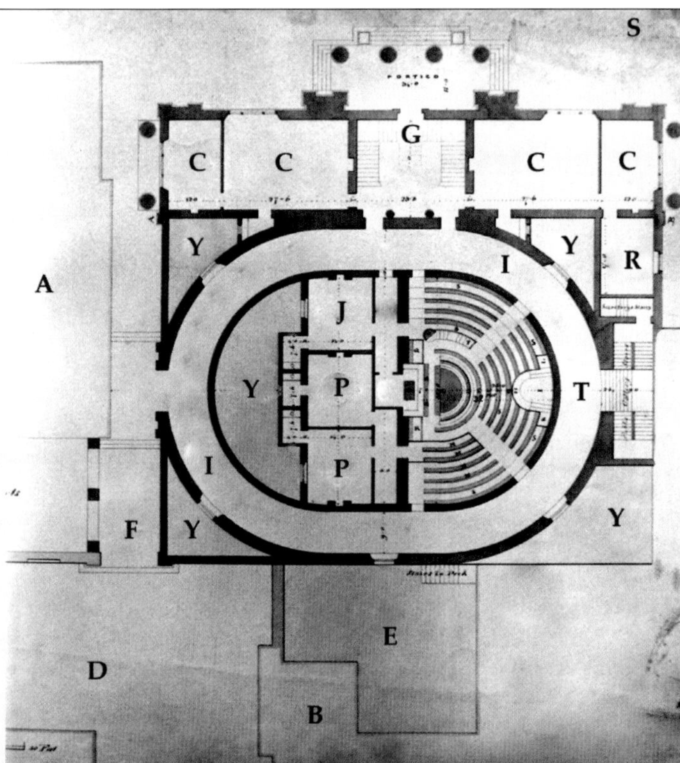

Fig. 3.26. Limerick city courthouse, ground-floor plan, unexecuted. Henry Hill, June 1834. Hill's adaptation of Morrison's arrangement of semi-circular courtrooms demonstrates the impact that the new courthouse at Tralee had on courthouse design in Ireland. Here the design provided only one courtroom, with the other half rather inefficiently used for judge and jury rooms and a lengthy curved corridor. (*Reproduced courtesy of the Allen family.*)

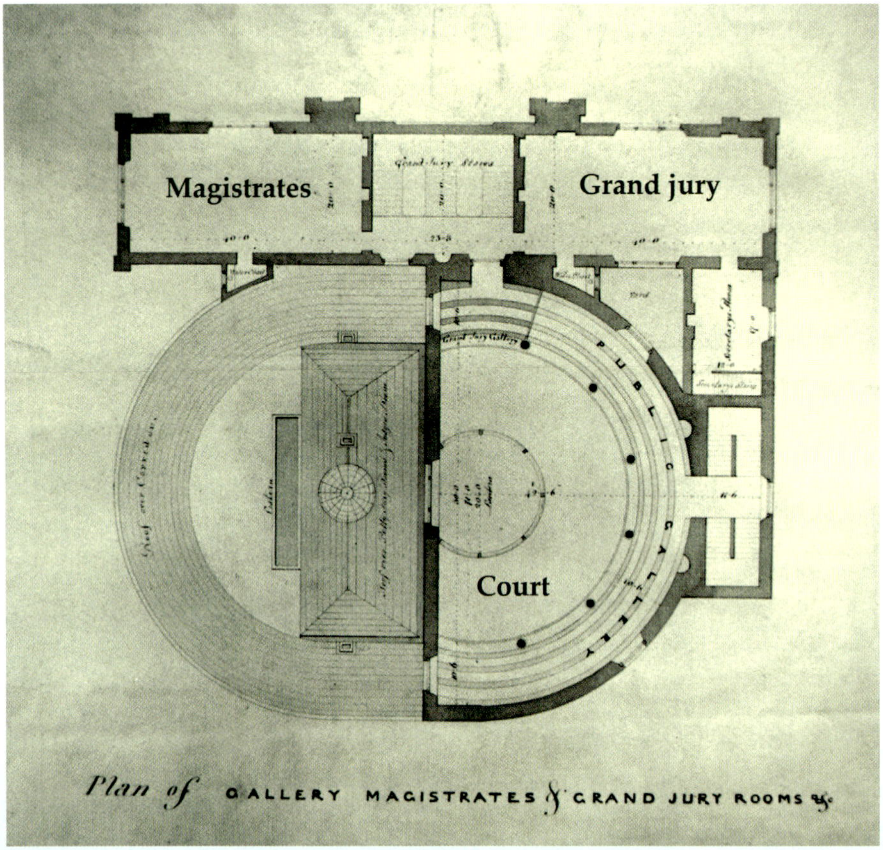

Fig. 3.27. Limerick city courthouse, first-floor plan, unexecuted. Henry Hill, June 1834. Hill proposed giving the most sumptuous views over the River Shannon to the magistrates and grand jurors. The roof of the low curved corridor and of the judge's chambers in the centre is visible in this view. As was done at Tralee and Carlow, Hill provided for a colonnaded public gallery surrounding the courtroom. (*Reproduced courtesy of the Allen family.*)

Fig. 3.28. Limerick city courthouse (left) and city gaol (right), as built, photograph *c.* 1950. These buildings were mostly demolished around 1990. The city courthouse was designed by James Pain in the 1840s in a simple and unornamented manner, unlike what Henry Hill had proposed a decade earlier. (*Reproduced courtesy of Sean Curtin and the 'Limerick: A stroll down memory lane' project.*)

The memory of O'Connell in Ennis

Across the Shannon the Clare grand jurors had been planning a new courthouse since the early 1830s if not before. Their existing building was a typical eighteenth-century combined market and courthouse (Fig. 3.29) with an open arcade at street level, a large central window on the first floor framed by engaged columns, and a simple pediment containing a clock.[79] This modest building witnessed one of the most important events in Irish and British political history when in the upstairs room overlooking the market in July 1828, election officers conceded that Daniel O'Connell had beaten William Vesey Fitzgerald to become MP for the county. Such was the ruckus that, as mentioned in the Introduction, the grand jurors had to pass a presentment for around £14 to 'make several repairs' to the building following what was noted as 'damage at the election'.[80]

In February 1836, the county surveyor Richard Grantham recommended that the county commit to 'the erection of a new [courthouse] or a thorough alteration and repair of the present building. [This] is becoming daily more … urgent so that suitable accommodation may be provided for the increasing business of your fine and improving county.'[81] His reference to increasing business is backed up by criminal-indictment figures for the county, which rose from an average of 320 between 1820 and 1830 to 481 between 1830 and 1835.[82] Yet at this time the grand jurors seem to have had other priorities. Though Ciarán Ó Murchadha has suggested that the memory of O'Connell's victory in 1828 may have led the predominantly Protestant landed elite to withdraw from adequately maintaining their courthouse – he fashions the grand jurors' neglect as 'an uncomfortable reminder … of the recent successes of Catholic nationalism' – we should ask why then did they not just demolish the building outright and start anew elsewhere?[83] Many other grand juries in less politically contentious environments had done something similar in the 1820s. Instead, however, we find that the Clare grand jurors entered into a seven-year contract starting in 1833 with a local craftsman to keep the courthouse clock in good working order.[84] Nothing would or did happen until this contract expired. Furthermore, in the late 1830s the finances of the grand jury were in a very grave position, and two acts of parliament were necessary to resolve the mess left by the death of a former county treasurer who had racked up debts of at least £15,000. The second of these acts gave the Clare grand jurors special permission to borrow this sum from central government so that they would remain solvent.[85] Thus it made sense for the grand jurors to follow those counties such as Sligo and Longford that had continued to use very old courthouses and to roll over small maintenance presentments.

Grantham's replacement as surveyor – James Boyd – continued to make critical remarks about the old courthouse in 1837 and 1838, and finally at the summer assizes in 1838 designs for a replacement were presented by John B. Keane, who later immodestly described them as combining 'solidity with convenience and utile beauty' – an arrangement that he had admittedly perfected elsewhere in the country.[86] Boyd thought that £12,000 would be required for the new building, but the 1840s were not the 1820s and grand juries had much less freedom to commit to such a large and ostentatious project without seeking the approval of cess-payers at special sessions. In 1841 a presentment was traversed that put a sudden stop to the whole affair.[87] As in many other counties, it took a series of negative comments from assize judges to restart the project, and in 1845 an architectural competition was staged to pick the best design, discounting Keane's earlier proposal.[88] Some eighteen architects submitted designs, including the familiar names of William Murray, George Papworth, William Tinsley,

Fig. 3.29. William Turner de Londe, 'The Market Square, Ennis' (1805), oil on canvas, 75.6 cm x 106 cm. Until around 1850 the grand jurors of County Clare used this old tholsel for their biannual meetings. It was also where Daniel O'Connell was formally elected an MP in 1828 to the dismay of the Protestant interest in the county. (*Reproduced courtesy of the Merrion Hotel, Dublin.*)

John B. Keane, and even the Englishman Sancton Wood. But the victor was the relatively young Henry Whitestone, who had trained with James Pain in Limerick and was thus well-connected among Shannonside jurors.[89]

His design (Fig. 3.30) was essentially borrowed from Keane at Tullamore in both plan and elevation, but the semi-circular courtrooms were rotated through ninety degrees so that the judge's benches were situated to the rear. The hexastyle portico was also a clear derivation from Keane. With hardly any ornamentation, the building conformed to the initial suggestions of the grand jurors in 1845 when they had called for it to be 'convenient, lasting, and to portray a sober dignity of character indicative of its intended use'. 'To this end,' they continued, 'the simple forms of the ancients are best adopted' (this implied that a Gothic Revival scheme would not be acceptable).[90] The details of the construction of the building have been recorded by Ó Murchadha, but the most salient points are that construction began in 1846 on a site at the edge of the town (Fig. 3.31), as in Waterford, and continued slowly through the Famine period, with numerous delays and disputes.[91] While the summer assizes of 1850 were held in the new building, it was not yet completely finished.[92] The *Clare Journal* suggested that the old courthouse, which interfered with traffic in the centre of the town, should be demolished, but it appears that there were attempts by a local Franciscan community to purchase the building. One historian has suggested that the grand jurors refused to entertain this idea, as they 'preferred to demolish it rather than sell' to this religious group.[93] Only a tiny fragment of the original edifice remains today – in the wall of an adjacent house – and a large column (Fig. 3.32) now stands on its site commemorating O'Connell's political victory in its former grand-jury room.

Fig. 3.30. Ennis courthouse, County Clare, from the south, *c.* 1900. Whitestone's design was remarkable not for its originality but for how similar it was to other new courthouses of the time. Like their Waterford colleagues, the Clare grand jurors elected to remove their new courthouse to the suburbs of the town and to demolish its predecessor, tainted since 1828 as the site of O'Connell's great political victory. (*Reproduced courtesy of the National Library of Ireland.*)

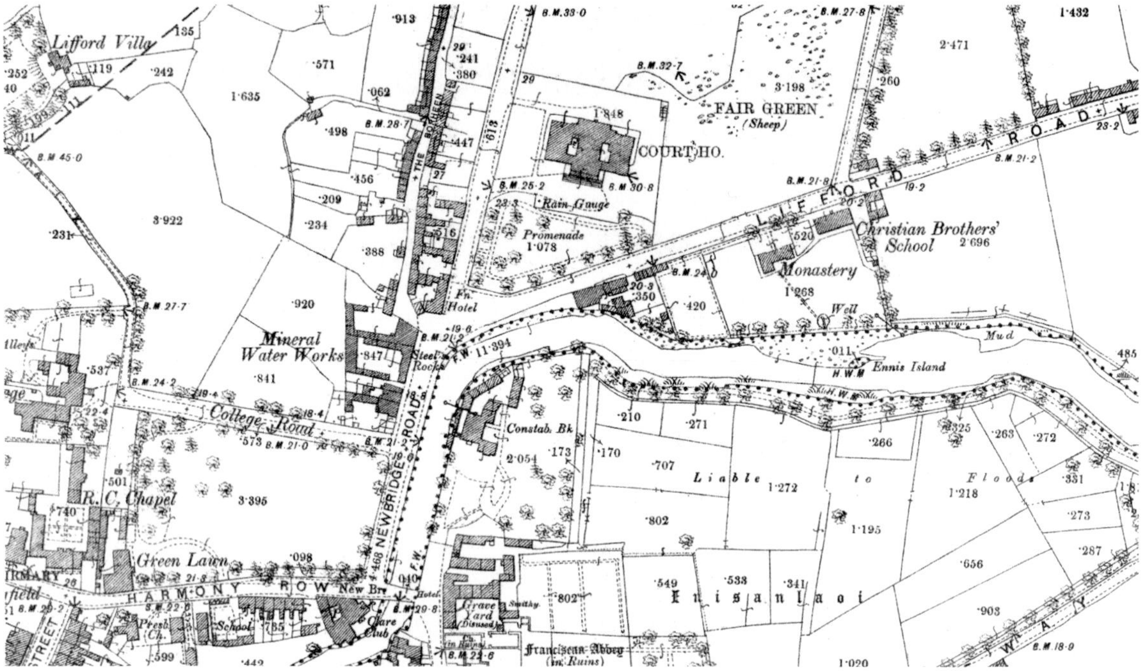

A new courthouse for an industrial city

Fig. 3.31. Ennis, showing the northern edge of the town. Ordnance Survey twenty-five-inch map, surveyed June 1894. As earlier in Waterford and Carlow, Clare's new courthouse was placed at the edge of the town and at the junction of two major roads. The arrangement of rooms was remarkably similar to that in other courthouses of the time designed by John B. Keane in Waterford and Tullamore. (*Reproduced courtesy of the Board of Trinity College Dublin.*)

The dynamic of courthouse building in Ulster was rather different to that in southern counties. Criminal indictments in County Antrim rose from an average of 451 between 1825 and 1835 to 602 between 1835 and 1845, and in County Down they increased from 359 to 505 over the same time period. Though greater increases were found in counties such as Tipperary, rising crime rates in the north-east were the result not of agrarian unrest but rather of rapid urban expansion and the continuation of sectarian conflict.[94] The need to rebuild courthouses there was thus much closer to the norm experienced in England, especially the northern cities, where the justice system had to accommodate a vastly increased urban population.[95] Neither grand jury received any government loans for the extensive work carried out to their courthouses after 1831; both were comfortably able to afford such large investments in their public buildings. By far the most important was the new courthouse at Crumlin Road in Belfast. The assizes for Antrim were held at Carrickfergus but there had been many attempts to have them removed to a much more convenient location and the rapidly growing city of Belfast was the obvious destination.[96] From 1839 these plans became more concrete, and a site was purchased in 1841 for the new building on Crumlin Road,

Fig. 3.32. The O'Connell Monument, Ennis, built 1859–65. Erected on the site of the former courthouse, of which only a tiny fragment survives to the left. (*Photograph by author, 2017.*)

to the west of the city, which had recently been laid out and planned (Figs 3.33, 3.34).[97] A large gaol for the county was to be situated directly opposite, with a tunnel under the road connecting the two (as discussed in Chapter 7). The commission for both the gaol and the courthouse went to Charles Lanyon, the county surveyor for Antrim.[98] If this position had weakened the hand of grand juries in the 1830s, by the 1840s it was also beginning to threaten the livelihood of the professional architect. The sense that these officials were claiming a monopoly on county building work was one of the reasons that led to the founding of the Royal Institute of the Architects of Ireland.[99] Lanyon brought forward plans for a new courthouse in 1847 (Fig. 3.35), but his ambitious design was checked by a grand-jury directive that the whole building must cost no more than £16,000 – still a very sizable amount. A surviving elevation drawing suggests that Lanyon proposed curved wings flanking a central portico in a manner similar to Morrison's design for Tralee and Carlow courthouses and also reminiscent of the curved screen of the Parliament Building on College Green in Dublin.

Lanyon returned with a reduced scheme in 1848 that was quickly approved, and construction then proceeded rapidly. The building was complete by 1850.[100] At the time of writing, Crumlin Road courthouse is one of the most spectacular ruins in Belfast (Fig. 3.36), and it is all but impossible to sense what Lanyon's original design was owing to extensive later alterations.[101] Old photographs show

Fig. 3.33. Ordnance Survey six-inch map of Belfast, showing Crumlin Road gaol, surveyed 1858. Charles Lanyon built a new gaol and a courthouse for the Antrim grand jurors in the 1840s that faced each other a little beyond Carlisle Circus. The site had been owned by the Belfast Charitable Society, whose Clifton poorhouse was situated nearby. (*Ordnance Survey of Northern Ireland (licence no. 14/09/2852).*)

Fig. 3.34. Sketch of Belfast by J.H. Connop, 1863, from his *Belfast, Part II*, plate 4. In the distance can be seen the distinctive radial cell blocks of Charles Lanyon's Crumlin Road gaol, with his new assize courthouse immediately opposite. The site, at the edge of the city, was seen as both healthy and convenient and was typical of courthouse- and gaol-building in mid-nineteenth-century Ireland. (*Reproduced courtesy of the Linen Hall Library, Belfast.*)

Fig. 3.35. Antrim assize courthouse, Belfast, front-elevation drawing, unexecuted. Charles Lanyon, 1847. This scheme was seen as too ostentatious by the Antrim grand jurors, who asked Lanyon to prepare a reduced design. He appears to have borrowed liberally from Morrison's semi-circular courtroom design and from the curved screens at the old Parliament Building on College Green in Dublin. This drawing should also be compared with John B. Keane's unexecuted design for Tullamore (Fig. 3.11). (*Reproduced courtesy of the Deputy Keeper of the Records, Public Record Office of Northern Ireland.*)

Lanyon's hexastyle Corinthian portico with a royal coat of arms in the pediment and a large statue on top (both of which still remain), flanked by short wings with projecting ends, the Corinthian order of the portico carrying through onto pilasters. Though the plan owes something to the Dublin Parliament Building, the language is thoroughly Roman throughout and constitutes a substantial break with the Greek tradition of courthouse building that had existed in Ireland from almost the beginning of the century.[102] Similarly, the extensive and unfortunate use of stucco instead of stone and the position directly facing a county gaol were unusual in the canon of Irish assize courthouse building of the time. Perhaps, then, Lanyon's courthouse is also a 'one-off' in an era of such buildings, but whose origins were markedly different.

This was the last new assize courthouse to be built in Ireland for more than twenty years, until the Sligo grand jurors planned a new courthouse in the late 1870s (Fig. 3.37). By that time Irish society had so fundamentally changed that the funding and erection of this building deserves a completely separate analysis that is outside the scope of this work.[103] The fallow period of assize-courthouse building in Ireland between around 1850 and 1875 stands in strong contrast with the enormous activity in Britain at the same time, especially in the northern cities.[104] It also stands out when compared to courthouse building in Ireland in the 1820s. A few years after Crumlin Road had opened, the Irish Whig MP Sir Denham Norreys introduced a bill in parliament that sought to abolish grand juries entirely and to replace them with elected councils.[105] It did not succeed, but it was the first serious attempt at grand-jury reform in more than a decade and was promoted by a new and younger generation of reformers. Nevertheless,

Fig. 3.36. Antrim courthouse, Crumlin Road, Belfast, from the east. Lanyon's original design was greatly altered and expanded in the early 1900s by Young & Mackenzie and has been abandoned since about the late 1990s. In recent years fires and vandalism have caused great damage to the interiors. (*Photograph by author, 2012.*)

Fig. 3.37. Sligo courthouse, from the east. The grand jurors finally decided to replace their eighteenth-century courthouse in the 1870s with a Gothic Revival building on the same site designed by James Rawson Carroll. (*Photograph by author, 2012.*)

the old oligarchical system of the grand jury, hollowed out and reformed but still otherwise intact, continued for several more decades. Norreys' proposal for councils – later known as county councils – was not adopted until 1898, when the grand-jury system, and a system of patronage of public architecture in provincial towns, finally came to an end.

PART II

The County Gaol

Cath
Edmond Byrne Esq

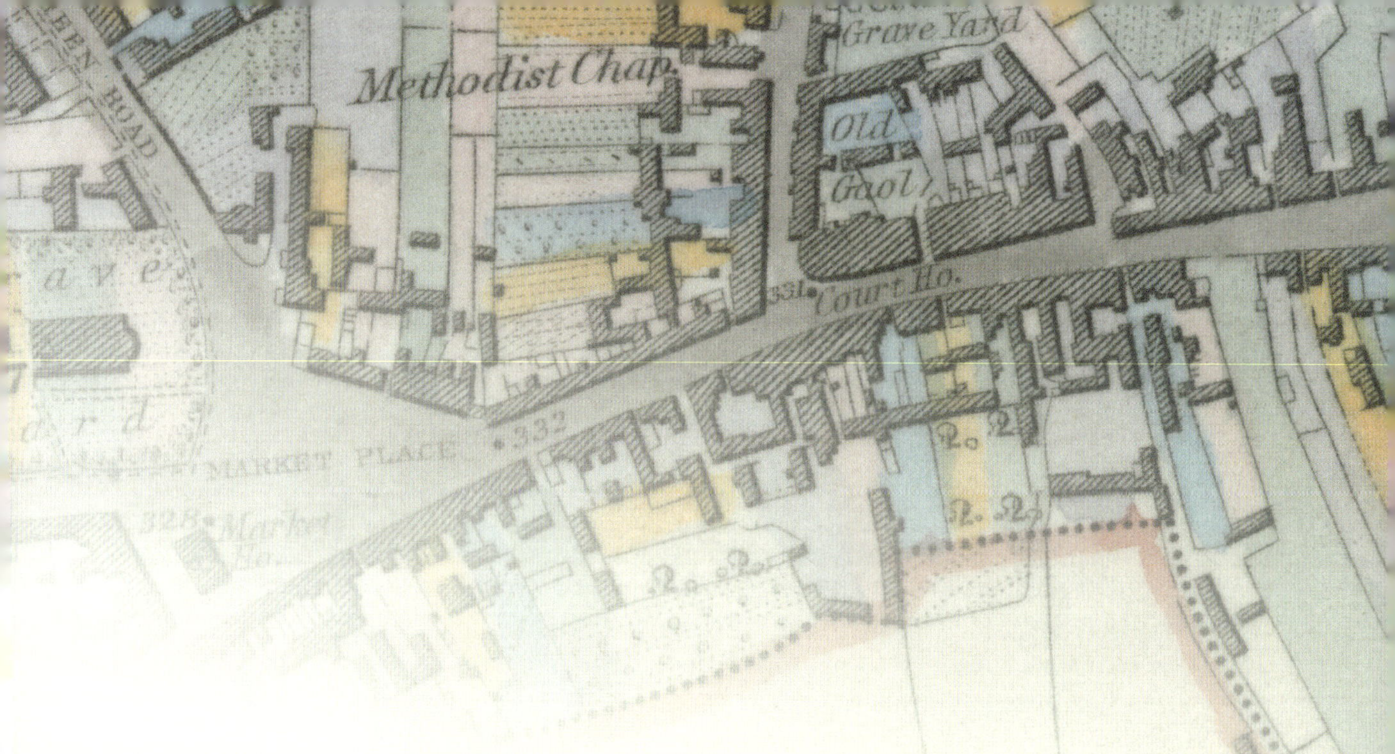

Chapter 4

Architecture before Reform:

Grand juries and the problem of implementing social reform, 1770–1810

Ireland's prisons provide a useful counterpoint to its courthouses. From an early date central government was more deeply involved in their planning and concerned itself primarily with their security, safety, and potential for effecting moral reformation. Often, the pressure from government on the grand juries was not aimed at reining in unnecessary spending, but at encouraging building work along the lines of the most enlightened penal-reform principles of the day. Before around 1760 Irish prisons were almost entirely local affairs, paid for and managed by grand juries. Gaolers charged fees for board and lodging from those they held in prison, and gaolers were entrusted by grand juries with one clear-cut responsibility: to prevent escapes. These gaolers operated like small private companies, often with the help of their families, and came in touch with the state – in the form of either assize judges or grand jurors – only when blame and punishment were doled out following an escape. Early gaols, then, had little if anything in common with the late Victorian penitentiary system, run, funded, and managed by the state, or with their geometrical layout, individual cells, torturous forced labour, and restrictions on speech and movement. It is the story of this transition from a highly decentralised and architecturally undistinguished prison system in the Georgian era to the modern prison regime developed by the Victorians that concerns this part of the book.[1] This first chapter in particular focuses on legal and administrative issues, and on developments in gaol design, within the constraints (as with courthouses in Chapter 1) of the relatively poor survival of eighteenth-century grand-jury correspondence and drawings.

There were as many different types of prisons in Ireland as there were opinions on how wrongdoers should be reformed. A 'gaol' was a county's main centre for the incarceration of persons awaiting trial at the assizes or serving time for less serious sentences. Though sometimes interchangeable with 'jail' or 'prison', the archaic spelling was preferred at the time for specific references to large county prisons (and is used here). Both felons (criminals) and debtors (bankrupts) were held there. Many gaols also developed adjacent 'houses of correction', where petty criminals and misdemeanants would ostensibly be 'reformed', and they were kept separate from their more hardened colleagues. The next stratum of prisons were the smaller provincial prisons, used – at least in theory – to hold accused persons only for a few days before their transfer to a gaol, or while awaiting the next quarter-sessions or (in later years) petty-sessions. These were known in Ireland as 'bridewells' (confusingly a different usage of the word than in Britain, where the term was synonymous with houses of correction). In Ireland gaols and bridewells were the concern of the grand juries. Corporations, manors, and some religious bodies also maintained smaller prisons, but here the definition of what constituted a prison begins to break down; often, these places were little more than a room with a locked door. They were variously known as 'lock-ups', 'dungeons', or simply '(black-)holes'.

Independent of the grand juries, central government also built prisons. In the early years of the prison-reform movement these were typically convict penitentiaries (used to imprison people who for various reasons would otherwise have been sent to the penal colonies in America or later Australia) and marshalseas (for debtors not accommodated in the county gaols). These prisons are also discussed in these chapters, but the main focus throughout is on the county gaol, the principal concern of each grand jury. In the period under study, gaols became immensely complicated palimpsests of penal-reform architecture from different generations and movements. Whereas most assize courthouses had a single definable period of construction, gaols were constantly subject to alteration and addition. In the more cramped city locations this phenomenon can make

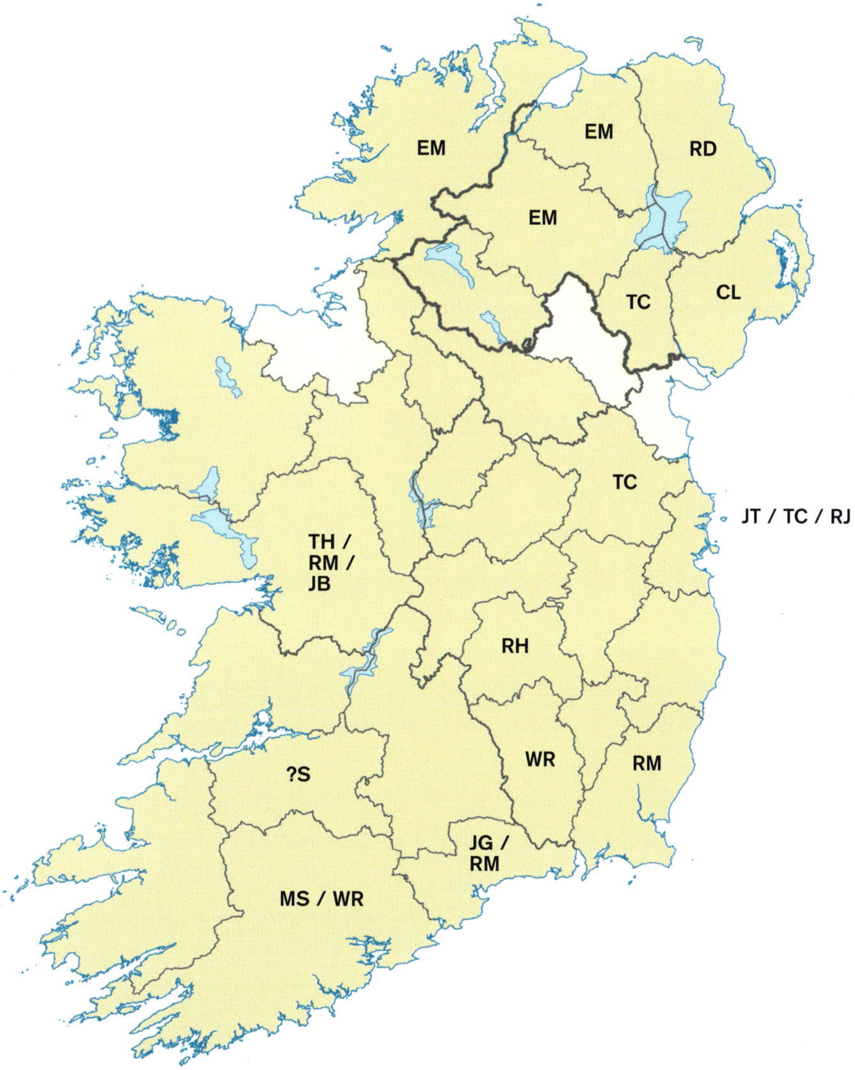

Fig. 4.1. A map showing new county gaols, or large additions made to existing gaols, in Ireland between 1780 and 1810, with the architect responsible named, where known. While only about a third of counties commissioned assize courthouses during each of the periods studied in chapters 1 to 3, it was rare for a county to escape some deep involvement in gaol-building work about every twenty years or so.

EM Edward Miller
RD Richard Drew
CL Charles Lilly
TC Thomas Cooley
TH Thomas Hardwick
RM Richard Morrison
JB John Behan
JT John Traile
RJ Richard Johnston
RH Richard Harman
WR William Robertson
?S ? Smyth
JG James Gandon
MS Michael Shanahan

disentangling their rich history a herculean task, and some questions inevitably remain unanswerable. It is not possible here to outline every architectural change to every gaol, for almost every existing building discussed in the following four chapters was either torn down or significantly altered many times. The 'model' prison was a constantly evolving and rather elusive architectural and intellectual goal – a moving target from the beginning of this period to the very end.

Prison building in Ireland during the period under study was not exceptional by British or European standards, though some aspects of central-government involvement were decades ahead of their time. Throughout Europe rising populations and growing cities and towns drove up crime figures. More unique to Ireland were distinct periods of agrarian and political unrest and rebellion that led to severe overcrowding in gaols for much of the 1790s and again in the 1820s and 1830s. The practice of imprisoning debtors from the eighteenth century onwards also greatly increased the number of prisoners held in gaols. By some estimates as many as half of all prisoners in Irish (and indeed British) gaols were debtors, and their presence created a uniquely uncomfortable mixture of different social classes.[2] The debtors' marshalsea was often the only part of a gaol that a middle-class person had genuine reason to fear. The earliest segregation of felons was almost always by gender (for moral purposes), but segregation for debtors was mostly by class. This had perhaps unintended consequences: R.B. McDowell argues that the more 'respectable' middle-class debtors furthered the prison-reform movement in the late eighteenth century by providing 'emphatic evidence' of deplorable prison conditions.[3]

But there were other factors contributing to the prison reform movement. One was the abrupt ending of penal transportation at the outbreak of the American War of Independence. Another was the concern over 'gaol fever' (as it was then termed; it is now understood as typhus). Together these events led to a widespread rebuilding programme from the 1780s onwards. Robin Evans has shown that some forty-five new gaols were built in England in the last quarter of the eighteenth century; in Ireland the figure was at least twenty-five, an impressive figure when the respective populations of the two islands are included (Fig. 4.1).[4] In this era the assize courthouse emerged out of its markethouse and tholsel origins, and so too the prison became for the first time a distinguishable type of building. As Evans has shown, the 'reformed prisons', as they were known, developed out of three perhaps counterintuitive but distinct needs: enclosure (for security), exposure and fragmentation (for ventilation and the health of prisoners), and compartmentalisation (for limiting 'moral contagion' and permitting reformation of character). It was this final requirement (generally known as 'classification') that was central to ideas of crime as a contagious social ill, the remedy for which was thought to be solitude, moral instruction, and contemplation. For this to be achievable, prisoners had to be segregated by gender, age, and type and severity of crime. Architecturally, this imperative meant, as Evans argues, that 'for the first time' the prison itself took 'full advantage of [its] latent powers' in a way that 'fixed the shape of experience'. Nevertheless, as the penal-reform debates evolved, almost all of these early new gaols were, he continues, 'declared failures' as soon as they were opened and 'never proved capable of delivering quite what was expected of them: they did not manufacture "goodness" in quantity'.[5] The dynamic was similar in Ireland.

Confinement before reform

We need to ask what the condition of Irish gaols was on the eve of the first great wave of prison rebuilding around 1782. Unsurprisingly, very few buildings survive unaltered. In the early 1770s there were attempts by some Antrim grand jurors to move the county's assizes and gaol from Carrickfergus to the more central town of Antrim. As in the other disputes outlined with regards to courthouses in Chapter 3, it is likely that the economic dividends of supplying the institution were a major consideration. However, in Antrim the proposal was voted down – as an earlier one had been in the 1750s – and soon afterwards Richard Drew was commissioned to build a new courthouse and gaol, which were erected between 1776 and 1779.[6] Such a financial outlay ensured that the assizes would remain at Carrickfergus and fortuitously led to the old gaol (subsequently given over to the town grand jury for its use in exchange for a site for the new county building) surviving long enough to be sketched by Samuel McSkimmin prior to its demolition in 1827 (Fig. 4.2).[7] Built around 1613, it was typical of the early gaols in being a labyrinthine, domestic-looking building. Commenting on coeval English gaols, Evans notes their 'fundamental ordinariness', with plenty of haphazard augmentations, with the gaol often distinguishable as a place of confinement only by its window bars.[8] There was no exercise yard for prisoners, and when John Howard, the noted English reformer, visited in July 1787, he found just one prisoner inside.[9] Despite the protestations of later government inspectors, the town grand jury continued to use the building as their own county gaol until 1826, by which time its archaic and primitive design was almost an object of curiosity.[10]

Fig. 4.2. Samuel McSkimmin, Carrickfergus old courthouse and gaol, *c.* 1811. Penal reformers of later years regarded this gaol (built in the early seventeenth century) as the absolute anathema of good prison design. From McSkimmin, *History … of Carrickfergus*, p. 151.

In Cork, the city's old north and south gates served respectively as the city and county gaols. The former was erected in 1715 (Fig. 4.3), soon after the old wooden north bridge had been rebuilt in stone.[11] The latter was put up in the 1720s (Fig. 4.4).[12] As late as 1823 there were still some prisoners kept at the north gate, described by Howard in 1787 as an unhealthy and squalid lock-up overseen by a lazy gaoler who permitted the free entry of alcoholic spirits.[13] He found confined around seventy debtors and fifty felons, of all ages and both genders. There had been many attempted escapes, and some prisoners had succeeded in fleeing by cutting the iron bars of the windows.[14] In the south gate a prisoner tunnelled through wooden floors but was pursued and recaptured.[15] The busy public thoroughfare running below, and the ease of conversation and admission of goods through the windows that opened onto it, were classed as threats to both physical security and moral correction by the reformers of the 1770s, and later prison architects more consciously shaped their designs with these concerns in mind.

City gates were convenient locations for keeping prisoners, and Dublin's Newgate and Derry's Ferrygate were also used at this time as county gaols.[16] Elsewhere it was common for existing buildings to be requisitioned and colonised as gaols.[17] The Louth grand jurors purchased Castlenyrooty Castle (in Dundalk) from Viscount Dungannon in 1667 and used it as their gaol until well into the nineteenth century.[18] In County Kildare the medieval White's Castle in the

Fig. 4.3. Nathaniel Grogan, 'North Gate Bridge', Cork, *c.* 1796. The imposing gatehouse on the city side of the bridge served as the city gaol from 1715 until the early 1820s. (*Reproduced courtesy of the Crawford Art Gallery, Cork.*)

Fig. 4.4. John Fitzgerald (after Nathaniel Grogan), 'The South Gate and Bridge, Cork, 1797', *c.* 1850. Similar in scale and composition to the city gaol, this gatehouse held the county prisoners from the 1720s until the early nineteenth century. The rusticated columns and broken pediment of the passageway gave the gaol a false appearance of solidity, but prisoners found it rather easy to escape. (*Reproduced courtesy of the Crawford Art Gallery, Cork.*)

centre of Athy served as a gaol for a century or more.[19] In County Donegal the cellars under Lifford's courthouse (see Chapter 1) constituted the county gaol for nearly fifty years until a free-standing gaol was built nearby. In 1787 there were thirty-two prisoners kept there in what Howard described as 'five dungeons' under the courthouse.[20] In County Galway the grand jurors had their first gaol at Loughrea, built around 1585, but after so much warfare and disturbance it was unsurprisingly described as 'old and ruinous' in 1671. When the county prisoners were evicted in 1686 from their temporary confinement in the Galway town gaol (an old tholsel), the grand jurors leased the nearby Blakes' Castle from the Morgan family.[21] Medieval tower houses, however, were ill suited to keeping prisoners, and the reformers almost always condemned their use. Blakes' Castle required heavy (and seemingly continual) financial intervention, and this expenditure was criticised by those who suspected jobbery and corruption in the grand jurors' private deals. An unfriendly letter in the *Dublin Evening Post* in 1786 claimed that this gaol, where Howard had seen all the felons kept in 'two long rooms with dirt floors and no fire-place', was costing more to maintain than 'the noblest prison in Petersburg or Amsterdam'.[22]

Early central-government reforms and Enlightenment thinking

In Britain and Ireland, the prison reformers of the eighteenth century looked to central government to set new standards for gaol design and administration. As early as 1635 an Irish act called for a house of correction to be built in every county, but it was not enforced or enforceable, and was widely ignored.[23] Similarly ineffective was a 1705 law that sought to curb grand-jury 'corruption' and jobbery. By setting out the types of presentments that were permissible, this law specifically allowed grand jurors, for the first time, to build courthouses (as analysed in Chapter 1) as well as to pay for the 'repairing and strengthening' of gaols and for the installation of bolts, stocks, whipping-posts, and pillories.[24] Furthermore, a House of Commons inquiry in 1729 revealed the horrors of Dublin's Newgate, a gaol never far from controversy.[25] As Oliver MacDonagh has shown, the problem with much early legislation was simply the difficulty in enforcing it, and specifically in overcoming the inertia and the prized independence of grand juries.[26] From the mid-1750s the pace of reform in Ireland became much more pronounced; by coincidence plans were also coming together for the first major new British gaol, a new Newgate for London, and this project exerted an influence in Ireland in subsequent years.[27] An Irish measure in 1756 concerning houses of correction noted that many presentments for these institutions 'hath been frequently abused and ... misapplied' by grand jurors; the new law limited their annual spending on all gaol-related concerns to just £10. It also stated that in future all houses of correction should be built 'distinct and separate' from the county gaol and should be designed to allow basic classification by gender.'[28] More ambitious were two acts in 1764 that dealt with both architecture and administration. Grand jurors were now required to build exercise yards for prisoners (to prevent gaol fever) and to segregate not only men from women but also 'lunatics' from all other prisoners. These acts also reformed the payment of gaol fees and set up a system of local inspection led by the Protestant clergy, who were to report regularly to the grand jurors.[29] MacDonagh argues that this kind of local inspection was an 'extraordinary' development for its time – many years ahead of similar provisions in Britain.[30] Yet the practical changes that resulted can be easily exaggerated, and as the act limited the amount of money that could be spent on effecting all these changes to just £230 per year, few new gaols were immediately begun.[31]

In the late 1760s there were other developments beyond the rarefied world of parliamentary statutes. In 1767 *An Essay on Crimes and Punishments*, written by the Milanese Enlightenment thinker and pioneering penologist Cesare Beccaria, was first published in Dublin. Decrying the death penalty and other cruel punishments, and calling for a rational system of criminal justice, Beccaria's treatise set the tone for the rapidly evolving penal-reform movement in both Ireland and Britain.[32] Howard began his tours of European prisons in 1773, following his appointment as high sheriff of Bedfordshire, and soon became a national celebrity and a key influence on British prison-reform legislation. In 1769 the Royal Dublin Society held a competition for the best design of a new county gaol with separate wards for felons and debtors, men and women, to cost between £1,000 and £3,000. It appears that none of the entries have survived, nor indeed has the identity of the winner, but such a degree of polite 'establishment' support for prison design at the same time that Dublin's most celebrated architectural competition was underway (for the new Royal Exchange) gives some indication of how far up the social and political spectrum the penal-reform agenda had progressed.[33] Howard made the first of his five Irish tours a few years later and publicised the miserable conditions in which he found prisoners. At Dublin's old Newgate in 1775 he saw 'numbers of poor creatures ill with the gaol-fever, unattended and disregarded'.[34] Over the next few years he penned at least two essays in the *Hibernian Magazine* – on gaol design and a call for greater classification (1776) and on Swiss prisons (1779).[35] In the first edition of his *The State of the Prisons* (1777), he sketched a 'model' county gaol (Fig. 4.5) that met all the safety, security, and segregation requirements of his evolving penal policy. It became the first of many 'models' over the next fifty years, giving primacy not only to the concept of a single 'perfect' design but also to the theories of a lay expert who was not a professional architect. By raising the cell blocks off the ground with an arcade, Howard hoped to counteract the poorly understood but deadly gaol fever that was devastating prison inmates at this time.[36] Yet within a few years his 'model' design – a rectilinear arrangement of cell blocks and irregularly sized yards – came to be seen as the very antithesis of good prison design. The local Irish authorities, however, moved rather slowly, and many of them rebuilt their gaols on 'Howardian' principles long after his proposed arrangement had been officially discredited.

A 'reformed' gaol for the city of Dublin

The growing intellectual depth of the prison-reform movement exerted its first impact on Irish prison architecture in the early 1770s. The problem of overcrowding and gaol fever was most acute in Dublin, and as the city's prisons were so visible to parliamentarians and the press, the reform movement naturally

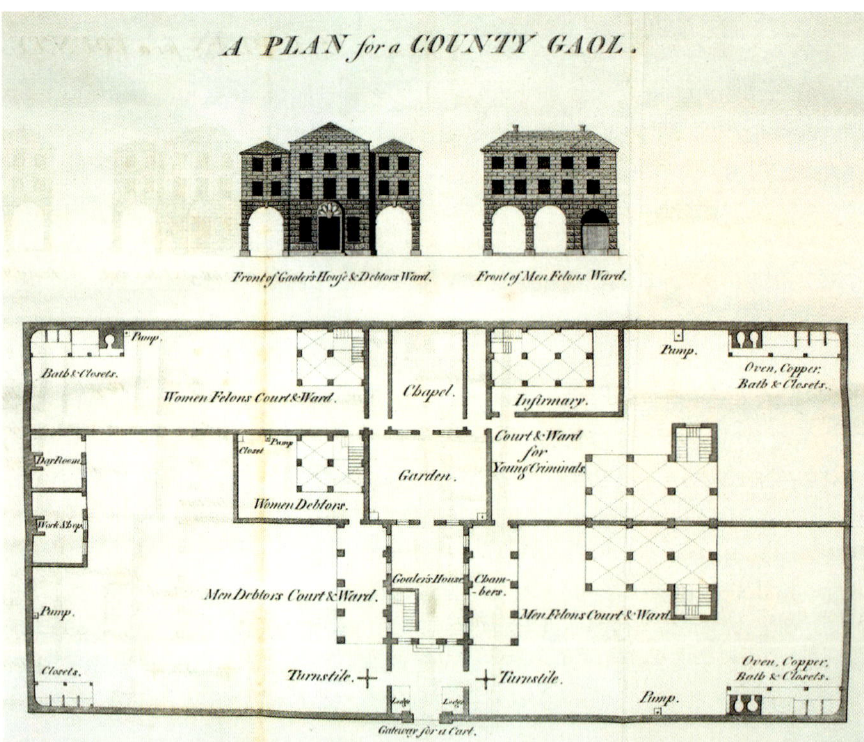

Fig. 4.5. 'A plan for a county gaol', by John Howard, from *The State of the Prisons* (1777). In order to educate British magistrates and local elites about the aims of the penal-reform movement, Howard drew a 'model' gaol that met all the requirements that he described in his writings. Though not architecturally distinguished, the plan provided answers to the main concerns of security, classification, and ventilation. Later reformers and more talented architects quickly realised its limitations.

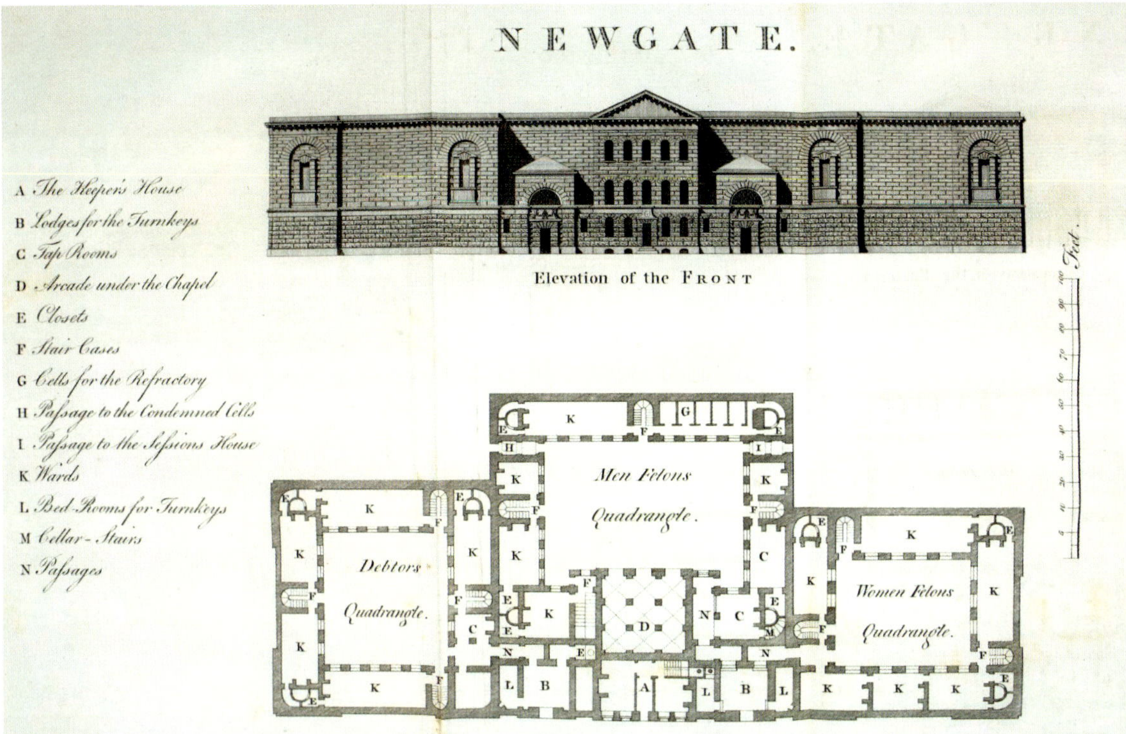

Fig. 4.6. Newgate Gaol, London. George Dance the younger, 1769. From Howard, *The State of the Prisons* (1777). Dance's heavily rusticated façade has won the admiration of generations of architectural historians, but the gaol itself was, like its namesake in Dublin, an abject failure from beginning to end.

began there. Dublin's Newgate was condemned as 'very ruinous' in a 1767 inquiry, which called for a new gaol to be built for the city and also promoted the idea of a new sheriff's prison (where some city debtors were to be incarcerated).[37] Though the latter facility would not appear for another twenty years, the 'new' Newgate, the first attempt made in Ireland to build a 'reformed' prison, became an eagerly watched building site after the foundation stone was laid in October 1773.[38] It closely mirrored the construction of its namesake in London under the architect George Dance (Fig. 4.6). The Dublin city grand jurors were given a site by the city corporation – a little green to the north of the Liffey (Fig. 4.7). The ground was cleared in 1773, but little happened until Thomas Cooley became involved two years later, and he is credited with the final design.[39] Cooley had come to Ireland from London after winning the aforementioned Royal Exchange competition, and he emerged as the foremost neo-classicist in the city in the 1770s. Such was the national importance of the new Newgate that central government made direct grants to aid in its construction; at least £2,000 was forwarded to the city grand jury.[40] Later commentators suggest that the final bill reached about £16,000, which would have made it Ireland's most expensive gaol at that time.[41] After it was completed around 1781, the 'old' Newgate was abandoned for a period and then served as a house of correction for prostitutes before its later demolition.[42]

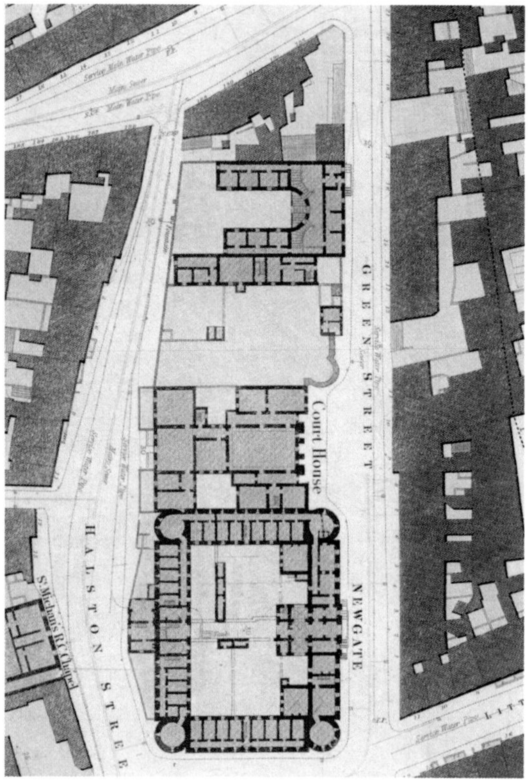

Fig. 4.7. Dublin city, showing the Green Street courthouse, Newgate gaol, the sheriff's city prison, and the city marshalsea. Ordnance Survey five-feet town map, surveyed 1847. Newgate was built on the site of a little green in the tightly packed north inner city, with many of the city's markets located nearby. (*Reproduced courtesy of the Board of Trinity College Dublin.*)

It is unlikely that Cooley had designed any gaols before leaving London, but he would naturally have looked, as so many British architects did, to Dance's Newgate for inspiration.[43] He adopted the same quadrangular design, with cells on four sides looking into exercise yards (Fig. 4.8). In his elevation he borrowed heavily from Dance's deeply rusticated stonework and protruding Mannerist keystones, broken pediments, and blind arches. These were most apparent in the granite centrepiece where the hanging apparatus was installed – a feature memorably described by Maurice Craig as 'a powerful piece of terroristic architecture' (Figs 4.9, 4.10).[44] The foreboding appearance of the gaol was heightened by the four corner Bastille-like turrets, which as late as 1809 served no real purpose and were entirely empty and open to the air.[45] This was not the only deceit of the new gaol; complaints soon arose of poor workmanship, of 'crumbling' cement and mortar, of an 'uncomfortable and insecure' gaol. Before it turned thirty years old the gaol was condemned as 'a disgrace to this metropolis'.[46] We need to ask what went so badly wrong. There was no clear answer for the poor workmanship, but many suspected jobbery on the part of the grand jurors (as they did when courthouse projects went astray – see chapters 1 and 2).[47] An incompetent and inefficient gaol keeper did little to help. In Cooley's defence his design had provided, with its two large yards and several smaller ones, for basic segregation by type of offence and gender. In July 1779 Howard had in fact praised the design, calling it ‘airy’ and ‘convenient’ and noting its allowance for gender segregation.[48] Furthermore, the corner turrets should have provided plenty of ventilation, and similar shafts had been deployed by Dance (and in an earlier Newgate scheme by William Jones) in London.[49] A healthy prison environment was certainly on the minds of the government, for in the same year that money was voted for Newgate, a law was passed (following an outbreak of gaol fever in Dublin) that encouraged grand juries to ventilate and whitewash their gaols and to avoid keeping prisoners underneath courthouses or in other insalubrious places.[5]

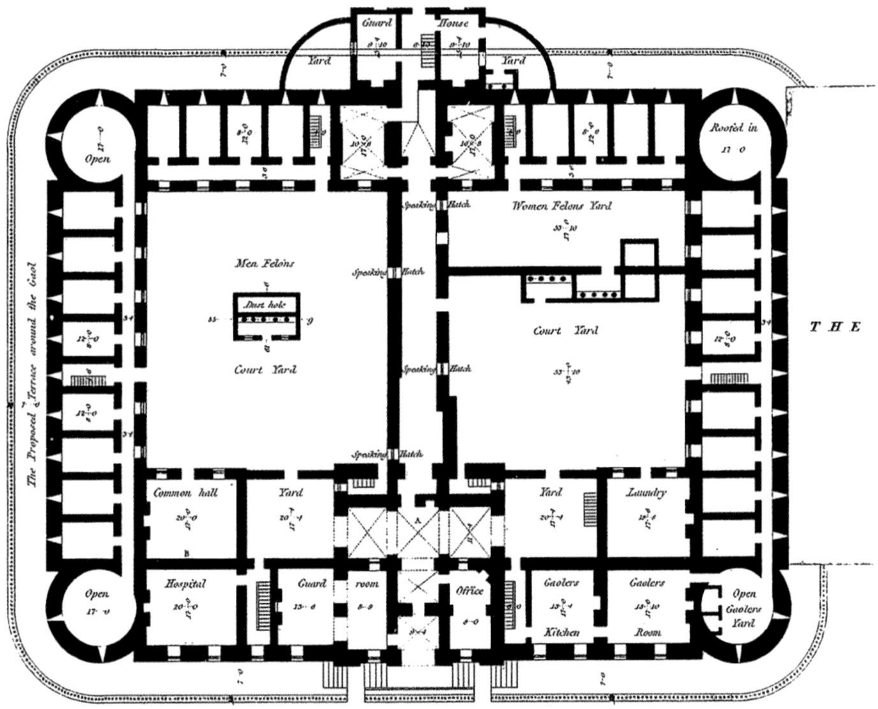

Fig. 4.8. Newgate gaol, Dublin, ground-floor plan. Thomas Cooley's design was like a scaled-down version of its London namesake. The 'rectilinear' design, as it became known, was later deemed unsuitable for prison building, as it failed to provide adequate classification, ventilation, and inspection. Drawn by Francis Johnston, December 1808, from *Report from the Commissioners Appointed To Inquire into … the State Prisons and Other Gaols in Ireland*, H.C. 1809 (265), vii.

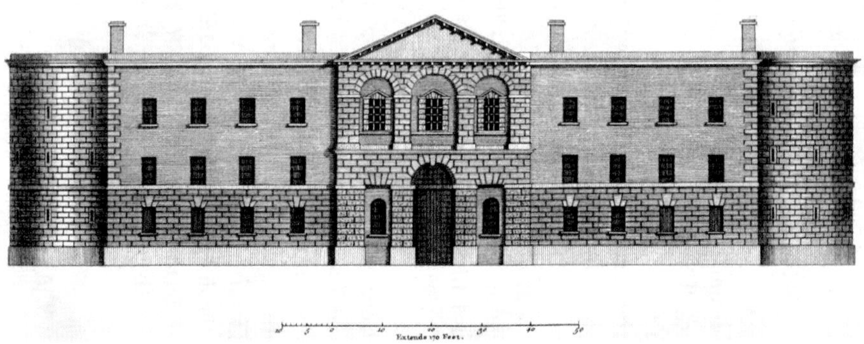

Fig. 4.9. Newgate gaol, Dublin, principal (east) elevation. Cooley also borrowed from the extensive rustication used to give an impregnable appearance to Dance's Newgate. From Robert Pool and John Cash, *Views of the Most Remarkable Public Buildings … in the City of Dublin* (1780).

Fig. 4.10. Newgate gaol, Dublin, principal (east) elevation, from a photograph taken before the gaol's demolition in 1893. On the first floor of this granite centrepiece was the hanging apparatus, still intact in this view. The façade was described by Maurice Craig as 'a powerful piece of terroristic architecture'. (*Reproduced courtesy of the Historical Picture Archive (Ireland).*)

There were, however, two great problems with Cooley's Newgate. First, it was simply too crowded from the outset and too small to afford a separate sleeping cell for every prisoner. Second, by 1782, when Howard did a *volte-face* and condemned it as 'in every respect the very reverse [of] a perfect and well-regulated gaol', the latest British 'model' gaol had already evolved beyond the confines of a simple rectilinear plan with a limited number of yards and methods for natural ventilation.[51] Newgate was old before its time. Howard's report in the following year was even more alarming: the gaoler permitted whiskey to be sold, there was no separation of the sexes, prisoners were robbed and stripped on admission, day-rooms were unused, cellars were used as cells, there was no hospital, and divine worship was not being celebrated.[52] Remarkably, Cooley's provincial business seems not to have been too badly affected by these scandals, and around 1780 he built new county gaols at Armagh and Trim (Fig. 4.11). Still, the running sore of Newgate was notorious in the capital and, revealingly, he gained few new commissions there after this time. In 1790 there was rioting and forty escapes from the gaol and for a moment the prisoners seemed poised to set it alight, emulating perhaps events at the Bastille in the previous year. The military was needed to restore order.[53] From almost the day it opened until it was finally abandoned as a city prison in 1851, Newgate was an allegory for the difficulties of translating well-meaning reforms into bricks and mortar. The story was much the same in London: apart from its celebrated façade, Evans has shown how Dance's new gaol was seen by contemporaries as 'a bad prison from any other point of view'; he calls it a 'botched but instructive prelude to the reform movement'. The two Newgates, then, shared more than a name.[54]

Fig. 4.11. The River Boyne, Trim, County Meath. Little survives today of Thomas Cooley's Meath county gaol except some masonry walls facing the river. Built in the 1780s, soon after the opening of Cooley's Dublin Newgate gaol, it was always too small for such a large county; it was extended three times before being abandoned in the 1830s upon the opening of a much larger county gaol nearby (see Chapter 6). (*Photograph by author, 2014.*)

The reaction from central government, 1780–4

Central government helped to pay for Newgate, and yet it turned out to be a great disappointment. Events beyond Ireland shaped the government's response at this time. The ending of transportation to America focused minds in Britain on the possibility of building large new penitentiaries for convicts at home. A key figure, perhaps second only to Howard, was William Eden, noted as an outspoken penal reformer and the author of *Principles of Penal Law* (1771). He had been vocal in parliament on reform issues before the American war began, and he became intimately involved in the drafting and redrafting of the Penitentiary Act (1779).[55] The effect of this British scheme in Ireland will be discussed in due course, but by good fortune Eden was appointed Irish chief secretary in 1780 and remained in Dublin for two years. His enthusiasm for penal reform meshed with that of like-minded Irish MPs such as Peter Holmes, comptroller of stamps, and John Parnell, commissioner of revenue, and together with the often-visiting Howard, the 'sanctified exemplar and authoritative source', these officials formed a new coterie just as Newgate's limitations were becoming apparent.[56]

Holmes voiced concerns about gaol fever in the Irish House of Commons in 1781. Any outbreak not only claimed lives and destroyed order in a gaol but also posed a grave threat to nearby dwellers, especially in larger cities.[57] In 1782 Howard made his third visit to Ireland, and after addressing a parliamentary inquiry, he was given an honorary degree by Trinity College Dublin.[58] The continuing problem for the reformers was how to enforce the existing laws; they tackled this difficulty in two important acts passed in 1782 and 1784. The first reinforced the existing power of assize judges to compel grand jurors to follow parliament's prison legislation. Now, for the first time, jurors who refused to make presentments to improve their gaols could be fined, and this money could then be used to help pay for the required works. Effectively, this meant in a roundabout way that judges could make presentments for gaol building.[59] As MacDonagh argued, it is striking that a law with such an important rebalancing of the relative power of central and local government could find its way onto the statute books in what was a tumultuous year – the beginning of 'Grattan's parliament'.[60] Yet the 1784 act was even more ambitious. It noted that Irish gaols 'continue in a ruinous state' and required grand jurors to make a detailed investigation of the state of their gaols and to repair, rebuild, or enlarge them if necessary. Their proposals had to be advertised in the newspapers. Classification was now more explicitly required, and not only by gender but also between the accused, the convicted, and petty criminals. Gaols were to have at least two yards, with water pumps and a toilet in each, and 'dry and airy cells' throughout to prevent fever. Magistrates were required to inspect gaols and report on their condition at the quarter-sessions. To curb the abuse of fees, gaolers' salaries were now to be paid directly by the grand jury, and penalties for supplying prisoners with alcohol (however naïve in practice) were greatly increased. The overall message to grand jurors was simple: spend money but spend it wisely.[61]

Though Howard praised Lord Temple, the viceroy in 1782–3, with spearheading the new energy for penal reform in Ireland, equally important were the roles played by Eden and various Irish MPs in drafting the new legislation.[62] Around 1786 there was an explosion in building activity (Fig. 4.12), with around a dozen new gaols begun. Some of these had been planned for several years but now moved beyond the drawing board. A few grand juries obtained local acts of parliament to clarify their building plans, but others simply forged ahead regardless.[63] A very similar boom started in Britain after a law was passed that allowed local authorities to mortgage their rates to help in covering the large expenditure of new gaols.[64] Such a measure did not take effect in Ireland for more than twenty years, but new Irish gaols could in any case be smaller and cheaper, and grand jurors had frequently been setting aside funds for such building work for many years. Despite this new energy there was little correlation between the quantity of the new gaols built and their quality. One of the first to be built was Waterford.

'Monuments to the unskillfulness of the architects'

By the mid-1780s a 'reformed' gaol provided at least some rudimentary system of classification, with prisoners sleeping alone at night but congregated in common halls or in exercise yards by day. The gaol had to be secure and well

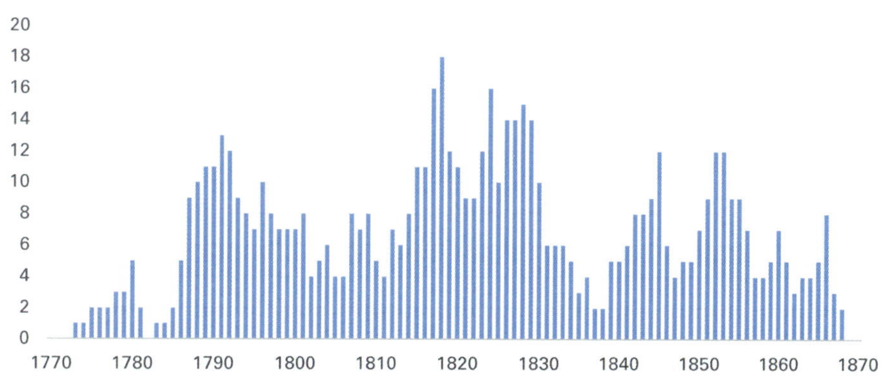

Fig. 4.12. Graph showing the number of gaols that were under construction in Ireland between 1770 and 1870. The building boom of the late 1780s and 1790s is immediately apparent, as are the later rebuilding programmes of the 1810s, 1820s, and 1840s. Compiled from Appendix A.

ventilated. Architecturally, to satisfy these requirements meant in general a rectilinear building of two-to-three storeys in height with little ornamentation. Waterford's courthouse and gaol were adjoining buildings, erected between 1784 and 1787 (the courthouse is discussed in Chapter 1). The design of prisons became an increasingly specialised task from this time onwards, and though the man responsible at Waterford, James Gandon, is now seen as one of Ireland's great architects – and in his own time Howard even reputedly called him 'an ingenious man, a treasure' – he was not an expert on prison architecture.[65] We know little about the design of his gaol building (it was demolished in 1861), only that the general outline was of a three-sided court open to the rear and that it was entirely hidden from view by the celebrated façade of his courthouse.[66] John Beresford asked Howard to inspect a plan for the gaol around 1784, but Howard brushed him aside, saying he was too busy with other work. Gandon's biographer records Howard's praise for the architect and claims that they had been friends since Gandon's work at London's Bethlehem Lunatic Hospital in the previous decade.[67] There is, however, no specific endorsement for his Waterford design in this often-quoted passage, and though Edward McParland claims that the gaol 'must have been planned on Howard's principles', it seems likely that the very opposite was the case.[68] Only a few months after the courthouse had been roofed in,[69] Howard visited Waterford and noticed what was taking place:

> A new county gaol, too splendid, and built on a bad plan, is not yet occupied. [In Ireland] the grand juries have granted very liberal presentments [for new gaols]. On seeing gentlemen so *liberal* and *benevolent*, I could not but reflect with great concern that many of the *prisons* now building will be monuments to the *unskillfulness* of the architects, who are ignorant of what constitutes a *secure* and *healthy* prison. The new gaols, having pompous fronts, appear like palaces to the lower class of people.[70]

Writing privately to a friend while on his travels, he was even more direct:

> There is a spirit of improvement [in Ireland], but it has to struggle with the vice of persons, from the highest to the lowest, who make a job of every public institution .... [Ireland] never can be a rich, united, or independent state. Many parts are as savage as the inland parts of Russia.[71]

However exaggerated these broader impressions may have been, the new Waterford gaol undoubtedly failed to match the constantly evolving standards set by Howard and the reformers. Twenty years later, it was condemned for its 'fraudulently executed' workmanship, the internal division of 'lath and plaster', and its subsiding boundary walls. At least £4,000 was needed to carry out essential repairs.[72] Half of the building was so dangerously unstable in the 1820s that it had to be temporarily abandoned.[73] Perhaps Gandon's contractor can be blamed for many of these faults, but the outdated design – seemingly oblivious to all the theoretical advances in prison design of the 1770s – was solely the responsibility of the architect and constituted further proof of ineffectiveness in the implementation of central government's more detailed pronouncements.

Jeremiah Fitzpatrick and the first building boom

The 1780s were a busy decade in Irish penal reform; the last major change came with the appointment of Sir Jeremiah Fitzpatrick (*c.* 1740–1810) (Fig. 4.13) as the first 'inspector general of prisons' in 1786.[74] In Dublin in the same year there were other changes, such as the creation of a new police force and the initial planning of a new county gaol for Kilmainham.[75] Nonetheless, it is likely that Fitzpatrick's appointment stemmed from events in the less accountable grand-jury rooms of the provincial towns. Though the law under which Fitzpatrick was appointed also created a new inspector specifically for the city of Dublin, Fitzpatrick's powers were far more extensive than those of this individual, especially after Fitzpatrick's position was made permanent in 1787 and was strengthened by the setting of penalties for interference with his work.[76] The importance of this new position in the broader narrative of British and Irish administrative history is beyond the scope of this chapter, but the essential issue is and was enforcement.[77] Fitzpatrick was a friend of Holmes and some other prison reformers and had testified before a House of Commons inquiry on gaols as a medical expert prior to his appointment. His intellectual debt to Howard is apparent in his *Essay on Gaol-abuses and on the Means of Redressing Them* (1784). As inspector-general, Fitzpatrick was obliged to visit all the country's prisons at least every two years, and to submit an annual report to parliament. The same law also put further pressure on grand jurors to improve their gaols. There was to be a common room or kitchen heated by a fire in every gaol, and there were threats of further 'fines' (or forced presentments) if jurors failed to act.[78] Finally, as some gaol enlargements were being delayed by 'exorbitant demands' for compensation from nearby landholders, grand jurors were granted the far-reaching land-acquisition powers of the Dublin Wide Streets Commissioners (established in 1757).[79] The *Dublin Journal* welcomed the reforms and praised Fitzpatrick's appointment as the first of its kind in Europe.[80]

Fig. 4.13. Sir Jeremiah Fitzpatrick (*c.* 1740–1810). Mezzotint by William Barnard, after Samuel Drummond, 1801. (*Reproduced courtesy of the National Portrait Gallery, London.*)

The building boom of the 1780s and 1790s was a response to growing interest in penal-reform issues both in parliament and in polite society, as well as to the impact of celebrated international self-styled experts such as Howard. It was also undoubtedly a reaction to the increase in crime and agrarian unrest that came with the Rightboy movement of 1785–8 in the south, sectarian violence in the north-east in subsequent years, and the uncertainty created by the outbreak of war with revolutionary France in 1793.[81] There were thus multiple reasons for rebuilding gaols – some practical (overcrowding), others political (control or repression), and still others 'humanitarian' (gaol fever, etc.). By 1788 the effects in the provincial towns of Ireland were obvious to see, with the *Freeman's Journal* – a keen supporter of the prison-reform movement from the early days – perhaps best encapsulating the mood of the time with its comment that there were 'more gaols at present building ... than any person living can recollect ..., and it may be concluded from the multiplicity and enormity of transgressions that they were never more necessary than now'.[82]

With Dublin's Newgate gaol open, attention naturally fell upon its sister gaol for the surrounding county at Kilmainham. As early as 1774, Edward Newenham, another of the reform MPs, had called for a replacement of the existing gaol.[83] In 1782 a Commons inquiry described it as 'extremely insecure', with 'narrow cells sunk underground'. The low windows allowed free

Fig. 4.14. William Ashford, 'A View of Dublin from Chapelizod', 1795–8 (detail). Ashford shows the recently completed Kilmainham gaol at the edge of the city, unobstructed by later buildings. (*Reproduced courtesy of the National Gallery of Ireland.*)

conversation with passers-by and the admission not only of alcohol but also of tools to effect escapes.[84] Approval of plans for the new gaol came in 1785, along with an act of the Irish parliament to assist in conveying a site at Gallows Hill (Fig. 4.14) from a local landlord to the grand jurors at a peppercorn rent.[85] The architect, John Traile, was very much an insider with the Dublin grand jurors as he was their high sheriff; surprisingly (or perhaps unsurprisingly), there appear to have been no accusations of jobbery.[86] Traile had no previous experience in designing gaols, but neither did many other architects at this time.[87] He had spent much of the previous decade in building canals and lighthouses; yet, however questionable his appointment might appear, the story of the new Kilmainham was the very opposite of that of Newgate. Howard's principles were now much more widely understood, at least in Dublin, and Fitzpatrick was at hand to see to their implementation. The *Freeman's Journal* was quick to note that the design was 'one of Mr Howard's most approved plans', and gave regular updates on the building work, including the comment at one point that the stones used were 'uncommonly large' and 'so ingrafted in each other as to beg defiance to escapes'.[88] Howard did not live long enough to see the gaol finished, but he commented in 1787 that it was 'a new prison in a fine situation'.[89] Construction proceeded slowly. The grand jurors had hoped to secure grants, just as their city colleagues had done with Newgate, but the government was unwilling to provide such funds, and it was August 1796 before the gaol finally opened.[90] By then the violence and intimidation associated with the United Irish movement were so acute that British army officers briefly considered occupying it with troops, as they considered it 'almost a fortress', and during the rebellion of 1798 cannon were placed around the entrances to the gaol.[91]

Kilmainham was the first gaol in Ireland to conform to Howard's principles of the early 1780s, however obsolete they became by the turn of the century. Virtually nothing, bar the main entranceway, has survived unaltered from the eighteenth century, but the original plan can be traced from old drawings and maps (Fig. 4.15). Its elevation was significantly more two-dimensional and plainer than later additions now make it appear. The only coherent façade, of two storeys with corner towers and a three-bay central block (Fig. 4.16), all heavily rusticated, faced north towards Inchicore Road. (Its western half partially survives today.) Over the main door with its powerful vermiculated rustication the architect

Fig. 4.15. Kilmainham gaol, ground-floor plan. John Traile designed the first prison in Ireland to exactly follow all the principles espoused by Howard. It was deemed at the time of its opening to be a success. Drawn by Francis Johnston, December 1808, from *Report from the Commissioners Appointed To Inquire into … the State Prisons and Other Gaols in Ireland*, H.C. 1809 (265), vii.

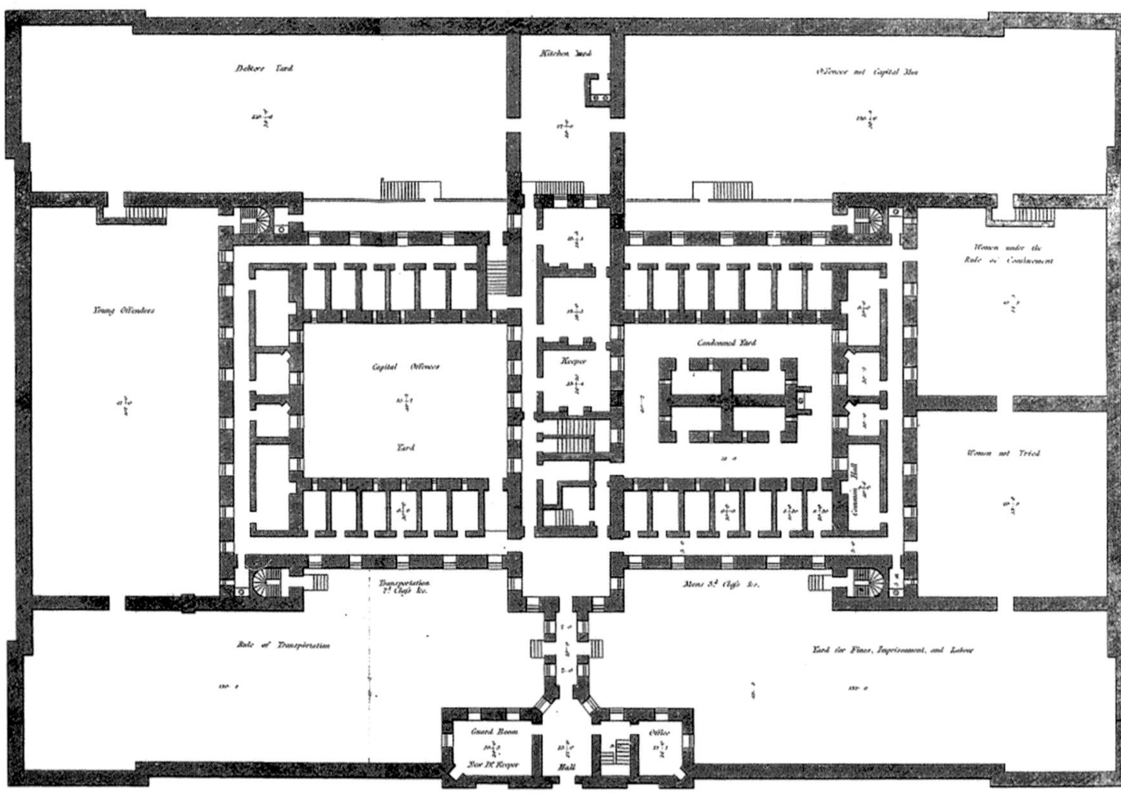

Fig. 4.16. Kilmainham courthouse and gaol, from the north-east, *c.* 1835. In this view the appearance of the gaol before substantial alterations in the 1840s and 1850s is visible, with the three-bay central block not deeply recessed as it now is. William Farrell's courthouse, from the late 1810s, is nearby. From *The Dublin Penny Journal*, vol. 4, no. 184, 9 January 1836, p. 221.

placed a tympanum carved with interwoven menacing snakes and serpents in chains; above was the ghoulish spectacle of the gallows (Fig. 4.17). But these details often meant little to the prison reformers, who concerned themselves with the more prosaic details of plan, utility, and construction. In this regard Kilmainham was a considerable advance on Newgate in terms of classification and security, but it left unanswered questions of ventilation and inspection. Whereas Newgate had yards only inside its quadrangle, Kilmainham had a suite of yards between the cell blocks and its outer insulating perimeter wall, which completely shut off prisoners from the outer world, from conversations, and from illicit goods and tools. To prevent conversations between classes of inmates, the cells, divided into seven classes, looked inwards and were separated from the outer yards by an arterial corridor. But the closed rectilinear arrangement did little to bring fresh air to the inner yards, and it was almost impossible for the gaoler to observe all his inmates at any one time. Nonetheless the classic Howardian design had an enduring appeal, and a somewhat reduced version served by the same underlying principles was built at Downpatrick by Charles Lilly between 1789 and 1796 (Fig. 4.18).[92] As late as 1820, Thomas Hopper designed a very similar gaol for the Wiltshire magistrates at Fisherton Anger (Fig. 4.19).[93]

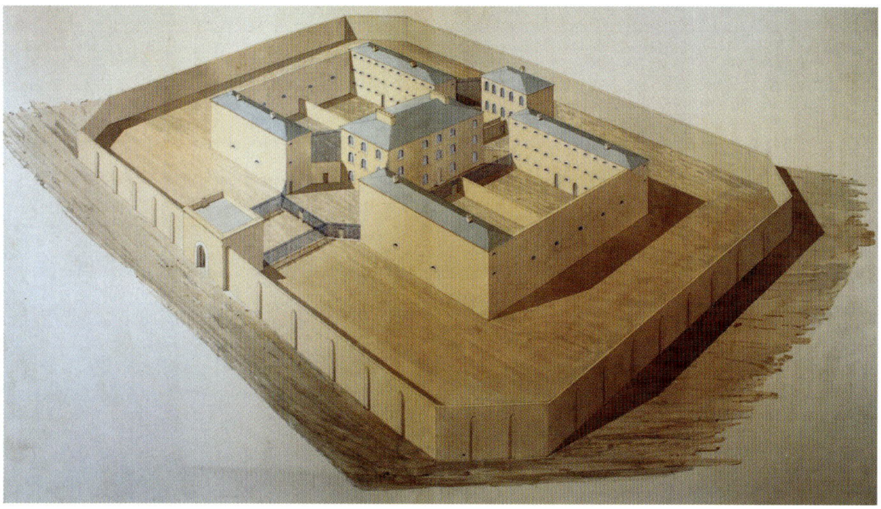

(clockwise from top left)
Fig. 4.17. Kilmainham gaol, tympanum over the main door. Above these snakes and serpents in chains was the ghoulish spectacle of the county gallows. (*Photograph by author, 2014.*)

Fig. 4.18. Downpatrick gaol, from the south-west. Built by Charles Lilly between 1789 and 1796, the new gaol for County Down was similar to Kilmainham in many aspects of its plan; both derived from the principles established by Howard in the previous decade. The gaol survives today as a museum, with the assize courthouse visible in the distance. (*Photograph by author, 2014.*)

Fig. 4.19. Fisherton Anger (Wiltshire), county gaol. Thomas Hopper, 1820. The design of a rectilinear gaol on Howardian principles as late as 1820, in a fashion similar to Kilmainham and Downpatrick in the 1790s, shows the enduring appeal of its simple layout. (*Reproduced courtesy of Wiltshire and Swindon Archives.*)

Provincial gaols in the late 1780s

In Waterford, as discussed in Chapter 1, the city and county grand juries came together to build a common courthouse, but they appear to have maintained separate gaols.[94] Cooperation was relatively rare at this time, and when it did occur, it often led to intractable financial disagreements. Providing an exception to this general rule is Limerick, where the city and county grand juries petitioned parliament in 1784 (and again in 1786) for legislation to allow them to build a common gaol.[95] Both the *Oxford Dictionary of National Biography* and the *Biographical Dictionary of British Architects* claim that this gaol was designed by the famous English prison architect William Blackburn in 1789, soon before his death, but this claim is based on an erroneous reading of Howard, the only known archival source, who actually stated that the Limerick grand jurors had 'sent for the ingenious architect Mr Blackburne to direct them in fixing on a spot' – or a site for the new gaol – but, Howard continued, 'at my last visit a much less eligible one was chosen'.[96] Not only, then, did Blackburn not design the gaol – a crude rectilinear plan condemned as obsolete by the inspector-general as early as 1801 – but the grand jurors did not even follow his advice in choosing the site.[97] Kilmainham and Downpatrick were exceptional at this time; elsewhere around the country grand jurors continued to build gaols increasingly at odds with Howardian philosophy. Limerick's new gaol was in fact designed by an anonymous 'Mr Smyth', of whom we know nothing. It was still under construction in 1801, and by 1807 the city grand jurors were already contemplating replacing their part of it; they did so between 1811 and 1814.[98] Like so many of the prison building projects of the period, accusations of jobbery were rife, and few considered the new Limerick gaol a 'success'.

The story was similar elsewhere. In Roscommon the grand jurors built a new gaol opposite their 1760s courthouse (see Chapter 1) between about 1786 and 1797 (Fig. 4.20). Howard saw it soon after construction had begun and condemned it as of 'the same bad construction' as he had seen elsewhere in Ireland.[99] Since the new Roscommon gaol had no insulating walls and only very small yards to the rear, the prisoners looked out directly onto the marketplace. Its deficient plan was concealed by a picturesque Gothic elevation, akin to an enlarged medieval tower house, with stepped battlements at both ends and a recessed folly-like wedding cake of chimneys, arches, and battlements in the middle. Around the same time in Queen's County (now Laois), the grand jurors planned to build a new gaol. Howard

Fig. 4.20. Roscommon gaol, from the south. Built in the 1780s and 1790s, this gaol complemented the new courthouse built opposite it by the county grand jurors in the 1760s. Apart from its broad and rather theatrical façade, little was said in favour of the gaol's design. (*Photograph by author, 2012.*)

warned them not to reuse the same cramped and low-lying site of their existing building but instead to occupy an old barracks nearby, which was near a river.[100] Neither he nor Fitzpatrick seem to have succeeded in this plea, and later that year Richard Harman, who had worked with Gandon in Dublin, advertised for a vast quantity of brick and cut stone in the town of Maryborough; he laid the foundation stone for the new gaol there in the summer of 1789.[101] Its main quadrangle, with an adjoining range to the street (Fig. 4.21), wholly ignored Howardian thinking in its lack of a boundary wall, its outward-facing cell windows, and its lack of yards.[102] Though Howard had little interest in what he termed the 'pompous fronts' of so many Irish gaols, Harman showed his refined compositional skill (and debt to Gandon) in his rusticated entrance façade (Figs 4.22, 4.23), with its vermiculated Ledoux stonework, heavy entablature, and carvings of fasces and a sceptre surrounded by chains.[103] One observer in 1813 thought these 'appropriate emblematic ornaments'.[104] Situated on a narrow street in a small provincial town (Fig. 4.24), this façade was a bold and monumental choice; nothing like it had been attempted in Ireland since Richard Castle's gateway at Leinster House (1747), to which it may owe an unacknowledged debt (Fig. 4.25).

The plans survive for two other 'unreformed' gaols that were built during what was ostensibly the first period of reform – those at Mullingar and Naas.

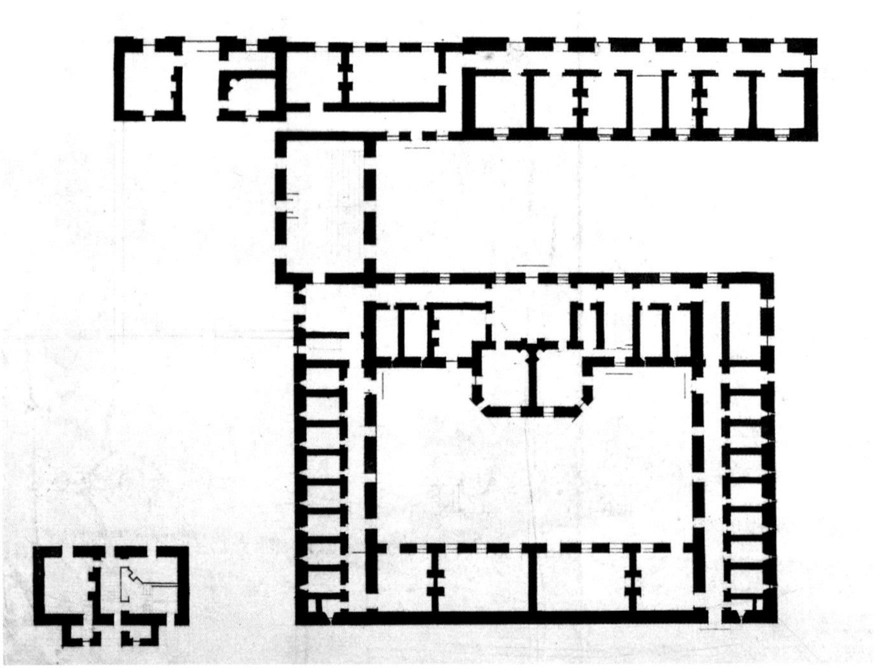

Fig. 4.21. Maryborough (Portlaoise) gaol, ground-floor plan. Richard Harman, *c.* 1789. This unsigned and undated drawing forms part of the Henry, Mullins & McMahon collection and is now at Tullynally Castle, County Westmeath. It shows Harman's Maryborough gaol. At the top-left is shown the sole surviving part, the monumental entrance gateway. Beside and behind it was a layout similar in many respects to Dublin's Newgate, a layout seen as increasingly outdated by this time. (*Reproduced courtesy of the Irish Architectural Archive.*)

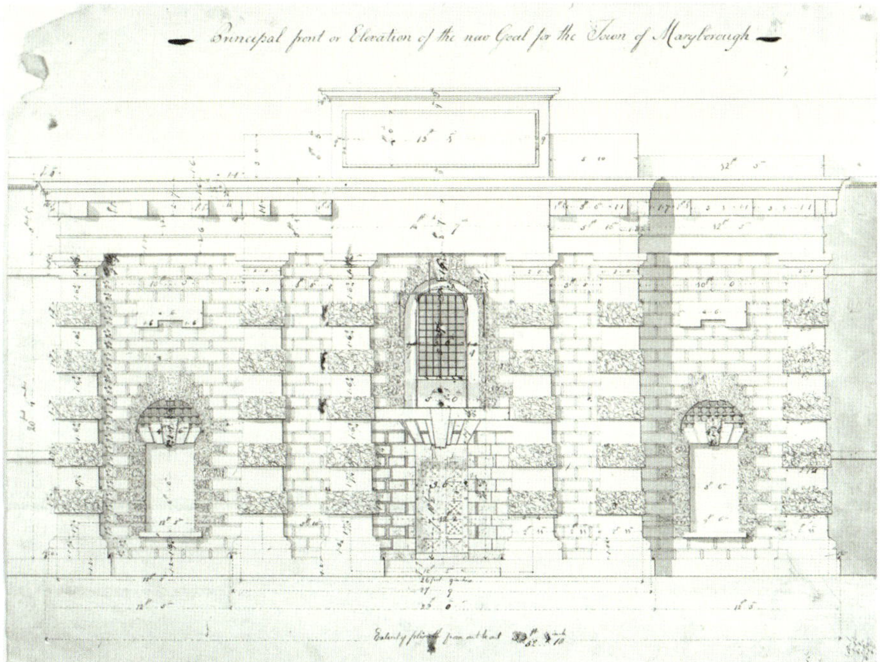

Fig. 4.22. Maryborough (Portlaoise) gaol, elevation of entrance gateway. Richard Harman, *c.* 1789. This unsigned and undated drawing, forming part of the Henry, Mullins & McMahon collection now at Tullynally Castle, County Westmeath, accompanies the plan drawing shown in Fig. 4.21. (*Reproduced courtesy of the Irish Architectural Archive.*)

Fig. 4.23. Maryborough (Portlaoise) gaol, from the west. The rusticated entrance gateway is today the sole surviving part of Harman's rectilinear-plan gaol from the 1790s. Like many other gaols of its time, its façade was its most commendable feature. (*Photograph by author, 2014.*)

They give us a sense of what a small county gaol typically looked like as late as 1790 – quite independent of the rhetoric of the Dublin reformers. The gaol at Mullingar was built between about 1786 and 1788. Situated at the south edge of the town, it was formed of two rectangular blocks that faced each other, separated

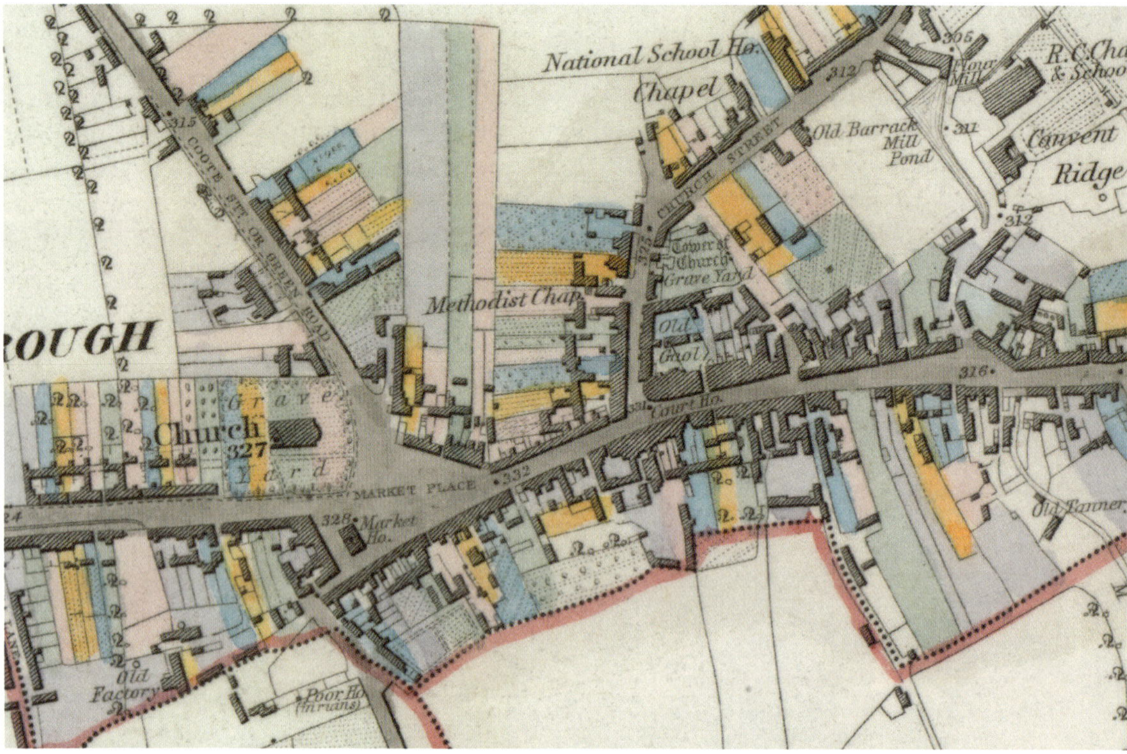

by three yards – one for debtors, a second for male felons, and a third for female felons (Fig. 4.26).[105] An outer perimeter wall, irregularly shaped, enclosed a large garden and service yards for the gaoler and was cleverly built over a river to the south (with arches protected by iron bars), which served as both the gaol's water supply and its sewerage system. The north block (Fig. 4.27), where the gaoler and debtors resided, was two storeys in height, with a simple façade of five bays, the centre three bays being somewhat recessed. The south block, similar in size but with an extra floor, housed felons of both genders. In total there were about thirteen cells of various sizes and around five day-rooms, in addition to rooms for the gaoler and his family. Howard praised the choice of site in 1787 and pointed to the fresh water supply as another asset, but he expressed fears that it would be too small for the county's needs, and that it would be impossible to give every prisoner a cell. (He noted an average of twenty prisoners at any one time in 1787–8.)[106] Though the gaol provided basic classification and sanitation, it was obsolete even before it opened, and later reports suggest that felons were formally segregated by gender only in the 1810s, by which time crowding was so severe that as many as 124 prisoners had been kept locked up at one time.[107]

Fig. 4.24. Maryborough (Portlaoise), Queen's County (County Laois). Ordnance Survey six-inch map, surveyed January 1839. The county's courthouse and gaol were located at the T-junction to the east of the marketplace. The rectilinear arrangement of Harman's gaol is visible to the north of the courthouse in this view. (*Reproduced courtesy of the Board of Trinity College Dublin.*)

Fig. 4.25. Richard Castle's gateway at Leinster House, Dublin, built around 1747, and since demolished. Harman may have been influenced by the heavy composition and extensive use of vermiculated rustication in Castle's now-lost gateway. From Henry F. Berry, *A History of the Royal Dublin Society* (1915).

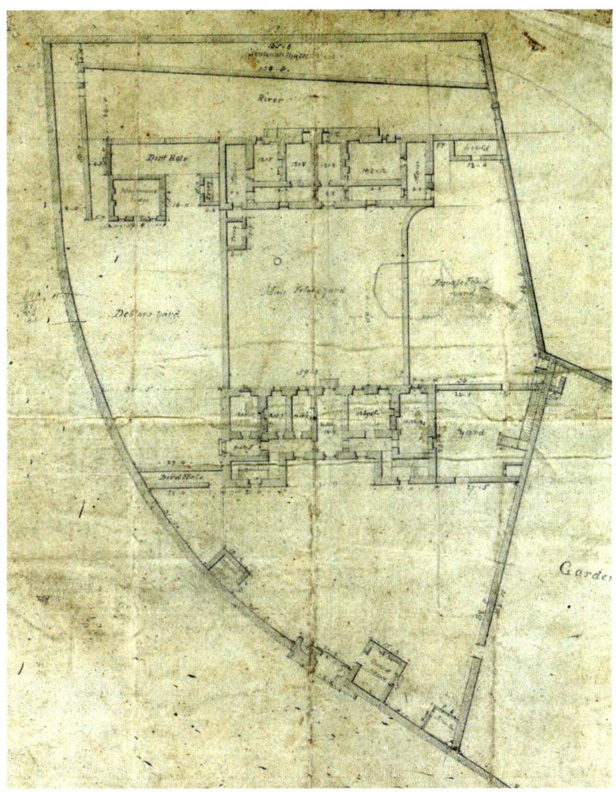

Fig. 4.26. Mullingar gaol, site plan, *c.* 1788. This very faded old sketch, which survives as part of the Guinness Collection of architectural drawings, shows the two blocks of the 1780s Westmeath county gaol, along with a series of yards between them and a curved outer perimeter wall. A river ran through the gaol, shown at the top of this sketch. (*Reproduced courtesy of the Irish Architectural Archive*).

The situation was rather similar in County Kildare. Naas' old gaol was notoriously insecure and described in the 1780s as 'an inconsiderable house' with no yards.[108] Its replacement, on the site of Old White's Castle in the centre of the town (Fig. 4.28), was built between 1787 and 1792.[109] We do not know the identity of the architect, but he seems not to have been aware of the design principles of the reformers. Howard condemned this gaol from the outset:

> A new county gaol is building at Naas .... The situation is *improper*, and the plan *bad*, the staircase narrow (two feet nine inches), the entrance and passages dark. The vaults in the passages must be offensive and unhealthy.[110]

We can deduce the plan from an 1824 survey drawing (Fig. 4.29).[111] The arrangements were like those at Mullingar in scale and classification, but instead of having the two blocks built parallel to each other we find them arranged at Naas in a 'T' shape. Three yards were situated to the rear (for males, females, and debtors). Howard's criticisms probably arose from the cramped site, where private dwellings surrounded the gaol on almost all four sides, and where

Fig. 4.27. Mullingar gaol, photograph taken *c.* 1900. This picture shows one half of the Westmeath county gaol that was built in the 1780s. Howard rightly believed that it would be too small for the county's needs. (*Reproduced courtesy of Westmeath County Library.*)

Fig. 4.28. Naas, County Kildare. Ordnance Survey six-inch map, surveyed January 1837. The old gaol, finished by 1792, is shown marked in the centre of the town. Further to the south is Richard Morrison's courthouse of the early 1800s. When a new gaol was eventually built in the 1820s, it was removed to the far western edge of the town, allowing plenty of room for future expansion, in contrast to its constricted predecessor. The old gaol later became a town hall. (*Reproduced courtesy of the Board of Trinity College Dublin.*)

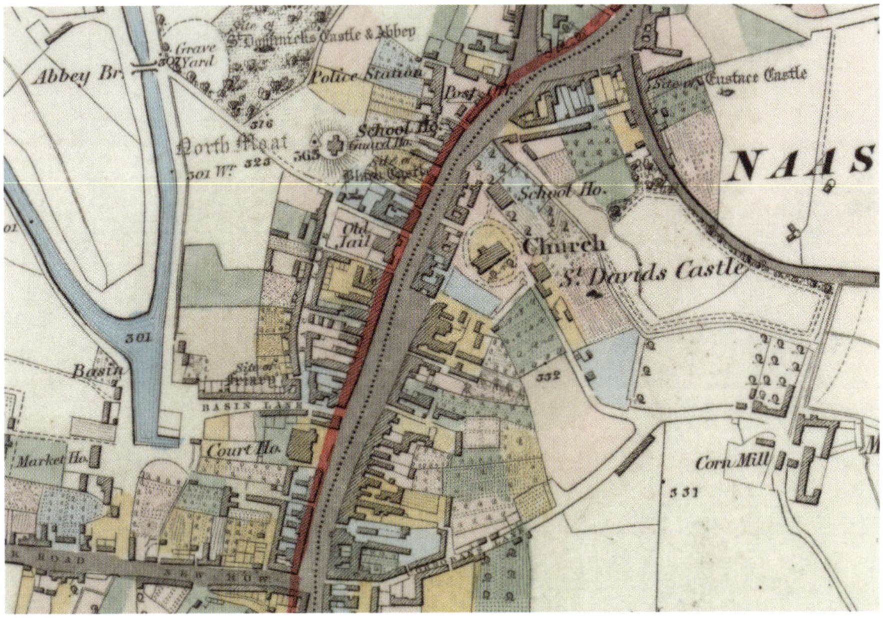

Fig. 4.29. John Longford, 'A Map of [the old gaol] at Naas … and Adjoining Concerns', 1824. The simple design and cramped site of the gaol, opened in the 1790s, are immediately apparent. Howard was critical of the design, though the grand jurors could plausibly have argued that their gaol was similar in many respects to the 'model' that Howard himself had put forward in the 1770s. (*Reproduced courtesy of the National Library of Ireland.*)

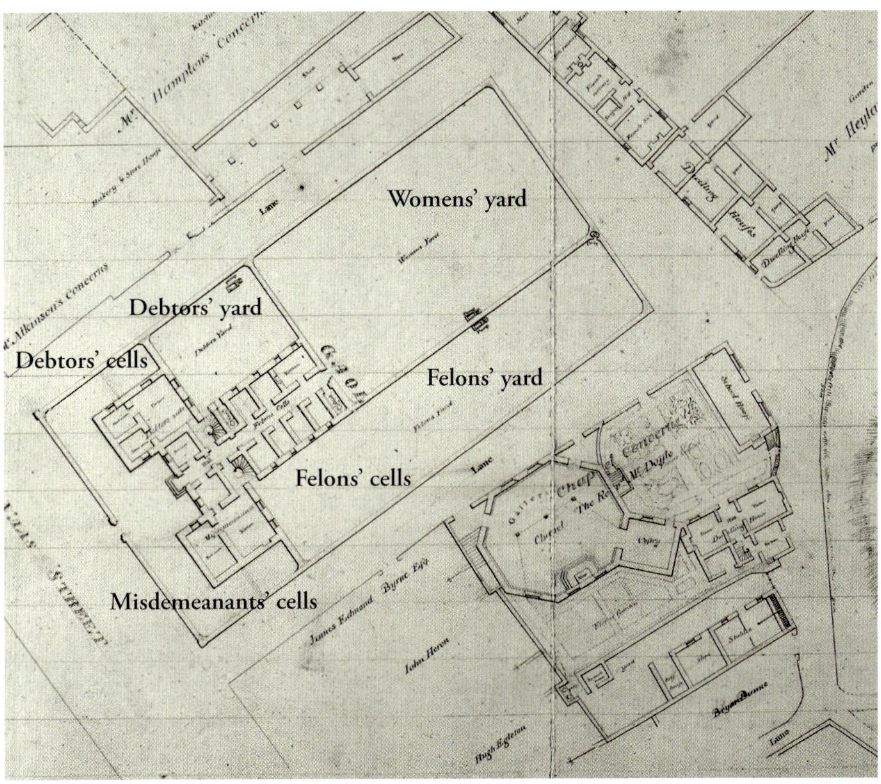

Fig. 4.30. Naas old gaol, from the east, as shown in an old photograph (*c.* 1900) before extensive alterations were carried out to transform the building into a town hall in c. 1904. From Stan Hickey and Liam Kenny (eds), *Nás na Ríogh from Poorhouse Road to the Fairy Flax: An illustrated history of Naas* (1990). (*Reproduced courtesy of the Naas Local History Group.*)

no future extensions could be added to increase the number of cells beyond about twenty-four; and from the T-plan, which provided little ventilation or possibilities for inspection. William Tyler had built a somewhat similar gaol in Dorchester in 1783 only to have Howard condemn it four years later. In response, the Dorset magistrates started all over again; they commissioned a gaol from Blackburn with a better situation and plan and abandoned Tyler's 'unreformed' building.[112] In Naas there was no such reaction, and little willingness among the grand jurors to start over; their little gaol continued to serve the county until the 1830s. The limitations of its plan were perhaps compensated by its forbidding elevation, visible in an old photograph but now drastically altered (Fig. 4.30). The architect emulated Dance's Newgate with his Mannerist blind arches and window surrounds, all heavily rusticated.

Penitentiaries and transportation

In the last quarter of the eighteenth century, the Irish government helped to pay for Dublin's Newgate but otherwise kept itself out of directly building or controlling prisons. In the years 1790–2 this pattern seemed briefly to change with the question of penitentiaries in place of transportation. In Britain in 1776, in order to deal with the immediate crisis caused by the American war, hard labour for convicts – often in the form of dredging rivers – was authorised by the government.[113] Westminster staged a competition for separate male and female penitentiaries and William Blackburn and Thomas Hardwick were declared the winners. Blackburn's scheme was to prove revolutionary in the history of prison architecture, and though no drawings have survived, we know that it was formed of blocks arranged radially around a central inspection building – the gaoler's residence (Fig. 4.31).[114] By separating the cell blocks from the centre, Blackburn at last resolved the long-standing issue of ventilation and enabled the gaoler to see into all the yards at any moment. With more blocks and more yards, classification could be dramatically increased. The impact of this scheme on Irish prison architecture was not felt for another thirty years (see Chapter 6). Predictably, the grand plans for state-run penitentiaries in Britain soon ran into financial opposition; Blackburn's original estimate for £149,982 was probably more than had been spent on all of Ireland's new gaols by this time. The entire scheme was shelved in 1784, and instead the transportation of convicts to Australia commenced.[115]

In the same year as the first ship left Britain for New South Wales, Jeremy Bentham invented the 'panopticon', an architectural device that brought together the concept of complete moral control of prisoners with its author's widely publicised utilitarian theories (Fig. 4.32). It was somewhat similar to

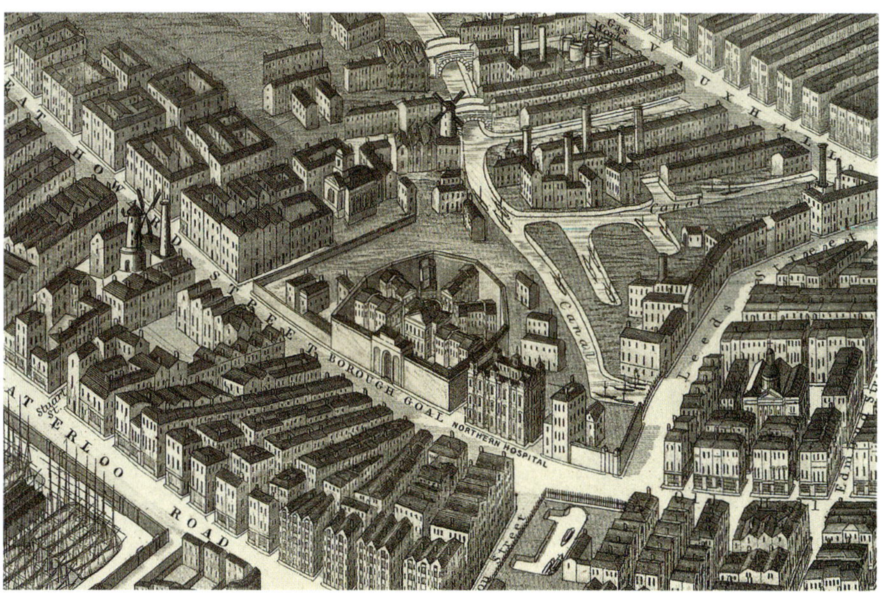

Fig. 4.31. Liverpool borough gaol. William Blackburn, built between 1785 and 1789. Blackburn's winning design for the British penitentiary competition has not survived, but other sources confirm that it was very similar (or even identical) to that for his gaol at Liverpool, built soon afterwards. Blackburn's key advance was to arrange the cell blocks in a radial fashion, an arrangement that became known as the 'radial-plan' gaol. From *Ackermann's Panoramic View of Liverpool*, 1847.

Blackburn's radial plan, but with the crucial difference that all the cells opened facing the inspection tower, allowing the gaoler to see not only the common yards but also – and critically – the entire interior of every cell.[116] The idea of the panopticon was to exercise great influence on the planning of British and later Irish prisons, but its inventor faced a constant struggle to gain the kind of government support that would allow him to actually build a prototype. By 1790 Irish convicts as well as British were being sent to Australia, but with the outbreak of war with France, the chartering of ships became increasingly difficult. At about the same time the British government toyed with the idea of building large regional penitentiaries where some convicts would be kept in Ireland instead of being sent abroad.[117] Fitzpatrick was very supportive of the idea; in 1790 he published his *Thoughts on Penitentiaries* and established a small

Fig. 4.32. Design for a penitentiary panopticon. Jeremy Bentham, Samuel Bentham, and Willey Reveley, 1791. The panopticon was different from Blackburn's radial-plan gaols in several key respects, including the alignment of the prisoners' cells. Such a penitentiary was almost built in Dublin in the early 1790s. From John Bowring (ed.), *The Works of Jeremy Bentham*, 11 vols. (Edinburgh: William Tait, 1838–43), vol. 4, p. 35.

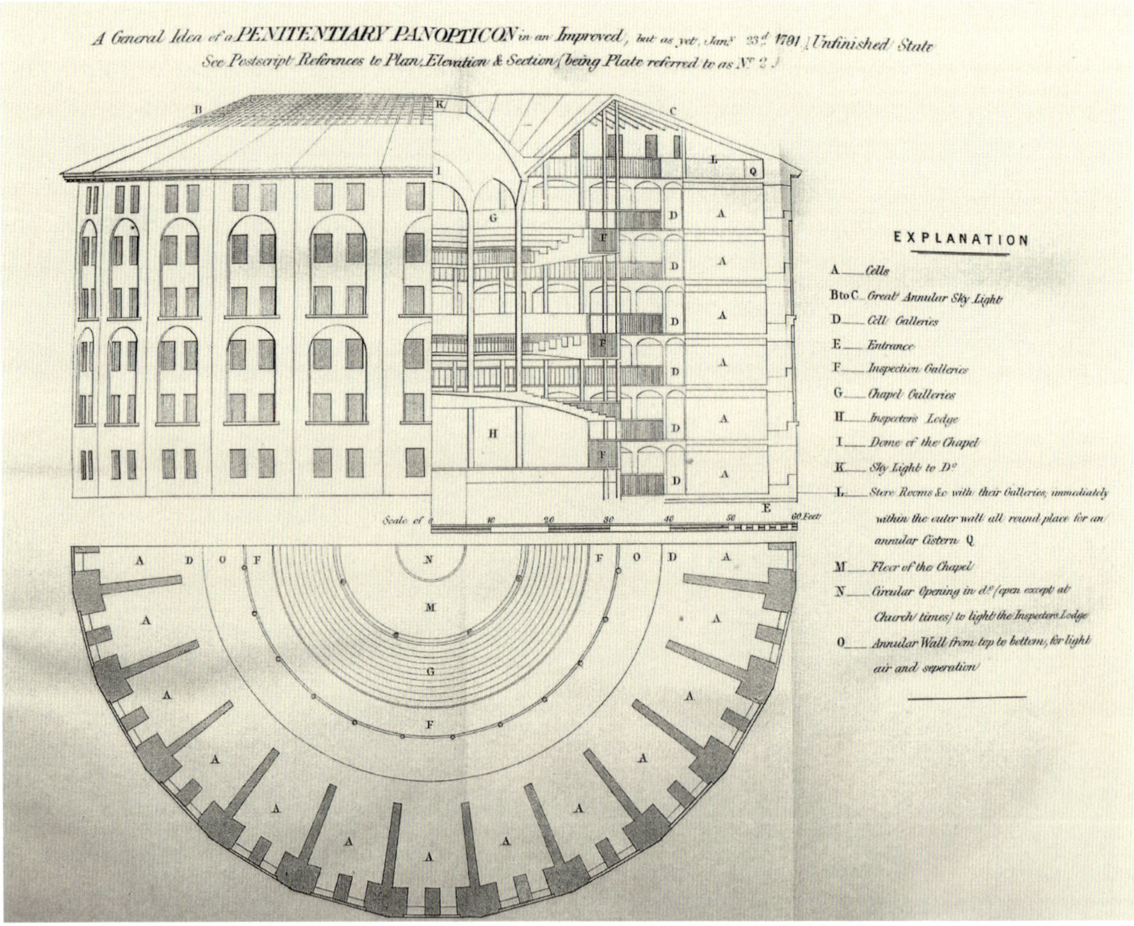

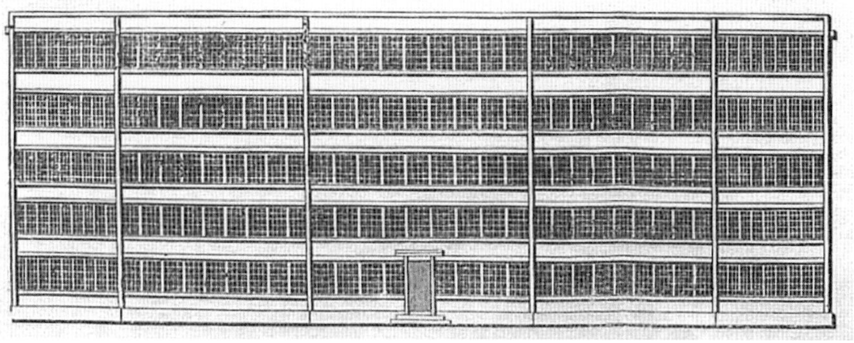

Fig. 4.33. Design for a panopticon house of industry. Samuel Bentham and Samuel Bunce, 1797. Though no drawings survive for Bentham's proposed glass-and-iron penitentiary for Dublin, it was probably very similar in design to this slightly later scheme. The Earl of Westmorland dismissed the plan by declaring that all the prisoners would escape. From John Bowring (ed.), *The Works of Jeremy Bentham*, 11 vols. (Edinburgh: William Tait, 1838–43), vol. 4, p. 35.

experimental penitentiary at the St James' Street bridewell in Dublin.[118] In the following year both Bentham and Blackburn made plans for a large penitentiary in Dublin along panoptic principles, and an act of 1792 gave legal standing to the project.[119] But relations with Bentham in particular soon deteriorated and this adverse development, coupled with financial concerns, caused the whole project to be abandoned. Bentham's design was remarkably ambitious for its time and made liberal use of glass and iron for almost all of its internal walls (Fig. 4.33). Just as significantly, the design had the explicit aim of eliminating any privacy that prisoners had heretofore maintained. Regardless of the ethical implications of this aim, the plan was intellectually (and architecturally) too radical for Irish eyes in the 1790s. The viceroy, the Earl of Westmorland, dismissed the design with the simple put-down, 'They will all get out.'[120] The idea of a state-run penitentiary did not resurface in Ireland until 1809 (as discussed below).

County gaols and the slow emergence of Howardian principles, 1790–1810

Joseph Starr has suggested that the outbreak of the French wars in 1789 put prison reform and prison rebuilding in Ireland on the back burner for a generation.[121] Nothing could be further from the truth. Many of the new county gaols of this era had been planned, at least tentatively, before 1789, but there was no downturn thereafter in building. In fact, in 1791 there were at least thirteen different gaols under construction all around the country (see Fig. 4.12). In Britain the fall-off in building was more pronounced at this time, but Evans has concluded that the war was just one factor; another equally important one was that 'the more active local authorities' had by then completed their gaol projects.[122] Fitzpatrick retired in 1793 to take up an army position, and his position remained vacant for three years, but before he left, he boasted to parliament that 'thirteen gaols have been lately built, eight are now building, three in part are presented for, [and] four have been in a great measure improved'.[123] Less clear, however, was how many of these Irish gaols conformed to the increasingly high standards set by the creative British architects and reformers who followed in Howard's footsteps.

The grand jurors of three neighbouring counties – Donegal, Tyrone, and Derry – employed Edward Miller to build new county gaols for them in the period 1787–1804. It appears that he used the same design throughout, barring some trifling details. In Derry the old gaol was, as previously mentioned, on top of one of the city's gates, and by 1787 it was seen as a public disgrace, with only six rooms, no classification, no fresh water, and no yards. Thomas Conolly, an MP for the county, took up the issue of its replacement, no doubt influenced by his marriage to the sister of one the leading aristocratic penal reformers of his time, Charles Lennox, 3rd Duke of Richmond.[124] The site chosen for the new gaol, built between 1787 and 1791, was spacious, well-aired, and outside the city walls (Fig. 4.34).[125] It has been completely demolished (part of a later addition has survived – see Chapter 6), but photographs and maps show that it was very similar to Cooley's Armagh gaol of ten years before – with a single large rectangular block, one cell deep, facing the street with some yards to the rear (Fig. 4.35). Miller preferred the façades of his gaols to be rigidly symmetrical and cloaked them with what one critic has described as 'cardboard-castle-style' Gothick arches, bays, and a surfeit of battlements.[126] Basic classification was established (four classes in Derry, five in Tyrone, and three in Donegal), but compared to the more advanced plans invented by Blackburn in England, and indeed compared to the letter of Irish prison law, these gaols cannot have been welcomed by the new prison inspector, the Rev. Forster Archer, on his taking office in 1795.[127] Donegal's gaol, built between 1791 and 1793 (Fig. 4.36), became notorious for its cracking masonry and settling walls; less than twenty years later, Archer suggested that some plaster might be applied to 'conceal, if possible, the bad materials and workmanship', but only a large addition in the 1820s relieved pressure on the institution.[128] The story was much the same at Omagh gaol, built between about 1796 and 1804 (mostly since demolished), where the inspector accused the Tyrone grand jurors of having erected the gaol 'by lump or contract', and declared that the 'workmanship has been fraudulently executed'.[129] For seasoned Irish penal reformers in parliament this scene was an unwelcome echo of the Newgate scandal that they had hoped would not be repeated. The fact that such a repetition occurred as late as the 1790s says much about the difficulties faced by central government in reshaping the grand juries' gaols.

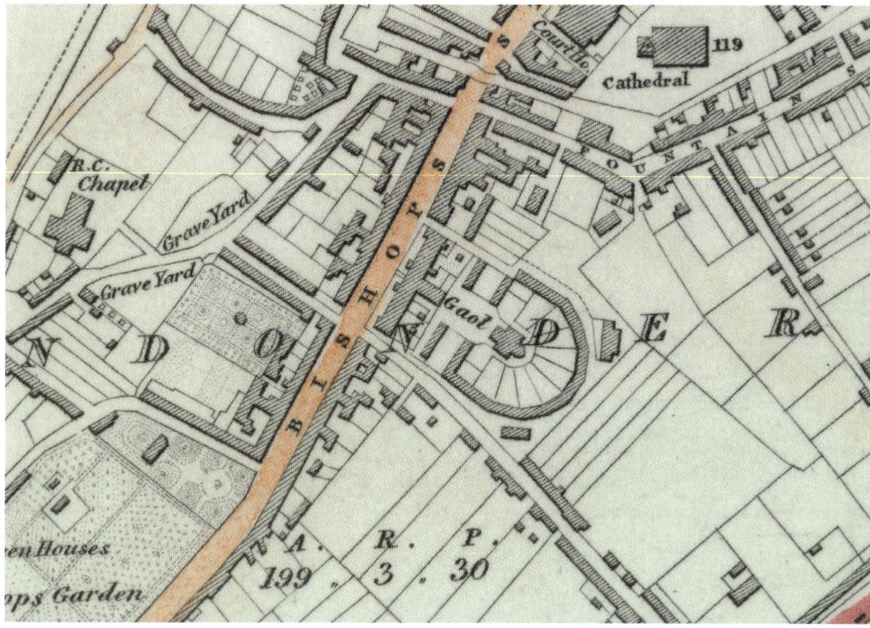

Fig. 4.34. Derry, outside of Bishop's-gate. Edward Miller's gaol, completed in 1791, was only a small part of the larger complex shown in this Ordnance Survey six-inch map surveyed in June 1830. It was simply the rectilinear block facing the street, with a few yards to the rear; the much larger polygonal-plan gaol to the rear was built in the 1820s. (*Reproduced courtesy of the Board of Trinity College Dublin.*)

Fig. 4.35. Derry gaol, from the south-west, *c.* 1900. The two fanciful Gothic Revival towers at either end of the façade (one survives) were additions made in the 1820s to Miller's original and much smaller gaol, distinguishable here by its plaster rather than stone veneer. (*Reproduced courtesy of the National Library of Ireland.*)

Fig. 4.36. Lifford gaol, County Donegal, *c.* 1900. Designed by Edward Miller and built between 1791 and 1793. In plan and appearance, this gaol was remarkably similar to Miller's other new gaols in Derry and Omagh. It paid little regard to the Howardian principles of prison design and was roundly criticised by the reformers and the government inspector Forster Archer. (*Reproduced courtesy of Donegal County Archives.*)

Archer was a Cork Protestant clergyman who knew little about prisons.[130] Yet by the turn of the century he could claim to have mastered the ideas of the penal reformers. For the time being, this was sufficient – until he was overtaken by the new energy of philanthropic organisations and by a second generation of reformers after about 1810. By the time of his (forced) early retirement in 1821 he was hopelessly out of touch. Even if he had been as passionate as Howard or Fitzpatrick, he still possessed few powers of enforcement, and his advice was often simply ignored. In 1801, he voiced his frustrations: 'Architects generally know how to build private houses & churches, but I have scarcely met one in Ireland that knew how to build [a] healthy, safe, or convenient prison.'[131]

After the rush of prison legislation between 1782 and 1787 there was little in the way of new gaol laws until the very end of the century, and when they arrived, they were a classic combination of give and take. The 'take' came first, with a 1796 act that limited commissions payable to overseers of new gaols to five per cent (as discussed in Chapter 1).[132] This was a rather blunt attempt to limit jobbery and corruption. The 'give' came three years later in 1799 with the 'Act to Promote the Building of New Gaols', undoubtedly a response to the destruction and lawlessness associated with the 1798 rebellion and its aftermath.[133] It was still common at this time for grand jurors to press for local acts of parliament to facilitate their rebuilding plans, but this time-consuming step was not obligatory, and the 1799 law attempted to clear a common path for building projects without the inevitable delay suffered in waiting for these measures; the new law noted that grand jurors could make presentments of up to £2,000 every year for their gaol funds. By this time, however, there were fewer gaols needing replacement for precisely the reasons identified by Evans with respect to England in the early 1790s: most of the gaols were new, and thus the 1799 act did not have as great an impact as perhaps its authors anticipated. And while not suggesting that the levels of crime and unrest in the country at large had no impact on the extent of gaol construction in the 1780s and 1790s, it is clear that there were other factors at play – such as administrative reform and changing ideas in prison design – that better explain the huge growth in building from the 1780s onwards than the short-lived lawlessness and chaos of the uprisings and rebellions around 1800 (1796, 1798, and 1803). In this respect, and however unlikely it might seem, the troubled years of the 1790s had a greater impact on the building of new courthouses (in many cases following destruction), as outlined in Chapter 1, than on the building of new gaols.

Around 1800 the main activity in gaol building shifted to Cork, Galway, and Kilkenny. There was also an unexecuted scheme for Sligo that is of particular architectural interest. In that town the old gaol had been built in 1766 and there was little attempt to improve it by the grand jurors until the end of the century.[134] Howard and Archer were both dismayed at conditions inside and called for repairs to be made at the very least, but a new gaol (discussed in Chapter 5) was not begun until 1816.[135] It appears that Bernard Mullins, later to be involved in building many new gaols through the Henry, Mullins & McMahon partnership, produced a design for a new gaol for Sligo in 1801 (Fig. 4.37).[136] His drawing appears in a book that shows other gaol-like buildings that continue to evade identification, and so it is entirely possible that this scheme was only a *capriccio* from a young and enthusiastic architect. Whatever its provenance, it is noteworthy for two reasons: first, its centrepiece is unmistakably derived from Harman's gaol at Maryborough, almost to the detail. This borrowing shows the wide appreciation of architects for his distinctive composition and more broadly indicates the deep interest held by architects in façades, something that

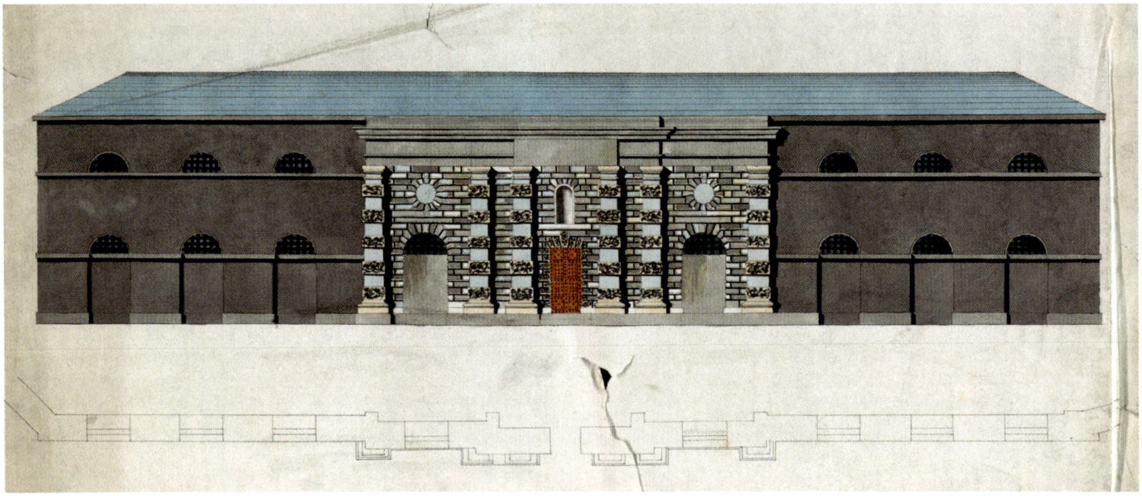

Fig. 4.37. Sligo gaol, elevation and partial plan, unexecuted. Bernard Mullins, *c.* 1801. This unsigned and undated drawing appears to show a clear debt to Harman's Maryborough gaol. (*Reproduced courtesy of the Irish Architectural Archive.*)

put them at odds with the reformers. Second, it is undoubtedly a problematic design in every other respect, and one that Howard would have condemned, in particular for its windows flush with the main façade (confirmed by the sketch of part of the plan) and therefore opening onto the street. The era when this kind of communication between prisoners and the public was permissible for architects to design into their new gaols was coming to an end by this time, and one of the last hearings came with the new gaol built in Kilkenny.

Sligo was never built. Kilkenny was built but no longer exists. For a fleeting moment in the early 1800s, it was the most celebrated 'reformed' gaol in Ireland. The city and county shared a series of dungeons under the courthouse that were so repellent to Archer in July 1801 (the prisoners appeared to him to suffer under 'all the miseries which the damn'd endure in hell') that he insisted that the county build a new gaol elsewhere.[137] A local committee had come to the same conclusion a few months previously, and plans were already in motion for a competition. Four architects entered, including Richard Morrison, who was soon to begin work on Galway's new gaol, but a local man, William Robertson, was declared the winner.[138] Construction began immediately, well outside the historic core of the city, and the gaol opened in 1809.[139] Robertson's plan is known only from written descriptions and Ordnance Survey maps (Fig. 4.38). It appears to have been a reduced Kilmainham with one quadrangle instead of two and surrounded by no fewer than ten exercise yards. To the front were the gaoler's house and six work-rooms, behind were cell blocks right and left, giving a total of forty-eight cells, and a marshalsea to the rear. Archer considered the new Kilkenny gaol, using the language of the 1770s, 'a model … to other counties in Ireland', but more exacting critics were less sure. Thomas Reid, who saw himself as a latter-day Howard, asserted in 1822 that the ventilation was poor, that the cell windows (six inches square) were too small, and that the quadrangular arrangement allowed prisoners 'to hold conversation the whole night' between adjacent blocks.[140] The *Kilkenny Moderator* suggested that the design was based on Blackburn's Dorchester prison, and there were certainly shared characteristics between the two, but Robertson was quick to refute the claim, saying that Howard's principles were only his guide, and he challenged anyone to find an identical prison in Britain or Ireland.[141] While the reformers called for uniformity and 'model' designs, architects were often less willing to surrender their prized mantle of creativity.

Galway and Cork: New designs and a scandal on a marsh

William Blackburn is credited not only with inventing the radial-plan gaol but also (in 1785) the first polygonal-plan gaol, for Northleach bridewell in Gloucestershire (Fig. 4.39). Here the central-inspection 'hub' of his earlier design remained, but instead of radial blocks he substituted a single polygonal (or semi-circular) range of cells.[142] These two competing arrangements became central to

Fig. 4.38. Kilkenny county gaol, at the edge of the city. Six-inch Ordnance Survey map, surveyed January 1839. The design, seemingly based on Kilmainham, and the healthy location were praised at the time of construction. (*Reproduced courtesy of the Board of Trinity College Dublin.*)

penal-reform debate for the next forty years. Neither design, however, appeared in Ireland until work began at Galway's county gaol in 1804. A replacement for Blakes' Castle (discussed above) (Fig. 4.40) had long been contemplated by the Galway grand jurors; as early as 1791 they had passed presentments for a new building.[143] Problems with the county treasurer delayed the project for several years, but in 1801 Archer examined three potential sites and recommended that the derelict county hospital should be expanded and used as a gaol. As in other counties, his advice was ignored; the grand jurors instead chose what they described as a 'healthful and convenient' site on an island between two channels of the River Corrib and petitioned parliament for a local act to clear the way for building to begin (Fig. 4.41).[144] At the same time the town grand jurors condemned their existing gaol (an old tholsel) and called for its demolition without giving any indication of what its replacement might be. After construction began at the county gaol, the town grand jurors proposed to follow suit with a new gaol at Bohermore at the eastern edge of the town, but they backtracked soon afterwards and instead negotiated an agreement with their county colleagues to build their new gaol adjacent to the county one. The deal, which was formalised in a second local act in 1807, was a marriage of convenience: the county grand jurors

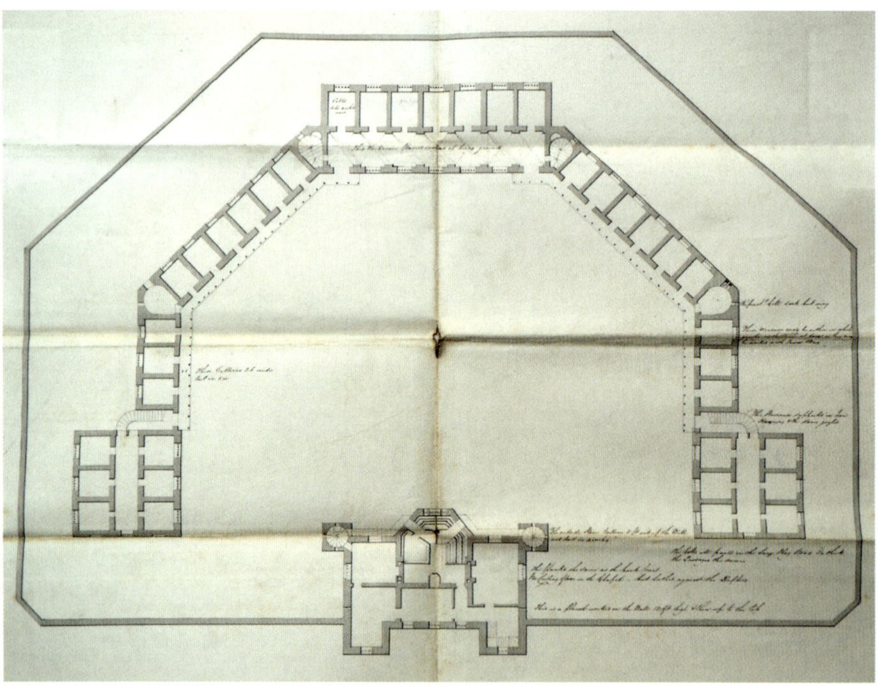

Fig. 4.39. Northleach bridewell, Gloucestershire, ground-floor plan. William Blackburn, 1785. This was the first polygonal-plan prison and served as the prototype for Galway's county gaol and for many other polygonal-plan gaols in Ireland built between 1800 and 1830. Northleach survives today as a museum. (*Reproduced courtesy of Gloucestershire Archives.*)

realised that they did not need all the land they had purchased, and the town jurors obviously required a site for their new gaol.[145] For much of the decade this large island was a hive of building activity, with the county gaol being built between 1804 and 1811, and the town gaol being erected between 1807 and 1810.[146] As outlined in chapters 1 and 2, the new gaols prompted further public buildings in subsequent years as both sets of grand jurors rebuilt their courthouses in the immediate vicinity, connecting them all with a new bridge.

Fig. 4.40. Blakes' Castle, Galway. This medieval tower house served as the county gaol from 1686 until 1811. It has been renovated for use as a hotel in recent years. (*Photograph by author, 2017.*)

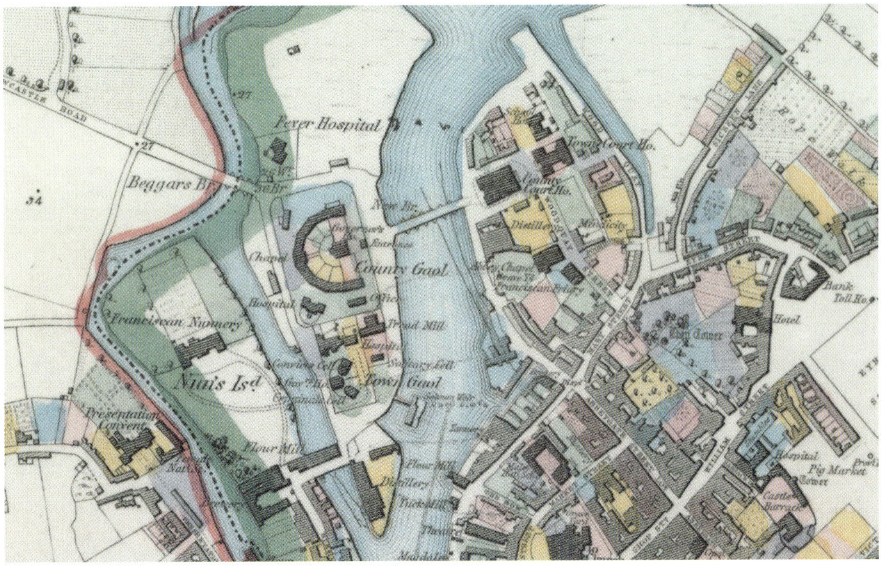

Fig. 4.41. Galway county and town gaols, separated by the River Corrib from their respective courthouses. Ordnance Survey six-inch map, surveyed January 1838. This view shows a series of later additions to both gaols, including a substantial radial-plan addition to the town gaol visible to the south. The original town gaol was much smaller and roundly criticised by the reformers for its inadequate design. (*Reproduced courtesy of the Board of Trinity College Dublin.*)

Galway's new gaols were an excellent example of 'reformed' and 'unreformed' designs being built at the same time (Fig. 4.42). The county gaol was a polygonal (semi-circular) plan designed by the renowned English architect Thomas Hardwick, who had won the premium for the best female penitentiary design in England back in 1782, and who later built a vast polygonal penitentiary at Millbank in London in the 1810s (Fig. 4.43).[147] In 1802 he exhibited his design for Galway at the Royal Academy, but it seems unlikely that he spent much time in the town during construction, owing to his many other commitments; Richard Morrison supervised the building of the gaol, with John Behan as the main contractor.[148] Both men used their Galway experience to gain further gaol commissions in the years ahead. Hardwick's polygonal plan allowed a much greater degree of inspection and ventilation than any previous gaol erected in Ireland. Because of its location on an island, fresh water was always available, and at least in theory the sewers should have been healthy and fast-flowing. A high boundary wall sealed the gaol off from all outside communications and potential imports. Only the austere entrance block and gallows, axially arranged with the courthouse and bridge (Fig. 4.44), provided a break in the otherwise monotonous presence of this new gaol in the town. Despite its advanced design incorporating almost all the principles of the penal-reform movement, Archer was unimpressed by its high cost and by the pretensions of the grand jurors, who had ignored his more modest plan; he pithily remarked that 'the costly plans on which English prisons are erected are not suited to this comparatively poor country'.[149]

By contrast, the adjacent town gaol, probably designed by Morrison or Behan without any input from Hardwick, was a simple three-storey T-shaped rectilinear block in the fashion of Naas from a generation earlier. The design provided for very basic classification by gender, but little else, and the new town gaol was condemned as too small, insecure, unhealthy, and lacking sufficient classification almost as soon as it was built (Figs 4.42, 4.45).[150] Within a few years it was labelled the 'most insecure prison in Ireland'.[151] Despite some small additions around 1820, an entirely new gaol was built nearby in the early 1830s (see Chapter 6).[152] We may rightly ask how two gaols could be erected at the same time adjacent to one another, with one following the prison laws but the other so clearly not. In the previous examples of small gaols built in the 1780s, it could plausibly be argued that there was no understanding locally of central government's latest penal legislation. But in Galway the extensive county gaol left no room for doubt that the local authorities understood the requirements

Fig. 4.42. (opposite page) General plan of Galway county and town gaols. Samuel Roberts, May 1866. Roberts was the county surveyor in Galway in the 1860s, and this drawing was produced when the decision had been made to amalgamate both gaols. Around 1810 the general outline would have been quite similar, but the two-pronged radial-plan town gaol to the left had not yet been built, and the cells within the polygonal-plan county gaol were interspersed with day-rooms throughout. By 1866 only half of the gaol still retained this original layout. The small T-shaped old town gaol appears utterly insignificant next to Hardwick's polygonal range. The building of the two gaols was a rare instance of the results of 'good' and 'bad' designs appearing beside each other at the same time. *(Reproduced courtesy of Galway County Council Archives.)*

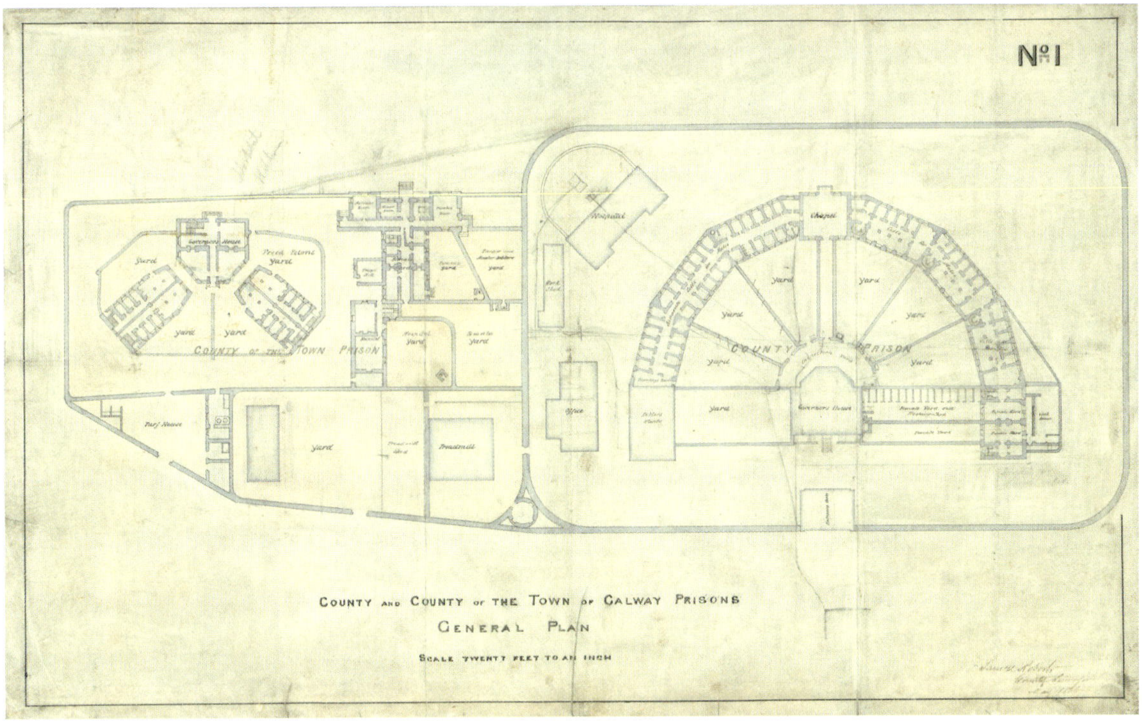

of the law, and so it must be concluded that the town grand jurors were aware of what was expected of them but chose to push on regardless. When new legislation followed in 1810, the example of Galway's illegal town gaol must have been a simmering background issue for the reformers. But a far greater scandal was playing out in Cork at the same time, which certainly focused their attention.

As noted earlier in this chapter, Cork's county and city gaols were seen by 1800 as out of step with the rest of the country. Both grand juries continued to use early eighteenth-century gatehouses on the city's north and south bridges. In 1788 the county jurors petitioned parliament for a local act to allow them to build a new gaol; this petition stated that the old gatehouse was to be demolished, and that a portion of the site was to be sold to help pay for the new gaol. When passed, the act explicitly stipulated that the new gaol would conform to all the prison legislation of the early 1780s regarding classification, ventilation, and exercise yards.[153] Michael Shanahan, an architect who had worked at Downhill in County Derry and on various public-works projects in Cork, was commissioned to build the new gaol at a site far outside the centre of the city. Building began

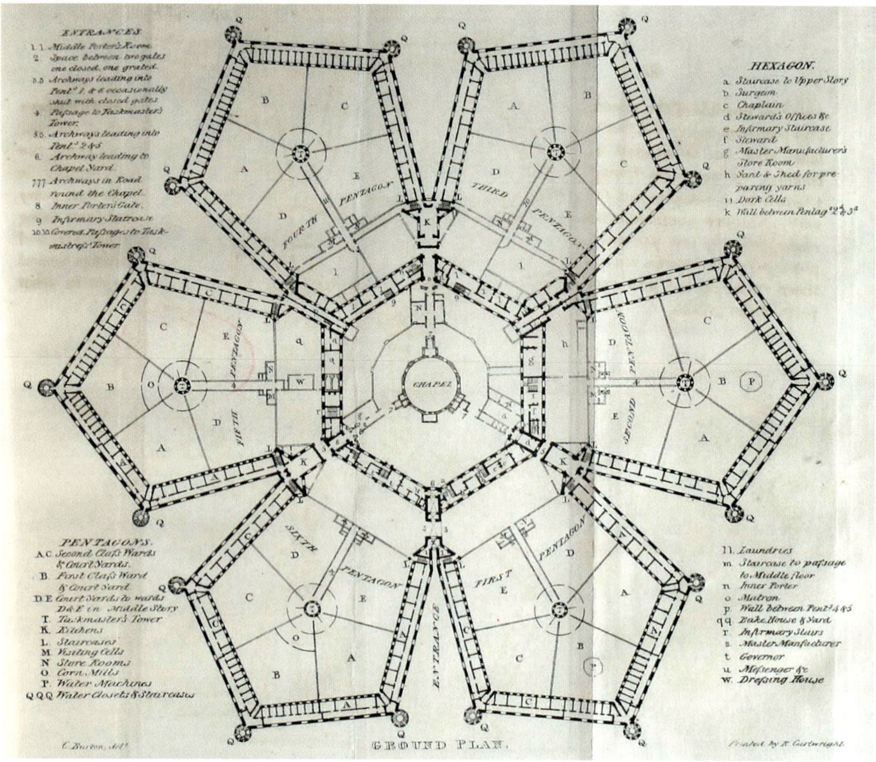

Fig. 4.43. Millbank penitentiary, London, ground-floor plan. William Williams and Thomas Hardwick, built between 1812 and 1818. This vast polygonal-plan gaol was the equivalent of seven Galway county gaols combined. Its building proved a financial and architectural scandal in late Georgian Britain. From George Holford, *An Account of the General Penitentiary at Millbank* (1828), p. 66.

Fig. 4.44. Galway county gaol, from the south-east, *c.* 1940. Hardwick and Morrison's entrance gateway was bleak and forbidding, as was the high perimeter wall that separated the polygonal-plan gaol from the town. From Geraldine Curtin, *The Women of Galway Jail* (2001), p. 40. (*Reproduced courtesy of Geraldine Curtin.*)

Fig. 4.45. Galway town gaol, from the west, *c.* 1940. In terms of design, planning, and administration, the diminutive town gaol was in every respect the poor cousin of the nearby county gaol. From Geraldine Curtin, *The Women of Galway Jail* (2001), p. 90. (*Reproduced courtesy of Geraldine Curtin.*)

in 1791 but was torturously slow, and ten years later, when some convicts nearly escaped from the old gaol by breaking down one of its walls, Shanahan's gaol was still not finished (Figs 4.46, 4.47).[154] John Carr, visiting the city in 1805, praised the 'healthy and beautiful situation' of the gaol then under construction in the western suburbs near the River Lee, but he noted that it was still only a building site and that the old gaol was 'a shocking place'.[155] By 1807 Archer had lost all patience with this seemingly never-ending project:

> I have so often reported on the frauds committed on the building of this [unfinished] gaol .... [The old gaol is still used] because the gaoler thinks it more secure than the costly new one. [I] learned that the architect who had [been] contracted for building this gaol was dismissed, [and] that it will require two years to complete it and to amend some of its imperfections. Had my advice been followed [in 1796] and that architect then dismissed, the gaol would have been long ago finished, and the county saved some thousand pounds expense.[156]

Shanahan's gaol was finally completed two years later, but only after William Deane and Abraham Hargrave had come onboard site to finish it.[157] Architecturally, the

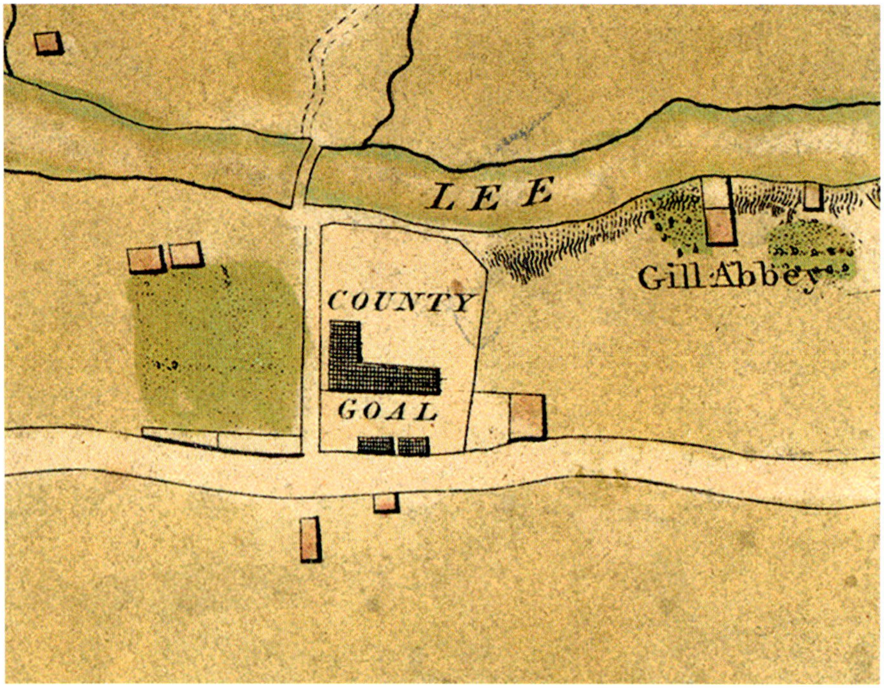

Fig. 4.46. A detail from William Beauford, 'A Map of the City and Suburbs of Cork', 1801. By 1801 Shanahan's new county gaol had been under construction for a decade but was still only partially built. Beauford's map shows that only around half of the structure had been completed by this time (compare with Figs 4.47 and 4.48). The gaol was situated just beyond the city boundaries in the western suburbs, near a channel of the River Lee. (*Reproduced courtesy of Cork City Libraries.*)

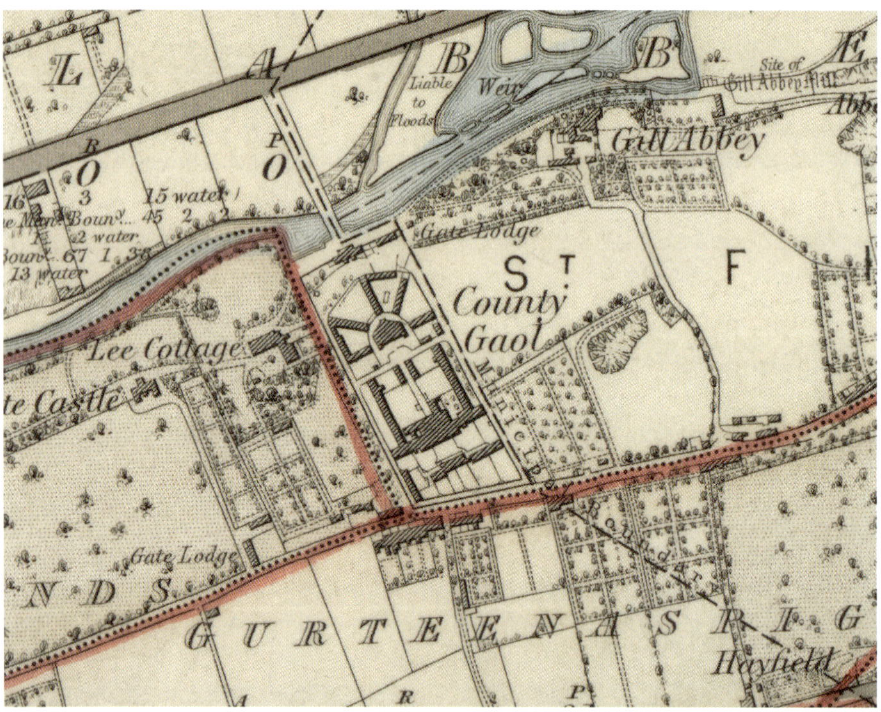

Fig. 4.47. Cork county gaol. Ordnance Survey six-inch map, surveyed January 1841. Shanahan's rectilinear gaol is shown to the south of the large radial-plan additions built by George Richard Pain around 1820. These later buildings took about five years to complete; Shanahan's earlier work had taken nearly twenty years and Forster Archer had accused the county jurors of corruption and waste. (*Reproduced courtesy of the Board of Trinity College Dublin.*)

gaol was a simple three-sided rectilinear structure with a small number of yards and an insulating wall. It was too small by half for this extensive and increasingly troubled county and was at odds with the latest gaol designs in Britain and elsewhere (Fig. 4.48). At one point during 1818 no fewer than 468 inmates were kept in its seventy-nine cells.[158] This scandalous project, which reeked of jobbery and inside deals (however ubiquitous these were in both British and Irish local government at the time), would have been even more of an issue at Westminster (where Archer's findings were published after 1800) were it not for the still more egregious actions of the city grand jurors at the same time.

From around 1804 the Cork city grand jurors also began raising money for a new gaol.[159] In 1805 they sponsored a competition and attracted entries from Morrison, fresh from his Galway work, and from William Robertson, then active in Kilkenny. In 1806 the grand jurors obtained a local act of parliament very similar in outline to what the county jurors had obtained in 1788. Robertson won the competition, and building began on a site known as Reilly's Marsh (the Mardyke) near Shanahan's new gaol.[160] By 1808, however, the entire project had to be abandoned, as the low-lying site was deemed unsuitable for such a large building and extremely unhealthy for future prisoners. Recriminations quickly erupted, with Archer, who was from the city and would have known many of the grand jurors from his earlier careers, caustically remarking:

Fig. 4.48. Cork county gaol, from the south-west, *c.* 1950. Shanahan's rectilinear gaol is visible in the foreground, with later radial-plan additions to the rear. The scandal surrounding Shanahan's work was one of many reasons why Westminster launched an investigation into Irish prisons in 1809.

> What an accumulated expence will be required by making a foundation in this swamp! What agues and fevers will be created! From this it appears jobbing and avarice have no bowels. A more improper site than this could have scarcely been found in this city.[161]

After reading Archer's report, Richard Sheridan, the Dublin-born MP for Ilchester, and one of the younger generation of politicians interested in prison reform in both Britain and Ireland, called for an inquiry into Irish prisons. As mentioned in Chapter 1, he quoted directly from Archer's criticisms of the aborted new gaol in Cork. Though William Wellesley-Pole, the Irish chief secretary, was unhappy that so few Irish MPs were present at Westminster to debate the motion, the government agreed to a commission of inquiry being established.[162] Archer had fulfilled the most basic of his responsibilities – to inform parliament of the state of Irish gaols – and now it remained to be seen if the inquiry would lead to more involvement from central government. The two Cork gaols, unfinished and abandoned, provided ample evidence that despite nearly forty years of prison legislation, grand jurors continued to evade or ignore the best efforts of the reformers.

The inquiry and the resulting Prisons Act of 1810 that followed have become associated with the 4th Duke of Richmond, lord lieutenant of Ireland from 1807 until 1813.[163] Richmond's uncle had been a passionate follower of Howard from the 1770s to the 1790s and had overseen the building of new gaols in West Sussex.[164] Nonetheless there were other actors such as Archer, Sheridan, and the group of Irish Whig MPs who had attempted (but failed) to pass grand-jury reform legislation in 1807 (see Chapter 1). The report of the inquiry, when it was printed in 1809, was something of a disappointment in that it focused greatly on Dublin's gaols at the expense of the rich litany of prison scandals in provincial towns.[165] This appears to have been because the bulk of prisoners locked up since the rebellion of 1798 – whose condition represented one of the main reasons why the inquiry was established – were incarcerated in Dublin's many prisons. Nonetheless, the report provided plenty of general evidence about the mismanagement of gaols and this was extrapolated to form national conclusions.[166] Wellesley-Pole considered it 'shocking to humanity that the evils detailed in [the] report had so long been permitted to exist without any steps having been taken to remove them'.[167] But even as a draft bill of the new act passed through parliament in the spring of 1810, the grand juries in Wexford and Waterford city (and perhaps others too) continued to build new gaols with no reference to the existing legislation. Archer regarded these buildings as 'illegally conducted', 'fraudulently executed', and 'extremely injudicious', but until the political balance shifted in favour of central government, there was little he could do.[168]

We may ask if the prison reform movement of 1770–1810 had achieved anything. It is easy to think not, in view of the many scandals and inadequate gaols built over this extended period. But the small battles that had been won – at Kilmainham, Galway, and Kilkenny – served as springboards for a younger generation of humanitarian public intellectuals and philanthropic societies that took up the issue of prison reform in Britain and Ireland where Howard, Eden, and the others had left off, and which are the subject of the next chapter. Of the small victories, undoubtedly the most important was the establishment of the office of the inspector-general, through which the increasing rigour of central-government legislation would inevitably flow. A few of the new gaols had been successful – relatively speaking – at the time of their building. They conformed to the established 'models' of prison design. After 1810 the idea of a 'model' prison again came under public debate, with several conflicting pronouncements as to what was the most effective way for architecture to be used to punish and to reform.

for the employment and exercise of the Prisoners being wholly in sight of the Keeper.
Court & Ward for ten Prisoners
Cells

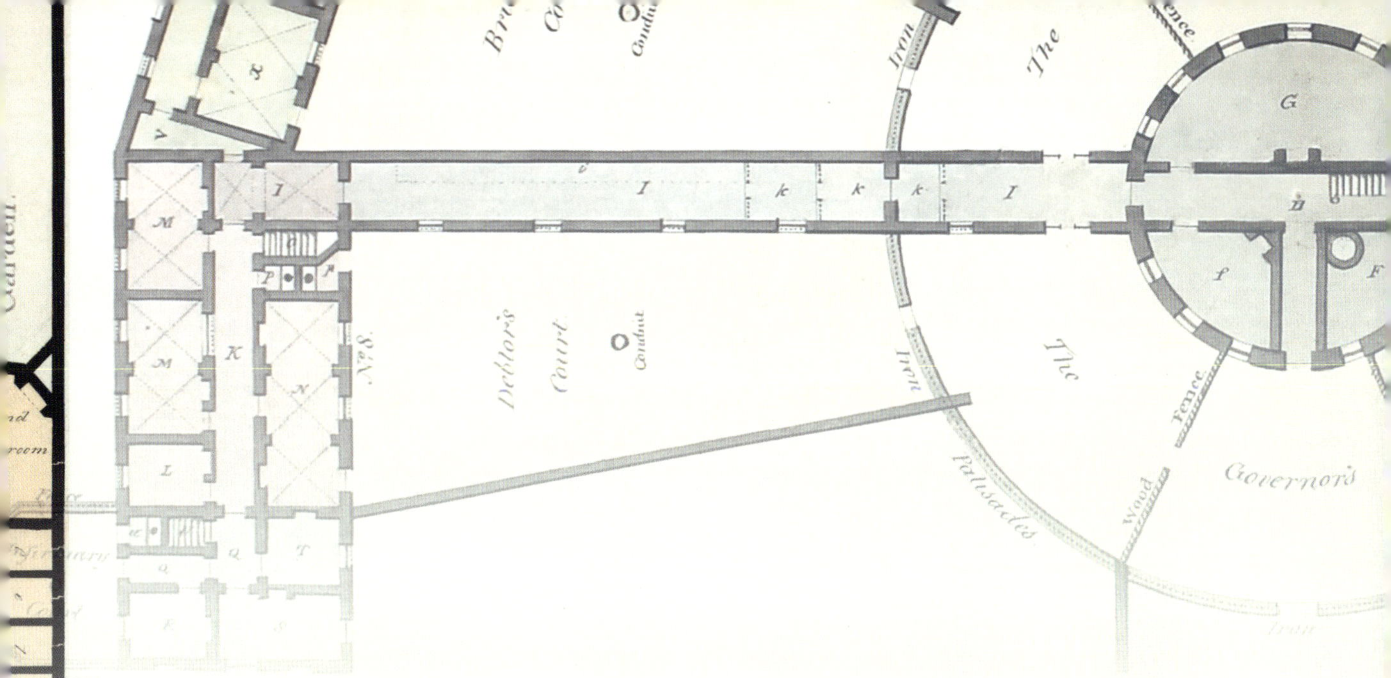

Chapter 5

Reform Revisited:

Central government, philanthropic societies, and disruptions to grand-jury patronage, 1810–21

Edward McParland commented, in his important study of Irish public architecture, that the Irish Prisons Act of 1810 'resulted in lasting improvement in the planning of Irish gaols'.[1] As outlined in the preceding chapter, the law emerged from a Commons inquiry held in the previous year and was supported by a lord lieutenant with a noted interest in penal reform. Its author, the chief secretary William Wellesley-Pole, prepared the draft bill with such finesse that it passed through parliament with no significant amendments – despite seeking to repeal no fewer than fourteen Irish acts dating back to the reign of Charles II.[2] The 1810 law tackled four key aspects of prison administration: design and construction, finance, classification, and inspection. First, it stated that no building work could begin before grand jurors had received approval from central government for their overall plan, location, and proposed contracts with builders; the grand jurors were also required to appoint a committee of between six and twelve persons to oversee the building work. This set of requirements represented a radical shift in the balance of power between Dublin Castle and local government. Second, central government would now directly pay for the operation of the Four Courts Marshalsea in Dublin and for any future penitentiaries that might be built for convicts (following a 1792 act – see previous chapter). This provision had little direct effect on the grand juries, but another clause, which allowed central government to offer loans to local bodies for gaol building, was a much more radical departure; in theory these loans could be for the whole sum required. This provision opened the floodgates to cheap capital and brought Ireland more closely in line with prison laws in Britain, where the mortgaging of rates (though not the availability of loans) had been permissible since Wray's Act of 1784. Once approval had been gained for the design of a new gaol, it was almost certain that a loan would follow if the grand jurors so required. Third, the 1810 law dealt with the issue of classification. The definition of what constituted a 'model' gaol was elaborated, directing not only that there should be segregation by gender and type of offence but also that in a gaol's design the cells must be dry and airy, and ideally used to sleep just one prisoner. Gaols were to have at least one solitary-confinement cell (for rebellious inmates), a chapel, an infirmary, a room for the reception of ill new prisoners, common rooms, yards, and at least one place where prisoners could work at manufacturing goods. Further detailed regulations set out prisoners' diet, a complete ban on all alcohol in prisons, and a ban on animals being kept by the gaoler within the walls of the gaol. It was quickly clear that many of the gaols built in the first construction boom of the 1780s and 1790s – as discussed in Chapter 4 – failed to meet these new standards, and it must have been apparent to Wellesley-Pole and others that the loans scheme would be an essential incentive for the second rebuilding programme. Fourth, and finally, the 1810 law took up the issue of inspection. Grand jurors were to inspect their prisons as before, and local Protestant clergymen were to continue to act as regular outside inspectors. Now, however, the inspector general – the Rev. Forster Archer – was to advise the lord lieutenant on what constituted an appropriate gaol and was to

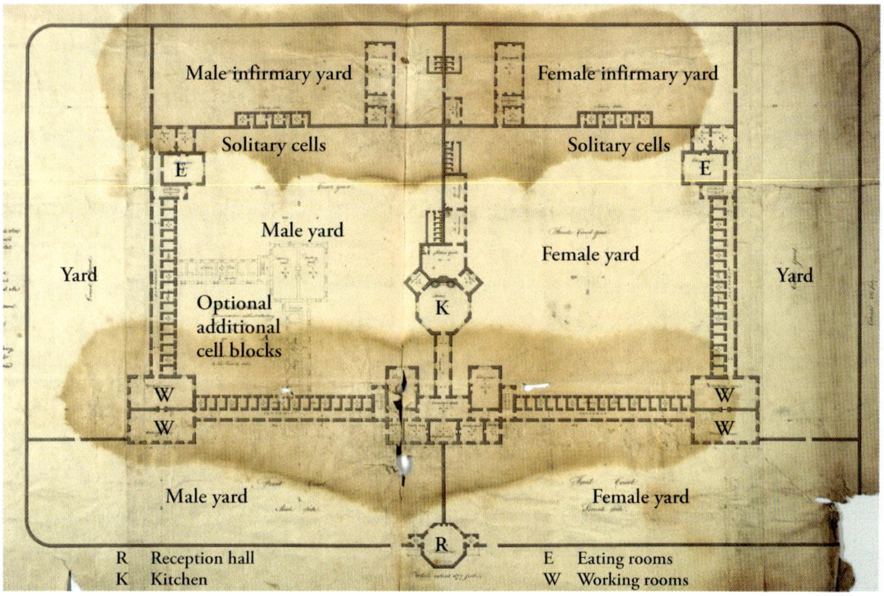

Fig. 5.1. Design for a general penitentiary, ground-floor plan, unexecuted. Francis Johnston, August 1810. Johnston's rectilinear model gaol, following in the wake of the Prisons Act of 1810, owed more to Howard's prison designs of the 1770s than to the more advanced plans of his own time. (*Reproduced courtesy of the Irish Architectural Archive.*)

work with government in processing requests for design approvals from grand-jury committees. Moreover, the act stated for the first time that Catholic and Dissenting ministers, like their Established Church counterparts, were to visit each gaol at least three times weekly, meet all the members of their flock, and perform services on Sundays.

The 1810 law was clearly intended to institute far-reaching reform, and the government did not again intervene with further significant prison legislation for over ten years. Of all the clauses in the 1810 law, the two most important advances were the requirement for approval of gaol designs and the offer of generous loans. In practice the latter was much easier to administer than the former; it took many years for government to develop the in-house expertise required to ensure that new gaols would be healthy, secure, and capable of effecting 'moral reformation'. In August 1810, however, only two months after the act received the royal assent, the government's architect, Francis Johnston – previously mentioned in Chapter 1 in connection with the building of Armagh's courthouse – was asked by an official within the Board of Works to prepare a 'model' prison design, emulating Howard's scheme of thirty years earlier, that conformed to 'the directions of the act'. The request stated that the design 'may serve as a general plan upon which all the new gaols in Ireland may be built, only varying it according to the size which may be suitable to the extent of the county'.[3] Later that year, Johnston prepared drawings for Dublin's new Richmond penitentiary, and his design for this institution and for his 'model' gaol (Fig. 5.1) can easily be mixed up. In fact, his unbuilt 'model' gaol design is more important for several reasons.[4] Johnston's assignment was to design a gaol that followed every clause in the new act and that could be used when designs for new county gaols from grand-jury committees arrived in Dublin Castle. We can imagine that this design was hung on the wall in the Board of Works office and was regularly consulted.

Johnston was an accomplished designer of many major public buildings and country houses and is now celebrated as one of Ireland's great architects. Yet he knew little about gaols and had not designed one before 1810.[5] This inexperience is reflected in the remarkably outdated design that he sketched. For any of the penal reformers of the previous generation who were aware of Blackburn's more advanced radial and polygonal designs in England, it must have appeared as an unwelcome throwback to the gaols of Howard's early years. Johnston's new role as the examiner of county-gaol designs must also have been a worrying prospect for the future of Irish penal reform. Indeed, his debt to Howard's 1777 model design is clearly apparent in the rectilinear geometry of the gaol and in its limited potential for inspecting prisoners or providing adequate ventilation. Johnston's scheme could, he claimed, accommodate 204 prisoners in its large three-storey courtyards. An additional smaller sub-courtyard could be formed inside, if required, and this alteration would have brought the capacity up to 300 persons. He stated that six different classes were provided for, but presumably this was true only if the members of each of the six classes took turns in sharing the two large exercise yards. The central range was to house the kitchen and chapel, and to the rear Johnston placed a large infirmary and some solitary cells, as required by the new prison act. The whole gaol was to have had no architectural ornamentation and its gigantic 512-foot-long, 42-bay façade (Fig. 5.2) was matched in terms of sheer bleakness only by the surrounding 677-foot-long perimeter wall, punctuated by two doors and a bay section in the centre. Had this 'model' been faithfully followed in Irish provincial towns, gaols in Ireland would have had little or no architectural character and would have appeared in the urban streetscape as simply high and blank perimeter walls. But the real problem with his design was not its architectural ornamentation; more worryingly, it was that despite fulfilling (in a technocratic sense) all the stipulations of the 1810 act, it represented an outdated 'model' by any other standard and a low base from which to launch the second rebuilding programme.

Fig. 5.2. Design for a general penitentiary, elevation, facing west, unexecuted. Francis Johnston, August 1810. Johnston's façade was little more ornamented than its bleak surrounding wall. Central-government officials paid little attention to the decorative details of prison buildings, preferring instead to concentrate on the function and adaptability of different plans. (*Reproduced courtesy of the Irish Architectural Archive.*)

Before grand jurors could push ahead with seeking government approval for their gaol design, they needed to know that it was within their means to see the project through to fruition. The new prison law simplified financial matters with its new system of generous loans. This largesse was undoubtedly the main factor behind the second great rebuilding programme of Irish gaols from 1810 onwards (Figs 5.3, 5.4). By 1855 a total of at least £600,000 had been loaned to grand jurors at favourable interest rates for gaol building; almost every county benefited at some stage. In the period covered by this chapter, nineteen grand juries had loans approved that eventually totalled some £222,000, or an average of £11,600 each (Fig. 5.5). These disbursements were significantly heavier than the courthouse loans detailed in chapters 2 and 3 and reflected the relative scale and complexity of prison architecture. The most handsomely rewarded were the Cork city grand jurors, whose incompetence had, not without some irony, sparked the inquiry that led to the passing of the act; they received over £40,000 for their new gaol from 1819 until its eventual completion in the mid-1820s. The larger cities of Dublin, Derry, and Limerick also received very significant loans. The smallest single loan was £727 for the Dublin county grand jurors to allow them to rebuild parts of Kilmainham gaol that had been damaged by a fire in 1817.[6] The availability of these loans was in general a more important factor in explaining the boom in gaol building than increases in crime and unrest: in some counties new gaols were built at a time when average crime rates were steady or even falling (Cork city); in others no building work occurred despite significant increases in crime (King's County). Moreover, there was almost always a delay of at least a couple of years between when grand jurors committed to building work and when it actually occurred; the spike in building in 1815–20 may therefore be more accurately attributed to a time-lagged reaction to the new capital provided by the 1810 act than to the undeniable increase in crime and unrest which was apparent in these years (especially 1813–16), and which closely tracked the agricultural depression and unemployment associated with the closing phase of the Napoleonic wars.[7] It would be a mistake to hastily attribute this construction boom to a straightforward reaction to the unrest of the period, however tempting and convenient the coincidence; in fact, its origins lay in the less dramatic administrative reforms of the preceding years.

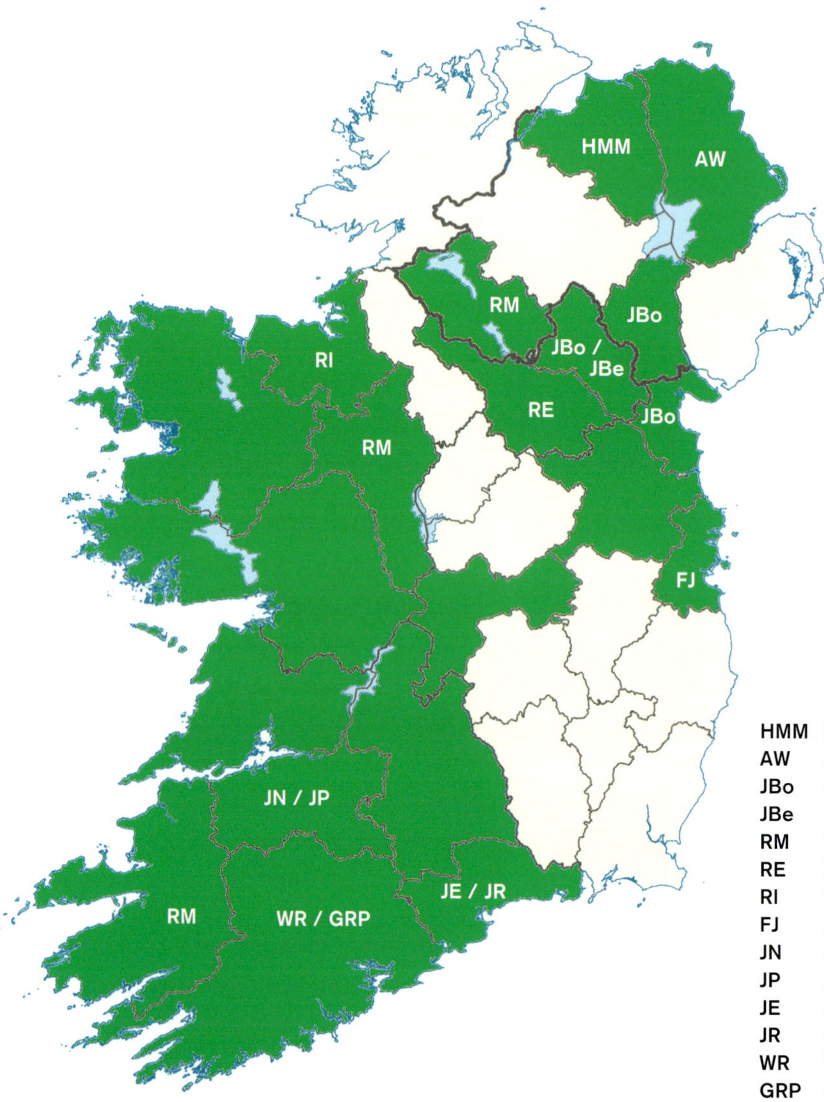

Fig. 5.3. A map showing new county gaols, or large additions made to existing gaols, in Ireland between 1810 and 1821, with the architect responsible marked, where known. Despite the extensive building boom of the preceding decades, the Prisons Act of 1810 and the input of philanthropic penal-reform societies later in the decade turned most county gaols into building sites once more.

HMM	Henry, Mullins & McMahon
AW	Alexander Wilson
JBo	John Bowden
JBe	John Behan
RM	Richard Morrison
RE	Richard Elsam
RI	Richard Ingleman
FJ	Francis Johnston
JN	John Nash
JP	James Pain
JE	James Elmes
JR	John Roberts
WR	William Robertson
GRP	George Richard Pain

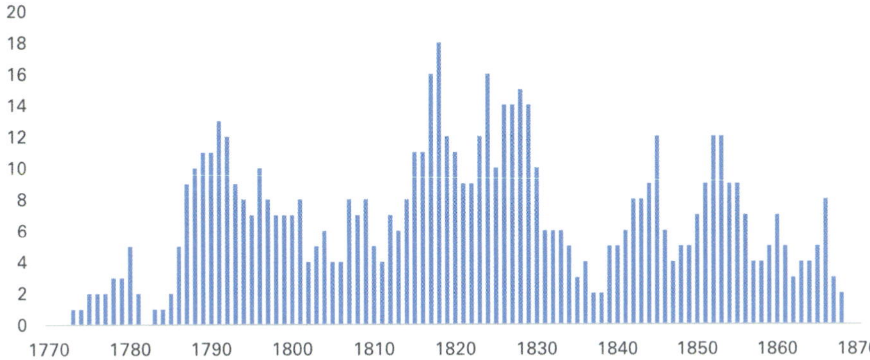

Fig. 5.4. Graph showing the number of gaols that were under construction in Ireland between 1770 and 1870. The building boom between 1810 and the early 1820s is apparent; at its peak in 1818 some eighteen gaols were being altered, extended, or built anew. Compiled from Appendix A.

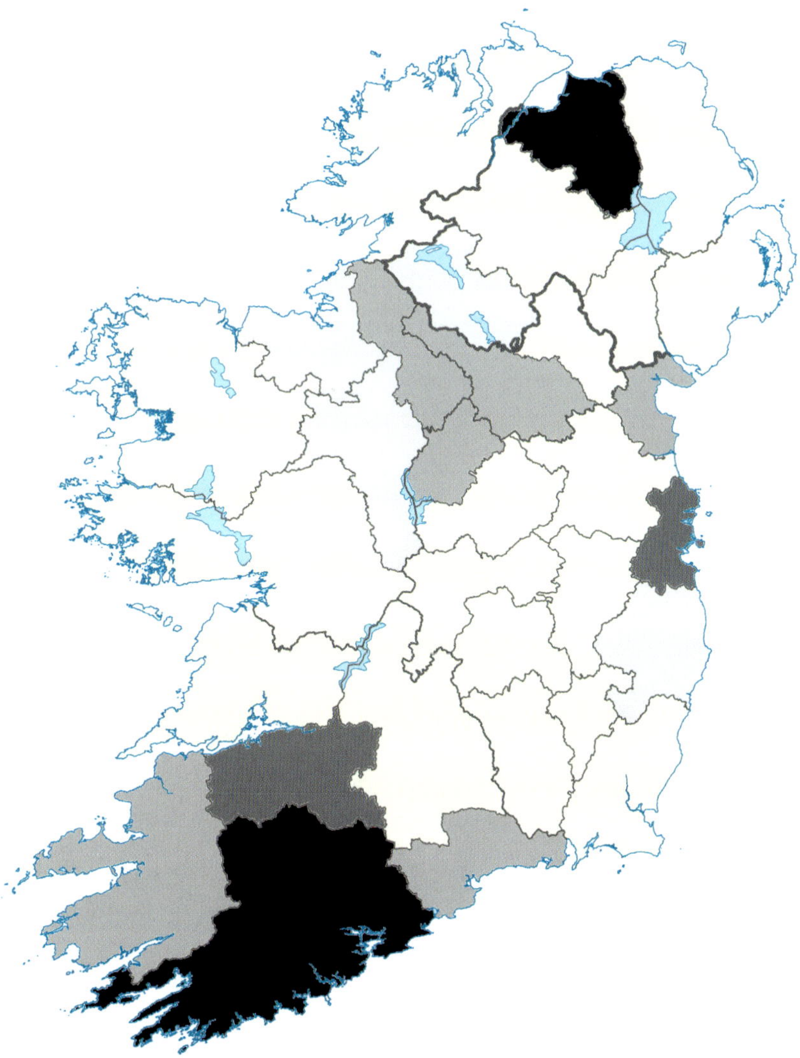

Fig. 5.5. A map showing central-government loans to Irish grand juries for gaol building between 1810 and 1821. Weightings are by percentage of the total sum: light grey (1–3%), grey (3–6%), dark grey (6–10%), and black (above 10%). Cork city received the greatest sum (£40,427) and Dublin county the least (£727); in both cases the neighbouring county or city also received sizeable amounts (Cork county, £14,768; Dublin city, £20,032).

Dublin's Richmond penitentiary and Richmond bridewell

Grand jurors were not the only beneficiaries of the new loan scheme. As briefly mentioned above, the 1810 act also set in motion plans for a large government penitentiary in Dublin that was paid for and built directly by the Board of Works, according to the designs of its architect Francis Johnston. The Board of Works was also loaned money for building this prison by Dublin Castle, and of the total sum of £41,200 loaned to this body in the years up to 1821, £32,415, or seventy-nine per cent of the total, was spent solely on the Richmond penitentiary.[8] Situated at Grangegorman in Dublin's north inner city, this penitentiary (Fig. 5.6) was an experiment in penal reform where convicts otherwise due to be transported would instead serve their sentences in a tightly managed prison environment. Initially, they were to be held in complete isolation and then gradually allowed to mingle with other prisoners while also engaging in hard labour. It was hoped that the moral reformation of prisoners would not only lessen the practical and financial burdens of transportation to Australia but would also demonstrate that through hard work and solitude it was indeed possible to 'improve' moral character. From the beginning this was a wildly ambitious aim, and the institution's first governor was quick to note that the penitentiary was operating in an 'age of theory and experiment'.[9] And the penitentiary was experimental in more ways than one: it was also the first

Fig. 5.6. Richmond penitentiary, Grangegorman, Dublin. Francis Johnston, 1810–20. Christine Casey has commented that the penitentiary's façade is 'as bald an expression of the late-Georgian penal code as one is likely to get … , plain and dour' (*Buildings of Ireland: Dublin*, p. 256). However, Johnston's earlier unexecuted design was even more sparsely ornamented. (*Photograph by author, 2014.*)

time that central government had managed and built such a large prison, a circumstance that, at least in theory, should have removed the evils of jobbery and incompetence so often attributed to grand jurors.

The design of this penitentiary was fundamentally different from that of a county gaol because its purpose and function were unique. Nonetheless, some of the well-established penal-reform principles applied equally to both types of prisons, including such issues as ventilation, classification, and inspection. In January 1811, Johnston submitted his proposed design (Figs 5.7, 5.8). Approval came quickly from the government; it was only a formality, of course, for Johnston was also the approver of designs.[10] His prison, at 630 feet by 312 feet, occupying a site of over two acres, was the largest such building ever planned in Ireland. A total of 250 cells, split evenly by gender, were arranged in two concentric polygonal ranges, with further adjoining radial blocks containing the solitary cells for new arrivals. This geometrical arrangement carved out twenty large and irregularly shaped exercise yards and – as in his earlier 'model' design – the chapel and kitchen were placed in the central range, though each was now segregated by gender. Likewise, the cell blocks were surrounded by an enormous perimeter wall, though Johnston made more of an effort to give it some architectural punctuation as it faced the street; he further elaborated this design in a later drawing, consistent with the way in which the penitentiary was eventually built (Fig. 5.9). Johnston's façade, articulated with a pedimented central block and a clock tower, was similar in outline to his district lunatic asylums of the early 1820s; it contained the governor's residence and associated offices and also served as a shop where the goods produced by the prisoners could be sold to the public.[11]

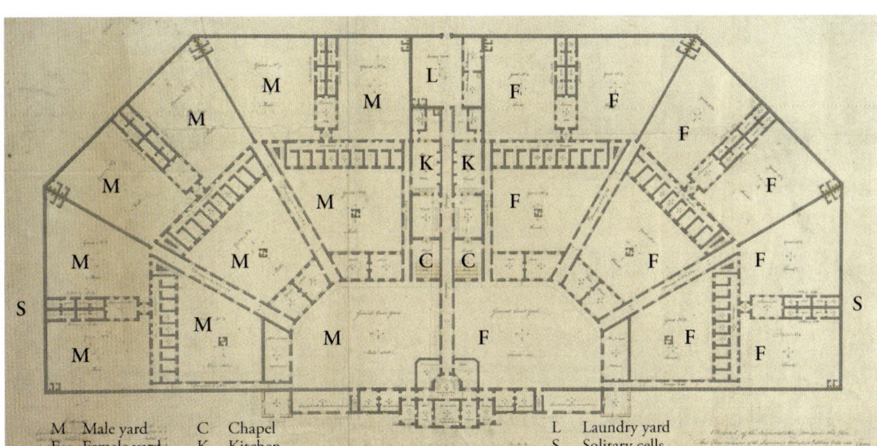

Fig. 5.7. Richmond general penitentiary, ground-floor plan, unexecuted. Francis Johnston, January 1811. The design combined elements of the rectilinear, polygonal, and radial plans, but in a manner that offered few of their individual advantages. A central passage divided the male (left) from the female (right) wards. (*Reproduced courtesy of the Irish Architectural Archive.*)

Fig. 5.8. (top) Richmond general penitentiary, elevation, facing west, unexecuted. Francis Johnston, January 1811. Johnston's projecting central and end bays, door surrounds, and central pediment were all the architectural ornamentation offered by his first scheme (compare with Figs 5.6, 5.9). (*Reproduced courtesy of the Irish Architectural Archive.*)

Fig. 5.9. (bottom) Richmond general penitentiary, elevation, facing west, as built. Francis Johnston, 1812. The clock tower and wind vane (inscribed with the year 1816) were similar to Johnston and William Murray's nine district lunatic asylums, built around the country from 1820 onwards. (*Reproduced courtesy of the Irish Architectural Archive.*)

We may ask how this design fitted into developing ideas of prison architecture at the time. First, it is curious that Johnston did not follow the general rectilinear outline of his 'model' scheme of only a few months earlier. Instead he chose a layout that combined elements of the radial and the polygonal plans – but with the disadvantages of both. There has been some scholarly disagreement over the design's merits, with McParland in 1969 acclaiming Johnston's 'triumph of planning'; six years later, he revised this opinion by noting that the scheme was 'in no sense revolutionary' and that it derived almost entirely from the polygonal plan built by Hardwick in Galway and elsewhere in Britain.[12] McParland's historiographical shift was probably influenced by an article by Henry Heaney published in 1974 that examined the penitentiary's design and administration; Heaney concluded that the design was 'far from adequate' and was seriously deficient in both classification and inspection.[13] More recently, Bernadette Goslin (1990) and Christine Casey (2005) have both described the design as radial, albeit with some polygonal features.[14] In fact, the design is a double polygon laid out in a rectilinear fashion. A single polygon, for example at Galway, allowed the gaoler to see all the prisoners at any moment from his central-inspection 'hub'; placing a second polygon behind the first destroyed this principle of inspection, and linking the two ranges with corridors prevented the free passage of air that was the polygon's other great advantage. Likewise, the radial blocks at the far extremities were perfectly useless in terms of inspection, as they were out of view of the governor. In these ways Johnston misunderstood the merits of the two main prison designs then being built throughout Britain

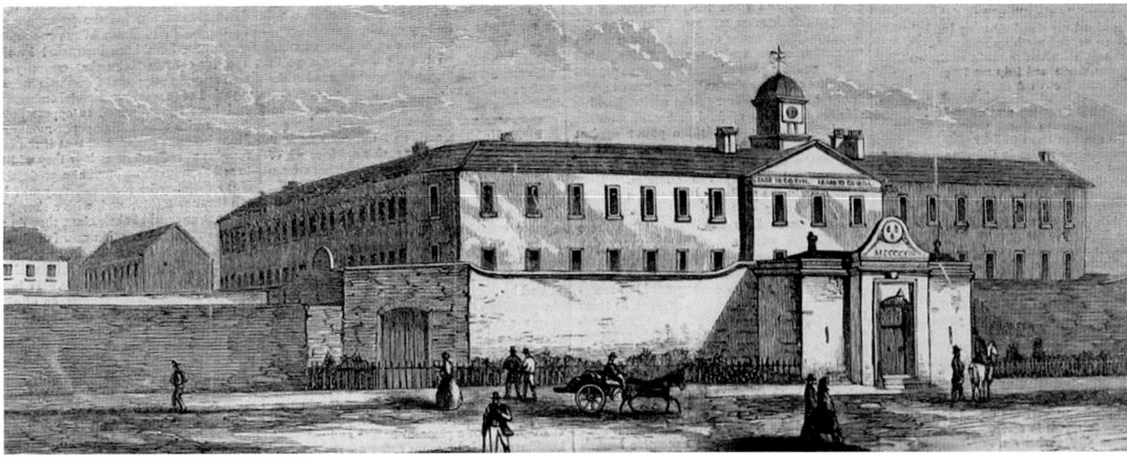

Fig. 5.10. Richmond bridewell, South Circular Road, Dublin, 1866. Designed by Johnston and built between 1813 and 1819, this institution served as an auxiliary prison for Dublin city's Newgate gaol. Visible in the entablature was the warning to both the free and the incarcerated: 'CEASE TO DO EVIL – LEARN TO DO WELL'. The bridewell later became a military barracks and is today a college. From *Harper's Weekly* (New York), vol. 10, no. 484, 7 April 1866.

and Europe, and in combining them, he managed to eliminate the usefulness of both. As soon as the penitentiary opened in 1820, it was heavily criticised by penal reformers for these reasons and stood as a giant folly in prison design throughout the 1820s and 1830s (see Chapter 6).[15]

Johnston's contribution to Irish gaols has thus far been presented in an entirely negative manner. Yet his design must be allowed to speak for his knowledge of penal-reform ideas, and in 1813 he completed his trio of antiquated gaol designs with another Dublin project, the Richmond bridewell on the South Circular Road (Fig. 5.10). Dublin city's Newgate, as outlined in Chapter 4, was exceptionally overcrowded from the 1780s onwards, and despite a series of small bridewells and houses of correction in the city (for beggars, prostitutes, children, etc.), it was clear from the 1809 inquiry that a major extension was required to meet the increasing population and rising crime levels in the capital.[16] One measure of this need is provided by the rolling three-year averages for criminal indictments in the city; these rose from 505 in 1805–7 to 634 in 1809–11.[17] It is debatable whether this increase would, by itself, have pushed the grand jurors into action; the large loans available after 1810 were probably the decisive factor. At a meeting of the city grand jurors in late 1811 a plan for a new bridewell costing £28,691 was approved, and a location was chosen at the edge of the city, near the Grand Canal.[18] Here 'bridewell' was understood in the English sense of the word, that is, a house of correction and not simply a holding-prison as it meant in rural Ireland; Johnston's design made explicit reference in its architectural detailing to this reformatory purpose. Inscribed in the entablature above the celebrated pylon-like main door was the phrase 'CEASE TO DO

EVIL – LEARN TO DO WELL' (Figs 5.11, 5.12).[19] Johnston's plan was less imaginative (Fig. 5.13): another rectilinear court with cross ranges inserted inside that prevented adequate ventilation, classification, and inspection. It was similar in outline to his Richmond Lunatic Asylum, built in Grangegorman between 1810 and 1814, and adjacent to his new penitentiary (see Figs 5.14, 5.15).

With the Richmond bridewell nearing completion in 1818, the Dublin historians Warburton, Whitelaw and Walsh commented that it presented a vista of 'appropriate gloom', more so than the new Richmond penitentiary at the other end of the city; they added that the bridewell 'is ponderous and massive and has a marked air of precautionary contrivance to prevent a crime or to punish it'.[20] This was an optimistic reading. In fact, the bridewell was a costly affair displaying old-fashioned prison design (at least £41,300 was expended in total), and like the Richmond penitentiary, it was heavily criticised almost as soon as it opened.[21] The Duke of Richmond had left Ireland in 1813 and both these prisons were named in his honour and to mark his interest in penal reform. However, it is unclear whether he approved of their out-of-date plans. The scale of building work was in itself remarkable – as was the sheer quantity of money expended – and by 1821 the Grangegorman quarter of the city had been transformed from the private orchard of Lord Monck into the institutional

Fig. 5.11. (left) 'Cease To Do Evil' doorway, Richmond bridewell, elevation and section, *c.* 1813. Johnston used a battered, Egyptian pylon-like composition, with an enormous overhanging cornice, to express the fearsome and impenetrable character of the institution. (*Reproduced courtesy of the Irish Architectural Archive.*)

Fig. 5.12. (right) 'Cease To Do Evil' doorway, Richmond bridewell. This impressive example of late Georgian abstract propaganda, cut from granite, is a rare survival from the original institution. Students and teachers now walk where prisoners once entered the bridewell. (*Photograph by author, 2013.*)

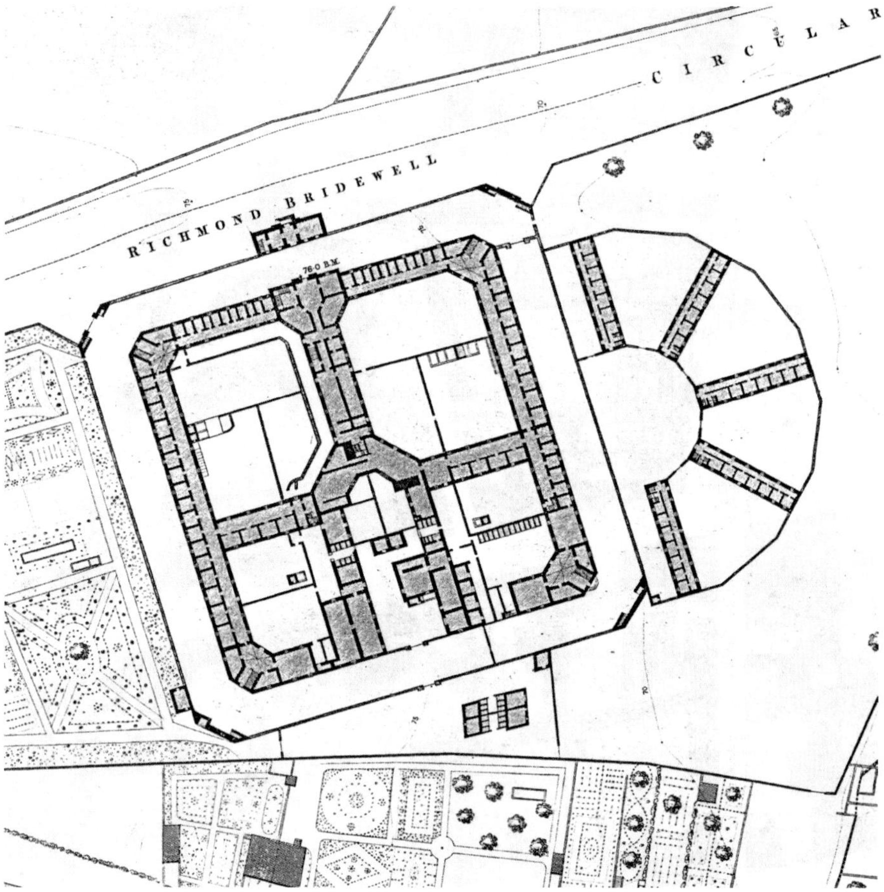

Fig. 5.13. Richmond bridewell. Ordnance Survey five-feet town map, 1847. Johnston's old-fashioned rectilinear plan provided little ventilation or opportunities for adequate classification and inspection of prisoners. The five radial blocks to the right are a later addition dating from 1836–9 (see Chapter 7). (*Reproduced courtesy of the Board of Trinity College Dublin.*)

capital of the city, with large government-run hospitals, lunatic asylums, and prisons – a character that it still retains today (Figs 5.14, 5.15).[22]

The quantity of new buildings, if not their quality, set a new standard for the grand jurors who were also building gaols at this time. But many of them looked to England rather than to Dublin for inspiration: George Byfield's Bury gaol in Suffolk (Fig. 5.16), built between 1802 and 1803, was an important revival of Blackburn's radial plan from the 1780s, with its cell blocks detached from the central building to permit more unobstructed inspection, and also to prevent prisoners from converging on the gaoler's residence in revolt. At both Southwell and Devizes (Fig. 5.17), the architect Richard Ingleman built large polygonal gaols in 1807 and 1808, and in the 1810s he brought this expertise to his work in Sligo (to be considered shortly).[23] Bentham's scheme for a British penitentiary continued to occupy parliamentary time at Westminster in the early 1810s, but after a final disagreement he was compensated and the scheme finally folded. In its place came Thomas Hardwick, designer of Galway's gaol, and William Williams, who proposed a vast polygonal penitentiary for Millbank, which was built between 1812 and 1822 (see Chapter 4).[24] James Neild (1744–1814), an acolyte of Howard, toured British gaols and published his *State of the Prisons* in 1812; he did not visit Ireland, though he was often requested to do so. Instead he read Archer's annual reports and concluded that Irish gaols were 'extremely defective'.[25] After 1810 it was very unusual for a new gaol to be built in Britain that was neither radial nor polygonal in design. Reformers and local gaolers confirmed the advantages of these plans after some years of use. There was a heated debate in Britain over which was the 'best' design as between the two, and the eventual resolution of this issue will be discussed in Chapter 6. Nonetheless, with these two competing plans so firmly adopted in Britain, it is unsurprising that they finally started to make significant inroads into Irish gaol design at this time.

Fig. 5.14. Grangegorman district, Dublin. Ordnance Survey six-inch map, surveyed January 1837. Before 1800 much of the district had been Lord Monck's private orchard. But by the time this map was produced, the north-western suburb of the city had developed a uniquely institutional character. It was home to, in a clockwise fashion, the Richmond penitentiary (later female penitentiary), the Dublin north workhouse (incorporating the Bedford asylum), the Hardwick fever hospital and lunatic asylum, the Whitworth hospital, the Richmond surgical hospital, a house of refuge, and the Richmond Lunatic Asylum. Several years later, Arbour Hill military prison and Broadstone railway terminus were built nearby. (*Reproduced courtesy of the Board of Trinity College Dublin.*)

Fig. 5.15. A part of the former Richmond Lunatic Asylum, Grangegorman district, Dublin. This quarter of Dublin is at the time of publication undergoing extensive rehabilitation. (*Photograph by author, 2013.*)

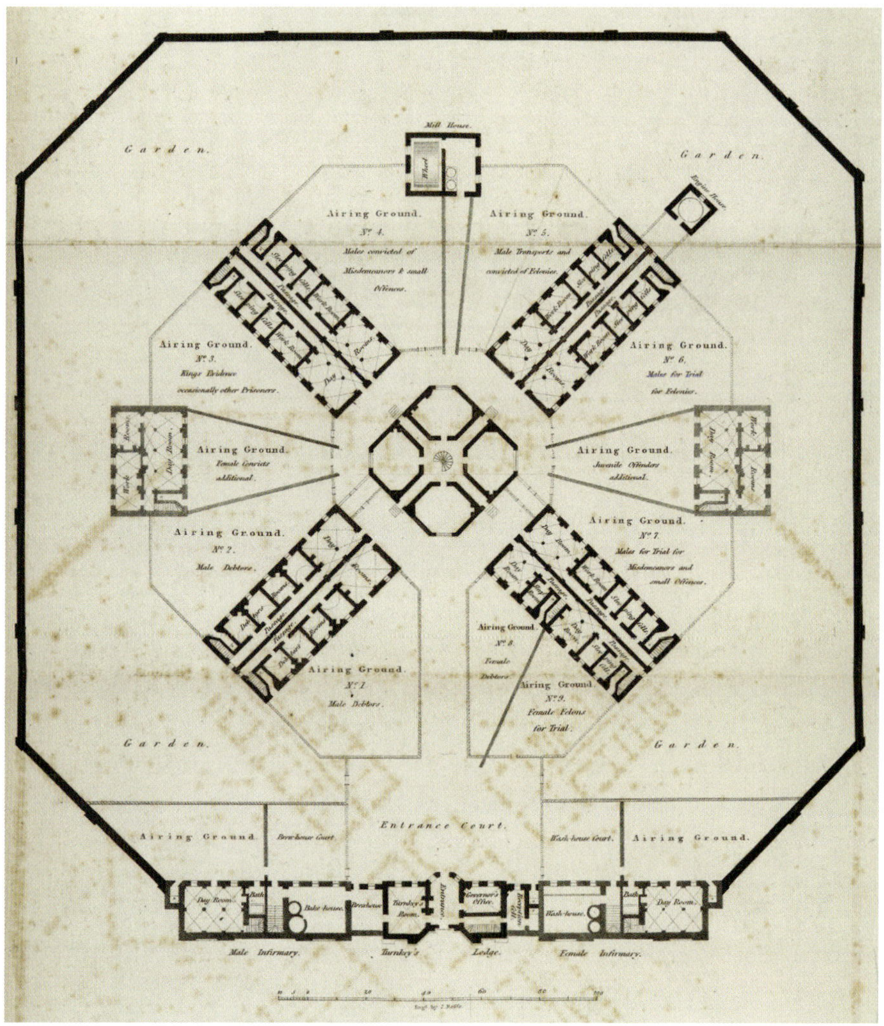

Fig. 5.16. Bury St Edmunds gaol, Suffolk, ground-floor plan. George Byfield and John Orridge, 1802–3. Bury gaol was originally composed only of the four radial blocks; the other pavilions are later additions. It was an influential early second-generation adaptation of Blackburn's radial-plan design of the1780s. From John Orridge, *Description of the Gaol at Bury Saint Edmunds* (London, 1819). (*Reproduced courtesy of the Royal Institute of British Architects Collection.*)

Fig. 5.17. Devizes house of correction, Wiltshire, ground-floor plan. Richard Ingleman, 1808–17. Competing with the radial plan was the polygonal, which had many supporters, including Ingleman, who built similar gaols in Southwell (Nottinghamshire) and in Sligo. Much of the penal-reform debate of the 1810s concerned the relative advantages of both plans. (*Reproduced courtesy of Wiltshire and Swindon Archives.*)

Ireland's first radial-plan county gaols and the issue of scale

In Cavan the old county gaol was built in the 1780s, but it was described as being ruinous within twenty years.[26] It appears to have been a very small building, and assize judges instructed the grand jurors to make a presentment for a new gaol several years before the 1810 act took effect. Nevertheless, Archer recommended that a site should not be chosen until the local landlord, the Earl of Farnham, made clear his plans for building a new wide street in the town (Fig. 5.18).[27] This issue had been resolved by 1810, when the grand jurors entered into a contract with the English architect Richard Elsam to build the new gaol on an elevated site on this new street. Building work was completed by 1812 (Fig. 5.19).[28] As outlined in Chapter 2, the reconstruction of Cavan's main public buildings continued into the following decade, when William Farrell's new assize courthouse was erected nearby.

Fig. 5.18. (right) Cavan town. Ordnance Survey six-inch map, surveyed January 1835. Around the turn of the century, the proprietor of the town, the Earl of Farnham, planned a wide and straight new street – Farnham Street – to the west of the historic town centre. In 1811–12 and in 1822–5 the county's gaol and courthouse, respectively, were rebuilt there. (*Reproduced courtesy of the Board of Trinity College Dublin.*)

Fig. 5.19. (below) Farnham Street, with Cavan's partially demolished gaol behind, May 1922. Situated on an elevated site, Elsam's gaol brought purpose, dignity, and architectural sophistication to the new street. The gaol closed in 1886 and was handed over to the Catholic Church in 1921; a school now occupies the site. From A.F. McEntee, *Memories of … Journalism in Cavan* (1991), pp. 56–7. (*Reproduced courtesy of* The Anglo-Celt.)

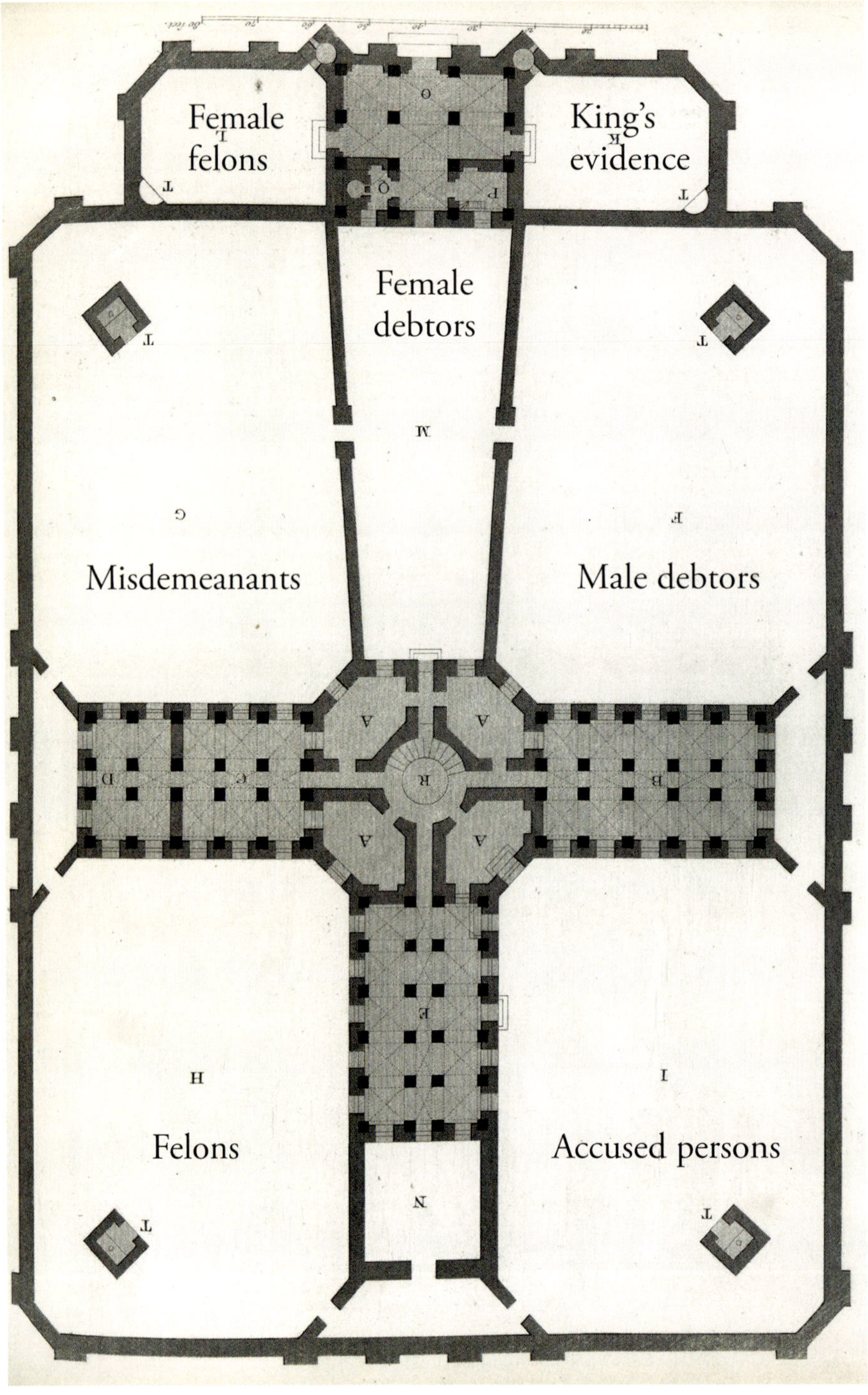

Fig. 5.20. Cavan gaol, ground-floor plan. Richard Elsam, 1810. Elsam thought that his three-wing radial-plan gaol would be suited to a relatively small county such as Cavan; in time it proved to be far too limited for the grand jurors' needs. He built an almost identical gaol at Dover in the late 1810s. From Peter Nicholson, *A Theoretical And Practical Treatise on the Five Orders of Architecture* (London, 1853), plate 64. (*Reproduced courtesy of the Royal Institute of British Architects Collection.*)

We know a great deal about Elsam's design because a series of drawings and a detailed description were published by the architect in 1810, and again in 1834, and because he built an identical gaol at Dover between 1818 and 1821.[29] Though the Cavan county gaol has been demolished, we know that it was a three-sided radial plan, with cell blocks adjoining the central hub, where the gaoler's living quarters, the chapel, and the infirmary were located (Fig. 5.20). Each of the three radial blocks had sixteen cells, the first for male debtors, the second for female felons, and the third for male felons. The architect envisaged that female debtors would be so rare that they could be kept in a few rooms in the central hub. Nonetheless, there were seven separate yards, which made enhanced segregation possible in the future if the grand jurors desired it. Even though the gaol was almost certainly designed before the 1810 act came into force, it followed all the new law's requirements. The erection of the gaol represented probably the first occasion that a set of grand jurors had been so fully attentive to the penal reformers' ideas since the Galway county gaol project of the previous decade.

Elsam was proud of his elegant design, which he labelled for British readers a 'small county prison'; its modest price-tag of £12,000, almost entirely offset by government loans, was designed to make the scheme attractive to other local authorities in Ireland and Britain.[30] But, at least in Ireland, this did not happen, probably for two reasons related to core elements of the design: first, the gaol was simply too small for many other counties, and second, it was unrealistic to divide a county gaol into equal numbers of cells for male and female felons; most Irish gaols had ratios closer to four-to-one or even six-to-one. In a replica built at Dover in 1818, Elsam 'managed by a bit of mathematical casuistry', according to Robin Evans, to prove that male and female prisoner numbers were roughly equal in the town, and therefore that his design was a perfect fit. But in Cavan the imbalance in accommodation was perfectly clear, especially as the time for the assizes drew close.[31] By 1817 criminal indictments in the county were one-third higher than when the gaol had opened; gaol fever erupted and 'soon infected the whole prison', with eight prisoners dying.[32] Despite these serious problems, Elsam remained a committed advocate of his radial plan, arguing the case in his *Brief Treatise on Prisons* (1818). But by then innovative reformers and architects had already developed more elaborate radial plans that could be expanded if necessary and had provided a more realistic gender division of cells. To achieve this, they generally either used radial blocks of irregular length, or they provided six, eight, ten, or more blocks instead of just three. But none of these shortcomings should diminish the importance of Cavan as Ireland's first radial-plan prison. Elsam's elevation, with its Sanmicheli-esque rusticated façade (Fig. 5.21), which he illustrated in all his promotional writings but executed in a somewhat reduced fashion at Cavan (Fig. 5.22), was later adopted by other Irish architects seeking to give the entrances to their gaols a sense of solidity and sobriety (see chapters 6 and 7).[33]

Other counties soon adopted Elsam's design, at least in principle; Richard Morrison began building two new radial-plan gaols at Tralee and Enniskillen in

Fig. 5.21. Cavan gaol, principal (south-east) elevation. Richard Elsam, 1810. This undated drawing, an exact copy of Elsam's original 1810 scheme (as published), was made by Henry, Mullins & McMahon and shows the high central-inspection hub that allowed uninterrupted inspection of the gaol's five principal exercise yards. (*Reproduced courtesy of the Irish Architectural Archive.*)

Fig. 5.22. Entrance gateway, Cavan gaol, 1938. In Elsam's original design, and at Dover, the rusticated pilasters had a triangular profile, in the manner of the Italian Renaissance architect Sanmicheli (compare with Figs 5.20, 5.21). In Cavan they were flat, with blank doorways and plaques adjacent to the main door. This façade and the gaol's boundary wall were demolished soon after this photograph was taken. (*Reproduced courtesy of the Irish Architectural Archive.*)

the following year (Figs 5.23–5.25).[34] Both were almost identical to Cavan in having three-sided radial plans, but under the new regulatory environment of the 1810 act, the designs now had to be submitted to Johnston and Archer for government approval before building could begin. Both men demanded a slew of small changes, involving such issues as the height of the gate-house and the exact location of the infirmary; this level of intervention prefigured much more detailed inspection of gaol design in the decades that followed.[35] Larger issues, however, such as the size of the gaol and the number of its cells, appear not to have been sufficiently addressed in early government examinations, and both gaols were too small for their respective counties when they opened. In Enniskillen there were 170 prisoners sharing around 65 cells in 1818; in Tralee there were 212 prisoners in 77 cells in the same year, and fever broke out among them.[36] The figures for criminal indictments are incomplete for Kerry, but in Fermanagh they show a rise of around a third in terms of a three-year rolling average between the years immediately prior to the gaol being constructed and its first three years of operation.[37] This increase in criminal indictments by itself does not account for the huge extent of overcrowding, and it must be concluded that both gaols were built on too small a scale at the outset, despite significant loans averaging £7,000 to both grand juries.[38] These shortcomings do not reflect well on the ability of central-government officials in this early period to ensure that adequately sized gaols were being built around the country.

The 1810 act did not specify that radial or polygonal plans had to be

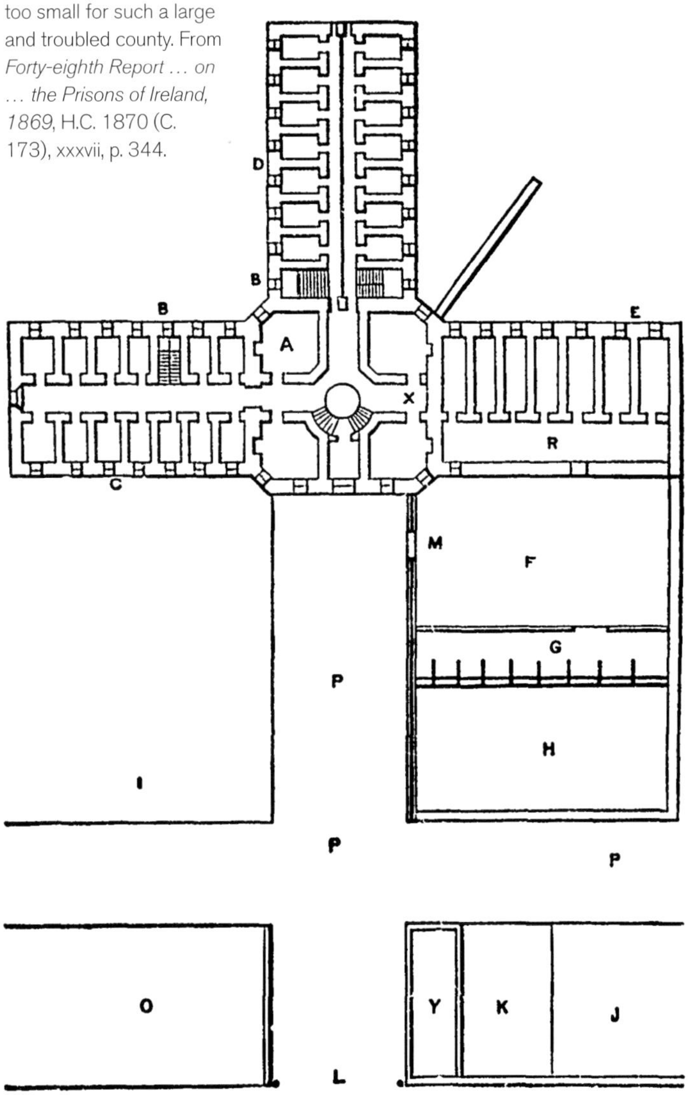

Fig. 5.23. Tralee gaol, ground-floor plan, 1870. Despite many alterations by this date, the original three-wing radial gaol, designed by Richard Morrison and built between 1812 and 1817, is still clearly apparent. From the outset Morrison's gaol was far too small for such a large and troubled county. From *Forty-eighth Report … on … the Prisons of Ireland, 1869*, H.C. 1870 (C. 173), xxxvii, p. 344.

Fig. 5.24. Tralee gaol, entrance gateway, from the west. Today only this block and part of the boundary wall survive. Morrison's use of rustication was plainer and less intimidating than that in many other gaols built at the same time. (*Photograph by author, 2013.*)

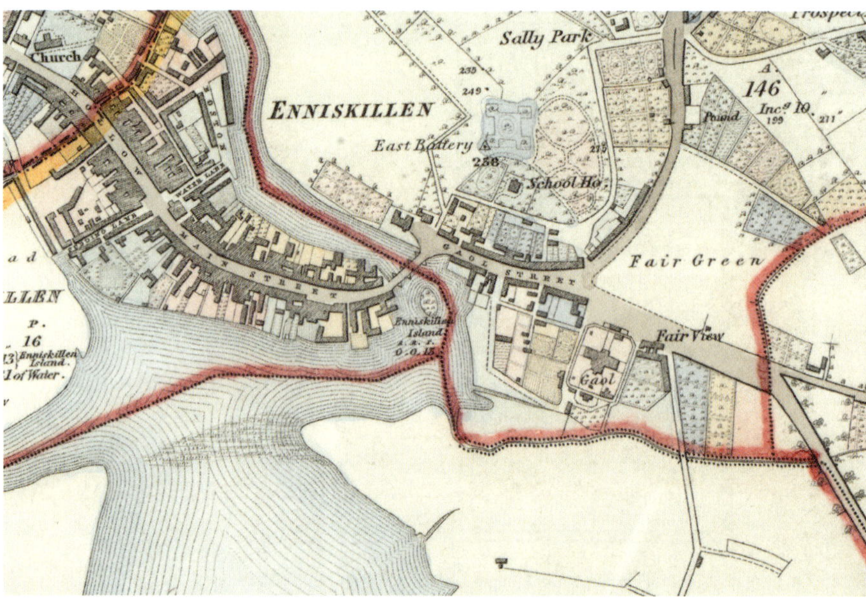

Fig. 5.25. Enniskillen, County Fermanagh. Ordnance Survey six-inch map, surveyed June 1834. Morrison's gaol, in the bottom right corner, was similar in scale and design to Tralee; it too required extensive enlargements in later years. (*Reproduced courtesy of the Board of Trinity College Dublin.*)

adopted by architects or grand juries, and in some cases, gaols continued to be built or extended using the old rectilinear arrangements of the eighteenth century. In Limerick the new gaol that was slowly built by the elusive 'Mr Smyth', as discussed in Chapter 4, was quickly followed by another building project: in 1807 the city grand jurors appointed a building committee and designs were drawn up by John Nash in conjunction with his assistant James Pain, an English architect who had recently arrived in the city to oversee the construction of Nash's Lough Cutra Castle (Fig. 5.26) near Gort for the prominent landlord and politician Charles Vereker.[39] An old-fashioned rectilinear plan was adopted, suggesting that the claim – made in 1866 by the local historian Maurice Lenihan – that Nash had 'perfected' the gaol's design was wild exaggeration, and that he probably had little or no direct involvement in the project.[40] Thomas Spring Rice was closer to the mark in 1819 when he admitted that the gaol's design was 'very imperfect'.[41] Nash had demonstrated a knowledge of more advanced gaol design in his radial-plan Hereford county gaol in the 1790s, but the small new Limerick city gaol (Fig. 5.27) was a rectilinear arrangement, and it is not clear if approval was even sought from government for the work. Some sources describe the work as completing the haphazard gaol left by Smyth rather than as a new building outright, and this discrepancy may help to explain how such a design was kept out of the view of Dublin Castle.[42] Meanwhile in Belfast, the Antrim grand jurors commissioned a new house of correction along rectilinear principles that was built between 1815 and 1817.[43] The prison was a definite improvement on its predecessor, described in 1807 by Archer as a 'miserable dungeon' and severely overcrowded, but there was little novelty in its architecture except for the imposing epitaph, 'WITHIN AMEND, WITHOUT BEWARE', said to

Fig. 5.26. Lough Cutra Castle near Gort, County Galway. John Nash and James and George Richard Pain, 1811–17. Viscount Gort's country house brought the Pain brothers to Ireland, where, adapting Nash's gaol designs from Wales and the west of England, they became engaged in the construction of both gaols and bridewells throughout the south of Ireland. (*Photograph by author, 2013.*)

Fig. 5.27. (left) A surviving entrance gateway to the former Limerick city gaol, probably dating from the 1790s. In the middle of the nineteenth century, a new city courthouse was built adjacent to the gaol (see Chapter 3). The majority of the former gaol site is now office accommodation. (*Photograph by author, 2014.*)

Fig. 5.28. (right) Entrance gateway and boundary wall, Drogheda gaol, from the south-west. John Bowden built a small rectilinear-plan gaol for the town grand jurors between 1814 and 1818; it was quickly condemned by the government inspector as totally inadequate. The gateway, built of hewn stone, is even plainer than those of Cavan or Tralee gaols and suited the town's limited finances. (*Photograph by author, 2013.*)

have been inscribed in a prominent location.[44] And in Drogheda the town grand jurors, representing one of the smallest and poorest counties in the whole country, built a new rectilinear gaol between 1814 and 1818 to the designs of John Bowden (Fig. 5.28).[45] Despite having received nearly £9,000 in loans, the Drogheda grand jurors apparently proceeded in contravention of the law, and Archer condemned the design for inadequate inspection of prisoners, insecure walls, and poor ventilation. He thought that the architect involved had little experience in gaol building, commenting that 'he that designs a gaol should be acquainted with the habits of prisoners and be prepared to meet them accordingly'.[46] Later inspectors continued to label this small gaol as one of the worst in the country until further substantial alterations occurred in the late 1850s.

Polygonal gaols after Galway

The 1810 act was certainly not a panacea for all prison-reform issues. Lack of enforcement was again widely evident and as many grand jurors seem to have consciously ignored the new law as conformed to it. Nonetheless, grand jurors were almost always rewarded for their lobbying with government loans for building work. It is perhaps surprising that an architect such as Morrison – who had overseen the building of Ireland's first polygonal gaol in Galway – should have reverted to rectilinear and basic radial-plan designs in the following decade at Waterford and Wexford (as noted in Chapter 4). In 1814, however, he began building his only known polygonal gaol at Roscommon after winning a competition in which two other architects had also submitted designs.[47] It appears that the grand jurors yielded their right to adjudicate on the three schemes to central government and asked Johnston to decide for them.

Though Morrison's design was not the cheapest, it was recommended as the best plan subject to some minor alterations. Thus, in the space of four years, Johnston moved from designing his own old-fashioned rectilinear 'model' gaol to choosing a polygonal design and even to suggesting some improvements. He had adjusted quickly to the role of expert. Unlike earlier gaol-building projects, the commission at Roscommon was tightly managed; the contract stated that if the gaol was not in use by 1 July 1819, the contractors would have to forfeit £2,000, or ten per cent of the agreed price.[48] Archer strongly approved of the gaol, noting that the polygonal range was of 'a very superior appearance', and that the workmanship throughout was 'extremely well executed'.[49] The new gaol provided for eight classes of prisoners, with eight exercise yards, arranged as adjacent sectors, between the gaoler's apartment and the cells (Figs 5.29, 5.30). The reconstruction of the county's main buildings was completed in the mid-1820s, when a new courthouse was built close by the gaol (see Chapter 2); the old gaol was thereafter used to detain 'lunatics' until the new district lunatic asylum opened at Ballinasloe in the early 1830s.[50] By all accounts the new gaol was a rare success story; even the more exacting inspectors of the following decade found little to criticise in its healthy, safe, and convenient design.[51] We should question what may have led the grand jurors to commit to the project.

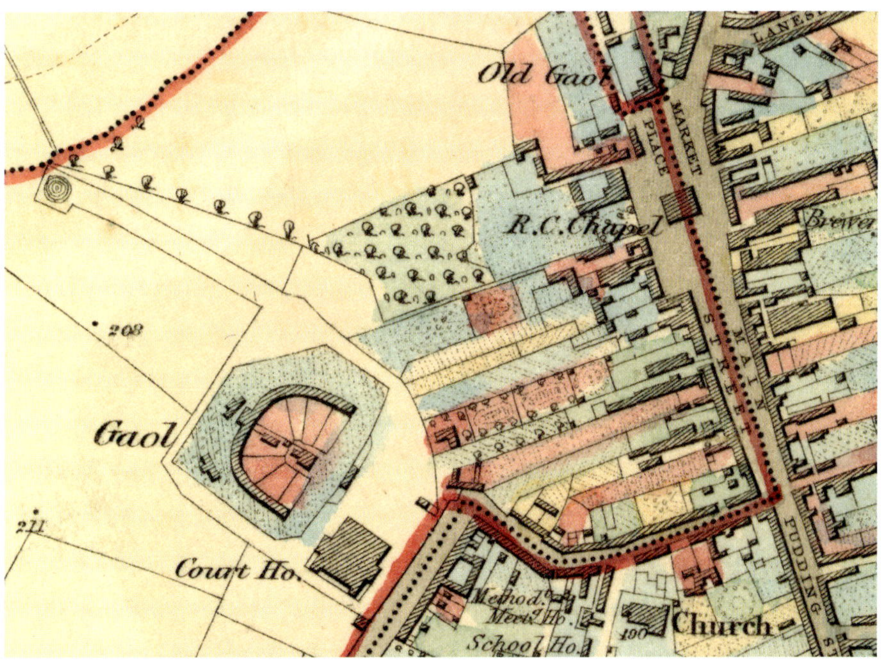

Fig. 5.29. Roscommon town, showing the old and new gaols, and old and new courthouses (the old marked 'R.C. Chapel'). Ordnance Survey six-inch map, surveyed January 1837. Following his Galway experience, Morrison built a polygonal-plan gaol for the county between 1814 and 1818. (*Reproduced courtesy of the Board of Trinity College Dublin.*)

There was no noticeable increase in the criminal-indictment rate in the county over the twenty years before the decision in 1814 to rebuild; ironically, the great increase occurred only when the gaol was nearly open, and this rise should be attributed to wider social and economic problems associated with the ending of the Napoleonic wars. Of significantly more importance must have been the £5,538 loaned to the grand jurors for the building, and for purchasing its site.[52]

One of the unsuccessful entrants in the competition for Roscommon's new gaol was John Behan, who had better luck soon afterwards in Monaghan. There, Johnston was again asked to adjudicate on the designs, and the list of competitors included Elsam and Bowden, both then active in gaol building in the region.[53] Behan possessed the advantage of having been the contractor for the building of Galway county gaol, and this experience would have made him intimately familiar with polygonal-design principles. For unknown reasons, however, the Monaghan grand jurors became dissatisfied with his work soon after construction began, and the gaol became a running sore throughout the 1810s. Bowden was brought in as a supervising architect in 1816 and was very critical of Behan's workmanship, but it was 1820 before Behan was finally dismissed.[54] After five years of building, no part of the main polygonal range was above ground level, and it was 1824 before the gaol finally opened (Fig. 5.31).[55] In the meantime typhus had ripped through the old gaol in 1817, and 27 of the 135 prisoners had died.[56] When the new gaol at last opened, penal reformers praised it in terms similar to what had been said about Roscommon. No significant further work occurred until the 1860s – a remarkable and highly unusual occurrence in Irish penal history. As in Roscommon and so many other towns, the building of a new prison in Monaghan can be seen as part of a broader process of urban improvement: once the new gaol was opened, the old

Fig. 5.30. Roscommon gaol, from the south-east, *c.* 1930. Morrison's entrance gateway was similar to his Tralee gaol, but the long polygonal range behind owed more to his and Hardwick's Galway county gaol of the previous decade. The gaol closed in 1886, and when this photograph of the county hunt was taken was probably still in use as a police station. It was demolished around 1945. (*Reproduced courtesy of the Irish Architectural Archive.*)

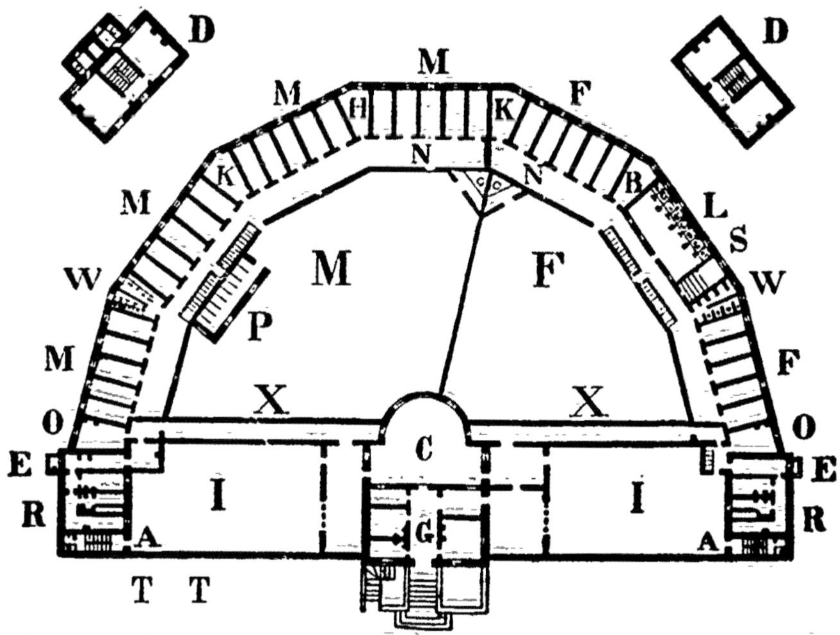

Fig. 5.31. Monaghan gaol, ground-floor plan, 1870. Morrison's plan was a reduced version of Galway, where the polygonal range was one row of cells deep instead of two, and where the chapel was relocated to the central inspection building. Two-thirds of the gaol was appropriated for males, one-third for females. From *Forty-ninth Report … on … the Prisons of Ireland, 1870*, H.C. 1871 (C. 359), xxx, p. 247.

C, chapel; G, Governor's house; E E, entrance for prisoners; R R, reception wards, with baths and every appliance required; M M M M and M, male prison; W W, lavatories and water-closets; P, pump; D D, debtors' prisons, male and female, or one might be used for lunatics; O O, officers' quarters, separate from the prison, but adjoining; N N, inspection halls for male and female prisons, with stairs and galleries; K, kitchen for both prisons; H, heating apparatus; L, laundry; B, boiler and steaming apparatus for ditto; S, clothes store and drying-room; A A, stairs leading to male and female infirmaries; I I, exercising yards for invalids; X X, passages to the two prisons; T T, line of sheds for prisoners employed at breaking stones, erected against the wall A—a tramway for a hand-truck is laid down in front of them.

gaol was demolished and its site was used for the county's controversial new assize courthouse, as planned from 1826 onwards (as discussed in Chapter 2).

The increasing scrutiny of designs and contracts by government officials meant that long-drawn-out building projects, such as that at Monaghan, were becoming increasingly rare. Despite some notable exceptions, many of the new gaols were highly praised for their architectural planning and (into the 1820s) for their management too. Irish grand jurors – by and large – followed British precedents, sometimes adopting British designs and at other times employing British architects directly. The last polygonal gaol begun before 1820 – at Sligo – fits neatly into this trend. Sligo's old gaol dated to the 1760s, and unexecuted plans to replace it at the beginning of the nineteenth century have already been noted (see Chapter 4).[57] Archer applied increasing pressure on the grand jurors in 1807, saying that a 'commodious gaol on an approved plan is much wanted'.

They responded immediately with a first presentment; in 1814 they organised a competition in which major figures such as Hardwick submitted schemes.[58] Richard Ingleman won the competition with a polygonal design that was almost identical to one that he later (unsuccessfully) attempted to build at Fisherton Anger in Wiltshire (Figs 5.32, 5.33).[59] The gaol's building placed a heavy burden on the Sligo grand jurors, who obtained a loan worth £3,700 but paid out at least £30,000 during the four years that it took to build their new gaol.[60] Like many other counties, Sligo witnessed a dramatic increase in crime on the eve of the project commencing, with the average rate of criminal indictments almost doubling, and this upsurge may have been the key factor pushing the grand jurors into action, but of course the rebuilding plan had been in the pipeline for many years.[61] For their new gaol the grand jurors chose a site at the eastern edge of the town, with plenty of space for an extensive boundary wall separating the gaol from the outside world (Figs 5.34, 5.35). Of crucial importance for the health and wellbeing of its future inmates, the gaol was the first polygonal-plan prison in Ireland that faced south and thereby allowed sunlight to enter each of the cells and yards throughout the day. And the high boundary wall won the praise of the penal reformers of the time, with one commentator in 1818 saying that at the old gaol the windows had:

> looked to the streets, [and prisoners spend the day] talking to persons outside, annoying the passengers, and singing indecent songs. [When] they received the notice of removal to the new prison, [they had] feelings similar to those evinced by convicts ordered out for transportation, and on their arrival there many of them exclaimed they had 'rather been sent to Botany Bay than' to so lonesome a place.[62]

Fig. 5.32. Fisherton Anger (Wiltshire) county gaol near Salisbury, principal elevation, unexecuted. Richard Ingleman, 1817. Unusually, Ingleman's design was rejected in favour of a rectilinear scheme by Thomas Hopper (see Fig. 4.19). Ingleman's Fisherton Anger design was almost identical to the gaol that he built at Sligo. (*Reproduced courtesy of Wiltshire and Swindon Archives.*)

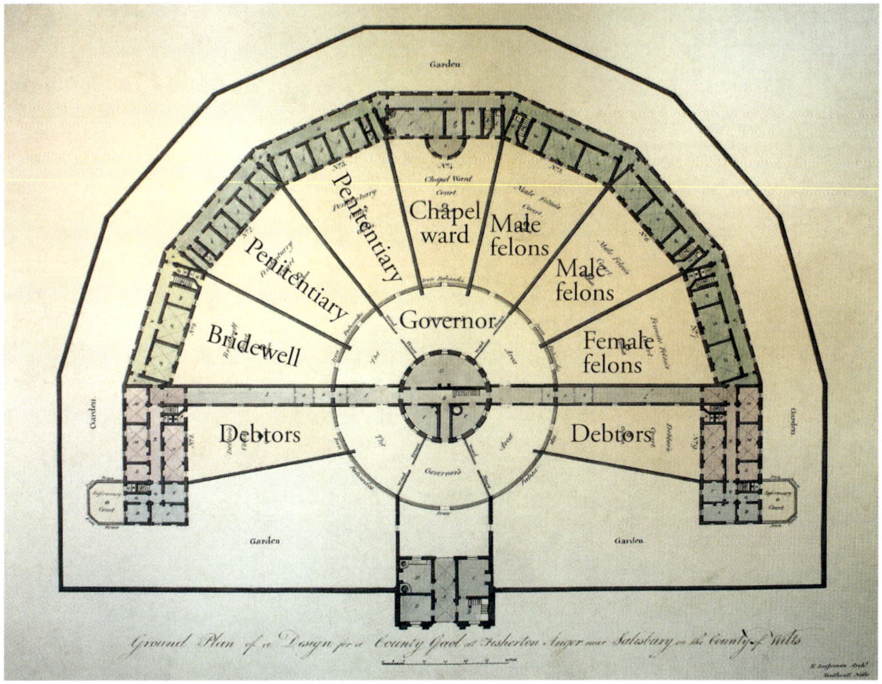

Fig. 5.33. Fisherton Anger (Wiltshire) county gaol near Salisbury, ground-floor plan, unexecuted. Richard Ingleman, 1817. The innovation of using radial corridors to link the cell blocks with the central hub allowed the gaoler to inspect prisoners unannounced, solving one of the problems identified with the polygonal plan. (*Reproduced courtesy of Wiltshire and Swindon Archives.*)

Fig. 5.34. (below) Sligo gaol, from the south, 1955. While Ingleman's design for Fisherton Anger was rejected on the grounds of cost in 1817, an almost identical scheme was built in Sligo between 1816 and 1818. One of the problems associated with the polygonal plan was ensuring that cells were adequately lighted and ventilated; Sligo gaol was the first in Ireland to solve this problem by having the polygonal range open to the south, bringing sunlight to the entire prison. The approach was originally from the river, but around 1850 a new wide street was built linking it directly with the county courthouse (compare with Fig. 5.35). (*Reproduced courtesy of the National Library of Ireland.*)

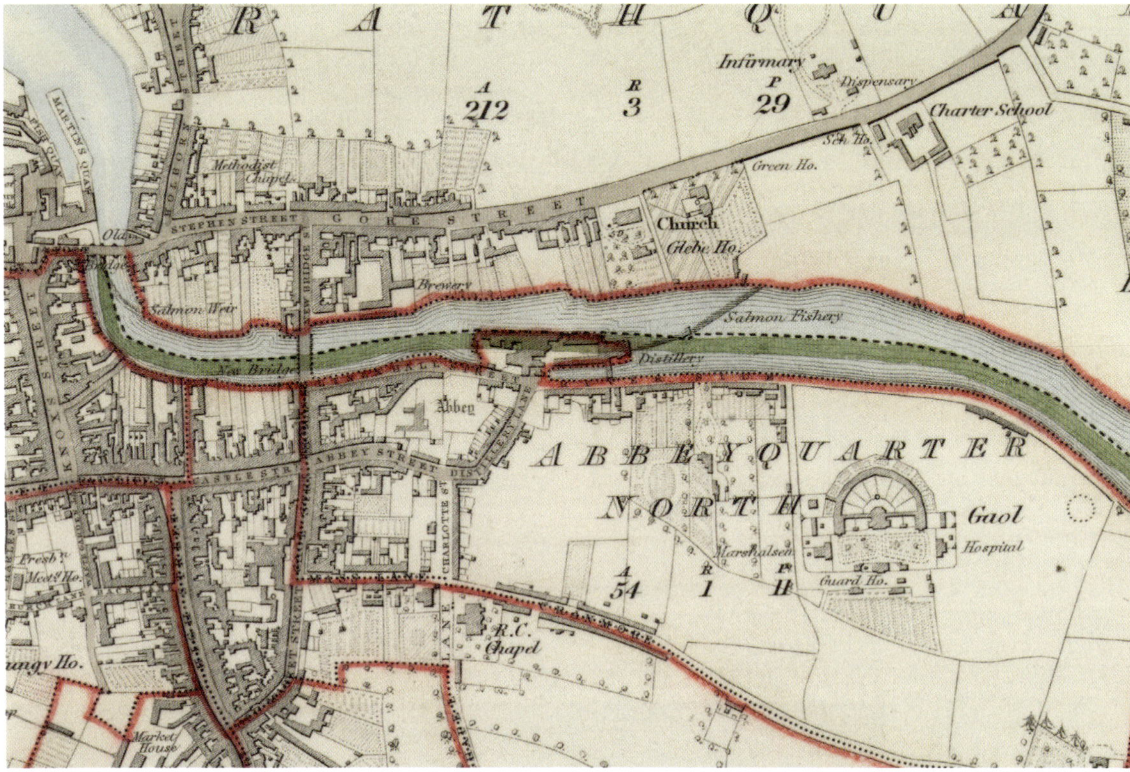

The Association for the Improvement of Prisons and of Prison Discipline in Ireland

Fig. 5.35. Sligo town, showing the gaol to the east. Ordnance Survey six-inch map, surveyed January 1837. The original circuitous approach road to the gaol is apparent – proof that having a south-facing gaol was a priority for both the architect and the grand jurors. (*Reproduced courtesy of the Board of Trinity College Dublin.*)

The preceding quote about Sligo's old and new gaols was printed in the first report of a new Irish philanthropic penal-reform organisation established in 1818 and known as the Association for the Improvement of Prisons and of Prison Discipline in Ireland (here called the AIPPD). It became one of the key drivers of the penal-reform movement from the late 1810s onwards;[63] it closely emulated the traditions and principles of its British equivalent, the Society for the Diffusion of Knowledge upon the Punishment of Death and the Improvement of Prison Discipline, founded in 1801, and the Society for Investigating the Cause of the Increase of Juvenile Delinquency, with which it had merged in 1816 to form the Society for the Improvement of Prison Discipline and for the Reformation of Young Offenders (here called the SIPD). The AIPPD has been overlooked by most historians of Irish prisons with the notable exception of Maria Luddy, who considered its background role in the formation of female philanthropic penal-reform societies in the 1820s (see Chapter 6). However, Luddy significantly understates the importance of the AIPPD when she claims that its purpose was simply to provide advice on penal issues (quoting from one of its pamphlets) for 'any who are willing to learn'.[64] In fact, at its first meeting held at 16 Upper Sackville Street in Dublin on 9 December 1818, a more ambitious primary aim was stated to be the collecting of 'a detailed account of the gaols in Ireland, with particulars respecting the objects of classification, labour, and solitary confinement'.[65] Their role was as much about gathering information as it was giving advice – though the two were obviously linked.

The problem for Archer was that this sounded remarkably like his own job description. For a variety of reasons, a younger penal-reform movement overtook Archer and the older generation of reformers and administrators in Britain and Ireland in the late 1810s. The shift became readily apparent in London in 1814 with a highly publicised government inquiry into the state of London's gaols, the first of three such endeavours in the years up to 1818.[66] In parliament the reform movement was now headed by such figures as Samuel Romilly, MP for Arundel in West Sussex, and George Holford, MP for the rotten borough of Lostwithiel in Cornwall and a leading figure in the Millbank penitentiary project. These men operated on both sides of the main political divide at Westminster and shared a common philanthropic and religious interest in prisons. They also had some Irish connections: their bills were generally supported by Irish Whigs such as John Newport, and Holford spent much time in Ireland, his wife's native country.[67] They sought to address one of the many scandals in London's gaols in 1814 with a bill to abolish the paying of fees by prisoners to their gaolers; this bill failed to receive support in the Lords, but a revised version became law in 1815.[68] They also proposed a bill requiring the formation of a committee to oversee London's gaols, similar to the Boards of Superintendence that were later encouraged in Irish gaols; this measure also failed to become law.[69] The merger of the adult and juvenile penal-reform societies to form the SIPD in 1816 must be seen in the light of these efforts in parliament. Both the SIPD and the AIPPD received support from the professional classes, the nobility and gentry, and leading politicians; Evans has noted that at the height of its influence in the mid-1820s the SIPD's vice-presidents included a duke, a marquess, eleven earls, four bishops, eleven other aristocrats, fifteen MPs, and the anti-slavery campaigner William Wilberforce.[70] At the core of the SIPD were an impassioned group of Protestant evangelicals and Quakers led by Samuel Hoare and by its most famous member, Hoare's sister-in-law Elizabeth Fry. In Ireland the AIPPD represented a similar stratum of polite elite society; on the founding committee were Joseph Pim, the wealthy Dublin Quaker, and Henry Joseph Monck Mason, the noted librarian, who at the same time founded the controversial Irish Society, dedicated to promoting Protestant evangelical teaching through the Irish language. Influential MPs such as John Leslie Foster and Henry Grattan served as vice-presidents, and the patron and president were respectively the newly arrived chief secretary Charles Grant and the Earl of Charlemont.[71]

Without Grant's involvement, it seems unlikely that the AIPPD would have been as effective as it proved to be. His arrival in Ireland in August 1818 to replace Robert Peel was a fortuitous coincidence, and he quickly accepted the status of patron of the AIPPD and joined as a life member.[72] The position of patron was not simply a revolving chair for the chief secretary of the day; Grant continued in this post long after he had resigned and left Ireland.[73] He was seen as a liberal within his own party and supported Catholic emancipation; he was also an evangelical Protestant who fitted very easily into the rarefied intellectual and religious environment of the AIPPD.[74] Grant's involvement in the AIPPD effectively confirmed the end of Archer's tenure as the government's prison inspector. Since Archer's appointment the penal-reform debate had moved on from simply gaol design and the old issues of ventilation and security to include discussions of the value of labour in gaols, the education of prisoners, the need for separate treatment of female prisoners, and the quest for greater and greater classification. The result of attempting to compartmentalise prisoners by the seriousness of their crimes had an inevitable result, namely that every crime would be seen as distinct and unique, and every prisoner as an individual case. In effect, then, classification meant prisoners not mingling at all in gaols. Examples of prisoners in England emerging from gaol as more toughened criminals than when they had entered provided ample proof that crime was contagious, and that the architecture of gaols needed to be used to limit its spread. The reformers earnestly believed that if all the conditions of incarceration were perfectly implemented, including the moral instruction of prisoners, an adequate diet, and a system of labour to punish wrongdoing, crime could be 'cured'.[75] The requirement of forced labour was revolutionised in 1818 by William Cubitt's invention of the treadmill, a device that became ubiquitous in British and (to a lesser extent) Irish gaols in the 1820s.[76] For a brief few years both the SIPD and the AIPPD cherished a utopian vision whereby crime could be treated as a scientific problem that could be 'solved'. Ingleman, the architect of Sligo's gaol, went so far as to propose a mathematical equation specifying that the rate of increase of 'vice and idleness' was directly proportional to the square of the number of prisoners kept in any class.[77] In time the mathematical certainty of this viewpoint came to seem hopelessly naïve, but around 1818 we can detect a critical combination of energy, enthusiasm, and influence in penal reform. 'The spirit of improvement,' the AIPPD optimistically stated in 1820, in a bid to shore up their perennially threadbare finances, 'is widely extending its influences, and it is gratifying to observe that the public confidence in [the organisation] advances in the same degree.'[78] Both the AIPPD and the SIPD were also aware of developments in America, where William Strickland began building the First Pittsburgh Penitentiary in 1818, a prison where every inmate was held in complete isolation; this arrangement became known as the 'solitary' system and was vigorously debated in Britain and Ireland in the 1830s.[79] Like the radial and polygonal plans of earlier generations, it failed to fulfil the high expectations thrust upon it and did not 'cure' crime, but it did provide plenty of experimental data for the reformers to analyse. Archer sat uneasily among these increasingly sophisticated, earnest, if somewhat mechanical reformers. He was shadowed by the AIPPD from 1818 onwards, and in several notable cases grand jurors chose to follow the AIPPD's advice rather than his (see Chapter 6).[80] Other grand jurors had grown to understand Archer's opinions and habits and had worked around them; the less enthusiastic among them felt threatened by the self-righteous pronouncements of the AIPPD and by its connections to government. There also appears to have been a concerted attempt from this time forward to have Archer replaced.

Charles Grant and the new zeal for reform

A Commons inquiry into British and Irish gaols in 1819 revealed the new settlement.[81] The chairman Charles Bathurst thoroughly interrogated Archer, highlighting his lack of attention to Irish gaols and especially to the smaller provincial bridewells. Over the course of five days Archer was subjected to a barrage of questions (often hostile) – more than any other witness except for an Australian clerk probed on the issue of transportation. Archer was asked if his report on Irish prisons was based on visits to all or just some of them, and when he had last visited a dozen or so named prisons. He had to admit that most bridewells were not built in accordance with legal requirements.[82] By way of contrast the other major Irish witness was Thomas Spring Rice, a key grand juror in Limerick and the driver behind the highly praised new radial gaol built for that county and then under construction. He was given an opportunity to highlight the diligence and humanitarian interest of his fellow grand jurors while lending little support to Archer, whom he accused of not taking an interest in the smaller bridewells.[83] The inquiry provided a wealth of information concerning seventeen of the forty Irish county gaols and many smaller bridewells too, but its final report made for uncomfortable reading. Despite a great financial outlay, decades of legislation, and two distinct rebuilding movements, there were still

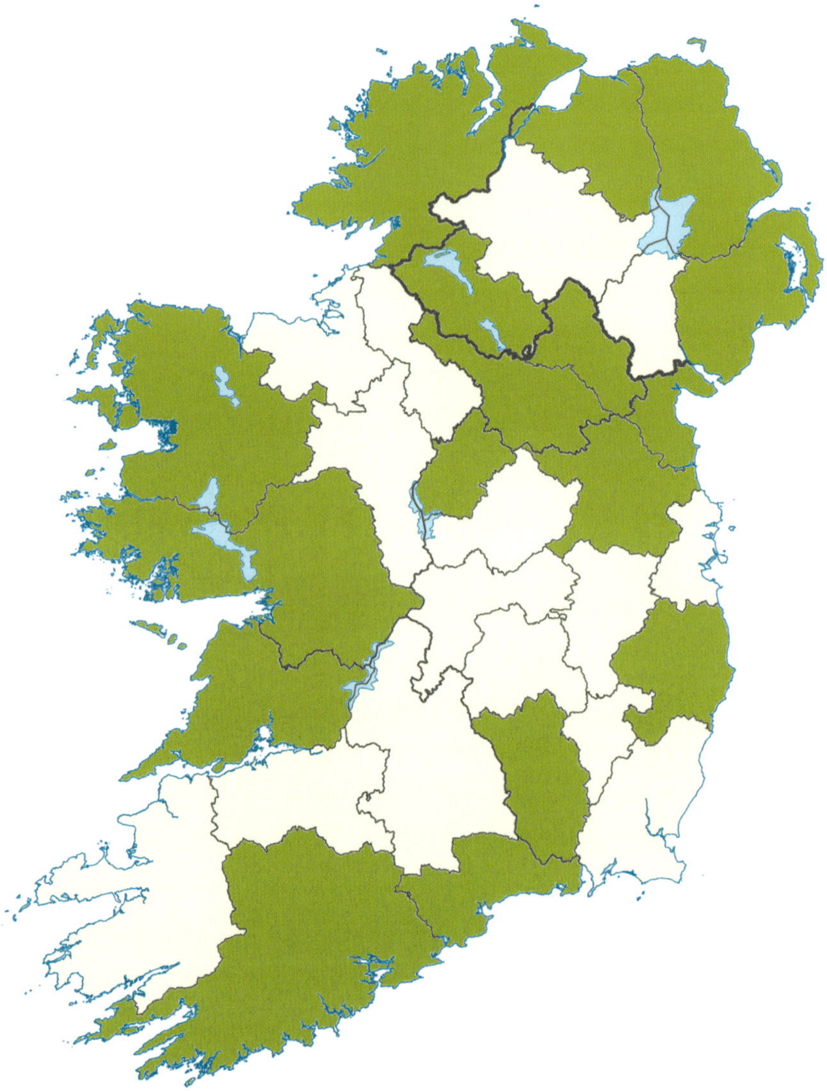

Fig. 5.36. A map showing the counties that replied to a request from the AIPPD in 1819 for information about the number, condition, management, and location of their gaols and bridewells. In all some eighteen of the forty bodies replied, a major achievement for a new private philanthropic society. This work was an obvious encroachment into the responsibilities held by Forster Archer, the increasingly discredited government prison inspector. Compiled from *First Report of the AIPPD*, p. 10.

major problems with both the architecture and the administration of gaols. Increasing crime numbers in the years after around 1813 only added to the difficulties, and the government even toyed with the idea of adding a third assize to lessen the numbers kept in gaols while awaiting trial.[84] At the same time the AIPPD published its own independent report based on information gathered from assize judges, barristers, and other interested persons all around the country. The AIPPD wrote to every county high sheriff asking for detailed descriptions and statistics pertaining to gaols and bridewells. Around half of these officials replied – a significant and unprecedented achievement for a new non-statutory agency (Fig. 5.36) – and the organisation followed up with further probing questions.[85]

The 1819 inquiry revealed the scale of the challenge facing Grant. At the same time the AIPPD usurped Archer's responsibilities and intensified the pressure on grand juries. When the Richmond penitentiary finally opened in 1819, Grant asked the AIPPD to comment on the design; its reply was damning, finding the penitentiary insecure and unhealthy and built to an antiquated and inefficient plan.[86] For a brief moment it seemed likely that Dublin's Newgate would be rebuilt, but objections from the city grand jurors put a halt to the project; in reply the AIPPD staged a competition to select the best design for a new gaol and awarded a prize to a polygonal plan (by an unknown architect).[87] Archer was far more conservative and suggested that with some minor alterations Cooley's old gaol might continue to be used.[88] Though the AIPPD's scheme was not proceeded with, the enthusiasm and proactive spirit of its leaders stood increasingly at odds with Archer's approach. Grant was the AIPPD's most valuable asset, and in 1819 he introduced the first of three Irish prison acts; this simply clarified the appointment of church ministers to gaols.[89] In 1821 he abolished gaol fees, carefully following the wording of the equivalent British act of 1815.[90] But his major achievement was a more extensive legislative measure that he had been planning since at least 1820, with the full endorsement of the AIPPD, which borrowed from one of the SIPD's most influential tracts, *Rules Proposed for the Government of Gaols* (1820).[91]

In May 1821 Grant published the latest version of his proposed major bill on Irish prisons. It noted, with thinly disguised reference to the 1819 inquiry, that 'many bridewells and houses for idiots or lunatics do not appear to have been so visited', and demanded that Archer provide a full list of every prison, large and small, in the country.[92] At the same time Grant listened attentively to the advice of the AIPPD, expressing his hope to one of its officers that he might 'perhaps be able to fulfil the wish of the society [and] shall on every account have pleasure in so doing'. While the leaders of the AIPPD were keen to include provisions for educating and employing prisoners, Grant asked them to reply quickly with their views on a much broader range of prison issues.[93] What Grant had originally described as 'a very short bill' grew with the AIPPD's help into a much more substantive measure. One of the key changes was the wording of the section that set out the role of government inspectors. Because the work of visiting every prison was deemed 'too extensive and arduous for the performance of one officer', the bill permitted the appointment of *two* 'inspectors-general of prisons', who were to divide up the country between them and to visit every prison at least biennially. Their detailed reports were to be sent to grand juries at each assize, and every year a national report was to be prepared for Dublin Castle that would be laid before parliament. The bill set out heavy penalties for inspectors who failed to carry out their duties, and their salaries were to be paid only after their annual reports had been received.[94] In carrying this prison bill through parliament, Grant established a distinctly modern model of prison inspection, based on clear responsibilities and penalties ('modern' being the word that one of the new inspectors himself later used to describe the system).[95] By also requiring the new inspectors to compile a list of all the smaller prisons, the act hinted that further powers could soon be granted to manage or even close notorious local centres of confinement. This possibility soon became reality (as discussed in Chapter 6). By extending the powers of the government inspectors, and by threatening embarrassment to grand jurors through the inspectors' detailed and elegantly composed reports to be laid before parliament, Grant shifted the ethos of Irish prison inspection from a voluntary to a more programmatic code. A clear signal of the dawning new regime appeared when Archer's son Robert failed to succeed his father upon his retirement in late 1821. Dublin Castle officials quickly made clear that Robert Archer would not be recommended, and that Grant had already decided to bring in new blood in order to buttress and consolidate the new powers of central government. 'I could not recommend you,' William Gregory informed Archer, adding that there were other candidates 'better qualified for the situation'.[96]

Gaol building on the eve of the new regime

Grant's 1821 act was the most important rebalancing of power between central and local government in penal issues since 1786 or 1810; the role played by the new inspectors will be discussed in the following chapter.[97] Before these reforms were implemented in Dublin and London, county gaol building continued in Irish provincial towns and cities. In fact, the year 1818 marked the all-time peak for Irish gaol building with no fewer than eighteen different projects underway, seventeen led by grand juries and one – the Richmond penitentiary – managed by central government (Fig. 5.37). Some of the new gaols of the late 1810s followed penal-reform ideas more closely than others. In Mayo an extra storey was added to the county's disgraceful old gaol in Castlebar (Fig. 5.38); it was so badly built that part of it collapsed during construction, killing one person and injuring three.[98] The AIPPD found scandals such as this completely inexplicable in the new era of reform. More promising was the new house of correction built for the Waterford city grand jurors at the edge of their city (Fig. 5.39). Its architect James Elmes was a keen advocate for the polygonal design and he used his small new building at Waterford as a springboard to gain further commissions for larger district penitentiaries in Ireland (a scheme then being considered by government but subsequently abandoned).[99] Nevertheless, with the SIPD and the AIPPD increasingly involved in the practicalities of gaol design, even Elmes

Fig. 5.37. Smithfield penitentiary, Dublin, 1968. Originally the residence of an eighteenth-century judge of the Court of Common Pleas, Robert French, the building was later used as a penitentiary by the Dublin city grand jurors for incarcerating young boys and prostitutes. In 1818, the peak year for gaol building in Irish history, Smithfield was one of eighteen construction projects countrywide; Francis Johnston was tasked with enlarging and altering the penitentiary. It was demolished around 1970. (*Reproduced courtesy of Dublin City Library and Archive.*)

Fig. 5.38. Castlebar, County Mayo, showing the old gaol (at the eastern corner of the green) and its replacement of the 1830s (to the south-west). Ordnance Survey six-inch map, surveyed January 1838. Archer pushed the Mayo grand jurors to build such a new gaol for many years, but they refused and instead added a third storey (which collapsed with disastrous results) around 1819–20 to their cramped, rectilinear-plan gaol built in the 1790s. (*Reproduced courtesy of the Board of Trinity College Dublin.*)

soon appeared out of touch, and within just five years the Waterford house of correction was seen as deficient and insecure.[100] Evans comments that Elmes' treatise *Hints for the Improvement of Prisons* (1817) was little more than a 'mixed bag of derivative nostrums' and that 'the specialized task of prison building was becoming institutionalized' by the new philanthropic societies.[101] Within fifteen years the inspectors proposed abandoning Waterford's new prison altogether, so far had the goalposts moved in the intervening years.[102]

Elsewhere there were more positive signs. In Cork the long-running scandal of the new city gaol was finally quelled in 1819 when construction began again in earnest on a much better (and less waterlogged) site.[103] With generous loans from central government, the city grand jurors made a clear statement of intent by building a gaol bigger than they needed: Nicholas Colthurst, a key figure in the project, estimated that the new gaol provided one-and-a-half times the number

Fig. 5.39. Waterford city house of correction, elevation and ground-floor plan. James Elmes, 23 September 1820. By 1818 the old city gaol near Gandon's courthouse was overcrowded, and the city jurors elected to commission an entirely separate polygonal-plan gaol from the English architect James Elmes; this was built at the edge of the city in 1820 and 1821. It was abandoned when a new joint gaol was built for the county and city in 1860–3, and it has since been demolished. (*Reproduced courtesy of the Director of the National Archives of Ireland.*)

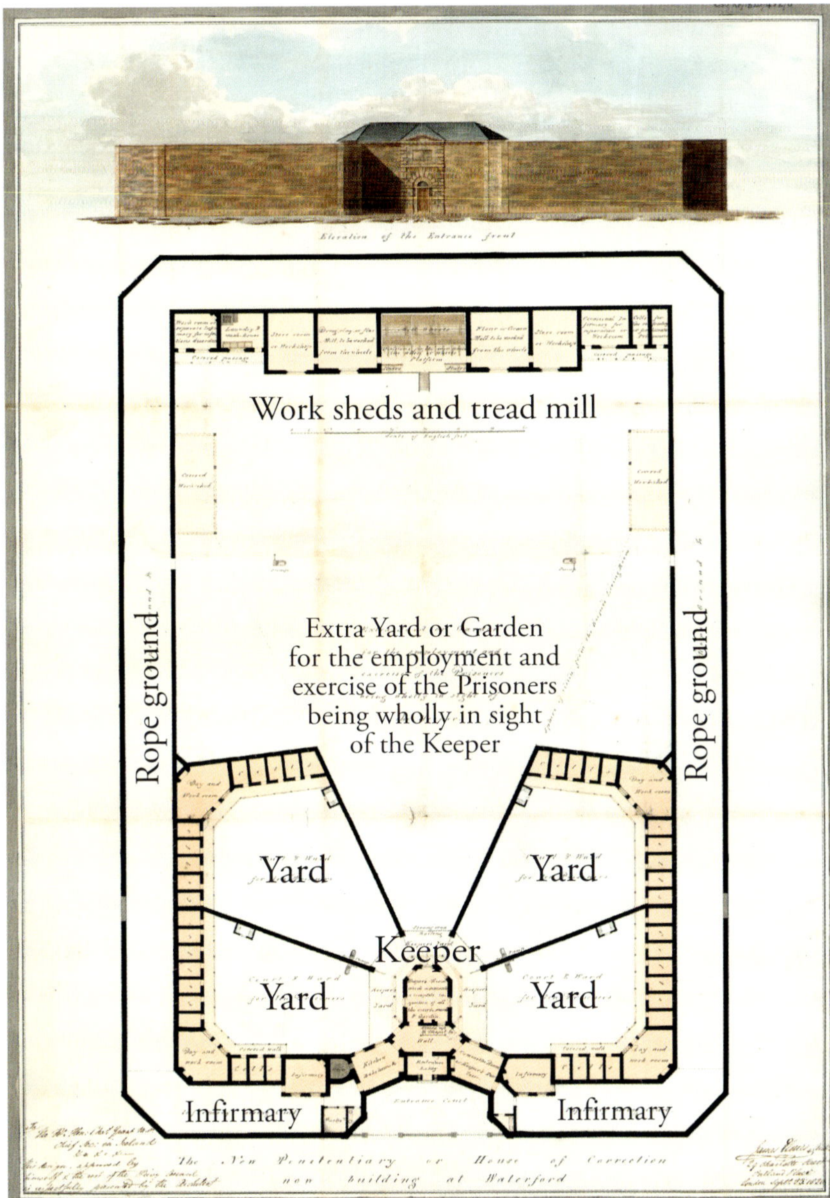

of cells required based on recent maximum-occupancy figures. The reason for this unusual approach was the hope of the grand jurors that they could earn revenues from using parts of the gaol to house convicts due for transportation from Cove (now Cobh).[104] In previous years the problem for central government had often been that of forcing reluctant grand juries to expand and improve their gaols; now central government tried to rein in an extravagant and oversized design. One of the new inspectors was glad in late 1822 that the building of the debtors' cells and the governor's house had not begun as the 'extent of the plan was preposterous'.[105] Five years and £40,400 worth of loans later, the gaol finally opened.[106] Its double-radial plan owed some debt to James Bevans' 1815 design for the Wakefield pauper lunatic asylum, but he appears not to have been involved in the Cork city project and the layout of corridors and cells within each of the radial blocks was in any case quite different (Figs 5.40, 5.41).[107] When the prisoners were moved in 1824, the old North Gate gaol, one of the very few gaols remaining from the early eighteenth century still in use, was finally abandoned and demolished. Robertson surrounded its replacement with a high boundary wall and a Gothic Revival gatehouse, praised by one contemporary observer for appearing like 'a great fortress' (Fig. 5.42).[108] The real achievement, however, was behind the façade, and after nearly twenty years of on-and-off building the city grand jurors finally had a gaol that provided adequate classification, ventilation, and inspection. Afterwards they committed themselves to little new building work until the 1850s.

On the other side of the Lee the Cork county grand jurors built a large addition to their relatively new gaol at the same time. After years of neglect and disinterest the issue of penal reform finally appeared on the jurors' agenda, and Johnston approved a design for a house of correction adjacent to Shanahan's rectilinear gaol in late 1818.[109] As previously noted, the gaol was so overcrowded, and the level of crime in the county so pronounced, that the addition could not

Fig. 5.40. Yorkshire West Riding (Wakefield) pauper lunatic asylum, ground-floor plan. James Bevans, 15 March 1815. Frederick O'Dwyer has suggested a link between this double-radial-plan design and William Robertson's Cork city gaol, but apart from a general similarity, they share few details, and there is no evidence that Bevans ever visited Cork. There were, however, strong similarities between the planning of prisons and of mental hospitals. From *Report … on Provisions for Better Regulation of Madhouses in England*, H.C. 1814–15 (295), iv, plate 5.

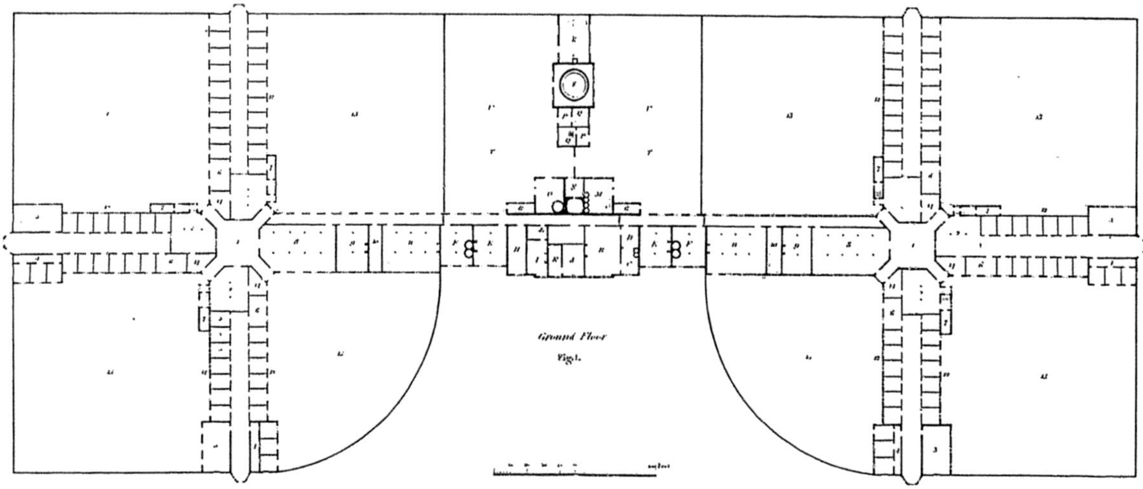

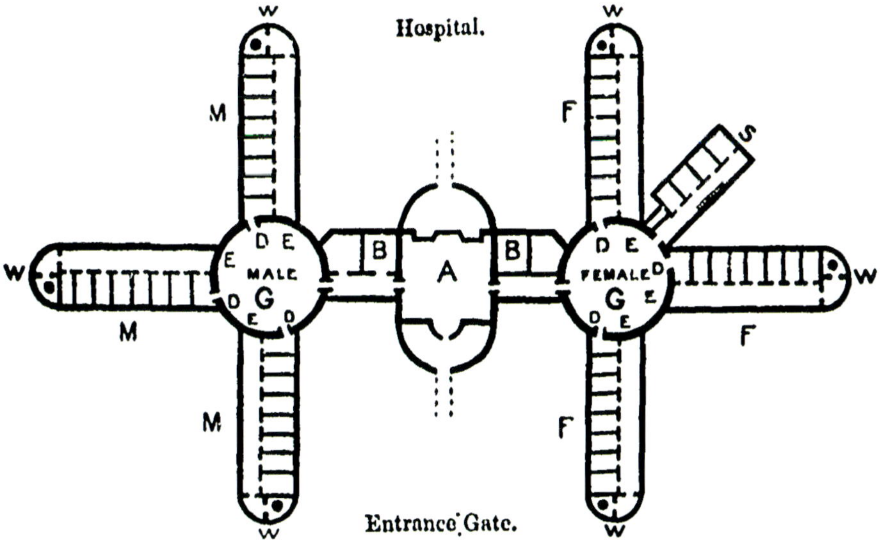

Fig. 5.41. Cork city gaol, ground-floor plan, 1870. Apart from the eight female separate-system cells added in 1851–2 (marked 'S'), this drawing shows the gaol as Robertson built it in 1819–24, and before the reconstruction of the west wing (marked 'W M') later in the nineteenth century. The completion of the gaol in the 1820s ended a twenty-year saga of misappropriated funds, jobbery, and incompetence. From *Forty-eighth Report … on … the Prisons of Ireland, 1869*, H.C. 1870 (C. 173), xxxvii, p. 307.

Fig. 5.42. Cork city gaol, from the south. Hermann von Puckler-Muskau, visiting in 1828, considered the prison a 'magnificent building' that 'has the appearance of a great fortress'. (*Photograph by author, 2017.*)

have come soon enough. The architects were James Pain, who had built a new city gaol in Limerick a few years earlier, and his brother George Richard. Though the decision to undertake the new addition predated the AIPPD's influence over gaol design, the Pains must have been following the latest trends in Britain, as they proposed a radial scheme that won the praise of contemporary critics.[110] For most of the 1820s the Cork county gaol was seen as one of the most distinguished such institutions in the south of Ireland, and coupled with the large-scale rebuilding of bridewells in the county that soon followed, it established the Cork grand jurors as leading rather than trailing in prison-reform circles. The Pains' house of correction provided seventy-eight additional cells in a relatively cramped site and was elegantly built in local limestone (Figs 5.43, 5.44). The Doric portico and its adjoining bridge, attributed to George Richard Pain alone

Fig. 5.43. Central-inspection building, house of correction, Cork county gaol, from the south-west, *c.* 1950. Between 1819 and 1824 George Richard Pain added a large radial-plan extension to Cork's overcrowded county gaol (compare with Fig. 4.48). For many years afterwards his design was seen as a model design for gaols throughout Ireland. From David Lee, *James Pain, Architect* (Limerick: Limerick Civic Trust, 2005), p. 77. (*Reproduced courtesy of Limerick Civic Trust.*)

Fig. 5.44. Cork county gaol, ground-floor plan, 1870. A vast, sprawling complex of buildings, the gaol was primarily composed of Shanahan's rectilinear-plan gaol from the early 1800s (top) and Pain's radial-plan gaol from the early 1820s (bottom). By 1870, Pain's blocks had been rebuilt to align with the 'separate system' (see Chapter 7). Today only the celebrated portico screen survives; the rest has been appropriated by University College Cork. From *Forty-eighth Report … on … the Prisons of Ireland, 1869*, H.C. 1870 (C. 173), xxxvii, p. 284.

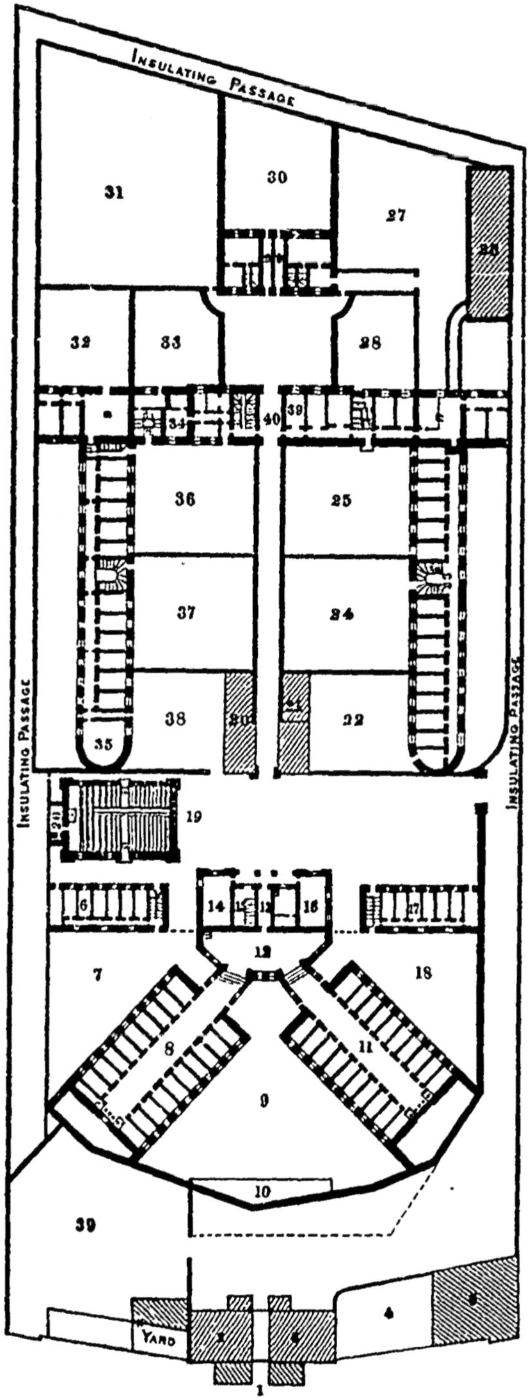

Reference to Ground Plan.

1. Entrance.
2. Guard-room. Gatekeeper's rooms overhead.
3. Lumber room. Warder's room overhead.
4. Governor's yard.
5. Do. house.
6. Block containing 15 cells.
7. Exercise yard.
. Block containing 60 cells for separate use.
9. Exercise yard.
10. Treadwheels.
11. Block containing 60 cells for separate use.
12. Inspection hall. Hospital rooms overhead.
13. Entrance to Inspection hall.
14. Gaol office, with two rooms overhead, latter approachable from Inspection hall.
15. Chief Warder's apartments.
16. Board-room and Governor's office, with two rooms overhead, latter approachable from Inspection hall.
17. Block containing 15 cells.
18. Exercise yard.
19 Chapel.
20. Vestry or robing room.
20. Building which will be probably fitted with baths, &c., for male prisoners.
21. Do. do. female prisoners.
22. Yard attached to do.
23. Female prison containing 41 cells for separate use.
24. Exercise yard.
25. Do.
26. Laundry block, with 12 stalls, and ironing room, and having 24 small cells overhead.
27. Laundry yard.
28. Yard which will probably be reserved for use of matron and sub-matron.
29. Block containing 27 small cells.
30. Yard.
31. Will be used as a garden.
32. Pauper deb'ors' yard.
33. Master debtors' yard.
34. Large block, with officers' apartments on ground and middle floors, with rooms for master and pauper debtors, also female hospital rooms. No communication between the different departments exists.
35. Block containing 34 large airy cells.
36. Exercise yard.
37. Do.
38. Yard attached to building No. 20.
39. Large yard containing coal, straw stores, &c., also ash-pit.

Fig. 5.45. (above) Cork county gaol, from the city gaol, looking south, 1831. Behind the Greek portico, which survives, we can see Pain's radial cell blocks and the central-inspection hub. These were demolished around 1960. From G.N. Wright, *Ireland Illustrated, from Original Drawings* (London: Fisher, Son & Jackson, 1831), pp. 66–7.

Fig. 5.46. (left) Cork county gaol, portico, screen, and bridge over one channel of the River Lee. One of the most powerful essays in prison architecture in Ireland, Pain's portico adopted the Delian Doric order (likely via Stuart and Revett's *The Antiquities of Athens* (1762)), while the corbelled arch over the main doorway was more Egyptian in inspiration. Contemporary observers as well as later critics have admired the composition. (*Photograph by author, 2013.*)

and built between 1824 and 1825, has won the approval of architectural historians for its powerful and sober design (Figs 5.45, 5.46). Even the new inspectors – not known for their interest in architectural ornamentation – commented that the façade was 'handsome'.[111]

At the same time James Pain built a new radial gaol for Limerick county (Figs 5.47, 5.48) that, more than his earlier city gaol, made explicit reference to Nash's radial gaols in Wales and Hereford of the 1790s. Government loans of £14,000 (two-thirds of the total cost) and the influence of Spring Rice and other prominent reformers in the area ensured that the Limerick county gaol would be built quickly and that Smyth's inadequate gaol in the city centre would be handed over for the city's use alone.[112] The new county gaol provided around 125 cells, divided into ten classes.[113] Thomas Reid, visiting in 1822, considered the design excellent and 'inferior to none in Europe'.[114] Rockite violence in the following years tested the gaol's capacity, but the inspectors remained broadly happy with its design until the mid-1830s.[115] Meanwhile in Derry, the grand jurors commissioned a large addition to their 1790s gaol from the firm of Henry, Mullins & McMahon (Figs 5.49, 5.50).[116] This addition took the form of a vast polygonal range to the rear of the existing building, and there were also Gothic Revival extensions facing the street on either side of it (of which one tower survives) (Fig. 5.51). When these additions were completed in 1824, the capacity of the gaol increased by 118 and the segregation of eleven different classes was possible; the old gaol became the county's marshalsea.[117] As an indicator of the increasing sophistication of gaol building from this time onwards, the total cost of the extension was over £33,000, a sum almost entirely financed by government loans.[118] One visitor in 1825 was perhaps only slightly exaggerating when he claimed the gaol was, 'as is usual in these days, … the most handsomest thing in the town'.[119]

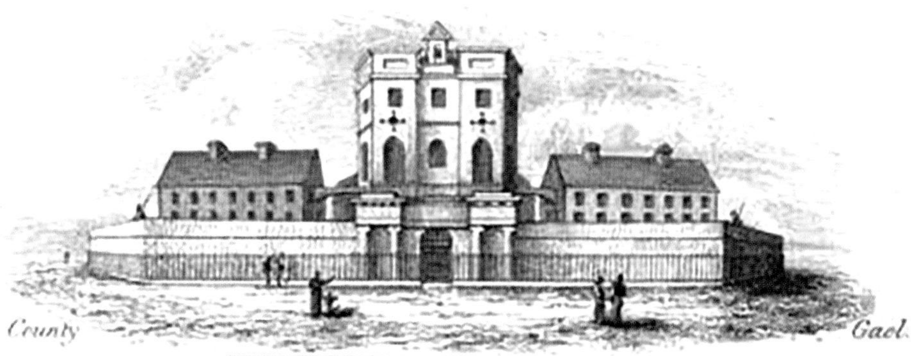

Fig. 5.47. Limerick county gaol, from the north. While his brother George Richard worked in Cork, James Pain built a new radial-plan gaol for the Limerick county grand jurors between 1817 and 1821. As it neared completion, the city of Limerick was marked by sustained unrest and labour struggle. While the façade was more restrained than that in Cork, the gaol won praise from all quarters for its plan and quality of construction. Unusually, it continues to serve as a prison today. From Patrick Fitzgerald and John James McGregor, *The History, Topography, and Antiquities of the County and City of Limerick*, 2 vols (Dublin: McKern, 1827), vol. 2, p. 578.

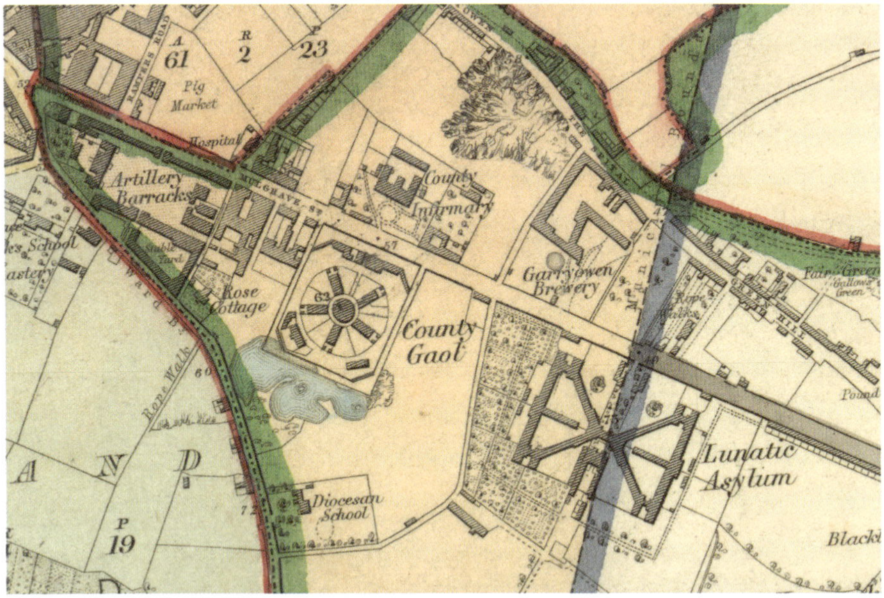

Fig. 5.48. Artillery barracks, county infirmary, county gaol, and district lunatic asylum, to the west of Limerick city. Ordnance Survey six-inch map, surveyed January 1840. Like Grangegorman in Dublin, the western suburbs of Limerick developed a pronounced institutional character in the early nineteenth century. The five radial blocks of Pain's county gaol, since greatly altered, are visible here. (*Reproduced courtesy of the Board of Trinity College Dublin.*)

Fig. 5.49. Derry gaol, from the west, *c.* 1960. Between 1820 and 1824 the firm of Henry, Mullins & McMahon added a vast polygonal extension to the rear of Miller's gaol of the 1790s. It was one of the most expensive projects of its time and benefited from nearly £30,000 in central-government loans. (*Reproduced courtesy of the Irish Architectural Archive.*)

Fig. 5.50. (left) Derry gaol, ground-floor plan, 1870. While the polygonal range was technically an extension, in which male prisoners were kept after 1824, it was so large (118 cells divided into eleven classes) that it might as easily be considered a wholly new gaol. The architects also added extensions on both sides of the original street-facing building. From *Forty-ninth Report ... on ... the Prisons of Ireland, 1870*, H.C. 1871 (C. 359), xxx, p. 169.

Fig. 5.51. (right) The surviving turret of Derry's gaol, from the north. After the expensive building works of the 1820s the Derry grand jurors hardly altered the gaol until it closed in 1953. Twenty years later, it was demolished to make way for social housing, leaving only this turret of 1824 by Henry, Mullins & McMahon (compare with Fig. 4.35). (*Photograph by author, 2014.*)

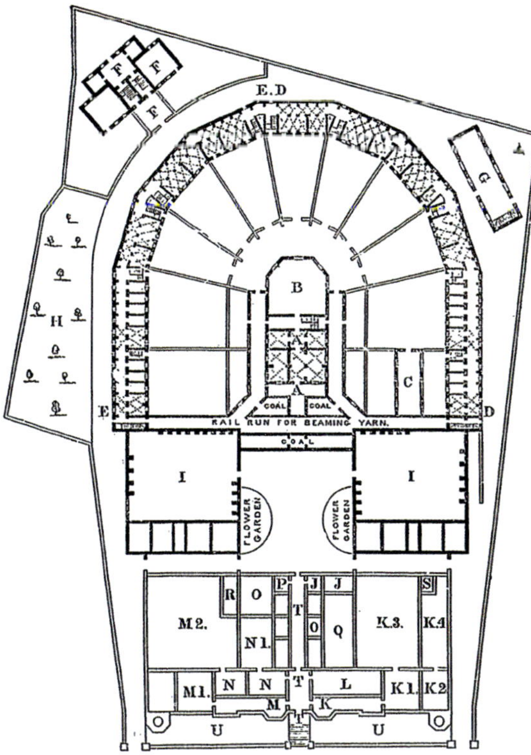

The new gaols in Cork, Limerick, and Derry were begun before the new central-government inspectors took office, but in general they were not completed until the mid-1820s. Though each of their designs was approved by Johnston, none received the detailed examination and pedantic scrutiny that the new inspectors Palmer and Woodward as well as the AIPPD would bring to gaol design in the years after Grant's reforms took effect in 1821. But these gaols were undoubtedly all costly and carefully considered projects; they were indicative of the growing specialisation in gaol building and showed that at least some grand jurors were taking more seriously the condition of their major prisons. This increased specialisation and greater attention given to technical aspects of prison design must count as the main achievement of the first two decades after the Act of Union, despite the constantly moving targets and sometimes conflicting opinions of the reformers, and despite the many deficient gaols that continued to be built elsewhere.

114 FT
Surrounding
Area
Pool
2nd Class
3rd Class
Day Room
1st Class
Inspection Room
IMPROVEMENTS
Pleasure Ground
Waste

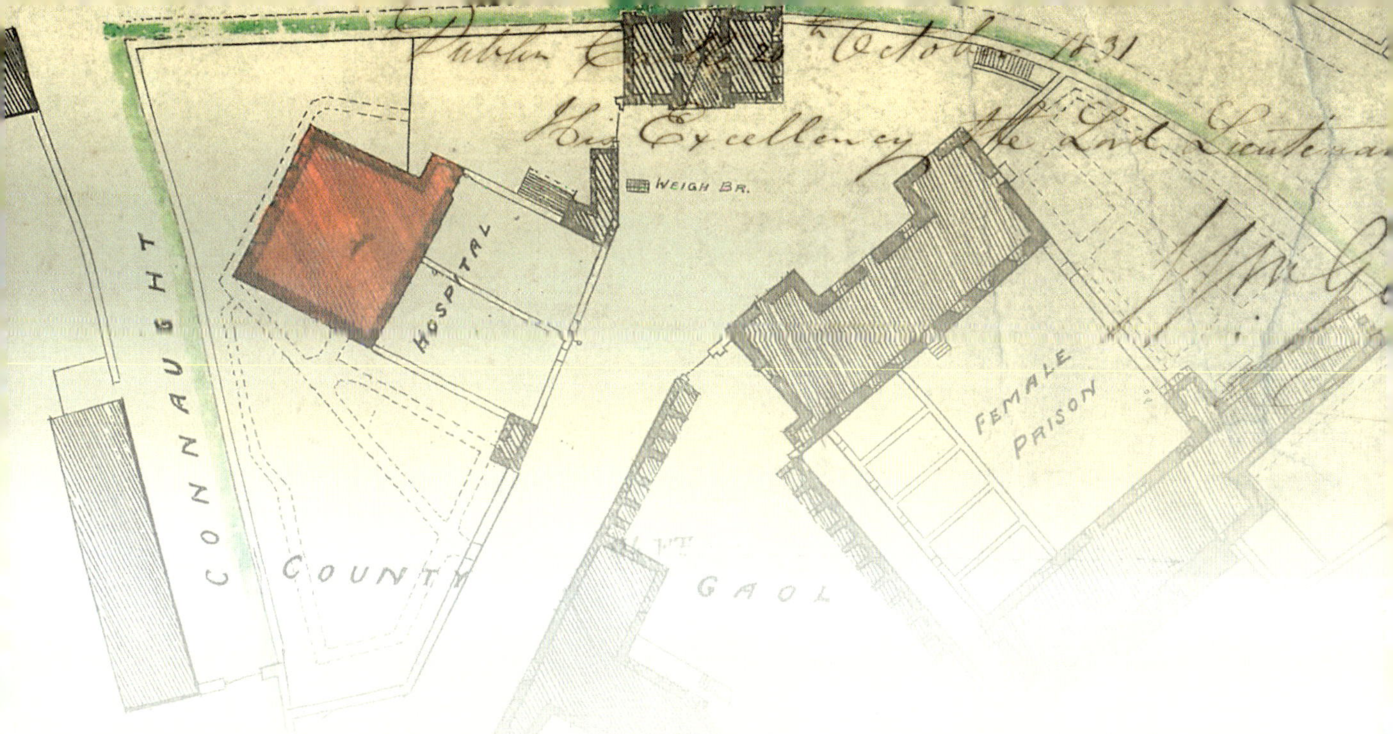

Chapter 6

The New Regime:

James Palmer, Benjamin Woodward, and grand-jury responses to the renewed call for penal reform, 1821-38

Charles Grant's Prisons Act of 1821 received the royal assent in the summer of 1821.[1] As noted in the preceding chapter, the measure allowed the Irish government to appoint two new prison inspectors to replace the discredited Forster Archer. These were James Palmer (*c.* 1780–1850) and Benjamin Blake Woodward (*c.* 1767–1841), and both were known to Grant before the new vacancies arose. Palmer (Fig. 6.1) was an army veteran, son of an archdeacon of the diocese of Ossory, and grandson of a former high sheriff of County Fermanagh. He retired with the rank of major in 1813 and secured a post as a collector of excise at Cove.[2] Keen to live in Dublin, he canvassed Robert Peel, unsuccessfully, for a surveyorship position at Ringsend in 1816. Another opportunity arose in 1820 when Grant set about reforming the Dublin House of Industry, replacing its five unpaid governors with a single salaried official.[3] Palmer lobbied for the position, and with the endorsement of Sir David Baird at the Royal Hospital in Kilmainham, he was appointed by Grant in October 1820 with a salary of £500.[4] Palmer spent fourteen months leading the House of Industry before being offered one of the new inspectorate positions. A devout high-church Protestant, he recognised how arduous the job was going to be, but considered that it was a providential calling and he enthusiastically acceded to Grant's request.[5] The other new inspector, Benjamin Woodward, was a son of the celebrated Protestant Bishop of Cloyne, Richard Woodward (1726–94), whose *Present State of the Church of Ireland* (1787) had established him as a leading voice of Protestant Ascendancy in late eighteenth-century Ireland.[6] Benjamin trained as a lawyer, held rank as an army major, had been MP for Midleton in the old Irish parliament between 1794 and 1800, and had served as a treasurer of the Cork infirmary.[7] His father was involved in the running of the House of Industry in Dublin, and this proved a useful institutional reference for his son, who was in turn appointed by Grant to the board of the Westmoreland Lock Hospital in Dublin in 1820.[8] Sixteen months later, he was asked to be the other new prison inspector, an opportunity that he quickly grasped, noting that it would be 'much more permanent than my present office', and came with a salary of £500 in addition to significant clerical and travel expenses.[9] Grant's appointments were one of his last actions as chief secretary, and within a few days he was replaced by Henry Goulburn (1784–1856), a close ally of Peel and

Fig. 6.1. James Palmer (*c.* 1780–1850), in an 1826 portrait. Palmer was one of the two new prison inspectors appointed by Charles Grant towards the end of his tenure as Irish chief secretary. (*Reproduced courtesy of the DuLong family.*)

someone who was less passionately interested in penal reform, but nevertheless set about completing the reforms initiated by his predecessor.[10]

One of the first issues facing Palmer and Woodward was the proposal to build one or more large provincial penitentiaries in Ireland to replace the existing county-gaol system.[11] Peel suggested similar radical reforms in Britain at this time – with counties coming together to jointly build and manage larger and more efficient prisons – but the scheme floundered amid local disagreements. His rationale was simple: if classification needed to be increased, and kitchens and hospitals and work-rooms provided for prisoners, it would make economic sense to amalgamate smaller old buildings into purpose-built large institutions.[12] In Ireland, the new provincial lunatic asylums built after 1817 were born out of the same principle of consolidation; these large institutions replaced the haphazard assortment of cells previously allocated to the insane in county gaols and infirmaries across the country. As noted in Chapter 5, architects such as James Elmes were keen to try and secure some of the large commissions for these new penitentiaries, and he repeatedly lobbied Grant in 1820 and 1821 but to no avail.[13] Like Peel, Goulburn backed down from this plan in the early 1820s, faced with potentially large central-government financial outlays, uncertain support from grand jurors, and the scale of renovations and additions to county gaols recently carried out all around the country. This can be regarded as the third great rebuilding programme of Irish gaols (Figs 6.2, 6.3). However, in some counties such as Queen's (now Laois), uncertainty over future penitentiaries had the effect of holding up plans for a new gaol for several years, and once the scheme was formally dropped, local building work proceeded rapidly.[14]

We should question how Palmer and Woodward managed to instigate such a renewed energy in Irish prison building. The answers are many. First, they were

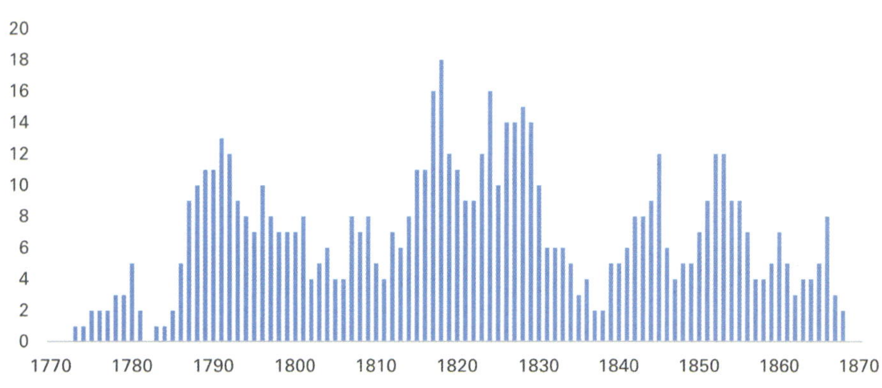

Fig. 6.2. Graph showing the number of gaols that were under construction in Ireland between 1770 and 1870. The third building boom between around 1821 and 1838 is apparent. At the peaks of building activity in 1824 and 1828, nearly half of all gaols were being altered, extended, or built anew. Compiled from Appendix A.

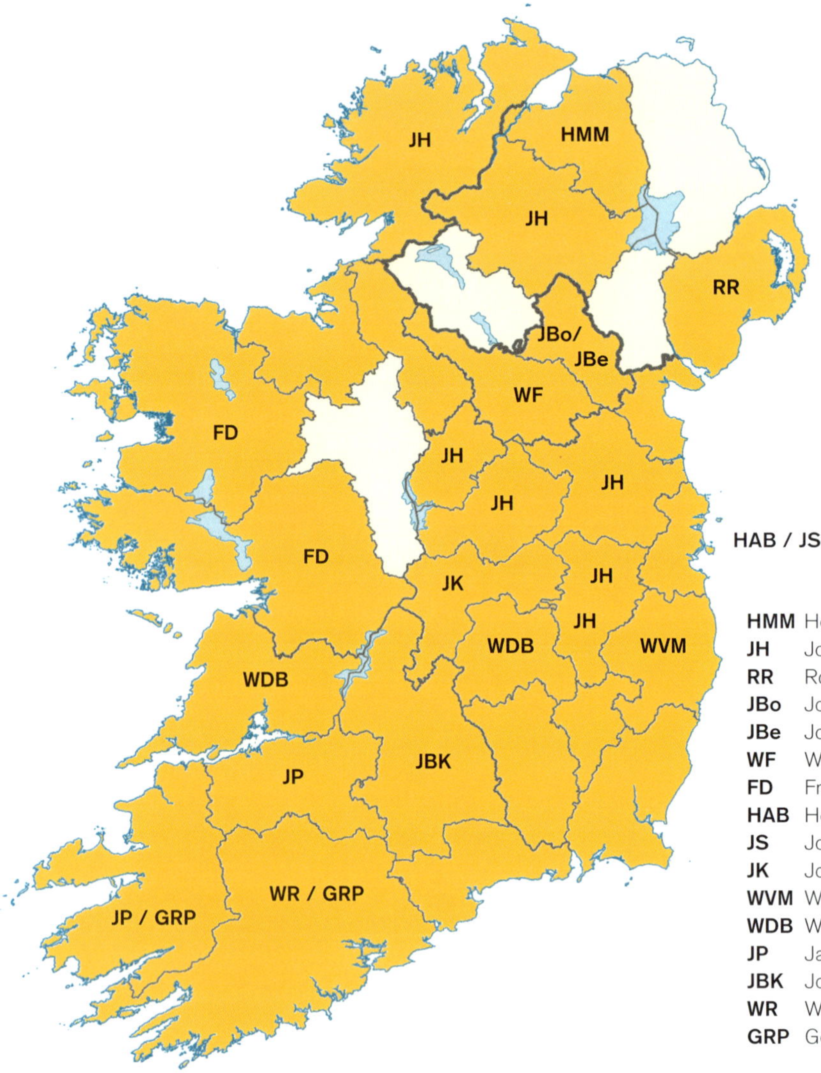

Fig. 6.3. A map showing new county gaols, or large additions made to existing gaols, in Ireland between 1821 and 1838, with the architect responsible marked, where known. Palmer and Woodward oversaw the third major rebuilding of Irish gaols in the space of sixty years; many of the additions that were built were so large that they can be seen as entirely new gaols in their own right. Generous loans from central government made the rebuilding programme possible.

HMM Henry, Mullins & McMahon
JH John Hargrave
RR Robert Reid
JBo John Bowden
JBe John Behan
WF William Farrell
FD Frederick Darley
HAB Henry Aaron Baker
JS John Semple
JK John Killaly
WVM William Vitruvius Morrison
WDB William Deane Butler
JP James Pain
JBK John B. Keane
WR William Robertson
GRP George Richard Pain

familiar with the new rhetoric of the Association for the Improvement of Prisons and of Prison Discipline (AIPPD), and its British counterpart – the SIPD – and they became spokespersons for these societies rather than – as Archer had been – the target of their criticisms. Both men were energetic, relatively young, and driven by an evangelical interest in the condition of prisoners and the poor. They travelled far more extensively around the country than Archer had in the preceding decades.[15] Their annual reports became documents of public notoriety at each assizes, with judges generally reading their conclusions and criticisms to each grand jury, and they were published at length in the national and provincial press (as briefly mentioned in Chapter 2). For the judges who sought to push grand jurors into action, these reports (the first of which appeared in February 1823) provided crucial evidence and ammunition, and formed the background to often rather spirited condemnations of deficient gaols.[16] Finally, the 1821 act clarified the preferred design and operation of gaols, and an amending measure the following year gave central government the power, for the first time, to shut down small bridewells that failed to meet the inspectors' approval. In some large counties, district bridewells were established as half-way houses between normal bridewells and county gaols; prisoners could be kept there for extended periods in order to reduce the cost of moving them to and from the county gaol. The 1822 act also allowed government to establish these bridewells wherever necessary, and explicitly restated the 1810 measure that no prison of any kind could be built without first being approved by the inspectors, the Board of Works, and the government.[17]

Large extra funds for public-works loans, a response to the economic failures and partial famine of the early 1820s, soothed the process of reform, with £250,000 granted in 1822, £100,000 the following year, and £300,000 more in 1825.[18] A significant portion of this went to gaol-building projects: between 1821 and 1838 a total of £262,000 was loaned to twenty-three grand juries for these projects, or an average of £11,400 each. This was broadly similar to what had occurred in the 1810s, but the geographical spread was now more even (Fig. 6.4). The largest single amount, totalling over £42,000, went to the Down grand jurors for their important large new radial gaol at Downpatrick (to be discussed shortly). Some Leinster counties clustered near Dublin were also major beneficiaries of loans, such as Kildare, where two new gaols were built, and Meath, where the grand jury erected a large radial gaol in Trim. The smallest loan, for just £100, was issued to the Dublin County grand jurors to allow them to pay an architect for some unexecuted drawings he had prepared for an addition to their gaol at Kilmainham.[19] Other small amounts, such as the £320 issued to the Leitrim grand jurors, were probably used to erect tread-wheels in gaols where prisoners were forced to exercise. This was a new idea in penal reform that was hastily adapted in the 1820s despite ample evidence that it was inhumane and injurious to prisoners' health.[20] Excluding these small amounts, the average loan was £13,000, and in those cases where entirely new gaols were built, this figure rose to £21,000. By way of comparison, this latter figure was about half the total amount taken in local (grand-jury) taxes in a mid-sized county such as Clare at this time.[21]

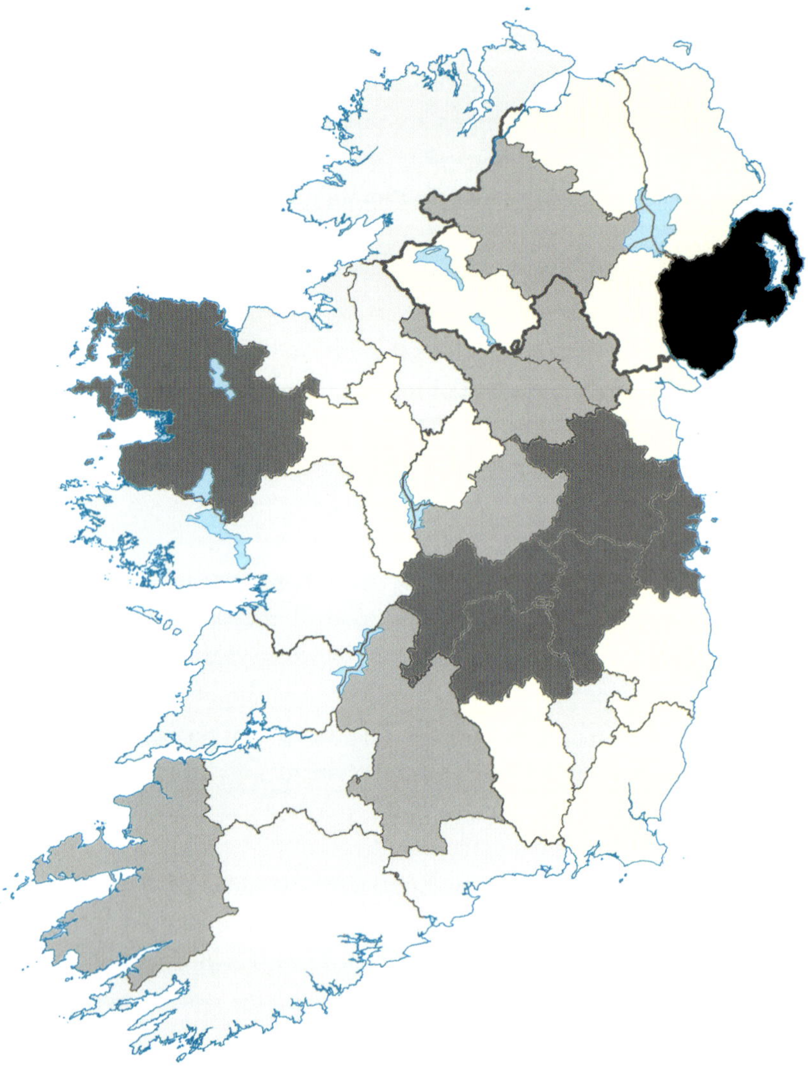

Fig. 6.4. A map showing central-government loans to Irish grand juries for gaol building between 1821 and 1838. Weightings are by percentage of the total sum: light grey (1–3%), grey (3–6%), dark grey (6–10%), and black (above 10%). County Down received the greatest sum (£42,461), and County Dublin the least (£100), but neighbouring Dublin city gained much more (£24,600), to help rebuild Richmond bridewell. The five Leinster counties of Dublin, Meath, Kildare, King's, and Queen's received almost half (£99,988) of the total amount loaned during this period; the populous counties in the south-west, who had benefited handsomely in the 1810s, received less at this time.

In their first report, Palmer and Woodward commented that Irish gaols had been 'principally erected prior to the enactment of those laws on which the modern principles of prison discipline are founded' and were thus defective in terms of the four key concerns of the AIPPD: classification, inspection, labour, and education. This was despite the fact that so many of these gaols were newly built and shows how penal reform was a constantly evolving science. Only the polygonal gaols at Sligo, Roscommon, and Galway met their highest approval, as well as the new radial gaol in Limerick. Many others did not provide sufficient classification (Antrim, Armagh, Louth), were too small (Fermanagh,

Cavan, Drogheda), or were half-ruined (Down, Westmeath, Carrickfergus). Worst of all were those gaols where grand jurors had failed to recognise that remedial work was required, such as in Meath and Kildare. Their report paints, it can be argued, a particularly negative picture of Irish gaols; perhaps this is slightly undeserved, as a number of the large extensions noted at the end of the preceding chapter, such as in Cork and Derry, were still under construction when Palmer and Woodward made their first national survey. Elsewhere in their report they remarked that during 1822 they had in fact made two tours of inspection, and they considered that 'very great improvement' had taken place in the meantime.[22]

The new inspectors recognised that healthy and safe gaols required more than good architectural designs. From the beginning of their tenure, they took up the other AIPPD issues such as employment and education and, in later years, the issue of female prisoners. 'Too much comparative importance,' they stated,

> has been attached to the nature of the building, too much want of prison discipline and order has been attributed to defective plans, and that grand juries have been often unnecessarily induced to expend large sums of money in the erection of new gaols [when instead there was] a want of conscientious and efficient officers, of attentive committees, of effectual inspection, and of order and cleanliness in the gaol.[23]

In other words, a 'good' gaol run by a 'bad' gaoler was still a 'bad' gaol. As the 1820s progressed, the issue of solving architectural problems proved far less burdensome than solving management issues, and in their second report they noted that the architectural plan of a gaol was 'but the machinery' by which a well-regulated institution should be run. To deal with these 'softer' problems, the inspectors scored an early success with the widespread establishment of what became known as Boards of Superintendence, comprised of committees of between six and twelve grand jurors or magistrates who took in hand the day-to-day management of a county's gaol and bridewells. Grant first proposed them as a reforming measure in his 1821 Prisons Act for certain counties where grand jurors were too occupied with 'public business of great importance' to take notice of their prisons. Boards of Superintendence also revolutionised the management of smaller bridewells in a way that surpassed even the inspectors' expectations.[24]

We may question the inspectors' apparent questioning of the importance of the architecture of prisons. Whatever about their pronouncement in their early reports, we should not overstate the focus that they put on the issues of management. The vast majority of each of their reports was still concerned with architecture, planning, and design. Throughout the 1820s, they ranked gaols every year into eight classes solely based on their architecture. If a bad gaoler made for a bad gaol, then the corollary was also true: a good gaoler could do little in a bad gaol. Administrative problems could only be tackled when the building itself was satisfactory. For example, if a gaol did not allow the separation of men and women, as was still – scandalously by this time – the case in Carrickfergus, Athy, and in many small bridewells, no amount of earnest instruction or employment could prevent the obvious moral hazards that vexed the inspectors. The Tyrone-born army surgeon Thomas Reid did a tour of Irish prisons in the early days of the new regime, in the summer of 1822, and though he was more interested in administrative issues, it was architecture and design that he most often commented upon on his travels. He thought the plan of Armagh's gaol was 'originally bad and no alteration can make it good'. In Kerry, the plan was bad and the gaol simply too small. In Limerick, the city gaol was old and bad: 'if I say the building is old,' Reid helpfully commented, 'it is almost unnecessary to add that [it] is bad.'[25]

Architecture – and especially the plan or layout of a gaol – was a hotly debated topic among British and Irish penal reformers in the early 1820s, as both sides argued over the relative advantages of the radial and polygonal plans.[26] Elevations, sections, and details of design were of much less significance. We see this in differing views at the time. Reid entered this debate only to implicitly support the polygonal plan when he praised the architect John Hargrave, who was then building many polygonal additions to Irish gaols.[27] Others were less equivocal. The AIPPD bluntly stated that once a design had been selected, a gaol 'can never afterwards be effectually corrected', and thus the issue needed to be settled from the outset. Referring to a similar debate then happening within the British SIPD, they noted a growing preference there for the radial design.[28] Robin Evans has tabulated that between 1801 and 1832, at least thirty radial gaols were built in England as opposed to just eight polygonal ones (Fig. 6.5).[29] The AIPPD felt somewhat behind the curve on developments on the other island. In their 1819 competition to select a design for a replacement to Dublin's Newgate, they had chosen a polygonal plan – which they quickly regretted. 'It is probable', they considered, that this decision 'has caused the adoption of the semi-circular plan, in some instances, in this kingdom'. In stating their preference for the radial plan, they listed three main reasons. First, the position of the gaoler in his free-standing central hub meant that whenever he wished to enter the day-rooms or corridors of the gaol, he first had to walk across a yard; he would thus be seen by prisoners, who would prepare themselves for his inspection. 'The important advantage,' the AIPPD argued, 'of having the prisoners under constant inspection, while they are themselves unconscious of being so, is in a great measure sacrificed.' Second, when polygonal gaols did not open to the south, they were liable to be unhealthy for prisoners simply because – especially in winter – the sun would rarely reach parts of the range of cells. At Brixton House of Correction in Surrey, the gaol had been built facing north and its yards were known to be 'damp and comfortless'. Third, it was difficult to expand a polygonal gaol to provide more cells, though some architects (such as Richard Ingleman at Sligo) attempted this by building ranges connecting the polygon itself to the central hub; this, of course, was little more than a radial arrangement by another name. In summary, the AIPPD recommended the radial design for all future gaols and even presented Goulburn with a 'model' radial gaol immediately upon its arrival in this country; the society later kept this model in their Dublin offices and urged grand jurors to visit and examine

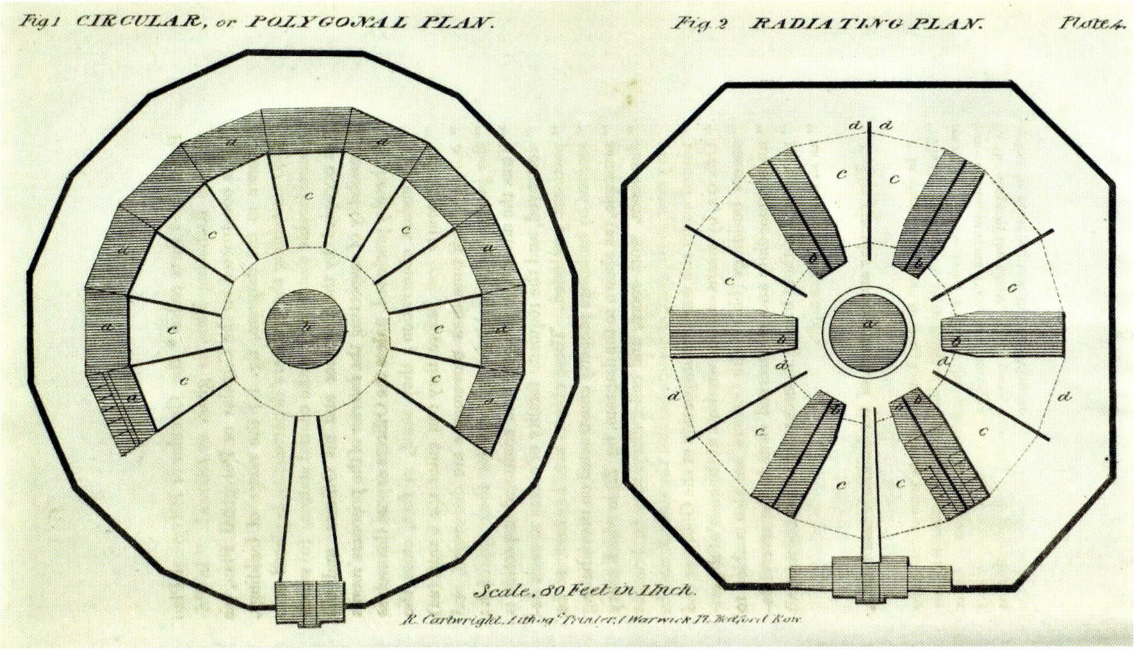

Fig. 6.5. The polygonal (left) and radial (right) plans. The relative advantages of both designs were hotly debated by penal reformers in the early 1820s, the latter eventually emerging as the preferred 'model'. From George Holford, *An Account of Millbank Penitentiary* (London: Rivington, 1828) p. 372.

it.[30] In their professionalising of the design of gaols, there was increasingly little flexibility for architects, or indeed for grand jurors.

The tussle between the two plans continued in London for some more years. The enormous Millbank penitentiary was under construction throughout the 1820s, and it was a polygonal gaol *par excellence*; its design had influential supporters in parliament such as George Holford. However, the issue was settled once and for all in 1826, when the SIPD published their *Remarks on the Form and Construction of Prisons*, which recommended only the radial plan (Fig. 6.6). In the many new gaols begun in Ireland in the early 1820s, we see an even balance between both plans, with the radial winning out by the middle of the decade. One architect – John Hargrave – emerged as the leading figure in the rebuilding movement and was endorsed by Reid as a man of 'first-rate talent, unwearied industry and inflexible integrity'.[31]

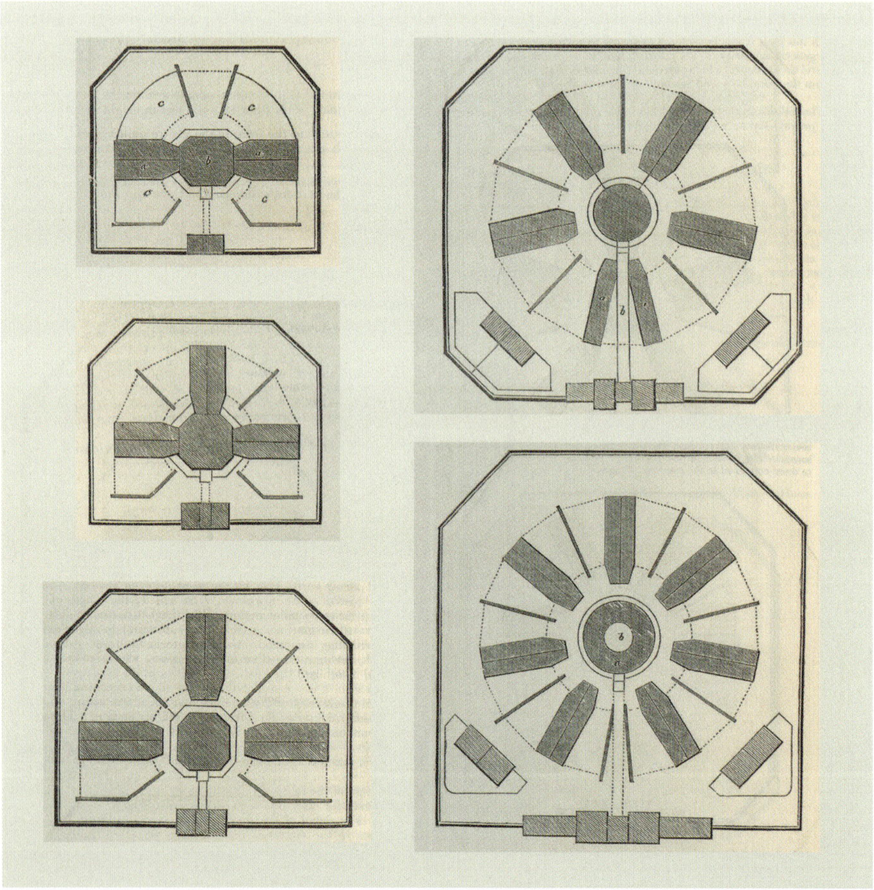

Fig. 6.6. Radial-plan gaols of different sizes, drawn by George Thomas Bullar. The SIPD came down in favour of the radial plan in 1826. Some Irish grand jurors (for example in Queen's County) agreed to polygonal-plan schemes in the early 1820s only to substitute them for radial plans once the SIPD had announced their decision. From SIPD, *Remarks on the Form and Construction of Prisons* (London: Arch, 1826), pp. 50–7. (*Reproduced courtesy of Cambridge University Library.*)

John Hargrave, the polygonal, and the radial

Evans has identified a three-year gap in the mid-1820s when no new gaols were begun in England.[32] There was no such fallow period in Ireland. As many grand jurors committed to new courthouses (see Chapter 2), they also made large presentments for either additions to gaols, or entirely new buildings, though the distinction was sometimes unclear, as many of the additions were so vast as to entirely dwarf the existing building. Hargrave (*c.* 1788–1833) was responsible for at least seven of these. The son of Abraham Hargrave, who we encountered in his remedial works at Cork county gaol around 1810 (see Chapter 4), Hargrave was a relative of the distinguished English neo-classical architect Thomas Harrison of Chester and trained with him before returning to Ireland in the mid-1810s, where he designed the new assize courthouse at Omagh and submitted an entry to the Wellington Testimonial competition in Dublin. Thereafter, he became the major figure for gaol architecture in Ireland under the new regime and had a promising and lucrative career until his tragic death in a sailing accident off the Welsh coast in 1833.[33]

Hargrave's master, Harrison, was an important gaol architect in his own right. He was an early adopter of Blackburn's polygonal design for Northleach bridewell and in his scheme for a new county gaol at Chester Castle, designed in 1786. This was occupied by the early 1790s, but Harrison was then commissioned to build a series of celebrated Greek Revival buildings nearby, including a new Shire Hall and a propylaeum (a gateway), and this work continued until the early 1820s (Fig. 6.7).[34] He also designed a polygonal male felons' prison at Lancaster, built between 1787 and 1793 (Fig. 6.8). It is very likely that Hargrave, articled to Harrison, was working on site in Chester during the course of the erection of the celebrated buildings there, and thus learned not only the intricacies of the polygonal layout, but also some of Harrison's flair for architectural massing and composition, and for the Greek style. Hargrave brought all these skills to Ireland.[35] His work can be divided into three categories: polygonal additions to existing gaols, new polygonal gaols, and, later in the decade, new radial gaols.

Hargrave built polygonal additions to existing gaols at Lifford, County Donegal, Omagh, County Tyrone, and Mullingar, County Westmeath. The architect of a very similar addition at Carrick-on-Shannon, County Leitrim, also built at this time, remains elusive but it is entirely possible, and indeed very probable, that Hargrave was responsible. The four schemes, here considered together, only differed slightly (Figs 6.9–6.12). In each case the existing gaols were small rectilinear blocks from the 1780s and 1790s; Lifford and Omagh

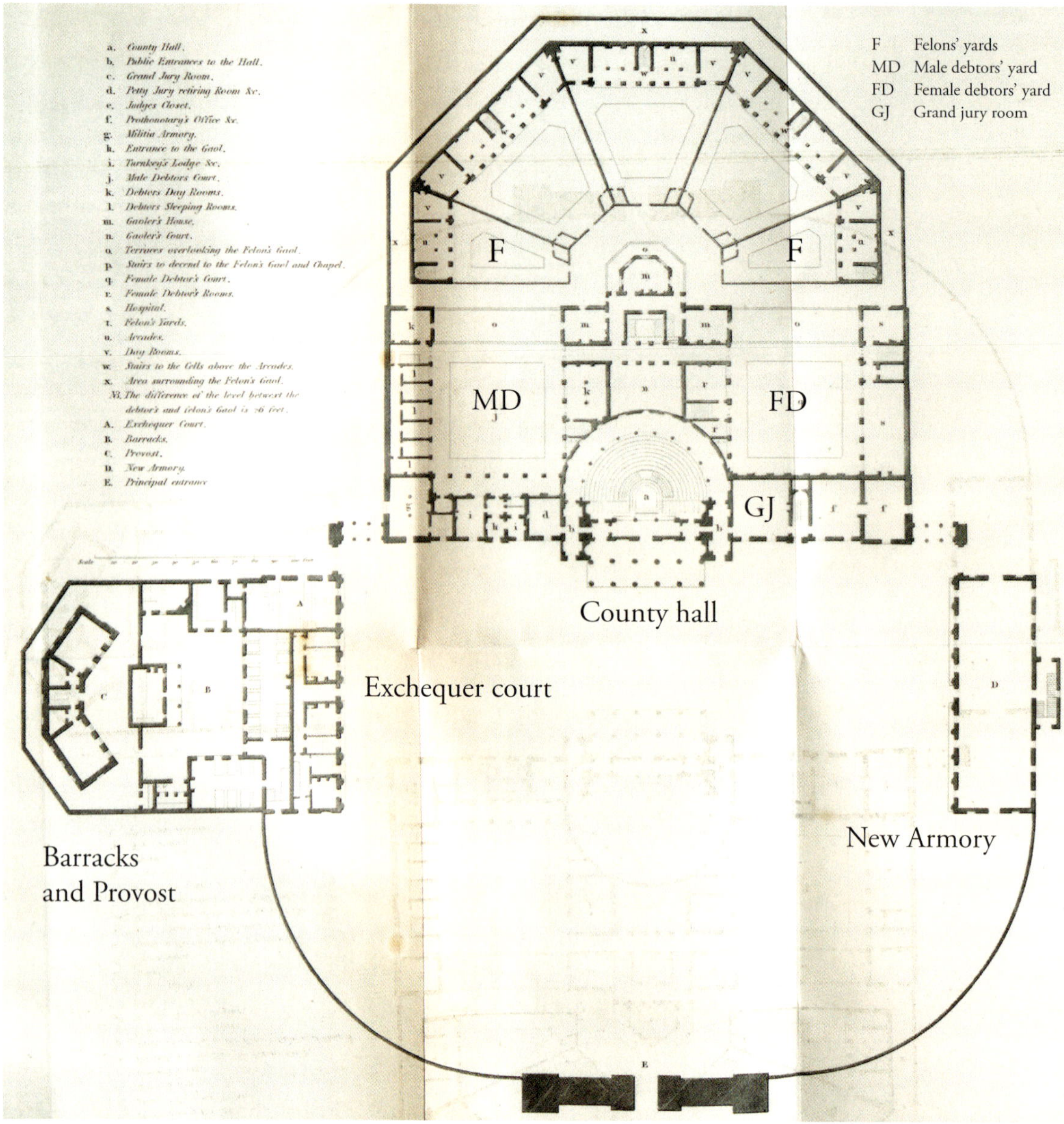

had been designed by Edward Miller, had been criticised soon afterwards for poor workmanship, and were both notoriously insecure. Lifford had some architectural pretensions, but the others, it would appear, did not, and were plain buildings (see Chapter 4). All were the fruits of the first reform movement, and all now appeared hopelessly inadequate. In Donegal, severe overcrowding

Fig. 6.7. (left) Plan of the county hall, gaol, etc., at Chester Castle, 1810. As well as a series of civic buildings, Harrison added a polygonal-plan gaol to the ensemble of buildings at Chester Castle. His pupil Hargrave used this gaol design extensively in Ireland in the 1820s. From Daniel and Samuel Lysons, *Magna Britannia, Being a Concise Topographical Account of the Several Counties of Great Britain … Volume the Second, Containing Cambridgeshire, and the County Palatine of Chester*, 6 vols (London: Cadell & Davies, 1810), vol. 2, p. 570. (*Reproduced courtesy of the University of Leicester.*)

around 1818, when at one time 230 persons were locked up and arranged into just three classes (felons, debtors, females), led the grand jurors to consider an addition. Archer noted that they had presented £900 for this purpose, but that the work was, in 1818, 'not yet finished'.[36] In fact nothing had happened at all, and Archer had to admit at the Commons inquiry the following year that his original proposal had been ignored by the grand jurors, and, having not bothered to travel to Donegal to see the alternative scheme for himself, he had learned of it simply through a verbal conversation with a local inspector.[37] This was clearly an unsatisfactory situation, but what Archer did not mention was that his original proposal had been superseded by one put forward by the AIPPD, then in discussion with the grand jurors directly. The AIPPD simply bypassed the old, discredited regime and communicated directly with the grand

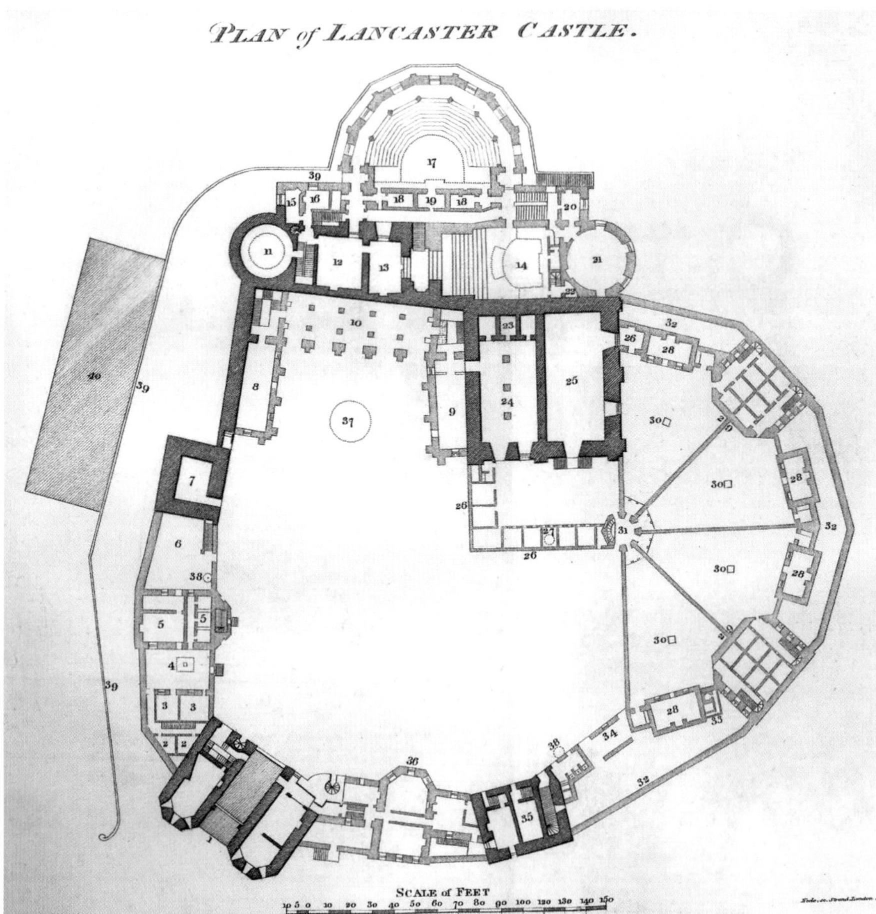

Fig. 6.8. (right) Lancaster Shire Hall and gaols. The additions made by the architect Thomas Harrison included the part-radial and part-polygonal male felons' prison visible to the right, built between 1787 and 1793. From Christopher Clark, *An Historical and Descriptive Account of the Town of Lancaster*, 2nd edn (Lancaster: Clark, 1811), p. 16.

jurors, the assize judge, local assistant barristers, and other interested officials in the county. The existing gaol in Lifford was crowded, they thought, on account of a series of recent 'atrocious murders' in the county, and because of many arrests for illegal distillation. These crimes were clearly not comparable in terms of severity, and the lack of proper classification in the gaol greatly troubled the reformers, who pronounced that 'through all the world, experience teaches, that no infection spreads so far as that of moral depravity' (a well-versed SIPD mantra). They blamed the gaol's defective original design, at least in part, for the hardening of criminals in the county and for its spiralling crime rates.[38] Something, they thought, had to be done to stem this tide, and the jurors sought help from the AIPPD. Soon after, plans came together for a large polygonal extension to the rear of the gaol. Hargrave appears to have been given the contract without competition, and by September 1820 he was advertising for builders, and in November 1821 the design was approved by the Board of Works. A loan for £5,500 followed soon after and the addition was built between 1822 and 1827.[39]

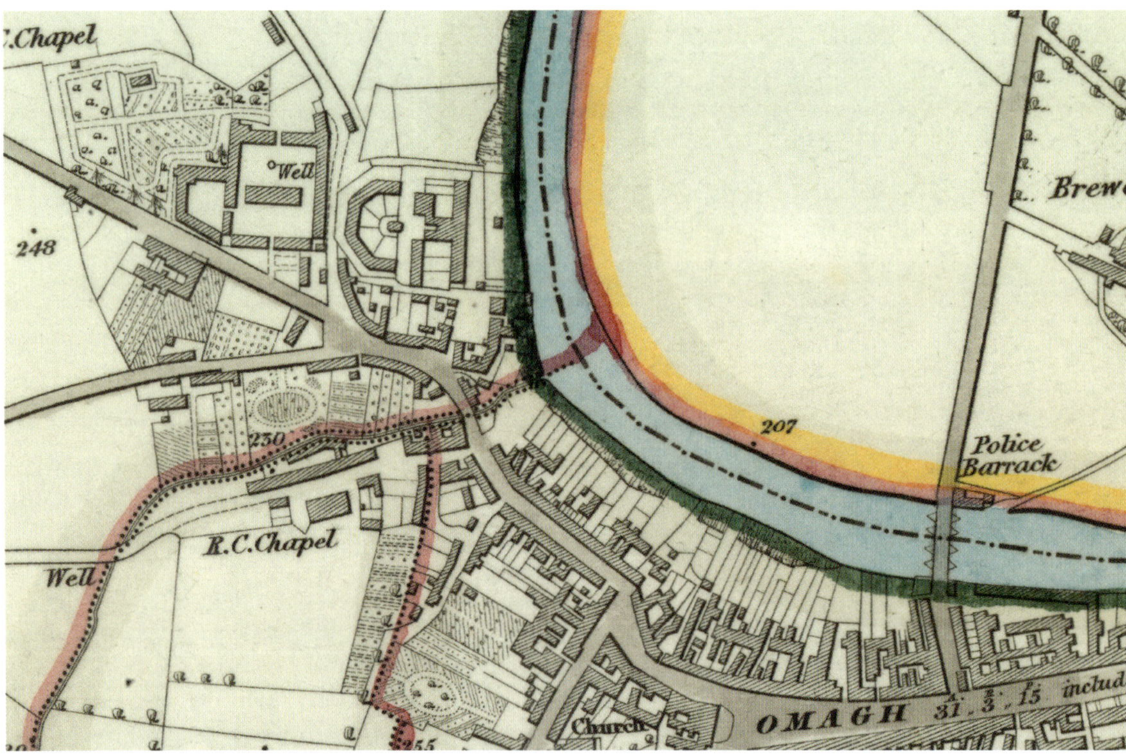

Fig. 6.9. Omagh, County Tyrone. Ordnance Survey six-inch map, surveyed June 1833. The original county gaol, shown as a H-shaped building near the banks of the River Strule, was greatly expanded in the 1820s with a polygonal-plan addition to the west by Hargrave. (*Reproduced courtesy of the Board of Trinity College Dublin.*)

Fig. 6.10. Carrick-on-Shannon gaol, County Leitrim. A small remaining part of the former county gaol, located adjacent to the assize courthouse. (*Photograph by author, 2012.*)

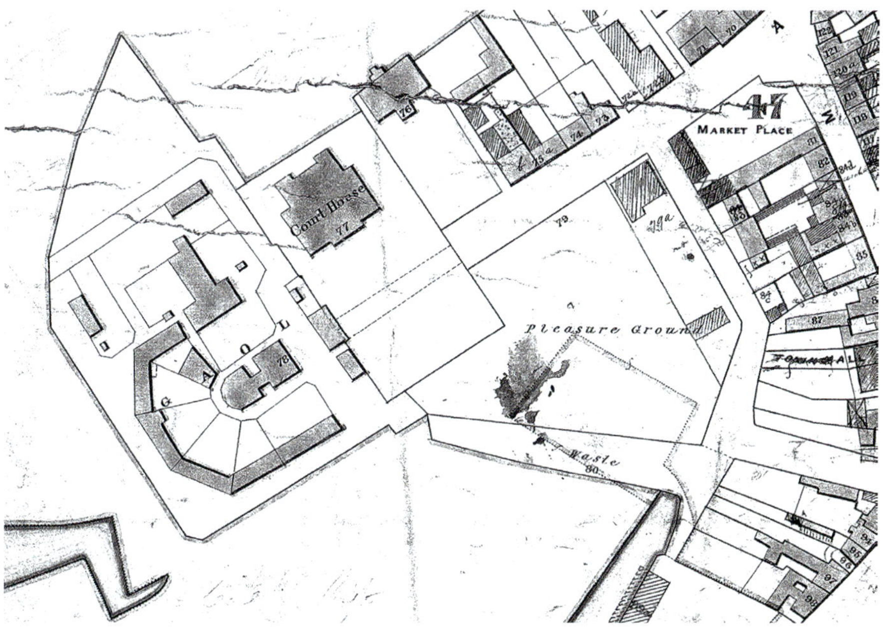

Fig. 6.11. Carrick-on-Shannon, County Leitrim. Ordnance Survey five-feet town map, *c.* 1850. Leitrim's old T-shaped gaol, near the courthouse that Farrell designed in the early 1820s, formed one range of a large polygonal-plan addition built at the same time. The architect responsible remains elusive. (*Reproduced courtesy of the Board of Trinity College Dublin.*)

The increase in crime in Donegal was clearly an important factor, but it may be questioned whether such a large addition would have been built in any case, on the back of the new energy encapsulated by the AIPPD, and the financial largesse provided by central-government loans. In other counties, the increase in

Fig. 6.12. The central inspection building, Omagh gaol, from the west, *c.* 1970. Now a domestic residence, this structure is the only surviving element of Hargrave's polygonal-plan additions to Omagh gaol in the 1820s. From its many windows, the gaoler could watch prisoners in the surrounding range of cells. (*Reproduced courtesy of the Irish Architectural Archive.*)

crime was less marked but the response was similar, if not identical.[40] The new addition at Lifford provided seventy cells arranged in six classes, with twelve day-rooms heated by fires, and six yards enclosed between the three-storey-high half-octagon of cells and the inspection building. Unlike the old gaol, thereafter given over only to debtors, Hargrave's addition was vaulted in stone throughout, reducing the risk of fire (as had killed two prisoners at Kilmainham in 1817) and making escape more difficult (Figs 6.13, 6.14).[41] Palmer and Woodward were so pleased with the harsh but more humanitarian new gaol, where prisoners were kept under surveillance at all times but had access to heated day-rooms and exercise yards, that they boasted in 1829 that it 'provided anything but comfort and relaxation to the prisoners .... In fact there is every reason to believe that the present reduction of numbers in the prison is much to be attributed to the gaol becoming odious to the people.'[42]

Fig. 6.13. Lifford gaol, County Donegal, *c.* 1900. From the roof of Miller's old rectilinear-plan gaol, this photographer was able to capture a classic image of Hargrave's standard polygonal design from the 1820s. The number of chimney stacks is indicative of the new humanitarian desire to improve the condition of prisoners. With this came the exacting punishment of being kept under strict control and observance. (*Reproduced courtesy of Donegal County Archives.*)

Fig. 6.14. Lifford gaol, County Donegal, under demolition, *c.* 1907. This rare photograph shows the stone and brick construction of Hargrave's walls and floors. These made the new gaols of the 1820s more secure and fireproof than earlier buildings. These men had much hard work ahead of them. (*Reproduced courtesy of Donegal County Archives.*)

Whatever their pronouncements about the administration of gaols, architecture still mattered greatly. However, any reduction in crime was elusive at best, and the inspectors soon lost their rather naïve mechanical correlation between bricks-and-mortar and the prevalence of crime in wider society. In the early 1820s, this optimism was palpable among the ranks of the AIPPD and the inspectors, and both felt that they were on the precipice of 'solving' crime. We need to bear this in mind when we consider the great wave of new buildings that were erected at the time. Government also played a large role in facilitating this new movement. In Omagh, the original presentment for Hargrave's polygonal extension had been £8,000, but in the end loans of more than £10,000 were forwarded to the grand jurors.[43] In Carrick-on-Shannon, the grand jury considered both a small and a large polygonal-plan addition to their existing gaol, and chose the latter, which was built between 1821 and 1824, and was in principle very similar to Omagh and Lifford. Their liberal financial commitment was backed up with at least £11,000 in central-government loans.[44] In Mullingar, the architect James Shiel had proposed a major transformation of the town centre with a new polygonal-plan gaol in 1817 and again (with an attached courthouse) in 1820 but the presentment was traversed at the assizes because, as the inspectors later stated, of 'a disagreement on the subject of estimate and [the] site'.[45] When work finally got underway in 1824, it was Hargrave who had the commission for the work, and for a new assize courthouse nearby (Figs 6.15–6.17). The old gaol had no more than thirteen cells (see Chapter 4); the new addition had 110, and soon became the county's male prison, with the females and debtors moved to the small old gaol nearby. It was such a substantial addition that it dwarfed entirely the existing gaol, and cost at least £11,626 (the amount presented by the grand jurors).[46] In the 1830s, there was further work to

Fig. 6.15. (left) Mullingar courthouse, County Westmeath, from the west. As well as erecting a large addition to the county gaol, Hargrave was commissioned to design a new assize courthouse in Mullingar, and both were built at the same time, with financial assistance from central government. (*Photograph by author, 2013.*)

Fig. 6.16. (right) Central inspection building, Mullingar gaol, County Westmeath, from the east. Hargrave used an almost identical design for all his polygonal-plan additions of the 1820s. A large library has been built on the site of the cell blocks in recent years. (*Photograph by author, 2017.*)

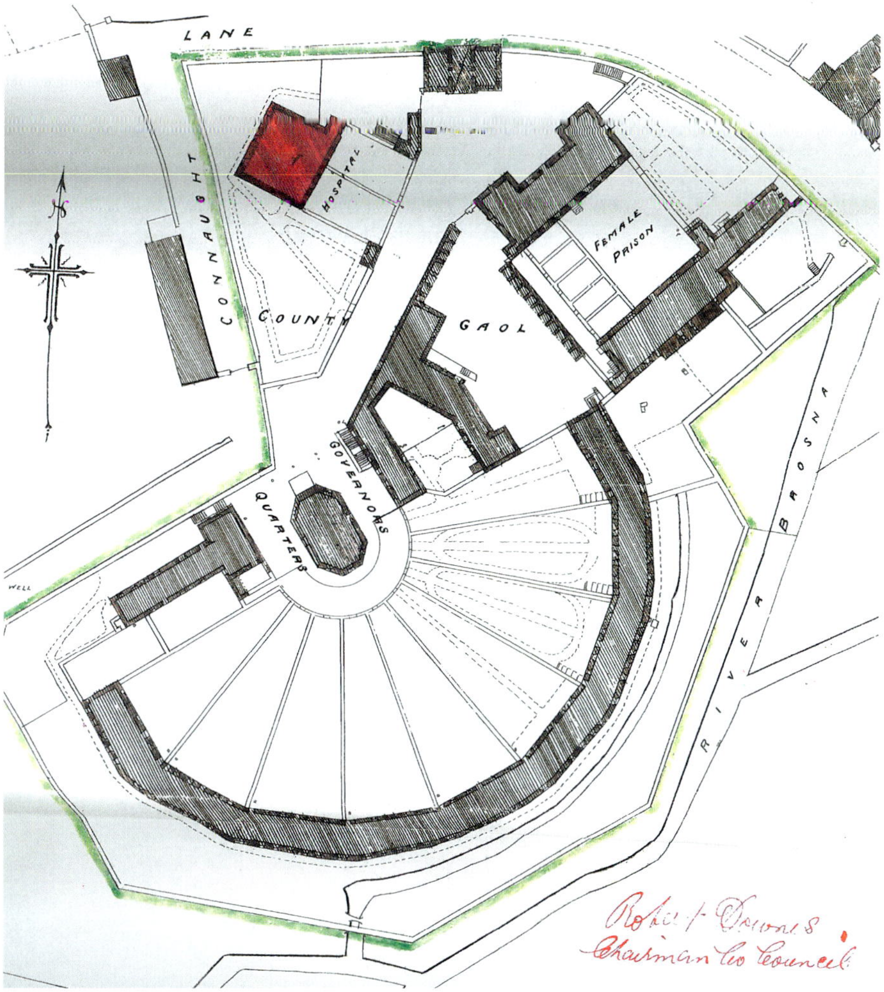

Fig. 6.17. Map of Mullingar gaol, *c.* 1910. The old rectilinear gaol (see Chapter 4) is marked 'Female Prison' in the top right. The scale of Hargrave's additions is evident. The assize courthouse, also by Hargrave, was built nearby. (*Reproduced courtesy of Westmeath County Library.*)

integrate better the old and new gaols, and to build, as an axial termination to the street and adjacent to the courthouse, an austere ashlar stone gatehouse with a pediment dated 1836 (since demolished) (Fig. 6.18).[47]

Hargrave built two entirely new polygonal gaols at this time, in Longford town, and in Athy, County Kildare. Both are interesting for the same reasons: first, the demonstrations from grand jurors of a new energy and enthusiasm for gaol building; and second, for the paternalistic interest shown by local elites, respectively Lord Forbes and the Duke of Leinster. Both new gaols were seen at the time of their opening as larger (and more expensive) than officially required; both counties exceeded the inspectors' expectations. In Longford, the small old gaol was described by Archer in 1819 as 'originally defective' and 'continually offensive' – the classic original-sin rhetoric of the time.[48] Initially, the grand jurors and Forbes planned to alter and make additions to this existing gaol, but they were convinced otherwise when Archer took them on an inspection, as he recalled in his annual report: 'when [Forbes] tasted [the gaol's drinking water], he declared that it was not fit for even cattle to drink [and] gave his decided opinion that a new gaol ought to be erected'.[49] The grand jurors were less keen for the financial outlay of building a new gaol, but Forbes eventually won the argument, and Hargrave's new gaol was built between 1821 and 1824.[50] It provided sixty-three cells and, excepting some minor reservations from the inspectors, the gaol was praised as a 'handsome building' but built 'upon a scale much larger than the object required, particularly in a small county' (Fig. 6.19).[51] It is unclear how much the final bill for the gaol was, but loans of nearly £13,000 were made available to the county. It is possible that Forbes contributed some funds directly, as the Duke of Leinster did in Kildare at this time. Furthermore, the AIPPD had a direct impact on the final design: the local gaol-building committee was specifically instructed by the grand jury at the spring assizes, 1819, to 'Communicate with the Association, for the better Regulation and Management of Gaols in Ireland'.[52]

Kildare had the unique standing of maintaining two county gaols in two different assize towns, Naas and Athy. By 1820, the medieval castle in Athy was

Fig. 6.18. The entrance gateway, Mullingar gaol, from the south, *c.* 1900. In the 1830s, the old and new parts of the gaol were brought together, and an entrance gateway rebuilt. This austere façade, since demolished, had a simple inscription in its pediment, 'MDCCCXXXVI'. (*Reproduced courtesy of Westmeath County Library.*)

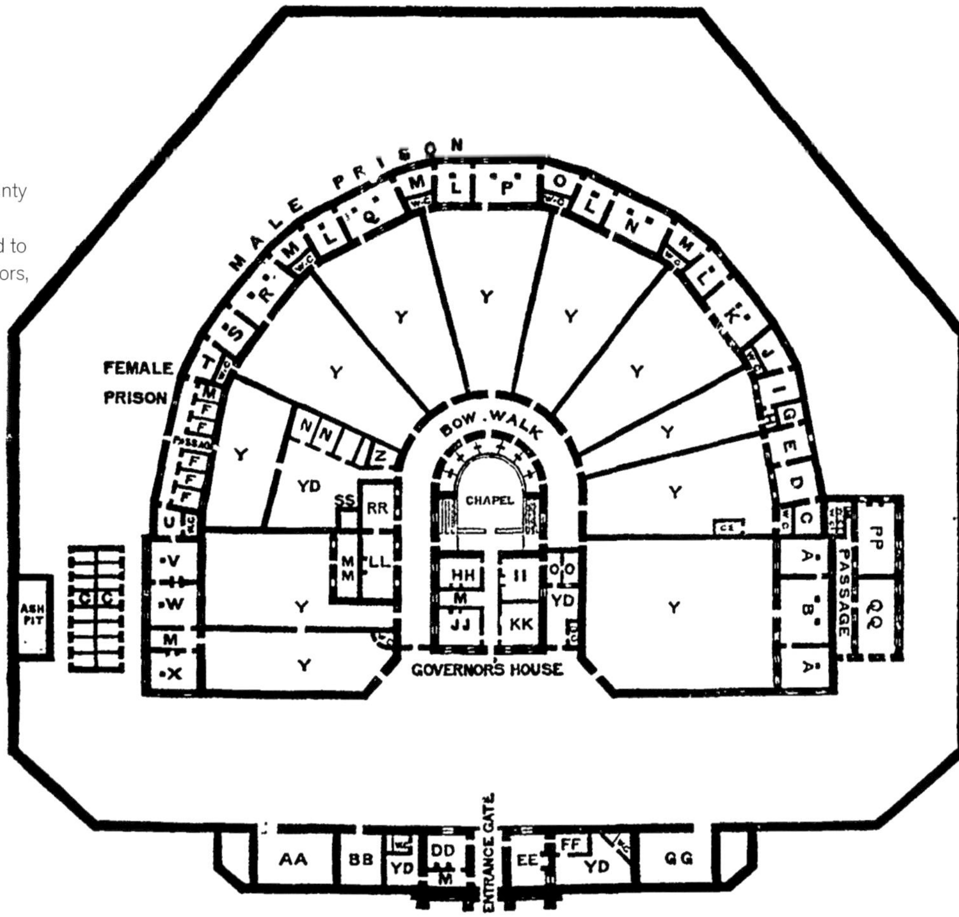

A, G G, Q Q, and R R, stores; B, pauper debtors' day-room; C, dead-house; D, hospital day-room; E and M, stairs; F, female prison; G, S, and T, baths; H, I, and J, reception wards for males; K and N, for untried males; L, turnkeys' rooms; O, dark cell; P, Q, and R, for convicted males; U, lavatory for females; V, furnace room; W, female reception ward; X, mistress debtors' room; Y, exercising yards; Z, well. A A, forge; B B, mill; C C, cells for stonebreakers; D D and K K, Deputy-Governor's apartments; E E and F F, Gate-porter's apartments; H H and I I, Governor's apartments; J J, prison office; L L, prison kitchen; M M, laundry; N N, treadwheel; O O, pantry; P P, carpenter's shop; S S, oven; Y D, small yards.

Fig. 6.19. Longford gaol, ground-floor plan, 1870. Hargrave's large polygonal-plan gaol in Longford town was larger and more expensive than the county required; the prison inspectors, accustomed to parsimonious grand jurors, were surprised at the liberality of the county. From *Forty-ninth Report … on … the Prisons of Ireland*, 1870, H.C. 1871 (C. 359), xxx, p. 184.

an object of curiosity for the prison reformers and seen as one of the most antiquated gaols still in regular use. It might have made for a useful museum piece showing the achievements of the earlier prison reform movement had it not continued to house prisoners in such terrible conditions. However, Palmer and Woodward were clear in their condemnation: nationally, 'there cannot be a worse county gaol'.[53] They urged the grand jurors to spend around £1,000 on a 'small bridewell' in the town.[54] However, after the Duke of Leinster took a personal interest in the county's gaols, probably influenced by the high standing of the AIPPD's governing committee and benefactors, and the fashionable humanitarianism of penal reform in the early 1820s, the project became much more ambitious. He donated a site, at the edge of the town, free of charge, and contributed £1,700 of the total building cost of £5,400, with loans from government making up the balance.[55] Hargrave built a small and elegant polygonal gaol of local limestone between 1826 and 1830 (Fig. 6.20), but before it was occupied, four prisoners managed to escape from the old castle by picking locks.[56] This must have provided proof to the duke and to the other reformers that the final expenditure, many times more than the inspectors initially called for, was a worthwhile investment for the county. The gaol continued in use until 1859 and a surviving section is now a private residence (Fig. 6.21).

Kildare's other gaol, at Naas, was also rebuilt at the same time. The building committee included the Duke of Leinster, and other local elites such as the Earl of Mayo, Lord Cloncurry and the MP Robert Latouche.[57] 'Nothing effectual

Fig. 6.20. Athy gaol, County Kildare. Ordnance Survey six-inch map, surveyed January 1837. Situated at the southern edge of the town, Athy's small polygonal-plan gaol benefited from a large private donation from the Duke of Leinster. The support of penal-reform projects became fashionable in elite circles for a brief period in the early 1820s, when this gaol was planned. (*Reproduced courtesy of the Board of Trinity College Dublin.*)

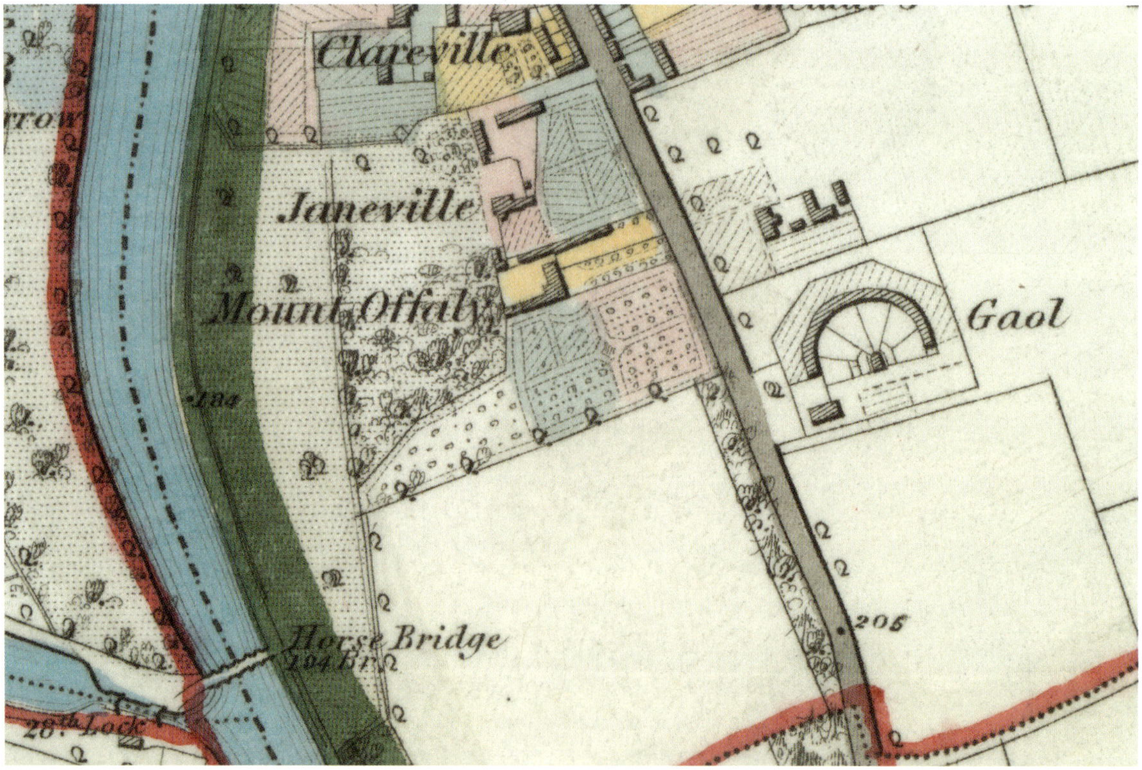

Fig. 6.21. Athy gaol, from the north-west. Hargrave's small, two-storey gaol was well built using local limestone. Today only a small portion of the cell block remains intact. Photograph by author, 2014. (*Reproduced with the permission of the present owners.*)

can be done' for tackling crime in the county, the inspectors noted in 1823, 'until [a] new [gaol] shall be built'.[58] The jurors approved plans at the summer assizes in 1825 and received approval for Hargrave's design from the Board of Works.[59] However, at this time, the design was to have been polygonal like all his earlier commissions.[60] In 1826, the jurors changed their mind, perhaps influenced by the publicity garnered by the SIPD's definitive ruling that year in favour of the radial design, and they asked Hargrave to submit a revised radial scheme to government for approval in 1827; the inspectors claimed credit for bringing about this last-minute change of mind.[61] Central-government loans began enriching the grand-jury bank balance in 1826, totalling nearly £13,000, and the new gaol opened in 1833.[62] Unlike its predecessor in the town centre, it was situated at the edge of the town, near the Grand Canal basin, and was connected with Richard Morrison's assize courthouse (see Chapter 1) via an alleyway that led to its imposing, Egyptian-style entrance gateway (Fig. 6.22).[63] Its construction shifted the gravitational centre of the town to the west. Inside the high boundary walls, Hargrave planned four free-standing radial blocks arranged around the governor's residence (Fig. 6.23). The gaol was one of a series of new, detached-wing radial gaols built in Ireland from the 1820s onwards, and this became the dominant and most highly approved design for nearly twenty years afterwards. The inspectors were certain that a properly arranged gaol, which met all the requirements set by the AIPPD, would lead to a reduction in crime. Upon the opening of Naas gaol, they issued a stern warning to the people who would administer the institution, commenting that 'a well-managed gaol will always produce a proportionate diminution of crime in a county, and should this effect not be produced in the new prison, blame will attach to the officers'.[64]

Fig. 6.22. Naas gaol, County Kildare, from the north-east, *c.* 1950. This photograph, taken from the Grand Canal basin, shows the gaol shortly before it was demolished. Hargrave's rusticated gateway is visible in the centre-left (compare with Fig. 6.29). From *The Leinster Leader*, 16 March 1985.

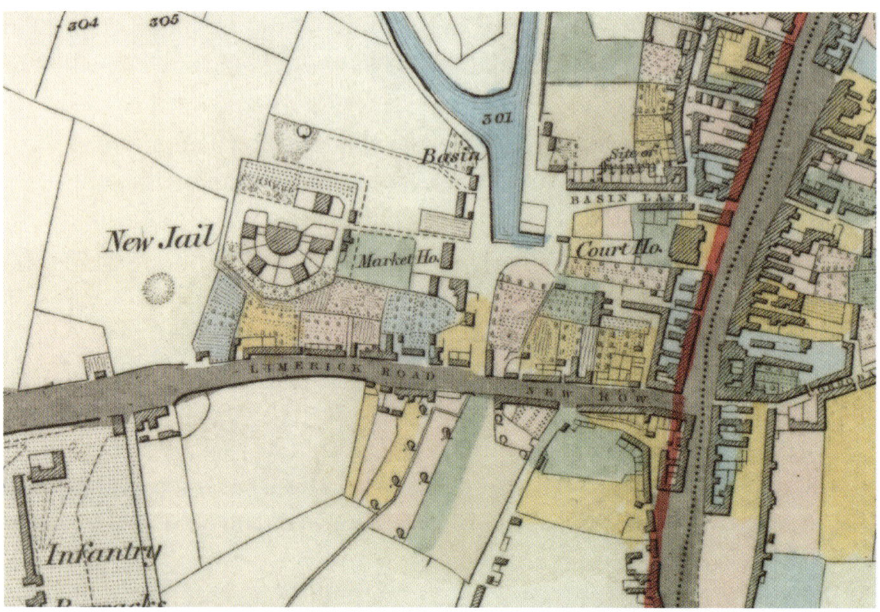

Fig. 6.23. Naas, County Kildare. Ordnance Survey six-inch map, surveyed January 1837. The relatively cramped site occupied by the old gaol (marked 'Old Jail') and the airier surroundings of its replacement ('New Jail') are clearly shown. A pathway connected the new jail with Morrison's assize courthouse. (*Reproduced courtesy of the Board of Trinity College Dublin.*)

The 1820s was arguably the most important decade for gaol construction, as it was for new courthouses (see Chapter 2). Two large radial-plan gaols were begun in the early 1820s, one by Hargrave at Trim, County Meath, and the other by the Scottish architect Robert Reid, at Downpatrick, County Down. Both are architectural achievements of national importance and are indicative of the sheer scale and complexity of gaol building under the new regime. Reid's gaol is considered here first. Charles Lilly's rectilinear-plan gaol in Downpatrick from the 1790s (see Chapter 4) was now seen as inadequate for the needs of the county, and the escape of five men through its sewers in the summer of 1817 focused minds on the need for improvement.[65] The grand jurors were divided between making additions to the existing gaol, including a separate infirmary, or building anew elsewhere.[66] When they decided in favour of the latter, they advertised for proposals but assumed an unrealistic estimate for the cost and received a meagre response from builders.[67] Then followed a series of unsuccessful attempts to cancel the project outright and instead extend the existing gaol. The contentious issue for the rebels appears to have been the decision at the outset to build big and the enthusiasm of some jurors for bringing in an expensive foreign architect (Reid mostly worked in Edinburgh); one deadline was even extended to allow certain unnamed 'distant architects' to submit plans.[68] The jurors also consulted with Archer, and with John Collingwood, an architect in Gloucester and Worchester who was involved in the building of the polygonal-plan lunatic asylum in the former town, built between 1819 and 1823.[69] Reid had designed the Morningside Asylum in Edinburgh and also built a military prison at Perth between 1810 and 1812.[70] When his plans for Downpatrick were eventually approved, the perhaps unprecedented extent of consultation and input from experts led Francis Johnston to claim that he had never before 'seen or met with a design so satisfactorily laid down nor so perfect and minute a detail'.[71] Despite Lord Glenawly and Robert Ward, local elites, claiming that the design was 'extravagant', the scheme was finally approved, with some reductions in scale, in 1823.[72] The enormous sum of £60,000 was presented by the county and at least £42,000 of this was loaned from central government.[73] This gaol alone consumed a large portion of the overall amount spent on new prisons in Ireland in the 1820s. The inspectors praised its design highly, calling it a 'splendid prison' with extensive classification, twenty-six work-rooms and 216 cells (Figs 6.24, 6.25).[74] From the outset it appears that a majority of the jurors were keen to make a major public statement with their new gaol and establish it as the leading such institution in the country. To confirm this, Reid built a monumental entrance gateway (that still survives), praised by McParland as 'a splendid composition [with] its cubic clarity and unifying Primitivist entablature … reminiscent of [James] Gandon [and] Sanmichaeli at Verona' (Fig. 6.26).[75]

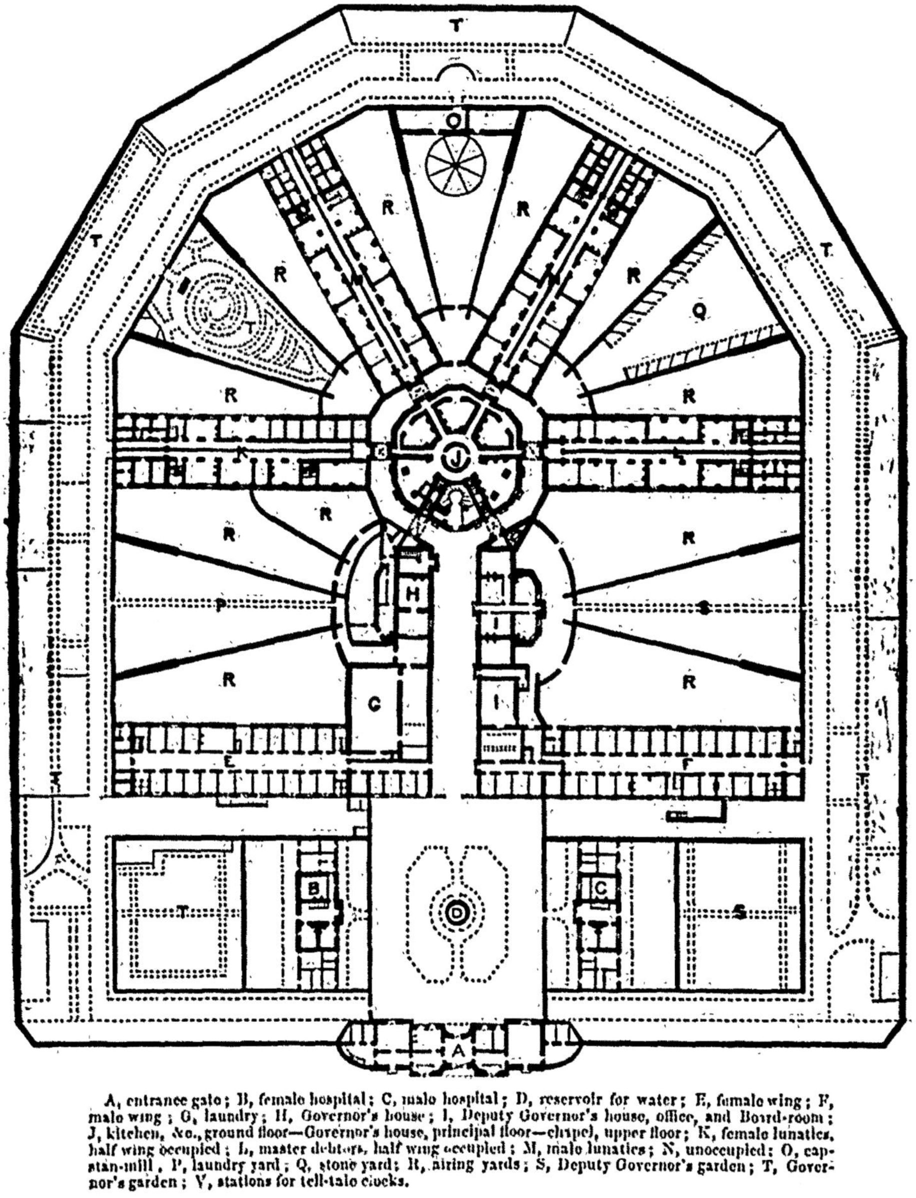

Fig. 6.24. Downpatrick gaol, ground-floor plan, 1870. Reid's radial-plan gaol was, by far, the most elaborate and expensive of its time, and was criticised for these reasons by grand jurors and cess-payers in County Down. From *Forty-ninth Report … on … the Prisons of Ireland, 1870*, H.C. 1871 (C. 359), xxx, p. 134.

Fig. 6.25. Downpatrick gaol, County Down, from the north-east, *c.* 1900. Reid's large central inspection building vies with Downpatrick Cathedral and the Mourne mountains in the skyline. Francis Johnston, at the Board of Works, commented that he had never 'seen or met with a design so satisfactorily laid down nor so perfect and minute a detail'. (*Reproduced courtesy of the National Library of Ireland.*)

Fig. 6.26. Entrance gateway, Downpatrick gaol, from the south-west. The public architectural language of Reid's gaol was one of impregnability and sobriety. Today this gateway and parts of the surrounding walls are the only surviving parts of one of Ireland's most elaborate prisons. (*Photograph by author, 2014.*)

In Meath there was notably less enthusiasm from the jurors for gaol building. While the Down jurors had set a high bar for other counties to follow, they also made others reluctant to commit to any building work whatsoever, for fear that it would cost as much as their new gaol at Downpatrick. At Trim, the old gaol was notoriously insecure and undersized, and yet the Meath grand jurors built several additions, first between 1801 and 1808, again between 1817 and 1818, and finally between 1822 and 1823.[76] One of these additions was a house of correction, aimed at relieving overcrowding at the same time as there was a peak in crime and rural unrest that followed a bad harvest and other issues, and there had been several houses damaged in attacks in the town.[77] However, the number of 'outrages' in the county soon subsided to an average of just twenty per year, as documented by Desmond Mooney, and this relieved pressure on the gaol.[78] It also provided a cloak-screen behind which the jurors could evade their responsibilities: 'it is greatly to be regretted', commented Palmer and Woodward in 1824, that 'this wealthy and enlightened county should now be the only one in the northern district that has not made some effort to render their county gaol capable of promoting prison discipline .... Nothing but a new prison can obtain the object.'[79] Three more years of persuasion ensued before the grand jurors finally presented the princely sum of £24,000 for a new gaol at the spring assizes in 1827.[80] Their old gaol had thirty-one cells; its replacement was to have 140, arranged in five radial blocks around a large governor's house and chapel (Fig. 6.27). It was built to Hargrave's design between 1828 and 1834.[81] Coincidentally, there was a great peak in agrarian unrest in the county from 1828 into the early 1830s, when the number of outrages rose ten-fold from around twenty to around 200 per year (Fig. 6.28); the gaol-building project preceded this change, however, and we should be slow to link the two in any way.[82] Architecturally, the design of the blocks and central hub was rather plain and typical for the time, but Hargrave's *tour de force* contribution to the architectural riches of Trim was his façade, which faces the Castle from an elevated site on the opposite side of the River Boyne (Fig. 6.29). Though the gaol's boundary wall edged upon a road to the rear, Hargrave deliberately chose the river-facing front to be the only entrance and built a long circuitous path to make this entryway possible. Developing further the heavy, Egyptian-like rustication that he used at Naas, his façade at Trim is an essay in impregnability and power. Deep channels of rustication and a heavy cornice run across the centre and the protruding end-bays, which appear like Egyptian pylons, and the monotony of the stone is only broken by sullen blank neoclassical plaques and the three doors for the turnkey and assistant governor. For no practical reason – a rare thing in gaol architecture – the façade is approached via a terraced arrangement of ramps, platforms, and steps, all battered and with inclined jambs (Figs 6.30, 6.31). It is a splendid example of what Robin Evans has termed 'exercises in abstract propaganda', where architects gave their buildings 'a voice that would transmit a universal language of emotion derived from the immutable bond between the substance of building and the sensations of the beholder'.[83] For the grand jurors, it was their most visible reward for such a large outlay and it usefully took shape in a period of high levels of crime and unrest. Once it was complete, they went back to their disinterested ways and did little or nothing else to improve their gaol until it was converted into an industrial school in the late 1880s.[84] Today only the monumental façade survives as a testament to the perseverance of the inspectors who lobbied for its building. Incidentally, in none of their reports did they say anything about the celebrated façade – they saw that as beyond their duties.

Fig. 6.27. Trim gaol, County Meath, from the south-east, 1959. This photograph shows the five radial cell blocks of Hargrave's gaol, minus the original boundary wall that would have shielded them. The façade facing Trim Castle, with offices and storerooms behind, is also visible.

Fig. 6.28. Number of 'outrages' in County Meath between 1815 and 1843. Though incomplete, this graph shows a peak in crime and unrest at the same time as the new gaol was nearing completion (in the early 1830s), and the relative calm of the years when the prison inspectors called for it to be built (in the early 1820s). Compiled from Mooney, 'Agrarian Violence in Meath, 1790–1828', and ibid., 'Agrarian Violence in Meath, 1828–1835'.

Fig. 6.29. (left) The entrance gateway and façade of Trim gaol, from the east. Like Hargrave's other radial-plan gaol, at Naas, the façade of Trim gaol was an excellent essay in 'abstract propaganda' and survives today as the only remaining part of the gaol. (*Photograph by author, 2014.*)

Fig. 6.30. (right) The terrace wall and steps leading to Trim gaol, from the north. Hargrave created a fearsome impression of strength without and punishment within by using an inclined, Egyptian-like terrace wall. (*Photograph by author, 2014.*)

Fig. 6.31. The entrance steps and terrace wall, Trim gaol, from the north-east, 1981. Carved into the earth, the double staircase was entered through a doorway with inclined jambs and gave access to the elevated main entrance to the gaol behind (visible in the top right). (*Reproduced courtesy of the Irish Architectural Archive (Photograph by Geoff White).*)

Cracks in the façade

The many new impressive gaols built in the first years of the new regime led by the AIPPD and the inspectors Palmer and Woodward may suggest a revolution in Irish penal history, with a new concern for prisoners' welfare, reformation through hard work, education, and moral guidance, and inspectors to hold corrupt grand jurors to account. There were certainly fewer scandals on the scale of Cork city's water-logged gaol site from this time onwards, and the inspectors had many achievements about which they could – and did – boast in their annual reports. In Britain in these years there was no comparable system of central-government inspection, and thereby no central agency pushing for uniformity and improvement, except of course the SIPD and its legion of followers. But by the mid-1820s the heyday of the SIPD, and the AIPPD, had passed, and along with them the utopian evangelical idealism of the early 1820s. The argument in favour of administrative and architectural uniformity had, in large measure, been won, as Robert Perceval commented at a meeting of the AIPPD in 1825: 'A uniformity of regulation implies a uniformity of construction, without which it is impossible that equal justice can be administered.'[85] Towards the end of the decade, the debate over prison design and management was taken over by more professional administrators, governors, and chaplains, and by 1835 the SIPD only had 100 subscribers and its secretary commented that numbers had 'fallen off very much of late years'.[86] In Ireland, the fact that seemingly 'perfect' new gaols did not lead to any noticeable decrease in crime levels put a damper on the naïve earnestness of the early AIPPD pronouncements. Their last surviving report dates from around 1828.[87] Vastly increasing crime figures – the origins of which are still debated by historians – reflected political violence attached to the campaign for Catholic emancipation, the Tithe War of the early 1830s, and widespread rural and urban unemployment and poverty, and these combined to fill many of the new gaols to capacity. This increase was, however, not unique to Ireland, and was also seen in many other countries, not least Britain.[88] Twelve years into their jobs – by the mid-1830s – the inspectors wearily noted that 'circumstances have changed' and they were now writing about a much more troubled country than when they were first appointed.[89]

High crime rates were just one issue facing the prison system (Fig. 6.32). In fact, it could plausibly be argued that Irish gaols were never very far from crisis, and of five major changes in these years, two were positive but three were very definitely negative. First, the achievements. From the mid-1820s the reformers, including the inspectors, began to consider female prisoners as a separate issue deserving of extra attention. The inspectors thought that lower-class female prisoners were especially susceptible to 'moral corruption', but also to reformation, and visiting groups of females of 'the higher classes' could use their leisure time to 'save', the reformers thought, some lower-class women from a life of crime. 'Ladies Visiting Committees' were established, following the encouragement of Elizabeth Fry and other celebrity reformers, who made occasional visits to Ireland, most notably in 1827. The high-minded Hibernian Ladies' Society for Promoting the Improvement of Female Prisoners was founded under Fry's tutelage, and closely modelled itself on the Ladies' Society in London.[90] In Armagh, the Ladies' Committee consisted of twelve women, one of whom visited every day and taught reading and writing. In Roscommon, three ladies visited the county gaol twice every week.[91] Of course female prisoners only occupied a small portion of gaols outside of the metropolis, and with so many new additions recently built, the inspectors pushed for the old gaols in each town to be given over entirely to females, where they could be housed away from the 'corrupting' influence of the male majority. The Hibernian Ladies' Society advocated for this throughout the late 1820s, with considerable success. The second achievement of the era was the removal of military guards from gaols in 1829. The inspectors had long viewed the presence of these young and idle men as a corrupting influence, and one that portrayed the wrong message: prison administration meant more than preventing escapes and 'open violence', they argued. 'Vigilance' and 'moral training' should replace the balder displays of military force. This change brought Irish gaols into line with their British counterparts.[92]

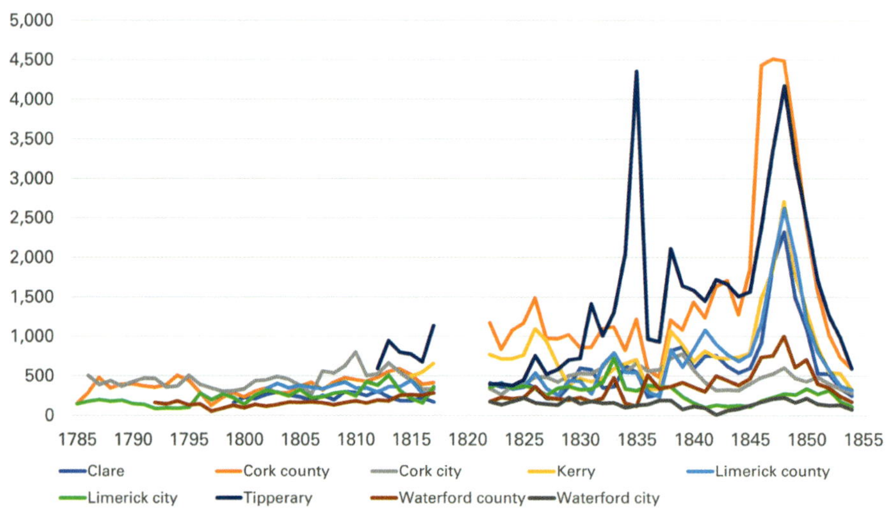

Fig. 6.32. Criminal indictments in Munster between 1785 and 1855. Despite the lack of data for the years 1819–22 (inclusive), the gradual increase in crimes is apparent, with a sudden peak in Tipperary in the mid-1830s. The effects of the Great Famine are also clear to see. The increase in crime in the 1830s challenged the utopian vision of the AIPPD and the two prison inspectors, and their belief in the virtues of a 'model' prison discipline system. Compiled from Appendix B.

Of the three crises, two were centred in Dublin. The most egregious was the Richmond penitentiary, which had opened in 1820 (see Chapter 4). Within a few months, the Catholic chaplain complained that his Protestant counterpart was proselytising boys sent to the experimental national penitentiary; the inspectors found no evidence this was true.[93] At the same time, Palmer and Woodward, based on an incorrect reading of a recent act of parliament, suggested that the inmates were being underpaid for their work; the issue was eventually resolved but not without some controversy.[94] The governor claimed that he was working in an age of 'theory and experiment', but the problems with his institution continued to mount. By 1823, Palmer and Woodward were very critical of the prison's design, and alterations costing £15,000 were briefly considered.[95] The terminal blow for the institution came in 1826 when the Catholic archbishop of Dublin, Daniel Murray, accused the governor of overseeing the forced conversion of seventeen inmates and of permitting the use of torture. Henry Heaney, the preeminent historian of the penitentiary, links this abuse to the 'fanatical evangelical[ism]' of 'second reformation' Protestant theology then gaining ground in the Irish church.[96] By the end of the decade, all sides were blaming each other, numbers at the institution were dwindling, and the inspectors publicly toyed with the idea of abandoning the whole experiment. It closed in April 1831 and found a later use as a cholera hospital and later again as a city gaol for females.[97] It must be remembered that this penitentiary consumed more than £32,000 in central-government loans in the 1810s, and was, by 1831, seen by all concerned as an abject failure and an ugly display of sectarianism at a delicate period in Irish political history. This did not reflect well on the Irish prison system.

The second crisis was Dublin's Newgate gaol, and the problem was simply that nothing had happened to improve Thomas Cooley's widely condemned building from the 1770s. The AIPPD's competition to select a replacement around 1819 has already been discussed, but nothing came of it, and Palmer and Woodward were clear in their first report that the Dublin city gaol was 'a public disgrace to the metropolis of Ireland' in these 'enlightened' days.[98] Both the inspectors and the AIPPD sparred off each other in the 1820s, attempting to find the strongest and most damning language to condemn the gaol – with the inspectors even claiming in 1826 that its disgraceful condition was 'a source of contagion to the prison system in general', but no-one could force the jurors into action except the assize judges, and this proved an impossible task. 'Crowding, filth, nakedness, blasphemy and disorder' characterised the condition of the gaol, the inspectors stated, and whatever about the risk of moral or medical contagion, this was certainly an embarrassing institution for the new regime.[99] The inspectors asked David Henry of the gaol-building firm Henry, Mullins & McMahon to design a new gaol, but they could not force the jurors to adopt his plan, which would have provided a total of 412 cells in twenty-three radial blocks around a vast governor's house and twelve turnkey's lodges (Fig. 6.33). Henry estimated it would have cost £83,500 – more than enough to scare the city jurors into inaction.[100] John Semple put forward another rebuilding plan in the late 1830s that remained mostly unbuilt amid heated opposition from some city cess-payers.[101] The condition of the gaol in these years made a mockery of the reformers' lobbying elsewhere: in 1832 the inspectors found fifty-two men in a yard a little over twenty feet square; the following year there were between 200 and 350 prisoners kept in just fifty-two cells.[102] An exasperated AIPPD concluded

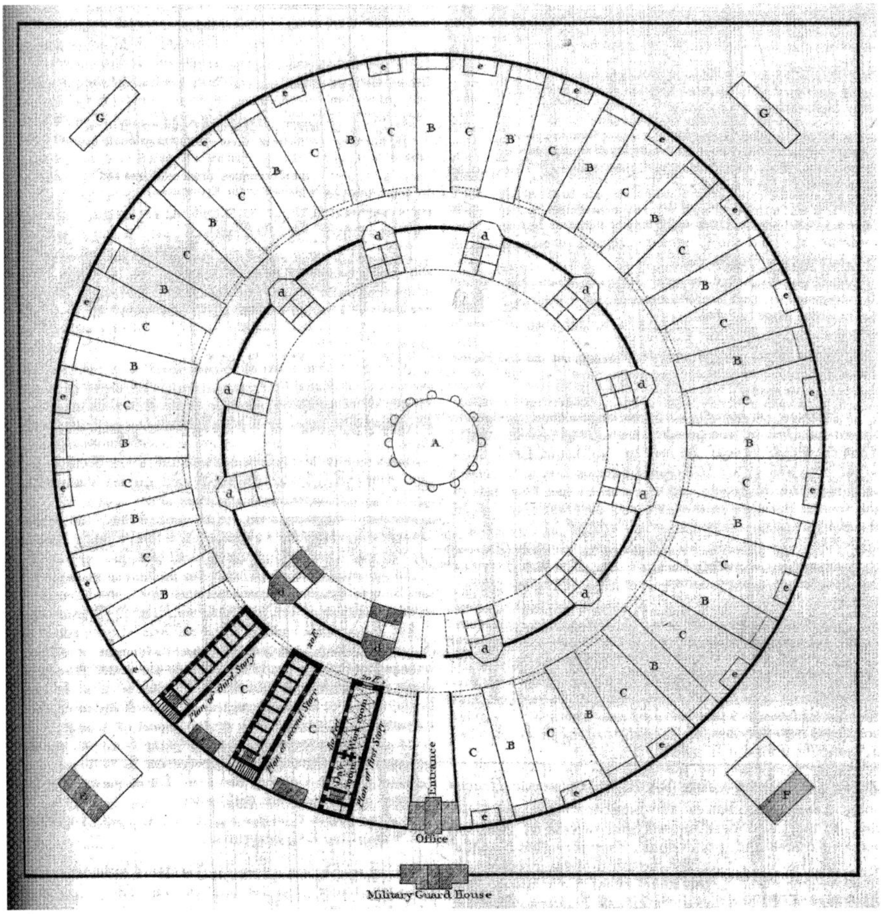

Fig. 6.33. 'General outline of a plan of prison', unexecuted. David Henry, 1826. The prohibitive cost of Henry's proposed replacement for Dublin's Newgate gaol, with its 412 cells arranged in an enormous radial plan, was enough to dissuade the city grand jurors from committing to the project. From *Journal of the House of Commons*, vol. 81, 21 March 1826, Plate B.

one of their reports by pleading: 'If crime and misery be encreased [sic], is there not every claim, of Humanity, of Justice, and of Christianity, *to hasten a remedy*, by building A NEW PRISON FOR THE CITY OF DUBLIN?'[103] Despite this, the gaol continued in use and ever-increasing squalor until April 1851.

The final crisis came out of the very success of the rebuilding effort. With heavy expenditure incurred throughout the country, there were accusations of waste and that some of the new gaols were palaces where the poor were better housed and fed than outside. This debate has obvious correlations with the furore about workhouses that occurred in the late 1830s and 1840s under the new Poor Law. Just as the *Freeman's Journal* attacked what they saw as unnecessary spending on new courthouses (see Chapter 2), they claimed that the 'caprice' of grand jurors extended to gaol building too. Often this criticism was ill-informed, such as when they claimed that Mullingar's small old gaol was sufficient for the county's needs, or that the insecure and unhealthy old gaol at Maryborough (see Chapter 5) was perfectly functional and not needing of replacement. It was undoubtedly true, however, that all this work was 'at great expense and taxation to the people'.[104] More stinging was the view of a barrister, who published an anonymous pamphlet in 1831 that claimed the poor 'prefer to go to gaols than live in the misery of their hovels'; this was in turn quoted in a Royal Dublin Society statistical survey.[105] On his travels, Reid heard a Dublin doctor claim that prisoners were too well fed and were committing crimes simply to get free meals in gaol.[106] In 1841, the travel writers Samuel Carter Hall and Anna Maria Fielding commented that Irish gaols were 'stately and elegant' buildings,

> so grand, 'graceful,' and inviting, … so clean and neat in the interiors, that a caustic observed remarked, 'it would seem as if all the gentry of Ireland expected some day or other to be among their inmates.'[107]

We need to ask how fair these criticisms are. It is difficult to say for sure, but the inspectors certainly felt hurt by the allegations and deplored the fact that 'an opinion has gone abroad that the present comfortable state of our gaols is productive of [an] increase in crime, an opinion wholly unfounded'. Their aim was to have gaols that were 'formidable and revolting to the depraved character and licentious habits of the persons likely to become inmates'.[108] From this time onwards, they stepped up their scrutiny of gaol accounts and recommended many downgrades in the quantity and quality of nourishment offered to prisoners. In many ways this was the paradoxical alter ego of the humanitarian reformers – 'severity and gentleness, rigid autocracy and dispassionate altruism' – and such actions were typical throughout the reform movement in these years in both Ireland and Britain.[109]

Meanwhile gaol building continued apace. In 1828, no fewer than fifteen were under construction all around the country, many already discussed. Four projects from the late 1820s will be briefly mentioned here, and all are indicative of the dominance of the radial plan by this time. First, we consider Cavan. There, the early radial gaol built by Elsam (discussed in Chapter 5) was barely sufficient at the time of its opening, but severe overcrowding in later years pushed the grand jurors into action. Fever broke out in 1817 and eight prisoners died.[110] Despite a lowering of the crime rate in the early 1820s, the inspectors convinced the jurors to push ahead with an addition, and in 1826 they presented £6,000 for forty new cells on a detached radial plan, designed by William Farrell, the architect of the nearby county courthouse (see Chapter 2).[111] The two new radial blocks were built adjacent to the existing gaol without the need for any demolition, and the first prisoners were kept there in 1828 (Fig. 6.34). By comparison, the building of a new radial-plan gaol in King's County, by the engineer John Killaly, was one episode in the long-running dispute between rival families (see Chapter 3). From 1820 a committee populated with allies of the Bury family had consulted with the AIPPD and received plans from several architects, including William Murray, for a polygonal-plan gaol (Fig. 6.35).[112] The old gaol at Philipstown was roundly condemned by the inspectors and the AIPPD, and building work there in *c.* 1818–19 had only worsened the situation: the gaol, commented the AIPPD, was 'so radically bad', and the recent addition was 'bad in execution and still more in design .... The original plan provided abundantly for the disease of the mind. The recent addition appears to have done so, for that of the body.'[113] The grand-jury committee visited other gaols then built or under construction and were especially impressed by James Pain's Limerick county gaol, which they took as their model. After much wrangling, a series of central-government loans arrived from 1826 onwards, and the foundation stone for the Gothic Revival gaol was laid with great pomp (and more than a few swipes at the Ponsonby family) by the Bury family later that year. Bonfires were lit to celebrate the coming of a regular income to the town through the supply of provisions to the new gaol, and Lord Tullamore paid for 'pipers and fiddlers' to play to the crowds and 'ale to be distributed', but warned that he expected there would be 'no fighting, no drunkenness, no broken heads', and no complaints from 'mothers, wives, or daughters' about the behaviour of their men the next morning.[114] The gaol, which opened in 1830, was larger than the county needed and provided enough classification, inspection, and opportunities for employment to satisfy the inspectors (Figs 6.36–6.38). As discussed in Chapter 2, its Gothic façade stood alongside the new classical courthouse and set up a new judicial quarter at the southern edge of the town on the road to Lord Tullamore's residence.[115]

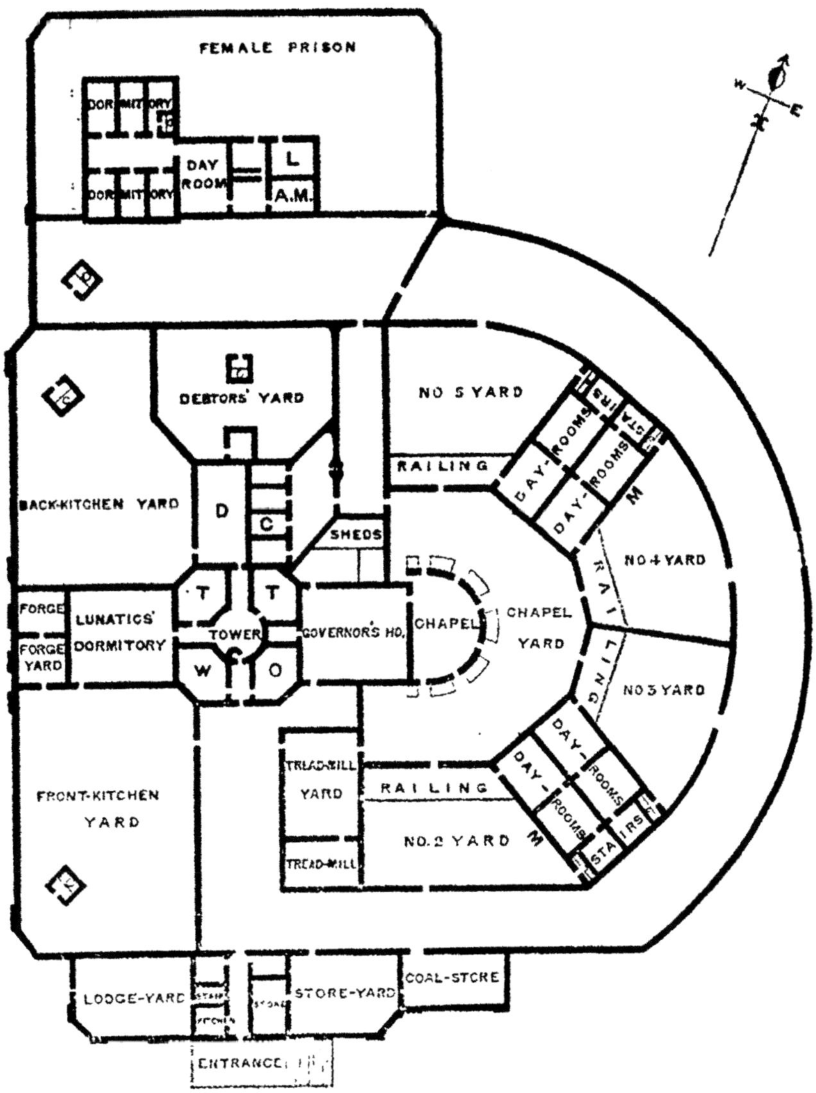

MM, male prisons; O, office; W, workshop; TT, turnkeys' rooms; D, day-room for the lunatic class; C, punishment cells; AM, Assistant Matron's room; L, laundry. The marshalsea for males, and the hospital for both sexes, are situate in the upper part of the central building, marked "Tower," T, W, O, C, and D, on the plan.

Fig. 6.34. Cavan gaol, ground-floor plan, 1870. Farrell's additions (to the right) radiated out of an existing wing of Elsam's gaol (compare with Fig. 5.20). The female prison in the top left was a later addition in 1845 and 1846. From *Forty-ninth report … on … the Prisons of Ireland, 1870*, H.C. 1871(C. 359), xxx, p. 108.

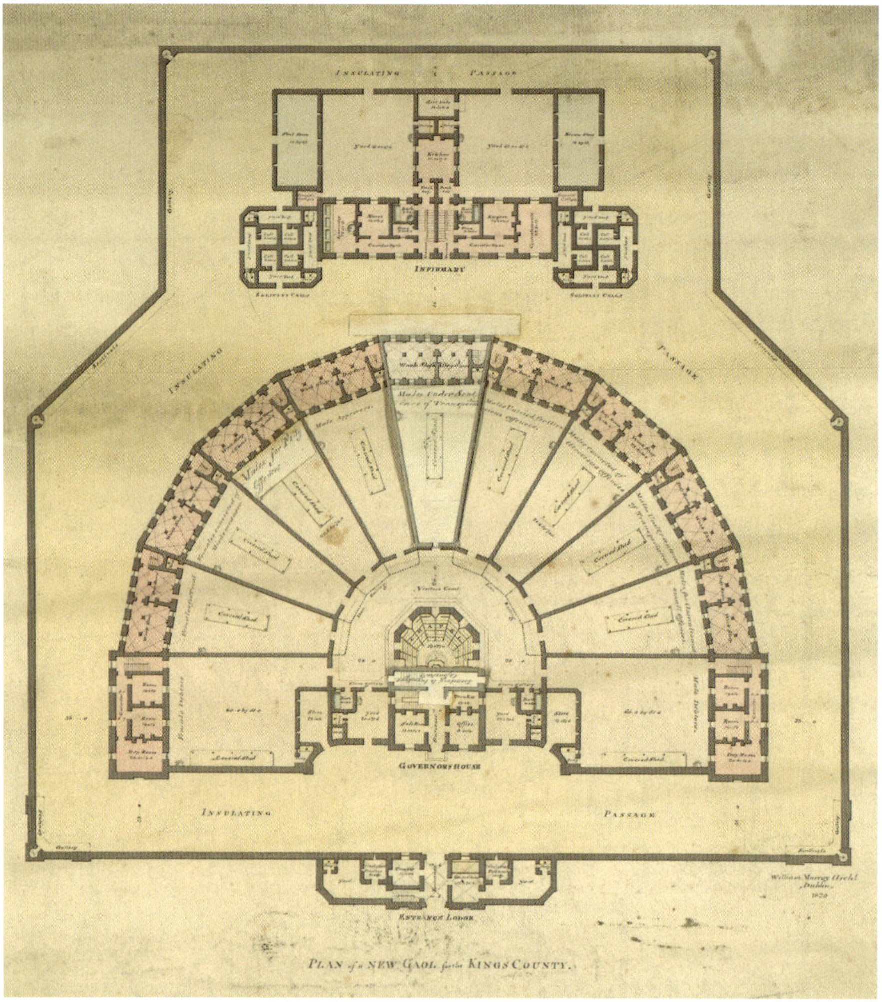

Fig. 6.35. Tullamore gaol, ground-floor plan, unexecuted. William Murray, 1820. The King's County grand jurors were more impressed with James Pain's radial-plan gaol for Limerick and chose that general outline for their new gaol; Murray's polygonal-plan gaol remained unexecuted. (*Reproduced courtesy of the Irish Architectural Archive.*)

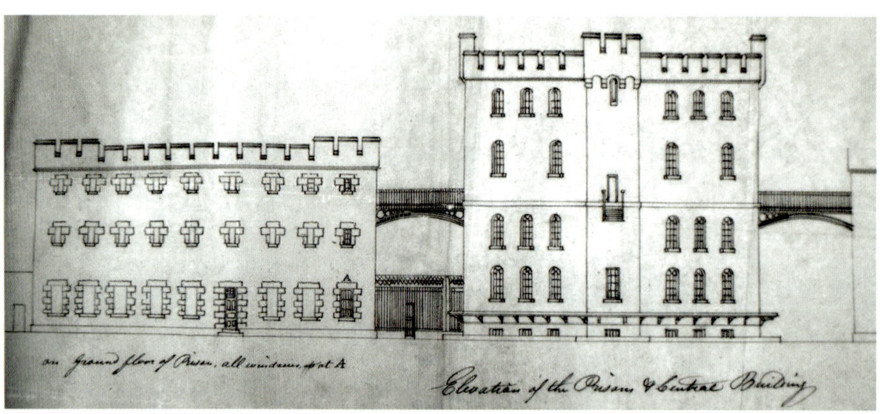

Fig. 6.36. Tullamore gaol, elevation drawing of central building and cell block, n.d. [*c.* 1826]. John Killaly's radial-plan gaol, similar to Pain's gaol in Limerick, won the favour of the King's County grand jurors. The building of the gaol brought economic prosperity to the town and was an important battle in the long war between the Bury and Ponsonby families in the county. (*Reproduced courtesy of the National Library of Ireland.*)

Fig. 6.37. Tullamore gaol, King's County (County Offaly), from the west, 1978. The engineer, builders, and grand-jury commissioners are commemorated in a plaque above the gateway. Lord Tullamore thought the Gothic detailing would clash with his new assize courthouse (see Chapter 3). The metal palisade railings, with fasces and axes, protected many courthouses and gaols built at this time (see Chapter 2). (*Reproduced courtesy of the Irish Architectural Archive.*)

Fig. 6.38. Tullamore gaol, *c.* 1930s. The half-ruined central inspection building, in a Gothic style matching the façade, was connected to the radial cell blocks by iron bridges, of which one is visible here. The gaol was demolished some years after it was damaged during the War of Independence and Civil War. (*Reproduced courtesy of Offaly County Library.*)

In neighbouring Queen's County (now Laois), a plan for a new polygonal gaol, to the designs of William Deane Butler, had been approved as early as 1821 but disagreements over the location and design of the gaol delayed building work for many years.[116] The inspectors rather oddly advocated for a cramped site close to the existing gaol, in the centre of the town, but in the end the jurors pushed instead for a more airy location in the far eastern suburbs.[117] The government's aborted plan for provincial penitentiaries, discussed above, also held up the building plans, and by the time the first loans were forwarded to the jurors, in 1826, Butler's design had transformed into a radial scheme.[118] This gaol, with its four radial blocks, is so similar in design and architectural style (Gothic Revival) that it has sometimes been mistakenly attributed to James Pain on account of his influence at Tullamore, but the architect was Butler, who went on to build many more additions to county gaols in the 1830s (Fig. 6.39).[119] At the same time as the Queen's County jurors were building a new gaol, their neighbours in Carlow decided upon a large radial-plan addition to the county's old gaol, built between 1828 and 1831. As discussed in Chapter 2, the caustic comments offered by assize judge Charles Bushe at the assizes in 1827 pushed the jurors into action. There, the building works were tied up with Morrison's new courthouse in the town, and it seems probable that the designer of the additions was the firm of Williams & Cockburn, contractors, who had also built Farrell's radial-plan additions at Cavan gaol.[120] The new addition at Carlow took the form of a series of radial blocks built around the existing T-shaped gaol; as in so many other radial gaols, the governor's house and the chapel were in the central hub building (Fig. 6.40). The small scale of the additions in Carlow reflected the peaceable situation in the county, and the gaol was very rarely, it would appear, overcrowded.

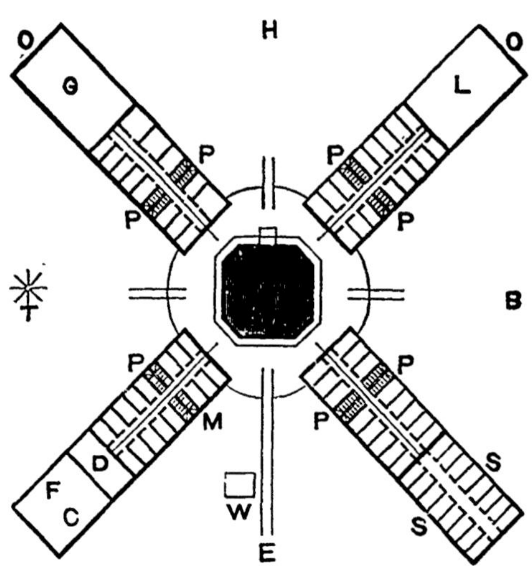

A, Governor's house; B, Matron's house; C, carpenter's shop; D, store; E, entrance; F, forge; G, turf yard; H, hospital; I, coal yard, store, and bath; M, marshalsea; O O, solitary cells; P P P, old prisons; S, separate prison; T, treadwheel; W, watch-house.

Fig. 6.39. Maryborough (Portlaoise) gaol, Queen's County (County Laois), ground-floor plan, 1870. In both architectural style (Gothic) and layout (radial-plan), the King's and Queen's county gaols were remarkably similar. In both cases, earlier polygonal plans had been superseded when the pendulum swung in favour of the radial plan in the mid-1820s. Maryborough gaol was designed by William Deane Butler. From *Forty-eighth Report … on … the Prisons of Ireland, 1869*, H.C. 1870 (C. 173), xxxvii, p. 431.

Fig. 6.40. Carlow gaol, central inspection building, governor's house, and chapel, from the south. Criticism from an assize judge in 1827 pushed the Carlow grand jurors to build a new courthouse (see Chapter 2) and a small radial-plan addition to their gaol. A durable local granite was used for door and window surrounds and for quoins. (*Photograph by author, 2014.*)

Grand-jury reform and the limits of classification

The wave of reforms to grand juries, and the Board of Works, in the early 1830s precipitated a dramatic reduction in assize-courthouse building, as outlined in chapters 2 and 3. But it had little effect on gaols, and this was for four main reasons. First, the principal reforms had been implemented in the earlier prison acts of 1810 and 1821. Second, most gaols had been rebuilt once or even twice within a single generation, and there was little appetite for more expenditure – and the penal reformers had little by way of new ideas, for now at least, in gaol design. Third, the loans scheme for gaol building operated somewhat independently of that for courthouses; it had been operating for longer; and it was less likely to be condemned as wasteful or unnecessary. Finally, it was still inherently in the interest of central government, which increasingly took upon itself the responsibility for humanitarian and social issues, to have grand jurors rebuild and improve their gaols. Perhaps the greatest change that came out of the 1833 and 1836 grand-jury reform acts was the reintroduction of the county surveyor as a salaried official.[121] As these men consolidated their hold over local patronage, they began to make regular reports on gaol conditions, and to gain commissions for required alterations and additions. Often a professional architect was paid the maximum amount permitted by the law (£50) for general drawings, but the actual building work was managed by the county surveyor.

This was the case for the additions to Ennis gaol in the 1830s.[122] Considering that both the engineer (John Killaly) and the building contractors (Henry, Mullins & McMahon) had built gaols in the 1820s, it is not all that surprising that the figure of the professional architect should have come under further pressure from the new county surveyors in the 1830s. Separately, there was the contentious issue of where new gaols were to be built, as the political debates in King's County proved. The clauses in the Assizes Act of 1835 and the Grand Jury Act of 1836 that gave central government, for the first time, the right to establish assize towns, with or without a majority vote from the affected grand jurors, opened up the possibility of new gaols being built.[123] The effect of this law on the division of Tipperary was considered in Chapter 3; the building of Nenagh gaol will be discussed in Chapter 7.

The decline in gaol building in the 1830s – when only a handful were begun – was not because of these reforms; instead it grew out of a wider, and international, crisis among the prison-reform community. After a decade of inspection, Palmer and Woodward put a brave face on events and could rightly claim that they had overseen a great rebuilding effort. They were confident that Irish gaols now possessed 'every moral advantage [that] architectural arrangement can give' and boasted that they had implemented a 'perfect *national* system of prison discipline'.[124] To prove their point, they assembled a table (Fig. 6.41):

Class	Type	1822	1831
1st	New radial-plan gaols	1	9
2nd	New polygonal-plan gaols	4	6
3rd	New non-panoptic-plan (rectilinear) gaols	7	7
4th	Radial-plan additions to gaols	0	6
5th	Polygonal-plan additions to gaols	0	5
6th	Non-panoptic-plan (rectilinear) additions to gaols	0	5
7th	Counties requiring entirely new gaols	12	2*
8th	Counties requiring additions to their gaols	16	0
	Total	**40**	**40**
	* The cities of Dublin (Newgate gaol) and Kilkenny		

Fig. 6.41. Table showing the condition of Irish county gaols in 1831 compared with 1822. From *Tenth Report … on … the Prisons of Ireland, 1832*, H.C. 1831–2 (152), xxiii, p. 5.

Palmer and Woodward were keen to draw attention to their successes, especially when many British penal reformers pushed to expand the Irish central-government inspection system to the entire United Kingdom. Palmer's rather immodest *Treatise on the Modern System of Government Gaols* (1832) was, in this regard, cleverly dedicated to the British magistrates, and oozed with praise for the Irish grand jurors (their 'liberality' and 'zeal'), leading members of the AIPPD (for their 'zeal' and 'usefulness'), and for himself and his colleague Woodward (a 'striking instance' of a 'completely accomplished' task).[125] Several British House of Commons inquiries heard celebrity reformers, such as Elizabeth Fry, praise the Irish inspectors in flowing language. For this and other reasons, five central-government inspectors were appointed in Britain in 1835 – the ultimate statement of approval for the Irish precedent.[126]

We should ask how this crisis was visible, if it can be said to have existed. Perhaps Palmer's treatise was aimed at securing one of the new British inspector positions, but his chances must have been dashed when, after some overindulgent speculation on property, he was declared bankrupt and ignominiously became the only prison inspector in Irish history to serve time in gaol, being kept in the debtors' ward at Kilmainham.[127] This was a personal and professional embarrassment, but a more systemic problem was the increasing crime rates of the 1830s. There was, at best, equivocal evidence that prisoners were being 'reformed' while serving out their punishments, and with this came the implication that the intricate system of prison discipline developed by the SIPD and AIPPD was simply not bearing fruit. 'Success', after all, only could be truly proclaimed if a gaol lay empty, and in Ireland this was never the case. As the provision of heated day-rooms, tread-wheels, hospitals, teaching and religious services, and a regulated diet became commonplace, the running costs of these institutions spiralled. In Clare in the early 1830s, the gaols and bridewells cost around £2,000 to run each year – five per cent of the county's budget. This was almost the same as the expenditure on the county's house of industry, infirmary, fever hospital, and share of the district lunatic asylum combined.[128] In some gaols there were now twelve or fifteen classes of prisoners, and the inspectors continued to believe that the risk of 'crime contagion' could be reduced by increasing this number even further. But classification could reach absurd levels, and in some British gaols, for example at Westminster bridewell, built between 1829 and 1832, there were twenty-four classes arranged in three adjoining radial-plan complexes (Fig. 6.42).[129] Clearly there would have to be a limit on this kind of sub-division – might someone build a gaol with fifty classes, or a hundred, or two hundred?

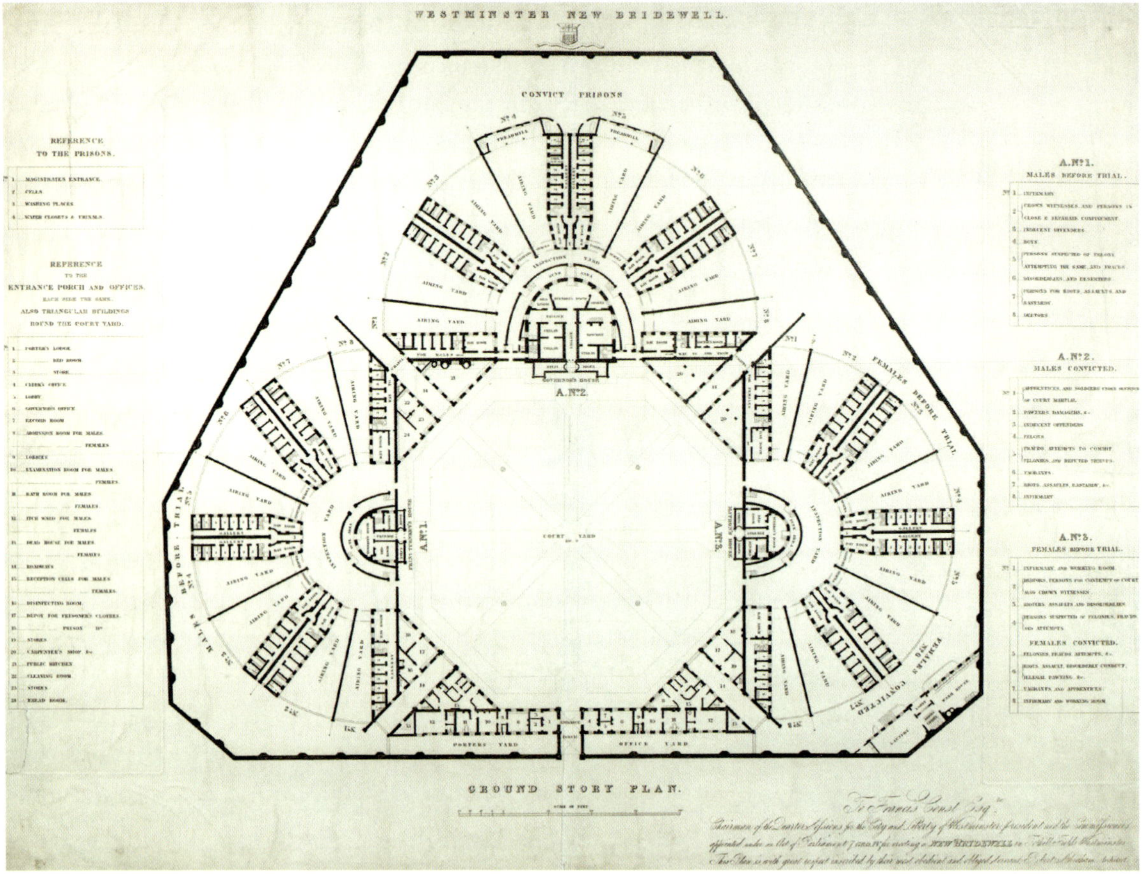

Fig. 6.42. Westminster new bridewell, Tothill Fields, London, ground-floor plan. Robert Abraham, 1829–32. At the same time as the desire for greater classification emerged in British gaols, the practical limits on achieving this architecturally became increasingly evident; this large prison was divided into twenty-four classes. (*Reproduced courtesy of the London Metropolitan Archives, City of London.*)

If ever-increasing classification did not lower crime rates, as was becoming apparent, might there be a plausible alternative discipline system? The solution came from developments in America, particularly in Pennsylvania and New York. A group of more radical reformers there had experimented with what was called the 'silent' and the 'separate' systems. The former insisted on prisoners keeping complete silence at all times, and thus removed the risk of 'contagion' simply by preventing speech. The latter brought classification to its logical if rather barbaric utilitarian conclusion by keeping every prisoner in a separate cell through day and night, with only short exercise breaks. Both systems brought a terrifying new prospect of mental derangement and anguish to prisons and made life within them one of silent reflection, contemplation, and suffering. Stories abounded of inmates losing their minds and attempting suicide.[130] For the dispirited idealists of the 1820s, the American experiments provided an unploughed furrow that was soon adopted as the new solution to crime and punishment. William Crawford's *Report on the Penitentiaries of the United States* (1834) brought the detail of American gaol design and operation to interested British and Irish readers. Palmer and Woodward summarised its findings in their 1836 report, and acknowledged that if 'separate' cells were to be provided for every Irish prisoner, a great deal of rebuilding work would be needed.[131] The reasons why this was the case will be discussed in Chapter 7, but the growing approval for the 'separate system' in the late 1830s is an important background factor when considering the few new gaols built at this time. These building projects fall into two distinct categories: first, long-overdue new gaols and additions planned since the previous decade, delayed for a variety of reasons; and second, the reconfiguration of Dublin's gaols following the closure of the discredited Richmond penitentiary in 1831.

Gaol building on the eve of separate confinement

Palmer and Woodward had been critical of old rectilinear-plan gaols in Castlebar (for the county of Mayo) and Galway (for the *town* of Galway) since assuming their positions. In the early 1830s, the Dublin architect Frederick Darley designed new radial-plan gaols for both grand juries; in Galway the addition to the town gaol was so large that it dwarfed the existing building, in Castlebar the gaol was a substantial free-standing structure at the edge of the town. These grand juries were the last in the west of Ireland to upgrade their gaols and had regularly pleaded their inability to pay. But once they finally committed to the work, the resulting buildings were highly accomplished and met with approval from the inspectors. In Galway, the new town gaol, built between 1832 and 1836, was divided into two radial blocks and four classes, with the old building given over to females and debtors (Figs 6.43, 6.44).[132] In Castlebar, the government forwarded loans totalling £23,000 to the grand jurors that allowed them to proceed with building a large four-wing radial-plan gaol for males, and a smaller adjacent radial-plan gaol for females, as well as a hospital, all built between 1831 and 1835 (Figs 6.45–6.47).[133] This was perhaps the first time that complete separation of male and female prisoners had been built into the design of a new gaol, following the advice of Elizabeth Fry and the Hibernian Ladies' Society. Contemporaries found little to criticise in the new gaol except perhaps its rather extravagant architectural detailing and high cost. The *Connaught Telegraph* carried many scathing editorials calling attention to what they saw as corruption and 'jobbery' among the grand jurors, and attacking the remuneration offered to Darley, who was also the Dublin police chief magistrate and a known leading member of the Orange Order. However, it is difficult to tell if these allegations should be given any weight, and in fact the cost of the gaol was within the normal bounds for the time and substantially less than, say, the expenditure at Downpatrick.[134] The splendid Gothic Revival gateway, inscribed, following Dublin's Richmond bridewell, with the warning 'WITHOUT BEWARE, WITHIN AMEND', became the reference for many travel writers' predictable contrasts of the wealth of the county's public buildings with the poverty of its inhabitants.[135] Even the inspectors shared these sentiments, and in a rare display of interest in architectural ornamentation called Darley's gaol 'splendid', 'handsome and imposing', and 'beautiful'.[136]

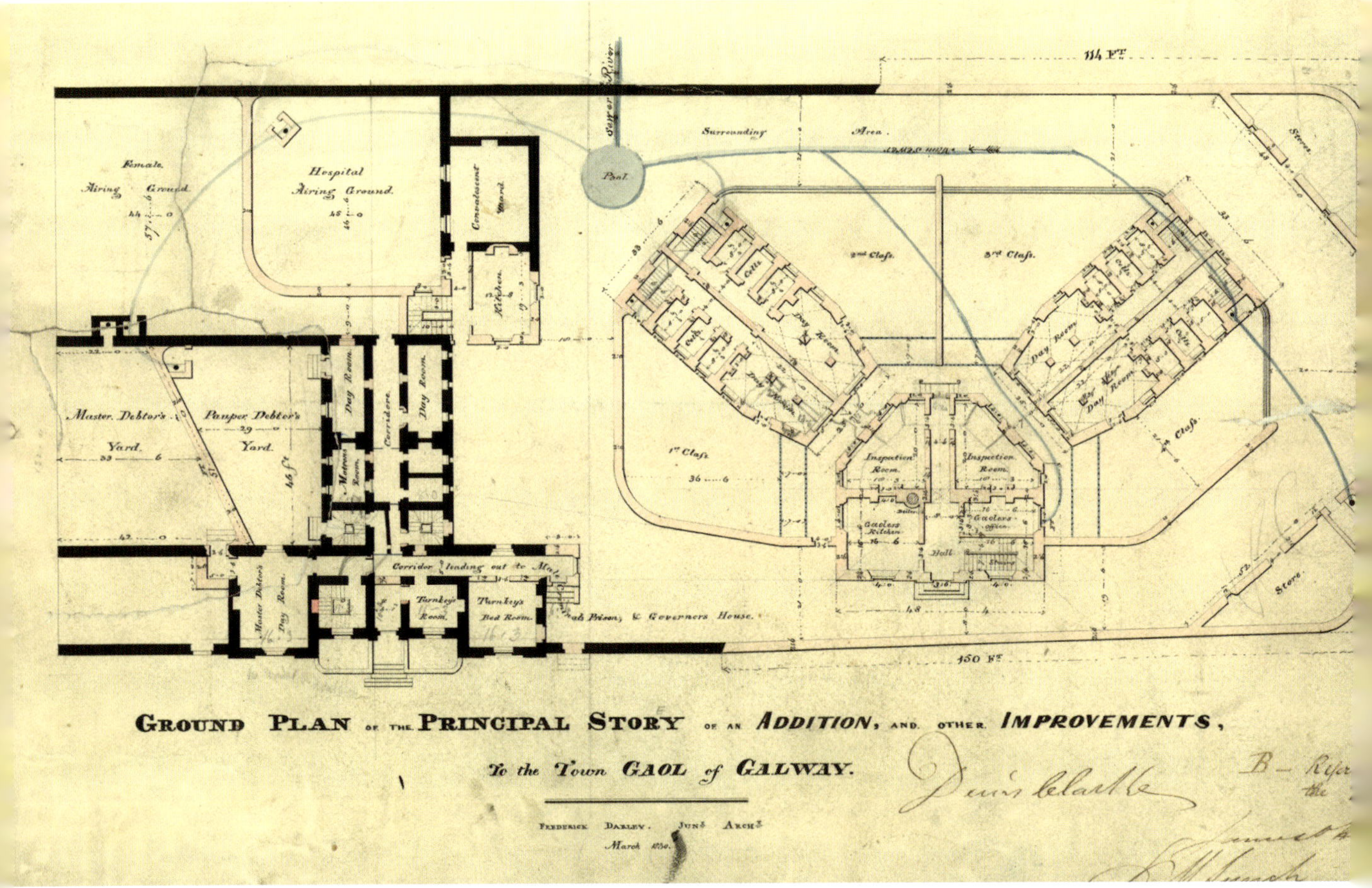

Fig. 6.43. Galway town gaol, ground-floor plan. Frederick Darley, Jnr, 1830. From the outset, Galway town's small rectilinear gaol (left) was seen as completely inadequate (see Chapter 4). In the early 1830s, the town grand jurors were eventually convinced to pay for a small radial-plan addition (right). (*Reproduced courtesy of Galway County Council Archives.*)

Fig. 6.11. Galway town gaol, from the south, *c.* 1940. Darley's small radial-plan addition is visible in the foreground; in the top left are some semi-circular cell windows of Hardwick and Morrison's county gaol from the 1800s (see Chapter 4). Both gaols were surrounded with a maze of yards and high walls. A Catholic cathedral occupies the site today. From Geraldine Curtin, *Women of Galway Jail* (2001), p. 37. (*Reproduced courtesy of Geraldine Curtin.*)

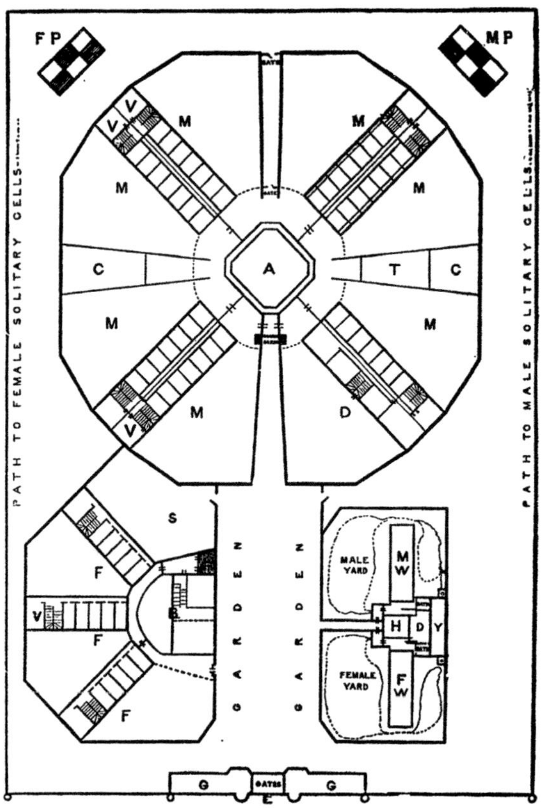

A Governor's house, chapel over it and offices. B Matron's house. CC cisterns. D debtors' prison. E entrance to the gaol. FF female prison. GG officers' quarters. H hospital. FW female ward. MW male ward. T treadwheel. MMM male prison. MP punishment cells for males; FP for females. S stone yard. VVVV baths lately erected.

Fig. 6.45. Castlebar gaol, County Mayo, ground-floor plan, 1870. Darley's large radial-plan prison provided complete segregation of the sexes (both in the cell blocks, and in the hospital (marked 'MW' and 'FW'). From *Forty-ninth Report … on … the Prisons of Ireland, 1870*, H.C. 1871 (C. 359), xxx, p. 218.

Fig. 6.46. Castlebar gaol, from the west, *c.* 1900 (by Thomas J. Wynne). The Mayo grand jurors were among the last in Ireland to rebuild their gaol in accordance with the new penal-reform and prison-discipline agendas. Darley provided them with an extravagant Gothic edifice at the outskirts of their county town. (*Reproduced courtesy of Source Photographic Archives (Wynne collection).*)

In counties Limerick and Tipperary, there were substantial additions made to the existing county gaols. James Pain added a female prison with ten cells to his Limerick county gaol in 1835, again following the new fashion for complete separation of the sexes.[137] In Clonmel, the county gaol was perennially overcrowded, and never more so than during the Tithe War of the early 1830s. The grand jurors eventually conceded to build a house of correction adjacent to their old rectilinear gaol, and the architect John B. Keane provided the design; it was built between 1831 and 1834 (Fig. 6.48).[138] During the building process, the purpose of this addition shifted from being simply a house of correction of 100 cells for both sexes, to being solely a male prison, and this somewhat relieved the

Fig. 6.47. (below) Castlebar gaol, inspection building and two radial blocks, *c.* 1900 (by Thomas J. Wynne). The large radial-plan gaol marked a revolutionary change in the county's prison system and allowed proper classification and inspection for the first time. It was built with extensive government loans, which, it would appear, were never fully repaid. The three figures, a lady and two men, remain unidentified. (*Reproduced courtesy of Source Photographic Archives (Wynne collection).*)

great burden then placed on the institution.[139] Keane's design was, of course for this time, radial in plan, but for his entrance gateway he borrowed from Elsam's design for Cavan – in what is the only part of the complex that still survives. Neither of these gaols, nor indeed Darley's buildings in Galway and Castlebar, were designed on the 'separate' system just then coming into fashion; the cells were too small and not properly heated and ventilated for round-the-clock inhabitation. They were instead responses to the older concerns for adequate classification and inspection and were thus old before their time when the shift came to formally adopt the 'separate' system at the end of the decade.

In Dublin, the vast empty Richmond penitentiary provided an opportunity for a shake-up of the city's prisons. The object was, by whatever means, to close and abandon the notorious Newgate, but this proved much more difficult than expected. Instead, Palmer and Woodward succeeded in shutting down the small house of correction for young offenders and vagrants at Smithfield and transferring them, and the entirety of the city's female prisoners, to the former penitentiary at Grangegorman.[140] The 'female penitentiary', as it was renamed, was a bold experiment in female incarceration, and one of the first of its kind; Fry and the Hibernian Ladies' Society had been advocating such an institution for many years. All of the officers were to be female.[141] To make better use of Johnston's inconvenient design, a series of extensive alterations were carried out between 1838 and 1840 by John Semple, including the building of a large block of additional cells within the gaol and the conversion of some of the large work-rooms into day-rooms for prisoners.[142] The work was just the first of many interventions to remedy the original defects of the gaol in subsequent years.

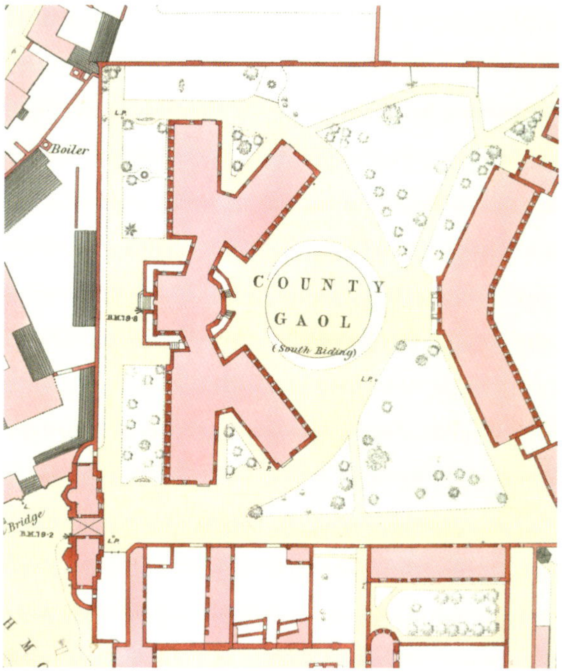

Fig. 6.48. Clonmel gaol, detail of house of correction, built between 1831 and 1834. Ordnance Survey five-feet town map, 1874. Tipperary's gaol was perennially overcrowded, and John B. Keane's large addition lessened pressure on the institution. The old rectilinear-plan gaol is visible at the bottom, as is the new entranceway that Keane built to link the two parts of the gaol. (*Reproduced courtesy of the Board of Trinity College Dublin.*)

Meanwhile, Semple was commissioned to build a large radial-plan addition to the Richmond bridewell at the other end of the city. The reconfiguration of the city's prisons meant that the bridewell was only to house men, and as they were so great in number, many more cells would be needed. With £14,000 in loans, the city jurors voted for an additional 214 cells, some carved out inside Johnston's old building, but most built in a series of low radial wings nearby (Fig. 6.49).[143] The inspectors insisted that these new cells would be large enough to permit the 'separate' system if it was in future adopted, and the design is distinctive in that it contains no day-rooms for prisoners, who were to be kept in their cells at all times. This addition, since demolished, may be regarded as Ireland's first 'separate-system' prison block but despite the intentions of the inspectors, when some problems with ventilation and labour were more fully understood in the early 1840s, they changed their stance and declared the early prototype incorrectly built as the cells were too small to meet the revised standards.[144]

By around 1840, the city's prisoners were concentrated in just three great institutions: Grangegorman (for females), South Circular Road (for males), and Newgate (for untried males, convicts, and an untidy miscellany of others). As previously noted, plans by Semple to rebuild Newgate were soon thereafter aborted and the Newgate Gaol Act, 1840, proposed that no more work should be carried out to remedy the gaol's many defects.[145] The inspectors also scored a significant victory in consolidating the city's debtors' prisons in 1842, with the passing of an act that declared only the Four Courts Marshalsea would remain open.[146] The city marshalsea and sheriff's prison closed in the years that followed.

However, the reconfiguration of Dublin's prisons, which had been on the mind of the inspectors for many years, was soon overtaken by a series of wider changes that affected the course of Irish prisons. First, the Poor Law in 1838 set up an entirely new system of local government and initiated the building of over one hundred workhouses in the early 1840s.[147] In many cases these institutions received the same class of persons who had previously ended up in county gaols. Second, all the new district lunatic asylums had opened their doors by 1835, and these had relieved most gaols of a historic function. Their design and use also contributed to debates about ventilation, the placing of corridors, and the division between larger and smaller rooms.[148] They also became an ever-increasing burden on the budgets of grand jurors. Third, the Criminal Lunatics Act of 1838 empowered magistrates and, if necessary, central government to keep 'dangerous' or convicted insane persons in lunatic asylums.[149] This was the first step in the plan to build a completely separate national criminal lunatic asylum that was later designed by Jacob Owen and built between 1847 and 1850, which formally ended a role for county gaols that, all observers agreed, had been continuing for far too long.[150] Fourth, and finally, the Irish Municipal Corporations Act of 1840 (some years after the passing of its British equivalent) brought widespread changes to local government and, in the field of prisons, allowed town and county grand jurors to combine their gaols – or as the inspectors often hoped – to use the smaller gaol only for females, and the larger for males.[151] The year 1838 is a useful time to draw this chapter to a close as there were just two gaols under construction in the entire country – both in Dublin – and the later adoption of the 'separate' system initiated a final rebuilding programme in the years through to the mid-1860s. This architectural coda to Irish prison building was more slow-paced and contested, and far less idealistic, than when Palmer and Woodward were catapulted into the crest of what had been, albeit temporarily, a fashionable penal-reform movement, and 'zeal' was harder to come by in the years after 1838.

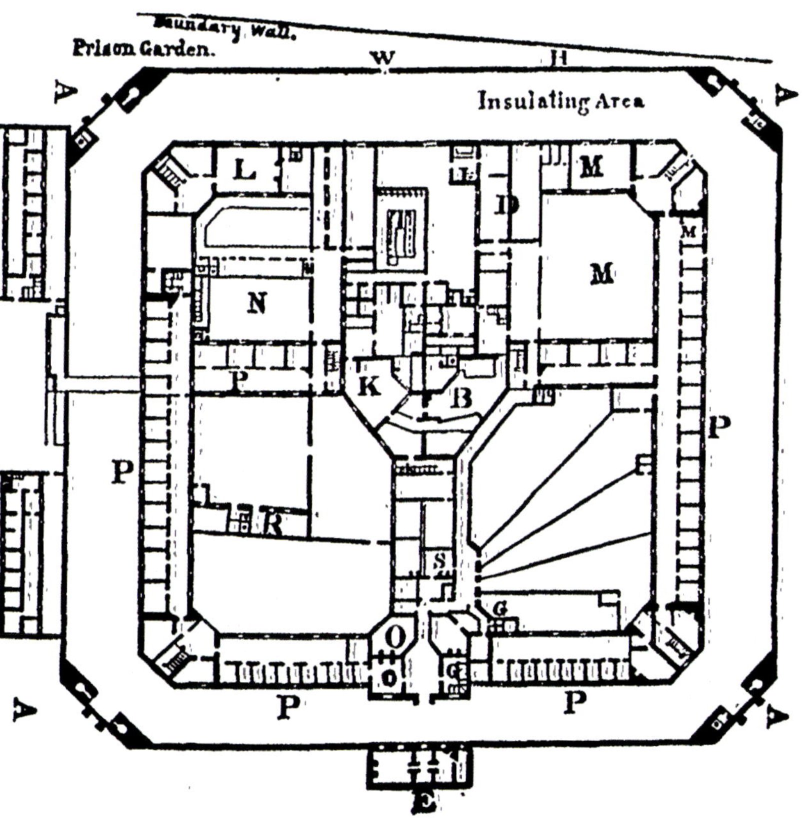

Fig. 6.49 Richmond bridewell, Dublin, ground-floor plan, 1870. John Semple added the five radial cell blocks to the left between 1838 and 1840. The inspectors hoped that the 'separate' system might be trialled in the new extension, but later changed their minds when they learned the individual cells were too small for this use, according to the rapidly evolving specifications of the time. From *Forty-ninth Report … on … the Prisons of Ireland, 1870*, H.C. 1871 (C. 359), xxx, p. 558.

- **A** ramparts for sentries
- **B** bakehouse
- **D** washhouse
- **E** entrance gate from the Circular-road
- **G** Governor's house
- **H** prison garden
- **W** prison garden
- **K** kitchen
- **L** apartments used as stores and for looms
- **O** offices
- **P** prison cells
- **R** workshops
- **S** store
- **M** hospital wards above school-room on ground floor
- **T** tread-wheel
- **M** hospital and exercising yard
- **N** exercising yard

KITCHEN
PANTRY
STORE
CENTRAL HALL
CORRIDOR
BATHS
BOXES
RECEPTION
OFFICE
YARD
VERANDAH
CHIEF CLERK
CLERKS
INCLINED PLANE
EXERCISE YARD

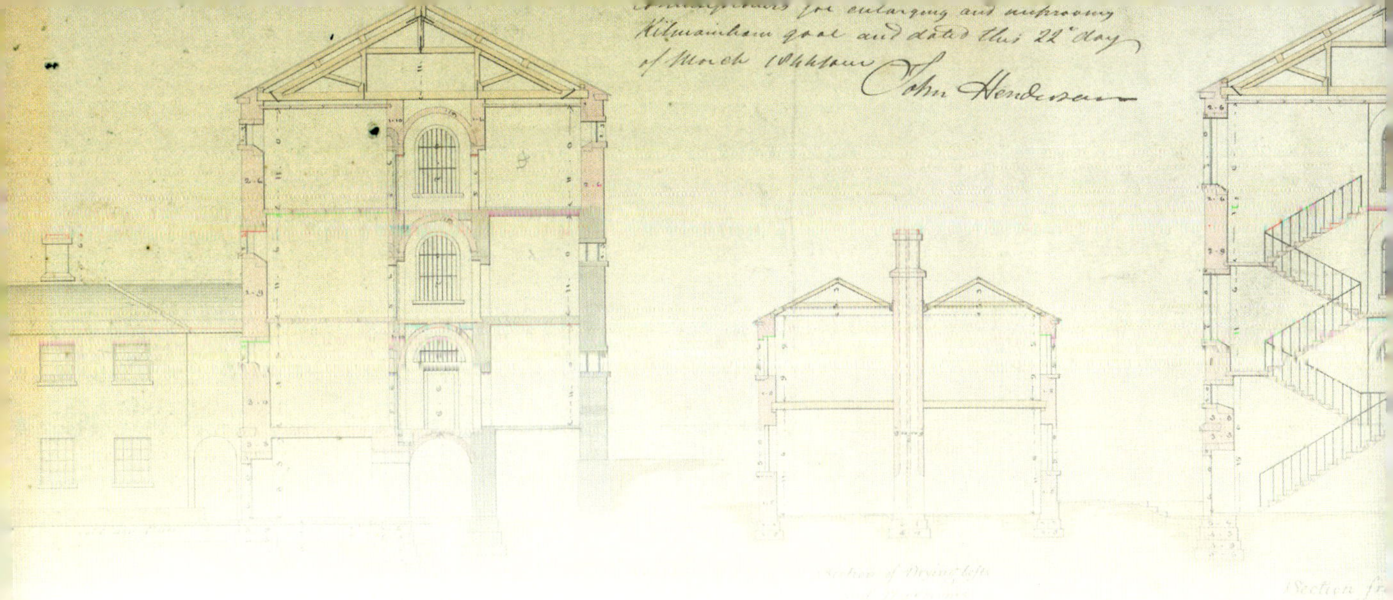

Chapter 7

A Separate Agenda:

Conformity, consolidation, the Famine, and its aftermath, 1838–55

Few could doubt the scale of rebuilding of gaols that had occurred in Ireland between 1810 and around 1838. A middle-aged adult at the turn of the nineteenth century could easily have seen three new iterations of their local county gaol – built and demolished – during their lifetime. This was unprecedented in Irish history, and with grand-jury budgets increasingly stretched – and heavy loans to repay – it must have seemed unlikely in these years that another rebuilding programme was about to begin (Figs 7.1, 7.2). Nonetheless, as noted in Chapter 6, the failure of the many new gaols to achieve any

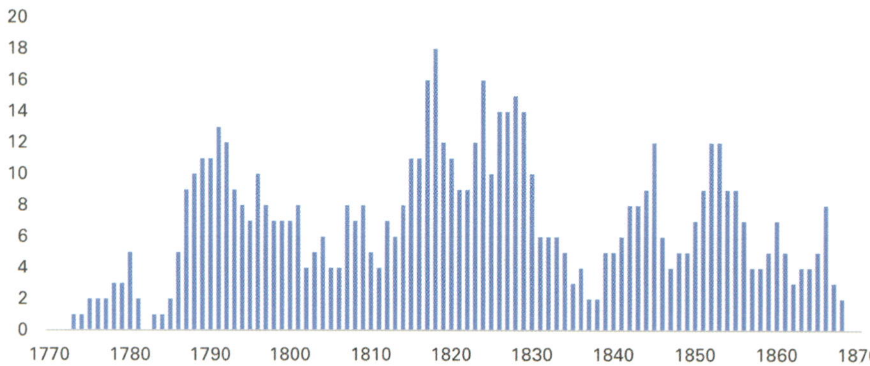

Fig. 7.1. Graph showing the number of gaols that were under construction in Ireland between 1770 and 1870. Building activity after around 1838 fell short of the peaks attained in the 1790s, 1810s and 1820s, and individual building projects tended to be less ambitious in size. Compiled from Appendix A.

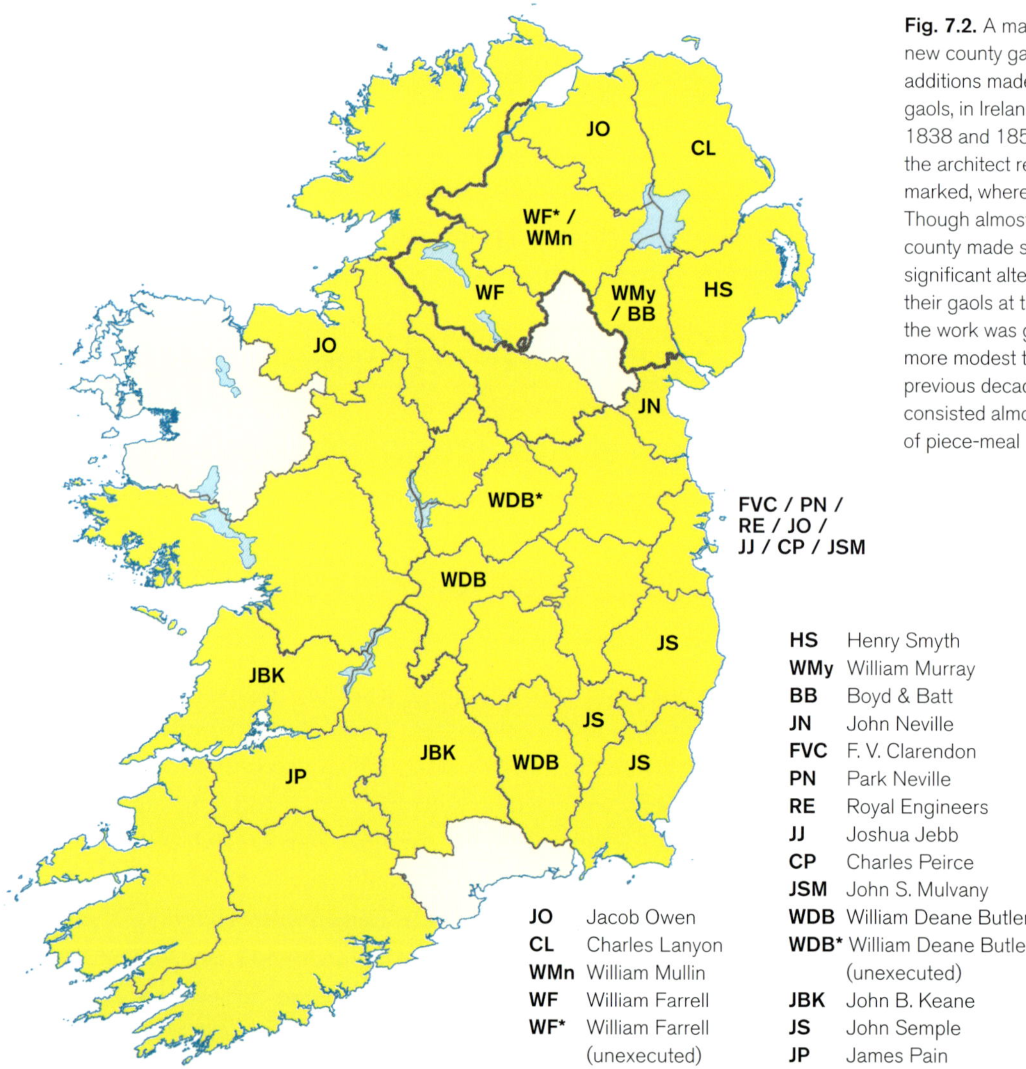

Fig. 7.2. A map showing new county gaols, or large additions made to existing gaols, in Ireland between 1838 and 1855, with the architect responsible marked, where known. Though almost every county made some significant alterations to their gaols at this time, the work was generally more modest than in previous decades and consisted almost entirely of piece-meal additions.

meaningful decrease in crime levels troubled the reformers who had advocated most for their building. The utopian idealism of the early 1820s – when for a brief time it was thought that an architecturally 'perfect' gaol would lead to a mathematical reduction in crime – failed to re-emerge in this last episode of building. Reformers in Britain and Ireland looked instead for new ideas and found them in the experimental prison-discipline systems then being established in the United States: the 'silent' and the 'separate' systems. The silent system was quickly abandoned by moderate voices (it was found to lead to insanity among prisoners), but certain Irish gaols, for example Lifford, used it to some extent in the 1830s, when the gaoler thought it impossible to provide adequate classification.[1]

Of far more influence was the separate system of confinement, pioneered at the Cherry Hill penitentiary in Pennsylvania, and built by an Englishman, John de Haviland, between 1821 and 1829 (Fig. 7.3).[2] This allowed prisoners to be kept in individual cells with little or no contact with the outside world or with other inmates. Isolation was seen by many as a solution to the perennial problem of 'moral contagion' among prisoners, and a logical conclusion of earlier theories of classification. To make the case that it was humane to keep a prisoner in such

Fig. 7.3. Cherry Hill penitentiary, Philadelphia, Pennsylvania, perspective view. John de Haviland, 1821–9. This pioneering separate-system prison attracted international attention, and brought great riches for its designer, who had emigrated from England and brought with him the radial designs of Blackburn and others. At Cherry Hill, prisoners spent almost their entire sentence in individual cells, separate from all other offenders. The design inspired London's Pentonville, and in turn large prisons in Belfast, Dublin, and elsewhere. (*Reproduced courtesy of The Library Company of Philadelphia.*)

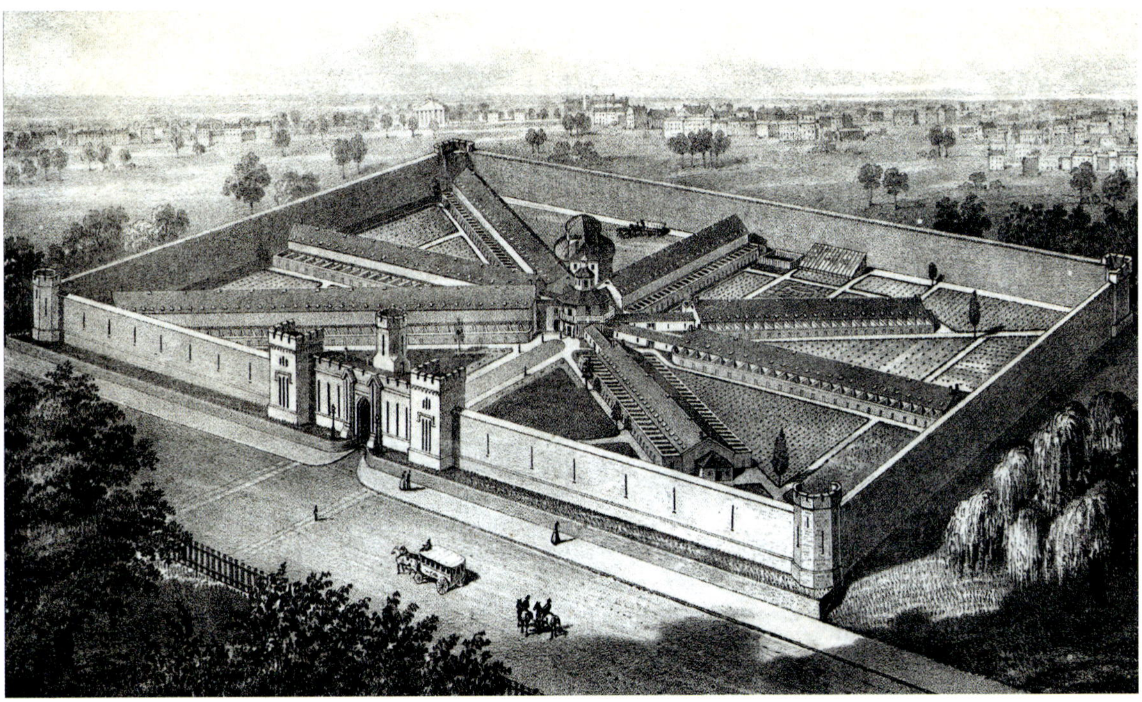

conditions for twenty-three or more hours a day, the American penal reformers realised that each cell would have to be larger than under the old system, where prisoners simply slept at night but spent their days in large communal work-rooms. They also realised the cells would need to be adequately heated and ventilated to ensure that fever did not emerge. In the gaols built to the standards set by the SIPD and the AIPPD in the 1820s, each cell was typically no larger than ten feet by seven (as at Downpatrick). By contrast, cells at the separate-system Pentonville prison in London were thirteen feet by seven, were higher, and included a privy, a sink, and a table (Fig. 7.4).[3] Enlarging cells by a few feet may not appear such a major undertaking, but when it is considered that in the new gaols the walls were generally built of thick, fireproof masonry construction – with brick vaults – and that some gaols had well in excess of 100 cells, the practical interventions required to adapt to the separate system were daunting and hugely expensive. The early experimental building of separate-system cells at Richmond bridewell, noted at the end of Chapter 6, was soon superseded by many additions and alterations to Irish gaols – some modest in scale, others much more extensive. Though this rebuilding programme was advocated by the inspectors, they relied upon international examples almost entirely for their 'models' and took great interest in William Crawford's report on American penitentiaries, and Joshua Jebb's appointment as surveyor general of prisons in Britain in 1837, and his designs for Pentonville that followed soon after (Figs 7.5, 7.6).[4]

Fig. 7.4. Pentonville (the 'model prison'), London, sections of a cell. Joshua Jebb, 1840–2. Under the separate system of confinement, cells were larger and more equipped for round-the-clock inhabitation; where older prisons had cells that were simply furnished with beds or hammocks, Jebb provided a privy, a sink and a table in each cell, and most importantly a centralised ventilation system to prevent fever. From *Report of the Surveyor-general of Prisons on the Construction, Ventilation and Details of Pentonville Prison, 1844*, H.C. 1844 (594), xxviii.

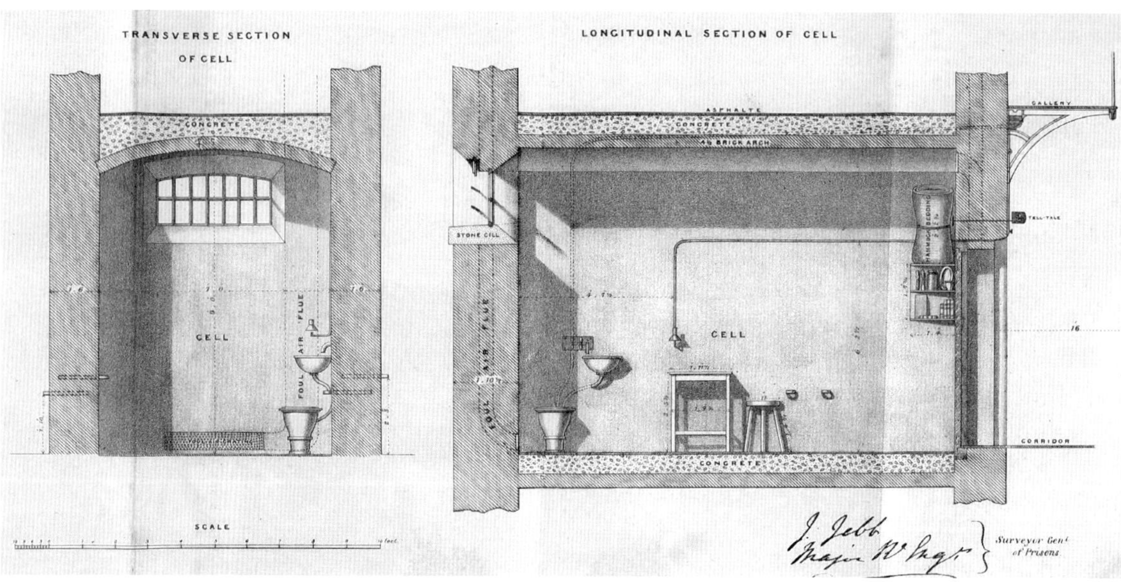

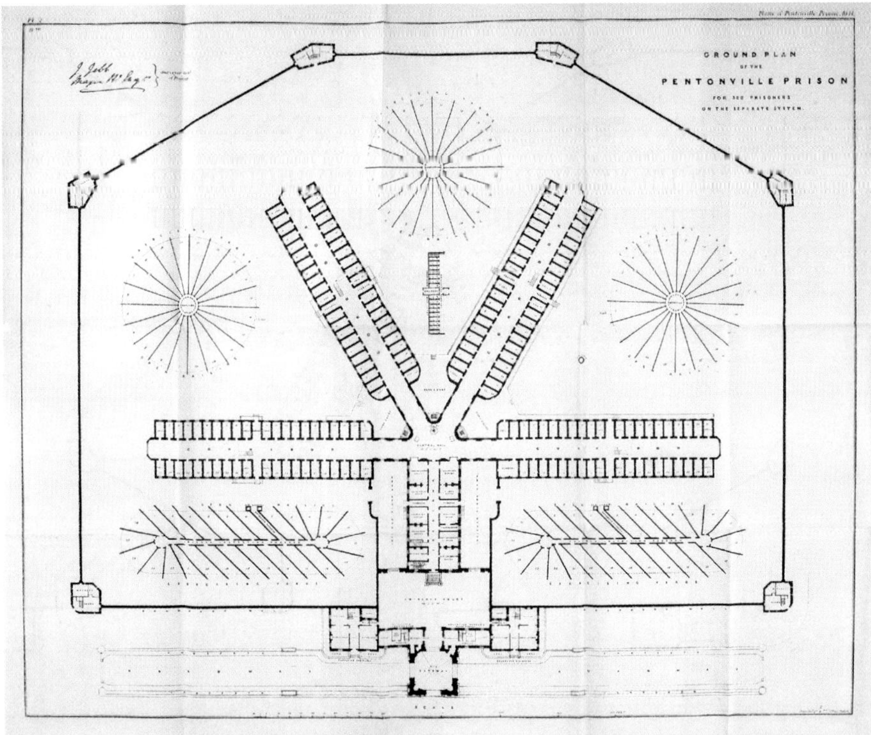

Fig. 7.5. Pentonville (the 'model prison'), London, ground-floor plan. Joshua Jebb, 1840–2. The 'model' separate-system prison differed from radial-plan classification-system prisons in two key respects: first, the cells were larger and individually heated and ventilated, and second, the corridors linking the inspection hub with the cells permitted unobstructed inspection of the entrance to each cell. Jebb's design thus took the earlier concepts of classification and inspection to their logical conclusion. The radial fan-like buildings placed between the wings of the prison were used to separate prisoners during work and exercise. From *Report of the Surveyor-general of Prisons on the Construction, Ventilation and Details of Pentonville Prison, 1844*, H.C. 1844 (594), xxviii.

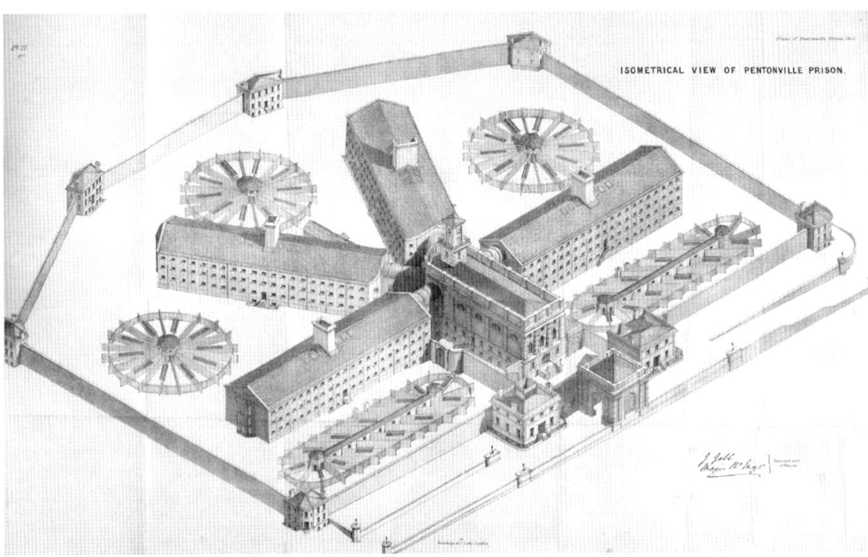

Fig. 7.6. Pentonville (the 'model prison'), London, perspective view. Joshua Jebb, 1840–2. This view shows how similar were, in general outline, the new prisons in Philadelphia and London (compare with Fig. 7.3). Jebb restricted any architectural ornamentation only to the entrance carriage porch, the governor's building behind, and the perimeter watch houses. From *Report of the Surveyor-general of Prisons on the Construction, Ventilation and Details of Pentonville Prison, 1844*, H.C. 1844 (594), xxviii.

In March 1837, Palmer and Woodward pronounced in favour of the separate system and pushed for its use in all future gaol building.[5] Three years later, an Irish prisons act – modelled closely on an English act of around the same time – gave unquestionable official endorsement to the separate system:

> In order to prevent the contamination arising from the association of prisoners in any prison in which rules for the individual separation of prisoners shall be in force, any prisoner may be separately confined during the whole or any part of the period of his or her imprisonment.[6]

The inspectors now had the unenviable task of attempting to convince grand jurors to make extensive alterations to their relatively new gaols, in order to implement this new system in penal administration. They were initially met with little enthusiasm, and a call from the Treasury in London at the same time to increase the interest rates payable on gaol loans only further weakened any appetite for building.[7] When the loans issue was resolved to the grand jurors' satisfaction, the building of a series of new separate-system additions to existing gaols began. One of the first was at Wicklow, a county with a relatively low crime rate that had long maintained an interest in penal-reform issues.[8] Around the time of the founding of the AIPPD, a separate organisation, the 'Association for Bettering the Condition of the Prisoners in the County Gaol of Wicklow', was also established, and the gaol was significantly expanded and rebuilt to the designs of William Vitruvius Morrison.[9] By 1836 there were, on average, just thirty prisoners kept in the gaol's thirty-two cells.[10] Still, the grand jurors pushed for around twenty more cells and, after consulting with the inspectors, they planned an annexe on the old-fashioned radial-classification system. However, the separate system was soon thereafter adopted, and when these plans were submitted for official approval in 1841, the design of the annexe had morphed

Fig. 7.7. (below left) Wicklow gaol, from the west. Despite a low crime rate, the Wicklow grand jurors funded several additions to their county gaol during the 1820s and 1830s. The dramatic entrance façade was likely part of William Vitruvius Morrison's work at the gaol from 1819 onwards. The 1840s separate-system addition is situated to the rear, and now forms part of a large heritage centre. (*Photograph by author, 2013.*)

Fig. 7.8. (below right) Wicklow gaol, separate-system cell block, by John Semple, from the south. Outwardly similar to prison cell blocks of earlier times, this wing was revolutionary in its internal arrangement of cells and mezzanines. (*Photograph by author, 2013.*)

Fig. 7.9. Wicklow gaol, separate-system cell block, by John Semple, from the west. Instead of a narrow series of corridors that led to single rows of cells, as in earlier radial-plan prisons, Wicklow's cell block was designed with an airy, top-lit hall and iron mezzanine walkways that gave access to large cells on both sides. Following Pentonville, this layout allowed new levels of separation and inspection of prisoners (compare with Fig. 7.10 below). (*Photograph by author, 2013.*)

Fig. 7.10. Pentonville (the 'model prison'), London, perspective view of interior. Joshua Jebb, 1840–2. On a much larger scale, Jebb demonstrated the logic and order of linking cells with the inspection hub via a large hall and a series of iron walkways (compare with Fig. 7.9). From *Report of the Surveyor-general of Prisons on the Construction, Ventilation and Details of Pentonville Prison, 1844*, H.C. 1844 (594), xxviii.

into a more ambitious block of forty-six cells on the separate system. The jurors presented the handsome sum of £6,000 to build the addition, and it was erected in 1842 and 1843 (Figs 7.7–7.9).[11] This cell block, by John Semple, is important for two reasons: first, it was the first separate-system addition in Ireland to follow precisely the dimensions and arrangement of Jebb's Pentonville.[12] Second, in order to facilitate continuous and unobstructed inspection, it provided access to the cells via a series of cast-iron mezzanine walkways, again borrowed from Pentonville (Fig. 7.10). The result was a new departure for the internal arrangement of an Irish gaol: instead of the labyrinthine passageways of the early rectilinear designs, or the narrow corridors of the radial- and polygonal-plan prisons of later years, we find instead a large high central hall, lit from above, surrounded by an outer shell of heated large cells. This design is typical of almost all the new gaols and additions to existing gaols built from around 1840 onwards.

Fits and starts

Several other counties followed with modest alterations and additions in the years before the Famine, including Fermanagh, Wexford, Dublin, Carlow, and Kildare. For the Fermanagh grand jurors, Richard Morrison's three-wing radial-plan gaol at Enniskillen was only just large enough for the county's needs. In 1815, when it opened, there were 252 criminal indictments in the county; however, by 1817 this had fallen to 217, and by 1823 it stood at 184 (Fig. 7.11).[13] For the next decade, faced with a fluctuating criminal-indictment rate, Palmer and Woodward vacillated over how many additional cells – if any – might be required. In 1827, Palmer called for twenty more cells; in 1828, Woodward said this was unnecessary, as there was an average of seventy prisoners for the gaol's sixty-nine beds.[14] In 1831 and 1832, in the midst of an unprecedented increase in crime, both inspectors agreed that some addition was necessary; however, a temporary abatement in this increase in 1835 led them to once again withdraw their request.[15] The surge reappeared the following year, and by 1838 Woodward was clear that no fewer than eighty new cells would be needed, and he recommended that the separate system should be employed.[16] The jurors were unwilling to meet the projected £10,000 bill, having only recently paid off the last of the loans for the original building, and the plans were only finally agreed, with a reduced budget, in 1843.[17] William Farrell, who had built a large addition to the gaol in neighbouring Cavan in the previous decade, and who had built courthouses in Cavan, Leitrim, and Fermanagh (see chapters 2, 5, and 6), drew up the design for seventy separate-system cells and a hospital block,

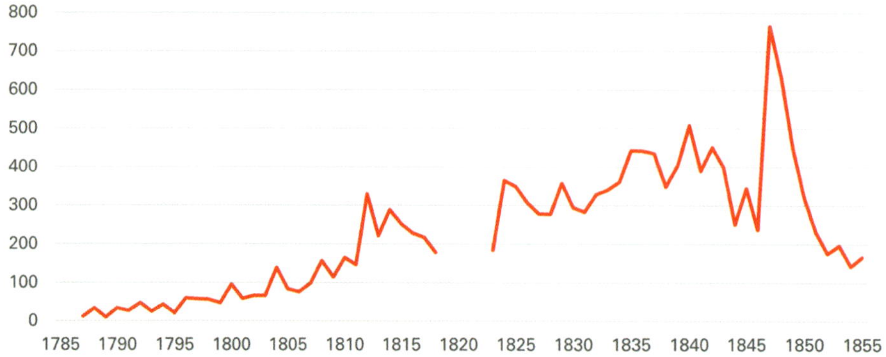

Fig. 7.11. Criminal indictments in County Fermanagh between 1787 and 1855 (where available). The periodic ebb and flow of crime in the county repeatedly delayed the enlargement of the county gaol; paradoxically, by the time that building work had finally begun in the early 1840s, the crime rate was falling rapidly. Compiled from Appendix B.

Fig. 7.12. (right) Enniskillen gaol, ground-floor plan, 1870. The original three-wing gaol designed by Richard Morrison in the 1810s (marked 'Old Prison') was greatly extended with William Farrell's separate-system block, infirmary, and work sheds to the rear in the 1840s. From *Forty-ninth Report … on … the Prisons of Ireland, 1870*, H.C. 1871 (C. 359), xxx, p. 146.

Fig. 7.13. (below) Enniskillen gaol, separate-system block and infirmary, from the east. Today, the older parts of the gaol have been demolished but Farrell's additions from the 1840s remain remarkably intact. The large central hall of the cell block to the right is apparent from the arrangement of windows at the gable wall, while the smaller windows of the cells run down either side of the façade. (*Photograph by author, 2014.*)

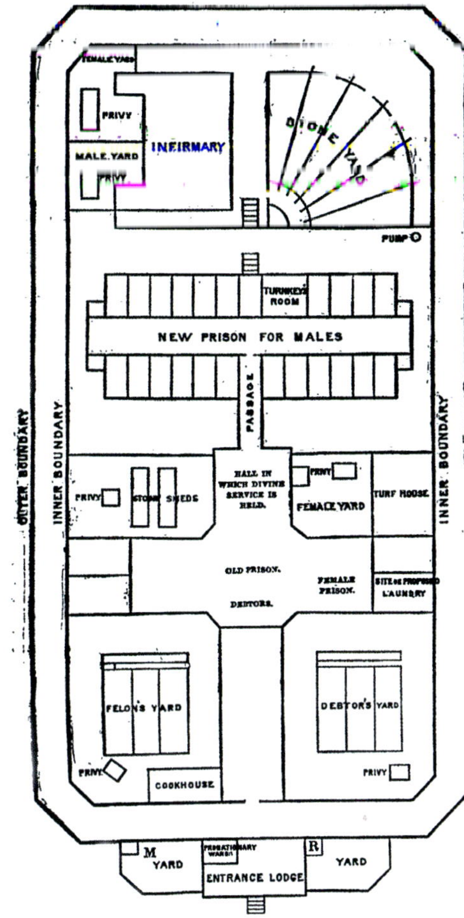

R, reception cell for females.

and they were erected to the rear of the old gaol between 1843 and 1845 (Figs 7.12, 7.13).[18] As the jurors had so long delayed their building plans, the extension opened at a time when – barring the exceptional years of the Famine (when the indictment rate exploded five-fold in the space of a year) – the level of crime in the county was in a steep decline; from a peak of 508 cases in 1840, it had fallen to 237 on the eve of the Famine, and just 142 by 1854. Indeed, Farrell's extension was begun when this fall-off was already clearly apparent, and its building may thus be more accurately attributed to the gradual increase in crime of earlier years, and perhaps most of all the enthusiasm of the inspectors for experimenting with the new separate-system design, than to the state of crime when it was finally erected.

The story was similar elsewhere. In Wexford, the county gaol, despite a series of extensions in the mid-1820s, was still too small for the county; by

1836 the inspectors found eighty prisoners occupying just forty-six cells.[19] As in Fermanagh, the late 1830s in Wexford was an exceptional period of tithe- and unemployment-related crime, and the broad reduction in crime that followed in the early 1840s lessened pressure on the grand jurors (Fig. 7.14). They also postponed any decision on additions while the four south-eastern counties of Wicklow, Wexford, Carlow, and Waterford considered combining forces to build a new house of correction in a central town such as Enniscorthy, County Wexford.[20] The moving or proposed moving of the assizes and county gaol in King's County, Tipperary, and Waterford, as discussed in Chapter 3, was a live issue in the 1830s but, apart from King's and Tipperary, it only served to delay the necessary rebuilding or expansion of existing gaols. The Wicklow jurors briefly flirted with the idea of moving their courthouse and gaol from Wicklow town to Rathdrum in 1840.[21] But when this and the south-eastern penitentiary scheme were soon abandoned, the Wexford jurors instead proposed a four-wing radial-plan addition to their gaol, with half of the cells to be designed according to the separate system, and the other half on the old classification system; this equivocal adoption of the new arrangement was typical of the time, and indicative of how the American separate system was still seen – despite the inspectors' lobbying – as somewhat experimental in nature.[22] As in Fermanagh, a series of delays and cuts – and the eventual threat of an imperative presentment from an assize judge – meant that a smaller, fifty-cell addition, on the separate system alone, designed by John Semple, was built between 1843 and 1846 (Fig. 7.15); when it opened the crime rate in the county was just half of what it had been a decade earlier.[23] The new cell block was hidden from the road by an extravagant Gothick gateway (Fig. 7.16), also by Semple, which served as the gaoler and turnkey's residence, and was described by one of the inspectors – in a rare show of artistic interest – as a 'very handsome' façade.[24] Asenath Nicholson, visiting during construction,

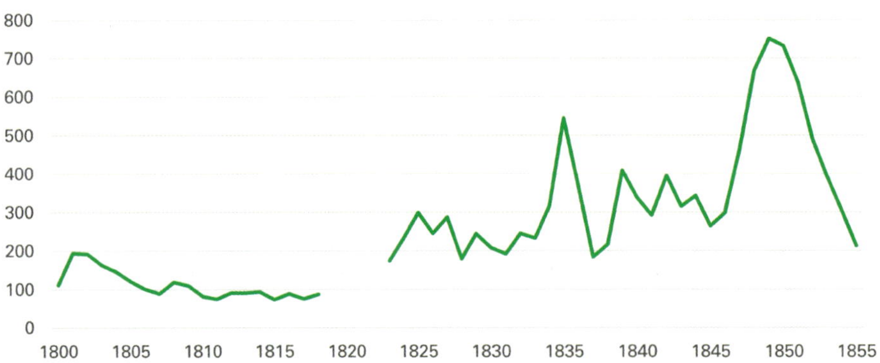

Fig. 7.14. Criminal indictments in County Wexford between 1800 and 1855 (where available). Fluctuating crime levels frustrated the prison inspectors' attempts to convince the Wexford grand jurors to expand their small gaol. When an addition was eventually completed, on the eve of the Famine, the indictment rate was at its lowest in many years. After the exceptional years that followed, it resumed its downward trend. Compiled from Appendix B.

thought the gaol 'looked little like a house of punishment', and suggested that the inmates were better housed and fed inside than out.[25] It remains a mystery why, at a time when extravagant grand-jury spending on 'palatial' gaol buildings was subject to increased public criticism, and when the proposed addition to Wexford's gaol had been repeatedly downsized and simplified, the jurors elected to fund this playful and theatrical façade, but it offers a revealing insight into their relative priorities.

Fig. 7.15. Wexford gaol, ground-floor plan, 1870. The confusing arrangement of the gaol arose from the piece-meal nature of at least seven different building periods. The separate-system block of the 1840s and its associated entrance gateway (see Fig. 7.16) are visible at the bottom of this drawing, marked 'K' and 'G' respectively. From *Forty-eighth Report … on … the Prisons of Ireland, 1869*, H.C. 1870 (C. 173), xxxvii, p. 489.

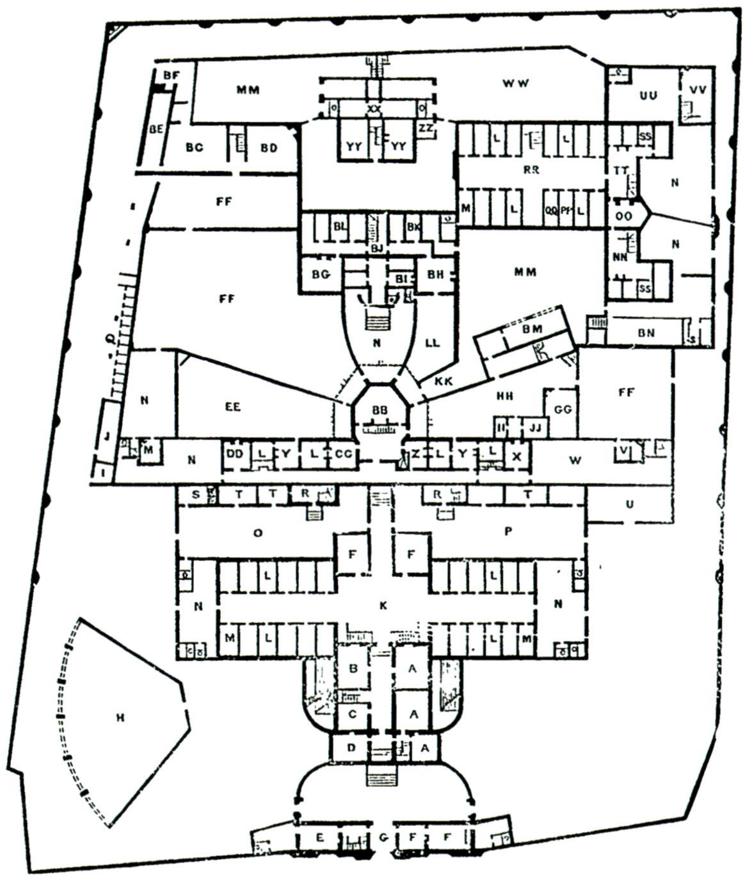

A, Governor's house; B, Clerk's office; C, Governor's office; D, Board-room; E, for visitors; F, warders' rooms; G, entrance to gaol; H, prisoners' exercising ground; I, stable; J, coal store; K, central hall of separate prison for males; L, separate prison for males; M, lavatories and water-closets; N, yards; O, yard for pauper debtors; P, yard for master debtors; Q, sheds for stone-breaking; R, entrance to marshalsea; S, bath; T, stores; U, straw store; V, photographic house; W, mistress debtors' exercising ground; X, mistress debtors; Y and Z, old prison cells; BC, wool carding room; BD, BG, BL, lunatic wards; BE, crank; BI, BJ, solitary cells; BF, tuck mill; BK, reception cells; BM, boiler house; BN, wash-house; BB, store; CC, apartment for Deputy Governor; DD, apartment for turnkey; EE, FF, exercising yards for lunatics; GG, kitchen; HH, cook-house yard; II, milk store; JJ, bread store; KK, entrance to female prison; LL, reception yard; MM, hospital yard; NN, SS, reception ward; OO, female warders' room; QQ, matron's apartments; RR, separate prison for females; TT, female school; UU, female laundry; VV, yard for laundry; WW, hospital yard; XX, YY, hospital; ZZ, dead-house.

Fig. 7.16. Wexford gaol, from the north. Designed by John Semple and built between 1843 and 1846, this extravagant two-dimensional Gothick gateway led to a much plainer separate-system cell block behind that was similar to those built in Wicklow and Enniskillen at this time. (*Photograph by author, 2014.*)

The inspectors faced an uphill struggle. Due to strong opposition from grand jurors, who claimed an inability to fund the required changes of the new prison system, the inspectors settled instead for a series of more piece-meal alterations. At Kilmainham, twenty-seven female separate-system cells were designed by the city architect, Park Neville, and built by 1845 (Fig. 7.17).[26] In Naas, the grand jury enlarged eighteen cells and fitted ventilation and piped heating.[27] In Clonmel, forty separate-system cells were added to the female prison.[28] In Cavan, a separate-system female prison was erected.[29] At the female penitentiary in Grangegorman, forty-five separate-system cells were built.[30] In Mullingar, the grand jurors employed William Deane Butler to enlarge some of the cells in Hargrave's polygonal gaol (Fig. 7.18).[31] In Carlow, John Semple added just eight separate-system cells, and a turnkey's lodge, to the county gaol.[32] To realise this, he changed the orientation of the gaol so that the main entrance now faced south instead of west; architecturally, he borrowed from Elsam's Sanmicheli-esque design for Cavan (Figs 7.19, 7.20). This quantity of building around the country may seem impressive, but it pales in comparison to the earlier full-blooded rebuilding programmes of the 1810s and late 1820s, and, on the eve of the Famine, most Irish gaols were still arranged on the increasingly discredited classification system. However, Ireland's first entirely new 'model' gaol, along the lines of Pentonville, opened in 1845 in Belfast. This was Crumlin Road gaol, and in contrast to earlier periods, it was one of only two entirely new gaols of this time – the other was at Nenagh. A comparative history of these two projects reveals some of the dynamics of the penal-reform movement on the eve of the Famine.

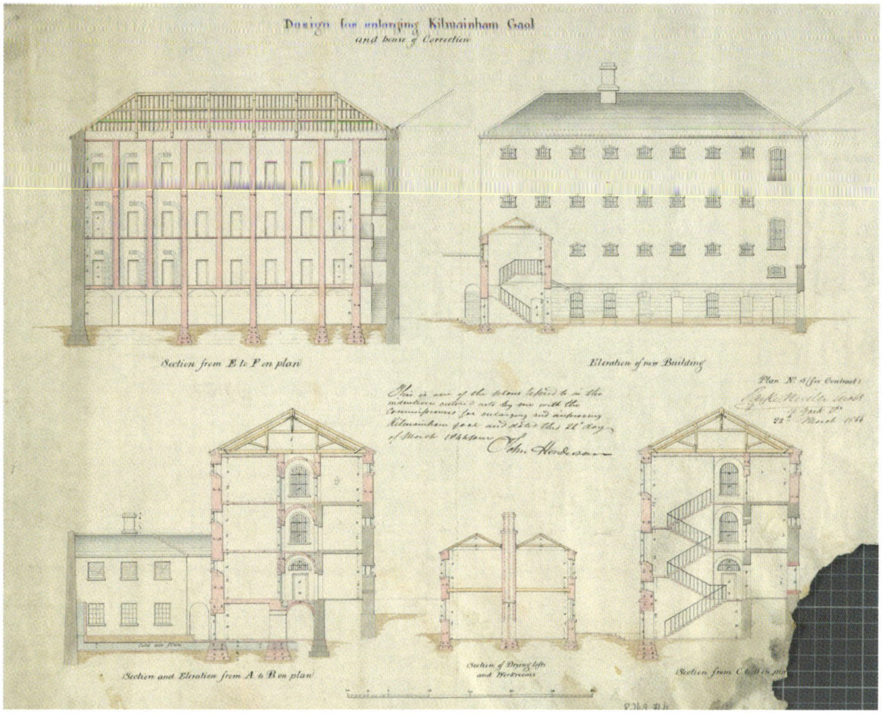

Fig. 7.17. 'Design for enlarging Kilmainham Gaol', consisting of a new cell block on the separate system for female prisoners. Park Neville, 22 March 1844. Neville was keen to point out that his design was closely modelled on Jebb's Pentonville scheme, especially in technical aspects such as heating and ventilation. The Dublin county jurors approved the plan in late 1843, and the block was built in 1844–5. (*Reproduced courtesy of the Irish Architectural Archive.*)

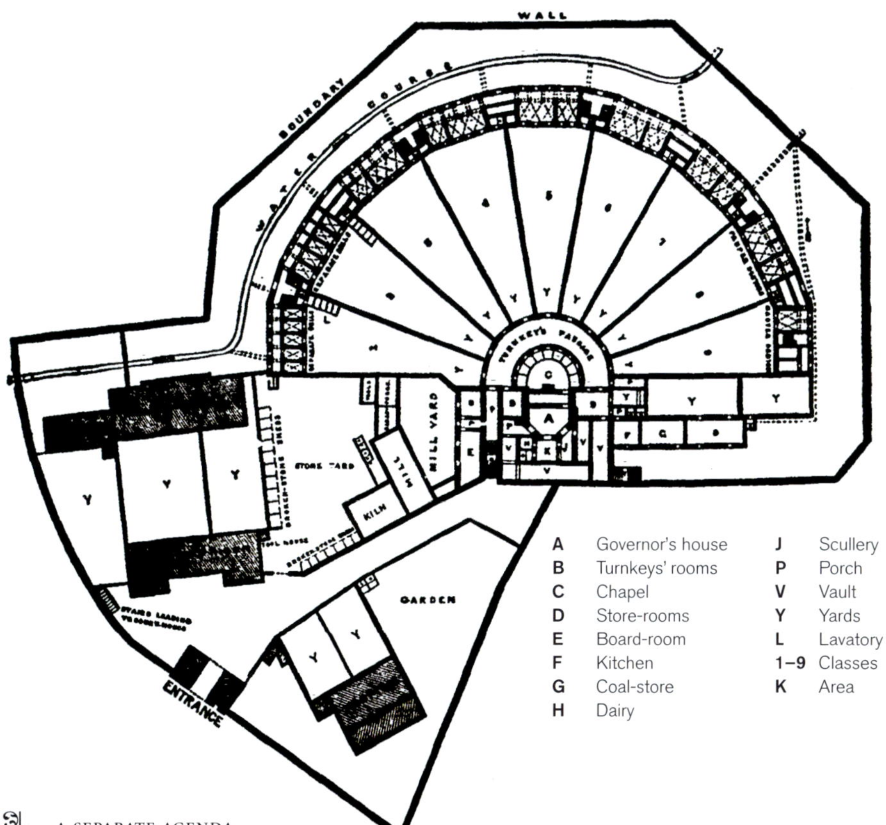

Fig. 7.18. Mullingar gaol, ground-floor plan, 1870. John Hargrave built the large polygonal-plan extension in the 1820s illustrated here (see Chapter 6); two of the ranges, in the bottom left (as marked), were modified for separate-system use by William Deane Butler in the early 1840s. The dark lines indicate walls that were added when day-rooms in these ranges were converted into cells; the remainder of the gaol was left unaltered. From *Forty-ninth Report … on … the Prisons of Ireland, 1870,* H.C. 1871 (C. 359), xxx, p. 299.

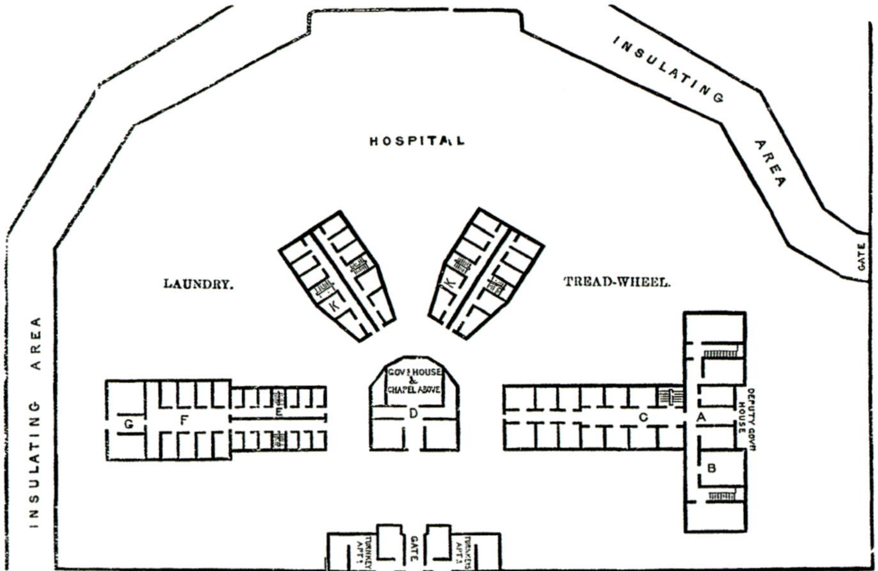

A, Deputy Governor's house; B, marshalsea; C, old prison; D, Governor's house and chapel; E, old female prison; F, separate prison for females; G. Matron's house; K K, male prisons.

Fig. 7.19. Carlow gaol, ground-floor plan, 1870. Before around 1828, the gaol consisted only of the T-shaped block in the bottom right; then, between 1828 and 1831, three radial blocks and a governor's house were added; finally, between 1841 and 1843, John Semple designed a small extension on the separate system (with larger cells, marked 'F'), and also built a new entranceway to the south (shown at the bottom). The near-symmetry of the final layout belies the gaol's complicated building history. From *Forty-eighth Report … on … the Prisons of Ireland, 1869*, H.C. 1870 (C. 173), xxxvii, p. 263.

Fig. 7.20. Carlow gaol, entrance gateway, from the south. When Semple reoriented Carlow gaol with this new entranceway in 1843, in a severe Italianate style, he borrowed from the designs used at many other Irish gaols, such as Cavan, Clonmel, and Nenagh. (*Photograph by author, 2012.*)

Nenagh and Belfast: A comparative history

The new gaols at Belfast and Nenagh shared much in terms of how and why they came to be built, despite their obvious contrast of urban and rural locations. In both cases, they were linked to campaigns within their respective counties to move the location of the assizes or the county gaol. In Belfast, as noted in Chapter 1, there were many attempts in the eighteenth century to relocate the courthouse from its historic location at Carrickfergus to a more central town such as Antrim town, Ballymena, or Belfast. The exponential growth of industry and commerce in the latter town in the early nineteenth century, and the growing sectarian and petty crime that, in part, derived from this growth, put further pressure on the grand jurors to reconsider the Carrickfergus question (Fig. 7.21).[33] At the spring assizes in 1813, an attempt was made to relocate the assizes to Belfast, but when local interests saw it defeated on the grounds that it would harm the economy of Carrickfergus, a small house of correction was instead built at the southern edge of Belfast.[34] This opened in 1817, and though it was technically considered a bridewell (with a quarter-sessions courthouse adjoining), it tended to hold almost half as many prisoners as did the county gaol, despite a significant expansion of cell numbers in the latter, and was in reality more akin to a district bridewell or a sub-county gaol. Palmer and Woodward were dissatisfied with the arrangement and called, in 1829, for a new county gaol to be built, as well as a large addition to the house of correction, or alternatively that Carrickfergus should hold all those persons awaiting trial, and Belfast all those convicted. The overcrowded state of the county's prisons – where they found around 90 prisoners in 36 cells in Belfast, and 168 prisoners in 50 cells in Carrickfergus – was proof enough for action.[35] But different factions within the grand jury wished to see the gaol built in their own town, and the inspectors lost almost a decade to indecision and aborted plans; in 1834, Woodward complained that 'we have been less successful in this county than in almost any other .... [Its] backwardness ... has been partly occasioned by a difficulty of deciding upon the most eligible mode of proceeding.'[36] The inspectors put forward different compromise solutions, including the addition of 100 cells to the existing house of correction.[37] However, following the intervention of an assize judge in 1837, the grand jury proposed to build a completely new bridewell in Belfast with 300 cells, and after further lobbying from the inspectors, the Antrim and Ballymena interests finally abandoned their campaigns in 1840, and the grand jury purchased a site for the prison on the newly laid-out Crumlin Road the following year.[38]

While the Antrim jurors had to address the needs of an expanding urban centre, their Tipperary colleagues had instead to deal with a swelling and deeply unsettled rural population. As noted in Chapter 3, the average per capita crime rate in Tipperary in 1825–35 was at least four times the national average. In 1836, a series of crop failures and the Tithe War pushed this rate higher than any county experienced during the worst years of the Famine (see Fig. 7.21), and this put enormous pressure on the county gaol in Clonmel, where an average of 500 prisoners were kept at any one time, in only around 200 cells.[39] In Chapter 3, we considered the radical rebalancing of power between central government and the Tipperary grand jury, with the resulting unpopular division of the county into two ridings after 1836. For the new north riding, the split represented an opportunity. As in Antrim, various north-riding towns such as Thurles and Nenagh vied for the right to host the new courthouse and gaol, keen to benefit from the prosperity it would bring, and once Palmer discounted the idea of expanding the small bridewell in Thurles, the privy council decided in favour of Nenagh.[40] The inspectors then lobbied to ensure that the gaol would be large enough for the north riding's needs, and pushed that the aforementioned house of correction in Clonmel (discussed in Chapter 6) could not be used by both ridings, nor that the small bridewell in Nenagh could be used as the nucleus for a larger gaol in that town.[41] They argued instead for an entirely new gaol, and pushed for the number of cells to be increased from 100 to nearly 200. The grand jury purchased sites for the new courthouse (see Chapter 3) and gaol in 1839, with a tunnel linking the two, and several new streets were laid out around the new buildings, which now represented the town's *raison d'être* (Fig. 7.22).[42]

The new gaols in Belfast and Nenagh – sombre symbols of crime and punishment, and which may not have been required in a less turbulent period – brought, paradoxically, many reasons for celebration. In Chapter 6, we saw the Bury family's sponsoring of bonfires, music, and partying in Tullamore, to celebrate the laying of the foundation stone of the new gaol there. Though it is unclear what, if anything, of substance occurred in Belfast, in Nenagh in September 1839 there were immense festivities to mark the foundation stone being laid. Lord Dunalley, a prominent local landlord and close relation of the Tullamore Bury family, funded the occasion, which saw him arrive with his wife

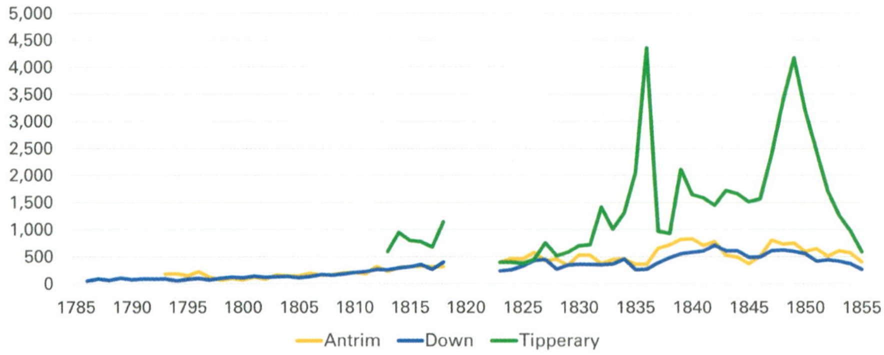

Fig. 7.21. Criminal indictments in counties Antrim, Down, and Tipperary between 1786 and 1855 (where available). Belfast's geographical location affected the criminal-indictment rates in both County Antrim and County Down, and though the exceptional nature of Tipperary is clearly apparent from this graph, the more gradual but still substantial increase found in north-east Ulster also put huge pressure on the gaols in Carrickfergus and Downpatrick, and the house of correction in Belfast. Compiled from Appendix B.

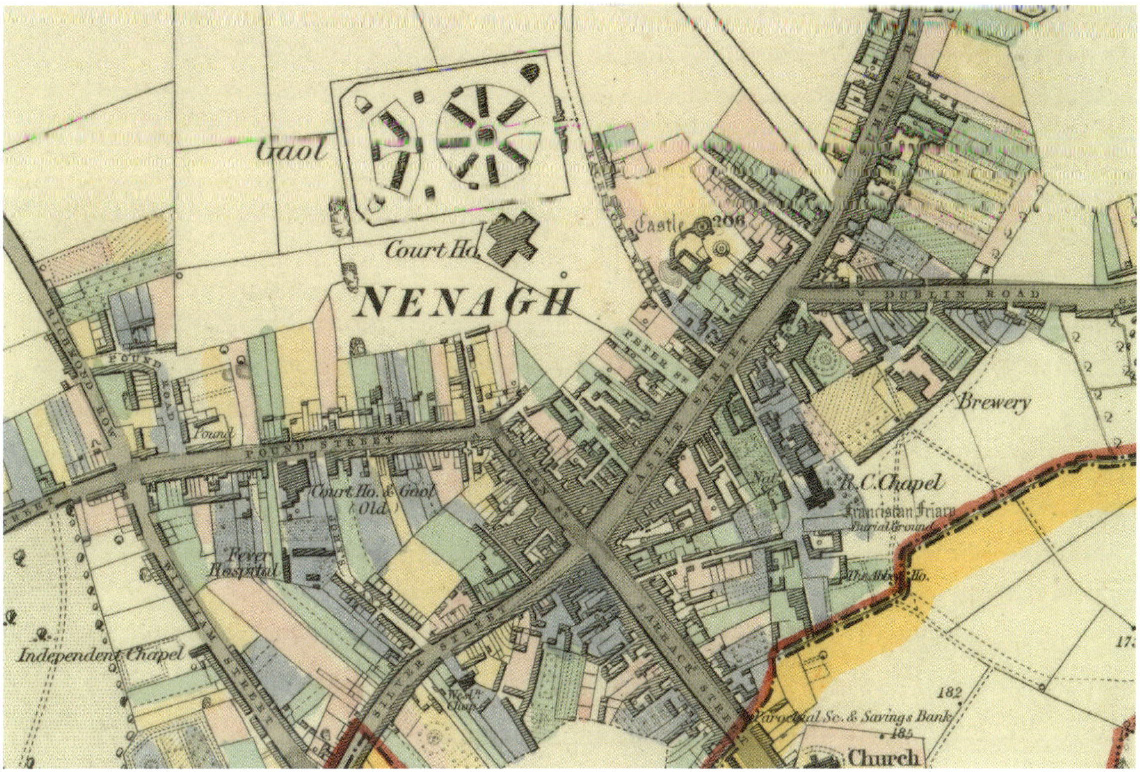

Fig. 7.22. Nenagh, County Tipperary. Ordnance Survey six-inch map, surveyed January 1840. The establishment of Nenagh as the assize town for Tipperary's north riding in 1838 had a dramatic impact on the urban landscape of the town, with new roads built to link the two great public buildings – courthouse and gaol – that appeared in the north-west suburbs in the early 1840s. (*Reproduced courtesy of the Board of Trinity College Dublin.*)

in a procession led by the architect and contractor of the new gaol carrying white wands. An amateur brass band performed for the crowds and there were 'hearty' cheers for Dunalley, who deftly ordered 'several barrels of beer' to be distributed. The new *Nenagh Guardian* summed up the mood by saying the cheerful crowds 'heartily joined in the manifestations of pleasure on the prospect now afforded of extensive employment to the people of the town and surrounding district'. Clearly even the most troubled of Irish counties found reason to celebrate the building of a new gaol.[43]

Nenagh's gaol was built between 1839 and 1842, Belfast's between 1843 and 1845. This chronology is important as it overlaps with the formal adoption of the separate system, and the growing understanding among the inspectors (and central government more generally) of the detail of its implementation. The first design for Belfast's new house of correction (as it was then known), by the renowned local architect and county surveyor Charles Lanyon, was not arranged for separate confinement.[44] By the time the last of the county disputes had been settled, and an issue with Treasury loans resolved, Lanyon (and Jacob Owen, a Board of Works architect instructed by Palmer) revised the design to comply with the principles established at Jebb's Pentonville (Fig. 7.23).[45] This meant larger cells, adequately heated and ventilated, and a more complicated and expensive building. The inspectors were desperate to avoid any last-minute hitches, and with the estimated cost ballooning from £20,000 to £38,000, they lavishly praised the design, calling it 'a perfect separate[-system] gaol'.[46] The eventual cost was around £46,000, for 350 cells, or £131 per cell (Fig. 7.24).[47] To put this in perspective, a small courthouse or bridewell typically cost around £1,000, and a commodious family house not more than £100. In the increasingly scientific penal-reform debates of the time, cost-per-cell became an important benchmark, and for critics it permitted a comprehensible 'cost per crime' calculator. To British observers, Belfast was relatively cheap: earlier polygonal (Millbank, £458, Devizes, £308) and radial (Bury St Edmunds, £212) gaols, as well as Pentonville (£158), had cost significantly more.[48]

After the new prison opened, the inspectors wished it to be a 'model' for all Irish grand juries, following in an established pattern of identifying 'perfect' architectural solutions. They called it 'beautiful …, [a] perfect model prison [without any unnecessary] eye-catching decoration'.[49] Unlike earlier periods, when the radial and polygonal plans had been openly debated, the radial separate-system gaol was now the only accepted design, and this led to a great

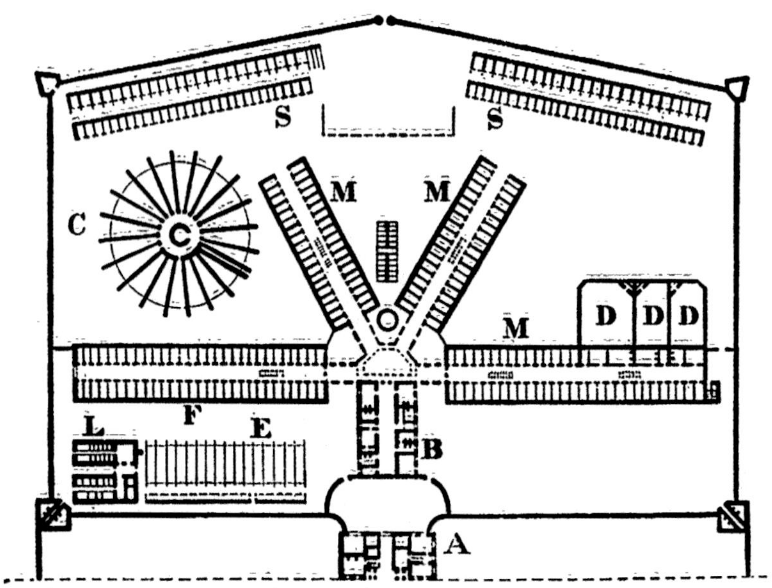

A Governor's house; **B** prison offices, over which are the chapel and hospital; **C** exercising yards for males; **D** debtors and male lunatics; **E** exercising yards for females; **M M** male prison; **F** female prison; **I** inspection hall; **G** gas works; **L** laundry; **S S** stone-breakers' sheds.

Fig. 7.23. Belfast (Crumlin Road) gaol, ground-floor plan, 1870. Charles Lanyon's design for what became Antrim's county gaol was blatantly derived from Jebb's Pentonville; its erection in the mid-1840s marked the first completely new separate-system prison in Ireland. From *Forty-ninth Report … on … the Prisons of Ireland, 1870*, H.C. 1871 (C. 359), xxx, p. 77.

Fig. 7.24. The cost of building certain prisons per cell, in England (red), and in Ireland (green), between c. 1800 and 1863. By the 1840s, prison reformers and government bureaucrats placed greater importance on reducing this figure, as it brought home the huge cost of prison building to the public, cess-payers, and politicians. Certain experimental prisons such as Millbank had proven ruinously expensive, and after Pentonville was built – the new 'model' prison that standardised design and reduced opportunities for extravagant spending – the cost-per-cell of prisons in Ireland became more homogenous and gradually decreased. The cost-per-cell in Kilkenny in 1853 (£55) was more than five times lower than in Galway in 1810 (£277). Irish figures for before 1826 (when the Irish currency was abolished) are shown in British pounds for consistency. Compiled from Evans, *Fabrication of Virtue*, p. 348, and Appendix A.

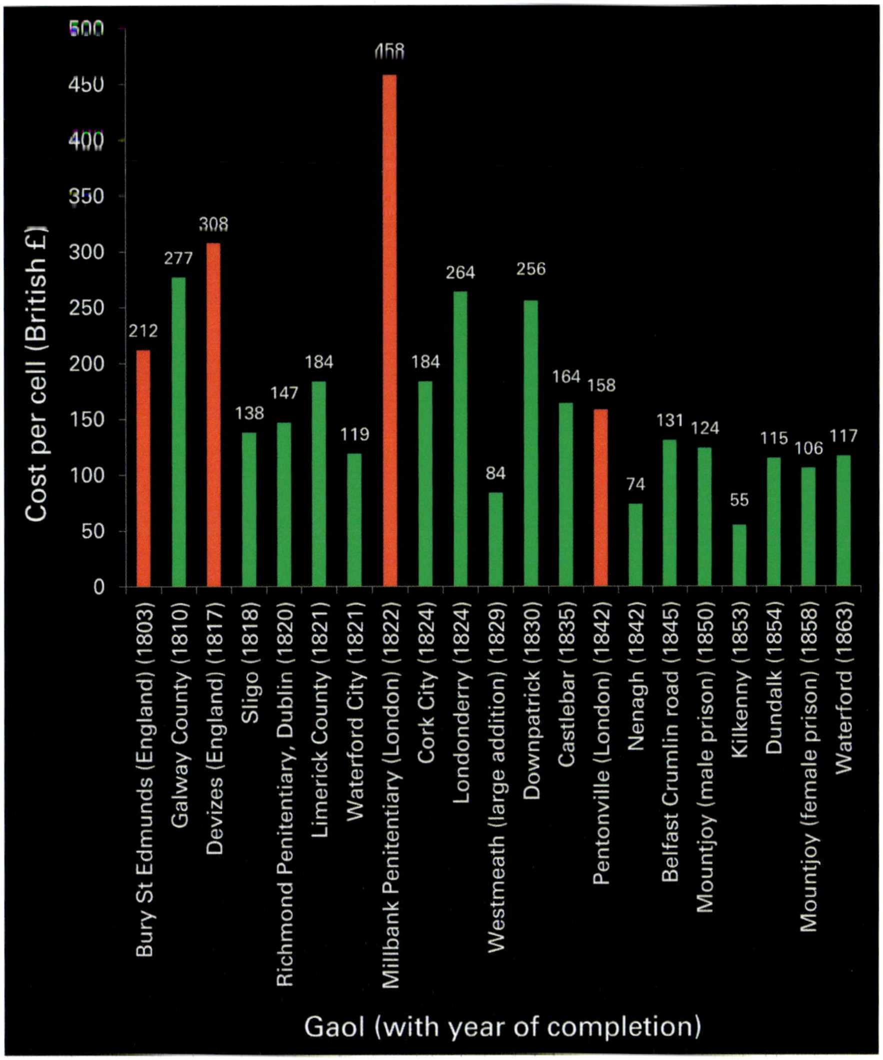

Fig. 7.25. Belfast (Crumlin Road) gaol, entrance building, from the south. Like Jebb's Pentonville prison, and perhaps Reid's Downpatrick gaol, Lanyon relied on heavily rusticated Italianate classicism to give his new prison a dignified as well as a stern appearance. He soon built a courthouse directly opposite in the same style, but without such heavy detailing. (*Photograph by author, 2013.*)

uniformity in gaol design. With layouts and details now precisely outlined, the architectural history of the post-Pentonville gaols is admittedly less stimulating, but the new settlement channelled an architect's creativity more towards the exterior appearance and gateway – the few remaining components of a prison that remained outside the watchful eye of central government and its inspectorate. The celebrated façade of Belfast's new prison (Fig. 7.25), facing the courthouse opposite, was an essay in Italianate classicism, perhaps derived from Reid's gaol at Downpatrick. The inspectors proposed that Belfast's prison should be a replacement for both the old house of correction and Carrickfergus' gaol. An 1846 prisons act facilitated its formal rebranding as a district bridewell, and once the courthouse opened in 1850, eighty-four prisoners were taken from Carrickfergus to Belfast, and the old gaol there was sold to the Board of Works.[50] With all of Antrim's quarter-session towns now linked by railways, Crumlin Road at the edge of Belfast was the obvious home for the county's courts and gaol, and it remained so until the early twentieth century.[51]

Like Belfast, Nenagh's new gaol was originally conceived on the old classification system. However, unlike Belfast, its foundation stone was laid before the separate system was formally adopted, and so the design was an uneasy compromise between the two competing ideologies. The inspectors argued that 'the principle' of separate confinement had been 'provided for' in the design, but like Semple's extension to Dublin's Richmond bridewell built at this time (see Chapter 6), in hindsight the inspectors realised that they had not anticipated the finer details of ventilating and heating that the system required.[52] When the new gaol opened in 1843, only the main six radial blocks, containing 192 cells, could be used; the fifty-two separate-system cells to the rear remained empty as the heating system failed to work (Figs 7.26–7.28).[53] Furthermore, the inspectors banned the use of eight solitary-confinement cells for punishing insubordinate prisoners, as they were deemed to be inadequately ventilated. The folly of attempting to combine the two discipline systems, and of the unfortunate timing of the gaol being commenced on the eve of the adoption of the separate system, was made clear to the inspectors within a few years. They condemned the solitary cells as 'very expensive, badly constructed [and] totally useless'.[54] Later, they admitted that the gaol's design was settled 'unfortunately before the true form of construction had been discovered'.[55] The final cost at Nenagh was £18,000 for 244 cells, or £74 per cell.[56] At half the cost of Belfast, this figure showed the stark difference between the simpler classification system and the new separate system. The architect of the gaol was John B. Keane, the undisputed king of courthouse and gaol building in the south midlands at this time, and as in Clonmel, his entrance gateway owed much to Elsam's Cavan and Dover gaols (Fig. 7.29). The *Nenagh Guardian* was impressed with its appearance, claiming that it displayed 'the appropriate character of a prison entrance [with] an iron-grated Diocletian window, having a series of massive arch-stones, representing, as it were, an awful brow over the aperture from which the fatal machinery [gallows] is to be constructed .... [It] altogether conveys to the observer an astounding effect.'[57]

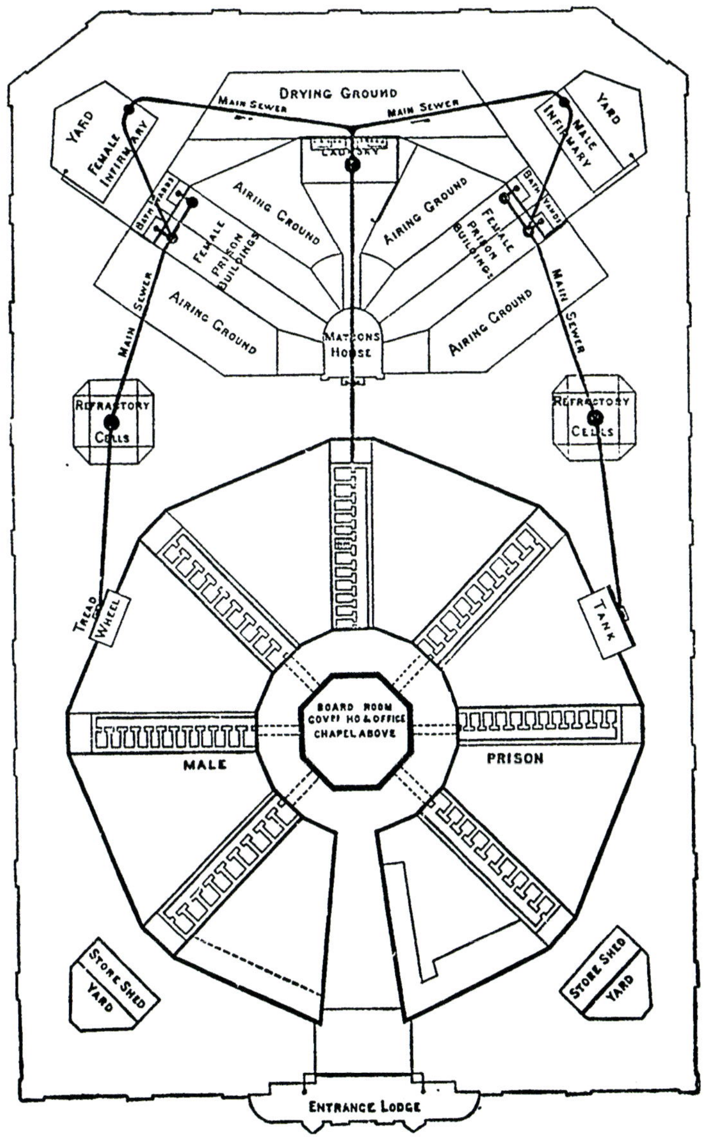

Fig. 7.26. Nenagh gaol, ground-floor plan, 1870. John B. Keane designed Nenagh gaol at the crossroads between the old classification system and the incoming separate system. His seven radial blocks (shown as 'Male Prison'), which were cheaper to build than Belfast's Crumlin Road gaol, were nonetheless seen as old-fashioned by the early 1840s, and the inspectors later stated the cells were too small for separate-system confinement. The two blocks shown in the top (overlaid with sewerage pipe schematics) were supposed to be ready for separate-system confinement, but problems with heating and ventilating meant that they could not be used as originally intended. Nenagh gaol was thus designed as a compromise between the two systems, and in the end this proved an unsuccessful experiment, and later gaols tended to follow instead Belfast's example. From *Forty-eighth Report ... on ... the Prisons of Ireland, 1869*, H.C. 1870 (C. 173), xxxvii, p. 442.

Problems with the central-government inspectors, and the effects of the Famine

The lukewarm enthusiasm from grand jurors for adopting the costly new separate system has already been discussed. Even Palmer was unconvinced by the design he was tasked with promoting, writing privately to a friend in New York in 1845 that 'I think [American gaols] have gone too far in [the] separate system [and] your confinements are too long.'[58] Were it not for the catastrophe of the Famine, the 1840s was otherwise the beginning of a long downward trend in crime rates, with the national figure falling from 23,833 in 1840 to 16,696 in 1845, or a fall of about a third.[59] The exact causes of this decline are beyond the scope of this book, but its effect on prison management will be obvious. Combined with the widespread decimation of grand-jury bank balances during the Famine, this waning of crime figures lessened the pressure on grand jurors to rebuild their gaols. Nonetheless some building work did occur, but this was generally more modest than in earlier periods.

In addition, there were other problems facing central government at this time. For twenty years, the inspectors Palmer and Woodward had – with the support of like-minded assize judges – led the charge to convince grand jurors to improve their gaols. Woodward died in June 1841, and was succeeded by Captain Francis White (1787–1859), a Catholic medical doctor and former

Fig. 7.27. (left) Nenagh gaol, governor's residence, inspection building and chapel, from the east. Unlike Belfast's Crumlin Road gaol, the governor's residence at Nenagh was a free-standing building, akin to Hargrave's gaols of the 1820s and early 1830s. (*Photograph by author, 2017.*)

Fig. 7.28. (right) Nenagh gaol, a surviving cell block, from the south. The narrowness of this block indicates its asymmetrical corridor-and-cell layout, while the alternating window-sill heights on the ground floor reveal the original intended function of the ground floor rooms as day-rooms rather than separate-system cells (compare with Figs 7.8, 7.13). When complete in 1843, this design was seen as old-fashioned and inconvenient. (*Photograph by author, 2017.*)

Fig. 7.29. Nenagh gaol, entrance gateway, from the east. The *Nenagh Guardian* commented upon its completion that the gateway, almost identical to that built by Keane in Clonmel, 'conveys to the observer an astounding effect'. A statue of Mary now occupies the former gallows. (*Photograph by author, 2017.*)

president of the Irish College of Surgeons.[60] He was an important witness at the Whately commission on the Irish poor in the 1830s, and was critical of Palmer and Woodward in a Commons investigation into grand-jury presentments in 1841, claiming that, among other problems, it was perfectly obvious to gaolers when the inspectors were about to make their biannual visits.[61] His working relationship with Palmer was rather poor from the outset: Palmer privately hoped that, if a proposed reform to the inspectorate went ahead in 1842, and a single inspector was appointed with two deputies, White would be bumped into a subordinate position.[62] Palmer had little sympathy with the pro-Catholic Whig administration under Thomas Drummond that had appointed White, and privately declared that 'I am turned a complete Tory', adding that White was 'a Roman & a nasty disagreeable man … self-conceited to a degree'.[63]

This unabridged loathing for his colleague arose because – soon after taking office – White exposed a series of allegations aimed at Palmer, which suggested he had been corruptly involved in the appointment of gaolers and turnkeys. Specifically, he was accused of arranging jobs for his brother-in-law and one of his illegitimate sons. Despite a stable and respectable income, Palmer needed some extra earnings to help repair his ruined personal finances, and, as noted in Chapter 6, he even served time as a debtor in Kilmainham gaol, whose head turnkey he later asked for a bail-out.[64] Finally, to add to his woes, he was tasked with managing the convict system by Drummond in 1836 with no extra pay, and a series of scandals in that agency came back to haunt him.[65] Though an investigation found no evidence of wrongdoing, Palmer's reputation was irrevocably destroyed, and his ability to lobby grand jurors greatly diminished. Friends of Palmer wrote that he had 'got into some scrape lately and lost his influence', that now he 'never will be able to do anything' to help them, and that his demise was a 'sad ca[ta]strophe'.[66]

Understandably for Palmer, after more than a dozen years promoting the classification system, and overseeing a vast rebuilding programme, it was hard to begin over again, and he lost all interest in his role, retiring in 1846.[67] In later life he was increasingly bitter and despondent, writing that 'in this land, we have nothing but strife, Popery, & folly – well for us there is another beyond the Flood', and, during the Famine, that 'poor Ireland is as bad as ever in starvation & wicked ways. Popery & potatoes are the ruin of Ireland.'[68] Around the same time, White took up a new role as the inspector of convict prisons. Thus, on the eve of the Famine, the prison inspectorate was left rudderless. Furthermore, one of the new inspectors, Major Edward Cottingham, died within months of taking office while overseeing building work at Spike Island in Cork, and five other inspectors came and went for various reasons during the Famine years.[69] This broke the continuity and close cooperation that marked the twenty years from roughly 1821 to 1841.

This crisis could not have happened at a worse moment. Along with the workhouses and county infirmaries, the gaols bore the brunt of the Famine's destitute. Though the history of Irish prisons during this period demands a study of its own, it is instructive to make a few general points here.[70] First, the exponential increase in prisoner numbers, and the widespread outbreak of gaol fever and other illnesses, completely destroyed the classification, silent, and separate systems operated by the local authorities. All the penal-reform ideas of earlier generations were simply thrown out the window, and what had slowly emerged as a carefully organised and disciplined system simply fell apart. In April 1847, the inspectors found a 100 per cent increase in prisoner numbers in certain gaols and called for a temporary prison of some kind for detaining convicts (to be discussed shortly).[71] By their next report the full extent of the crisis was obvious, and they began their report by saying:

> No task can well be more discouraging and, indeed, melancholy than that of attempting to detail the history of the Irish prisons .... The terrible catastrophe, which has disorganized the whole framework of

society in Ireland, fell with its full force upon the establishments under our charge .... Classification [is] destroyed, separation unattempted, and disease and death increasing to a degree that could never have been contemplated.[72]

The Inspectors thought that there were too many minor debtors (for sums under £10 or £20) in gaols and called for the adoption in Ireland of an English act that removed the penalty of imprisonment for these persons (as it was the following year). Too many children, they felt, and especially young boys, lingered in gaols, mostly for petty offences such as stealing food. The inspectors' solution had little humanity: they suggested that these boys should be whipped and sent back to the nearest workhouse, and that the diet for children in gaols should be reduced to match that provided by the Poor Law (a change that affected adult gaol diets too).[73] By the following year the inspectors reported that there had been 34,105 *more* cases in 1848 than in 1847, and commented that 'the annals of this country never before exhibited such a numerical array'.[74] With prisoner numbers still exceptionally high in 1849, they recommended for the first time the complete abandonment of the classification system, suggesting that twenty or more hammocks could be erected in each cell, and they accepted that grand jurors were simply unable to fund the kinds of large extensions that might otherwise be required.[75] The financial burden that the Famine placed on county treasurers is apparent if we consider the state of Munster's prisons during the period 1845–52, compiled from the annual reports of the prison inspectors (Fig. 7.30). For the purposes of this graph, the city and county jurisdictions in Cork,

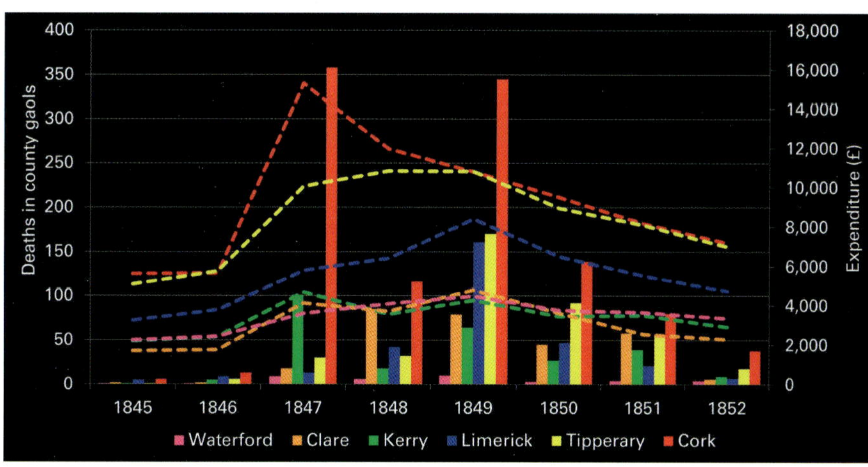

Fig. 7.30. A graph showing the number of prisoner deaths in county gaols in Munster between 1845 and 1852 (shown as solid bars), and the expenditure on prisons during this time (shown as dotted lines). The grim human and financial cost of the Famine is clearly apparent. Compiled from the annual reports of the Irish prison inspectors.

Limerick and Waterford have been combined, and so have the two ridings of Tipperary. Plotted against the cost of running gaols are the number of prisoner deaths in each institution; this shows without any ambiguity the devastating human cost of these years. In 1845, there were six deaths in Cork's city and county gaols; two years later there were 358. In Kerry, the number rose from just one to 101. Nationally, the criminal-indictment rate reflected the crisis of these years, with the long-term average of around 20,000 per year rising to over 40,000 in 1849; in truth the actual figure was probably much higher, and in certain counties there appears to have been significant under-reporting of cases, where the system of justice collapsed.

As commented above, there was inevitably a time lag between when grand jurors committed to gaol-building work and when this work commenced. The Famine was so dramatic in its effects, and so ruinous to county bank balances, that there was no new spurt in building activity to house the multitudes of the destitute. Instead, some counties continued to slowly adjust their gaol to the separate system, and others finally began building new gaols that had been planned for many decades. The fall-off in crime after the Famine was just as fast as its earlier increase, and by 1855 the indictment rate was lower than at any period since around 1817. This reflected a vastly reduced population (perhaps two million less than before the Famine), as well as broader changes to Irish rural society. By the mid-1850s, the view from Dublin Castle – however briefly – was of a country 'almost entirely without crime'.[76] From around 1852 until the Fenian unrest of the mid-1860s, there was little pressure on gaol numbers, and during this time we find the first of a series of gaol amalgamations (to be discussed shortly).

Mountjoy and Spike Island: Central government re-emerges as a builder of prisons

Before looking at gaol building during and after the Famine, two other prisons need to be briefly analysed. They are Mountjoy convict prison, in north Dublin, and Spike Island convict depot, in Cork harbour. Both represent the first time since the controversial (and unsuccessful) Richmond penitentiary in the 1810s that central government built large new gaols independent of the grand juries. During the worst years of the Famine, these prisons represented – by far – the most significant financial outlays on prison-building work in Ireland. In the worst year of the Famine – 1847 – only one grand jury (Armagh) was engaged in gaol building, the quietest year in gaol building since at least 1783. By comparison, central government was building large new gaols in both Dublin and Cork, and the army Royal Engineers were also erecting a military prison (beyond the scope of this book), on the separate system, at Arbour Hill (Fig. 7.31).[77] Both Mountjoy and Spike Island convict prisons grew out of problems with the transportation of convicts to Australia. Traditionally, these prisoners had been gathered in Dublin's Kilmainham and Newgate gaols, and at the seventeenth-century Elizabeth Fort in Cork city, which had been fitted up as a convict depot by the Board of Works in 1818.[78] The history of mid-nineteenth-century transportation is beyond the scope of this study, but in short, the transportation of convicts to New South Wales ceased in May 1840. For a while after, and not without heated objections from the colonial authorities, convicts were instead sent to Van Diemen's Land. This proved unsatisfactory and instead government proposed the idea of attempting to 'reform' prisoners in a large separate-system prison, copying the similar experiment then underway at Pentonville.[79] There was also a sense in government that a large convict prison in Dublin might, at last, solve the city's prison problems by allowing the city grand jurors to finally abandon their Newgate gaol.[80]

The Cork convict depot was the more straightforward of the two. Palmer and Woodward, and the AIPPD, were unhappy with the arrangements at Elizabeth Fort from almost the time that they were appointed, and they both independently suggested as early as 1822 that a penitentiary might be built on Spike Island.[81] They remarked that Elizabeth Fort was only kept in good repair 'with difficulty'.[82] Generally there were more females than males among the inmates, and by the mid-1830s only females were being kept there, though increasing crime rates had swelled their numbers to 250. The inspectors protested and insisted on a new large depot.[83] Meanwhile, the Board of Ordnance were happy to give up Fort Westmorland on Spike Island and, in 1846, they handed it over to the government for use as a depot. Initially, the convicts were held in the old barracks buildings (Fig. 7.32), but during the Famine years a succession of more temporary structures, of wood and iron, were erected by the Royal Engineers using convict labour.[84] By 1851, the depot's capacity was a staggering 1,500 persons, making it by far Ireland's largest prison, and after transportation completely ceased around this time, the buildings became a normal convict prison like Mountjoy and Pentonville, and remained in use for this purpose until very recent years.[85]

The building of Mountjoy convict prison was of greater significance. Before the project got off the ground, various wings of central government liaised

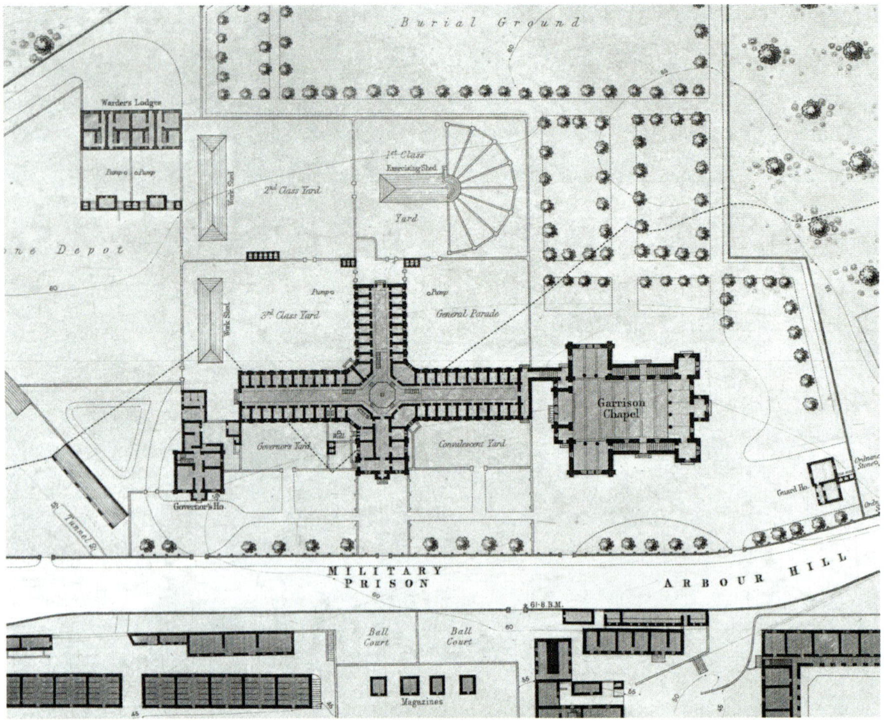

Fig. 7.31. Arbour Hill military prison, Dublin. Ordnance Survey five-feet town map, 1847. This prison, with its connecting corridors and large cells, built to the designs of Royal Engineers between 1845 and 1848, shows the far reach of the separate-system design introduced by Jebb at Pentonville. The institution, greatly altered and expanded, now serves as a state prison. (*Reproduced courtesy of the Board of Trinity College Dublin.*)

Fig. 7.32. Spike Island, County Cork, Fort Westmorland, part of barracks buildings, later used as a convict prison. Unlike Arbour Hill and Mountjoy, the prisoners on Spike Island were kept in buildings not initially designed for use as a prison. Many temporary prison buildings were erected on the site in the 1840s and 1850s. (*Photograph by author, 2017.*)

over where it should be located. Initially, government planned to reuse the old Smithfield penitentiary, which had closed in 1840 when Dublin city's prisons were rearranged (see Chapter 6), and the Board of Works undertook some alterations to fit up this building for convict use around 1843–4.[86] However, Palmer and White made it clear that while Smithfield was a welcome addition, it was not suited for use as a convict prison, and they would ideally like to see a completely new convict prison built in the city to the design of Pentonville or Belfast's Crumlin Road gaol.[87] The next move was for government to purchase a site by the River Liffey at the Point Depot, but this was later abandoned on the grounds that it would be prone to flooding and was simply too small. Another site at Merrion in the south suburbs was also briefly considered but ruled out for the same reasons.[88] Eventually the Board of Works settled on a site offered by Lord Rathdowne and the Mountjoy family to the north of the city, near the Royal Canal.[89] Meanwhile, the Board of Works and the prison inspectors (especially Cottingham) communicated with the directors of the English convict system and their architect Jebb, and they requested Jebb to prepare a design in early 1847.[90] Architecturally, there was little that separated his proposed scheme (Fig. 7.33) from what was built at Pentonville: it had almost exactly the same number of cells as built (520 versus 522), and the cost was similar (£64,975 versus £82,271) – indeed the prison was initially named 'New Pentonville'. The Board of Works boasted that the cost-per-cell was £124, a tenth cheaper than Lanyon's gaol in Belfast.[91]

As soon as the prison opened, the Board of Works planned a female convict prison to be built nearby; this time the architect was one of their own staff members, James Higgins Owen. The female prison provided another 360 cells to a similar layout (Fig. 7.34), cost around £38,000 (£106 per cell) and was built between 1855 and 1858.[92] Unlike the deficient design and controversial management of the Richmond penitentiary, Mountjoy was truly a 'model' gaol for the grand juries to follow, in, of course, much reduced and scaled-down formats. The example of Mountjoy also paved the way for more complete central-government control over county gaols and bridewells. To allow the Board of Works to build the prison, a special Land for Prisons Act was passed in 1847; this gave the board the power, for Mountjoy and for all future prison-building projects, to purchase land, contract with architects, pay bills, purchase or rent existing buildings, and obtain loans from government – in other words, to completely emulate and indeed supersede the historic functions of the grand juries.[93]

Gaol building during the Famine: Continuity during an exceptional time

The opening of Mountjoy lessened pressure on the other large prisons in Dublin, notably Kilmainham and Richmond bridewell. It also allowed central government to at last shut down Newgate – the most heavily criticised gaol in the

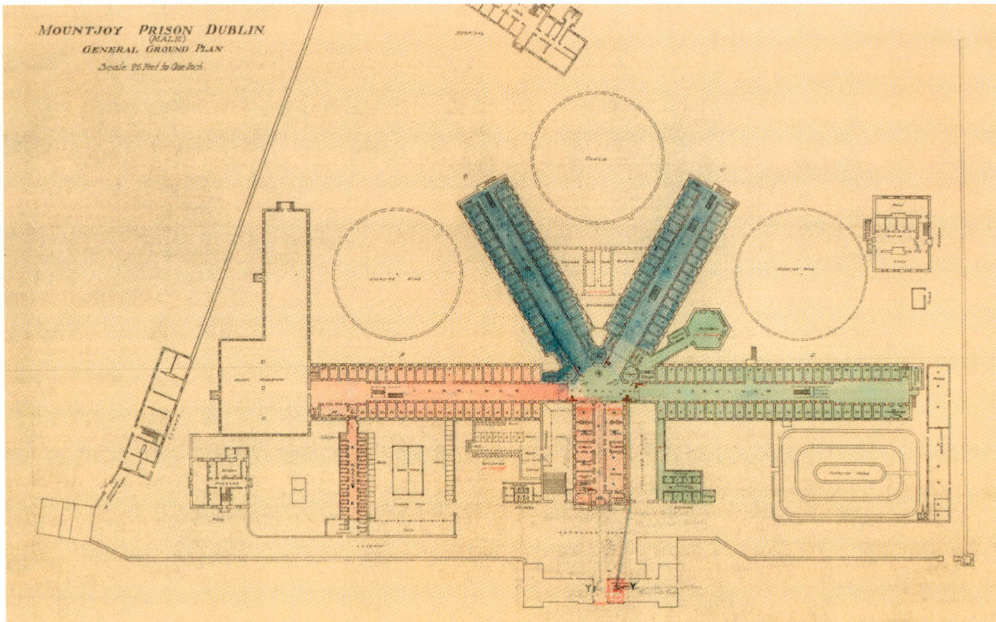
MOUNTJOY PRISON DUBLIN
(MALE)
GENERAL GROUND PLAN
Scale 25 Feet to One Inch

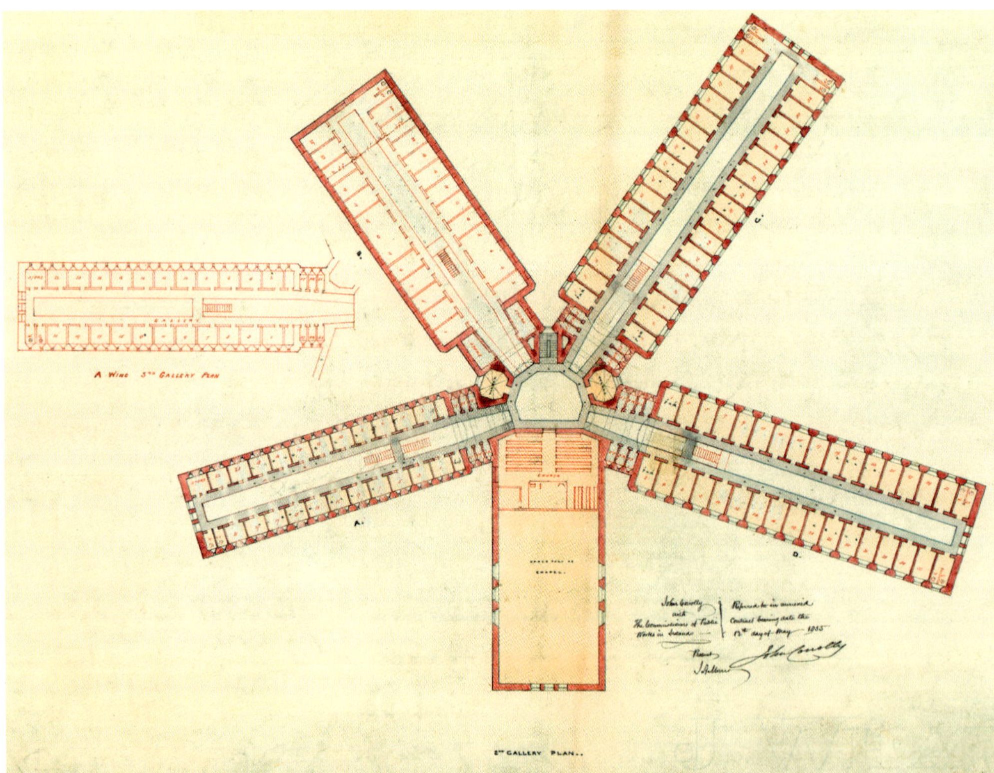
A WING 3RD GALLERY PLAN
2ND GALLERY PLAN.

Fig. 7.33. (opposite top) Mountjoy (male) convict prison, Dublin. Jacob Owen, Joshua Jebb, and Charles Peirce, 1847–50. Dublin's answer to Pentonville was so remarkably similar in size and layout that it was initially termed 'New Pentonville'. Jebb's 'model' prison brought about a homogeneity in prison design that had escaped all previous 'models', back to Howard's time. (*Reproduced courtesy of the Director of the National Archives of Ireland.*)

Fig. 7.34. (opposite bottom) Mountjoy (female) convict prison, Dublin, 1855. James Higgins Owen, built 1855–8. Owen's design was a response to a constricted site adjacent to the male convict prison but was otherwise similar to Pentonville in its arrangement of separate-system cells and central inspection hub. (*Reproduced courtesy of the Director of the National Archives of Ireland.*)

entire country. One of the inspectors described it in 1848 as 'a disgrace to a civilized community, and is more like what prisons may be fancied to have been 200 years ago than what we should expect to find them in the present day'.[94] Newgate's twilight years were spent housing some convicts, but the government abandoned it entirely in 1863 and it thereafter became a fruit and vegetable market, with only the base of one turret (heavily rebuilt) surviving today (Fig. 7.35).[95] Newgate's closure was uniquely long in the making, and the few other gaol-building projects of the Famine years – in neighbouring Armagh and Dundalk – were also the fruits of remarkably drawn-out campaigns by the inspectors and assize judges for improvement in prison conditions in those counties.

The condition of Armagh gaol was a continual source of frustration to Palmer and Woodward, whose repeated calls for a large additional building were ignored by the county's disinterested grand jurors. Like the many other rectilinear gaols of Howard's time – for example at Lifford, Omagh, and Derry – the addition that the inspectors promoted would have been a series of radial blocks to the rear of the old building. But this would have entailed the purchase of additional land, and even the inspectors were unsure if an entirely new gaol on a different site might not be a better proposition.[96] By the mid-1830s, when the crime rate soared dramatically, the gaol still only contained twenty-seven cells – not much bigger than a large bridewell – and a radial-plan addition by William Farrell to provide fifty more cells was rejected by the grand jurors.[97] By 1836, the criminal-indictment rate had jumped by 150 per cent in the space of just two years (Fig. 7.36), and the gaol was woefully overcrowded; at last, the grand jurors commissioned a design from William Murray, who had been involved in the building of the district lunatic asylum in the city, and this scheme provided

Fig. 7.35. (right) St Michan's Park, Green Street, Dublin, from the south-east. Dublin's Newgate gaol stood on this site between 1773 and 1893; today only the base of one of the corner turrets remains (though heavily rebuilt; compare with Figs 4.7–4.9). (*Photograph by author, 2014.*)

for seventy-seven additional cells in four radial blocks (Fig. 7.37).[98] Woodward thought that the addition would be too small, and the proposed £6,000 cost was unrealistic; instead, he asked Murray to prepare an alternative scheme that would give 123 cells in five radial blocks, two of which would be designed with larger cells to allow for the future use of the separate system.[99] This plan (Fig. 7.38) was more architecturally coherent than the first proposal and necessitated the purchase of

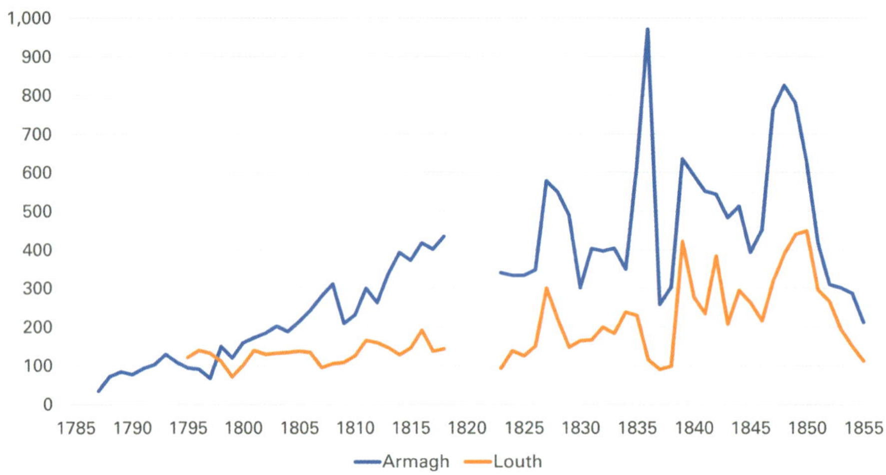

Fig. 7.36. Criminal indictments in County Armagh and County Louth between 1787 and 1855 (where available). Both counties had small old rectilinear-plan gaols that were condemned as inadequate by the prison inspectors in the troubled years of the late 1820s and again in the late 1830s; in both cases, by the time extensions or new gaols were under construction, the rate of crime was falling. Compiled from Appendix B.

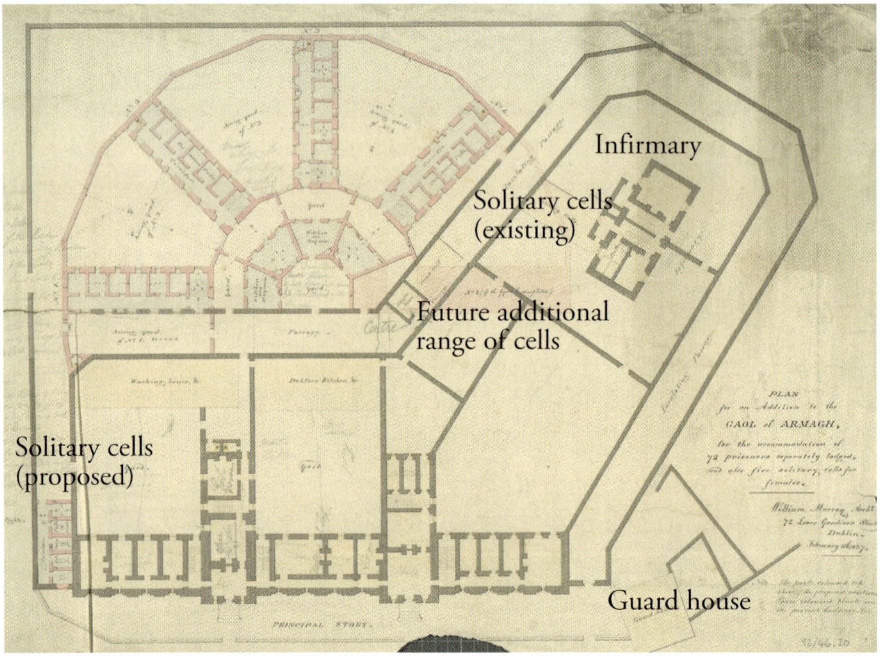

Fig. 7.37. 'Plan for an addition to the gaol of Armagh', ground-floor plan, unexecuted. William Murray, 11 February 1837. Overcrowding in Armagh gaol in the mid-1830s pushed the grand jurors into asking Murray for a design for a large addition. His idiosyncratic proposal was the result of an awkward and confined site, and it was soon opposed by the prison inspectors who felt that it was too small for the county's needs. (*Reproduced courtesy of the Irish Architectural Archive.*)

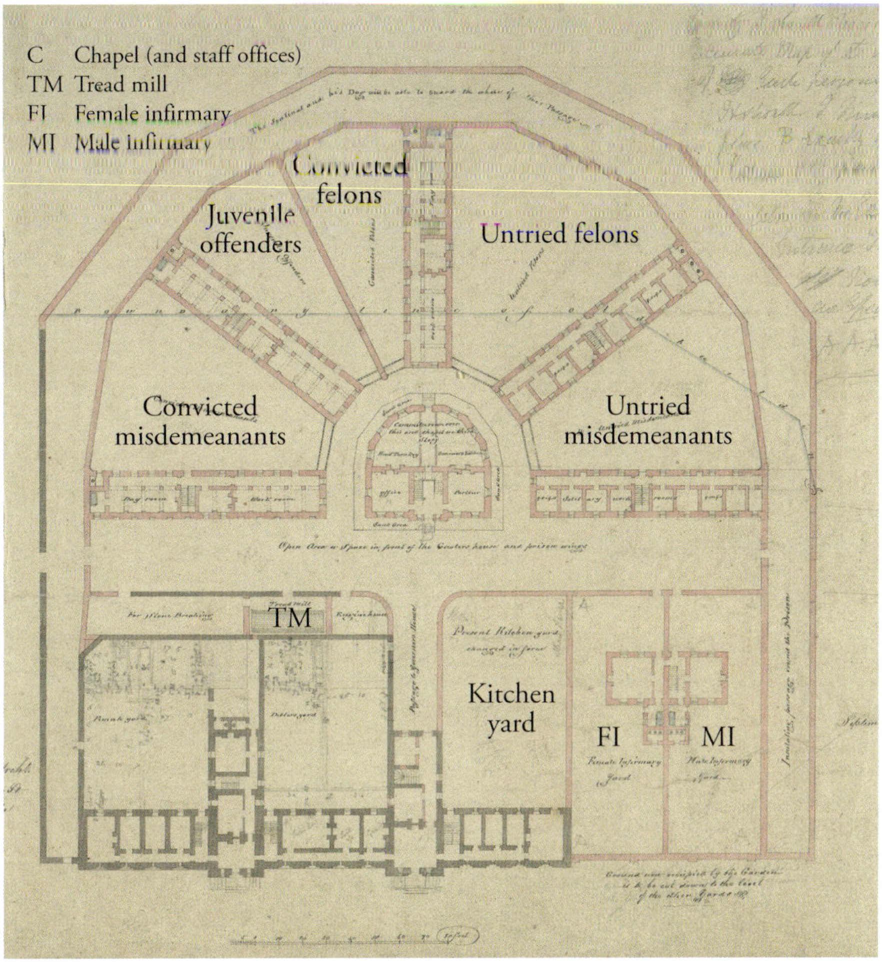

Fig. 7.38. 'Plan of Armagh gaol with proposed additions', ground-floor plan, unexecuted. William Murray, 22 September 1837. Woodward requested Murray to prepare this alternative design that would have provided a much greater number of cells (some of which would be equipped for separate confinement) as well as a new infirmary. The county's cess-payers were unconvinced and refused to fund the project. (*Reproduced courtesy of the Irish Architectural Archive.*)

some more land, and the rebuilding of the gaol's infirmary. Presumably in order to tempt the jurors to agree to the £10,000 cost, Murray also proposed two schemes for adding Gothick detailing to the main façade to, in Woodward's words, render the gaol 'a handsome ornament to the town' (Fig. 7.39).[100]

Woodward's request for a partial adoption of the separate system was as problematic in Armagh as it had been in Nenagh and in Dublin's Richmond bridewell. Once the separate system became law in 1840, and there was the possibility of an increase in interest rates charged by the Treasury, Murray's design was thrown in doubt.[101] Moreover, with the crime rate now falling, the inspectors had great trouble convincing the grand jurors to act, and there was strong opposition to the financial burden that would be placed on cess-payers.[102]

Fig. 7.39. Three elevation drawings for the main façade of Armagh gaol, William Murray, 22 September 1837: top (as the gaol appeared in 1837), middle (Murray's proposed classical rebuilding), and bottom (Murray's less extensive Gothick rebuilding scheme). Neither scheme was built. Presumably in order to tempt the Armagh grand jurors and cess-payers to fund a large addition to the county gaol, Murray suggested that the gaol's façade might be rebuilt in a fashionable Gothick style. His rather Palladian classical scheme showed little development from the era of Dance's Newgate. (*Reproduced courtesy of the Irish Architectural Archive.*)

At the spring assizes in 1845, the comments of two assize judges, Philip Crampton and Robert Torrens, saved the inspectors from further lobbying:

> The number of cases on the calendar is considerable; but with the exception of a very few cases, they are not of a serious nature .... There is one subject, gentlemen, on which I cannot avoid congratulating you. When attending your county on a former occasion, I had reason to complain of the state of your jail [, which] was in a lamentable state, it being utterly impossible to procure accommodation for the safety – the moral safety – of those persons deposited in it for trial, or those undergoing their punishment. I am, however, happy to understand that, since then, you have granted a presentment amounting to five thousand pounds for its improvement; and I trust that all consequent measures ... will be adopted, and followed up with spirit, for I know of nothing in which the gentlemen of a county should feel a greater interest, than having a proper jail for the accommodation of prisoners.

> In this matter there has been a vast improvement in modern times, and the system of jail management adopted in England, and followed up in this country, has had the effect of making jails rather a school for teaching morality and religion, than as formerly, a school for demoralising the habits, and teaching vice.[103]

This plea finally pushed the jurors into action. Murray prepared another scheme, this time entirely on the separate system, which provided for sixty-one cells in one large three-storey block (Fig. 7.40).[104] It will be apparent that this

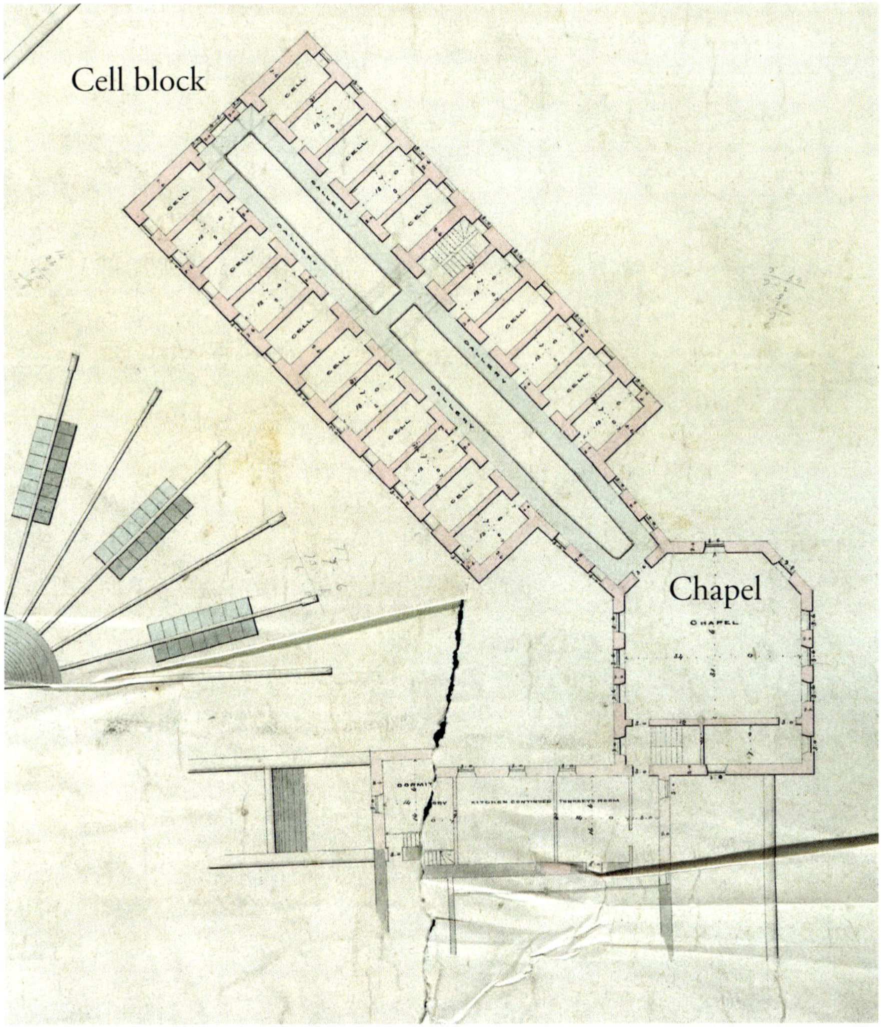

Fig. 7.40. Armagh gaol, separate-system cell block, second-floor plan. William Murray, January 1846. After years of delays and unexecuted plans, the comments from two assize judges and continued pressure from the prison inspectors pushed the grand jurors into action. Murray's scheme cleverly allowed for a symmetrical future addition; otherwise, his design was similar to other cell blocks built at this time. (*Reproduced courtesy of the Irish Architectural Archive.*)

was a smaller number of cells than the scheme Woodward had rejected back in 1838, but with a falling crime rate, this was not seen as a major issue. Murray cleverly arranged the cell block at an angle to allow for a symmetrical extension in future if so required; building began in 1846 and the wing opened three years later. In 1852, the firm of Boyd and Batt of Belfast was commissioned to erect a symmetrical wing in the space that Murray had envisioned, and this provided another forty separate-system cells for females (Fig. 7.41).[105] The scheme was completed in 1864–6 when the same firm rebuilt the main façade (Fig. 7.42) and, after public hangings had been abolished, took down the 'hateful gallows'. The *Armagh Guardian* commented that the façade now appeared more 'palatial' than penal, and was 'an ornament to the locality', as Murray had intended twenty years earlier.[106]

Fig. 7.41. Armagh gaol, female separate-system cell block, from the east. The space that Murray left in his cell block design of 1846–9 was later filled by another range of cells, shown here, designed by Boyd and Batt of Belfast, and built in 1853–6. (*Photograph by author, 2017.*)

Fig. 7.42. Armagh gaol, from the north. Murray had first proposed rebuilding the façade of the gaol, which mostly dated to c. 1780, in the late 1830s, but it was not until the mid-1860s that Boyd and Batt carried out some alterations, in the Italianate rather than the Gothic style (compare with Fig. 7.39 above). (*Photograph by author, 2014.*)

Two aspects of Murray's separate-system extension are striking: first, that its building merely coincided with the Famine, but was not born of, or in any meaningful manner influenced by, its effects. And second, that it explicitly allowed for a convenient future extension. This was a new departure in prison design and had not been possible with the radial- and polygonal-plan gaols of the previous generation, which both vied for acceptance as the 'model' arrangement. We find similar factors at work in the building of Dundalk's new gaol, designed by the county surveyor, John Neville, and built between 1849 and 1854.[107] For over twenty years, the inspectors lobbied without success for the grand jurors to improve their gaol. Instead, the grand jurors engaged in a series of cul-de-sac debates. They considered three options at length: first, piece-meal additions

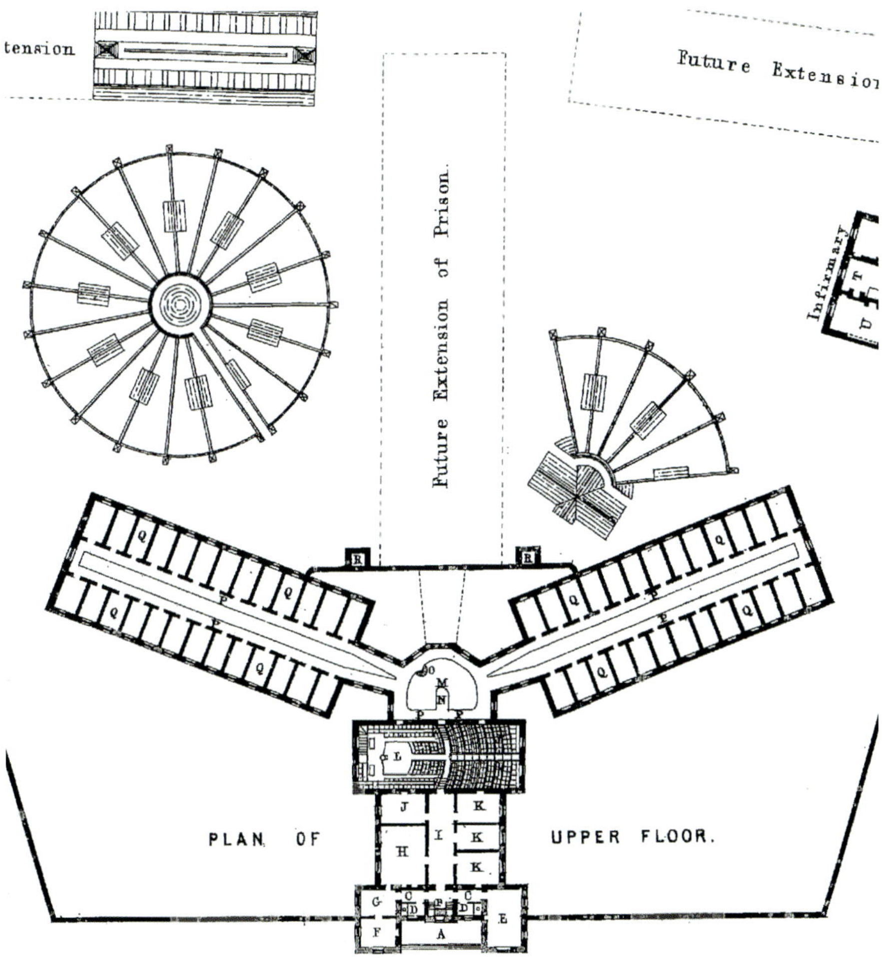

Fig. 7.43. Dundalk gaol, ground-floor plan, 1853. John Neville's new gaol for County Louth was built between 1849 and 1854, and cleverly followed Armagh in allowing for future additions (as marked) if they proved necessary; no such work was, however, carried out. From *Civil Engineer and Architect's Journal*, vol. 16, no. 229, April 1853, p. 121.

to the existing gaol; second, a combined gaol for Louth and its neighbouring counties; and third, the possibility of an entirely new building.[108] Louth did not experience the kind of exponential increase in unrest that marked many other counties during the Famine years, and after many years of a falling crime rate (see Fig. 7.36), the grand jurors finally appointed a committee to build a new gaol 'outside the town' in 1847.[109] Neville's design provided for 126 separate-system cells in two radial blocks; similar to Murray in Armagh, he left a space for a future additional wing if the county so required (Fig. 7.43). This new gaol was completed in 1854, at a cost of £14,500, or £115 per cell – a respectable figure for the time, and proof of the financial efficiency of the county-surveyor system that grand jurors had railed against two generations before.[110] To reduce the cost, Neville eliminated the living quarters for the governor and the chaplain (he argued that Irish gaols tended to have at least three chaplains of different faiths and housing them all was impractical).[111] His façade in turn won the admiration of contemporary and more recent critics for its severe Italianate classicism, including a fanciful belvedere inspection tower that faced onto a green (and which served no real purpose other than to look menacing) (Figs 7.44, 7.45). In former times, the effect was enhanced with a cast-iron railing of fasces – mostly since removed – which were similar to those that surrounded Tullamore gaol and Carlow courthouse (see Chapter 2).[112]

Fig. 7.44. Dundalk gaol, perspective drawing, 1853. Neville used careful massing and rustication to give his Italianate façade a uniquely severe and repressive character. To the far right is the first bay of one of the cell blocks, hidden from view by a boundary wall as built. From *Civil Engineer and Architect's Journal*, vol. 16, no. 229, April 1853, p. 121.

Fig. 7.15. Dundalk gaol, from the east, c. 1900. The effect of Neville's memorable and evocative entrance building to his gaol was enhanced by its raised location and surrounding cast-iron railings, mostly since removed. The building now serves as a police station and as the county archives. (*Reproduced courtesy of the National Library of Ireland.*)

Central government and the process of consolidation: The last of the new gaols

The building work in Armagh and Dundalk resolved the long-standing problems at two county gaols, but three others – the old gaols in Drogheda, Kilkenny, and Waterford – had to wait until the post-Famine years for new buildings that met separate-system requirements. Elsewhere, the process of slowly adapting and rebuilding existing gaols – which had begun before the Famine – continued to be implemented in a piece-meal fashion. All of this building work, without exception, occurred in an age of rapidly falling crime rates and none of it can be attributed to any severe overcrowding or periods of unrest.[113] Furthermore, with the separate system now firmly established, and symbolised in the new large prisons in Belfast and Dublin, there was little room left for manoeuvre by either grand jurors or architects. We find little variation in the few new gaols, or large additions, built in the decade or so after the Famine, except in minor details of ventilation and heating systems, and, of course, the eclectic and highly ornamented gateways and façades that these institutions projected into the urban landscape of the towns in which they were sited. However, behind these architectural displays lay rigid conformity and mathematical exactitude. A new corps of younger prison inspectors used the perceived success of the new separate-system prisons to lobby for greater centralisation and control. They questioned whether, for example, it made sense for grand jurors to maintain their own gaols. Back in the 1820s, the proposal to build a series of large central-government penitentiaries was abandoned because of worries over cost and the objections from certain grand jurors (see Chapter 6); now, the issue of consolidation and efficiency re-emerged. At the 1842 inquiry into grand-jury presentments, mentioned above, a Commons committee suggested that it did not make sense for county and town/city gaols to exist as entirely separate institutions as they often shared adjoining sites. The committee thought that most of these gaols should be merged and closed.[114] Reforms to the Irish municipal corporations around this time also made possible such a radical intrusion into the historic powers of grand juries.[115] The Assizes Act of 1850 confirmed the right of central government to merge gaols (and courthouses), if both affected grand juries agreed to the idea.[116] This cleared the way for the mergers that followed in the 1860s in Galway, Kildare, Kilkenny, and Waterford.

The inspectors ensured that gaols would only be allowed to merge if there were sufficient numbers of suitable cells in the larger of the two. As such they blocked the Limerick city grand jurors' plans to give up their old gaol and keep their prisoners in the county gaol. The county jurors, in turn, refused to back the plan unless their city colleagues paid for the required additions. In the end, the city backtracked and diverted their attention towards building a new courthouse (see Chapter 3), to the great annoyance of the inspectors, and the issue was not revisited until the late 1860s.[117] In Drogheda, an inspector threatened to close the small gaol and move the prisoners to Dundalk if the grand jurors did not rebuild their prison. However, as the two Louth towns were some distance apart, a merger would have been difficult, though the opening of the railway in 1849 made it distinctly possible. In the end, the jurors elected not to lose their economically valuable right to maintain a gaol, and commissioned John Neville to oversee a rebuilding of Bowden's existing building to comply with the separate system. This new cell block, with thirty-five cells, was built between 1859 and 1861.[118]

Cell blocks of around this size were typical of the post-Famine years. The Queen's County (Laois) jurors added thirty cells for females in 1851–3; their colleagues in King's County (Offaly) and Roscommon soon thereafter added eight and sixteen cells, respectively, for females.[119] One of the wings of Downpatrick gaol was rebuilt for separate-system confinement by the county surveyor, Henry Smyth, between 1852 and 1860.[120] His more ambitious plan to convert two wings was abandoned when cess-payers objected, saying that the merits of the separate system and its effectiveness in decreasing crime have 'not been proved'. The inspectors countered that British penal reformers proclaimed the layout the most desirable, but in the end the grand jurors were not able to convince the people who funded them.[121] Considering that the last repayments for Reid's enormously expensive gaol were only made in the late 1840s, it is unsurprising there was so little enthusiasm locally for yet more building work.[122] However, there were fewer problems at Dublin's Kilmainham gaol, where John McCurdy won a commission to take down the eastern half of the building and erect a new separate-system block (Figs 7.46, 7.47); he also extended the street-facing façade of the gaol with a curved wall punctuated with Gothic turrets (Fig. 7.48).[123] McCurdy used his Dublin commission – which the *Dublin Builder* praised lavishly – to win other commissions around the country.[124] He also could point to his work at Naas, where he took down one of the radial wings of Hargrave's gaol and put up a new block with ninety-six cells between 1857 and 1860 (Fig. 7.49).[125] The governor of the gaol was a keen supporter of the separate system and during the Famine years he made a wooden model of a proposed twenty-two-cell addition, but this plan was put aside for the tried and trusted scheme offered by McCurdy.[126] Its cost was offset by the closure of Athy gaol at the same time; this small gaol was built at the height of local enthusiasm for penal-reform issues in the early 1820s, but by all accounts it had a remarkably short lifetime of just thirty years.[127] Many of the more senior townspeople of Athy must surely have remembered not only the old gaol in the medieval castle, but the building of its replacement, and in turn its abandonment.

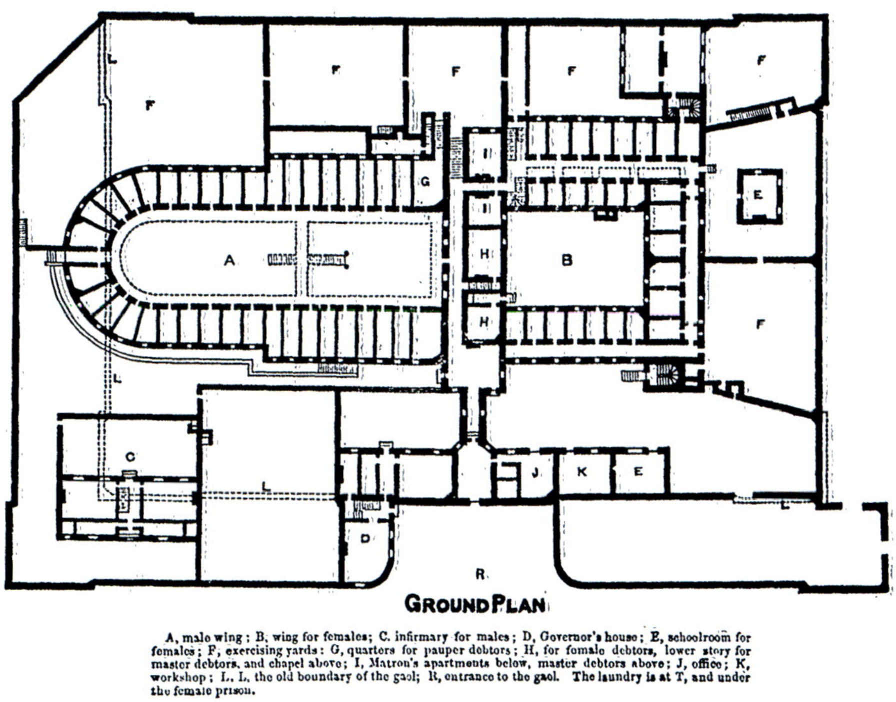

Fig. 7.46. Kilmainham gaol, Dublin, ground-floor plan, 1870. Between 1858 and 1863, John McCurdy demolished the eastern (left) half of the original gaol building, and built a large separate-system block in its place (marked 'A'). He also enlarged the gaol's boundary wall and provided more yards (in the bottom left and right, compare with Fig. 4.15). From *Forty-ninth Report … on … the Prisons of Ireland, 1870,* H.C. 1871 (C. 359), xxx, p. 545.

Fig. 7.47. (above) Kilmainham gaol, separate-system block. McCurdy's celebrated rebuilding of Kilmainham gaol provided a distinctly Victorian image for an Irish prison, marked by its delicate iron brackets, arches, stairways, airy proportions, and roof lights. (*Reproduced courtesy of the National Library of Ireland.*)

Fig. 7.48. (left) Kilmainham gaol, Dublin, boundary wall, north-east corner, from the east. While rebuilding half of this gaol in the early 1860s, McCurdy also enlarged the boundary wall and built a pair of matching Norman-Gothic corner towers facing Inchicore Road. In an era marked by conformity and standardisation in prison design, façades and boundary walls gave architects an opportunity for creativity. (*Photograph by author, 2014.*)

Fig. 7.49. Naas gaol, County Kildare, ground-floor plan, 1870. In addition to his Kilmainham work, McCurdy won many other commissions in the provincial towns for alterations to existing gaols. At Naas, he demolished one wing of Hargrave's radial-plan gaol and rebuilt it for separate-system confinement between 1857 and 1860. From *Forty-eighth Report … on … the Prisons of Ireland, 1869*, H.C. 1870 (C. 173), xxxvii, p. 361.

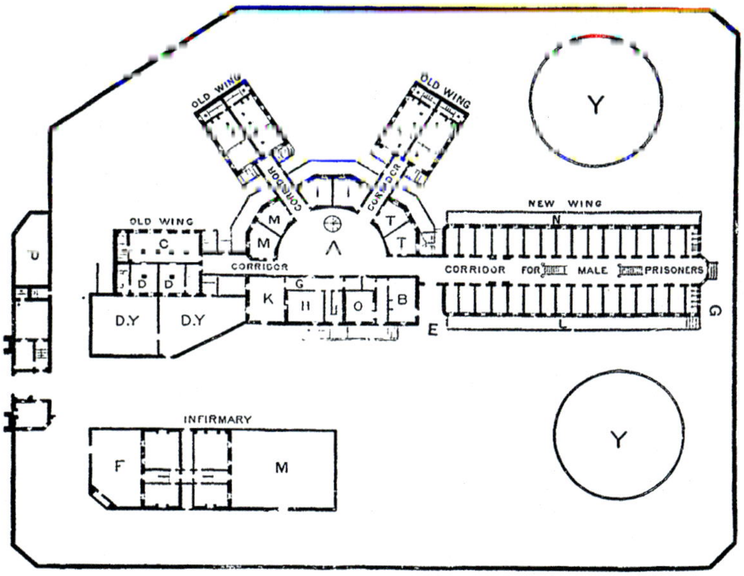

A, central inspection hall; B, board-room; C, chapel; DD, marshalsea for debtors; DY, exercising yard for debtors; GKH, Governor's apartments; O, office; MM, Head Warder's apartments. Matron's rooms over head; TT, prison officers and turnkeys' rooms; P, apartment for Head Warder; L, entrance to kitchen and other offices for males in the basement; N, entrance to laundry and other offices for females in the basement. In the infirmary the males are placed on the side marked M on the plan; the females on the side marked F; E, entrance to the prison; G, shed in which the crank pump is placed, so that supervision can be exercised over the prisoners from the hall of the prison.

When some adjacent gaols merged, it was logical that the smaller of the two should become a female prison, and the larger a male prison. Between 1859 and 1866, Samuel Ussher Roberts, the county surveyor for Galway, rebuilt part of the Galway county gaol in accordance with the separate system, and he later merged the two institutions.[128] Much later, the city gaols in Limerick and Cork became female-only institutions, with the larger county gaols appropriated to the combined population of males.[129] This met the long-standing desire to keep the sexes segregated at all times, but central government pushed for amalgamations *and* new gaols where possible; this would allow a 'model' gaol to be built from the outset, and would bring about significant financial savings in the long run.

Merging gaols was increasingly common in the post-Famine years, for example at Kilkenny and Waterford. The old gaol in Kilkenny was praised back in 1818 by Archer as a 'model' institution, but by 1830 was regarded by Palmer and Woodward as 'in the worst class of prisons'.[130] A series of plans for a replacement gaol fell through around 1841, which would have seen separate-system cell blocks built with eighty-four cells, to the designs of William Deane Butler and Charles Frederick Anderson; the grand jurors thought both schemes too expensive.[131] The Kilkenny county grand jurors took little interest in their gaol, and in 1848, the government inspectors used their example as an argument for greater central-government control over prison building. At the same time, an assize judge was also frustrated with the condition of the gaol, and warned that he would force the funding of a new gaol if there were any more delays.[132] This pushed the jurors into action, and they committed to spending £11,000 on the addition of three separate-system blocks, to Butler's design.[133] The work was so extensive that there was little of Robertson's old gaol left when the new gaol opened in 1853 (Fig. 7.50). After so much strife, the inspectors thought the new gaol a success, and its 200 cells (at just £55 per cell) allowed the disgraced city gaol under the courthouse – described by the inspectors in 1859 as 'a school of corruption' – to close finally in 1861.[134] Nothing remains of Butler's gaol today, but written and photographic descriptions show that it boasted two asymmetrical neo-Norman towers (only one of which was intact by the 1940s (see Fig. 7.51), with much less ornate radial cell blocks behind.[135]

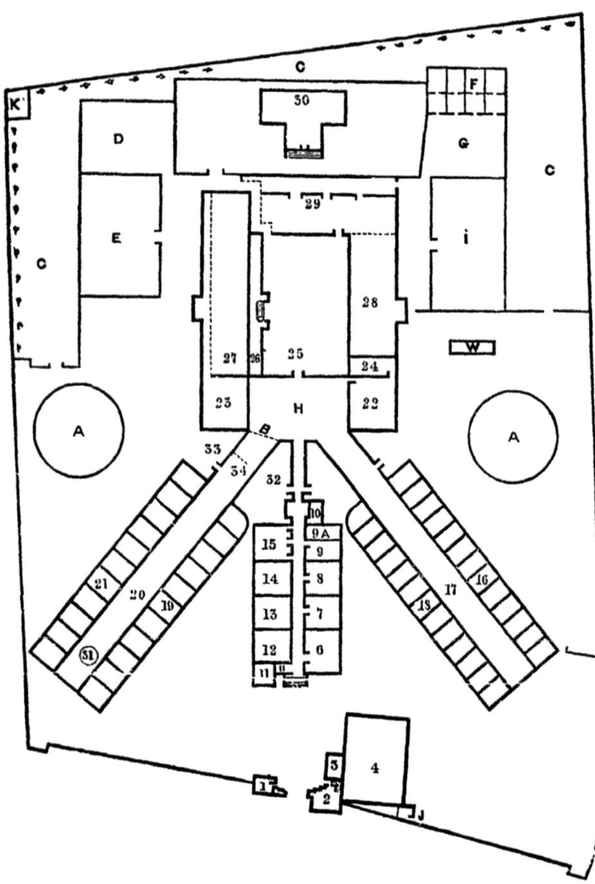

1. Guard-room
2. Tower and Entrance to Execution-room
3. Guards' Bedroom
4. Governor's Residence

6–9. Turnkeys' Rooms

9A. Store-room

10. Water-closet
11. Entrance to Chapel
12. Office
13. Board-room
14. Paint-room
15. Room for visitors to prisoners
16. New range of male cells (52 in number)
17. Passage
18. Same as No. 16 (52 cells)
19. New range of female cells (44 in number)
20. Passage
21. Same as No. 19 (44 cells)
22. Cooking-house
23. Laundry
24. Bathhouse
25. Shot-drill yard
26. Tread-wheel or mill
27. Old cells
28. Same
29. Debtors' prison
30. Prison hospital
31. Entrance to solitary cells
32. Proposed entrance to female prison
33. Proposed entrance to the laundry
34. Railing

H. Central hall
A. Exercising rings
B. Partition between male and female prison
C. Governor's garden
D & E Yards
F. Cells
G. Master Debtors' yard
I. Pauper Debtors' yard
W. Wheel-pump

Fig. 7.50. Kilkenny county and city gaol, ground-floor plan, 1870. The outline of Robertson's rectilinear-plan gaol is visible in the upper half of this drawing; Butler added two large separate-system cell blocks and a shorter third wing with work rooms and offices. His Norman-style gateway (see Fig. 7.51) is shown at the bottom. From *Forty-eighth Report … on … the Prisons of Ireland, 1869*, H.C. 1870 (C. 173), xxxvii, p. 374.

Fig. 7.51. Kilkenny county and city gaol, entrance gateway, from the east, date unknown but likely during demolition, c. 1948; by this time, the larger central tower had been demolished. William Deane Butler extensively rebuilt Kilkenny's old county gaol between 1850 and 1853; his entrance façade was, like McCurdy's work at Kilmainham, inspired by Norman sources. Photograph by Billy Brett (reproduced in Walsh, 'Hard labour', p. 232). (*Reproduced with the permission of the journal editor.*)

While Kilkenny's new gaol was being built, its prisoners were kept in part of the old gaol. This was a less-than-ideal situation, and in 1850 the inspectors commented that 'the confusion occasioned by the works renders the place very insecure'.[136] In neighbouring County Waterford, as outlined in Chapter 3, plans for an entirely new gaol on a new site occupied much of the grand jurors' time throughout the 1830s and early 1840s. Even after the Dungarvan proposal had been finally defeated, the inspectors called for 'a new model gaol for the south of Ireland', on 'a new site'.[137] They implied that neither the existing labyrinth of county and city gaol buildings near Gandon's courthouse, nor the city's suburban house of correction, were suitable for further alterations or additions. In 1844, the county and city grand jurors agreed to build a new shared courthouse (see Chapter 3) as well as a combined gaol.[138] With Gandon's courthouse vacant from around 1850 onwards, the jurors proposed appropriating its site to expand the gaol; however, the Board of Superintendence and the inspectors continued to push for an entirely new site.[139] After the crisis of the Famine years, the criminal-indictment rate in both the county and city fell dramatically – the former in particular collapsed from just over 1,000 in 1849 to 173 in 1855 (Fig. 7.52).[140] With less pressure on the existing gaols, the grand jurors were less inclined to vote for a large new gaol, and various proposals for such a building, one of which would have cost £21,000, were rejected at assizes throughout the 1850s. As at Carlow in previous decades, an assize judge intervened to make the case to the grand jurors: at the summer assizes in 1856, Baron Pennefather focused his attention on the inadequate female prison. The prison inspector, he commented,

> alludes to other wants, gentlemen, he mentions the want of ventilation, the want of the means of cleanliness, and other things to which, gentlemen,

> your attention ought to be directed. But mainly I would impress on your minds, gentlemen, the situation of the female prisoners; young persons, general speaking, committed for small offences, obliged to mix with the hardened sinners who are there imprisoned; their morals, gentlemen, can scarcely escape corruption and contagion. I would say that those who have it in their power to provide for the separate classification, especially of the female prisoners, and who neglect the exercise of that power, and who cause, by the mixing of the two classes of female prisoners I have named, the young to receive contagion from the old, are deeply responsible for those results. I cannot, gentlemen, impress the consideration of this matter too forcibly on your minds, in order that you may nurse it, and as soon as may be remedy, as far as you can, this serious defect in your county prison, and which tends to contaminate the females in it.[141]

The same words had been uttered by Howard and Fry in earlier generations. Remarkably, it was another four years before plans were finally agreed. The jurors thought that a smaller gaol would suffice, with 120 cells instead of 170 as originally proposed.[142] Charles Tarrant, the county surveyor, drew up plans for this gaol, and after the demolition of almost all the existing buildings, his gaol was erected between 1860 and 1863 (Figs 7.53, 7.54).[143] During the construction period, the county and city prisoners were conveniently kept at the old city house of correction. When the first prisoners were moved to Tarrant's gaol in

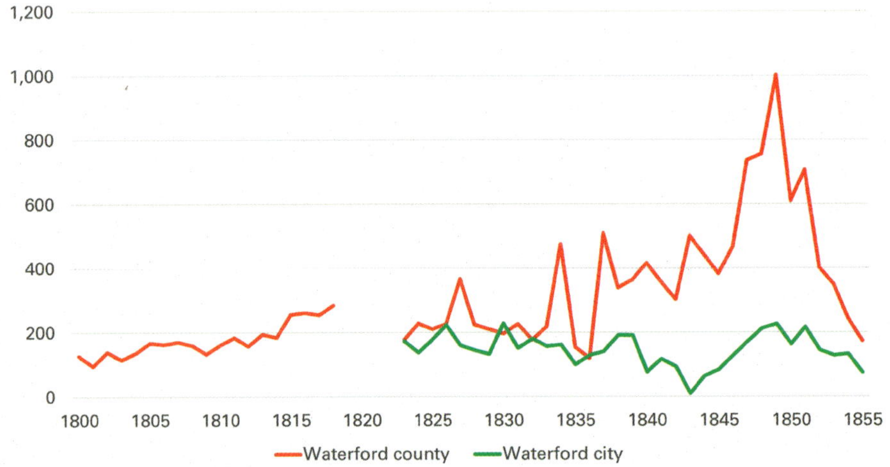

Fig. 7.52. A graph showing the number of criminal indictments in Waterford county and city between 1800 and 1855 (where available). Certain factions within the Waterford county grand jury wished to see a new gaol built in Dungarvan from the mid-1830s onwards, but an agreement to build a combined gaol for the county and city in Waterford was only reached in 1844. When designs for this gaol were being discussed in the years after the Famine, combined criminal-indictment rates were at historic lows, and plans for the gaol were correspondingly scaled back, with the number of cells reduced from 170 to 120. Compiled from Appendix B.

June 1863, the grand jurors and inspectors praised the fact that three old gaols (two on rectilinear plans and one on a polygonal plan) had been replaced by a single separate-system institution. Architecturally, the new gaol followed Kilkenny, Dundalk, and all the other small separate-system gaols of the 1840s and 1850s and was composed of two cell blocks of unequal length (the larger for males).[144] Tarrant deployed a highly ornate Gothic Revival style for the entrance gateway (Fig. 7.55), and for the chapel behind, but the cell blocks were left much sparser. His design is known only today from a series of photographs and drawings, as it was demolished in the early 1950s.[145]

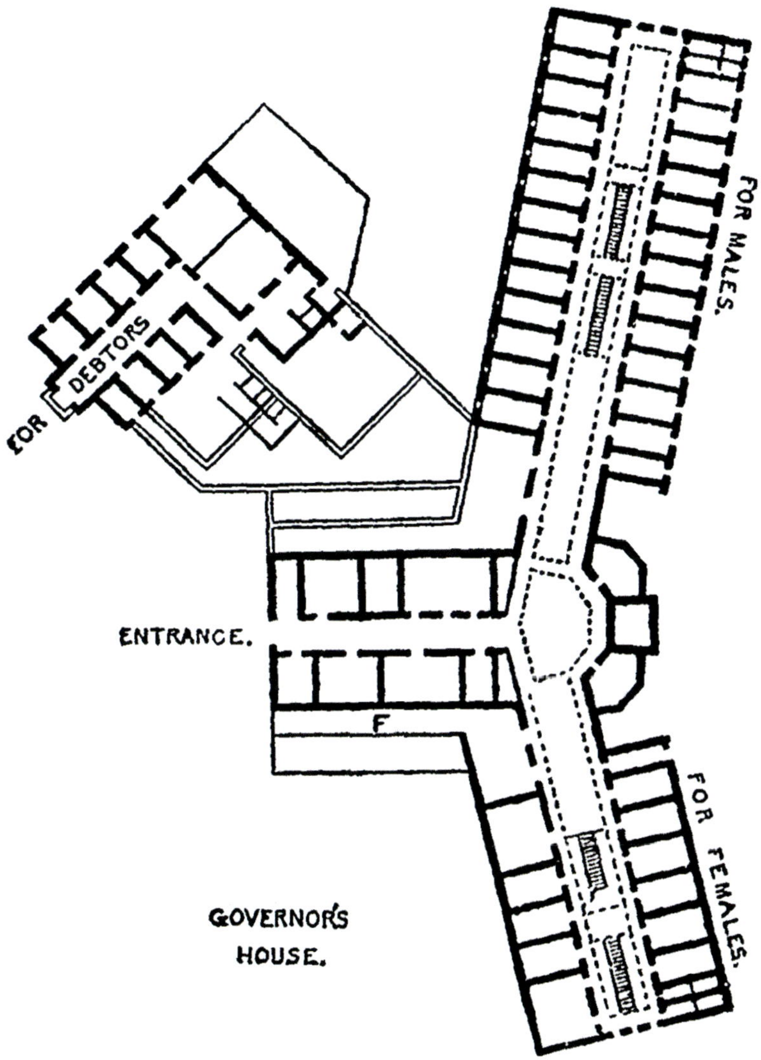

Fig. 7.53. Waterford county and city gaol, ground-floor plan, 1870. Charles Tarrant's design for Waterford gaol was similar to other small gaols built after 1840, such as Dundalk and Kilkenny. The length of the two wings corresponds to the proportion of crime by gender in the county when the design was approved. The gaol was built between 1860 and 1863. From *Forty-eighth Report … on … the Prisons of Ireland, 1869*, H.C. 1870 (C. 173), xxxvii, p. 474.

Fig. 7.54. Waterford county and city gaol, aerial photograph, from the south-west, *c.* 1933. Tarrant's gaol, demolished around 1950, featured a Gothick gateway and chapel. It was built on the site of Gandon's courthouse and the old county and city gaols. (*Reproduced courtesy of the Waterford Museum of Treasures.*)

Fig. 7.55. Waterford county and city gaol, entrance gateway, from the south-west, undated but likely *c.* 1950 during demolition. Tarrant gave his gaol – which may be considered Ireland's last county gaol – a picturesque Gothick composition. (*Reproduced courtesy of the Waterford Museum of Treasures.*)

It is fitting to end with Tarrant's Waterford gaol, built on the same site as Gandon's courthouse. This corner of Ballybricken Green featured not only the beginning of one building type but arguably also the end of another. In the intervening eighty years, we see a transformation in prison (and courthouse) architecture in Ireland. Moreover, we see a revolution in how and why prisons were built, from the small rectilinear-plan gaol to the rear of Gandon's courthouse that had disappointed Howard almost as soon as it was begun, to the conformity of the government-approved separate-system institution. As outlined in chapters 4 to 7, the rebalancing of power between central government and the grand juries is arguably the most important dynamic of this entire time period. One effect of this was that when Tarrant's gaol was planned, there was no ambiguity over the layout or organisation of the institution; also, this exacting rigidity meant that an in-house engineer, rather than a professional architect, could design such a building.

In the years after 1860, the management of Ireland's gaols pushed further towards central-government control. In 1877, the establishment of the General Prisons Board formally ended the historic role that grand juries had played in running county gaols.[146] However, and in contrast to Britain, there was little gaol-building activity in the latter decades of the nineteenth century; with a falling population, and a continued decline in crime rates (with certain short-term exceptions), there was less impetus to rebuild, and no new architectural arrangements that challenged the separate system.[147] The next chapter in the architectural history of the Irish prison was not their rebuilding or enlargement but their widespread destruction during the revolutionary period of 1916–23.

Reflections:

Identities, Actors, Towns

This book suggests a range of questions for further debate and research, not least whose legacy is represented in the building of Ireland's courthouses and prisons. How 'Irish' are they?[1] Are they the product of an imperial – even colonial – government, firmly forcing the mark of its authority on the urban landscape of the poorest and most troubled outpost of the Union, or do they have a more local meaning?[2] Judith Hill, for example, has recently identified the colonial hybridity evident in the interplay between architecture, sculpture, and distinctly Protestant political agendas in the rebuilding of the Viceregal Chapel in Dublin in the years immediately after the Act of Union.[3] And Barclay has noted how grand jurors sometimes encouraged architects to furnish courtrooms with 'Irish' designs to encourage, she argued, 'familiarity with the court amongst locals, as well as underlining that this was "Irish", and so legitimate, justice'.[4] Alistair Rowan, by contrast, has written that the many new courthouses of this time were 'monumental and repressive' and 'totally foreign in their point of reference', and hints at a post-colonial interpretation; 'grand juries', he added, 'voted funds to reinforce the rule of law'.[5] There are grounds for accepting his viewpoint, not least because of the pivotal role, as outlined here, that generous central-government loans played in actually making possible these (re)building programmes, especially from 1817 onwards. But it is also evident that however much the imperial government and the grand juries cooperated in their administration of Ireland at this time, there is a clear need to drive a wedge between their differing political viewpoints and agendas: their relationship was in fact closer to one of alliance and enmity, cooperation and discord, acceptance and frustration. In the field of public architecture, the new courthouses and prisons owed as much to local agendas and the influence of key grand jurors as they did to any kind of overarching central-government policy. This is not to suggest that Westminster played no role in the history of these buildings, of course, but rather that there is a highly individual and local character to each of the decisions taken by grand juries to either build or rebuild. This is perhaps unsurprising considering that grand jurors retained a final say over these projects, but bringing their role into central focus suggests that the imperial legacy of these buildings needs to be reconsidered. In its place may be substituted or appended more provincial and local meanings.

Historians familiar with the course of twentieth-century Irish history may be surprised to hear debate of provincial or local meanings for Ireland's courthouses and prisons. It is easy to understand why these have been all but forgotten today: at times of high political drama, and in particular during rebellions and uprisings, these buildings became emblematic of 'the state' – the British imperial state – more generally. In the case of prisons, this was in many ways a fair assessment: after 1877 all Irish prisons were brought under central-government control and many of the smaller bridewells were closed.[6] The grand juries lost their ancient right to control their own prisons, but they did keep their courthouses. Nevertheless, whatever subtle or nuanced local meanings survived were lost in the polarising political rancour that came with the Land War in the 1880s, the Maamtrasna executions, and, of course, the War of Independence and Civil War.[7] At this time many courthouses were burned, such as at Tullamore in County Offaly. Jason Knirck argues that these burnings represented legible sequences of contested claims of ownership and possession over the judicial and political power that these buildings embodied, or in other words, that attacks on these buildings were meant to be seen as attacks on the colonial or imperial state.[8] During the Northern Irish 'troubles' this cycle of destruction reached a new apogee, and with it the complete polarisation of whatever political meanings these buildings embodied. It is easy to lose sight of the very different political and social environment in which these courthouses and prisons were built, and especially the aims and mentalities of those who built them. One of the aims of this book is to attempt to recover some of these older meanings, and in some ways to 'rescue' these buildings from the legacy of their subsequent history.

The grand juries, as patrons, coalesced around certain political and sectarian viewpoints. As argued here, they were for the most part conservative, oligarchical, high-church Protestant organisations that resisted central-government reform and especially the granting of Catholic emancipation. The economic and political high-water mark of their power and influence occurred under the ascendancy parliament of the eighteenth century; after the Act of Union they were constantly faced with reforms and new limitations from a proactive central government based not in Dublin but in Westminster. The tenor of some of the speeches of their more spirited defenders in parliament – such as Vereker of Limerick – hints not at their strength but at their growing weakness. From the 1810s onwards, it is readily apparent that they were, as elsewhere in Europe, *ancien régime* institutions under siege. A clear example of this is the method by which Tipperary was divided in the 1830s, as outlined in Chapter 3: this saga demonstrated how the authority and autonomy of grand juries had been fatally undermined. Furthermore, it is evident from the views of key politicians such as Robert Peel that many grand jurors had foreseen the decline of their prized institutions, and that even in the 1810s there was a pervasive mentalité of resignation and defeat. Nonetheless, at the exact same time we find a great peak in grand-jury patronage of new large, expensive, impressive public buildings. We should see this as a rich period of architectural patronage in the twilight years of grand-jury power. The extent of their indulgence in building, fuelled by loans, was perhaps a reaction to the loss of real power and influence in a changing society. The great granite porticos and rusticated quoins of provincial public buildings are then more the legacy of reactionary politics – of a system of local authority under siege – than they are of a dominant imperial government.

This, however, does not fully explain the distinct patterns in regional patronage that characterise courthouse and prison building in these years. The debate was more than simply a binary one between central government and the grand juries: it was also a discourse played out within, and between, grand juries. The former, *intra*-county disputes, are evident in counties where stark divisions emerged over broader political issues, such as in Monaghan in the 1820s, but also in King's County, Tipperary, and Waterford, where patronage was tied up with the prosperity or decline of individual towns, and the standing of the grand jurors who represented them. The latter, however – *inter*-county competition – is found in many of the patronage decisions of the period. The history of the building of Ireland's courthouses and prisons cannot be told without reference to these local jealousies and to a distinct competitive culture that convinced grand jurors to emulate the consumerism of their neighbours and rivals. The most distinguished of the new courthouses – at Carlow, Tralee, and Cork –

grew out of this sense of competition. This book shows how assize judges, prison inspectors, and newspaper reporters, amongst others, contributed to this competitive dynamic, which peaked in the years before grand-jury patronage was restricted by government reforms. In the case of prisons, assize judges and prison inspectors realised the usefulness of this sense of competition and used it to attempt to eliminate the last of the ancient county gaols.

We should ask what importance we can attribute to issues of crime and unrest. It is undeniable that Ireland had acute levels of agrarian unrest and sectarian violence in the pre-Famine period, and indisputable also that this culture of violence and insurrection must have played a part in shaping the mentalité and outlook of the grand jurors and central-government politicians that concerned themselves with crime and punishment and the public buildings where these concerns were played out. But it is remarkable that many of the most resplendent new courthouses, and expensive, intricately planned new prisons were built during periods of either steady or declining rates of crime at a county level. Carlow's new courthouse emerged in the context of praise from assize judges for the uniquely peaceable character of the county; Cork's new county gaol was quickly filled with Rockite activists in the 1820s, but the grand-jury decision to commit to the project occurred long before this spike in unrest. Tipperary's uniquely troubled history had little impact on the size and condition of the county buildings in Clonmel for many decades; only from the perspective of the mid-1840s was it clear that crime levels had influenced the decision to split the county in two. Neighbouring counties Roscommon, Sligo, and Longford experienced broadly similar increases in crime in the early nineteenth century, but only one of them committed to build a new courthouse. All three built new gaols, but at different times, and at different points in their cyclical increasing and decreasing levels of crime. On balance, it is clear that the availability of government loans was almost always more influential in instigating courthouse building than the particular crime levels in a given county at a given time; for prisons, these loans, and the reorganised central-government inspectorate of the early 1820s, played a larger role than the specifics of crime levels. Histories of Ireland's courthouses and prisons need to give more credence to issues of financial wherewithal, political reform, local elites, and inter-county competition: the factors that help to explain patronage decisions and the consumption of architecture.

In the field of prison building, this book analyses the impact of the Irish philanthropic penal-reform society, the Association for the Improvement of

Prisons and of Prison Discipline in Ireland (AIPPD). The AIPPD has escaped the attention of almost all scholars who have worked on the subject, yet it is clear from their correspondence and their publications that they were close to Charles Grant, Irish chief secretary, and to his drafting of the Prisons Act of 1821. They influenced not only prison design but also broader issues of administration and inspection. Learning from their London-based sister organisation, they contributed to the confluence of reforms in the early 1820s that led to the widespread rebuilding of gaols and bridewells all around the country.

By the mid-1820s the annual reports of the AIPPD had been superseded and they exerted less influence. This was certainly not because every prison now met the government's improved standards. Rather it was because the revived prison inspectorate, who the AIPPD had been involved in founding, had usurped their work and carried it on with a degree of rigour and professionalism that a small voluntary society could not match. It is remarkable how much the inspectors Palmer and Woodward achieved in the first decade of work, and how their reports were so widely publicised in the provincial newspapers and taken up by assize judges. The inspectors were acutely aware of their own success, of course, and Palmer's expansive treatise on prisons in 1832, with its call to British magistrates to emulate his approach, must have appeared more than a little patronising on the other side of the Irish Sea. Palmer's portfolio was emblematic of his predecessor: MacDonagh shows how Fitzpatrick, as Ireland's first prison inspector, grew his role to take in much more than what was originally expected of him. Furthermore, both MacDonagh and Henriques, in their studies of inspectors as a new addition to the civil service of government administrations, conclude that the idea of the position – whatever about its success or failure in practice – had a huge impact on the development of the bureaucratic structures that we associate with nineteenth-century government.[9] For Palmer and Woodward, this was also true: their opinions were called upon in the 1830s to help decide the location of assize towns, which had a direct impact on the rise or fall of the economy of these provincial towns. The history of Tullamore, Nenagh, or Dungarvan can hardly be written without reference to the influence and impact of these inspectors. A future avenue of research, building on this book, might be to study the economic development of these towns in much greater detail, and analyse the role that the state played in promoting urban growth and prosperity by the gain or loss of key public buildings.

We may also consider the role of the architect, whose skill and creativity can easily be lost in histories that focus on patronage and consumption. The object of reforms to grand-jury spending on public architecture was, fundamentally, to lessen corruption, jobbery, and waste. But the unreformed system worked particularly well for architects, who were able to earn a generous living from large projects and subsequent follow-up work. Richard Morrison profited from perhaps a dozen new courthouse and gaol commissions around 1810, but many ended in scandal, overruns, or were completed only to be quickly condemned by the government inspectors. The scandals surrounding Cork's county and city gaols were proof enough that where lax accountability existed, architects (and contractors) would too easily reap great rewards from their work. It is therefore unsurprising that one of the key aspects of grand-jury reform from the 1830s onwards was to take away jurors' ability to make contracts with the architect of their choice; instead, the Board of Works took this responsibility. With its own architects, the Board of Works began to monopolise more and more of the architecture market, depriving architects of much of the traditional source of income. For central-government officials, this represented better value for money; for architects, it was a more worrying trend. This book considers two of the four great programmes of public architecture from the pre-Famine period, deliberately excluding the building of lunatic asylums and workhouses. But it is hardly surprising that the design of the new lunatic asylums of the 1820s was entrusted to just two architects (themselves prolific courthouse and gaol builders), or that the stream of new workhouses were given without competition to one man – George Wilkinson of Oxford – much to the chagrin of the Irish architectural establishment.[10] Existing histories of these buildings say little about the way in which the reforms to courthouse and prison building in the preceding decades had an impact on the formation of monopolies in these later programmes. Though the establishment of the Royal Institute of the Architects of Ireland (RIAI) in 1839 has been seen in the light of the workhouse controversy, there is little written about the prelude offered by the earlier building programmes.[11]

It was not just the Board of Works that came to threaten the individuality and independence of the architecture profession. O'Donoghue shows how county surveyors, within grand juries, came to take over many of the roles traditionally filled by architects.[12] In the case of courthouse and prison building, it is evident that from the mid-1830s onwards, an increasing proportion of grand-jury architectural work was controlled by these surveyors. This must be seen within a broader European context, where the primacy of the architect was threatened by resourceful (and competitive) engineers and contractors.[13] But in terms of prison building, architects also had to contend with new government inspectors (with architectural ideas of their own), philanthropic societies (with good connections), and even prison staff (such as at Naas where the governor built his own model for a new gaol). As prisons became increasing complicated in design, their construction went beyond the skills of traditional architects and into a closed group of professional engineers and bureaucrats. In the 1790s an architect designed every inch of a prison; by the 1820s there were set models that the inspectors assumed would be followed, and by the 1840s he had only the façade to embellish. Freed from these more onerous responsibilities, architects of this era produced some of the most distinguished façades and entrance gateways within the canon of Irish public architecture. Their colleagues designing courthouses faced fewer restrictions, particularly in the 1820s, and it was here – in the great triumphs of Tralee and Carlow in particular – that skill and creativity was most keenly received. But the effects of grand-jury reform went far beyond the confines of the grand-jury room, and architects were by no means immune to the shifting sands around them.

This book suggests little by way of a systematic engagement among grand-jury patrons with architectural style. In the excitement that surrounded Morrison's designs for Tralee and Carlow courthouses we can certainly see a strong interest in the neo-classical, but the exact reasons why this was so remain rather elusive. Only in the Tullamore courthouse competition do we gain an insight into one grand juror's views on what would be an appropriate style for a public building, and even then, his comments are strongly influenced, as argued in this book, by political and financial considerations. But it is surely more than a coincidence that every Irish assize courthouse of the early nineteenth century was built in the neo-classical style, often with a Doric or an Ionic portico, and that we must wait until Sligo in the 1870s for the first hints of the Gothic Revival. We can speculate that this was because of the influential precedents set by Gandon in Waterford and at the Four Courts, and his sway over a younger generation of architects, not least the Morrisons. It may also be that the neo-classical style, such as at Tullamore, was seen as cheaper and better value for grand jurors than the more ornate Gothic Revival. But most of all it suggests that the neo-classical style carried certain meanings for grand jurors – strength, dignity, eloquence, sophistication – and that these were seen as the most appropriate for the grand-jury system of local government and justice.[14]

In the case of prisons, we find much greater architectural variety. The majority are, again, in the neo-classical style, but perhaps a dozen were built in various

Gothic Revival idioms and some later prisons such as Crumlin Road, Belfast, and Dundalk adopted Italianate motifs. Interestingly, the few Gothic style prisons that were built span the whole period from Roscommon and Lifford in the late eighteenth century to Castlebar, Wexford, and Kilkenny in the 1830s and 1840s. The main façade of a prison was undoubtedly a noteworthy aspect and was commented upon by prison inspectors, travellers, and sometimes by grand jurors. The neo-classical style, often with extensive use of rustication, was likely popular in prison building for the same reasons that it was for courthouses, namely its impression of strength, impregnability, and sophistication.

Architects and grand-jury patrons were of course operating within a broader world of architectural styles and meanings. The neo-classical style appears in many British colonial courthouses and government buildings – not least in nineteenth-century Calcutta. This style was almost *de rigueur* for public or institutional buildings in Ireland before the late 1830s: not only in assize courthouses and county gaols but also in the great majority of quarter-session courthouses and bridewells. Furthermore, the first wave of lunatic asylums, built by Johnston and Murray in the 1820s, all adopted a restrained neo-classical style. Curiously, though, the fashion for the neo-classical in public buildings did not extend across all areas of government architecture at the time: for example, the vast majority of the Board of First Fruits Protestant churches were built in a rather severe Gothic Revival style. Ironically, it was the Roman Catholic Church in these years that was most enthusiastic about Palladian and neo-classical designs.[15] In terms of institutions, it was only with the building of the workhouses to the standard designs of Wilkinson in the 1840s that the Tudor Gothic style overtook the neo-classical, and afterwards we see this used in many (though not all) asylums and school buildings. For the many new country houses, there was a more balanced use of neo-classical and Gothic Revival ideas – some houses, such as Castle Ward in County Down, famously combined the two. Within this complicated and multi-layered world of architectural practice it is hard to discern clear trends and meanings, but the dominance of the neo-classical style in the design of assize courthouses and county gaols comes as close as is possible to a unified statement of architectural meaning and symbol. As Barclay has recently commented,

> neoclassical architecture embodied the masculine virtues valued during the era, self-control, truthfulness, responsibility, whilst acknowledging the law's role in producing rights and justice. Such messages tied

> courthouses, and the practice of law, into the wider Enlightenment project of nation and Empire building, improvement and the expansion of the polity. This was not dissimilar from the messages conveyed by court buildings across the British Empire.[16]

The new courthouses and prisons were situated within existing – mostly eighteenth-century – urban landscapes, and they deserve greater recognition for their role in promoting town development in the early nineteenth century.[17] This was as much morphological as it was economic: often courthouses in particular formed the focal point at the end of new streets, such as at Nenagh. The new public buildings also transformed the local economy, often spurring on speculative housing development, gas lighting, and the establishment of local newspapers. In Galway, the relocation of the town's duo of courthouses and prisons formed a new quarter in the city, enclosing a square and bound together by a new bridge. In Sligo the new prison set out a network of new streets and affected the spatial layout of the eastern half of the town; in Belfast, Limerick, Tullamore, and Dublin new courthouses and prisons carved out institutional suburbs at the edge of the city, giving these quarters a distinct character that they maintain to this day. In Cork too the new courthouse was the centrepiece of a new street. In each of these cities and towns the economic dividend provided by these public buildings was very substantial, though sometimes rather difficult to quantify. By focusing on Nenagh and Tullamore, this book begins to shed light on what remain much under-researched topics, but further questions beckon, and the role that new public buildings played in promoting speculative housing development seems a particularly inviting subject for future research. It may even be that this history could significantly disrupt the existing narrative of decline in Irish provincial towns in the mid-nineteenth century.

Stepping further back, we should ask what exactly, if anything, was unique about the Irish experience in the period under question, and what comparisons or contrasts can be made with developments in Britain. Ireland was not unique in its great rebuilding of courthouses and prisons in the late eighteenth and early nineteenth centuries: Evans and Graham, in their respective studies, find similar levels of architectural activity in England. But these buildings were, by and large, funded in different ways: as outlined in Chapter 2, Irish grand juries benefited disproportionately from government loans, which in England went mostly to aid private companies. In terms of courthouse building, for every government loan in England there were ten or twenty such loans in Ireland. But this did not make for larger or more impressive courthouses in Ireland – instead it propped up a poorer country with a smaller tax base and allowed Irish grand jurors to compete on a level playing field with their wealthier English counterparts. It is hard to overstate the importance of this economic divide: just as spending restrictions and stagnation in Ireland called a halt to courthouse building in the 1830s and 1840s, the new urban prosperity in England permitted courthouses and municipal halls – such as St George's Hall in Liverpool, built between 1841 and 1854 – on a scale that no Irish grand juror could even begin to conceive.

With prisons, it would likewise be a mistake to see the Irish experience as entirely without precedent or comparison. For all the agrarian unrest, economic stagnation, and political controversy in Ireland – the sense that Ireland *needed* many large and impressive prisons – there was little of the explosive urban growth that forced so many local authorities to build new prisons in Britain. As with courthouses, government loans had a large impact, but the average Irish county gaol was rather small compared with those in England, Wales, or Scotland. Belfast and Mountjoy may be compared with Pentonville, but the other new prisons in London, Manchester, Liverpool, and Edinburgh stand without any obvious Irish brother or sister. To find common ground, we need to look at those agricultural counties in England that were to some degree insulated from the industrial revolution: the county gaol at Lincoln, for example, is on an 'Irish' scale, and may be compared with Enniskillen, Kilkenny, or Waterford. However, this is not to suggest that there is nothing unique or fascinating about Irish prison building – as outlined in this book, the political and social world in which these prisons were built had its own unique dynamic, the system of inspection was different, and the sectarian problems and historical legacy was without any parallel. These buildings have their own identity and their own story.

Much of their uniqueness was down to the oddities of the grand-jury system. This book attempts to explore the mentality, or mentalities, of Irish grand jurors in the early nineteenth century. The building of courthouses and prisons gives us an insight into Irish life more generally in the years before the Great Famine. It presents a picture of an oligarchy that was pessimistic and in decline, faced with great changes in the society that it had so convincingly controlled in the eighteenth century. The grand jurors' social composition, their sectarian biases, and their cavalier use of large government loans to prop up their building programmes speaks to a key stratum of Irish society that failed to engage with the majority of the population. The civic society that they embodied –

Norbury's 'proud aristocracy of Ireland' was a weak and deeply fractured one, and the extent of these fissures became plain for all to see during the Great Famine. By bringing together Protestant political outlook and mentalities, and the coeval peaks and troughs in the building of new courthouses and prisons, this book argues that politics and architecture were deeply intertwined, that one reflected the other, was affected by it, and helped shape it. It has therefore adopted a more general principle: that we can understand patrons and their world by studying the buildings that they have left us, and by studying how and why these buildings were erected. Architectural historians have been happy to take this almost as an axiom and apply it universally, and political historians have little hesitation in looking to architecture, or visual culture more generally, for a fleeting glimpse of the world in which their debates played out. The Palace of Westminster, for example, tells us a huge amount about British politics and culture in the 1830s, just as New Delhi speaks for British imperialism in the 1910s and 1920s. But in Ireland we need much more research into the other new buildings of the early nineteenth century – country houses, asylums, schools, unexecuted streets, squares and harbours, among others – to expand our understanding of mentalities and agendas. This book attempts to present a more complete insight into the world of one of these patrons – the grand juries – and it suggests that Irish political, social, and cultural historians should better integrate the discoveries of architectural and urban history into their general narratives, something they have often been slow to do. Grand juries, as the largest and arguably the most controversial patrons of public architecture in the period under study, deserve this broader recognition.

Notes

Introduction

1 Maurice Craig, *The Architecture of Ireland from the Earliest Times to 1880* (London: Batsford, 1982), pp. 200–31, 257–325; Ruth Delany, *A Celebration of 250 Years of Ireland's Inland Waterways* (Belfast: Appletree, 1992); Andrew Carpenter, Rolf Loeber, Hugh Campbell, Livia Hurley, and Ellen Rowley (eds), *Art and Architecture of Ireland: Volume IV: Architecture 1600–2000* (Dublin, New Haven and London: Yale University Press, 2014), pp. 148–50, 159–62, 214–17, 240–4, 288–95, 302–9; and Christine Casey, 'Art and Architecture in the Long Eighteenth Century', in James Kelly (ed.), *The Cambridge History of Ireland: Volume III, 1730–1880* (Cambridge: Cambridge University Press, 2018), pp. 406–64, at pp. 459–63.

2 Markus Reuber, *Staats- und Privatanstalten in Irland: Irre, ärzte und idioten, 1600–1900* (Cologne: Verlag, 1994); John O'Connor, *The Workhouses of Ireland: The fate of Ireland's poor* (Dublin: Anvil, 1995); Loeber, et al., *Art and Architecture of Ireland: Volume IV: Architecture 1600–2000*, pp. 171, 178–9, 181–4, 200–6, 212–14; and Pierce Grace, 'Patronage and Health Care in Eighteenth-century Irish County Infirmaries', *Irish Historical Studies*, vol. 41, no. 159, May 2017, pp. 1–21.

3 Daire Hogan and W.N. Osborough (eds), *Brehons, Serjeants and Attorneys: Studies in the history of the Irish legal profession* (Dublin: Irish Academic Press, 1990), pp. 111–19, 125, 153, 173, 181–3, 189, 196–7, 202; Neal Garnham, *The Courts, Crime and the Criminal Law in Ireland, 1692–1760* (Dublin: Irish Academic Press, 1996), pp. 71–86, 104–8, 119–32. For contemporary descriptions, see Edward Wakefield, *An Account of Ireland, Statistical and Political* (2 vols, London: Longman, 1812), vol. 2, pp. 342–4; C.J. Woods, 'Johann Friedrich Hering's Description of Connacht, 1806–7', *Irish Historical Studies*, vol. 25, no. 99, May 1987, pp. 315–21, at p. 320; and *Freeman's Journal*, 25 March 1826.

4 Terence M. Dunne, 'The Law of Captain Rock', in Kyle Hughes and Donald M. MacRaild (eds), *Crime, Violence and the Irish in the Nineteenth Century* (Liverpool: Liverpool University Press, 2017), pp. 38–52, at p. 48. See also Desmond MacCabe, '"The part that laws or kings can cause or cure": Crown prosecution and jury trial at Longford assizes, 1830–45', in Raymond Gillespie and Gerard Moran (eds), *Longford: Essays in county history* (Dublin: Lilliput Press, 1991), pp. 153–72, at p. 160; Brendán Mac Suibhne, *The End of Outrage: Post-Famine adjustment in rural Ireland* (Oxford: Oxford University Press, 2017), p. 155; and Barclay, *Men on Trial*, pp. 70–1.

5 P.J. Meghen, 'The Administrative Work of the Grand Jury', *Administration: Journal of the Institute of Public Administration of Ireland*, vol. 6, no. 3, Autumn 1958, pp. 247–64; C.E.B. Brett, *Court Houses and Market Houses of the Province of Ulster* (Belfast: Ulster Architectural Heritage Society, 1973), pp. 15–20; Christine Casey, 'Courthouses, Markethouses and Townhalls of Leinster', MA thesis, University College Dublin, 1982, pp. 15–22; Virginia Crossman, *Local Government in Nineteenth-century Ireland* (Belfast: Institute of Irish Studies, 1994), pp. 33–41; W.E. Vaughan, *Murder Trials in Ireland, 1836–1914* (Dublin: Four Courts Press, 2009), pp. 86–115; David Dickson, *Dublin: The making of a capital city* (Cambridge, MA: Belknap Press, 2014), pp. 45, 244, 262–3.

6 K. Theodore Hoppen, *Governing Hibernia: British politicians and Ireland, 1800–1921* (Oxford: Oxford University Press, 2016), p. 3. See also Mac Suibhne, *The End of Outrage*, p. 64.

7 See David Eastwood, *Governing Rural England: Tradition and transformation in local government, 1780–1840* (Oxford: Clarendon Press, 1994). For Irish grand and petty juries more broadly, see Niamh Howlin, 'Irish Jurors: Passive observers or active participants?', *Journal of Legal History*, vol. 35, no. 2, 2014, pp. 143–71; and Niamh Howlin, *Juries in Ireland: Laypersons and law in the long nineteenth century* (Dublin: Four Courts Press, 2017).

8 Brett, *Court Houses and Market Houses*, pp. 18–20; Brendan O'Donoghue, *The Irish County Surveyors, 1834–1944: A biographical dictionary* (Dublin: Four Courts Press, 2007), pp. 3–25.

9 See, for example, David Nolan's analysis of the Cork grand jury: David M. Nolan, 'The County Cork Grand Jury, 1836–1899', MA thesis, University College Cork, 1974, Chapter 2; and David Broderick, *Local Government in Nineteenth-century County Dublin: The grand jury* (Dublin: Four Courts Press, 2007), p. 14.

10 See for example speeches by George Dawson and Daniel O'Connell in the House of Commons: *Hansard*, vol. 1, 3rd ser., 9 December 1830, cols 909–32. See also Broderick, *Local Government in Nineteenth-century County Dublin*, p. 10.

11 Craig, *Architecture of Ireland*, p. 266.

12 Hoppen, *Governing Hibernia*, pp. 21–2, 42.

13 Barclay, *Men on Trial*, p. 72.

14 As suggested by Livia Hurley amongst others; see Loeber, et al., *Art and Architecture of Ireland: Volume IV: Architecture 1600–2000*, p. 182.

15 Norman Gash, *Mr Secretary Peel: The life of Sir Robert Peel to 1830* (London & New York: Longman, 1985), pp. 521–8.

16 Clare grand-jury presentment book, summer assizes 1828 (Cambridge University Library). See also, for Cork county and city courthouse, *Southern Reporter*, 11 April 1844.

17 See for example Virginia Crossman, 'Local Government in Nineteenth-century Ireland', in Terrence McDonough (ed.), *Was Ireland a Colony? Economics, politics and culture in nineteenth-century Ireland* (Dublin: Irish Academic Press, 2005), pp. 102–16.

18 See for example Gavin Stamp, 'British Architecture in India, 1857–1947', *Journal of the Royal Society of Arts*, vol. 129, no. 5298, May 1981, pp. 357–79; Costas Douzinas and Lynda Nead (eds), *Law and the Image: The authority of art and the aesthetics of law* (Chicago: University of Chicago Press, 1999); and Linda Mulcahy, *Legal Architecture: Justice, due process and the place of law* (Oxford and New York: Routledge, 2011).

19 For an excellent recent overview of this subject, see G.A. Bremner, *Imperial Gothic: Religious architecture and high Anglican culture in the British empire, c. 1840–1870* (New Haven and London: Yale University Press, 2013), pp. 350–63. See also Judith Hill, 'Architecture in the Aftermath of Union: Building the Viceregal Chapel in Dublin Castle, 1801–15', *Architectural History*, vol. 60, 2017, pp. 182–217; Barry Crosbie, 'Ireland and the Empire in the Nineteenth Century', in Kelly, *The Cambridge History of Ireland: Volume III, 1730–1880*, pp. 617–36, at p. 624; and Barclay, *Men on Trial*, p. 84.

20 Patrick Carroll, *Science, Culture and Modern State Formation* (Berkeley, CA: University of California Press, 2006), pp. 11–27, 150–63; Ciaran O'Neill, 'Bourgeois Ireland, or, on the benefits of keeping one's hands clean', in Kelly, *The Cambridge History of Ireland: Volume III*, pp. 517–41, at pp. 523–6. See also Richard J. Butler, 'Urban Governance and Prison Building in Pre-Famine Ireland, 1820–1845', in Simon Gunn and Tom Hulme (eds), *New Approaches to Governance and Rule in Urban Europe since 1500* (Routledge, forthcoming).

21 Christine Casey (ed.), *The Eighteenth-century Dublin Town House* (Dublin: Four Courts Press, 2010), and in particular Conor Lucey, 'Classicism or Commerce? The town house interior as commodity', pp. 236–48; Kathleen James-Chakraborty, 'Neo-classical Commodities: From Coade Stone to the fall of the Wall and beyond', in Lynda Mulvin (ed.), *The Fusion of Neo-classical Principles* (Dublin: Wordwell, 2011), pp. 1–10; Andrew Tierney, 'Architectures of Gentility in Nineteenth-century Ireland,' in Ciaran O'Neill (ed.), *Irish Elites in the Nineteenth Century* (Dublin: Four Courts Press, 2013), pp. 31–50. See also Barbara Arciszewska and Elizabeth McKellar (eds), *Articulating British Classicism: New approaches to eighteenth-century architecture* (London: Ashgate, 2004).

22 Edward McParland, 'The Public Work of Architects in Ireland during the Neo-classical Period', PhD thesis, Cambridge University, 1975; Craig, *Architecture of Ireland*.

23 Brett, Casey, and O'Donoghue consider grand jurors generally as patrons but say less about the modes and methods of their patronage. See Brett, *Court Houses and Market Houses*, pp. 18–20; Casey, 'Courthouses', pp. 15–22; and O'Donoghue, *Irish County Surveyors*, pp. 3–25.

24 Toby Barnard, *Making the Grand Figure: Lives and possessions in Ireland, 1641–1770* (New Haven and London: Yale University Press, 2004), pp. 21–9, 35–43, 57–78; Martyn J. Powell, *The Politics of Consumption in Eighteenth-century Ireland* (Basingstoke: Palgrave Macmillan, 2005); Toby Barnard, *A Guide to the Sources for the History of Material Culture in Ireland, 1500–2000* (Dublin: Four Courts Press, 2005); Stephanie Rains, *Commodity Culture and Social Class in Dublin, 1850–1916* (Dublin: Irish Academic Press, 2010), pp. 1–8; Susan Flavin, *Consumption and Culture in Sixteenth-century Ireland: Saffron, stockings and silk* (Woodbridge: Boydell, 2014), pp. 4–7, 244–6; and Alison Fitzgerald, *Silver in Georgian Dublin: Making, selling, consuming* (Abingdon: Routledge, 2017), pp. 159–90.

25 Barnard, *Making the Grand Figure*, p. 22.

26 John Howard, *An Account of the Principal Lazarettos in Europe* (1st ed. 1789, 2nd ed., London: Johnson, Dilly & Cadell, 1791), p. 78. See also Johnston, *Forms of Constraint*, pp. 42–6.

27 *Freeman's Journal*, 23 April 1828.

28 Galen Broeker, *Rural Disorder and Police Reform in Ireland, 1812–36* (London: Routledge, 1970), pp. 20–38ff; Gash, *Mr Secretary Peel*, pp. 108–37ff; Stanley H. Palmer, *Police and Protest in England and Ireland, 1780–1850* (New York: Cambridge University Press, 1988), pp. 193–236ff; Gearóid Ó Tuathaigh, *Ireland before the Famine, 1798–1848* (Dublin: Gill & Macmillan, 1990), pp. 29–41, 80–93; Shane Kilcommins, et al., *Crime, Punishment and the Search for Order in Ireland* (Dublin: Institute of Public Administration, 2004), pp. 1–37; Hoppen, *Governing Hibernia*, pp. 51–3.

29 The only surviving materials from grand-jury meetings are usually statements of their biannual presentments and query-books; for a discussion, see Casey, 'Courthouses', p. 15. Private correspondence, central-government correspondence, and newspaper reports allow for a more rounded view of grand-jury activity.

30 See Brian Griffin, *Sources for the Study of Crime in Ireland, 1801–1921* (Dublin: Four Courts Press, 2005).

31 For an introduction, see Kyle Hughes and Donald M. MacRaild, 'Introduction: Crime, violence and the Irish in the nineteenth century; themes and perspectives', in Hughes and MacRaild, *Crime, Violence and the Irish in the Nineteenth Century*, pp. 1–12, at pp. 1–3.

32 Some parts of these chapters formed the basis for my article: Richard J. Butler, '"The radicals in these reform times": Politics, grand juries, and Ireland's unbuilt assize courthouses, 1800–50', *Architectural History*, vol. 58, 2015, pp. 109–40.

33 In terms of design, see for example Marion MacRae and Anthony Adamson, *Cornerstones of Order: Courthouses and town halls of Ontario, 1784–1914* (Toronto: C. Irwin, 1983); Margaret Carter, *Early Canadian Court Houses* (Ottawa: Canadian Parks Service, 1983); William B. Robinson, *The People's Architecture: Texan courthouses, jails and municipal buildings* (Austin: Texan State Historical Association, 1983); and Robert J. Brink (ed.), *Courthouses of the Commonwealth*

(Amherst: University of Massachusetts, 1984).

34 Clare Graham, *Ordering Law: An architectural and social history of the English law court to 1914* (Aldershot, Hampshire: Ashgate, 2003), chapters 2–4; and Christopher Chalklin, *English Counties and Public Building, 1650–1830* (London: Hambledon, 1998).

35 Martha J. McNamara, *From Tavern to Courthouse: Architecture and ritual in American law, 1658–1860* (Baltimore and London: Johns Hopkins University Press, 2004), pp. 81–102; Judith Resnik and Dennis E. Curtis, *Representing Justice: Invention, controversy, and rights in city-states and democratic courtrooms* (New Haven and London: Yale University Press, 2011), chapters 7–12, quote at p. 226; see also Mulcahy, *Legal Architecture*.

36 Katie Barclay, *Men on Trial: Performing emotion, embodiment and identity in Ireland, 1800–45* (Manchester: Manchester University Press, 2019), especially pp. 59–91. See also Katie Barclay, 'Singing and lower-class masculinity in the Dublin Magistrate's Court, 1800–1845', *Journal of Social History*, vol. 47, no. 3, 2014, pp. 746–68.

37 Barclay, *Men on Trial*, p. 84.

38 Ibid., pp. 50–60, 63–9, 71–2, 77–84.

39 McNamara, *From Tavern to Courthouse*, p. 5.

40 Mulcahy, *Legal Architecture*, p. 83; Graham, *Ordering Law*, pp. 315–34; Linda Mulcahy, 'Putting the Defendant in their Place: Why do we still use the dock in criminal proceedings?', *The British Journal of Criminology*, vol. 53, no. 6, November 2013, pp. 1139–56.

41 Patrick Polden, *A History of the County Court, 1846–1971* (Cambridge: Cambridge University Press, 1991). See also Graham, *Ordering Law*, pp. 157–315; and Jonathan Simon, Nicholas Temple, and Renée Tobe (eds), *Architecture and Justice: Judicial meanings in the public realm* (Aldershot, Hampshire: Ashgate, 2013).

42 Carl Lounsbury, 'From Tavern to Courthouse: Architecture and ritual in American law, 1658–1860, by Martha J. McNamara (review)', *Journal of the Society of Architectural Historians*, vol. 64, no. 2, June 2005, pp. 254–5.

43 Claire Priest, 'From Tavern to Courthouse: Architecture and ritual in American law, 1658–1860, by Martha J. McNamara (review)', *Law and History Review*, vol. 25, no. 3, Fall 2007, pp. 635–7.

44 Barclay suggests a more extensive role was played by barristers and petty juries in courthouse design – see Barclay, *Men on Trial*, pp. 71–2.

45 Brett, *Court Houses and Market Houses*, pp. 15–20; Casey, 'Courthouses', pp. 15–22.

46 Graham, *Ordering Law*, pp. 73–114, especially pp. 91–3.

47 As Barclay comments in relation to Wexford courthouse, see *Men on Trial*, p. 72.

48 For an overview of this subject, see the extensive work of Proudfoot and Graham in particular: Lindsay J. Proudfoot and B.J. Graham, 'The Nature and Extent of Urban and Village Foundation and Improvement in Eighteenth and Early Nineteenth Century Ireland', *Planning Perspectives*, vol. 8, no. 3, 1993, pp. 259–81; B.J. Graham and Lindsay J. Proudfoot, *Urban Improvement in Provincial Ireland, 1700–1840* (Athlone: Temple Printing, 1994); Lindsay J. Proudfoot, *Urban Patronage and Social Authority: The management of the Duke of Devonshire's towns in Ireland, 1764–1891* (Washington, DC: Catholic University of America Press, 1995); and Lindsay J. Proudfoot, *Property Ownership and Urban and Village Improvement in Provincial Ireland, ca. 1700–1845* (London: Historical Geography Research Group, 1997).

49 Barclay, *Men on Trial*, p. 71.

50 Transnational aspects of penal reform, touched upon in these chapters, are discussed in further detail in Richard J. Butler, 'Rethinking the Origins of the British Prisons Act of 1835: Ireland and the development of central-government prison inspection, 1820–35', *The Historical Journal*, vol. 59, no. 3, September 2016, pp. 721–46.

51 Robin Evans, *The Fabrication of Virtue: English prison architecture, 1750–1840* (Cambridge: Cambridge University Press, 1982).

52 Norman Johnston, *Forms of Constraint: A history of prison architecture* (Urbana, IL: University of Illinois Press, 2000); Margaret Heather Tomlinson, 'Victorian Prisons: Administration and architecture, 1835–1877', PhD thesis, University of London, Bedford College, 1975. For Irish prison architecture, see McParland, 'Public Work of Architects', pp. 136–40, 250–3; Loeber, et al., *Art and Architecture of Ireland: Volume IV: Architecture 1600–2000*, pp. 202–6.

53 Michel Foucault, *Discipline and Punish. The birth of the prison* (1st pub. 1975, trans. Alan Sheridan, New York: Pantheon, 1977), Johnston, *Forms of Constraint*, pp. 1–2.

54 R.B. McDowell, *The Irish Administration, 1801–1914* (London: Faber & Faber, 1964), pp. 145–63; Ursula R.Q. Henriques, 'The Rise and Decline of the Separate System of Prison Discipline', *Past & Present*, vol. 54, 1972, pp. 61–93; Ursula R.Q. Henriques, *Before the Welfare State: Social administration in early industrial Britain* (London: Longman, 1979), pp. 155–97; Oliver MacDonagh, *The Inspector General: Sir Jeremiah Fitzpatrick and the politics of social reform, 1783–1802* (London: Croom Helm, 1981) (hereafter cited as *Jeremiah Fitzpatrick*); Simon Devereaux, 'In Place of Death: Transportation, penal practices, and the English state, 1770–1830', in Carolyn Strange (ed.), *Qualities of Mercy: Justice, punishment, and discretion* (Vancouver: University of British Columbia Press, 1996), pp. 52–76; Simon Devereaux, 'The Making of the Penitentiary Act, 1775–1779', *The Historical Journal*, vol. 42, no. 2, 1999, pp. 405–33; Joanna Innes, 'Prisons for the Poor: English bridewells, 1666–1800', in Francis Snyder and Douglas Hay (eds), *Labour, Law, and Crime: An historical perspective* (London: Tavistock, 1987), pp. 42–122; Joanna Innes, 'What Would a "Four Nations" Approach to the Study of Eighteenth-century British Social Policy Entail?', in S.J. Connolly (ed.), *Kingdoms United?*

Great Britain and Ireland since 1500: Integration and diversity (Dublin: Four Courts Press, 1999), pp. 181–99, at pp. 190–2.

55 V.A.C. Gatrell, *The Hanging Tree: execution and the English people, 1770–1868* (Oxford: Oxford University Press, 1994); Miles Ogborn, 'Discipline, Government and Law: Separate confinement in the prisons of England and Wales, 1830–1877', *Transactions of the Institute of British Geographers*, vol. 20, no. 3, new series, 1995, pp. 295–311; Patrick Carroll-Burke, *Colonial Discipline: The making of the Irish convict system* (Dublin: Four Courts Press, 2000); James J. Willis, 'Transportation versus Imprisonment in Eighteenth- and Nineteenth-century Britain: Penal power, liberty, and the state', *Law & Society Review*, vol. 39, no. 1, 2005, pp. 171–210.

56 J.R.S. Whiting, *Prison Reform in Gloucestershire, 1776–1820: A study of the work of Sir George Onesiphorus Paul, Bart.* (London: Phillimore, 1975); Margaret DeLacy, *Prison Reform in Lancashire, 1700–1850: A study in local administration* (Stanford, CA: Stanford University Press, 1986); Brian Henry, *Dublin Hanged: Crime, law enforcement and punishment in late eighteenth-century Dublin* (Dublin: Irish Academic Press, 1994); Caroline Windrum, 'The Provision and Practice of Prison Reform in County Down, 1745–1894', in Lindsay Proudfoot (ed.), *Down: History & society* (Dublin: Geography Publications, 1997), pp. 327–52; Virginia Crossman, 'The Growth of the State in the Nineteenth Century', in Kelly, *The Cambridge History of Ireland: Volume III*, pp. 542–66, at pp. 546–7.

57 Mary Rogan, *Prison Policy in Ireland: Politics, penal-welfarism and political imprisonment* (London: Routledge, 2011).

58 Some preliminary explorations in this field can be found in: Richard J. Butler, 'Bagenalstown Courthouse (1826)', *Carloviana*, vol. 63, 2015, pp. 201–4; Richard J. Butler, 'Cork's Courthouses, the Landed Elite and the Rockite Rebellion: Architectural responses to agrarian violence, 1820–27', in Hughes and MacRaild (eds), *Crime, Violence, and the Irish in the Nineteenth Century*, pp. 87–111; and Barclay, *Men on Trial*, p. 76. See also Judith Hill, 'Irish Court Houses: A brief architectural history to 1998', in Paul Burns, Ciaran O'Connor, and Colum O'Riordan (eds), *Ireland's Court Houses* (Dublin: Irish Architectural Archive, 2019), pp. 18–37.

Chapter 1 – The Spoils of War: Upheaval and rebellion at home and abroad, 1786–1817

1 Building of Law Courts Act, 1790, 30 Geo. III, c. 41; Building of Law Courts Act, 1794, 34 Geo. III, c. 6; *Return of All Sums of Money … in Aid of Public Works in Ireland, since the Union*, H.C. 1839 (540), xxxxiv, p. 12. See Appendix A.

2 4 Anne, c. 6.

3 Graham, *Ordering Law*, pp. 73–4.

4 7 Geo. III, c. 4.

5 The architect's name and the date 1746 are inscribed above the door. See Donegal grand-jury presentment book, 1754 (Donegal County Library).

6 Donegal grand-jury presentment books, 1756–7, 1760 (Donegal County Library); Alistair Rowan, 'The Irishness of Irish Architecture', *Architectural History*, vol. 40, 1997, pp. 1–23, at pp. 9–10; McParland, 'Public Work of Architects', p. 195.

7 Donegal grand-jury presentment books, 1793–4 (Donegal County Library).

8 *Report of the Commissioners Appointed to Take the Census of Ireland for the Year 1841*, H.C. 1843 (504), xxiv, p. 308; Six-inch Ordnance Survey map for Lifford, County Donegal, surveyed January 1834.

9 See Appendix B.

10 Though Brett notes that 'substantial additions' were made in the 1830s, this claim is not supported by the annual returns of the Donegal grand jury for courthouse-building work: just £70 was spent throughout the entire county in this decade. See Brett, *Court Houses and Market Houses*, p. 62; Appendix C.

11 Henry David Inglis, *Ireland in 1834: A journey throughout Ireland, during the spring, summer, and autumn of 1834*, 2 vols (London: Whittaker, 1834), vol. 2, pp. 188–9.

12 Charles Gavan Duffy, *The League of North and South: An episode in Irish history, 1850–1854* (London: Chapman & Hall, 1886), p. 95, quoted in Mac Suibhne, *The End of Outrage*, p. 153.

13 For example, Wicklow in 1774, 13 & 14 Geo. III, c. 18; and Down in 1787, 27 Geo. III, c. 21. For an overview, see W.N. Osborough, 'Eighteenth-century Ireland's Legislative Deficit', in Michael Brown and Seán Patrick Donlan (eds), *The Laws and other Legalities of Ireland, 1689–1850* (Farnham, Surrey: Ashgate, 2011), pp. 75–96.

14 L.M. Cullen, *An Economic History of Ireland since 1660* (London: Batsford, 1972), pp. 50–76; T.W. Freeman, 'Irish Towns in the Eighteenth and Nineteenth Centuries', in R.A. Butlin (ed.), *The Development of the Irish Town* (London: Croom Helm, 1977), pp. 101–38, at pp. 101–21; David Dickson, *Old World Colony: Cork and south Munster, 1630–1830* (Madison, WI: University of Wisconsin Press, 2005), pp. 411–36.

15 W. Moran, 'Tullamore', *Ríocht na Midhe*, vol. 2, no. 4, 1962, pp. 44–54, at pp. 49–51.

16 The new courthouse was built between 1777 and 1779 by Richard Drew. See the inscription above the door. See also Samuel McSkimmin, *The History and Antiquities of the County of the Town of Carrickfergus*, 1st ed., 1811, rev. ed. E.J. McCrum (Belfast: Mullan et al., 1909), pp. 151, 170–3, 511–14.

17 Kilkenny Corporation minute books, 1 December 1758, 20 February 1759 (NLI, microfilm, p. 5137); John Hogan, 'The Three Tholsels of Kilkenny', *Journal of the Royal Historical and Archaeological Association of Ireland*, vol. 5, no.

41, 4th ser., January 1880, pp. 236–52; McParland, 'Public Work of Architects', p. 11; John Newman and Nikolaus Pevsner, *The Buildings of England: Dorset* (Harmondsworth: Penguin, 1972), p. 97. Drogheda's new tholsel was built between 1765 and 1770 by George Darley. See Drogheda Corporation minute books, 9, 23 August 1765, 10 October 1766 (NLI, microfilm, n. 4120).

18 Longford courthouse was built in *c.* 1791. See Anon. [W.P.], 'Sketch of a Journey through Part of Ireland', in *Walker's Hibernian Magazine*, October 1807, pp. 616–19, at p. 618. Sligo courthouse was complete by 1785. See Nehemiah Curnock (ed.), *The Journal of the Rev. John Wesley, A.M.*, 8 vols (London: Epworth Press, 1909–16), vol. 7, p. 82, Samuel Lewis, *A Topographical Dictionary of Ireland*, 2 vols (London: S. Lewis, 1837), vol. 2, p. 570. As at Lifford, increasing criminal indictments at Sligo had little architectural effect, and the courthouse survived until the 1870s. See Appendix B.

19 G. Wills to Thomas Mahon, 23 June 1762 (NLI, MS 10,770(1)).

20 McParland, 'Public Work of Architects', pp. 11–12.

21 G. Wills to Thomas Mahon, 23 June 1762 (NLI, MS 10,770(1)).

22 A clause in a 1796 act (36 Geo. III, c. 55, s. 97) allowed the Roscommon grand jurors to acquire this small market space 'for the benefits of the court and the grand jury'. A separate market house was built elsewhere at this time, thereby completing the judicial take-over of the building. See drawings and contract, dated 27 April 1762 (NLI, MS 10,770(1)–(3)). Another scheme, very close to the executed design and presumably also by Ensor, survives in this collection.

23 Butler, 'Politics, Grand Juries, and Ireland's Unbuilt Assize Courthouses', pp. 113–14; Arthur Gibney, Livia Hurley and Edward McParland (eds), *The Building Site in Eighteenth-century Ireland* (Dublin: Four Courts Press, 2017), pp. 26, 42, 48, 55.

24 Edward McParland, *James Gandon: Vitruvius Hibernicus* (London: Zwemmer, 1985), pp. 144–65; Maurice Craig, *Dublin. 1660–1860: The shaping of a city*, 1st ed., 1952 (Dublin: Liberties Press, 2006), pp. 267–82; John Summerson, *Architecture in Britain, 1530–1830* (New Haven and London: Yale University Press, 1993), pp. 412–14; Christine Casey, *The Buildings of Ireland: Dublin* (New Haven and London: Yale University Press, 2005), pp. 92–8.

25 McParland, *Gandon*, p. 163. Gandon's work has been associated with the French architect Marie-Joseph Peyre, author of *Oeuvres d'Architecture* (Paris, 1765). See Robin Middleton, 'Some Pages from Marie-Joseph Peyre's Roman Album', in Frank Salmon (ed.), *The Persistence of the Classical: Essays on architecture presented to David Watkin* (London: Philip Wilson, 2008), pp. 73–97.

26 Thomas J. Mulvany and James Gandon, *The Life of James Gandon* (Dublin: Hodges & Smith, 1846), pp. 68–74.

27 McParland, 'Public Work of Architects', p. 159.

28 John Martin Robinson, *James Wyatt: Architect to George III* (New Haven and London: Yale University Press, 2012), pp. 115–16.

29 Mulvany and Gandon, *Gandon*, pp. 69–71.

30 Such professional disputes were common at the time, as the monopoly held by professional architects came under attack from an increasingly skilled cohort of builders and craftsmen. See John Wilton-Ely, 'The Adam Style: Reflections on a revolution in design', in Mulvin, *Fusion of Neo-classical Principles*, pp. 105–30, at pp. 105–8; Conor Lucey, 'British Agents of the Irish Adamesque', *Architectural History*, vol. 56, 2013, pp. 135–70.

31 Craig, *Architecture of Ireland*, pp. 267–71; John Woolfe and James Gandon, *Vitruvius Britannicus, volume 5* (London: Woolfe & Gandon, 1771), p. 8, plates 72–7.

32 George Wilkinson, *Practical Geology and Ancient Architecture of Ireland* (London: Murray, 1845), pp. 183–4.

33 Mulvany and Gandon, *Gandon*, p. 69.

34 Henry Heaney (ed.), *A Scottish Whig in Ireland, 1835–1838: The Irish journals of Robert Graham of Redgorton* (Dublin: Four Courts Press, 1999), p. 83.

35 The Green Street courthouse was built by Whitmore Davis between 1792 and 1797. See Dublin City grand-jury presentment books, 1793–1803 (NLI, MS 16,223); McParland, 'Public Work of Architects', p. 105; Gibney, Hurley and McParland, *Building Site in Eighteenth-century Ireland*, pp. 220–1.

36 The use of a single courthouse by more than one grand jury had been permitted, presumably for the convenience of the Waterford grand jurors, in a 1788 act (28 Geo. III, c. 38); this formed the template for the 1795 act for Dublin city's new courthouse (35 Geo. III, c. 25).

37 Casey, 'Courthouses', pp. 17–18.

38 Hoppen, *Governing Hibernia*, p. 12.

39 36 Geo. III, c. 55. The problems with this act were first noted by Casey. See her 'Courthouses', pp. 17–18.

40 R.B. McDowell, 'The Age of the United Irishmen: Revolution and the Union, 1794–1800', in T.W. Moody and W.E. Vaughan (eds), *A New History of Ireland: Volume IV: Eighteenth-century Ireland, 1791–1800* (Oxford: Oxford University Press, 2009), pp. 339–73.

41 Mulvany and Gandon, *Gandon*, pp. 170–3; Craig, *Architecture of Ireland*, pp. 247–8.

42 R.B. McDowell, 'Ireland in 1800', in Moody and Vaughan, *A New History of Ireland: Volume IV*, pp. 657–711, at pp. 666–70.

43 *Dictionary of Irish Architects* (www.dia.ie).

44 Ruan O'Donnell, 'The Rebellion of 1798 in County Wicklow', in Ken Hannigan and William Nolan (eds), *Wicklow: History & society* (Dublin: Geography Publications, 1994), pp. 341–78.

45 See Appendix B.

46 John Carr, *The Stranger in Ireland* (London: Phillips, 1805), p. 271.

47 Woods, 'Johann Friedrich Hering's Description of Connacht', p. 316.

48 Anon., *Journal of a Tour through Several of the Southern Counties of Ireland during the Autumn of 1809* (London: McDowall, 1810), pp. vi, 34–5.

49 Cork (*c.* 1806, Richard Morrison); Carlow (*c.* 1800, unknown architect); Philipstown (now Daingean, *c.* 1807, unknown architect); Clonmel (*c.* 1801, Richard Morrison); Trim (*c.* 1809, Richard Morrison); Athy (*c.* 1804–7, additions to an existing markethouse, likely by Richard Morrison); Naas (*c.* 1804–7, Richard Morrison); and Limerick (1807–9, Nicholas and William Hannan). See Appendix A; and Andrew Tierney, *The Buildings of Ireland: Central Leinster, the counties of Kildare, Laois, and Offaly* (New Haven and London: Yale University Press, 2019), pp. 96, 302–3, 510–11.

50 The new courthouse at Maryborough was built in *c.* 1805 by Richard Morrison. See Appendix B.

51 *Journal of the Irish House of Commons*, vol. 23, 1786, p. 194; *Hansard*, vol. 13, 3rd ser., 30 May 1832, cols 209–10; Casey, 'Courthouses', pp. 98–9; Michael Byrne, *Legal Offaly: The county courthouse at Tullamore and the legal profession in County Offaly from the 1820s to the present day* (Tullamore: Esker, 2008), p. 390.

52 The new courthouse in Galway was built between 1812 and 1815, by Richard Morrison.

53 Jarlath Glynn, *Wexford: Then & now* (Dublin: History Press, 2013), pp. 60–1, 88–9.

54 Anon., *Journal of a Tour through Several of the Southern Counties of Ireland*, pp. 42–3; James Glassford, *Notes of Three Tours in Ireland in 1824 and 1826* (Bristol: Strong & Chilcott, 1832), p. 127.

55 Terence Denman, *A Lonely Grave: The life and death of William Redmond* (Dublin: Irish Academic Press, 1995), p. 18; *Accounts of Presentments by Grand Juries in Ireland ... in 1807*, H.C. 1808 (205), xiii, pp. 419–34; Thomas Lacy, *Sights and Scenes of our Fatherland* (London: Simpkin, 1863), p. 408; George Griffiths, *Chronicles of the County Wexford* (Enniscorthy: Watchman, 1877), pp. 268–72.

56 Griffiths, *Wexford*, p. 272.

57 McParland, 'Public Work of Architects', p. 240.

58 Griffiths, *Wexford*, p. 272; *Dublin Builder*, vol. 4, no. 61, 1 July 1862, p. 172.

59 Cornwallis to Portland, 16 September 1798, in Charles Ross (ed.), *Correspondence of Charles, First Marquis Cornwallis*, 3 vols (London: Murray, 1859), vol. 2, p. 404, quoted in Hoppen, *Governing Hibernia*, p. 13. The Dublin County grand jurors also maintained a picture of William III in the magistrates' room of their courthouse – see Dublin County grand-jury minutes, 9 May 1821 (Fingal County Council Archives, GJ/1/1).

60 Disused Public Buildings (Ireland) Act, 1808, 48 Geo. III, c. 113.

61 Ó Tuathaigh, *Ireland before the Famine*, pp. 82–8; Gash, *Mr Secretary Peel*, pp. 11–13.

62 *Journal of the House of Commons*, vol. 62, 20 April 1807, p. 346. See also Hill, 'Architecture in the Aftermath of Union', pp. 186–91.

63 *Hansard*, vol. 9, 1st ser., 20 April 1807, cols 499–502.

64 *Journal of the House of Commons*, vol. 63, 2 July 1808, p. 480; *Hansard*, vol. 11, 1st ser., 2 July 1808, cols 1131–4.

65 *Accounts of Presentments by Grand Juries in Ireland ... in 1807*, H.C. 1808 (205), xiii; Highways (Ireland) Act, 1809, 49 Geo. III, c. 84.

66 Edward Cooper to Robert Peel, 21 May 1817 (British Library, Add. MS 40265, f. 234).

67 *Journal of the House of Commons*, vol. 64, 24 May 1809, p. 341; *Hansard*, vol. 14, 1st ser., 24 May 1809, cols 668–70; *Journal of the House of Commons*, vol. 65, 21 February 1810, p. 113; *A Bill to Amend the Laws in Ireland Respecting ... Grand Juries*, H.C. 1810 (118), i.

68 Prisons (Ireland) Act, 1810, 50 Geo. III, c. 103.

69 *Journal of the House of Commons*, vol. 66, 20 May 1811, p. 350; *Journal of the House of Lords*, vol. 48, 10 June 1811, p. 400.

70 *Journal of the House of Commons*, vol. 6, 21 February 1812, p. 136; *Journal of the House of Lords*, vol. 49, 9 April 1812, p. 684.

71 For Derry, see *Accounts of Presentments by Grand Juries in Ireland ... in 1807*, H.C. 1808 (205), xiii, p. 205; for Dundalk, see P.J. Geraghty, 'Urban Improvement and the Erection of Municipal Buildings in County Louth during the Eighteenth and Nineteenth Centuries', *Journal of the County Louth Archaeological and Historical Society*, vol. 23, no. 3, 1995, pp. 295–317, at p. 312.

72 John Leslie Foster to Robert Peel, 26 February 1813 (British Library, Add. MS 40223, f. 121).

73 Drawings by Francis Johnston, 1805–8 (Irish Architectural Archive, RIAI Murray Collection, Acc.92/46.4–18). See also Armagh grand-jury presentment book, 1810 (PRONI, ARM/4/1/18).

74 Edward McParland, 'Francis Johnston, Architect', *Irish Georgian Society Bulletin*, vol. 12, nos. 3–4, 1969, pp. 61–139.

75 For a full discussion, see Butler, 'Politics, Grand Juries, and Ireland's Unbuilt Assize Courthouses', pp. 115–19.

76 Francis Johnston to James Norris Brewer, 29 February 1820, printed in Patrick Henchy, 'Francis Johnston, Architect, 1760–1829', *Dublin Historical Record*, vol. 11, no. 1, December 1949–February 1950, pp. 1–16, at pp. 12–13; McParland, 'Public Work of Architects', p. 241.

77 *Journal of the House of Commons*, vol. 67, 14 April 1812, p. 265.

78 George Beresford, son of the 1st Marquis of Waterford, who had brought Gandon to Waterford in the 1780s, and a sometime MP for Derry, also helped to draft this local act.

79 Londonderry Court House Act, 1812, 52 Geo. III, c. clxxxii.

80 See, for example, Brett, *Court Houses*, pp. 88–90; McParland, 'Public Work of Architects', pp. 241–4; Casey, 'Courthouses', pp. 17–19; Crossman, *Local Government in Nineteenth-century Ireland*, p. 27.

81 As suggested by Crossman, *Local Government in Nineteenth-century Ireland*, p. 27.

82 Richard Elsam submitted a design that was exhibited at the Society of Artists of Ireland in 1809, no. 67. See drawings by John Bowden and building contract, dated 20 August 1813 (PRONI, LA/5/8/JA/2).

83 *Dictionary of Irish Architects* (www.dia.ie)

84 Lewis, *Topographical Dictionary*, vol. 2, p. 303.

85 Salaries of County Officials (Ireland) Act, 1823, 4 Geo. IV, c. 43.

86 Alistair Rowan, *The Buildings of Ireland: North west Ulster: The counties of Londonderry, Donegal, Fermanagh, and Tyrone* (Harmondsworth, Middlesex: Penguin, 1979), p. 389.

87 John Christian Curwen, *Observations on the State of Ireland*, 2 vols (London: Baldwin, Cradock & Joy, 1818), vol. 1, p. 224; John Forbes, *Memorandums Made in Ireland in the Autumn of 1852*, 2 vols (London: Smith, Elder & Co., 1853), vol. 2, p. 111.

88 Londonderry Court House Act, 1812, 52 Geo. III, c. clxxxii.

89 *Journal of the House of Commons*, vol. 67, 22 April 1812, p. 311.

90 Ibid., vol. 68, 23 February 1813, p. 210; Robert Peel to Edward Synge Cooper, 15 May 1817 (British Library, Add. MS 40265, f. 175).

91 John Leslie Foster to Robert Peel, 26 February 1813 (British Library, Add. MS 40223, ff. 119, 121); *Journal of the House of Commons*, vol. 68, 1 June 1813, p. 536; Gash, *Peel*, p. 232.

92 Court House (Ireland) Act, 1813, 53 Geo. III, c. 131; Barclay, *Men on Trial*, p. 72. For more on contracts in the Irish building trade, see Gibney, Hurley and McParland, *Building Site in Eighteenth-century Ireland*, pp. 33–56.

93 Geraghty, 'Urban Improvement', p. 311; for Morrison's work, see memorandum by Robert Page, 27 September 1811 (PRONI, D/562/12762); John Foster to Robert Page, 4 October 1811 (PRONI, D/562/12766); memorandum by Richard Morrison, 22 October 1812 (PRONI, T/2519/4/13).

94 McParland, 'Francis Johnston', pp. 64–74.

95 For the contract, see Harold O'Sullivan, 'The Courthouse, Dundalk, and the Contract for Its Erection Dated 30th April 1813', *Journal of the County Louth Archaeological Society*, vol. 15, no. 2, 1962, pp. 131–43; Christine Casey, 'The Greek Revival Courthouse, Dundalk, County Louth', *Irish Arts Review*, vol. 3, no. 2, Summer 1986, pp. 16–20; *Journal of the House of Commons*, vol. 76, 12 April 1821, p. 256; Dundalk Court House Act, 1821, 1 & 2 Geo. IV, c. cxxiv.

96 See Appendix B.

97 Casey, 'Greek Revival Courthouse, Dundalk', p. 17.

98 A.P.W. Malcomson, *John Foster: The politics of the Anglo-Irish ascendancy* (Oxford: Oxford University Press, 1978), pp. 18–20; A.P.W. Malcomson, 'John Foster', in James McGuire and James Quinn (eds), *Dictionary of Irish Biography*, 9 vols (Cambridge: Cambridge University Press, 2009), vol. 3, p. 1070; John Leslie Foster, *A Letter on the Fittest Style and Situation for the Wellington Trophy about To Be Erected in Dublin* (Dublin: Graisberry & Campbell, 1815).

99 O'Sullivan, 'Courthouse, Dundalk', pp. 131–43; Casey, 'Greek Revival Courthouse, Dundalk', p. 16; McParland, 'Public Work of Architects', p. 173; James Stuart and Nicholas Revett, *The Antiquities of Athens* (London: Haberkorn, 1762). I am grateful to Anthony Malcomson for sharing with me his detailed research into the history of Dundalk's courthouse.

100 John Jocelyn to John Foster, 10 March 1819 (NLI, MS 4128), quoted in Christine Casey, 'John Neville: Louth county surveyor', *Journal of the County Louth Archaeological and Historical Society*, vol. 21, no. 1, 1985, pp. 23–30, at p. 23.

101 As shown in Casey, 'Greek Revival Courthouse, Dundalk', pp. 16–20.

102 A. Atkinson, *Ireland Exhibited to England in a Political and Moral Survey of Her Population*, 2 vols (London: Baldwin, Cradock & Joy, 1823), vol. 1, pp. 91–2.

Chapter 2 – Judging the Neighbours: Grand juries, rivalry, and the peak years of courthouse building, 1817–31

1 Londonderry Court House Act, 1812, 52 Geo. III, c. clxxxii; Court House (Ireland) Act, 1813, 53 Geo. III, c. 131.

2 *Report … on Grand Jury Presentments of Ireland, Minutes of Evidence, and Appendix*, H.C. 1814–15 (283), vi; *Report … on Grand Jury Presentments of Ireland*, H.C. 1816 (374), ix; *Second Report … on Grand Jury Presentments of Ireland*, H.C. 1816 (435), ix.

3 *Journal of the House of Commons*, vol. 70, 28 April 1815, p. 253; ibid., vol. 71, 29 April 1816, p. 317; ibid., vol. 72, 23 May 1817, p. 306.

4 *Hansard*, vol. 36, 1st ser., 30 June 1817, col. 1277; O'Donoghue, *Irish County Surveyors*, pp. 6–9.

5 Hoppen, *Governing Hibernia*, pp. 21–2, 29–31.

6 *Hansard*, vol. 36, 1st ser., 30 June 1817, cols 1270–75; Grand Jury Presentments (Ireland) Act, 1817, 57 Geo. III, c. 107.

7 *Journal of the House of Commons*, vol. 73, 29 January 1818, p. 13; Grand Jury Presentments (Ireland) Act, 1818, 58 Geo. III, c. 2; O'Donoghue, *Irish County Surveyors*, pp. 8–9.

8 *Hansard*, vol. 37, 1st ser., 3 February 1818, cols 145–6; *Accounts of Presentments by Grand Juries in Ireland … in 1807*, H.C. 1808 (205), xiii, p. 419.

9 Grand Jury Presentments (Ireland) Act, 1818, 58 Geo. III, c. 67.

10 Gash, *Peel*, pp. 135–7; Cullen, *Economic History of Ireland*, pp. 100–20.

11 Public Works Loan Act, 1817, 57 Geo. III, c. 34; Ruth Heard, 'Public Works in Ireland, 1800–1831', MA thesis, Trinity College Dublin, 1977; John Cunningham, '"Compelled to Their Bad Acts by Hunger": Three Irish urban crowds, 1817–45', Éire-*Ireland*, vol. 45, nos. 1–2, Spring–Summer 2010, pp. 128–51, at p. 140.

12 Public Works Loan (Ireland) Act, 1818, 58 Geo. III, c. 88; Employment of the Poor (Ireland) Act, 1822, 3 Geo. IV, c. 34; Public Works Loans (Ireland) Act, 1822, 3 Geo. IV, c. 112.

13 *Hansard*, vol. 7, 2nd ser., 23 May 1822, col. 727; M.W. Flinn, 'The Poor Employment Act of 1817', *Economic History Review*, vol. 14, no. 1, 1961, pp. 82–92.

14 See Appendix D.

15 *Account (since the Union) of all Sums of Money … for Public Works … for England and Scotland*, H.C. 1847 (718), liv, pp. 160–1.

16 See Appendix D.

17 Gash, *Peel*, pp. 145–8; Gerard O'Brien, 'Robert Peel and the Pursuit of Catholic Emancipation, 1813–17', *Archivium Hibernicum*, vol. 43, 1988, pp. 135–41.

18 Gash, *Peel*, pp. 205–10; Richard A. Gaunt, *Sir Robert Peel: The life and legacy* (London: Tauris, 2010), p. 24.

19 Robert Saunders, 'God and the Great Reform Act: Preaching against reform, 1831–32', *Journal of British Studies*, vol. 53, no. 2, April 2014, pp. 378–99, at p. 397.

20 Gash, *Peel*, pp. 204–5.

21 Robert Peel to Charles Whitworth, 19 May 1817 (Kent History and Library Centre, Sackville [Whitworth] papers, U269/022525), quoted in O'Brien, 'Robert Peel', p. 140.

22 Gash, *Peel*, p. 210; Resolution of the Dublin city grand jury, 14 May 1817 (British Library, Add. MS 40265, f. 317).

23 Drawings by Henry, Mullins & McMahon, 5 October 1817 (Irish Architectural Archive, Guinness Collection, Acc. 96.68.5.1.1-4); Dublin County grand-jury presentment books, Mich. 1817 (Fingal County Council Archives, GJ/5/1); Brett, *Court Houses*, p. 88; Butler, 'Politics, Grand Juries, and Ireland's Unbuilt Assize Courthouses', pp. 120–5.

24 A similar entranceway, though not entirely analogous, appears in Dublin's Green Street courthouse, built between 1792 and 1797 for the Dublin city grand jury. See Casey, *Buildings of Ireland: Dublin*, pp. 99–100.

25 A.J. Nowlan, 'Kilmainham Jail', *Dublin Historical Record*, vol. 15, no. 4, January 1960, pp. 105–15, at p. 110. See also Dublin County grand-jury minute book, 22 April 1818, 27 April 1818, 9 May 1820 and 14 November 1820 (Fingal County Council Archives, GJ/1/1), and Dublin County grand-jury presentments, Mich. 1818 (ibid., GJ/5/1).

26 See Appendix D.

27 Dublin County grand-jury presentments, spring 1819 (Fingal County Council Archives, GJ/5/1). The use of government loans to purchase sites was prohibited by the Public Works Loan (Ireland) Act, 1820, 1 Geo. IV, c. 81, s. 13.

28 Baker exhibited drawings at the Royal Hibernian Academy in 1826 – nos. 245, 253, 259, and 265; a plaque in the grand-jury room gives the architect's name and the date of opening, 3 October 1820; in Casey, *Buildings of Ireland: Dublin*, p. 686, the architect is given as Isaac Farrell, William Farrell's brother, but this is a typo (clarified in correspondence with Christine Casey). See elevation drawing by William Farrell, n.d. (Houghton Library, Harvard University, William Farrell album, MS Typ 788). The Irish Architectural Archive has copies. See also Appendix D.

29 Ground-floor and first-floor plans, dated 16 February 1920 (NAI, OPW 5HC/4/400).

30 See Appendix D.

31 George Kelly to William Gregory, August 1822 (NAI, CSORP 1822/730); John Parker Lawson, *The Gazetteer of Ireland* (Edinburgh: Edinburgh Printing and Publishing Co., 1842), p. 714; Appendix D.

32 Lewis, *Topographical Dictionary*, vol. 2, p. 526.

33 *Dublin Evening Post*, 9 May 1822; *Connaught Journal*, 16 January 1823; *Galway Advertiser*, 7 June 1823; James Mitchell, 'The Tholsel at Galway, 1639–1822', *Journal of the Galway Archaeological and Historical Society*, vol. 35, 1976, pp. 77–85, at pp. 83–5.

34 *Galway Advertiser*, 12 April 1823, quoted in Mitchell, 'Tholsel', p. 84.

35 *Connaught Journal*, 19 June 1823; *Dictionary of Irish Architects* (www.dia.ie).

36 See Appendix D.

37 *Inspector General's Report of … the Prisons in Ireland for … 1807*, H.C. 1808 (239), ix, p. 4.

38 See Appendix B.

39 Fergus D'Arcy, 'Wages of Labourers in the Dublin Building Industry, 1667–1918', *Saothar: Journal of the Irish Labour History Society*, vol. 14, 1989, pp. 17–32, at p. 29; Gibney, Hurley and McParland, *Building Site in Eighteenth-century Ireland*, pp. 36–7.

40 An unexecuted design by William Deane Butler was exhibited at the Royal Hibernian Academy in 1826, nos. 252, 258; Henry Westenra to William Gregory, 25 July 1827 (NAI, CSORP 1827/1453); Obituary for Joseph Welland, *Dublin Builder*, vol. 2, no. 14, 1 April 1860, p. 232; *Dictionary of Irish Architects* (www.dia.ie).

41 Henry Westenra to William Gregory, 25 July 1827 (NAI, CSORP 1827/1453).

42 Kevin V. Mulligan, *The Buildings of Ireland: South Ulster, the counties of Armagh, Cavan, and Monaghan* (New Haven and London: Yale University Press, 2013), pp. 470–1.

43 See Appendix B.

44 D.R. Fisher, *The History of Parliament: The House of Commons, 1820–1832*, 7 vols (Cambridge: Cambridge University Press, 2009), vol. 7, pp. 696–700.

45 *Journal of the House of Commons*, vol. 82, 11 June 1827, p. 541.

46 *Freeman's Journal*, 2 April 1827. For an overview of the revival of Protestant political militancy in these years, see Irene Whelan, *The Bible War in Ireland: The 'second reformation' and the polarization of Protestant–Catholic relations, 1800–40* (Madison, WI: University of Wisconsin Press, 2005).

47 Henry Westenra to Richard Wellesley, 25 March 1827 (NAI, CSORP 1827/445).

48 Westenra to Wellesley, 25, 27 March 1827 (ibid.).

49 Ann Martha Rowan (ed.), *The Architecture of Richard Morrison (1767–1849) & William Vitruvius Morrison (1794–1838)* (Dublin: Irish Architectural Archive, 1989), pp. 149–53; *Dictionary of Irish Architects* (www.dia.ie).

50 Henry Westenra to William Gregory, 25 July 1827 (NAI, CSORP 1827/1453).

51 McParland, 'Public Work of Architects', p. 246.

52 Brett, *Court Houses*, pp. 95–7.

53 *Freeman's Journal*, 23 April 1828.

54 Some attempt to limit grand-jury expenditure was made in the Salaries of County Officials (Ireland) Act, 1823, 4 Geo. IV, c. 43. See James Ebenezer Bicheno, *Ireland and Its Economy, Being the Result of Observations Made in a Tour through the Country in the Autumn of 1829* (London: Murray, 1830), p. 137.

55 Ian d'Alton, *Protestant Society and Politics in Cork, 1812–1844* (Cork: Cork University Press, 1980), pp. 27, 110.

56 Jonathan Binns, *The Miseries and Beauties of Ireland*, 2 vols (London: Longman, 1837), vol. 1, p. 304.

57 *Freeman's Journal*, 13 July 1827.

58 See, for example, *Freeman's Journal*, 30 March 1819, 4 August 1824.

59 Ronan Keane, 'John Toler, First Earl of Norbury', in H.C.G. Matthew and Brian Harrison (eds), *Oxford Dictionary of National Biography*, 60 vols (Oxford: Oxford University Press, 2004), vol. 54, p. 900.

60 *Freeman's Journal*, 30 July 1822.

61 Ibid.

62 Ibid., 4 August 1824.

63 Ibid., 29 March 1825. *The Ghost of the Catholic Association of Ireland* was printed and published by W.J. Battersby, Winetavern Street, Dublin in 1825.

64 Ibid., 6 June 1827.

65 Ibid., 3 August 1831. In early nineteenth-century Ireland, 'Orangeism' within grand juries was more the rule than the exception – see for example Barclay's comments on the politics of the Wexford grand jurors in *Men on Trial*, p. 72.

66 *Journal of the House of Commons*, vol. 81, 5 May 1826, p. 328.

67 *Freeman's Journal*, 25 March 1826.

68 Barclay, *Men on Trial*, p. 77.

69 *Finn's Leinster Journal*, 11 April 1827.

70 Charles Burke to William Gregory, 19 July 1828 (NAI, CSORP 1828/556).

71 Butler, 'Bagenalstown Courthouse', pp. 201–4.

72 *Freeman's Journal*, 27 July 1827, 15 March 1828; *Finn's Leinster Journal*, 28 July 1827, 26 March 1828.

73 *Finn's Leinster Journal*, 19 July 1828.

74 *Fifth Report … on the … Prisons of Ireland, 1827*, H.C. 1826–7 (471), xi, p. 51. See also Butler, 'Cork's Courthouses, the Landed Elite and the Rockite Rebellion: Architectural responses to agrarian violence, 1820–27'.

75 John Morrison, 'The Late William Vitruvius Morrison, Architect', *Dublin Builder*, vol. 1, no. 6, 1 June 1859, p. 73; Rowan, *Morrison*, pp. 10, 46–7, 168–9.

76 Rowan, *Morrison*, p. 10; McParland, 'Public Work of Architects', pp. 246–7.

77 Diaries of Charles Robert Cockerell, 24 October 1823 (Royal Institute of British Architects, prints and drawings collection); see also Lynda Mulvin, 'Charles Robert Cockerell's Encounter with Ireland: Drawings, observations, and buildings', *Irish Architectural and Decorative Studies*, vol. 12, 2009, pp. 131–57.

78 This was 7,000 British pounds, for the separate Irish currency had been abolished in 1826. The exchange rate had been £1 Irish = £0.923 British.

79 See Appendix D. Lewis claimed that the final cost was £14,000. See *Topographical Dictionary*, vol. 2, p. 641.

80 *Western Herald*, 17 January 1833. I am grateful to Marc Caball for this reference.

81 *Copy of Memorials to the Irish Government on the Subject of Advances for Building a Court House in the County of Kerry*, H.C. 1830 (240), xxvi, pp. 1–2. See also Copy of County Kerry presentments for 1828 (NAI, CSORP 1828/1340); Treasury advances to County Kerry (NAI, CSORP 1832/6100); *Tralee Mercury*, 6 February, 17 March 1830, 31 August, 2 October 1833; Inglis, *Ireland in 1834*, vol. 1, pp. 262–3. Morrison's name appears on the architrave of the portico.

82 William Vitruvius Morrison's Royal Academy exhibits were 1828 (no. 1048), and 1834 (no. 874). John B. Keane, who had trained with Morrison, also exhibited a design at the Royal Hibernian Academy in 1830 (nos. 269, 280).

83 The interior has since been drastically remodelled, and the original roof of the courtrooms replaced. See also McParland, 'Public Work of Architects', pp. 245–6.

84 *Inspector General's Report on … the Prisons in Ireland for … 1807*, H.C. 1808 (239), ix, p. 10.

85 See Victoria M. McCarthy, 'The Denny Family in Tralee: An analysis of the Denny family's role in Tralee and Denny Street', MUBC thesis, University College Dublin, 2007.

86 Charles Burke to William Gregory, 19 July 1828 (NAI, CSORP 1828/556).

87 Williams and Cockburn, contractors, to Carlow courthouse commissioners, 14 May 1828 (Carlow County Library, P2/0053).

88 Carlow courthouse commissioners to chief justice of Ireland, 17 July 1828 (NAI, CSORP 1828/556).

89 Mary Teehan, 'The Emergence of County Courthouses: A socio-archaeological study of Co. Kilkenny and Co. Carlow', MA thesis, University College Cork, 2004, p. 85. The date appears on the cathedral's foundation stone.

90 William Ellis, 'Battle for the Courthouse', *Carloviana*, vol. 48, 2000, pp. 44–5, citing *The Nationalist and Leinster Times*, 29 December 1888.

91 Anon. [J.K.], *Letters to the North, from a Traveller in the South, Republished from the Ulster Times* (Belfast: Hodgson, 1837), p. 16.

92 Rowan, *Morrison*, pp. 137–9; Cathleen Delaney, 'Oak Park House and the Bruen Family', *Carloviana*, vol. 50, 2001, pp. 20–3.

93 *Tralee Mercury*, 12 July 1834.

94 Carlow courthouse commissioners to chief justice of Ireland, 17 July 1828 (NAI, CSORP 1828/556). Morrison exhibited drawings of the building at the Royal Academy in 1828 (no. 1078), and in 1833 (no. 962); and at the Royal Hibernian Academy in 1829 (no. 255), and 1832 (no. 286). See plan and section drawings by W.V. Morrison for Carlow courthouse, *c.* 1832 (Carlow County Library, P2/0048); Articles of agreement between Williams & Cockburn and Carlow courthouse commissioners, 20 July 1832 (ibid., GJ/9/9); Documents in relation to alterations in plans in Board of Works minutes, 30 June 1832 (NAI, Board of Works files, 2D/56/98); *First Report of the Commissioners on Public Works, Ireland*, H.C. 1833 (75), xvii, p. 8; *Second Report of the Commissioners on Public Works, Ireland*, H.C. 1834 (240), xxxx, p. 12. See also Appendix D.

95 Morrison's tetrastyle scheme is shown in an undated ground-floor plan, *c.* 1827 (Carlow County Library, P2/48). See also Contract between Williams & Cockburn and Carlow courthouse commissioners, 21 August 1828 (ibid., GJ/9/7); McParland, 'Public Work of Architects', pp. 245–6.

96 Lydia Fisher, *Letters from the Kingdom of Kerry in the Year 1845* (Dublin: Webb & Chapman, 1847), p. 9.

97 Carlow courthouse was the scene of a notorious political disturbance at an election in August 1837; see Elizabeth Malcolm, '"The Reign of Terror in Carlow": The politics of policing Ireland in the late 1830s', *Irish Historical Studies*, vol. 32, no. 125, May 2000, pp. 59–74.

98 Patrick Holohan, 'Cork Courthouse: The Pains, the Deanes, the stonecutters', *Journal of the Cork Historical and Archaeological Society*, vol. 111, 2006, pp. 77–106; Louise Harrington, 'The Work of Cork's Wide Streets Commissioners on Washington Street', *Irish Architectural and Decorative Studies*, vol. 15, 2012, pp. 98–117.

99 Henry Westenra to William Gregory, 25 July 1827 (NAI, CSORP 1827/1453); *Southern Reporter*, 27 February, 23 August 1827, as quoted in Holohan, 'Cork Courthouse', p. 94.

100 Memorial of Cork county grand jury to Richard Wellesley, Spring 1827 (NAI, CSORP 1827/508); Holohan, 'Cork Courthouse', pp. 77–106.

101 Harrington, 'Cork's Wide Streets Commissioners', pp. 102–6; Holohan, 'Cork Courthouse', p. 79.

102 *Cork Constitution*, 6 April 1830, as quoted in Holohan, 'Cork Courthouse', pp. 80–1.

103 Craig, *Architecture of Ireland*, p. 272.

104 Holohan, 'Cork Courthouse', pp. 82, 89. Holohan refers to government loans that were delayed in 1830–1 and cites a letter from the chief secretary Edward Stanley printed in the *Southern Reporter*, 3 March 1831, but there appear to be no records of these loans in the parliamentary papers.

105 Harrington, 'Cork's Wide Streets Commissioners', p. 106.

106 Ian d'Alton, 'Remembering the Future, Imagining the Past: How Southern Irish Protestants survived', in F.M. Larkin (ed.), *Librarians, Poets and Scholars: A festschrift for Dónall Ó Luanaigh* (Dublin: Four Courts Press, 2007), p. 217. I am grateful to Ian d'Alton for this reference. See also *Freeman's Journal*, 4 June 1829.

Chapter 3 – Against the Tide: Grand-jury reform, economic opportunism, and the last of Ireland's new assize courthouses, 1831–55

1 *Dictionary of Irish Architects* (www.dia.ie).

2 *Journal of the House of Commons*, vol. 86, no. 1, 16 March 1831, p. 388.

3 *Hansard*, vol. 1, 3rd ser., 9 December 1830, cols 909–32.

4 *Journal of the House of Commons*, vol. 86, no. 2, 11 October 1831, p. 907.

5 Public Works Act, 1831 (Ireland), 1 & 2 Will. IV, c. 33.

6 Nisi Prius Court House Act, 1832 (Dublin), 2 Will. IV, c. 32; *Fourth Report of the Commissioners of Public Works, Ireland*, H.C. 1836 (314), xxxvi, p. 4, and appendix with drawings by Jacob Owen.

7 Grand Jury Act, 1833 (Ireland), 3 & 4 Will. IV, c. 78; Meghen, 'The Administrative Work of the Grand Jury', p. 261.

8 Special sessions had been occurring in some parts of the country before 1833. The King's County grand-jury presentment book for 1821 (Cambridge University Library) lists the location of all special sessions to take place in the county that year. The 1833 act simply removed any doubts about the necessity of holding these meetings with cess-payers.

9 *Journal of the House of Commons*, vol. 88, 9 March 1833, p. 152.

10 Hoppen, *Governing Hibernia*, pp. 64–6, 69–70. Hoppen is more sceptical about the origins of grand-jury reform in these years, seeing the government's Irish legislative agenda as a 'colourful medley of significant and marginal odds and ends' (p. 70).

11 Civil Bill Courts Act, 1836 (Ireland), 6 & 7 Will. IV, c. 75; Grand Jury Act, 1836 (Ireland), 6 & 7 Will. IV, c. 116.

12 Public Works Act, 1839 (Ireland), 2 & 3 Vict., c. 50.

13 Cullen, *Economic History of Ireland*, pp. 105–12, 119–22.

14 Byrne, *Legal Offaly*, pp. 15, 390, and passim; Tierney, *The Buildings of Ireland: Central Leinster*, pp. 622–4.

15 Thomas Bernard to Charles Grant, 15 March 1820; Charles Grant to Thomas Bernard, 29 March 1820, printed in King's County grand-jury presentment book, 1820 (Cambridge University Library).

16 King's County grand-jury presentment book, 1821 (Cambridge University Library).

17 Byrne, *Legal Offaly*, pp. 13, 15, 18–22, 391–5; Charles Bury to Francis Leveson Gower, 19 October 1829 (NAI, CSORP 1829/5045); Bury to Leveson Gower, 17 November 1829 (NAI, CSORP 1829/6040); Nikolaus Pevsner and Bridget Cherry, *The Buildings of England: Devon* (New Haven and London: Yale University Press, 2004), p. 401.

18 John Ponsonby to Leveson Gower, 12 November 1829 (NAI, CSORP 1829/6040).

19 Charles Bury to Catherine Bury, 17 November 1829 (University of Nottingham Library, Charles Brinsley Marlay papers), quoted in Byrne, *Legal Offaly*, p. 22. Ponsonby was an influential diplomat and often resident abroad during these years.

20 *Freeman's Journal*, 19 March 1830; King's County grand-jury presentments, spring assizes 1830 (Offaly County Library, GJ/1/1/1); Byrne, *Legal Offaly*, p. 15.

21 Charles Bury to Catherine Bury, 3 September 1830 (University of Nottingham Library, Charles Brinsley Marlay papers), quoted in Byrne, *Legal Offaly*, p. 26.

22 Bury to Bury, March 1830 (ibid.), quoted in Byrne, *Legal Offaly*, p. 28.

23 See Appendix B. An exception to this tranquillity came in 1831, when an assize judge made some unfavourable comments about the state of crime in the county. See *Freeman's Journal*, 22 July 1831.

24 M.L. Ferrar (ed.), *The Diary of Colour-Sergeant George Calladine, 19th Foot, 1793–1837* (London: Eden, Fisher & Co., 1922), p. 194.

25 *Journal of the House of Commons*, vol. 87, 19 April 1832, p. 290, and passim.

26 Norfolk Assizes Act, 1832, 2 Will. IV, c. 47; *Journal of the House of Commons*, vol. 87, 23 May 1832, p. 334; *Hansard*, vol. 12, 3rd ser., 23 May 1832, cols 1411–14.

27 Ibid., cols 1414–16.

28 *Hansard*, vol. 13, 3rd ser., 30 May 1832, cols 209–10; King's County Assizes Act, 1832 (Ireland), 2 Will. IV, c. 60; Byrne, *Legal Offaly*, pp. 15–30.

29 Letter from overseers of courthouse competition at Tullamore to William Murray, 15 November 1832 (Irish Architectural Archive, RIAI Murray Collection, Acc. 92/46.1174); Byrne, *Legal Offaly*, p. 31.

30 Theresa Cornwallis West, *A Summer Visit to Ireland in 1846* (London: Bentley, 1847), p. 167.

31 A few months earlier, Bury had been in London communicating with Smirke directly on the new building, but it appears that their plans came to nothing. See Byrne, *Legal Offaly*, p. 32.

32 Morrison, 'William Vitruvius Morrison', p. 7; Charles Bury to Catherine Bury, 3 September 1833 (University of Nottingham Library, Charles Brinsley Marlay papers, My 463/1-3). William Deane Butler exhibited a design for this courthouse at the Royal Hibernian Academy in 1834 (nos. 273, 278).

33 Bernadette Goslin, 'A History and Descriptive Catalogue of the Murray Collection of Architectural Drawings in the Collection of the Royal Institute of the Architects of Ireland', MA thesis, University College Dublin, 1990, p. 338; Unexecuted drawings for Tullamore courthouse by William Murray, December 1832 (Irish Architectural Archive, RIAI Murray Collection, Acc.92/46.1174–93); Butler, 'Politics, Grand Juries, and Ireland's Unbuilt Assize Courthouses', pp. 125–31.

34 French haunched segmental windows were used by Charles Robert Cockerell around this time. See David Watkin, *The Life and Work of C.R. Cockerell* (London: Zwemmer, 1974), p. 228.

35 Charles Bury to Catherine Bury, 17 January, 3 September 1833 (University of Nottingham Library, Charles Brinsley Marlay papers, My 454/1-4 and My 463/1-3).

36 J. Mordaunt Crook, *The Greek Revival: Neo-classical attitudes in British architecture* (London: Murray, 1995), p. 133.

37 Drawings for Tullamore courthouse, by John B. Keane, 1833 (Irish Architectural Archive, Lismore Castle Collection, Acc.97/107.3.1-4 (photocopies)); Appendix D.

38 Elevation drawing for Tullamore courthouse, n.d., by John B. Keane (private collection of Michael Byrne, Tullamore, County Offaly). The Irish Architectural Archive has a copy.

39 'Thoughts for a Square at Tullamoore [sic] Ireland, Facing the Courthouse, To Be Called "The Beaujolois"', sketch of *c.* 1835 (Irish Architectural Archive, photograph collection); Byrne, *Legal Offaly*, p. 13.

40 Donal A. Murphy, *The Two Tipperarys: The national and local politics … of the unique 1838 division into two ridings* (Nenagh, County Tipperary: Relay, 1994), pp. 27–30, 57. See also Appendix B.

41 John B. Keane to William Gosset, 2 July 1833 (NAI, CSORP 1833/3124).

42 Assizes (Ireland) Act, 1835, 5 & 6 Will. IV, c. 26; The English version is the Assizes Act, 1833, 3 & 4 Will. IV, c. 71.

43 *Journal of the House of Commons*, vol. 90, 17 August 1835, p. 559.

44 Ibid., vol. 90, 27 March 1835, p. 170. See also *Hansard*, vol. 27, 3rd ser., 26 March 1835, cols 303–5; ibid., 27 March 1835, cols 187–94; Murphy, *Two Tipperarys*, pp. 36–8.

45 Murphy, *Two Tipperarys*, pp. 52–6.

46 Ibid., pp. 38–43.

47 Grand Jury Act, 1836 (Ireland), 6 & 7 Will. IV, c. 116, ss. 176–7.

48 Murphy, *Two Tipperarys*, p. 87.

49 Privy Council minute book, 16 June 1837 (NAI, PCO MB 8, ff. 63–5); Privy Council proclamation book, 8 November 1838 (NAI, PRO PB 1); *Clonmel Advertiser*, 21 June 1837. See also Murphy, *Two Tipperarys*, pp. 87–91.

50 Murphy, *Two Tipperarys*, pp. 104–5.

51 *Clonmel Advertiser*, 17 March 1838.

52 *Nenagh Guardian*, 8 December 1838, 23 March 1839.

53 Murphy, *Two Tipperarys*, p. 128.

54 *Nenagh Guardian*, 17 March 1841.

55 *Nenagh Guardian*, 3 August 1839; 10 June 1841; Appendix B; Murphy, *Two Tipperarys*, pp. 122, 128.

56 Court Houses Act, 1841 (Ireland), 4 & 5 Vict., c. 31, s. 1.

57 Murphy, *Two Tipperarys*, pp. 128–9.

58 *Nenagh Guardian*, 6 May 1840.

59 Craig, *Architecture of Ireland*, p. 272.

60 In the 1841 census the population of Waterford city stood at 23,216 persons while the population of Dungarvan was just 8,625. See *Report of the Commissioners Appointed to Take the Census of Ireland for the Year 1841*, H.C. 1843 (504), xxiv, pp. 240, 246.

61 William Fraher, 'The Reconstruction of Dungarvan, 1807–*c.* 1830: A political ploy', *Decies*, vol. 25, January 1984, pp. 4–21; Proudfoot, *Urban Patronage and Social Authority*; *Hansard*, vol. 28, 3rd ser., 27 May 1835, cols 187–94; Murphy, *Two Tipperarys*, pp. 284–6. A statue of O'Loghlen was unveiled inside the new courthouse at Ennis in 1850. See *The Builder*, vol. 8, no. 395, 31 August 1850, p. 416.

62 *Tipperary Free Press*, 15 July 1835.

63 *Waterford Mirror*, 17 July 1835.

64 Privy Council minute book, 18 August, 30 September, 27 October and 3 November 1836 (NAI, PCO MB 7, ff. 465–6, 482–4, 489–92 and 493–7); *Waterford Chronicle*, 3 November, 8 November 1836; *Clonmel Advertiser*, 9 November 1836. See also Murphy, *Two Tipperarys*, pp. 289–91, 294–7.

65 William Makepeace Thackeray, *The Irish Sketch Book 1842*, 1st ed. (London: Chapman & Hall, 1843, repub. Dublin: Gill & Macmillan, 1990), p. 49.

66 Privy Council minute book, 12 May 1837 (NAI, PCO MB 8, ff. 51–2); *Clonmel Advertiser*, 17 May 1837. See also Murphy, *Two Tipperarys*, pp. 298–9.

67 *Twenty-third Report … on … the Prisons of Ireland, 1844*, H.C. 1845 (620), xxv, p. 78.

68 Royal Hibernian Academy exhibits for 1846 (no. 458); J.D. Forbes, *Victorian Architect: The life and work of William Tinsley* (Bloomington, IN: Indiana University Press, 1953), p. 45.

69 While no drawings for Waterford have survived, the attribution to Keane rests on the many similarities between this courthouse and his buildings at Tullamore and Nenagh.

70 *Correspondence Explanatory of the Measures Adopted … for the Relief of Distress Arising from the Failure of the Potato Crop in Ireland*, H.C. 1846 (735), xxxvii, p. 326; *Twenty-seventh Report … on … the Prisons of Ireland, 1849*, H.C. 1849 (1069), xxvi, p. 101. The Assizes (Ireland) Act, 1850, 13 & 14 Vict., c. 85, was probably introduced to facilitate this Waterford project.

71 Judith Hill, *The Building of Limerick* (Dublin: Amer, 1991), pp. 51–2; Lewis, *Topographical Dictionary*, vol. 2, p. 272.

72 John McGrath, 'Organised Labour in Limerick City, 1819–1821: Violence and the struggle for legitimacy', in Hughes and MacRaild, *Crime, Violence, and the Irish in the Nineteenth Century*, pp. 67–86, at p. 69; Cunningham, 'Three Irish Urban Crowds', pp. 128–51.

73 *Freeman's Journal*, 8 March 1833, 2 August 1833, 17 July 1834, 12 July 1836. See also Appendix B.

74 Henry H. Hill (ed.), 'Diary of a Tour in Cos. Waterford, Kilkenny, and Tipperary, 29 August–6 Sep[t]. 1831', *Journal of the Cork Historical and Archaeological Society*, vol. 38, 1933, pp. 30–7; Dagmar Ó Riain-Raedel, '"Rambles Throughout the South of Ireland": An antiquarian's journey', *Journal of the Cork Historical and Archaeological Society*, vol. 113, 2008, pp. 40–52.

75 Drawings for Limerick City courthouse, June 1834, by Henry Hill (private collection of the Allen family, Shanagarry, County Cork). The Irish Architectural Archives has copies. See also Butler, 'Politics, Grand Juries and Ireland's Unbuilt Assize Courthouses', pp. [illegible].

76 Drawing of a design for a public building, n.d., by Henry Hill (private collection of the Allen family, Shanagarry, County Cork). The Irish Architectural Archive has a copy.

77 Cunningham, 'Three Irish Urban Crowds', pp. 136–7.

78 *Limerick Chronicle*, 26 July 1843; *Twenty-third Report ... on ... the Prisons of Ireland, 1845*, H.C. 1845 (620), xxv, pp. 69–70. The minutes of the Board of Superintendence printed in this report refer to an 'original plan alongside the county court-house' – very probably Hill's scheme. See Appendix D.

79 Brian Ó Dálaigh, 'The Old Courthouse of Ennis', *The Other Clare*, vol. 10, 1986, pp. 5–12, at p. 8.

80 Clare grand-jury presentment book, summer assizes 1828 (Cambridge University Library).

81 Clare grand-jury presentment book, spring assizes 1836 (ibid.). Lewis was equally explicit: the courthouse was in a 'dilapidated state [and] requires to be rebuilt'. See *Topographical Dictionary*, vol. 1, p. 600.

82 See Appendix B.

83 Ciarán Ó Murchadha, *Sable Wings over the Land: Ennis, County Clare, and its wider community during the Great Famine* (Ennis: Clasp, 1998), p. 8. The Clare grand jurors were selected overwhelmingly from the Protestant landed class – see 'Grand Juries of the County of Clare from 1784 [to 1877]' (Clare County Archives, GJ/CC).

84 Clare grand-jury presentment book, summer assizes 1833 (Cambridge University Library).

85 County Treasurers Act, 1837 (Ireland), 1 Vict., c. 54, s. 20; County of Clare Treasurer Act, 1838 (Ireland), 1 & 2 Vict., c. 104.

86 Clare grand-jury presentment books, 1837–9 (Cambridge University Library); *Connaught Journal*, 17 February 1840, quoted in Ó Murchadha, *Sable Wings*, p. 255.

87 *Connaught Journal*, 24 February 1842, quoted in Ó Murchadha, *Sable Wings*, p. 255.

88 *Connaught Journal*, 10 February 1842, 29 February, 8 July 1844, 18 September 1845, quoted in Ó Murchadha, *Sable Wings*, p. 255.

89 *Clare Journal*, 27 October 1845, quoted in Ó Murchadha, *Sable Wings*, p. 255; *Dictionary of Irish Architects* (www.dia.ie).

90 Clare grand-jury presentment books for summer assizes 1845 (NAI, 1D/40/90), quoted in McParland, 'Public Work of Architects', p. 249.

91 Ó Murchadha, *Sable Wings*, pp. 255–8.

92 *The Builder*, vol. 8, no. 395, 31 August 1850, p. 416.

93 *Clare Journal*, 1 July 1850, quoted in Ó Murchadha, *Sable Wings*, p. 258; *Limerick Chronicle*, 22 May 1852, quoted in Tim Kelly, 'Ennis Courthouse', *The Other Clare*, vol. 5, 1981, pp. 20–1.

94 See Appendix B.

95 Graham, *Ordering Law*, pp. 93–105, 115; Frank Salmon, *Building on Ruins: The rediscovery of Rome and English architecture* (Aldershot, Hampshire: Ashgate, 2000), pp. 210–26.

96 McSkimmin, *Carrickfergus*, pp. 170–3.

97 Ibid., pp. 511–14; Emrys Jones, *A Social Geography of Belfast* (Oxford: Oxford University Press, 1960), pp. 246–7.

98 McSkimmin, *Carrickfergus*, pp. 511–14; O'Donoghue, *Irish County Surveyors*, pp. 232–3.

99 O'Donoghue, *Irish County Surveyors*, pp. 19–22, 75–9; *Civil Engineer and Architect's Journal*, vol. 3, no. 35, August 1840, p. 285.

100 Brett, *Court Houses*, pp. 47–50; McSkimmin, *Carrickfergus*, pp. 511–14. According to a writer in *The Builder*, the new courthouse was then only 'completed'; the final cost was reportedly £20,000. See *The Builder*, vol. 10, no. 496, 7 August 1852, pp. 495–6.

101 Alterations were made to the courthouse in *c.* 1905 by Young and Mackenzie. See C.E.B. Brett, *Buildings of Belfast, 1700–1914* (Belfast: Friar's Bush Press, 1985), pp. 29–31.

102 McParland, 'Public Work of Architects', p. 249.

103 *The Irish Builder*, vol. 16, no. 349, 1 July 1874, p. 189. See Appendix B.

104 Graham, *Ordering Law*, p. 157, and passim.

105 *Journal of the House of Commons*, vol. 110, 20 March 1855, p. 134, and passim.

Chapter 4 – Architecture before Reform: Grand juries and the problem of implementing social reform, 1770–1810

1 MacDonagh, *Jeremiah Fitzpatrick*, pp. 42–61; Evans, *Fabrication of Virtue*, pp. 9–93.

2 Kilcommins, *Crime, Punishment and the Search For Order*, p. 15; Evans, *Fabrication of Virtue*, p. 19.

3 McDowell, *Irish Administration*, pp. 148–9.

4 Evans, *Fabrication of Virtue*, p. 94.

5 Ibid., pp. 6–7, 142–3.

6 McSkimmin, *Carrickfergus*, pp. 170–3; John Dubourdieu, *Statistical Survey of the County of Antrim* (Dublin: Graisberry & Campbell, 1812), p. 486.

7 McSkimmin, *Carrickfergus*, pp. 151, 397; *Fifth Report … on the … Prisons of Ireland, 1827*, H.C. 1826–7 (471), xi, p. 7.

8 McSkimmin, *Carrickfergus*, pp. 151, 171; Charter for the town of Carrickfergus by James I, dated 14 December 1612 (Rolls of Patents, 10 James I, p. 3, m. 16); Evans, *Fabrication of Virtue*, p. 16.

9 Howard, *Lazarettos*, p. 98.

10 McSkimmin, *Carrickfergus*, p. 151.

11 Francis H. Tuckey, *The County and City of Cork Remembrancer* (Cork: Savage, 1837), p. 125; *Inspector General's Report of … the Prisons in Ireland for … 1818*, H.C. 1819 (534), xii, p. 6. Painted as 'North Gate Bridge' by Nathaniel Grogan in *c.* 1796 (Crawford Art Gallery, Cork). See also Gibney, Hurley and McParland, *Building Site in Eighteenth-century Ireland*, p. 166.

12 Tuckey, *Cork Remembrancer*, p. 128. Painted as 'South Gate Bridge' by Nathaniel Grogan in *c.* 1796 (Crawford Art Gallery, Cork).

13 *Prisons of Ireland: Report of inspectors general, 1823*, H.C. 1823 (342), x, p. 47; Howard, *Lazarettos*, p. 89.

14 Tuckey, *Cork Remembrancer*, pp. 165, 168–9.

15 Ibid., p. 177.

16 Dublin's old Newgate was located at Thomas Street and was in use until 1781. Derry's Ferrygate gaol was built in 1676 and was in use until 1791. See Robert Simpson, *Annals of Derry* (Londonderry: Hempton, 1847), pp. 242–3, and Charles McNeill, 'New Gate, Dublin', *Journal of the Royal Society of Antiquaries of Ireland*, vol. 11, no. 2, 1921, pp. 152–65 (illus.).

17 Evans, *Fabrication of Virtue*, p. 56.

18 John D'Alton and J.R. O'Flanagan, *The History of Dundalk* (Dundalk: William Tempest, 1864), p. 162; John Bowden to John Foster, 9 August 1814 (PRONI, D/562/13002).

19 John Carr, *Stranger in Ireland*, p. 272; Tierney, *The Buildings of Ireland: Central Leinster*, pp. 98–9.

20 See Chapter 1; Howard, *Lazarettos*, pp. 96–7.

21 James Hardiman, *The History of the Town and County of the Town of Galway* (Dublin: Folds, 1820), p. 313; Hely Dutton, A *Statistical and Agricultural Survey of the County of Galway* (Dublin: Graisberry, 1824), pp. 205, 212. See also M.J. Blake (ed.), 'An Account of the Lynch Family', *Journal of the Galway Archaeological and Historical Society*, vol. 8, 1913–14, p. 91; J. Rabbitte, 'Galway Corporation MS. C', ibid., vol. 12, 1924, pp. 57–84, at p. 82; James Mitchell, 'The Prisons of Galway: Background to the inspector general's reports, 1796–1818', ibid., vol. 49, 1997, pp. 1–21.

22 Howard, *Lazarettos*, p. 93; *Dublin Evening Post*, 19 July 1786.

23 10 & 11 Car. 1, c. 4; Dickson, *Dublin*, p. 58.

24 4 Anne, c. 6.

25 *Journal of the Irish House of Commons*, vol. iii, 1729, pp. ccclxxxvi–ix; McDowell, *Irish Administration*, p. 149.

26 MacDonagh, *Jeremiah Fitzpatrick*, pp. 42–7.

27 Evans, *Fabrication of Virtue*, p. 104.

28 29 Geo. II, c. 14.

29 3 Geo. III, c. 5; 3 Geo. III, c. 28.

30 MacDonagh, *Jeremiah Fitzpatrick*, p. 43.

31 Another act in 1768 (7 Geo. III, c. 4, s. 3) restricted presentments for the building of new houses of correction to just £200 per annum; and in 1774, another law (13 & 14 Geo. III, c. 32, s. 15) limited the overseer of gaol-building work to a wage of 12d.

32 Cesare Beccaria, *An Essay on Crimes and Punishments, Translated from the Italian* (Dublin: Exshaw, 1767). Joseph Starr, 'Prison Reform in Ireland in the Age of Enlightenment', *History Ireland*, vol. 3, no. 2, 1995, pp. 21–5.

33 Royal Dublin Society, Minutes and proceedings of the Dublin Society, 1767–9 (RDS/MAN), 9 February 1769; Henry F. Berry, *A History of the Royal Dublin Society* (London: Longmans, Green & Co., 1915), pp. 144–5; McParland, 'Public Work of Architects', p. 137.

34 John Howard, *The State of the Prisons in England and Wales* (Warrington: Eyres, 1784 [1st ed., 1777]), p. 203.

35 *Hibernian Magazine*, August 1776, pp. 540–1; ibid., April 1779, pp. 224–5; McParland, 'Public Work of Architects', p. 137.

36 Evans, *Fabrication of Virtue*, pp. 114–15 (illus.).

37 *Journal of the Irish House of Commons*, vol. viii, 1767, part 1, app. clxx. Thomas King Moylan, 'The Little Green: Part I', *Dublin Historical Record*, vol. 8, no. 3, June–August 1946, pp. 81–91, at p. 89.

38 Carr, *Stranger in Ireland*, p. 72.

39 *Hibernian Magazine*, September 1773, p. 504; ibid., May 1774, p. 301; *Freeman's Journal*, 1–3 June 1775; William Gregory, *The Picture of Dublin, Being a Description of the City* (Dublin: Carrick, 1817 [1st ed., 1811]), p. 177; Moylan, 'Little Green: Part I', p. 89; McParland, 'Public Work of Architects', pp. 43–4.

40 17 & 18 Geo. III, c. 1, s. 17; 19 & 20 Geo. III, c. 7, s. 24.

41 Carr, *Stranger in Ireland*, p. 72; Gregory, *Picture of Dublin*, p. 177.

42 Bernadette Doorly, 'Newgate Prison', in David Dickson (ed.), *The Gorgeous Mask: Dublin, 1700–1850* (Dublin: Trinity History Workshop, 1987), pp. 121–31, at p. 122.

43 Ruth Thorpe, 'Thomas Cooley before the Dublin Royal Exchange', *Irish Architectural and Decorative Studies*, vol. 8, 2005, pp. 71–85.

44 Craig, *Dublin*, p. 198.

45 *Report from the Commissioners Appointed To Inquire into … the State Prisons and Other Gaols in Ireland*, H.C. 1809 (265), vii, p. 142, Plate 1.

46 *Journal of the Irish House of Commons*, vol. xi, 1785, part 1, app. cclxxxv; ibid., xii (1787), part 2, app. dxxv; *Report from the Commissioners Appointed To Inquire into … the State Prisons and Other Gaols in Ireland*, H.C. 1809 (265), vii, pp 4–8, 33.

47 The gaol's structural problems were outlined in detail by Francis White in *Twentieth Report … on … the Prisons of Ireland, 1842*, H.C. 1842 (377), xxii, p. 37.

48 Howard, *State of the Prisons*, pp. 202–3.

49 Evans, *Fabrication of Virtue*, pp. 102–11 (illus.).

50 17 & 18 Geo. III, c. 28; MacDonagh, *Jeremiah Fitzpatrick*, pp. 48–9.

51 With the gaol only 170 by 130 feet and spread over three floors, Howard counted on average 200 prisoners in Newgate in 1787–8. See *Journal of the Irish House of Commons*, vol. x, 1782, part 2, app. dxxxiii–dxxxiv; Howard, *Lazarettos*, p. 79.

52 Howard, *State of the Prisons*, pp. 206–8.

53 Dickson, *Dublin*, pp. 216, 233.

54 Evans, *Fabrication of Virtue*, p. 109.

55 Devereaux, 'Making of the Penitentiary Act', pp. 410–18.

56 MacDonagh, *Jeremiah Fitzpatrick*, pp. 50–3.

57 Ibid.

58 *Journal of the Irish House of Commons*, vol. x, 1782, part 2, app. dxxxiii–dxxxiv.

59 21 & 22 Geo. III, c. 42.

60 MacDonagh, *Jeremiah Fitzpatrick*, p. 53.

61 23 & 24 Geo. III, c. 41. Other minor prison laws passed in the same year included 23 & 24 Geo. III, c. 26 (accountability for money advanced for building) and 23 & 24 Geo. III, c. 42 (penalties for malicious damage).

62 Howard, *State of the Prisons*, p. 208.

63 See for example 23 & 24 Geo. III, c. 44, for Limerick, and Subscriptions of County Wicklow gentry to appeal for funds for building a new gaol, 1786 (NLI, MS 15,303), for Wicklow.

64 24 Geo. III, c. 54; Evans, *Fabrication of Virtue*, p. 135.

65 Quoted in Gandon and Mulvany, *Gandon*, pp. 69–72.

66 See Appendix A.

67 Gandon and Mulvany, *Gandon*, pp. 69–72.

68 McParland, 'Public Work of Architects', p. 138.

69 Waterford Council minute book, 1770–1801, for 29 March 1787 (NLI, microfilm, p. 5559, f. 115), quoted in McParland, *Gandon*, p. 207.

70 Howard, *Lazarettos*, pp. 78–9, 87–8.

71 John Howard to Samuel Whitbread, 8 June 1787 and 6 July 1787, quoted in John Stoughton, *Howard the Philanthropist, and His Friends* (London: Hodder & Stoughton, 1884), pp. 260–1.

72 *Inspector General's Report of … the Prisons in Ireland for … 1807*, H.C. 1808 (239), ix, p. 16; Affidavit of John Roberts, architect, 26 June 1813 (NAI, SPO 554/403/5).

73 *Prisons of Ireland: Report of inspectors general, 1823*, H.C. 1823 (342), x, pp. 63–4.

74 26 Geo. III, c. 27, ss. 30–1; Crossman, 'The Growth of the State in the Nineteenth Century', p. 547.

75 26 Geo III, c. 14; Dickson, *Dublin*, pp. 216.

76 26 Geo. III, c. 27, ss. 4–7; 27 Geo. III, c. 39, ss. 6, 12; Kilcommins, *Crime, Punishment and the Search for Order*, p. 16, significantly understates the duties of the inspector general.

77 MacDonagh, *Jeremiah Fitzpatrick*, pp. 294–329. See also Carroll, *Science, Culture and Modern State Formation*, pp. 157–8.

78 26 Geo. III, c. 27, ss. 22, 32, 40–3, etc.

79 26 Geo. III, c. 27, s. 44.

80 *Dublin Journal*, 4–6 July 1786.

81 James S. Donnelly, Jr, 'The Rightboy Movement 1785–8', *Studia Hibernica*, nos. 17–18, 1977–8, pp. 120–202; Hoppen, *Governing Hibernia*, p. 12. For an overview of English and Irish crime at this time, see Palmer, *Police and Protest in England and Ireland*, pp. 35–162. The figures in Appendix B are very incomplete, but even so the increase in criminal indictments in 1787–8 is clear.

82 *Freeman's Journal*, 14–16 August 1788, quoted in McParland, 'Public Work of Architects', p. 139; MacDonagh, *Jeremiah Fitzpatrick*, pp. 46–7; Starr, 'Prison Reform in Ireland', p. 22. Starr erroneously claims that prison building at this time was 'half-hearted'.

83 Freida Kelly, *A History of Kilmainham Gaol: The dismal house of little ease* (Cork: Mercier, 1988), p. 23.

84 *Journal of the Irish House of Commons*, vol. x, 1782, part 2, app. dxxxiii–dxxxiv.

85 26 Geo. III, c. 14; Nowlan, 'Kilmainham Jail', pp. 105–6.

86 Nowlan, 'Kilmainham Jail', p. 107.

87 His transition to being seen as an expert was very rapid; he went on to build a new sheriff's prison for Dublin city in 1789–94, winning the commission at the expense of the city's own surveyor, Samuel Byron. See John T. Gilbert (ed.), *Calendar of the Ancient Records of Dublin in the Possession of the Municipal Corporation of that City*, 19 vols (Dublin: Dollard, 1889–1944), vol. 14, pp. 346–7; *Report from the Commissioners Appointed To Inquire into … the State Prisons and Other Gaols in Ireland*, H.C. 1809 (265), vii, pp. 21–3; Plan drawings for Kilmainham gaol, n.d., n.s. [before 1817] (NLI, AD 2663–4); *Dictionary of Irish Architects* (www.dia.ie). See Appendix A.

88 *Freeman's Journal*, 21–4 April, 4–6 September 1787.

89 Howard, *Lazarettos*, p. 83.

90 *Faulkner's Dublin Journal*, 13 August 1796; Nowlan, 'Kilmainham Jail', pp. 106–7.

91 John T. Gilbert (ed.), *Documents Relating to Ireland, 1795–1804* (Dublin: Dollard, 1893), p. 94; Dickson, *Dublin*, p. 294.

92 *Belfast Newsletter*, 19 May 1789; *Journal of the Irish House of Commons*, vol. xvii, 1797, p. ccvi; Appendix A.

93 Evans, *Fabrication of Virtue*, pp. 291, 294 (illus.).

94 *Inspector General's Report of … the Prisons in Ireland for … 1807*, H.C. 1808 (239), ix, p. 16.

95 23 & 24 Geo. III, c. 44; 26 Geo. III, c. 59.

96 Howard, *Lazarettos*, p. 91; M.H. Port, 'William Blackburn', in Matthew and Harrison, *Oxford Dictionary of National Biography*, vol. 5, pp. 931–2; Howard Colvin, *A Biographical Dictionary of British Architects, 1600–1840* (New Haven and London: Yale University Press, 2008), pp. 126–8.

97 'Forster Archer's Tour of Ireland in 1801' (British Library, Add. MS 35920, f. 4v), quoted in P.J. Dowling, 'Forster Archer's Tour of Ireland in 1801', *Irish Ecclesiastical Record*, vol. 62, 1943, pp. 22–8, at p. 26.

98 The architect was named by Charles Coquebert de Montbret in 1791. See Sighle Ní Chinnéide (ed.), 'A Frenchman's Impressions of Limerick, Town and People, in 1791', *North Munster Antiquarian Journal*, vol. 5, no. 4, 1948, pp. 96–101, at p. 100; *Accounts of Presentments by Grand Juries in Ireland … in 1807*, H.C. 1808 (205), xiii, p. 220; Maurice Lenihan, *History of Limerick* (Dublin: Duffy, 1866), pp. 428, 431.

99 Howard, *Lazarettos*, p. 92.

100 Ibid., p. 86.

101 *Freeman's Journal*, 27–31 October 1787; 4–6 August 1789; 1–3 February 1791; Tierney, *The Buildings of Ireland: Central Leinster*, pp. 547–8.

102 Elevation and plan drawings, n.s., n.d., in Henry, Mullins & McMahon collection (M37), now in the possession of Thomas Pakenham, Tullynally Castle, County Westmeath. The Irish Architectural Archive has copies.

103 Howard, *Lazarettos*, p. 78.

104 Diaries of Sir Vere Hunt, 10 March to 31 December 1813 (NLI, microfilm, pp. 5527–8), entry for 10 May 1813. The Limerick City Library has the original diaries.

105 *Dublin Journal*, 21 July 1787; General survey plan and floor plans of Mullingar gaol, n.s., n.d., watermark 1818 (Irish Architectural Archive, Guinness Collection, Acc. 96/68.5/5/1–2); Plan drawing for the old gaol at Mullingar, n.d., n.s. [*c.* 1824] (NLI, AD 2643).

106 Howard, *Lazarettos*, p. 94.

107 *Inspector General's Report of … the Prisons in Ireland, for … 1818*, H.C. 1819 (534), xii, p. 27; *Account of all Gaols … in the … United Kingdom*, H.C. 1819 (137), xvii, pp. 18–19. The same report spuriously claimed that the capacity of this gaol was 150 and that the number of separate classes was 18.

108 Liam Price (ed.), *An Eighteenth-century Antiquary: The sketches, notes, and diaries of Austin Cooper, 1759–1830* (Dublin: Falconer, 1942), p. 28; Anon., 'Notes on Naas Gaol', *Journal of the County Kildare Archaeological Society*, vol. 14, no. 3, 1968, pp. 333–5.

109 *Journal of the Irish House of Commons*, vol. xvii, 1797, p. ccvi; Cornelius Costello, 'Naas and the Country in General, from 1800–48', *Journal of the County Kildare Archaeological Society*, vol. 13, no. 3, 1960, pp. 432–4.

110 Howard, *Lazarettos*, p. 86.

111 John Longfield, 'A Map of Naas Gaol and Adjoining Concerns', 1824 (NLI, MS 21 F 35, no. 44); Tierney, *The Buildings of Ireland: Central Leinster*, pp. 509–10.

112 Evans, *Fabrication of Virtue*, pp. 132–5 (illus.).

113 16 Geo. III, c. 56.

114 Evans, *Fabrication of Virtue*, pp. 120–31 (illus.).

115 Ibid.

116 Evans, *Fabrication of Virtue*, pp. 195–235. The term 'panopticon' is often mistakenly applied to radial or separate-system prison designs, see for example Dublin's Kilmainham jail in Hughes and MacRaild, 'Introduction: Crime, violence and the Irish in the nineteenth century', p. 7.

117 Kilcommins, *Crime, Punishment and the Search for Order*, p. 16; Bob Reece, *The Origins of Irish Convict Transportation to New South Wales* (Houndmills: Palgrave, 2001).

118 MacDonagh, *Jeremiah Fitzpatrick*, pp. 132–41.

119 32 Geo. III, c. 27; Jeremy Bentham to John Parnell, n.d. [September 1790]; Jeremy Bentham to Robert Adam, 28 May 1791 (University College London, Bentham MSS, box 119a, nos. 12, 14); Evans, *Fabrication of Virtue*, pp. 197, 211, 220.

120 John Bowring (ed.), *The Works of Jeremy Bentham*, 11 vols (Edinburgh: William Tait, 1838–43), vol. 11, p. 104 (supplement); Evans, *Fabrication of Virtue*, pp. 218–24.

121 Starr, 'Prison Reform in Ireland', p. 25.

122 Evans, *Fabrication of Virtue*, p. 185.

123 *Journal of the Irish House of Commons*, vol. xv, 1793, p. 2, app. ccccviii. These figures match this author's research.

124 Howard, *Lazarettos*, p. 97; Evans, *Fabrication of Virtue*, pp. 73, 132, 141.

125 Simpson, *Annals of Derry*, pp. 242–3; *Journal of the Irish House of Commons*, vol. xviii, 1799, p. ccxxxiii.

126 With reference to Lifford gaol, County Donegal, see Rowan, *Buildings of Ireland: North west Ulster*, p. 348.

127 *Account of All Gaols … in the … United Kingdom*, H.C. 1819 (137), xvii, pp. 6–7, 12–13, 16–17.

128 *Inspector General's Report on … the Prisons in Ireland for … 1818*, H.C. 1819 (534), xii, pp. 6–7.

129 *Inspector General's Report on … the Prisons in Ireland for … 1807*, H.C. 1808 (239), ix, p. 16. For commentary on this type of building contract, see Gibney, Hurley and McParland, *Building Site in Eighteenth-century Ireland*, pp. 38–56.

130 Brian Inglis, *The Freedom of the Press in Ireland, 1784–1841* (London: Faber & Faber, 1954), pp. 88–9.

131 'Forster Archer's Tour of Ireland in 1801' (British Library, Add. MS 35920, f. 15), quoted in Dowling, 'Forster Archer's Tour', p. 26.

132 36 Geo. III, c. 55, s. 38.

133 39 Geo. III, c. 55.

134 William Gregory Wood-Martin, *History of Sligo, County and Town* (Dublin: Hodges, Figgis & Co., 1892), pp. 156–7.

135 Howard, *Lazarettos*, p. 92; *Inspector General's Report of … Prisons in Ireland for … 1807*, H.C. 1808 (239), ix, p. 15.

136 *Dictionary of Irish Architects* (www.dia.ie); 'Elevation of Front of a Large Gaol', n.d. [*c.* 1801], by Bernard Mullins (Irish Architectural Archive, ICEI Collection, Acc. 2005/095).

137 'Forster Archer's Tour of Ireland in 1801' (British Library, Add. MS 35920, f. 4v), quoted in Dowling, 'Forster Archer's Tour', p. 23.

138 *Finn's Leinster Journal*, 18 April 1801; *Kilkenny Moderator*, 15 August 1801; Walter Walsh, 'Hard Labour, Hard Board, and Hard Fare: Kilkenny gaols, 1770–1900', *Ossory, Laois, and Leinster*, vol. 3, 2008, pp. 209–39, at pp. 209–10.

139 *Leinster Journal*, 13 September 1809; Walsh, 'Kilkenny Gaols', p. 211.

140 Forster Archer, 'Report of the State of Gaols of Ireland for the Year 1802', f. 8 (Houses of the Oireachtas Library, Dublin, MS.7H28); *Inspector General's Report on … the Prisons in Ireland for … 1807*, H.C. 1808 (239), ix, pp. 10–11; Thomas Reid, *Travels in Ireland* (London: Longman, 1823), pp. 245–6.

141 *Kilkenny Moderator*, 5 May 1814; Evans, *Fabrication of Virtue*, p. 173 (illus.).

142 Evans, *Fabrication of Virtue*, pp. 144–7 (illus.); Johnston, *Forms of Constraint*, pp. 53–8.

143 Hardiman, *Galway*, p. 313; Mitchell, 'Prisons of Galway', p. 6.

144 *Journal of the Irish House of Commons*, vol. xvii, 1797, p. ccvi; 'Forster Archer's Tour of Ireland in 1801' (British Library, Add. MS 35920, f. 9); Forster Archer, 'Report of the State of Gaols of Ireland for the Year 1802', f. 6 (Houses of the Oireachtas Library, Dublin, MS.7H28); Galway County Gaol Act, 1802, 42 Geo. III, c. xviii; Hardiman, *Galway*, pp. 313–14; Mitchell, 'Prisons of Galway', p. 10.

145 Galway Corporation Minute Book K, ff 309–10, 351–3 (NUI Galway); Galway County Gaol and Sessions House Act, 1807, 47 Geo. III, sess. 2, c. cxii; Mitchell, 'Prisons of Galway', pp. 10–11.

146 Hardiman, *Galway*, pp. 312–13; Dutton, *Statistical … Survey … of Galway*, pp. 212, 321, 382; Marguirite Hayes-McCoy, 'The Eyre Documents', *Journal of the Galway Archaeological and Historical Society*, vol. 20, 1943, pp. 151–79, at p. 154.

147 Evans, *Fabrication of Virtue*, pp. 121, 131, 247–8.

148 Thomas Hardwick, 'A Design for a Gaol To Be Built in Ireland', R.A. 1802, no. 895; Journal of Daniel Augustus Beaufort, 1808, f. 88 (Trinity College Library, Dublin); Hardiman, *Galway*, p. 313; Dutton, *Statistical … Survey … of Galway*, p. 205.

149 *Inspector General's Report on … the Prisons in Ireland for … 1807*, H.C. 1808 (239), ix, p. 9.

150 Forster Archer, 'Report of the State of Gaols of Ireland for the Year 1811' (Houses of the Oireachtas Library, Dublin, MS.4E63); *Report … on the State of Gaols*, H.C. 1819 (579), vii, pp. 210–11.

151 *Account of all Gaols … in the United Kingdom*, H.C. 1819 (137), xvii, pp. 8–9.

152 Hardiman, *Galway*, p. 312; Reid, *Travels*, p. 306.

153 28 Geo. III, c. 39.

154 Tuckey, *Cork Remembrancer*, pp. 205, 217; *Dictionary of Irish Architects* (www.dia.ie).

155 Carr, *Stranger in Ireland*, p. 260.

156 *Inspector General's Report on … the Prisons in Ireland for … 1807*, H.C. 1808 (239), ix, p. 5. See also Forster Archer, 'Report of the State of Gaols of Ireland for the Year 1802', f. 3 (Houses of the Oireachtas Library, Dublin, MS.7H28).

157 Copy book of bills, estimates, bills of measurement, valuations, etc., kept by William Deane, 1797–1809 (Irish Architectural Archive, Acc. 2009/91); Tuckey, *Cork Remembrancer*, p. 234; *Accounts of Presentments by Grand Juries in Ireland … in 1807*, H.C. 1808 (205), xiii, p. 86.

158 *Account of all Gaols … in the United Kingdom*, H.C. 1819 (137), xvii, pp. 4–5.

159 Forster Archer, 'Report of the State of Gaols of Ireland for the Year 1802', f. 3 (Houses of the Oireachtas Library, Dublin, MS.7H28); *Report … on the State of Gaols*, H.C. 1819 (579), vii, pp. 205–7.

160 George Papworth, Design for Cork city gaol (1805), exhibited at the Society of Artists, Dublin, 1809, no. 79; *Accounts of Presentments by Grand Juries in Ireland … in 1807*, H.C. 1808 (205), xiii, pp. 90, 94; Anon., 'Site for [city] Gaol',

Journal of the Cork Historical and Archaeological Society, vol. 35, no. 141, January–June 1940, p. 55; Cork City Gaol Act, 1806, 46 Geo. III, c. xxxviii.

161 *Inspector General's Report on … the Prisons in Ireland for … 1807*, H.C. 1808 (239), ix, p. 5.

162 *Hansard*, vol. 11, 1st ser., 2 July 1808, cols 1131–4; R.G. Thorne, *The History of Parliament: The House of Commons, 1790–1820*, 5 vols (London: Secker & Warburg, 1986), vol. 5, pp. 143–69 (Richard Sheridan).

163 McParland, 'Public Work of Architects', pp. 140, 250.

164 The family's association with penal reform continued on to the 5th duke, who chaired a House of Lords inquiry in 1835 that saw central-government inspectors, along Irish lines, appointed throughout Britain. See Evans, *Fabrication of Virtue*, pp. 73, 132, 141.

165 *Report from the Commissioners Appointed To Inquire into … the State Prisons and Other Gaols in Ireland*, H.C. 1809 (265), vii, pp. 4–8, 26, 52, 64, and passim.

166 Ibid., pp. 31–3.

167 *Hansard*, vol. 15, 1st ser., 19 February 1810, col. 468. See also Anon., 'Irish Prisons', *The Hibernia Magazine*, vol. 1, no. 6, June 1810, pp. 394–400; and Anon., 'Prison Abuses in Ireland', *The Examiner*, 14 October 1810.

168 Both new gaols in Waterford city and Wexford were built by Richard Morrison. See *Accounts of Presentments by Grand Juries in Ireland … in 1807*, H.C. 1808 (205), xiii, pp. 412, 429, 433; *Inspector General's Report on … the Prisons in Ireland for … 1807*, H.C. 1808 (239), ix, pp. 16–17. For commentary on the legacy of eighteenth-century building contracts, see Gibney, Hurley and McParland, *Building Site in Eighteenth-century Ireland*, pp. 33–56.

Chapter 5 – Reform Revisited: Central government, philanthropic societies, and disruptions to grand-jury patronage, 1810–21

1 McParland, 'Public Work of Architects', p. 250.

2 50 Geo. III, c. 103; *Hansard*, vol. 15, 1st ser., 19 February 1810, cols 468–9; *Journal of the House of Commons*, vol. 65, 10 February 1810, p. 103, and passim.

3 Board of Works letterbooks, 3 August 1810 to 20 December 1816, for August 1810, p. 5 (NAI, Board of Works files, 2D/57/35).

4 Drawings for a penitentiary, August 1810, by Francis Johnston (Irish Architectural Archive, RIAI Murray Collection, Acc.92/46.424–6).

5 *Dictionary of Irish Architects* (www.dia.ie).

6 Dublin County grand-jury minute book, 22 April 1818 and 9 May 1820 (Fingal County Council Archives, GJ/1/1); Nowlan, 'Kilmainham Jail', p. 110. See Appendix D.

7 See Appendix B.

8 See Appendix D.

9 Henry Heaney, 'Ireland's Penitentiary, 1820–1831: An experiment that failed', *Studia Hibernica*, vol. 14, 1974, pp. 28–39, at p. 39.

10 Board of Works letterbooks, 3 August 1810 to 20 December 1816, for August 1810, p. 65 (NAI, Board of Works files, 2D/57/35); Goslin, 'Descriptive Catalogue of the Murray Collection', pp. 154–7; Drawings for Richmond penitentiary, January 1811 and 1812, by Francis Johnston (Irish Architectural Archive, RIAI Murray Collection, Acc.92/46.428–31).

11 McParland, 'Francis Johnston', p. 131.

12 Ibid., p. 130; McParland, 'Public Work of Architects', pp. 250–1.

13 Heaney, 'Ireland's Penitentiary', pp. 30, 36.

14 Goslin, 'Descriptive Catalogue of the Murray Collection', p. 156; Casey, *The Buildings of Ireland: Dublin*, pp. 256–8.

15 T. Taylor to Charles Grant, 'Report on the Richmond General Penitentiary', n.d. [1819] (NAI, CSORP 1819 106P).

16 *Inspector General's Report on … the Prisons in Ireland for … 1807*, H.C. 1808 (239), ix, p. 7; *Report from the Commissioners Appointed To Inquire into … the State Prisons and Other Gaols in Ireland*, H.C. 1809 (265), vii, p. 26, and passim; John Warburton, James Whitelaw, and Robert Walsh, *History of the City of Dublin*, 2 vols (London: Cadell & Davies, 1818), vol. 1, p. 583.

17 See Appendix B.

18 *Accounts of All Sums Presented To Be Raised off the City of Dublin … from … 1807 … to 1821*, H.C. 1821 (477), xx, p. 32; Site map for Richmond bridewell, n.d. [1811], n.s. (Irish Architectural Archive, RIAI Murray Collection, Acc. 92/46.325); McParland, 'Public Work of Architects', p. 250; Goslin, 'Descriptive Catalogue of the Murray Collection', p. 130.

19 Drawings for Richmond bridewell, 1813–16, by Francis Johnston (Irish Architectural Archive, RIAI Murray Collection, Acc. 92/46.327–39; Francis Johnston to J.N. Brewer, 29 February 1820, quoted in Henchy, 'Francis Johnston', at p. 13; McParland, 'Francis Johnston', p. 130.

20 Warburton, Whitelaw, and Walsh, *History of … Dublin*, vol. 2, p. 1062.

21 *Paper Relating to the Prisons in Dublin*, H.C. 1819 (195), xii, p. 2; AIPPD, *Fifth Report of the Association for the Improvement of Prisons and of Prison Discipline in Ireland, for 1823* (Dublin: Goodwin, 1824), p. 23 (hereafter cited as *Fifth Report of the AIPPD*).

22 Site map for Grangegorman, Dublin, n.d. [1809], n.s. (Irish Architectural Archive, RIAI Murray Collection, Acc. 92/46.401); Thomas King Moylan, 'The District of Grangegorman: Part II', *Dublin Historical Record*, vol. 7, no. 2, March–May 1945, pp. 55–68, at p. 55; Dickson, *Dublin*, p. 288; Sinéad Gargan, 'How Not To "Encourage People To Take Lotts for Building": The 18th-century non-development of Grangegorman by the Monck estate', *Irish Architectural and Decorative Studies*, vol. 18, 2015, pp. 106–29; Katherine Fennelly, 'The Institution and the City: The impact of hospitals and workhouses on the development of Dublin's north inner city, *c.* 1773–1911', *Urban History* (forthcoming).

23 Evans, *Fabrication of Virtue*, pp. 237, 241.

24 Ibid., pp. 227–8, 244–50.

25 James Neild, *State of the Prisons in England, Scotland, and Wales* (London: Nichols, 1812), pp. 617–18; Evans, *Fabrication of Virtue*, pp. 242–3.

26 Howard, *Lazarettos*, p. 95; *Journal of the Irish House of Commons*, vol. xvii, 1798, p. dcxxxii; Forster Archer, 'Report of the State of Gaols of Ireland for the Year 1802', f. 2 (Houses of the Oireachtas Library, Dublin, MS.7H28).

27 *Inspector General's Report of … the Prisons in Ireland for … 1807*, H.C. 1808 (239), ix, p. 4.

28 Design for Cavan gaol by Richard Elsam, described as 'now erecting', exhibited at the Society of Artists, Dublin, 1809 (nos. 81, 132); *Accounts of Presentments by Grand Juries in Ireland … in 1807*, H.C. 1808 (205), xiii, pp. 39–40.

29 Richard Elsam, *A Description of Cavan Gaol: With Neild's observations on the law of civil imprisonment: with his report of Gloucester county gaol: together with cursory hints for the internal regulation of prisons … to which is annexed an abstract of the statutes of Geo. III for the information of grand juries, in building and repairing of prisons in Ireland* (Dublin: Carrick, 1810); Nicholson, *A Theoretical and Practical Treatise on the Five Orders of Architecture*, p. 156, plates 64, 65; Evans, *Fabrication of Virtue*, p. 274.

30 Nicholson, *A Theoretical and Practical Treatise on the Five Orders of Architecture*, p. 156.

31 Evans, *Fabrication of Virtue*, p. 271.

32 *Inspector General's Report of … the Prisons in Ireland, for … 1818*, H.C. 1819 (534), xii, pp. 4–5; *Account of All Gaols … in the … United Kingdom*, H.C. 1819 (137), xvii, pp. 4–5.

33 Copies of Elsam's plan and elevation drawings for Cavan appear in an album book owned by the gaol contractors Henry, Mullins & McMahon, see elevation drawing, n.d., n.s. (Irish Architectural Archive, ICEI Collection, Acc. 2005/095).

34 Tralee county gaol was built between 1812 and 1817; Enniskillen county gaol between 1812 and 1815. See 'An Account of the Several Presentments Made … on which Advances Have Been Made by Government for Gaols' (NAI, SPO 588 AAB 944); Charge of judge Robert Day to the Kerry grand jurors, March 1812 (Royal Irish Academy, Day papers, MS 12W12); William Irvine to Charles Saxton, 1 June 1812, and Francis Johnston to Richard Morrison, July 1812 (NAI, SPO 552/382/14); Richard Morrison to William Vesey-Fitzgerald, 5 February 1814 (NLI, Vesey-Fitzgerald papers, MS 7823, pp. 267–8). I am grateful to Anthony Malcomson for several of these references.

35 Francis Johnston to R. Robinson, 16 July 1812 (NAI, SPO 552/382/15); *Limerick Evening Post*, 28 March 1817.

36 *Inspector General's Report of … the Prisons in Ireland, for … 1818*, H.C. 1819 (534), xii, pp. 13–14; *Account of All Gaols … in the … United Kingdom*, H.C. 1819 (137), xvii, pp. 8–9; *Faulkner's Dublin Journal*, 30 August 1817.

37 See Appendix B.

38 See Appendix D.

39 *Accounts of Presentments by Grand Juries in Ireland … in 1807*, H.C. 1808 (205), xiii, p. 220; Lenihan, *Limerick*, pp. 428, 431.

40 Lenihan, *Limerick*, p. 428.

41 *Report … on the State of Gaols*, H.C. 1819 (579), vii, p. 174.

42 John Alexander Staples, *A Tour in Ireland in 1813 & 1814* (Dublin: Gough, 1817), p. 210; Evans, *Fabrication of Virtue*, pp. 146, 151.

43 *Belfast Newsletter*, 13 June 1815; *Inspector General's Report of … the Prisons in Ireland, for … 1818*, H.C. 1819 (534), xii, p. 3; Reid, *Travels*, pp. 176–7; George Benn, *A History of the Town of Belfast from 1799 till 1810*, 2 vols (London: Ward, 1880), vol. 2, p. 79.

44 *Accounts of Presentments by Grand Juries in Ireland … in 1807*, H.C. 1808 (205), xiii, p. 3; Benn, *Belfast*, vol. 2, p. 79.

45 John Leslie Foster to Robert Peel, 15 March 1813 (British Library, Add. MS 40225, ff. 227–30); Drogheda grand-jury presentment books, spring assizes, 1814 (NAI, SPO 588 YY 910); John Foster to Robert Peel, 1 September 1814 (NAI, SPO 558/423/23).

46 *Inspector General's Report of … the Prisons in Ireland for … 1818*, H.C. 1819 (534), xii, pp. 7–8; Appendix D. Bowden also built significant additions to the gaols at Dundalk and Armagh at this time, see Appendix A.

47 Francis Johnston to R. Robinson, 21 April 1814 (NAI, SPO 558/423/32); Rowan, *Morrison*, pp. 148–9.

48 Rowan, *Morrison*, p. 148; McParland, 'Public Work of Architects', p. 250.

49 *Inspector General's Report of … the Prisons in Ireland for … 1818*, H.C. 1819 (534), xii, pp. 23–4.

50 *Twelfth Report … on … the Prisons of Ireland, 1834*, H.C. 1834 (63), xl, p. 49.

51 *Prisons of Ireland: Report of Inspectors General, 1823*, H.C. 1823 (342), x, p. 5.

52 See Appendix B and Appendix D.

53 John Bowden to John Foster, 29 January 1814 (PRONI, D/562/4227); Henry Westenra to William Gregory, 3 August 1814 (NAI, SPO 558/423/31); Memorandum of John Behan of Dublin, n.d. [1821] (NAI, CSORP 1821/547).

54 Andrew Blayney to Charles Grant, 20 May 1822 (NAI, CSORP 1822/22); *Inspector General's Report of … the Prisons in Ireland for … 1818*, H.C. 1819 (534), xii, pp. 21–2.
55 *Belfast Newsletter*, 23 June 1820; *Prisons of Ireland: Report of inspectors general, 1824*, H.C. 1824 (294), xxii, p. 5.
56 *Inspector General's Report of … the Prisons in Ireland for … 1818*, H.C. 1819 (534), xii, pp. 21–2.
57 Wood-Martin, *Sligo*, pp. 156–7.
58 Memorandum from Francis Johnston, 8 November 1814 (NAI, SPO 558/423/33); Edward Cooper to Robert Peel, 19 November 1815 (NAI, SPO 560/439/28); *Inspector General's Report of … Prisons in Ireland for … 1807*, H.C. 1808 (239), ix, p. 15.
59 Notes on designs for a county gaol at Salisbury, 10 September 1817, by Richard Ingleman (Wiltshire County Records Office); Plan drawings for Sligo gaol, n.d., n.s. [*c.* 1816] (NLI, AD 2661); Evans, *Fabrication of Virtue*, pp. 292–3 (illus.).
60 Lewis, *Topographical Dictionary*, vol. 2, p. 570; Appendix D.
61 See Appendix B.
62 AIPPD, *First Report of the Association for the Improvement of Prisons and of Prison Discipline in Ireland, for 1819* (Dublin: Goodwin, 1820), pp. 22–5 (hereafter cited as *First Report of the AIPPD*).
63 Anon., *An Account of the Origin and Object of the Society for the Diffusion of Knowledge upon the Punishment of Death and the Improvement of Prison Discipline* (London: Taylor, 1812); *First Report of the AIPPD*, p. 11; Evans, *Fabrication of Virtue*, p. 239. A Scottish society, the Society for the Improvement of Prison Discipline in Scotland, was also founded *c.* 1830; see Anon., *Address by the Committee of Directors of the Society for the Improvement of Prison Discipline in Scotland* (Edinburgh: Neill, 1835), pp. iii–xvi.
64 Maria Luddy, *Women and Philanthropy in Nineteenth-century Ireland* (Cambridge: Cambridge University Press, 1995), pp. 149–75; see also Robert Alan Cooper, 'The English Quakers and Prison Reform, 1809–23', *Quaker History*, vol. 68, no. 1, Spring 1979, pp. 3–19.
65 AIPPD, *A Statement of the Objects of the Association for the Improvement of Prisons and of Prison Discipline in Ireland* (Dublin: Bentham, 1819), p. 12.
66 *Report … on the State of the Gaols of the City of London*, H.C. 1813–14 (157), iv; *Report … on the King's Bench, Fleet, and Marshalsea Prisons*, H.C. 1814–15 (152), iv; *Report … on the Prisons within the city of London and Borough of Southwark*, H.C. 1818 (275), viii.
67 Thorne, *History of Parliament: The House of Commons, 1790–1820*, vol. 5, pp. 36–43 (Samuel Romilly); Fisher, *History of Parliament: The House of Commons, 1820–1832*, vol. 5, pp. 676–8 (George Holford).
68 *Journal of the House of Commons*, vol. 69, 8 July 1814, p. 443.
69 *A Bill for the Better Regulation of the Prisons or Gaols within the Jurisdiction of the city of London*, H.C. 1813–14 (263), ii.
70 Evans, *Fabrication of Virtue*, pp. 239–41; Johnston, *Forms of Constraint*, pp. 44–6.
71 *First Report of the AIPPD*, p. 4.
72 Ibid., p. 30.
73 AIPPD, *Third Report of the Association for the Improvement of Prisons, and of Prison Discipline in Ireland, for 1821* (Dublin: Goodwin, 1822), pp. 4, 19 (hereafter cited as *Third Report of the AIPPD*); *Fifth Report of the AIPPD*, p. 3.
74 Charles Grant was a member of the British and Foreign Bible Society. See *The Inquirer* (April 1822), pp. 320–5, at p. 321.
75 Evans, *Fabrication of Virtue*, pp. 261–71.
76 Ibid., p. 295.
77 Quoted in ibid., p. 266.
78 AIPPD, Appeal for support [sent to the Earl Fitzwilliam], 17 August 1820 (Sheffield City Archives, Wentworth Woodhouse Muniments collection: WWM/H/206).
79 Ibid., pp. 318–19.
80 See Chapter 6.
81 *Report … on the State of Gaols*, H.C. 1819 (579), vii, pp. 195–235.
82 Ibid., pp. 195, 201, 204.
83 Ibid., pp. 173–4, 193.
84 *Belfast Newsletter*, 18 April 1820.
85 *First Report of the AIPPD*, pp. 11–27.
86 T. Taylor to Charles Grant, 'Report on the Richmond General Penitentiary', n.d. [1819] (NAI, CSORP 1819 106P).
87 George Warner to Charles Grant, 4 January 1819, printed in *Paper Relating to the Prisons in Dublin*, H.C. 1819 (195), xii, p. 1; *Fifth Report of the AIPPD*, p. 19.
88 *Report … on the State of Gaols*, H.C. 1819 (579), vii, p. 220.
89 Prisons Act, 1819 (Ireland), 59 Geo. III, c. 100.
90 Gaols Fees Abolition Act, 1821 (Ireland), 1 & 2 Geo. IV, c. 77.
91 *Journal of the House of Commons*, vol. 75, 25 May 1820, p. 238; *Third Report of the AIPPD*, p. 14.
92 *A Bill to Amend an Act … Relating to Prisons in Ireland*, H.C. 1821 (493), iii, p. 4.
93 Charles Grant to Charles Fox, 6 June 1820 (NAI, CSORP 1820/552).
94 Prisons Act, 1821 (Ireland), 1 & 2 Geo. IV, c. 57, ss. 8–15.

95 James Palmer, *A Treatise on the Modern System of Government Gaols, Penitentiaries, and Houses of Correction, with a View to Moral Improvement and Reformation of Character; also a Detail of the Duties of Each Department of a Prison, Together with Some Observations on the State of Prison Discipline, at Home and Abroad, and on the Management of Lunatic Asylums* (Dublin: Holden, 1832), p. 91.

96 William Gregory to Robert Archer, 25 November 1821 (NAI, CSORP/SC 1821/53).

97 Butler, 'Rethinking the Origins of the British Prisons Act'.

98 Henry Pasley to Forster Archer, 19 November 1819 (NAI, CSORP 1819/212); Reid, *Travels*, pp. 316–18.

99 James Elmes to Charles Grant, 25 September 1820, 19 February 1821, 18 April 1821, 4 June 1821, 27 July 1821, 16 November 1821 (NAI, CSORP 1819/990, 1820/432, and 1820/1328); elevation and plan drawings for Waterford city house of correction, 23 September 1820, by James Elmes (NAI, CSORP 1820/432/6).

100 *Prisons of Ireland: Report of inspectors general, 1824*, H.C. 1824 (294), xxii, p. 64.

101 Evans, *Fabrication of Virtue*, pp. 275–6.

102 *Fifteenth Report … on … the Prisons of Ireland, 1837*, H.C. 1837 (123), xxxi, p. 47.

103 Francis Johnston to the commissioners of the Board of Works, 17 December 1818 (NAI, CSORP 1818/180).

104 *Report … on the State of Gaols*, H.C. 1819 (579), vii, pp. 205–7.

105 Benjamin Woodward to Henry Goulburn, 4 December 1822 (NAI, CSORP 1822/3061).

106 *Prisons of Ireland: Report of inspectors general, 1824*, H.C. 1824 (294), xxii, p. 47; Appendix D.

107 *Report … on Provisions for Better Regulation of Madhouses in England*, H.C. 1814–15 (295), iv, plate 5; Frederick O'Dwyer, 'Public Works Architecture in Ireland, 1829–1923', PhD thesis, Trinity College Dublin, 1996, p. 152 (hereafter cited as 'Public Works Architecture').

108 Hermann von Puckler-Muskau, *Tour in England, Ireland and France in the Years 1828 & 1829*, 2 vols, trans. Sarah Austin (London: Effingham, 1832), vol. 2, p. 16.

109 Francis Johnston to the chief secretary's office, 3 September 1819 (NAI, CSORP 1819/187).

110 Reid, *Travels*, p. 269; *Prisons of Ireland: Report of inspectors general, 1823*, H.C. 1823 (342), x, p. 43.

111 *Prisons of Ireland: Report of inspectors general, 1824*, H.C. 1824 (294), xxii, pp. 7, 43; Memorandum of James Chatterton of Cork, n.d. [1824] (NAI, CSORP 1824/8009).

112 *Limerick Gazette*, 5 April and 25 March 1816; *Report … on the State of Gaols*, H.C. 1819 (579), vii, pp. 173–4; Lenihan, *Limerick*, pp. 447–8; Evans, *Fabrication of Virtue*, p. 408; Appendix D.

113 *Prisons of Ireland: Report of inspectors general, 1823*, H.C. 1823 (342), x, p. 56.

114 Reid, *Travels*, pp. 293–4.

115 One of the first prisoners to be executed in front of the new gaol was a Mr Daniel O'Connell in August 1823, for a conviction related to Rockite agrarian unrest. See Lenihan, *Limerick*, p. 438.

116 Thomas Colby, *Ordnance Survey of the County of Londonderry: Memoir of the city and north-western liberties of Londonderry: parish of Templemore* (Dublin: Hodges & Smith, 1837), p. 116; Lewis, *Topographical Dictionary*, vol. 2, p. 303; Simpson, *Annals of Derry*, pp. 242–3.

117 *Prisons of Ireland: Report of inspectors general, 1824*, H.C. 1824 (294), xxii, p. 34.

118 Simpson, *Annals of Derry*, p. 243; Appendix D.

119 Journal of a visit to Ireland by Fred Amherst, 1825 (NLI, MS 16,539), as quoted in McParland, 'Public Work of Architects', p. 136.

Chapter 6 – The New Regime: James Palmer, Benjamin Woodward, and grand-jury responses to the renewed call for penal reform, 1821–38

1 Prisons Act, 1821 (Ireland), 1 & 2 Geo. IV, c. 57.

2 Biographical information from Dr John and Mrs Patricia DuLong, Lansing, Michigan; confirmation of arms to the descendants of Henry Palmer, 4 December 1908 (NLI, MS 111, pp. 235–6); James Palmer to Robert Peel, 17 December 1817 (British Library, Add. MS 40232, f. 177); James Palmer to Robert Peel, 5 August 1816 (British Library, Add. MS 40257, ff. 176–7). I am grateful to the DuLong family for all their assistance.

3 James Palmer to Robert Peel, 28 September 1816 (British Library, Add. MS 40258, f. 271); House of Industry Dublin Act, 1820, 1 Geo. IV, c. 49.

4 David Baird to Charles Grant, 15 September 1820 (NAI, CSORP 1820/200); James Palmer to Charles Grant, 18 October 1820 (NAI, CSORP 1820/739).

5 James Palmer to Charles Grant, 15 December 1821 (NAI, CSORP 1821/932).

6 Donnelly, 'Rightboy Movement', pp. 140–7, and passim; James Kelly, 'Richard Woodward', in McGuire and Quinn, *Dictionary of Irish Biography*, vol. 9, pp. 1036–9.

7 Henry MacDougall, *Sketches of Irish Political Characters of the Present Day Shewing the Parts they Respectively Take on the Question of the Union* (London: Davison, 1799), p. 230.

8 Benjamin Blake Woodward to Charles Grant, 17 July 1820 (NAI, CSORP 1820/1391).

9 Benjamin Blake Woodward to Charles Grant, 28 December 1821 (NAI, CSORP 1821/875). The Prisons Act, 1822

(Ireland), 3 Geo. IV, c. 64, s. 20, increased the basic salary of each inspector to £600.

10 G.F.R. Barker and David Eastwood, 'Henry Goulburn', in Matthew and Harrison, *Oxford Dictionary of National Biography*, vol. 23, pp. 62–6; Ged Martin, 'Charles Grant', ibid., vol. 23, pp. 293–5; Martin McElroy, 'Henry Goulburn', in McGuire and Quinn, *Dictionary of Irish Biography*, vol. 4, pp. 168–70; Daniel Beaumont, 'Charles Grant', ibid., vol. 4, pp. 195–7; Melinda D. Grimsley-Smith, 'Politics, Professionalization, and Poverty: Lunatic asylums for the poor in Ireland, 1817–1920', PhD thesis, University of Notre Dame, 2011, p. 93 (hereafter cited as 'Lunatic asylums') incorrectly states that the new inspectors were appointed by Goulburn as they shared his Protestant Ascendancy politics, when in fact they were appointed by the pro-Catholic Grant.

11 *Journal of the House of Commons*, vol. 76, 1 May 1821, p. 299, and passim; Anon., *Observations on the Expediency of Erecting Provincial Penitentiaries in Ireland Which May Receive all Criminals Who Are Sentenced to Confinement and Hard Labour or Are Under the Rule of Transportation* (London: Belch, 1821). For the British SIPD's take on this, see *The Inquirer* (April 1822), article 15, 'Prison Discipline', pp. 203–20, at pp. 213–14.

12 *Report from the Select Committee Appointed To Consider the Laws Relating to Prisons*, H.C. 1822 (300), iv, pp. 3–4; Prisons Act, 1823 (4 Geo. IV, c. 64); *Hansard*, vol. 10, 2nd ser., 19 February 1824, col. 242; Gash, *Peel*, pp. 315–17.

13 James Elmes to Charles Grant, 18 April 1821 (NAI, CSORP 1820/432); James Elmes to Charles Grant, 16 November 1821 (NAI, CSORP 1821/110).

14 Commissioners for building a new gaol at Maryborough to William Gregory, 2 July 1824 (NAI, CSORP 1824/9669).

15 Joseph Robins, *Fools and Mad: A history of the insane in Ireland* (Dublin: Institute of Public Administration, 1986), p. 34, incorrectly claims that Grant appointed a Catholic and a Protestant to the new positions of prison inspectors for political reasons, when in fact both new inspectors were evangelical high church Protestants.

16 *Prisons of Ireland: Report of inspectors general, 1823*, H.C. 1823 (342), x. An English Act of 1823 set up the less-onerous responsibility on magistrates to send an annual report concerning their gaol to the secretary of state, but the principle of information-gathering by central government was analogous, see Butler, 'Rethinking the Origins of the British Prisons Act'.

17 Prisons Act, 1822 (Ireland), 3 Geo. IV, c. 64, ss. 31–2, 49.

18 Public Works Loans Act, 1822 (Ireland), 3 Geo. IV, c. 112; Support of Commercial Credit Act, 1823 (Ireland), 4 Geo. IV, c. 42; Public Works Loans Act, 1825 (Ireland), 6 Geo. IV, c. 35.

19 John Semple to James Palmer and Benjamin Blake Woodward, 1 September 1838 (NAI, CSORP 1838/2333).

20 Evans, *Fabrication of Virtue*, pp. 295–309.

21 Appendix D; Clare grand-jury presentment books, 1825 (Cambridge University Library).

22 *Prisons of Ireland: Report of inspectors general, 1823*, H.C. 1823 (342), x, pp. 5–7. See also *Third Report of the AIPPD*, pp. 22–49.

23 Ibid., p. 7.

24 Prisons Act, 1821 (Ireland), 1 & 2 Geo. IV, c. 57, s. 29; *Prisons of Ireland: Report of inspectors general, 1825*, H.C. 1825 (493), xxii, pp. 10–11.

25 Reid, *Travels*, pp. 165, 289, 292.

26 Johnston, *Forms of Constraint*, pp. 44–63.

27 Ibid., p. 208.

28 *Fifth Report of the AIPPD*, pp. 19–20.

29 Evans, *Fabrication of Virtue*, p. 286.

30 *Fifth Report of the AIPPD*, pp. 19–20; AIPPD, *Seventh Report of the Association for the Improvement of Prisons and of Prison Discipline in Ireland, for 1826* (Dublin: Goodwin, 1826), pp. 10–12 (hereafter cited as *Seventh Report of the AIPPD*). Robert Perceval, a medical doctor who addressed the annual meetings of the AIPPD in 1825 and 1826, took a dissenting view, preferring a particular type of the polygonal plan, which he confusingly termed a 'panoptic radiated plan' – see AIPPD, *Speech Delivered by Robert Perceval, at the Seventh Annual General Meeting of the Association for the Improvement of Prisons and of Prison Discipline in Ireland, 27 June 1826* (Dublin: Bentham, 1826), pp. 12–13.

31 Reid, *Travels*, p. 208.

32 Evans, *Fabrication of Virtue*, p. 440.

33 *Dictionary of Irish Architects* (www.dia.ie).

34 John Champness, *Thomas Harrison: Georgian architect of Chester and Lancaster, 1744–1829* (Lancaster: Lancaster University, 2005), p. 58.

35 John Hargrave to Henry Goulburn, 6 February 1826 (NAI, CSORP 1826/14,307); Evans, *Fabrication of Virtue*, pp. 146, 152, 165 (illus.).

36 *Account of All Gaols … in the … United Kingdom*, H.C. 1819 (137), xvii, pp. 6–7.

37 *Report … on the State of Gaols*, H.C. 1819 (579), vii, pp. 208–9.

38 *First Report of the AIPPD*, pp. 21–2.

39 *Belfast Newsletter*, 12 September 1820; Francis Johnston to R. Robinson, 30 November 1821 (NAI, CSORP 1822/573); Reid, *Travels*, pp. 211–12; Appendix D.

40 See Appendix B.

41 *Fourth Report … on … the Prisons of Ireland, 1826*, H.C. 1826 (173), xxiii, p. 27; photographs taken *c.* 1900 (Donegal

County Archives).

42 *Seventh Report … on … the Prisons of Ireland, 1829*, H.C. 1829 (10), xiii, p. 35.

43 Reid, *Travels*, pp. 206–7; AIPPD, *Fourth Report of the Association for the Improvement of Prisons, and of Prison Discipline in Ireland, for 1822* (Dublin: Goodwin, 1823), pp. 41–2 (hereafter cited as *Fourth Report of the AIPPD*), Appendix D.

44 Plan, elevation and section drawings for a new gaol in Carrick-on-Shannon, as built, n.d., n.s. [*c.* 1821] (NLI, AD 2646–7, 2650–1); Plan, elevation and section drawings for a smaller new gaol in Carrick-on-Shannon, unexecuted, n.d., n.s. [*c.* 1821] (NLI, AD 2659–60); *Third Report of the AIPPD*, p. 42; *Prisons of Ireland: Report of inspectors general, 1825*, H.C. 1825 (493), xxii, p. 33; Appendix D.

45 James Shiel to William Gregory, 24 December 1817 (NAI, SPO 570/494/21); Drawings for a new gaol (1817) and a new gaol and courthouse (February 1820) in Mullingar, by James Shiel (see photographic copies in the Irish Architectural Archive, 088/063: C. 15/403–8); Commissioners of the Board of Works to William Gregory, 10 March 1821 (NAI, CSORP 1821/1247); Westmeath grand-jury presentment book, summer 1822 (Westmeath County Library, WMGJ/AP/11); *Prisons of Ireland: Report of inspectors general, 1823*, H.C. 1823 (342), x, pp. 6, 39.

46 Francis Johnston to Robert Robinson, 4 November 1823 (NAI, CSORP 1823/7131); *Freeman's Journal*, 17 March 1823; *Westmeath Journal*, 20 March 1823; Plan drawings for Mullingar gaol, n.d., n.s. [*c.* 1824] (NLI, AD 2649); *Sixth Report … on … the Prisons of Ireland, 1828*, H.C. 1828 (68), xii, p. 50; Appendix D.

47 *Westmeath Guardian & Longford Newsletter*, 17 March 1836; Plan drawing for Mullingar gaol, n.d. [*c.* 1836], n.s. (Irish Architectural Archive, Guinness Collection, Acc.96/68.5/5/3); photograph of the entrance gateway of Mullingar gaol, n.d. [*c.* 1900] (Westmeath County Library, Westmeath Photographic Collection, M/1 (33)).

48 *Report … on the State of Gaols*, H.C. 1819 (579), vii, p. 214.

49 *Inspector General's Report of … the Prisons in Ireland for … 1818*, H.C. 1819 (534), xii, pp. 18–19.

50 Lord Forbes to William Gregory, 17 December 1820 (NAI, CSORP 1820/592); Lord Longford to Henry Goulburn, 22 January 1826 (NAI, CSORP 1825/12,783); Plan, elevation and section drawings for Longford gaol and surrounding buildings, n.d., n.s. [*c.* 1821] (NLI, AD 2652–7); Appendix D.

51 *Prisons of Ireland: Report of inspectors general, 1825*, H.C. 1825 (493), xxii, pp. 50–1.

52 Longford grand-jury presentment books, 1818–23 (Longford County Library, LGJ/2/3–6).

53 *Prisons of Ireland: Report of inspectors general, 1823*, H.C. 1823 (342), x, pp. 6, 32. Alterations and additions by Richard Robinson in 1820–1 did little to allay the inspectors' concerns – see Kildare grand-jury presentment books, 1820–1 (Kildare County Library, GJ). See also *Third Report of the AIPPD*, p. 39.

54 *Prisons of Ireland: Report of Inspectors General, 1824*, H.C. 1824 (294), xxii, p. 33.

55 *Fourth Report … on … the Prisons of Ireland, 1826*, H.C. 1826 (173), xxiii, pp. 29–30; Kildare grand-jury presentment books, 1824–5 (Kildare County Library, GJ); Appendix D.

56 J.M. Bagot to William Gregory, 5 March 1825 (NAI, CSORP 1825/11,066); John Hamilton to William Gregory, 16 August 1825 (NAI, CSORP 1825/12,000); *Freeman's Journal*, 27 November 1827; Tierney, *The Buildings of Ireland: Central Leinster*, pp. 96–7.

57 *Prisons of Ireland: Report of inspectors general, 1824*, H.C. 1824 (294), xxii, pp. 32–3.

58 *Prisons of Ireland: Report of inspectors general, 1823*, H.C. 1823 (342), x, p. 6.

59 Presentments passed at Kildare summer assizes, 1825, 14 July 1825 (NAI, SPO 588 AAB 944); Kildare grand-jury presentment books, 1824–5 (Kildare County Library, GJ).

60 R. Robinson to Henry Goulburn, 23 August 1825 (NAI, CSORP 1825/12,000).

61 William Murray to R. Robinson, 2 August 1827 (NAI, CSORP 1827/572); *Sixth Report … on … the Prisons of Ireland, 1828*, H.C. 1828 (68), xii, p. 42.

62 *Eleventh Report … on … the Prisons of Ireland, 1833*, H.C. 1833 (67), xvii, p. 39; Appendix D.

63 Site map for the new gaol at Naas, Co. Kildare, 1825, by John Longford (NLI, MS 21 F 35, no. 44); photographs of the new gaol (Naas Local History Group).

64 *Tenth Report … on … the Prisons of Ireland, 1832*, H.C. 1831–2 (152), xxiii, p. 26.

65 *Belfast Newsletter*, 5 August 1817.

66 Ibid., 28 July 1818 and 10 August 1819.

67 Ibid., 13 August, 1 October 1819, and 7 January 1820.

68 Ibid., 18 April 1820.

69 David Verey and Alan Brooks, *The Buildings of England: Gloucestershire 2: the Vale and the Forest of Dean*, 3rd ed. (New Haven and London: Yale University Press, 2002), pp. 464–5.

70 Colvin, *Biographical Dictionary*, pp. 847–9.

71 Bundle of ten letters, including reports by Francis Johnston, Robert Reid and James Palmer, and a memorandum prepared by Justice Arthur Moore, 1821–3 (NAI, CSORP 1823/6726); Drawing showing Downpatrick gaol, n.d., n.s. [*c.* 1820] (NLI, AD 2641).

72 *Prisons of Ireland: Report of inspectors general, 1823*, H.C. 1823 (342), x, p. 6.

73 James Waddell, 'Account of Money … Expended on the New Gaol at Downpatrick', 17 May 1827 (NAI, CSORP 1827/1956); *Prisons of Ireland: Report of inspectors general, 1825*, H.C. 1825 (493), xxii, p. 28; Appendix D.

74 *Eighth Report … on … the Prisons of Ireland, 1830*, H.C. 1830 (48), xxiv, p. 35; *Eleventh Report … on … the Prisons of*

Ireland, 1833, H.C. 1833 (67), xvii, pp. 37–8. For a more complete analysis see Windrum, 'Provision and Practice of Prison Reform in County Down', pp. 334–47.

75 McParland, 'Public Work of Architects', p. 252.

76 *Fifth Report of the AIPPD*, p. 33; Appendix A.

77 *Inspector General's Report of … the Prisons in Ireland for … 1807*, H.C. 1808 (239), ix, p. 14; *Accounts of Presentments by Grand Juries in Ireland … in 1807*, H.C. 1808 (205), xiii, pp. 272, 306; *Inspector General's Report of … the Prisons in Ireland, for … 1818*, H.C. 1819 (534), xii, p. 21. *Account of All Gaols … in the … United Kingdom*, H.C. 1819 (137), xvii, pp. 6–7. See also Johnston, *Forms of Constraint*, pp. 58–9.

78 Desmond Mooney, 'The Origins of Agrarian Violence in Meath, 1790–1828', *Ríocht na Midhe – Records of Meath Archaeological and Historical Society*, vol. 8, no. 1, 1987, pp. 45–67, at pp. 57, 60, 67.

79 *Prisons of Ireland: Report of inspectors general, 1824*, H.C. 1824 (294), xxii, p. 6.

80 *Sixth Report … on … the Prisons of Ireland, 1828*, H.C. 1828 (68), xii, pp. 46–7; William Murray to R. Robinson, 22 October 1827 (NAI, CSORP 1827/1508); William Murray to R. Robinson, 10 January 1828 (NAI, CSORP 1828/110).

81 *Eighth Report … on … the Prisons of Ireland, 1830*, H.C. 1830 (48), xxiv, pp. 40–1; *Thirteenth Report … on … the Prisons of Ireland, 1835*, H.C. 1835 (114), xxxvi, p. 30.

82 Mooney, 'Agrarian Violence in Meath, 1790–1828', p. 67; Desmond Mooney, 'A Society in Crisis: Agrarian violence in Meath, 1828–1835', *Ríocht na Midhe – Records of Meath Archaeological and Historical Society*, vol. 8, no. 2, 1988–9, pp. 102–28.

83 Evans, *Fabrication of Virtue*, p. 251.

84 *The Architect*, vol. 40, 7 December 1888, supplement, p. 1; and ibid., 28 December 1888, supplement, p. 5.

85 AIPPD, *Speech Delivered by Robert Perceval, at the Sixth Annual General Meeting of the Association for the Improvement of Prisons and of Prison Discipline in Ireland, 27 June 1825* (Dublin: Goodwin, 1825), p. 8.

86 Evans, *Fabrication of Virtue*, p. 331.

87 AIPPD, *Analysis of the Inspectors Generals' Report on the Prisons … of Ireland for the Year 1827* (Dublin: publisher unknown, *c.* 1828). The National Library of Ireland has a copy of this booklet.

88 Hoppen, *Governing Hibernia*, pp. 46–8, 48–9, 71. See also Virginia Crossman, 'Emergency Legislation and Agrarian Disorder in Ireland, 1821–41', *Irish Historical Studies*, vol. 27, no. 108, November 1991, pp. 309–23.

89 *Twelfth Report … on … the Prisons of Ireland, 1834*, H.C. 1834 (63), xl, p. 5. The effectiveness of the inspectors was questioned by some contemporary writers – see for example Alexander Wilson, *Outlines of a Plan for the Improvement of Prison Discipline* (Dublin: Milliken, 1830), pp. 7–9. Wilson was a deputy-governor of the Richmond bridewell.

90 See for example Hibernian Ladies' Society for Promoting the Improvement of Female Prisoners, *Second Report of the Hibernian Ladies' Society for Promoting the Improvement of Female Prisoners* (Dublin: Bentham, 1828).

91 *Seventh Report … on … the Prisons of Ireland, 1829*, H.C. 1829 (10), xiii, pp. 16–20; Elizabeth Fry and Joseph John Gurney, *Report Addressed to the Marquess Wellesley, Lord Lieutenant of Ireland, Respecting Their Late Visit to that Country* (London: Arch, 1827); *The Kilkenny Independent*, 27 November 1827.

92 *Eighth Report … on … the Prisons of Ireland, 1830*, H.C. 1830 (48), xxiv, p. 7. Other progressive developments of the time included the consolidation of the prison-reform acts in 1826 by Henry Goulburn (Prisons Act, 1826 (Ireland), 7 Geo. IV, c. 74) and the praise for the Irish central-government inspectors in various British prison inquiries, including a call from the Inverness gentry for a similar system to be adopted in Scotland – see *Report … on the State of Prisons in Scotland*, H.C. 1826 (381), v, p. 81; *Report … on Criminal Commitments and Convictions*, H.C. 1828 (545), vi, p. 90.

93 John Sealy Townsend and Benjamin Blake Woodward to William Gregory, 26 March 1821 (NAI, CSORP 1821/1134).

94 Heaney, 'Ireland's Penitentiary', pp. 30–4; Wilson, *Outlines of a Plan for the Improvement of Prison Discipline*.

95 *Prisons of Ireland: Report of inspectors general, 1823*, H.C. 1823 (342), x, pp. 10–11; *Prisons of Ireland: Report of inspectors general, 1825*, H.C. 1825 (493), xxii, p. 8.

96 Heaney, 'Ireland's Penitentiary', p. 32; Whelan, *Bible War in Ireland*.

97 *Sixth Report … on … the Prisons of Ireland, 1828*, H.C. 1828 (68), xii, pp. 23–6; *Eleventh Report … on … the Prisons of Ireland, 1833*, H.C. 1833 (67), xvii, p. 16.

98 *Prisons of Ireland: Report of inspectors general, 1823*, H.C. 1823 (342), x, pp. 14–20.

99 *Prisons of Ireland: Report of inspectors general, 1825*, H.C. 1825 (493), xxii, pp. 18–19; *Fourth Report … on … the Prisons of Ireland, 1826*, H.C. 1826 (173), xxiii, p. 13.

100 *Journal of the House of Commons*, vol. 81, 21 March 1826, pp. 191, 755–76, and plate B: general outline of a plan of a prison, n.d., by David Henry of Dublin.

101 Report by John Semple, Jnr, 10 November 1836 (NAI, SPO OP 1837/86); *Freeman's Journal*, 6 October 1838; Newgate Gaol Dublin Act, 1840 (3 & 4 Vict., c. 53); Newgate Gaol Dublin Act, 1842 (5 & 6 Vict., c. 6).

102 *Eleventh Report … on … the Prisons of Ireland, 1833*, H.C. 1833 (67), xvii, p. 16; *Twelfth Report … on … the Prisons of Ireland, 1834*, H.C. 1834 (63), xl, p. 18.

103 *Analysis of the Inspectors Generals' Report on the Prisons … of Ireland for the Year 1827*, p. 12.

104 *Freeman's Journal*, 23 April 1828.

105 Isaac Weld, *Statistical Survey of the County of Roscommon* (Dublin: Graisberry, 1832), p. 420.

106 Reid, *Travels*, pp. 374–5.

107 Mr & Mrs Samuel Carter Hall, *Ireland: Its scenery, character, etc.*, 3 vols (London: How & Parsons, 1841–3), vol. 3, p. 183.

108 *Twelfth Report … on … the Prisons of Ireland, 1834*, H.C. 1834 (63), xl, pp. 5–6.

109 Evans, *Fabrication of Virtue*, p. 92. They reduced the diet, for example, at Carrick on Shannon in 1823 and Lifford in 1824, see *Prisons of Ireland: Report of inspectors general, 1823*, H.C. 1823 (342), xi, p. 34; *Prisons of Ireland. Report of inspectors general, 1824*, H.C. 1824 (294), xxii, p. 31.

110 *Inspector General's Report of … the Prisons in Ireland, for … 1818*, H.C. 1819 (534), xii, p. 4–5.

111 *Prisons of Ireland: Report of Inspectors General, 1825*, H.C. 1825 (493), xxii, pp. 39–40; *Fourth Report … on … the Prisons of Ireland, 1826*, H.C. 1826 (173), xxiii, p. 25; *Seventh Report … on … the Prisons of Ireland, 1829*, H.C. 1829 (10), xiii, pp. 34–5; Appendix B.

112 King's County presentments books, spring and summer assizes 1821 (Cambridge University Library); Plan drawings for Tullamore gaol, 1820, by William Murray (Irish Architectural Archive, RIAI Murray Collection, Acc.92/46.1194–6); Plan and elevation drawings for Tullamore gaol as built, n.d, n.s. [*c.* 1826] (NLI, AD 2642–5, 2662).

113 *Third Report of the AIPPD*, p. 40.

114 Lord Tullamore to Henry Goulburn, 14 September 1826 (NAI, CSORP 1826/13,514); Printed notice explaining the procession at the laying of the foundation stone of Tullamore's new gaol, 13 September 1826 (Westmeath County Library, Howard Bury papers, P1/28), Byrne, *Legal Offaly*, pp. 391–5; Appendix D.

115 Tierney, *The Buildings of Ireland: Central Leinster*, pp. 303, 621–2.

116 Queen's County presentments books, summer assizes 1821 (Cambridge University Library); *Prisons of Ireland: Report of inspectors general, 1824*, H.C. 1824 (294), xxii, p. 7.

117 Memorandum of the inhabitants of Queen's County to the Lord Lieutenant, n.d. [1823] (NAI, CSORP 1823/6075); Robert Vicars to William Gregory, 18 February 1824 (NAI, CSORP 1823/6075); *Fourth Report … on … the Prisons of Ireland, 1826*, H.C. 1826 (173), xxiii, p. 50.

118 *Fifth Report … on … the Prisons of Ireland, 1827*, H.C. 1826–7 (471), xi, p. 7; Appendix D.

119 Dan Cruickshank, *A Guide to the Georgian Buildings of Great Britain and Ireland* (London: Rizzoli, 1985), p. 159; Tierney, *The Buildings of Ireland: Central Leinster*, p. 548.

120 William Murray to R. Robinson, 25 April 1828 (NAI, CSORP 1828/556); *Dublin Builder*, vol. 4, no. 52, 15 February 1862, p. 43; *Seventh Report … on … the Prisons of Ireland, 1829*, H.C. 1829 (10), xiii, pp. 9, 46; *Tenth Report … on … the Prisons of Ireland, 1832*, H.C. 1831–2 (152), xxiii, pp. 34–5.

121 Grand Jury Act, 1833 (Ireland), 3 & 4 Will. IV, c. 78; Grand Jury Act, 1836 (Ireland), 6 & 7 Will. IV, c. 116.

122 Clare grand-jury presentment books, summer assizes 1839 (Cambridge University Library).

123 Assizes Act, 1835 (Ireland), 5 & 6 Will. IV, c. 26; Grand Jury Act, 1836 (Ireland), 6 & 7 Will. IV, c. 116, ss. 176–7.

124 *Eleventh Report … on … the Prisons of Ireland, 1833*, H.C. 1833 (67), xvii, pp. 6–7.

125 Palmer, *Treatise on the Modern System of Government Gaols*, pp. vi, 85, 90, 91.

126 *Report … on Secondary Punishments*, H.C. 1831–2 (547), vii, pp. 119, 127–8; *Second Report from the Select Committee of the House of Lords Appointed To Inquire into the Present State of the Several Gaols and Houses of Correction in England and Wales*, H.C. 1835 (439), xi, pp. 329, 341–2; Prisons Act, 1835, 5 & 6 Will. IV, c. 38; Butler, 'Rethinking the Origins of the British Prisons Act'.

127 *Returns of Reports … on Complaints Forwarded to the Irish Government … and of Evidence Relative to the Mode of Conducting the Convict Service in Ireland*, H.C. 1843 (547), xlii, pp. 41, 53, 74.

128 Clare grand-jury presentment books, spring and summer assizes 1833 (Cambridge University Library).

129 Evans, *Fabrication of Virtue*, pp. 310–17 (illus.).

130 Ibid., pp. 318–23, 386–7.

131 *Fourteenth Report … on … the Prisons of Ireland, 1836*, H.C. 1836 (118), xxxv, pp. 7–8.

132 *Eighth Report … on … the Prisons of Ireland, 1830*, H.C. 1830 (48), xxiv, pp. 53–4; *Eleventh Report … on … the Prisons of Ireland, 1833*, H.C. 1833 (67), xvii, p. 23; *Fifteenth Report … on … the Prisons of Ireland, 1837*, H.C. 1837 (123), xxxi, pp. 36–7; Plan drawings for an addition to the town gaol of Galway, March 1830, by Frederick Darley, Jnr (Galway County Archives, GS11-02-1).

133 *Tenth Report … on … the Prisons of Ireland, 1832*, H.C. 1831–2 (152), xxiii, p. 5; *Fourteenth Report … on … the Prisons of Ireland, 1836*, H.C. 1836 (118), xxxv, pp. 40–1; Frederick Darley to William Gregory, 19 May 1829 (NAI, CSORP 1829/671); *The Mayo Constitution*, 7 June 1830, 14 October 1830, and 5 March 1835; Appendix D.

134 *The Connaught Telegraph*, 6 August 1834, 19 August 1835, 19 July 1837, and 7 March 1838; Dickson, *Dublin*, pp. 271, 301; Gibney, Hurley and McParland, *Building Site in Eighteenth-century Ireland*, pp. 135–6.

135 Binns, *Miseries and Beauties*, vol. 1, p. 373; Thackeray, *Irish Sketch Book*, p. 241; Lacy, *Sights and Scenes*, pp. 281–2.

136 *Twenty-second Report … on … the Prisons of Ireland, 1844*, H.C. 1844 (535), xxviii, p. 51; *Twenty-eighth Report … on … the Prisons of Ireland, 1850*, H.C. 1850 (1229), xxix, p. 58.

137 H.R. Paine to William Gossey, 9 July 1834 (NAI, CSORP 1834/2880); *Thirteenth Report … on … the Prisons of Ireland, 1835*, H.C. 1835 (114), xxxvi, p. 41; *Fourteenth Report … on … the Prisons of Ireland, 1836*, H.C. 1836 (118), xxxv, pp. 38–9.

138 John B. Keane to the Lord Lieutenant, 22 August 1831 (NAI, CSORP 1831/2229); *Clonmel Advertiser*, 8 February 1832; *Seventh Report … on … the Prisons of Ireland, 1829*, H.C. 1829 (10), xiii, pp. 60–1; Appendix D.

139 *Fourteenth Report … on … the Prisons of Ireland, 1836*, H.C. 1836 (118), xxxv, p. 42.

140 Ibid., pp. 11–12.

141 Richmond Penitentiary Act, 1836 (Ireland), 6 & 7 Will. IV, c. 51; *Fifteenth Report … on … the Prisons of Ireland, 1837*, H.C. 1837 (123), xxxi, p. 6.

142 *Sixteenth Report … on … the Prisons of Ireland, 1838*, H.C. 1837–8 (186), xxix, pp. 8, 20–1; *Eighteenth Report … on … the Prisons of Ireland, 1840*, H.C. 1840 (240), xxvi, pp. 7, 20; *Freeman's Journal*, 13 November 1837 and 28 September 1838. I am grateful to Frank Keohane for several of these references.

143 *Fifteenth Report … on … the Prisons of Ireland, 1837*, H.C. 1837 (123), xxxi, pp. 16–17; *Seventeenth Report … on … the Prisons of Ireland, 1839*, H.C. 1839 (91), xx, pp. 18–19; Appendix D.

144 *Twentieth Report … on … the Prisons of Ireland, 1842*, H.C. 1842 (377), xxii, p. 22.

145 Newgate Gaol Dublin Act, 1840, 3 & 4 Vict., c. 53.

146 Four Courts Marshalsea Act, 1842 (Ireland), 5 & 6 Vict., c. 95.

147 Poor Relief Act, 1838 (Ireland), 1 & 2 Vict., c. 56.

148 Markus Reuber, 'Moral Management and the "Unseen Eye": Public lunatic asylums in Ireland, 1800–1845', in Elizabeth Malcolm and Greta Jones (eds), *Medicine, Disease, and the State in Ireland, 1650–1940* (Cork: Cork University Press, 1999), pp. 208–33.

149 Criminal Lunatics Act, 1838 (Ireland), 1 & 2 Vict., c. 27.

150 Criminal Lunatic Act, 1845 (Ireland), 8 & 9 Vict., c. 107; *Civil Engineer and Architect's Journal*, vol. 14, 15 February 1851, p. 133.

151 Municipal Corporations Act, 1840 (Ireland), 3 & 4 Vict., c. 108; Dickson, *Dublin*, pp. 338–9.

Chapter 7 – A Separate Agenda: Conformity, consolidation, the Famine, and its aftermath, 1838–55

1 *Eighteenth Report … on … the Prisons of Ireland, 1840*, H.C. 1840 (240), xxvi, p. 29; Evans, *Fabrication of Virtue*, pp. 318–20.

2 Evans, *Fabrication of Virtue*, pp. 320–5 (illus.).

3 Ibid., pp. 349–67 (illus.).

4 Johnston, *Forms of Constraint*, pp. 89–98.

5 *Fifteenth Report … on … the Prisons of Ireland, 1837*, H.C. 1837 (123), xxxi, p. 5.

6 Prisons Act, 1840 (Ireland), 3 & 4 Vict., c. 44, s. 3.

7 O'Dwyer, 'Public Works Architecture', p. 181; Johnston, *Forms of Constraint*, pp. 97–8.

8 See, for example, Subscriptions of County Wicklow gentry to appeal for funds for building a new gaol, 1786 (NLI, MS 15,303).

9 Anon., *First Report of the Association for Bettering the Condition of the Prisoners in the County Gaol of Wicklow* (Dublin: Goodwin, 1820); Forster Archer to William Gregory, 2 March 1819 (NAI, CSORP 1819/14); John Revell to William Gregory, 5 September 1820 (NAI, CSORP 1820/1080); Wicklow grand-jury presentment books, summer 1820, and summer 1823 (Wicklow County Archives, GJ).

10 *Fourteenth Report … on … the Prisons of Ireland, 1836*, H.C. 1836 (118), xxxv, pp. 45–6.

11 *Sixteenth Report … on … the Prisons of Ireland, 1838*, H.C. 1837–8 (186), xxix, p. 54; *Seventeenth Report … on … the Prisons of Ireland, 1839*, H.C. 1839 (91), xx, pp. 56–7; *Nineteenth Report … on … the Prisons of Ireland, 1841*, H.C. 1841 (299), xi, pp. 59–60; *Twenty-first Report … on … the Prisons of Ireland, 1843*, H.C. 1843 (462), xxvii, pp. 3, 85.

12 Wicklow grand-jury presentment books, spring and summer 1840 (Wicklow County Archives, GJ).

13 See Appendix B.

14 *Fifth Report … on … the Prisons of Ireland, 1827*, H.C. 1826–7 (471), xi, p. 31; *Sixth Report … on … the Prisons of Ireland, 1828*, H.C. 1828 (68), xii, p. 41.

15 *Ninth Report … on … the Prisons of Ireland, 1831*, H.C. 1830–1 (172), iv, p. 26; *Tenth Report … on … the Prisons of Ireland, 1829*, H.C. 1831–2 (152), xxiii, p. 25; *Thirteenth Report … on … the Prisons of Ireland, 1835*, H.C. 1835 (114), xxxvi, p. 26.

16 *Fourteenth Report … on … the Prisons of Ireland, 1836*, H.C. 1836 (118), xxxv, p. 24; *Sixteenth Report … on … the Prisons of Ireland, 1838*, H.C. 1837–8 (186), xxix, pp. 27–8.

17 *Eighteenth Report … on … the Prisons of Ireland, 1840*, H.C. 1840 (240), xxvi, pp. 30–1; *Twentieth Report … on … the Prisons of Ireland, 1842*, H.C. 1842 (377), xxii, pp. 6, 70–1; *Twenty-first Report … on … the Prisons of Ireland, 1843*, H.C. 1843 (462), xxvii, pp. 3, 36–7; see Appendix D.

18 *Twenty-third Report … on … the Prisons of Ireland, 1845*, H.C. 1845 (620), xxv, pp. 20–1; Contract drawings, letters, and accounts, 1841–6, by William Farrell (PRONI, FER/4/6/7-50); *Dublin Evening Mail*, 3 February 1843.

19 For the house of correction and other additions built in Wexford between 1823 and 1829, see *Prisons of Ireland: Report of inspectors general, 1825*, H.C. 1825 (493), xxii, pp. 37–8; *Seventh Report … on … the Prisons of Ireland, 1829*, H.C. 1829 (10), xii, pp. 9, 64; Bundle of five letters between Arthur Walker, William Gregory, and R. Robinson, 31 March to 9 May 1827 (NAI, CSORP 1827/481). See also *Freeman's Journal*, 15 March 1820; *Fourteenth Report … on … the Prisons of Ireland, 1836*, H.C. 1836 (118), xxxv, p. 45.

20 *Sixteenth Report … on … the Prisons of Ireland, 1838*, H.C. 1837–8 (186), xxix, pp. 52–3.
21 Wicklow grand-jury presentment book, spring 1840 (Wicklow County Archives, GJ)
22 *Seventeenth Report … on … the Prisons of Ireland, 1839*, H.C. 1839 (91), xx, pp. 55–6; *Freeman's Journal*, 8 July 1839.
23 *Saunders' Newsletter*, 2 March 1841; Charles Walker to H.R. Paine (NAI, CSORP 1841/G15264); H.R. Paine, memo re Wexford gaol, 24 August 1843 (ibid., CSORP 1843/G11630); *Twenty-first Report … on … the Prisons of Ireland, 1843*, H.C. 1843 (462), xxvii, pp. 83–5; *Twenty-second Report … on … the Prisons of Ireland, 1844*, H.C. 1844 (535), xxviii, pp. 98–9; *Twenty-third Report … on … the Prisons of Ireland, 1845*, H.C. 1845 (620), xxv, pp. 79–81; *Twenty-fourth Report … on … the Prisons of Ireland, 1846*, H.C. 1846 (697), xx, pp. 89–90.
24 *Twenty-fifth Report … on … the Prisons of Ireland, 1847*, H.C. 1847 (805), xxix, p. 101. D.S. Richardson misleadingly states that this façade was built in 1812 – see *Gothic Revival Architecture in Ireland* (New York and London: Garland, 1983), p. 313, plate 175.
25 Asenath Nicholson, *Ireland's Welcome to the Stranger, or, Excursions through Ireland in 1844 & 1845, for the Purpose of Personally Investigating the Condition of the Poor* (London: Gilpin, 1847), pp. 220–1.
26 *Twenty-third Report … on … the Prisons of Ireland, 1845*, H.C. 1845 (620), xxv, pp. 39–41; Contract drawings for enlarging Kilmainham gaol, 22 March 1844, by Park Neville (Irish Architectural Archive, McCurdy and Mitchell Collection, Acc. 82/49/71/1).
27 *Twentieth Report … on … the Prisons of Ireland, 1842*, H.C. 1842 (377), xxii, p. 71.
28 *Twenty-second report … on … the Prisons of Ireland, 1844*, H.C. 1844 (535), xxviii, pp. 7, 94–6.
29 *Twenty-fourth Report … on … the Prisons of Ireland, 1846*, H.C. 1846 (697), xx, pp. 23–5.
30 Ibid., pp. 13–17.
31 *Twenty-first report … on … the Prisons of Ireland, 1843*, H.C. 1843 (462), xxvii, pp. 54–5; *Twenty-second Report … on … the Prisons of Ireland, 1844*, H.C. 1844 (535), xxviii, pp. 67–8.
32 *Twenty-first Report … on … the Prisons of Ireland, 1843*, H.C. 1843 (462), xxvii, pp. 56–7. See also O'Dwyer, 'Public Works Architecture', p. 180; Teresa Kelly, 'The Old Gaol, Now Hanover Works', *Carloviana*, vol. 1, no. 9, December 1960, pp. 38–9.
33 See Appendix B.
34 *Belfast Newsletter*, 13 March 1813 and 13 June 1815; *Inspector General's Report of … the Prisons in Ireland for … 1818*, H.C. 1819 (534), xii, p. 3; Reid, *Travels*, pp. 176–7; Lewis, *Topographical Dictionary*, vol. 1, p. 197; McSkimmin, *Carrickfergus*, p. 173; Benn, *Belfast*, vol. 2, p. 79.
35 *Sixth Report … on … the Prisons of Ireland, 1828*, H.C. 1828 (68), xii, pp. 36–7; *Ninth Report … on … the Prisons of Ireland, 1831*, H.C. 1830–1 (172), iv, p. 22; *Eleventh Report … on … the Prisons of Ireland, 1833*, H.C. 1833 (67), xvii, pp. 35–6.
36 *Twelfth Report … on … the Prisons of Ireland, 1834*, H.C. 1834 (63), xxxx, p. 38.
37 *Fifteenth Report … on … the Prisons of Ireland, 1837*, H.C. 1837 (123), xxxi, p. 19.
38 *Sixteenth Report … on … the Prisons of Ireland, 1838*, H.C. 1837–8 (186), xxix, p. 8, 24; 54; McSkimmin, *Carrickfergus*, p. 512. See also O'Dwyer, 'Public Works Architecture', p. 184.
39 *Seventeenth Report … on … the Prisons of Ireland, 1839*, H.C. 1839 (91), xx, pp. 52–3; see also Appendix B.
40 Murphy, *Two Tipperarys*, pp. 61–104.
41 Ibid., p. 122. See also *Seventeenth Report … on … the Prisons of Ireland, 1839*, H.C. 1839 (91), xx, pp. 52–3.
42 *Nenagh Guardian*, 17 March 1841, 30 September 1843; Murphy, *Two Tipperarys*, pp. 122, 125.
43 *Nenagh Guardian*, 4 September 1839; Murphy, *Two Tipperarys*, pp. 114–18.
44 Bundle of letters concerning the building of Belfast house of correction, 1845 (NAI, CSORP 1845/G3238); McSkimmin, *Carrickfergus*, p. 511; O'Dwyer, 'Public Works Architecture', p. 181.
45 Eleven contract drawings, 1842–3, by Charles Lanyon (Northern Ireland Prison Service Agency); Three drawings, showing various details of the prison, 1843–50, by Charles Lanyon (PRONI, LA/1/8/JA/111, 113–14); O'Dwyer, 'Public Works Architecture', pp. 181–5.
46 McSkimmin, *Carrickfergus*, p. 512; O'Dwyer, 'Public Works Architecture', pp. 181–2.
47 O'Dwyer, 'Public Works Architecture', p. 184.
48 Evans, *Fabrication of Virtue*, p. 348.
49 *Twenty-fifth Report … on … the Prisons of Ireland, 1847*, H.C. 1847 (805), xxix, pp. 31–6.
50 *Twenty-second Report … on … the Prisons of Ireland, 1844*, H.C. 1844 (535), xxviii, pp. 7, 29–30; *Twenty-third Report … on … the Prisons of Ireland, 1845*, H.C. 1845 (620), xxv, pp. 6, 12–14; Prisons Act, 1846 (Ireland), 9 & 10 Vict., c. 61; *Twenty-eighth Report … on … the Prisons of Ireland, 1850*, H.C. 1850 (1229), xxix, pp. 33–8; *Belfast Newsletter*, 1 September 1850; McSkimmin, *Carrickfergus*, pp. 109, 512; O'Dwyer, 'Public Works Architecture', p. 184.
51 The inspectors noted the usefulness of the railway for transporting prisoners – see *Twenty-fifth Report … on … the Prisons of Ireland, 1847*, H.C. 1847 (805), xxix, p. 33.
52 *Eighteenth Report … on … the Prisons of Ireland, 1840*, H.C. 1840 (240), xxvi, pp. 7, 58.
53 *Twenty-first Report … on … the Prisons of Ireland, 1843*, H.C. 1843 (462), xxvii, pp. 77–8; *Twenty-second Report … on … the Prisons of Ireland, 1844*, H.C. 1844 (535), xxviii, pp. 7, 93–4; *Nenagh Guardian*, 27 July 1843.
54 *Twenty-third Report … on … the Prisons of Ireland, 1845*, H.C. 1845 (620), xxv, pp. 72–4.

55 *Twenty-seventh Report … on … the Prisons of Ireland, 1849*, H.C. 1849 (1069), xxvi, pp. 96–7.

56 Murphy, *Two Tipperarys*, pp. 122, 125.

57 *Nenagh Guardian*, 10 June 1841.

58 James Palmer to James Buchanon, 14 August 1845 (University of Michigan Bentley Historical Library, Ann Arbor, MI, DuLong family collection).

59 See Appendix B.

60 *Twentieth Report … on … the Prisons of Ireland, 1842*, H.C. 1842 (377), xxii, p. 5; Patrick Long, 'Francis White', in McGuire and Quinn, *Dictionary of Irish Biography*, vol. 9, pp. 884–5; Grimsley-Smith, 'Lunatic Asylums', pp. 95–118.

61 Francis White, *Report and Observations on the State of the Poor of Dublin* (Dublin: Joshua Porter, 1833); *First Report of Commissioners for Inquiring into the Condition of the Poorer Classes in Ireland*, H.C. 1836 (35), xxxi, p. ii; *Report of the Commissioners Appointed to Revise the Several Laws Under … Which Moneys Are Now Raised by Grand Jury Presentment in Ireland*, H.C. 1842 (386), xxiv, pp. 98–99.

62 James Palmer to Thomas W. Palmer, 4 April 1842 (University of Michigan Bentley Historical Library, Ann Arbor, MI, DuLong family collection).

63 Ibid.

64 *Returns of Reports … on Complaints Forwarded to the Irish government … and of Evidence Relative to the Mode of Conducting the Convict Service in Ireland*, H.C. 1843 (547), xlii, pp. 41, 53, 74. See also Grimsley-Smith, 'Lunatic Asylums', pp. 110–13.

65 McDowell, *Irish Administration*, p. 147.

66 Hungerford Hoskyns to John Arkwright, 4 January and 6 April 1843 (University of Michigan Bentley Historical Library, Ann Arbor, MI, DuLong family collection).

67 *Twenty-fourth Report … on … the Prisons of Ireland, 1846*, H.C. 1846 (697), xx, p. 8.

68 James Palmer to James Buchanon, 14 August 1845 and 7 May 1847; James Palmer to Thomas W. Palmer, 26 February 1848 (University of Michigan Bentley Historical Library, Ann Arbor, MI, DuLong family collection). Palmer died in London on 1 May 1850 – see *The Nation*, 25 May 1850.

69 *Twenty-sixth Report … on … the Prisons of Ireland, 1847–48*, H.C. 1847–8 (952), xxiv, pp. 11–12. The other inspectors were Captain Clement Johnson, Sir Nicholas Fitzsimon, Frederic Beckford Long, James Galwey, and J. Corry Connellan. The year 1850 was the first since 1845 in which there were no new prison inspectors appointed.

70 James S. Donnelly, Jr, *The Great Irish Potato Famine* (Stroud, Gloucestershire: Sutton Publishing, 2001), and John Crowley, William J. Smyth and Mike Murphy (eds), *Atlas of the Great Irish Famine* (Cork: Cork University Press, 2012).

71 *Twenty-fifth Report … on … the Prisons of Ireland, 1847*, H.C. 1847 (805), xxix, pp. 10–11.

72 *Twenty-sixth Report … on … the Prisons of Ireland, 1847–48*, H.C. 1847–8 (952), xxiv, pp. 5–6.

73 Ibid., pp. 7–8.

74 *Twenty-seventh Report … on … the Prisons of Ireland, 1849*, H.C. 1849 (1069), xxvi, p. 5.

75 *Twenty-eighth Report … on … the Prisons of Ireland, 1850*, H.C. 1850 (1229), xxix, pp. 7–11.

76 Carlisle (viceroy), diary, 1 January 1856, quoted in Hoppen, *Governing Hibernia*, p. 94.

77 Casey, *The Buildings of Ireland: Dublin*, pp. 246–7.

78 Francis Johnston to William Gregory, 18 April 1818 (NAI, CSORP 1818/84); Lewis, *Topographical Dictionary*, vol. 1, p. 420; see Appendix D.

79 Tim Carey, *Mountjoy: The story of a prison* (Cork: Collins Press, 2000), pp. 37, 41–2 (citing NAI, CSORP 1849/G8196); Evans, *Fabrication of Virtue*, pp. 346–87; Rena Lohan, 'The Management of Female Convicts Sentenced to Transportation and Penal Servitude, 1790–1898', PhD thesis, Trinity College Dublin, 1989; Carroll-Burke, *Colonial Discipline*.

80 *Nineteenth Report … on … the Prisons of Ireland, 1841*, H.C. 1841 (299), xi, pp. 17–18.

81 James Elmes to Arthur Moore, 7 April 1821 (NAI, CSORP 1823/7065); *Fourth Report of the AIPPD*, pp. 20–1; *Prisons of Ireland: Report of inspectors general, 1823*, H.C. 1823 (342), x, pp. 10–11.

82 *Fourth Report … on … the Prisons of Ireland, 1826*, H.C. 1826 (173), xxiii, p. 42.

83 *Fourteenth Report … on … the Prisons of Ireland, 1836*, H.C. 1836 (118), xxxv, pp. 34–5; Lewis, *Topographical Dictionary*, vol. 1, p. 420.

84 *Twenty-sixth Report … on … the Prisons of Ireland, 1847–48*, H.C. 1847–8 (952), xxiv, pp. 6, 8, 11–12; *Twenty-seventh Report … on … the Prisons of Ireland, 1849*, H.C. 1849 (1069), xxvi, p. 9; *Twenty-eighth Report … on … the Prisons of Ireland, 1850*, H.C. 1850 (1229), xxix, pp. 15–16; O'Dwyer, 'Public Works Architecture', p. 193.

85 Mac Suibhne, *The End of Outrage*, p. 176.

86 *Twentieth Report … on … the Prisons of Ireland, 1842*, H.C. 1842 (377), xxii, p. 7; *Twenty-second Report … on … the Prisons of Ireland, 1844*, H.C. 1844 (535), xxviii, p. 8; *Eleventh Report of the Commissioners on Public Works, Ireland … for the Year 1842*, H.C. 1843 (467), xxviii, p. 4; *Twelfth Report of the Commissioners on Public Works, Ireland … for the Year 1843*, H.C. 1844 (555), xxx, pp. 5–6; *Thirteenth Report of the Commissioners on Public Works, Ireland … for the Year 1844*, H.C. 1845 (640), xxvi, p. 5; O'Dwyer, 'Public Works Architecture', p. 67, 186–7; Appendix D.

87 *Twenty-second Report … on … the Prisons of Ireland, 1844*, H.C. 1844 (535), xxviii, p. 8.

88 Registry of Deeds, for the purchase of a site at the Point Depot by the Board of Works, 1846 (NAI, Registry of Deeds, 1846/19/6); O'Dwyer, 'Public Works Architecture', p. 187; Carey, *Mountjoy*, pp. 38–9.

89 *Sixteenth Report of the Commissioners on Public Works, Ireland … for the Year 1847*, H.C. 1848 (983), xxxvii, pp. 16–17; Bundle of letters relating to the purchase of a site for and the construction of Mountjoy convict prison, Dublin, 1843–9 (NAI, CSORP 1849/G8196); O'Dwyer, 'Public Works Architecture', p. 188; Carey, *Mountjoy*, p. 39.

90 *Sixteenth Report of the Commissioners on Public Works, Ireland … for the Year 1847*, H.C. 1848 (983), xxxvii, pp. 16–17; Bundle of letters relating to the building of Mountjoy convict prison, 1847 (NAI, CSORP 1847/G5458); O'Dwyer, 'Public Works Architecture', p. 187; Carey, *Mountjoy*, p. 37.

91 *Nineteenth Report of the Commissioners on Public Works, Ireland … for the Year 1850*, H.C. 1851 (1414), xxv, pp. 41–2.

92 *Twenty-first Report of the Commissioners on Public Works, Ireland … for the Year 1852*, H.C. 1852–3 (1651), xli, p. 24; *Twenty-second Report of the Commissioners on Public Works, Ireland … for the Year 1853*, H.C. 1854 (1820), xx, p. 25; *Twenty-seventh Report of the Commissioners on Public Works, Ireland … for the Year 1858*, H.C. 1859 (2545), xiv, p. 18; Convict Prisons Act, 1854 (Ireland), 17 & 18 Vict., c. 76; Four contract drawings for the Mountjoy female convict depot, 12 May 1855, by James Higgins Owen (NAI, OPW 5HC/4/412); see also O'Dwyer, 'Public Works Architecture', p. 190.

93 Land for Prisons Act, 1847 (Ireland), 10 & 11 Vict., c. 26.

94 *Twenty-sixth Report … on … the Prisons of Ireland, 1847–48*, H.C. 1847–8 (952), xxiv, p. 32.

95 Newgate Gaol (Dublin) Act, 1849, 12 & 13 Vict., c. 55; *Twenty-ninth Report … on … the Prisons of Ireland, 1851*, H.C. 1851 (1364), xxviii, p. 3; Moylan, 'Little Green: Part I', pp. 90–1.

96 *Prisons of Ireland: Report of Inspectors General, 1825*, H.C. 1825 (493), xxii, p. 26; *Fifth Report … on … the Prisons of Ireland, 1827*, H.C. 1826–7 (471), xi, pp. 7, 26–7.

97 *Fourth Report … on … the Prisons of Ireland, 1826*, H.C. 1826 (173), xxiii, p. 21.

98 Drawings for alterations and additions to Armagh gaol, first scheme, 11 February 1837, by William Murray (Irish Architectural Archive, RIAI Murray Collection, Acc. 92/46.20); Goslin, 'Descriptive Catalogue of the Murray Collection', p. 55.

99 *Sixteenth Report … on … the Prisons of Ireland, 1838*, H.C. 1837–8 (186), xxix, pp. 8, 24–5; Plan drawings for alterations and additions to Armagh gaol, second scheme, 22 September 1837, by William Murray (Irish Architectural Archive, RIAI Murray Collection, Acc. 92/46.22).

100 *Sixteenth Report … on … the Prisons of Ireland, 1838*, H.C. 1837–8 (186), xxix, pp. 8, 24–5; Plan, elevation, and section drawings for alterations and additions to Armagh gaol, second scheme, 22 September 1837 and 11 January 1838, by William Murray (Irish Architectural Archive, RIAI Murray Collection, Acc. 92/46.25–7, 30, 33).

101 O'Dwyer, 'Public Works Architecture', p. 181.

102 *Twenty-first Report … on … the Prisons of Ireland, 1843*, H.C. 1843 (462), xxvii, pp. 3, 28–9.

103 *Armagh Guardian*, 4 March 1845.

104 Ibid., 14 January, 11 February, 4 March, 3 June, 24 June and 15 July 1845; *Twenty-fourth Report … on … the Prisons of Ireland, 1846*, H.C. 1846 (697), xx, pp. 21–2; Plan drawings for alterations and additions to Armagh gaol, final scheme, January 1846, by William Murray (Irish Architectural Archive, RIAI Murray Collection, Acc. 92/46.48); Goslin, 'Descriptive Catalogue of the Murray Collection', p. 55.

105 *Twenty-eighth Report … on … the Prisons of Ireland, 1850*, H.C. 1850 (1229), xxix, pp. 40; *Thirty-third Report … on … the Prisons of Ireland, 1855*, H.C. 1854–5 (1956), xxvi, pp. 15, 44–7; *Armagh Guardian*, 20 March, 10 July 1852; 12 February, 23 March 1853; 28 March 1856; *The Builder*, vol. 11, no. 547, 30 July 1853, p. 484.

106 *Forty-first Report … on … the Prisons of Ireland, 1863*, H.C. 1863 (3214), xxiii, pp. 128–9; *Forty-second Report … on … the Prisons of Ireland, 1864*, H.C. 1864 (3377), xxvii, p. 78; *Forty-fourth Report … on … the Prisons of Ireland, 1866*, H.C. 1866 (3690), xxxiv, p. 81; *Armagh Guardian*, 2 September 1864, 20 April 1866; *Dublin Builder*, vol. 7, no. 133, 1 July 1865, p. 170; ibid., vol. 8, no. 152, 15 April 1866, p. 106.

107 John Neville, 'Dundalk County Prison', *Civil Engineer and Architect's Journal*, vol. 16, no. 229, April 1853, p. 121 (illus.).

108 *Prisons of Ireland: Report of Inspectors General, 1825*, H.C. 1825 (493), xxii, p. 51; *Seventh Report … on … the Prisons of Ireland, 1829*, H.C. 1829 (10), xii, p. 40; *Sixteenth Report … on … the Prisons of Ireland, 1838*, H.C. 1837–8 (186), xxix, p. 31; *Nineteenth Report … on … the Prisons of Ireland, 1841*, H.C. 1841 (299), xi, p. 36.

109 *Twenty-fifth Report … on … the Prisons of Ireland, 1847*, H.C. 1847 (805), xxix, p. 54; D'Alton and O'Flanagan, *Dundalk*, p. 335; Appendix B.

110 *Twenty-eighth Report … on … the Prisons of Ireland, 1850*, H.C. 1850 (1229), xxix, pp. 55; *Thirty-second Report … on … the Prisons of Ireland, 1854*, H.C. 1854 (1803), xxxii, pp. 20, 86; Neville, 'Dundalk County Prison', p. 121; O'Donoghue, *Irish County Surveyors*, p. 267.

111 Neville, 'Dundalk County Prison', p. 121.

112 *Dublin Builder*, vol. 5, no. 87, 1 August 1863, p. 121; Lacy, *Sights and Scenes*, pp. 223–4; Casey, 'John Neville', p. 25; Christine Casey and Alistair Rowan, *The Buildings of Ireland: North Leinster, the counties of Longford, Louth, Meath and Westmeath* (London: Penguin, 1993), p. 247.

113 See Appendix B.

114 *Report of the Commissioners Appointed To Revise the Several Laws under … which Moneys Are Now Raised by Grand Jury Presentment in Ireland*, H.C. 1842 (386), xxiv, p. xliv.

115 Municipal Corporations Act, 1840 (Ireland), 3 & 4 Vict., c. 108.

116 Assizes Act, 1850 (Ireland), 13 & 14 Vict., c. 85.

117 *Twentieth Report … on … the Prisons of Ireland, 1842*, H.C. 1842 (377), xxii, p. 108; *Twenty-second Report … on … the Prisons of Ireland, 1844*, H.C. 1844 (535), xxviii, p. 89; *Twenty-third Report … on … the Prisons of Ireland, 1845*, H.C. 1845 (620), xxv, pp. 69–70; *Twenty-fourth Report … on … the Prisons of Ireland, 1846*, H.C. 1846 (697), xx, pp. 81–2; *Thirty-third Report … on … the Prisons of Ireland, 1855*, H.C. 1854–5 (1956), xxvi, p. 182; *Dublin Builder*, vol. 8, no. 158, 15 February 1866, p. 53; *Irish Builder*, vol. 10, no. 201, 1 May 1868, p. 116.

118 *Thirty-second Report … on … the Prisons of Ireland, 1854*, H.C. 1854 (1803), xxxii, pp. 93–8; *Thirty-ninth Report … on … the Prisons of Ireland, 1861*, H.C. 1861 (2861), xxix, p. 148; *The Builder*, vol. 10, no. 493, 17 July 1852, p. 460; ibid., vol. 12, no. 592, 10 June 1854, p. 305; ibid., vol. 16, no. 782, 30 January 1858, p. 73; *Dublin Builder*, vol. 3, no. 29, 1 March 1861, p. 448.

119 For Queen's County, see *Thirtieth Report … on … the Prisons of Ireland, 1852*, H.C. 1852 (1531), xxv, pp. 17, 204; for King's County, see *Thirty–second Report … on … the Prisons of Ireland, 1854*, H.C. 1854 (1803), xxxii, p. 171; for Roscommon, see ibid., p. 112; *Thirty-third Report … on … the Prisons of Ireland, 1855*, H.C. 1854–5 (1956), xxvi, pp. 18, 95; *The Builder*, vol. 11, no. 553, 10 September 1853, p. 584.

120 *Thirty-fourth Report … on … the Prisons of Ireland, 1856*, H.C. 1856 (2113), xxxiv, p. 21; Drawings for a proposed new wing at Downpatrick gaol, 20 December 1853, and other dates between 1853 and 1859, by Henry Smyth (PRONI, D/2992/B/3–4A).

121 *Thirty-second Report … on … the Prisons of Ireland, 1854*, H.C. 1854 (1803), xxxii, pp. 64–7; *Thirty-third Report … on … the Prisons of Ireland, 1855*, H.C. 1854–5 (1956), xxvi, p. 59.

122 See Appendix D.

123 *Saunders' Newsletter*, 24 March 1857; *The Builder*, vol. 15, no. 750, 20 June 1859, p. 353; ibid., vol. 15, no. 754, 18 July 1857, p. 409; ibid., vol. 17, no. 856, 2 July 1859, p. 444; Nowlan, 'Kilmainham Jail', p. 112.

124 *Dublin Builder*, vol. 4, no. 60, 15 June 1862, p. 155. McCurdy later won commissions in Clonmel, Lifford, Monaghan, and Tralee, as well as Naas – see Appendix A.

125 *The Builder*, vol. 14, no. 709, 6 September 1856, p. 490; ibid., vol. 15, no. 754, 18 July 1857, p. 409; *Civil Engineer and Architect's Journal*, vol. 19, no. 271, October 1856, p. 358; *Dublin Builder*, vol. 3, no. 39, 1 August 1861, p. 591; *Thirty-seventh Report … on … the Prisons of Ireland, 1859*, H.C. 1859 (2557), xiii, pp. 257–8; *Thirty-eighth Report … on … the Prisons of Ireland, 1860*, H.C. 1860 (2691), xxxvi, pp. 266–9.

126 *Twenty-sixth Report … on … the Prisons of Ireland, 1847–48*, H.C. 1847–8 (952), xxiv, p. 93; *Twenty-seventh Report … on … the Prisons of Ireland, 1849*, H.C. 1849 (1069), xxvi, p. 86.

127 *Thirty-seventh Report … on … the Prisons of Ireland, 1859*, H.C. 1859 (2557), xiii, p. 257.

128 *The Builder*, vol. 17, no. 867, 17 September 1859, p. 615; *Dublin Builder*, vol. 4, no. 55, 1 April 1862, p. 73; John Brady to Samuel Roberts, 16 September 1864 (Galway County Archives, GS/11/2); Nine drawings showing the partial rebuilding of Galway county gaol to provide for the separate system, and the later amalgamation of the county and town gaols, July 1858 to May 1866, by Samuel Ussher Roberts (ibid., GS/11/2/2–9).

129 The date for this change in Limerick is unclear, but in Cork the city gaol was female-only from 1878 – see John L. O'Sullivan, *The Cork City Gaol* (Midleton: Litho Press, 1996), pp. 15–17.

130 *Inspector General's Report of … the Prisons in Ireland for … 1818*, H.C. 1819 (534), xii, p. 15; *Eighth Report … on … the Prisons of Ireland, 1830*, H.C. 1830 (48), xxiv, p. 11.

131 Kilkenny County grand-jury presentment books, 1840–2 (Bodleian Library, Oxford); *Eighteenth Report … on … the Prisons of Ireland, 1840*, H.C. 1840 (240), xxvi, p. 49; *Twentieth Report … on … the Prisons of Ireland, 1842*, H.C. 1842 (377), xxii, pp. 6, 103; *Twenty-first Report … on … the Prisons of Ireland, 1843*, H.C. 1843 (462), xxvii, pp. 3, 70; *Kilkenny Moderator*, 17 July 1841; *Kilkenny Journal*, 16 March 1842; Walsh, 'Hard Labour', p. 216, and passim.

132 *Twenty-sixth Report … on … the Prisons of Ireland, 1847–48*, H.C. 1847–8 (952), xxiv, p. 10; *Twenty-seventh Report … on … the Prisons of Ireland, 1849*, H.C. 1849 (1069), xxvi, pp. 87–8; *Kilkenny Moderator*, 24 March 1849; Walsh, 'Hard Labour', p. 217.

133 *Kilkenny Journal*, 13, 20 June 1849 and 4 August 1849; *Twenty-ninth Report … on … the Prisons of Ireland, 1851*, H.C. 1851 (1364), xxviii, p. 14, 79; *Thirty-second Report … on … the Prisons of Ireland, 1854*, H.C. 1854 (1803), xxxii, p. 164; Walsh, 'Hard Labour', p. 218. As Walsh argues, *The Builder* incorrectly attributes the final design to William D'Esterre Smith, when it was actually by William Deane Butler – see vol. 8, no. 394, 24 August 1850, p. 404.

134 *Thirty-seventh Report … on … the Prisons of Ireland, 1859*, H.C. 1859 (2557), xiii, pp. 262–71; *Fortieth Report … on … the Prisons of Ireland, 1862*, H.C. 1862 (3020), xxvi, p. 281; *Kilkenny Moderator*, 1 February 1862.

135 Lacy, *Sights and Scenes*, p. 139; Walsh, 'Hard Labour', pp. 232, 235.

136 *Twenty-ninth Report … on … the Prisons of Ireland, 1851*, H.C. 1851 (1364), xxviii, p. 79.

137 *Twentieth Report … on … the Prisons of Ireland, 1842*, H.C. 1842 (377), xxii, pp. 6, 113–15; *Twenty-second Report … on … the Prisons of Ireland, 1844*, H.C. 1844 (535), xxviii, pp. 96–8.

138 *Twenty-third Report … on … the Prisons of Ireland, 1845*, H.C. 1845 (620), xxv, pp. 76–9.

139 *Twenty-seventh Report … on … the Prisons of Ireland, 1849*, H.C. 1849 (1069), xxvi, pp. 100–1; *Twenty-ninth Report … on … the Prisons of Ireland, 1851*, H.C. 1851 (1364), xxviii, pp. 103–10; *Thirtieth Report … on … the Prisons of Ireland,*

1852, H.C. 1852 (1531), xxv, pp. 17, 215–19, 223–4; *Thirty-third Report … on … the Prisons of Ireland, 1855*, H.C. 1854–5 (1956), xxvi, pp. 205–10.

140 See Appendix B.

141 Extracts from reports of the inspectors-general of prisons, etc., [1851–6] (NLI, Lismore papers, MS 43,456/13).

142 *Thirty-eighth Report … on … the Prisons of Ireland, 1860*, H.C. 1860 (2691), xxxvi, pp. 314–22; Waterford County grand-jury presentment book, summer assizes 1860 (Waterford City and County Archives).

143 *Freeman's Journal*, 3 August 1860; *The Builder*, vol. 18, no. 914, 11 August 1860, p. 512; Waterford County grand-jury presentment books, spring and summer assizes 1860, and summer assizes 1863 (Waterford City and County Archives); *Thirty-ninth Report … on … the Prisons of Ireland, 1861*, H.C. 1861 (2861), xxix, pp. 280–4; *Fortieth Report … on … the Prisons of Ireland, 1862*, H.C. 1862 (3020), xxvi, pp. 344–6; *Forty-second Report … on … the Prisons of Ireland, 1864*, H.C. 1864 (3377), xxvii, p. 356.

144 There had been significant opposition to a separate-system design on cost and utility grounds in the 1850s – see Report of the committee appointed by the grand juries, to select a plan for the alteration or erection of a joint prison, for the county and city of Waterford, 19 February 1855 (NLI, Lismore papers, MS 43,456/13).

145 The gaol closed around 1938 – see *Irish Independent*, 5 March, 26 March 1943; *Irish Examiner*, 6 March 1943.

146 McDowell, *Irish Administration*, pp. 158–60.

147 For British gaol-building of this time, see Tomlinson, 'Victorian Prisons', pp. 98–154; Evans, *Fabrication of Virtue*, pp. 367–401.

Reflections: Identities, Actors, Towns

1 Rowan, 'Irishness of Irish Architecture'.

2 See in addition David Fitzpatrick, 'Ireland in Empire', in A. Porter (ed.), *The Oxford History of the British Empire*, 5 vols (Oxford: Oxford University Press, 1999), vol. 3, pp. 494–521; Bremner, *Imperial Gothic*, pp. 350–63; Hoppen, *Governing Hibernia*, pp. 1–2; Crosbie, 'Ireland and the Empire in the Nineteenth Century', p. 624. See also Richard J. Butler, 'The Architecture of the State in Ireland: The colonial question, 1800-1922', in G.A. Bremner and Daniel Maudlin (eds), *Inner Empire: Architecture and imperialism in the British Isles, 1560–2000* (Manchester: Manchester University Press, forthcoming).

3 Hill, 'Architecture in the Aftermath of Union', pp. 184–6 and 201–11.

4 Barclay, *Men on Trial*, p. 73.

5 Rowan, 'Irishness of Irish Architecture', p. 18.

6 General Prisons Act, 1877 (Ireland), 40 & 41 Vict., c. 49.

7 See, for example, Patrick Joyce, *The State of Freedom: A history of the British state since 1800* (Cambridge: Cambridge University Press, 2013), pp. 303–7, and Margaret Kelleher, *The Maamtrasna Murders: Language, life and death in nineteenth-century Ireland* (Dublin: University College Dublin Press, 2018).

8 Jason Knirck, *Afterimage of the Revolution: Cumann na nGaedheal and Irish politics, 1922–1932* (Madison, WI: University of Wisconsin Press, 2004), pp. 63–8. See also Hughes and MacRaild, 'Introduction: Crime, violence and the Irish in the nineteenth century', pp. 6–7.

9 Ursula R.Q. Henriques, 'An Early Factory Inspector: James Stuart of Dunearn', *The Scottish Historical Review*, vol. 50, no. 149, April 1971, pp. 18–46; MacDonagh, *Jeremiah Fitzpatrick*.

10 See Richard J. Butler, 'British Solutions to Irish Problems: Representations of Ireland in the British architectural press, 1837–53', *Victorian Periodicals Review*, vol. 47, no. 4, Winter 2014, pp. 577–96, at pp. 583–6.

11 See for example Frederick O'Dwyer, 'The Foundation and Early Years of the RIAI', in John Graby (ed.), *150 Years of Architecture in Ireland: The Royal Institute of the Architects of Ireland, 1839–1989* (Dublin: RIAI, 1989), pp. 8–21.

12 O'Donoghue, *Irish County Surveyors*, pp. 3–25.

13 See Andrew Saint, *Architect and Engineer: A study in sibling rivalry* (New Haven and London: Yale University Press, 2008); Gibney, Hurley and McParland, *Building Site in Eighteenth-century Ireland*, pp. 1–56.

14 Barclay, *Men on Trial*, pp. 60–1, 71–2, 84.

15 Craig, *Architecture of Ireland*, pp. 257–62.

16 Barclay, *Men on Trial*, p. 84.

17 Ibid., pp. 71–2; Casey, 'Art and Architecture in the Long Eighteenth Century', pp. 444–63.

Appendix A
Buildings Histories

Part 1: Assize Courthouses

ANTRIM (and later TOWN OF CARRICKFERGUS)
Carrickfergus, no. 1

High St. & Market Place
Lat. 54°42'52.42" N.; Long. 5°48'24.58" W.

Planned 1612; built 1612–13; partially rebuilt (*Hugh Darley and John Gibson*) 1727; handed over to the Town of Carrickfergus 1776; ceased to be used as a courthouse 1817; demolished 1827; foundation stone of new courthouse laid 1828; soon thereafter abandoned and demolished; later buildings now occupy the site.

Site for a gaol granted in the charter for the town of Carrickfergus, 1612. Gaol (and presumably courthouse) built for the county, 1612–13. E. part rebuilt (*Hugh Darley and John Gibson*), 1727. Handed over to the Town of Carrickfergus, 1776. Baron McClelland, assize judge, refused to use courthouse for the town's public business, 1817; assizes thereafter held in county courthouse, 1817 (see 'Antrim: Carrickfergus, no. 2'). Petition to parliament from the mayor, etc., of Carrickfergus, claiming an inability to pay for the upkeep of the town's public buildings, 1824. Prisoners moved from adjacent gaol to the Antrim county gaol, 1827. Town courthouse and gaol demolished, 1827. Foundation for a new town courthouse laid on the same site, 1828; this abandoned when two storeys in height and about to be roofed in, and materials sold for £35, 1828. County and town courthouse abandoned, 1850 (see 'Antrim: Carrickfergus, no. 2'); town assizes thereafter held in markethouse and elsewhere in the town. Later buildings now occupy the site.

Archival and primary sources:

Charter for the town of Carrickfergus by James I, dated 14 December 1612 (Rolls of Patents, 10 James I, p. 3, m. 16); Dubourdieu, *Statistical Survey of the County of Antrim*, p. 486; G.N. Wright, *Tours in Ireland*, 3 vols (London: Baldwin, Cradock & Joy, 1823), vol. 3, p. 17; *Journal of the House of Commons*, vol. 79, 19 May 1824, p. 386; *Fifth Report … on … the Prisons of Ireland, 1827*, H.C. 1826–7 (471), xi, pp. 7, 25; McSkimmin, *Carrickfergus*, pp. 151, 170–3 (illus.); Ordnance survey maps, 1832 (PRONI, OS/6/1/52/1); Lewis, *Topographical Dictionary*, vol. 1, p. 273.

Secondary sources:

Brett, *Court Houses*, pp. 29–30, 106; Anngret Simms (ed.), *Irish Historic Towns Atlas: Volume 1: Kildare, Carrickfergus, Bandon, Kells, Mullingar, Athlone* (Dublin: Royal Irish Academy, 1996), no. 2, p. 11.

ANTRIM (and site of earlier TOWN OF CARRICKFERGUS)
Carrickfergus, no. 2

Antrim St. & High St.
Lat. 54°42'56.51" N.; Long. 5°48'19.25" W.

Planned 1776; built (*Richard Drew*) 1777–9; alterations and additions (*James Hunter*) 1781–3; repairs (*Duff and Jackson*) 1832; alterations 1836; plans for a replacement 1839; abandoned *c.* 1850; sold to the Board of Public Works 1851; leased to the government 1852; in use by the military 1856–96; purchased by the military 1896; adjacent gaol demolished 1897; ordnance stores built 1900; in use also as a town hall 1935; extant.

Site of former Franciscan friary, 1232–*c.* 1560. Partly site of the Earl of Donegall's former Joymount Palace, 1618–1768. Partly site of Castle Worraigh, the Town of Carrickfergus' courthouse and gaol, *c.* 1699–1776. Petition to move assizes to Ballymena, 1707, 1712. Petition to move assizes to Antrim town, 1753, 1771, 1774. Old county courthouse and gaol nearby handed over to the Town of Carrickfergus, 1776 (see 'Antrim: Carrickfergus, no. 1'). New courthouse and gaol built together (*Richard Drew*), at a total cost of £5,785, 1777–9. Addition of a boundary wall to the S., and alterations to the Crown courtroom (*James Hunter*), 1781–3. Scene of the trial of William Orr, United Irishman, 1797. Petition to move assizes to Belfast, 1813. Town of Carrickfergus assizes also held in county courthouse, 1817 onwards. Serious malicious damage to Crown courtroom, 1831; repaired (*Thomas J. Duff and Thomas Jackson*), 1832. Sitting-room added, 1836. Plans for a replacement courthouse in Belfast (see 'Antrim: Belfast'), 1839. Replacement courthouse built, *c.* 1848–50. Courthouse and gaol abandoned, 1850. Sold to the Board of Public Works for use as a convict prison, for £390, 1851. Prison plan abandoned, 1852. Government lease, 1852 onwards. Alterations for use by the military, 1856. Purchased by the military, 1896. Adjacent gaol demolished, 1897; ordnance stores built on site, 1900. Courthouse used as a town hall, 1935 onwards. Listed, 1976. Extant.

Archival and primary sources:

Inscription in pediment above doorway ('1779'); Antrim grand-jury presentment books, 1778–9, and 1781–1837 (PRONI, ANT/4); McSkimmin, *Carrickfergus*, pp. 151, 170–3, 511–14; Dubourdieu, *Statistical Survey of the County of Antrim*, p. 486; G.N. Wright, *Tours in Ireland*, 3 vols, (London: Baldwin, Cradock & Joy, 1823), vol. 3, p. 17; Ordnance survey maps, 1832, 1857, 1901–2 (PRONI, OS/6/1/52/1–3); Lewis, *Topographical Dictionary*, vol. 1, p. 273; *The Builder*, vol. 9, no. 461, 6 December 1851, p. 775.

Secondary sources:

Francis Joseph Bigger, 'The Franciscan Friary at Carrigfergus, with a Photograph of the Courthouse at Carrickfergus after the Trial of William Orr, 18 Sept. 1797', *Ulster Journal of Archaeology*, vol. 15, no. 2, May 1909, p. 53 (illus.); Brett, *Court Houses*, pp. 27, 29–30, 106 (illus.); McParland, 'Public Work of Architects', p. 158; Gordon Campbell and Susan Crowther, *Historic Buildings … in the Town of Carrickfergus* (Belfast: Ulster Architectural Heritage Society, 1978), p. 25; Sheela Speers, *Under the Big Lamp: Historic photographs of … Carrickfergus* (Belfast: Friar's Bush Press, 1989), p. 25 (illus.); Charles McConnell, *Carrickfergus: A stroll through time* (Carrickfergus: Carrickfergus Publications, 1994); Simms, *Irish Historic Towns Atlas: Volume 1: Kildare, Carrickfergus, Bandon, Kells, Mullingar, Athlone*, no. 2, p. 11; Northern Ireland Environmental Agency (NIEA), Listed Buildings Database (www.doeni.gov.uk).

ANTRIM

Belfast

Crumlin Rd.
Lat. 54°36'29.95" N.; Long. 5°56'33.84" W.

Planned 1839; site purchased 1841; large gaol built nearby (*Charles Lanyon*) 1843–5; unexecuted design (*Charles Lanyon*) 1847; built (*Charles Lanyon*) *c.* 1848–50; Antrim County assizes held for the first time 1850; extensive alterations and additions (*Robert Young and John Mackenzie*) 1905–7; abandoned 1998; damaged by fire 2009; extant, though partially ruined.

Petition to move assizes to Belfast, 1813. Small courthouse built in Belfast for quarter-sessions, 1817. Crumlin Road laid out, 1836. Plans for a replacement for the old courthouse at Carrickfergus (see 'Antrim: Carrickfergus, no. 1'), 1840. Site on Crumlin Road purchased from the Belfast Charitable Society, 1841. New district bridewell (later Antrim county gaol) built opposite the site of the future courthouse (*Charles Lanyon*), 1843–5. Unexecuted design (*Charles Lanyon*), 1847; rejected on grounds of cost (not to exceed £16,000). Second design (*Charles Lanyon*) submitted and agreed to by the grand jury, to cost £16,500, 1848. Built (*Charles Lanyon*), *c.* 1848–50. Old Carrickfergus courthouse and gaol abandoned, 1850. Extensive alterations and additions (*Robert Young and John Mackenzie*), at a cost of £12,500, 1905–7. Listed, 1988. Abandoned, 1998. Extensively damaged by a series of malicious fires, 2009. Extant, though partially ruined. The future of this building is now very uncertain.

Archival and primary sources:

Unexecuted drawings for Crumlin Road courthouse, 1847, by Charles Lanyon (PRONI, LA/1/8/JA/119/1–14); Unexecuted drawings for Crumlin Road courthouse, *c.* 1847–8, by Charles Lanyon (Belfast City Council), Drawings for Crumlin Road courthouse, *c.* 1848–50, by Charles Lanyon (PRONI, LA/1/8/JA/107-1-6 and 113); McSkimmin, *Carrickfergus*, pp. 511–14; Lewis, *Topographical Dictionary*, vol. 1, pp. 197, 273; *Belfast Newsletter*, 19 July 1850; *The Builder*, vol. 10, no. 496, 7 August 1852, pp. 495–6; J.B. Doyle, *Tours in Ulster* (Dublin: Hodges & Smith, 1855), pp. 27–8; Ordnance survey maps, 1858, 1872 (PRONI); William McComb, *McComb's Guide to Belfast* (Belfast: McComb, 1861), p. 35; View of Belfast looking west, by J.H. Connop, 1863, from his *Belfast, part II* (NIEA); Watercolour showing courthouse before later additions and alterations, attributed to W.H. Lynn (Ulster Museum, Local history collection, no. 6/1956); *Irish Builder*, vol. 47, 12 August, 26 August, 23 September, 7 October, 18 November 1905, pp. 524, 594, 676, 685, 830; Schedule of quantities for additions and alterations to the county courthouse, Belfast, July 1905 (PRONI, D/2194/99/1); Unexecuted drawings for alterations and additions, 1904, by J.C.M. Browne (Belfast City Council); *Irish Builder and Engineer*, vol. 49, no. 7, 6 April 1907, p. 252; *The Builder*, vol. 92, no. 3347, 30 March 1907, p. 605; R.M. Young, *Belfast and the Province of Ulster* (Brighton: Pike, 1909), p. 127 (illus.).

Secondary sources:

W.G. Strickland, *A Dictionary of Irish Artists*, 2 vols (Dublin: Maunsel, 1913), vol. 1, no. 593; *Northern Whig and Belfast Post*, 23 April 1928; Jones, *Social Geography of Belfast*, pp. 246–7 (illus.); Brett, *Court Houses*, pp. 47, 49–50, 106 (illus.); McParland, 'Public Work of Architects', pp. 239–40, 249; Richardson, *Gothic Revival Architecture in Ireland*, p. 325; Brett, *Buildings of Belfast*, pp. 29, 31, plate 24; Paul Larmour, *Belfast: An illustrated architectural guide* (Belfast: Friar's Bush Press, 1987), p. 16 (illus.); Paul Larmour, 'Lanyon', *Belfast Telegraph*, 30 December 1989, p. 7; O'Dwyer, 'Architecture of the Board of Works', pp. 184–5; O'Donoghue, *Irish County Surveyors*, p. 232–3; Northern Ireland Environmental Agency (NIEA), Listed Buildings Database (www.doeni.gov.uk).

ARMAGH

Armagh, no. 1

Market St. & Market Place
Lat. 54°20'52.26" N.; Long. 6°39'13.80" W.

Unknown date of construction; damaged by fire 1704; rebuilt 1735; attached gaol abandoned 1780; new courthouse planned from at least 1804; new courthouse built 1807–10; old courthouse abandoned 1810; demolished; markethouse built (probably *Thomas J. Duff*) 1815.

Date of construction unknown. Combined assize courthouse and gaol (beneath), located 'at the foot of Market-street', damaged by fire, 1704. Rebuilt, 1735. New gaol (*Thomas Cooley*) built at the south end of the Mall, 1780; old gaol thereafter abandoned. New courthouse planned from at least 1804; old courthouse described as 'very inconvenient'. New courthouse built (*Francis Johnston*) at the north end of the Mall, 1807–10 (see 'Armagh: Armagh, no. 2'); old courthouse thereafter abandoned, and soon after demolished. 'His grace [the primate] intends the site of the present [courthouse] for that of the market-house', 1804. Markethouse built (probably *Thomas J. Duff*), 1815.

Archival and primary sources:

Gentleman's Magazine, 5 (September 1735), p. 557; Charles Coote, *Statistical Survey of the County of Armagh* (Dublin: Graisberry & Campbell, 1804), pp. 321–2; James Stuart, *Historical Memoirs of the City of Armagh* (Newry: Wilkinson, 1819), pp. 530–1.

Secondary sources:

Brett, *Court houses,* p. 36; Goslin, 'Descriptive Catalogue of the Murray Collection', p. 54; Catherine McCullough and W.H. Crawford, *Irish Historic Towns Atlas, No. 18: Armagh* (Dublin: Royal Irish Academy, 2007), section 13.

ARMAGH

Armagh, no. 2

The Mall
Lat. 54°21'2.38" N.; Long. 6°39'9.99" W.

New courthouse planned from at least 1804; series of unexecuted designs (*Francis Johnston*) 1805–7; new courthouse built (*Francis Johnston*) 1807–10; reported as dilapidated 1835; alterations and additions, including a new wing (*Henry Davison, Thomas Turner and Thomas Ross*) 1859–63; addition of offices (*Richard Henry Dorman*) *c.* 1909; repairs and alterations (*Albert Neill*) 1965–71; damaged by a bomb 1993; rebuilt (*Stephen Leighton*) 1994–9; threatened with closure 2015; extant.

Old courthouse on Market St. & Market Place, rebuilt, 1735 (see 'Armagh: Armagh, no. 1'). New courthouse planned from at least 1804. Series of unexecuted designs (*Francis Johnston*), 1805–7. Johnston paid £27.6.0 for these designs, 1807. New courthouse built (*Francis Johnston*) at the north end of the Mall, at a cost of at least £6,000, 1807–10. County surveyor (*H.L. Lindsay*) reports that courthouse is in a dilapidated state and that the roof is leaking, 1835. Alterations and additions, including a new wing to the rear (*Henry Davison, Thomas Turner and Thomas Ross*), at a cost of £2,500, 1859–63. Addition of offices (*Richard Henry Dorman*), *c.* 1909. Extensive repairs and alterations (*Albert Neill*), 1965–71. Listed, 1975. Damaged by a bomb, 1993. Extensively rebuilt (*Stephen Leighton*), at a cost of £8 million, 1994–9. Threatened with closure, 2015. Extant.

Archival and primary sources:

Coote, *Statistical Survey of the County of Armagh*, pp. 321–2; Stuart, *Armagh*, pp. 530–1; Armagh grand-jury presentment books, 1805–89 (PRONI, ARM/4/1/12-161); Armagh grand-jury presentment books, 1821–99 (Armagh County Museum); Series of drawings for Armagh courthouse, unexecuted and as built, 1805–8, by Francis Johnston (Irish Architectural Archive, RIAI Murray Collection, Acc. 92/46.4–18); Series of drawings for Armagh courthouse, mostly copies of material in the IAA, 1805–7, by Francis Johnston (PRONI, T/1554/1); 'City of Armagh', painting by James Black, 1810 (Armagh County Museum, ARMCM.156.1958); Francis Johnston to James Norris Brewer, 29 February 1820, printed in Patrick Henchy, 'Francis Johnston', pp. 12–13; The same letter in Anon., 'A Letter from Francis Johnston', *Quarterly Bulletin of the Irish Georgian Society*, vol. 6, no. 1, 1963, p. 4; Reid, *Travels*, pp. 165–8; Lewis, *Topographical Dictionary*, vol. 1, nos. 68–9; Map of Armagh City by James O'Hagan, 1851 (Armagh County Museum); *Armagh Guardian*, 15 June, 6 July 1860; *The Builder*, vol. 18, no. 910, 14 July 1860, p. 447; *Dublin Builder*, vol. 2, no. 11, 1 July 1860, p. 301; *The Builder*, vol. 96, no. 3447, 27 February 1909, p. 257.

Secondary sources:

John Betjeman, 'Francis Johnston, Irish architect', in M. Evans (ed.), *The Pavilion: A contemporary collection of British art and architecture* (London: I.T. Publications, 1946), pp. 20–38, at pp. 24–5; Henchy, 'Francis Johnston', pp. 7, 12–13; Brett, *Court Houses*, p. 37–9, 106; Hugh Dixon, *An Introduction to Ulster Architecture* (Belfast: Ulster Architectural Heritage Society, 1975), p. 53; McParland, 'Public Work of Architects', pp. 241, 244; Craig, *Architecture of Ireland*, p. 271; Goslin, 'Descriptive

Catalogue of the Murray Collection', p. 44–7; Robert McKinstry, et al., *The Buildings of Armagh* (Belfast: Ulster Architectural Heritage Society, 1992), pp. 148, 145, 153–4; C.E.B. Brett, *The Buildings of Armagh* (Belfast: Ulster Architectural Heritage Society, 1999), pp. 219–20; O'Donoghue, *Irish County Surveyors*, pp. 144–5, 241–2, 315; McCullough and Crawford, *Irish Historic Towns Atlas, No. 18: Armagh*, section 13; Mulligan, *Buildings of Ireland: South Ulster*, pp. 120–1; Rolf Loeber, et al., *Art and Architecture of Ireland: Volume IV: Architecture 1600–2000*, pp. 181–2, 446; Butler, 'Politics, Grand Juries, and Ireland's Unbuilt Assize Courthouses', pp. 115–19; Northern Ireland Environmental Agency (NIEA), Listed Buildings Database (www.doeni.gov.uk).

CARLOW

Carlow, no. 1

Burrin St. & Kennedy St.
Lat. 52°50'9.75" N.; Long. 6°55'57.13" W.

Site of a former gaol, destroyed 1798; gaol rebuilt elsewhere *c.* 1800; courthouse built *c.* 1799–1801; criticised by assize judge 1827; replacement planned 1827; new courthouse built 1830–4; old courthouse abandoned 1834; demolished 1837; Dreighton Memorial Hall (extant) built on site thereafter.

Site of a former gaol that was mostly destroyed during unrest, 1798. Gaol rebuilt elsewhere, *c.* 1800. Courthouse built on the site of this gaol, *c.* 1799–1801. Severely criticised by the assize judge Charles Kendal Bushe, 1827. New courthouse planned, 1827 (see 'Carlow: Carlow, no. 2'). New courthouse built, 1830–4; old courthouse thereafter abandoned. Partially or completely demolished, 1837. Dreighton Memorial Hall (extant) built on its site, sometime afterwards. Listed.

Archival and primary sources:

A. Atkinson, *The Irish Tourist* (Dublin: Thomas Courtney, 1815), p. 376; Brewer, *Beauties of Ireland*, vol. 2, p. 8; *Finn's Leinster Journal*, 11 April 1827.

Secondary sources:

M.C. Douglas, 'Carlow's Old Inns: Churches, gaol, and castle', *Carloviana*, vol. 1, no. 4, 1951, pp. 173–4; William Garner, *Carlow: Architectural heritage* (Dublin: Foras Forbartha, 1980), p. 45; Alan Doran, 'Carlow Criminal Court', *Carloviana*, vol. 2, no. 29, new series, 1981, pp. 23–4; Mary Teehan, 'The Emergence of County Courthouses: A socio-archaeological study of Co. Kilkenny and Co. Carlow', MA thesis, University College Cork, 2004, pp. 47–8.

CARLOW

Carlow, no. 2

Athy Rd. & Court Pl.
Lat. 52°50'20.56" N.; Long. 6°55'48.29" W.

Old courthouse criticised by assize judge 1827; replacement planned 1827; first design and site chosen 1828; alterations to site 1828; alterations to design 1828–32; new courthouse built (*William Vitruvius Morrison* with *Jacob Owen*) 1832–4; opened 1834; alterations (*John C. Bower*) 1867. Reopened after extensive refurbishments 2002. Extant.

Old courthouse (see 'Carlow: Carlow, no. 1') severely criticised by the assize judge Charles Kendal Bushe, 1827. New courthouse planned, 1827. First design and site chosen, 1828. Alteration to site, 1828. Alterations to design, 1828–32. New courthouse built (*William Vitruvius Morrison* with suggestions from *Jacob Owen*), 1832–4. Opened, 1834. Alterations (*John C. Bower*), 1867. Reopened after extensive refurbishments, 2002. Listed. Extant.

Archival and primary sources:

Finn's Leinster Journal, 11 April 1827 and 19 July 1828; Royal Academy exhibits by Morrison, 1828 (no. 1078), and 1833 (no. 962); Royal Hibernian Academy exhibits by Morrison, 1829 (no. 255) and 1832 (no. 286); Charles Burke to William Gregory, 19 July 1828 (NAI, CSORP 1828/556); Carlow courthouse commissioners to chief justice of Ireland, 17 July 1828 (NAI, CSORP 1828/556); Williams & Cockburn, contractors, to Carlow courthouse commissioners, 14 May 1828 (Carlow County Library, P2/0053); Articles of agreement between Williams & Cockburn and Carlow courthouse commissioners, 21 August 1828 (Carlow County Library, GJ/9/7); Specifications for Carlow courthouse, 1828 (NAI, PRO MS 1C.12.56); Registry of Deeds, 1829, no. 565292 (NAI); Plan and section drawings by Morrison for Carlow courthouse, *c.* 1828–32 (Carlow County Library, P2/48); Articles of agreement between Williams & Cockburn and Carlow courthouse commissioners, 20 July 1832 (Carlow County Library, GJ/9/9); Documents in relation to alterations in plans in Board of Works minutes, 30 June 1832 (NAI, Board of Works files, 2D/56/98); *First Report of the Commissioners on Public Works, Ireland*, H.C. 1833 (75), xvii, p. 8; *Second Report of the Commissioners on Public Works, Ireland*, H.C. 1834 (240), xxxx, p. 12; *Tralee Mercury*, 12 July 1834; Lewis, *Topographical Dictionary*, vol. 1, p. 262; Binns, *Miseries and Beauties*, vol. 2, p. 223; Thackeray, *Irish Sketch-book*, p. 35; Morrison, 'William Vitruvius Morrison', p. 7; West, *Summer Visit to Ireland*, p. 45; Fisher, *Letters from the Kingdom of Kerry*, p. 9; Anon. [J.K.], *Letters to the North*, p. 16; *Dublin Builder*, vol. 1, no. 6, 1 June 1859, p. 73; ibid., vol. 4, no. 52, 15 February 1862, p. 43; *The Nationalist and Leinster Times*, 29 December 1888; John Price O'Hagan, 'Leinster and Munster in the Summer of 1844', *Irish Monthly*, vol. 40, 1912, pp. 454–70, at p. 455.

Secondary sources:

Douglas, 'Carlow's Old Inns', p. 173; Alice Tracey, 'A Short Account of Carlow Courthouse', *Carloviana*, vol. 1, no. 2, 1953, p. 39; Edward McParland, 'Carlow Courthouse and Railings', *Carloviana*, vol. 2, no. 22, new series, 1973, p. 9; Sean O'Leary, 'Courthouse Railings', *Carloviana*, vol. 2, no. 23, new series, 1974, p. 35; McParland, 'Public Work of Architects', pp. 3, 238–40, 245–6; Matthew J. McDermott, 'Notable Irish Architectural Families, 2: the Morrisons', *RIAI Yearbook* (1977), pp. 81–91; Garner, *Carlow: Architectural heritage*, p. 15; Craig, *Architecture of Ireland*, pp. 272, 274; Casey, 'Courthouses', pp. 39–40; Rowan, *Morrison*, pp. 46–7, 137–9; Edward McParland, 'Carlow Courthouse and Railings', *Carloviana*, vol. 47, 1999, p. 51; William Ellis, 'Battle for the Courthouse', *Carloviana*, vol. 48, 2000, p. 44; William Ellis, 'Snippets from the Past', *Carloviana*, vol. 48, 2000, pp. 44–5; Cathleen Delaney, 'Oak Park House and the Bruen Family', *Carloviana*, vol. 50, 2001, pp. 20–3; Teehan, 'Emergence of County Courthouses', pp. 47–8, 52, 62, 64, 84–6; Lee, *James Pain*, p. 185; Michael J. Conry, *Carlow Granite: Years of history written in stone* (Chapelstown, Co. Carlow: Chapelstown Press, 2006), pp. 173–5; O'Donoghue, *Irish County Surveyors*, p. 106; Loeber, et al., *Art and Architecture of Ireland: Volume IV: Architecture 1600–2000*, p. 182.

CAVAN

Cavan, no. 1

Unknown, likely Main St.

Combined courthouse and gaol, described as built by 1744; replacement gaol, described as 'lately built' 1787; replacement planned 1822; new courthouse built 1824–5; old courthouse presumably demolished; not extant.

A combined courthouse and gaol, described as 'a large stone building', location unknown, built by 1744. A replacement gaol, described as 'lately built', 1787. Further mention of old courthouse, 1801, 1806. Replacement planned, 1822. New courthouse built, 1824–5. Old courthouse presumably demolished soon after. Not extant.

Archival and primary sources:

Isaac Butler, 'A Journey to Lough Derg', *Journal of the Royal Society of Antiquaries of Ireland*, vol. [illegible], no. [illegible], 5th series, July 1892 pp. 126–36, at p. 132; Howard, *Lazarettos*, p. 95; Charles Coote, *Statistical Survey of the County of Cavan* (Dublin: Graisberry & Campbell, 1802), p. 93; Joseph Robertson, *The Traveller's Guide through Ireland* (Edinburgh: Denham & Dick, 1806), p. 165; Cavan grand-jury presentment books, 1809–17 (Cavan County Library, GJ/2) (currently inaccessible awaiting conservation).

Secondary sources:

Brett, *Court Houses*, p. 56, 106.

CAVAN

Cavan, no. 2

Farnham St.
Lat. 53°59'36.43" N.; Long. 7°21'43.67" W.

Farnham St. laid out *c.* 1810; planned 1822; first loan 1822; possible unexecuted design (*John Bowden*) 1822; built (*William Farrell*) 1824–5; additions and alterations 1866; alterations (*Patrick J. Brady*) 1928; coat of arms removed *c.* 1930s; large extension *c.* 1985; alterations (*Charles D. Ellisson & Sons*) 1987; reopened 1989; extant.

Farnham St. laid out, *c.* 1810. Replacement courthouse planned, 1822. First loan from central government obtained, 1822. Possibility that an unexecuted design was drawn up (*John Bowden*), 1822. New courthouse built (*William Farrell*, contractors *Williams & Cockburn*), at a cost of at least £11,000, 1824–5. Additions and alterations, 1866. Internal alterations (*Patrick J. Brady*), 1928. Coat of arms removed from pediment, *c.* 1930s. Large extension to the rear, *c.* 1985. Further alterations (*Charles D. Ellisson & Sons*), 1987. Reopened, 1989. Extant.

Archival and primary sources:

Pigot & Co's Provincial Directory of Ireland, 1824, p. 368; Plan and elevation drawings for Carrick-on-Shannon courthouse (identical to Cavan), n.d., by William Farrell (Houghton Library, Harvard University, William Farrell album, MS Typ 788); John Gorton and G.N. Wright, *A Topographical Dictionary of Great Britain and Ireland*, 3 vols (London: Chapman & Hall, 1831–3), vol. 1, p. 402; Binns, *Miseries and Beauties*, vol. 1, p. 304; Lewis, *Topographical Dictionary*, vol. 2, p. 318; J.P. Lawson, *Gazetteer of Ireland* (Edinburgh: Lawson, 1842), p. 231; Wilkinson, *Practical Geology And Ancient Architecture of Ireland*, pp. 300–1; *An Account of Loans Advanced … for Public Works in Ireland … since 1800*, H.C. 1847 (718), liv, pp. 20–1; Cavan grand-jury presentment books, 1856–9 (Cavan County Library, GJ/9) (currently inaccessible awaiting conservation); *Dublin Builder*, vol. 8, no. 158, 15 July 1866, p. 185; *Irish Builder*, vol. 70, no. 3, 4 February 1928, p. 95.

Secondary sources:

Brett, *Court Houses*, pp. 55–6, 106; McParland, 'Public Work of Architects', p. 240; William Garner, *Historic Buildings … in the Town of Cavan* (Belfast: Ulster Architectural Heritage Society, 1978), p. 12; Anon., 'Cavan Courthouse: Official opening' (Cavan: Good News Promotions, 1989) (copy in Cavan County Library); Mulligan, *Buildings of Ireland: South Ulster*, p. 252.

CLARE

Ennis, no. 1

High St. & Market Place
Lat. 52°50'39.73" N.; Long. 8°58'57.26" W.

An ancient courthouse at the Franciscan friary in use 1571; a markethouse/courthouse built *c.* 1616–42; damaged 1690; replacement (possibly by *Francis Bindon*) *c.* 1733–40; significant alterations and enlargement *c.* 1787–91; repairs, alterations and additions 1815–17; repairs (*James Pain*) 1820–1; alterations (*Michael Fitzgerald*) 1825; repairs (*Michael Fitzgerald*) 1828; reported as in very poor condition with a replacement recommended 1836, 1837, 1838; unexecuted scheme (*John B. Keane*) 1838; rejected by cess-payers 1841; condemned by assize judge who calls for a new courthouse 1845; competition staged 1845; site bought 1846; new courthouse built to winning design 1846–50; old courthouse abandoned 1850; offer from Franciscan order to purchase site rejected 1852; old courthouse demolished 1852; O'Connell Monument built (*John Neville, William Carroll, and James Cahill*) on site of old courthouse 1859–67; only a fragment of the old courthouse wall survives.

An ancient courthouse at the Franciscan friary, in use, 1571. A markethouse/courthouse built, *c.* 1616–42. Damaged, 1690. Courthouse and markethouse built (possibly by *Francis Bindon*) by *c.* 1733–40. Significant alterations and enlargement, *c.* 1787–91. Repairs, alterations and additions, 1815–17. Repairs (*James Pain*), 1820–1; Alterations (*Michael Fitzgerald*), 1825. Repairs after Daniel O'Connell's election (*Michael Fitzgerald*), 1828. County surveyor, James Boyd, reports that courthouse is in very poor condition and a new building is required, 1836. County surveyor repeats these comments, 1837, 1838. Two acts of parliament to rescue the Clare grand jury from insolvency, 1837–8. Unexecuted scheme (*John B. Keane*), 1838. County surveyor states that a new courthouse will likely cost £12,000, 1838. Scheme rejected by cess-payers, 1841. Assize judge condemns courthouse and states that a replacement is required, 1845. Competition staged, 1845. Competition winner selected, 1845. Site bought, 1846. New courthouse built (see 'Clare: Ennis, no. 2'), at a cost of at least £12,000 (likely £16,000), 1846–50. Old courthouse abandoned, 1850. Offer from Franciscan order to purchase old courthouse, 1852; rejected by grand jurors, 1852. Demolished, 1852. O'Connell Monument built on the site of the old courthouse (*John Neville, William Carroll,* and *James Cahill*), 1859–67. Only a small wall fragment of the old courthouse survives.

Archival and primary sources:

Thomas Dineley, 'Observations in a Voyage through the Kingdom of Ireland, 1675–80' (NLI, MS 392); Thomas Conway to Sir Donough O'Brien, 1690 (NLI, MS 45, 302/5); Clare grand-jury presentment books, 1786–91, and spring assizes 1815 (Clare County Archives, GJ/AP/42 and GJ/AP/43); Clare grand-jury presentment books, 1799–1839 (Cambridge University Library); *Journal of the Irish House of Commons*, vol. iv, 1733, p. 142; William Turner de Londe, 'The Market Square, Ennis' 1805, oil on canvas, 75.6 cm x 106 cm (The Merrion Hotel, Dublin); Clare grand-jury presentment books, 1830–98 (Clare County Archives); Inglis, *Ireland in 1834*, vol. 1, pp. 276–7, 280–93; Heaney, *Scottish Whig in Ireland*, p. 219; Lewis, *Topographical Dictionary*, vol. 1, p. 600; County Treasurers Act, 1837 (Ireland), 1 Vict., c. 54, s. 20; County of Clare Treasurer Act, 1838 (Ireland), 1 & 2 Vict., c. 104; *Connaught Journal*, 17 February, 27 February 1840, 24 February 1842, 29 February, 8 July 1844, 18 September, 27 October 1845; Clare grand-jury presentment books, 1845 (NAI, 1D/40/90); Royal Hibernian Academy exhibits by Kirk, 1845 (no. 461) and 1851 (nos. 345–7); *Clare Journal*, 27 October 1845, 6 July 1848, 19 June 1850, 1 July 1850, 10 May 1852 and 26 March 1866; *Limerick Chronicle*, 15 February, 29 October, 1 November, 26 November 1845, 11 March 1846, 27 June 1849, 22 May 1852; S. Godolphin Osborne, *Gleanings in the West of Ireland* (London: Boone, 1850), pp. 34–6; James Caird, *The Plantation Scheme, or, the West of Ireland as a Field for Investment* (Edinburgh and London: Blackwood, 1850), p. 51; *The Builder*, vol. 8, no. 395, 31 August 1850, p. 416; ibid., vol. 9, no. 420, 22 February 1851, p. 124; *Dublin Builder*, vol. 1, no. 4, 1 April 1859, p. 43; ibid., vol. 4, no. 57, 1 May 1862, p. 113; ibid., vol. 5, no. 76, 15 February 1863, p. 34; ibid., vol. 6, no. 106, 15 May 1864, p. 100; Lacy, *Sights and Scenes*, p. 687; Royal Hibernian Academy exhibits by Cahill, 1864 (no. 439); *Clare Almanac* (1878).

Secondary sources:

Strickland, *Dictionary of Irish Artists*, vol. 1, no. 148; McParland, 'Public Work of Architects', pp. 244–5, 247–9; Kelly, 'Ennis Courthouse', pp. 20–1; William Garner, *Ennis: Architectural Heritage* (Dublin: An Foras Forbartha, 1981), pp. 16, 18–19, 21, 31; Craig, *Architecture of Ireland*, p. 272; Jeremy Williams, *A Companion Guide to Architecture in Ireland, 1837–1921* (Dublin: Irish Academic Press, 1994), p. 51; Ó Dálaigh, 'The Old Courthouse of Ennis', pp. 5–12; Ó Murchadha, *Sable Wings over the Land*, pp. 8–9, 236, 240, 255–9; Lee, *James Pain*, pp. 190, 328; O'Donoghue, *Irish County Surveyors*, pp. 89, 108, 268; Paula Murphy, *Nineteenth-century Irish Sculpture: Native genius reaffirmed* (New Haven and London: Yale

University Press, 2010), p. 182; Brian Ó Dálaigh, *Irish Historic Towns Atlas, No. 25: Ennis* (Dublin: Royal Irish Academy, 2012), pp. 15–16.

CLARE

Ennis, no. 2

Gort Rd. & Lifford Rd.
Lat. 52°50'55.56" N.; Long. 8°58'49.29" W.

Old courthouse reported as in very poor condition with a replacement recommended 1836, 1837, 1838; unexecuted scheme (*John B. Keane*) 1838; rejected by cess-payers 1841; condemned by assize judge who calls for a new courthouse 1845; competition staged 1845; site bought 1846; new courthouse built to winning design (*Henry Whitestone*) 1846–50; O'Loghlen Testimonial (*Joseph R. Kirk*) installed 1850; alterations (*Arthur Charles Adair*) to new courthouse *c.* 1860; refurbished (*Dermot & Sean Merry*) 2002–4; extant.

County surveyor, James Boyd, reports that old courthouse (see 'Clare: Ennis, no. 1') is in very poor condition and a new building is required, 1836. County surveyor repeats these comments, 1837, 1838. Two acts of parliament to rescue the Clare grand jury from insolvency, 1837–8. Unexecuted scheme (*John B. Keane*), 1838. County surveyor states that a new courthouse will likely cost £12,000, 1838. Scheme rejected by cess-payers, 1841. Assize judge condemns courthouse and states that a replacement is required, 1845. Competition staged, 1845; seventeen entries (by *William Atkins, John B. Keane, Charles Frederick Anderson, James Boyd, Edward Henry Carson, Thomas J. Duff, George Fowler Jones, William Grady, William D'Esterre Smith, William Deane Butler, William Murray, George Papworth, Sancton Wood, William Tinsley*, etc.). Competition winner selected (*Henry Whitestone*), 1845. Site bought, 1846. New courthouse built (*Henry Whitestone*), at a cost of at least £12,000 (likely £16,000), 1846–50. O'Loghlen Testimonial (*Joseph R. Kirk*) installed in the entrance hall of the new courthouse, at a cost of £1,500, 1850. Alterations (*Arthur Charles Adair*), *c.* 1860. Refurbished (*Dermot & Sean Merry*), at a cost of €10 million, 2002–4. Extant.

Archival and primary sources:

Clare grand-jury presentment books, 1799–1839 (Cambridge University Library); Clare grand-jury presentment books, 1830–98 (Clare County Library); Lewis, *Topographical Dictionary*, vol. 1, p. 600; County Treasurers Act, 1837 (Ireland), 1 Vict., c. 54, s. 20; County of Clare Treasurer Act, 1838 (Ireland), 1 & 2 Vict., c. 104; *Connaught Journal*, 17 February, 27 February 1840, 24 February 1842, 29 February, 8 July 1844, 18 September, 27 October 1845; Clare grand-jury presentment books, 1845 (NAI, 1D/40/90); *Clare Journal*, 27 October 1845, 6 July 1848, 19 June 1850, 1 July 1850, and 10 May 1852; *Limerick Chronicle*, 15 February, 29 October, 1 November, 26 November 1845, 11 March 1846, 27 June 1849, 22 May 1852; S. Godolphin Osborne, *Gleanings in the West of Ireland* (London: Boone, 1850), pp. 34–6; James Caird, *The Plantation Scheme, or, the West of Ireland as a Field for Investment* (Edinburgh and London: Blackwood, 1850), p. 51; *The Builder*, vol. 8, no. 395, 31 August 1850, p. 416; ibid., vol. 9, no. 420, 22 February 1851, p. 124; Lacy, *Sights and Scenes*, p. 687; *Clare Almanac* (1878).

Secondary sources:

McParland, 'Public Work of Architects', pp. 244–5, 247–9; Kelly, 'Ennis Courthouse', pp. 20–1; Garner, *Ennis: Architectural heritage*, pp. 16, 18–19, 21, 31; Craig, *Architecture of Ireland*, p. 272; Williams, *Companion Guide to Architecture in Ireland*, p. 51; Ó Dálaigh, 'The Old Courthouse of Ennis', pp. 5–12; Ó Murchadha, *Sable Wings over the Land*, pp. 8–9, 236, 240, 255–9; Lee, *James Pain*, pp. 190, 328; O'Donoghue, *Irish County Surveyors*, pp. 89, 108, 268; Ó Dálaigh, *Irish Historic Towns Atlas, No. 25: Ennis*, pp. 15–16.

CORK COUNTY

Cork, no. 1

Grand Parade & St Patrick's St.
Lat. 51°53'54.55" N.; Long. 8°28'33.22" W.

An earlier courthouse on the same site by 1750; new courthouse built (*Richard Morrison,* builder *Abraham Hargrave*) *c.* 1806–7; damaged by fire 1827; criticised by an assize judge 1827; a replacement considered 1827; petition to build a joint courthouse for the city and county 1827; decision to build a joint courthouse 1829; competition staged 1830; new joint courthouse built 1830–5; old courthouse thereafter demolished; business premises (*Henry Hill*) erected on its site *c.* 1835; extant.

An earlier courthouse on the same site, facing Castle St., built by 1750. A new courthouse built (*Richard Morrison,* builder *Abraham Hargrave*), reportedly at a cost of £20,000 (probably a wild exaggeration), *c.* 1806–7. Damaged by fire, 1827. Condition criticised by an assize judge, 1827. A new courthouse considered by the county grand jury, 1827. County and city grand juries petition government to be allowed to build a single courthouse, 1827. County and city grand juries combine to build a joint courthouse, 1829. Competition staged, 1830. Replacement courthouse built (see 'Cork County and City: Cork, no. 2'), 1830–5; old courthouse thereafter demolished. Business premises (*Henry Hill*) erected on site, *c.* 1835. This survives, with many later alterations, as 'Queen's Old Castle'. It has been suggested by Patrick Holohan that the surviving attached portico is a remnant of Morrison's courthouse, but proof remains elusive.

Archival and primary sources:

Charles Smith, 'A Plan [map] of the City of Cork … in 1750' (Cork City and County Archives); William Beauford, 'A Map of the City and Suburbs of Cork', 1801 (ibid.); Thomas Holt, 'A Plan [map] of the City of Cork … in 1832' (ibid.); *Accounts of the Presentments Passed by the Grand Juries of Ireland … in … 1807*, H.C. 1808 (205), xiii, pp. 85, 87; Henry Westenra to William Gregory, 25 July 1827 (NAI, CSORP 1827/1453); Memorial of Cork county grand jury to Richard Wellesley, Spring 1827 (NAI, CSORP 1827/508); *Southern Reporter*, 27 February, 23 August, 30 August 1827, 5 December, 8 December 1829, and 20 October 1846; Lewis, *Topographical Dictionary*, vol. 1, p. 419; John Windele, *Historical and Descriptive Notices of the City of Cork and its Vicinity* (Cork: Bolster, 1839), p. 26; *Irish Builder*, vol. 29, no. 659, 1 June 1887, p. 150.

Secondary sources:

McParland, 'Public Work of Architects', pp. 239, 240–1, 246; Craig, *Architecture of Ireland*, p. 272; Rowan, *Morrison*, p. 76; Patrick Holohan, 'Cork Courthouses', pp. 77–8, 94; Gibney, Hurley and McParland, *Building Site in Eighteenth-century Ireland*, pp. 178–9.

CORK CITY

Cork, no. 1

Castle St. & North Main St.
Lat. 51°53'54.35" N.; Long. 8°28'37.99" W.

Built (*Twiss Jones*), 1708–9; described as in a dilapidated condition 1829; plans for repair work abandoned 1829; petition to build a joint courthouse for the city and county 1827; decision to build a joint courthouse for the city and county 1829; competition staged 1830; new courthouse built 1830–5; demolished *c.* 1835; later buildings now occupy the site.

Built (*Twiss Jones*), 1708–9. Described as in a dilapidated condition, 1829. Plans for repair work abandoned, 1829. County and city grand juries petition government to be allowed to build a single courthouse, 1827. County and city grand juries combine to build a joint courthouse, 1829. Competition staged, 1830. Replacement courthouse built (see 'Cork

County and Cork City: Cork, no. 2'), 1830–5. Old city courthouse described as a 'small and ill-considered building', 1834. Demolished, c.1835. Later buildings now occupy the site.

Archival and primary sources:

Charles Smith, 'A Plan [map] of the City of Cork … in 1750' (Cork City and County Archives); Nathaniel Grogan, 'Cork Exchange', 1796 (Crawford Art Gallery, Cork); William Beauford, 'A Map of the City and Suburbs of Cork', 1801 (ibid.), Thomas Holt, 'A Plan [map] of the City of Cork … in 1832' (ibid.); Two perspective sketches of the old city courthouse (exchange), n.d. (ibid.); Carr, *Stranger in Ireland*, pp. 264–5; *Accounts of the Presentments Passed by the Grand Juries of Ireland … in … 1807*, H.C. 1808 (205), xiii, pp. 85, 87; Memorial of Cork county grand jury to Richard Wellesley, Spring 1827 (NAI, CSORP 1827/508); *Irish Penny Magazine*, vol. 2, no. 1, 4 January 1834, p. 2; *Southern Reporter*, 30 August 1827, 5 December, 8 December 1829; Lewis, *Topographical Dictionary*, vol. 1, p. 419; Tuckey, *Cork Remembrancer*, p. 125.

Secondary sources:

S.F. Pettit, *This City of Cork, 1700–1900* (Cork: Studio Publications, 1977), p. 164; Patrick Holohan, 'Cork Courthouses', pp. 77–8, 94; Barclay, *Men on Trial*, p. 71.

CORK COUNTY and CITY

Cork, no. 2

Washington (Great George's) St.
Lat. 51°53'52.33" N.; Long. 8°28'43.71" W.

Old county courthouse damaged by fire 1827; county courthouse criticised by an assize judge 1827; a replacement considered by the county grand jury 1827; petition to build a joint courthouse for the city and county 1827; old city courthouse described as in a dilapidated condition 1829; plans for repair work to old city courthouse abandoned 1829; decision to build a joint courthouse 1829; various potential sites investigated 1829–30; competition staged 1830; new joint courthouse built (*James and George Richard Pain* with *Thomas Kirk*) 1830–5; offices furnished (*Thomas Deane*) 1836; repairs to the roof (possibly by *Jacob Owen*) 1839; gutted by fire 1891; competition staged to rebuild courthouse 1891; courthouse rebuilt (*William Henry Hill*) 1891–5; additions (*William Henry Hill*) 1904, 1907; external refurbishment work (*Neil Hegarty* and *Michael Russell*) 1997–9; internal alterations and refurbishment (*Neil Hegarty, Michael Russell*, etc.) 2003–5; extant.

Old county courthouse (see 'Cork County: Cork, no. 1') damaged by fire, 1827. County courthouse criticised by an assize judge, 1827. A new courthouse considered by the county grand jury, 1827. County and city grand juries petition government to be allowed to build a single courthouse, 1827. Washington (Great George's) St. laid out, 1827 onwards. Old city courthouse (see 'Cork City: Cork, no. 1') described as in a dilapidated condition, 1829. Plans for repair work to old city courthouse abandoned, 1829. County and city grand juries combine to build a joint courthouse, 1829. Various potential sites investigated, 1829–30. Competition staged, 1830; sixteen entries (by *William Vitruvius Morrison, Thomas Deane, Kearns Deane, James and George Richard Pain, John B. Keane*, etc.). Competition joint winners (*James and George Richard Pain* and *Thomas Deane*), 1835. Replacement courthouse built (*James and George Richard Pain*, with sculptural work by *Thomas Kirk*), at a cost of £22,000, 1830–5. Offices furnished (*Thomas Deane*), 1836. Repairs to the roof (possibly by *Jacob Owen*), 1839. Minor damage following political meeting, 1844. Gutted by fire, 1891. Competition staged to rebuild courthouse, 1891; at least two entries (by *Thomas Newenham Deane* and *William Henry Hill*). Courthouse rebuilt (*William Henry Hill*), 1891–5. Additions (*William Henry Hill*), 1904, 1907. External refurbishment work (*Neil Hegarty* and *Michael Russell*), 1997–9; Internal alterations and refurbishment (*Neil Hegarty, Michael Russell*, etc.), at a cost of €26 million, 2003–5. Extant.

Archival and primary sources:

Henry Westenra to William Gregory, 25 July 1827 (NAI, CSORP 1827/1453); Memorial of Cork county grand jury to Richard Wellesley, Spring 1827 (NAI, CSORP 1827/508); Correspondence relating to the building of Cork courthouse (NAI, CSORP 1831/2951); *Irish Penny Magazine*, vol. 1, no. 14, 6 April 1833, pp. 105–7 (illus.); ibid., vol. 2, no. 1, 4 January 1834, p. 2; *Southern Reporter*, 27 February, 23 August, 30 August 1827; 5 December, 8 December 1829; 3 March 1831; 11 April 1844; and 20 October 1846; Royal Hibernian Academy exhibit by John B. Keane, 1829 (no. 275); *Cork Constitution*, 6 April 1830; Cork County grand-jury presentment books, summer assizes 1834 (Cork City and County Archives, GJ/CO/PR/1); Correspondence relating to work by Thomas Deane at Cork courthouse (NAI, CSORP 1837/100); Lewis, *Topographical Dictionary*, vol. 1, p. 419; Binns, *Miseries and Beauties*, vol. 2, p. 146; *Limerick Chronicle*, 10 June, 14 June 1837; *Cork Constitution*, 11 July 1839; Windele, *Historical and Descriptive Notices of the City of Cork*, p. 21; *A Return of the Sums Paid to Jacob Owen … for … Each Year since His Appointment, up to April 1842*, H.C. 1842 (323), xxxviii, p. 3; *Irish Examiner*, 30 May 1845; Wilkinson, *Practical Geology and Ancient Architecture of Ireland*, p. 176; *Irish Builder*, vol. 5, no. 78, 15 March 1863, p. 49; ibid., vol. 33, no. 763, 1 October 1891, pp. 215, 239; vol. 33, no. 765, 1 November 1891, p. 247; ibid., vol. 34, no. 776, 15 April 1892, pp. 98–9; ibid., vol. 34, no. 777, 1 May 1892, p. 136; ibid., vol. 37, no. 846, 15 March 1895, pp. 80, 94; ibid., vol. 38, no. 882, 15 September 1896, p. 195; ibid., vol. 43, no. 987, 27 February 1901, p. 643; ibid., vol. 46, no. 1073, 2 July 1904, p. 422; ibid., vol. 46, no. 1074, 16 July 1904, p. 458; ibid., vol. 46, no. 1075, 30 July 1904, p. 496; ibid., vol. 48, no. 11, 2 June 1906, p. 444; ibid., vol. 49, no. 5, 9 March 1907, p. 178; *The Builder*, vol. 87, no. 3204, 2 July 1904, p. 28; Drawings for rebuilding Cork courthouse, 1891, by William Henry Hill (Cork City and County Archives, CCS02); Other drawings for rebuilding Cork courthouse, 1891, by William Henry Hill (sold at auction, 4 December 2012; copy in Irish Architectural Archive, RP.C.107.5); *The Irish Times*, 9 February 1895. There are further archival sources in Holohan's comprehensive history (see below).

Secondary sources:

Henry H. Hill, 'Cork Architecture', *Journal of the Cork Historical and Archaeological Society*, vol. 48, 1943, pp. 94–8; Maurice Craig, 'A Note on Courthouses', *Quarterly Bulletin of the Irish Georgian Society*, vol. 1, January–March 1958, pp. 8–12, at p. 11; Mark Bence-Jones, 'Two Pairs of Architect Brothers', *Country Life*, vol. 142, no. 3675, 10 August 1967, pp. 306–9; McParland, 'Public Work of Architects', pp. 246–9; Craig, *Architecture of Ireland*, p. 272; Rowan, *Morrison*, p. 76; O'Dwyer, 'Public Works Architecture', p. 59; Frederick O'Dwyer, *The Architecture of Deane and Woodward* (Cork: Cork University Press, 1997), pp. 16–18, 127–9, 551–2; Patrick Holohan, 'Cork Courthouses', p. 77–107; Lee, *James Pain*, pp. 4, 185–9, 191, 197, 225; Harrington, 'Work of Cork's Wide Streets Commissioners', pp. 98–117; Loeber, et al., *Art and Architecture of Ireland: Volume IV: Architecture 1600–2000*, pp. 183, 451; Barclay, *Men on Trial*, pp. 71, 73, 88.

DONEGAL

Lifford

The Diamond
Lat. 54°49'59.26" N.; Long. 7°28'43.17" W.

Planned 1743; built (*Michael Priestley*) 1746–54; alterations and repairs 1756, 1757, 1760; new gaol planned 1787; new gaol built *c.* 1791–3; repairs to courthouse (*Edward Miller*) 1793–4; further possible alterations and additions 1830s; alterations and additions (*William Harte*) 1868; improvements (*William James Doherty*) 1931; ceases to be a courthouse 1938; used as a library 1940s–80s; renovated and opened as a heritage centre 1994.

Planned, 1743. Built (*Michael Priestley*), 1746–54. County gaol was situated in the cellar of the courthouse. Alterations, 1756. Repairs to the 'battlements' (now vanished), 1757. Repairs to the ceilings, 1760. County gaol noted as 'five dungeons' under the courthouse, 1787. A replacement gaol is planned, 1787. Replacement gaol built nearby (*Edward Miller*), *c.* 1791–3. Repairs to courthouse (*Edward Miller*), 1793–4. Possible alterations and additions, 1830s. Alterations and additions

(*William Harte*), 1868. Improvements (*William James Doherty*), 1931. In use as a courthouse until 1938. In use as a library, 1940s–80s. Renovated and opened as a heritage centre, 1994.

Archival and primary sources:

Plaque above doorway ('designed & executed by Michael Priestley, A.D. 1746'); Donegal grand-jury presentment books, 1754, 1756–7, 1760, 1793–4 (copies) (Donegal County Library); Donegal grand-jury presentment books, 1754, 1756–7, 1760, 1793–4 (Donegal County Archives); Howard, *Lazarettos*, pp. 96–7; Angelique Day and Patrick McWilliams (eds), *Ordnance Survey Memoirs of Ireland: Volume 39: Donegal* (Belfast: Institute of Irish Studies, 1997), p. 12; Inglis, *Ireland in 1834*, vol. 2, pp. 188–9; Lewis, *Topographical Dictionary*, vol. 2, no. 260; *Irish Builder*, vol. 10, no. 196, 15 February 1868, p. 40; ibid., vol. 73, 24 October 1931, p. 929; Charles Gavan Duffy, *The League of North and South: An episode in Irish history, 1850–1854* (London: Chapman & Hall, 1886), p. 95.

Secondary sources:

Brett, *Court houses*, pp. 60–2, 106; McParland, 'Public Work of Architects', p. 195; Rowan, *Buildings of Ireland: North West Ulster*, pp. 43, 348; Craig, *Architecture of Ireland*, p. 202; Rowan, 'Irishness of Irish Architecture', pp. 9–10; O'Donoghue, *Irish County Surveyors*, p. 205; Billy Patton, *The Court Will Rise: A short history of the old courthouse, Lifford, Co. Donegal* (Lifford, Co. Donegal, 2004), pp. 12–21, 53, 68–70, 78, 82, 83–5; Loeber, et al., *Art and Architecture of Ireland: Volume IV: Architecture 1600–2000*, p. 181; Mac Suibhne, *The End of Outrage*, pp. 153–5; Gibney, Hurley and McParland, *Building site in Eighteenth-century Ireland*, p. 168.

DOWN

Downpatrick

English St. & Mount Crescent
Lat. 54°19'43.79" N.; Long. 5°43'7.81" W.

An earlier courthouse elsewhere in use by 1570; a new courthouse built by 1708; replacement built (*Hugh Darley*) 1737; repaired 1787, 1819, 1839; reported as in poor condition 1832; alterations and enlargements (*John. B. Keane*) 1832–4; committee room added 1841; damaged by fire 1855; extensive rebuilding, including a new crown courtroom and a tunnel to the county gaol (*Henry Smyth*) 1855–9; addition of a porch, etc. (*Bernard Murray*) 1870; bombed 1971; refurbished 1989–91; future as a courthouse uncertain 2015; extant.

An earlier courthouse, site unknown, in use by 1570. A courthouse built at (or near to) this location by 1708. Built (*Hugh Darley*), 1737. Repaired, 1787. Repair work to the roof, 1819, 1829. The grand jurors reported that the courthouse is in poor repair and deficient in accommodation, 1832. Alterations and enlargements (*John B. Keane*; contractor *John Lynn*), at a cost of at least £3,000, 1832–4. Grand-jury committee room added, 1841. Damaged in a fire, 1855. Extensive rebuilding, including a new crown courtroom, and a tunnel linking the courthouse with the county gaol to the north (*Henry Smyth*; contractor *George Stockdale*), at a cost of at least £4,000, 1855–9. Addition of a porch and other alterations (*Bernard Murray*), 1870. Bombed, 1971. Listed, 1976. Refurbished, 1989–91. Tunnel filled in, *c.* 1991. Future as a courthouse uncertain, 2015.

Archival and primary sources:

Walter Harris and Charles Smith, *The Antient and Present State Of The County of Down* (Dublin: Reilly, 1744), p. 43; *Walker's Hibernian Magazine*, May 1777, p. 332; *The Compleat Irish Traveler* (London, 1788), p. 218; 27 Geo. III, c. 21 (1787); Down grand-jury presentment books, 1819, 1829–33, 1841, 1855, 1856–7, 1859, and 1870 (PRONI, DOW/4/2); Reid, *Travels*, p. 186; Binns, *Miseries and Beauties*, pp. 145–6; *Belfast Newsletter*, 5 August 1828; Lewis, *Topographical Dictionary*, vol. 1, p. 493; J.A. Pilson, *Notices of the Most Important Events Connected with the County of Down* (Belfast: Phillips, 1842),

p. 22; *The Builder*, vol. 13, no. 654, 18 August 1855, p. 395; ibid., vol. 14, no. 676, 19 January 1856, p. 36; ibid., vol. 14, no. 704, 2 August 1856, p. 425; ibid., vol. 16, no. 807, 24 July 1858, p. 511; James O'Laverty, *An Historical Account of the Diocese of Down and Connor Ancient and Modern*, 5 vols (Dublin: Duffy, 1878), vol. 1, p. 261.

Secondary sources:

D. Dunleath, P.J. Rankin and A.J. Rowan, *Historic Buildings in the Town of Downpatrick* (Belfast: Ulster Architectural Heritage Society, 1970), p. 11; Brett, *Court Houses*, pp. 65–7; McParland, 'Public Work of Architects', pp. 247–8; Maureen Hunter, 'Downpatrick's Dungeons Rediscovered', *Lecale Miscellany*, vol. 9, 1991, pp. 21–5, at p. 21; Gordon Wheeler, 'John Lynn: Architect, contractor, engineer', *Lecale Miscellany*, vol. 15, 1997, pp. 24–46, at p. 38; O'Donoghue, *Irish County Surveyors*, p. 301; Anthony M. Wilson, *Saint Patrick's Town: A history of Downpatrick and the barony of Lecale* (Belfast: Isabella Press, 1995), pp. 124–5, 161, 176–7, 221; R.H. Buchanan and Anthony Wilson, *Irish Historic Towns Atlas, No. 8: Downpatrick* (Dublin: Royal Irish Academy, 1997), section 13; Northern Ireland Environmental Agency (NIEA), Listed Buildings Database (www.doeni.gov.uk); Barclay, *Men on Trial*, p. 88.

DUBLIN COUNTY

Kilmainham

Inchicore Rd. & South Circular Rd.
Lat. 53°20'30.27" N.; Long. 6°18'30.82" W.

Planned 1817; unexecuted designs (*Henry, Mullins & McMahon* and *Henry Aaron Baker*) *c.* 1818–19; built (*William Farrell*) *c.* 1819–20; proposed (executed?) alterations to the courtroom (*John McCurdy*) *c.* 1856–61; closed as a courthouse 2008; renovated 2014–16; extant.

New courthouse planned, 1817. First presentment (£9,572), 1817. Unexecuted design (*Henry, Mullins & McMahon*), 1817. First central-government loan received by grand jury, 1818. Unexecuted design (*Henry Aaron Baker*), *c.* 1819. Built (*William Farrell*), at a cost of at least £8,679, 1819–20. Minor alterations, 1823. Stone wall built at rear, 1826. Iron railings installed, 1828. Minor alterations, 1828. Alterations to the courtroom, 1835. Interior alterations, 1841. Proposed (executed?) alterations to the courtroom (*John McCurdy*), *c.* 1856–61. Closed as a courthouse, 2008. Renovated to form part of Kilmainham gaol museum, 2014–16.

Archival and primary sources:

Plaque in grand-jury room ('Architect William Farrell. Opened 3 October 1820'); Drawings by Henry, Mullins & McMahon, 5 October 1817 (Irish Architectural Archive, Guinness Collection, Acc. 96.68.5.1.1-4); Dublin County grand-jury presentment books, 1817–41, see in particular Mich. 1817, Mich. 1818, Easter 1821, Easter 1823, Easter 1826, Easter 1827 (Fingal County Council Archives, GJ/5/1-9); Dublin County grand-jury minute book, 22 April 1818, 11 May 1819, 9 November 1819, 21 November 1820, 9 May 1821, 24 November 1821 (Fingal County Council Archives, GJ/1/1); Elevation drawing by William Farrell, n.d. (Houghton Library, Harvard University, William Farrell album, MS Typ 788) (the Irish Architectural Archive has copies); *Saunders' Newsletter*, 27 November 1821; Royal Hibernian Academy exhibits by Henry Aaron Baker, 1826 (nos. 245, 253, 259, 265); *Dublin Penny Journal*, vol. 4, no. 184, 9 January 1836, p. 221 (illus.); *Returns of All Sums of Money … in Aid of Public Works in Ireland, since the Union*, H.C. 1839 (540), xliv, p. 12; Plan drawings and specifications for works for alterations to the courtroom in Kilmainham courthouse, by John McCurdy, n.d. [*c.* 1856–61] (NLI, AD 1702–5); Ground-floor and first-floor plans, dated 16 February 1920 (NAI, OPW 5HC/4/400).

Secondary sources:

Brett, *Court Houses*, p. 88; Casey, *Buildings of Ireland: Dublin*, p. 686; Butler, 'Politics, Grand Juries, and Ireland's Unbuilt Assize Courthouses', pp. 120–5; Willy Cumming, 'Kilmainham Gaol', National Inventory of Architectural Heritage Building of the Month, May 2016 (www.buildingsofireland.ie); Barclay, *Men on Trial*, p. 88.

DUBLIN CITY

Dublin, no. 1

Christ Church Pl. & Nicholas St.
Lat. 53°20'34.00" N.; Long. 6°16'17.19" W.

An earlier tholsel replaced as early as 1311; reported as decayed 1611; decision to build a new tholsel 1674; built 1682–3; damaged in a storm 1728; tower removed before 1791; building partially abandoned 1791; replacement courthouse built 1792–7; demolished 1809; not extant, but fragments survive.

An earlier tholsel replaced as early as 1311. Reported as decayed, 1611. Decision taken to build a new tholsel, with the old tholsel reported as dilapidated, 1674. New tholsel built, 1682–3. Damaged in a storm, 1728. Tower removed before 1791. City meetings held elsewhere due to unstable condition of tholsel, 1791. Replacement courthouse built, 1792–7 (see 'Dublin City: Dublin, no. 2'). Old tholsel demolished, 1809. Statues and coat of arms survive in the crypt of Christchurch Cathedral.

Archival and primary sources:

Walter Harris, *The History and Antiquities of the City of Dublin* (Dublin: Flinn & Williams, 1766), pp. 110–11, 472; James Malton, 'The Tholsel, Dublin', 1792 (National Gallery of Ireland); Dublin City grand-jury presentment books, 1793–1803 (NLI, MS 16,223); 35 Geo. III, c. 25 (1795); Warburton, Whitelaw, and Walsh, *History of … Dublin*, vol. 1, pp. 534–5; A. Peter, *Sketches of Old Dublin* (Dublin: Sealy, Bryers, & Walker, 1907), pp. 80–6.

Secondary sources:

Thomas King Moylan, 'The Little Green: Part I', *Dublin Historical Record*, vol. 8, no. 3, June–August 1946, pp. 81–91; Thomas King Moylan, 'The Little Green: Part II', *Dublin Historical Record*, vol. 8, no. 4, September–November 1946, pp. 141–4; McParland, 'Public Work of Architects', p. 105; Dickson, *Dublin*, pp. 22, 95–6, 232–3, 268–9; Gibney, Hurley and McParland, *Building Site in Eighteenth-century Ireland*, pp. 32, 86, 220–1 (illus.).

DUBLIN CITY

Dublin, no. 2

Green St. & Halston St.
Lat. 53°20'59.26" N.; Long. 6°16'15.62" W.

An earlier tholsel built 1682–3; damaged in a storm 1728; tower removed before 1791; building partially abandoned 1791; replacement courthouse built (*Whitmore Davis*) 1792–7; alterations and additions (*John Semple*) 1837, 1842; proposal to enlarge *c.* 1842–3; alterations (*Murray and Denney*) 1850; alterations and improvements (*Charles James McCarthy*) 1893; Special Criminal Court ceases use of building 2010; extant.

An earlier tholsel (see 'Dublin City: Dublin, no. 1') built, 1682–3. Damaged in a storm, 1728. Tower removed before 1791. City meetings held elsewhere due to unstable condition of tholsel, 1791. New city gaol (Newgate) built 1773–81 (see Part II). New courthouse built adjacent to this gaol (*Whitmore Davis*), 1792–7. Staged the trial of Robert Emmet, 1803. Alterations and additions (*John Semple*), 1837, 1842. Proposal to extend courthouse into adjoining city marshalsea and sheriff's prison, *c.* 1842–3. Staged the trial of John Mitchell, 1848. Alterations (*Murray and Denney*), 1850. Alterations and improvements (*Charles James McCarthy*), 1893. Special Criminal Court ceases use of building, 2010.

Archival and primary sources:

Brian Bolger papers (NAI, PRO 1A/58/128); Dublin City grand-jury presentment books, 1793–1803 (NLI, MS 16,223); 35

Geo. III, c. 25 (1795); Warburton, Whitelaw, and Walsh, *History of… Dublin*, vol. 1, pp. 534–5; Wright, *Historical Guide to the City of Dublin*, p. 255; *Twenty-first Report … on … the Prisons of Ireland, 1843*, H.C. 1843 (462), xxvii, p. 20; *The Builder*, vol. 8, no. 391, 3 August 1850, p. 368; A. Peter, *Sketches of Old Dublin* (Dublin: Sealy, Bryers, & Walker, 1907), pp. 80–6; J.J. Reynolds, Photograph of interior, 1903, from 'Footprints of Emmet' collection (South Dublin County Libraries); *The Irish Times*, 14 June 1898.

Secondary sources:

Moylan, 'Little Green: Part I', pp. 81–91; Moylan, 'Little Green: Part II', pp. 141–4; Edward McParland, 'The Papers of Bryan Bolger, Measurer', *Dublin Historical Record*, vol. 25, no. 4, September 1972, pp. 120–31, at p. 124; McParland, 'Public Work of Architects', p. 105; Desmond Guinness, *Georgian Dublin* (London: Batsford, 1979), p. 57; Casey, 'Courthouses', p. 48; Casey, *Buildings of Ireland: Dublin*, pp. 99–100; Dickson, *Dublin*, pp. 22, 95–6, 232–3, 268–9; Barclay, *Men on Trial*, pp. 60–70.

THE FOUR COURTS*

Dublin

Inns Quay
Lat. 53°20'45.11" N.; Long. 6°16'25.06" W.

Planned 1776; part of west courtyard built (*Thomas Cooley*) 1776–84; remainder built (*James Gandon* and *Henry Aaron Baker*) 1785–1804; proposal to build a new Nisi Prius courtroom 1832; Nisi Prius courtroom and other alterations (*Jacob Owen*) 1835–9; addition of a records depository (*James Higgins Owen*) 1861–6; gutted by fire 1922; extensively rebuilt (*Thomas Joseph Byrne*, etc.) 1925–32; ceases to hold criminal trials 2010.

**Note: this entry provides only a very brief summary of the history of the Four Courts. Its list of sources is only a representative sample of the vast amount of literature pertaining to this internationally renowned building. Further information can be found at the Dictionary of Irish Architects (www.dia.ie), in Edward McParland's* James Gandon*, and elsewhere.*

Unexecuted proposal (*Robert Mack*), 1765. Planned, 1776. North and west ranges of the west courtyard built (*Thomas Cooley*), 1776–84. Project taken over by James Gandon on Cooley's death, 1784. Remainder built (*James Gandon* and *Henry Aaron Baker*), 1785–1804. Series of loans from central government, 1801–9. Work to Prerogative Court, etc. (*Francis Johnston*), 1818. Alterations (*Francis Johnston*), *c.* 1821. Proposal for a bar library (*William Farrell*), 1825–6; Proposed alterations and additions (*William Murray*), 1827. Proposal to build a new Nisi Prius courtroom and for other improvements to the Four Courts, 1832; these additions and other works built (*Jacob Owen*), 1835–9; New Landed Estates and Probate courts, etc. (*James Higgins Owen*), 1858–60. New record repository (*James Higgins Owen*), 1861–6. Additions (*Enoch Trevor Owen*), 1864, 1866. Additions (*McCurdy & Mitchell*), 1873–4. Additions and repairs (*James Higgins Owen*), 1879. Additions (*Albert Edward Murray*), 1887. Additions (*Thomas Drew*), 1894–6. Held by rebels during the Easter Rising, 1916. Occupied by anti-Treaty rebels, 1922. Gutted by fire, 1922. Extensively rebuilt (*Thomas Joseph Byrne, Harold Leask*, etc.), 1925–32. All criminal trials moved elsewhere, 2010.

Archival and primary sources:

Society of Artists (Ireland) exhibit by Robert Mack, 1765; Drawings for the new Four Courts, 1776–84, by Thomas Cooley (Irish Architectural Archive, Acc. 2007/10.2/1-7, on loan from the King's Inns Library); Copies of drawings, 1785, by James Gandon (Irish Architectural Archive); 30 Geo. III, c. 41 (1790); 34 Geo. III, c. 6 (1794); 35 Geo. III, c. 25 (1795); Board of Works minutes, 28 March 1804 (NAI, Board of Works files, 2D/56/93); Estimates and contract agreements for a bar library, 1825–6, by William Farrell (King's Inns Archives, H/3-1); Nisi Prius Court House Dublin Act, 1832, 2 Will. IV, c. 32; *Fourth Report of the Commissioners on Public Works, Ireland … for the Year 1835*, H.C. 1836 (314), xxxvi, p. 4 and plan and elevation drawings by Jacob Owen: *Returns of All Sums of Money … in Aid of Public Works in Ireland, since the Union*, H.C. 1833 (540), xlii, pl. 11; 'Hall of the Four Courts, Dublin', *Illustrated London News* 27 Jan. 1844; Mulvany and Gandon, *James Gandon*, pp. 68–74 and passim; *The Builder*, vol. 16, no. 784, 13 February 1858, p. 111; ibid., vol. 24, no. 1219 (16 June 1866), pp. 450–1; *Dublin Builder*, vol. 1, no. 12, 1 December 1859, p. 164; ibid., vol. 2, no. 20, 1 April 1860, p. 241; ibid., vol. 3, no. 48, 15 December 1861, p. 712; ibid., vol. 4, no. 53, 1 March 1862, p. 58; vol. 8, no. 157, 1 July 1866, p. 166; *Irish Builder*, vol. 29, no. 666, 15 September 1887, p. 266; ibid., vol. 67, no. 15, 25 July 1925, p. 617.

Secondary sources:

C.P. Curran, 'Cooley, Gandon and the Four Courts', *Journal of the Royal Society of Antiquaries of Ireland*, vol. 19, 7th ser., 1949, pp. 20–5; Craig, *Dublin*, pp. 267–82; J.A. Culliton, 'The Four Courts, Dublin', *Dublin Historical Record*, vol. 21, no. 4, 1967, pp. 116–26; McParland, 'Public Work of Architects', pp. 90–1; Guinness, *Georgian Dublin*, pp. 54–5; Edward McParland, 'The Early History of James Gandon's Four Courts', *Burlington Magazine*, vol. 122, no. 932, November 1980, pp. 727–35; McParland, *James Gandon*, pp. 144–65; Summerson, *Architecture in Britain*, pp. 412–14; Frederick O'Dwyer, 'Building Empires: Architecture, politics and the Board of Works 1760–1860', *Irish Architectural and Decorative Studies*, vol. 5, 2002, pp. 109–75, at p. 154; Casey, *Buildings of Ireland: Dublin*, pp. 92–8; Dickson, *Dublin*, p. 225; Loeber, et al., *Art and Architecture of Ireland: Volume IV: Architecture 1600–2000*, p. 181; Barclay, *Men on Trial*, pp. 60–70.

FERMANAGH

Enniskillen

East Bridge St.
Lat. 54°20'37.96" N.; Long. 7°38'10.23" W.

Probably built *c.* 1785; county gaol rebuilt elsewhere 1812–15; reroofed 1816; remodelled and extensively altered, probably also a porch added (*William Farrell*) 1821–2; alterations and additions (*Roderick Gray*) *c.* 1860–2; redundant 1973; refurbished 1982; future as a courthouse uncertain 2015.

Probably built *c.* 1785. County gaol situated in the cellars under the courthouse. A new gaol built elsewhere in the town (see Part II), 1812–15. Reroofed, at a cost of £900, 1816. Remodelled (*William Farrell* and *Henry Lambert*; contractors *Williams & Cockburn*), probably including a new porch, at a cost of at least £3,500, 1821–2. Alterations and additions (*Roderick Gray*), *c.* 1860–2. Redundant, 1973. Refurbished, at a cost of £1 million, 1982. Listed, 1977. Future as a courthouse uncertain, 2015.

Archival and primary sources:

Howard, *Lazarettos*, pp. 95–6; Fermanagh grand jury presentment books, 1815–22 (PRONI, FER/4); *Pigot & Co's Provincial Directory of Ireland, 1824*, p. 448; Angelique Day and Patrick McWilliams (eds), *Ordnance Survey Memoirs of Ireland: Volume 4: Fermanagh* (Belfast: Institute of Irish Studies, 1990), p. 54; Gorton and Wright, *Topographical Dictionary*, vol. 1, p. 739; Lewis, *Topographical Dictionary*, vol. 1, p. 606; *The Builder*, vol. 18, no. 891, 3 March 1860, p. 141; *Dublin Builder*, vol. 2, no. 14, 1 March 1860, p. 225; ibid., vol. 4, no. 53, 1 March 1862, p. 58; *General Advertiser*, 4 February 1860.

Secondary sources:

W. Copeland Trimble, *The History of Enniskillen*, 3 vols (Enniskillen: Trimble, 1921), vol. 3, pp. 868–91; Hugh Dixon, *List of Historic Buildings … in the Town of Enniskillen* (Belfast: Ulster Architectural Heritage Society, 1973), p. 22; Brett, *Court Houses*, pp. 78–80, 107; McParland, 'Public Work of Architects', p. 244; Rowan, *Buildings of Ireland: North west Ulster*, p. 281; Breege McCusker, 'The County Gaol and Some Past Crimes and Punishments in County Fermanagh', *Clogher Record*, vol. 13, no. 1, 1988, pp. 50–5, at p. 50; O'Donoghue, *Irish County Surveyors*, p. 195; Northern Ireland Environmental Agency (NIEA), Listed Buildings Database (www.doeni.gov.uk).

GALWAY COUNTY

Galway, no. 1

Druid Ln. (Court House Ln.), near Quay St. and Flood St.
Lat. 53°16'15.71" N.; Long. 9°3'13.03" W.

Unknown date of construction; a replacement courthouse built 1812–15; old courthouse thereafter used as a Catholic chapel, *c.* 1815–21; not extant.

Unknown date of construction. A new county gaol built (see Part II), 1804–11. A new courthouse planned, 1808. A new courthouse built (see 'Galway County: Galway, no. 2'), 1812–15. Old county courthouse used as a Catholic chapel, *c.* 1815–21. Not extant.

Archival and primary sources:

Freeman's Journal, 29 June 1812; Hardiman, *Galway*, pp. 47, 264, 310–11; Dutton, *Statistical ... Survey ... of Galway*, pp. 205–6, 250–1, 322.

Secondary sources:

Patrick J. Kennedy, 'The County of the Town of Galway', *Journal of the Galway Archaeological and Historical Society*, vol. 30, nos. 3–4, 1963, pp. 90–101, at pp. 91, 95; Mitchell, 'Tholsel', p. 83.

GALWAY COUNTY

Galway, no. 2

Courthouse Square
Lat. 53°16'33.31" N.; Long. 9°3'17.95" W.

Newtownsmith quarter laid out, *c.* 1780s–90s; a new county gaol built 1804–11; new courthouse planned 1808; various sites considered *c.* 1811; new courthouse built (*Richard Morrison*) 1812–15; nearby bridge built (*John Behan*) 1818–19; alterations to the Crown courthouse (*William Deane Butler*) 1839; extensive alterations (*James Perry*) *c.* 1895–7; coat of arms removed, etc. *c.* 1922; refurbished (*O'Riain & Yates*) *c.* 2005–13; extant.

An earlier courthouse built at an unknown date (see 'Galway County: Galway, no. 1'). Newtownsmith quarter laid out, *c.* 1780s–90s. A new county gaol built (see Part II), 1804–11. A new courthouse planned, 1808. Various sites considered for this new courthouse, *c.* 1811. A new courthouse built (*Richard Morrison*), at a cost of at least £7,500, on the site of a former Franciscan abbey, 1812–15. Bridge connecting new courthouse with new county gaol built (*John Behan*), 1818–19. Temporarily used to stage the town assizes, *c.* 1823. Alterations, *c.* 1823, *c.* 1826, *c.* 1829. Alterations to the Crown courtroom (*William Deane Butler*), 1839. Extensive alterations, including a new roof and more accommodation for jurors, witnesses, and clerks (*James Perry*), *c.* 1895–7. Coat of arms, etc., removed, situated in the lawns of University College Galway, *c.* 1922. Courthouse extensively refurbished (*O'Riain & Yates*), *c.* 2005–13. Extant.

Archival and primary sources:

Freeman's Journal, 29 June 1812; Account of work at Galway courthouse, n.d. (NAI, Brian Bolger papers, PRO 1A/58/124 and 2/476/15,17); Galway County grand-jury presentment books, 1805, 1807–8, 1811–14, 1818, 1823, 1826, 1829, 1839–40 (NAI); Registry books of Erasmus Smith school, 22 June 1793 to 25 November 1822, no. 2, for 18 June 1812 (NLI); Hardiman, *Galway*, pp. 47, 264, 310–11 (illus.); Dutton, *Statistical ... Survey ... of Galway*, pp. 205–6, 250–1, 322, 382; *Galway Patriot*, 27 March 1829; Heaney, *Scottish Whig in Ireland*, p. 254; Lewis, *Topographical Dictionary*, vol. 1, p. 648;

Five drawings of Galway courthouse, *c.* 1870s (Galway County Library); *Irish Builder*, vol. 37, no. 851, 1 June 1895, p. 134; ibid., vol. 39, no. 903, 1 August 1897, p. [illegible]

Secondary sources:

Kennedy, 'County of the Town of Galway', p. 91; McParland, 'Public Work of Architects', pp. 161, 241; Mitchell, 'Tholsel', p. 83; Richardson, *Gothic Revival Architecture in Ireland*, p. 136; Maurice Semple, *From Where the River Corrib Flows* (Galway, 1988), p. 41; Rowan, *Morrison*, p. 98; Fionnuala May, 'The County Courthouse at Galway by Richard Morrison', MUBC thesis, University College Dublin, 1993, pp. 12, 22–33, 38–72, 140–62, 168–75; Loeber, et al., *Art and Architecture of Ireland: Volume IV: Architecture 1600–2000*, p. 463; Barclay, *Men on Trial*, p. 88.

TOWN OF GALWAY

Galway, no. 1

Shop St. & Church Yard St.
Lat. 53°16'21.26" N.; Long. 9°3'11.60" W.

An earlier tholsel built nearby *c.* 1580; a new tholsel planned 1639; foundations laid 1641; left unfinished; finally complete *c.* 1707–9; condemned as unsafe *c.* 1822; plans for a new courthouse 1822; demolished *c.* 1822; new courthouse built 1824–5; site later used as a fruit market; not extant.

An earlier tholsel built nearby, *c.* 1580. A new tholsel planned, 1639. Foundation of a new tholsel laid, 1641. Left unfinished. Still incomplete, 1685. Finally completed, *c.* 1707–9. Old tholsel used as a town gaol (see Part II), 1709–1810. Condemned as unsafe, *c.* 1822. Plans for a new courthouse (see 'Town of Galway: Galway, no. 2'), 1822. New courthouse built (*Alexander Hay*), 1824–5. Tholsel demolished, *c.* 1822. Site later used as a fruit market. Not extant.

Archival and primary sources:

Thomas Phillips, 'Ground-plaine of Galway', 1685 (NLI, MS. 3137 (28)); Sketch of tholsel, *c.* 1820, by James Hardiman (Galway County Archives); Hardiman, *Galway*, pp. 298–9; *Dublin Evening Post*, 9 May 1822; Dutton, *Statistical … Survey … of Galway*, pp. 208, 212.

Secondary sources:

Blake, 'Account of the Lynch Family', p. 91; Patrick J. Kennedy, 'The County of the Town of Galway', *Journal of the Galway Archaeological and Historical Society*, vol. 30, nos. 3–4, 1963, pp. 90–101; Mitchell, 'Tholsel', pp. 77–85 (illus.); Mitchell, 'Prisons of Galway', pp. 1–3.

TOWN OF GALWAY

Galway, no. 2

Courthouse Square
Lat. 53°16'34.14" N.; Long. 9°3'14.65" W.

Tholsel built *c.* 1707–9; condemned as unsafe *c.* 1822; demolished *c.* 1822; plans for a new courthouse 1822; new courthouse built (*Alexander Hay*) 1824–5; in use as a town hall 1894; and as a cinema *c.* 1950s; dilapidated state 1990s; refurbished 1993–5; in use as a theatre.

Tholsel completed (see 'Town of Galway: Galway, no. 1'), *c.* 1707–9. Condemned as unsafe, *c.* 1822. Demolished, *c.* 1822.

Plans for a new courthouse, 1822. County courthouse temporarily used to stage the town assizes, *c.* 1823. First central-government loan, 1823. Further loan to add a portico to the new courthouse, 1825. New courthouse built (*Alexander Hay*), 1824–5. In use as a town hall, 1894. Converted into a cinema, *c.* 1950s. In a dilapidated state, 1990s. Refurbished as a municipal theatre, 1993–5. In use as a theatre.

Archival and primary sources:

Thomas Phillips, 'Ground-plaine of Galway', 1685 (NLI, MS. 3137 (28)); Hardiman, *Galway*, pp. 298–9; *Dublin Evening Post*, 9 May 1822; *Connaught Journal*, 16 January, 19 June 1823; *Galway Advertiser*, 12 April, 7 June 1823; Dutton, *Statistical … Survey … of Galway*, pp. 208, 212; Galway town grand-jury presentment books, 1826–38 (location unknown, quoted in Kennedy, 'County of the Town of Galway' below); *Galway Patriot*, 27 March 1829; Heaney, *Scottish Whig in Ireland*, p. 254; Lewis, *Topographical Dictionary*, vol. 1, p. 648; *An Account of Loans Advanced … for Public Works in Ireland … since 1800*, H.C. 1847 (718), liv, pp. 20–3.

Secondary sources:

Patrick J. Kennedy, 'The County of the Town of Galway', *Journal of the Galway Archaeological and Historical Society*, vol. 30, nos. 3–4, 1963, pp. 90–101; McParland, 'Public Work of Architects', p. 244; Mitchell, 'Tholsel', pp. 77–85 (illus.); Mitchell, 'Prisons of Galway', pp. 1–3; Loeber, et al., *Art and Architecture of Ireland: Volume IV: Architecture 1600–2000*, p. 463; Barclay, *Men on Trial*, p. 88.

KERRY

Tralee, no. 1

Market Square
Lat. 52°16'10.42" N.; Long. 9°42'22.83" W.

Date of construction unknown; replacement gaols built *c.* 1788, 1812–17; a new courthouse planned 1827; old courthouse described as 'unsafe' and 'inconvenient' 1830; built 1830–3; later buildings now occupy the site; not extant.

Date of construction unknown. Shown on Smith's 1756 map as 'The courthouse, gaol, and markethouse', at the north of Market Square. The gaol was built over a river. A new gaol built elsewhere (see Part II), *c.* 1788. Call from Forster Archer for a new gaol and courthouse, 1807. Another new gaol built elsewhere (see Part II), 1812–17. A new courthouse planned, 1827. Old courthouse described as 'unsafe' and 'inconvenient', 1830. New courthouse built (see 'Kerry: Tralee, no. 2'), 1830–3. Later buildings now occupy the site.

Archival and primary sources:

Charles Smith, 'A Plan [map] of Tralee', 1756 (Kerry County Library); Gerald J. Lyne (ed.), 'Rev. Daniel A.B. Beaufort's Tour of Kerry in 1788', *Journal of the Kerry Archaeological and Historical Society*, vol. 18, 1985, pp. 183–214, at pp. 201, 203; Howard, *Lazarettos*, p. 91; *Inspector General's Report of … the Prisons in Ireland for … 1807*, H.C. 1808 (239), ix, p. 10; A.B. Rowan, n.t., *The Kerry Magazine*, vol. 3, no. 25, January 1856, p. 13.

Secondary sources:

Gerald O'Carroll, 'Penal Reform and Gaol Construction: A case study of Tralee', *North Munster Antiquarian Journal*, vol. 39, 1998–9, pp. 7–11, at pp. 7, 9.

KERRY

Tralee, no. 2

Ashe (Nelson) St.
Lat. 52°16'11.42" N.; Long. 9°42'12.73" W.

The site of a former gaol, built *c.* 1788; a new courthouse planned 1827; new courthouse built (*William Vitruvius Morrison*) 1830–3; repairs (*Donald Alfred Tyndall*) 1952–3; extensively rebuilt 1980s; extant.

Former courthouse on Market Square (see 'Kerry: Tralee, no. 1'). A gaol built on the site of the future second courthouse (see Part II), *c.* 1788. Call from Forster Archer for a new gaol and courthouse, 1807. Another new gaol built elsewhere (see Part II), 1812–17. A new courthouse planned, 1827. Exhibits by Morrison of design for new courthouse, 1828, 1834. Exhibits by John B. Keane of design for new courthouse, 1830. Commissioners appointed, 1828. First application for a central-government loan rejected, 1828. First central-government loan received, 1830. New courthouse built (*William Vitruvius Morrison*), at a cost of at least £9,350, 1830–3. Repairs (*Donald Alfred Tyndall*), 1952–3; partially disused, 1960s; extensively rebuilt, 1980s; extant.

Archival and primary sources:

Gerald J. Lyne (ed.), 'Rev. Daniel A.B. Beaufort's Tour of Kerry in 1788', *Journal of the Kerry Archaeological and Historical Society*, vol. 18, 1985, pp. 183–214, at pp. 201, 203; Howard, *Lazarettos*, p. 91; *Inspector General's Report of … the Prisons in Ireland for … 1807*, H.C. 1808 (239), ix, p. 10; Royal Academy exhibits by Morrison, 1828 (no. 1048) and 1834 (no. 874); Royal Hibernian Academy exhibits by John B. Keane, 1830 (nos. 269, 280); Henry Westenra to William Gregory, 25 July 1827 (NAI, CSORP 1827/1453); Charles Burke to William Gregory, 19 July 1828 (NAI, CSORP 1828/556); *An Account of All Sums of Money … for Public Works, During the Last Four Years*, H.C. 1828 (464), xxii, p. 3; *Copy of Memorials to the Irish Government on the Subject of Advances for Building a Court House in the County of Kerry*, H.C. 1830 (240), xxvi, pp. 1–2; Copy of County Kerry presentments for 1828 (NAI, CSORP 1828/1340); Treasury advances to County Kerry (NAI, CSORP 1832/6100); *Tralee Mercury*, 6 February, 17 March 1830, 10 March 1832, 31 August 1833, 2 October 1833; Lewis, *Topographical Dictionary*, vol. 2, p. 641; Morrison's name inscribed on the architrave of the portico; Inglis, *Ireland in 1834*, vol. 1, nos. 262–3; *Returns of All Sums of Money … in Aid of Public Works in Ireland, since the Union*, H.C. 1839 (540), xliv, p. 13; *Tralee Chronicle*, 2 August 1845; Fisher, *Letters from the Kingdom of Kerry*, p. 9; *Dublin Builder*, vol. 1, no. 6, 1 June 1859, p. 73; *Irish Builder*, vol. 94, no. 12, 7 June 1952, p. 600; ibid., vol. 95, no. 6, 14 March 1953, p. 274.

Secondary sources:

McParland, 'Public Work of Architects', pp. 3, 245–46; Craig, *Architecture of Ireland*, pp. 272–4; Richardson, *Gothic Revival Architecture in Ireland*, p. 136; Rowan, *Morrison*, pp. 10, 46–7, 168–9; O'Carroll, 'Penal Reform', pp. 7, 9; Lee, *James Pain*, p. 227; Loeber, et al., *Art and Architecture of Ireland: Volume IV: Architecture 1600–2000*, p. 182; Barclay, *Men on Trial*, p. 88.

KILDARE

Athy

Emily Square
Lat. 52°59'30.08" N.; Long. 6°58'59.42" W.

Probably built *c.* 1740; noted as 'new' 1752; additions (probably by *Richard Morrison*) *c.* 1804–9; bell tower added *c.* 1845; attic storey added 1913; in use as a factory and a fire station *c.* 1950s; in disrepair 1960s; purchased by Kildare County Council 1976; renovated 1983–90; in use as a town hall and heritage centre; extant.

Probably built *c.* 1740. Noted as 'new', 1752. Additions (probably by *Richard Morrison*), probably the north range with Morrison-esque sculptured panels, *c.* 1804–9. Unexecuted proposal to use the courthouse as a temporary barracks, *c.* 1804. Minor work (*Richard Richards*), 1822. Bell tower added, *c.* 1845. An unused portion rented to the Athy Town Commissioners, 1862. Attic storey added, cupola taken down, and other works, 1913. In use as a factory and a fire station, *c.* 1950s. In disrepair, 1960s. Purchased by Kildare County Council from the Duke of Leinster, 1976. Renovated, 1983–90. In use as a town hall and heritage centre. Extant.

A nearby corn exchange, built by Frederick Darley, *c.* 1857, and refurbished in 1999–2001, now in use as a courthouse.

Archival and primary sources:

Anon., 'Ancient and Present State of Athy', *Anthologica Hibernica*, May 1793, pp. 325–8; Richard Pococke, *Tour in Ireland* (1st edn 1752, repub. Dublin: Hodges, Figgis, & Co., 1891), pp. 165–6; Kildare grand-jury presentment books, summer 1809, spring 1822, and spring 1862 (Kildare County Library, GJ); Photograph showing the building before an attic storey was added, taken *c.* 1900 (NLI, Lawrence Collection).

Secondary sources:

Casey, 'Courthouses', p. 57; Denis Cogan, 'Athy Town Hall', *Journal of the County Kildare Archaeological Society*, vol. 17, 1987–91, pp. 99–105; Arnold Horner, 'A Note on the Fate of the "Factory" at Maynooth', *Journal of the County Kildare Archaeological Society*, vol. 19, no. 3, 2004–5, pp. 562–4; Andrew Tierney, *The Buildings of Ireland: Central Leinster, the Counties of Kildare, Laois, and Offaly* (New Haven and London: Yale University Press, 2019), p. 96.

KILDARE

Naas, no. 1

South Main St.
Lat. 53°13'4.27" N.; Long. 6°39'48.74" W.

Unknown date of construction (built by 1682); plans to build a new courthouse on the same site (*Simon Vierpyle*) 1797; work abandoned 1798; new courthouse built nearby *c.* 1804–7; Presbyterian church built on the site 1866–7; not extant.

Unknown date of construction (built by 1682). Plans to build a new courthouse on the same site (*Simon Vierpyle*), 1797. Work abandoned and destroyed, 1798. New courthouse built nearby (see 'Kildare: Naas, no. 2'), *c.* 1804–7. Presbyterian church built on the site, 1866–7. Not extant.

Archival and primary sources:

Accounts of Presentments by Grand Juries in Ireland … in 1807, H.C. 1808 (205), xiii, p. 177; Map of Naas, 1805, by George Taylor (NLI); *Dublin Builder*, vol. 6, no. 114, 15 September 1864, p. 188; ibid., vol. 8, no. 150, 15 March 1866, pp. 67, 78; ibid., vol. 9, no. 176, 15 April 1867, p. 102; *Freeman's Journal*, 27 January 1866.

Secondary sources:

William H. Gibson, 'The North and South Moats of Naas', *Journal of the County Kildare Archaeological Society*, vol. 17, 1987–91, p. 49; Sheena Meagher, 'South Main Street, Naas', ibid., vol. 18, no. 3, 1996–7, pp. 367–96; Con Costello, 'Thomas Sherrard's Map of Naas, 1787', ibid., vol. 18, no. 4, 1998–9, pp. 589–97; Con Costello, 'Thomas Sherrard's Map of Naas, 1787', ibid., vol. 19, no. 1, 2000–1, p. 229; Barnard, *Making the Grand Figure*, p. 27.

KILDARE

Naas, no. 2

South Main St.
Lat. 53°13'4.27" N.; Long. 6°39'48.74" W.

Plans to build a new courthouse on the same site as the old tholsel (*Simon Vierpyle*) 1797; work abandoned 1798; new courthouse built nearby (*Richard Morrison*) *c.* 1804–7; extensive alterations and additions, including a new portico (*John McCurdy*) 1858–61; alterations and additions (*John Henry Brett*) 1871–3, 1876; damaged by fire 1952; renovations (*Deaton Lysaght Architects*) 1997; extant.

Plans to build a new courthouse on the same site as the old tholsel (*Simon Vierpyle*) (see 'Kildare: Naas, no. 1'), 1797. Work abandoned and destroyed, 1798. New courthouse built nearby (*Richard Morrison*), *c.* 1804–7. Minor alterations (*John Yeates*), 1838. Extensive alterations and additions, including a new portico (*John McCurdy*), 1858–61. Alterations and additions (*John Henry Brett*), 1871–3, 1876. Coat of arms removed from pediment, *c.* 1930s. Damaged by fire, 1952. Extensive renovations, at a cost of €2.25 million (*Deaton Lysaght Architects*), 1997. Extant.

Archival and primary sources:

Accounts of Presentments by Grand Juries in Ireland ... in 1807, H.C. 1808 (205), xiii, p. 177; Map of Naas, 1805, by George Taylor (NLI); Kildare grand-jury presentment books, summer 1838, spring 1858, and spring 1862 (Kildare County Library, GJ); Lacy, *Sights and Scenes*, p. 187; *Leinster Express*, 19 March 1859; *Dublin Builder*, vol. 3, no. 31, 1 April 1861, p. 472; ibid., vol. 3, no. 39, 1 August 1861, p. 591; Survey drawings, including plans, elevations, and sections, of Naas courthouse, 8 December 1870, by R.J. Stirling and J.H. Mellon (NAI, OPW 5HC/4/402); *Irish Builder*, vol. 13, no. 279, 1 August 1871, pp. 201–2; ibid., vol. 13, no. 281, 1 September 1871, p. 230.

Secondary sources:

McParland, 'Public Work of Architects', p. 241; Craig, *Architecture of Ireland*, p. 271; Casey, 'Courthouses', p. 62; Rowan, *Morrison*, pp. 136–7; Gibson, 'The North and South Moats of Naas', *Journal of the County Kildare Archaeological Society*, vol. 17, 1987–91, p. 49; Sheena Meagher, 'South Main Street, Naas', ibid., vol. 18, no. 3, 1996–7, pp. 367–96; Con Costello, 'Thomas Sherrard's Map of Naas, 1787', ibid., vol. 18, no. 4, 1998–9, pp. 589–97; Con Costello, 'Thomas Sherrard's Map of Naas, 1787', ibid., vol. 19, no. 1, 2000–1, p. 229; Maureen Gill-Cummins, 'The Evolution of the Court House at Naas, Co. Kildare', ibid., vol. 20, no. 1, 2008–9, pp. 66–75; Hickey and Kenny, *Nás na Ríogh*, p. 74 and passim; Loeber, et al., *Art and Architecture of Ireland: Volume IV: Architecture 1600–2000*, p. 182; Barclay, *Men on Trial*, p. 69; Tierney, *The Buildings of Ireland: Central Leinster*, pp. 510–11.

KILKENNY COUNTY

Kilkenny

Parliament St.
Lat. 52°39'15.17" N.; Long. 7°15'13.93" W.

Site of a former castle; in use as a gaol perhaps as early as 1568; county gaol shown on map 1758; courthouse built on site *c.* 1790–5; replacement county gaol built elsewhere 1801–9; extensive alterations and repairs (*William Robertson*) 1824–5; additions and alterations (*Richard Burnham*, etc.) 1855; condemned as 'disgusting and abominable' 1875; partially destroyed by fire 1895; rebuilt 1895; additions 1920s; extensive refurbished and extended (*Bluett & O'Donoghue*) 2009–10; extant.

Assizes were formerly held, perhaps, at Black Abbey. Site of a former castle, known as Grace's Castle. Gaol located on the site perhaps as early as 1568. County gaol shown on map, 1758. Courthouse built on site, with gaol below, *c.* 1790–5.

Replacement county gaol built (see Part II), 1801–9. Alterations and repairs to courthouse, including façade (*William Robertson*), 1824–5. Additions and alterations (*Richard Burnham*, etc.), 1855. Condemned by a judge as 'disgusting and abominable', 1875. Partially destroyed by fire, 1895. Rebuilt, 1895. Additions, 1920s. Extensively refurbished and extended (*Bluett & O'Donoghue*), 2009–10. Listed. Extant.

Archival and primary sources:

G. Evans, Memorial of Deed. No. 116066 (NAI, Registry of Deeds); 'A Survey of the City of Kilkenny', 1758, by John Rocque (NLI); William Tighe, *Statistical Observations Relative to the County of Kilkenny Made in the Years 1800 and 1801* (Dublin: Graisberry & Campbell, 1802), p. 42; Reid, *Travels*, p. 243; Brewer, Beauties of Ireland, vol. 1, p. 444; Kilkenny County grand-jury presentment book, spring 1824 (Bodleian Library, Oxford); Kilkenny County grand-jury presentment books, 1836–98 (Kilkenny County Library, GJ/1-63A); Lewis, *Topographical Dictionary*, vol. 1, pp. 110–11; *The Builder*, vol. 13, no. 651, 28 July 1855, p. 359; *Irish Builder*, vol. 17, no. 375, 1 August 1875, p. 216; *The Architect*, vol. 53, 8 February 1895, supplement, p. 17.

Secondary sources:

May Sparks and Eric Bligh, *Kilkenny: Pen and picture pages of its story* (Kilkenny: Kilkenny People, 1926), pp. 30, 50; McParland, 'Public Work of Architects', p. 158; Katherine M. Lanigan, Gerald Tyler and Margery Brady, *Kilkenny: Its architecture & history* (Belfast: Appletree, 1987), pp. 66, 83; Craig, *Architecture of Ireland*, pp. 267–8; Teehan, 'Emergence of County Courthouses', pp. 46–7, 59–60, 90–2; John Bradley, *Irish Historic Towns Atlas, No. 10: Kilkenny* (Dublin: Royal Irish Academy, 2000), section 13; Loeber, et al., *Art and Architecture of Ireland: Volume IV: Architecture 1600–2000*, pp. 172, 181, 465.

KILKENNY CITY

Kilkenny, no. 1

High St. & Pudding Ln.
Lat. 52°39'3.67" N.; Long. 7°15'9.23" W.

Unknown date of construction; probably built by the fifteenth century; noted as under repair 1517; noted as intact 1628; city gaol nearby shown on map 1758; replaced by another tholsel nearby *c.* 1700; demolished *c.* 1800; later housing on site; not extant.

Unknown date of construction. Probably built by the fifteenth century. Noted as under repair, 1517. Noted as intact, 1628. The old city gaol was nearby. City gaol shown on map, 1758. Replaced (to a certain extent) by a tholsel elsewhere on High Street, *c.* 1700. Assizes still held in old tholsel, 1793. Demolished, *c.* 1800. Later housing on site, extended, 1836. Only minor fragments appear to survive as spolia in later buildings. Not extant.

Archival and primary sources:

'A Survey of the City of Kilkenny', 1758, by John Rocque (NLI); other sources noted in Hogan, 'Three Tholsels', below.

Secondary sources:

John Hogan, 'The Three Tholsels of Kilkenny', *Journal of the Royal Historical and Archaeological Association of Ireland*, vol. 5, no. 41, 4th series, January 1880, pp. 236–52, at pp. 236, 238–40, 242; Sparks and Bligh, *Kilkenny*, pp. 30, 50; Bradley, *Irish Historic Towns Atlas, No. 10: Kilkenny*, section 13.

KILKENNY CITY

Kilkenny, no. 2

High St.
Lat. 52°39'7.08" N.; Long. 7°15'10.53" W.

An earlier tholsel on the same site built *c.* 1600; noted as 'new' 1619; plans submitted for a replacement (*Ambrose Evans*) 1758; demolished *c.* 1760; a replacement built on the same site (possibly by *Davis Ducart* or more likely *William Colles*) *c.* 1759–64; alterations (*William Robertson*) 1807; alterations 1825; additions *c.* 1829–30; 'almost ruinous' 1842; alterations 1849; extensive renovations 1951; damaged by fire 1985; extensively rebuilt *c.* 1985–90; in use as a town hall; extant.

An earlier tholsel on the same site, built *c.* 1600, itself replacing the first tholsel in the town (see 'Kilkenny City; Kilkenny, no. 1'); Noted as 'the new tholsel', 1619. Noted as 'remarkable, though small [and] very neat', 1757. Plans submitted for a replacement (*Ambrose Evans*), 1758. Demolished, *c.* 1760. A third tholsel erected (possibly by *Davis Ducart* or more likely *William Colles*), at a cost of £1,315, *c.* 1759–64. Alterations (*William Robertson*), 1807. Alterations, 1825. Additions, *c.* 1829–30. Described by the County Surveyor as 'almost ruinous', 1842. Alterations to cellars, 1849. Minor alterations, 1851. Repairs and minor alterations, 1855. Extensive renovations, 1951. Damaged by fire, 1985. Extensively rebuilt, *c.* 1985–90. In use as a town hall. Listed. Extant.

Archival and primary sources:

'A Survey of the City of Kilkenny', 1758, by John Rocque (NLI); Plans by Ambrose Evans for a new tholsel in Kilkenny, 1758 (NLI, microfilm, Pos. 5136); Kilkenny Corporation Minute Book (NLI, microfilm P5137, entries for 1 December 1758, 20 February 1759, etc.); Kilkenny City grand-jury presentment books, 1807–55 (Bodleian Library, Oxford); Kilkenny City grand-jury presentment books, 1836–98 (Kilkenny County Library, GJ/1-63A); Lewis, *Topographical Dictionary*, vol. 1, pp. 110–11; *Irish Builder and Engineer*, vol. 92, no. 13, 24 June 1950, p. 653 (illus.); other sources noted in Hogan, 'Three Tholsels', below.

Secondary sources:

Hogan, 'Three Tholsels of Kilkenny', pp. 243–9; Sparks and Bligh, *Kilkenny*, pp. 30, 50; McParland, 'Public Work of Architects', p. 11; Lanigan, Tyler and Brady, *Kilkenny*, p. 66; Craig, *Architecture of Ireland*, pp. 201–2; Casey, 'Courthouses, p. 67; Teehan, 'Emergence of County Courthouses', pp. 46–7, 59–60, 90–2; Bradley, *Irish Historic Towns Atlas, No. 10: Kilkenny*, section 13; Loeber, et al., *Art and Architecture of Ireland: Volume IV: Architecture 1600–2000*, pp. 178, 465.

KING'S COUNTY (OFFALY)

Philipstown (Daingcan)

Main St. & Church Rd.
Lat. 53°17'40.16" N.; Long. 7°17'31.84" W.

An earlier courthouse probably on the same site, built *c.* 1760; plans to move assizes to Tullamore 1786; a new courthouse built (possibly by *James Gandon*) *c.* 1807; new gaol built at Tullamore 1826–30; commissioners appointed to build a new courthouse at Tullamore 1829; act of parliament to move assizes to Tullamore 1832; act takes effect 1835; courthouse built at Tullamore 1833–5; extensive alterations *c.* 1930; being renovated 2012–; extant.

An earlier courthouse, probably on the same site, built *c.* 1760. Plans to move assizes to Tullamore, 1786. Replaced by a new courthouse (possibly by *James Gandon*), *c.* 1807. Renewed plans to move the county gaol to Tullamore, 1820–1. Minor repairs, 1821. Described as 'lately erected', 1821. New gaol built in Tullamore (see Part II), 1826–30. Commissioners appointed to build a new courthouse at Tullamore, 1829. Repaired after damage during an election, 1831. Act of parliament passed to move assizes to Tullamore, 1832. Act takes effect, 1835. Courthouse built in Tullamore (see 'King's County: Tullamore'), 1833–5. Furniture, etc. removed to Tullamore courthouse, 1835. Later used as a quarter-sessions courthouse. Extensive alterations, including the taking down of a part of the central section of the building, blocking up windows, etc., *c.* 1930. Being renovated, 2012–. Listed. Extant.

Archival and primary sources:

Design for Philipstown courthouse, *c.* 1760 (NLI, MS 10,770(1)); *Journal of the Irish House of Commons*, vol. xxiii, 1786, p. cxciv; *Accounts of the Presentments Passed by the Grand Juries of Ireland … in … 1807*, H.C. 1808 (205), xiii, p. 218; King's County grand-jury presentments, 1821 (Cambridge University Library); King's County grand-jury presentments, spring assizes 1830, summer assizes 1831, and spring assizes 1835 (Offaly County Library, GJ/1/1/1-2); Memorandum from Lord Downshire to the lord lieutenant, 17 May 1824 (PRONI, D/671/c/12); *Hansard*, vol. 13, 3rd ser., 30 May 1832, cols 209–10; King's County Assizes Act, 1832 (Ireland), 2 Will. IV, c. 60; Lewis, *Topographical Dictionary*, vol. 2, no. 460.

Secondary sources:

McParland, 'Public Work of Architects', p. 11, 162; Casey, 'Courthouses', pp. 98–9; Byrne, *Legal Offaly*, pp. 22, 67, and passim; Tierney, *The Buildings of Ireland: Central Leinster*, pp. 302–3.

KING'S COUNTY (OFFALY)

Tullamore

Charleville Rd.
Lat. 53°16'13.35" N.; Long. 7°29'48.30" W.

Plans to move assizes to Tullamore 1786; a new courthouse built in Philipstown *c.* 1807; a new gaol built at Tullamore 1826–30; commissioners appointed (*John Killaly*) 1829; blocked by rival grand-jury interests in Philipstown 1829–32; act of parliament to move assizes to Tullamore 1832; act takes effect 1835; courthouse built at Tullamore (*John B. Keane*) 1833–5; unexecuted designs (*William Murray, William Vitruvius Morrison*, etc.) *c.* 1832; Gutted by fire 1922. Rebuilt (*Thomas Francis McNamara*) 1925–7; coat of arms removed *c.* 1927; extensively refurbished (*Newenham Mulligan Associates*) 2005–7; listed; extant.

Plans to move assizes to Tullamore, 1786. A new courthouse built in Philipstown (see 'King's County: Philipstown'), *c.* 1807. Renewed plans to move the county gaol to Tullamore, 1820–1. New gaol built in Tullamore (see Part II), 1826–30. Commissioners appointed to build a new courthouse in Tullamore (*John Killaly*), 1829. Grand-jury presentment – traversed – for £11,350, for a new courthouse, 1830. Act of parliament passed to move assizes to Tullamore, 1832. Act takes effect, 1835. Courthouse built in Tullamore (*John B. Keane*), at a cost of at least £9,890, 1833–5. Unexecuted designs by a series of other architects (*William Murray, William Vitruvius Morrison, William Deane Butler*, etc.), *c.* 1832. Gutted by fire, 1922. Rebuilt (*Thomas Francis McNamara*), 1925–7. Coat of arms removed, *c.* 1927. Extensively refurbished (*Newenham Mulligan Associates*), at a cost of €15 million, 2005–7; Listed. Extant.

Archival and primary sources:

Journal of the Irish House of Common, vol. xxiii, 1786, p. cxciv; King's County grand-jury presentments, 1821 (Cambridge University Library); King's County grand-jury presentments, spring assizes 1830, spring assizes 1833, and spring assizes 1835 (Offaly County Library, GJ/1/1/1-2); Memorandum from Lord Downshire to the lord lieutenant, 17 May 1824 (PRONI, D/671/c/12); Charles Bury to Francis Leveson Gower, 19 October 1829 (NAI, CSORP 1829/5045); Bury to Leveson Gower, 17 November 1829 (NAI, CSORP 1829/6040); John Ponsonby to Leveson Gower, 12 November 1829 (NAI, CSORP 1829/6040); Charles Bury to Catherine Bury, 17 November 1829, March 1830, 3 September 1830 (University of Nottingham

Library, Charles Brinsley Marlay papers); Charles Bury to Catherine Bury, 3 September 1833 (ibid., My 454/1-4 and My 463/1-3), *Freeman's Journal*, 19 March 1830; Letter from overseers of courthouse competition at Tullamore to William Murray, 15 November 1832 (Irish Architectural Archive, RIAI Murray Collection, Acc. 92/46.1174); Drawings for Tullamore courthouse by William Murray, unexecuted, December 1832 (ibid., Acc. 92/46.1174-93); *Hansard*, vol. 13, 3rd ser., 30 May 1832, cols 209–10; King's County Assizes Act, 1832 (Ireland), 2 Will. IV, c. 68; Drawings for Tullamore courthouse, by John B. Keane, 1833 (Irish Architectural Archive, Lismore Castle Collection, Acc. 97/107.3.1-4 (photocopies); Elevation drawing for Tullamore courthouse, n.d., by John B. Keane (private collection of Michael Byrne, Tullamore, Co. Offaly); Royal Hibernian Academy exhibits by William Deane Butler, 1834 (nos. 273, 278), Ferrar, *Diary of Colour-Sergeant George Calladine*, p. 194; Lewis, *Topographical Dictionary*, vol. 2, no. 652; West, *Summer Visit to Ireland in 1846*, p. 167; Morrison, 'William Vitruvius Morrison', p. 7; *An Account of Loans Advanced … for Public Works in Ireland … since 1800*, H.C. 1847 (718), liv, p. 3; Drawings for the reconstruction of Tullamore courthouse, 1925, by Thomas Francis McNamara (NAI, OPW collection); *Irish Builder*, vol. 67, no. 15, 8 August 1925, p. 650; ibid., vol. 67, no. 19, 19 September 1925, p. 766; *The Builder*, vol. 129, no. 4306, 14 August 1925, p. 264.

Secondary sources:

W. Moran, 'Tullamore', *Ríocht na Midhe – Records of the Meath Archaeological and Historical Society*, vol. 2, no. 4, 1962, pp. 44–54; McParland, 'Public Work of Architects', pp. 244–5, 248; Michael Byrne, *A Walk through Tullamore* (Tullamore: Esker, 1980); Casey, 'Courthouses', pp. 98–9; Richardson, *Gothic Revival Architecture*, p. 137; Craig, *Architecture of Ireland*, pp. 272, 275; Rowan, *Morrison*, p. 181; Goslin, 'Descriptive Catalogue of the Murray Collection', pp. 335–8; Michael Byrne, 'Tullamore: The growth process, 1785–1841', in William Nolan and Timothy P. O'Neill (eds), *Offaly: History & society* (Dublin: Geography Publications, 1998), pp. 569–626, at pp. 596 and passim; Michael Byrne, 'The County Courthouse at Tullamore and the Making of a County Town', *Journal of the Offaly Historical and Archaeological Society*, vol. 1, 2003, pp. 108–25; Byrne, *Legal Offaly*, pp. 15, 18–22, 67, 391–5, and passim; Loeber, et al., *Art and Architecture of Ireland: Volume IV: Architecture 1600–2000*, p. 182; Butler, 'Politics, Grand Juries, and Ireland's Unbuilt Assize Courthouses', pp. 125–31; Barclay, *Men on Trial*, pp. 60–1; Tierney, *The Buildings of Ireland: Central Leinster*, pp. 622–4.

LEITRIM

Carrick-on-Shannon, no. 1

Unknown

Old gaol and courthouse were adjoining buildings; a new gaol built *c.* 1796–1802; a new courthouse built *c.* 1820; presumably not extant.

Old gaol and courthouse were adjoining buildings. A new gaol built elsewhere, *c.* 1796–1802 (see Part II). Courthouse described as 'a large building [that] formerly served as [a] jail and sessions house', but that a replacement gaol had since been built elsewhere, 1807. A new courthouse built near the new gaol (see 'Leitrim: Carrick-on-Shannon, no. 2'), *c.* 1820. Later condition of old courthouse not known. Presumably not extant.

Archival and primary sources:

Howard, *Lazarettos*, p. 92; James McParlan, *Statistical Survey of the County of Leitrim* (Dublin: Graisberry & Campbell, 1802), p. 46; Anon. ['W.P.'], 'Sketch of a Journey through Part of Ireland', in *Walker's Hibernian Magazine*, November 1807, pp. 675–80, at p. 677.

No secondary sources.

LEITRIM

Carrick-on-Shannon, no. 2

St George's Terrace
Lat. 53°56'41.45" N.; Long. 8°5'52.36" W.

Old gaol and courthouse were adjoining buildings; a new gaol built *c.* 1796–1802; a new courthouse built (*William Farrell*) *c.* 1820; Repairs (*Thomas Dugall Hall*) 1837–8; repairs 1845; portico removed *c.* 1980; ceased to be used as a courthouse 1994; renovated for use as a theatre 2005; extant.

Old gaol and courthouse were adjoining buildings (see 'Leitrim: Carrick-on-Shannon, no. 2'). A new gaol built elsewhere, *c.* 1796–1802 (see Part II). A new courthouse built near the new gaol (*William Farrell*), *c.* 1820. A tunnel links the courthouse and gaol, probably also built *c.* 1820. Repairs to the roof and other sundry works (*Thomas Dugall Hall*), 1837–8. Further repairs, 1845. Portico removed, *c.* 1980. Ceased to be used as a courthouse, 1994. Renovated for use as a theatre (The Dock), 2005. Extant.

Archival and primary sources:

Howard, *Lazarettos*, p. 92; James McParlan, *Statistical Survey of the County of Leitrim* (Dublin: Graisberry & Campbell, 1802), p. 46; Anon. ['W.P.'], 'Sketch of a Journey through Part of Ireland', in *Walker's Hibernian Magazine*, November 1807, pp. 675–80, at p. 677; Ferrar, D*iary of Colour-Sergeant George Calladine*, p. 120; Plan and elevation drawings for Carrick-on-Shannon courthouse, n.d., by William Farrell (Houghton Library, Harvard University, William Farrell album, MS Typ 788); *Pigot & Co's Provincial Directory of Ireland, 1824*; Gorton and Wright, *Topographical Dictionary*, vol. 1, p. 383; Lewis, *Topographical Dictionary*, vol. 1, p. 276; *Roscommon and Leitrim Gazette*, 17 June 1837, 6 July 1839, and 22 February 1845; Thomas Dugall Hall, *Report on the State and Progress of Public Buildings … in the County of Leitrim* (Dublin: Hodges & Smith, 1838), p. 5; Wilkinson, *Practical Geology and Ancient Architecture of Ireland*, pp. 294–5.

Secondary sources:

McParland, 'Public Work of Architects', p. 240; Craig, *Architecture of Ireland*, pp. 272, 274; T.W. Freeman, 'Land and People, *c.* 1841', in W.E. Vaughan (ed.), *A New History of Ireland: Volume 5: Ireland under the Union, I, 1801–70* (Oxford: Oxford University Press, 1989), pp. 242–71, at p. 247; Sean Gill, 'Historical Introduction to the Dock', n.d. (Leitrim County Library, Ballinamore).

LIMERICK COUNTY

Limerick, no. 1

Meatmarket Ln. & Sheep St.
Lat. 52°40'5.26" N.; Long. 8°37'16.00" W.

On the site of a former Franciscan friary; built 1732; a new courthouse built elsewhere 1807–14; demolished *c.* 1820; a corn store on the site *c.* 1850; not extant.

Old county courthouse built outside the city walls, on the site of a former Franciscan friary. Built, 1732. A new courthouse built elsewhere (see 'Limerick County: Limerick, no. 2'), 1807–14. Demolished, *c.* 1820. A corn store built on the site, *c.* 1850. Not extant.

Archival and primary sources:

John Ferrar, *The History of Limerick … from the Earliest Records to the Year 1787* (Limerick: Watson, 1787), pp. 200–3; Patrick Fitzgerald and John James McGregor, *The History, Topography, and Antiquities of the County and City of Limerick*, 2 vols (Dublin: McKern, 1827), vol. 2, pp. 579–81; Lenihan, *Limerick*, pp. 341, 419–20, 433, 654, 670.

Secondary sources:

Judith Hill, *The Building of Limerick* (Cork: Mercier, 1991), p. 35; Eamonn O'Flaherty, *Irish Historic Towns Atlas, No. 21: Limerick* (Dublin: Royal Irish Academy, 2010), pp. 27–8; Loeber, et al., *Art and Architecture of Ireland: Volume IV. Architecture 1600–2000*, p. 467.

LIMERICK COUNTY

Limerick, no. 2

Merchants Quay
Lat. 52°40'3.71" N.; Long. 8°37'30.11" W.

Built (*Nicholas and William Hannan*) 1807–9; additions 1813; portico completed 1814; additions (*James and George Richard Pain*) 1820; renovations and proposals for a new courthouse elsewhere (*Patrick Joseph Sheahan*) 1936–9; extensively rebuilt (*Patrick Joseph Sheahan*) 1953–5; refurbished (*Murray O'Laoire Associates*) 2001–3; extant.

Old county courthouse built (see 'Limerick County: Limerick, no. 1'), 1732. A new courthouse built (*Nicholas and William Hannan*), 1807–9. Gallery added to Crown courthouse, 1813. Portico completed, 1814. Total cost of building works, at least £13,700. Additions (*James and George Richard Pain*), 1820. Renovations (*Patrick Joseph Sheahan*), 1936. Unexecuted proposal for a new county courthouse elsewhere (*Patrick Joseph Sheahan*), 1938–9. Extensively rebuilt (*Patrick Joseph Sheahan*), 1953–5. Refurbished (*Murray O'Laoire Associates*), at a cost of €10 million, 2001–3. Listed. Extant.

Archival and primary sources:

Ferrar, *The History of Limerick*, pp. 200–3; Limerick County grand-jury presentments, 1807, 1808, 1810–14, 1820 (Limerick City Library); John Alexander Staples, *A Tour in Ireland in 1813 & 1814* (Dublin: Gough, 1817), p. 219; William Turner de Londe, 'A View from Bank Place, Limerick', *c.* 1821 (Private collection); Fitzgerald and McGregor, *History, Topography and Antiquities of the County and City of Limerick*, vol. 2, pp. 579–81 (illus.); Lewis, *Topographical Dictionary*, vol. 2, pp. 272–3; W.H. Bartlett, Nathaniel Parker Willis and Joseph Stirling Coyne, *The Scenery and Antiquities of Ireland*, 2 vols (London: George Virtue, 1842), vol. 1, p. 106 (illus.); *Limerick Reporter*, 23 August 1842; Lenihan, *Limerick*, pp. 341, 419–20, 433, 654, 670; *Irish Builder*, vol. 78, 12 December 1936, p. 1133; ibid., vol. 80, 8 January 1938, p. 30; ibid., vol. 95, no. 4, 14 February 1953, p. 171; ibid., vol. 97, no. 24, 19 November 1955, p. 1224; ibid., vol. 97, no. 25, 3 December 1955, p. 1270; ibid., vol. 97, no. 26, 17 December 1955, p. 1314.

Secondary sources:

Hill, *The Building of Limerick*, pp. 35, 51–2, 87, 103, 142, 144–6; Lee, *James Pain*, pp. 18, 37, 46, 53, 190, 244, 266, 317, 328, 267; O'Flaherty, *Irish Historic Towns Atlas, No. 21: Limerick*, pp. 27–8; Loeber, et al., *Art and Architecture of Ireland: Volume IV: Architecture 1600–2000*, p. 467; Barclay, *Men on Trial*, p. 88.

LIMERICK CITY

Limerick, no. 1

Quay Ln.
Lat. 52°40'3.34" N.; Long. 8°37'22.74" W.

Replaced an earlier city courthouse on the same site, built 1640; additions and alterations to old courthouse 1685; a new courthouse built 1763–6; unexecuted proposal for a new courthouse elsewhere 1834; new courthouse built elsewhere 1843–5; old courthouse purchased by the Christian Brothers 1845; in use as a school; extant.

A city courthouse built at the corner of Quay Lane, 1640. Court cases moved from old tholsel to this building at this time. Additions and alterations, 1685. A new courthouse built on the same site, at a cost of at least £700, 1763–6. Unexecuted proposal for a new courthouse (see 'Limerick City: Limerick, no. 2'), 1834. A new courthouse built elsewhere, 1843–5. Old courthouse purchased by the Christian Brothers for use as a school, 1845. Still in use as a school. Extant.

Archival and primary sources:

Ferrar, *The History of Limerick*, pp. 200–3; Fitzgerald and McGregor, *History, Topography, and Antiquities of the County and City of Limerick*, vol. 2, pp. 579–81; Lewis, *Topographical Dictionary*, vol. 2, p. 272; Lenihan, *Limerick*, pp. 205, 210, 226, 355, 358, 419–20, 427, 433, 642, 670.

Secondary sources:

Judith Hill, *The Building of Limerick* (Cork: Mercier, 1991), pp. 35, 51–2, 87, 103, 142, 144–6; Lee, *James Pain*, pp. 18, 37, 46, 53, 190, 244, 266, 317, 328, 267; O'Flaherty, *Irish Historic Towns Atlas, No. 21: Limerick*, pp. 27–8; Loeber, et al., *Art and Architecture of Ireland: Volume IV: Architecture 1600–2000*, p. 467.

LIMERICK CITY

Limerick, no. 2

Merchants Quay
Lat. 52°40'5.18" N.; Long. 8°37'29.62" W.

An earlier courthouse built nearby 1763–6; unexecuted proposal for a new courthouse (*Henry Hill*) 1834; new courthouse built partially on site of city gaol (*James Pain*) 1843–5; repaired (*Joseph J. Peacocke*) 1911; demolished *c.* 1988; not extant.

An earlier courthouse built nearby, 1763–6 (see 'Limerick City: Limerick, no. 1'). Unexecuted proposal for a new courthouse to have been situated between the existing county courthouse and city gaol (*Henry Hill*), 1834. A new courthouse built partially on the site of the city gaol (*James Pain*), 1843–5. Repaired (*Joseph J. Peacocke*), 1911. Demolished, *c.* 1988. City council buildings thereafter built on the site. Not extant.

Archival and primary sources:

Drawings for Limerick City courthouse, June 1834, by Henry Hill (private collection of the Allen family, Shanagarry, Co. Cork); *Limerick Chronicle*, 26 July 1843; ibid., vol. 25, November 1843; *Twenty-third Report … on … the Prisons of Ireland, 1845*, H.C. 1845 (620), xxv, pp. 69–70; *Twenty-fourth Report … on … the Prisons of Ireland, 1846*, H.C. 1846 (697), xx, pp. 81–2; *Twenty-fifth Report … on … the Prisons of Ireland, 1847*, H.C. 1847 (805), xxix, p. 93; *An Account of Loans Advanced … for Public Works in Ireland … since 1800*, H.C. 1847 (718), liv, pp. 40–1; *Twenty-first Report of the Commissioners on Public Works, Ireland … for the Year 1852*, H.C. 1852–3 (1651), xli, pp. 42–3; *Irish Architect and Craftsman*, vol. 1, no. 14, 29 April 1911, p. 197; Photographs taken before demolition, by Joe Ranson, *c.* 1988 (Limerick City and County Archives, Ranks Community Collection (Joe Ranson photography collection), P/90/23/6 and P/90/23/10).

Secondary sources:

Judith Hill, *The Building of Limerick* (Cork: Mercier, 1991), pp. 144–6; Lee, *James Pain*, pp. 18, 37, 46, 53, 190, 244, 266, 317, 328, 267; O'Flaherty, *Irish Historic Towns Atlas, No. 21: Limerick*, pp. 27–8; Butler, 'Politics, Grand Juries, and Ireland's Unbuilt Assize Courthouses', pp. 131–5; Barclay, *Men on Trial*, p. 88.

LONDONDERRY (DERRY)

Derry

Bishop St.
Lat. 54°59'38.15" N.; Long. 7°19'26.04" W

Old town hall/exchange used for the assizes, built 1691; presentments for a new courthouse 1807; unexecuted proposal (*Richard Elsam*) 1809; local act of parliament 1812; new courthouse built (*John Bowden*; contractors *Henry, Mullins & McMahon*) 1813–17; additions 1836; alterations and additions (*Arthur Charles Adair*) 1896–7; alterations and repairs (*Charles Littleboy Boddie*) 1902–3; bombed *c.* 1990; rebuilt; extant.

Old town hall/exchange used for staging court cases, built 1691. Grand-jury presentments to repair old town hall/exchange, as well as build a new courthouse, 1807. Unexecuted proposal for a new courthouse (*Richard Elsam*), 1809. Local act of parliament obtained for building a new courthouse, 1812. New courthouse built (*John Bowden*; contractors *Henry, Mullins & McMahon*), at a cost of at least £30,000, 1813–17; Addition of offices to the south, 1836. Extensive alterations and additions (*Arthur Charles Adair*), 1896–7. Criticised as inadequate in terms of accommodation for judges, jurors, etc., 1899. Repairs (*Matthew Alexander Robinson*), 1902. Alterations and repairs (*Charles Littleboy Boddie*), 1902–3. Listed, 1976. Bombed, *c.* 1990; thereafter extensively refurbished. Extant.

Archival and primary sources:

Londonderry grand-jury presentment books, 1788–1899 (PRONI, LOND/4/1); *Accounts of the Presentments Passed by the Grand Juries of Ireland … in … 1807*, H.C. 1808 (205), xiii, p. 231; Society of Artists (Ireland) exhibit by Richard Elsam, 1809 (no. 67); *Journal of the House of Commons*, vol. 66, 20 May 1811, p. 350, and passim; ibid., vol. 67, 14 April 1812, pp. 265–6 and passim; Londonderry Court House Act, 1812 (52 Geo. III, c. clxxxii); Drawings for Derry courthouse, 20 August 1813, by John Bowden (PRONI, LA/5/8/JA/2); Contract for the building of Derry courthouse, 20 August 1813 (PRONI, LA/5/8/JA/2); John Christian Curwen, *Observations on the State of Ireland*, 2 vols (London: Baldwin, Cradock, & Joy, 1818), vol. 1, p. 224; *Pigot & Co's Provincial Directory of Ireland, 1824*, p. 395–6; Memorandum from David Henry, 19 January 1826 (NAI, CSORP 1825/12,887); Anon., *Notes of a Journey in the North of Ireland in the Summer of 1827* (London: Baldwin, Cradock, & Joy, 1828), p. 58; Gorton and Wright, *Topographical Dictionary*, vol. 1, p. 591; John Barrow, *A Tour Round Ireland … in the Autumn of 1835* (London: Murray, 1836), p. 98; Lewis, *Topographical Dictionary*, vol. 2, p. 303; Thomas Colby, *Ordnance Survey of the County of Londonderry: Memoir of the city and north western liberties of Londonderry, parish of Templemore* (Dublin: Hodges & Smith, 1837), pp. 115–16; Simpson, *Derry*, pp. 189, 240–3; Bartlett, Willis and Coyne, *The Scenery and Antiquities of Ireland*, vol. 1, p. 54; John Forbes, *Memorandums Made in Ireland in the Autumn of 1852*, 2 vols (London: Smith, Elder, & Co, 1853), vol. 2, p. 111; *The Irish Times*, 10 July 1896; *Irish Builder*, vol. 38, no. 878, 15 July 1896, pp. 156, 164; ibid., vol. 43, no. 1017, 8 May 1902, p. 1241; *Londonderry Sentinel*, 1 January 1898; ibid., vol. 30, May 1899; ibid., vol. 30, December 1899.

Secondary sources:

Alistair Rowan, John Tracey and W.S. Ferguson, *List of Historic Buildings … in and Near the City of Derry* (Belfast: Ulster Architectural Heritage Society, 1970), pp. 17, 19, Brett, *Court Houses*, pp. 17, 86, 88, 90, 107; McParland, 'Public Work of Architects', pp. 240, 244; Rowan, *Buildings of Ireland: North west Ulster*, p. 389; Craig, *Architecture of Ireland*, pp. 271, 273; O'Donoghue, *Irish County Surveyors*, pp. 90, 102, 315; Avril Thomas, *Irish Historic Towns Atlas, No. 15: Derry-Londonderry* (Dublin: Royal Irish Academy, 2005), section 13; Loeber, et al., *Art and Architecture of Ireland: Volume IV: Architecture 1600–2000*, pp 181–2, 471; Northern Ireland Environmental Agency (NIEA), Listed Buildings Database (www.doeni.gov.uk); Barclay, *Men on Trial*, pp. 73–4.

LONGFORD

Longford

Main St.
Lat. 53°43'41.63" N.; Long. 7°48'4.64" W.

An earlier courthouse noted as in existence 1737, 1743; repaired 1760; substantial additions or a new building *c.* 1791–3; grand-jury discussion over possibility of building a new courthouse 1858–9; enlarged and altered (*James Bell*) 1859–61; disused 2004; refurbished 2006; extant.

An earlier courthouse noted as in existence, 1737, 1743. Repaired, 1760. A new courthouse (or substantial additions), *c.* 1791–3. Grand-jury discussion over possibility of building a new courthouse, 1858–9. Enlarged and altered, including an extra storey (*James Bell*), 1859–61. Disused, 2004. Refurbished, 2006. In use as a courthouse. Extant.

Archival and primary sources:

Registry of Deeds (1737, 1743): 90/94/63077 and 106/382/74252; Longford grand-jury presentment book, summer 1793 (Longford County Library, LGJ/1/1); Longford grand-jury presentment books, 1858–61 (ibid., LGJ/2/35–8); Anon. [W.P.], 'Sketch of a Journey through Part of Ireland', in *Walker's Hibernian Magazine*, October 1807, p. 618; *Dublin Builder*, vol. 1, no. 6, 1 June 1859, p. 75; ibid., vol. 2, no. 14, 1 April 1860, p. 239; *The Builder*, vol. 17, no. 856, 2 July 1859, p. 444.

Secondary sources:

Michael Ó Finn, 'History of Longford, Ancient and Modern', *Teathbha: Journal of the Longford Historical Society*, vol. 1, no. 1, December 1969, pp. 10–16, at p. 14; Casey, 'Courthouses', pp. 82–3; Christine Casey and Alistair Rowan, *The Buildings of Ireland: North Leinster, the counties of Longford, Louth, Meath and Westmeath* (London: Penguin, 1993), p. 381; O'Donoghue, *Irish County Surveyors*, p. 95; Sarah Gearty, Martin Morris and Fergus O'Ferrall, *Irish Historic Towns Atlas, No. 22: Longford* (Dublin: Royal Irish Academy, 2010), p. 11.

LOUTH

Dundalk

Market Square
Lat. 54°0'16.18" N.; Long. 6°24'5.12" W.

Site of a previous assize courthouse built (*William Elgee*) 1736–40; plans to build a new courthouse 1802; unexecuted schemes (*Richard Morrison* and *John Behan*) 1804, 1810, 1812; contract signed to build a new courthouse 1813; new courthouse built (*John Bowden* and *Edward Parke*; contractor *William Moore*) 1813–21; alterations to agreed design *c.* 1813–18; contractor dismissed; legal action; contractor awarded damages; local act of parliament to resolve financial problems 1821; additions (*John Neville*) 1846; repairs and improvements (*John Neville*) 1855; additions (*Thomas Walsh*) 1930; extensively refurbished (*Brian O'Halloran & Associates*) 1998–2003; extant.

Site of a previous assize courthouse, built (*William Elgee*), 1736–40. Plans to build a new courthouse, 1802. Unexecuted scheme (*Richard Morrison*), 1804. Further unexecuted schemes (*Richard Morrison* and *John Behan*), 1810. More unexecuted schemes (*Richard Morrison*), 1812. Contract to build a new courthouse (*John Bowden* and *Edward Parke*; contractor *William Moore*), 1813. Built (*John Bowden* and *Edward Parke*), at a cost of at least £16,190, 1813–21. Alterations to the agreed design, *c.* 1813–18. Grand jury unhappy with the progress of building and move to dismiss the contractor (*William Moore*), 1818. Legal action by contractor (*William Moore*) for damages, 1819. Case tried, with Moore awarded £3,500 with costs, 1820. Local act of parliament passed to resolve financial problems with the grand jury, 1821. Additions (*John Neville*), 1846. Repairs and improvements (*John Neville*), 1855. Additions (*Thomas Walsh*), 1930. Extensively refurbished (*Brian O'Halloran & Associates*), 1998–2003. Listed. Extant.

Archival and primary sources:

Series of drawings for Dundalk courthouse, n.d. [c. 1813], by Owen Fahy (Dundalk County Archives / Old Dundalk Society); *Journal of the House of Commons*, vol. 66, 20 May 1811, p. 350, and passim; ibid., vol. 67, 14 April 1812, pp. 265–6 and passim; ibid., vol. 68, 1 June 1813, p. 536, and passim; Londonderry Court House Act, 1812, 52 Geo. III, c. clxxxii; Court House (Ireland) Act, 1813, 53 Geo. III, c. 131; Memorandum from Edward Parke, 16 September 1812 (PRONI, T/2519/4/1387); John Leslie Foster to Robert Peel, 26 February 1813 (British Library, Add. MS 40223, ff. 119, 121); Memorandum by Robert Page, 27 September 1811 (PRONI, D/562/12762); John Foster to Robert Page, 4 October 1811 (PRONI, D/562/12766); memorandum by Richard Morrison, 22 October 1812 (PRONI, T/2519/4/13); Harold O'Sullivan, 'The Courthouse, Dundalk, and the Contract for Its Erection Dated 30th April 1813', *Journal of the County Louth Archaeological Society* vol. 15, no. 2, 1962, pp. 131–43; John Leslie Foster, *A Letter on the Fittest Style and Situation for the Wellington Trophy about to be Erected in Dublin* (Dublin: Graisberry & Campbell, 1815); John Jocelyn to John Foster, 10 March 1819 (NLI, MS 4128); Memorandum from John Bowden (PRONI, D/207/23/98); *Journal of the House of Commons*, vol. 76, 12 April 1821, p. 256; Dundalk Court House Act, 1821, 1 & 2 Geo. IV, c. cxxiv; A. Atkinson, *Ireland Exhibited to England in a Political and Moral Survey of Her Population*, 2 vols (London: Baldwin, Cradock & Joy, 1823), vol. 1, pp. 91–2; Diary of Charles Robert Cockerell, 24 October 1823 (RIBA, Prints and drawings collection, C.R. Cockerell diary); Gorton and Wright, *Topographical Dictionary*, vol. 1, p. 657; *Louth Free Press*, 18 March 1829; Lewis, *Topographical Dictionary*, vol. 1, p. 571; Wilkinson, *Practical Geology and Ancient Architecture of Ireland*, p. 307; Louth grand-jury presentment books, 1846, 1855 (Louth County Archives, GJ/005); *Fifteenth Report of the Commissioners on Public Works, Ireland … for the Year 1846*, H.C. 1847 (847), xvii, p. 26; M.W. Savage (ed.), *Sketches, Legal and Political, by … Richard Lalor Sheil*, 2 vols (London: Colburn, 1855), vol. 1, pp. 172–3; *Architect & Building News*, vol. 123, 21 March 1930, p. 398.

Secondary sources:

McParland, 'Public Work of Architects', pp. 3, 173, 241–5; A.P.W. Malcomson, *John Foster: The politics of the Anglo-Irish ascendancy* (Oxford: Oxford University Press, 1978), pp. 18–20; Craig, *Architecture of Ireland*, pp. 261, 271, 273; Casey, 'Courthouses', pp. 89–91; Christine Casey, 'John Neville: Louth county surveyor', *Journal of the County Louth Archaeological and Historical Society*, vol. 21, no. 1, 1985, pp. 23–30; Christine Casey, 'The Greek Revival Courthouse, Dundalk, County Louth', *Irish Arts Review*, vol. 3, no. 2, Summer 1986, pp. 16–20; Casey and Rowan, *The Buildings of Ireland: North Leinster*, pp. 268–9; Virginia Crossman, *Local Government in Nineteenth-century Ireland* (Belfast: Institute of Irish Studies, 1994), p. 27; P.J. Geraghty, 'Urban Improvement and the Erection of Municipal Buildings in County Louth during the Eighteenth and Nineteenth Centuries', *Journal of the County Louth Archaeological and Historical Society*, vol. 23, no. 3, 1995, pp. 295–317, at pp. 310–14; Harold O'Sullivan, *Irish Historic Towns Atlas, No. 16: Dundalk* (Dublin: Royal Irish Academy, 2006), section 13; O'Donoghue, *Irish County Surveyors*, pp. 267–8; A.P.W. Malcomson, 'John Foster', in James McGuire and James Quinn (eds), *Dictionary of Irish Biography*, 9 vols (Cambridge: Cambridge University Press, 2009), vol. 3, p. 1070; Loeber, et al., *Art and Architecture of Ireland: Volume IV: Architecture 1600–2000*, p. 183.

TOWN OF DROGHEDA

Drogheda

West St. & Shop St.
Lat. 53°42'53.21" N.; Long. 6°21'1.58" W.

An earlier tholsel replaced (*George Darley*) 1765–70; alterations and improvements (*John Neville*) 1861; courts moved to a nearby cornmarket building (*Patrick John Lynam*) *c.* 1887–9; tholsel converted into a bank 1890; both buildings are extant.

Earlier tholsel was a wooden structure with battlements and a colonnade. A new tholsel built, presumably on the same site (*George Darley*), 1765–70. Alterations and improvements (*John Neville*), 1861. Cornmarket building, built (*Francis Johnston*), 1796, located nearby, remodelled as the town's courthouse (*Patrick John Lynam*), *c.* 1887–9. Tholsel converted into a bank (*William Henry Byrne*), 1890. Repairs to this later courthouse (*Patrick John Lynam*), 1901. Both buildings are listed and extant.

Archival and primary sources:

Drogheda Corporation minute books, 9 August, 23 August 1765, and 10 October 1766 (NLI, microfilm, n. 4120); Robertson, *The Traveller's Guide through Ireland*, pp. 246–7; Lewis, *Topographical Dictionary*, vol. 1, p. 501; Charlotte Elizabeth Tonna, *Letters from Ireland, MDCCCXXXVII* (London: Seeley & Burnside, 1838), p. 172; *Dublin Builder*, vol. 3, no. 29, 1 March 1861, p. 448; Drawings showing alterations to Drogheda's cornmarket to fit it up as a courthouse, 3 January 1887 (NAI, OPW 5HC/4/401); *The Irish Times*, 12 August, 13 August, 19 August, 20 August 1890; *Irish Builder*, vol. 43, no. 1000, 29 August 1901, p. 845.

Secondary sources:

McParland, 'Francis Johnston', pp. 77, 79; James Garry, 'The Tholsel, Drogheda', *Journal of the County Louth Archaeological and Historical Society*, vol. 17, no. 3, 1971, pp. 164–8; Casey, 'Courthouses', p. 86; Casey and Rowan, *The Buildings of Ireland: North Leinster*, pp. 243, 268–9; Geraghty, 'Urban Improvement and the Erection of Municipal Buildings in County Louth', pp. 300, 305–6; O'Donoghue, *Irish County Surveyors*, p. 247; Peter Geraghty, 'P.J. Lynam, the Last County Surveyor for Louth Grand Jury (1886–1912)', *Journal of the County Louth Archaeological and Historical Society*, vol. 27, no. 2, 2010, p. 293; Loeber, et al., *Art and Architecture of Ireland: Volume IV: Architecture 1600–2000*, pp. 63, 178, 453; Barclay, *Men on Trial*, p. 71.

MAYO

Ballinrobe

Market St. & Abbey St.
Lat. 53°37'26.30" N.; Long. 9°13'20.80" W.

Probably built *c.* 1752; in use as a venue for the Mayo assizes until *c.* 1840; extant.

In the early nineteenth century, the Mayo assizes were held in both Castlebar and Ballinrobe. This appears to have been a long-standing historical practice in this extensive western county, and some sources refer to the assizes being held in Ballinrobe as early as 1716, but it is unclear when Castlebar became the sole venue. This appears to have happened by 1840, and after this time Ballinrobe's courthouse and markethouse was only used for quarter- and petty-session cases. It remains largely intact and is included in this list on account of its historic use as a venue for assizes.

Probably built *c.* 1752. Account of a tourist attending the assizes in the town, 1807. Repairs, 1823–4. Comment that the town no longer holds the assizes, 1840. A visitor comments that the assizes have ceased to be held in the town, 1846. In use as a courthouse until *c.* 1970. Used as a public house, *c.* 1970–2000. In use as a boxing club. Extant.

Archival and primary sources:

Hibernian Journal, 8 April 1807; C.J. Woods (ed.), 'Johann Friedrich Hering's Description of Connacht, 1806–7', *Irish Historical Studies*, vol. 25, no. 99, May 1987, pp. 315–21, at p. 320; Lewis, *Topographical Dictionary*, vol. 1, p. 116; *Sixth Annual Report of the Poor Law Commissioners*, H.C. 1840 (253), xvii, p. 369; Asenath Nicholson, *Lights and Shades of Ireland in Three Parts* (London: Gilpin, 1850), p. 351; *Statement of All Issues of Public Money Made for … Public Works in … Mayo*, H.C. 1850 (158), li, pp. 2–3.

Secondary sources:

Historical Ballinrobe (www.historicalballinrobe.com).

MAYO

Castlebar

The Green
Lat. 53°51'14.59" N.; Long. 9°17'49.02" W.

Probably built *c.* 1807; extensive alterations and additions (*George Papworth*) *c.* 1820–2; further extensive alterations and additions (*George Wilkinson*) 1858–60; refurbished (*Mayo County Council*) *c.* 2002–4; extant.

Probably built *c.* 1807. Extensive alterations and additions (*George Papworth*), *c.* 1820–2. Unexecuted scheme for alterations and additions (*Edward Henry Carson*), 1858. Further extensive alterations and additions (*George Wilkinson*), 1858–60. Refurbished (*Mayo County Council*), *c.* 2002–4. Extant.

Archival and primary sources:

Accounts of the Presentments Passed by the Grand Juries of Ireland … in … 1807, H.C. 1808 (205), xiii, p. 241; Reid, *Travels*, p. 318; William Hamilton Maxwell, *Wild Sports of the West of Ireland* (London: Bentley, 1832), p. 31; Lewis, *Topographical Dictionary*, vol. 1, p. 289; Lawson, *Gazetteer of Ireland*, p. 220; Nicholson, *Lights and Shades of Ireland*, p. 351; *Statement of All Issues of Public Money Made for … Public Works in … Mayo*, H.C. 1850 (158), li, pp. 2–3; Forbes, *Memorandums Made in Ireland*, vol. 1, pp. 288–9; *The Builder*, vol. 13, no. 634, 31 March 1855, p. 150; ibid., vol. 16, no. 799, 29 May 1858, p. 381; ibid., vol. 16, no. 828, 18 December 1858, p. 857; ibid., vol. 18, no. 914, 11 August 1860, p. 512; *Dublin Builder*, vol. 2, no. 20, 1 August 1860, p. 308.

Secondary sources:

J.F. Quinn, *History of Mayo*, 5 vols (Ballina: Brendan Quinn, 1993), vol. 1, p. 368; Andrew Saint, 'Three Oxford Architects', *Oxoniensia*, vol. 35, 1970, pp. 53–102, at p. 56; McParland, 'Public Work of Architects', p. 244; Desmond MacCabe, 'Magistrates, Peasants, and the Petty Sessions Courts: Mayo, 1823–50', *Cathair na Mart: Journal of the Westport Historical Society*, vol. 5, no. 1, 1985, pp. 45–53; Loeber, et al., *Art and Architecture of Ireland: Volume IV: Architecture 1600–2000*, p. 76.

MEATH

Trim

Market St. & Castle St.
Lat. 53°33'19.75" N.; Long. 6°47'27.66" W.

Site of a former friary; repaired 1806; a new courthouse built, or extensive additions to an existing building (*Richard Morrison*) *c.* 1809; unexecuted plans for a replacement *c.* 1828; extensively refurbished (*Newenham Mulligan Architects*) *c.* 1999–2001; extant.

The site of a former friary, used for staging the assizes previous to a new courthouse being built. An older courthouse noted on the site, 1782. Repaired, 1806. Committee appointed by grand jury to consider the 'present state' of the county courthouse, 1806. A new courthouse built, or perhaps extensive alterations to an existing building (*Richard Morrison*), *c.* 1809. An unexecuted scheme (*Mr [Francis?] Johnston*), *c.* 1809. An unexecuted plan to build a new courthouse, *c.* 1828. Extensively refurbished (*Newenham Mulligan Architects*), at a cost of €6.4 million, *c.* 1999–2001. Extant.

Archival and primary sources:

Registry of Deeds (1782), 347/148/231477; Meath grand-jury presentment book, summer 1806 (University of Illinois at Urbana-Champaign Rare Book and Manuscript Library, Champaign, IL.); 'Plan of the Principal Story of the Court House at Trim with the Proposed Additions and Improvements', n.d., by Richard Morrison (NLI, Gun Cuninghame Collection,

AD 3568 (48)); Meath grand-jury presentment books, 1798–1809 (NAI, IC/33/71); Meath grand-jury presentment books, 1803, 1806–7, 1847, 1867, 1882, 1884, 1887, 1889–91, 1893–8 (incomplete) (Meath County Archives, GJ); Atkinson, *Ireland Exhibited to England*, pp. 243–4; *Freeman's Journal*, 23 April 1828; Richard Butler, *Some Notices of the Castle and of the Abbies and Other Religious Houses at Trim* (Trim: Henry Griffith, 1835), p. 20; Lewis, *Topographical Dictionary*, vol. 2, p. 644.

Secondary sources:

Casey, 'Courthouses', p. 97; Rowan, *Morrison*, p. 171; Casey and Rowan, *The Buildings of Ireland: North Leinster*, p. 520; Mark Hennesy, *Irish Historic Towns Atlas, No. 14: Trim* (Dublin: Royal Irish Academy, 2004), section 13.

MONAGHAN

Monaghan, no. 1

The Diamond (Old Diamond)
Lat. 54°14'54.17" N.; Long. 6°58'8.81" W.

Probably built in the eighteenth century; minor repairs 1810–11; a replacement planned from at least 1826; new courthouse built elsewhere 1827–30; demolished; not extant.

Probably built in the eighteenth century. Minor repairs, 1810–11. A new county gaol built (see Part II), 1815–24. The site of the old county gaol thereafter used for building a new courthouse (see 'Monaghan: Monaghan, no. 2'). Unexecuted design for a new courthouse, 1826. New courthouse built, 1827–30. Plan of old courthouse shown in 1831 drawing. Demolished. Later buildings now occupy the site. Not extant.

Archival and primary sources:

Charles Coote, *Statistical Survey of the County of Monaghan* (Dublin: Graisberry & Campbell, 1801), p. 170; Reid, *Travels*, p. 199; Monaghan grand-jury presentment book, summer 1811 (Monaghan County Library, 352.0417); Plan drawing of the old courthouse at Monaghan, 27 April 1831, by Alexander Fleming (Monaghan County Museum).

Secondary sources:

Brett, *Court Houses*, pp. 94, 96–7, 107; Theresa Loftus, 'Monaghan Courthouse', National Inventory of Architectural Heritage Building of the Month, May 2014 (www.buildingsofireland.ie).

MONAGHAN

Monaghan, no. 2

Church Square (New Diamond)
Lat. 54°14'51.51" N.; Long. 6°58'12.34" W.

The site of a former county gaol; new courthouse planned from at least 1826; unexecuted scheme (*William Deane Butler*) 1826; unexecuted scheme, sought by Henry Westenra (*William Vitruvius Morrison*) *c.* 1827; new courthouse built (*Joseph Welland*) 1827–30; repairs (*Joseph Welland*) 1837–8; alterations and additions (*John P. McArdle*) 1930; gutted by fire 1981; partially restored 1985–6; extensively refurbished (*Office of Public Works*) 2009–10; extant.

An earlier courthouse existed in a nearby square (see 'Monaghan: Monaghan, no. 1'). A new county gaol built (see Part II), 1815–24. New courthouse built on the site of this former county gaol. Unexecuted design for a new courthouse (*William Deane Butler*), 1826. Proposal from a grand juror, Henry Westenra, to have *William Vitruvius Morrison* design a new courthouse in the town, unexecuted, 1827. New courthouse built (*Joseph Welland*), at a cost of at least £10,000, 1827–30.

Repairs (*Joseph Welland*), 1837–8. Occupied by Free State forces, 1921–3. Alterations and additions (*John P. McArdle*), 1930. Gutted by fire, 1981. Partially restored, 1985–6. Extensively refurbished (*Office of Public Works, Michael Haugh, Seán Moylan, etc.*), at a cost of €8.5 million, 2009–10. Extant.

Archival and primary sources:

Coote, *Statistical Survey of the County of Monaghan*, p. 170; Reid, *Travels*, p. 199; Royal Hibernian Academy exhibits by William Deane Butler, 1826 (nos. 252, 258); *Freeman's Journal*, 2 April 1827; Henry Westenra to William Gregory, 25 March, 27 March, and 25 July 1827 (NAI, CSORP 1827/445 and 1827/1453); Lewis, *Topographical Dictionary*, vol. 2, p. 383; Monaghan grand-jury presentment books, 1837 (Monaghan County Museum) (microfilm copy in Monaghan County Library, B6129M); William Stevens Balch, *Ireland as I Saw It: The character, condition, and prospects of the people* (New York: Putnam, 1850), p. 417; *Dublin Builder*, vol. 2, no. 14, 1 April 1860, p. 232; *Irish Builder*, vol. 72, no. 12, 7 June 1930, p. 532.

Secondary sources:

C.E.B. Brett, *List of Historic Buildings … in the Town of Monaghan* (Belfast: Ulster Architectural Heritage Society, 1970), pp. 14–15; Brett, *Court Houses*, pp. 94, 96–7, 107; McParland, 'Public Work of Architects', pp. 240, 246, 248; Fisher, *History of Parliament: The House of Commons*, 1820–1832, vol. 7, pp. 696–700; Mulligan, *Buildings of Ireland: South Ulster*, pp. 470–1; Grainne Shaffrey, 'Projects: Monaghan courthouse: Classical tradition with Miesian rigour, review', *Architecture Ireland*, vol. 270, July–August 2013, pp. 46–9; Loftus, 'Monaghan Courthouse', National Inventory of Architectural Heritage Building of the Month.

QUEEN'S COUNTY (LAOIS)

Maryborough (Portlaoise)

Main St. & Church St.
Lat. 53°2'3.16" N.; Long. 7°17'59.16" W.

Built (*Richard Morrison*) *c.* 1805; an unexecuted plan to build a new courthouse *c.* 1828; addition of offices *c.* 1830–5; enlargements and alterations (*James Rawson Carroll*) 1875–6; refurbished (*David Slattery*) 2001–2; alterations 2010; future as a courthouse in doubt 2015; extant.

New courthouse built (*Richard Morrison*), *c.* 1805. Remarked as being new, 1813. Petition from the Queen's County grand jury to parliament, calling for a third assize to be held each year, 1823. An unexecuted plan to build a new courthouse, *c.* 1828. Addition of offices, from adjacent vacated old county gaol (see Part II), *c.* 1830–5. Enlargements and alterations (*James Rawson Carroll*), at a cost of at least £2,000, 1875–6. Refurbished (*David Slattery*), at a cost of €2.75 million, 2001–2. Alterations, 2010. Future as a courthouse in doubt, 2015. Extant.

Archival and primary sources:

Queen's County grand-jury presentment book (abstracts), 1805 (NLI, Ir. 94137.c.2); Diaries for Sir Vere Hunt, 10 May 1813 (Limerick City and County Archives, Vere Hunt Diaries, 10 March to 31 December 1813; NLI microfilm copy, pp. 5527–8); *Journal of the House of Commons* 78 (29 April 1823), p. 264; *Freeman's Journal*, 23 April 1828; Lewis, *Topographical Dictionary*, vol. 2, pp. 345–6; Lacy, *Sights and Scenes*, p. 187; Queen's County grand-jury presentment books (copies), summer assizes 1874 and spring assizes 1875 (Laois County Library, 352.1 LH); *Irish Builder*, vol. 17, no. 368, 15 April 1875, pp. 112–13; ibid., vol. 18, no. 385, 1 January 1876, p. 14; *Forty-fourth Report of the Commissioners on Public Works, Ireland … for the Year 1875–76*, H.C. 1876 (1509), xxi, p. 9.

Secondary sources:

McParland, 'Public Work of Architects', pp. 240–1; Casey, 'Courthouses', pp. 77–8; Craig, *Architecture of Ireland*, p. 271; McParland, *James Gandon*, pp. 46, 193; Rowan, *Morrison*, pp. 146–7; O'Donoghue, *Irish County Surveyors*, pp. 204;

Loeber, et al., *Art and Architecture of Ireland: Volume IV: Architecture 1600–2000*, p. 182; Tierney, *The Buildings of Ireland: Central Leinster*, pp. 546–7.

ROSCOMMON

Roscommon, no. 1

Market Square
Lat. 53°37'52.11" N.; Long. 8°11'26.19" W.

A former courthouse and markethouse collapsed *c.* 1718; new courthouse built (*George Ensor*) *c.* 1762; unexecuted design for the same (probably *Oliver Crawford*) *c.* 1762; a new markethouse built elsewhere *c.* 1796; a new county gaol built elsewhere 1814–18; a new courthouse built *c.* 1824–7; old courthouse thereafter used as a Catholic chapel, and a bank; many later alterations; extant.

Old courthouse and markethouse collapsed in *c.* 1718, killing and injuring people. A new courthouse and markethouse built (*George Ensor*), *c.* 1762. Unexecuted design for the same (probably *Oliver Crawford*), *c.* 1762. Market functions of the building cease; new markethouse built elsewhere, *c.* 1796. A new county gaol built elsewhere (see Part II), 1814–18. A new courthouse built elsewhere (see 'Roscommon: Roscommon, no. 2'), *c.* 1824–7. Old courthouse thereafter used as a Catholic chapel. Now in use as a bank. Extensive alterations and additions. Extant.

Archival and primary sources:

Anon., ['E.S.'], *Account of How the Court House in Roscommon Fell Down* (Dublin: C.C., 1718–19) (Cambridge University Library); G. Wills to Thomas Mahon, 23 June 1762 (NLI, MS 10,770(1)); Drawings and contract for Roscommon courthouse, dated 27 April 1762, by George Ensor and Oliver Crawford (NLI, MS 10,770(1)–(3)); 36 Geo. III, c. 55, s. 97.

Secondary sources:

McParland, 'Public Work of Architects', pp. 11–12, 159; Butler, 'Politics, Grand Juries, and Ireland's Unbuilt Assize Courthouses', pp. 113–14; Gibney, Hurley and McParland, *Building Site in Eighteenth-century Ireland*, pp. 24, 26, 37, 42, 48, 55, 83, 199, 217.

ROSCOMMON

Roscommon, no. 2

Courthouse Square
Lat. 53°37'45.43" N.; Long. 8°11'36.06" W.

A former courthouse built *c.* 1762; a new county gaol built 1814–18; a new courthouse planned from at least 1820; a new courthouse built (*Richard Richards*) *c.* 1824–7; destroyed by fire 1882; unexecuted designs for a replacement (*William Kaye-Parry, Henry A. Cheers*, etc.) 1883; a replacement built (*Christopher John Mulvany*) 1883; alterations 1904; repairs 1950; additions *c.* 1965; refurbishments planned 2015; extant.

A former courthouse and markethouse built (see 'Roscommon: Roscommon, no. 1'), *c.* 1762. Market functions of the building ceased, and a new markethouse built elsewhere, *c.* 1796. A new county gaol built (see Part II), 1814–18. A new courthouse planned from at least 1820. A new courthouse built adjacent to this gaol (*Richard Richards*), at a cost of at least £5,310, *c.* 1824–7. Loans from central government for building a new courthouse, 1824–6. Destroyed by fire, 1882. A temporary courthouse erected (*James Perry*), 1882. Unexecuted designs for a courthouse to replace the building destroyed by fire (*William Kaye-Parry, Henry A. Cheers, William Hague, William Sterling*, etc.), 1883. New courthouse built on the same site (*Christopher John Mulvany*), at a cost of over £11,000, 1883. Alterations (*Christopher John Mulvany*), 1904. Repairs (*Michael Scott*), 1950. Additions, *c.* 1965. Refurbishments planned, 2015. Extant.

Archival and primary sources:

George Kelly to William Gregory, August 1822 (NAI, CSORP 1822/730), Lewis, *Topographical Dictionary*, vol. 2, p. 526; Lawson, *Gazetteer of Ireland*, p. 714; *An Account of Loans Advanced for Public Works in Ireland … since 1800*, H.C. 1847 (718), liv, pp. 22–3; *Irish Builder*, vol. 24, no. 543, 1 August 1882, p. 228; ibid., vol. 25, no. 569, 1 September 1883, pp. 270, 275 (illus.); ibid., vol. 46, no. 1085, 17 December 1904, p. 870; ibid., vol. 92, no. 15, 22 July 1950, p. 776; *Roscommon Messenger*, 18 October 1919.

Secondary sources:

McParland, 'Public Work of Architects', p. 244.

SLIGO

Sligo

Teeling St. & Chapel St.
Lat. 54°16'11.18" N.; Long. 8°28'19.63" W.

At least two earlier courthouses in other parts of the town; a courthouse on the site of the present building, described as 'new' in 1785; noted as too small 1837; a new courthouse built (*James Rawson Carroll*) 1874–80; refurbished (*McCullough Mulvin Architects*) 1998–2001; extant.

An earlier courthouse existed near the present-day building. Another courthouse also existed on High Street, at the corner of Back Lane. A third courthouse described as 'new' in 1785. An unfounded suggestion that a new courthouse and gaol was built in 1807. Further uncertainties about building work and possible extensions, 1809, 1816. Noted as too small, 1837. A new courthouse built on the site of an earlier courthouse (*James Rawson Carroll*), at a cost of at least £17,500, 1874–80. Refurbished (*McCullough Mulvin Architects*), at a cost of €7.3 million, 1998–2001. Extant.

Archival and primary sources:

Sligo grand-jury presentment books, 1809–96 (incomplete) (Sligo County Library, LGOV 769-78); Lewis, *Topographical Dictionary*, vol. 2, p. 570; Heaney, *Scottish Whig in Ireland*, pp. 339–43; *Irish Builder*, vol. 16, no. 349, 1 July 1874, p. 189; *Forty-fourth Report of the Commissioners on Public Works, Ireland … for the Year 1875–6*, H.C. 1876 (1509), xxi, p. 9; Terence O'Rorke, *The History of Sligo: Town and county*, 2 vols (Dublin: Duff, 1889), vol. 1, p. 389; William Gregory Wood-Martin, *History of Sligo, County and Town, from the Close of the Revolution of 1688 to the Present Time* (Dublin: Hodges, Figgis, & Co., 1892), pp. 156–8; Nehemiah Curnock (ed.), *The Journal of the Rev. John Wesley, A.M.*, 8 vols (London: Culley, 1909–16), vol. 7, p. 82; Tadhg Kilgannon, *Sligo and Its Surroundings* (Sligo: Kilgannon, 1926), p. 141.

Secondary sources:

McParland, 'Public Work of Architects', p. 158; John McTernan, *In Sligo Long Ago: Aspects of town and county over two centuries* (Sligo, 1998), p. 171; Derry O'Connell, 'The Arrival at Sligo: Early approaches to Sligo in the 19th century', in Martin A. Timoney (ed.), *A Celebration of Sligo: First essays for Sligo Field Club* (Sligo: Sligo Field Club, 2002), pp. 257–61; Lynda Mulvin, 'Sligo Courthouse', National Inventory of Architectural Heritage Building of the Month, August 2007 (www.buildingsofireland.ie); Lynda Mulvin, 'Administering Justice in Gothic Revival Ireland: A study of the Sligo assizes courthouse', in Michael McCarthy and Karina O'Neill (eds), *Studies in the Gothic Revival* (Dublin: Four Courts Press, 2008), pp. 180–94; Fíona Gallagher and Marie-Louise Legg, *Irish Historic Towns Atlas, No. 24: Sligo* (Dublin: Royal Irish Academy, 2012), pp. 14–15.

TIPPERARY

Clonmel, no. 1

Sarsfield (Johnston) St. & O'Connell (Main) St.
Lat. 52°21'10.65" N.; Long. 7°42'5.01" W.

Built 1674–5; a new courthouse built elsewhere *c.* 1801; divided into shops, arches blocked up, etc., *c.* 1810; listed as a national monument 1994; extensively restored (*Margaret Quinlan Architects* and the *Office of Public Works*) *c.* 2004–10; extant.

Tholsel, known as the Main Guard, built 1674–5. A replacement courthouse built nearby (see 'Tipperary: Clonmel, no. 2') *c.* 1801. Tholsel divided into shops, arches blocked up, etc., *c.* 1810. Listed as a national monument, 1994. Extensively restored (*Margaret Quinlan Architects* and the *Office of Public Works*), at a cost of €2 million, *c.* 2004–10. In use as an exhibition centre and museum. Extant.

Archival and primary sources:

Lewis, *Topographical Dictionary*, vol. 1, p. 370.

Secondary sources:

Craig, *Architecture of Ireland*, p. 202; Loeber, et al., *Art and Architecture of Ireland: Volume IV: Architecture 1600–2000*, pp. 175, 181.

TIPPERARY (and later TIPPERARY SOUTH RIDING)

Clonmel, no. 2

Nelson St. & Wellington St.
Lat. 52°21'10.64" N.; Long. 7°41'53.38" W.

Assizes formerly held at the Main Guard; new courthouse built (*Richard Morrison*) *c.* 1801; Tipperary divided into two ridings 1838; partially refurbished 1980s; refurbished (*Deaton Lysaght Architects*) 1996–8; extant.

Assizes were formerly held in the Main Guard (see 'Tipperary: Clonmel, no. '1); New courthouse built (*Richard Morrison*), *c.* 1801. Tipperary formally divided into two ridings, 1838 (see 'Tipperary: Nenagh'). Partially refurbished, 1980s. Refurbished (*Deaton Lysaght Architects*), 1996–8. Extant.

Archival and primary sources:

Society of Artists (Ireland) exhibit by Richard Morrison, 1801 (no. 144); Plan sketch of Clonmel courthouse, n.d., n.s. (NLI, Portfolio 8); 'Forster Archer's Tour of Ireland in 1801' (British Library, Add. MS 35920); Journal of Daniel Augustus Beaufort, 1806 (Trinity College Library, Dublin, f. 72); James Hall, *A Tour through Ireland*, 2 vols (London: Moore, 1813), vol. 1, pp. 142–4; Staples, *Tour in Ireland in 1813 & 1814*, p. 245; Lewis, *Topographical Dictionary*, vol. 1, p. 370; Morrison, 'William Vitruvius Morrison', p. 2; Thackeray, *Irish sketch-book*, pp. 9–14, 55; *Limerick Reporter*, 26 March 1844; Tipperary South Riding grand-jury presentment books, 1855–91 (incomplete) (Tipperary Libraries Local Studies and Archives, TL/LG/29); Survey drawings of Clonmel courthouse, 1986, by Tipperary South Riding County Engineer's Department (copies in Irish Architectural Archive, Acc. 86/72.1/1).

Secondary sources:

McParland, 'Public Work of Architects', pp. 161–2; Craig, *Architecture of Ireland*, p. 271. Richardson, *Gothic Revival Architecture in Ireland*, p. 136; Rowan, *Morrison*, pp. 70–1; Photograph of main façade, 12 February 1966 (Tipperary

Libraries Local Studies and Archives); Loeber, et al., *Art and Architecture of Ireland: Volume IV: Architecture 1600–2000*, pp. 181–2, Gibney, Hurley and McParland, *Building Site in Eighteenth-century Ireland*, p. 171; Barclay, *Men on Trial*, p. 88.

TIPPERARY NORTH RIDING

Nenagh

Kickham (Peter) St. & Ashe Rd. (Banba Square)
Lat. 52°51'53.74" N.; Long. 8°12'1.71" W.

Proposal to divide Tipperary since at least 1828; unexecuted scheme for a new courthouse and gaol in Nenagh (*John B. Keane*) 1833; act passed to divide the county 1836; Nenagh to be the assize town 1837; division takes effect 1838; assizes temporarily held in the town's old quarter-sessions courthouse 1838–44; first government loan secured 1839; new street laid out nearby *c.* 1839–40; new gaol built 1839–42; new courthouse built (*John B. Keane*) 1840–4; portico rebuilt (*John Moynan* and *Walter G. Doolin*) 1890s; reconstructed 1966; closed for safety reasons 1999; extensively refurbished (*CMB Architects*) *c.* 2004–6; extant.

Proposal to divide Tipperary into two ridings debated from at least 1828 (see 'Tipperary: Clonmel, no. 2'). Unexecuted scheme (*John B. Keane*) for a new courthouse and gaol in Nenagh, 1833. Act passed that permitted the division of Tipperary into two ridings, 1836. Privy Council hears representations from Nenagh and Thurles, 1837. Privy Council decides in favour of Nenagh as the new assize town for the North Riding, 1837. Division of the county takes effect, 1838. Assizes held in Nenagh's small old quarter-sessions courthouse (since demolished), 1838–44. Central-government loan secured for a new courthouse, 1839. New street (Peter Street) laid out, *c.* 1839–40. New gaol built (see Part II), 1839–42. New courthouse built (*John B. Keane*), at a cost of at least £7,000, 1840–4. A tunnel built between the new courthouse and new gaol, *c.* 1843. Portico rebuilt (*John Moynan* and *Walter G. Doolin*), 1890s. Alterations and repairs (*John Moynan*), 1909–10. Reconstructed, 1966. Closed for safety reasons, 1999. Extensively refurbished (*CMB Architects*), at a cost of €11.5 million, *c.* 2004–6. Extant.

Archival and primary sources:

Reid, *Travels*, p. 299; *Limerick Evening Herald*, 16 September 1833; John B. Keane to William Gosset, 2 July 1833 (NAI, CSORP 1833/3124); Assizes (Ireland) Act, 1835, 5 & 6 Will. IV, c. 26; *Journal of the House of Commons*, vol. 90, 17 August 1835, p. 559, and passim; *Hansard*, vol. 27, 3rd ser., 26 March 1835, cols 303–5; ibid., 27 March 1835, cols 187–94; Grand Jury Act, 1836 (Ireland), 6 & 7 Will. IV, c. 116; *Clonmel Advertiser*, 10 August 1836 and 21 June 1837; *Clonmel Herald*, 30 November 1836; *Tipperary Constitution*, 30 December 1836; Lewis, *Topographical Dictionary*, vol. 2, p. 423; Privy Council minute book, 16 June 1837 (NAI, PCO MB 8, ff. 63–5); Privy Council proclamation book, 8 November 1838 (NAI, PRO PB 1); *Nenagh Guardian*, 8 December 1838, 23 March 1839, 3 August 1839, 6 May 1840, 17 March 1841, 10 June 1841, 19 June 1842, 30 September 1843; Royal Hibernian Academy exhibits by John B. Keane, 1840 (no. 340); *Eighth Report of the Commissioners on Public Works, Ireland ... for the Year 1839*, H.C. 1840 (327), xxviii, p. 23; Court Houses Act, 1841 (Ireland), 4 & 5 Vict., c. 31, s. 1; Mr & Mrs S.C. Hall, *Ireland: Its scenery, character, etc.*, 3 vols (London: How & Parsons, 1841–3), vol. 2, p. 113; Tipperary North Riding grand-jury presentment books, 1842–1910 (incomplete) (Tipperary Libraries Local Studies and Archives, TL/LG/28); John Price Durbin, *Observations in Europe, Principally in France and Great Britain*, 2 vols (New York: Harper & Brothers, 1844), vol. 2, p. 223; *An Account of Loans Advanced ... for Public Works in Ireland ... since 1800*, H.C. 1847 (718), liv, pp. 34–5; Plan shown in Ordnance Survey five-feet town map, 1879 (copy in Tipperary County Library, Thurles); *Irish Builder*, vol. 51, no. 15, 24 July 1909, p. 470; *The Builder*, vol. 99, no. 3522, 6 August 1910, p. 169.

Secondary sources:

Postcards showing Nenagh courthouse and gaol, n.d. (Tipperary Libraries Local Studies and Archives); McParland, 'Public Work of Architects', pp. 247–8; Craig, *Architecture of Ireland*, p. 272; Donal A. Murphy, *The Two Tipperarys: The national and local politics … of the unique 1838 division into two ridings* (Nenagh, Co. Tipperary: Relay, 1994), pp. 27–30, 36–43, 52–7, 87–91, 104–5, 122, 128–9, and passim; O'Dwyer, 'Public Works Architecture', p. 368; O'Donoghue, *Irish County Surveyors*, p. 257; Loeber, et al., *Art and Architecture of Ireland: Volume IV: Architecture 1600–2000*, p. 182.

TYRONE

Omagh

High St. & George's St.
Lat. 54°36'0.0" N.; Long. 7°18'16.14" W.

A former courthouse destroyed by fire in 1742; a new courthouse built on the site of a former gaol; built (*John Hargrave*) 1814–20; portico added (*John Hargrave*) 1820–2; sundry works 1827, 1829; alterations 1837; additions and alterations (*William Joseph Barre*) 1863; further additions 1867, 1869; repairs and alterations (*William Henry Byrne*) 1906; refurbished 2000s; extant.

A former courthouse destroyed by fire in 1742. A new gaol built, 1796–1804 (see Part II). Courthouse built on the site of the former gaol. Built (*John Hargrave*), at a cost of at least £17,000, 1814–20. Portico added (*John Hargrave*), 1820–2. Sundry works, 1827, 1829. Alterations, 1837. Additions and alterations (*William Joseph Barre*), 1863. Further additions, 1867, 1869. Repairs and alterations (*William Henry Byrne*), 1906. Listed, 1976. Refurbished, 2000s. Extant.

Archival and primary sources:

Belfast Mercury, 21 September 1786; Reid, *Travels*, p. 209; *Pigot & Co's Provincial Directory of Ireland, 1824*, p. 415; Tyrone grand-jury presentment books, 1799–1897 (PRONI, TYR/4/1); *Morning Register* (Dublin), 18 August 1827; Angelique Day and Patrick McWilliams (eds), *Ordnance Survey Memoirs of Ireland: Volume 5: Tyrone* (Belfast: Institute for Irish Studies, 1990), p. 104; Binns, *Miseries and Beauties*, vol. 1, p. 261; Lewis, *Topographical Dictionary*, vol. 2, p. 449; *Parliamentary Gazetteer of Ireland* (1845), vol. 3, p. 50; *Tyrone Constitution*, 10 September 1847; *Dublin Builder*, vol. 5, no. 95, 1 December 1863, p. 197; ibid., vol. 8, no. 156, 15 June 1866, p. 161; *Irish Builder*, vol. 48, no. 18, 30 June 1906, p. 526; ibid., vol. 48, no. 17, 25 August 1906, p. 690.

Secondary sources:

W.T. Latimer, *Presbyterianism in Omagh* (Belfast: reprinted from The Witness, 1913), p. 16; Brett, *Court Houses*, pp. 100, 102–3, 107; McParland, 'Public Work of Architects', p. 244; Rowan, *Buildings of Ireland: North West Ulster*, p. 446; Dixon, *Introduction to Ulster Architecture*, p. 137; Audrey M. Hodge, *Gallows and Turnkeys: A short history of Omagh gaol* (Omagh: West Tyrone Historical Society, 1993), p. 6; Williams, *Companion Guide to Architecture in Ireland*, p. 357; Northern Ireland Environmental Agency (NIEA), Listed Buildings Database (www.doeni.gov.uk).

WATERFORD COUNTY and CITY

Waterford, no. 1

Ballybricken Green and Mayor's Walk
Lat. 52°15'37.12" N.; Long. 7°6'55.55" W.

Earlier (separate) county and city courthouses on High St. and Broad St. respectively, shown on map 1764; new combined county and city courthouse, and county gaol, built (*James Gandon*) 1786–7; unsuccessful proposal to move the county assizes to Dungarvan 1835; plan to build a new combined county and city courthouse 1844; new courthouse built *c.* 1848–50; vestibule and grand-jury room of old courthouse used as chapel and work-room for adjoining gaol 1852–60; demolished; new combined county and city gaol built on its site 1860–3; this demolished *c.* 1949–54; police station now occupies the site; not extant.

Earlier (separate) county and city courthouses on High St. and Broad St. respectively, shown on map, 1764. New combined county and city courthouse, and county gaol (see Part II), built (*James Gandon*), 1786–7. Minor work (*Richard Morrison*), 1811. Unsuccessful proposals to move the county assizes to Dungarvan, 1835–7. Plans to build a new combined county and city courthouse agreed, 1844. New courthouse built (see 'Waterford County and City: Waterford, no. 2'), *c.* 1848–50. Vestibule of the old courthouse used as a chapel for the adjoining gaol, 1852–60. Grand-jury room of the old courthouse used as a work-room for female prisoners, 1853–60. Demolished. New combined county and city gaol (see Part II) built on its site, 1860–3. Gaol demolished, *c.* 1949–54. Police station now occupies the site. Not extant.

Archival and primary sources:

Bernard Scale and William Richards, 'A Plan of the City and Suburbs of Waterford' (1764) (copy in Waterford Museum of Treasures), John Woolfe and James Gandon, *Vitruvius Britannicus, volume 5* (London: Woolfe & Gandon, 1771), p. 8, plates 72–7, *Freeman's Journal*, 12–13 October 1786; Howard, *Lazarettos*, pp. 87–8, Waterford Council minute book, 1770–1801, for 29 March 1787 (NLI, microfilm, p. 5559, f. 115); 28 Geo. III, c. 38; View of Waterford courthouse entrance hall, n.d., by Thomas Malton (National Gallery of Ireland); Elevation drawing reconstructed by Conor Rochford, based on a surviving copper plate (NLI, prints and drawings collection) (reproduced in Loeber, *Art and Architecture of Ireland: Volume IV: Architecture 1600–2000*, p. 17); Waterford County grand-jury presentments, spring 1811 (Waterford City and County Archives, Dungarvan, GJ/31); *Waterford News*, 20 July 1829; *Waterford Mirror*, 17 July 1835; Assizes (Ireland) Act, 1835, 5 & 6 Will. IV, c. 26; Grand Jury Act, 1836 (Ireland), 6 & 7 Will. IV, c. 116, ss. 176–7; Privy Council minute book, 18 August, 30 September, 27 October and 3 November 1836, and 12 May 1837 (NAI, PCO MB 7, ff. 465–6, 482–4, 489–92 and 493–7, and PCO MB 8, ff. 51–2); *Waterford Chronicle*, 3 November, 8 November 1836; *Clonmel Advertiser*, 9 November 1836, 17 May 1837; Heaney, *Scottish Whig in Ireland*, p. 83; Lewis, *Topographical Dictionary*, vol. 2, pp. 689–90; Thackeray, *Irish Sketch-book*, p. 49; Mulvany and Gandon, *James Gandon*, pp. 68–74; Wilkinson, *Practical Geology and Ancient Architecture*, pp. 183–4; *Twenty-third Report … on … the Prisons of Ireland, 1845*, H.C. 1845 (620), xxv, pp. 76–9; *Twenty-seventh Report … on … the Prisons of Ireland, 1849*, H.C. 1849 (1069), xxvi, p. 101; *Twenty-eighth Report … on … the Prisons of Ireland, 1850*, H.C. 1850 (1229), xxix, p. 100; *Thirtieth Report … on … the Prisons of Ireland, 1852*, H.C. 1852 (1531), xxv, pp. 17, 215–19; *Thirty-first Report … on … the Prisons of Ireland, 1853*, H.C. 1853 (1657), liii, p. 18.

Secondary sources:

Craig, 'Note on Courthouses', pp. 8–12; McParland, 'Public Work of Architects', pp. 90, 159; Craig, *Architecture of Ireland*, pp. 267–71, 273; McParland, *James Gandon*, pp. 10–15, 144–9, 207; Murphy, *The Two Tipperarys*, pp. 283–314; Loeber, et al., *Art and Architecture of Ireland: Volume IV: Architecture 1600–2000*, pp. 17, 181; Donnchadh Ó Ceallacháin, 'The Old Jail in Ballybricken', 2016 (copy in Waterford Museum of Treasures); Exhibition on Waterford courthouse and jail, opened March 2016 (Waterford Museum of Treasures); Barclay, *Men on Trial*, p. 88.

WATERFORD COUNTY and CITY

Waterford, no. 2

Catherine St.
Lat. 52°15'26.43" N.; Long. 7°6'22.79" W.

An earlier combined city and county courthouse built 1786–7; unsuccessful proposal to move the county assizes to Dungarvan 1835; agreement to build a new combined city and county courthouse 1844; application for public-works loans 1846; unexecuted scheme (*William Tinsley*) *c.* 1846; new courthouse built (*John B. Keane*) *c.* 1848–50; extensive refurbishments and additions 2012–18; extant.

Combined county and city courthouse, and county gaol (see 'Waterford Count and City: Waterford, no. 1' and Part II), built, 1786–7. Unsuccessful proposal to move the county assizes to Dungarvan, 1835. Issue of the location of the assizes discussed at the Privy Council, 1836, 1837; decided in favour of the status quo. Plans to build a new combined county and city courthouse agreed, 1844. County and city grand juries submit applications for public-works loans, 1846. Unexecuted scheme (*William Tinsley*), *c.* 1846. New courthouse built (*John B. Keane*), *c.* 1848–50. Extensive refurbishments and additions, 2012–18. Extant.

Archival and primary sources:

Tipperary Free Press, 15 July 1835; *Waterford Mirror*, 17 July 1835; Assizes (Ireland) Act, 1835, 5 & 6 Will. IV, c. 26; Grand Jury Act, 1836 (Ireland), 6 & 7 Will. IV, c. 116, ss. 176–7; Privy Council minute book, 18 August, 30 September, 27 October and 3 November 1836, and 12 May 1837 (NAI, PCO MB 7, ff. 465–6, 482–4, 489–92 and 493–7, and PCO MB 8, ff. 51–2); *Waterford Chronicle*, 3 November, 8 November 1836; *Clonmel Advertiser*, 9 November 1836, 17 May 1837; *Twenty-third Report … on … the Prisons of Ireland, 1845*, H.C. 1845 (620), xxv, pp. 76–9; Royal Hibernian Academy exhibits by William Tinsley, 1846 (no. 458); *Correspondence Explanatory of the Measures Adopted … for the Relief of Distress Arising from the Failure of the Potato Crop in Ireland*, H.C. 1846 (735), xxxvii, p. 326; *Twenty-seventh Report … on … the Prisons of Ireland, 1849*, H.C. 1849 (1069), xxvi, p. 101; Assizes (Ireland) Act, 1850, 13 & 14 Vict., c. 85.

Secondary sources:

J.D. Forbes, *Victorian Architect: The life and work of William Tinsley* (Bloomington, IN: Indiana University Press, 1953), p. 45; McParland, 'Public Work of Architects', pp. 248–9; Craig, *Architecture of Ireland*, pp. 272, 275–6; Murphy, *The Two Tipperarys*, pp. 38–43, 52–6, 283–314; Loeber, et al., *Art and Architecture of Ireland: Volume IV: Architecture 1600–2000*, pp. 181, 474; Donnchadh Ó Ceallacháin, 'The Old Jail in Ballybricken', 2016 (copy in Waterford Museum of Treasures); Exhibition on Waterford courthouse and jail, opened March 2016 (Waterford Museum of Treasures).

WESTMEATH

Mullingar

Mount St.
Lat. 53°31'27.44" N.; Long. 7°20'24.81" W.

An earlier courthouse nearby, built *c.* 1682; described as 'excellent' and 'a large building' 1807; plans for a new courthouse 1819; unexecuted scheme for a new courthouse and gaol (*James Shiel*) 1820; new courthouse built (*John Hargrave*) 1824–9; loans for this building 1825–8; large additions to the nearby county gaol 1825–9; extensively refurbished and extended 2015–17; extant.

An earlier courthouse nearby, built *c.* 1682. This courthouse described as 'excellent …, a large building which makes a good appearance in the principal street', 1807. Minor alterations, 1812–13. Grand-jury plans for a new courthouse, 1819. Unexecuted scheme for a new courthouse and gaol (*James Shiel*) (see Part II), 1820. Plans for a new courthouse and gaol received by Francis Johnston at the Board of Works, 1821. Grand-jury presentment for a new combined courthouse and gaol (*James Shiel*) (see Part II), at a cost of £21,000, traversed, 1822. Grand-jury presentment for a new courthouse, 1823. New courthouse built (*John Hargrave*), at a cost of at least £11,626, 1824–9. Central-government loans received for courthouse building, 1825–8. Large addition to the county gaol nearby (see Part II), 1825–9. Extensively refurbished and extended, 2015–17. Extant.

Archival and primary sources:

Anon. ['W.P.'], 'Sketch of a Journey through Part of Ireland', in *Walker's Hibernian Magazine*, September 1807, pp. 545–7, at p. 546; Westmeath grand-jury presentment books, 1812–13, and 1822–6 (Westmeath County Library, WMGJ/AP/8–10, and WMGJ/AP/11–18); *Dublin Evening Post*, 14 December 1819; Plans for a new courthouse in Mullingar, February 1820, by James Shiel (Westmeath County Library) (there are copies in the Irish Architectural Archive: 088/063, C.15/403–8); Francis Johnston to the Commissioners of the Board of Works, 5 March 1821 (NAI, CSORP 1821/1205); Commissioners of the Board of Works to William Gregory, 10 March 1821 (NAI, CSORP 1821/1247); Francis Johnston to R. Robinson, 4 November 1823 (NAI, CSORP 1823/7131); *Westmeath Journal*, 20 March 1823; ibid., 29 April 1824; ibid., 12 March

1829, ibid., 19 January 1832; James Gibbons to Henry Goulburn, 29 January 1826 (NAI, CSORP 1825/12,783); Catalogue of auction of architectural drawings, etc., by John Hargrave, 1 December 1836, lots 8, 12, 35, 50; Westmeath grand-jury presentment book (abstracts), 1826–8 (NLI); Lewis, *Topographical Dictionary*, vol. 2, p. 412.

Secondary sources:

McParland, 'Public Work of Architects', p. 240; Casey, 'Courthouses', pp. 108–9; Rowan and Casey, *Buildings of Ireland: North Leinster*, pp. 240–1; Anngret Simms (ed.), *Irish Historic Towns Atlas: Volume 1: Kildare, Carrickfergus, Bandon, Kells, Mullingar, Athlone* (Dublin: Royal Irish Academy, 1996), no. 5, p. 10.

WEXFORD

Wexford

Commercial Quay & Wexford Bridge
Lat. 52°20'29.04" N.; Long. 6°27'43.81" W.

A former courthouse was located in the Bullring, presumably destroyed in the rebellion of 1798, when the square was used by rebels for making armaments; new courthouse planned from at least 1802; new courthouse built at Wexford Bridge (*Richard Morrison*) *c.* 1803–7; additions *c.* 1810–11; extensive alterations and enlargement (*James Barry Farrell*) 1862; gutted by fire 1922; partially rebuilt (*William Fitz-gerald Barry*) 1929–30; demolished; not extant.

A former courthouse was located in the Bullring. This was used by rebels to make armaments during the rebellion of 1798, and was presumably destroying during the fighting of that year. A new courthouse planned from at least 1802. A new courthouse built at the termination of Wexford Bridge (*Richard Morrison*), *c.* 1803–7. Old courthouse to be demolished and its materials sold off, 1807. Many later alterations and repairs, including additions of *c.* 1810–11. Extensive alterations, including reconstruction of the main façade, and enlargement, and the removal of pictures of kings George III and William III from the two roundels in the façade (*James Barry Farrell*), 1862. Gutted by fire, 1922. Partial reconstruction (*William Fitz-gerald Barry*), 1929–30. Later demolished. Not extant.

Archival and primary sources:

Accounts of the Presentments Passed by the Grand Juries of Ireland … in … 1807, H.C. 1808 (205), xiii, pp. 167, and passim; Brewer, *Beauties of Ireland*, vol. 1, p. 351; Lewis, *Topographical Dictionary*, vol. 2, p. 710; *Wexford Independent*, 9 June 1841; Lacy, *Sights and Scenes*, pp. 187, 408; Wexford grand-jury presentment book, summer assizes 1859 (Wexford County Archives, GJ); Drawings for alterations to Wexford courthouse by James Barry Farrell, September 1860 (Wexford County Archives, P387); *Dublin Builder*, vol. 4, no. 61, 1 July 1862, p. 172; *Irish Builder*, vol. 71, no. 26, 21 December 1929, pp. 1139; ibid., vol. 72, no. 2, 18 January 1930, p. 45; George Griffiths, *Chronicles of the County Wexford* (Enniscorthy: Watchman, 1877), pp. 268–72.

Secondary sources:

McParland, 'Public Work of Architects', pp. 240–1; Casey, 'Courthouses', p. 105; Rowan, *Morrison*, pp. 172–3; O'Donoghue, *Irish County Surveyors*, p. 167; Jarlath Glynn, *Wexford: Then & now* (Dublin: History Press, 2013), pp. 60–1, 88–9.

WICKLOW

Wicklow

Market Square & Kilmartin Hill
Lat. 52°58'45.61" N.; Long. 6°2'15.25" W.

Older building enlarged and altered 1774; substantially altered and enlarged (*William Vitruvius Morrison*) 1817–20; repaired 1824; alterations 1830; noted as 'dilapidated' 1840; unexecuted proposal to move assize town from Wicklow to Rathdrum 1840; alterations and repairs (*John Edwards*) 1842; alterations and improvements (*Henry Brett*) 1866; further work, including a new courtroom (*John Henry Brett*) 1876; enlarged 1943; closed 2010; future uncertain; extant.

Described as 'too narrow and confined', 1774. Act of parliament obtained for 'enlarging and rendering … more convenient' the courthouse, 1774. Courthouse and gaol located where they exist today, 1788. Courthouse substantially altered and enlarged (*William Vitruvius Morrison*), at a cost of £3,996, 1817–20. Repaired, 1824. Alterations, 1830. Grand-jury note courthouse as 'dilapidated', and that 'it may even be necessary to re-build the greater part of it at no distant period', 1840. Unexecuted proposal to move assize town from Wicklow to Rathdrum, 1840. Alterations and repairs (*John Edwards*), 1842. Alterations and improvements (*Henry Brett*), 1866. Further alterations and improvements, including a new courtroom (*John Henry Brett*), at a cost of at least £1,800, 1876. Enlarged, 1943. Closed for 'safety reasons', 2010. Future uncertain. Extant.

Archival and primary sources:

13 & 14 Geo. III, c. 18, s. 16; Howard, *Lazarettos*, p. 84; Wicklow grand-jury presentment books, 1818–42 (Wicklow County Archives, GJ); Wicklow grand-jury presentment book, spring 1830 (NLI); Lewis, *Topographical Dictionary*, vol. 2, p. 722; *Irish Builder*, vol. 18, no. 398, 15 July 1876, p. 214.

Secondary sources:

Casey, 'Courthouses', p. 125; O'Donoghue, *Irish County Surveyors*, p. 113.

Part 2: County Gaols, Penitentiaries, and Prisons in Dublin

ANTRIM (and later TOWN OF CARRICKFERGUS)

Carrickfergus, no. 1

High St. & Market Place
Lat. 54°42'52.42" N.; Long. 5°48'24.58" W.

Planned 1612; built 1612–13; partially rebuilt (*Hugh Darley* and *John Gibson*) 1727; handed over to the Town of Carrickfergus 1776; unexecuted replacement 1824; prisoners moved to Antrim county gaol 1827; demolished 1827; foundation stone of new courthouse laid 1828; soon thereafter abandoned and demolished; later buildings now occupy the site.

Site for a gaol granted in the charter for the town of Carrickfergus, 1612. Gaol (and presumably also courthouse) built for the county, 1612–13. E. part rebuilt (*Hugh Darley* and *John Gibson*), 1727. Handed over to the Town of Carrickfergus, 1776. Forster Archer, prison inspector, says town gaol is 'very ruinous and a disgrace to the corporation', 1818. Petition to parliament from the mayor, etc., of Carrickfergus, claiming an inability to pay for the upkeep of the town's public buildings, 1824. Unexecuted proposal for a new town gaol, to cost around £1,000, 1824. Prisoners moved from adjacent gaol to the Antrim county gaol, 1827. Town courthouse and gaol demolished, 1827. Foundation for a new town courthouse laid on the same site, 1828; this abandoned when two storeys in height and about to be roofed in, and materials sold for £35, 1828. Combined county and town gaol abandoned, 1850 (see 'Antrim: Carrickfergus, no. 2'); town prisoners remain in old Antrim county gaol for an uncertain period of time, 1851. Later buildings now occupy the site.

Archival and primary sources:

Charter for the town of Carrickfergus by James I, dated 14 December 1612 (Rolls of Patents, 10 James I, p. 3, m. 16); Howard, *Lazarettos*, p. 98; Forster Archer, 'Report of the State of Gaols of Ireland for the Year 1811' (Houses of the Oireachtas Library,

Dublin, MS.4E63); Dubourdieu, *Statistical Survey of the County of Antrim*, p. 486; Wright, *Tours in Ireland*, vol. 3, p. 17; *Journal of the House of Commons*, vol. 79, 19 May 1824, p. 386; McSkimmin, *Carrickfergus*, pp. 151, 170–3 (illus.); Ordnance survey maps, 1832 (PRONI, OS/6/1/52/1); Lewis, *Topographical Dictionary*, vol. 1, p. 273.

Prison reports:

Inspector General's Report of … the Prisons in Ireland for … 1818, H.C. 1819 (534), xii, p. 3;

Prisons of Ireland: Report of Inspectors General, 1823, H.C. 1823 (342), x, pp. 6, 25;

Prisons of Ireland: Report of Inspectors General, 1824, H.C. 1824 (294), xxii, pp. 6, 28;

Prisons of Ireland: Report of Inspectors General, 1825, H.C. 1825 (493), xxii, p. 24;

Fourth Report … on … the Prisons of Ireland, 1826, H.C. 1826 (173), xxiii, p. 23;

Fifth Report … on … the Prisons of Ireland, 1827, H.C. 1826–7 (471), xi, p. 7, 25;

Ninth Report … on … the Prisons of Ireland, 1831, H.C. 1830–1 (172), iv, pp. 22–3;

Twenty-ninth Report … on … the Prisons of Ireland, 1851, H.C. 1851 (1364), xxviii, pp. 16, 20–1.

Secondary sources:

Brett, *Court Houses*, p. 29; Simms, *Irish Historic Towns Atlas: Volume 1: Kildare, Carrickfergus, Bandon, Kells, Mullingar, Athlone*, no. 2, p. 11.

ANTRIM (and site of earlier TOWN OF CARRICKFERGUS)

Carrickfergus, no. 2

Antrim St. & High St.
Lat. 54°42'56.51" N.; Long. 5°48'19.25" W.

Planned 1776; built (*Richard Drew*) 1777–9; expanded, 1792; large addition built (*Alexander Wilson*) 1815–19; calls for a new prison 1823; used for keeping county as well as town prisoners 1827; new gaol in Belfast suggested 1837; prisoners moved to Belfast 1850; abandoned *c.* 1850; sold to the Board of Public Works 1851; leased to the government 1852; in use by the military 1856–96; purchased by the military 1896; gaol demolished 1897; partially extant.

Site of former Franciscan friary, 1232–*c.* 1560. Partly site of the Earl of Donegall's former Joymount Palace, 1618–1768. Partly site of Castle Worraigh, the Town of Carrickfergus' courthouse and gaol, *c.* 1699–1776. Petition to move assizes to Ballymena, 1707, 1712. Petition to move assizes to Antrim town, 1753, 1771, 1774. Old county courthouse and gaol nearby handed over to the Town of Carrickfergus, 1776 (see 'Antrim: Carrickfergus, no. 1'). New courthouse and gaol built together (*Richard Drew*), at a total cost of £5,785, 1777–9. A wing added to the south, 1792. Forster Archer recommends alterations for purposes of classification, and suggests a large bridewell should be built in Belfast, 1807. Presentments for an addition, termed a house of correction, costing £5,200–£7,437, 1814–15. Tenders invited for altering and enlarging gaol, 1815. Large additions including new wings to the west (*Alexander Wilson*), costing £16,000, 1815–19. James Palmer, prison inspector, calls for a new prison for the county, 1823. Town of Carrickfergus prisoners also kept in county gaol, 1827 onwards. Unexecuted proposal for a new radial-plan gaol in Antrim town, 1828. Palmer and Woodward suggest an addition of 100 cells to the rear of the existing county gaol, 1837. Later that year, they suggest instead a new house of correction in Belfast (see 'Antrim: Belfast'), 1837. Prisoners moved to new Belfast gaol, 1850. Courthouse and gaol abandoned, 1850. Sold to the Board of Public Works for use as a convict prison, for £390, 1851. Prison plan abandoned, 1852. Government lease, 1852 onwards. Alterations for use by the military, 1856. Purchased by the military, 1896. Gaol demolished, 1897. Only small portions of the original walls, etc., survive. Partially extant.

Archival and primary sources:

Antrim grand-jury presentment books, 1778–9, 1781–1837 (PRONI, ANT/4); Howard, *Lazarettos*, p. 98; McSkimmin, *Carrickfergus*, pp. 151, 170–3, 511–14; Dubourdieu, *Statistical Survey of the County of Antrim*, p. 486; Forster Archer, 'Report of the State of Gaols of Ireland for the Year 1811' (Houses of the Oireachtas Library, Dublin, MS.4E63); *Belfast Newsletter*, 10 February 1815; An account of the several presentments made … on which advances have been made by government for gaols, n.d. (NAI, SPO OP 1832–38, 1A/77/4); Wright, *Tours in Ireland*, vol. 3, p. 17; Reid, *Travels*, pp. 173–4; *First Report of the AIPPD*, pp. 25–6; *Third Report of the AIPPD*, p. 22; Ordnance survey maps, 1832, 1857, 1901–2 (PRONI, OS/6/1/52/1–3); Lewis, *Topographical Dictionary*, vol. 1, pp. 270–3; Collection of drawings purportedly by William Vitruvius Morrison for proposed additions to Carrickfergus gaol, n.d. (PRONI, LA/1/8/JA/109 – said now to be lost); *The Builder*, vol. 9, no. 461, 6 December 1851, p. 775.

Prison reports:

Inspector General's Report of … the Prisons in Ireland for … 1807, H.C. 1808 (239), ix, p. 3;

Account of All Gaols … in the … United Kingdom, H.C. 1819 (137), xvii, pp. 2–3;

Inspector General's Report of … the Prisons in Ireland for … 1818, H.C. 1819 (534), xii, p. 3;

Prisons of Ireland: Report of Inspectors General, 1823, H.C. 1823 (342), x, pp. 5–6, 25;

Prisons of Ireland: Report of Inspectors General, 1824, H.C. 1824 (294), xxii, pp. 6, 27–8;

Fourth Report … on … the Prisons of Ireland, 1826, H.C. 1826 (173), xxiii, pp. 22–3;

Fifth Report … on … the Prisons of Ireland, 1827, H.C. 1826–7 (471), xi, p. 7, 25;

Seventh Report … on … the Prisons of Ireland, 1829, H.C. 1829 (10), xiii, pp. 8, 31;

Eighth Report … on … the Prisons of Ireland, 1830, H.C. 1830 (48), xxiv, p. 30;

Tenth Report … on … the Prisons of Ireland, 1832, H.C. 1831–2 (152), xxiii, p. 20;

Eleventh Report … on … the Prisons of Ireland, 1833, H.C. 1833 (67), xvii, p. 35;

Twelfth Report … on … the Prisons of Ireland, 1834, H.C. 1834 (63), xl, p. 38;

Fifteenth Report … on … the Prisons of Ireland, 1837, H.C. 1837 (123), xxxi, pp. 8, 19;

Sixteenth Report … on … the Prisons of Ireland, 1838, H.C. 1837–8 (186), xxix, pp. 8, 24;

Seventeenth Report … on … the Prisons of Ireland, 1839, H.C. 1839 (91), xx, p. 22;

Eighteenth Report … on … the Prisons of Ireland, 1840, H.C. 1840 (240), xxvi, pp. 7, 25–6;

Nineteenth Report … on … the Prisons of Ireland, 1841, H.C. 1841 (299), xi, pp. 24–5;

Twenty-ninth Report … on … the Prisons of Ireland, 1851, H.C. 1851 (1364), xxviii, pp. 16, 20–1.

Secondary sources:

Brett, *Court Houses*, p. 29; O'Dwyer, 'Public Works Architecture', p. 407; Simms, *Irish Historic Towns Atlas: Volume 1: Kildare, Carrickfergus, Bandon, Kells, Mullingar, Athlone*, no. 2, p. 11.

ANTRIM

Belfast

Crumlin Rd.
Lat. 54°36'33.88" N.; Long. 5°56'31.70" W.

A small prison built in Belfast 1803; calls for a new bridewell 1807; new house of correction built 1815–17; call for large additions 1831–3; new gaol planned 1837; unexecuted design (*Charles Lanyon*) not on separate-system principles 1839; new prison built (*Charles Lanyon* and assistants) 1843–5; prisoners moved to new gaol 1850; additions (*Alexander Tate*) 1873; closed 1996; refurbished as a tourist attraction, etc., 2010–12; extant

A small prison opened in Belfast, 1803. Forster Archer, prison inspector, calls for a new bridewell for Belfast, 1807. Tenders invited for building a new house of correction in Belfast, 1815. New house of correction built, 1815–17. James Palmer, prison inspector, calls for large additions to existing house of correction, 1831–3. Crumlin Road laid out, 1836. Palmer and Woodward call for a 100 cell addition to the existing house of correction, 1837. Assize Judge forces grand jury to build a new gaol for the county, 1837. Unexecuted proposal for a new bridewell not arranged to separate system requirements (*Charles Lanyon*), 1839. Palmer and Woodward announce that Belfast's new bridewell will be built on separate-system principles, 1840. Presentment for new prison agreed by grand jury, 1840. Site on Crumlin Road purchased from the Belfast Charitable Society, 1841. New district bridewell (later Antrim county gaol) built (*Charles Lanyon* and *Thomas Ellis Owen* and *Thomas Turner*), at a cost of £41,000, 1843–5. New prison deemed a district bridewell, 1847. New courthouse built opposite (*Charles Lanyon*), *c.* 1848–50. Prisoners moved to new prison, 1850. Old Carrickfergus courthouse and gaol abandoned, 1850. In use as Antrim county gaol, 1850. Additions (*Alexander Tate*), 1873. Closed, 1996. Refurbished as a tourist attraction and conference centre, 2010–12. Listed. Extant.

Archival and primary sources:

Accounts of the Presentments Passed by the Grand Juries of Ireland … in … 1807, H.C. 1808 (205), xiii, pp. 17; Forster Archer, 'Report of the State of Gaols of Ireland for the Year 1811' (Houses of the Oireachtas Library, Dublin, MS.4E63); *Belfast Newsletter*, 13 March 1813; ibid., 13 June 1815; ibid., 1 September 1850; Reid, *Travels in Ireland*, pp. 176–7; Lewis, *Topographical Dictionary*, vol. 1, p. 197; Letters and accounts (NAI, CSORP 1845/G.3238); *The Builder*, vol. 2, no. 59, 23 March 1844, p. 162; ibid., vol. 10, no. 496, 7 August 1852, pp. 495–6; Collection of eleven contract drawings, *c.* 1842–3 (Belfast, Northern Ireland Prison Service Agency); Collection of three drawings, *c.* 1843–50 (PRONI, LA/1/8JA/111–14); Doyle, *Tours in Ulster*, pp. 26–7; McComb, *McComb's Guide to Belfast*, pp. 34–5; George Benn, *A History of the Town of Belfast from 1799 till 1810*, 2 vols (London: Marcus Ward, 1877–80), vol. 2, p. 79; McSkimmin, *Carrickfergus*, pp. 109, 173, 511–12; Young, *Belfast and the Province of Ulster*, p. 93 (illus.); Survey drawing by the Department of Works and Public Buildings, 1924 (Belfast, Northern Ireland Prison Service Agency).

Prison reports:

Inspector General's Report of … the Prisons in Ireland for … 1807, H.C. 1808 (239), ix, p. 3;

Account of All Gaols … in the … United Kingdom, H.C. 1819 (137), xvii, pp. 2–3;

Inspector General's Report of … the Prisons in Ireland for … 1818, H.C. 1819 (534), xii, p. 3;

Sixth Report … on … the Prisons of Ireland, 1828, H.C. 1828 (68), xii, pp. 36–7;

Seventh Report … on … the Prisons of Ireland, 1829, H.C. 1829 (10), xiii, pp. 31–2;

Eighth Report … on … the Prisons of Ireland, 1830, H.C. 1830 (48), xxiv, p. 30;

Ninth Report … on … the Prisons of Ireland, 1831, H.C. 1830–1 (172), iv, p. 22;

Eleventh Report … on … the Prisons of Ireland, 1833, H.C. 1833 (67), xvii, pp. 35–6;

Twelfth Report … on … the Prisons of Ireland, 1834, H.C. 1834 (63), xl, p. 38;

Thirteenth Report … on … the Prisons of Ireland, 1835, H.C. 1835 (114), xxxvi, p. 22;

Fifteenth Report … on … the Prisons of Ireland, 1837, H.C. 1837 (123), xxxi, p. 19;

Sixteenth Report … on … the Prisons of Ireland, 1838, H.C. 1837–8 (186), xxix, pp. 8, 24;

Seventeenth Report … on … the Prisons of Ireland, 1839, H.C. 1839 (91), xx, p. 22;

Eighteenth Report … on … the Prisons of Ireland, 1840, H.C. 1840 (240), xxvi, pp. 7, 25–6;

Nineteenth Report … on … the Prisons of Ireland, 1841, H.C. 1841 (299), xi, pp. 24–5;

Twentieth Report … on … the Prisons of Ireland, 1842, H.C. 1842 (377), xxii, pp. 5–6, 48–50;

Twenty-first report … on … the Prisons of Ireland, 1843, H.C. 1843 (462), xxvii, pp. 1, 26–7;
Twenty-second report … on … the Prisons of Ireland, 1844, H.C. 1844 (535), xxviii, pp. 7, 29–30;
Twenty-third report … on … the Prisons of Ireland, 1844, H.C. 1845 (620), xxv, pp. 6, 12–14;
Twenty-fourth Report … on … the Prisons of Ireland, 1846, H.C. 1846 (697), xx, pp. 20–1;
Twenty-fifth Report … on … the Prisons of Ireland, 1847, H.C. 1847 (805), xxix, pp. 31–6;
Twenty-sixth Report … on … the Prisons of Ireland, 1847–48, H.C. 1847–8 (952), xxiv, pp. 45–8;
Twenty-seventh Report … on … the Prisons of Ireland, 1849, H.C. 1849 (1069), xxvi, p. 40;
Twenty-eighth Report … on … the Prisons of Ireland, 1850, H.C. 1850 (1229), xxix, p. 35;
Twenty-ninth Report … on … the Prisons of Ireland, 1851, H.C. 1851 (1364), xxviii, pp. 16, 20–1;
Forty-ninth Report … on … the Prisons of Ireland, 1870, H.C. 1871 (C. 359), xxx, p. 77.

Secondary sources:

Belfast Newsletter, 9 July 1936; R.W. Magill Strain, 'The History and Associations of the Belfast Charitable Institute', PhD thesis, Queen's University Belfast, 1955, vol. 1, pp. 354–60; Jones, *Social Geography of Belfast*, pp. 245–7 (illus.); McParland, 'Public Work of Architects', p. 252; Richardson, *Gothic Revival Architecture in Ireland*, p. 325; Brett, *Buildings of Belfast*, pp. 29, plate 23; Larmour, *Belfast: An illustrated architectural guide*, p. 12; Paul Larmour, 'Sir Charles Lanyon', *Irish Arts Review Yearbook* (1989–90), pp. 200–6, at pp. 201–2; O'Dwyer, 'Public Works Architecture', pp. 181–5, 407; Loeber, et al., *Art and Architecture of Ireland: Volume IV: Architecture 1600–2000*, pp. 205–6; Northern Ireland Environmental Agency (NIEA), Listed Buildings Database (www.doeni.gov.uk).

ARMAGH

Armagh, no. 1

Market St. & Market Place
Lat. 54°20'52.26" N.; Long. 6°39'13.80" W.

Unknown date of construction; damaged by fire 1704; rebuilt 1735; replacement gaol built elsewhere 1780; new courthouse built elsewhere 1807–10; abandoned 1810; demolished; markethouse built (probably *Thomas J. Duff*) 1815.

Date of construction unknown. Combined assize courthouse and gaol (beneath), located 'at the foot of Market-street', damaged by fire, 1704. Rebuilt, 1735. Replacement gaol (*Thomas Cooley*) built, 1780; old gaol thereafter abandoned. Replacement courthouse built (*Francis Johnston*) at the north end of the Mall, 1807–10 (see Part I); old courthouse and gaol abandoned, soon after demolished. 'His grace [the primate] intends the site of the present [courthouse and gaol] for that of the market-house', 1804. Markethouse built (probably *Thomas J. Duff*), 1815.

Archival and primary sources:

Gentleman's Magazine, vol. 5, September 1735, p. 557; Coote, *Statistical Survey of the County of Armagh*, pp. 321–2; Stuart, *Historical Memoirs of the City of Armagh*, pp. 530–1.

Secondary sources:

Brett, *Court Houses*, p. 36; Goslin, 'Descriptive Catalogue of the Murray Collection', p. 54; McCullough and Crawford, *Irish Historic Towns Atlas, No. 18: Armagh*, section 13.

ARMAGH

Armagh, no. 2

The Mall
Lat. 54°20'48.51" N.; Long. 6°38'50.37" W.

Gaol built on site of former barracks; built (*Thomas Cooley*) 1780; addition of five bays and an infirmary (*John Bowden*) 1817–19; call for a new prison on a new site 1825; unexecuted proposal for a large addition (*William Farrell*) 1825; first unexecuted scheme for a large addition to the rear (*William Murray*) 1837; large separate-system wing built (*William Murray*) 1846–9; second separate-system wing built (*Boyd and Batt*) 1853–6; façade extensively rebuilt (*Boyd and Batt*) 1864–6; in use as a women's prison 1920; closed 1988; derelict; extant.

Old gaol on Market St. & Market Place, rebuilt, 1735 (see 'Armagh: Armagh, no. 1'). A site to the south of the Mall cleared of a steep mound and a former barracks to make way for a new gaol, 1780. Gaol built (*Thomas Cooley*), 1780. New courthouse built (*Francis Johnston*) at the north end of the Mall, 1807–10. Forster Archer notes a 'newly erected female courtyard', 1813. Unexecuted designs for additions or alterations (*John Bowden*), 1816. Francis Johnston requests changes to these designs, 1817. Tenders invited for enlarging gaol and building an infirmary (*John Bowden*), 1817. Five bays to the north added, as well as an infirmary (*John Bowden*), 1817–19. James Palmer, prison inspector, calls for a new prison on a new site, 1825. Unexecuted proposal (*William Farrell*) for a radial-plan extension to the rear, to cost £9,000, 1825. A large yard added to the rear of the gaol, 1828–30. Unexecuted proposal for a large radial-plan extension (*William Murray*), 1837. Additional land purchased to allow for a large extension, 1837. Unexecuted second proposal for an even larger radial-plan extension (*William Murray*), 1837. Unexecuted proposals for rebuilding the gaol façade (*William Murray*), 1837. Woodward, prison inspector, suggests a new gaol or a large extension, the latter to be built partially on separate-system requirements, 1838. Further unexecuted proposals (*William Murray*), 1837–40. Decision that addition will be on separate-system plan only, 1840. Assize judge urges the grand jury to commit to expanding the gaol, but refused by cess-payers, 1842. Assize judge urges grand jury to proceed, 1845. Addition of a chapel and a single large wing on a separate-system plan (*William Murray*), 1846–9. Prison inspectors call for a further wing to be added, 1850. Competition held for designs of a second wing, with forty cells, for females, 1852. Second wing built (*Boyd and Batt*), 1853–6. Unexecuted proposal to alter the gaol façade, 1855. Façade extensively rebuilt and gallows removed (*Boyd and Batt*), 1864–6. In use as a women's prison, 1920. Closed, 1988. Currently derelict. Extant.

Archival and primary sources:

Gentleman's Magazine, vol. 5, September 1735, p. 557; Howard, *Lazarettos*, p. 99; Coote, *Statistical Survey of the County of Armagh*, p. 319; Stuart, *Armagh*, pp. 449, 530–2; 'City of Armagh', painting by James Black, 1810 (Armagh County Museum, ARMCM.156.1958); Forster Archer, 'Report of the State of Gaols of Ireland for the Year 1811' (Houses of the Oireachtas Library, Dublin, MS.4E63); John Bowden to William Gregory, 30 November 1816 (NAI, SPO 563/462/21); *Belfast Newsletter*, 13 June 1817; Drawings for Armagh gaol, showing additions as built in 1817–19, n.d., n.s. [*c.* 1817] (NLI, AD 2665); Board of Works letterbooks, 29 January 1817 to 18 May 1826 (NAI, 2D/57/36); William Ball to Forster Archer, 31 May 1819 (NAI, CSORP 1819/27); *Third Report of the AIPPD*, p. 25; Armagh grand-jury presentment books, 1821–99 (Armagh County Museum); Reid, *Travels in Ireland*, pp. 165–7; *Newry Telegraph*, 22 February 1828; Lewis, *Topographical dictionary*, vol. 1, p. 69; Drawings for Armagh gaol by William Murray, various schemes, 1837–52 (Irish Architectural Archive, RIAI Murray Collection, Acc. 92/46.19–62); *Armagh Guardian*, 14 January, 11 February, 4 March, 3 June, 24 June, 15 July 1845; ibid., 20 March, 10 July 1852, 12 February, 25 March 1853; ibid., 28 March 1856; ibid., 2 September 1864, 20 April 1866; *The Builder*, vol. 11, no. 547, 30 July 1853, p. 484; Map of Armagh City by James O'Hagan, 1851 (Armagh County Museum); Edward Rogers, *A Record of the City of Armagh from the Earliest Period to the Present Time* (Armagh: Armagh Guardian, 1861), photograph of Armagh by Abraham Talbot, *c.* 1861; *Dublin Builder*, vol. 7, no. 133, 1 July 1865, p. 170; ibid., vol. 8, no. 152, 15 April 1866, p. 106; Ordnance Survey map of Armagh, *c.* 1870 (Armagh County Museum, 5.2014.16).

Prison reports:

Inspector General's Report of ... the Prisons in Ireland for ... 1807, H.C. 1808 (239), ix, p. 3;
Account of All Gaols ... in the ... United Kingdom, H.C. 1819 (137), xvii, pp. 2–3;
Inspector General's Report of ... the Prisons in Ireland for ... 1818, H.C. 1819 (534), xii, pp. 3–4;
Report from the Select Committee on the State of Gaols, H.C. 1819 (579), vii, p. 203;
Prisons of Ireland: Report of Inspectors General, 1823, H.C. 1823 (342), x, pp. 5–6, 27;
Prisons of Ireland: Report of Inspectors General, 1824, H.C. 1824 (294), xxii, pp. 6, 29;
Fourth Report ... on ... the Prisons of Ireland, 1826, H.C. 1826 (173), xxiii, p. 21;
Fifth Report ... on ... the Prisons of Ireland, 1827, H.C. 1826–7 (471), xi, pp. 7, 26–7;
Sixth Report ... on ... the Prisons of Ireland, 1828, H.C. 1828 (68), xii, pp. 8, 37–8;
Seventh Report ... on ... the Prisons of Ireland, 1829, H.C. 1829 (10), xiii, pp. 9, 32;
Eighth Report ... on ... the Prisons of Ireland, 1830, H.C. 1830 (48), xxiv, pp. 31–2;
Ninth Report ... on ... the Prisons of Ireland, 1831, H.C. 1830–1 (172), iv, p. 23;
Tenth Report ... on ... the Prisons of Ireland, 1832, H.C. 1831–2 (152), xvii, p. 21;
Twelfth Report ... on ... the Prisons of Ireland, 1834, H.C. 1834 (63), xl, p. 39;
Thirteenth Report ... on ... the Prisons of Ireland, 1835, H.C. 1835 (114), xxxvi, p. 23;
Fifteenth Report ... on ... the Prisons of Ireland, 1837, H.C. 1837 (123), xxxi, pp. 8, 20–1;
Sixteenth Report ... on ... the Prisons of Ireland, 1838, H.C. 1837–8 (186), xxix, pp. 8, 24–5;
Seventeenth Report ... on ... the Prisons of Ireland, 1839, H.C. 1839 (91), xx, pp. 23–4;
Eighteenth Report ... on ... the Prisons of Ireland, 1840, H.C. 1840 (240), xxvi, pp. 7, 27;
Nineteenth Report ... on ... the Prisons of Ireland, 1841, H.C. 1841 (299), xi, pp. 26–7;
Twenty-first Report ... on ... the Prisons of Ireland, 1843, H.C. 1843 (462), xxvii, pp. 3, 28;
Twenty-second Report ... on ... the Prisons of Ireland, 1844, H.C. 1844 (535), xxviii, pp. 30–2;
Twenty-third Report ... on ... the Prisons of Ireland, 1844, H.C. 1845 (620), xxv, pp. 6, 14;
Twenty-fourth Report ... on ... the Prisons of Ireland, 1846, H.C. 1846 (697), xx, p. 22;
Twenty-fifth Report ... on ... the Prisons of Ireland, 1847, H.C. 1847 (805), xxix, p. 36;
Twenty-sixth Report ... on ... the Prisons of Ireland, 1847–48, H.C. 1847–8 (952), xxiv, p. 50;
Twenty-seventh Report ... on ... the Prisons of Ireland, 1849, H.C. 1849 (1069), xxvi, p. 43;
Twenty-eighth Report ... on ... the Prisons of Ireland, 1850, H.C. 1850 (1229), xxix, p. 40;
Thirtieth Report ... on ... the Prisons of Ireland, 1852, H.C. 1852 (1531), xxv, p. 15;
Thirty-first Report ... on ... the Prisons of Ireland, 1853, H.C. 1853 (1657), liii, pp. 15, 73;
Thirty-second Report ... on ... the Prisons of Ireland, 1854, H.C. 1854 (1803), xxxii, p. 18;
Thirty-third Report ... on ... the Prisons of Ireland, 1855, H.C. 1854–5 (1956), xxvi, pp. 15, 45–7;
Thirty-fourth Report ... on ... the Prisons of Ireland, 1856, H.C. 1856 (2113), xxxiv, p. 63;
Forty-first Report ... on ... the Prisons of Ireland, 1863, H.C. 1863 (3214), xxiii, pp. 128–9;
Forty-second Report ... on ... the Prisons of Ireland, 1864, H.C. 1864 (3377), xxvii, p. 78;
Forty-third Report ... on ... the Prisons of Ireland, 1865, H.C. 1865 (3522), xxiv, p. 84;
Forty-fourth Report ... on ... the Prisons of Ireland, 1866, H.C. 1866 (3690), xxxiv, p. 81;
Forty-fifth Report ... on ... the Prisons of Ireland, 1867, H.C. 1867 (3915), xxxv, p. 85;
Forty-ninth Report ... on ... the Prisons of Ireland, 1870, H.C. 1871 (C. 359), xxx, p. 94.

Secondary sources:

Aerial photograph of Armagh Gaol, June 1975 (copy) (Armagh County Museum); Goslin, 'Descriptive Catalogue of the Murray Collection', pp. 48–55; Robert McKinstry, et al., *Buildings of Armagh*, pp. 138–42; O'Dwyer, 'Public Works Architecture', pp. 181, 192, 407; McCullough and Crawford, *Irish Historic Towns Atlas, No. 18: Armagh*, section 13; Mulligan, *Buildings of Ireland: South Ulster*, pp. 123–4; Rolf Loeber, et al., *Art and Architecture of Ireland: Volume IV: Architecture 1600–2000*, pp. 203, 446; Northern Ireland Environmental Agency (NIEA), Listed Buildings Database (www.doeni.gov.uk); Sean Barden and Sarah Millsopp (eds), *Mad or Bad: An exhibition about crime, gender and mental health in Victorian Ireland: Armagh County Museum, 5th October 2016 – 18th February 2017* (Armagh: Armagh County Museum, 2016); Gibney, Hurley and McParland, *Building Site in Eighteenth-century Ireland*, p. 171.

CARLOW

Carlow, no. 1

Burrin St. & Kennedy St.
Lat. 52°50'9.75" N.; Long. 6°55'57.13" W.

Possibly the site of a former gaol, said to have been built *c.* 1750, or *c.* 1783, destroyed 1798; gaol rebuilt elsewhere *c.* 1800; a courthouse built on site *c.* 1799–1801; another new courthouse built elsewhere 1830–4; old courthouse abandoned 1834; demolished 1837; Dreighton Memorial Hall (extant) built on site thereafter.

Possibly the site of a former gaol, said to have been built *c.* 1750, or *c.* 1783, mostly destroyed during unrest, 1798. Gaol rebuilt elsewhere, *c.* 1800 (see 'Carlow: Carlow, no. 3'). Courthouse built on this site, *c.* 1799–1801. Dreighton Memorial Hall (extant) built on its site, sometime afterwards. Listed.

Archival and primary sources:

Howard, *Lazarettos*, p. 86; Atkinson, *Irish Tourist*, p. 376; Brewer, *Beauties of Ireland*, vol. 2, p. 8; *Finn's Leinster Journal*, 11 April 1827.

Secondary sources:

Douglas, 'Carlow's Old Inns: Churches, gaol, and castle', pp. 173–4; Teresa Kelly, 'The Old Gaol, now Hanover Works', *Carloviana*, vol. 1, no. 9, new series, December 1960, pp. 38–9; Garner, *Carlow: Architectural heritage*, p. 45; Peter Thomas, 'Carlow Gaol', *Carloviana*, vol. 2, no. 31, new series, 1983, pp. 8–9; Doran, 'Carlow Criminal Court', pp. 23–4; Teehan, 'The Emergence of County Courthouses', pp. 47–8.

CARLOW

Carlow, no. 2

Bridewell Ln.
Lat. 52°50'4.69" N.; Long. 6°55'45.25" W.

Possibly the site of a former gaol, said to have been built *c.* 1750, or *c.* 1783; gaol rebuilt elsewhere *c.* 1800; site sold by grand jury 1809; site later known as Gillespie's Corn Store; extant in 1983; demolished.

Possibly the site of a former gaol, said to have been built *c.* 1750, or *c.* 1783. Gaol rebuilt elsewhere, *c.* 1800 (see 'Carlow: Carlow, no. 3'). Site sold by grand jury, 1809. Site later known as Gillespie's Corn Store. Still extant, 1983. Later demolished.

Archival and primary sources:

Howard, *Lazarettos*, p. 86; Atkinson, *Irish Tourist*, p. 376; Carlow grand-jury presentment book, spring assizes 1809

(Carlow County Library, GJ/2/1); Brewer, *Beauties of Ireland*, vol. 2, p. 8; *Finn's Leinster Journal*, 11 April 1827.

Secondary sources:

Douglas, 'Carlow's Old Inns: Churches, gaol, and castle', pp. 173–4; Kelly, 'The Old Gaol, now Hanover Works', pp. 38–9; Garner, *Carlow: Architectural heritage*, p. 45; Thomas, 'Carlow Gaol', pp. 8–9; Doran, 'Carlow Criminal Court', pp. 23–4; Teehan, 'The Emergence of County Courthouses', pp. 47–8.

CARLOW

Carlow, no. 3

Barrack St. & Kennedy Ave.
Lat. 52°50'4.74" N.; Long. 6°55'38.85" W.

An earlier gaol built *c.* 1750 or *c.* 1783; condemned by Howard 1788; new gaol built 1797–1800; condemned by Palmer and Woodward 1825; condemned by assize judge 1827; radial-plan additions (*Williams & Cockburn*, contractors) 1828–31; new gatehouse and several separate-system cells (*John Semple*) 1841–3; additions to female ward 1853–4; closed *c.* 1860; in use as a factory 1901; mostly demolished *c.* 1910; incorporated into a shopping centre 1994; partially extant.

An earlier gaol built *c.* 1750, or *c.* 1783. Condemned by Howard while visiting, 1788. Grand jury appoint a committee to receive plans for altering the gaol, 1789. New gaol built, a T-shaped structure, on a new site, 1797–1800. Gaol condemned by Forster Archer as too small and in the wrong location, 1803. Forster Archer notes alterations and improvements 'nearly perfected', 1813. Gaol condemned by prison inspectors, 1825. Assize judge urges grand jury to improve county gaol and courthouse, 1827. Grand-jury presentment of £7,000 for additions to gaol, 1827. New courthouse built elsewhere (see Part I), 1827–33. Contract for additions to the gaol (*Williams & Cockburn*, contractors), 1828. Large radial-plan additions made to gaol (architect unknown), 1828–31. Grand-jury presentment of £6,000 for a new gate house, and a small number of separate-system cells (*John Semple*), 1840. Gate house and cells built (*John Semple*), 1841–3. Additions and alterations to female ward of prison, 1853–4. Closed, *c.* 1860. Sold to Mr Molloy, for £1,200, 1897. Used by Mr T. Thompson as a factory, known as Hanover Works, 1901. Mostly demolished, *c.* 1910. Incorporated into a shopping centre, 1994. Gate house and governor's house survive. Listed. Extant.

Archival and primary sources:

Finn's Leinster Journal, 18–22 April 1789; ibid., 11 April, 27 July, 28 July 1827; ibid., 28 March, 19 July 1828; Howard, *Lazarettos*, p. 86; *Journal of the Irish House of Commons*, vol. xvii, 1797, p. ccvi; ibid., vol. xviii, 1799, p. cclxxxix; Hall, *Tour through Ireland*, vol. 1, p. 73; *Accounts of the Presentments Passed by the Grand Juries of Ireland ... in ... 1807*, H.C. 1808 (205), xiii, p. 29; Forster Archer, 'Report of the State of Gaols of Ireland for the Year 1802', f. 2 (Houses of the Oireachtas Library, Dublin, MS.7H28); Forster Archer, 'Report of the State of Gaols of Ireland for the Year 1811' (Houses of the Oireachtas Library, Dublin, MS.4E63); *Freeman's Journal*, 4 August 1824; ibid., 29 March 1825; ibid., 25 March 1826; ibid., 15 March 1828; ibid., 17 March 1834; letters relating to Carlow gaol, 1828–30 (Carlow County Library, P2/0053); William Murray to R. Robinson, 25 April 1828 (NAI, CSORP 1828/556); *Dublin Builder*, vol. 4, no. 52, 15 February 1862, p. 43; Joseph Jameson, *The following rules and regulations shall be strictly observed and carried into force and effect in every gaol, house of correction, marshalsea, bridewell, penitentiary house, sheriff's prison, and other prisons throughout Ireland, as directed by statute, 50 Geo. III, c. 103* (Dublin, 1822, copy in NLI with hand-written comments on Carlow gaol); A map of Carlow, *c.* 1832 (source unknown, available online).

Prison reports:

Inspector General's Report of ... the Prisons in Ireland for ... 1807, H.C. 1808 (239), ix, p. 4;
Account of All Gaols ... in the ... United Kingdom, H.C. 1819 (137), xvii, pp. 2–3;

Inspector General's Report of … the Prisons in Ireland for … 1818, H.C. 1819 (534), xii, p. 4;
Prisons of Ireland: Report of Inspectors General, 1823, H.C. 1823 (342), x, p. 40;
Prisons of Ireland: Report of Inspectors General, 1824, H.C. 1824 (294), xxii, pp. 7, 40;
Prisons of Ireland: Report of Inspectors General, 1825, H.C. 1825 (493), xxii, p. 27;
Fourth Report … on … the Prisons of Ireland, 1826, H.C. 1826 (173), xxiii, p. 40;
Fifth Report … on … the Prisons of Ireland, 1827, H.C. 1826–7 (471), xi, pp. 42–3;
Sixth Report … on … the Prisons of Ireland, 1828, H.C. 1828 (68), xii, pp. 51;
Seventh Report … on … the Prisons of Ireland, 1829, H.C. 1829 (10), xiii, pp. 9, 46;
Eighth Report … on … the Prisons of Ireland, 1830, H.C. 1830 (48), xxiv, p. 46;
Ninth Report … on … the Prisons of Ireland, 1831, H.C. 1830–1 (172), iv, p. 34;
Tenth Report … on … the Prisons of Ireland, 1832, H.C. 1831–2 (152), xvii, pp. 5, 34–5;
Nineteenth Report … on … the Prisons of Ireland, 1841, H.C. 1841 (299), xi, p. 44;
Twentieth Report … on … the Prisons of Ireland, 1842, H.C. 1842 (377), xxii, pp. 6, 94–5;
Twenty-first Report … on … the Prisons of Ireland, 1843, H.C. 1843 (462), xxvii, pp. 56–7;
Twenty-second Report … on … the Prisons of Ireland, 1844, H.C. 1844 (535), xxviii, p. 69;
Twenty-third Report … on … the Prisons of Ireland, 1844, H.C. 1845 (620), xxv, p. 42;
Thirtieth Report … on … the Prisons of Ireland, 1852, H.C. 1852 (1531), xxv, p. 147;
Thirty-first Report … on … the Prisons of Ireland, 1853, H.C. 1853 (1657), liii, p. 15;
Thirty-second Report … on … the Prisons of Ireland, 1854, H.C. 1854 (1803), xxxii, pp. 18, 129–30;
Thirty-third Report … on … the Prisons of Ireland, 1855, H.C. 1854–5 (1956), xxvi, pp. 16, 111–14;
Forty-eighth Report … on … the Prisons of Ireland, 1869, H.C. 1870 (C. 173), xxxvii, p. 263.

Secondary sources:

Douglas, 'Carlow's Old Inns: Churches, gaol, and castle', pp. 172–4; Maurice Craig and the Knight of Glin, *Ireland Observed: A handbook to the buildings and antiquities* (Cork: Mercier, 1970), p. 23; Kelly, 'The Old Gaol, now Hanover Works', pp. 38–9; McParland, 'Public Work of Architects', p. 252; Garner, *Carlow: Architectural heritage*, p. 45; Thomas, 'Carlow Gaol', pp. 8–9; O'Dwyer, 'Public Works Architecture', pp. 176, 180, 407; Doran, 'Carlow Criminal Court', pp. 23–4; Teehan, 'The Emergence of County Courthouses', pp. 47–8; Rolf Loeber, et al., *Art and Architecture of Ireland: Volume IV: Architecture 1600–2000*, p. 203.

CAVAN

Cavan, no. 1

Unknown, likely Main St.

Combined courthouse and gaol, described as built by 1744, replacement gaol, described as 'lately built' 1787, replacement courthouse built 1824–5; not extant.

A combined courthouse and gaol, described as 'a large stone building', location unknown, built by 1744. A replacement gaol, described as 'lately built', 1787. Further mention of old gaol, 1801. Strongly criticised by Forster Archer, who suggested a new plan and noted a recent grand-jury presentment, 1803. Replacement gaol built elsewhere (see 'Cavan: Cavan, no. 2'), 1811–12. Replacement courthouse built 1824–5 (see Part I); not extant.

Archival and primary sources:

Butler, 'Journey to Lough Derg', p. 132; Howard, *Lazarettos*, p. 95; Coote, *Statistical Survey of the County of Cavan*, p. 93; Price, *Eighteenth-century Antiquary*, p. 119; Forster Archer, 'Report of the State of Gaols of Ireland for the Year 1802', f. 2 (Houses of the Oireachtas Library, Dublin, MS.7H28); Cavan grand-jury presentment books, 1809–17 (Cavan County Library, GJ/9) (currently inaccessible awaiting conservation).

Secondary sources:

Brett, *Court Houses*, pp. 56, 106.

CAVAN

Cavan, no. 2

Farnham St.
Lat. 53°59'27.90" N.; Long. 7°21'49.76" W.

Old gaol described as ruinous 1798; new gaol built on newly laid-out street (*Richard Elsam*) 1811–12; condemned as too small 1818; large radial-plan additions (*William Farrell*) 1826–8; new female prison built 1845–6; extended (*William Hague*) *c.* 1860s; closed 1886; mostly demolished 1938–42; school built on site; not extant.

An old gaol, built *c.* 1780. Described as ruinous, 1798, and not large enough, 1801. Condemned by assize judge, 1807. Grand-jury presentment of £1,000 towards a new prison, 1807. Design for Cavan gaol (*Richard Elsam*) exhibited at Society of Artists of Ireland, 1809. Designs (*Richard Elsam*) published, 1810. New street, Farnham Street, laid out, *c.* 1810. New prison built on Farnham Street (*Richard Elsam*), at a cost of £12,000, 1811–12. Condemned as too small, 1818. New courthouse built (see Part I) nearby, 1822–5. Grand-jury presentment to enlarge the gaol, at a cost of £5,200, 1824. Large radial-plan additions, including forty cells, at a cost of £6,000 (*William Farrell*), 1826–8. Prison inspectors call for a separate female prison, 1841. A new female prison, on separate-system principles, built, 1845–6. Extended (*William Hague*), *c.* 1860s. Closed, 1886. Handed over to Cavan County Council, 1911. Handed over to the Catholic Church, *c.* 1921. Mostly demolished, 1938–42. School built on site. Not extant.

Archival and primary sources:

Butler, 'Journey to Lough Derg', p. 132; Howard, *Lazarettos*, p. 95; *Journal of the Irish House of Commons*, vol. xvii, 1798, p. dcxxxii; Coote, *Statistical Survey of the County of Cavan*, p. 90; Forster Archer, 'Report of the State of Gaols of Ireland for the Year 1802', f. 2 (Houses of the Oireachtas Library, Dublin, MS.7H28); *Accounts of the Presentments Passed by the Grand Juries of Ireland … in … 1807*, H.C. 1808 (205), xiii, pp. 39–40; Richard Elsam, *Description of Cavan Gaol: With Neild's observations on the law of civil imprisonment: with his report of Gloucester county gaol: together with cursory hints for the internal regulation of prisons … to which is annexed an abstract of the statutes of Geo. III for the information of grand juries, in building and repairing of prisons in Ireland* (Dublin: Carrick, 1810); Price, *Eighteenth-century Antiquary*, p. 119; Forster Archer, 'Report of the State of Gaols of Ireland for the Year 1811' (Houses of the Oireachtas Library, Dublin, MS.4E63); Elevation drawing, n.d. (Irish Architectural Archive, ICEI collection, Henry, Mullins & McMahon album, Acc. 2005/095, IEI 5190); An account of the several presentments made … on which advances have been made by government for gaols, n.d. (NAI, SPO OP 1832-38, 1A/77/4); Nicholson, *A Theoretical and Practical Treatise on the Five Orders of Architecture*, p. 156, pls. 64–5; Colonel Barry to Charles Grant, 17 December 1818 (NAI, CSORP 1818/190); Cavan grand-jury presentment books, 1856–9 (Cavan County Library, GJ/9) (currently inaccessible awaiting conservation); Letter concerning Cavan gaol, n.d. (NAI, CSORP 1824/4831); Lewis, *Topographical Dictionary*, vol. 1, p. 319; *Dublin Builder*, vol. 4, no. 52, 15 February 1862, p. 43; Department of Justice papers, 1939 (NAI, JUS/3/16, 90/16/308).

Prison reports:

Inspector General's Report of … the Prisons in Ireland for … 1807, H.C. 1808 (239), ix, p. 4;

Account of All Gaols … in the … United Kingdom, H.C. 1819 (137), xvii, pp. 4–5;
Inspector General's Report of … the Prisons in Ireland for … 1818, H.C. 1819 (534), xii, pp. 4–5;
Prisons of Ireland: Report of Inspectors General, 1823, H.C. 1823 (342), x, pp. 6, 28;
Prisons of Ireland: Report of Inspectors General, 1824, H.C. 1824 (294), xxii, pp. 39–40;
Fourth Report … on … the Prisons of Ireland, 1826, H.C. 1826 (173), xxiii, p. 25;
Fifth Report … on … the Prisons of Ireland, 1827, H.C. 1826–7 (471), xi, pp. 27–8;
Sixth Report … on … the Prisons of Ireland, 1828, H.C. 1828 (68), xii, p. 39;
Seventh Report … on … the Prisons of Ireland, 1829, H.C. 1829 (10), xiii, pp. 9, 34–5;
Eighth Report … on … the Prisons of Ireland, 1830, H.C. 1830 (48), xxiv, pp. 33–4;
Fourteenth Report … on … the Prisons of Ireland, 1836, H.C. 1836 (118), xxxv, p. 22;
Nineteenth Report … on … the Prisons of Ireland, 1841, H.C. 1841 (299), xi, pp. 28–9;
Twentieth Report … on … the Prisons of Ireland, 1842, H.C. 1842 (377), xxii, pp. 6, 60;
Twenty-first report … on … the Prisons of Ireland, 1843, H.C. 1843 (462), xxvii, pp. 31–2;
Twenty-second report … on … the Prisons of Ireland, 1844, H.C. 1844 (535), xxviii, p. 34;
Twenty-third report … on … the Prisons of Ireland, 1844, H.C. 1845 (620), xxv, p. 15;
Twenty-fourth Report … on … the Prisons of Ireland, 1846, H.C. 1846 (697), xx, p. 23;
Twenty-fifth Report … on … the Prisons of Ireland, 1847, H.C. 1847 (805), xxix, p. 40;
Forty-ninth Report … on … the Prisons of Ireland, 1870, H.C. 1871 (C. 359), xxx, pp. 108–9.

Secondary sources:

McEntee, *Memories of the Lifetime in Journalism in Cavan*, pp. 56–7; O'Dwyer, 'Public Works Architecture', pp. 175–6, 407; Noleen O'Connell-Toal, 'County Cavan Gaol: A nineteenth-century prison', *Breifne Journal: Journal of Cumann Seanchas Bhreifne*, vol. 9, no. 35, 1998, pp. 922–36; Johnston, *Forms of Constraint*, p. 173; Colvin, *Biographical Dictionary of British Architects*, pp. 355–6; Mulligan, *Buildings of Ireland: South Ulster*, p. 245; Rolf Loeber, et al., *Art and Architecture of Ireland: Volume IV: Architecture 1600–2000*, p. 203.

CLARE

Ennis, no. 1

Arthur's Row, off Gaol (O'Connell) St.
Lat. 52°50'34.71" N.; Long. 8°58'58.63" W.

An ancient gaol in the Franciscan friary, in use, 1585; another early gaol built *c.* 1591; replaced by a new gaol nearby built 1779–81.

An ancient gaol in the Franciscan friary, in use, 1585. Another early gaol, built on Arthur's Row, near old county courthouse, *c.* 1591. Replaced by a new gaol nearby, 1779–81 (see 'Clare: Ennis, no. 2')

Archival and primary sources:

None.

Secondary sources:

Tim Kelly, 'Ennis County Jail', *North Munster Antiquarian Journal*, vol. 16, 1973–4, pp. 66–9, at p. 66; Ó Dálaigh, *Irish Historic Towns Atlas, No. 25: Ennis*, pp. 15–16.

CLARE

Ennis, no. 2

Gaol (O'Connell) St.
Lat. 52°50'32.43" N.; Long. 8°58'59.23" W.

An early gaol built *c.* 1591; replaced by a new gaol on Gaol St. built 1779–81; superseded by another new gaol 1814–18; used as a police barracks *c.* 1837; used as a temporary auxiliary prison during the Famine; mostly demolished; Town Hall built on site; currently in use as a hotel; partially extant.

An early gaol, built on Arthur's Row, near old county courthouse, *c.* 1591 (see 'Clare: Ennis, no. 1'). Replaced by a new gaol nearby, on Gaol St., 1779–81. Grand jury decision to build a new gaol, 1811. Superseded by another new gaol elsewhere, 1814–18 (see 'Clare: Ennis, no. 3'). Used as a police barracks, *c.* 1837. Used as a temporary auxiliary prison during the Famine, 1849. Mostly demolished. Town Hall built on the site. Currently in use as a hotel. Partially extant.

Archival and primary sources:

Clare Journal, 13 August 1778; Howard, *Lazarettos*, p. 93; *Journal of the Irish House of Commons*, vol. xvii, 1797, p. ccvi; Forster Archer, 'Report of the State of Gaols of Ireland for the Year 1811' (Houses of the Oireachtas Library, Dublin, MS.4E63); Clare grand-jury presentment books, 1786–91 (Clare County Archives, GJ/AP/42); Clare grand-jury presentment books, 1799–1839 (Cambridge University Library); Clare grand-jury presentment books, spring assizes 1813 and spring assizes 1815 (Clare County Archives, GJ/AP/43 and GJ/AP/44).

Prison reports:

Twenty-eighth Report ... on ... the Prisons of Ireland, 1850, H.C. 1850 (1229), xxix, p. 72.

Secondary sources:

Kelly, 'Ennis County Jail', pp. 66–9; Ó Dálaigh, *Irish Historic Towns Atlas, No. 25: Ennis*, pp. 15–16.

CLARE

Ennis, no. 3

Gaol (Station) Rd.
Lat. 52°50'25.58" N.; Long. 8°58'49.94" W.

Earlier gaols elsewhere in town centre; plans for a new gaol 1814; new polygonal-plan gaol built (*Richard Morrison* or *John Behan*) 1814–18; front building added 1824–7; new female prison and marshalsea (*William Deane Butler*) 1832–4; large additions, partially on separate-system principles (*John B. Keane*) 1839–42; closed 1880; in use again during the Land War 1882; re-opened as the Ennis Inebriate Reformatory 1889; factories later built on site; partially demolished 1960; further demolished *c.* 2000; not extant.

Earlier gaols on Arthur's Row and on Gaol St. (see 'Clare: Ennis, no. 1' and 'Clare: Ennis, no. 2'). Grand jury decision to build a new gaol, 1811. Plans approved for a new gaol, and a presentment of £14,000 passed, 1814. New polygonal-plan gaol built (*Richard Morrison* or *John Behan*), at a cost of around £16,000, 1814–18. Condemned by Forster Archer as built on a poor site, 1818. Palmer and Woodward suggest that gaol is too small for the county, and propose a new district bridewell in Kilrush, 1824. Front building added, with kitchens, offices, etc., 1824–7. Series of unexecuted proposals (*William Deane Butler*) for a new marshalsea and/or female prison and/or infirmary, 1825–32. New female prison and marshalsea built (*William Deane Butler*), 1832–4. Unexecuted proposal to add another story to main buildings, 1838. Large additions, partially on separate-system principles (*John B. Keane*), 1839–42. New courthouse built for the county, 1846–51. Gaol closed, 1880. In use as a prison during the Land War, 1882. Re-opened as the Ennis Inebriate Reformatory, 1889. Used as a military barracks, 1921. Sold, 1929. Factories established on site, *c.* 1932–7 and *c.* 1951–2. Entrance gateway demolished, 1960. Further demolition, *c.* 2000. Not extant.

Archival and primary sources:

Clare grand-jury presentment books, 1799–1839 (Cambridge University Library); 'Forster Archer's tour of Ireland in 1801' (British Library, Add. MS 35920); Forster Archer, 'Report of the state of gaols of Ireland for the year 1811' (Houses of the Oireachtas Library, Dublin, MS.4E63); Letter from Francis Johnston, 24 May 1814 (NAI, SPO 558/123/30); An account of the several presentments made … on which advances have been made by government for gaols, n.d. (NAI, SPO OP 1832–8, 1A/77/4); Richard Morrison to William Vesey Fitzgerald, 6 February 1814 (NLI, Vesey Fitzgerald papers, MS 7823, pp. 267–8); Plan drawings for Ennis gaol, n.d., n.s. [*c.* 1814] (NLI, AD 2666–7); Clare grand-jury presentment books, spring assizes 1813 and spring assizes 1815 (Clare County Archives, GJ/AP/43 and GJ/AP/44), Reid, *Travels in Ireland*, p. 302, *Fourth Report of the AIPPD*, p. 29; *Tralee Mercury*, 10 March 1832; Ordnance Survey ten-feet maps for Ennis, sheet 21 (surveyed 1879) (Clare County Archives); *Clare Journal*, 22 January 1880; ibid., 23 January 1882; Plan drawing of Ennis gaol, 27–31 August 1880 (NAI, OPW 5HC/4/416); *Saturday Record* (Ennis), 28 September 1929; *The Irish Times*, 17 March 1937; Ennis Urban District Council papers for the lease and sale of portions of Ennis gaol, *c.* 1932–7 and *c.* 1951–2 (NAI, Department of the Environment and Local Government papers, ENV/3, 2013/94/41, 469); *Clare Champion*, 28 May 1960 (illus.).

Prison reports:

Inspector General's Report of … the Prisons in Ireland for … 1807, H.C. 1808 (239), ix, pp. 4–5;

Account of All Gaols … in the … United Kingdom, H.C. 1819 (137), xvii, pp. 4–5;

Inspector General's Report of … the Prisons in Ireland for … 1818, H.C. 1819 (534), xii, p. 5;

Report from the Select Committee on the State Of Gaols, H.C. 1819 (579), vii, p. 196;

Prisons of Ireland: Report of Inspectors General, 1823, H.C. 1823 (342), x, pp. 6, 41;

Prisons of Ireland: Report of Inspectors General, 1824, H.C. 1824 (294), xxii, pp. 7, 41;

Prisons of Ireland: Report of Inspectors General, 1825, H.C. 1825 (493), xxii, pp. 40–1;

Fourth Report … on … the Prisons of Ireland, 1826, H.C. 1826 (173), xxiii, p. 39;

Fifth Report … on … the Prisons of Ireland, 1827, H.C. 1826–7 (471), xi, p. 47;

Seventh Report … on … the Prisons of Ireland, 1829, H.C. 1829 (10), xiii, pp. 46–7;

Eighth Report … on … the Prisons of Ireland, 1830, H.C. 1830 (48), xxiv, pp. 46–7;

Ninth Report … on … the Prisons of Ireland, 1831, H.C. 1830–1 (172), iv, p. 34;

Tenth Report … on … the Prisons of Ireland, 1832, H.C. 1831–2 (152), xvii, p. 35;

Eleventh Report … on … the Prisons of Ireland, 1833, H.C. 1833 (67), xvii, p. 20;

Twelfth Report … on … the Prisons of Ireland, 1834, H.C. 1834 (63), xl, p. 23;

Fourteenth Report … on … the Prisons of Ireland, 1836, H.C. 1836 (118), xxxv, p. 32;

Fifteenth Report … on … the Prisons of Ireland, 1837, H.C. 1837 (123), xxxi, p. 32;

Sixteenth Report … on … the Prisons of Ireland, 1838, H.C. 1837–8 (186), xxix, pp. 7, 37–8;

Seventeenth Report … on … the Prisons of Ireland, 1839, H.C. 1839 (91), xx, pp. 39–40;

Eighteenth Report … on … the Prisons of Ireland, 1840, H.C. 1840 (240), xxvi, pp. 7, 43;

Nineteenth Report … on … the Prisons of Ireland, 1841, H.C. 1841 (299), xi, pp. 44–5;

Twentieth Report … on … the Prisons of Ireland, 1842, H.C. 1842 (377), xxii, pp. 6, 95;

Twenty-second Report … on … the Prisons of Ireland, 1844, H.C. 1844 (535), xxviii, pp. 7, 70–1;

Twenty-third Report ... on ... the Prisons of Ireland, 1844, H.C. 1845 (620), xxv, pp. 6, 44–6;
Twenty-eighth Report ... on ... the Prisons of Ireland, 1850, H.C. 1850 (1229), xxix, p. 72;
Forty-eighth Report ... on ... the Prisons of Ireland, 1869, H.C. 1870 (C. 173), xxxvii, p. 272.

Secondary sources:

Kelly, 'Ennis County Jail', pp. 66–9; O'Dwyer, 'Public Works Architecture', p. 407; Ó Murchadha, *Sable Wings over the Land*, p. 21; Ó Dálaigh, *Irish Historic Towns Atlas, No. 25: Ennis*, pp. 15–16.

CORK COUNTY

Cork, no. 1

South Main St. & South Gate Bridge
Lat. 51°53'44.69" N.; Long. 8°28'34.52" W.

Earliest recorded mention of a gaol in Cork 1326; South Gate Bridge rebuilt in stone 1713; gaol built at South Gate 1728–30; new gaol built elsewhere 1791–5; old gaol demolished; not extant.

Earliest recorded mention of a gaol in Cork, 1326. South Gate Bridge rebuilt in stone, 1713. South Gate gaol built, 1728–30. Minor alterations to this gaol, 1775. Escape of prisoner from gaol by cutting through floors, 1778. Howard visits and notes alcohol in gaol, and that its windows face the street, 1787. New gaol built elsewhere (see 'Cork County: Cork, no. 2'), 1791–5. Old gaol depicted in Nathaniel Grogan drawing, 1796. Later demolished. Not extant.

Archival and primary sources:

Tuckey, *Cork Remembrancer*, pp. 20, 125, 128, 171, 177; Howard, *Lazarettos*, p. 89; Nathaniel Grogan, 'The South Gate and Bridge, Cork', *c.* 1796 (Crawford Art Gallery, Cork); Forster Archer, 'Report of the State of Gaols of Ireland for the Year 1802', f. 3 (Houses of the Oireachtas Library, Dublin, MS.7H28); Watercolours of Cork North Gate Bridge and Cork South Gate Bridge, by John Fitzgerald, based on Nathaniel Grogan's originals, mid-1800s (Crawford Art Gallery, Cork).

Secondary sources:

Pettit, *This City of Cork*, unnumbered plate; Gibney, Hurley and McParland, *Building Site in Eighteenth-century Ireland*, p. 166.

CORK COUNTY

Cork, no. 2

Western Rd. & Gaol Walk
Lat. 51°53'35.09" N.; Long. 8°29'38.70" W.

Early gaol built 1728–30; superseded by a new gaol built (*Michael Shanahan*) 1791–5; lengthy building process with accusations of corruption and jobbery 1795–1809; sundry works to complete gaol (*William Deane* and *Abraham Hargrave*) 1809; large house of correction built (*James and George Richard Pain*) 1819–22; adjoining bridge built (*George Richard Pain*) 1822–4; additions to female prison and marshalsea (*George Richard Pain*) 1827–9; new governor's residence and chapel 1851; separate-system alterations (*Williams Atkins*) 1865–7; mostly demolished *c.* 1950; parts now survive in UCC campus; conservation work 2017; partially extant.

Early gaol built (see 'Cork County: Cork, no. 1'), 1728–30. Minor alterations to this gaol, 1775. Escape of prisoner from gaol by cutting through floors, 1778. Howard visits and notes alcohol in gaol, and that its windows face the street, 1787.

Act of parliament to appoint commissioners to build a new gaol, 1788. New gaol built, an L-shaped building (*Michael Shanahan*), 1791–5. Described as still in progress, 1797. Convicts attempt an escape from the new gaol, 1801. Described as unfinished, 1805. Condemned by Forster Archer as a fraudulent building project in very strong language, 1807. Further work to complete gaol (*Michael Shanahan*), 1807–9. Sundry works at gaol (*William Deane* and *Abraham Hargrave*), 1809. Plans for a house of correction approved by Francis Johnston, 1818. Addition of a three-wing house of correction (*James and George Richard Pain*), 1819–22. Adjoining bridge built (*George Richard Pain*), 1822–4. Additions to female prison and marshalsea (*George Richard Pain*), 1827–9. Proposal to merge county and city gaols, 1847. Prison inspectors suggest building a new large gaol in the west of the county, 1850. Unexecuted proposal for two new district bridewells (Mallow and Skibbereen), to relieve pressure on the county gaol, 1851. Addition of a governor's residence, 1851. Extensive alterations to introduce separate-system confinement, and a new chapel (*William Atkins*), 1865–7. Mostly demolished, *c.* 1950. Bridge, parts of boundary wall and Doric portico survive as part of UCC campus. Conservation work to portico (*Frank Murphy & Partners Architects*), 2017. Partially extant.

Archival and primary sources:

28 Geo. III, c. 39; Tuckey, *Cork Remembrancer*, pp. 20, 125, 128, 171, 177, 205, 217, 234; Carr, *Stranger in Ireland*, p. 260; Howard, *Lazarettos*, p. 89; *Journal of the Irish House of Commons*, vol. xvii, 1797, p. ccvi; William Beaufort map of Cork city, 1801 (NLI); Forster Archer, 'Report of the State of Gaols of Ireland for the Year 1802', f. 3 (Houses of the Oireachtas Library, Dublin, MS.7H28); *Accounts of the Presentments Passed by the Grand Juries of Ireland … in … 1807*, H.C. 1808 (205), xiii, p. 86; Reid, *Travels in Ireland*, p. 269; *First Report of the AIPPD*, pp. 17–18; Forster Archer to William Gregory, 19 July 1819 (NAI, CSORP 1819/35); Francis Johnston to Robert Robinson, 5 July 1819 (NAI, CSORP 1819/108); Bundle of letters pertaining to the addition of a house of correction to Cork county gaol, 1819 (NAI, CSORP 1819/187); Francis Johnston to Robert Robinson, 30 March 1819 (NAI, CSORP 1819/465); Francis Johnston to Robert Robinson, 17 May 1819 (NAI, CSORP 1819/467); Richard Griffith to Henry Goulburn, 30 August 1822 (NAI, CSORP, 1822/298); Richard B. Cotter to Henry Goulburn, 23 August 1822 (NAI, CSORP 1822/628); Statement of James Chatterton, n.d. (NAI, CSORP 1824/8009); Davys Tuckey to William Gregory, 19 February 1819 (NAI, CSORP 1819/868); Expenditure on addition to Cork county gaol, March 1827 (NAI, SPO 588/AAB/944); Wright, *Ireland Illustrated*, pp. 66–7; Windele, *Historical and Descriptive Notices of the City of Cork*, pp. 25–6; von Puckler-Muskau, *Tour in England, Ireland and France*, vol. 2, p. 16; *Seventh Report of the AIPPD*, p. 12; Heaney, *Scottish Whig in Ireland*, pp. 144–6; bills, estimates, etc., by William Deane, 1797–1809 (Irish Architectural Archive, Acc. 2009/91); Thackeray, *Irish Sketch-book*, pp. 77, 83, 90; Walter Berwick, memo (re proposed district bridewells), 18 January 1851 (NLI, Lismore papers, MS 43,456/13); *The Builder*, vol. 24, no. 1247, 29 December 1866, p. 964; *Irish Builder*, vol. 9, no. 170, 1 January 1867, p. 14; ibid., vol. 9, no. 171, 15 January 1867, p. 25.

Prison reports:

Inspector General's Report of … the Prisons in Ireland for … 1807, H.C. 1808 (239), ix, p. 5;

Account of All Gaols … in the … United Kingdom, H.C. 1819 (137), xvii, pp. 4–5;

Report from the Select Committee on the State of Gaols, H.C. 1819 (579), vii, p. 204;

Prisons of Ireland: Report of Inspectors General, 1823, H.C. 1823 (342), x, pp. 7, 43;

Prisons of Ireland. Report of Inspectors General, 1824, H.C. 1824 (294), xxii, pp. 7, 43;

Fourth Report … on … the Prisons of Ireland, 1826, H.C. 1826 (173), xxiii, p. 41;

Fifth Report … on … the Prisons of Ireland, 1827, H.C. 1826–7 (471), xi, pp. 43–4;

Sixth Report … on … the Prisons of Ireland, 1828, H.C. 1828 (68), xii, pp. 52–3;

Seventh Report … on … the Prisons of Ireland, 1829, H.C. 1829 (10), xiii, p. 48;

Eighth Report … on … the Prisons of Ireland, 1830, H.C. 1830 (48), xxiv, p. 48;

Seventeenth Report … on … the Prisons of Ireland, 1839, H.C. 1839 (91), xx, pp. 40–1;

Eighteenth Report … on … the Prisons of Ireland, 1840, H.C. 1840 (240), xxvi, p. 44;

Nineteenth Report … on … the Prisons of Ireland, 1841, H.C. 1841 (299), xi, p. 45;

Twentieth Report ... on ... the Prisons of Ireland, 1842, H.C. 1842 (377), xxii, pp. 96–7;
Twenty-fifth Report ... on ... the Prisons of Ireland, 1847, H.C. 1847 (805), xxix, p. 77;
Twenty-eighth Report ... on ... the Prisons of Ireland, 1850, H.C. 1850 (1229), xxix, pp. 11, 75;
Twenty-ninth Report ... on ... the Prisons of Ireland, 1851, H.C. 1851 (1364), xxviii, pp. 18, 58–63;
Thirty-first Report ... on ... the Prisons of Ireland, 1853, H.C. 1853 (1657), liii, p. 157;
Thirty-fourth Report ... on ... the Prisons of Ireland, 1856, H.C. 1856 (2113), xxxiv, pp. 20–1;
Forty-eighth Report ... on ... the Prisons of Ireland, 1869, H.C. 1870 (C. 173), xxxvii, p. 284.

Secondary sources:

The Builder, vol. 100, no. 3568, 23 June 1911, pp. 771–3 (illus.); A.E. Richardson, *Monumental Classic Architecture in Great Britain and Ireland during the Eighteenth & Nineteenth Centuries* (London: Batsford, 1914), p. 47 (illus.); Photograph of Cork county gaol, *c.* 1950 (Cork City and County Archives); Craig, *Architecture of Ireland*, p. 261; O'Dwyer, 'Public Works Architecture', pp. 192, 407; Lee, *James Pain, Architect*, pp. 77–9 (illus.); McParland, 'Public Work of Architects', p. 252; Mark Bence-Jones, 'Two Pairs of Architect Brothers', *Country Life*, vol. 142, no. 3675, 10 August 1967, pp. 306–9; Jeremy Williams, 'William Atkins 1812–1887, a Forgotten Cork Pre-Raphaelite', in Agnes Bernelle (ed.), *Decantations: A tribute to Maurice Craig* (Dublin: Lilliput Press, 1992), pp. 240–9, at p. 249; Johnston, *Forms of Constraint*, p. 173; Rolf Loeber, et al., *Art and Architecture of Ireland: Volume IV: Architecture 1600–2000*, p. 451; Gibney, Hurley and McParland, *Building Site in Eighteenth-century Ireland*, pp. 30, 139.

CORK CONVICT DEPOT

Cork, no. 1

Fort St. & Keyser's Hill (Elizabeth Fort)
Lat. 51°53'40.45" N.; Long. 8°28'40.43" W.

Built *c.* 1601; converted into a convict depot (*Board of Works*) 1817–18; used for females only 1827; a replacement depot built at Fort Westmorland, Spike Island, 1846–50s; Elizabeth Fort abandoned *c.* 1850; later used as a Garda station; derelict 2013; under redevelopment as a tourism heritage site 2014; extant.

Elizabeth Fort built, *c.* 1601. Forster Archer suggests a convict depot should be established in Cork, 1811. Elizabeth Fort converted into a convict depot (*Board of Works*), 1817–18. Unexecuted plans for regional penitentiaries around Ireland (*James Elmes* and others), 1821–4. The AIPPD suggest a new convict penitentiary on Spike Island, unexecuted, 1822. Palmer and Woodward consider a new convict penitentiary on Spike Island, unexecuted, 1824. Existing depot used for females only, 1827. Palmer and Woodward call for a new depot in Cork, 1836. Fort Westmorland handed over to the government for the purposes of establishing a convict depot there, 1846. Convict depot buildings erected at Fort Westmorland, Spike Island, 1846–50s (see 'Cork Convict Depot: Cork, no. 2'). Elizabeth Fort abandoned, *c.* 1850. Later used as a Garda station. Derelict, 2013. Under redevelopment as a tourism heritage site, 2014. Extant.

Archival and primary sources:

Forster Archer, 'Report of the State of Gaols of Ireland for the Year 1811' (Houses of the Oireachtas Library, Dublin, MS.4E63); Charles Bushe to William Gregory, 23 March 1818 (NAI, CSORP 1818/78); Francis Johnston to William Gregory, 18 April 1818 (NAI, CSORP 1818/84); James Elmes to Arthur Moore, 7 April 1821 (NAI, CSORP 1823/7065); *Fourth Report of the AIPPD*, pp. 20–1; Henry Goulburn to James Elmes, 17 April 1823 (NAI, CSORP 1823/7065); Lewis, *Topographical Dictionary*, vol. 1, p. 420; Windele, *Historical and Descriptive Notices of the City of Cork*, p. 34; Nicholson, *Lights and Shades of Ireland in Three Parts*, pp. 377–8.

Prison reports:

Report from the Select Committee on the State of Gaols, H.C. 1819 (579), vii, pp. 204–7;
Prisons of Ireland: Report of Inspectors General, 1823, H.C. 1823 (342), x, pp. 10–11;
Prisons of Ireland: Report of Inspectors General, 1824, H.C. 1824 (294), xxii, pp. 9–10;
Fourth Report … on … the Prisons of Ireland, 1826, H.C. 1826 (173), xxiii, p. 42;
Fifth Report … on … the Prisons of Ireland, 1827, H.C. 1826–7 (471), xi, p. 46;
Fourteenth Report … on … the Prisons of Ireland, 1836, H.C. 1836 (118), xxxv, pp. 34–5;
Twenty-sixth Report … on … the Prisons of Ireland, 1847–48, H.C. 1847–8 (952), xxiv, pp. 6, 8, 11–12;
Twenty-seventh Report … on … the Prisons of Ireland, 1849, H.C. 1849 (1069), xxvi, p. 9;
Twenty-eighth Report … on … the Prisons of Ireland, 1850, H.C. 1850 (1229), xxix, pp. 15–16.

Secondary sources:

Heard, 'Public Works in Ireland, 1800–1831', p. 88; O'Dwyer, 'Public Works Architecture', pp. 177, 193; Carey, *Mountjoy*, p. 41; Rolf Loeber, et al., *Art and Architecture of Ireland: Volume IV: Architecture 1600–2000*, p. 205.

CORK CONVICT DEPOT

Cork, no. 2

Fort Westmorland (Fort Mitchell), Spike Island
Lat. 51°50'0.45" N.; Long. 8°17'3.11" W.

Converted into a convict depot, 1846–1850s; given up by British forces 1938; in use as a prison and military base, later a youth correctional facility; closed 2004; transferred to Cork County Council for use as a heritage centre 2009; subject of a major research project and archaeological excavations, 2012–; extant.

Former convict depot at Elizabeth Fort (see 'Cork Convict Depot: Cork, no. 1'). Unexecuted plans for regional penitentiaries around Ireland (*James Elmes* and others), 1821–4. The AIPPD suggest a new convict penitentiary on Spike Island, unexecuted, 1822. Palmer and Woodward consider a new convict penitentiary on Spike Island, unexecuted, 1824. Palmer and Woodward call for a new depot in Cork, 1836. Fort Westmorland handed over to the government for the purposes of establishing a convict depot there, 1846. Convict depot buildings erected at Fort Westmorland, Spike Island, 1846–1850s. Given up by British forces, 1938. In use as a prison and military base. Later used as a youth correctional facility. Closed, 2004. Transferred to Cork County Council for use as a heritage centre, 2009. Subject of a major research project (UCC) and archaeological excavations, 2012–. Extant.

Archival and primary sources:

Charles Bushe to William Gregory, 23 March 1818 (NAI, CSORP 1818/78); Francis Johnston to William Gregory, 18 April 1818 (NAI, CSORP 1818/84); James Elmes to Arthur Moore, 7 April 1821 (NAI, CSORP 1823/7065); *Fourth Report of the AIPPD*, pp. 20–1; Henry Goulburn to James Elmes, 17 April 1823 (NAI, CSORP 1823/7065); Lewis, *Topographical Dictionary*, vol. 1, p. 420; Windele, *Historical and Descriptive Notices of the City of Cork*, p. 34; Nicholson, *Lights and Shades of Ireland in Three Parts*, pp. 377–8.

Prison reports:

Report from the Select Committee on the State of Gaols, H.C. 1819 (579), vii, pp. 204–7;

Prisons of Ireland: Report of Inspectors General, 1823, H.C. 1823 (342), x, pp. 10–11;

Prisons of Ireland: Report of Inspectors General, 1824, H.C. 1824 (294), xxii, pp. 9–10;

Fourth Report … on … the Prisons of Ireland, 1826, H.C. 1826 (173), xxiii, p. 42;

Fifth Report … on … the Prisons of Ireland, 1827, H.C. 1826–7 (471), xi, p. 46;

Fourteenth Report … on … the Prisons of Ireland, 1836, H.C. 1836 (118), xxxv, pp. 34–5;
Twenty-sixth Report … on … the Prisons of Ireland, 1847–48, H.C. 1847–8 (952), xxiv, pp. 6, 8, 11–12;
Twenty-seventh Report … on … the Prisons of Ireland, 1849, H.C. 1849 (1069), xxvi, p. 9;
Twenty-eighth Report … on … the Prisons of Ireland, 1850, H.C. 1850 (1229), xxix, pp. 15–16.

Secondary sources:

Heard, 'Public Works in Ireland, 1800–1831', p. 88; O'Dwyer, 'Public Works Architecture', pp. 177, 193; Carey, *Mountjoy*, p. 41; Rolf Loeber, et al., *Art and Architecture of Ireland: Volume IV: Architecture 1600–2000*, p. 205.

CORK CITY

Cork, no. 1

North Main St. & North Gate Bridge
Lat. 51°54'3.51" N.; Long. 8°28'45.88" W.

Earliest recorded mention of a gaol in Cork 1326; North Gate Bridge rebuilt in stone 1712; gaol built at North Gate 1715; new gaol built elsewhere 1819–24; old gaol demolished; not extant.

Earliest recorded mention of a gaol in Cork, 1326. North Gate Bridge rebuilt in stone, 1712. North Gate gaol built, 1715. Attempted and successful escapes of prisoner from gaol, 1773, 1774. Howard visits and notes alcohol in gaol, and that gaol is extremely defective, 1787. Old gaol depicted in Nathaniel Grogan drawing, 1796. New gaol built elsewhere (see 'Cork City: Cork, no. 2'), 1819–24. Old gaol later demolished. Not extant.

Archival and primary sources:

Tuckey, *Cork Remembrancer*, pp. 20, 125, 165, 168–9; Howard, *Lazarettos*, p. 89; Nathaniel Grogan, 'North Gate Bridge, Cork', 1796 (Crawford Art Gallery); Forster Archer, 'Report of the State of Gaols of Ireland for the Year 1802', f. 3 (Houses of the Oireachtas Library, Dublin, MS.7H28); Cork City Gaol Act, 1806 (46 Geo. III., c. xxxviii); Watercolours of Cork North Gate Bridge and Cork South Gate Bridge, by John Fitzgerald, based on Nathaniel Grogan's originals, mid-1800s (Crawford Art Gallery, Cork).

Secondary sources:

Pettit, *This City of Cork*, unnumbered plate; Gibney, Hurley and McParland, *Building Site in Eighteenth-century Ireland*, p. 166.

CORK CITY

Cork, no. 2

Convent Ave. (City Gaol Rd.)
Lat. 51°53'57.89" N.; Long. 8°29'56.28" W.

Former gaol built 1715; new gaol begun at Reilly's Marsh (*William Robertson*) 1805; abandoned with only boundary walls built 1809–10; plans for a new gaol elsewhere approved 1818; new gaol built (*William Robertson*, with *Thomas Deane*) 1819–24; addition of female cells 1851–2; reconstruction of the west range on separate-system principles *c.* 1870s–80s; in use as a women's prison 1878; used to hold republican prisoners *c.* 1919–23; closed *c.* 1923; in use as a radio station and later a post office 1927–80s; opened as a museum 1993; extant but mostly derelict.

Former gaol built, 1715 (see 'Cork City: Cork, no. 1'). Attempted and successful escapes of prisoner from gaol, 1773, 1774.

Howard visits and notes alcohol in gaol, and that gaol is extremely defective, 1787. City grand-jury presentments for a new gaol, 1804. Competition for designs for a new city gaol on Reilly's Marsh, 1805. Building begun on Reilly's Marsh (*William Robertson*), 1805–6. Act of parliament to build a new city gaol, 1806. Fraudulent building work condemned by Forster Archer, 1807. Erection of foundations and boundary wall at Reilly's Marsh (*William Robertson*), then site abandoned, 1809–10. Plans for a new gaol on a different site approved by Francis Johnston, 1818. New gaol built (*William Robertson*, with *Thomas Deane*), 1819–24. James Palmer, prison inspector, recommends the introduction of the separate system throughout the gaol, 1840. Introduced in one corridor with eighteen cells, 1841. Unexecuted proposal to merge county and city gaols, 1847. Addition of eight female solitary cells, and eight female separate-system cells, 1851–2. Reconstruction of the west range on separate-system principles, *c.* 1870s–80s. In use as a women's prison, 1878. Separate system implemented in full, *c.* 1880. Stairs from gateway to prison, 1900. Used to hold republican prisoners, *c.* 1919–23. Closed, *c.* 1923. In use as offices for a radio station, 1927. Fittings and furniture disposed at auction, 1934. Radio station ceases use of buildings, 1959. In use as a post office, 1950s–80s. First section opened as a museum (*Frank Murphy & Partners Architects*), 1993. In use as a museum. Extant but mostly derelict.

Archival and primary sources:

Tuckey, *Cork Remembrancer*, pp. 20, 125, 165, 168–9, 228; Howard, *Lazarettos*, p. 89; Cork City Gaol Act, 1806 (46 Geo. III, c. xxxviii); *Accounts of the Presentments Passed by the Grand Juries of Ireland … in … 1807*, H.C. 1808 (205), xiii, pp 90, 94; Forster Archer, 'Report of the State of Gaols of Ireland for the Year 1802', f. 3 (Houses of the Oireachtas Library, Dublin, MS.7H28); Forster Archer, 'Report of the State of Gaols of Ireland for the Year 1811' (Houses of the Oireachtas Library, Dublin, MS.4E63); *Report … on Provisions for Better Regulation of Madhouses in England*, H.C. 1814–15 (295), iv, plate 5; Charles Bushe to William Gregory, 23 March 1818 (NAI, CSORP 1818/78); Nicholas Colthurst to Charles Grant, 21 November 1818 (NAI, CSORP 1818/177); Correspondence relating to Cork city gaol, December 1818 (NAI, CSORP 1818/180); Nicholas Colthurst to Charles Grand, 20 December 1818 (NAI, CSORP 1818/182); Benjamin Woodward to Henry Goulburn, 4 December 1822 (NAI, CSORP 1822/3061); Correspondence relating to Cork city gaol, 1823 (NAI, CSORP 1823/5230); Richard Griffith to Henry Goulburn, 2 April 1823 (NAI, CSORP 1823/5745); Reid, *Travels in Ireland*, p. 269; Affidavit of Thomas Deane, 28 July 1825 (NAI, CSORP 1825/11,933); Recollections of Cork, 1833 (TCD, Thomas Crofton Croker papers, MS 1206, p. 11); von Puckler-Muskau, *Tour in England, Ireland and France*, vol. 2, p. 16; Windele, *Historical and Descriptive Notices of the City of Cork*, p. 43; Anon., 'Site for [City] Gaol', *Journal of the Cork Historical and Archaeological Society*, vol. 35, no. 141, January–June 1940, p. 55; *Irish Examiner*, 26 March 1843; ibid., 12 April 1850; ibid., 29 July 1850.

Prison reports:

Inspector General's Report of … the Prisons in Ireland for … 1807, H.C. 1808 (239), ix, p. 5;

Account of All Gaols … in the … United Kingdom, H.C. 1819 (137), xvii, pp. 6–7;

Inspector General's Report of … the Prisons in Ireland for … 1818, H.C. 1819 (534), xii, p. 6;

Report from the Select Committee on the State of Gaols, H.C. 1819 (579), vii, pp. 205–7;

Prisons of Ireland: Report of Inspectors General, 1823, H.C. 1823 (342), x, pp. 7, 47–8;

Prisons of Ireland: Report of Inspectors General, 1824, H.C. 1824 (294), xxii, pp. 7, 47–8;

Prisons of Ireland: Report of Inspectors General, 1825, H.C. 1825 (493), xxii, p. 44;

Fourth Report … on … the Prisons of Ireland, 1826, H.C. 1826 (173), xxiii, p. 41;

Fifth Report … on … the Prisons of Ireland, 1827, H.C. 1826–7 (471), xi, p. 46;

Sixth Report … on … the Prisons of Ireland, 1828, H.C. 1828 (68), xii, p. 55;

Ninth Report … on … the Prisons of Ireland, 1831, H.C. 1830–1 (172), iv, p. 37;

Fifteenth Report … on … the Prisons of Ireland, 1837, H.C. 1837 (123), xxxi, p. 34;

Sixteenth Report … on … the Prisons of Ireland, 1838, H.C. 1837–8 (186), xxix, p. 39;

Seventeenth Report … on … the Prisons of Ireland, 1839, H.C. 1839 (91), xx, p. 41;

Eighteenth Report ... on ... the Prisons of Ireland, 1840, H.C. 1840 (240), xxvi, p. 45;
Nineteenth Report ... on ... the Prisons of Ireland, 1841, H.C. 1841 (299), xi, p. 47;
Twentieth Report ... on ... the Prisons of Ireland, 1842, H.C. 1842 (377), xxii, p. 98;
Twenty-first Report ... on ... the Prisons of Ireland, 1843, H.C. 1843 (462), xxvii, pp. 61–2;
Twenty–second report ... on ... the Prisons of Ireland, 1844, H.C. 1844 (535), xxviii, p. 74;
Twenty-fourth Report ... on ... the Prisons of Ireland, 1846, H.C. 1846 (697), xx, p. 68;
Twenty-fifth Report ... on ... the Prisons of Ireland, 1847, H.C. 1847 (805), xxix, p. 78;
Twenty-ninth Report ... on ... the Prisons of Ireland, 1851, H.C. 1851 (1364), xxviii, pp. 18, 68;
Thirtieth Report ... on ... the Prisons of Ireland, 1852, H.C. 1852 (1531), xxv, pp. 15, 164;
Forty-eighth Report ... on ... the Prisons of Ireland, 1869, H.C. 1870 (C. 173), xxxvii, p. 307.

Secondary sources:

O'Dwyer, 'Public Works Architecture', pp. 152, 407; Lee, *James Pain, Architect*, p. 82; O'Sullivan, *Cork City Gaol*, pp. 15–17; Sean Rothery, *A Field Guide to the Buildings of Ireland, Illustrating the Smaller Buildings of Town and Countryside* (Dublin: Lilliput Press, 1997), p. 160; Johnston, *Forms of Constraint*, p. 173; O'Dwyer, *Architecture of Deane and Woodward*, pp. 15, 550–1; Loeber, et al., *Art and Architecture of Ireland: Volume IV: Architecture 1600–2000*, p. 204; Cork City Gaol Heritage Centre leaflet (available at museum).

DONEGAL

Lifford, no. 1

The Diamond
Lat. 54°49'59.26" N.; Long. 7°28'43.17" W.

Planned 1743; built (*Michael Priestley*), 1746–54; new gaol planned 1787; new gaol built *c.* 1791–3; ceases to be a courthouse 1938; used as a library 1940s–80s; renovated and opened as a heritage centre 1994.

Planned, 1743. Built (*Michael Priestley*), 1746–54. County gaol was situated in the cellar of the courthouse. County gaol visited by Howard, who noted it as 'five dungeons' under the courthouse, 1787. A replacement gaol is planned, 1787. Replacement gaol built nearby (see 'Donegal: Lifford, no. 2'), *c.* 1791–3. In use as a courthouse until 1938. In use as a library, 1940s–80s. Renovated and opened as a heritage centre, 1994.

Archival and primary sources:

Plaque above doorway ('designed & executed by Michael Priestley, A.D. 1746'); Donegal grand-jury presentment books, 1754, 1756–7, 1760, 1793–4 (copies) (Donegal County Library); Donegal grand-jury presentment books, 1754, 1756–7, 1760, 1793–4 (Donegal County Archives); Howard, *Lazarettos*, pp. 96–7; Day and McWilliams, *Ordnance Survey Memoirs of Ireland: Volume 39: Donegal*, p. 12; Lewis, *Topographical Dictionary*, vol. 2, p. 260; Gavan Duffy, *The League of North and South*, p. 95.

Secondary sources:

Brett, *Court Houses*, pp. 60–2, 106; McParland, 'Public Work of Architects', p. 195; Rowan, *Buildings of Ireland: North west Ulster*, pp. 43, 348; Craig, *Architecture of Ireland*, p. 202; Rowan, 'Irishness of Irish Architecture', pp. 9–10; Patton, *The Court Will Rise*, pp. 12–21, 53, 68–70, 78, 82, 83–5; Loeber, et al., *Art and Architecture of Ireland: Volume IV: Architecture 1600–2000*, p. 181; Mac Suibhne, *The End of Outrage*, pp. 56–7, 153–5, 175; Gibney, Hurley and McParland, *Building Site in Eighteenth-century Ireland*, p. 168.

DONEGAL

Lifford, no. 2

The Diamond
Lat. 54°50'0.85" N.; Long. 7°28'42.13" W.

Earlier gaol built 1746–54; new gaol planned 1787; new gaol built (*Edward Miller*) *c.* 1791–3; large polygonal extension to the rear (*John Hargrave*) 1822–7; five separate-system cells and a new chapel 1845–6; new hospital 1852; separate system introduced (*John McCurdy*) 1866–8; abandoned *c.* 1890; demolished 1907; not extant.

Earlier gaol built (see 'Donegal: Lifford, no. 1'), 1746–54. Visited by Howard, who condemned its condition, 1787. Howard notes that a new gaol is planned, 1787. New gaol built (*Edward Miller*), at a cost of £11,032, *c.* 1791–3. Forster Archer, prison inspector, criticises street-facing location, 1803. Forster Archer, prison inspector, states gaol is too small, 1818. Grand-jury presentment for an addition, 1818. Grand jury seek advice from the Association for the Improvement of Prisons and of Prison Discipline, 1818–19. New polygonal gaol to the rear of the older building (*John Hargrave*), 1822–7. Five separate-system cells and a new chapel added, 1845–6. New hospital, 1852. Separate system introduced (*John McCurdy*), 1866–8. Abandoned, *c.* 1890. Demolished, 1907. Housing built on site. Not extant.

Archival and primary sources:

Howard, *Lazarettos*, pp. 96–7; Forster Archer, 'Report of the State of Gaols of Ireland for the Year 1802', f. 4 (Houses of the Oireachtas Library, Dublin, MS.7H28); *First Report of the AIPPD*, pp. 21–2; *Third Report of the AIPPD*, p. 30; Day and McWilliams, *Ordnance Survey Memoirs of Ireland: Volume 39: Donegal*, p. 12; Lewis, *Topographical Dictionary*, vol. 2, p. 260; *Journal of the Irish House of Commons*, vol. xviii, 1799, p. ccxxxiii; Francis Johnston to Robert Robinson, 30 November 1821 (NAI, CSORP 1822/573); Reid, *Travels in Ireland*, pp. 211–12; *Belfast Newsletter*, 12 September 1820; *Dublin Builder*, vol. 8, no. 150, 15 March 1866, p. 78; *Irish Builder*, vol. 10, no. 196, 15 February 1868, p. 40; Gavan Duffy, *The League of North and South*, p. 95; Photographs of Donegal county gaol, before and during demolition, *c.* 1907 (Donegal County Library).

Prison reports:

Inspector General's Report of … the Prisons in Ireland for … 1807, H.C. 1808 (239), ix, p. 6;
Account of All Gaols … in the … United Kingdom, H.C. 1819 (137), xvii, pp. 6–7;
Inspector General's Report of … the Prisons in Ireland for … 1818, H.C. 1819 (534), xii, pp. 6–7;
Report from the Select Committee on the State of Gaols, H.C. 1819 (579), vii, pp. 208–9;
Prisons of Ireland: Report of Inspectors General, 1823, H.C. 1823 (342), x, pp. 5, 30;
Prisons of Ireland: Report of Inspectors General, 1824, H.C. 1824 (294), xxii, pp. 6, 31;
Prisons of Ireland: Report of Inspectors General, 1825, H.C. 1825 (493), xxii, pp. 27–8;
Fourth Report … on … the Prisons of Ireland, 1826, H.C. 1826 (173), xxiii, p. 27;
Fifth Report … on … the Prisons of Ireland, 1827, H.C. 1826–7 (471), xi, pp. 28–9;
Sixth Report … on … the Prisons of Ireland, 1828, H.C. 1828 (68), xii, pp. 8, 39–40;
Seventh Report … on … the Prisons of Ireland, 1829, H.C. 1829 (10), xiii, p. 25;
Eighth Report … on … the Prisons of Ireland, 1830, H.C. 1830 (48), xxiv, p. 34;
Sixteenth Report … on … the Prisons of Ireland, 1838, H.C. 1837–8 (186), xxix, p. 26;
Eighteenth Report … on … the Prisons of Ireland, 1840, H.C. 1840 (240), xxvi, p. 29;
Twenty-second Report … on … the Prisons of Ireland, 1844, H.C. 1844 (535), xxviii, p. 36;
Twenty-third Report … on … the Prisons of Ireland, 1844, H.C. 1845 (620), xxv, pp. 6, 17–18;

Twenty-fourth Report ... on ... the Prisons of Ireland, 1846, H.C. 1846 (697), xx, p. 26;
Twenty-fifth Report ... on ... the Prisons of Ireland, 1847, H.C. 1847 (805), xxix, p. 41;
Thirtieth Report ... on ... the Prisons of Ireland, 1852, H.C. 1852 (1531), xxv, p. 16;
Forty-ninth Report ... on ... the Prisons of Ireland, 1870, H.C. 1871 (C. 359), xxx, p. 120.

Secondary sources:

Brett, *Court Houses*, p. 62; Rowan, *Buildings of Ireland: North west Ulster*, pp. 348–9; O'Dwyer, 'Public Works Architecture', p. 407; Patton, *The Court Will Rise*, pp. 12–21, 53, 68–70, 78, 82, 83–5; Loeber, et al., *Art and Architecture of Ireland: Volume IV: Architecture 1600–2000*, p. 203; Mac Suibhne, *The End of Outrage*, pp. 56–7, 153–5, 175.

DOWN

Downpatrick, nos. 1 and 2

English St.?

An early gaol built by *c.* 1708; another gaol built nearby, in use 1708–46; a third new gaol built *c.* 1746, on site of first institution; an entirely new gaol built elsewhere 1789–96; closed; later demolished; not extant.

Until *c.* 1708, a house of correction served as the county gaol. Superseded by 'Castle Dorras', nearby, 1708–46. Another gaol built, *c.* 1746, seemingly on the site of the earlier house of correction. Outbreak of fire kills four/six prisoners, 1792. Several escapes, *c.* 1780s–90s. Superseded by a new gaol (see 'Down: Downpatrick, no. 3'), built 1789–96. Closed, 1796. Later demolished. Site used for extension to county courthouse (see Part I). Not extant.

Archival and primary sources:

Belfast Newsletter, 12 August 1746; ibid., 23 May 1792; Howard, *Lazarettos*, p. 98; Angelique Day and Patrick McWilliams (eds), *Ordnance Survey Memoirs of Ireland: Volume 12: Down* (Belfast: Institute of Irish Studies, 1992), pp. 41–2; Roger Johnson Smyth to the Marquess of Downshire, 1 October 1795 (PRONI, D/607/C/145).

Secondary sources:

R.E. Parkinson, *The City of Downe from Its Earliest Days* (Belfast: Erskine Mayne, 1927), p. 89; Wilson, *Saint Patrick's Town: A history of Downpatrick and the barony of Lecale*, pp. 116–17, 134, 143; Caroline Windrum, 'The Provision and Practice of Prison Reform in County Down, 1745–1894', in Proudfoot, *Down: History & society*, p. 330; Buchanan and Wilson, *Irish Historic Towns Atlas, No. 8: Downpatrick*, section 13.

DOWN

Downpatrick, no. 3

English St.
Lat. 54°19'42.63" N.; Long. 5°43'10.89" W.

An earlier gaol built *c.* 1746; a new gaol built (*Charles Lilly*) 1789–96; perimeter wall increased in height 1798; new gaol built nearby 1824–30; closed 1831; sold 1832; later used as a military barracks *c.* 1838; reopened as St Patrick's Heritage Centre *c.* 1990; partially extant.

An earlier gaol built (see 'Down: Downpatrick, nos. 1 and 2'), *c.* 1746, partially on the site of a former gaol. Outbreak of fire kills four/six prisoners, 1792. Several escapes, *c.* 1780s–90s. Superseded by a new gaol on English

Street (*Charles Lilly*), built at a cost of £13,378, 1789–96. Perimeter wall increased in height, 1798. United Irishman Thomas Russell executed in front of gaol, 1803. Unexecuted proposal for alterations, 1807. Unexecuted proposal to build a new infirmary at old gaol, 1818. New gaol built nearby (see 'Down: Downpatrick, no. 4'), 1824–30. Closed, 1831. Old gaol sold to John Saul, for £650, 1832. Later used as a military barracks, *c.* 1838. Reopened as St Patrick's Heritage Centre, *c.* 1990. Partially extant.

Archival and primary sources:

Belfast Newsletter, 12 August 1746; ibid., 19 May 1789; ibid., 23 May 1792; ibid., 5 August 1817; ibid., 28 July 1818; Howard, *Lazarettos*, p. 98; *Journal of the Irish House of Commons*, vol. xvii, 1797, p. ccvi; ibid., vol. xviii, 1798, app. cclxii, xxxviii; Roger Johnson Smyth to the Marquess of Downshire, 1 October 1795 (PRONI, D/607/C/145); Robertson, *Traveller's Guide through Ireland*, p. 65; Aynsworth Pilson, 'Memoirs of Notable Inhabitants of Downpatrick', 1838 (PRONI, T/2986/2, f. 118); Day and McWilliams, *Ordnance Survey Memoirs of Ireland: Volume 12: Down*, pp. 41–2.

Prison reports:

Inspector General's Report of … the Prisons in Ireland for … 1807, H.C. 1808 (239), ix, p. 6;

Account of All Gaols … in the … United Kingdom, H.C. 1819 (137), xvii, pp. 6–7;

Inspector General's Report of … the Prisons in Ireland for … 1818, H.C. 1819 (534), xii, p. 7.

Secondary sources:

E.R.R. Green and F.M. Jope, 'Patron and Architect: An example of relations in the late 18th century', *Ulster Journal of Archaeology*, vols 24–5, third series, 1961–2, pp. 145–51, at p. 146; Dunleath, Rankin, and Rowan, *Historic Buildings in the Town of Downpatrick*, pp. 17, 31; McParland, 'Public Work of Architects', p. 140; Wilson, *Saint Patrick's Town: A history of Downpatrick and the barony of Lecale*, pp. 116–17, 134, 142–3, 156, 222; Caroline Windrum, 'The Provision and Practice of Prison Reform in County Down, 1745–1894', in Proudfoot, *Down: History & society*, pp. 330–4, 345; Buchanan and Wilson, *Irish Historic Towns Atlas, No. 8: Downpatrick*, section 13; Colvin, *Biographical Dictionary of British Architects*, pp. 847–9.

DOWN

Downpatrick, no. 4

Mount Crescent
Lat. 54°19'47.69" N.; Long. 5°43'6.26" W.

An earlier gaol built 1789–96; unexecuted proposal to build a new infirmary at old gaol 1818; decision to build a new gaol 1819; delays over scale and cost of new gaol 1819–22; new gaol built at Mount Crescent (*Robert Reid*, contractor *John Lynn*) 1824–30; extensive alterations to introduce separate-system confinement (*Henry Smyth*) *c.* 1852–60; converted into a convict depot 1884; closed 1891; mostly demolished 1927–9; Down High School built on site 1933; partially extant.

Old gaol built on English Street (see 'Down: Downpatrick, no. 3'), 1789–96. Unexecuted proposal to build a new infirmary at old gaol, 1818. Grand jury decide that a new gaol is needed, 1819. Disagreements over scale and cost of proposed new gaol (*Robert Reid*), 1819–22. New gaol built nearby (*Robert Reid*, contractor *John Lynn*), at a cost of £60,000, 1824–30. Palmer and Woodward call for several cells to be adapted to separate system confinement, 1839. Extensive alterations to introduce separate-system confinement, including rebuilding one wing (*Henry Smyth*), *c.* 1852–60. A tunnel dug from gaol to courthouse (see Part I), *c.* 1855–7. Converted into a convict depot, 1884. Closed, 1891. Mostly demolished, 1927–9. Down High School built on site, 1933. Tunnel filled in, *c.* 1991. Partially extant.

Archival and primary sources:

Belfast Newsletter, 5 August 1817; ibid., 28 July 1818; ibid., 10 August, 13 August, 1 October 1819; ibid., 7 January, 18

April 1820; ibid., 14 May 1822; ibid., 18 March 1828; ibid., 10 September 1830; Reid, *Travels in Ireland*, pp. 185–6; Day and McWilliams, *Ordnance Survey Memoirs of Ireland: Volume 12: Down*, pp. 41–2; Down grand-jury presentments, spring assizes 1821 (PRONI, DOW 4/2/10); *Fourth Report of the AIPPD*, p. 31; Correspondence relating to Downpatrick gaol, 1821–3 (NAI, CSORP 1823/6726); Account of money received and ... expended on the new gaol at Downpatrick, by James Waddell, 17 May 1827 (NAI, CSORP 1827/1956); Lewis, *Topographical Dictionary*, vol. 1, p. 493; Matthew Forde to Lord Downshire, January 1824 (PRONI, D/671/C/12/286); J.R. Moore to W. Freeman, 10 November 1839 (PRONI, D1854/6/1); Drawings for Downpatrick gaol by Robert Reid, *c.* 1820 (PRONI, D/2992); Drawing showing Downpatrick gaol, n.d., n.s. [*c.* 1820] (NLI, AD 2641); Drawings for Downpatrick gaol by Henry Smyth, 5 November 1853 (PRONI, D/2992/B/4A); *Down Recorder*, 4 April 1891; ibid., 10 August 1929; ibid., 9 September 1933.

Prison reports:

Inspector General's Report of ... the Prisons in Ireland for ... 1807, H.C. 1808 (239), ix, p. 6;

Account of All Gaols ... in the ... United Kingdom, H.C. 1819 (137), xvii, pp. 6–7;

Inspector General's Report of ... the Prisons in Ireland for ... 1818, H.C. 1819 (534), xii, p. 7;

Prisons of Ireland: Report of Inspectors General, 1823, H.C. 1823 (342), x, pp. 6, 29;

Prisons of Ireland: Report of Inspectors General, 1824, H.C. 1824 (294), xxii, pp. 5, 30–1;

Prisons of Ireland: Report of Inspectors General, 1825, H.C. 1825 (493), xxii, p. 28;

Fourth Report ... on ... the Prisons of Ireland, 1826, H.C. 1826 (173), xxiii, p. 26;

Fifth Report ... on ... the Prisons of Ireland, 1827, H.C. 1826–7 (471), xi, p. 30;

Sixth Report ... on ... the Prisons of Ireland, 1828, H.C. 1828 (68), xii, pp. 8, 41;

Seventh Report ... on ... the Prisons of Ireland, 1829, H.C. 1829 (10), xiii, pp. 9, 36;

Eighth Report ... on ... the Prisons of Ireland, 1830, H.C. 1830 (48), xxiv, p. 35;

Ninth Report ... on ... the Prisons of Ireland, 1831, H.C. 1830–1 (172), iv, p. 25;

Tenth Report ... on ... the Prisons of Ireland, 1832, H.C. 1831–2 (152), xvii, pp. 24–5;

Twelfth Report ... on ... the Prisons of Ireland, 1834, H.C. 1834 (63), xl, pp. 37–8;

Sixteenth Report ... on ... the Prisons of Ireland, 1838, H.C. 1837–8 (186), xxix, pp. 7, 27;

Eighteenth Report ... on ... the Prisons of Ireland, 1840, H.C. 1840 (240), xxvi, p. 30;

Twentieth Report ... on ... the Prisons of Ireland, 1842, H.C. 1842 (377), xxii, p. 67;

Twenty-first Report ... on ... the Prisons of Ireland, 1843, H.C. 1843 (462), xxvii, p. 35;

Thirtieth Report ... on ... the Prisons of Ireland, 1852, H.C. 1852 (1531), xxv, p. 16;

Thirty-second Report ... on ... the Prisons of Ireland, 1854, H.C. 1854 (1803), xxxii, pp. 64, 67;

Thirty-third Report ... on ... the Prisons of Ireland, 1855, H.C. 1854–5 (1956), xxvi, p. 59;

Thirty-fourth Report ... on ... the Prisons of Ireland, 1856, H.C. 1856 (2113), xxxiv, p. 21;

Forty-ninth Report ... on ... the Prisons of Ireland, 1870, H.C. 1871 (C. 359), xxx, p. 134.

Secondary sources:

Dunleath, Rankin, and Rowan, *Historic Buildings in the Town of Downpatrick*, pp. 17, 31; McParland, 'Public Work of Architects', pp. 140, 252; Craig, *Architecture of Ireland*, p. 304; Wilson, *Saint Patrick's Town: A history of Downpatrick and the barony of Lecale*, pp. 116–17, 134, 142–3, 156, 161, 222; Hunter, 'Downpatrick's Dungeons Rediscovered', pp. 21–5; Windrum, 'The Provision and Practice of Prison Reform in County Down, 1745–1894', in Proudfoot, *Down: History & society*, pp. 330–47; O'Dwyer, 'Public Works Architecture', pp. 149, 184, 407; Wheeler, 'John Lynn – architect/contractor/engineer', pp. 28–31; Buchanan and Wilson, *Irish Historic Towns Atlas, No. 8: Downpatrick*, section 13; Colvin, *Biographical Dictionary of British Architects*, pp. 847–9.

DUBLIN – ARBOUR HILL

Dublin

Arbour Hill
Lat. 53°21'0.04" N.; Long. 6°17'15.89" W.

Built as a military prison (*Royal Engineers*) 1845–8; converted into a state prison *c.* 1975; extant.

Secondary sources:

O'Dwyer, 'Public Works Architecture', p. 192; Casey, *Buildings of Ireland: Dublin*, pp. 246–7.

DUBLIN – FOUR COURTS MARSHALSEA

Dublin

Bridgefoot St. & Marshal Lane
Lat. 53°20'38.68" N.; Long. 6°16'58.16" W.

Built (likely *Francis Sandys*) 1775; extensive additions and repairs (*Board of Works: Francis Johnston*) 1809–12; extra yard added 1824–6; used for all Dublin debtors 1842; three punishment cells added and a new yard *c.* 1852–3; closed 1874; in use as a barracks; demolished *c.* 1975; only small parts survive.

Built (likely *Francis Sandys*) 1775. Howard visits and is very critical of running of establishment, 1787. Forster Archer, prison inspector, calls for a new prison, 1807. Extensive additions and repairs (*Board of Works: Francis Johnston*), 1809–12. Forster Archer recommends an entirely new building, 1818. An extra yard enclosed and sundry repairs, 1824–6. All Dublin debtors now confined in this prison following an act of parliament, 1842. Three punishment cells added, and a new yard for females, *c.* 1852–3. Closed, 1874. Later used as a barracks. Demolished, *c.* 1975. Only small parts survive.

Archival and primary sources:

Finn's Leinster Journal, 15–19 July 1775; Howard, *State of the Prisons in England and Wales*, p. 205; Howard, *Lazarettos*, p. 80; *Freeman's Journal*, 8 December 1809; ibid., 18 January 1816; Forster Archer, 'Report of the State of Gaols of Ireland for the Year 1811' (Houses of the Oireachtas Library, Dublin, MS.4E63); James Palmer to Henry Goulburn, 21 September 1822 (NAI, CSORP 1822/1527); Four Courts Marshalsea (Ireland) Act, 1842 (5 & 6 Vict., c. 95).

Prison reports:

Inspector General's Report of … the Prisons in Ireland for … 1807, H.C. 1808 (239), ix, p. 8;

Report from the Commissioners Appointed To Inquire into … the State Prisons and Other Gaols in Ireland, H.C. 1809 (265), vii, pp. 13–21, 91–2;

Inspector General's Report of … the Prisons in Ireland for … 1818, H.C. 1819 (534), xii, pp. 10–11;

Prisons of Ireland: Report of Inspectors General, 1823, H.C. 1823 (342), x, p. 22;

Prisons of Ireland: Report of Inspectors General, 1824, H.C. 1824 (294), xxii, p. 25;

Prisons of Ireland: Report of Inspectors General, 1825, H.C. 1825 (493), xxii, p. 21;

Fourth Report … on … the Prisons of Ireland, 1826, H.C. 1826 (173), xxiii, pp. 18–19;

Fifth Report ... on ... the Prisons of Ireland, 1827, H.C. 1826–7 (471), xi, p. 21;
Sixth Report ... on ... the Prisons of Ireland, 1828, H.C. 1828 (68), xii, p. 32;
Seventh Report ... on ... the Prisons of Ireland, 1829, H.C. 1829 (10), xiii, p. 28;
Eighth Report ... on ... the Prisons of Ireland, 1830, H.C. 1830 (48), xxiv, p. 21;
Thirteenth Report ... on ... the Prisons of Ireland, 1835, H.C. 1835 (114), xxxvi, p. 21;
Fifteenth Report ... on ... the Prisons of Ireland, 1837, H.C. 1837 (123), xxxi, p. 18;
Sixteenth Report ... on ... the Prisons of Ireland, 1838, H.C. 1837–8 (186), xxix, p. 22;
Nineteenth Report ... on ... the Prisons of Ireland, 1841, H.C. 1841 (299), xi, p. 22;
Twenty-first report ... on ... the Prisons of Ireland, 1843, H.C. 1843 (462), xxvii, p. 21;
Thirty-first report ... on ... the Prisons of Ireland, 1853, H.C. 1853 (1657), liii, p. 63;
Forty-ninth Report ... on ... the Prisons of Ireland, 1870, H.C. 1871 (C. 359), xxx, p. 586.

Secondary sources:

McDowell, *Irish Administration*, p. 146.

DUBLIN – GRANGEGORMAN LANE (RICHMOND PENITENTIARY)

Dublin

Grangegorman Lane
Lat. 53°21'17.97" N.; Long. 6°16'41.19" W.

Unexecuted proposal for a panopticon penitentiary in Dublin (*Jeremy Bentham*) 1790; penitentiary built (*Francis Johnston*) 1812–20; closed 1831; in use as a fever hospital 1832; opened as Dublin City female prison 1836; additions and alterations (*John Semple*) 1838–40; forty-five separate-system cells added 1844–5; additions and alterations (*John Skipton Mulvany*) 1850–1; further alterations and additions (*Edward Henry Carson*) 1863–6; handed over to the Richmond Lunatic Asylum 1897; alterations 1898; mostly demolished; only the front range survives; partially extant.

Unexecuted proposal for a panopticon penitentiary in Dublin (location unknown) (*Jeremy Bentham*), 1790. Irish Penitentiary Act, 1792. Jeremiah Fitzpatrick, prison inspector, opens a small penitentiary at James Street bridewell in Dublin, 1792. Land for a penitentiary near the Dublin House of Industry purchased, 1810. Design for penitentiary approved, 1811. Penitentiary built (*Francis Johnston*), 1812–20. Sectarian scandal, 1821. Palmer and Woodward very critical of establishment, 1823. Major sectarian scandal, 1826. Management of penitentiary disintegrates, 1826–30. Closed, 1831. Used as a fever hospital, 1832. Act of parliament to transfer prison to Dublin City grand jury, 1836. In use as city female prison, 1836. Additions and alterations, including ninety-six new cells, kitchens, infirmary, etc. (*John Semple*), 1838–40. Forty-five separate-system cells added, 1844–5. Additions and alterations (*John Skipton Mulvany*), 1850–1. Further alterations and additions (*Edward Henry Carson*), 1863–6. Handed over to the Richmond Lunatic Asylum, 1897. Alterations, 1898. Mostly demolished. Only the front range survives. Partially extant.

Archival and primary sources:

Jeremy Bentham to Robert Adam, 28 May 1791 (University College London, Bentham papers, box 119a, paper 12); 32 Geo. III, c. 27 (1792); *Journal of the Irish House of Commons*, vol. xv, 1793, p. ccccviii; Date on weather vane ('1816'); *Gentleman's and Citizen's Almanack* (1819), p. 176; T. Taylor, 'Report on the Richmond General Penitentiary', n.d. (NAI, CSORP 1819/106P); Anon., 'A Letter from Francis Johnston', *Quarterly Bulletin of the Irish Georgian Society*, vol. 6, no. 1, 1963, pp. 1–5, at p. 3; Drawings by Francis Johnston for the Richmond General Penitentiary, 1810–12 (Irish Architectural Archive, RIAI Murray Collection, Acc. 92/46.424–33); Thomas Kitson Cromwell, *Excursions through Ireland: Comprising topographical and historical delineations of each province*, 3 vols (London: Longman, 1820), vol. 1, pp. 129–30; Warburton,

Whitelaw and Walsh, *History of the City of Dublin*, vol. 2, pp. 1061–2; John Townsend to William Gregory, 26 March 1821 (NAI, CSORP 1821/1134 and 1821/1140); Benjamin Woodward to William Gregory, 3 August 1822 (NAI, CSORP 1822/927); Board of Works letterbooks, 3 August 1810 to 20 December 1816 (NAI); Richmond Penitentiary, &c. Act (Ireland), 1836 (6 & 7 Will. IV, c. 51); *Freeman's Journal*, 13 November 1837; ibid., 28 September 1838; ibid., 16 May 1863; *The Builder*, vol. 8, no. 391, 3 August 1850, p. 368, ibid., vol. 8, no. 395, 31 August 1850, p. 416; ibid., vol. 9, no. 445, 16 August 1851, p. 517; ibid., vol. 24, no. 1238, 27 October 1866, p. 800; *The Irish Times*, 20 October 1863; ibid., 12 March 1864; ibid., 4 March 1898; *Dublin Builder*, vol. 5, no. 92, 15 October 1863, p. 170; ibid., vol. 6, no. 105, 1 May 1864, p. 87; ibid., vol. 6, no. 111, 1 August 1864, p. 149; ibid., vol. 8, no. 164, 15 October 1866, p. 253; ibid., vol. 9, no. 170, 15 January 1867, p. 24; ibid., vol. 9, no. 179, 1 June 1867, p. 140.

Prison reports:

Prisons of Ireland: Report of Inspectors General, 1823, H.C. 1823 (342), x, pp. 10–11, 19;

Prisons of Ireland: Report of Inspectors General, 1824, H.C. 1824 (294), xxii, pp. 10–11;

Prisons of Ireland: Report of Inspectors General, 1825, H.C. 1825 (493), xxii, p. 8;

Fourth Report … on … the Prisons of Ireland, 1826, H.C. 1826 (173), xxiii, p. 12;

Sixth Report … on … the Prisons of Ireland, 1828, H.C. 1828 (68), xii, pp. 23–6;

Ninth Report … on … the Prisons of Ireland, 1831, H.C. 1830–1 (172), iv, p. 17;

Tenth Report … on … the Prisons of Ireland, 1832, H.C. 1831–2 (152), xvii, p. 16;

Eleventh Report … on … the Prisons of Ireland, 1833, H.C. 1833 (67), xvii, p. 16;

Twelfth Report … on … the Prisons of Ireland, 1834, H.C. 1834 (63), xl, p. 18;

Fourteenth Report … on … the Prisons of Ireland, 1836, H.C. 1836 (118), xxxv, pp. 11–12;

Fifteenth Report … on … the Prisons of Ireland, 1837, H.C. 1837 (123), xxxi, p. 6;

Sixteenth Report … on … the Prisons of Ireland, 1838, H.C. 1837–8 (186), xxix, pp. 8, 20–1;

Seventeenth Report … on … the Prisons of Ireland, 1839, H.C. 1839 (91), xx, p. 17;

Eighteenth Report … on … the Prisons of Ireland, 1840, H.C. 1840 (240), xxvi, pp. 7, 20;

Nineteenth Report … on … the Prisons of Ireland, 1841, H.C. 1841 (299), xi, p. 20;

Twenty-second Report … on … the Prisons of Ireland, 1844, H.C. 1844 (535), xxviii, p. 17;

Twenty-fourth Report … on … the Prisons of Ireland, 1846, H.C. 1846 (697), xx, pp. 15–16;

Forty-ninth Report … on … the Prisons of Ireland, 1870, H.C. 1871 (C. 359), xxx, p. 575.

Secondary sources:

Moylan, 'District of Grangegorman: Part II', pp. 55–8; Betjeman, 'Francis Johnston', in Myfanwy Evans, *Pavilion*, pp. 24–5; Henchy, 'Francis Johnston', pp. 7, 13; McParland, 'Francis Johnston', pp. 62, 78, 126, 130–1; Heaney, 'Ireland's Penitentiary', pp. 28–39; McParland, 'Public Work of Architects', pp. 250–1; Goslin, 'Descriptive Catalogue of the Murray Collection', pp. 154–7; 'O'Dwyer, 'Public Works Architecture', pp. 192, 407; Casey, *Buildings of Ireland: Dublin*, pp. 256–8; Loeber, et al., *Art and Architecture of Ireland: Volume IV: Architecture 1600–2000*, pp. 275–6, 288; Sinéad Gargan, 'How Not To "Encourage People To Take Lotts for Building": The 18th-century non-development of Grangegorman by the Monck estate', *Irish Architectural and Decorative Studies*, vol. 18, 2015, pp. 106–29.

DUBLIN – MOUNTJOY

Dublin

North Circular Rd.
Lat. 53°21'42.56" N.; Long. 6°16'2.41" W.

Transportation to New South Wales ceases 1840; Smithfield Penitentiary abandoned 1841; unexecuted plans for a new convict prison at Smithfield 1842–4; site for a convict prison purchased near the Point Depot 1845; all transportation to Australia, etc., suspended 1846; plans for a prison near the Point Depot abandoned 1846; act of parliament to allow the Board of Works to build prisons 1847; site purchased 1847; convict prison built (*Joshua Jebb, Jacob Owen, Charles Peirce*) 1847–50; female convict prison built (*James Higgins Owen*) 1855–8; in use as a state prison; extant.

Palmer and Woodward suggest a new prison is required in Dublin, with at least 400 cells, 1829. Transportation to New South Wales ceases, 1840. Smithfield Penitentiary abandoned, 1841. Unexecuted plans for a new convict prison at Smithfield, 1842–4. Site for a convict prison purchased near the Point Depot, 1845. All transportation to Australia, etc., suspended, 1846. Plans for a prison near the Point Depot abandoned, 1846. Board of Works begins plans to build a convict prison at Mountjoy, 1846. Act of parliament to allow the Board of Works to build prisons, 1847. Site purchased from Lord Rathdowne and the Mountjoy family, 1847. Convict prison built (*Joshua Jebb, Jacob Owen, Charles Peirce*), at a cost of at least £60,000, 1847–50. Newgate gaol closed, 1850. Board of Works prepares a design for an adjoining female convict prison, 1851. Female convict prison built (*James Higgins Owen*), 1855–8. In use as a state prison. Extant.

Archival and primary sources:

Land for Prisons (Ireland) Act, 1847 (10 & 11 Vict., c. 26); Newgate Gaol (Dublin) &c. Act, 1849 (12 & 13 Vict., c. 55); Convict Prisons (Ireland) Act, 1854 (17 & 18 Vict., c. 76); *The Builder, vol.*, vol. 8, no. 400, 5 October 1850, p. 473; *Dublin Evening Post*, 26 March 1850; Papers relating to Mountjoy prison, including correspondence from the prison inspectors and maps of Dublin, 1843–9 (NAI, CSORP 1847/G5458 and 1849/G8196 (further bundles of files exist beyond these)); Purchase of land by the Board of Works (NAI, Registry of deeds, 1846/19/6); Drawings for Mountjoy female convict prison, by James Higgins Owen, 12 May 1855 (NAI, OPW 5HC/4/412); Drawings of Mountjoy male convict prison, 5 August 1924 (NAI, OPW 5HC/4/412).

Prison reports:

Seventh Report … on … the Prisons of Ireland, 1829, H.C. 1829 (10), xiii, p. 26;

Nineteenth Report … on … the Prisons of Ireland, 1841, H.C. 1841 (299), xi, p. 18;

Twentieth Report … on … the Prisons of Ireland, 1842, H.C. 1842 (377), xxii, p. 7;

Twenty-first Report … on … the Prisons of Ireland, 1843, H.C. 1843 (462), xxvii, pp. 3–4;

Twenty-second Report … on … the Prisons of Ireland, 1844, H.C. 1844 (535), xxviii, p. 8;

Twenty-fourth Report … on … the Prisons of Ireland, 1846, H.C. 1846 (697), xx, p. 18;

Twenty-fifth Report … on … the Prisons of Ireland, 1847, H.C. 1847 (805), xxix, p. 11;

Twenty-eighth Report … on … the Prisons of Ireland, 1850, H.C. 1850 (1229), xxix, p. 15.

Public works reports:

Sixteenth Report of the Commissioners on Public Works, Ireland … for the Year 1847, H.C. 1848 (983), cxxvii, pp. 16–17;

Seventeenth Report of the Commissioners on Public Works, Ireland … for the Year 1848, H.C. 1849 (1098), xxiii, pp. 24–5;

Eighteenth Report of the Commissioners on Public Works, Ireland … for the Year 1849, H.C. 1850 (1235), xxv, p. 34;

Nineteenth Report of the Commissioners on Public Works, Ireland … for the Year 1850, H.C. 1851 (1414), xxv, p. 34;

Twenty-first Report of the Commissioners on Public Works, Ireland … for the Year 1852, H.C. 1852–3 (1651), xli, p. 24;

Twenty-second Report of the Commissioners on Public Works, Ireland … for the Year 1853, H.C. 1854 (1820), xx, p. 25;

Twenty-third Report of the Commissioners on Public Works, Ireland … for the Year 1854, H.C. 1854–5 (1929), xvi, p. 23;

Twenty-fourth Report of the Commissioners on Public Works, Ireland … for the Year 1855, H.C. 1856 (2140), xvi, p. 26;

Twenty–fifth Report of the Commissioners on Public Works, Ireland … for the Year 1856, H.C. 1857 (2228), xvii, p. 21;

Twenty-sixth Report of the Commissioners on Public Works, Ireland … for the Year 1857, H.C. 1857–8 (2412), xxvi, p. 17;

Twenty seventh Report of the Commissioners on Public Works, Ireland … for the Year 1858, H.C. 1859 (2545), xiv, p. 18.

Secondary sources:

O'Dwyer, 'Public Works Architecture', pp. 187–91, 407; Johnston, *Forms of Constraint*, p. 98; Carey, *Mountjoy*; Casey, *Buildings of Ireland: Dublin*, pp. 279–81; Loeber, et al., *Art and Architecture of Ireland. Volume IV: Architecture 1600–2000*, p. 205.

DUBLIN – SMITHFIELD PENITENTIARY

Dublin

Smithfield Square
Lat. 53°20'57.58" N.; Long. 6°16'38.95" W.

Built as a private residence; in use as a bridewell by Dublin police 1787; a penitentiary for young male criminals 1801; enlarged and altered (*Francis Johnston*) 1818; alterations and additions (*Henry Aaron Baker*) 1823–4; institution repeatedly opened and closed 1836–47; unexecuted plans to convert building into a male convict prison (*John Semple*) 1838; further work to convert building into this purpose (*Board of Works: F.V. Clarendon*) 1843–4; closed and abandoned 1869; still intact in 1968; demolished; social housing on site; not extant.

Built as the house of Justice French. Bought by the police for use as a bridewell and house of correction, 1787. In use as a penitentiary for young male criminals, 1801. Women also kept at institution, 1807. Penitentiary for adult female convicts formally established, 1809. Enlarged and altered (*Francis Johnston*), 1818. Boys moved to new Richmond Penitentiary, 1821. Alterations and additions, including solitary cells, raising walls, etc. (*Henry Aaron Baker*), 1823–4. Prison inspectors suggest the penitentiary should close, 1831. Act of parliament states institution to close, 1836. Handed over to government as a female convict prison, 1836. Unexecuted plans to convert prison into a full convict prison (*John Semple*), 1838. Shut down and abandoned, 1841. In use as a convict prison again, 1842. Alterations and additions to use building as a male convict penitentiary (*Board of Works: F.V. Clarendon*), 1843–4. Building abandoned, 1847. Formally closed and abandoned, 1869. Derelict when photographed (see above), 1968. Demolished. Social housing on the site. Not extant.

Archival and primary sources:

Freeman's Journal, 9–11 January 1787; ibid., 24 April 1823; Forster Archer, 'Report of the State of Gaols of Ireland for the Year 1811' (Houses of the Oireachtas Library, Dublin, MS.4E63); Warburton, Whitelaw and Walsh, *History of the City of Dublin*, vol. 1, pp. 627–8; Reid, *Travels in Ireland*, p. 152; *Analysis of the Grand Jury Presentments for the City of Dublin, from the Year 1822 to 1834 Inclusive* (Dublin: Graisberry, 1835, copy in Oireachtas Library); Richmond Penitentiary, &c. Act (Ireland), 1836 (6 & 7 Will. IV, c. 51); Photograph, *c.* 1968 (Dublin City Libraries, Strumpet City collection, SC019); Papers relating to Smithfield penitentiary, 1846 (NAI, CSORP 1846/G12952).

Prison reports:

Inspector General's Report of … the Prisons in Ireland for … 1807, H.C. 1808 (239), ix, p. 8;

Report from the Commissioners Appointed to Inquire into … the State Prisons and Other Gaols in Ireland, H.C. 1809 (265), vii, pp. 26–8;

Prisons of Ireland: Report of Inspectors General, 1823, H.C. 1823 (342), x, pp. 21–2;

Prisons of Ireland: Report of Inspectors General, 1824, H.C. 1824 (294), xxii, pp. 23–4;

Ninth Report … on … the Prisons of Ireland, 1831, H.C. 1830–1 (172), iv, p. 17;

Fourteenth Report ... on ... the Prisons of Ireland, 1836, H.C. 1836 (118), xxxv, pp. 11–12;
Fifteenth Report ... on ... the Prisons of Ireland, 1837, H.C. 1837 (123), xxxi, p. 17;
Sixteenth Report ... on ... the Prisons of Ireland, 1838, H.C. 1837–8 (186), xxix, p. 21;
Seventeenth Report ... on ... the Prisons of Ireland, 1839, H.C. 1839 (91), xx, p. 19;
Eighteenth Report ... on ... the Prisons of Ireland, 1840, H.C. 1840 (240), xxvi, p. 21;
Nineteenth Report ... on ... the Prisons of Ireland, 1841, H.C. 1841 (299), xi, pp. 18;
Twentieth Report ... on ... the Prisons of Ireland, 1842, H.C. 1842 (377), xxii, p. 7;
Twenty-first Report ... on ... the Prisons of Ireland, 1843, H.C. 1843 (462), xxvii, pp. 3–4;
Twenty-second Report ... on ... the Prisons of Ireland, 1844, H.C. 1844 (535), xxviii, p. 8;
Twenty-third Report ... on ... the Prisons of Ireland, 1844, H.C. 1845 (620), xxv, pp. 10–11;
Twenty-fourth Report ... on ... the Prisons of Ireland, 1846, H.C. 1846 (697), xx, p. 18;
Twenty-fifth Report ... on ... the Prisons of Ireland, 1847, H.C. 1847 (805), xxix, p. 11;
Twenty-sixth Report ... on ... the Prisons of Ireland, 1847–48, H.C. 1847–8 (952), xxiv, pp. 6, 8, 11.

Public works reports:

Eleventh Report of the Commissioners on Public Works, Ireland ... for the Year 1842, H.C. 1843 (467), xxviii, p. 4;
Twelfth Report of the Commissioners on Public Works, Ireland ... for the Year 1843, H.C. 1844 (555), xxx, pp. 5–6;
Thirteenth Report of the Commissioners on Public Works, Ireland ... for the Year 1844, H.C. 1845 (640), xxvi, p. 5.

Secondary sources:

McDowell, *Irish Administration*, p. 156; Heaney, 'Ireland's Penitentiary', p. 30; Frederick O'Dwyer, *Lost Dublin* (Dublin: Gill & Macmillan, 1981), p. 87 (illus.); O'Dwyer, 'Public Works Architecture', pp. 67, 180, 186, 407; Carey, *Mountjoy*, p. 39; Loeber, et al., *Art and Architecture of Ireland: Volume IV: Architecture 1600–2000*, p. 205.

DUBLIN COUNTY

Dublin, no. 1

Old Kilmainham Rd. & Brookfield Rd.
Lat. 53°20'27.03" N.; Long. 6°18'10.81" W.

First mention of a gaol in Kilmainham district *c.* 1212; a gaol active in Old Kilmainham *c.* 18th century; campaign for a new gaol 1774; gaol condemned 1782; plans for a replacement approved 1785; gaol again condemned (by Howard) 1787; new gaol built 1787–96; old gaol later demolished; not extant.

First mention of a gaol at Kilmainham, used by the Hospitallers of St John of Jerusalem, *c.* 1212. A gaol in Old Kilmainham, *c.* 18th century. Campaign for a new county gaol, by Edward Newenham MP, 1774. Gaol condemned in Irish House of Commons reports, 1782. Plans for a new gaol approved by the grand jury, 1785. Gaol condemned by Howard, 1787. New gaol built (see 'Dublin County: Dublin, no. 2'), 1787–96. Old gaol later demolished. Not extant.

Archival and primary sources:

Howard, *State of the Prisons in England and Wales*, p. 208; Howard, *Lazarettos*, p. 83; 26 Geo. III, c. 14 (1786); *Faulkner's Dublin Journal*, 13 August 1796.

Secondary sources:

Charles McNeill, 'The Hospitallers at Kilmainham and Their Guests', *Journal of the Royal Society of Antiquaries of Ireland*, vol. 14, no. 1, 6th series, June 1924, pp. 15–30, at p. 17; Nowlan, 'Kilmainham Gaol', p. 105; Kelly, *History of Kilmainham Gaol*, pp. 15, 18, 23; Pat Cooke, *A History of Kilmainham Gaol, 1796–1924* (Dublin: Government of Ireland, 1995), p. 7; Cumming, 'Kilmainham Gaol', National Inventory of Architectural Heritage Building of the Month.

DUBLIN COUNTY

Dublin, no. 2

Inchicore Rd.
Lat. 53°20'30.20" N.; Long. 6°18'34.37" W.

First mention of a gaol in Kilmainham district *c.* 1212; a gaol active in Old Kilmainham *c.* 18th century; campaign for a new gaol 1774; gaol condemned 1782; plans for a replacement approved 1785; gaol again condemned (by Howard) 1787; new gaol built (*Sir John Traile*) 1787–96; courthouse built nearby 1817–20; fire destroys western half 1817; this rebuilt (*William Farrell*) 1819–20; unexecuted designs (*John Semple*) for an adjacent convict depot 1838; addition of twenty-seven female separate-system cells and a kitchen (*Park Neville*) 1844–5; extensive rebuilding of gaol, especially eastern half, with new boundary walls, corner towers, etc. (*John McCurdy*) 1858–63; used for keeping Fenian prisoners, gaol strengthened at the same time 1865; Land War prisoners kept 1881–2; Easter 1916 executions 1916; last political prisoner (de Valera) released 1923; closed 1924; derelict; reopened as a museum; extant.

First mention of a gaol at Kilmainham, used by the Hospitallers of St John of Jerusalem, *c.* 1212. A gaol in Old Kilmainham, *c.* 18th century (see 'Dublin County: Dublin, no. 1'). Campaign for a new county gaol, by Edward Newenham MP, 1774. Gaol condemned in Irish House of Commons reports, 1782. Plans for a new gaol approved by the grand jury, 1785. Act of parliament for new gaol, 1786. Land secured for new gaol, from Sir Nicholas Lawless, 1786. Old gaol condemned by Howard, 1787. New gaol built (*Sir John Traile*), at a cost of around £22,000, 1787–96. Canon situated outside gaol during rebellion, 1798. Courthouse built nearby (see Part I), 1817–20. Fire destroys western half of gaol, 1817. Rebuilding of western half of gaol (*William Farrell*) and other repairs and minor alterations, 1819–20. Minor alterations, 1821. Flagging of yards, 1823. Palmer and Woodward unhappy with arrangements at gaol, especially holding of convicts there, 1823–7. Alterations to female gaol, 1825. Flagging of yards, 1826. Construction of new solitary cells, 1830. Repairs to roofs, 1831, 1833. Unexecuted design for a new convict depot adjacent to gaol (*John Semple*), 1838. Palmer and Woodward call for construction of separate-system cells, 1841. Plans approved for twenty-seven female separate-system cells, 1842. Addition of twenty-seven female separate-system cells and a kitchen (*Park Neville*), 1844–5. Chapel enlarged and two female solitary cells built, 1852. Competition announced for extensive rebuilding of gaol on separate-system requirements, 1857. Extensive rebuilding of gaol, especially eastern half, with new boundary walls, corner towers, etc. (*John McCurdy*), 1858–63. Gaol used for keeping Fenian prisoners, gaol strengthened at the same time, 1865. Back in use as an ordinary county gaol, 1870. Land War prisoners kept, 1881–2. Easter 1916 executions, 1916. Last political prisoner (de Valera) released, 1923. Closed, 1924. Derelict. Reopened as a museum. Extant.

Archival and primary sources:

Howard, *State of the Prisons in England and Wales*, p. 208; Howard, *Lazarettos*, p. 83; 26 Geo. III, c. 14 (1786); *Freeman's Journal*, 21–4 April 1787; ibid., July 1787; ibid., 4–6 September 1787; ibid., 5 December 1817; ibid., 18 March 1822; *Faulkner's Dublin Journal*, 13 August 1796; ibid., 5 December 1817; William Ashford, 'A View of Dublin from Chapelizod', 1795–8 (National Gallery of Ireland); *Saunders' Newsletter*, 5 December 1817; ibid., 24 March 1837; *Hansard*, vol. 11, 1st ser., 2 July 1808, cols 1131–2; Plan drawings for Kilmainham gaol, n.d., n.s. [before 1817] (NLI, AD 2663–4); Dublin County grand-jury minute book, 22 April 1818, 27 April 1818, 18 November 1818, 11 May 1819, 9 May 1820, 12 May 1820, 14 November 1820, 2 November 1839 (Fingal County Council Archives, GJ/1/1); Dublin County grand-jury presentment books, 1818–41, see especially spring 1818, spring 1819, spring 1825, spring 1826, spring 1831, and spring 1833 (ibid., GJ/5/1–5); *First Report of the AIPPD*, p. 27; *Dublin Penny Journal*, vol. 4, no. 184, 9 January 1836, p. 221; John Semple to the Inspectors General of Prisons, 1 September 1838 (NAI, CSORP 1838/2333); Designs for enlarging Kilmainham gaol by

Parke Neville, 22 March 1844 (Irish Architectural Archive, McCurdy and Mitchell collection, Acc. 82/49.71.1); *The Builder*, vol. 15, no. 750, 20 June 1857, p. 353; ibid., vol. 15, no. 754, 18 July 1857, p. 409; ibid., vol. 17, no. 856, 2 July 1859, p. 444; *Dublin Builder*, vol. 1, no. 7, 1 July 1859, p. 89; ibid., vol. 4, no. 60, 15 June 1862, p. 155; Gilbert, *Documents Relating to Ireland*, p. 94; Drawing of Kilmainham gaol, 22 March 1920 (NAI, OPW 5HC/4/423).

Prison reports:

Inspector General's Report of … the Prisons in Ireland for … 1807, H.C. 1808 (239), ix, p. 7;

Report from the Commissioners Appointed To Inquire into … the State Prisons and Other Gaols in Ireland, H.C. 1809 (265), vii, pp. 8–13, 64, plan drawings;

Account of All Gaols … in the … United Kingdom, H.C. 1819 (137), xvii, pp. 8–9;

Inspector General's Report of … the Prisons in Ireland for … 1818, H.C. 1819 (534), xii, pp. 8–9;

Prisons of Ireland: Report of Inspectors General, 1823, H.C. 1823 (342), x, p. 18;

Prisons of Ireland: Report of Inspectors General, 1824, H.C. 1824 (294), xxii, p. 22;

Prisons of Ireland: Report of Inspectors General, 1825, H.C. 1825 (493), xxii, pp. 17–18;

Fourth Report … on … the Prisons of Ireland, 1826, H.C. 1826 (173), xxiii, p. 16;

Fifth Report … on … the Prisons of Ireland, 1827, H.C. 1826–7 (471), xi, p. 18;

Sixth Report … on … the Prisons of Ireland, 1828, H.C. 1828 (68), xii, p. 29;

Seventh Report … on … the Prisons of Ireland, 1829, H.C. 1829 (10), xiii, p. 25;

Eighth Report … on … the Prisons of Ireland, 1830, H.C. 1830 (48), xxiv, pp. 11, 25;

Eleventh Report … on … the Prisons of Ireland, 1833, H.C. 1833 (67), xvii, pp. 15–16;

Thirteenth Report … on … the Prisons of Ireland, 1835, H.C. 1835 (114), xxxvi, p. 17;

Fifteenth Report … on … the Prisons of Ireland, 1837, H.C. 1837 (123), xxxi, pp. 15–16;

Seventeenth Report … on … the Prisons of Ireland, 1839, H.C. 1839 (91), xx, p. 16;

Eighteenth Report … on … the Prisons of Ireland, 1840, H.C. 1840 (240), xxvi, p. 18;

Nineteenth Report … on … the Prisons of Ireland, 1841, H.C. 1841 (299), xi, pp. 16–17;

Twentieth Report … on … the Prisons of Ireland, 1842, H.C. 1842 (377), xxii, pp. 7, 16;

Twenty-first Report … on … the Prisons of Ireland, 1843, H.C. 1843 (462), xxvii, pp. 3–4;

Twenty-second Report … on … the Prisons of Ireland, 1844, H.C. 1844 (535), xxviii, pp. 7–8, 15;

Twenty-third Report … on … the Prisons of Ireland, 1844, H.C. 1845 (620), xxv, pp. 6, 39;

Twenty-fourth Report … on … the Prisons of Ireland, 1846, H.C. 1846 (697), xx, p. 62;

Twenty-sixth Report … on … the Prisons of Ireland, 1847–48, H.C. 1847–8 (952), xxiv, pp. 8, 11, 30;

Thirtieth Report … on … the Prisons of Ireland, 1852, H.C. 1852 (1531), xxv, pp. 16, 33;

Thirty-first Report … on … the Prisons of Ireland, 1853, H.C. 1853 (1657), liii, p. 46;

Forty-ninth Report … on … the Prisons of Ireland, 1870, H.C. 1871 (C. 359), xxx, p. 545.

Secondary sources:

McNeill, 'The Hospitallers at Kilmainham and Their Guests', p. 17; Nowlan, 'Kilmainham Gaol', pp. 105–15; McParland, 'Public Work of Architects', p. 139; Guinness, *Georgian Dublin*, pp. 61–2; Kelly, *History of Kilmainham Gaol*; Cooke, *History of Kilmainham Gaol*; O'Dwyer, 'Public Works Architecture', pp. 180, 191, 407; Johnston, *Forms of Constraint*, pp. 172–4; Carey, *Mountjoy*, p. 41; Niamh O'Sullivan, *Every Dark Hour: A history of Kilmainham jail* (Dublin: Liberties Press, 2007); Broderick, *Local Government in Nineteenth-century County Dublin*, pp. 20–2, 38–43; Rory O'Dwyer, *The Bastille of Ireland: Kilmainham gaol, from ruin to restoration* (Dublin: History Press, 2010); Loeber, et al., *Art and Architecture of*

Ireland: Volume IV: Architecture 1600–2000, p. 203; Dickson, *Dublin*, pp. 215, 254, 382; Cumming, 'Kilmainham Gaol', National Inventory of Architectural Heritage Building of the Month.

DUBLIN CITY – OLD NEWGATE

Dublin

Thomas St. & Francis St.
Lat. 53°20'35.82" N.; Long. 6°16'32.57" W.

Medieval Newgate to the west of the city; references to Newgate being used as a city prison *c.* 1660s; parliamentary report highlights abuses within prison 1729; Government committee recommends a new prison 1767; news reports that a new gaol is being planned 1771; Howard visits old Newgate and condemns it 1775, 1779; new Newgate built 1773–81; old Newgate abandoned, partially demolished, later used as a prison for prostitutes, then later again demolished entirely; not extant.

Medieval Newgate to the west of the city. References to Newgate being used as a city prison, *c.* 1660s. Parliamentary report highlights abuses within prison, 1729. Government committee recommends a new prison, 1767. News reports that a new gaol is being planned, 1771. Howard visits old Newgate and condemns it, 1775, 1779. New Newgate (see 'Dublin City – Newgate') built, 1773–81. Old Newgate abandoned, partially demolished, later used as a prison for prostitutes, then later again demolished entirely. Not extant.

Archival and primary sources:

Journal of the Irish House of Commons, vol. viii, 1767, part 1, App. clxx; *Freeman's Journal*, 29–31 January 1771; Howard, *State of the Prisons in England and Wales*, pp. 202–3.

Secondary sources:

Charles McNeill, 'New Gate, Dublin', *Journal of the Royal Society of Antiquaries of Ireland*, vol. 11, no. 2, 1921, pp. 152–65 (illus.); Bernadette Doorly, 'Newgate Prison', in Dickson, *Gorgeous Mask: Dublin, 1700–1850*, pp. 121–31, at pp. 121–2; Moylan, 'The Little Green: Part I', p. 89; Dickson, *Dublin*, p. 118.

DUBLIN CITY – NEWGATE

Dublin

Green St. & Halston St.
Lat. 53°20'57.95" N.; Long. 6°16'15.93" W.

Medieval Newgate to the west of the city; references to old Newgate being used as a city prison *c.* 1660s; parliamentary report highlights abuses within prison 1729; Government committee recommends a new prison 1767; news reports that a new gaol is being planned 1771; Howard visits old Newgate and condemns it 1775, 1779; new Newgate built (*Thomas Cooley*) 1773–81; [illegible] 1780; courthouse built nearby 1792–7; AIPPD competition to select a design for a new gaol (unexecuted) 1819; unexecuted proposal for a new gaol (*David Henry*) 1826; unexecuted plans for rebuilding gaol (*John Semple*) 1836–9; abandoned 1851; in use as a convict prison; abandoned finally 1863; fruit and vegetable market; demolished 1893; only the base of one of the corner towers survives; not extant.

Medieval Newgate to the west of the city. References to old Newgate being used as a city prison, *c.* 1660s. Parliamentary report highlights abuses within prison, 1729. Government committee recommends a new prison, 1767. News reports that a new gaol is being planned, 1771. Howard visits old Newgate and condemns it, 1775, 1779. New Newgate built (*Thomas*

Cooley), at a cost of at least £16,000, 1773–81. Howard visits and is very critical of new gaol, 1782, 1783, 1787. Quality of building criticised in parliament, 1785, 1787. Riot leading to forty escapes, with gaol threatened with destruction, 1790. Green Street courthouse built nearby (see Part I), 1792–7. Reinforced with canon during rebellion, 1798. Forster Archer, prison inspector, notes a recent addition of a house for the gaoler, and a new roof, 1803. Gaol severely criticised in government inquiry, 1809. Alterations to kitchens and hospital, *c.* 1810. Competition held by Association for the Improvement of Prisons and of Prison Discipline (AIPPD) for a new gaol, 1819. Prize given to a polygonal-plan design, 1819. Proposal unexecuted. Gaol criticised by Palmer and Woodward, 1823, 1825, 1826, etc. Unexecuted proposal for a new gaol with 412 cells in 23 classes, on a radial plan (*David Henry*), 1826. Following acquisition of Richmond Penitentiary, Newgate only used for untried prisoners and convicts awaiting transportation, 1836. Unexecuted plans for rebuilding gaol (*John Semple*), at a cost of at least £16,000, 1836–9. Palmer and Woodward give up hopes of a new gaol, 1841. Abandoned, 1851. Handed over to Government for use as a convict prison, 1851. Use ceases, 1863. A fruit and vegetable market thereafter. Demolished, 1893. Only the base of a corner tower survives. Not extant.

Archival and primary sources:

Journal of the Irish House of Commons, vol. viii, 1767, part 1, App. clxx; ibid., vol. ix, 1775, part 1, p. cxcvii; ibid., vol. x, 1782, part 2, App. dxxxiii–dxxxiv; ibid., vol. xi, 1785, part 1, App. cclxxxv; ibid., vol. xii, 1787, part 2, App. dxxv; *Freeman's Journal*, 29–31 January 1771; ibid., 1–3 June 1775; *Hibernian Magazine*, September 1773, p. 504; ibid., May 1774, p. 301; *Faulkner's Dublin Journal*, 18–21 September 1773; 17 & 18 Geo. III, c. 1 (1778); 19 & 20 Geo. III, c. 7 (1779); 26 Geo. III, c. 27, s. 24 (1786); Pool and Cash, *Views of the Most Remarkable Public Buildings … in the City of Dublin*, pp. 55–8; Howard, *State of the Prisons in England and Wales*, pp. 202–3, 206–8; Howard, *Lazarettos*, p. 79; Forster Archer, 'Report of the State of Gaols of Ireland for the Year 1802', f. 5 (Houses of the Oireachtas Library, Dublin, MS.7H28); Anon., *Journal of a Tour in Ireland … Performed in August 1804* (London: Phillips, 1806), p. 9; Carr, *Stranger in Ireland*, pp. 72–4; Forster Archer, 'Report of the State of Gaols of Ireland for the Year 1811' (Houses of the Oireachtas Library, Dublin, MS.4E63); Gregory, *Picture of Dublin*, p. 177; Warburton, Whitelaw and Walsh, *History of the City of Dublin*, vol. 2, p. 1047; George Warner to Charles Grant, 4 January 1819, printed in *Accounts Relating to Prisons in Dublin*, H.C. 1819 (195), xii, p. 1; Plan drawings of Newgate, n.d., printed in ibid.; James Palmer to Alexander Mangin, 19 June 1822 (NAI, CSORP 1822/1653); Report of subcommittee [appointed to visit Newgate] of the Association for the Improvement of Prisons and Prison Discipline in Ireland, 7 October 1822 (NAI, CSORP 1822/1533); *Fifth Report of the AIPPD*, pp. 19–20; Reid, *Travels in Ireland*, p. 151; General outline of a prison for Dublin city by David Henry, 21 March 1826 (printed in *Journal of the House of Commons*, vol. 81, 21 March 1826); *Analysis of the Grand Jury Presentments for the City of Dublin, from the Year 1822 to 1834 Inclusive* (Dublin: Graisberry, 1835, copy in Oireachtas Library); Report on Newgate gaol by John Semple, 10 November 1836 (NAI, SPO OP 1837/86); Survey drawings of Newgate, by John Semple, April 1837 (Dublin City Libraries, Wide Streets Commissioners maps, WSC-067); *Freeman's Journal*, 6 October 1838; ibid., 3 August 1839; ibid., 22 November 1839; ibid., 30 January 1840; *Journal of the House of Commons*, vol. 94, 30 July 1839, p. 494; ibid., vol. 94, 7 August 1839, p. 523; ibid., vol. 94, 12 August 1839, p. 528; ibid., vol. 94, 26 August 1839, p. 583; Newgate Gaol, Dublin Act, 1840 (3 & 4 Vict., c. 53); Newgate Gaol (Dublin) &c. Act, 1849 (12 & 13 Vict., c. 55); *Irish Examiner*, 3 September 1850; *The Builder*, vol. 8, no. 400, 5 October 1850, p. 473; *Dublin Builder*, vol. 1, no. 9, 1 September 1859, p. 114; Gilbert, *Calendar of the Ancient Records of Dublin*, vol. 13, p. 33.

Prison reports:

Inspector General's Report of … the Prisons in Ireland for … 1807, H.C. 1808 (239), ix, p. 7;

Report from the Commissioners Appointed To Inquire into … the State Prisons and Other Gaols in Ireland, H.C. 1809 (265), vii, pp. 4–8, 52, plan drawings;

Report from the Select Committee on the State of Gaols, H.C. 1819 (579), vii, p. 220;

Prisons of Ireland: Report of Inspectors General, 1823, H.C. 1823 (342), x, pp. 14, 19–20;

Prisons of Ireland: Report of Inspectors General, 1824, H.C. 1824 (294), xxii, pp. 19, 22–3;

Prisons of Ireland: Report of Inspectors General, 1825, H.C. 1825 (493), xxii, pp. 18–19;

Fourth Report … on … the Prisons of Ireland, 1826, H.C. 1826 (173), xxiii, p. 13;

Sixth Report … on … the Prisons of Ireland, 1828, H.C. 1828 (68), xii, pp. 21–3, 29–30;
Seventh Report … on … the Prisons of Ireland, 1829, H.C. 1829 (10), xiii, p. 26;
Eighth Report … on … the Prisons of Ireland, 1830, H.C. 1830 (48), xxiv, pp. 25–6;
Ninth Report … on … the Prisons of Ireland, 1831, H.C. 1830–1 (172), iv, p. 17;
Tenth Report … on … the Prisons of Ireland, 1832, H.C. 1831–2 (152), xvii, p. 16;
Eleventh Report … on … the Prisons of Ireland, 1833, H.C. 1833 (67), xvii, p. 16;
Twelfth Report … on … the Prisons of Ireland, 1834, H.C. 1834 (63), xl, p. 18;
Fourteenth Report … on … the Prisons of Ireland, 1836, H.C. 1836 (118), xxxv, pp. 11–12;
Fifteenth Report … on … the Prisons of Ireland, 1837, H.C. 1837 (123), xxxi, p. 16;
Seventeenth Report … on … the Prisons of Ireland, 1839, H.C. 1839 (91), xx, p. 16;
Eighteenth Report … on … the Prisons of Ireland, 1840, H.C. 1840 (240), xxvi, pp. 18–19;
Nineteenth Report … on … the Prisons of Ireland, 1841, H.C. 1841 (299), xi, pp. 17–18;
Twentieth Report … on … the Prisons of Ireland, 1842, H.C. 1842 (377), xxii, pp. 17–21, 37;
Twenty-first Report … on … the Prisons of Ireland, 1843, H.C. 1843 (462), xxvii, p. 15;
Twenty-second Report … on … the Prisons of Ireland, 1844, H.C. 1844 (535), xxviii, p. 17;
Twenty-third Report … on … the Prisons of Ireland, 1844, H.C. 1845 (620), xxv, p. 4;
Twenty-fifth Report … on … the Prisons of Ireland, 1847, H.C. 1847 (805), xxix, p. 19;
Twenty-sixth Report … on … the Prisons of Ireland, 1847–48, H.C. 1847–8 (952), xxiv, p. 32;
Twenty-eighth Report … on … the Prisons of Ireland, 1850, H.C. 1850 (1229), xxix, pp. 15, 20;
Twenty-ninth Report … on … the Prisons of Ireland, 1851, H.C. 1851 (1364), xxviii, p. 3.

Secondary sources:

Charles McNeill, 'New Gate, Dublin', *Journal of the Royal Society of Antiquaries of Ireland*, vol. 11, no. 2, 1921, pp. 152–65; Moylan, 'The Little Green: Part I', pp. 81–91; Moylan, 'Little Green: Part II', pp. 135–57; Craig, *Dublin*, pp. 197–9 and plate 33; McParland, 'Public Work of Architects', pp. 43–4; Bernadette Doorly, 'Newgate prison', in Dickson, *Gorgeous Mask: Dublin, 1700–1850*, pp. 121–31; Johnston, *Forms of Constraint*, p. 43; O'Dwyer, 'Public Works Architecture', pp. 178, 407; Carey, *Mountjoy*, p. 41; Colvin, *Biographical Dictionary of British Architects*, pp. 126–8; Dickson, *Dublin*, pp. 118, 215–16, 233, 254–5; Loeber, et al., *Art and Architecture of Ireland: Volume IV: Architecture 1600–2000*, pp. 202–3.

DUBLIN CITY – CITY MARSHALSEA and SHERIFF'S PRISON

Dublin

Green St. & Halston St.
Lat. 53°21'1.41" N.; Long. 6°16'14.92" W.

Government committee recommends a new Sheriff's Prison 1767; advert for tenders (unexecuted) for building a new City Marshalsea 1788; new Sheriff's Prison built adjacent to Newgate Gaol (*Sir John Traile*) 1789–94; new City Marshalsea built adjacent to Newgate and Sheriff's Prison (*Richard Johnston*) 1803–4; City Marshalsea condemned by Forster Archer 1818; unexecuted plans (*Arthur Neville*) for repairing both prisons 1842; Sheriff's Prison closed 1843; City Marshalsea closed *c.* 1845; both prisons bought by Government for use as stores for adjacent Newgate 1854; Sheriff's Prison converted into a police station 1869; ceased use as a Garda station 1946; derelict; extant.

Government committee recommends a new Sheriff's Prison, 1767. Newgate Gaol built, 1773–81. Howard visits City Marshalsea and condemns it, 1787. Advert for tenders (unexecuted) for building a new City Marshalsea, 1788. New

Sheriff's Prison built adjacent to Newgate Gaol (*Sir John Traile*), at a cost of £3,000, 1789–94. Designs requested for a new City Marshalsea, 1802. New City Marshalsea built adjacent to Newgate and Sheriff's Prison (*Richard Johnston*), 1803–4. New City Marshalsea said to be incomplete, 1807. Minor alterations, *c.* 1810. City Marshalsea condemned by Forster Archer, 1818. Palmer and Woodward claim City Marshalsea and Sheriff's Prison are 'the principal blot remaining within the extensive range of our inspection', 1830. Unexecuted plans (*Arthur Neville*) for repairing both prisons, 1842. Both prisons to close by act of parliament, 1842. Sheriff's Prison closed, 1843. City Marshalsea closed, *c.* 1845. Both prisons bought by Government for use as stores for adjacent Newgate, 1854. Sheriff's Prison converted into a police station, 1869. Ceased use as a Garda station, 1946. Derelict. Extant.

Archival and primary sources:

Howard, *State of the Prisons in England and Wales*, p. 205; Howard, *Lazarettos*, pp. 80–1; *Dublin Journal*, 10–12 June 1788; *Freeman's Journal*, 22–4 September 1789; ibid., 8 May 1802; ibid., 12 February 1803; Forster Archer, 'Report of the State of Gaols of Ireland for the Year 1811' (Houses of the Oireachtas Library, Dublin, MS.4E63); Reid, *Travels in Ireland*, pp. 151–2; *Analysis of the Grand Jury Presentments for the City of Dublin, from the Year 1822 to 1834 Inclusive* (Dublin: Graisberry, 1835, copy in Oireachtas Library); Lewis, *Topographical Dictionary*, vol. 1, p. 543; Four Courts Marshalsea (Ireland) Act, 1842 (5 & 6 Vict., c. 95); Gilbert, *Calendar of the Ancient Records of Dublin*, vol. 14, pp. 346–7; ibid., vol. 16, p. 411; ibid., vol. 17, p. 100; ibid., vol. 18, p. 150.

Prison reports:

Inspector General's Report of … the Prisons in Ireland for … 1807, H.C. 1808 (239), ix, p. 8;

Report from the Commissioners Appointed To Inquire into … the State Prisons and Other Gaols in Ireland, H.C. 1809 (265), vii, pp. 21–9;

Inspector General's Report of … the Prisons in Ireland for … 1818, H.C. 1819 (534), xii, pp. 9–10;

Report from the Select Committee on the State of Gaols, H.C. 1819 (579), vii, pp. 222–4;

Prisons of Ireland: Report of Inspectors General, 1823, H.C. 1823 (342), x, p. 23;

Prisons of Ireland: Report of Inspectors General, 1824, H.C. 1824 (294), xxii, pp. 19, 25;

Prisons of Ireland: Report of Inspectors General, 1825, H.C. 1825 (493), xxii, p. 22;

Fourth Report … on … the Prisons of Ireland, 1826, H.C. 1826 (173), xxiii, pp. 18–19;

Fifth Report … on … the Prisons of Ireland, 1827, H.C. 1826–7 (471), xi, p. 21;

Sixth Report … on … the Prisons of Ireland, 1828, H.C. 1828 (68), xii, pp. 31–2;

Seventh Report … on … the Prisons of Ireland, 1829, H.C. 1829 (10), xiii, p. 28;

Eighth Report … on … the Prisons of Ireland, 1830, H.C. 1830 (48), xxiv, p. 21;

Ninth Report … on … the Prisons of Ireland, 1831, H.C. 1830–1 (172), iv, pp. 18–19;

Eighteenth Report … on … the Prisons of Ireland, 1840, H.C. 1840 (240), xxvi, p. 23;

Twenty-first Report … on … the Prisons of Ireland, 1843, H.C. 1843 (462), xxvii, pp. 3, 20;

Twenty-second Report … on … the Prisons of Ireland, 1844, H.C. 1844 (535), xxviii, p. 27;

Twenty-third Report … on … the Prisons of Ireland, 1844, H.C. 1845 (620), xxv, pp. 8, 10.

Secondary sources:

Moylan, 'The Little Green: Part I', pp. 81–91; Moylan, 'The Little Green: Part II', pp. 135–57; Nowlan, 'Kilmainham Jail', p. 107; Casey, *Buildings of Ireland: Dublin*, p. 100.

DUBLIN CITY – RICHMOND BRIDEWELL

Dublin

South Circular Rd.
Lat. 53°19'52.04" N., Long. 6°16'43.19" W.

South Circular Road laid out 1763; old bridewell at James' Street condemned by Forster Archer 1807, 1809; new bridewell built on South Circular Road (*Francis Johnston*) 1813–19; additions 1821; Palmer and Woodward call for an additional 250 cells 1824; bridewell only to hold convicted males 1836; extensive additions, including a radial building to the east, planned on separate-system principles, and another large wing (in total more than 200 new cells) 1836–9; extensive alterations to further implement separate-system principles (*John Skipton Mulvany*) 1850–1; handed over to the army, renamed Wellington Barracks, later Griffith Barracks 1877; now Griffith College, partially demolished.

South Circular Road laid out, 1763. Old bridewell at James' Street condemned by Forster Archer, 1807, 1809. Dublin city grand-jury presentment for a new large bridewell, 1811. New bridewell built on South Circular Road (*Francis Johnston*), at a cost of at least £41,300, 1813–19. Additions, 1821. Design condemned by the Association for the Improvement of Prisons and of Prison Discipline, 1823. Palmer and Woodward call for an additional 250 cells, 1824. Bridewell only to hold convicted males, 1836. Extensive additions, including a radial building to the east, planned on separate-system principles, and another large wing (in total more than 200 new cells), at a cost of at least £10,600, 1836–9. Extensive alterations to further implement separate-system principles (*John Skipton Mulvany*), 1850–1. Handed over to the army, renamed Wellington Barracks, later Griffith Barracks, 1877. Now Griffith College. Partially demolished.

Archival and primary sources:

Accounts of All Sums Presented To Be Raised off the City of Dublin … from the Year 1807 … to … 1821, H.C. 1821 (477), xx, pp. 32, 71, 88, 94; Papers concerning Richmond bridewell, 1811–18 (NAI, SPO 570/494/23); *Freeman's Journal*, 29 January 1812; Anon., 'A Letter from Francis Johnston', p. 3; Drawings by Francis Johnston for Richmond bridewell, 1811–14 (Irish Architectural Archive, RIAI Murray Collection, Acc. 92/46.325–39); Cromwell, *Excursions through Ireland*, vol. 1, p. 156; Warburton, Whitelaw and Walsh, *History of the City of Dublin*, vol. 1, p. 583, vol. 2, p. 1062; *Third Report of the AIPPD*, p. 34; *Fifth Report of the AIPPD*, p. 23; *Analysis of the Grand Jury Presentments for the City of Dublin, from the Year 1822 to 1834 Inclusive* (Dublin: Graisberry, 1835, copy in Oireachtas Library); Richmond Penitentiary, &c. Act (Ireland), 1836 (6 & 7 Will. IV, c. 51); James Grant, *Impressions of Ireland and the Irish*, 2 vols (London: Cunningham, 1844), vol. 1, pp. 66–7; *The Builder*, vol. 8, no. 391, 3 August 1850, p. 368; General Prisons (Ireland) Act, 1877 (40 & 41 Vict., c. 49).

Prison reports:

Inspector General's Report of … the Prisons in Ireland for … 1807, H.C. 1808 (239), ix, p. 7;

Report from the Commissioners Appointed To Inquire into … the State Prisons and Other Gaols in Ireland, H.C. 1809 (265), vii, p. 26;

Inspector General's Report of … the Prisons in Ireland for … 1818, H.C. 1819 (534), xii, p. 9;

Prisons of Ireland: Report of Inspectors General, 1823, H.C. 1823 (342), x, p. 21;

Prisons of Ireland: Report of Inspectors General, 1824, H.C. 1824 (294), xxii, pp. 18–19, 24;

Prisons of Ireland: Report of Inspectors General, 1825, H.C. 1825 (493), xxii, pp. 20–1;

Fourth Report … on … the Prisons of Ireland, 1826, H.C. 1826 (173), xxiii, p. 18;

Fifth Report … on … the Prisons of Ireland, 1827, H.C. 1826–7 (471), xi, p. 20;

Sixth Report … on … the Prisons of Ireland, 1828, H.C. 1828 (68), xii, p. 31;

Seventh Report … on … the Prisons of Ireland, 1829, H.C. 1829 (10), xiii, p. 27;

Ninth Report … on … the Prisons of Ireland, 1831, H.C. 1830–1 (172), iv, p. 17;

Twelfth Report … on … the Prisons of Ireland, 1834, H.C. 1834 (63), xl, pp. 18–19;
Thirteenth Report … on … the Prisons of Ireland, 1835, H.C. 1835 (114), xxxvi, pp. 11–12;
Fifteenth Report … on … the Prisons of Ireland, 1837, H.C. 1837 (123), xxxi, pp. 16–17;
Sixteenth Report … on … the Prisons of Ireland, 1838, H.C. 1837–8 (186), xxix, p. 19;
Seventeenth Report … on … the Prisons of Ireland, 1839, H.C. 1839 (91), xx, pp. 18–19;
Eighteenth Report … on … the Prisons of Ireland, 1840, H.C. 1840 (240), xxvi, pp. 7, 21–2;
Nineteenth Report … on … the Prisons of Ireland, 1841, H.C. 1841 (299), xi, pp. 18–19;
Twentieth Report … on … the Prisons of Ireland, 1842, H.C. 1842 (377), xxii, p. 22;
Twenty-second Report … on … the Prisons of Ireland, 1844, H.C. 1844 (535), xxviii, p. 17;
Twenty-sixth Report … on … the Prisons of Ireland, 1847–48, H.C. 1847–8 (952), xxiv, pp. 8, 11;
Twenty-seventh Report … on … the Prisons of Ireland, 1849, H.C. 1849 (1069), xxvi, pp. 27–8;
Twenty-eighth Report … on … the Prisons of Ireland, 1850, H.C. 1850 (1229), xxix, p. 21;
Twenty-ninth Report … on … the Prisons of Ireland, 1851, H.C. 1851 (1364), xxviii, p. 3;
Forty-ninth Report … on … the Prisons of Ireland, 1870, H.C. 1871 (C. 359), xxx, p. 558.

Secondary sources:

John Betjeman, 'Francis Johnston', in Evans, *The Pavilion*, pp. 24–5; Henchy, 'Francis Johnston', pp. 7, 13; McParland, 'Francis Johnston', pp. 126, 130; P.D. O'Donnell, 'Dublin Military Barracks', *Dublin Historical Record*, vol. 25, no. 5, September 1972, pp. 152–3; McParland, 'Public Work of Architects', p. 250; Goslin, 'Descriptive Catalogue of the Murray Collection', pp. 128–31; O'Dwyer, 'Public Works Architecture', p. 407; Carey, *Mountjoy*, p. 41; Casey, *Buildings of Ireland: Dublin*, pp. 645–6; Dickson, *Dublin*, pp. 44, 58, 117–18, 120, 226, 238, 275–6; Loeber, et al., *Art and Architecture of Ireland: Volume IV: Architecture 1600–2000*, p. 203.

FERMANAGH

Enniskillen, no. 1

East Bridge St.
Lat. 54°20'37.96" N.; Long. 7°38'10.23" W.

Reported that there was no county gaol in Fermanagh 1610; unexecuted plans for a courthouse and gaol in Lisgoole *c.* 1610; Captain Cole, on obtaining a grant for lands around Enniskillen, is obliged to build a gaol there, 1613; a later combined courthouse and gaol probably built *c.* 1785; county gaol situated in the cellars under the courthouse; sundry works *c.* 1787; noted as 'very old' 1797; strongly criticised by Forster Archer 1803; grand-jury presentment for a new gaol 1811; a new gaol built elsewhere in the town 1812–15; in use as a courthouse; redundant 1973; refurbished 1982; listed 1977; future as a courthouse uncertain 2015.

Reported that there was no county gaol in Fermanagh, 1610. Unexecuted plans for a courthouse and gaol in Lisgoole, *c.* 1610. Captain Cole, on obtaining a grant for lands around Enniskillen, is obliged to build a gaol there, 1613. A later combined courthouse and gaol probably built *c.* 1785; county gaol situated in the cellars under the courthouse. Sundry works, *c.* 1787. Noted as 'very old', 1797. Strongly criticised by Forster Archer, prison inspector, 1803. Grand-jury presentment for a new gaol, 1811. A new gaol built elsewhere in the town (see 'Fermanagh: Enniskillen, no. 2'), 1812–15. In use as a courthouse (see Part I). Redundant, 1973. Refurbished, at a cost of £1 million, 1982. Listed, 1977. Future as a courthouse uncertain, 2015.

Archival and primary sources:

Howard, *Lazarettos*, pp. 95–6; *Journal of the Irish House of Commons*, vol. xvii, 1797, p. ccvi; Forster Archer, 'Report of the

State of Gaols of Ireland for the Year 1802', f. 6 (Houses of the Oireachtas Library, Dublin, MS.7H28); Forster Archer, 'Report of the State of Gaols of Ireland for the Year 1811' (Houses of the Oireachtas Library, Dublin, MS.4E63); *Pigot & Co's Provincial Directory of Ireland, 1824*, p. 448; Day and McWilliams, *Ordnance Survey Memoirs of Ireland: Volume 4: Fermanagh*, p. 54; Gorton and Wright, *Topographical Dictionary*, vol. 1, no. 739; Lewis, *Topographical Dictionary*, vol. 1, p. 606.

Secondary sources:

Copeland Trimble, *History of Enniskillen*, vol. 3, pp. 868–91; Dixon, *List of Historic Buildings … in the Town of Enniskillen*, p. 22; Brett, *Court Houses*, pp. 78–80, 107; McParland, 'Public Work of Architects', p. 244; Rowan, *Buildings of Ireland: North west Ulster*, p. 281; McCusker, 'The County Gaol and Some Past Crimes and Punishments in County Fermanagh', pp. 50–5; O'Donoghue, *Irish County Surveyors*, p. 195; Northern Ireland Environmental Agency (NIEA), Listed Buildings Database (www.doeni.gov.uk).

FERMANAGH

Enniskillen, no. 2

Dublin Rd. (Gaol St.)
Lat. 54°20'37.71" N.; Long. 7°37'52.92" W.

Reported that there was no county gaol in Fermanagh 1610; unexecuted plans for a courthouse and gaol in Lisgoole *c.* 1610; Captain Cole, on obtaining a grant for lands around Enniskillen, is obliged to build a gaol there, 1613; a combined courthouse and gaol probably built *c.* 1785; county gaol situated in the cellars under the courthouse; noted as 'very old' 1797; strongly criticised by Forster Archer 1803; grand jury plan for a new gaol 1807; grand-jury presentment 1811; a new gaol built elsewhere in the town (*Richard Morrison*) 1812–15; uncertainty over necessity of an addition 1827–38; large addition to the rear of the gaol, comprising separate-system cells (*William Farrell*) 1843–5; closed as a gaol; Morrison wings demolished *c.* 1902; Farrell wings used as part of a new technical school built 1902–11; new buildings erected on site of Morrison part of gaol, 1969; Farrell wings are still intact; partially extant.

Reported that there was no county gaol in Fermanagh, 1610. Unexecuted plans for a courthouse and gaol in Lisgoole, *c.* 1610. Captain Cole, on obtaining a grant for lands around Enniskillen, is obliged to build a gaol there, 1613. A later combined courthouse and gaol probably built *c.* 1785; county gaol situated in the cellars under the courthouse. Noted as 'very old', 1797. Strongly criticised by Forster Archer, prison inspector, 1803. Forster Archer recommends a new gaol on a new site, 1807. Grand jury plan for a new gaol, 1807. Grand-jury presentment for a new gaol, 1811. A new gaol built elsewhere in the town (*Richard Morrison*), at a cost of at least £14,846, 1812–15. Renovations and sundry works at old gaol (county courthouse) (*William Farrell*) (see Part I), 1821–2. James Palmer calls for twenty more cells, 1827. Benjamin Woodward states that no addition is necessary, 1828. Palmer calls for additional cells, 1831. Palmer confident that low crime rates in the county mean that the gaol is sufficient for the time being, 1835. On an increase in crime, the prison inspectors call for an addition, 1836. Woodward calls for 80 additional cells, on the separate system, 1838. Large addition to the rear of the gaol, comprising separate-system cells (*William Farrell*), at a cost of £8,000, 1843–5. Minor alterations, *c.* 1852–3. Closed as a gaol. Morrison wings demolished, *c.* 1902. Farrell wings used as part of a new technical school, built 1902–11. New buildings erected on site of Morrison part of gaol, 1969. Farrell wings are still intact. Partially extant.

Archival and primary sources:

Howard, *Lazarettos*, pp. 95–6; *Journal of the Irish House of Commons*, vol. xvii, 1797, p. ccvi; Forster Archer, 'Report of the State of Gaols of Ireland for the Year 1802', f. 6 (Houses of the Oireachtas Library, Dublin, MS.7H28); *Accounts of the Presentments Passed by the Grand Juries of Ireland … in … 1807*, H.C. 1808 (205), xiii, p. 172; Forster Archer, 'Report of the State of Gaols of Ireland for the Year 1811' (Houses of the Oireachtas Library, Dublin, MS.4E63); An account of the several presentments made … on which advances have been made by government for gaols, n.d. (NAI, SPO OP 1832–8, 1A/77/4);

Correspondence relating to the building of Enniskillen gaol, 1812 (NAI, SPO 552/382/14–15); Richard Morrison to William Vesey Fitzgerald, 6 February 1814 (NLI, Vesey Fitzgerald papers, MS 7823, pp. 267–8); Letter by Richard Morrison, 22 January 1816 (NAI, SPO 564/468/5); Reid, *Travels in Ireland*, p. 323; *Pigot & Co's Provincial Directory of Ireland, 1824*, p. 448; Glassford, *Notes of Three Tours in Ireland*, p. 88; Day and McWilliams, *Ordnance Survey Memoirs of Ireland: Volume 4: Fermanagh*, p. 54; Gorton and Wright, *Topographical Dictionary*, vol. 1, p. 739; Lewis, *Topographical Dictionary*, vol. 1, p. 606; Contract drawings and letters for Enniskillen gaol, by William Farrell, 1841–2 (PRONI, FER/4/6/8–20, 44–50); *Irish Builder*, vol. 43, no. 1009, 16 January 1902, p. 999; ibid., vol. 51, no. 4, 20 February 1909, p. 114; ibid., vol. 53, no. 23, 11 November 1911, p. 758.

Prison reports:

Inspector General's Report of … the Prisons in Ireland for … 1807, H.C. 1808 (239), ix, p. 9;

Account of All Gaols … in the … United Kingdom, H.C. 1819 (137), xvii, pp. 8–9;

Inspector General's Report of … the Prisons in Ireland for … 1818, H.C. 1819 (534), xii, p. 11;

Prisons of Ireland: Report of Inspectors General, 1823, H.C. 1823 (342), x, pp. 6, 31;

Prisons of Ireland: Report of Inspectors General, 1824, H.C. 1824 (294), xxii, pp. 6, 32;

Prisons of Ireland: Report of Inspectors General, 1825, H.C. 1825 (493), xxii, p. 29;

Fourth Report … on … the Prisons of Ireland, 1826, H.C. 1826 (173), xxiii, p. 28;

Fifth Report … on … the Prisons of Ireland, 1827, H.C. 1826–7 (471), xi, pp. 30–1;

Sixth Report … on … the Prisons of Ireland, 1828, H.C. 1828 (68), xii, pp. 40–2;

Seventh Report … on … the Prisons of Ireland, 1829, H.C. 1829 (10), xiii, pp. 36–7;

Eighth Report … on … the Prisons of Ireland, 1830, H.C. 1830 (48), xxiv, pp. 11, 35–6;

Ninth Report … on … the Prisons of Ireland, 1831, H.C. 1830–1 (172), iv, pp. 25–6;

Tenth Report … on … the Prisons of Ireland, 1832, H.C. 1831–2 (152), xvii, p. 25;

Eleventh Report … on … the Prisons of Ireland, 1833, H.C. 1833 (67), xvii, p. 38;

Thirteenth Report … on … the Prisons of Ireland, 1835, H.C. 1835 (114), xxxvi, p. 26;

Fourteenth Report … on … the Prisons of Ireland, 1836, H.C. 1836 (118), xxxv, p. 24;

Fifteenth Report … on … the Prisons of Ireland, 1837, H.C. 1837 (123), xxxi, p. 23;

Sixteenth Report … on … the Prisons of Ireland, 1838, H.C. 1837–8 (186), xxix, pp. 27–8;

Eighteenth Report … on … the Prisons of Ireland, 1840, H.C. 1840 (240), xxvi, p. 31;

Nineteenth Report … on … the Prisons of Ireland, 1841, H.C. 1841 (299), xi, p. 31;

Twentieth Report … on … the Prisons of Ireland, 1842, H.C. 1842 (377), xxii, pp. 6, 70–1;

Twenty-first Report … on … the Prisons of Ireland, 1843, H.C. 1843 (462), xxvii, pp. 6, 36–7;

Twenty-second Report … on … the Prisons of Ireland, 1844, H.C. 1844 (535), xxviii, pp. 7, 39–40;

Twenty-third Report … on … the Prisons of Ireland, 1844, H.C. 1845 (620), xxv, p. 20;

Twenty-fourth Report … on … the Prisons of Ireland, 1846, H.C. 1846 (697), xx, p. 30;

Twenty-fifth Report … on … the Prisons of Ireland, 1847, H.C. 1847 (805), xxix, p. 45;

Twenty-sixth Report … on … the Prisons of Ireland, 1847–48, H.C. 1847–8 (952), xxiv, p. 58;

Thirty-first Report … on … the Prisons of Ireland, 1853, H.C. 1853 (1657), liii, p. 16;

Forty-ninth Report … on … the Prisons of Ireland, 1870, H.C. 1871 (C. 359), xxx, p. 146.

Secondary sources:

Copeland Trimble, *History of Enniskillen*, vol. 3, pp. 868–91; Dixon, *List of Historic Buildings … in the Town of Enniskillen*, [illegible] Brett, *Court Houses*, pp. [illegible]; McParland, 'Public Works of Architecture', p. 244; Rowan, *Buildings of Ireland: North west Ulster*, p. 284; McCusker, 'The County Gaol and Some Past Crimes and Punishments in County Fermanagh', pp. 50–5; Rowan, *Architecture of Richard Morrison*, pp. 89–90; O'Dwyer, 'Public Works Architecture', pp. 181, 407; Johnston, *Forms of Constraint*, p. 173; O'Donoghue, *Irish County Surveyors*, p. 195; Northern Ireland Environmental Agency (NIEA), Listed Buildings Database (www.doeni.gov.uk).

GALWAY COUNTY

Galway, no. 1

Quay St.
Lat. 53°16'14.80" N.; Long. 9°3'16.28" W.

First county gaol built in Loughrea 1585; described as 'old and ruinous' 1671; decision to move county gaol to Galway town, 1671; town gaol used for county prisoners 1671–86; town grand jury refuses the use of their gaol 1686; Blakes' Castle acquired for use as a county gaol 1686; first presentment for a new gaol *c.* 1791; new gaol built elsewhere 1804–10; old gaol thereafter derelict; later used as part of a distillery; shown as disused *c.* 1900; later incorporated into a hotel *c.* 1990; extant.

First county gaol built in Loughrea, 1585. Described as 'old and ruinous', 1671. Decision to move county gaol to Galway town, 1671. Town gaol used for county prisoners, 1671–86. Town grand jury refuses the use of their gaol, 1686. Blakes' Castle acquired from a Mr Morgan of Monksfield for use as a county gaol, 1686. Critical article in the press about the state of the gaol, 1786. Visited by Howard, and condemned, 1788. First presentment for a new gaol, *c.* 1791. New gaol built elsewhere (see 'Galway County: Galway, no. 2'), 1804–10. Old gaol thereafter derelict. Later used as part of a distillery. Shown as disused, *c.* 1900. Later incorporated into a hotel, *c.* 1990. Extant.

Archival and primary sources:

Howard, *Lazarettos*, p. 93; *Dublin Evening Post*, 19 July 1786; *Journal of the Irish House of Commons*, vol. xvii, 1797, p. ccvi; ibid., vol. xix, 1800, p. dccxc; Galway county grand-jury payments book, 1794–6, 1799 (NLI, MS 19,803); Hardiman, *History of the Town and County of the Town of Galway*, p. 313; Dutton, *Statistical … Survey … of Galway*, p. 205; J. Rabbitte, 'Galway Corporation MS. C', *Journal of the Galway Archaeological and Historical Society*, vol. 12, 1924, p. 82; Pencil sketch of Blakes' Castle, Galway, n.d. (NLI, TX 1995).

Secondary sources:

Mitchell, 'Prisons of Galway', pp. 1, 2, 5, 6, 12, 18, 19.

GALWAY COUNTY

Galway, no. 2

Gaol Rd.
Lat. 53°16'29.92" N.; Long. 9°3'26.68" W.

First county gaol built in Loughrea 1585; described as 'old and ruinous' 1671; decision to move county gaol to Galway town, 1671; town gaol used for county prisoners 1671–86; town grand jury refuses the use of their gaol 1686; Blakes' Castle acquired for use as a county gaol 1686; first presentment for a new gaol *c.* 1791; disagreements over proposed site *c.* 1801–2; new gaol built (*Thomas Hardwick* and *Richard Morrison*) 1804–10; new courthouse and bridge built nearby 1812–15, 1818–19; alterations 1853; further alterations (*Samuel Ussher Roberts*) *c.* 1859–60; gaols merged *c.* 1866; closed 1939; demolished *c.* 1950; Catholic cathedral built on the site 1957–65; not extant.

First county gaol built in Loughrea, 1585. Described as 'old and ruinous', 1671. Decision to move county gaol to Galway town, 1671. Town gaol used for county prisoners, 1671–86. Town grand jury refuses the use of their gaol, 1686. Blakes' Castle acquired from a Mr Morgan of Monksfield for use as a county gaol, 1686. Critical article in the press about the state of the gaol, 1786. Visited by Howard, and condemned, 1788. First presentment for a new gaol, *c.* 1791. Forster Archer recommends that the unfinished and derelict county hospital building should be used as a new gaol, 1801. Grand jury commissioners decide against Archer's proposal and agree on an island site, 1802. Act of parliament for a new county gaol, 1802. New gaol built (*Thomas Hardwick* and *Richard Morrison*; contractor *John Behan*), 1804–10. Town grand jury decides to build a new gaol adjacent to the new county gaol (see 'Town of Galway'), 1806. Second act of parliament for new gaols, 1807. Old county gaol abandoned, 1811. New county courthouse built (see Part I), 1812–15. Bridge connecting gaol and courthouse built, 1818–19. Minor alterations, 1818. Inspectors call for 30–40 separate-system cells, 1842. Unexecuted plan to merge county and town gaols, 1843. Alterations to female ward to partially introduce separate-system confinement, 1853. Further alterations to gaol to permit separate-system confinement (*Samuel Ussher Roberts*), *c.* 1859–60. Alterations to tread-wheels, 1864. County and town gaols merged; alterations to permit this (*Samuel Ussher Roberts*), *c.* 1866. Gaol closed, 1939. Site handed over to the Catholic Church, 1941. Gaol demolished, *c.* 1950. Catholic cathedral built on the site, 1957–65. Not extant.

Archival and primary sources:

Howard, *Lazarettos*, p. 93; *Dublin Evening Post*, 19 July 1786; *Journal of the Irish House of Commons*, vol. xvii, 1797, p. ccvi; ibid., vol. xix, 1800, p. dccxc; Galway county grand-jury payments book, 1794–6, 1799 (NLI, MS 19803); 'Forster Archer's Tour of Ireland in 1801' (British Library, Add. MS 35920); Forster Archer, 'Report of the State of Gaols of Ireland for the Year 1802', f. 6 (Houses of the Oireachtas Library, Dublin, MS.7H28); Report of the State of Gaols of Ireland for the Year 1811 by the Inspector General of prisons (ibid., MS.4E63); *Journal of the House of Commons*, vol. 57, 3 February 1802, p. 82, passim; ibid., vol. 62, 1 July 1807, p. 606; Galway County Gaol Act (Local Act), 1802 (42 Geo. III, c. xviii); Galway County Gaol and Sessions House Act, 1807 (47 Geo. III, sess. 2, c. cxii); Royal Academy exhibits, 1802 (no. 895); Daniel Augustus Beaufort diary, 1806–8, for 1808, p. 88 (Trinity College Library, Dublin); Brian Bolger papers (NAI, Brian Bolger papers: 1A/58/128); *Accounts of the Presentments Passed by the Grand Juries of Ireland … in … 1807*, H.C. 1808 (205), xiii, p. 175; Hardiman, *History of the Town and County of the Town of Galway*, pp. 308–14 (illus.); Dutton, *Statistical … Survey … of Galway*, pp. 203–5, 382; Reid, *Travels in Ireland*, p. 305; *Freeman's Journal*, 31 March 1823; J. Rabitte, 'Galway Corporation MS. C', *Journal of the Galway Archaeological and Historical Society*, vol. 12, 1924, p. 82; Marguirite Hayes-McCoy, 'The Eyre Documents', ibid., vol. 20, 1943, p. 154; *Pigot and Co's Directory of Ireland* (1824), p. 205; Pencil sketch of Blakes' Castle, Galway, n.d. (NLI, TX 1995); Lewis, *Topographical Dictionary*, vol. 1, no. 648; Anon., *The Sportsman in Ireland, with His Summer Route through the Highlands of Scotland, by a Cosmopolite*, 2 vols (London: Colburn, 1840), vol. 2, pp. 24–6; Osborne, *Gleanings in the West of Ireland*, p. 51; *The Builder*, vol. 17, no. 867, 17 September 1859, p. 615; *Dublin Builder*, vol. 4, no. 55, 1 April 1862, p. 73; Correspondence and drawings relating to work at Galway county gaol, mostly by Samuel Ussher Roberts, county surveyor, 1858–66 (Galway County Archives, GS-11-02); Galway County Council minutes, 1 November 1916 (Galway County Archives, GC-1-2, p. 763); Galway prison closing order, 1 May 1939 (NAI, Statutory Instrument no. 87/1939); Correspondence relating to the handover of Galway gaol to the Department of Justice and then to the Galway Diocesan Trustees, 1940 (Galway County Archives, 109/38/72); *The Connacht Tribune*, 6 May 1939; ibid., 31 May 1941; *City Tribune* (Galway), 6 September 1996; Photographs of old county gaol and new Catholic cathedral, *c.* 1963 (Galway County Library, Donal Taheny collection).

Prison reports:

Inspector General's Report of … the Prisons in Ireland for … 1807, H.C. 1808 (239), ix, p. 9;

Account of All Gaols … in the … United Kingdom, H.C. 1819 (137), xvii, pp. 8–9;

Inspector General's Report of … the Prisons in Ireland for … 1818, H.C. 1819 (534), xii, p. 12;

Prisons of Ireland: Report of Inspectors General, 1823, H.C. 1823 (342), x, pp. 6, 48;

Prisons of Ireland: Report of Inspectors General, 1824, H.C. 1824 (294), xxii, pp. 7, 48;

Prisons of Ireland: Report of Inspectors General, 1825, H.C. 1825 (493), xxii, pp. 45–6;

Fourth Report … on … the Prisons of Ireland, 1826, H.C. 1826 (173), xxiii, p. 43;
Fifth Report … on … the Prisons of Ireland, 1827, H.C. 1826–7 (471), xi, p. 48;
Sixth Report … on … the Prisons of Ireland, 1828, H.C. 1828 (68), xii, p. 56;
Seventh Report … on … the Prisons of Ireland, 1829, H.C. 1829 (10), xiii, p. 52;
Eighth Report … on … the Prisons of Ireland, 1830, H.C. 1830 (48), xxiv, pp. 51–2;
Fifteenth Report … on … the Prisons of Ireland, 1837, H.C. 1837 (123), xxxi, pp. 35–6;
Sixteenth Report … on … the Prisons of Ireland, 1838, H.C. 1837–8 (186), xxix, pp. 40–1;
Eighteenth Report … on … the Prisons of Ireland, 1840, H.C. 1840 (240), xxvi, p. 46;
Twentieth Report … on … the Prisons of Ireland, 1842, H.C. 1842 (377), xxii, p. 100;
Twenty-first Report … on … the Prisons of Ireland, 1843, H.C. 1843 (462), xxvii, p. 63;
Twenty-ninth Report … on … the Prisons of Ireland, 1851, H.C. 1851 (1364), xxviii, pp. 14, 69;
Thirty-second Report … on … the Prisons of Ireland, 1854, H.C. 1854 (1803), xxxii, pp. 20, 147;
Thirty-third Report … on … the Prisons of Ireland, 1855, H.C. 1854–5 (1956), xxvi, p. 139;
Thirty-fourth Report … on … the Prisons of Ireland, 1856, H.C. 1856 (2113), xxxiv, p. 202;
Forty-eighth Report … on … the Prisons of Ireland, 1869, H.C. 1870 (C. 173), xxxvii, p. 324.

Secondary sources:

S.J. Maguire, 'Galway Jail', *The Galway Reader* (published by Galway County Libraries), vol. 3, no. 3, 1951, pp. 47–51; Anon., 'From Jail to Cathedral', *The Mantle* (Galway), vol. 1, 1958, pp. 30–2; McParland, 'Public Work of Architects', p. 250; Mitchell, 'The Tholsel at Galway', pp. 77–8, 83; May, 'County Courthouse at Galway by Richard Morrison', pp. 27, 145–7; Mitchell, 'Prisons of Galway', pp. 1–21; O'Dwyer, 'Public Works Architecture', pp. 176, 407; Geraldine Curtin, *The Women of Galway Jail: Female criminality in nineteenth-century Ireland* (Galway: Arlen House, 2001), pp. 37, 40, 76, 90, 101–4 (illus.); Johnston, *Forms of Constraint*, p. 174; Geraldine Curtin, 'Female Prisoners in Galway Gaol in the Late Nineteenth Century', *Journal of the Galway Archaeological and Historical Society*, vol. 54, 2002, pp. 175–82; Loeber, et al., *Art and Architecture of Ireland: Volume IV: Architecture 1600–2000*, pp. 203, 463.

TOWN OF GALWAY

Galway, no. 1

An early tholsel built with a gaol beneath *c.* 1580; a new tholsel planned 1639; foundations laid 1641; left unfinished; finally complete *c.* 1707–9; old tholsel used as a town gaol 1709–1810; also used as a county gaol 1671–86; new town gaol built 1807–10; old tholsel demolished *c.* 1810; not extant.

An early tholsel built with a gaol beneath, *c.* 1580. A new tholsel planned (see Part I), 1639. Foundation of new tholsel laid, 1641. Left unfinished. Still incomplete, 1685. Finally completed, *c.* 1707–9. Old tholsel used as a town gaol, 1709–1810. Old tholsel also used as a county gaol, 1671–86. Escape of all prisoners, 1741. Forster Archer suggests old county gaol (see 'Galway County: Galway, no. 1') could serve as a new town gaol, 1796, 1801. Unexecuted proposal to demolish old tholsel and gaol, 1802. New town gaol built elsewhere (see 'Town of Galway: Galway, no. 2'), 1807–10. Old tholsel demolished *c.* 1810. Not extant.

Archival and primary sources:

Thomas Phillips, 'Ground-plaine of Galway', 1685 (NLI, MS 3137 (28)); *Pue's Occurrences* (Dublin), 31 October–3 November 1741; Howard, *Lazarettos*, p. 93; *Journal of the Irish House of Commons*, vol. xvii, 1797, p. ccvi; ibid., vol. xix, 1800, p. dccxc; 'Forster Archer's Tour of Ireland in 1801' (British Library, Add. MS 35920); Forster Archer, 'Report of the State of Gaols of

Ireland for the Year 1811' (Houses of the Oireachtas Library, Dublin, MS.4E63); Galway County Gaol and Sessions House Act, 1807 (47 Geo. III, sess. 2, c. cxii); Galway Corporation minute book, K (1802), ff. 309–10, 351–3 (NUI Galway); *Inspector General's Report of … the Prisons in Ireland for … 1807*, H.C. 1808 (239), ix, p. 9; Daniel Augustus Beaufort diary, 1806–8, for 1808, p. 88 (Trinity College Library, Dublin); Hardiman, *Galway*, pp. 308–12; Dutton, *Statistical … Survey … of Galway*, pp. 212, 321, 382; Blake, 'An Account of the Lynch Family', p. 91; Rabbitte, 'Galway Corporation MS. C', p. 82.

Secondary sources:

Blake, 'Account of the Lynch Family', p. 91; Kennedy, 'County of the Town of Galway', pp. 90–101; Mitchell, 'Tholsel', pp. 77–85 (illus.); Mitchell, 'Tholsel at Galway', pp. 77–8, 83; Mitchell, 'Prisons of Galway', pp. 1–21.

TOWN OF GALWAY

Galway, no. 2

Gaol Rd.
Lat. 53°16'27.43" N.; Long. 9°3'25.60" W.

An early tholsel and gaol built *c.* 1580; a new tholsel planned 1639; foundations laid 1641; left unfinished; finally complete *c.* 1707–9; old tholsel used as a town gaol 1709–1810; also used as a county gaol 1671–86; unexecuted new gaol at Bohermore 1806; act of parliament 1807; new town gaol built (unknown architect, possibly *Richard Morrison* or *John Behan*) 1807–10; minor alterations *c.* 1820–1; large radial-plan additions (effectively a new gaol) (*Frederick Darley*) 1832–6; town and county gaols merged (*Samuel Ussher Roberts*) 1866; in use as a female prison 1884; closed 1939; demolished *c.* 1950; Catholic cathedral built on the site 1957–65; not extant.

An early tholsel and gaol built, *c.* 1580. A new tholsel planned (see Part I), 1639. Foundation of new tholsel laid, 1641. Left unfinished. Still incomplete, 1685. Finally completed, *c.* 1707–9. Old tholsel used as a town gaol, 1709–1810. Old tholsel also used as a county gaol, 1671–86. Escape of all prisoners, 1741. Forster Archer suggests old county gaol (see 'Galway County: Galway, no. 1') could serve as a new town gaol, 1796, 1801. Unexecuted proposal to demolish old tholsel and gaol, 1802. Act of parliament to permit new county gaol (see 'Galway County: Galway, no. 2'), 1802. Unexecuted plan to build a new town gaol at Bohermore, 1806. Town grand jury change proposed site and combine with county grand jury to petition for a second act of parliament, 1807. New town gaol built adjacent to new county gaol (unknown architect, possibly *Richard Morrison* or *John Behan*), 1807–10. Forster Archer recommends many alterations, and notes that six prisoners recently escaped, 1818. Minor alterations, *c.* 1820–1. New town court house (see Part I), 1822–5. Inspectors call for large additions or an entirely new gaol, 1826–9. Large radial-plan addition, effectively a new gaol, built alongside town gaol (*Frederick Darley*), 1832–6. Town and county gaols merged, with many alterations (*Samuel Ussher Roberts*), 1866. Old town gaol in use as a female prison, 1884. Closed, 1939. Site handed over to the Catholic Church, 1941. Gaol demolished, *c.* 1950. Catholic cathedral built on the site, 1957–65. Not extant.

Archival and primary sources:

Thomas Phillips, 'Ground-plaine of Galway', 1685 (NLI, MS. 3137 (28)); *Pue's Occurrences* (Dublin), 31 October–3 November 1741; Howard, *Lazarettos*, p. 93; *Journal of the Irish House of Commons*, vol. xvii, 1797, p. ccvi; ibid., vol. xix, 1800, p. dccxc; 'Forster Archer's Tour of Ireland in 1801' (British Library, Add. MS 35920); Forster Archer, 'Report of the State of Gaols of Ireland for the Year 1811' (Houses of the Oireachtas Library, Dublin, MS.4E63); *Journal of the House of Commons*, vol. 62, 1 July 1807, p. 606; Galway County Gaol Act (Local Act), 1802 (42 Geo. III, c. xviii); Galway County Gaol and Sessions House Act, 1807 (47 Geo. III, sess. 2, c. cxii); Galway Corporation minute book, K (1802), ff. 309–10, 351–3 (NUI Galway); Daniel Augustus Beaufort diary, 1806–8, for 1808, p. 88 (Trinity College Library, Dublin); Brian Bolger papers (NAI, Brian Bolger papers: 1A/58/128); Hardiman, *Galway*, pp. 308–12; Sketch drawing of Galway town gaol, *c.* 1812–30, by James Hardiman (Galway County Archives, GS-01-02); Plan drawing of Galway town gaol as built in 1807–10, n.d., n.s. (Irish Architectural Archive, Henry Mullins & McMahon collection, Acc. 2005/095); Dutton, *Statistical*

… *Survey … of Galway*, pp. 111, 311, 381; Reid, *Travels in Ireland*, pp. 306–7; *Third Report of the AIFFD*, p. 38; Blake, 'An Account of the Lynch Family', p. 91; Rabbitte, 'Galway Corporation MS. C', p. 82; Lewis, *Topographical Dictionary*, vol. 1, no. 648; Plan drawing for a large addition to Galway town gaol, by Frederick Darley, March 1830 (Galway County Archives, GS-11-02-01); Drawings relating to the merger of Galway county and town gaols, by Samuel Ussher Roberts, May 1866 (ibid., GS-11-02-6 and GS-11-02-7); Galway County Council minutes, 1 November 1916 (ibid., GC-1-2, p. 763); Galway prison closing order, 1 May 1939 (NAI, Statutory Instrument no. 87/1939); Correspondence relating to the handover of Galway gaol to the Department of Justice and then to the Galway Diocesan Trustees, 1940 (Galway County Archives, 109/38/72); *The Connacht Tribune*, 6 May 1939; ibid., 31 May 1941; *City Tribune* (Galway), 6 September 1996; Photographs of old town gaol and new Catholic cathedral, *c.* 1963 (Galway County Library, Donal Taheny collection).

Prison reports:

Inspector General's Report of … the Prisons in Ireland for … 1807, H.C. 1808 (239), ix, p. 9;

Account of All Gaols … in the … United Kingdom, H.C. 1819 (137), xvii, pp. 8–9;

Inspector General's Report of … the Prisons in Ireland for … 1818, H.C. 1819 (534), xii, pp. 12–13;

Report from the Select Committee on the State of Gaols, H.C. 1819 (579), vii, pp. 210–11;

Prisons of Ireland: Report of Inspectors General, 1823, H.C. 1823 (342), x, p. 50;

Fourth Report … on … the Prisons of Ireland, 1826, H.C. 1826 (173), xxiii, p. 45;

Fifth Report … on … the Prisons of Ireland, 1827, H.C. 1826–7 (471), xi, p. 50;

Sixth Report … on … the Prisons of Ireland, 1828, H.C. 1828 (68), xii, p. 57;

Seventh Report … on … the Prisons of Ireland, 1829, H.C. 1829 (10), xiii, p. 53;

Eighth Report … on … the Prisons of Ireland, 1830, H.C. 1830 (48), xxiv, pp. 53–4;

Tenth Report … on … the Prisons of Ireland, 1832, H.C. 1831–2 (152), xvii, p. 40;

Eleventh Report … on … the Prisons of Ireland, 1833, H.C. 1833 (67), xvii, p. 23;

Twelfth Report … on … the Prisons of Ireland, 1834, H.C. 1834 (63), xl, p. 26;

Thirteenth Report … on … the Prisons of Ireland, 1835, H.C. 1835 (114), xxxvi, p. 38;

Fourteenth Report … on … the Prisons of Ireland, 1836, H.C. 1836 (118), xxxv, pp. 35–6;

Fifteenth Report … on … the Prisons of Ireland, 1837, H.C. 1837 (123), xxxi, pp. 36–7;

Sixteenth Report … on … the Prisons of Ireland, 1838, H.C. 1837–8 (186), xxix, p. 42;

Seventeenth Report … on … the Prisons of Ireland, 1839, H.C. 1839 (91), xx, p. 44;

Twentieth Report … on … the Prisons of Ireland, 1842, H.C. 1842 (377), xxii, pp. 100–1;

Twenty-first Report … on … the Prisons of Ireland, 1843, H.C. 1843 (462), xxvii, p. 63;

Twenty-second Report … on … the Prisons of Ireland, 1844, H.C. 1844 (535), xxviii, p. 78;

Thirty-third Report … on … the Prisons of Ireland, 1855, H.C. 1854–5 (1956), xxvi, p. 144.

Secondary sources:

Blake, 'Account of the Lynch Family', p. 91; Maguire, 'Galway Jail', p. 18; Kennedy, 'County of the Town of Galway', p. 96; Mitchell, 'Tholsel', pp. 77–85 (illus.); Mitchell, 'Tholsel at Galway', pp. 77–8, 83; May, 'County Courthouse at Galway by Richard Morrison', pp. 27, 145–7; Mitchell, 'Prisons of Galway', pp. 1–11; Curtin, *Women of Galway Jail*, pp. 37, 40, 76, 90, 101–4 (illus.); Curtin, 'Female Prisoners in Galway Gaol in the Late Nineteenth Century', pp. 175–82; Loeber, et al., *Art and Architecture of Ireland: Volume IV: Architecture 1600–2000*, p. 463; Dickson, *Dublin*, pp. 271, 301.

KERRY

Tralee, no. 1

Market Square
Lat. 52°16'10.42" N.; Long. 9°42'22.83" W.

Unknown date of construction; shown on 1756 map; escape of prisoners 1767, 1784; a replacement gaol built *c.* 1788; abandoned; not extant.

Earliest known gaol was on Market Square. Shown on the north-west side of Market Square, beside the Big River in Charles Smith's map of Tralee, as a combined courthouse, gaol and market-house, 1756. Escape of eight prisoners, 1767. Escape of a large number of Rightboys, 1784. Another gaol built on Nelson Street (see 'Kerry: Tralee, no. 2'), *c.* 1788. Old gaol thereafter abandoned. Not extant.

Archival and primary sources:

Charles Smith, 'A Plan [Map] of Tralee', 1756 (Kerry County Library); *Belfast Newsletter*, 27 October 1767; *Hibernian Journal*, 10 May 1784; Lyne, 'Rev. Daniel A.B. Beaufort's Tour of Kerry in 1788', pp. 201, 203; Howard, *Lazarettos*, p. 91; *Journal of the Irish House of Commons*, vol. xvii, 1797, p. ccvi; A.B. Rowan, n.t., *The Kerry Magazine*, vol. 3, no. 25, January 1856, p. 13; Mrs Morgan John O'Connell, *The Last Colonel of the Irish Brigade: Count O'Connell and old Irish life at home and abroad, 1745–1833*, 2 vols (London: Paul, 1892), vol. 1, p. 310.

Secondary sources:

O'Carroll, 'Penal Reform and Gaol Construction: A case study of Tralee', pp. 7–9.

KERRY

Tralee, no. 2

Ashe (Nelson) St.
Lat. 52°16'11.42" N.; Long. 9°42'12.73" W.

An earlier gaol on Market Square, shown on 1756 map; escape of prisoners 1767, 1784; a replacement gaol built on Nelson St. *c.* 1788; described as 'new' 1797; Forster Archer recommends a new gaol 1807; new gaol built elsewhere 1812–17; old gaol thereafter demolished; a new county courthouse built on the site 1830–3; not extant.

An earlier gaol on Market Square, shown on 1756 map. Escape of eight prisoners, 1767. Escape of a large number of Rightboys, 1784. A new gaol built on Nelson Street, *c.* 1788. Noted as under construction by Howard and by Daniel Beaufort, 1788. Described as 'new', 1797. Forster Archer recommends that a new gaol be built elsewhere, 1807. A new gaol built elsewhere (see 'Kerry: Tralee, no. 3'), 1812–17. Old gaol thereafter demolished. A new courthouse planned on the site of this old gaol, 1827. Courthouse built on site (see Part I), 1830–3. Not extant.

Archival and primary sources:

Charles Smith, 'A Plan [Map] of Tralee', 1756 (Kerry County Library); *Belfast Newsletter*, 27 October 1767; *Hibernian Journal*, 10 May 1784; Lyne, 'Rev. Daniel A.B. Beaufort's Tour of Kerry in 1788', pp. 201, 203; Howard, *Lazarettos*, p. 91; *Journal of the Irish House of Commons*, vol. xvii, 1797, p. ccvi; 'Forster Archer's Tour of Ireland in 1801' (British Library, Add. MS 35920); *Inspector General's Report of … the Prisons in Ireland for … 1807*, H.C. 1808 (239), ix, p. 10; *Tralee Mercury*, 10 March 1832; A.B. Rowan, n.t., *The Kerry Magazine*, vol. 3, no. 25, January 1856, p. 13; O'Connell, *The Last Colonel of the Irish Brigade*, vol. 1, p. 310.

Secondary sources:

Pádraig de Brún, 'Rev. Forster Archer's Account of Kerry in 1801', *Journal of the Kerry Archaeological and Historical Society*, vol. 14, 1981, pp. 26–30, at p. 29; O'Carroll, 'Penal Reform and Gaol Construction: A case study of Tralee', pp. 7–9.

KERRY

Tralee, no. 3

Ballymullen Rd.
Lat. 52°15'49.79" N.; Long. 9°41'40.47" W.

An earlier gaol on Nelson St., built *c.* 1788; described as 'new' 1797; Forster Archer recommends a new gaol 1807; critical comments from assize judge 1811; site selected 1811; new gaol built (*Richard Morrison*) 1812–17; large extensions and alterations (*James and George Richard Pain;* contractor *Thomas Deane*) 1828–31; additions 1844–5; new kitchen 1852; new boundary wall, gateway and lodge 1854; extensive separate-system alterations (*John McCurdy*) 1873; closed; mostly demolished; partly extant.

An earlier gaol on Nelson Street built, *c.* 1788. Described as 'new', 1797. Forster Archer recommends that a new gaol be built elsewhere, 1807. Grand jury select site for new gaol, 1811. Local inspector criticises proposed site and design of new gaol, 1811. Assize judge very critical of old gaol, 1811. A new gaol built (*Richard Morrison*), 1812–17. Palmer and Woodward complain that this gaol is too small, 1823–6. New courthouse built in Tralee (see Part I), 1827–34. Large extensions and alterations, including a new female prison, kitchen, chapel, etc. (*James and George Richard Pain*; contractor *Thomas Deane*), 1828–31. Inspectors call for additional cells, on separate-system principles, 1840–4. Additions to female prison, 1844–5. New kitchen, 1852. A new boundary wall, gateway, and lodge, 1854. Extensive alterations to introduce separate-system confinement throughout (*John McCurdy*), 1873. Closed. Mostly demolished. Gate house survives, as well as part of boundary wall.

Archival and primary sources:

'Forster Archer's Tour of Ireland in 1801' (British Library, Add. MS 35920); *Limerick General Advertiser*, 23 April 1811; Forster Archer, 'Report of the State of Gaols of Ireland for the Year 1811' (Houses of the Oireachtas Library, Dublin, MS.4E63); Charge of Judge Robert Day to the Kerry grand jury, March 1812 (Royal Irish Academy, Dublin, Day papers, MS12w12); Correspondence involving the building of Tralee gaol, 1812 (NAI, SPO 552/382/14); *Limerick Evening Post*, 28 March 1812; Richard Morrison to William Vesey Fitzgerald, 6 February 1814 (NLI, Vesey Fitzgerald papers, MS 7823, pp. 267–8); An account of the several presentments made … on which advances have been made by government for gaols, n.d. (NAI, SPO OP 1832–8, 1A/77/4); *Faulkner's Dublin Journal*, 30 August 1817; Reid, *Travels in Ireland*, pp. 286–9; *Third Report of the AIPPD*, p. 38; *Southern Reporter*, 30 June, 14 July 1827; ibid., 26 March 1835; Statement by Thomas Deane, 31 August 1829 (NAI, SPO 588 AAB 944); William Murray to R. Robinson, 11 October 1827 (NAI, CSORP 1827/1722); *Western Herald*, 1 November 1830; *Tralee Mercury*, 10 March 1832; Return of sums advanced by the Treasury to the Kerry grand jury, 17 November 1832 (NAI, CSORP 1832/6100); A.B. Rowan, n.t., *The Kerry Magazine*, vol. 3, no. 25, January 1856, p. 13; Ground plan drawing for Tralee gaol by McCurdy and Mitchell, 17 June 1873 (NAI, OPW 5HC/4/422); Second-floor plan drawing for Tralee gaol by McCurdy and Mitchell, n.d. (but likely also 17 June 1873) (Tralee County Council offices, copy in Irish Architectural Archive); Ballymullen estate map, 1877 (Kerry County Library); postcard showing entrance to the gaol, n.d. (Kerry County Library).

Prison reports:

Inspector General's Report of … the Prisons in Ireland for … 1807, H.C. 1808 (239), ix, p. 10;

Account of All Gaols … in the … United Kingdom, H.C. 1819 (137), xvii, pp. 8–9;

Inspector General's Report of … the Prisons in Ireland for … 1818, H.C. 1819 (534), xii, pp. 13–14;

Report from the Select Committee on the State of Gaols, H.C. 1819 (579), vii, pp. 175, 213;
Prisons of Ireland: Report of Inspectors General, 1823, H.C. 1823 (342), x, pp. 50–1;
Prisons of Ireland: Report of Inspectors General, 1824, H.C. 1824 (294), xxii, pp. 7, 50–1;
Prisons of Ireland: Report of Inspectors General, 1825, H.C. 1825 (493), xxii, p. 48;
Fourth Report … on … the Prisons of Ireland, 1826, H.C. 1826 (173), xxiii, p. 45;
Fifth Report … on … the Prisons of Ireland, 1827, H.C. 1826–7 (471), xi, p. 50;
Seventh Report … on … the Prisons of Ireland, 1829, H.C. 1829 (10), xiii, pp. 53–4;
Eighth Report … on … the Prisons of Ireland, 1830, H.C. 1830 (48), xxiv, p. 54;
Ninth Report … on … the Prisons of Ireland, 1831, H.C. 1830–1 (172), iv, p. 40;
Tenth Report … on … the Prisons of Ireland, 1832, H.C. 1831–2 (152), xvii, p. 40;
Seventeenth Report … on … the Prisons of Ireland, 1839, H.C. 1839 (91), xx, pp. 44–5;
Eighteenth Report … on … the Prisons of Ireland, 1840, H.C. 1840 (240), xxvi, pp. 48–9;
Nineteenth Report … on … the Prisons of Ireland, 1841, H.C. 1841 (299), xi, p. 49;
Twentieth Report … on … the Prisons of Ireland, 1842, H.C. 1842 (377), xxii, p. 6;
Twenty-second Report … on … the Prisons of Ireland, 1844, H.C. 1844 (535), xxviii, pp. 7, 79;
Twenty-third Report … on … the Prisons of Ireland, 1844, H.C. 1845 (620), xxv, p. 56;
Twenty-ninth Report … on … the Prisons of Ireland, 1851, H.C. 1851 (1364), xxviii, p. 75;
Thirtieth Report … on … the Prisons of Ireland, 1852, H.C. 1852 (1531), xxv, p. 16;
Thirty-second Report … on … the Prisons of Ireland, 1854, H.C. 1854 (1803), xxxii, pp. 20, 153;
Forty-eighth Report … on … the Prisons of Ireland, 1869, H.C. 1870 (C. 173), xxxvii, p. 344.

Secondary sources:

de Brún, 'Rev. Forster Archer's Account of Kerry in 1801', p. 29; Rowan, *Architecture of Richard Morrison*, p. 170; O'Carroll, 'Penal Reform and Gaol Construction: A case study of Tralee', pp. 7–11; O'Dwyer, 'Public Works Architecture', pp. 192, 407; Johnston, *Forms of Constraint*, p. 173.

KILDARE

Athy, no. 1

Leinster St. & Cromaboo Bridge
Lat. 52°59'32.16" N.; Long. 6°59'4.28" W.

Medieval castle; condemned by prison inspectors in 1818, 1823, 1824; condemned by the AIPPD 1821; alterations and additions 1820–1; a new gaol built 1826–30; extant.

Medieval castle, used as one of the two Kildare county gaols from early times. Condemned by prison inspectors, 1818, 1823, 1824. Condemned by the AIPPD, 1821. Alterations and additions, including to roof and to privies (*Richard Robinson*), 1820–1. Escape of four prisoners from the old gaol, 1827. A new gaol built (see 'Kildare: Athy, no. 2'), 1826–30. Extant.

Archival and primary sources:

Journal of the Irish House of Commons, vol. xvii, 1797, p. ccvi; Carr, *Stranger in Ireland*, p. 272; Robertson, *Traveller's Guide through Ireland*, p. 266; Kildare grand-jury presentment books, 1820–1 (Kildare County Library, GJ); *Third Report of the AIPPD*, p. 39.

Prison reports:

Inspector General's Report of … the Prisons in Ireland for … 1807, H.C. 1808 (239), ix, p. 10;

Account of All Gaols … in the … United Kingdom, H.C. 1819 (137), xvii, pp. 10–11;

Inspector General's Report of … the Prisons in Ireland for … 1818, H.C. 1819 (534), xii, p. 14;

Prisons of Ireland: Report of Inspectors General, 1823, H.C. 1823 (342), x, pp. 6, 32;

Prisons of Ireland. Report of Inspectors General, 1824, H.C. 1824 (294), xxii, p. 33.

Secondary sources:

Tierney, *The Buildings of Ireland: Central Leinster*, pp. 98–9.

KILDARE

Athy, no. 2

Carlow Rd. (Offaly St.)
Lat. 52°59'21.42" N.; Long. 6°58'48.69" W.

Medieval castle served as the old gaol; this condemned by prison inspectors in 1818, 1823, 1824; a new gaol built (*John Hargrave*) 1826–30; chapel enlarged and two cells added *c.* 1855–6; closed 1860; mostly demolished; partially extant.

A medieval castle, used as one of the two Kildare county gaols, from early times. This condemned by prison inspectors, 1818, 1823, 1824. Site for a new gaol donated by the Duke of Leinster, 1824. A new polygonal-plan gaol built (*John Hargrave*), at a cost of £5,400, 1826–30. Escape of four prisoners from the old gaol, 1827. Inspectors suggest that Athy gaol might be used for holding females only, unexecuted, 1838. Inspectors suggest altering gaol to comply with separate-system requirements, unexecuted, 1841. Chapel enlarged, and two cells added, *c.* 1855–6. Closed, 1860. Mostly demolished. Governor's house and a portion of the polygonal range survive.

Archival and primary sources:

Journal of the Irish House of Commons, vol. xvii, 1797, p. ccvi; Carr, *Stranger in Ireland*, p. 272; Robertson, *Traveller's Guide through Ireland*, p. 266; Kildare grand-jury presentment book, summer 1824 (Kildare County Library, GJ); Report by Francis Johnston on Athy gaol, 9 February 1825 (NAI, CSORP 1825/11,066); J.M. Bagot to William Gregory, 5 March 1825 (ibid.); John Hamilton to William Gregory, 16 August 1825 (ibid., 1825/12,00); *Freeman's Journal*, 27 November 1827; Lewis, *Topographical Dictionary*, vol. 1, nos. 90–1; *Leinster Express*, 31 January 1857.

Prison reports:

Inspector General's Report of … the Prisons in Ireland for … 1807, H.C. 1808 (239), ix, p. 10;

Account of All Gaols … in the … United Kingdom, H.C. 1819 (137), xvii, pp. 10–11;

Inspector General's Report of … the Prisons in Ireland for … 1818, H.C. 1819 (534), xii, p. 14;

Prisons of Ireland: Report of Inspectors General, 1823, H.C. 1823 (342), x, pp. 6, 32;

Prisons of Ireland: Report of Inspectors General, 1824, H.C. 1824 (294), xxii, p. 33;

Prisons of Ireland: Report of Inspectors General, 1825, H.C. 1825 (493), xxii, p. 32;

Fourth Report … on … the Prisons of Ireland, 1826, H.C. 1826 (173), xxiii, pp. 29–30;

Fifth Report … on … the Prisons of Ireland, 1827, H.C. 1826–7 (471), xi, p. 32;

Sixth Report … on … the Prisons of Ireland, 1828, H.C. 1828 (68), xii, p. 43;

Seventh Report ... on ... the Prisons of Ireland, 1829, H.C. 1829 (10), xiii, p. 38;
Eighth Report ... on ... the Prisons of Ireland, 1830, H.C. 1830 (48), xxiv, p. 36;
Ninth Report ... on ... the Prisons of Ireland, 1831, H.C. 1830–1 (172), iv, p. 26;
Sixteenth Report ... on ... the Prisons of Ireland, 1838, H.C. 1837–8 (186), xxix, pp. 28–9;
Seventeenth Report ... on ... the Prisons of Ireland, 1839, H.C. 1839 (91), xx, p. 28;
Eighteenth Report ... on ... the Prisons of Ireland, 1840, H.C. 1840 (240), xxvi, p. 32;
Nineteenth Report ... on ... the Prisons of Ireland, 1841, H.C. 1841 (299), xi, p. 33;
Thirty-fourth Report ... on ... the Prisons of Ireland, 1856, H.C. 1856 (2113), xxxiv, pp. 21, 221;
Thirty-seventh Report ... on ... the Prisons of Ireland, 1859, H.C. 1859 (2557), xiii, p. 257;
Thirty-eighth Report ... on ... the Prisons of Ireland, 1860, H.C. 1860 (2691), xxxvi, pp. 268–9.

Secondary sources:

Tierney, *The Buildings of Ireland: Central Leinster*, pp. 96–7.

KILDARE

Naas, no. 1

North Main St.

Location of ancient gaol unknown; eighteenth-century gaol located on North Main St., shown on map 1787; noted as insecure or defective or both *c.* 1747, 1782, 1783; a new gaol built elsewhere 1787–92; demolished; not extant.

Naas made a garrison and assize town in the twelfth century. Escape of prisoners from an ancient gaol noted, 1562. By the eighteenth century, gaol was a small building located 'near the North Main Street/Sallins Road junction'. This gaol shown on Thomas Sherrard map of Naas, 1787. Gaol noted as not secure, *c.* 1747. Attempted escape, 1759. Described as 'an inconsiderable house', 1782. Described as insecure and unsatisfactory, 1783. Old White's Castle demolished elsewhere in the town, offering a site for a new gaol, 1786. New gaol built (see 'Kildare: Naas, no. 2'), 1787–92. Ancient gaol thereafter demolished. Not extant.

Archival and primary sources:

James Freney, *The Life and Adventures of James Freney: Commonly called Captain Freney ... written by himself* (Dublin: S. Powell, 1754), pp. 50–1; *Sleator's Public Gazeteer*, 22 May 1759; Price, *Eighteenth-century Antiquary*, p. 28; Thomas Sherrard's map of Naas, 1787 (see secondary sources); 'Report from the Committee Appointed To Inquire into the Present State, Situation and Management of the Public Prisons, Jails and Bridewell of this Kingdom', *Journal of the Irish House of Commons*, vol. xi, 1783–5, app. cxxi, appendix & index, 1797.

Secondary sources:

Costello, 'Naas and the Country in General', pp. 423, 432–4; Costello, 'Thomas Sherrard's Map of Naas: 1787', pp. 589–97; Hickey and Kenny, *Nás na Ríogh from Poorhouse Road to the Fairy Flax*, pp. 7, 74–5; Anon., 'Notes on Naas Gaol', pp. 333–5.

KILDARE

Naas, no. 2

South Main St.
Lat. 53°13'5.43" N.; Long. 6°39'49.98" W.

Old White's Castle demolished elsewhere in the town, offering a site for a new gaol 1786; new gaol built 1787–92; visited by Howard and condemned, though not yet finished 1787; Inspectors call for a new gaol 1823 onwards; new gaol built elsewhere 1828–33; in use as a depot for the Kildare Militia arms 1838; sold to the Naas Town Commissioners and converted into a town hall 1857–61; façade rebuilt (*John Eacret*) 1904; Extant.

Old White's Castle demolished elsewhere in the town, offering a site for a new gaol, 1786. New gaol built, 1787–92. Visited by Howard and condemned, though not yet finished, 1787. Inspectors call for a new gaol, 1823 onwards. New gaol built elsewhere (see 'Kildare: Naas, no. 3'), 1828–33. In use as a 'a depot for the arms of the County of Kildare Militia', 1838. Sold to the Naas Town Commissioners and converted into a town hall, 1857–61. Façade rebuilt (*John Eacret*), 1904. Extant.

Archival and primary sources:

Freney, *The Life and Adventures of James Freney*, pp. 50–1; *Sleator's Public Gazeteer*, 22 May 1759; Thomas Sherrard's map of Naas, 1787 (see secondary sources); 'Report from the Committee Appointed To Inquire into the Present State, Situation and Management of the Public Prisons, Jails and Bridewell of this Kingdom', *Journal of the Irish House of Commons*, vol. xi, 1783–5, app. cxxi, appendix & index, 1797; Howard, *Lazarettos*, p. 86; *Journal of the Irish House of Commons*, vol. xvii, 1797, p. ccvi; *First Report of the AIPPD*, p. 19; Map of old gaol of Naas, by John Longford, 1824 (NLI, MS 21 F 35, no. 44); Lewis, *Topographical Dictionary*, vol. 2, p. 418; Kildare grand-jury presentment books, summer 1838, and spring 1858 (Kildare County Library, GJ); *Dublin Builder*, vol. 3, no. 39, 1 August 1861, p. 591.

Prison reports:

Inspector General's Report of … the Prisons in Ireland for … 1807, H.C. 1808 (239), ix, p. 10;

Account of All Gaols … in the … United Kingdom, H.C. 1819 (137), xvii, pp. 10–11;

Inspector General's Report of … the Prisons in Ireland for … 1818, H.C. 1819 (534), xii, p. 14;

Prisons of Ireland: Report of Inspectors General, 1823, H.C. 1823 (342), x, pp. 6, 31–2;

Prisons of Ireland: Report of Inspectors General, 1824, H.C. 1824 (294), xxii, pp. 5, 32–3;

Prisons of Ireland: Report of Inspectors General, 1825, H.C. 1825 (493), xxii, p. 32;

For later years, see 'Kildare: Naas, no. 3'.

Secondary sources:

Costello, 'Naas and the Country in General', pp. 423, 432–4; Costello, 'Thomas Sherrard's Map of Naas: 1787', pp. 589–97; Hickey and Kenny, *Nás na Ríogh from Poorhouse Road to the Fairy Flax*, pp. 7, 74–5 (illus.); Anon., 'Notes on Naas Gaol', pp. 333–5; Patrick and Maura Shaffrey, *Buildings of Irish Towns: Treasures of everyday architecture* (Dublin: O'Brien Press, 1983), p. 79 (illus.); Mick Mulvey, *From Castle Keep to Council Chamber: The story of Naas town hall* (Naas: Naas Printing Ltd., 2013); Tierney, *The Buildings of Ireland: Central Leinster*, pp. 509–10.

KILDARE

Naas, no. 3

Limerick Rd.
Lat. 53°13'1.42" N.; Long. 6°40'8.93" W.

Former gaol built 1787–92; visited by Howard and condemned, though not yet finished 1787; Inspectors call for a new gaol 1823 onwards; new gaol built (*John Hargrave*) 1828–33; eighteen separate-system cells built 1841–2; unexecuted plan by the governor for further separate-system alterations 1848–9; extensive alterations including a new wing (*John McCurdy*) 1857–60; minor alterations 1866; closed 1890s; used for social housing 1940s–50s; acquired by Naas Urban Council for social housing 1951; gaol demolished 1951–66; housing estate built on site 1966–7; not extant.

Former gaol built, 1787–92. Visited by Howard and condemned, though not yet finished, 1787. New courthouse in Naas (see Part I), *c.* 1807. Inspectors call for a new gaol, 1823 onwards. Grand jury appoints committee to decide on future of gaol, 1824. Grand jury approves plans for a new polygonal-plan gaol, 1825. A revised radial-plan gaol submitted, 1827. New radial-plan gaol built (*John Hargrave*), at a cost of £14,000, 1828–33. Inspectors suggest separate-system confinement could be partially introduced, 1841. Eighteen cells converted for separate-system use, with heating and ventilation, 1841–2. Unexecuted plan by the governor of the gaol for a separate-system addition of twenty-two cells, 1848–9. Extensive alterations including a new separate-system wing (*John McCurdy*), 1857–60. Athy gaol closed, 1860. Minor alterations, 1866. Closed, 1890s. Unsuccessful sale of buildings, 1893, 1924. Used for social housing, 1940s–50s. Naas Urban Council acquire site and demolish all gaol buildings, 1951–66. Housing estate built on site, 1966–7. Not extant.

Archival and primary sources:

Accounts of the Presentments Passed by the Grand Juries of Ireland … in … 1807, H.C. 1808 (205), xiii, p. 176; Lewis, *Topographical Dictionary*, vol. 2, p. 418; Kildare grand-jury summer presentments, 14 July 1825 (NAI, SPO 588 AAB 944); Kildare grand-jury presentment books, 1824–5, and spring 1858 (Kildare County Library, GJ); A map of a piece of ground proposed as a site for a new gaol at Naas, by John Longfield, 1825 (NLI, MS 21 F 35, no. 44); R. Robinson to Henry Goulburn, 23 August 1825 (NAI, CSORP 1825/12,000); William Murray to R. Robinson, 2 August 1827 (NAI, CSORP 1827/572); *The Builder*, vol. 14, no. 709, 6 September 1856, p. 490; ibid., vol. 15, no. 754, 18 July 1857, p. 409; *Civil Engineer and Architect's Journal*, vol. 19, no. 271, October 1856, p. 358; *Dublin Builder*, vol. 3, no. 39, 1 August 1861, p. 591; Lacy, *Sights and Scenes in Our Fatherland*, p. 187; *Irish Builder*, vol. 8, no. 163, 1 October 1866, p. 242; ibid., vol. 24, no. 551, 15 December 1882, p. 358; *Leinster Leader*, 6 January 1951; photos of Naas gaol during demolition, n.d. (Naas Local History Group).

Prison reports:

Prisons of Ireland: Report of Inspectors General, 1823, H.C. 1823 (342), x, pp. 6, 31–2;

Prisons of Ireland: Report of Inspectors General, 1824, H.C. 1824 (294), xxii, pp. 5, 32–3;

Prisons of Ireland: Report of Inspectors General, 1825, H.C. 1825 (493), xxii, p. 32;

Fourth Report … on … the Prisons of Ireland, 1826, H.C. 1826 (173), xxiii, p. 29;

Fifth Report … on … the Prisons of Ireland, 1827, H.C. 1826–7 (471), xi, pp. 7, 31;

Sixth Report … on … the Prisons of Ireland, 1828, H.C. 1828 (68), xii, pp. 7, 42;

Seventh Report … on … the Prisons of Ireland, 1829, H.C. 1829 (10), xiii, pp. 9, 37–8;

Eighth Report … on … the Prisons of Ireland, 1830, H.C. 1830 (48), xxiv, p. 36;

Ninth Report … on … the Prisons of Ireland, 1831, H.C. 1830–1 (172), iv, p. 26;

Tenth Report … on … the Prisons of Ireland, 1832, H.C. 1831–2 (152), xvii, p. 26;

Eleventh Report … on … the Prisons of Ireland, 1833, H.C. 1833 (67), xvii, p. 39;

Twelfth Report … on … the Prisons of Ireland, 1834, H.C. 1834 (63), xl, pp. 43–4;

Sixteenth Report … on … the Prisons of Ireland, 1838, H.C. 1837–8 (186), xxix, p. 28;

Seventeenth Report … on … the Prisons of Ireland, 1839, H.C. 1839 (91), xx, p. 28;

Eighteenth Report … on … the Prisons of Ireland, 1840, H.C. 1840 (240), xxvi, p. 32;

Nineteenth Report … on … the Prisons of Ireland, 1841, H.C. 1841 (299), xi, p. 32;

Twentieth Report … on … the Prisons of Ireland, 1842, H.C. 1842 (377), xxii, p. 71;

Twenty-second Report … on … the Prisons of Ireland, 1844, H.C. 1844 (535), xxviii, p. 7;

Twenty-sixth Report … on … the Prisons of Ireland, 1847–48, H.C. 1847–8 (952), xxiv, p. 93;

Twenty-seventh Report … on … the Prisons of Ireland, 1849, H.C. 1849 (1069), xxvi, p. 86;

Thirty-seventh Report … on … the Prisons of Ireland, 1859, H.C. 1859 (2557), xiii, pp. 257–8;

Thirty-eighth Report … on … the Prisons of Ireland, 1860, H.C. 1860 (2691), xxxvi, pp. 266–9; *Forty-eighth Report … on … the Prisons of Ireland, 1869*, H.C. 1870 (C. 173), xxxvii, p. 361.

Secondary sources:

Costello, 'Naas and the Country in General', pp. 423, 432–4, Hickey and Kenny, *Nás na Rìogh from Poorhouse Road to the Fairy Flax*, pp. 7, 74–5 (illus.); Anon., 'Notes on Naas Gaol', pp. 333–5; O'Dwyer, 'Public Works Architecture', pp. 191, 407; Con Costello, 'St. Patrick's Day in Naas Jail', *Leinster Leader*, 16 March 1985; Johnston, *Forms of Constraint*, p. 173; James Durney, *In the Shadow of Kings: Social housing in Naas, 1898–1984* (Naas: Naas Printing Ltd., 2007), pp. 78, 93–5; Tierney, *The Buildings of Ireland: Central Leinster*, pp. 509–10.

KILKENNY COUNTY

Kilkenny, no. 1

Parliament St.
Lat. 52°39'15.17" N.; Long. 7°15'13.93" W.

Site of a former castle; in use as a gaol perhaps as early as 1568; county gaol shown on map 1758; courthouse built on site *c.* 1790–5; replacement county gaol built elsewhere 1801–9; extant.

Assizes were formerly held, perhaps, at Black Abbey. Site of a former castle, known as Grace's Castle. Gaol located on the site perhaps as early as 1568. County gaol shown on map, 1758. Escapes, 1770, 1772. Courthouse built on site, with gaol below, *c.* 1790–5. Replacement county gaol built (see 'Kilkenny County: Kilkenny, no. 2'), 1801–9. For later history, see Part I. Extant.

Archival and primary sources:

G. Evans, Memorial of Deed. No. 116066 (NAI, Registry of Deeds); 'A Survey of the City of Kilkenny', 1758, by John Rocque (NLI); *Finn's Leinster Journal*, 12 September 1770 and 18 February 1772; Tighe, *Statistical Observations Relative to the County of Kilkenny*, p. 42; Forster Archer, 'Report of the State of Gaols of Ireland for the Year 1802', f. 8 (Houses of the Oireachtas Library, Dublin, MS.7H28); Reid, *Travels*, p. 243; Brewer, Beauties of Ireland, vol. 1, p. 444; Kilkenny County grand-jury presentment books, 1836–98 (Kilkenny County Library, GJ/1-63A); Lewis, *Topographical Dictionary*, vol. 1, pp. 110–11.

Secondary sources:

Sparks and Bligh, *Kilkenny: Pen and picture pages of its story*, pp. 30, 50; McParland, 'Public Work of Architects', p. 158; Lanigan, Tyler and Brady, *Kilkenny*, pp. 66, 83; Craig, *Architecture of Ireland*, pp. 267–8; Teehan, 'Emergence of County Courthouses', pp. 46–7, 59–60, 90–2; Walsh, 'Hard Labour', p. 209; Bradley, *Irish Historic Towns Atlas, No. 10: Kilkenny*, section 13; Loeber, et al., *Art and Architecture of Ireland: Volume IV: Architecture 1600–2000*, pp. 172, 181, 465.

KILKENNY COUNTY

Kilkenny, no. 2

Gaol Rd.
Lat. 52°38'55.93" N.; Long. 7°15'39.36" W.

Former gaol at Grace's Castle. Courthouse built on site, with gaol below *c.* 1790–5; replacement county gaol built (*William Robertson*) 1801–9; tread mill added 1824; solitary cells added 1825–6; road leading to gaol built 1829; inspectors urge the building of a new house of correction 1835 onwards; see 'Kilkenny County and City: Kilkenny, no. 1' for later history.

Former gaol at Grace's Castle. Courthouse built on site, with gaol below, *c.* 1790–5. Grand jury committee investigate gaol, recommends an entirely new building, 1801. Competition for design won by William Robertson, 1801. Replacement county gaol built (*William Robertson*), 1801–9. New gaol described by Forster Archer, prison inspector, as 'a perfect model for this part of the United Kingdom', 1803. Further praise from Forster Archer for gaol's design, 1811. Tread mill added (*William Robertson*), 1824. Solitary cells added, 1825–6. Former House of Correction (on Kells Rd.) used as a combined female prison for county and city, by agreement of both grand juries, 1829. Road leading to gaol built, 1829. Inspectors urge the construction of a new house of correction, 1835. See 'Kilkenny County and City: Kilkenny no. 1' for later history.

Archival and primary sources:

Kilkenny County grand-jury presentment books, 1801–8, 1824–9 (Bodleian Library, Oxford); 'Forster Archer's Tour of Ireland in 1801' (British Library, Add. MS 35920); *Finn's Leinster Journal*, 18 April 1801; *Kilkenny Moderator*, 15 August 1801; ibid., 5 May 1814; ibid., 18 November 1829; Tighe, *Statistical Observations Relative to the County of Kilkenny*, pp. 42, 519; Forster Archer, 'Report of the State of Gaols of Ireland for the Year 1802', f. 8 (Houses of the Oireachtas Library, Dublin, MS.7H28); *Accounts of the Presentments Passed by the Grand Juries of Ireland … in … 1807*, H.C. 1808 (205), xiii, pp. 191, 200; *Leinster Journal*, 13 September 1809; Atkinson, *Irish Tourist*, pp. 425–6; Forster Archer, 'Report of the State of Gaols of Ireland for the Year 1811' (Houses of the Oireachtas Library, Dublin, MS.4E63); Reid, *Travels in Ireland*, pp. 245–6; Kilkenny County grand-jury presentment books, 1836–98 (Kilkenny County Library, GJ/1-63A); Lewis, *Topographical Dictionary*, vol. 1, pp. 110–11.

Prison reports:

Inspector General's Report of … the Prisons in Ireland for … 1807, H.C. 1808 (239), ix, pp. 10–11;
Account of All Gaols … in the … United Kingdom, H.C. 1819 (137), xvii, pp. 10–11;
Inspector General's Report of … the Prisons in Ireland for … 1818, H.C. 1819 (534), xii, p. 15;
Report from the Select Committee on the State of Gaols, H.C. 1819 (579), vii, pp. 197–8;
Prisons of Ireland: Report of Inspectors General, 1823, H.C. 1823 (342), x, pp. 53–4;
Prisons of Ireland: Report of Inspectors General, 1824, H.C. 1824 (294), xxii, pp. 7, 52–4;
Prisons of Ireland: Report of Inspectors General, 1825, H.C. 1825 (493), xxii, p. 31;
Fourth Report … on … the Prisons of Ireland, 1826, H.C. 1826 (173), xxiii, p. 47;
Fifth Report … on … the Prisons of Ireland, 1827, H.C. 1826–7 (471), xi, pp. 51–2;
Seventh Report … on … the Prisons of Ireland, 1829, H.C. 1829 (10), xiii, p. 54;
Eighth Report … on … the Prisons of Ireland, 1830, H.C. 1830 (48), xxiv, p. 11;
Ninth Report … on … the Prisons of Ireland, 1831, H.C. 1830–1 (172), iv, pp. 55–6;
Eleventh Report … on … the Prisons of Ireland, 1833, H.C. 1833 (67), xvii, p. 25;
Thirteenth Report … on … the Prisons of Ireland, 1835, H.C. 1835 (114), xxxvi, pp. 39–40;
For later years, see 'Kilkenny County and City: Kilkenny, no. 1'.

Secondary sources:

Dowling, 'Forster Archer's Tour in Ireland in 1801', p. 23; O'Dwyer, 'Public Works Architecture', pp. 181, 407; Walsh, 'Hard Labour', pp. 209–13; Bradley, *Irish Historic Towns Atlas, No. 10: Kilkenny*, section 13.

KILKENNY CITY

Kilkenny, no. 1

High St. & Pudding Ln.
Lat. 52°39'3.67" N.; Long. 7°15'9.23" W.

Unknown date of construction; probably built by the fifteenth century; noted as under repair 1517; noted as intact 1628; city gaol nearby shown on map 1758; new combined city and county gaol built *c.* 1792; demolished *c.* 1800; later housing on site; not extant.

Unknown date of construction. Probably built by the fifteenth century. Noted as under repair, 1517. Noted as intact, 1628. The old city gaol was nearby. City gaol shown on map, 1758. New combined city and county gaol built, *c.* 1792. Demolished, *c.* 1800. Later housing on site, extended, 1836. Only minor fragments appear to survive as spolia in later buildings. Not extant.

Archival and primary sources:

'A Survey of the City of Kilkenny', 1758, by John Rocque (NLI); Forster Archer, 'Report of the State of Gaols of Ireland for the Year 1802', f. 8 (Houses of the Oireachtas Library, Dublin, MS.7H28); other sources noted in Hogan, 'Three Tholsels', below.

Secondary sources:

Hogan, 'Three Tholsels of Kilkenny', pp. 236, 238–40, 242; Sparks and Bligh, *Kilkenny*, pp. 30, 50; Bradley, *Irish Historic Towns Atlas, No. 10: Kilkenny*, section 13.

KILKENNY CITY

Kilkenny, no. 2

Parliament St.
Lat. 52°39'15.17" N.; Long. 7°15'13.93" W.

Site of a former castle; in use as a gaol perhaps as early as 1568; county gaol shown on map 1758; courthouse and combined county and city gaol built on site *c.* 1790–5; replacement county gaol built elsewhere 1801–9; repairs (*William Robertson*) 1807; city grand jury consider purchasing old workhouse for new city gaol (unexecuted) 1855; continued in use as a city gaol until 1861; thereafter a courthouse; extant.

Assizes were formerly held, perhaps, at Black Abbey. Site of a former castle, known as Grace's Castle. Gaol located on the site perhaps as early as 1568. County gaol shown on map, 1758. Escapes, 1770, 1772. Courthouse built on site, with gaol below, *c.* 1790–5. Replacement county gaol built (see 'Kilkenny County: Kilkenny, no. 2'), 1801–9. Minor alterations and repairs to city gaol (*William Robertson*), 1807. Inspectors highlight severe problems with gaol, 1823 onwards. For later history, see 'Kilkenny County and City: Kilkenny, no. 1'. Former House of Correction (on Kells Rd.) used as a combined female prison for county and city, by agreement of both grand juries, 1829. Presentment for a new fever hospital in the city gaol, 1847, 1850. Minor works, 1851. City grand jury consider purchasing old workhouse for new city gaol, unexecuted, 1855. City grand jury advertise for plans for a new city gaol, unexecuted, 1859. New combined gaol in use, 1861. Building thereafter used as a courthouse. For later history in this regard, see Part I. Extant.

Archival and primary sources:

G. Evans, Memorial of Deed. No. 116066 (NAI, Registry of Deeds); 'A Survey of the City of Kilkenny', 1758, by John Rocque (NLI); *Finn's Leinster Journal*, 12 September 1770 and 18 February 1772; Howard, *Lazarettos*, p. 85; *Journal of the Irish House of Commons*, vol. xvii, 1797, p. ccvi; 'Forster Archer's Tour of Ireland in 1801' (British Library, Add. MS 35920); Tighe, *Statistical Observations Relative to the County of Kilkenny*, p. 519; Forster Archer, 'Report of the State of Gaols of Ireland for the Year 1802', f. 8 (Houses of the Oireachtas Library, Dublin, MS.7H28); Kilkenny City grand-jury presentment books, 1807–61 (Bodleian Library, Oxford); *Accounts of the Presentments Passed by the Grand Juries of Ireland … in … 1807*, H.C. 1808 (205), xiii, p. 203; Reid, *Travels*, p. 243–4; Brewer, Beauties of Ireland, vol. 1, p. 444; Kilkenny County grand-jury presentment books, spring 1829 (Bodleian Library, Oxford); Kilkenny City grand-jury presentment books, 1836–98 (Kilkenny County Library, GJ/1-63A); Kilkenny City grand-jury presentment books, 1855–61 (Bodleian Library, Oxford); Lewis, *Topographical Dictionary*, vol. 1, pp. 110–11.

Prison reports:

Inspector General's Report of … the Prisons in Ireland for … 1807, H.C. 1808 (239), ix, p. 11;

Account of All Gaols … in the … United Kingdom, H.C. 1819 (137), xvii, pp. 10–11;

Inspector General's Report of … the Prisons in Ireland for … 1818, H.C. 1819 (534), xii, p. 15;

Prisons of Ireland: Report of Inspectors General, 1823, H.C. 1823 (342), x, pp. 54–5;

Prisons of Ireland: Report of Inspectors General, 1824, H.C. 1824 (294), xxii, pp. 7, 54;

Prisons of Ireland: Report of Inspectors General, 1825, H.C. 1825 (493), xxii, p. 32;

Fourth Report … on … the Prisons of Ireland, 1826, H.C. 1826 (173), xxiii, pp. 47–8;

Fifth Report … on … the Prisons of Ireland, 1827, H.C. 1826–7 (471), xi, p. 53;

Sixth Report … on … the Prisons of Ireland, 1828, H.C. 1828 (68), xii, pp. 59–60;

Seventh Report … on … the Prisons of Ireland, 1829, H.C. 1829 (10), xiii, p. 55;

Eighth Report … on … the Prisons of Ireland, 1830, H.C. 1830 (48), xxiv, p. 56;

Fourteenth Report … on … the Prisons of Ireland, 1836, H.C. 1836 (118), xxxv, pp. 37–8;

For later years, see 'Kilkenny County and City: Kilkenny, no. 1'.

Secondary sources:

Hogan, 'Three Tholsels of Kilkenny', pp. 239, 242; Dowling, 'Forster Archer's Tour in Ireland in 1801', p. 23; Sparks and Bligh, *Kilkenny: Pen and picture pages of its story*, pp. 30, 50; McParland, 'Public Work of Architects', p. 158; Lanigan, Tyler and Brady, *Kilkenny*, pp. 66, 83; Craig, *Architecture of Ireland*, pp. 267–8; Teehan, 'Emergence of County Courthouses', pp. 46–7, 59–60, 90–2; Walsh, 'Hard Labour', p. 209; Bradley, *Irish Historic Towns Atlas, No. 10: Kilkenny*, section 13; Loeber, et al., *Art and Architecture of Ireland: Volume IV: Architecture 1600–2000*, pp. 172, 181, 465.

KILKENNY COUNTY and CITY

Kilkenny, no. 1

Gaol Rd.
Lat. 52°38'55.93" N.; Long. 7°15'39.36" W.

New county gaol built (*William Robertson*) 1801–9; solitary cells added 1825–6; road leading to gaol built 1829; inspectors urge the building of a new house of correction 1835 onwards; unexecuted plans (*William Deane Butler*, and later *Charles Frederick Anderson*) 1841–2; inspectors suggest merger of county and city gaols 1842 onwards; intervention from assize judge 1849; unexecuted scheme for an addition (*William D'Esterre Smith*) 1849; a large new gaol built (*William Deane Butler*) 1850–3; county and city gaols merged 1861; closed 1929; demolished 1948; social housing built on site; not extant.

New county gaol built (*William Robertson*), 1801–9. Solitary cells added, 1825–6. Road leading to gaol built, 1829. Inspectors urge the construction of a new house of correction, 1835. Unexecuted plans for large additions (*William Deane Butler*, and later *Charles Frederick Anderson*), 1841–2. Objections from grand jurors to projected expenditure, 1841–2. Inspectors suggest merger of county and city gaols, 1842 onwards. Further objections, 1842–9. Assize judge intervenes and urges an enlargement of the gaol, 1849. Unexecuted scheme for an addition (*William D'Esterre Smith*), 1849. Effectively a new gaol, for the county and city (*William Deane Butler*), built at a cost of £11,000, 1850–3. Disagreements over proposed merger of county and city gaols, 1854–9. City grand jury consider purchasing old workhouse for new city gaol, unexecuted, 1855. City grand jury advertise for plans for a new city gaol, unexecuted, 1859. Agreement reached to merge gaols, 1860. County and city gaols merged, 1861. Closed, 1929. Demolished, 1948. Social housing built on site. Not extant.

Archival and primary sources:

'Forster Archer's Tour of Ireland in 1801' (British Library, Add. MS 35920); *Finn's Leinster Journal*, 18 April 1801; *Kilkenny Moderator*, 15 August 1801; ibid., 5 May 1814; ibid., 18 November 1829; Tighe, *Statistical Observations Relative to the County of Kilkenny*, pp. 42, 519; *Accounts of the Presentments Passed by the Grand Juries of Ireland … in … 1807*, H.C. 1808 (205), xiii, pp. 191, 200, 203; *Leinster Journal*, 13 September 1809; Atkinson, *Irish Tourist*, pp. 425–6; An account of the several presentments made … on which advances have been made by government for gaols, n.d. (NAI, SPO OP 1832–8, 1A/77/4); Reid, *Travels in Ireland*, pp. 243–6; Kilkenny County and Kilkenny City grand-jury presentment books, 1836–98 (Kilkenny County Library, GJ/1-63A); Kilkenny County grand-jury presentment books, 1840–2 (Bodleian Library, Oxford); Kilkenny City grand-jury presentment books, 1855–61 (Bodleian Library, Oxford); Lewis, *Topographical Dictionary*, vol. 1, pp. 110–11; *Kilkenny Moderator*, 17 July 1841; *Kilkenny Journal*, 16 March 1842; ibid., 29 August 1847; ibid., 20 February, 1 July 1848; ibid., 24 March 1849; ibid., 13, 20 June, 4 August 1849; *The Builder*, vol. 8, no. 394, 24 August 1850, p. 404; *Kilkenny Journal*, 26 July 1854; *Kilkenny Moderator*, 25 August 1852; Report of the committee appointed by the grand juries, to select a plan for the alteration or erection of a joint prison, for the county and city of Waterford, 19 February 1855 (NLI, Lismore papers, MS 43,456/13); 1 February 1862; Lacy, *Sights and Scenes in our Fatherland*, p. 139; *Kilkenny Prison Closing Order* (Dublin: Stationary Office, 1929); *Kilkenny People*, 6 August 1949.

Prison reports:

Inspector General's Report of … the Prisons in Ireland for … 1807, H.C. 1808 (239), ix, pp. 10–11;

Account of All Gaols … in the … United Kingdom, H.C. 1819 (137), xvii, pp. 10–11;

Inspector General's Report of … the Prisons in Ireland for … 1818, H.C. 1819 (534), xii, p. 15;

Report from the Select Committee on the State of Gaols, H.C. 1819 (579), vii, pp. 197–8;

Prisons of Ireland: Report of Inspectors General, 1823, H.C. 1823 (342), x, pp. 53–5;

Prisons of Ireland: Report of Inspectors General, 1824, H.C. 1824 (294), xxii, pp. 7, 52–4;

Prisons of Ireland: Report of Inspectors General, 1825, H.C. 1825 (493), xxii, pp. 31–2;

Fourth Report … on … the Prisons of Ireland, 1826, H.C. 1826 (173), xxiii, pp. 47–8;

Fifth Report … on … the Prisons of Ireland, 1827, H.C. 1826–7 (471), xi, pp. 51–3;

Seventh Report … on … the Prisons of Ireland, 1829, H.C. 1829 (10), xiii, pp. 54–5;

Eighth Report … on … the Prisons of Ireland, 1830, H.C. 1830 (48), xxiv, pp. 11, 56;

Ninth Report … on … the Prisons of Ireland, 1831, H.C. 1830–1 (172), iv, pp. 41, 55–6;

Eleventh Report … on … the Prisons of Ireland, 1833, H.C. 1833 (67), xvii, p. 23;

Thirteenth Report … on … the Prisons of Ireland, 1835, H.C. 1835 (114), xxxvi, pp. 39–40;

Fourteenth Report … on … the Prisons of Ireland, 1836, H.C. 1836 (118), xxxv, pp. 6, 37–8;

Fifteenth Report … on … the Prisons of Ireland, 1837, H.C. 1837 (123), xxxi, pp. 8, 39;

Sixteenth Report … on … the Prisons of Ireland, 1838, H.C. 1837–8 (186), xxix, pp. 43–4;

Seventeenth Report … on … the Prisons of Ireland, 1839, H.C. 1839 (91), xx, pp. 46–7;

Eighteenth Report … on … the Prisons of Ireland, 1840, H.C. 1840 (240), xxvi, pp. 49–50;

Nineteenth Report … on … the Prisons of Ireland, 1841, H.C. 1841 (299), xi, pp. 50–1;
Twentieth Report … on … the Prisons of Ireland, 1842, H.C. 1842 (377), xxii, pp. 6, 8, 103–5;
Twenty-first Report … on … the Prisons of Ireland, 1843, H.C. 1843 (462), xxvii, pp. 3, 5, 70;
Twenty-second Report … on … the Prisons of Ireland, 1844, H.C. 1844 (535), xxviii, p. 83;
Twenty-third Report … on … the Prisons of Ireland, 1844, H.C. 1845 (620), xxv, p. 61;
Twenty-fourth Report … on … the Prisons of Ireland, 1846, H.C. 1846 (697), xx, pp. 75, 77;
Twenty-fifth Report … on … the Prisons of Ireland, 1847, H.C. 1847 (805), xxix, pp. 88–9;
Twenty-sixth Report … on … the Prisons of Ireland, 1847–48, H.C. 1847–8 (952), xxiv, pp. 10, 94–5;
Twenty-seventh Report … on … the Prisons of Ireland, 1849, H.C. 1849 (1069), xxvi, pp. 87–8;
Twenty-eighth Report … on … the Prisons of Ireland, 1850, H.C. 1850 (1229), xxix, pp. 11, 86, 88;
Twenty-ninth Report … on … the Prisons of Ireland, 1851, H.C. 1851 (1364), xxviii, pp. 14, 79–83;
Thirtieth Report … on … the Prisons of Ireland, 1852, H.C. 1852 (1531), xxv, pp. 16, 184–7;
Thirty-first Report … on … the Prisons of Ireland, 1853, H.C. 1853 (1657), liii, p. 192;
Thirty-second Report … on … the Prisons of Ireland, 1854, H.C. 1854 (1803), xxxii, pp. 163–4, 170;
Thirty-third Report … on … the Prisons of Ireland, 1855, H.C. 1854–5 (1956), xxvi, pp. 161–4, 168;
Thirty-seventh Report … on … the Prisons of Ireland, 1859, H.C. 1859 (2557), xiii, pp. 262–71;
Thirty-ninth Report … on … the Prisons of Ireland, 1861, H.C. 1861 (2861), xxix, pp. 236–7;
Fortieth Report … on … the Prisons of Ireland, 1862, H.C. 1862 (3020), xxvi, p. 281;
Forty-eighth Report … on … the Prisons of Ireland, 1869, H.C. 1870 (C. 173), xxxvii, p. 374.

Secondary sources:

Dowling, 'Forster Archer's Tour of Ireland in 1801', p. 23; Forbes, *Victorian Architect*, p. 45; Daniel Wilson Randle, 'A Question of Style: The architectural competition for the central building for the university of the south', MA thesis, University of Texas, 1978, pp. 241–5; O'Dwyer, 'Public Works Architecture', pp. 181, 407; Tom Boyle and Michael O'Dwyer, *Kilkenny County Council: A century of local government* (Kilkenny: Kilkenny County Council, 1999), p. 44; Walsh, 'Hard Labour', pp. 209–39 (illus.); Bradley, *Irish Historic Towns Atlas, No. 10: Kilkenny*, section 13; Michael O'Dwyer, *St. Rioch's Graveyard Inscriptions with Historical Notes on the Area* (Kilkenny: St Rioch's, 2007), p. 30.

KING'S COUNTY (OFFALY)

Philipstown (Daingean)

Molesworth St. & Grand Canal
Lat. 53°17'56.65" N.; Long. 7°17'36.47" W.

Philipstown established as the assize town of King's County 1557; unsuccessful petition to move assizes to Tullamore 1786; new gaol built 1797–1801; strongly criticised by Forster Archer 1803; minor additions *c.* 1818–19; disagreements over location of proposed new gaol 1820–6; condemned by the AIPPD, 1821; new gaol built in Tullamore 1826–30; old gaol closed *c.* 1830; reopened for convicts *c.* 1852; iron prison built 1855–6; closed 1861; dismantled 1869; reopened as a reformatory for young boys *c.* 1870–*c.* 1973; original gaol building demolished; not extant.

Philipstown established as an assize town, 1557. Petition to move the assizes and gaol to Tullamore, unsuccessful, 1786. Howard visits and notes that gaol was built around 1763, 1788. A new gaol built to the rear of the barracks, rectilinear in plan, 1797–1801. Strongly criticised for design, quality of construction, and site, by Forster Archer, prison inspector,

1803. New courthouse in Philipstown, *c.* 1807. Gaol condemned by Forster Archer, 1807, 1818. Some minor additions and solitary cells, at a cost of at least £1,000, *c.* 1818–19. Disagreement within grand jury about location of a new gaol, 1820–6. Condemned by the AIPPD, 1821. New gaol built in Tullamore (see 'King's County: Tullamore'), 1826–30. Gaol in Philipstown closed, *c.* 1830. Reopened for convicts, *c.* 1852. Iron prison built, at a cost of at least £5,250, 1855–6. Prison closed, 1861. Iron buildings dismantled, 1869. Old gaol and barracks reopened as a reformatory for young boys, *c.* 1870–*c.* 1973. Original gaol building demolished. Not extant.

Archival and primary sources:

3 & 4 Ph. and M., c. 2 (1557); Howard, *Lazarettos*, p. 87; *Journal of the Irish House of Commons*, vol. xxiii, 1786, p. 194; ibid., vol. xvii, 1797, p. ccvi; Charles Coote, *General View of the Agriculture and Manufactures of the King's County: With observations on the means of their improvement* (Dublin: Graisberry & Campbell, 1801), pp. 150, 177; Forster Archer, 'Report of the State of Gaols of Ireland for the Year 1802', f. 9 (Houses of the Oireachtas Library, Dublin, MS.7H28); *Freeman's Journal*, 27 March 1821; *Third Report of the AIPPD*, p. 40; *Fourth Report of the AIPPD*, p. 35; King's County grand-jury presentments, 1821 (Cambridge University Library); Printed notice relating to Tullamore gaol, 13 September 1826 (Westmeath County Library, Howard Bury papers, P1/28); King's County grand-jury presentments, spring assizes 1830 (Offaly County Library, GJ/1/1/1); Lord Ponsonby to Lord Francis Leveson Gower, 12 November 1829 (NAI, CSORP 1829/10140); *The Builder*, vol. 10, no. 514, 11 December 1852, p. 786; *Twenty-fifth Report of the Commissioners on Public Works, Ireland … for the Year 1856*, H.C. 1857 (2228), xvii, p. 21; Correspondence relating to Philipstown iron prison, 1855–6 (NAI, Board of Works files, 2D/61/80 and 2D/61/81).

Prison reports:

Inspector General's Report of … the Prisons in Ireland for … 1807, H.C. 1808 (239), ix, p. 11;

Account of All Gaols … in the … United Kingdom, H.C. 1819 (137), xvii, pp. 15–16;

Report from the Select Committee on the State of Gaols, H.C. 1819 (579), vii, pp. 10–11;

Prisons of Ireland: Report of Inspectors General, 1823, H.C. 1823 (342), x, pp. 55–6;

Prisons of Ireland: Report of Inspectors General, 1824, H.C. 1824 (294), xxii, pp. 7, 54;

Prisons of Ireland: Report of Inspectors General, 1825, H.C. 1825 (493), xxii, p. 30;

Fourth Report … on … the Prisons of Ireland, 1826, H.C. 1826 (173), xxiii, p. 46;

Fifth Report … on … the Prisons of Ireland, 1827, H.C. 1826–7 (471), xi, pp. 53–4;

Sixth Report … on … the Prisons of Ireland, 1828, H.C. 1828 (68), xii, p. 60;

Seventh Report … on … the Prisons of Ireland, 1829, H.C. 1829 (10), xiii, p. 56;

Eighth Report … on … the Prisons of Ireland, 1830, H.C. 1830 (48), xxiv, p. 57.

Secondary sources:

O'Dwyer, 'Public Works Architecture', pp. 193–8, 407; Byrne, 'The County Courthouse at Tullamore', p. 112; Byrne, *Legal Offaly*, pp. 21, 387–95; Loeber, et al., *Art and Architecture of Ireland: Volume IV: Architecture 1600–2000*, p. 205; Tierney, *The Buildings of Ireland: Central Leinster*, p. 303.

KING'S COUNTY (OFFALY)

Tullamore

Charleville Rd.
Lat. 53°16'10.84" N.; Long. 7°29'51.78" W.

Assizes and gaol in Philipstown 1557; great fire in Tullamore 1785; unsuccessful petition to move assizes and gaol to

Tullamore 1786; unexecuted proposal for a new polygonal-plan gaol in Tullamore (*William Murray*) 1820; new radial-plan gaol built in Tullamore (*John Killaly*) 1826–30; act of parliament to move the assizes to Tullamore 1832, to take effect 1835; alterations and sundry works (*William Deane Butler*) *c.* 1845; eight female separate-system cells built 1853–4; further alterations 1860s; occupied by British forces, then by republicans 1921–2; ruined 1922; mostly demolished *c.* 1937; factory established on site *c.* 1930s; partially extant.

Assizes and gaol in Philipstown, 1557. Great fire in Tullamore, 1785. Rebuilding of town, 1786 onwards. Unsuccessful petition to move assizes and gaol to Tullamore, 1786. Disagreements within grand jury about location of new gaol, 1820–6. Unexecuted proposal for a new polygonal-plan gaol in Tullamore (*William Murray*), 1820. New radial-plan gaol built in Tullamore (*John Killaly*), 1826–30. New courthouse built nearby (see Part I), 1829–35. Act of parliament to move the assizes to Tullamore, 1832, to take effect, 1835. Alterations and sundry works (*William Deane Butler*), *c.* 1845. Eight female separate-system cells built, 1853–4. Further alterations, 1860s. Occupied by British forces, then by republicans, 1919–22. Ruined, 1922. Mostly demolished, 1937. Factory established on site, late 1930s. Partially extant.

Archival and primary sources:

3 & 4 Ph. and M., c. 2 (1557); *Journal of the Irish House of Commons*, vol. xxiii, 1786, p. 194; Coote, *General View of … the King's County*, pp. 150, 177; R. Warwick Bond (ed.), *The Marlay Letters, 1778–1820* (London: Constable, 1937), p. 111; Drawings by William Murray for Tullamore gaol, 1820 (Irish Architectural Archive, RIAI Murray Collection, Acc. 92/46.1194–6); Plan and elevation drawings for Tullamore gaol as built, n.d, n.s. [*c.* 1826] (NLI, AD 2642–5, 2662); King's County grand-jury presentment books, 1821 (Cambridge University Library); *Fourth Report of the AIPPD*, p. 35; King's County grand-jury presentments, spring assizes 1830 (Offaly County Library, GJ/1/1/1); Printed notice relating to Tullamore gaol, 13 September 1826 (Westmeath County Library, Howard Bury papers, P1/28); Correspondence relating to Tullamore gaol, 1826 (NAI, CSORP 1826/13,514); Lord Ponsonby to Lord Francis Leveson Gower, 12 November 1829 (NAI, CSORP 1829/10140); *Journal of the House of Commons*, vol. 87, 19 April 1832, p. 290 and passim; *Hansard*, vol. 12, 3rd ser., 23 May 1832, cols 1414–16 and passim; King's County Assizes Act, 1832 (2 Will. IV, c. 60); Royal Hibernian Academy exhibits, 1845 (no. 430); Charles Bury to Catherine Bury, 17 January 1833 (University of Nottingham, Charles Brinsley Marlay papers, My 454/1–4); Charles Bury to Catherine Bury, 3 September 1833 (ibid., My 463/1–3); Plan drawing of Tullamore gaol showing new laundry and stores, etc., by William Deane Butler, July 1843 (Offaly County Library, P123); *Midland Tribune*, 4 March 1922; Photographs taken during demolition, *c.* 1937 (Offaly County Library, P50/14, and acc. nos. 434–5); *Offaly Independent*, 25 September 1937.

Prison reports:

Fourth Report … on … the Prisons of Ireland, 1826, H.C. 1826 (173), xxiii, p. 46;

Fifth Report … on … the Prisons of Ireland, 1827, H.C. 1826–7 (471), xi, pp. 7, 53–4;

Sixth Report … on … the Prisons of Ireland, 1828, H.C. 1828 (68), xii, p. 60;

Seventh Report … on … the Prisons of Ireland, 1829, H.C. 1829 (10), xiii, pp. 9, 56;

Eighth Report … on … the Prisons of Ireland, 1830, H.C. 1830 (48), xxiv, p. 57;

Ninth Report … on … the Prisons of Ireland, 1831, H.C. 1830–1 (172), iv, p. 42;

Fourteenth Report … on … the Prisons of Ireland, 1836, H.C. 1836 (118), xxxv, p. 38;

Seventeenth Report … on … the Prisons of Ireland, 1839, H.C. 1839 (91), xx, p. 47;

Eighteenth Report … on … the Prisons of Ireland, 1840, H.C. 1840 (240), xxvi, pp. 50–1;

Nineteenth Report … on … the Prisons of Ireland, 1841, H.C. 1841 (299), xi, p. 52;

Twentieth Report … on … the Prisons of Ireland, 1842, H.C. 1842 (377), xxii, pp. 105–6;

Twenty-third Report … on … the Prisons of Ireland, 1844, H.C. 1845 (620), xxv, p. 64;

Thirty-first Report … on … the Prisons of Ireland, 1853, H.C. 1853 (1657), liii, p. 17;

Thirty-second Report … on … the Prisons of Ireland, 1854, H.C. 1854 (1803), xxxii, p. 171;

Thirty-third Report … on … the Prisons of Ireland, 1855, H.C. 1854–5 (1956), xxvi, p. 17,

Forty-eighth Report … on … the Prisons of Ireland, 1869, H.C. 1870 (C. 173), xxxvii, pp. 388–9.

Secondary sources:

Moran, 'Tullamore', pp. 49–50; Photographs, 1978 (Irish Architectural Archive, photos collection, nos. 3/46 x 1); Byrne, *Walk through Tullamore*, p. 297; William Garner, *Tullamore Architectural Heritage* (Dublin: An Foras Forbartha, 1980), pp. 13–14; Craig, *Architecture of Ireland*, p. 304; Niall McCullough and Valerie Mulvin, *A Lost Tradition: The nature of architecture in Ireland* (Dublin: Gandon Editions, 1987), p. 112; Goslin, 'History and Descriptive Catalogue of the Murray Collection', pp. 339–40; O'Dwyer, 'Public Works Architecture', pp. 176, 407; Michael Byrne, 'Tullamore: The growth process, 1784–1841', in William Nolan and Timothy P. O'Neill (eds), *Offaly: History and society* (Dublin: Geography Publications, 1998), pp. 569–626; Lee, *James Pain, Architect*, p. 65; Byrne, *Legal Offaly*, pp. 15, 21, 33–5, 41, 51, 54, 66, 387–95; O'Dwyer, 'Building Empires', p. 146; Byrne, 'County Courthouse at Tullamore', pp. 112, 121, 123; Loeber, et al., *Art and Architecture of Ireland: Volume IV: Architecture 1600–2000*, p. 203; Tierney, *The Buildings of Ireland: Central Leinster*, pp. 621–2.

LEITRIM

Carrick-on-Shannon

St George's Terrace
Lat. 53°56'39.94" N.; Long. 8°5'53.0" W.

Gaol reported by Howard to be adjacent to the courthouse, and partially below ground 1788; a new gaol built nearby 1796–1802; unexecuted smaller polygonal-plan addition (unknown architect, perhaps *John Hargrave*) *c.* 1821; a large polygonal-plan addition to the rear (unknown architect, but likely *John Hargrave*) 1821–4; minor alterations to female prison 1840; unexecuted plan to convert gaol to separate-system confinement *c.* 1842; additions to female prison 1852–4; closed *c.* 1900; reopened as a gaol during War of Independence 1919–21; mostly demolished 1968; a marina occupies much of the site; partially extant.

Gaol reported by Howard to be adjacent to the courthouse, and partially below ground, 1788. A new gaol built nearby, 1796–1802. Unexecuted smaller polygonal-plan addition (unknown architect, perhaps *John Hargrave*), *c.* 1821. A larger polygonal-plan addition to the rear (unknown architect, but likely *John Hargrave*), 1821–4. New courthouse nearby (see Part I), *c.* 1820. Minor alterations to female prison, 1840. Unexecuted plan to convert gaol to separate-system confinement, *c.* 1842. Additions to female prison, 1852–4. Closed, *c.* 1900. Reopened as a gaol during War of Independence, 1919–21. Mostly demolished, 1968. A marina occupies much of the site. Partially extant.

Archival and primary sources:

Howard, *Lazarettos*, p. 92; *Journal of the Irish House of Commons*, vol. xvii, 1797, p. ccvi; McParlan, *Statistical Survey of … Leitrim*, p. 46; Hall, *Tour through Ireland*, vol. 2, p. 35; *Accounts of the Presentments Passed by the Grand Juries of Ireland … in … 1807*, H.C. 1808 (205), xiii, p. 219; W. P. [Anon.], 'Sketch of a Journey through Part of Ireland', in *Walker's Hibernian Magazine*, November 1807, pp. 675–80, at p. 677; Forster Archer, 'Report of the State of Gaols of Ireland for the Year 1802', f. 9 (Houses of the Oireachtas Library, Dublin, MS.7H28); Robert Robinson to William Gregory, 16 May 1820, and Francis Johnston to Robert Robinson, 9 May 1820 (NAI, CSORP 1820/1051); Plan, elevation and section drawings for a new gaol in Carrick-on-Shannon, as built, n.d., n.s. [*c.* 1821] (NLI, AD 2646–7, 2650–1); Plan, elevation and section drawings for a smaller new gaol in Carrick-on-Shannon, unexecuted, n.d., n.s. [*c.* 1821] (NLI, AD 2659–60); *Third Report of the AIPPD*, p. 42; *Fourth Report of the AIPPD*, p. 36; Lewis, *Topographical Dictionary*, vol. 1, p. 276; *The Builder*, vol. 9, no. 428, 19 April 1851, p. 254.

Prison reports:

Inspector General's Report of … the Prisons in Ireland for … 1807, H.C. 1808 (239), ix, p. 11;

Account of All Gaols … in the … United Kingdom, H.C. 1819 (137), xvii, pp. 10–11;

Inspector General's Report of … the Prisons in Ireland for … 1818, H.C. 1819 (534), xii, pp. 16–17;
Report from the Select Committee on the State of Gaols, H.C. 1819 (579), vii, pp. 196–7;
Prisons of Ireland: Report of Inspectors General, 1823, H.C. 1823 (342), x, pp. 5, 34;
Prisons of Ireland: Report of Inspectors General, 1824, H.C. 1824 (294), xxii, pp. 5, 35;
Prisons of Ireland: Report of Inspectors General, 1825, H.C. 1825 (493), xxii, p. 33;
Fourth Report … on … the Prisons of Ireland, 1826, H.C. 1826 (173), xxiii, p. 33;
Eighteenth Report … on … the Prisons of Ireland, 1840, H.C. 1840 (240), xxvi, p. 33;
Twentieth Report … on … the Prisons of Ireland, 1842, H.C. 1842 (377), xxii, p. 72;
Twenty-first Report … on … the Prisons of Ireland, 1843, H.C. 1843 (462), xxvii, p. 37;
Twenty-second Report … on … the Prisons of Ireland, 1844, H.C. 1844 (535), xxviii, p. 43;
Twenty-fifth Report … on … the Prisons of Ireland, 1847, H.C. 1847 (805), xxix, p. 47;
Thirty-first Report … on … the Prisons of Ireland, 1853, H.C. 1853 (1657), liii, pp. 17, 94;
Thirty-second Report … on … the Prisons of Ireland, 1854, H.C. 1854 (1803), xxxii, p. 20;
Forty-ninth Report … on … the Prisons of Ireland, 1870, H.C. 1871 (C. 359), xxx, p. 156.

Secondary sources:

Des Smith (ed.), *Shannonside: A parochial magazine* (1988) (copy in Leitrim County Library, Ballinamore), p. 44; T.W. Freeman, 'Land and People, *c.* 1841', in Vaughan, *New History of Ireland: Volume 5*, pp. 242–71, at p. 247; O'Dwyer, 'Public Works Architecture', p. 407; Anon., 'A Sign-posted Walking Tour of Carrick-on-Shannon' (n.d.) (copy in Leitrim County Library, Ballinamore), pp. 11–12.

LIMERICK CITY

Limerick

Mary St. & Gaol Lane
Lat. 52°40'3.00" N.; Long. 8°37'16.09" W.

An ancient gaol in use 1673; (re)built 1750; superseded by a new combined county and city gaol *c.* 1788–1801; sold 1804; described as ruined 1866; demolished; not extant.

An ancient gaol in use, 1673. City gaol built on the site of a former tholsel, at the corner of Mary Street and Gaol Lane, 1750. Superseded by a new combined county and city gaol (see 'Limerick County and City: Limerick'), *c.* 1788–1801. Sold, 1804. Described as a 'ruin', 1866. Thereafter demolished. Not extant.

Archival and primary sources:

Lenihan, *History of Limerick*, pp. 341, 704; Registry of Deeds (1804), 564/52/376014; Forster Archer, 'Report of the State of Gaols of Ireland for the Year 1802', f. 10 (Houses of the Oireachtas Library, Dublin, MS.7H28).

Secondary sources:

Hill, *Building of Limerick*, p. 87; O'Flaherty, *Irish Historic Towns Atlas, No. 21: Limerick*, pp. 27–8; Loeber, et al., *Art and Architecture of Ireland: Volume IV: Architecture 1600–2000*, p. 467.

LIMERICK COUNTY and CITY (and later LIMERICK CITY)

Limerick

Merchants Quay & Bow Ln.
Lat. 52°40′5.94″ N.; Long. 8°37′29.47″ W.

A former city gaol located nearby, built 1750; act of parliament to build a new combined county and city gaol 1784; second act of parliament, with a change of site 1786; Howard visits and comments that county and city gaols are 'one prison', and that 'a new gaol is proposed' 1787; new rectilinear-plan county and city gaol (a *Mr Smyth*) *c.* 1788–1801; grand-jury presentment for a new city gaol 1807; new city gaol on the same site as the previous combined gaol (*John Nash* and *James Pain*), 1811–14; new county gaol built elsewhere 1817–21; both buildings merged to form a single city gaol, with alterations (*James Pain*) 1826–7; new city courthouse built on part of site of city gaol to the displeasure of the inspectors *c.* 1845–7; introduction of separate-system confinement and other alterations (*William Edward Corbett*) 1866–8; in use as a female prison *c.* 1900; demolished (except for small portions) *c.* 1990; City Council offices on site; partially extant.

A former city gaol located nearby (see 'Limerick City: Limerick'), built 1750. Unknown location of former county gaol. New city courthouse (see Part I) built, 1763–6. Act of parliament to build a new combined county and city gaol, 1784. Second act of parliament, with a change of site, 1786. Howard visits and comments that county and city gaols are 'one prison', and that 'a new gaol is proposed', 1787. New rectilinear-plan county and city gaol (a *Mr Smyth*), *c.* 1788–1801. Unexecuted proposals for a new gaol, or perhaps the completion of a gaol (*Robert Woodgate*), *c.* 1799–1802. County and city gaols described as 'one building', 1807. Grand-jury presentment for a new city gaol, 1807. New city gaol built on the same site as the previous combined gaol, at a cost of £7,500 (*John Nash* and *James Pain*), 1811–14. New county gaol built elsewhere (see 'Limerick County: Limerick'), 1817–21. Inspectors urge the purchase of the old county gaol for use by city prisoners, 1824 onwards. Both buildings merged to form a single city gaol, with alterations (*James Pain*), 1826–7. Unexecuted proposal for a new city courthouse (see Part I), 1834. Inspectors say it 'probable' that the county and city gaols will again merge, 1842. New city courthouse built on part of site of city gaol (see Part I), to the displeasure of the inspectors, *c.* 1845–7. Large additions to city gaol (*James Pain*), unexecuted, 1853–5. Introduction of separate-system confinement and other alterations (*William Edward Corbett*), 1866–8. In use as a female prison, *c.* 1900. Demolished (except for small portions), *c.* 1990. City Council offices on site. Partially extant.

Archival and primary sources:

23 & 24 Geo. III, c. 44 (1784); 26 Geo. III, c. 59 (1786); Howard, *Lazarettos*, p. 91; 'Forster Archer's Tour of Ireland in 1801' (British Library, Add. MS 35920); *Accounts of the Presentments Passed by the Grand Juries of Ireland … in … 1807*, H.C. 1808 (205), xiii, p. 220; *Limerick Gazette*, 9 February 1816; Robert Woodgate to John Soane, 18 November 1799 (Sir John Soane's Museum, London, XV.A.2.5); Forster Archer, 'Report of the State of Gaols of Ireland for the Year 1802', f. 10 (Houses of the Oireachtas Library, Dublin, MS.7H28); Staples, *Tour in Ireland*, p. 210; *Limerick City [Grand Jury]: Returns to orders of the … House of Commons, dated 8th February 1821*, H.C. 1821 (175), xx, pp. 5–7; *Limerick Chronicle*, 13 April 1822; ibid., 25 November 1843; Reid, *Travels in Ireland*, pp. 292–3; Accounts of Nicholas Hannan and Timothy Mackey, 1826 (NAI, SPO 588 AAB 944); *The Builder*, vol. 11, no. 536, 14 May 1853, p. 315; Bartlett, Willis and Coyne, *Scenery and Antiquities of Ireland*, vol. 1, p. 106; *Dublin Builder*, vol. 8, no. 148, 15 February 1866, p. 53; *Irish Builder*, vol. 10, no. 201, 1 May 1868, p. 116; Lenihan, *History of Limerick*, pp. 341, 428, 431, 704; Ní Chinnéide, 'Frenchman's Impressions of Limerick', p. 100; Photographs taken before demolition, by Joe Ranson, *c.* 1988 (Limerick City and County Archives, Ranks Community Collection (Joe Ranson photography collection), P/90/23/6 and P/90/23/10).

Prison reports:

Inspector General's Report of … the Prisons in Ireland for … 1807, H.C. 1808 (239), ix, p. 12;
Account of All Gaols … in the … United Kingdom, H.C. 1819 (137), xvii, pp. 12–13;

Inspector General's Report of … the Prisons in Ireland for … 1818, H.C. 1819 (534), xii, p. 17;
Report from the Select Committee on the State of Gaols, H.C. 1819 (579), vii, p. 174;
Prisons of Ireland: Report of Inspectors General, 1823, H.C. 1823 (342), x, p. 59;
Prisons of Ireland: Report of Inspectors General, 1824, H.C. 1824 (294), xxii, pp. 7, 57;
Prisons of Ireland: Report of Inspectors General, 1825, H.C. 1825 (493), xxii, p. 50;
Fourth Report … on … the Prisons of Ireland, 1826, H.C. 1826 (173), xxiii, p. 49;
Fifth Report … on … the Prisons of Ireland, 1827, H.C. 1826–7 (471), xi, pp. 56–7;
Sixth Report … on … the Prisons of Ireland, 1828, H.C. 1828 (68), xii, p. 62;
Seventh Report … on … the Prisons of Ireland, 1829, H.C. 1829 (10), xiii, p. 59;
Eleventh Report … on … the Prisons of Ireland, 1833, H.C. 1833 (67), xvii, p. 28;
Twentieth Report … on … the Prisons of Ireland, 1842, H.C. 1842 (377), xxii, p. 108;
Twenty-first Report … on … the Prisons of Ireland, 1843, H.C. 1843 (462), xxvii, p. 74;
Twenty-second Report … on … the Prisons of Ireland, 1844, H.C. 1844 (535), xxviii, p. 89;
Twenty-third Report … on … the Prisons of Ireland, 1844, H.C. 1845 (620), xxv, pp. 69–70;
Twenty-fourth Report … on … the Prisons of Ireland, 1846, H.C. 1846 (697), xx, pp. 81–2;
Twenty-fifth Report … on … the Prisons of Ireland, 1847, H.C. 1847 (805), xxix, p. 93;
Twenty-sixth Report … on … the Prisons of Ireland, 1847–48, H.C. 1847–8 (952), xxiv, p. 99;
Twenty-eighth Report … on … the Prisons of Ireland, 1850, H.C. 1850 (1229), xxix, pp. 92–3;
Twenty-ninth Report … on … the Prisons of Ireland, 1851, H.C. 1851 (1364), xxviii, p. 94;
Thirty-second Report … on … the Prisons of Ireland, 1854, H.C. 1854 (1803), xxxii, p. 179;
Thirty-third Report … on … the Prisons of Ireland, 1855, H.C. 1854–5 (1956), xxvi, p. 182;
Forty-eighth Report … on … the Prisons of Ireland, 1869, H.C. 1870 (C. 173), xxxvii, p. 418.

Secondary sources:

Hill, *Building of Limerick*, pp. 87, 142; O'Dwyer, 'Public Works Architecture', p. 407; Lee, *James Pain, Architect*, pp. 17, 51; Colvin, *Biographical Dictionary of British Architects*, pp. 126–8; O'Flaherty, *Irish Historic Towns Atlas, No. 21: Limerick*, pp. 27–8; Loeber, et al., *Art and Architecture of Ireland: Volume IV: Architecture 1600–2000*, pp. 203, 467.

LIMERICK COUNTY

Limerick

Mulgrave St.
Lat. 52°39'31.68" N.; Long. 8°37'0.93" W.

Former combined county and city gaol on Merchants Quay built *c.* 1788–1801; new radial-plan county gaol built (*James Pain*, contractors *Nicholas and William Hannan*) 1817–21; new female prison added (*James Pain*) 1835–6; alterations to one of the wings, possibly to introduce separate-system confinement (*James Pain*) 1841–2; further additions to female prison, and a hospital (*James Pain*) *c.* 1848–50; extensive alterations to introduce separate-system confinement (*William Atkins*) *c.* 1865; alterations 1900; in use as a state prison; extant.

Former combined county and city gaol on Merchants Quay (see 'Limerick County and City: Limerick'), built, *c.* 1788–1801. New county courthouse (see Part I), built, 1807–14. New radial-plan county gaol built (*James Pain*, contractors *Nicholas and William Hannan*), at a cost of at least £23,000, 1817–21. Inspectors call for more female accommodation,

1827, 1829. Sundry works (*James Pain*), 1829. New female prison added (*James Pain*), 1835–6. Alterations to one of the wings, possibly to introduce separate-system confinement (*James Pain*), 1841–2. Further additions to female prison, and a hospital (*James Pain*), *c.* 1848–50. Inspectors suggest that county and city gaols should merge, 1855. Extensive alterations to introduce separate-system confinement (*William Atkins*), *c.* 1865. Alterations, 1900. In use as a state prison. Extant.

Archival and primary sources:

An account of the several presentments made … on which advances have been made by government for gaols, n.d. (NAI, SPO OP 1832–8, 1A/77/4); Limerick County grand-jury presentment books, 1815–16, 1818, 1820, 1821, 1829, etc. (Limerick City Library); *Limerick Gazette*, 9 February, 25 March, 5 April 1816; ibid., 7 March, 15 August, 16 August 1817; William Thomas Monsell to William Gregory, 6 August 1822 (NAI, CSORP 1822/702); Reid, *Travels in Ireland*, pp. 293–4; *Seventh Report of the AIPPD*, pp. 25–6; H.R. Paine to William Gossey, 9 July 1834 (NAI, CSORP 1834/2880); Fitzgerald and McGregor, *History … of the County and City of Limerick*, vol. 2, pp. 583–8; Lewis, *Topographical Dictionary*, vol. 2, p. 273; Lenihan, *History of Limerick*, pp. 341, 438, 447–8, 704; *Dublin Builder*, vol. 5, no. 76, 15 February 1863, p. 33; ibid., vol. 5, no. 84, 15 June 1863, p. 107; ibid., vol. 7, no. 125, 1 March 1865, p. 58; *The Builder*, vol. 23, no. 1154, 18 March 1865, p. 197; *Irish Builder*, vol. 42, no. 976, 16 September 1900, p. 1004.

Prison reports:

Account of All Gaols … in the … United Kingdom, H.C. 1819 (137), xvii, pp. 12–13;

Inspector General's Report of … the Prisons in Ireland for … 1818, H.C. 1819 (534), xii, p. 17;

Report from the Select Committee on the State of Gaols, H.C. 1819 (579), vii, pp. 173–4;

Prisons of Ireland: Report of Inspectors General, 1823, H.C. 1823 (342), x, pp. 6–7, 56;

Prisons of Ireland: Report of Inspectors General, 1824, H.C. 1824 (294), xxii, pp. 7, 56;

Prisons of Ireland: Report of Inspectors General, 1825, H.C. 1825 (493), xxii, p. 49;

Fifth Report … on … the Prisons of Ireland, 1827, H.C. 1826–7 (471), xi, pp. 54–5;

Sixth Report … on … the Prisons of Ireland, 1828, H.C. 1828 (68), xii, pp. 60–1;

Seventh Report … on … the Prisons of Ireland, 1829, H.C. 1829 (10), xiii, pp. 56–7;

Eighth Report … on … the Prisons of Ireland, 1830, H.C. 1830 (48), xxiv, p. 58;

Ninth Report … on … the Prisons of Ireland, 1831, H.C. 1830–1 (172), iv, pp. 42–3;

Eleventh Report … on … the Prisons of Ireland, 1833, H.C. 1833 (67), xvii, p. 26;

Thirteenth Report … on … the Prisons of Ireland, 1835, H.C. 1835 (114), xxxvi, p. 41;

Fourteenth Report … on … the Prisons of Ireland, 1836, H.C. 1836 (118), xxxv, pp. 38–9;

Seventeenth Report … on … the Prisons of Ireland, 1839, H.C. 1839 (91), xx, p. 48;

Nineteenth Report … on … the Prisons of Ireland, 1841, H.C. 1841 (299), xi, p. 52;

Twentieth Report … on … the Prisons of Ireland, 1842, H.C. 1842 (377), xxii, pp. 106–7;

Twenty-first Report … on … the Prisons of Ireland, 1843, H.C. 1843 (462), xxvii, pp. 1, 74;

Twenty-second Report … on … the Prisons of Ireland, 1844, H.C. 1844 (535), xxviii, p. 7;

Twenty-third Report … on … the Prisons of Ireland, 1844, H.C. 1845 (620), xxv, pp. 66–7;

Twenty-sixth Report … on … the Prisons of Ireland, 1847–48, H.C. 1847–8 (952), xxiv, pp. 97–8;

Twenty seventh Report … on … the Prisons of Ireland, 1849, H.C. 1849 (1069), xxvi, pp. 91–2;

Thirtieth Report … on … the Prisons of Ireland, 1852, H.C. 1852 (1531), xxv, p. 17;

Thirty-third Report … on … the Prisons of Ireland, 1855, H.C. 1854–5 (1956), xxvi, p. 177;

Forty-eighth Report … on … the Prisons of Ireland, 1869, H.C. 1870 (C. 173), xxxvii, p. 404.

Secondary sources:

McParland, 'Public Work of Architects', p. 251; Hill, *Building of Limerick*, pp. 87, 142; Williams, 'William Atkins', pp. 246, 249; O'Dwyer, 'Public Works Architecture', pp. 192, 407; Johnston, *Forms of Constraint*, p. 173; Lee, *James Pain, Architect*, pp. 31, 51–6, 364–8; O'Flaherty, *Irish Historic Towns Atlas, No. 21: Limerick*, pp. 27–8; Loeber, et al., *Art and Architecture of Ireland: Volume IV: Architecture 1600–2000*, pp. 203, 467.

LONDONDERRY (DERRY)

Derry, no. 1

Ferryquay St.
Lat. 54°59'40.68" N.; Long. 7°19'12.91" W.

An early gaol on the Diamond, at the west corner of Butcher's Street, unknown date of construction; a new gaol at Ferry Gate 1676; visited by Howard, who described it as 'six rooms over a gateway' 1787; Howard notes a new gaol is planned 1787; new gaol built *c.* 1787–91; not extant.

An early gaol on the Diamond, at the west corner of Butcher's Street, unknown date of construction. A new gaol at Ferry Gate, 1676. Visited by Howard, who described it as 'six rooms over a gateway', 1787. Howard notes a new gaol is planned, 1787. New gaol built (see 'Londonderry: Derry, no. 2'), *c.* 1787–91. Noted as still intact, though a 'most miserable building', 1827. Demolished. Not extant.

Archival and primary sources:

Londonderry Journal, 27 October 1772; Howard, *Lazarettos*, p. 97; Colby, *Ordnance Survey of the County of Londonderry*, p. 116; Simpson, *Annals of Derry*, p. 242; J.C. Beresford, 'General Statement or Description Book Containing Names of Lessees of the Honorable Irish Society', 1827 (London Metropolitan Archives, Corporation of London Records, MS IS/E/5, f. 126).

Secondary sources:

Thomas, *Irish Historic Towns Atlas, No. 15: Derry-Londonderry*, section 13.

LONDONDERRY

Derry, no. 2

Bishop St.
Lat. 54°59'34.24" N.; Long. 7°19'30.75" W.

An earlier gaol at Ferry Gate built 1676; Howard notes that a new gaol is planned 1787; new gaol built outside the city walls (*Edward Miller*) *c.* 1787–91; large polygonal-plan extension to the rear (*Henry, Mullins and McMahon*) with additions to the Miller façade as well, built at a cost of at least £31,125, 1820–4; repairs to part of foundations (*Jacob Owen*) 1844–5; alterations (*Stewart Gordon*) *c.* 1850s; alterations 1887; closed 1953; demolished 1971; only one tower survives; social housing on site; partially extant.

An earlier gaol at Ferry Gate (see 'Londonderry: Derry, no. 1'), built 1676. Howard notes that a new gaol is planned, 1787. New gaol built outside the city walls (*Edward Miller*), *c.* 1787–91. New courthouse (see Part I), 1813–17. Large polygonal-plan extension to the rear (*Henry, Mullins and McMahon*), with additions to the Miller façade as well, built at a cost of at least £31,125, 1820–4. Repairs to part of foundations (*Jacob Owen*), 1844–5. Alterations (*Stewart Gordon*), *c.* 1850s. Alterations, 1887. Closed, 1953. Demolished, 1971. Only one tower survives. Social housing on site. Partially extant.

Archival and primary sources:

Londonderry grand-jury presentment books, 1788–1899 (PRONI, LOND/4/1); Howard, *Lazarettos*, p. 97; *Journal of the Irish House of Commons*, vol. xvii, 1798, p. dcxxxii; ibid., app. cclxii, cccviii; ibid., xviii, 1799, p. ccxxxiii; George Vaughan Sampson, *Statistical Survey of the County of Londonderry, with Observations on the Means of Improvement* (Dublin: Graisberry & Campbell, 1802), p. 284; Colby, *Ordnance Survey of the County of Londonderry*, p. 116; Simpson, *Annals of Derry*, pp. 242–3; George Fitzgerald Hill to William Gregory, 6 April 1820 (NAI, CSORP 1820/604); Board of Works to William Gregory, 19 May 1820 (NAI, CSORP 1820/832); Fred Amherst journal, 1825 (NLI, MS 16,539); Reid, *Travels in Ireland*, p. 218; *Third Report of the AIPPD*, p. 43; *Fourth Report of the AIPPD*, p. 37; *Fifth Report of the AIPPD*, p. 32; Lewis, *Topographical Dictionary*, vol. 2, p. 303, *Londonderry Sentinel*, 31 December 1887.

Prison reports:

Inspector General's Report of … the Prisons in Ireland for … 1807, H.C. 1808 (239), ix, p. 12;
Account of All Gaols … in the … United Kingdom, H.C. 1819 (137), xvii, pp. 12–13;
Inspector General's Report of … the Prisons in Ireland for … 1818, H.C. 1819 (534), xii, p. 18;
Prisons of Ireland: Report of Inspectors General, 1823, H.C. 1823 (342), x, pp. 5, 33;
Prisons of Ireland: Report of Inspectors General, 1824, H.C. 1824 (294), xxii, pp. 5, 34;
Prisons of Ireland: Report of Inspectors General, 1825, H.C. 1825 (493), xxii, p. 33;
Fourth Report … on … the Prisons of Ireland, 1826, H.C. 1826 (173), xxiii, pp. 31–2;
Fifth Report … on … the Prisons of Ireland, 1827, H.C. 1826–7 (471), xi, p. 35;
Sixth Report … on … the Prisons of Ireland, 1828, H.C. 1828 (68), xii, pp. 43–4;
Seventh Report … on … the Prisons of Ireland, 1829, H.C. 1829 (10), xiii, p. 39;
Eighth Report … on … the Prisons of Ireland, 1830, H.C. 1830 (48), xxiv, p. 37;
Eighteenth Report … on … the Prisons of Ireland, 1840, H.C. 1840 (240), xxvi, p. 34;
Nineteenth Report … on … the Prisons of Ireland, 1841, H.C. 1841 (299), xi, pp. 34–5;
Twentieth Report … on … the Prisons of Ireland, 1842, H.C. 1842 (377), xxii, p. 74;
Twenty-first Report … on … the Prisons of Ireland, 1843, H.C. 1843 (462), xxvii, p. 39;
Twenty-second Report … on … the Prisons of Ireland, 1844, H.C. 1844 (535), xxviii, p. 43;
Twenty-third Report … on … the Prisons of Ireland, 1844, H.C. 1845 (620), xxv, p. 23;
Twenty-fourth Report … on … the Prisons of Ireland, 1846, H.C. 1846 (697), xx, p. 34;
Forty-ninth Report … on … the Prisons of Ireland, 1870, H.C. 1871 (C. 359), xxx, p. 169.

Secondary sources:

McParland, 'Public Work of Architects', pp. 136, 140; Photographs of Derry gaol, n.d. (Irish Architectural Archive, photographs collection nos. 37/11 v2 and 67/56 x1); Rowan, *Buildings of Ireland: North west Ulster*, p. 390; Colm M. Kavanagh, *Derry Jail* (Derry: Guildhall Press, 1990), pp. 18, 20, 23, 31–2; O'Dwyer, 'Public Works Architecture', p. 407; Thomas, *Irish Historic Towns Atlas, No. 15: Derry-Londonderry*, section 13; O'Donoghue, *Irish County Surveyors*, p. 77; Loeber, et al., *Art and Architecture of Ireland: Volume IV: Architecture 1600–2000*, p. 471.

LONGFORD

Longford, no. 1

Battery Rd.
Lat. 53°43'54.98" N.; Long. 7°48'0.07" W.

An earlier gaol built *c.* 1730; Howard visits old gaol and condemns it, and notes plans for a new gaol 1787; new rectilinear-plan gaol built *c.* 1792–6; a new gaol planned 1818; another new gaol built 1821–4; offered for sale 1840; demolished by 1874; not extant.

An earlier gaol built, *c.* 1730. Howard visits old gaol and condemns it, and notes plans for a new gaol, 1787. New rectilinear-plan gaol built, *c.* 1792–6. Forster Archer, prison inspector, notes it as a 'new and strongly built gaol', 1803. A new gaol planned, 1818. Another new gaol built, 1821–4 (see 'Longford: Longford, no. 2'). Offered for sale, 1840. Demolished by 1874. Not extant.

Archival and primary sources:

Howard, *Lazarettos*, p. 95; Longford grand-jury presentment books, spring 1792 (Longford County Library, LGJ/1/1); *Journal of the Irish House of Commons*, vol. xvii, 1797, p. ccvi; Forster Archer, 'Report of the State of Gaols of Ireland for the Year 1802', f. 11 (Houses of the Oireachtas Library, Dublin, MS.7H28); *Inspector General's Report of … the Prisons in Ireland for … 1807*, H.C. 1808 (239), ix, p. 13; Longford grand-jury presentment book, spring 1818 (Longford County Library, LGJ/2/3); *Longford Journal*, 18 August 1840; J.P. Farrell, *Historical Notes and Stories of the County Longford* (Dublin: Dollard, 1886), p. 147.

Secondary sources:

Gearty, Morris and O'Ferrall, *Irish Historic Towns Atlas, No. 22: Longford*, p. 11.

LONGFORD

Longford, no. 2

Battery Rd.
Lat. 53°43'58.39" N.; Long. 7°48'9.26" W.

Howard visits old gaol and condemns it, and notes plans for a new gaol 1787; a rectilinear-plan gaol built *c.* 1788–96; a new gaol planned 1818; unexecuted designs (*William Farrell*, and *Richard Richards*) 1818–19; another new gaol built (*John Hargrave*) 1821–4; addition of some school rooms and other sundry works 1845; alterations and additions to kitchens and wash-house 1851; work to entrance lodge (*James Bell*) 1861; closed before *c.* 1900; mostly demolished *c.* 1900; in use as a school 1974; partially extant.

Howard visits an old gaol and condemns it, and notes plans for a new gaol, 1787. A rectilinear-plan gaol built (see 'Longford: Longford, no. 1'), *c.* 1788–96. Forster Archer notes regular repairs and that the prison was 15 years old in 1811. Grand jury discussions over whether to make additions to existing gaol, or build an entirely new building, 1818. Unexecuted designs (*William Farrell*, and *Richard Richards*), 1818–19. Another new gaol built (*John Hargrave*), at a cost of £14,000, 1821–4. Addition of some school rooms and other sundry works, 1845. Alterations and additions to kitchens and wash-house, 1851. Work to entrance lodge (*James Bell*), 1861. Closed before *c.* 1900. Mostly demolished, *c.* 1900. Parts of gaol in use as Leamore Park house and lodge. Site and buildings sold, 1973. Converted to St Christopher's School, 1974. In use as a school. Partially extant.

Archival and primary sources:

Howard, *Lazarettos*, p. 95; *Journal of the Irish House of Commons*, vol. xvii, 1797, p. ccvi; Forster Archer, 'Report of the State of Gaols of Ireland for the Year 1811' (Houses of the Oireachtas Library, Dublin, MS.4E63); Longford grand-jury presentment books, 1818–23 (Longford County Library, LGJ/2/3-6); Lord Forbes to William Gregory, 17 December 1820 (NAI, CSORP 1820/592); George Fetherston to Henry Goulburn, 11 September 1822 (NAI, CSORP 1822/1666); Lord Longford to Henry Goulburn, 22 January 1826 (NAI, CSORP 1825/12,783); Plan, elevation and section drawings for Longford gaol and surrounding buildings, n.d., n.s. [*c.* 1821] (NLI, AD 2652–7); *Third Report of the AIPPD*, p. 43; *Fourth*

Report of the AIPPD, p. 37; *Fifth Report of the AIPPD*, p. 32; Lewis, *Topographical Dictionary*, vol. 2, p. 311; Morrison, 'Life of the Late William Vitruvius Morrison', p. 7; *Parliamentary Gazetteer of Ireland*, 1846, vol. 2, p. 689; *The Builder*, vol. 17, no. 856, 2 July 1859, p. 444; *Dublin Builder*, vol. 1, no. 6, 1 June 1859, p. 75, ibid., vol. 2, no. 24, 1 December 1860, p. 388.

Prison reports:

Inspector General's Report of … the Prisons in Ireland for … 1807, H.C. 1808 (239), ix, p. 13;

Account of All Gaols … in the … United Kingdom, H.C. 1819 (137), xvii, pp. 12–13;

Inspector General's Report of … the Prisons in Ireland for … 1818, H.C. 1819 (534), xii, pp. 18–19;

Report from the Select Committee on the State of Gaols, H.C. 1819 (579), vii, p. 214;

Prisons of Ireland: Report of Inspectors General, 1823, H.C. 1823 (342), x, pp. 5, 35;

Prisons of Ireland: Report of Inspectors General, 1824, H.C. 1824 (294), xxii, p. 5;

Prisons of Ireland: Report of Inspectors General, 1825, H.C. 1825 (493), xxii, pp. 50–1;

Fifth Report … on … the Prisons of Ireland, 1827, H.C. 1826–7 (471), xi, pp. 33–4;

Sixth Report … on … the Prisons of Ireland, 1828, H.C. 1828 (68), xii, p. 45;

Seventeenth Report … on … the Prisons of Ireland, 1839, H.C. 1839 (91), xx, p. 30;

Eighteenth Report … on … the Prisons of Ireland, 1840, H.C. 1840 (240), xxvi, p. 33;

Nineteenth Report … on … the Prisons of Ireland, 1841, H.C. 1841 (299), xi, p. 34;

Twenty-first Report … on … the Prisons of Ireland, 1843, H.C. 1843 (462), xxvii, p. 41;

Twenty-fourth Report … on … the Prisons of Ireland, 1846, H.C. 1846 (697), xx, p. 36;

Thirtieth Report … on … the Prisons of Ireland, 1852, H.C. 1852 (1531), xxv, p. 17;

Forty-ninth Report … on … the Prisons of Ireland, 1870, H.C. 1871 (C. 359), xxx, p. 184.

Secondary sources:

Rowan, *Architecture of Richard Morrison*, p. 181; O'Dwyer, 'Public Works Architecture', p. 407; Sylvia Dawson, *Saint Christopher's: The first crucial years, 1964–1975*, 2nd edn (Longford, 2001), pp. 34, 37; O'Donoghue, *Irish County Surveyors*, p. 95; Gearty, Morris and O'Ferrall, *Irish Historic Towns Atlas, No. 22: Longford*, p. 11.

LOUTH

Dundalk, no. 1

Crowe St.
Lat. 54°0'16.70" N.; Long. 6°24'1.72" W.

Castlenyrooty Castle purchased by the Louth grand jury for use as a gaol 1667; another gaol was likely built sometime in the eighteenth century; Forster Archer, prison inspector, suggests many additions and alterations (seemingly unexecuted) 1803; extensive additions, or perhaps an entirely new gaol (*John Bowden*) 1815–20; inspectors call for additions 1824–34; commissioners appointed to build a new gaol elsewhere 1847; new gaol built elsewhere 1849–54; old gaol abandoned 1854; demolished; purchased by Dundalk Exchange and Market Company 1856, corn exchange, etc., built on site 1856–61, gaol not extant.

Castlenyrooty Castle purchased by the Louth grand jury for use as a gaol, 1667. Another gaol was likely built sometime in the eighteenth century. Forster Archer, prison inspector, suggests many additions and alterations (seemingly unexecuted), 1803, 1812. A new courthouse (see Part I), 1813–21. Extensive additions, or perhaps an entirely new gaol (*John Bowden*), built at a cost of at least £12,922, 1815–20. Inspectors call for additions, 1824–34. Inspectors promote the idea of a common house of correction for Louth and neighbouring counties, 1838. Commissioners appointed to build a new gaol elsewhere, 1847. New gaol built elsewhere (see 'Louth: Dundalk, no. 2'), 1849–54. Old gaol abandoned, 1854. Demolished. Purchased by Dundalk Exchange and Market Company, 1856. Corn exchange, etc., built on site, 1856–61. Gaol not extant.

Archival and primary sources:

Howard, *Lazarettos*, p. 97; John Bowden to John Foster, 9 August 1814 (PRONI, D/562/13002); John Foster to Robert Peel, 1 September 1814 (NAI, SPO 558/423/23); An account of the several presentments made … on which advances have been made by government for gaols, n.d. (NAI, SPO OP 1832–8, 1A/77/4); Forster Archer, 'Report of the State of Gaols of Ireland for the Year 1802', f. 11 (Houses of the Oireachtas Library, Dublin, MS.7H28); Forster Archer, 'Report of the State of Gaols of Ireland for the Year 1811' (Houses of the Oireachtas Library, Dublin, MS.4E63); Atkinson, *Ireland Exhibited to England*, vol. 1, pp. 92–3; Reid, *Travels in Ireland*, p. 231; *Fourth Report of the AIPPD*, p. 38; Thackeray, *Irish Sketch Book*, pp. 282–3; D'Alton and O'Flanagan, *History of Dundalk*, pp. 162, 169, 335; Lacy, *Sights and Scenes in Our Fatherland*, pp. 223–4; Photographs of old gaol, n.d. (Louth County Archives).

Prison reports:

Inspector General's Report of … the Prisons in Ireland for … 1807, H.C. 1808 (239), ix, p. 13;

Account of All Gaols … in the … United Kingdom, H.C. 1819 (137), xvii, pp. 14–15;

Inspector General's Report of … the Prisons in Ireland for … 1818, H.C. 1819 (534), xii, pp. 19–20;

Prisons of Ireland: Report of Inspectors General, 1823, H.C. 1823 (342), x, pp. 5–6, 32–3;

Prisons of Ireland: Report of Inspectors General, 1824, H.C. 1824 (294), xxii, pp. 6, 34;

Prisons of Ireland: Report of Inspectors General, 1825, H.C. 1825 (493), xxii, p. 51;

Fifth Report … on … the Prisons of Ireland, 1827, H.C. 1826–7 (471), xi, p. 32;

Sixth Report … on … the Prisons of Ireland, 1828, H.C. 1828 (68), xii, p. 45;

Seventh Report … on … the Prisons of Ireland, 1829, H.C. 1829 (10), xiii, p. 40;

Eighth Report … on … the Prisons of Ireland, 1830, H.C. 1830 (48), xxiv, pp. 39–40;

Ninth Report … on … the Prisons of Ireland, 1831, H.C. 1830–1 (172), iv, p. 29;

Tenth Report … on … the Prisons of Ireland, 1832, H.C. 1831–2 (152), xvii, p. 29;

Eleventh Report … on … the Prisons of Ireland, 1833, H.C. 1833 (67), xvii, p. 41–2;

Twelfth Report … on … the Prisons of Ireland, 1834, H.C. 1834 (63), xl, p. 47;

Thirteenth Report … on … the Prisons of Ireland, 1835, H.C. 1835 (114), xxxvi, p. 29;

Fourteenth Report … on … the Prisons of Ireland, 1836, H.C. 1836 (118), xxxv, p. 27;

Fifteenth Report … on … the Prisons of Ireland, 1837, H.C. 1837 (123), xxxi, p. 27;

Sixteenth Report … on … the Prisons of Ireland, 1838, H.C. 1837–8 (186), xxix, p. 31;

Seventeenth Report … on … the Prisons of Ireland, 1839, H.C. 1839 (91), xx, p. 32;

Eighteenth Report … on … the Prisons of Ireland, 1840, H.C. 1840 (240), xxvi, p. 35;

Nineteenth Report … on … the Prisons of Ireland, 1841, H.C. 1841 (299), xi, p. 36;

Twenty-second Report … on … the Prisons of Ireland, 1844, H.C. 1844 (535), xxviii, p. 48;

Twenty-third Report … on … the Prisons of Ireland, 1844, H.C. 1845 (620), xxv, p. 26.

Secondary sources:

O'Dwyer, 'Public Works Architecture', p. 407; O'Sullivan, *Irish Historic Towns Atlas, No. 16: Dundalk*, section 13.

LOUTH

Dundalk, no. 2

The Crescent
Lat. 53°59'58.0" N.; Long. 6°24'35.18" W.

Extensive additions, or perhaps an entirely new gaol 1815–20; inspectors call for additions 1824–34; commissioners appointed to build a new gaol elsewhere 1847; new gaol built (*John Neville*) 1849–54; closed 1931; in use as a Garda station 1945 onwards; also in use as Louth County Archives *c.* 2000 onwards; extant.

Extensive additions, or perhaps an entirely new gaol built (see 'Louth: Dundalk, no. 1'), 1815–20. Inspectors call for additions, 1824–34. Inspectors promote the idea of a common house of correction for Louth and neighbouring counties, 1838. Commissioners appointed to build a new gaol elsewhere, 1847. New gaol built (*John Neville*), at a cost of £23,000, 1849–54. Closed, 1931. In use as a Garda station, 1945 onwards. Also in use as Louth County Archives, *c.* 2000 onwards. Extant.

Archival and primary sources:

Thackeray, *Irish Sketch Book*, pp. 282–3; D'Alton and O'Flanagan, *History of Dundalk*, pp. 162, 169, 335; Louth grand-jury presentment books, 1847–99 (Louth County Archives, GJ/005); *Civil Engineer and Architect's Journal*, vol. 16, no. 229, April 1853, p. 121 (illus.); Lacy, *Sights and Scenes in Our Fatherland*, pp. 223–4; *Dublin Builder*, vol. 5, no. 87, 1 August 1863, p. 131; *Dundalk Prison Closing Order* (Dublin: Stationary Office, 1931).

Prison reports:

Prisons of Ireland: Report of Inspectors General, 1824, H.C. 1824 (294), xxii, pp. 6, 34;

Prisons of Ireland: Report of Inspectors General, 1825, H.C. 1825 (493), xxii, p. 51;

Fifth Report … on … the Prisons of Ireland, 1827, H.C. 1826–7 (471), xi, p. 32;

Sixth Report … on … the Prisons of Ireland, 1828, H.C. 1828 (68), xii, p. 45;

Seventh Report … on … the Prisons of Ireland, 1829, H.C. 1829 (10), xiii, p. 40;

Eighth Report … on … the Prisons of Ireland, 1830, H.C. 1830 (48), xxiv, pp. 39–40;

Ninth Report … on … the Prisons of Ireland, 1831, H.C. 1830–1 (172), iv, p. 29;

Tenth Report … on … the Prisons of Ireland, 1832, H.C. 1831–2 (152), xvii, p. 29;

Eleventh Report … on … the Prisons of Ireland, 1833, H.C. 1833 (67), xvii, p. 41–2;

Twelfth Report … on … the Prisons of Ireland, 1834, H.C. 1834 (63), xl, p. 47;

Thirteenth Report … on … the Prisons of Ireland, 1835, H.C. 1835 (114), xxxvi, p. 29;

Fourteenth Report … on … the Prisons of Ireland, 1836, H.C. 1836 (118), xxxv, p. 27;

Fifteenth Report … on … the Prisons of Ireland, 1837, H.C. 1837 (123), xxxi, p. 27;

Sixteenth Report … on … the Prisons of Ireland, 1838, H.C. 1837–8 (186), xxix, p. 31;

Seventeenth Report … on … the Prisons of Ireland, 1839, H.C. 1839 (91), xx, p. 32;

Eighteenth Report … on … the Prisons of Ireland, 1840, H.C. 1840 (240), xxvi, p. 35;

Nineteenth Report … on … the Prisons of Ireland, 1841, H.C. 1841 (299), xi, p. 36;

Twenty-second Report … on … the Prisons of Ireland, 1844, H.C. 1844 (535), xxviii, p. 48;

Twenty-third Report … on … the Prisons of Ireland, 1844, H.C. 1845 (620), xxv, p. 26;

Twenty-fifth Report … on … the Prisons of Ireland, 1847, H.C. 1847 (805), xxix, p. 54;

Twenty-sixth Report … on … the Prisons of Ireland, 1847–48, H.C. 1847–8 (952), xxiv, pp. 10, 64;

Twenty-seventh Report ... on ... the Prisons of Ireland, 1849, H.C. 1849 (1069), xxvi, p. 57;
Twenty-eighth Report ... on ... the Prisons of Ireland, 1850, H.C. 1850 (1229), xxix, pp. 11, 55;
Twenty-ninth Report ... on ... the Prisons of Ireland, 1851, H.C. 1851 (1364), xxviii, p. 37;
Thirtieth Report ... on ... the Prisons of Ireland, 1852, H.C. 1852 (1531), xxv, pp. 108–12;
Thirty-first Report ... on ... the Prisons of Ireland, 1853, H.C. 1853 (1657), liii, p. 106;
Thirty-second Report ... on ... the Prisons of Ireland, 1854, H.C. 1854 (1803), xxxii, pp. 20, 86;
Forty-ninth Report ... on ... the Prisons of Ireland, 1870, H.C. 1871 (C. 359), xxx, p. 196.

Secondary sources:

Casey, 'John Neville', pp. 23–5; O'Dwyer, 'Public Works Architecture', p. 407; Casey and Rowan, *Buildings of Ireland: North Leinster*, p. 247; O'Sullivan, *Irish Historic Towns Atlas, No. 16: Dundalk*, section 13; O'Donoghue, *Irish County Surveyors*, p. 267.

TOWN OF DROGHEDA

Drogheda

Scarlet St.
Lat. 53°43'8.12" N.; Long. 6°20'49.84" W.

A former gaol was located on James' Street, and had underground cells; Forster Archer calls for a new prison 1803, 1807; new gaol built (*John Bowden*) 1814–18; design and construction condemned by Forster Archer 1818; conversion of one day-room into four additional cells 1827; financial problems within the town grand jury lead to a suspension of funding of the gaol *c.* 1839–42; inspectors threaten to close gaol and move prisoners to Dundalk 1848, 1851; assize judge threatens the same 1851; extensive alterations and additions (*John Neville*) comprising thirty-five cells in total built 1859–61; closed before *c.* 1900; in use as a hardware store; partially extant.

A former gaol was located on James' Street, and had underground cells. Forster Archer calls for a new prison, 1803, 1807, 1812. New gaol built (*John Bowden*), at a cost of around £12,000, 1814–18. Design and construction condemned by Forster Archer, 1818. Conversion of one day-room into four additional cells, 1827. Financial problems within the town grand jury lead to a suspension of funding of the gaol, *c.* 1839–42. Inspectors threatened to close gaol and move prisoners to Dundalk, 1848, 1851. Assize judge threatens the same, 1851. Extensive alterations and additions (*John Neville*), comprising thirty-five cells in total, built, 1859–61. Closed before *c.* 1900. In use as a hardware store. Partially extant.

Archival and primary sources:

Forster Archer, 'Report of the State of Gaols of Ireland for the Year 1802', f. 4 (Houses of the Oireachtas Library, Dublin, MS.7H28); Forster Archer, 'Report of the State of Gaols of Ireland for the Year 1811' (Houses of the Oireachtas Library, Dublin, MS.4E63); John Leslie Foster to Robert Peel, 15 March 1813 (British Library, Add. MS 40225, ff. 227–30); John Bowden to William Gregory, 25 July 1814, and John Foster to Robert Peel, 1 September 1814 (NAI, SPO 558/423/23); Town of Drogheda grand-jury presentments book, spring assizes 1814 (NAI, SPO 588 YY 910); An account of the several presentments made ... on which advances have been made by government for gaols, n.d. (NAI, SPO OP 1832–8, 1A/77/4); Reid, *Travels in Ireland*, p. 234; *Third Report of the AIPPD*, p. 43; Lewis, *Topographical Dictionary*, vol. 1, p. 501; Grand Juries (Ireland) Act, 1843 (6 & 7 Vict., c. 32); Grand-jury presentments, Ireland Act, 1843 (6 & 7 Vict., c. 71); *The Builder*, vol. 10, no. 493, 17 July 1852, p. 460; ibid., vol. 12, no. 592, 10 June 1854, p. 305; ibid., vol. 16, no. 782, 30 January 1858, p. 73; *Dublin Builder*, vol. 3, no. 29, 1 March 1861, p. 448.

Prison reports:

Inspector General's Report of ... the Prisons in Ireland for ... 1807, H.C. 1808 (239), ix, p. 6;

Account of All Gaols … in the United Kingdom, H.C. 1819 (137), xvii, pp. 14–15;
Inspector General's Report of the Prisons in Ireland for … 1818, H.C. 1819 (534), xii, pp. [illegible];
Prisons of Ireland: Report of Inspectors General, 1823, H.C. 1823 (342), x, pp. 6, 33;
Prisons of Ireland: Report of Inspectors General, 1824, H.C. 1824 (294), xxii, pp. 6, 34;
Prisons of Ireland: Report of Inspectors General, 1825, H.C. 1825 (493), xxii, p. 52;
Fourth Report … on … the Prisons of Ireland, 1826, H.C. 1826 (173), xxiii, p. 31;
Sixth Report … on … the Prisons of Ireland, 1828, H.C. 1828 (68), xii, pp. 45–6;
Thirteenth Report … on … the Prisons of Ireland, 1835, H.C. 1835 (114), xxxvi, p. 30;
Sixteenth Report … on … the Prisons of Ireland, 1838, H.C. 1837–8 (186), xxix, p. 32;
Seventeenth Report … on … the Prisons of Ireland, 1839, H.C. 1839 (91), xx, p. 32;
Eighteenth Report … on … the Prisons of Ireland, 1840, H.C. 1840 (240), xxvi, pp. 35–6;
Nineteenth Report … on … the Prisons of Ireland, 1841, H.C. 1841 (299), xi, p. 37;
Twentieth Report … on … the Prisons of Ireland, 1842, H.C. 1842 (377), xxii, pp. 82–3;
Twenty-first Report … on … the Prisons of Ireland, 1843, H.C. 1843 (462), xxvii, p. 43;
Twenty-second Report … on … the Prisons of Ireland, 1844, H.C. 1844 (535), xxviii, p. 50;
Twenty-fourth Report … on … the Prisons of Ireland, 1846, H.C. 1846 (697), xx, p. 41;
Twenty-fifth Report … on … the Prisons of Ireland, 1847, H.C. 1847 (805), xxix, p. 56;
Twenty-sixth Report … on … the Prisons of Ireland, 1847–48, H.C. 1847–8 (952), xxiv, pp. 66–7;
Twenty-ninth Report … on … the Prisons of Ireland, 1851, H.C. 1851 (1364), xxviii, p. 39;
Thirtieth Report … on … the Prisons of Ireland, 1852, H.C. 1852 (1531), xxv, p. 114;
Thirty-first Report … on … the Prisons of Ireland, 1853, H.C. 1853 (1657), liii, pp. 17, 110;
Thirty-second Report … on … the Prisons of Ireland, 1854, H.C. 1854 (1803), xxxii, pp. 93–8;
Thirty-third Report … on … the Prisons of Ireland, 1855, H.C. 1854–5 (1956), xxvi, p. 82;
Thirty-fourth Report … on … the Prisons of Ireland, 1856, H.C. 1856 (2113), xxxiv, p. 117;
Thirty-seventh Report … on … the Prisons of Ireland, 1859, H.C. 1859, session 2 (2557), xiii, p. 174;
Thirty-eighth Report … on … the Prisons of Ireland, 1860, H.C. 1860 (2691), xxxvi, p. 178;
Thirty-ninth Report … on … the Prisons of Ireland, 1861, H.C. 1861 (2861), xxix, p. 148;
Fortieth Report … on … the Prisons of Ireland, 1862, H.C. 1862 (3020), xxvi, p. 172;
Forty-ninth Report … on … the Prisons of Ireland, 1870, H.C. 1871 (C. 359), xxx, p. 207.

Secondary sources:

Ned McHugh, 'Drogheda Jail during the Period of the Famine', *Journal of the Old Drogheda Society*, vol. 5, 1986, pp. 47–58;
Casey and Rowan, *Buildings of Ireland: North Leinster*, p. 247.

MAYO

Castlebar, no. 1

The Green
Lat. 53°51'16.58" N.; Long. 9°17'49.04" W.

An ancient gaol visited by Howard, and condemned 1788; a new gaol being planned 1788; new gaol built on The Green *c.* 1796; Forster Archer calls for a new gaol 1818; collapse of part of the gaol, killing one prisoner 1819; third story added to gaol *c.* 1819–20; inspectors call for a new gaol 1824 onwards; new radial-plan gaol built 1831–5; old gaol abandoned 1835; problems disposing of the site 1838 onwards; still intact, though ruined 1850; demolished; county council offices now occupy the site; not extant.

An ancient gaol visited by Howard, and condemned, 1788. A new gaol being planned, 1788. New gaol built on The Green, *c.* 1796. Forster Archer calls for additions and alterations, 1803. Forster Archer notes grand-jury presentments to improve the interior of the gaol, 1812. Forster Archer calls for a new gaol, 1818. Collapse of part of the gaol, killing one prisoner, 1819. Third story added to gaol, *c.* 1819–20. Inspectors call for a new gaol, 1824 onwards. New radial-plan gaol (see 'Mayo: Castlebar, no. 2'), built, 1831–5. Old gaol abandoned, 1835. Problems disposing of the site, 1838 onwards. Still intact, though ruined, 1850. Demolished. County council offices now occupy the site. Not extant.

Archival and primary sources:

Howard, *Lazarettos*, p. 93; *Journal of the Irish House of Commons*, vol. xvii, 1797, p. ccvi; 'Forster Archer's Tour of Ireland in 1801' (British Library, Add. MS 35920); Forster Archer, 'Report of the State of Gaols of Ireland for the Year 1802', f. 12 (Houses of the Oireachtas Library, Dublin, MS.7H28); Forster Archer, 'Report of the State of Gaols of Ireland for the Year 1811' (Houses of the Oireachtas Library, Dublin, MS.4E63); Henry Pasley to Forster Archer, 19 November 1819 (NAI, CSORP 1819/212); Reid, *Travels in Ireland*, pp. 316–18; Lewis, *Topographical Dictionary*, vol. 1, p. 289; *Mayo Constitution*, 5 March 1835; *Connaught Telegraph*, 7 March 1838; John Hervey Ashworth, *The Saxon in Ireland; or, the rambles of an Englishman in search of a settlement in the west of Ireland* (London: Murray, 1851), pp. 113–14.

Prison reports:

Inspector General's Report of … the Prisons in Ireland for … 1807, H.C. 1808 (239), ix, p. 13;
Account of All Gaols … in the … United Kingdom, H.C. 1819 (137), xvii, pp. 14–15;
Inspector General's Report of … the Prisons in Ireland for … 1818, H.C. 1819 (534), xii, pp. 20–1;
Prisons of Ireland: Report of Inspectors General, 1823, H.C. 1823 (342), x, pp. 59–60;
Prisons of Ireland: Report of Inspectors General, 1824, H.C. 1824 (294), xxii, pp. 7, 58–9;
Prisons of Ireland: Report of Inspectors General, 1825, H.C. 1825 (493), xxii, pp. 52–3;
Fourth Report … on … the Prisons of Ireland, 1826, H.C. 1826 (173), xxiii, p. 49;
Fifth Report … on … the Prisons of Ireland, 1827, H.C. 1826–7 (471), xi, p. 57;
Sixth Report … on … the Prisons of Ireland, 1828, H.C. 1828 (68), xii, pp. 62–3;
Seventh Report … on … the Prisons of Ireland, 1829, H.C. 1829 (10), xiii, pp. 9, 59–60;
Eighth Report … on … the Prisons of Ireland, 1830, H.C. 1830 (48), xxiv, pp. 60–1;
Ninth Report … on … the Prisons of Ireland, 1831, H.C. 1830–1 (172), iv, p. 45;
Tenth Report … on … the Prisons of Ireland, 1832, H.C. 1831–2 (152), xvii, pp. 5, 45;
Eleventh Report … on … the Prisons of Ireland, 1833, H.C. 1833 (67), xvii, p. 28;
Twelfth Report … on … the Prisons of Ireland, 1834, H.C. 1834 (63), xl, pp. 31–2;
Thirteenth Report … on … the Prisons of Ireland, 1835, H.C. 1835 (114), xxxvi, p. 43;
Fourteenth Report … on … the Prisons of Ireland, 1836, H.C. 1836 (118), xxxv, p. 40.

Secondary sources:

O'Dwyer, 'Public Works Architecture', p. 407.

MAYO

Castlebar, no. 1

Church St.
Lat. 53°51'6.67" N ; Long. 9°18'16.58" W

A gaol built on The Green *c.* 1796; Forster Archer calls for a new gaol 1818; collapse of part of the gaol, killing one prisoner 1819; third story added to gaol *c.* 1819–20; inspectors call for a new gaol 1824 onwards; new radial-plan gaol built (*Frederick Darley*) 1831–5; alterations to the female prison to allow separate-system confinement (*Enoch Trevor Owen*) *c.* 1879; occupied by the Black and Tans *c.* 1921; partially destroyed by the IRA, soon after; site purchased by Mayo County Board of Health 1932–3; demolished *c.* 1932–3; a hospital built on the site; not extant.

A gaol built on The Green, *c.* 1796. Forster Archer calls for a new gaol, 1818. Collapse of part of the gaol, killing one prisoner, 1819. Third story added to gaol, *c.* 1819–20. Inspectors call for a new gaol, 1824 onwards. New radial-plan gaol (*Frederick Darley*), built at a cost of around £23,000, 1831–5. Alterations to the female prison to allow separate-system confinement (*Enoch Trevor Owen*), *c.* 1879. Status of gaol downgraded, 1915. Occupied by the Black and Tans, *c.* 1921. Partially destroyed by the IRA, soon after. Site purchased by Mayo County Board of Health, 1932–3. Demolished, *c.* 1932–3. A hospital built on the site. Not extant.

Archival and primary sources:

Howard, *Lazarettos*, p. 93; *Journal of the Irish House of Commons*, vol. xvii, 1797, p. ccvi; 'Forster Archer's Tour of Ireland in 1801' (British Library, Add. MS 35920); Henry Pasley to Forster Archer, 19 November 1819 (NAI, CSORP 1819/212); Reid, *Travels in Ireland*, pp. 316–18; Frederick Darley to William Gregory, 19 May 1829 (NAI, CSORP 1829/671); William Murray to R. Robinson, 26 July 1830 (NAI, CSORP 1830/3042); Lewis, *Topographical Dictionary*, vol. 1, p. 289; Binns, *Miseries and Beauties of Ireland*, vol. 1, p. 373; *Mayo Constitution*, 7 June, 14 October 1830; ibid., 5 March 1835; *Connaught Telegraph*, 6 August 1834; ibid., 19 August 1835; ibid., 19 July 1837; ibid., 7 March 1838; Thackeray, *Irish Sketch Book*, p. 241; *Dublin Builder*, vol. 2, no. 18, 1 August 1860, p. 308; Lacy, *Sights and Scenes in Our Fatherland*, pp. 281–2; Plan and section drawings for Castlebar gaol, 8 October 1879 (NAI, OPW 5HC/4/415); Survey drawings of Castlebar gaol, 1920 (NAI, OPW 5HC/4/415); *Connaught Telegraph*, 31 July 1915; ibid., 30 January 1932; ibid., 24 January 1933; *Western People*, 3 March 1932; Photographs of Castlebar gaol, n.d. (Mayo County Archive).

Prison reports:

Inspector General's Report of … the Prisons in Ireland for … 1807, H.C. 1808 (239), ix, p. 13;
Account of All Gaols … in the … United Kingdom, H.C. 1819 (137), xvii, pp. 14–15;
Inspector General's Report of … the Prisons in Ireland for … 1818, H.C. 1819 (534), xii, pp. 20–1;
Prisons of Ireland: Report of Inspectors General, 1823, H.C. 1823 (342), x, pp. 59–60;
Prisons of Ireland: Report of Inspectors General, 1824, H.C. 1824 (294), xxii, pp. 7, 58–9;
Prisons of Ireland: Report of Inspectors General, 1825, H.C. 1825 (493), xxii, pp. 52–3;
Fourth Report … on … the Prisons of Ireland, 1826, H.C. 1826 (173), xxiii, p. 49;
Fifth Report … on … the Prisons of Ireland, 1827, H.C. 1826–7 (471), xi, p. 57;
Sixth Report … on … the Prisons of Ireland, 1828, H.C. 1828 (68), xii, pp. 62–3;
Seventh Report … on … the Prisons of Ireland, 1829, H.C. 1829 (10), xiii, pp. 9, 59–60;
Eighth Report … on … the Prisons of Ireland, 1830, H.C. 1830 (48), xxiv, pp. 60–1;
Ninth Report … on … the Prisons of Ireland, 1831, H.C. 1830–1 (172), iv, p. 45;
Tenth Report … on … the Prisons of Ireland, 1832, H.C. 1831–2 (152), xvii, pp. 5, 45;

Eleventh Report ... on ... the Prisons of Ireland, 1833, H.C. 1833 (67), xvii, p. 28;
Twelfth Report ... on ... the Prisons of Ireland, 1834, H.C. 1834 (63), xl, pp. 31–2;
Thirteenth Report ... on ... the Prisons of Ireland, 1835, H.C. 1835 (114), xxxvi, p. 43;
Fourteenth Report ... on ... the Prisons of Ireland, 1836, H.C. 1836 (118), xxxv, p. 40;
Seventeenth Report ... on ... the Prisons of Ireland, 1839, H.C. 1839 (91), xx, p. 49;
Nineteenth Report ... on ... the Prisons of Ireland, 1841, H.C. 1841 (299), xi, p. 54;
Twentieth Report ... on ... the Prisons of Ireland, 1842, H.C. 1842 (377), xxii, p. 109;
Twenty-second Report ... on ... the Prisons of Ireland, 1844, H.C. 1844 (535), xxviii, p. 51;
Twenty-seventh Report ... on ... the Prisons of Ireland, 1849, H.C. 1849 (1069), xxvi, p. 60;
Twenty-eighth Report ... on ... the Prisons of Ireland, 1850, H.C. 1850 (1229), xxix, p. 58;
Forty-ninth Report ... on ... the Prisons of Ireland, 1870, H.C. 1871 (C. 359), xxx, pp. 218–19.

Secondary sources:

Quinn, *History of Mayo*, pp. 368–9; O'Dwyer, 'Public Works Architecture', p. 407; Ivor Hamrock, 'Notes on Castlebar Gaol, 1830–1932' (unpublished manuscript, 2002, copy in Mayo County Library); Dickson, *Dublin*, pp. 271, 301.

MEATH

Trim, no. 1

Bridge St. & Mill St.
Lat. 53°33'23.27" N.; Long. 6°47'28.74" W.

Presentment towards building an earlier gaol 1681; a new gaol built (*Thomas Cooley*) *c.* 1780–5; extensive additions (*William Robertson*) *c.* 1801–8; bridewell built adjacent to gaol 1817–18; new female prison added 1822–3; inspectors call for a new gaol 1823 onwards; new gaol built elsewhere 1828–34; old gaol thereafter used for private housing; old gaol occupied by police forces during the War of Independence 1920–1; sold to Meath County Council 1982; opened as Meath Heritage Centre 1993–4; mostly extant.

Presentment towards building an earlier gaol, 1681. This gaol complete by 1684. A new gaol built (*Thomas Cooley*), *c.* 1780–5. Extensive additions (*William Robertson*), *c.* 1801–8. Forster Archer, prison inspector, recommends an entirely new prison near the Yellow Steeple, Trim, 1803. New courthouse built (see Part I), *c.* 1809. Bridewell built adjacent to gaol, 1817–18. Addition of a new female prison, 1822–3. Inspectors call for a new gaol, 1823 onwards. Grand jury consider building a new gaol, 1823 onwards. New gaol built elsewhere (see 'Meath: Trim, no. 2'), 1828–34. Old gaol thereafter used for private housing. Old gaol occupied by police forces during the War of Independence, 1920–1. Sold to Meath County Council, 1982. Opened as Meath Heritage Centre, 1993–4. Mostly extant.

Archival and primary sources:

Trim Corporation assembly minutes, 1760–1841, for 16 March 1760 (NLI, MS 2998, p. 131); Howard, *State of the Prisons*, p. 207; Howard, *Lazarettos*, p. 99; Forster Archer, 'Report of the State of Gaols of Ireland for the Year 1802', f. 12 (Houses of the Oireachtas Library, Dublin, MS.7H28); Richard Colt Hoare, *Journal of a Tour in Ireland, A.D. 1806* (London: Miller, 1807), p. 20; Meath grand-jury presentment book, summer 1806 (University of Illinois at Urbana-Champaign Rare Book and Manuscript Library, Champaign, IL); *Accounts of the Presentments Passed by the Grand Juries of Ireland ... in ... 1807*, H.C. 1808 (205), xiii, pp. 272, 306; Atkinson, *Irish Tourist*, pp. 243–5; Price, *Eighteenth-century Antiquary*, p. 99; *Fourth Report of the AIPPD*, p. 39; *Fifth Report of the AIPPD*, p. 33.

Prison reports:

Inspector General's Report of … the Prisons in Ireland for … 1807, H.C. 1808 (239), ix, p. 14;
Account of All Gaols … in the … United Kingdom, H.C. 1819 (137), xvii, pp. 14–15;
Inspector General's Report of … the Prisons in Ireland for … 1818, H.C. 1819 (534), xii, p. 21;
Prisons of Ireland: Report of Inspectors General, 1823, H.C. 1823 (342), x, p. 6;
Prisons of Ireland: Report of Inspectors General, 1824, H.C. 1824 (294), xxii, pp. 6, 36;
Prisons of Ireland: Report of Inspectors General, 1825, H.C. 1825 (493), xxii, pp. 53–4;
Fourth Report … on … the Prisons of Ireland, 1826, H.C. 1826 (173), xxiii, pp. 34–5;
Fifth Report … on … the Prisons of Ireland, 1827, H.C. 1826–7 (471), xi, p. 37;
Sixth Report … on … the Prisons of Ireland, 1828, H.C. 1828 (68), xii, pp. 46–7;
Seventh Report … on … the Prisons of Ireland, 1829, H.C. 1829 (10), xiii, pp. 9, 41;
Eighth Report … on … the Prisons of Ireland, 1830, H.C. 1830 (48), xxiv, p. 40;
Ninth Report … on … the Prisons of Ireland, 1831, H.C. 1830–1 (172), iv, p. 29;
Tenth Report … on … the Prisons of Ireland, 1832, H.C. 1831–2 (152), xvii, p. 30;
Eleventh Report … on … the Prisons of Ireland, 1833, H.C. 1833 (67), xvii, p. 42;
Twelfth Report … on … the Prisons of Ireland, 1834, H.C. 1834 (63), xl, p. 48;
Thirteenth Report … on … the Prisons of Ireland, 1835, H.C. 1835 (114), xxxvi, p. 30.

Secondary sources:

Hennesy, *Irish Historic Towns Atlas, No. 14: Trim*, section 13.

MEATH

Trim, no. 2

Patrick St.
Lat. 53°33'9.82" N.; Long. 6°47'22.81" W.

An earlier gaol built *c.* 1780; extensive additions 1804–8; bridewell built adjacent to gaol 1817–18; new female prison added 1822–3; inspectors call for a new gaol 1823 onwards; grand jury consider building a new gaol 1823 onwards; new gaol built (*John Hargrave*) 1828–34; sundry works to roof of central building 1855; closed *c.* 1880s; converted into a school for pauper children (*Anthony Scott*) *c.* 1888–9; mostly demolished 1953; the boundary walls survive in part.

An earlier gaol built, *c.* 1780. Extensive additions, 1804–8. New courthouse built (see Part I), *c.* 1809. Bridewell built adjacent to gaol, 1817–18. Inspectors call for a new gaol, 1823 onwards. Grand jury consider building a new gaol, 1823 onwards. Presentment for a new gaol, 1827. New gaol built (*John Hargrave*), at a cost of least £24,000, 1828–34. Sundry works to roof of central building, 1855. Closed, *c.* 1880s. Converted into a school for pauper children (*Anthony Scott*), *c.* 1888–9. Mostly demolished, 1953. The boundary walls survive in part.

Archival and primary sources:

Meath grand-jury presentment books, 1803, 1806–7, 1847, 1867, 1882, 1884, 1887, 1889–91, 1893–8 (incomplete) (Meath County Archives, GJ); *Fourth Report of the AIPPD*, p. 39; *Fifth Report of the AIPPD*, p. 33; William Murray to R. Robinson, 22 October 1827 (NAI, CSORP 1827/1508); William Murray to R. Robinson, 10 January 1828 (NAI, CSORP 1828/110); Lewis, *Topographical Dictionary*, vol. 2, p. 644; *The Architect*, vol. 40, 7 December 1888, suppl., p. 1; ibid., vol. 40, 28 December 1888, suppl., p. 5; *Irish Builder*, vol. 31, no. 697, 1 January 1889, p. 15; *Meath Chronicle*, 27 June 1953; Photographs of Trim gaol, *c.* 1950s (Noel French private collection, Trim, Co. Meath).

Prison reports:

Inspector General's Report of … the Prisons in Ireland for … 1807, H.C. 1808 (239), ix, p. 14;
Account of All Gaols … in the … United Kingdom, H.C. 1819 (137), xvii, pp. 14–15;
Inspector General's Report of … the Prisons in Ireland for … 1818, H.C. 1819 (534), xii, p. 21;
Prisons of Ireland: Report of Inspectors General, 1823, H.C. 1823 (342), x, p. 6;
Prisons of Ireland: Report of Inspectors General, 1824, H.C. 1824 (294), xxii, pp. 6, 36;
Prisons of Ireland: Report of Inspectors General, 1825, H.C. 1825 (493), xxii, pp. 53–4;
Fourth Report … on … the Prisons of Ireland, 1826, H.C. 1826 (173), xxiii, pp. 34–5;
Fifth Report … on … the Prisons of Ireland, 1827, H.C. 1826–7 (471), xi, p. 37;
Sixth Report … on … the Prisons of Ireland, 1828, H.C. 1828 (68), xii, pp. 46–7;
Seventh Report … on … the Prisons of Ireland, 1829, H.C. 1829 (10), xiii, pp. 9, 41;
Eighth Report … on … the Prisons of Ireland, 1830, H.C. 1830 (48), xxiv, p. 40;
Ninth Report … on … the Prisons of Ireland, 1831, H.C. 1830–1 (172), iv, p. 29;
Tenth Report … on … the Prisons of Ireland, 1832, H.C. 1831–2 (152), xvii, p. 30;
Eleventh Report … on … the Prisons of Ireland, 1833, H.C. 1833 (67), xvii, p. 42;
Twelfth Report … on … the Prisons of Ireland, 1834, H.C. 1834 (63), xl, p. 48;
Thirteenth Report … on … the Prisons of Ireland, 1835, H.C. 1835 (114), xxxvi, p. 30.
Fourteenth Report … on … the Prisons of Ireland, 1836, H.C. 1836 (118), xxxv, p. 28;
Fifteenth Report … on … the Prisons of Ireland, 1837, H.C. 1837 (123), xxxi, pp. 27–8;
Sixteenth Report … on … the Prisons of Ireland, 1838, H.C. 1837–8 (186), xxix, p. 32;
Seventeenth Report … on … the Prisons of Ireland, 1839, H.C. 1839 (91), xx, p. 33;
Nineteenth Report … on … the Prisons of Ireland, 1841, H.C. 1841 (299), xi, p. 38;
Twentieth Report … on … the Prisons of Ireland, 1842, H.C. 1842 (377), xxii, p. 84;
Twenty-first Report … on … the Prisons of Ireland, 1843, H.C. 1843 (462), xxvii, p. 46;
Thirty-fourth Report … on … the Prisons of Ireland, 1856, H.C. 1856 (2113), xxxiv, p. 22;
Forty-ninth Report … on … the Prisons of Ireland, 1870, H.C. 1871 (C. 359), xxx, p. 234.

Secondary sources:

Craig and Glin, *Ireland Observed*, p. 102; McParland, 'Public Work of Architects', pp. 251–2; Craig, *Architecture of Ireland*, p. 305; Mooney, 'The Origins of Agrarian Violence in Meath, 1790–1828', pp. 45–67; Mooney, 'A Society in Crisis: Agrarian violence in Meath, 1828–1835', pp. 102–28; Casey and Rowan, *Buildings of Ireland: North Leinster*, pp. 519–20; Noel. E. French, *Trim Gaol* (Trim: Meath Heritage Centre, 1994); O'Dwyer, 'Public Works Architecture', p. 407; Johnston, *Forms of Constraint*, pp. 58–9 (illus.); Hennesy, *Irish Historic Towns Atlas, No. 14: Trim*, section 13.

MONAGHAN

Monaghan, no. 1

Church Square (New Diamond)
Lat. 54°14'51.51" N.; Long. 6°58'12.34" W.

Former gaol was located where courthouse now stands; visited and condemned by Howard 1787; Forster Archer calls for a new gaol 1807; first grand-jury presentment for a new gaol 1807; described by John Gamble 1810; Forster Archer calls for a new gaol and suggests a site 1812; further grand-jury presentment for a new gaol 1813, outbreak of fever in the old gaol, with at least twenty-seven deaths, 1817; new gaol built elsewhere 1815–24; old gaol demolished *c.* 1825; new courthouse built on its site 1826–30. Not extant.

Former gaol was located where courthouse now stands (see Part I). Visited and condemned by Howard, 1787. Forster Archer calls for a new gaol, and suggests a suitable site, 1807, 1812. First grand-jury presentment for a new gaol, 1807. Described by John Gamble, 1810. Further grand-jury presentment for a new gaol, 1813. Outbreak of fever in the old gaol, with at least twenty-seven deaths, 1817. New gaol built elsewhere (see 'Monaghan: Monaghan, no. 2'), 1815–24. Old gaol demolished, *c.* 1825. New courthouse built on its site (see Part I), 1826–30. Not extant.

Archival and primary sources:

Howard, *Lazarettos*, p. 99; John Gamble, *Sketch of the History, Politics and Manners, Taken in Dublin, and the North of Ireland, in the Autumn of 1810* (London: Cradock & Joy, 1811), p. 155; Forster Archer, 'Report of the State of Gaols of Ireland for the Year 1811' (Houses of the Oireachtas Library, Dublin, MS.4E63); Monaghan grand-jury presentment books, 1811–12 (Monaghan County Library, 352.0417); Forster Archer to William Gregory, 28 November 1819 (NAI, CSORP 1819/46); Reid, *Travels in Ireland*, pp. 198–9.

Prison reports:

Inspector General's Report of … the Prisons in Ireland for … 1807, H.C. 1808 (239), ix, p. 14;

Account of All Gaols … in the … United Kingdom, H.C. 1819 (137), xvii, pp. 14–15;

Inspector General's Report of … the Prisons in Ireland for … 1818, H.C. 1819 (534), xii, pp. 21–2;

Prisons of Ireland: Report of Inspectors General, 1823, H.C. 1823 (342), x, pp. 5, 36;

Prisons of Ireland: Report of Inspectors General, 1824, H.C. 1824 (294), xxii, pp. 5, 37;

Prisons of Ireland: Report of Inspectors General, 1825, H.C. 1825 (493), xxii, p. 35.

Secondary sources:

None.

MONAGHAN

Monaghan, no. 2

High St.
Lat. 54°14'59.13" N.; Long. 6°58'26.25" W.

Former gaol was located where courthouse now stands; visited and condemned by Howard 1787; Forster Archer calls for a new gaol 1807, 1812; first grand-jury presentment for a new gaol 1807; described by John Gamble 1810; committee appointed to select site 1812, further grand-jury presentment for a new gaol 1813; outbreak of fever in the old gaol, with at least twenty-seven deaths, 1817; contract signed for building a new gaol (*John Behan*) 1815; first part of new gaol built (*John Behan*, supervising architect *John Bowden* from 1818) 1815–20; John Behan dismissed as architect 1820; plan adopted to complete gaol, mostly according to original design, 1820; gaol building completed (*John Bowden*) 1820–4; alterations to introduce separate-system confinement (*John McCurdy*) 1859–61; gaol used as a county infirmary *c.* 1894; partially demolished *c.* 1900; plan to build a new hospital 1933; demolished 1937; Monaghan County Hospital built on site *c.* 1938 onwards; not extant.

Former gaol was located where courthouse now stands (see Part I). Visited and condemned by Howard, 1787. Forster Archer calls for a new gaol, and suggests a suitable site, 1807, 1812. First grand-jury presentment for a new gaol, 1807. Described by John Gamble, 1810. Grand-jury committee appointed to select 'a proper site for a new gaol', 1812. Further grand-jury presentment for a new gaol, 1813. Outbreak of fever in the old gaol, with at least twenty-seven deaths, 1817. Contract signed for building a new gaol (*John Behan*), 1815. First part of new gaol built (*John Behan*, supervising architect *John Bowden* from 1816), 1815–20. John Behan dismissed as architect, 1820. Plan adopted to complete gaol, mostly according to original design, 1820. Gaol building completed (*John Bowden*), 1820–4. New courthouse built (see Part I), 1826–30. Alterations to introduce separate-system confinement (*John McCurdy*), 1859–61. Gaol used as a county infirmary, *c.* 1894. Partially demolished, *c.* 1900. Plan to build a new hospital, 1933. Demolished, 1937. Monaghan County Hospital built on site, *c.* 1938 onwards. Not extant.

Archival and primary sources:

Howard, *Lazarettos*, p. 99; Gamble, *Sketch of the History*, p. 155; Memorandum and drawings relating to Monaghan gaol, March 1811 (NAI, SPO 547/353/5); An account of the several presentments made … on which advances have been made by government for gaols, n.d. (NAI, SPO OP 1832–38, 1A/77/4); Forster Archer, 'Report of the State of Gaols of Ireland for the Year 1811' (Houses of the Oireachtas Library, Dublin, MS.4E63); Monaghan grand-jury presentment books, 1811–12, and 1859 (Monaghan County Library, 352.0417); John Bowden to John Foster, 29 January 1814 (PRONI, D/562/4227); Letter by Francis Johnston, 2 June 1814, and also Henry Westenra to William Gregory, 3 August 1814 (NAI, SPO 558/423/31); Forster Archer to William Gregory, 28 November 1819 (NAI, CSORP 1819/46); *Belfast Newsletter*, 23 June 1820; Memorandum of John Behan, n.d. (NAI, CSORP 1821/547); Andrew Blayney to Charles Grant, 20 May 1822 (NAI, CSORP 1822/22); Report by Francis Johnston, April 1821 (NAI, CSORP 1821/1194); Reid, *Travels in Ireland*, pp. 198–9; *Third Report of the AIPPD*, p. 45; *Fourth Report of the AIPPD*, p. 40; *Fifth Report of the AIPPD*, p. 33; Glassford, *Notes of Three Tours in Ireland*, p. 79; Lewis, *Topographical Dictionary*, vol. 2, p. 383; *Dublin Builder*, vol. 2, no. 14, 1 April 1860, p. 232; ibid., vol. 3, no. 41, 1 September 1861, p. 620; Anon., 'The New County Hospital, Monaghan', n.d. (copy in Monaghan County Museum); Photograph of Monaghan gaol and hospital, *c.* 1938 (Monaghan County Museum).

Prison reports:

Inspector General's Report of … the Prisons in Ireland for … 1807, H.C. 1808 (239), ix, p. 14;

Account of All Gaols … in the … United Kingdom, H.C. 1819 (137), xvii, pp. 14–15;

Inspector General's Report of … the Prisons in Ireland for … 1818, H.C. 1819 (534), xii, pp. 21–2;

Prisons of Ireland: Report of Inspectors General, 1823, H.C. 1823 (342), x, pp. 5, 36;

Prisons of Ireland: Report of Inspectors General, 1824, H.C. 1824 (294), xxii, pp. 5, 37;

Prisons of Ireland: Report of Inspectors General, 1825, H.C. 1825 (493), xxii, p. 35;

Nineteenth Report … on … the Prisons of Ireland, 1841, H.C. 1841 (299), xi, pp. 38–9;

Twentieth Report … on … the Prisons of Ireland, 1842, H.C. 1842 (377), xxii, p. 84;

Forty-ninth Report … on … the Prisons of Ireland, 1870, H.C. 1871 (C. 359), xxx, pp. 247–8.

Secondary sources:

O'Dwyer, 'Public Works Architecture', pp. 191, 407; Mulligan, *Buildings of Ireland: South Ulster*, p. 461.

QUEEN'S COUNTY (LAOIS)

Maryborough (Portlaoise), no. 1

Church St.
Lat. 53°2'4.12" N.; Long. 7°17'59.20" W.

Old gaol visited by Howard, who noted that a new gaol was planned, 1787; new gaol built (*Richard Harman*) *c.* 1789–91; another new gaol planned 1818 onwards; a new gaol built elsewhere 1827–30; old gaol thereafter used as county offices, a police barracks, etc.; largely extant.

Old gaol visited by Howard, who noted that a new gaol was planned, 1787. New gaol built (*Richard Harman*), *c.* 1789–91. New courthouse built nearby (see Part I), *c.* 1805–13. Forster Archer recommends additions and alterations, 1812. Another new gaol planned, 1818 onwards. A new gaol built elsewhere (see 'Queen's County (Laois): Maryborough (Portlaoise), no. 2'), 1827–30. Old gaol thereafter used as county offices, a police barracks, etc. Largely extant.

Archival and primary sources:

Howard, *Lazarettos*, p. 86; *Finn's Leinster Journal*, 27–31 October 1787; *Freeman's Journal*, 4–6 August 1789; ibid., 1–3 February 1791; Elevation and plan drawings for Maryborough gaol, n.d., n.s. (Irish Architectural Archive, Thomas Pakenham Tullynally Castle collection (copies), M37); Charles Coote, *Statistical Survey of the Queen's County* (Dublin: Graisberry & Campbell, 1801), pp. 107, 194; Forster Archer, 'Report of the State of Gaols of Ireland for the Year 1811' (Houses of the Oireachtas Library, Dublin, MS.4E63); Diaries for Sir Vere Hunt, 10 May 1813 (Limerick City and County Archives, Vere Hunt Diaries, 10 March to 31 December 1813; NLI microfilm copy, pp. 5527–8); *Fourth Report of the AIPPD*, p. 40; Lewis, *Topographical Dictionary*, vol. 2, pp. 345–6.

Prison reports:

Inspector General's Report of … the Prisons in Ireland for … 1807, H.C. 1808 (239), ix, p. 14;

Account of All Gaols … in the … United Kingdom, H.C. 1819 (137), xvii, pp. 14–15;

Inspector General's Report of … the Prisons in Ireland for … 1818, H.C. 1819 (534), xii, pp. 22–3;

Prisons of Ireland: Report of Inspectors General, 1823, H.C. 1823 (342), x, pp. 60–1;

Prisons of Ireland: Report of Inspectors General, 1824, H.C. 1824 (294), xxii, pp. 7, 59;

Prisons of Ireland: Report of Inspectors General, 1825, H.C. 1825 (493), xxii, pp. 35–6;

Fourth Report … on … the Prisons of Ireland, 1826, H.C. 1826 (173), xxiii, p. 50;

Fifth Report … on … the Prisons of Ireland, 1827, H.C. 1826–7 (471), xi, pp. 7, 57;

Sixth Report … on … the Prisons of Ireland, 1828, H.C. 1828 (68), xii, pp. 7, 63;

Seventh Report … on … the Prisons of Ireland, 1829, H.C. 1829 (10), xiii, pp. 9, 60;

Eighth Report … on … the Prisons of Ireland, 1830, H.C. 1830 (48), xxiv, p. 61;

Ninth Report … on … the Prisons of Ireland, 1831, H.C. 1830–1 (172), iv, p. 45.

Secondary sources:

Tierney, *The Buildings of Ireland: Central Leinster*, pp. 547–8.

QUEEN'S COUNTY (LAOIS)

Maryborough (Portlaoise), no. 2

Dublin Rd.
Lat. 53°2'13.93" N : Long. 7°17'21.14" W.

Former gaol built *c.* 1789–91; another new gaol planned 1818 onwards; plan for new polygonal-plan gaol agreed (*William Deane Butler*) 1821; disagreement over location of new gaol 1821–7; a revised radial-plan gaol (*William Deane Butler*) 1827; a new gaol built (*William Deane Butler*) 1827–30; addition of thirty separate-system female cells 1851–3; alterations and additions (*Enoch Trevor Owen*) 1879; additions (*Max Green*) 1898–9; in use as a state prison; extant.

Former gaol built, *c.* 1789–91. New courthouse built nearby (see Part I), *c.* 1805–13. Another new gaol planned, 1818 onwards. Plan for new polygonal-plan gaol agreed (*William Deane Butler*), 1821. Disagreement over location of new gaol, 1821–7. A revised radial-plan gaol (*William Deane Butler*), 1827. A new gaol built (*William Deane Butler*), at a cost of at least £18,500, 1827–30. Addition of thirty separate-system female cells, 1851–3. Alterations and additions (*Enoch Trevor Owen*), 1879. Additions (*Max Green*), 1898–9. In use as a state prison. Extant.

Archival and primary sources:

Coote, *Statistical Survey of the Queen's County*, pp. 107, 194; Queen's County grand-jury presentment books, summer assizes 1821 (Cambridge University Library); *Fourth Report of the AIPPD*, p. 40; *Fifth Report of the AIPPD*, p. 34; Correspondence relating to Maryborough gaol, 1823–4 (NAI, CSORP 1823/6075); Commissioners for Maryborough gaol to William Gregory, 2 July 1824 (NAI, CSORP 1824/9669); Memorandum of David Henry, 19 January 1826 (NAI, CSORP 1827/12,887); *Freeman's Journal*, 28 June 1826, 23 April 1828; William Deane Butler plans for Maryborough Gaol and Stradbally bridewell, 7 August 1827 (NAI CSORP 1827/1396); J. Rockfort to William Gregory, 7 August 1827 (NAI, CSORP 1827/1135); William Murray to R. Robinson, 11 August 1827 (NAI, CSORP 1827/1913); Lewis, *Topographical Dictionary*, vol. 2, pp. 345–6; *Irish Builder*, vol. 17, no. 368, 15 April 1875, p. 112; ibid., vol. 18, no. 385, 1 January 1876, p. 14; Sketch of Maryborough gaol, 28 October 1879, by Enoch Trevor Owen (NAI, OPW old ref. E.12.4).

Prison reports:

Inspector General's Report of ... the Prisons in Ireland for ... 1807, H.C. 1808 (239), ix, p. 14;

Account of All Gaols ... in the ... United Kingdom, H.C. 1819 (137), xvii, pp. 14–15;

Inspector General's Report of ... the Prisons in Ireland for ... 1818, H.C. 1819 (534), xii, pp. 22–3;

Prisons of Ireland: Report of Inspectors General, 1823, H.C. 1823 (342), x, pp. 60–1;

Prisons of Ireland: Report of Inspectors General, 1824, H.C. 1824 (294), xxii, pp. 7, 59;

Prisons of Ireland: Report of Inspectors General, 1825, H.C. 1825 (493), xxii, pp. 35–6;

Fourth Report ... on ... the Prisons of Ireland, 1826, H.C. 1826 (173), xxiii, p. 50;

Fifth Report ... on ... the Prisons of Ireland, 1827, H.C. 1826–7 (471), xi, pp. 7, 57;

Sixth Report ... on ... the Prisons of Ireland, 1828, H.C. 1828 (68), xii, pp. 7, 63;

Seventh Report ... on ... the Prisons of Ireland, 1829, H.C. 1829 (10), xiii, pp. 9, 60;

Eighth Report ... on ... the Prisons of Ireland, 1830, H.C. 1830 (48), xxiv, p. 61;

Ninth Report ... on ... the Prisons of Ireland, 1831, H.C. 1830–1 (172), iv, p. 45.

Tenth Report ... on ... the Prisons of Ireland, 1832, H.C. 1831–2 (152), xvii, p. 46;

Eleventh Report ... on ... the Prisons of Ireland, 1833, H.C. 1833 (67), xvii, p. 29;

Twelfth Report ... on ... the Prisons of Ireland, 1834, H.C. 1834 (63), xl, p. 32;

Fourteenth Report ... on ... the Prisons of Ireland, 1836, H.C. 1836 (118), xxxv, p. 41;

Sixteenth Report ... on ... the Prisons of Ireland, 1838, H.C. 1837–8 (186), xxix, p. 48;

Seventeenth Report ... on ... the Prisons of Ireland, 1839, H.C. 1839 (91), xx, p. 50;

Nineteenth Report ... on ... the Prisons of Ireland, 1841, H.C. 1841 (299), xi, p. 55;

Twentieth Report ... on ... the Prisons of Ireland, 1842, H.C. 1842 (377), xxii, pp. 110–11;

Thirtieth Report ... on ... the Prisons of Ireland, 1852, H.C. 1852 (1531), xxv, p. 17, 204;

Thirty-first Report ... on ... the Prisons of Ireland, 1853, H.C. 1853 (1657), liii, pp. 17, 215;

Forty-eighth Report ... on ... the Prisons of Ireland, 1869, H.C. 1870 (C. 173), xxxvii, p. 431.

Secondary sources:

Cruickshank, *Guide to the Georgian Buildings of Great Britain and Ireland*, p. 159; O'Dwyer, 'Public Works Architecture', p. 407; Lee, *James Pain, Architect*, pp. 65, 365; Loeber, et al., *Art and Architecture of Ireland: Volume IV: Architecture 1600–2000*, p. 205; Matthew Keenan, 'Queen's County Gaols: The people and their crimes', D.GNL thesis, University College Cork, 2017, pp. 14–28; Tierney, *The Buildings of Ireland: Central Leinster*, p. 548.

ROSCOMMON

Roscommon, no. 1

Market Square
Lat. 53°37'54.16" N.; Long. 8°11'26.96" W.

Courthouse built in Roscommon 1761–3; Howard visits, and notes that a new gaol is building 1787; new gaol built *c.* 1786–97; presentment to build another new gaol 1814; new gaol built elsewhere 1814–18; old gaol in use as a lunatic asylum 1818–*c.* 1834; thereafter lunatics moved to Ballinasloe District Lunatic Asylum; later refurbished as a shopping centre; extant.

Courthouse built in Roscommon (see Part I), 1761–3. Howard visits, and notes that a new gaol is building, 1787. New gaol built, *c.* 1786–97. Forster Archer notes a direction from an assize judge for the grand jury to visit and report on the poor condition of their gaol, 1812. Presentment to build another new gaol, 1814. New gaol built elsewhere (see 'Roscommon: Roscommon, no. 2'), 1814–18. Old gaol in use as a lunatic asylum, 1818–*c.* 1834; thereafter, lunatics moved to Ballinasloe District Lunatic Asylum. Later refurbished as a shopping centre. Extant.

Archival and primary sources:

Howard, *Lazarettos*, p. 92; *Accounts of the Presentments Passed by the Grand Juries of Ireland … in … 1807*, H.C. 1808 (205), xiii, p. 326; Forster Archer, 'Report of the State of Gaols of Ireland for the Year 1811' (Houses of the Oireachtas Library, Dublin, MS.4E63); Weld, *Statistical Survey of the County of Roscommon*, pp. 394, 414, 419.

Prison reports:

Inspector General's Report of … the Prisons in Ireland for … 1807, H.C. 1808 (239), ix, p. 15;
Account of All Gaols … in the … United Kingdom, H.C. 1819 (137), xvii, pp. 16–17;
Inspector General's Report of … the Prisons in Ireland for … 1818, H.C. 1819 (534), xii, pp. 23–4;
Report from the Select Committee on the State of Gaols, H.C. 1819 (579), vii, p. 196;
Prisons of Ireland: Report of Inspectors General, 1823, H.C. 1823 (342), x, pp. 5, 36–7;
Fifth Report … on … the Prisons of Ireland, 1827, H.C. 1826–7 (471), xi, p. 39;
Sixth Report … on … the Prisons of Ireland, 1828, H.C. 1828 (68), xii, p. 49;
Twelfth Report … on … the Prisons of Ireland, 1834, H.C. 1834 (63), xl, p. 49.

Secondary sources:

O'Dwyer, 'Public Works Architecture', p. 153.

ROSCOMMON

Roscommon, no. 2

Courthouse Square
Lat. 53°37'47.66" N.; Long. 8°11'37.56" W.

Howard visits ancient gaol, and notes that a new gaol is building 1787; gaol built *c.* 1786–97; presentment to build another new gaol 1814; new gaol built (*Richard Morrison*) 1814–18; inspectors suggest a new female prison 1836; extensive addition to female prison, with sixteen separate-system cells built 1854–5; plans to convert to RIC barracks 1878–9; closed 1886; in use as a Garda station 1925–42; demolished *c.* 1945; Garda station now on site; not extant.

Howard visits ancient gaol, and notes that a new gaol is building, 1787. Gaol built, *c.* 1786–97. Forster Archer notes a direction from an assize judge for the grand jury to visit and report on the poor condition of their gaol, 1812. Presentment to build another new gaol, 1814. New gaol built (*Richard Morrison*), at a cost of £19,930, 1814–18. Inspectors suggest a new female prison, 1836. Extensive addition to female prison, with sixteen separate-system cells built, 1854–5. Plans to convert to RIC barracks, 1878–9. Closed, 1886. In use as a Garda station, 1925–42. Demolished, *c.* 1945. Garda station now on site. Not extant.

Archival and primary sources:

Howard, *Lazarettos*, p. 92; *Accounts of the Presentments Passed by the Grand Juries of Ireland … in … 1807*, H.C. 1808 (205), xiii, p. 326; Weld, *Statistical Survey of the County of Roscommon*, pp. 394, 414, 419; An account of the several presentments made … on which advances have been made by government for gaols, n.d. (NAI, SPO OP 1832–8, 1A/77/4); Forster Archer, 'Report of the State of Gaols of Ireland for the Year 1811' (Houses of the Oireachtas Library, Dublin, MS.4E63); Correspondence relating to Roscommon gaol, 1814 (NAI, SPO 558/423/32); *The Builder*, vol. 11, no. 553, 10 September 1853, p. 584; Drawings for plans to convert Roscommon gaol to an RIC barracks, 1878–9 (NAI, OPW, old ref. D.3.9); Survey plans for Roscommon gaol by Kevin F. Loughlin, 26 June 1943 (NAI, OPW collection, copy in Irish Architectural Archive, Acc. 88/20); Photograph of Roscommon gaol, *c.* 1930s (from Rowan, *Morrison*, p. 148, copy in Roscommon County Library).

Prison reports:

Inspector General's Report of … the Prisons in Ireland for … 1807, H.C. 1808 (239), ix, p. 15;
Account of All Gaols … in the … United Kingdom, H.C. 1819 (137), xvii, pp. 16–17;
Inspector General's Report of … the Prisons in Ireland for … 1818, H.C. 1819 (534), xii, pp. 23–4;
Report from the Select Committee on the State of Gaols, H.C. 1819 (579), vii, p. 196;
Prisons of Ireland: Report of Inspectors General, 1823, H.C. 1823 (342), x, pp. 5, 36–7;
Prisons of Ireland: Report of Inspectors General, 1824, H.C. 1824 (294), xxii, p. 6;
Prisons of Ireland: Report of Inspectors General, 1825, H.C. 1825 (493), xxii, pp. 54–5;
Fifth Report … on … the Prisons of Ireland, 1827, H.C. 1826–7 (471), xi, pp. 38–9;
Sixth Report … on … the Prisons of Ireland, 1828, H.C. 1828 (68), xii, pp. 48–9;
Seventh Report … on … the Prisons of Ireland, 1829, H.C. 1829 (10), xiii, pp. 42–3;
Eighth Report … on … the Prisons of Ireland, 1830, H.C. 1830 (48), xxiv, p. 41;
Ninth Report … on … the Prisons of Ireland, 1831, H.C. 1830–1 (172), iv, p. 31;
Tenth Report … on … the Prisons of Ireland, 1832, H.C. 1831–2 (152), xvii, p. 31;
Twelfth Report … on … the Prisons of Ireland, 1834, H.C. 1834 (63), xl, p. 49;
Fourteenth Report … on … the Prisons of Ireland, 1836, H.C. 1836 (118), xxxv, p. 29;
Fifteenth Report … on … the Prisons of Ireland, 1837, H.C. 1837 (123), xxxi, p. 28;
Sixteenth Report … on … the Prisons of Ireland, 1838, H.C. 1837–8 (186), xxix, pp. 33–4;
Seventeenth Report … on … the Prisons of Ireland, 1839, H.C. 1839 (91), xx, p. 35;
Eighteenth Report … on … the Prisons of Ireland, 1840, H.C. 1840 (240), xxvi, p. 38;
Nineteenth Report … on … the Prisons of Ireland, 1841, H.C. 1841 (299), xi, pp. 39–40;
Twentieth Report … on … the Prisons of Ireland, 1842, H.C. 1842 (377), xxii, p. 88;
Thirty-second Report … on … the Prisons of Ireland, 1854, H.C. 1854 (1803), xxxii, p. 112;
Thirty-third Report … on … the Prisons of Ireland, 1855, H.C. 1854–5 (1956), xxvi, pp. 8, 95;
Forty-ninth Report … on … the Prisons of Ireland, 1870, H.C. 1871 (C. 359), xxx, p. 279.

Secondary sources:

McParland, 'Public Work of Architects', p. 250; Rowan, *Architecture of Richard Morrison*, pp. 148–9; O'Dwyer, 'Public Works Architecture', pp. 153, 407.

SLIGO

Sligo, no. 1

Teeling St. & Chapel St.
Lat. 54°16'11.18" N.; Long. 8°28'19.63" W.

In the seventeenth century, a gaol existed on Teeling Street near the corner of Castle Street; nothing further is known about this building; another courthouse and gaol built near Teeling Street, it would appear, in 1766; visited by Howard 1788; noted as in poor repair 1796; unexecuted design (*Bernard Mullins*) for a new gaol 1801; Forster Archer calls for a new gaol 1807, 1812; presentments for a new gaol 1808, 1814; new gaol built elsewhere 1816–18; unknown later history; not extant.

In the seventeenth century, a gaol existed on Teeling Street near the corner of Castle Street; nothing further is known about this building. Another courthouse and gaol built near Teeling Street, it would appear, in 1766. Visited by Howard, 1788. Noted as in poor repair, 1796. Unexecuted design (*Bernard Mullins*) for a new gaol, 1801. Forster Archer calls for a new gaol, 1807. Presentments for a new gaol, 1808, 1814. New gaol built elsewhere (see 'Sligo: Sligo, no. 2'), 1816–18. Unknown later history. Not extant.

Archival and primary sources:

Howard, *Lazarettos*, p. 92; *Journal of the Irish House of Commons*, vol. xvii, 1797, p. ccvi; Wood-Martin, *History of Sligo*, pp. 156–7; Elevation and partial plan drawing for Sligo gaol by Bernard Mullins, n.d. [1801] (Irish Architectural Archive, Henry, Mullins & McMahon collection, Acc. 2005/095); Forster Archer, 'Report of the State of Gaols of Ireland for the Year 1811' (Houses of the Oireachtas Library, Dublin, MS.4E63).

Prison reports:

Inspector General's Report of … the Prisons in Ireland for … 1807, H.C. 1808 (239), ix, p. 15;

Account of All Gaols … in the … United Kingdom, H.C. 1819 (137), xvii, pp. 16–17;

Inspector General's Report of … the Prisons in Ireland for … 1818, H.C. 1819 (534), xii, p. 24.

Secondary sources:

Kilgannon, *Sligo and Its Surroundings*, p. 141; Gallagher and Legg, *Irish Historic Towns Atlas, No. 24: Sligo*, pp. 14–15.

SLIGO

Sligo, no. 2

Chapel St. & Gaol Rd.
Lat. 54°16'12.19" N.; Long. 8°27'40.51" W.

A courthouse and gaol built near Teeling Street, it would appear, in 1766; visited by Howard 1788; noted as in poor repair 1796; unexecuted design (*Bernard Mullins*) for a new gaol 1801; Forster Archer calls for a new gaol 1807, 1812; presentments for a new gaol 1808, 1814; new gaol built elsewhere (*Richard Ingleman*, contractor *John Lynn*) 1816–18; addition of an infirmary and a marshalsea, and a sixteen-cell house of correction, and some solitary cells 1825–9; addition of some solitary cells, and a new road from the courthouse to the gaol (*Jacob Owen*) 1839–43; alterations *c.* 1854; enlarged 1885; closed 1956; partially demolished *c.* 1963, 1978; partially extant.

A courthouse and gaol built near Teeling Street, it would appear, in 1766. Visited by Howard, 1788. Noted as in poor repair, 1796. Unexecuted design (*Bernard Mullins*) for a new gaol, 1801. Forster Archer calls for a new gaol, 1807, 1812. Presentments for a new gaol, 1808, 1814. New gaol built elsewhere (*Richard Ingleman*, contractor *John Lynn*), at a cost of around £38,000, 1816–18. Addition of an infirmary and a marshalsea, and a sixteen-cell house of correction, and some solitary cells, 1825–9. Addition of some solitary cells, and a new road from the courthouse to the gaol (*Jacob Owen*), 1839–43. Governor's house remodelled, *c.* 1854. Enlarged, 1885. Closed, 1956. Partially demolished, *c.* 1963, 1978. County council offices. Partially extant (and with active conservation plans at the time of writing).

Archival and primary sources:

Howard, *Lazarettos*, p. 92; *Journal of the Irish House of Commons*, vol. xvii, 1797, p. ccvi; Wood-Martin, *History of Sligo*, pp. 156–7; Elevation and partial plan drawing for Sligo gaol by Bernard Mullins, n.d. [*c.* 1801] (Irish Architectural Archive, Henry, Mullins & McMahon collection, Acc. 2005/095); An account of the several presentments made … on which advances have been made by government for gaols, n.d. (NAI, SPO OP 1832–8, 1A/77/4); Sligo grand-jury presentment books, 1809–96 (incomplete) (Sligo County Library, LGOV 769–78); Forster Archer, 'Report of the State of Gaols of Ireland for the Year 1811' (Houses of the Oireachtas Library, Dublin, MS.4E63); Correspondence relating to Sligo gaol, 1814 (NAI, SPO 558/423/33); Edward Cooper to Robert Peel, 19 November 1815 (NAI, SPO 560/439/28); Richard Ingleman, 'Notes on Designs for a County Gaol at Salisbury', and various drawings, 10 September 1817 (Chippenham, Wiltshire and Swindon Archives and History Centre, Richard Ingleman papers, A1/509/2); Plan drawings for Sligo gaol, n.d., n.s. [*c.* 1816] (NLI, AD 2661); *First Report of the AIPPD*, pp. 22–5; Reid, *Travels in Ireland*, pp. 320–1; William Murray to R. Robinson, 15 September 1826 (NAI, CSORP 1826/14,900); William Murray to R. Robinson, 24 April 1828 (NAI, CSORP 1828/558); Lewis, *Topographical Dictionary*, vol. 2, p. 570; *A Return of the Sums Paid to Jacob Owen … for … Each Year since His Appointment, up to April 1842*, H.C. 1842 (323), xxxviii, p. 4; Photograph, 1955 (NLI, Morgan Aerial Photographic Collection).

Prison reports:

Inspector General's Report of … the Prisons in Ireland for … 1807, H.C. 1808 (239), ix, p. 15;
Account of All Gaols … in the … United Kingdom, H.C. 1819 (137), xvii, pp. 16–17;
Inspector General's Report of … the Prisons in Ireland for … 1818, H.C. 1819 (534), xii, p. 24;
Report from the Select Committee on the State of Gaols, H.C. 1819 (579), vii, p. 196;
Prisons of Ireland: Report of Inspectors General, 1823, H.C. 1823 (342), x, pp. 5, 38;
Prisons of Ireland: Report of Inspectors General, 1824, H.C. 1824 (294), xxii, p. 6;
Fourth Report … on … the Prisons of Ireland, 1826, H.C. 1826 (173), xxiii, p. 36;
Fifth Report … on … the Prisons of Ireland, 1827, H.C. 1826–7 (471), xi, p. 39;
Sixth Report … on … the Prisons of Ireland, 1828, H.C. 1828 (68), xii, p. 49;
Seventh Report … on … the Prisons of Ireland, 1829, H.C. 1829 (10), xiii, pp. 43–4;
Eighth Report … on … the Prisons of Ireland, 1830, H.C. 1830 (48), xxiv, p. 43;
Eleventh Report … on … the Prisons of Ireland, 1833, H.C. 1833 (67), xvii, p. 45;
Fourteenth Report … on … the Prisons of Ireland, 1836, H.C. 1836 (118), xxxv, p. 30;
Eighteenth Report … on … the Prisons of Ireland, 1840, H.C. 1840 (240), xxvi, p. 39;
Nineteenth Report … on … the Prisons of Ireland, 1841, H.C. 1841 (299), xi, p. 41;
Twentieth Report … on … the Prisons of Ireland, 1842, H.C. 1842 (377), xxii, p. 89;
Twenty-first Report … on … the Prisons of Ireland, 1843, H.C. 1843 (462), xxvii, p. 51;
Forty-ninth Report … on … the Prisons of Ireland, 1870, H.C. 1871 (C. 359), xxx, p. 275.

Secondary sources:

Kilgannon, *Sligo and Its Surroundings*, p. 141; McParland, 'Public Work of Architects', p. 251; Evans, *Fabrication of Virtue*, pp. 292–3, 441; O'Dwyer, 'Public Works Architects', pp. 39, 176, 407; John McTernan, *Olde Sligo: Aspects of town and county over 750 years* (Sligo, 1995), p. 259; Johnston, *Forms of Constraint*, p. 54 (illus.); Fíona Gallagher, *The Streets of Sligo: Urban evolution over the course of seven centuries* (Sligo, 2008), p. 262; Gallagher and Legg, *Irish Historic Towns Atlas, No. 24: Sligo*, pp. 14–15, Loeber, et al., *Art and Architecture of Ireland: Volume IV: Architecture 1600–2000*, p. 203; Siobhán Ryan, 'Sligo Gaol', National Inventory of Architectural Heritage Building of the Month, Oct. 2018 (www.buildingsofireland.ie).

TIPPERARY (and later TIPPERARY SOUTH RIDING)

Clonmel

Emmet St.
Lat. 52°21'17.58" N.; Long. 7°41'58.61" W.

An ancient county gaol recorded as early as 1655; visited and condemned by Howard, who noted a new gaol was building 1787; new gaol built *c.* 1786–8; Forster Archer notes presentments for additions 1812; new marshalsea and hospital *c.* 1817–18; inspectors critical of size of gaol 1823 onwards; inspectors propose a house of correction to be built 1829; house of correction, including a new gateway (*John B. Keane*) 1831–4; political debates over proposed division of Tipperary 1820s–38; Tipperary formally divided into two ridings 1838; new gaol built in Nenagh 1839–42; alterations and additions to debtors part of Clonmel gaol, forty new separate-system cells, and a new female prison, built 1842–4; separate-system alterations (*John McCurdy*) 1864–5; partly given over to an RIC barracks; a borstal occupying the other portions of the gaol *c.* 1906–56; extensive renovations and some demolition *c.* 1947; in industrial use *c.* 1956–68; almost entirely demolished 1972; only the gateway and parts of the boundary wall survive; partially extant.

An ancient county gaol recorded as early as 1655. Visited and condemned by Howard, who noted a new gaol was building, 1787. New gaol built, *c.* 1786–8. New courthouse built (see Part I), *c.* 1801. Attempted escapes, 1807. Forster Archer notes presentments for additions, of £8,000 (seemingly unexecuted), 1812. New marshalsea and hospital, *c.* 1817–18. Inspectors critical of size of gaol, 1823 onwards. Inspectors propose a house of correction to be built, 1829. House of correction, including a new gateway (*John B. Keane*), built at a cost of at least £12,875, 1831–4. Political debates over proposed division of Tipperary, 1820s–38. Tipperary formally divided into two ridings, 1838. New gaol built in Nenagh (see 'Tipperary North Riding: Nenagh'), 1839–42. Alterations and additions to debtors part of Clonmel gaol, forty new separate-system cells, and a new female prison, built, 1842–4. Separate-system alterations (*John McCurdy*), 1864–5. Partly given over to an RIC barracks. A borstal occupying the other portions of the gaol, *c.* 1906–56. Briefly taken over by Free State forces, 1922. Extensive renovations and some demolition, *c.* 1947. Used by Clonmel Industries Ltd., *c.* 1956–68. Almost entirely demolished, 1972. Only the gateway and parts of the boundary wall survive. Partially extant.

Archival and primary sources:

Howard, *Lazarettos*, p. 88; 'Forster Archer's Tour of Ireland in 1801' (British Library, Add. MS 35920); *Freeman's Journal*, 9 October 1807; Forster Archer, 'Report of the State of Gaols of Ireland for the Year 1811' (Houses of the Oireachtas Library, Dublin, MS.4E63); Reid, *Travels in Ireland*, pp. 257–8; *Limerick Evening Post & Clare Sentinel*, 26 August 1828; John B. Keane to the Lord Lieutenant, 22 August 1831 (NAI, CSORP 1831/2229); *Clonmel Advertiser*, 8 February 1832, 10 August 1836, and 21 June 1837; Assizes (Ireland) Act, 1835 (5 & 6 Will. IV, c. 26); *Hansard*, vol. 27, 3rd ser., 16 March 1835, cols 303–5 and passim; Grand Jury (Ireland) Act, 1836 (6 & 7 Will. IV, c. 116); *Tipperary Constitution*, 30 December 1836; Lewis, *Topographical Dictionary*, vol. 1, p. 370; Privy Council minute book, 16 June 1837 (NAI, PCO MB 8, ff. 63–5); Privy Council proclamation book, 8 November 1838 (NAI, PRO PB 1); *Nenagh Guardian*, 8 December 1838; *The Irish Times*, 5 April, 10 May 1864; Tipperary South Riding grand-jury presentment books, 1855–91 (incomplete) (Tipperary Libraries Local Studies and Archives, TL/LG/29); *General Advertiser*, 16, 23, 30 April 1864; Ordnance Survey maps for Clonmel, 1874 (Tipperary Libraries Local Studies and Archives); Photographs of Clonmel gaol (borstal) before demolition, by Donal Wylde (copies), *c.* 1970s (Tipperary County Museum).

Prison reports:

Inspector General's Report of … the Prisons in Ireland for … 1807, H.C. 1808 (239), ix, p. 15;
Account of All Gaols … in the … United Kingdom, H.C. 1819 (137), xvii, pp. 16–17;
Inspector General's Report of … the Prisons in Ireland for … 1818, H.C. 1819 (534), xii, p. 25;
Prisons of Ireland: Report of Inspectors General, 1823, H.C. 1823 (342), x, p. 61;
Prisons of Ireland: Report of Inspectors General, 1824, H.C. 1824 (294), xxii, pp. 60–1;
Prisons of Ireland: Report of Inspectors General, 1825, H.C. 1825 (493), xxii, p. 56;
Fourth Report … on … the Prisons of Ireland, 1826, H.C. 1826 (173), xxiii, p. 51;
Fifth Report … on … the Prisons of Ireland, 1827, H.C. 1826–7 (471), xi, p. 58;
Sixth Report … on … the Prisons of Ireland, 1828, H.C. 1828 (68), xii, p. 64;
Seventh Report … on … the Prisons of Ireland, 1829, H.C. 1829 (10), xiii, pp. 60–1;
Eighth Report … on … the Prisons of Ireland, 1830, H.C. 1830 (48), xxiv, pp. 11, 62–3;
Ninth Report … on … the Prisons of Ireland, 1831, H.C. 1830–1 (172), iv, pp. 46–7;
Tenth Report … on … the Prisons of Ireland, 1832, H.C. 1831–2 (152), xvii, pp. 5, 47;
Eleventh Report … on … the Prisons of Ireland, 1833, H.C. 1833 (67), xvii, p. 29;
Twelfth Report … on … the Prisons of Ireland, 1834, H.C. 1834 (63), xl, p. 33;
Thirteenth Report … on … the Prisons of Ireland, 1835, H.C. 1835 (114), xxxvi, p. 45;
Fourteenth Report … on … the Prisons of Ireland, 1836, H.C. 1836 (118), xxxv, p. 42;
Sixteenth Report … on … the Prisons of Ireland, 1838, H.C. 1837–8 (186), xxix, p. 49;
Seventeenth Report … on … the Prisons of Ireland, 1839, H.C. 1839 (91), xx, p. 52;
Eighteenth Report … on … the Prisons of Ireland, 1840, H.C. 1840 (240), xxvi, p. 57;
Twenty-first Report … on … the Prisons of Ireland, 1843, H.C. 1843 (462), xxvii, pp. 1, 79;
Twenty-second Report … on … the Prisons of Ireland, 1844, H.C. 1844 (535), xxviii, pp. 7, 94–5;
Thirtieth Report … on … the Prisons of Ireland, 1852, H.C. 1852 (1531), xxv, p. 17;
Forty-eighth Report … on … the Prisons of Ireland, 1869, H.C. 1870 (C. 173), xxxvii, p. 457.

Secondary sources:

McParland, 'Public Work of Architects', p. 252; Murphy, *Two Tipperarys*, pp. 9, 27–8, 36–7, 52–3, 57, 69, 83, 89, 104, 137; O'Dwyer, 'Public Works Architecture', pp. 176, 191–2, 407; Seán O'Donnell, *Clonmel, 1840–1900: Anatomy of an Irish town* (Dublin: Geography Publications, 1998), pp. 31–2; Johnston, *Forms of Constraint*, p. 173; Conor Reidy, *Ireland's 'Moral Hospital': The Irish Borstal system, 1906–1956* (Dublin: Irish Academic Press, 2009); Michael Ahern, *Clonmel County Gaol* (Clonmel: Ardo, 2010); Peter McNiff (ed.), *The Times & the Joys: Donal Wylde: Images of Clonmel & Tipperary South Riding* (Clonmel: Wylde, 2013), pp. 26–31; Loeber, et al., *Art and Architecture of Ireland: Volume IV: Architecture 1600–2000*, p. 203.

TIPPERARY NORTH RIDING

Nenagh

Bachelors Walk (O'Rahilly St.)
Lat. 52°51'56.45" N.; Long. 8°12'2.65" W.

A small bridewell on Pound Street, described by Forster Archer, 1818, Thomas Reid, 1822, and James Palmer, 1823; Palmer and Woodward suggest Nenagh would be an attractive location for a district bridewell 1824; assize judge recommends relocation of Tipperary assizes to a more central location 1828; unexecuted proposal (*John B. Keane*) for a new courthouse and gaol in Nenagh 1833; political debate over division of Tipperary *c.* 1820s–38; Tipperary divided into two ridings 1838; Nenagh picked as the assize town for the north riding 1838; new radial-plan gaol (*John B. Keane*) 1839–42; inspectors critical of construction and design of new gaol 1849, 1854; disused *c.* 1900; in use as a convent; later a heritage centre; partially demolished.

A small bridewell on Pound Street, described by Forster Archer, 1818, Thomas Reid, 1822, and James Palmer, 1823. Palmer and Woodward suggest Nenagh would be an attractive location for a district bridewell, 1824. Assize judge recommends relocation of Tipperary assizes to a more central location, 1828. Unexecuted proposal (*John B. Keane*) for a new courthouse and gaol in Nenagh, 1833. Political debate over division of Tipperary, *c.* 1820s–38. Tipperary divided into two ridings, 1838. Nenagh picked as the assize town for the north riding, 1838. New radial-plan gaol (*John B. Keane*), built at a cost of £18,000, 1839–42. New courthouse built (see Part I), 1840–4. New streets laid out near courthouse and gaol, 1840s. Inspectors critical of construction and design of new gaol, 1849, 1854. Disused, *c.* 1900. In use as a convent. Later a heritage centre. Partially demolished.

Archival and primary sources:

Reid, *Travels in Ireland*, p. 299; *Limerick Evening Post & Clare Sentinel*, 26 August 1828; *Clonmel Herald*, 19 November 1828; *Clonmel Advertiser*, 26 November 1828; *Limerick Evening Herald*, 16 September 1833; Correspondence relating to Nenagh courthouse and gaol, 1833 (NAI, CSORP 1833/3124); Assizes (Ireland) Act, 1835 (5 & 6 Will. IV, c. 26); *Hansard*, vol. 27, 3rd ser., 26 March 1835, cols 303–5 and passim; Grand Jury (Ireland) Act, 1836 (6 & 7 Will. IV, c. 116); *Clonmel Advertiser*, 10 August, 17 December, 21 December 1836; *Clonmel Herald*, 30 November 1836; *Tipperary Constitution*, 30 December 1836; Lewis, *Topographical Dictionary*, vol. 1, p. 423; Privy Council minute book, 16 June 1837 (NAI, PCO MB 8, ff. 63–5); Privy Council proclamation book, 8 November 1838 (NAI, PRO PB 1); *Clonmel Advertiser*, 21 June 1837; *Nenagh Guardian*, 8 December 1838; ibid., 19 June, 17 July, 24 July, 31 August, 4 September 1839; ibid., 20 February, 17 March, 10 June 1841; ibid., 17, 24 August 1842; ibid., 27 July, 30 September 1843; Tipperary North Riding grand-jury presentment books, 1842–1910 (incomplete) (Tipperary Libraries Local Studies and Archives, TL/LG/28).

Prison reports:

Inspector General's Report of … the Prisons in Ireland for … 1818, H.C. 1819 (534), xii, p. 25;

Prisons of Ireland: Report of Inspectors General, 1823, H.C. 1823 (342), x, p. 63;

Prisons of Ireland: Report of Inspectors General, 1824, H.C. 1824 (294), xxii, p. 62;

Prisons of Ireland: Report of Inspectors General, 1825, H.C. 1825 (493), xxii, p. 57;

Fourth Report … on … the Prisons of Ireland, 1826, H.C. 1826 (173), xxiii, p. 52;

Fifth Report … on … the Prisons of Ireland, 1827, H.C. 1826–7 (471), xi, p. 59;

Sixth Report … on … the Prisons of Ireland, 1828, H.C. 1828 (68), xii, p. 65;

Seventh Report … on … the Prisons of Ireland, 1829, H.C. 1829 (10), xiii, pp. 9, 32;

Eighth Report … on … the Prisons of Ireland, 1830, H.C. 1830 (48), xxiv, pp. 31–2;

Seventeenth Report … on … the Prisons of Ireland, 1839, H.C. 1839 (91), xx, pp. 52–3;

Eighteenth Report … on … the Prisons of Ireland, 1840, H.C. 1840 (240), xxvi, pp. 7, 58;

Nineteenth Report … on … the Prisons of Ireland, 1841, H.C. 1841 (299), xi, p. 57;

Twentieth Report … on … the Prisons of Ireland, [illegible], H.C. [illegible] [illegible];

Twenty-first Report … on … the Prisons of Ireland, 1843, H.C. 1843 (462), xxvii, pp. 77–8;

Twenty-second Report … on … the Prisons of Ireland, 1844, H.C. 1844 (535), xxviii, pp. 7, 93;

Twenty-third Report … on … the Prisons of Ireland, 1844, H.C. 1845 (620), xxv, p. 73;

Twenty-fifth Report … on … the Prisons of Ireland, 1847, H.C. 1847 (805), xxix, p. 96;

Twenty-seventh Report … on … the Prisons of Ireland, 1849, H.C. 1849 (1069), xxvi, pp. 96–7;

Thirty-second Report … on … the Prisons of Ireland, 1854, H.C. 1854 (1803), xxxii, p. 21;
Forty-eighth Report … on … the Prisons of Ireland, 1869, H.C. 1870 (C. 173), xxxvii, p. 442.

Secondary sources:

Postcards showing Nenagh courthouse and gaol, n.d. (Tipperary Libraries Local Studies and Archives); McParland, 'Public Work of Architects', p. 252; Murphy, *Two Tipperarys*, pp. 9, 27–30, 36–7, 41–2, 52–3, 57, 61, 66–7, 69, 83, 87–9, 104–18, 122, 125, 128, 137; O'Dwyer, 'Public Works Architecture', pp. 176, 191–2, 407; Nancy Murphy, *Guilty or Innocent? The Cormack brothers – trial, execution and exhumation* (Nenagh: Relay, 1998), pp. viii, 33–43, 144–5 (illus.); Loeber, et al., *Art and Architecture of Ireland: Volume IV: Architecture 1600–2000*, p. 203.

TYRONE

Omagh, no. 1

High St. & George's St.
Lat. 54°36'0.0" N.; Long. 7°18'16.14" W.

Unknown date of construction; visited by Howard, who noted the intention of the county to build a new gaol 1787; new gaol built elsewhere 1796–1804; courthouse built on the site of the former gaol 1814–20; See Part I for later history; gaol not extant.

Unknown date of construction. Visited by Howard, who noted the intention of the county to build a new gaol, 1787. New gaol built elsewhere (see 'Tyrone: Omagh, no. 2'), 1796–1804. Courthouse built on the site of the former gaol (see Part I), 1814–20. See Part I for later history. Gaol not extant.

Archival and primary sources:

Howard, *Lazarettos*, p. 96; Day and McWilliams, *Ordnance Survey Memoirs of Ireland: Volume 5: Tyrone*, p. 104.

Secondary sources:

Hodge, *Gallows and Turnkeys: A short history of Omagh gaol*, p. 6.

TYRONE

Omagh, no. 2

Derry Rd. & Castle Pl.
Lat. 54°36'9.95" N.; Long. 7°18'24.75" W.

Unknown date of construction; visited by Howard, who noted the intention of the county to build a new gaol 1787; new gaol built (*Edward Miller*) 1796–1804; new gaol condemned by Archer, 1807; extensive polygonal-plan additions (effectively a new gaol) (*John Hargrave*) 1822–30; inspectors call for additions, especially to debtors ward and to chapel and kitchen 1833–40; unexecuted scheme (*William Farrell*) for additions and alterations 1840; extensive alterations and additions, including a new female prison, chapel, marshalsea, etc. (*William Mullin*, builder) 1854–7; male prison converted for separate-system confinement (*Boyd and Batt*) 1862–3; closed; mostly demolished; governor's house survives.

Unknown date of construction. Visited by Howard, who noted the intention of the county to build a new gaol, 1787. New gaol built elsewhere (*Edward Miller*), 1796–1804. New gaol condemned by Archer, 1803, 1807. New courthouse (see Part I), 1814–20. Extensive polygonal-plan additions (effectively a new gaol) (*John Hargrave*), built at a cost of at least £6,000, 1822–30. Inspectors call for additions, especially to debtors ward and to chapel and kitchen, 1833–40. Unexecuted scheme

(*William Farrell*) for additions and alterations, 1840. Extensive alterations and additions, including a new female prison, chapel, marshalsea, etc. (*William Mullin*, builder), 1854–7. Male prison converted for separate-system confinement (*Boyd and Batt*), 1862–3. Closed. Mostly demolished. Governor's house survives.

Archival and primary sources:

Howard, *Lazarettos*, p. 96; Tyrone grand jury presentment books, 1799–1897 (PRONI, TYR/4/1), especially spring assizes 1854 (TYR/4/1/84) and spring and summer assizes 1857 (TYR/4/1/90–1); *Journal of the Irish House of Commons*, vol. xviii, 1799, p. ccxxxiii; *Accounts of the Presentments Passed by the Grand Juries of Ireland … in … 1807*, H.C. 1808 (205), xiii, p. 364; Forster Archer, 'Report of the State of Gaols of Ireland for the Year 1802', f. 14 (Houses of the Oireachtas Library, Dublin, MS.7H28); *First Report of the AIPPD*, pp. 19–21; Francis Johnston to R. Robinson, 15 February 1822 (NAI, CSORP 1822/572); Reid, *Travels in Ireland*, pp. 206–8; *Fourth Report of the AIPPD*, pp. 41–2; Day and McWilliams, *Ordnance Survey Memoirs of Ireland: Volume 5: Tyrone*, pp. 104–6; Glassford, *Notes of Three Tours*, p. 69; Lewis, *Topographical Dictionary*, vol. 2, p. 449; *Armagh Guardian*, 19 April 1861; *Dublin Builder*, vol. 4, no. 60, 1 June 1862, p. 142; ibid., vol. 4, no. 60, 1 October 1862, p. 254; Lacy, *Sights and Scenes in Our Fatherland*, p. 350.

Prison reports:

Inspector General's Report of … the Prisons in Ireland for … 1807, H.C. 1808 (239), ix, p. 16;

Account of All Gaols … in the … United Kingdom, H.C. 1819 (137), xvii, pp. 16–17;

Inspector General's Report of … the Prisons in Ireland for … 1818, H.C. 1819 (534), xii, pp. 25–6;

Prisons of Ireland: Report of Inspectors General, 1823, H.C. 1823 (342), x, pp. 5, 38–9;

Prisons of Ireland: Report of Inspectors General, 1824, H.C. 1824 (294), xxii, pp. 6, 39;

Prisons of Ireland: Report of Inspectors General, 1825, H.C. 1825 (493), xxii, pp. 36–7;

Fourth Report … on … the Prisons of Ireland, 1826, H.C. 1826 (173), xxiii, pp. 36–7;

Fifth Report … on … the Prisons of Ireland, 1827, H.C. 1826–7 (471), xi, p. 40;

Sixth Report … on … the Prisons of Ireland, 1828, H.C. 1828 (68), xii, p. 49;

Seventh Report … on … the Prisons of Ireland, 1829, H.C. 1829 (10), xiii, p. 44;

Eighth Report … on … the Prisons of Ireland, 1830, H.C. 1830 (48), xxiv, p. 44;

Ninth Report … on … the Prisons of Ireland, 1831, H.C. 1830–1 (172), iv, p. 32;

Tenth Report … on … the Prisons of Ireland, 1832, H.C. 1831–2 (152), xvii, p. 33;

Eleventh Report … on … the Prisons of Ireland, 1833, H.C. 1833 (67), xvii, p. 45;

Fifteenth Report … on … the Prisons of Ireland, 1837, H.C. 1837 (123), xxxi, p. 30;

Sixteenth Report … on … the Prisons of Ireland, 1838, H.C. 1837–8 (186), xxix, p. 35;

Seventeenth Report … on … the Prisons of Ireland, 1839, H.C. 1839 (91), xx, p. 37;

Eighteenth Report … on … the Prisons of Ireland, 1840, H.C. 1840 (240), xxvi, p. 39;

Nineteenth Report … on … the Prisons of Ireland, 1841, H.C. 1841 (299), xi, p. 42;

Twentieth Report … on … the Prisons of Ireland, 1842, H.C. 1842 (377), xxii, p. 89;

Thirtieth Report … on … the Prisons of Ireland, 1852, H.C. 1852 (1531), xxv, pp. 136–7;

Thirty-second Report … on … the Prisons of Ireland, 1854, H.C. 1854 (1803), xxxii, p. 21, 120;

Thirty-third Report … on … the Prisons of Ireland, 1855, H.C. 1854–5 (1956), xxvi, pp. 18, 119;

Thirty-fourth Report … on … the Prisons of Ireland, 1856, H.C. 1856 (2113), xxxiv, p. 148;

Thirty-fifth Report … on … the Prisons of Ireland, 1857, H.C. 1857 (2236), xvii, p. 124;

Thirty-sixth Report … on … the Prisons of Ireland, 1858, H.C. 1857–8 (2394), xxx, p. 78;

Thirty-seventh Report … on … the Prisons of Ireland, 1859, H.C. 1859 (2557), xiii, p. 203;
Fortieth Report … on … the Prisons of Ireland, 1862, H.C. 1862 (3020), xxvi, pp. 203–6;
Forty-first Report … on … the Prisons of Ireland, 1863, H.C. 1863 (3214), xxiii, p. 254;
Forty-second Report … on … the Prisons of Ireland, 1864, H.C. 1864 (3377), xxvii, p. 179;
Forty-ninth Report … on … the Prisons of Ireland, 1870, H.C. 1871 (C. 359), xxx, p. 287.

Secondary sources:

O'Dwyer, 'Public Works Architecture', p. 407; Rowan, *Buildings of Ireland: North west Ulster*, pp. 448–9; Hodge, *Gallows and Turnkeys: A short history of Omagh gaol*, p. 6; Loeber, et al., *Art and Architecture of Ireland: Volume IV: Architecture 1600–2000*, p. 203.

WATERFORD COUNTY and WATERFORD CITY (and later WATERFORD COUNTY and CITY)

Waterford

Ballybricken Green and Mayor's Walk
Lat. 52°15'37.12" N.; Long. 7°6'55.55" W.

A city gaol built (*Thomas Roberts*), location uncertain, 1727; a combined county and city courthouse built (*James Gandon*), on the site of a former fort and barracks 1784–7; a new county gaol built as part of this scheme (*James Gandon*) 1784–7; a new city gaol built adjacent to Gandon's buildings (*Richard Morrison*) 1807–11; additions and alterations to county gaol (*John Roberts* and *Richard Morrison*) 1812–13; city house of correction built 1820–1; unexecuted plan to move county gaol to Dungarvan *c.* 1821–4; an unstable wing of the county gaol rebuilt 1823–4; addition of a house of correction to the county gaol 1828–30; political debate over proposed move of county gaol to Dungarvan 1834–8; agreement between county and city grand juries to build a combined courthouse and a combined gaol 1844; new combined courthouse built 1848–50; discussions over location of new gaol 1853–9; new combined county and city gaol built (*Charles Tarrant*) 1860–3; old city house of correction closed 1863; gaol closed 1938; collapse of part of wall, killing nine, 1943; gaol demolished *c.* 1949 onwards; Garda station now on site; not extant.

A city gaol built (*Thomas Roberts*), location uncertain, 1727. A combined county and city courthouse built (*James Gandon*) (see Part I), on the site of a former fort and barracks, 1784–7. A new county gaol built as part of this scheme (*James Gandon*), 1784–7. Condition criticised by Forster Archer, prison inspector, 1803. A new city gaol built adjacent to Gandon's buildings (*Richard Morrison*), 1807–11. Workmanship of old gaol and proposed new gaol condemned by Forster Archer, 1807, 1812. Additions and alterations to county gaol (*John Roberts* and *Richard Morrison*), 1812–13. City house of correction built (see 'Waterford City: Waterford'), 1820–1. Unexecuted plan to move county gaol to Dungarvan, *c.* 1821–4. An unstable wing of the county gaol rebuilt, 1823–4. Addition of a house of correction to the county gaol, at a cost of at least £7,150, 1828–30. Political debate over proposed move of county gaol to Dungarvan, 1834–8. Sundry works to county gaol, 1838. Agreement between county and city grand juries to build a combined courthouse and a combined gaol, 1844. New combined courthouse built (see Part I), 1848–50. Discussions over location of new gaol, 1853–9. Unexecuted proposals (*Mr Derrick, Mr Gahan*, others), 1854–5. New combined county and city gaol built (*Charles Tarrant*), 1860–3. Old city house of correction closed, 1863. Gaol closed, 1938. Collapse of part of wall, killing nine, 1943. Gaol demolished, *c.* 1949 onwards. Garda station now on site. Not extant.

Archival and primary sources:

Bernard Scale and William Richards, 'A Plan of the City and Suburbs of Waterford' (1764) (copy in Waterford Museum of Treasures); *Freeman's Journal*, 10–12 October 1786; Howard, *Lazarettos*, pp. 87–8; Waterford Council minute book, 1770–1801, for 29 March 1787 (NLI, microfilm, p. 5559, f. 115); 28 Geo. III, c. 38 (1788); Forster Archer, 'Report of the State of Gaols of Ireland for the Year 1802', ff. 14–15 (Houses of the Oireachtas Library, Dublin, MS.7H28); *Accounts of the*

Presentments Passed by the Grand Juries of Ireland … in … 1807, H.C. 1808 (205), xiii, p. 412; Forster Archer, 'Report of the State of Gaols of Ireland for the Year 1811' (Houses of the Oireachtas Library, Dublin, MS.4E63); Memorandum of John Roberts, 26 June 1813 (NAI, SPO 554/403/5); An account of the several presentments made … on which advances have been made by government for gaols, n.d. (NAI, SPO OP 1832–8, 1A/77/4); *Freeman's Journal*, 28 March 1811; Waterford County grand-jury presentments, spring 1811 (Waterford City and County Archives, Dungarvan, GJ/31); Reid, *Travels in Ireland*, pp. 251–2; Francis Johnston to R. Robinson, 5 February 1827 (NAI, CSORP 1827/129); Heaney, *Scottish Whig in Ireland*, p. 83; Waterford County grand-jury presentments, 1827 (NAI, CSORP 1827/1709); *Waterford Mail*, 6 August 1834; *Waterford Chronicle*, 4 July 1835, 12, 19 July, 3 November 1836, 7 March 1837, 3 March 1838; *Waterford Mirror*, 17 July 1835; *Freeman's Journal*, 12 July 1836; *Clonmel Advertiser*, 9 November 1836, 17 May 1837; Assizes (Ireland) Act, 1835 (5 & 6 Will. IV, c. 26); *Hansard*, vol. 27, 3rd ser., 26 March 1835, cols 303–5 and passim; Grand Jury (Ireland) Act, 1836 (6 & 7 Will. IV, c. 116); Privy Council minute book, 18 August, 30 September, 27 October and 3 November 1836, and 12 May 1837 (NAI, PCO MB 7, ff. 465–6, 482–4, 489–92 and 493–7, and PCO MB 8, ff. 51–2); Gandon and Mulvany, *Life of James Gandon*, pp. 69, 72; Waterford County Grand Jury, memo respecting the enlargement of bridewells in the county, 10 March 1849 (NLI, Lismore papers, MS 43,456/13); Report of the committee appointed by the grand juries, to select a plan for the alteration or erection of a joint prison, for the county and city of Waterford, 19 February 1855 (NLI, Lismore papers, MS 43,456/13); Extracts from reports of the inspectors-general of prisons, etc. [1851–6] (NLI, Lismore papers, MS 43,456/13); Amalgamation of county and city gaols: […] Report of the united boards of superintendence of [Waterford] county and city […], Spring Assizes, 1857 (NLI, Lismore papers, MS 43,456/13); Waterford County grand-jury presentment books, 1859–63 (Waterford City and County Archives); *Freeman's Journal*, 3 August 1860; *The Builder*, vol. 18, no. 914, 11 August 1860, p. 512; *Irish Independent*, 5, 26 March 1943; *Irish Examiner*, 6 March 1943; Photographs of Waterford gaol, 1943 (Waterford City and County Archives); Photographs of Waterford gaol, 1930s–50s (Waterford Museum of Treasures); Donnchadh Ó Ceallacháin, 'The Old Jail in Ballybricken', 2016 (copy in Waterford Museum of Treasures); Exhibition on Waterford courthouse and jail, opened March 2016 (Waterford Museum of Treasures).

Prison reports:

Inspector General's Report of … the Prisons in Ireland for … 1807, H.C. 1808 (239), ix, p. 16;

Account of All Gaols … in the … United Kingdom, H.C. 1819 (137), xvii, pp. 18–19;

Inspector General's Report of … the Prisons in Ireland for … 1818, H.C. 1819 (534), xii, pp. 26–7;

Prisons of Ireland: Report of Inspectors General, 1823, H.C. 1823 (342), x, pp. 7, 63–5;

Prisons of Ireland: Report of Inspectors General, 1824, H.C. 1824 (294), xxii, pp. 7, 62–4;

Prisons of Ireland: Report of Inspectors General, 1825, H.C. 1825 (493), xxii, pp. 57–8;

Fourth Report … on … the Prisons of Ireland, 1826, H.C. 1826 (173), xxiii, pp. 52–3;

Fifth Report … on … the Prisons of Ireland, 1827, H.C. 1826–7 (471), xi, p. 60;

Sixth Report … on … the Prisons of Ireland, 1828, H.C. 1828 (68), xii, pp. 65–6;

Seventh Report … on … the Prisons of Ireland, 1829, H.C. 1829 (10), xiii, pp. 9, 62–3;

Eighth Report … on … the Prisons of Ireland, 1830, H.C. 1830 (48), xxiv, pp. 64–5;

Tenth Report … on … the Prisons of Ireland, 1832, H.C. 1831–2 (152), xvii, pp. 48–9;

Eleventh Report … on … the Prisons of Ireland, 1833, H.C. 1833 (67), xvii, p. 31;

Twelfth Report … on … the Prisons of Ireland, 1834, H.C. 1834 (63), xl, p. 35;

Thirteenth Report … on … the Prisons of Ireland, 1835, H.C. 1835 (114), xxxvi, p. 46;

Fourteenth Report … on … the Prisons of Ireland, 1836, H.C. 1836 (118), xxxv, p. 43;

Fifteenth Report … on … the Prisons of Ireland, 1837, H.C. 1837 (123), xxxi, pp. 45–6;

Sixteenth Report … on … the Prisons of Ireland, 1838, H.C. 1837–8 (186), xxix, p. 51;

Eighteenth Report … on … the Prisons of Ireland, 1840, H.C. 1840 (240), xxvi, pp. 59–60;

Nineteenth Report ... on ... the Prisons of Ireland, 1841, H.C. 1841 (299), xi, pp. 58–9;
Twentieth Report ... on ... the Prisons of Ireland, 1842, H.C. 1842 (377), xxii, pp. 6, 8, 113–15;
Twenty-first Report ... on ... the Prisons of Ireland, 1843, H.C. 1843 (462), xxvii, pp. 5, 82–3;
Twenty-second Report ... on ... the Prisons of Ireland, 1844, H.C. 1844 (535), xxviii, pp. 96–8;
Twenty-third Report ... on ... the Prisons of Ireland, 1844, H.C. 1845 (620), xxv, pp. 76–8;
Twenty-fifth Report ... on ... the Prisons of Ireland, 1847, H.C. 1847 (805), xxix, p. 100;
Twenty-seventh Report ... on ... the Prisons of Ireland, 1849, H.C. 1849 (1069), xxvi, pp. 100–1;
Twenty-eighth Report ... on ... the Prisons of Ireland, 1850, H.C. 1850 (1229), xxix, p. 100;
Twenty-ninth Report ... on ... the Prisons of Ireland, 1851, H.C. 1851 (1364), xxviii, pp. 103–10;
Thirtieth Report ... on ... the Prisons of Ireland, 1852, H.C. 1852 (1531), xxv, pp. 17, 215–19, 223;
Thirty-first Report ... on ... the Prisons of Ireland, 1853, H.C. 1853 (1657), liii, pp. 18, 242;
Thirty-third Report ... on ... the Prisons of Ireland, 1855, H.C. 1854–5 (1956), xxvi, pp. 205–10;
Thirty-fourth Report ... on ... the Prisons of Ireland, 1856, H.C. 1856 (2113), xxxiv, p. 22;
Thirty-eighth Report ... on ... the Prisons of Ireland, 1860, H.C. 1860 (2691), xxxvi, pp. 314–32;
Thirty-ninth Report ... on ... the Prisons of Ireland, 1861, H.C. 1861 (2861), xxix, pp. 280–4;
Fortieth Report ... on ... the Prisons of Ireland, 1862, H.C. 1862 (3020), xxvi, pp. 343–9;
Forty-first Report ... on ... the Prisons of Ireland, 1863, H.C. 1863 (3214), xxiii, p. 386;
Forty-second Report ... on ... the Prisons of Ireland, 1864, H.C. 1864 (3377), xxvii, p. 356;
Forty-third Report ... on ... the Prisons of Ireland, 1865, H.C. 1865 (3522), xxiv, p. 402;
Forty-eighth Report ... on ... the Prisons of Ireland, 1869, H.C. 1870 (C. 173), xxxvii, p. 474.

Secondary sources:

Mark Girouard, 'The Reign of the Building Families: City of Waterford, Ireland – II', *Country Life*, vol. 140, no. 3641, 15 December 1966, pp. 1626–9, at p. 1627; McParland, 'Public Work of Architects', pp. 90, 138; Daniel Wilson Randle, 'A Question of Style: The architectural competition for the central building for the university of the south', MA thesis, University of Texas, 1978, pp. 241–5; McParland, *James Gandon*, pp. 10–13, 144–5, 207; William Fraher, 'The Reconstruction of Dungarvan, 1807–*c.* 1830: A political ploy', *Decies: Journal of the Old Waterford Society*, vol. 25, 1984, pp. 2–21; Anon. ['CARA'], *Ballybricken & Thereabouts* (Waterford: Waterford Graphics, 1991), pp. 10–26 (illus.); Murphy, *Two Tipperarys*, pp. 283–302; O'Dwyer, 'Public Works Architecture', p. 407; Rolf Loeber, et al., *Art and Architecture of Ireland: Volume IV: Architecture 1600–2000*, p. 17.

WATERFORD CITY

Waterford

Hennessy's Rd.
Lat. 52°15'6.91" N.; Long. 7°7'18.21" W.

Forster Archer claims city gaol is too small 1818; new city house of correction built at some distance from the city gaol (*James Elmes*) 1820–1; new inspectors Palmer and Woodward suggest the building should be abandoned 1823; inspectors critical of design and construction of prison, 1824 onwards; inspectors again recommend abandoning the prison, 1837, 1840; used for county and city prisoners while new combined gaol being constructed 1860–3; abandoned 1864; demolished; not extant.

Forster Archer claims city gaol is too small, 1818. New city house of correction built at some distance from the city gaol

(*James Elmes*), at a cost of at least £4,990, 1820–1. New inspectors Palmer and Woodward suggest the building should be abandoned, 1823. Inspectors critical of design and construction of prison, 1824 onwards. Inspectors again recommend abandoning the prison, 1837, 1840. Used for county and city prisoners while new combined gaol being constructed, 1860–3. Abandoned, 1864. Demolished. Not extant.

Archival and primary sources:

Correspondence relating to Waterford city house of correction, 1819–21 (NAI, CSORP 1819/990, 1820/432, 1820/1328); Drawings for Waterford city house of correction by James Elmes, 23 September 1820 (NAI, CSORP 1820/432); Reid, *Travels in Ireland*, pp. 253–4; Lewis, *Topographical Dictionary*, vol. 2, p. 690.

Prison reports:

Inspector General's Report of … the Prisons in Ireland for … 1818, H.C. 1819 (534), xii, p. 27;
Prisons of Ireland: Report of Inspectors General, 1823, H.C. 1823 (342), x, pp. 7, 65;
Prisons of Ireland: Report of Inspectors General, 1824, H.C. 1824 (294), xxii, p. 64;
Prisons of Ireland: Report of Inspectors General, 1825, H.C. 1825 (493), xxii, p. 59;
Fourth Report … on … the Prisons of Ireland, 1826, H.C. 1826 (173), xxiii, p. 53;
Fifth Report … on … the Prisons of Ireland, 1827, H.C. 1826–7 (471), xi, p. 62;
Sixth Report … on … the Prisons of Ireland, 1828, H.C. 1828 (68), xii, pp. 8, 37–8;
Seventh Report … on … the Prisons of Ireland, 1829, H.C. 1829 (10), xiii, p. 63;
Eighth Report … on … the Prisons of Ireland, 1830, H.C. 1830 (48), xxiv, p. 65;
Ninth Report … on … the Prisons of Ireland, 1831, H.C. 1830–1 (172), iv, p. 49;
Tenth Report … on … the Prisons of Ireland, 1832, H.C. 1831–2 (152), xvii, p. 48;
Fifteenth Report … on … the Prisons of Ireland, 1837, H.C. 1837 (123), xxxi, p. 47;
Seventeenth Report … on … the Prisons of Ireland, 1839, H.C. 1839 (91), xx, p. 55;
Eighteenth Report … on … the Prisons of Ireland, 1840, H.C. 1840 (240), xxvi, pp. 60–1;
Nineteenth Report … on … the Prisons of Ireland, 1841, H.C. 1841 (299), xi, p. 59;
Twentieth Report … on … the Prisons of Ireland, 1842, H.C. 1842 (377), xxii, pp. 6, 8, 115;
Twenty-first Report … on … the Prisons of Ireland, 1843, H.C. 1843 (462), xxvii, pp. 5, 83;
Twenty-second Report … on … the Prisons of Ireland, 1844, H.C. 1844 (535), xxviii, p. 98;
Twenty-ninth Report … on … the Prisons of Ireland, 1851, H.C. 1851 (1364), xxviii, pp. 107–10;
Thirtieth Report … on … the Prisons of Ireland, 1852, H.C. 1852 (1531), xxv, pp. 223–4;
Thirty-first Report … on … the Prisons of Ireland, 1853, H.C. 1853 (1657), liii, p. 18;
Thirty-fourth Report … on … the Prisons of Ireland, 1856, H.C. 1856 (2113), xxxiv, p. 22;
Thirty-eighth Report … on … the Prisons of Ireland, 1860, H.C. 1860 (2691), xxxvi, pp. 314–22;
Thirty-ninth Report … on … the Prisons of Ireland, 1861, H.C. 1861 (2861), xxix, pp. 280–4;
Fortieth Report … on … the Prisons of Ireland, 1862, H.C. 1862 ([illegible]), xxvi, pp. 343–9;
Forty-second Report … on … the Prisons of Ireland, 1864, H.C. 1864 ([illegible]), xxvii, p. [illegible].

Secondary sources:

O'Dwyer, 'Public Works Architecture', p. 407.

WESTMEATH

Mullingar

Mount St.
Lat. 53°31'24.12" N.; Long. 7°20'26.41" W.

Howard visited and noted that a gaol was under construction 1787; rectilinear-plan gaol built (to the east of the later polygonal-plan extension) *c.* 1786–8; emergency works during Rebellion in 1798; grand-jury committee report on poor condition of gaol 1812–13; unexecuted plan for a new gaol (*James Shiel*) 1817; assize judge urges grand jury to expand their gaol 1818; grand jury plan new gaol 1819; unexecuted scheme for a new combined gaol and courthouse (*James Shiel*) 1820; grand-jury presentment for a new gaol, 1823; disputes over the location of the proposed extension (effectively a new gaol) *c.* 1823–4; assize judge intervenes 1823; large polygonal-plan addition (*John Hargrave*) 1824–9; yard walls rebuilt, a new entrance added, and alterations to the old gaol 1836; unexecuted proposal (*William Deane Butler*) to introduce separate-system confinement throughout the gaol 1843–4; closed; transferred to Westmeath County Council *c.* 1910; County council offices built on the site of the old gaol *c.* 1910 onwards; polygonal-plan gaol demolished *c.* 1980–90; large county council offices built on the site of this building *c.* 2000 onwards; governor's house and some other small buildings survive; partially extant.

Howard visited and noted that a gaol was under construction, 1787. Rectilinear-plan gaol built (to the east of the later polygonal-plan extension), *c.* 1786–8. Emergency works to secure gaol during Rebellion, 1798. Grand-jury committee report on poor condition of gaol, 1812–13. Unexecuted plan for a new gaol (*James Shiel*), 1817. Assize judge urges grand jury to expand their gaol, 1818. Grand jury plan new gaol, 1819. Unexecuted scheme for a new combined gaol and courthouse (*James Shiel*), 1820. New courthouse nearby (see Part I), 1820–5. Grand-jury presentment for a new combined courthouse and gaol (*James Shiel*) (see Part I), at a cost of £21,000, traversed, 1822. Grand-jury presentment for a new gaol, 1823. Disputes over the location of the proposed extension (effectively a new gaol), *c.* 1823–4. Assize judge intervenes, 1823. Additional land near old gaol purchased, 1824. Large polygonal-plan addition (*John Hargrave*), built at a cost of at least £11,626, 1824–9. Yard walls rebuilt, a new entrance added, and alterations to the old gaol, 1836. Unexecuted proposal (*William Deane Butler*) to introduce separate-system confinement throughout the gaol, 1843–4. Closed. Transferred to Westmeath County Council, *c.* 1910. County council offices built on the site of the old gaol, *c.* 1910 onwards. Polygonal-plan gaol demolished, *c.* 1980–90. Large county council offices built on the site of this building, *c.* 2000 onwards. Governor's house and some other small buildings survive. Partially extant.

Archival and primary sources:

Howard, *Lazarettos*, p. 94; *Dublin Journal*, 21 July 1787; *Journal of the Irish House of Commons*, vol. xvii, 1797, p. ccvi; Westmeath grand-jury presentment books, 1800–26 (Westmeath County Library, WMGJ/AP/1–18); James Shiel to William Gregory, 24 December 1817 (NAI, SPO 570/494/21); *Dublin Evening Post*, 4 December 1819; Plans for Mullingar gaol by James Shiel (two schemes), 1817 and February 1820 (Westmeath County Library) (there are copies in the Irish Architectural Archive: 088/063, C. 15/403–8); Francis Johnston to the Commissioners of the Board of Works, 5 March 1821 (NAI, CSORP 1821/1205); Commissioners of the Board of Works to William Gregory, 10 March 1821 (NAI, CSORP 1821/1247); *Fourth Report of the AIPPD*, p. 42; *Fifth Report of the AIPPD*, pp. 35–6; *Freeman's Journal*, 17 March 1823; *Westmeath Journal*, 20 March 1823; ibid., 22 April 1824; Francis Johnston to Robert Robinson, 4 November 1823 (NAI, CSORP 1823/7131); Plan drawings for old and new gaols at Mullingar, n.d., n.s. [*c.* 1824] (NLI, AD 2643, 2649); James Gibbons to Henry Goulburn, 29 January 1826 (NAI, CSORP 1825/12,783); *Freeman's Journal*, 23 April 1828; *Westmeath Guardian & Longford Newsletter*, 17 March 1836; Survey drawings of Mullingar old gaol, and also proposed changes to yard walls, entrance gateway, etc., n.d. [*c.* 1830s] (Irish Architectural Archive, Guinness Collection, Acc. 96/68.5/5/1–3); Lewis, *Topographical Dictionary*, vol. 2, p. 412; Osborne, *Gleanings in the West of Ireland*, pp. 51–2; Photographs of Mullingar old gaol, *c.* 1900 (Westmeath County Library, Westmeath Photographic Collection, M/1); Drawings and correspondence relating to plans for new Westmeath County Council buildings, *c.* 1910 (Westmeath County Library).

Prison reports.

Inspector General's Report of … the Prisons in Ireland for … 1807, H.C. 1808 (239), iv, p. 17;
Account of All Gaols … in the … United Kingdom, H.C. 1819 (137), xvii, pp. 18–19,
Inspector General's Report of … the Prisons in Ireland for … 1818, H.C. 1819 (534), xii, p. 27;
Prisons of Ireland: Report of Inspectors General, 1823, H.C. 1823 (342), x, pp. 6, 39;
Prisons of Ireland: Report of Inspectors General, 1824, H.C. 1824 (294), xxii, pp. 5, 39–40;
Prisons of Ireland: Report of Inspectors General, 1825, H.C. 1825 (493), xxii, p. 59;
Fourth Report … on … the Prisons of Ireland, 1826, H.C. 1826 (173), xxiii, p. 38;
Fifth Report … on … the Prisons of Ireland, 1827, H.C. 1826–7 (471), xi, p. 41;
Sixth Report … on … the Prisons of Ireland, 1828, H.C. 1828 (68), xii, p. 50;
Seventh Report … on … the Prisons of Ireland, 1829, H.C. 1829 (10), xiii, p. 45;
Eighth Report … on … the Prisons of Ireland, 1830, H.C. 1830 (48), xxiv, p. 45;
Ninth Report … on … the Prisons of Ireland, 1831, H.C. 1830–1 (172), iv, p. 33;
Tenth Report … on … the Prisons of Ireland, 1832, H.C. 1831–2 (152), xvii, pp. 5, 33–4;
Eleventh Report … on … the Prisons of Ireland, 1833, H.C. 1833 (67), xvii, p. 46;
Twelfth Report … on … the Prisons of Ireland, 1834, H.C. 1834 (63), xl, p. 51;
Thirteenth Report … on … the Prisons of Ireland, 1835, H.C. 1835 (114), xxxvi, p. 33;
Fourteenth Report … on … the Prisons of Ireland, 1836, H.C. 1836 (118), xxxv, p. 31;
Fifteenth Report … on … the Prisons of Ireland, 1837, H.C. 1837 (123), xxxi, p. 31;
Sixteenth Report … on … the Prisons of Ireland, 1838, H.C. 1837–8 (186), xxix, pp. 35–6;
Eighteenth Report … on … the Prisons of Ireland, 1840, H.C. 1840 (240), xxvi, p. 41;
Nineteenth Report … on … the Prisons of Ireland, 1841, H.C. 1841 (299), xi, p. 43;
Twenty-first Report … on … the Prisons of Ireland, 1843, H.C. 1843 (462), xxvii, pp. 54–5;
Twenty-second Report … on … the Prisons of Ireland, 1844, H.C. 1844 (535), xxviii, p. 67;
Thirty-third Report … on … the Prisons of Ireland, 1855, H.C. 1854–5 (1956), xxvi, pp. 18, 109;
Thirty-fourth Report … on … the Prisons of Ireland, 1856, H.C. 1856 (2113), xxxiv, p. 22;
Forty-ninth Report … on … the Prisons of Ireland, 1870, H.C. 1871 (C. 359), xxx, p. 299.

Secondary sources:

Casey and Rowan, *Buildings of Ireland: North Leinster*, p. 420; O'Dwyer, 'Public Works Architecture', p. 407; Anngret Simms (ed.), *Irish Historic Towns Atlas: Volume 1: Kildare, Carrickfergus, Bandon, Kells, Mullingar, Athlone* (Dublin: Royal Irish Academy, 1996), no. 5, p. 10; Shane O'Toole, writing in *The Sunday Times*, 9 August 2009; Raymond Ryan, 'Westmeath County Buildings & Library', *Irish Architecture: The RIAI Annual Review*, vol. 1, 2010–11, pp. 46–51.

WEXFORD

Wexford

West Gate & Hill St.
Lat. 52°20'30.62" N.; Long. 6°28'6.56" W.

A new gaol noted as building 1785; visited by Howard 1788; gaol built *c.* 1785–8; noted as repaired after the 1798 Rebellion 1803; new gaol built (*Richard Morrison*) *c.* 1807–9; condemned by Forster Archer 1818; grand-jury presentment for alterations and additions to gaol 1819; extensive alterations and additions, including a thirty-two-cell house of correction (used as a female prison) 1823–9; inspectors call for more cells 1836 onwards; unexecuted plan to build a common house of correction for south-eastern counties 1838; extensive addition, comprising two wings of separate-system cells and a large new Gothick entrance building (*John Semple*) 1843–6; fifty female cells added 1851–3; closed 1904; lent to the Sisters of St John of God for use as St Brigid's Home for Inebriate Women 1908; closed 1920; used by the RIC 1921–2; used by county council 1922; used by Free State Army forces 1923–4; given back to county council 1931; mostly intact.

A new gaol noted as building, 1785. Visited by Howard, 1788. Gaol built, *c.* 1785–8. Noted as repaired after the 1798 Rebellion, 1803. Forster Archer, prison inspector, recommends a site for a new gaol, 1803. New courthouse (see Part I), 1803–7. New gaol built (*Richard Morrison*), at a cost of around £10,000, *c.* 1807–9. Condemned by Forster Archer, 1818. Grand-jury presentment for alterations and additions to gaol, 1819. Extensive alterations and additions, including a thirty-two-cell house of correction (used as a female prison), 1823–9. Inspectors call for more cells, 1836 onwards. Unexecuted plan to build a common house of correction for south-eastern counties, 1838. Extensive addition, comprising two wings of separate-system cells and a large new Gothick entrance building (*John Semple*), 1843–6. Fifty female cells added, 1851–3. Closed, 1904. Lent to the Sisters of St John of God for use as St Brigid's Home for Inebriate Women, 1908. Closed, 1920. Used by the RIC, 1921–2. Used by county council, 1922. Used by Free State Army forces, 1923–4. Given back to county council, 1931. Mostly intact.

Archival and primary sources:

Howard, *Lazarettos*, p. 85; Forster Archer, 'Report of the State of Gaols of Ireland for the Year 1802', f. 16 (Houses of the Oireachtas Library, Dublin, MS.7H28); *Accounts of the Presentments Passed by the Grand Juries of Ireland … in … 1807*, H.C. 1808 (205), xiii, pp. 429, 433; Forster Archer, 'Report of the State of Gaols of Ireland for the Year 1811' (Houses of the Oireachtas Library, Dublin, MS.4E63); John Bernard Trotter, *Walks through Ireland in the Years 1812, 1814 and 1817; described in a series of letters to an English gentleman* (London: Phillips, 1819), pp. 126–7; *Freeman's Journal*, 15 March 1820; Correspondence relating to Wexford house of correction, 1827 (NAI, CSORP 1827/481); Inglis, *Ireland in 1834*, vol. 1, p. 46; *Freeman's Journal*, 8 July 1839; Heaney, *Scottish Whig in Ireland*, p. 64; *Saunders' Newsletter*, 2 March 1841; Charles Walker to H.R. Paine (NAI, CSORP 1841/G15264); H.R. Paine, Memo re Wexford gaol, 24 August 1843 (ibid., CSORP 1843/G11630); Nicholson, *Ireland's Welcome to the Stranger*, pp. 220–1; *The Builder*, vol. 9, no. 448, 6 September 1851, p. 565; Ground plan of Wexford gaol, by James Barry Farrell, January 1866 (Wexford County Archives).

Prison reports:

Inspector General's Report of … the Prisons in Ireland for … 1807, H.C. 1808 (239), ix, p. 17;

Account of All Gaols … in the … United Kingdom, H.C. 1819 (137), xvii, pp. 18–19;

Inspector General's Report of … the Prisons in Ireland for … 1818, H.C. 1819 (534), xii, p. 28;

Prisons of Ireland: Report of Inspectors General, 1823, H.C. 1823 (342), x, pp. 7, 66;

Prisons of Ireland: Report of Inspectors General, 1824, H.C. 1824 (294), xxii, pp. 8, 64;

Prisons of Ireland: Report of Inspectors General, 1825, H.C. 1825 (493), xxii, pp. 37–8;

Fourth Report … on … the Prisons of Ireland, 1826, H.C. 1826 (173), xxiii, pp. 53–4;

Fifth Report … on … the Prisons of Ireland, 1827, H.C. 1826–7 (471), xi, pp. 62–3;

Sixth Report … on … the Prisons of Ireland, 1828, H.C. 1828 (68), xii, p. 67;

Seventh Report … on … the Prisons of Ireland, 1829, H.C. 1829 (10), xiii, pp. 9, 64;

Eighth Report … on … the Prisons of Ireland, 1830, H.C. 1830 (48), xxiv, pp. 65–6;

Ninth Report … on … the Prisons of Ireland, 1831, H.C. 1830–1 (172), iv, p. 49;

Eleventh Report … on … the Prisons of Ireland, 1833, H.C. 1833 (67), xvii, p. 32;

Twelfth Report … on … the Prisons of Ireland, 1834, H.C. 1834 (63), xl, p. 36;

Fourteenth Report … on … the Prisons of Ireland, 1836, H.C. 1836 (118), xxxv, p. 45;

Fifteenth Report … on … the Prisons of Ireland, 1837, H.C. 1837 (123), xxxi, pp. 8, 47;
Sixteenth Report … on … the Prisons of Ireland, 1838, H.C. 1837–8 (186), xxix, pp. 52–3;
Seventeenth Report … on … the Prisons of Ireland, 1839, H.C. 1839 (91), xx, pp. 55–6;
Eighteenth Report … on … the Prisons of Ireland, 1840, H.C. 1840 (240), xxvi, pp. 7, 61;
Nineteenth Report … on … the Prisons of Ireland, 1841, H.C. 1841 (299), xi, p. 59;
Twentieth Report … on … the Prisons of Ireland, 1842, H.C. 1842 (377), xxii, pp. 6, 115–16;
Twenty-first Report … on … the Prisons of Ireland, 1843, H.C. 1843 (462), xxvii, pp. 3, 83–4;
Twenty-second Report … on … the Prisons of Ireland, 1844, H.C. 1844 (535), xxviii, pp. 7, 98–9;
Twenty-third Report … on … the Prisons of Ireland, 1844, H.C. 1845 (620), xxv, p. 79;
Twenty-fourth Report … on … the Prisons of Ireland, 1846, H.C. 1846 (697), xx, p. 89;
Twenty-fifth Report … on … the Prisons of Ireland, 1847, H.C. 1847 (805), xxix, p. 101;
Twenty-sixth Report … on … the Prisons of Ireland, 1847–48, H.C. 1847–8 (952), xxiv, p. 108;
Twenty-eighth Report … on … the Prisons of Ireland, 1850, H.C. 1850 (1229), xxix, p. 103;
Twenty-ninth Report … on … the Prisons of Ireland, 1851, H.C. 1851 (1364), xxviii, pp. 14, 112;
Thirtieth Report … on … the Prisons of Ireland, 1852, H.C. 1852 (1531), xxv, p. 18;
Thirty-first Report … on … the Prisons of Ireland, 1853, H.C. 1853 (1657), liii, p. 18;
Forty-eighth Report … on … the Prisons of Ireland, 1869, H.C. 1870 (C. 173), xxxvii, p. 489.

Secondary sources:

Richardson, *Gothic Revival Architecture*, p. 313; O'Dwyer, 'Public Works Architecture', pp. 181, 407; William P. Creedon (ed.), *Exemplar Hiberniae: 100 years of local government in County Wexford* (Dublin: Institute of Public Administration, 1999), p. 121; Glynn, *Wexford*, pp. 22–3.

WICKLOW

Wicklow

Kilmartin Hill
Lat. 52°58'43.92" N.; Long. 6°2'13.92" W.

Act of parliament to extend Wicklow courthouse, makes reference to an adjoining gaol 1774; Howard visits and notes that a new gaol is proposed 1788; new gaol built *c.* 1789–91; Forster Archer criticises condition of prison walls 1803; Forster Archer notes plans for additions 1818; extensive additions and alterations, probably including an entirely new façade (*William Vitruvius Morrison*) 1819–26; unexecuted proposal to move assize town (and gaol) from Wicklow to Rathdrum 1840; a new separate-system block built to the rear of the old gaol (*John Semple*, with contractor *John Edwards*) 1840–3; additions and alterations to female prison (*John Sayers*) 1855–6; now a museum; almost entirely intact.

Act of parliament to extend Wicklow courthouse, makes reference to an adjoining gaol, 1774. Howard visits and notes that a new gaol is proposed, 1788. New gaol built, *c.* 1789–91. Forster Archer, prison inspector, criticises condition of prison walls, 1803, 1811. Forster Archer notes plans for additions, 1818. Grand-jury committee appointed to consider the state of the gaol, 1818. Execution platform erected, 1820. Extensive additions and alterations, probably including an entirely new façade (*William Vitruvius Morrison*), at a cost of £4,500, 1819–26. Inspectors call for additional cells, 1837. Grand-jury note that 'an immediate expenditure of £6,000' would be required 'to afford legal and sufficient accommodation', 1840. Unexecuted proposal to move assize town (and gaol) from Wicklow to Rathdrum, 1840. A new separate-system block built to the rear of the old gaol (*John Semple*, with contractor *John Edwards*), at a cost of £6,000, 1840–3. Additions and alterations to female prison (*John Sayers*), 1855–6. Now a museum. Almost entirely intact.

Archival and primary sources:

13 & 14 Geo. III, c. 18 (1774); Subscriptions of County Wicklow gentry to appeal for funds for building a new gaol, 1786 (NLI, MS 15,303); Howard, *Lazarettos*, p. 84; *Journal of the Irish House of Commons*, vol. xvii, 1797, p. ccvi; Forster Archer, 'Report of the State of Gaols of Ireland for the Year 1802', f. 17 (Houses of the Oireachtas Library, Dublin, MS.7H28); Forster Archer, 'Report of the State of Gaols of Ireland for the Year 1811' (Houses of the Oireachtas Library, Dublin, MS.4E63); *The Traveller's New Guide*, 1815, p. 62; Atkinson, *Irish Tourist*, pp. 592–3; Wicklow grand-jury presentment books, 1818–56 (Wicklow County Archives, GJ); Forster Archer to William Gregory, 2 March 1819 (NAI, CSORP 1819/14); John Revell to William Gregory, 5 September 1820 (NAI, CSORP 1820/1080); Anon., *First Report of the Association for Bettering the Condition of the Prisoners in the County Gaol of Wicklow* (Dublin: Goodwin, 1820); *Third Report of the AIPPD*, p. 49; *Fourth Report of the AIPPD*, p. 44; Morrison, 'Life of the late William Vitruvius Morrison', p. 7.

Prison reports:

Inspector General's Report of … the Prisons in Ireland for … 1807, H.C. 1808 (239), ix, p. 18;

Account of All Gaols … in the … United Kingdom, H.C. 1819 (137), xvii, pp. 20–1;

Inspector General's Report of … the Prisons in Ireland for … 1818, H.C. 1819 (534), xii, p. 28;

Prisons of Ireland: Report of Inspectors General, 1823, H.C. 1823 (342), x, pp. 7, 68;

Prisons of Ireland: Report of Inspectors General, 1824, H.C. 1824 (294), xxii, pp. 8, 65–6;

Prisons of Ireland: Report of Inspectors General, 1825, H.C. 1825 (493), xxii, p. 39;

Fourth Report … on … the Prisons of Ireland, 1826, H.C. 1826 (173), xxiii, p. 55;

Fifth Report … on … the Prisons of Ireland, 1827, H.C. 1826–7 (471), xi, p. 64;

Seventh Report … on … the Prisons of Ireland, 1829, H.C. 1829 (10), xiii, p. 65;

Eighth Report … on … the Prisons of Ireland, 1830, H.C. 1830 (48), xxiv, p. 67;

Fourteenth Report … on … the Prisons of Ireland, 1836, H.C. 1836 (118), xxxv, pp. 45–6;

Fifteenth Report … on … the Prisons of Ireland, 1837, H.C. 1837 (123), xxxi, p. 48;

Sixteenth Report … on … the Prisons of Ireland, 1838, H.C. 1837–8 (186), xxix, p. 54;

Seventeenth Report … on … the Prisons of Ireland, 1839, H.C. 1839 (91), xx, pp. 56–7;

Eighteenth Report … on … the Prisons of Ireland, 1840, H.C. 1840 (240), xxvi, p. 62;

Nineteenth Report … on … the Prisons of Ireland, 1841, H.C. 1841 (299), xi, p. 59;

Twentieth Report … on … the Prisons of Ireland, 1842, H.C. 1842 (377), xxii, pp. 6, 117;

Twenty-first Report … on … the Prisons of Ireland, 1843, H.C. 1843 (462), xxvii, pp. 3, 85;

Twenty-second Report … on … the Prisons of Ireland, 1844, H.C. 1844 (535), xxviii, pp. 7, 100;

Twenty-third Report … on … the Prisons of Ireland, 1844, H.C. 1845 (620), xxv, p. 82;

Thirtieth Report … on … the Prisons of Ireland, 1852, H.C. 1852 (1531), xxv, p. 18, 229;

Thirty-first Report … on … the Prisons of Ireland, 1853, H.C. 1853 (1657), liii, p. 18;

Thirty-third Report … on … the Prisons of Ireland, 1855, H.C. 1854–5 (1956), xxvi, p. 19;

Thirty-fourth Report … on … the Prisons of Ireland, 1856, H.C. 1856 (2113), xxxiv, p. 22;

Forty-eighth Report … on … the Prisons of Ireland, 1869, H.C. 1870 (C. 173), xxxvii, p. 504.

Secondary sources:

Rowan, *Architecture of Richard Morrison*, p. 173; O'Dwyer, 'Public Works Architecture', p. 407; Anon., *Wicklow's Historic Gaol, 1702–1924: A story of crime, cruelty, exile and misery* (Wicklow: n.d. [*c.* 1999]).

Appendix B

Criminal Indictments by County, 1786–1855

(where available)

	Antrim	Armagh	Carlow	Cavan	Clare	Cork county	Cork city	Donegal	Down	Dublin county	Dublin city
1786			57			150			56		
1787		34	38	22		285	505		93		
1788		72	25	37		479	387		66		
1789		84	50	38		346	440		106		
1790		77		51		394	368		79		
1791		93	39	29		400	426		92		
1792		103	32	51		371	470		88		
1793	183	129		44		355	465		92		
1794	188	109		52		383	358		59		
1795	149	94		52		505	369		83		
1796	225	91		64		443	504		101		
1797	122	67	9	67		292	391		73		
1798	71	150	11	92		126	346		104		
1799	98	120	21	72		225	305		123		
1800	74	159	33	120	160	288	310	154	111		
1801	125	172	63	91	227	232	335	149	141		
1802	86	184	56	70	210	304	436	171	120		
1803	162	202	55	122	262	345	448	156	129		
1804	147	188	81	110	293	284	492	177	134		
1805	145	214	69	129	255	286	456	150	113	235	508
1806	193	243	47	135	233	363	378	177	131	195	467
1807	158	279	56	155	186	419	274	230	169	252	540
1808	165	311	53	155	252	323	559	233	156	194	568
1809	201	209	43	146	197	418	534	255	180	139	688
1810	212	231	44	156	300	476	624	252	208	116	580
1811	184	300	48	[illegible]	[illegible]	419	801	280	226	131	635
1812	218	[illegible]	46	196	218	430	502	287	202	138	[illegible]
1813	229	339	19	184	304	[illegible]	[illegible]	229	[illegible]	122	693
1814	295	393	68	177	230	554	663	302	290	92	654
1815	318	373	68	235	186	590	542	287	313		
1816	324	418	43	217	184	517	442	244	352		

	Antrim	Armagh	Carlow	Cavan	Clare	Cork county	Cork city	Donegal	Down	Dublin county	Dublin city
1817	312	402	45	193	223	393	330	254	264		
1818	315	435	65	193	168	412	334	232	399		
1819											
1820											
1821											
1822											
1823	396	341	163	531	406	1,175	339	190	237	273	2,065
1824	464	334	127	569	357	836	264	314	257	448	2,123
1825	459	334	159	540	365	1,075	374	465	326	393	2,120
1826	577	348	199	359	412	1,172	385	557	426	418	2,091
1827	427	578	273	461	344	1,488	490	542	446	506	2,122
1828	454	549	228	301	215	976	483	472	270	393	1,982
1829	338	490	158	280	215	969	423	527	346	366	2,096
1830	533	301	220	304	370	1,021	502	487	358	450	2,128
1831	528	403	195	306	598	859	534	445	355	413	2,312
1832	373	397	236	202	578	861	529	353	350	410	2,384
1833	450	404	351	236	349	1,098	611	472	364	456	2,005
1834	455	350	343	228	364	1,123	792	479	455	493	2,371
1835	363	616	248	619	626	825	546	433	260	322	2,432
1836	360	971	264	611	545	1,221	659	640	269	475	2,675
1837	653	258	307	263	235	581	562	237	388	405	2,799
1838	718	303	283	183	263	485	580	215	482	374	3,267
1839	819	635	355	671	816	1,210	722	455	555	597	3,901
1840	829	593	387	731	867	1,081	777	465	580	494	3,052
1841	708	552	270	653	593	1,438	572	301	606	431	2,147
1842	778	544	294	682	747	1,239	418	326	709	375	1,637
1843	527	483	340	688	757	1,631	316	365	609	336	1,322
1844	493	513	349	568	621	1,709	324	297	608	343	1,414
1845	369	394	350	453	536	1,278	317	289	489	253	1,330
1846	509	452	344	415	597	1,852	401	391	496	332	1,550
1847	804	764	634	754	919	4,430	482	488	612	410	1,844
1848	735	826	678	1,108	1,908	4,511	526	614	624	436	1,597
1849	750	780	737	1,008	2,320	4,487	602	616	597	410	1,435
1850	597	627	646	741	1,489	3,535	471	534	555	493	1,197
1851	648	419	467	433	1,098	2,409	429	469	418	372	1,339
1852	508	310	301	330	529	1,589	485	370	441	306	1,164
1853	611	301	278	316	524	1,023	399	296	419	337	1,271
1854	573	287	145	203	341	733	335	263	370	265	1,229
1855	407	212	125	174	247	591	284	217	269	170	744

	Fermanagh	Galway county	Galway town	Kerry	Kildare	Kilkenny county	Kilkenny city	King's	Leitrim
1786						162	109		
1787	11					170	99		
1788	33					267	110		
1789	9					197	133		
1790	33				50	237	139	51	
1791	26				63	213	142	115	
1792	47				82	211	90	56	
1793	24				86	127	108	91	
1794	43				65	177	91	44	
1795	20				54	175	140	48	
1796	59				53	216	122	84	
1797	57				74	194	87	72	
1798	56				5	56	98	54	94
1799	47				13	83	98	258	79
1800	95				48	112	86	244	85
1801	58				45	117	53	119	133
1802	66				72	116	64	183	245
1803	66				114	157	111	184	176
1804	138				79	164	79	255	149
1805	83				79	187	74	181	172
1806	76	142			102	204	88	199	243
1807	98	197			87	191	119	255	160
1808	156	179			114	179	111	240	172
1809	114	156			88	194	67	264	214
1810	164	200			126	269	132	355	180
1811	146	176			98	273	81	428	339
1812	329	158			94	276	112	323	237
1813	221	112			153	235	103	378	259
1814	288	161			194	229	146	459	169
1815	252	225			176	367	180	467	237
1816	228	234		496	160	48[illegible]	176	309	275
1817	217	207		548	192	391	149	286	254
1818	178	348		[illegible]	[illegible]	508	146	263	[illegible]
1819									
1820									
1821									
1822									
1823	184	611	72	772	381	328	61	358	230

	Fermanagh	Galway county	Galway town	Kerry	Kildare	Kilkenny county	Kilkenny city	King's	Leitrim
1824	364	486	167	716	328	400	64	316	431
1825	349	536	168	719	289	304	87	267	520
1826	307	577	109	766	357	311	91	334	511
1827	278	451	73	1,099	138	364	137	543	391
1828	277	458	136	944	78	221	115	563	380
1829	357	394	337	639	325	174	109	576	372
1830	294	483	127	389	135	221	153	313	282
1831	283	529	141	468	174	171	116	273	209
1832	328	489	107	431	277	199	127	271	293
1833	340	481	113	467	490	367	151	428	389
1834	361	640	145	592	546	408	190	505	330
1835	443	1,000	126	656	215	735	66	530	891
1836	442	1,308	105	709	208	498	49	431	727
1837	435	307	147	332	257	218	77	277	176
1838	348	311	112	338	231	201	69	346	209
1839	405	1,160	131	1,070	256	321	99	705	488
1840	508	932	154	900	230	404	75	512	455
1841	390	763	77	683	277	293	69	584	416
1842	451	781	88	817	284	347	62	559	457
1843	400	722	89	734	213	299	61	526	484
1844	251	821	47	721	173	378	26	465	317
1845	344	580	63	740	207	212	54	339	361
1846	237	607	54	787	204	276	73	465	344
1847	765	1,392	132	1,485	476	341	89	704	610
1848	632	2,446	242	1,847	542	574	166	1,037	677
1849	449	2,365	199	2,706	821	723	127	1,194	508
1850	320	1,243	186	1,796	562	678	104	751	310
1851	231	977	244	1,332	493	613	103	640	243
1852	175	602	150	870	347	371	90	474	210
1853	196	547	133	545	284	278	34	337	191
1854	142	312	70	532	251	208	43	187	168
1855	166	263	76	331	225	171	70	169	170

	Limerick county	Limerick city	Londonderry	Longford	Louth	Town of Drogheda	Mayo	Meath	Monaghan
1786		144	143						
1787		179	255						
1788		200	381						
1789		180	361						

	Limerick county	Limerick city	Londonderry	Longford	Louth	Town of Drogheda	Mayo	Meath	Monaghan
[illegible]		[illegible]	[illegible]						[illegible]
1791		148	375						118
1792		139	379						197
1793		86	282						116
1794		93	292						136
1795		89	270		121				128
1796		102	326		139				96
1797		279	202		132		41	67	60
1798		197	297		111		61	98	75
1799		269	244		71		19	44	119
1800		225	307		101		31	69	123
1801		140	265		139		38	93	137
1802		255	107		129		74	117	180
1803	338	318	163		132		101	109	153
1804	401	291	149		134		141	118	145
1805	346	247	280	130	137		118	136	186
1806	378	326	200	216	134		178	135	230
1807	353	224	245	204	95		121	177	193
1808	337	234	237	217	105		95	157	162
1809	382	281	201	176	108		110	121	153
1810	418	299	316	184	125		169	147	139
1811	345	246	283	187	165		119	146	211
1812	344	425	302	203	159		94	173	189
1813	293	381	265	206	146	55	163	217	177
1814	361	506	257	191	128	107	210	152	235
1815	360	315	368	192	145	88	184	225	226
1816	441	214	334	203	191	100	179	205	234
1817	277	158	321	200	137	40	95	114	208
1818	282	359	314	194	143	52	84	152	177
1819									
1820									
1821									
1822									
1823	368	358	385	322	93	39		281	465
1824	410	401	314	416	138	61	152	287	376
1825	332	348	314	321	125	64	260	269	366
1826	356	376	301	334	150	65	229	322	365
1827	536	345	405	389	300	61	319	320	447

	Limerick county	Limerick city	Londonderry	Longford	Louth	Town of Drogheda	Mayo	Meath	Monaghan
1828	337	255	237	330	218	66	346	212	352
1829	255	346	292	404	147	34	387	243	321
1830	441	365	260	429	164	48	829	247	310
1831	431	326	268	300	166	43	1,235	288	361
1832	272	336	217	391	199	34	705	240	279
1833	640	420	351	409	183	80	973	284	386
1834	789	726	303	590	238	113	1,487	361	455
1835	545	337	319	279	229	130	880	739	507
1836	539	313	425	189	115	92	789	627	628
1837	300	379	192	141	90	67	947	269	299
1838	234	363	258	202	98	86	916	307	301
1839	829	360	324	388	422	61	984	502	526
1840	613	237	385	376	277	62	814	485	492
1841	834	158	400	361	234	40	750	404	489
1842	1,079	99	478	419	384	76	805	408	462
1843	897	132	343	299	207	32	975	329	489
1844	767	114	402	269	294	45	918	297	391
1845	683	128	288	306	263	50	750	287	286
1846	770	111	326	232	216	50	892	264	275
1847	1,169	188	477	521	319	84	1,406	469	640
1848	1,933	228	475	721	390	126	1,781	548	766
1849	2,619	275	405	490	440	121	2,058	659	893
1850	2,019	261	397	327	449	78	1,128	537	545
1851	1,190	339	392	356	296	64	835	460	391
1852	799	269	266	183	266	77	561	270	330
1853	566	318	253	240	194	84	629	247	230
1854	370	175	224	110	150	55	468	197	203
1855	320	113	254	90	112	41	350	200	170

	Queen's	Roscommon	Sligo	Tipperary	Tyrone	Waterford county	Waterford city	Westmeath	Wexford	Wicklow
1786	63							25		
1787	43							28		
1788	21							56		
1789	46							49		
1790	50							55		
1791	65							140		
1792	87							108		

	Queen's	Roscommon	Sligo	Tipperary	Tyrone	Waterford county	Waterford city	Westmeath	Wexford	Wicklow
1793	60					163		176		
1794	27					144		128		
1795	33					183		143		
1796	62					133		113		
1797	45	188				145		117		210
1798	50	148				54		92		
1799	42	167				89		137		
1800	107	166				127		147	112	
1801	131	132				95		211	194	
1802	74	182				139		242	192	131
1803	116	225				115		234	163	
1804	112	191				136		264	146	
1805	148	142				167		359	121	
1806	190	178				163		366	101	141
1807	213	170	193			170		383	89	215
1808	110	132	178			160		283	119	185
1809	89	207	197			133		227	110	140
1810	143	254	173			161		259	82	104
1811	52	169	178		255	184		275	75	133
1812	34	233	195		269	157		287	91	160
1813	63	169	196	592	245	194		283	91	156
1814	157	283	279	944	242	184		279	94	133
1815	219	253	278	797	335	255		350	74	148
1816	196	250	356	773	235	261		391	89	152
1817	160	327	343	675	308	254		345	76	138
1818	281	304	336	1,137	250	284		425	88	174
1819										
1820										
1821										
1822										
1823	222	385	591	395	443	177	173	486	174	162
1824	267	[illegible]	[illegible]	336	411	228	137	[illegible]	231	181
1825	265	445	600	376	347	210	178	403	299	144
1826	298	535	575	450	379	226	223	436	245	147
1827	373	424	427	755	410	366	160	342	287	214
1828	189	456	402	519	330	224	145	288	179	103
1829	388	455	559	581	289	210	133	336	244	156

	Queen's	Roscommon	Sligo	Tipperary	Tyrone	Waterford county	Waterford city	Westmeath	Wexford	Wicklow
1830	454	438	532	700	394	196	228	347	208	133
1831	456	528	505	720	226	226	151	320	192	138
1832	582	470	360	1,414	228	177	180	404	245	128
1833	528	544	423	1,005	309	218	157	543	233	111
1834	699	603	482	1,305	377	475	162	583	316	147
1835	541	1,120	276	2,043	487	154	100	526	545	216
1836	633	827	492	4,352	627	119	129	660	368	284
1837	301	369	154	965	210	509	141	242	184	131
1838	296	682	271	928	268	338	192	296	217	147
1839	642	865	578	2,110	558	364	191	458	409	450
1840	561	922	540	1,642	560	416	77	582	339	427
1841	570	788	458	1,584	473	357	117	410	292	254
1842	721	765	510	1,448	535	302	93	434	395	344
1843	625	713	477	1,720	466	500	10	389	315	306
1844	557	663	535	1,661	486	442	64	338	343	424
1845	395	555	449	1,508	440	382	84	289	264	331
1846	408	580	478	1,565	440	466	128	307	298	300
1847	767	838	684	2,372	693	736	171	573	461	506
1848	917	1,145	862	3,363	785	755	212	658	668	463
1849	1,130	850	804	4,170	892	1,002	226	719	751	651
1850	881	633	595	3,202	944	609	163	538	732	451
1851	583	663	332	2,470	575	707	217	391	637	409
1852	382	467	199	1,711	620	401	145	350	489	271
1853	316	376	182	1,263	560	349	128	265	392	232
1854	295	264	160	975	381	243	133	232	304	192
1855	219	220	169	593	330	173	75	154	213	135

	Total
1786	909
1787	1,762
1788	2,134
1789	2,039
1790	2,313
1791	2,484
1792	2,511
1793	2,581
1794	2,389
1795	2,656
1796	2,933
1797	2,991
1798	2,446
1799	2,743
1800	3,594
1801	3,635
1802	4,205
1803	4,856
1804	4,998
1805	5,853
1806	6,552
1807	6,870
1808	6,831
1809	6,742
1810	7,598
1811	8,105
1812	8,312
1813	8,758
1814	10,106
1815	9,628
1816	9,910
1817	8,936
1818	10,165
1819	
1820	
1821	
1822	
1823	14,632
1824	15,258
1825	15,515
1826	16,318
1827	18,031
1828	14,683
1829	15,271
1830	15,794
1831	16,192
1832	16,056
1833	17,819
1834	21,381
1835	21,925
1836	25,375
1837	14,804
1838	15,723
1839	26,392
1840	23,833
1841	20,796
1842	21,352
1843	20,126
1844	19,448
1845	16,696
1846	18,492
1847	31,209
1848	38,522
1849	41,989
1850	31,326
1851	24,684
1852	17,678
1853	15,144
1854	11,788
1855	9,012

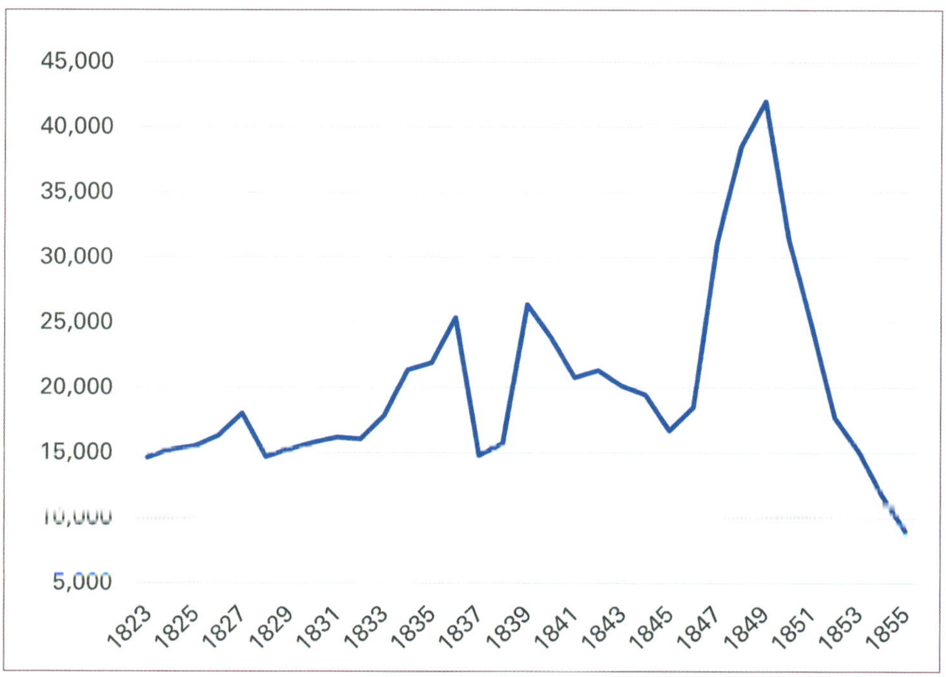

The blue line indicates total national criminal indictments during the period for which all county figures are available, 1823 through to 1855.

Notes

Criminal indictments are one of many possible ways of measuring crime in Ireland. It is difficult to find any other barometer that is, for the most part, as consistently recorded over such a long period spanning from *c.* 1780 through to 1855. Indictment figures are the number of persons sent forward for trial and should not be mistaken for conviction rates or indeed the number of persons in prisons at any time. They also do not take account of civil cases in the courts system, debtors of all kinds, and certain types of agrarian unrest punished in special sessions hearings. The statistics have gaps, for example, when counties failed to report their numbers to central government (the pink shaded boxes). Similarly, the figures for 1835 and 1836 are open to debate and revision as they are taken from a different source to that used elsewhere, presenting an unavoidable inconsistency (the orange shaded boxes). The figures for the county of Antrim and the county of the town of Carrickfergus are reported together because both grand juries merged their gaols as early as 1827 and because the indictment figures for the town of Carrickfergus are so small. These tables offer a guide to crime rates in Ireland during the period under study and are especially striking for the enormous numbers during the Famine and the sudden and unprecedented fall-off immediately afterwards. These figures are compiled from the following House of Commons papers:

For 1786 through to 1819

Return of the Number of Indictments, &c. Entered for Trial … in the Several Counties of Ireland … from 1786–1819, H.C. 1818–19 (15), iii

For 1805 through to 1812 for certain counties missing from the above report

Return of Number of Persons Committed for Trial in Ireland, 1805–12, H.C. 1813–14 (264), xiii

For 1819 through to 1822

I have been unable to locate any figures for criminal indictments for these years

For 1823 through to 1829

Eighth Report … on … the Prisons of Ireland, 1830, H.C. 1830 (48), xxiv, p. 81

For 1830 through to 1834

Thirteenth Report … on … the Prisons of Ireland, 1835, H.C. 1835 (114), xxxvi, pp. 54–5

For 1835 and 1836

Return from Clerks … of the Several Counties … in Ireland of Number of Persons Committed to the Different Gaols Thereof for Trial in the Year 1835, H.C. 1836 (97), xlii

Return from Clerks … of the Several Counties … in Ireland of Number of Persons Committed to the Different Gaols Thereof for Trial in the Year 1836, H.C. 1837 (158), xlv

For 1837 through to 1844

Fifteenth Report … on … the Prisons of Ireland, 1837, H.C. 1837 (123), xxxi, p. 67
Sixteenth Report … on … the Prisons of Ireland, 1838, H.C. 1837–8 (186), xxix, p. 69
Seventeenth Report … on … the Prisons of Ireland, 1839, H.C. 1839 (91), xx, p. 75
Eighteenth Report of … on … the Prisons of Ireland, 1840, H.C. 1840 (240), xxvi, p. 75
Nineteenth Report of … on … the Prisons of Ireland, 1841, H.C. 1841 (299), xi, p. 129
Twentieth Report of … on … the Prisons of Ireland, 1842, H.C. 1842 (377), xxii, p. 113
Twenty-first Report … on … the Prisons of Ireland, 1843, H.C. 1843 (462), xxvii, p. 111
Twenty-second Report … on … the Prisons of Ireland, 1844, H.C. 1844 (535), xxviii, p. 101

For 1845 through to 1855

Tables Showing the Number of Criminal Offenders Committed for Trial … in Ireland … in the Year 1845, H.C. 1846 (696), xxv, p. 9
Tables Showing the Number of Criminal Offenders Committed for Trial … in Ireland … in the Year 1846, H.C. 1847 (94), lvi, p. 9
Tables Showing the Number of Criminal Offenders Committed for Trial … in Ireland … in the Year 1847, H.C. 1847–8 (146), lvii, p. 7
Tables Showing the Number of Criminal Offenders Committed for Trial … in Ireland … in the Year 1848, H.C. 1849 (72), xliv, p. 7
Tables Showing the Number of Criminal Offenders Committed for Trial … in Ireland … in the Year 1849, H.C. 1850 (190), li, p. 7
Tables Showing the Number of Criminal Offenders Committed for Trial … in Ireland … in the Years 1850 and 1851, H.C. 1852 (192), xlvii, p. 7
Tables Showing the Number of Criminal Offenders Committed for Trial … in Ireland … in the Year 1852, H.C. 1852–3 (340), lxxxi, p. 7
Tables Showing the Number of Criminal Offenders Committed for Trial … in Ireland … in the Year 1853, H.C. 1854 (138), lviii, p. 7
Tables Showing the Number of Persons Committed … for Trial at the Assizes and Quarter Sessions in Each County in the Year 1854 … in Ireland, H.C. 1854–5 (1930), xliii, p. xxiii
Tables Showing the Number of Persons Committed … for Trial at the Assizes and Quarter Sessions in Each County in the Year 1855 … in Ireland, H.C. 1856 (2116), xlix, p. xxiii

Appendix C

Grand-Jury Presentments for Courthouse- and Prison-Building Work, 1822–55

(where available)

	Antrim	Armagh	Carlow	Cavan	Town of Carrickfergus	Clare	Cork county	Cork city	Donegal	Down
1822							75			
1823	0	26	54	25	0	10	46	91	0	0
1824	30	597	0	1,333	0	0	1,433	13	0	0
1825	14	27	100	1,869	0	32	953	22	0	0
1826	128	0	114	135	0	50	872	71	0	0
1827	0	0	374	81	175	94	3,900	22	0	73
1828	126	4	681	2,375	0	45	978	62	0	14
1829	7	279	589	2,379	0	68	1,869	63	0	28
1830	40	0	571	500	0	429	1,650	78		17
1831	320	0	1,490	1,396	17	392	4,040	496	0	1,040
1832	467	0	2,343	407	10	152	4,243	485	0	1,000
1833	19	94	1,837	593	4	43	7,463	455	0	1,150
1834	18	0	1,409	253	0	63	4,101	438	0	1,000
1835	72	0	0	171	0	26	0	674	0	0
1836	66	210	278	66	0		1,298	754	0	0
1837	141	0	407	650	0	43	570	541	0	5
1838	455	0	1,266	217	0	1,981	455	447	55	338
1839	585	0	235	194	0	59	50	603	15	716
1840	333	1,307	45	177	0	117	86	719	66	1,044
1841	310	29	21	147	0	73	251	42	0	535
1842	49	234	632	183	0	117	0	57	185	10
1843	131	15	90	0	0	183	570	660	0	46
1844	137	20	45	211	0	195	525	380	349	42
1845	145	20	75	0	0	64	0	86	0	118
1846	293	45	7	0	0	1,270	1,598	102	270	177
1847	2,050	173	0	0	0	2,479	165	0	0	240
1848	758	12	54	162	0	2,450	0	219	0	102
1849	5,828	9	49	155	0	2,436	1,005	63	0	656

	Antrim	Armagh	Carlow	Cavan	Town of Carrickfergus	Clare	Cork county	Cork city	Donegal	Down
1850	3,755	20	0	186	0	3,119	594	41	0	607
1851	778	136	0	122	0	548	120	47	0	86
1852	5	79	0	152	0	23	100	50	0	269
1853	0	11	605	20	0	27	299	51	0	13
1854	59	169	429	163	0	0	226		0	260
1855	0	4	70	22	0	43	111	74	0	2,538
Total	**17,119**	**3,520**	**13,870**	**14,344**	**206**	**16,631**	**39,646**	**7,906**	**940**	**12,124**

	Town of Drogheda	Dublin county	Dublin city	Fermanagh	Galway county	Galway town	Kerry	Kildare
1822		55						
1823	0	201	86	548	0	230	71	387
1824	0	0	414	439	203	0	29	228
1825	0	665	0	90	321	0	82	144
1826	0	0	367	131	78	332	127	91
1827	0	479	0	19	0	523	949	239
1828	0	123	0	839	862	24	56	91
1829	0	14	40		456	84	56	370
1830	0	0			0	40	20	845
1831	0	0	54		265	80	50	130
1832	0	0	232	102	268	32	52	302
1833	0	40	109		60	234	2102	92
1834	0	0	42		206	378	52	44
1835	0	0	95		0	186	834	82
1836	0	0	117		232	30	87	37
1837	0	108	0		331	77	276	78
1838	0	15	1,128	52	378	100	9	113
1839	0	31	0	69	429	270	0	221
1840	0	25	28	34	742	100	0	168
1841	0	398	92	1,163	994	252	528	162
1842	0	0	135	55	484	93	162	405
1843	0	19	1,877	8	300	30	32	101
1844	0	64	67	10	500	47	25	25
1845	0	0	141	0	614	0	196	99
1846	0	935	132	0	393	47	14	60

	Town of Drogheda	Dublin county	Dublin city	Fermanagh	Galway county	Galway town	Kerry	Kildare
[illegible]	[illegible]	[illegible]	[illegible]	[illegible]	[illegible]	[illegible]	[illegible]	[illegible]
1848	0	51	222	27	0	51	0	108
1849	0	1,013	522	30	0	0	0	19
1850	0	49	247	14	0	0	0	65
1851	0	24	147	150	0	0	65	362
1852	0	26	127	12	0	45	18	127
1853	75	50	193	32	439	4	40	
1854	0	25	67	51	47	38	0	108
1855	63	54	49	25	0	120	70	91
Total	138	4,464	6,796	3,907	9,302	3,517	6,007	5,559

	Kilkenny county	Kilkenny city	King's	Leitrim	Limerick county	Limerick city	Londonderry	Longford	Louth
1822				267				65	3,172
1823	237	56	0	0	285	9	172	96	1,616
1824	364	0	61	69	700	7	141	44	853
1825	28	0	53	48	0	60	0	16	0
1826	91	0	63	39	229	22	384	4	1,060
1827	89	0	0	0	388	15	319	1,022	839
1828	314	0	66	0	0	0	406	1,013	245
1829	28	0		20		0	394	61	89
1830	13			41		0	638	48	0
1831	3			242		13	568	28	0
1832	0			450		29	477	0	0
1833	0			126		3	152	30	0
1834	0			114		13	138	28	0
1835	0			100		10	348	28	0
1836	0			50		0	270	28	0
1837	0			428		0	344	1,309	49
1838	29			208		0	166	[illegible]	[illegible]
1839	5			250		0	829	200	8
1840	2			215	0	0	108	348	35
1841	0	3	22	185	0	0	142	52	25
1842	0	0	61	103	0	0	1	52	0
1843	97	0	182	46	0	0	85	52	0

	Kilkenny county	Kilkenny city	King's	Leitrim	Limerick county	Limerick city	Londonderry	Longford	Louth
1844	34	0	76	50	0	0	75	58	23
1845	19	0	6	18	0	0	21	58	9
1846	170	0	16	416	0	0	129	58	47
1847	0	0	58	0	0	550	25	72	507
1848	0	0	48	20	120	0	50	204	264
1849	177	0	14	0	0	0	65	98	20
1850	213	0	131	0	0	0	47	125	20
1851	0	0	13	0	0	0	574	132	34
1852	0	0	2	9	0	0	313	133	0
1853	0	0	19	480	0	0	37	145	45
1854	0	0	10	100	0	0	103	132	0
1855	0	0	83	50	0	0	1,085	140	700
Total	**1,913**	**59**	**984**	**4,234**	**1,722**	**731**	**8,606**	**6,775**	**9,710**

	Mayo	Meath	Monaghan	Queen's	Roscommon	Sligo	Tipperary	Tyrone
1822					1,264		277	
1823	830	94	10	130	1,052	0	296	23
1824	275	0	100	57	1,020	0	114	0
1825	483	6	91	60	15	83	114	738
1826	633	809	0	339	0	0	212	461
1827	1,318	644	537	348	1,236	60	1,331	489
1828	345	128	1,246	628	7	832	355	759
1829	613	254	1,747		1,906	59	111	693
1830	626	516	1,292	1,137	11	4	233	361
1831	664	14	594	222	29	423	645	451
1832	539	81	95	504	12	410	762	1,085
1833	312	850	150	512	74	620	212	136
1834	1,062	21	32	379	0	123	49	252
1835	288	8	0	493	28	126	150	
1836	417	11	423	1,861	32	678	8	39
1837	622	60	73	427	0	178	207	181
1838	656	882	218	20	158	496	203	292
1839	1,539	190	104	432	53	111	950	226
1840	720	228	350	1,179	32	402	6,094	162
1841	135	96	418	287	320	254	2,723	168
1842	78	94	392	425	303	117	1,538	221
1843	45	63	300	120	7	21	2,143	143

	Mayo	Meath	Monaghan	Queen's	Roscommon	Sligo	Tipperary	Tyrone
1844	32	214	370	144	2	77	1,120	128
1845	51	4	50	115	0	28	1,279	157
1846	95	280	347	114	380	98	957	170
1847	24	64	140	1,292	0	0	776	126
1848	314	4	188	10	217	67	111	104
1849	77	71	147	34	4	78	334	126
1850	82	18	140	10	30	10	37	60
1851	106	47	140	12	0	13	58	125
1852	97	164	139	14	0	101	2	32
1853	15	192	343	24	35	60	600	100
1854	49	28	180	24	38	66	195	171
1855	82	62	213	24	12	0	129	130
Total	13,224	6,197	10,569	11,377	8,277	5,595	24,325	8,309

	Waterford county	Waterford city	Westmeath	Wexford	Wicklow	National
1822	112					5,287
1823	167	125	5	117	30	7,225
1824	0	0	1,817	419	54	10,814
1825	134	25	637	364	30	7,304
1826	5	57	602	506	17	8,029
1827	323	35	682	543	28	17,174
1828	3	13	778	630	3	14,051
1829	2	0	1,219	471	259	14,228
1830	0	6	2,286	197	6	11,605
1831	0	24	1,467	333	38	15,528
1832	0	70	989	695	45	16,338
1833	116	32	578	622	6	18,826
1834	0	15	578	470	15	11,293
1835	26	30	603	329	35	4,742
1836	0	0	25	355	6	7,378
1837	51	64	600	419	45	8,284
1838	0	[illegible]	[illegible]	[illegible]	0	[illegible]
1839	[illegible]	[illegible]	0	[illegible]	[illegible]	8,773
1840	2	37	0	282	293	15,480
1841	6	5	0	383	870	11,091
1842	0	0	0	375	1,223	7,784
1843	298	2	0	321	801	8,788

	Waterford county	Waterford city	Westmeath	Wexford	Wicklow	National
1844	5	0	66	287	247	5,650
1845	0	0	3	618	35	4,029
1846	5	0	0	1,153	121	9,899
1847	1,872	1,595	0	232	5	13,458
1848	1,826	1,595	0	287	230	9,875
1849	1,194	798	40	452	0	15,514
1850	159	182	0	677	24	10,662
1851	164	70	56	58	22	4,209
1852	413	0	9	65	58	2,584
1853	22	0	14	60	0	4,050
1854	82	0	0	289	0	3,109
1855	118	0	35	269	191	6,657
Total	7,194	4,831	13,089	12,885	4,769	331,331

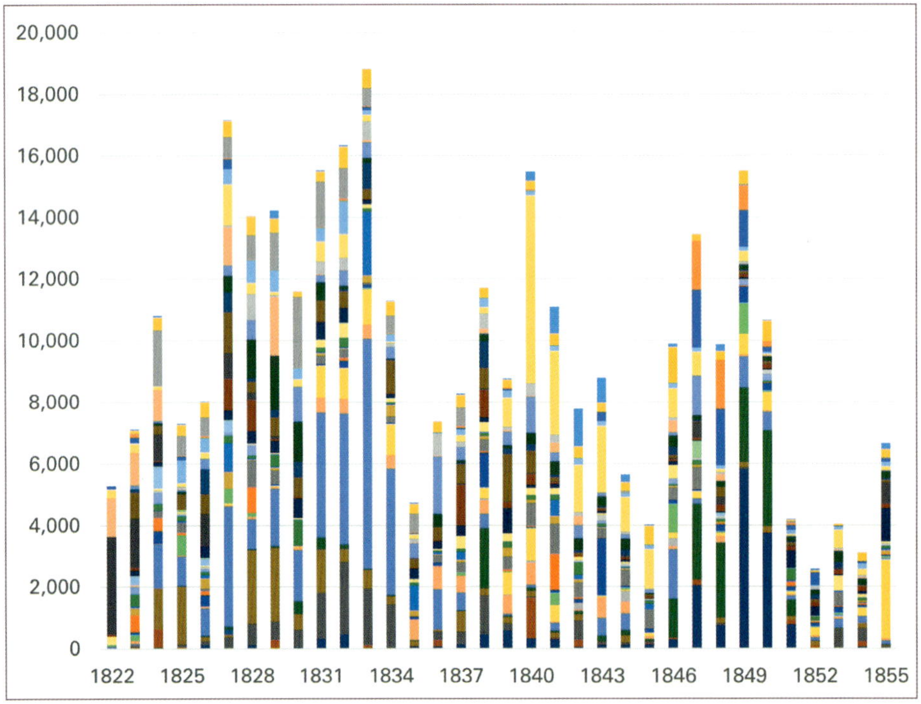

This graph shows the total amount presented by grand juries for the building and/or repairing of courthouses in Ireland between 1822 and 1855, where such figures exist. The likely true figure is almost certainly greater, particularly during the 1830s when several counties failed in their obligation to report their expenditure. The colour coding in the bar chart gives some indication of the extent to which the total figure could depend on a single large presentment by a large county – for example the peak in

1832 (£18,826) relies on the County of Cork grand juror's single presentment of £7,463 for nearly half of the national total (shown in blue for this year). The total amount presented for prisons in the period under study was forty per cent higher than the total amount presented for courthouses.

Part 2: Presentments for the erection and/or repair of prisons

	Antrim	Armagh	Carlow	Cavan	Town of Carrickfergus	Clare	Cork county	Cork city	Donegal	Down
1822							122		360	
1823	0	167	7	0	0	21	46	51	0	4,320
1824	100	15	72	5,200	124	0	5,981	27	1,023	4,000
1825	100	255	18	6,304	2	930	2,358	18	473	4,000
1826	101	89	346	2,792	1	222	2,567	0	1,425	3,846
1827	142	578	500	188	0	334	3,176	0	21	4,192
1828	192	2,250	1,430	1,680	0	427	1,692	2,381	1,237	4,592
1829	692	0	1,221	1,445	0	497	0	2,219	300	4,192
1830	435	150	853	1,150	0	538	0	2,218		3,692
1831	256	150	1,438	1,950	0	155	596	2,058	500	3,692
1832	197	21	0	50	0	217	0	2,058	500	3,692
1833	294	306	0	0	0	135	0	1,597	0	3,692
1834	0	41	0	0	0	125	0	858	0	3,692
1835	75	41	0	0	0	182	1,846	627	0	3,692
1836	140	41	0	0	0		0	437	0	0
1837	27	41	0	295	0	63	0	559	166	0
1838	92	41	0	17	0	366	0	558	647	0
1839	20	41	157	412	0	741	37	0	60	52
1840	34	41	460	66	0	508	0	0	96	0
1841	1,102	87	200	0	0	493	0	0	328	0
1842	6	41	0	0	0	631	0	100	385	0
1843	12	43	0	0	0	535	0	400	38	43
1844	900	166	34	0	0	493	8	0	12	23
1845	1,050	291	0	0	0	493	969	0	0	32
1846	2,091	1,021	0	784	0	493	0	0	73	0
1847	[illegible]	[illegible]	[illegible]	[illegible]	[illegible]	[illegible]	[illegible]	[illegible]	[illegible]	[illegible]
1848	0	1,521	0	0	0	368	0	200	0	0
1849	0	148	0	0	0	368	0	400	0	356
1850	0	0	0	5	0	368	0	500	639	370
1851	0	0	600	0	0	368	3,000	100	0	358
1852	50	0	49	0	0	368	124	0	0	366

	Antrim	Armagh	Carlow	Cavan	Town of Carrickfergus	Clare	Cork county	Cork city	Donegal	Down
1853	0	0	249	12	0	368	232	50	0	362
1854	499	500	0	15	0	368	170		0	307
1855	37	600	0	0	0	368	0	100	16	1,311
Total	**11,344**	**8,748**	**7,634**	**22,365**	**127**	**12,036**	**22,971**	**17,516**	**8,299**	**54,874**

	Town of Drogheda	Dublin county	Dublin city	Fermanagh	Galway county	Galway town	Kerry	Kildare
1822		55						
1823	0	406	2,989	0	0	100	44	47
1824	46	531	958	0	1,561	100	655	64
1825	120	2,910	0	636	758	65	500	134
1826	9	0	604	0	14	5	610	940
1827	49	0	0	366	20	40	1,951	1,315
1828	0	2,921	0	745	118	480	0	1,461
1829	0	0	748	650	330	115	482	1,060
1830	7	124		972	13	150	0	1,129
1831	30	200	288	800	205	0	0	1,174
1832	0	58	286	572	12	0	0	1,724
1833	0	227	202	650	355		0	596
1834	0	154	102	757	500	460	0	230
1835	0	112	491	496	1,534	701	0	620
1836	0	41	182	738	457	0	0	439
1837	0	557	0		349	0	0	17
1838	0	55	1,324		320	0	0	13
1839	0	108	3,362		0	0	513	65
1840	0	4	3,226		489	0	130	54
1841	0	27	144		200	0	256	0
1842	0	440	0		48	0	5	0
1843	0	0	0		170	0	44	0
1844	0	720	335		132	11	0	0
1845	0	110	0		152	0	0	0
1846	0	450	125		0	11	0	20
1847	0	300	323		300	11	350	0
1848	0	340	834		0	14	0	0
1849	0	65	681	0	0	0	0	0

	Town of Drogheda	Dublin county	Dublin city	Fermanagh	Galway county	Galway town	Kerry	Kildare
1850	0	15	1,647	0	0	0	0	0
1851	60	22	322	0	0	0	0	0
1852	95	25	686	0	0	0	0	0
1853	0	40	950	1,621	119	0	0	
1854	150	0	838	0	136	0	0	400
1855	0	200	590	0	0	0	0	126
Total	**566**	**11,217**	**22,237**	**9,003**	**8,292**	**2,263**	**5,540**	**11,628**

Year	Kilkenny county	Kilkenny city	King's	Leitrim	Limerick county	Limerick city	Londonderry	Longford	Louth
1822				382					
1823	188	0	0	0	285	44	419	319	50
1824	175	14	0	266	330	0	0	1,236	120
1825	50	326	53	0	600	206	0	305	100
1826	0	0	0	1,657	0	30	432	107	92
1827	0	0	0	0	950	2	662	40	415
1828	0	0		0	265	376	368	0	0
1829	0	0		287	0	45	841	0	0
1830	0			0	253	0	1,606	19	0
1831	0			28	0	100	1,477	19	0
1832	0			0	102	0	1,771	28	0
1833	0			0	1,581	0	1,485	923	0
1834	0			48	212	0	1,477	375	51
1835	0			0	515	0	1,477	375	0
1836	5			0	267	0	1,477	375	110
1837	0			200	156	0	1,610	356	0
1838	0			30	400	0	1,477	356	0
1839	0			0	200	0	1,630	356	0
1840	0			254	1,150	0	133	0	0
1841	[illegible]			[illegible]	[illegible]	[illegible]	[illegible]	[illegible]	[illegible]
1842	0			130	345	0	63	356	50
1843	0		9	0	0	0	69	676	20
1844	0	0	0	0	0	0	1,135	356	0
1845	0	0	100	0	0	0	0	356	50
1846	0	0	205	0	1,267	0	5	356	0

Year	Kilkenny county	Kilkenny city	King's	Leitrim	Limerick county	Limerick city	Londonderry	Longford	Louth
1847	0	0	0	0	0	0	50	178	0
1848	3,458	0	0	0	0	0	10	0	1,150
1849	1,372	50	0	0	0	706	131	9	42
1850	0	0	0	0	0	79	3	0	4
1851	1,355	0	0	30	0	0	61	0	30
1852	0	0	0	790	0	0	0	0	0
1853	0	0	0	120	0	0	300	144	130
1854	0	0	8	420	0	0	69	19	150
1855	0	0	0	0	0	0	483	19	11
Total	**6,607**	**390**	**375**	**4,642**	**9,159**	**1,588**	**20,736**	**8,014**	**2,628**

Year	Mayo	Meath	Monaghan	Queen's	Roscommon	Sligo	Tipperary	Tyrone
1822			1,772		729		277	
1823	415	216	1,772	1,282	1,200	193	104	267
1824	3,494	0	853	2,280	263	461	201	0
1825	3,660	63	100	1,000	671	0	1,000	379
1826	0	646	0	953	0	23	120	1,966
1827	0	1,822	250	1,423	21	9	695	7
1828	1,021	2,057	36	2,611	0	1,103	0	268
1829	1,100	1,822	108	1,945	406	2,203	0	103
1830		1,898	90	2,663	246	4	498	873
1831		1,511	25	357	0	1,129	562	1,377
1832		1,769	34	1,133	3	1,155	471	1,016
1833		640	58	1,043	0	60	383	1,029
1834		75	35	923	41	31	385	898
1835		0	0	1,071	0	0	778	
1836	1,000	0	46	923	0	0	791	0
1837	2,038	0	0	923	42	0	775	180
1838	25	44	10	0	252	200	814	35
1839	103	45	6	923	0	127	2,000	110
1840	0	438	249	923	13	0	2,349	50
1841	0	10	43	923	5	0	1,265	138
1842	242	13	0	923	9	0	1,606	222
1843	57	9	0	923	0	34	1,316	71
1844	97	0	0	0	0	0	1,315	2
1845	452	22	135	0	0	0	1,315	45

Year	Mayo	Meath	Monaghan	Queen's	Roscommon	Sligo	Tipperary	Tyrone
1846	0	0	0	0	0	22	1,315	88
1847	24	91	0	0	204	0	1,315	377
1848	83	0	0	0	0	0	1,315	293
1849	0	0	0	0	0	0	1,315	114
1850	0	26	0	0	0	0	1,315	52
1851	0	0	0	450	0	0	1,315	97
1852	0	0	0	0	0	0	1,370	0
1853	43	22	0	0	0	0	1,225	70
1854	0	11	0	0	120	0	1,225	52
1855	0	22	180	0	180	0	1,250	52
Total	13,854	13,272	5,802	25,595	4,405	6,754	31,980	10,231

Year	Waterford county	Waterford city	Westmeath	Wexford	Wicklow	National
1822	1,138			1,484		**6,319**
1823	0	0	0	3,282	0	**18,234**
1824	0	123	0	1,108	0	**31,381**
1825	86	0	698	2,526	484	**31,888**
1826	0	0	671	3,824	126	**24,218**
1827	250	0	702	1,586	67	**21,773**
1828	50	0	702	1,396	90	**31,949**
1829	285	0	1,674	742	27	**25,539**
1830	0	150	779	107	83	**20,700**
1831	0	0	1,303	167	0	**21,547**
1832	0	25	702	83	0	**17,679**
1833	100	40	702	318	0	**16,416**
1834	150	0	702	0	138	**12,463**
1835	7	0	702	0	928	**16,270**
1836	0	0	702	0	513	**8,684**
1837	0	0	821	50	0	**9,225**
1838	12	0	702	0	0	**7,790**
1839	0	0	165	0	597	**11,830**
1840	0	55	58	27	0	**10,807**
1841	0	0	58	0	688	**6,585**
1842	0	0	0	[illegible]	[illegible]	**[illegible]**
1843	2	0	58	739	0	**5,268**
1844	85	0	829	32	0	**6,685**
1845	0	0	58	0	0	**5,630**
1846	0	0	58	0	200	**8,584**

Year	Waterford county	Waterford city	Westmeath	Wexford	Wicklow	National
1847	0	0	28	0	0	**6,853**
1848	320	26	0	0	1	**9,933**
1849	0	0	0	0	0	**5,757**
1850	320	0	180	0	0	**5,523**
1851	0	0	5	0	0	**8,173**
1852	0	0	0	0	0	**3,923**
1853	99	0	0	29	0	**6,185**
1854	120	0	0	0	251	**5,828**
1855	0	0	0	0	346	**5,891**
Total	3,024	419	13,059	17,875	5,674	442,743

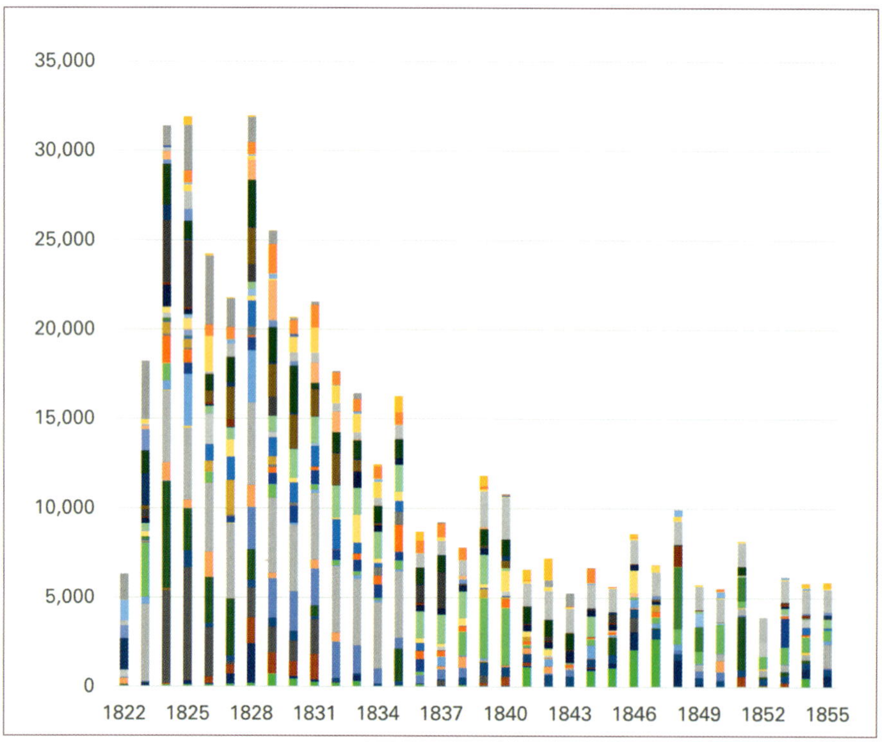

This graph shows the total amount presented by grand juries for the building and/or repairing of prisons in Ireland between 1822 and 1855, where such figures exist. The likely true figure is almost certainly greater, particularly for the 1830s where counties failed to report their expenditure. The figures are rather incomplete for 1849, which may be on account of the severity of the Famine at the time, and the general break-down in Irish administration. The colour coding in the bar chart gives some indication of the extent to which the total figure in each year depended upon both small and large presentments from individual grand juries. The largest total presentments were in

1828 (£31,949), the smallest for which a complete set of figures exist was 1852 (£3,923). The total amount presented for prisons in the period under study was forty per cent higher than the total amount presented for courthouses.

These two graphs attempt to present a summary of all courthouse- and prison-related presentments during the period under study. The first graph shows the total amounts spent in

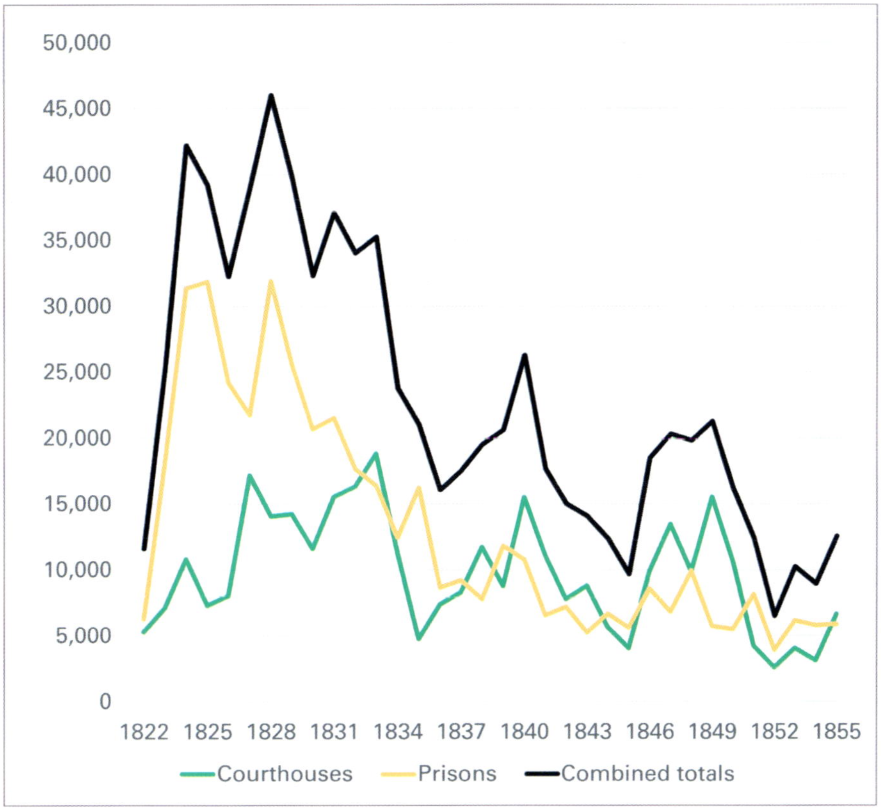

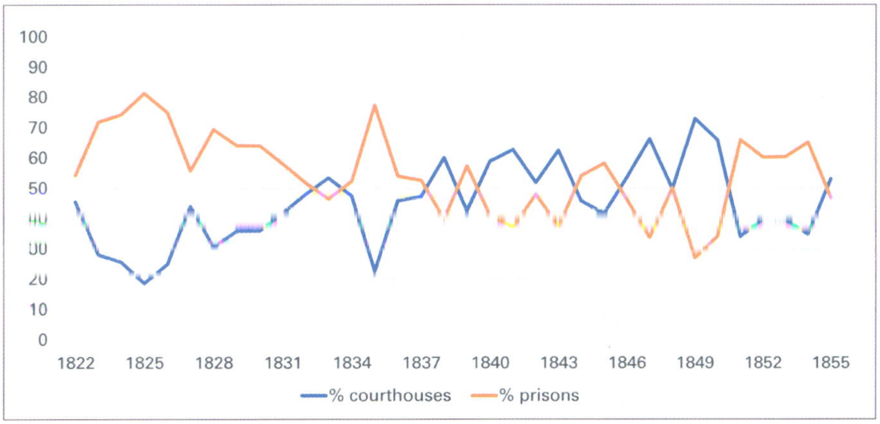

each of these fields of building, and the second shows the balance between the two. It must be remembered that the larger prisons, county gaols, built primarily in the 1820s and 1830s, were, by their nature, more complicated and expensive than even the most ornate of assize courthouses.

Notes

Annual returns to parliament of a summary of grand-jury presentments had been introduced as part of the Highways Act, 1809 (Ireland), 49 Geo. III, c. 84. However, in practice, this was widely ignored, and these returns were only gathered and published on a continuous basis from 1823 onwards, following the lengthy debate, controversy, and aftermath of the Grand Jury Presentments Act, 1817 (Ireland), 57 Geo. III, c. 107. A settlement was reached in the County Treasurers Act, 1823 (Ireland), 4 Geo. IV, c. 33, which set out a template for reporting these figures. However, even after this time some counties failed to report their presentments according to the law, some claimed the figures had been misplaced, and others reported them incorrectly. Like any other statistical source in early nineteenth-century government, there are many caveats that need to be attached to these figures. In some cases, for example, figures for the construction of new gaols were combined with the running costs of these institutions, and in these cases, and where other consistency issues appear, the relevant figures have been coloured in orange. In cases where no returns were submitted to parliament, the cells have been coloured in pink. All figures are rounded to the nearest pound.

In interpreting these figures, it must be remembered that repeated large presentments of the same amount were almost always related to the paying back of instalments of a government loan for building work. There was thus a time lag between when a county decided to build a new courthouse or gaol and when their peak expenditure on the project occurred. In some cases, counties were still paying back large sums a decade or more after the building had come into operation. Despite these caveats, the graphs show a general national trend that supports the arguments made throughout chapters 1 to 7, namely that the peaks in courthouse-related expenditure occurred following the boom in building assize courthouses in the 1820s, and the building of smaller courthouses in the 1840s. Similarly, prison-related expenditure correlates with the building boom in both county gaols and bridewells in the 1810s and 1820s, with relatively small amounts spent thereafter in the slow introduction of the 'separate system' of confinement.

These figures are compiled from the following House of Commons papers:

Abstracts of the Accounts of Presentments Made by the Grand Juries of Several Counties, Cities and Towns of Ireland, in the Year 1823, H.C. 1824 (258), xxii

Abstracts of the Accounts of Presentments Made by the Grand Juries of Several Counties, Cities and Towns of Ireland, in the Year 1824, H.C. 1825 (117), xxii

Abstracts of the Accounts of Presentments Made by the Grand Juries of Several Counties, Cities and Towns of Ireland, in the Year 1825, H.C. 1826 (290), xxiii

Abstracts of the Accounts of Presentments Made by the Grand Juries of Several Counties, Cities and Towns of Ireland, in the Year 1826, H.C. 1826–7 (200), xx

Abstracts of the Accounts of Presentments Made by the Grand Juries of Several Counties, Cities and Towns of Ireland, in the Year 1827, H.C. 1828 (118), xxii

Abstracts of the Accounts of Presentments Made by the Grand Juries of Several Counties, Cities and

Towns of Ireland, in the Year 1828*, H.C. 1829 (35), xxii

Abstracts of the Accounts of Presentments Made by the Grand Juries of Several Counties, Cities and Towns of Ireland, in the Year 1829, H.C. 1830 (196), xxvi

Abstracts of the Accounts of Presentments Made by the Grand Juries of Several Counties, Cities and Towns of Ireland, in the Year 1830, H.C. 1830–1 (293), xiv

Abstracts of the Accounts of Presentments Made by the Grand Juries of Several Counties, Cities and Towns of Ireland, in the Year 1831, H.C. 1831–2 (298), xlv

Abstracts of the Accounts of Presentments Made by the Grand Juries of Several Counties, Cities and Towns of Ireland, in the Year 1832, H.C. 1833 (19), xxxv

Abstracts of the Accounts of Presentments Made by the Grand Juries of Several Counties, Cities and Towns of Ireland, in the Year 1833, H.C. 1834 (174), xlviii

Abstracts of the Accounts of Presentments Made by the Grand Juries of Several Counties, Cities and Towns of Ireland, in the Year 1834, H.C. 1835 (220), xxxvii

Abstracts of the Accounts of Presentments Made by the Grand Juries of Several Counties, Cities and Towns of Ireland, in the Year 1835, H.C. 1836 (119), xlvii

Abstracts of the Accounts of Presentments Made by the Grand Juries of Several Counties, Cities and Towns of Ireland, in the Year 1836, H.C. 1837 (110), li

Abstracts of the Accounts of Presentments Made by the Grand Juries of Several Counties, Cities and Towns of Ireland, in the Year 1837, H.C. 1837–8 (207), xlvi

Abstracts of the Accounts of Presentments Made by the Grand Juries of Several Counties, Cities and Towns of Ireland, in the Year 1838, H.C. 1839 (104), xlvii

Abstracts of the Accounts of Presentments Made by the Grand Juries of Several Counties, Cities and Towns of Ireland, in the Year 1839, H.C. 1840 (41), xlviii

Abstracts of the Accounts of Presentments Made by the Grand Juries of Several Counties, Cities and Towns of Ireland, in the Year 1840, H.C. 1841 (143), xxvii

Abstracts of the Accounts of Presentments Made by the Grand Juries of Several Counties, Cities and Towns of Ireland, in the Year 1841, H.C. 1842 (90), xxxviii

Abstracts of the Accounts of Presentments Made by the Grand Juries of Several Counties, Cities and Towns of Ireland, in the Year 1842, H.C. 1843 (146), l

Abstracts of the Accounts of Presentments Made by the Grand Juries of Several Counties, Cities and Towns of Ireland, in the Year 1843, H.C. 1844 (194), xliii

Abstracts of the Accounts of Presentments Made by the Grand Juries of Several Counties, Cities and Towns of Ireland, in the Year 1844, H.C. 1845 (92), xlv

Abstracts of the Accounts of Presentments Made by the Grand Juries of Several Counties, Cities and Towns of Ireland, in the Year 1845, H.C. 1846 (45), xlii

Abstracts of the Accounts of Presentments Made by the Grand Juries of Several Counties, Cities and Towns of Ireland, in the Years 1846 and 1847, H.C. 1847–8 (150), lvii

Abstracts of the Accounts of Presentments Made by the Grand Juries of Several Counties, Cities and Towns of Ireland, in the Year 1848, H.C. 1849 (177), xlix

Abstracts of the Accounts of Presentments Made by the Grand Juries of Several Counties, Cities and Towns of Ireland, in the Year 1849, H.C. 1850 (164), li

Abstracts of the Accounts of Presentments Made by the Grand Juries of Several Counties, Cities and Towns of Ireland, in the Year 1850, H.C. 1852 (20), xlvii

Abstracts of the Accounts of Presentments Made by the Grand Juries of Several Counties, Cities and Towns of Ireland, in the Year 1851, H.C. 1852 (152), xlvii

Abstracts of the Accounts of Presentments Made by the Grand Juries of Several Counties, Cities and Towns of Ireland, in the Year 1852, H.C. 1852–3 (366), xciv

Abstracts of the Accounts of Presentments Made by the Grand Juries of Several Counties, Cities and Towns of Ireland, in the Year 1853, H.C. 1854 (207), lviii

Abstracts of the Accounts of Presentments Made by the Grand Juries of Several Counties, Cities and Towns of Ireland, in the Year 1854, H.C. 1854–5 (475), xlvii

Abstracts of the Accounts of Presentments Made by the Grand Juries of Several Counties, Cities and Towns of Ireland, in the Year 1855, H.C. 1856 (394), liii

Note: this series continues until at least 1872.

Appendix D

Central-Government Loans for the Building of Courthouses and Prisons, 1801–55

Part 1: Loans for building assize courthouses

Year	Loan issued to	Proposed object	Town	County	Amount	Notes
1801	John Ganden [sic]	Law Courts [The Four Courts]	Dublin	Dublin City	5,538	
1803	James Grandan [sic]	Law Offices, Dublin [The Four Courts]	Dublin	Dublin City	3,692	
1805	Board of Works	Law Offices, Dublin [The Four Courts]	Dublin	Dublin City	9,241	Made up of 11 separate loans between 1805 and 1809.
1818	Dublin County grand jury, H. and A. Baker	A new courthouse	Kilmainham	Dublin County	7,952	5% interest, with instalments of £431 twice every year. Paid off by 1847. Made up of 4 separate loans between 1818 and 1820.
1819	Dublin County grand jury	Land for a new court-house	Kilmainham	Dublin County	727	5% interest, with instalments of £50 twice every year. Paid off by 1847.
1822	Cavan grand jury	A new courthouse	Cavan	Cavan	5,538	5% interest, with instalments of £300 twice every year. Paid off by 1847. Made up of 2 separate loans in 1822 and 1823.
1822	Mayo grand jury	To improve a court-house	Castlebar	Mayo	2,222	5% interest, with instalments of £120 twice every year. £186 outstanding by 1847.
1823	Town of Galway grand jury	A new courthouse	Galway	Town of Galway	2,769	5% interest, with instalments of £150 per year. Paid off by 1847. Made up of 5 separate loans between 1823 and 1825. This loan is incorrectly shown in one parliamentary report as being issued to the Galway County grand jury.
1824	Roscommon grand jury	A new courthouse	Roscommon	Roscommon	5,310	5% interest, with instalments of £288 per year for 20 years. Paid off by 1847. Made up of 5 separate loans between 1824 and 1826.
1825	Westmeath grand jury	A new courthouse	Mullingar	Westmeath	5,309	5% interest, with instalments of £338 per year for 20 years. Paid off by 1847. Made up of 3 separate loans between 1825 and 1828. An earlier application for £6,428 for the same proposed work was rejected because the presentment was 'defective'.
1825	Town of Galway grand jury	A portico for a court-house	Galway	Town of Galway	554	5% interest, with instalments of £30 per year for 20 years. Paid off by 1847. This loan is incorrectly shown in one parliamentary report as being issued to the Galway County grand jury.

1830	Kerry grand jury	A new courthouse	Tralee	Kerry	9,350	5% interest. Paid off by 1847. Security offered was a mortgage of the county cess. An earlier application for £7,000 for the same proposed work was rejected because the security offered was 'insufficient'.
1832	Carlow grand jury	A new courthouse	Carlow	Carlow	5,000	5% interest. Paid off by 1847.
1833	King's County grand jury	A new courthouse	Tullamore	King's County	9,800	5% interest, later reduced to 4%. Paid off by 1847.
1839	Tipperary North grand jury	A new courthouse	Nenagh	Tipperary (N. Riding)	6,000	5% interest, repayable over 10 years. Still being repaid in 1847.
1845	Limerick City grand jury	A new courthouse	Limerick	Limerick City	1,250	5% interest, repayable over 10 years. No repayments whatsoever by 1847. £397 due by 1 January 1853.
1846	Waterford City grand jury	A new courthouse	Waterford	Waterford City	4,000	It is unclear when exactly this loan was issued, but an application was submitted in May 1846. The new courthouse was built between 1848 and 1850.
1846	Waterford County grand jury	A new courthouse	Waterford	Waterford County	4,000	It is unclear when exactly this loan was issued, but an application was submitted in May 1846. The new courthouse was built between 1848 and 1850.
1846	Louth grand jury	Alterations to the courthouse at Dundalk	Dundalk	Louth	1,200	
1849	Antrim grand jury	A new courthouse	Belfast	Antrim	6,786	Shown as £4,000 in the Board of Works annual report for 1850, but £6,786 in their 1853 report.

Part 2: Loans for building quarter-session and petty-session courthouses

Year	Loan issued to	Proposed object	Town	County	Amount	Notes
1818	The Earl of Clancarty	A new markethouse and store	Ballinasloe	Galway County	554	5% interest, with instalments of £30 every year. Paid off by 1832.
1819	Wexford grand jury and W. Harvey	A sessions house	Enniscorthy	Wexford	1,409	5% interest, with instalments of £354 twice every year. Paid off by 1847. Made up of 3 separate loans in 1819 and 1820.
1823	Mayo grand jury	To repair a courthouse	Ballinrobe	Mayo	478	5% interest, repayable over 20 years. Made up of 2 separate loans in 1823 and 1824. £54 outstanding by 1847.
1824	Kilkenny County grand jury	A new courthouse	Thomastown	Kilkenny County	692	This loan does not appear consistently in all the parliamentary reports.

Year	Borrower	Purpose	Town	County	Amount	Notes
1824	Cork County grand jury	Seven new courthouses and bridewells	Bantry, Clonakilty, Kanturk, Macroom, Midleton, Mallow, and Skibbereen	Cork County	8,723	5% interest, repayable over 20 years. Made up of 19 separate loans in 1824 and 1825. It is unclear what, if any proportion, of this amount was intended solely for the county's new quarter-session courthouses, and what was intended for the adjoining bridewells built at the same time. The total for the former appears to have been at least £8,000 (different calculating methods produce different results).
1824	Lord Kingston	New markethouses	Mitchelstown and Ballyporeen	Cork County	2,769	5% interest, repayable over 3 years. In arrears by 1828 but paid off by 1847.
1825	Waterford County grand jury	A new courthouse	Dungarvan	Waterford County	1,562	5% interest, with instalments of £85 twice every year for 20 years. Paid off by 1847. Made up of 3 separate loans between 1825 and 1827.
1825	Carlow grand jury	A new courthouse	Tullow	Carlow	702	5% interest, with instalments of £38 twice every year for 20 years. Paid off by 1847. Made up of 3 separate loans in 1825 and 1826.
1827	Roscommon grand jury	A new courthouse	Boyle	Roscommon	800	5% interest, with instalments of £40 twice every year for 20 years. Paid off by 1847. Made up of 2 separate loans in 1827 and 1828. Some parliamentary reports show the total amount issued as £1,400.
1827	Tyrone grand jury	A new courthouse	Dungannon	Tyrone	1,535	5% interest, with instalments of £102 twice every year for 10 years. Paid off by 1847. Made up of 2 separate loans between 1827 and 1829.
1828	Queen's County grand jury	New courthouses	Borris-in-Ossory and Stradbally	Queen's County	3,000	5% interest, with instalments of £150 twice every year. Paid off by 1847. Made up of 2 separate loans between 1828 and 1830.
1828	Roscommon grand jury	A new courthouse	Strokestown	Roscommon	800	5% interest, with instalments of £40 twice every year. Paid off by 1847. Made up of 2 separate loans in 1828 and 1829.
1828	Wexford grand jury	A new courthouse	New Ross	Wexford	534	This loan does not appear consistently in all the parliamentary reports.
1830	Kerry grand jury	A new courthouse	Killarney	Kerry	1,400	5% interest. Paid off by 1847. Security offered was a mortgage of the county cess.
1837	Antrim grand jury	A new courthouse	Ballymoney	Antrim	1,100	Paid off by 1847.
1839	Galway County grand jury	A new courthouse	Clifden	Galway County	1,888	5% interest, repayable over 15 years. Paid off by 1847.
1839	Kilkenny County grand jury	A new courthouse and bridewell	Callan	Kilkenny County	1,200	5% interest, repayable over 5 years. Paid off by 1847.
1839	Kilkenny County grand jury	A new courthouse and bridewell	Urlingford	Kilkenny County	1,200	5% interest, repayable over 5 years. Paid off by 1847.

1839	Galway County grand jury	A new courthouse	Oughterard	Galway County	1,000	5% interest, repayable over 10 years. Paid off by 1847.
1839	Kerry grand jury	A new courthouse	Listowel	Kerry	1,500	5% interest, repayable over 10 years. Still being repaid in 1847.
1841	Donegal grand jury	A new courthouse and bridewell	Buncrana	Donegal	950	5% interest, repayable over 5 years. Paid off by 1847.
1842	Donegal grand jury	A new courthouse and bridewell	Glenties	Donegal	750	5% interest, repayable over 10 years. Paid off (except for a very small amount) by 1847.
1842	Board of Public Works	A new courthouse	Newcastle West	Limerick County	991	Work undertaken by Board of Public Works, thereafter charged to the Limerick County grand jury. Made up of 3 separate loans between 1842 and 1848.
1842	Board of Public Works	A new courthouse	Bray	Wicklow	437	Work undertaken by Board of Public Works, thereafter charged to the Wicklow grand jury. Made up of (at least) 2 separate loans in 1842 and 1843.
1842	Board of Public Works	A new courthouse	Clones	Monaghan	150	Work undertaken by Board of Public Works, thereafter charged to the Monaghan grand jury. Made up of (at least) 2 separate loans in 1842 and 1843.
1843	Kerry grand jury	A new courthouse	Dingle	Kerry	742	5% interest, repayable over 5 years. Still being repaid in 1847.
1843	Mayo grand jury	A new courthouse and bridewell	Westport	Mayo	400	5% interest, with instalments of £20 twice every year. Still being repaid in 1847.
1844	Galway County grand jury	A new courthouse and bridewell	Portumna	Galway County	1,659	5% interest, repayable over 5 years. Still being repaid in 1847. £28 due by 1 January 1853.
1845	Roscommon grand jury	A new courthouse	Castlerea	Roscommon	1,284	5% interest, repayable over 5 years. Still being repaid in 1847.
1845	Antrim grand jury	A new courthouse	Ballymena	Antrim	3,000	5% interest, repayable over 10 years. Still being repaid in 1847.
1845	Mayo grand jury	A new courthouse and bridewell	Swinford	Mayo	100	Repayments of more than original amount (£160) by 1 January 1846, 'in anticipation of further loan'. The final amount issued is unclear.
1846	Board of Public Works and J. Rosborough	A new courthouse	Swords	Dublin County	446	Work undertaken by Board of Public Works, thereafter charged to the Dublin County grand jury. Made up of (at least) 3 separate loans between 1846 and 1849.
1848	Board of Public Works	A new courthouse	Balbriggan	Dublin County	608	Work undertaken by Board of Public Works, thereafter charged to the Dublin County grand jury. Made up of (at least) 2 separate loans in 1848 and 1849.
1848	Board of Public Works	A new courthouse	Youghal	Cork County	927	Work undertaken by Board of Public Works, thereafter charged to the Cork County grand jury. Made up of (at least) 2 separate loans in 1848 and 1849.

Part 3: Loans for building county gaols, penitentiaries, and prisons in Dublin

Year	Loan issued to	Proposed object	Town	County	Amount	Notes
1810	Board of Works	The Four Courts Marshalsea	Dublin	Dublin City	1,594	Additions.
1811	Board of Works	Four Courts Marshalsea and Newgate Gaol	Dublin	Dublin	297	Additions and alterations.
1811	Cavan grand jury	County gaol	Cavan	Cavan	10,154	A new gaol. Made up of 4 separate loans between 1811 and 1813.
1811	Board of Works	Richmond Penitentiary	Dublin	Dublin City	32,415	A new penitentiary. Made up of 11 separate loans between 1811 and 1818.
1812	Board of Works	The Four Courts Marshalsea	Dublin	Dublin City	729	Additions and alterations.
1812	Limerick City grand jury	City gaol	Limerick	Limerick City	5,272	A new gaol. Made up of 3 separate loans in 1812 and 1813.
1812	Waterford County grand jury	County gaol	Waterford	Waterford County	7,322	Additions. Made up of 3 separate loans in 1812 and 1813.
1812	Kerry grand jury	County gaol	Tralee	Kerry	9,230	A new gaol. Made up of 2 separate loans in 1812 and 1813.
1812	Board of Works	The Four Courts Marshalsea	Dublin	Dublin City	761	Alterations.
1813	Fermanagh grand jury and W. Hassard	County gaol	Enniskillen	Fermanagh	5,538	A new gaol. Made up of 2 separate loans in 1813.
1813	Dublin City grand jury and William Darley	Richmond bridewell	Dublin	Dublin City	15,460	A new gaol. Made up of 7 separate loans between 1813 and 1820. The final 3 loans in 1819 and 1820 were for a 'boundary wall, subdividing several apartments, providing a clock and other necessaries'.
1816	Board of Works	A 'depôt prison at Cork'	Cork	Cork City	5,470	Made up of 3 separate loans between 1816 and 1818. Unclear what exactly was the proposed work.
1817	Town of Drogheda grand jury and Henry Pentland	Town gaol	Drogheda	Town of Drogheda	8,933	Made up of 3 separate loans in 1817 and 1818.
1817	Limerick County grand jury	County gaol	Limerick	Limerick County	14,004	A new gaol. Made up of 3 separate loans in 1817 and 1818.
1817	Louth grand jury	County gaol	Dundalk	Louth	12,922	Additions. Made up of 3 separate loans between 1817 and 1819.
1817	Roscommon grand jury	County gaol	Roscommon	Roscommon	5,538	A new gaol. Made up of 2 separate loans in 1817 and 1819, the latter was for 'purchasing ground for the site of the new gaol'
1818	Sligo grand jury	County gaol	Sligo	Sligo	3,692	A new gaol.
1818	Dublin City grand jury	A gaol in Dublin city, likely the Richmond Bridewell	Dublin	Dublin City	4,572	Shown incorrectly as issued to the Dublin County grand jury.

1819	Dublin County grand jury	County gaol	Kilmainham	Dublin County	727	Repairs.
1819	Cork City grand jury	City gaol	Cork	Cork City	40,427	A new gaol. Made up of 14 separate loans between 1819 and 1825. The final 6 loans in 1824 and 1825 were for 'enlarging and additions' to the new gaol.
1819	Cavan grand jury	County gaol	Cavan	Cavan	569	Addition of an infirmary.
1819	Wicklow grand jury	County gaol	Wicklow	Wicklow	4,154	Additions and alterations. Made up of 3 separate loans between 1819 and 1821.
1820	Longford grand jury	County gaol	Longford	Longford	12,922	A new gaol. Made up of 3 separate loans between 1820 and 1822.
1820	Leitrim grand jury	County gaol	Carrick-on-Shannon	Leitrim	11,112	Large additions. Made up of 4 separate loans between 1820 and 1822.
1820	Londonderry grand jury	County gaol	Londonderry	Londonderry	29,537	Large additions. Made up of 5 separate loans between 1820 and 1823. Loans issued to build addition as well as purchase a site.
1820	Cork County grand jury	County gaol	Cork	Cork County	14,768	Addition of a House of Correction. Made up of 4 separate loans in 1820 and 1821.
1820	Waterford City grand jury	City House of Correction	Waterford	Waterford City	5,179	A new House of Correction. Made up of 3 separate loans between 1820 and 1822.
1822	Monaghan grand jury	County gaol	Monaghan	Monaghan	8,169	A new gaol. Made up of 4 separate loans between 1822 and 1824.
1822	Tyrone grand jury	County gaol	Omagh	Tyrone	7,564	Large additions. Made up of 3 separate loans between 1822 and 1825.
1822	Donegal grand jury	County gaol	Lifford	Donegal	5,538	Large additions. Made up of 2 separate loans in 1822 and 1823.
1823	Waterford County grand jury	County gaol	Waterford	Waterford County	2,122	The sum spent altering the county gaol was less than the amount shown as the loan was issued for building work to a 'part of [the] Dungarvan road, and [for] altering [the] gaol'.
1823	Cork City grand jury	A city bridewell	Cork	Cork City	1,107	A new city bridewell. Made up of 2 separate loans in 1823 and 1824.
1824	Westmeath grand jury	County gaol	Mullingar	Westmeath	10,087	Large additions. Made up of 3 separate loans between 1824 and 1826.
c. 1824	Galway County grand jury	County gaol	Galway	Galway County	532	Additions. The date of the loan is unclear.
1825	Kildare grand jury	County gaol	Athy	Kildare	3,658	A new gaol. Made up of 4 separate loans between 1825 and 1829.
1825	Down grand jury	County gaol	Downpatrick	Down	42,461	A new gaol. Made up of 4 separate loans between 1825 and 1828.

1826	Limerick City grand jury	City gaol	Limerick	Limerick City	3,252	For 'purchasing [the] old county gaol, and adding it to the present city gaol' and 'alterations and improvements in the cells'. Made up of 4 separate loans between 1826 and 1828.
1826	King's County grand jury	County gaol	Tullamore	King's County	15,721	A new gaol. Made up of 3 separate loans between 1826 and 1828.
1826	Queen's County grand jury	County gaol	Maryborough	Queen's County	20,769	A new gaol. Made up of 4 separate loans between 1826 and 1829.
1826	Cavan grand jury	County gaol	Cavan	Cavan	10,500	Alterations and additions. Made up of 4 separate loans between 1826 and 1829.
1826	Kildare grand jury	County gaol	Naas	Kildare	12,940	A new gaol. Made up of 7 separate loans between 1826 and 1831.
1826	Cork County grand jury	County gaol	Cork	Cork County	5,414	Addition of 'wards and day-rooms to [the] county gaol'. Made up of 3 separate loans between 1826 and 1828.
1827	Waterford County grand jury	County gaol	Waterford	Waterford County	1,150	Addition of a bridewell to the county gaol. Made up of 2 separate loans in 1827 and 1828.
1827	Tyrone grand jury	County gaol	Omagh	Tyrone	2,757	Alterations and additions. Made up of 4 separate loans between 1827 and 1831.
1828	Carlow grand jury	County gaol	Carlow	Carlow	4,500	For 'enlarging, repairing, altering [and] procuring ground'. Made up of 2 separate loans in 1828 and 1830.
1828	Meath grand jury	County gaol	Trim	Meath	22,200	A new gaol. Made up of 5 separate loans between 1828 and 1831.
1828	Kerry grand jury	County gaol	Tralee and other towns	Kerry	14,129	The sum spent altering the county gaol was less than the amount shown as the loan was issued for 'altering and enlarging' the county gaol as well as building work at the bridewells in Killarney, Milltown, Dingle, Tarbert, Listowel, Kenmare, Cahersiveen, and Castleisland.
1828	Sligo grand jury	County gaol	Sligo	Sligo	3,300	Additions and alterations. Made up of 3 separate loans in 1828 and 1829.
1830	Mayo grand jury	County gaol	Castlebar	Mayo	23,000	A new gaol. Made up of 5 separate loans between 1830 and 1835. £9,675 remained outstanding by 1 January 1846, with no further interest to be charged.
1831	Clare grand jury	County gaol	Ennis	Clare	2,125	Additions. Made up of 3 separate loans between 1831 and 1833.
1832	Galway County grand jury	County gaol	Galway	Galway County	4,200	Additions. Made up of 3 separate loans between 1832 and 1834.
1832	Tipperary grand jury	County gaol	Clonmel	Tipperary	12,875	Addition of a House of Correction. Made up of 3 separate loans between 1832 and 1835.
1833	Cavan grand jury	County gaol	Cavan	Cavan	200	Alterations and additions.

1833	Leitrim grand jury	County gaol	Carrick-on-Shannon	Leitrim	320	Alterations and additions.
1833	Monaghan grand jury	County gaol	Monaghan	Monaghan	125	Alterations and additions.
1836	Dublin City grand jury	Richmond bridewell	Dublin	Dublin City	14,000	Large additions and alterations. Made up of 2 separate loans in 1836 and 1837.
1837	Dublin City grand jury	A Dublin City prison, likely the Female Penitentiary at Grangegorman	Dublin	Dublin City	10,600	Likely to be large additions and alterations to the Richmond Penitentiary to bring it into use as the city's Female Penitentiary. Made up of 2 separate loans in 1837 and 1838.
1838	Dublin County grand jury	County gaol	Kilmainham	Dublin County	100	Payment of architect's fees.
1839	Galway County grand jury	County gaol	Galway	Galway County	305	Alterations and additions.
1842	Board of Works	Smithfield Penitentiary	Dublin	Dublin City	7,404	Large alterations and additions. Made up of 4 separate loans between 1842 and 1845.
1847	Board of Works	Mountjoy Male Convict Prison	Dublin	Dublin City	64,975	A new prison.
1855	Board of Works	Mountjoy Female Convict Prison	Dublin	Dublin City	37,900	A new prison.

Part 4: Loans for building bridewells outside of Dublin

Year	Loan issued to	Proposed object	Town	County	Amount	Notes
1805	Major General A. Campbell	A 'guardhouse and prison' in Belfast	Belfast	Antrim	255	For defraying 'the expense of fitting up a guardhouse and prison at Belfast in 1803'.
1812	Kilkenny County or City grand jury	A bridewell	Unknown	Kilkenny County or City	738	Location unclear.
1823	Wicklow grand jury	A bridewell	Baltinglass	Wicklow	622	For 'building improvements to the bridewell and barracks'. Made up of 3 separate loans in 1823 and 1824.
1823	Kilkenny County grand jury	A bridewell	Thomastown	Kilkenny	923	A new bridewell.
1824	Cork County grand jury	Seven new courthouses and bridewells	Bantry, Clonakilty, Kanturk, Macroom, Midleton, Mallow, and Skibbereen	Cork County	8,723	5% interest, repayable over 20 years. Made up of 19 separate loans in 1824 and 1825. It is unclear what, if any proportion, of this amount was intended solely for the county's new bridewells and what was intended for the adjoining courthouses built at the same time. See below for specific loans for bridewells.
1825	Cork County grand jury	A bridewell	Charleville	Cork County	92	
1825	Cork County grand jury	A bridewell	Dunmanway	Cork County	184	Made up of 2 separate loans between 1825 and 1827.

1825	Cork County grand jury	A bridewell	Bandon	Cork County	646	Made up of 3 separate loans between 1825 and 1827.
1825	Cork County grand jury	A bridewell	Bantry	Cork County	769	Made up of 3 separate loans between 1825 and 1827.
1825	Cork County grand jury	A bridewell	Mallow	Cork County	769	Made up of 3 separate loans between 1825 and 1827.
1825	Cork County grand jury	A bridewell	Kanturk	Cork County	769	Made up of 3 separate loans between 1825 and 1827.
1825	Cork County grand jury	A bridewell	Midleton	Cork County	769	Made up of 3 separate loans between 1825 and 1827.
1825	Cork County grand jury	A bridewell	Macroom	Cork County	769	Made up of 3 separate loans between 1825 and 1827.
1825	Cork County grand jury	A bridewell	Clonakilty	Cork County	769	Made up of 3 separate loans between 1825 and 1827.
1825	Cork County grand jury	A bridewell	Skibbereen	Cork County	769	Made up of 3 separate loans between 1825 and 1827.
1825	Waterford County grand jury	A bridewell	Dungarvan	Waterford County	622	Made up of 3 separate loans in 1825 and 1826.
1825	Clare grand jury	A district bridewell	Kilrush	Clare	647	Made up of 3 separate loans between 1825 and 1827.
1825	Clare grand jury	A bridewell	Ennistimon	Clare	461	For 'enlarging and extending' a bridewell. Made up of 2 separate loans in 1825 and 1826.
1825	Clare grand jury	A bridewell	Tulla	Clare	288	Made up of 2 separate loans in 1825 and 1827.
1826	Clare grand jury	A bridewell	Sixmilebridge	Clare	461	Made up of 2 separate loans in 1826 and 1827.
1826	Monaghan grand jury	A bridewell	Castleblayney	Monaghan	231	
1826	Roscommon grand jury	A bridewell	Boyle	Roscommon	1,127	Made up of 3 separate loans between 1826 and 1828.
1827	Roscommon grand jury	A bridewell	Castlerea	Roscommon	462	Made up of 2 separate loans in 1827 and 1828.
1827	Westmeath grand jury	A bridewell	Moate	Westmeath	1,157	Made up of 2 separate loans in 1827 and 1828.
1827	Tyrone grand jury	A bridewell	Dungannon	Tyrone	1,263	Made up of 3 separate loans in 1827 and 1829.
1827	Antrim grand jury	A bridewell	Ballymoney	Antrim	531	Made up of 2 separate loans in 1827 and 1831.
[illegible]	Wexford grand jury	A bridewell	New Ross	Wexford	800	
1828	Roscommon grand jury	A bridewell	Strokestown	Roscommon	450	Made up of 2 separate loans in 1828 and 1830.

1828	Cork County grand jury	Ten new courthouses and bridewells	Bantry, Clonakilty, Kanturk, Macroom, Midleton, Mallow, Skibbereen, Charleville, Bandon and Dunmanway	Cork County	1,000	For 'completing the bridewells and sessions houses lately built'.
1828	Kerry grand jury	Eight new bridewells	Killarney, Milltown, Dingle, Tarbert, Listowel, Kenmare, Cahersiveen and Castleisland	Kerry	14,129	The sum spent building bridewells throughout the county was less than the amount shown here as the loan was issued for 'altering and enlarging' the county gaol as well as the building of bridewells.
1828	Meath grand jury	A bridewell	Kells	Meath	1,089	Made up of 2 separate loans in 1828 and 1829.
1828	Meath grand jury	A bridewell	Navan	Meath	1,400	Made up of 2 separate loans in 1828 and 1829.
1829	Galway County grand jury	A bridewell	Tuam	Galway County	400	
1829	Galway County grand jury	A bridewell	Clifden	Galway County	280	
1829	Armagh grand jury	A bridewell	Lurgan	Armagh	533	Made up of 2 separate loans in 1829 and 1831.
1829	Galway County grand jury	A bridewell	Loughrea	Galway County	743	Made up of 2 separate loans in 1829 and 1831.
1831	Leitrim grand jury	A bridewell	Ballinamore	Leitrim	800	Made up of 2 separate loans in 1831 and 1832.
1831	Cavan grand jury	A bridewell	Ballyconnell	Cavan	550	Made up of 3 separate loans in 1831 and 1832.
1831	Galway County grand jury	A bridewell	Eyrecourt	Galway County	400	Made up of 2 separate loans in 1831.
1831	Antrim grand jury	A bridewell	Ballymena	Antrim	200	
1831	Cavan grand jury	A bridewell	Cootehill	Cavan	600	Made up of 3 separate loans in 1831 and 1832.
1831	Monaghan grand jury	A bridewell	Carrickmacross	Monaghan	300	Made up of 2 separate loans in 1831.
1831	Tyrone grand jury	A bridewell	Clogher	Tyrone	600	Made up of 2 separate loans in 1831 and 1832.
1832	Youghal Corporation	A bridewell	Youghal	Cork County	1,000	Loan application rejected for unknown reasons. A new bridewell was not built until around 1840.
1832	Cavan grand jury	A bridewell	Bailieborough	Cavan	600	Made up of 2 separate loans in 1832.
1836	Tipperary grand jury	A bridewell	Carrick-on-Suir	Tipperary	500	Made up of 2 separate loans in 1836 and 1837.

1839	Kilkenny County grand jury	A new bridewell and courthouse	Callan	Kilkenny County	1,200	5% interest, repayable over 5 years. Paid off by 1847
1839	Kilkenny County grand jury	A new bridewell and courthouse	Urlingford	Kilkenny County	1,200	5% interest, repayable over 5 years. Paid off by 1847.
1841	Donegal grand jury	A new bridewell and courthouse	Buncrana	Donegal	950	5% interest, repayable over 5 years. Paid off by 1847.
1842	Donegal grand jury	A new bridewell and courthouse	Glenties	Donegal	750	5% interest, repayable over 10 years. Paid off (except for a very small amount) by 1847.
1843	Mayo grand jury	A new bridewell and courthouse	Westport	Mayo	400	5% interest, with instalments of £20 twice every year. Still being repaid in 1847.
1844	Galway County grand jury	A new bridewell and courthouse	Portumna	Galway County	1,659	5% interest, repayable over 5 years. Still being repaid in 1847. £28 due by 1 January 1853.
1845	Mayo grand jury	A new bridewell and courthouse	Swinford	Mayo	100	Repayments of more than original amount (£160) by 1 January 1846, 'in anticipation of further loan'. The final amount issued is unclear.

Notes

In certain cases, there are overlaps between loans, such as when a grand jury proposed to build adjoining courthouses and bridewells at the same time. These figures appear in both relevant tables.

The above information is based on data from the following parliamentary papers:

Account of Payments … out of Votes of Credit for Ireland, 1805, H.C. 1810 (291), xii

Sixth Report of the Commissioners for Auditing Public Accounts in Ireland, 1816, H.C. 1818 (154), x

Seventh Report of the Commissioners for Auditing Public Accounts in Ireland, 1817, H.C. 1819 (422), xii

Eighth Report of the Commissioners for Auditing Public Accounts in Ireland, 1818, H.C. 1820 (107), viii

An Account of All Sums of Money … for Public Works … in Ireland, during the Last Four Years, H.C. 1828 (464), xxii

Accounts of All Sums Advanced … to Grand Juries in Ireland, during the Last Ten Years, H.C. 1829 (327), xxii

First Report of the Commissioners on Public Works, Ireland … for the Year 1832, H.C. 1833 (75), xvii

Second Report of the Commissioners on Public Works, Ireland … for the Year 1833, H.C. 1834 (240), xl

Third Report of the Commissioners on Public Works, Ireland … for the Year 1834, H.C. 1835 (76), xxxvi

Fourth Report of the Commissioners on Public Works, Ireland … for the Year 1835, H.C. 1836 (314), xxxvi

Fifth Report of the Commissioners on Public Works, Ireland … for the Year 1836, H.C. 1837 (483), xxxiii

Sixth Report of the Commissioners on Public Works, Ireland … for the Year 1837, H.C. 1837–8 (462), xxxv

Seventh Report of the Commissioners on Public Works, Ireland … for the Year 1838, H.C. 1839 (120), xx

Returns of All Sums of Money … in Aid of Public Works in Ireland, since the Union, H.C. 1839 (540), xliv

Eighth Report of the Commissioners on Public Works, Ireland … for the Year 1839, H.C. 1840 (327), xxviii

Ninth Report of the Commissioners on Public Works, Ireland … for the Year 1840, H.C. 1841 (252), xii

Tenth Report of the Commissioners on Public Works, Ireland … for the Year 1841, H.C. 1842 (384), xxiv

Eleventh Report of the Commissioners on Public Works, Ireland … for the Year 1842, H.C. 1843 (467), xxviii

Twelfth Report of the Commissioners on Public Works, Ireland … for the Year 1843, H.C. 1844 (555), xxx

Thirteenth Report of the Commissioners on Public Works, Ireland ... for the Year 1844, H.C. 1845 (640), xxvi
Correspondence Explanatory of the Measures Adopted ... for the Relief of Distress Arising from the Failure of the Potato Crop in Ireland, H.C. 1846 (735), xxxvii
Fourteenth Report of the Commissioners on Public Works, Ireland ... for the Year 1845, H.C. 1846 (762), xvii
An Account of Loans Advanced ... for Public Works ... since 1800, H.C. 1847 (718), liv
Fifteenth Report of the Commissioners on Public Works, Ireland ... for the Year 1846, H.C. 1847 (847), xvii
Sixteenth Report of the Commissioners on Public Works, Ireland ... for the Year 1847, H.C. 1848 (983), xxxvii
Seventeenth Report of the Commissioners on Public Works, Ireland ... for the Year 1848, H.C. 1849 (1098), xxiii
Eighteenth Report of the Commissioners on Public Works, Ireland ... for the Year 1849, H.C. 1850 (1235), xxv
Statement of All Issues of Public Money Made for ... Public Works in ... Mayo, H.C. 1850 (158), li
Nineteenth Report of the Commissioners on Public Works, Ireland ... for the Year 1850, H.C. 1851 (1414), xxv
Twentieth Report of the Commissioners on Public Works, Ireland ... for the Year 1851, H.C. 1852–3 (1569), xli
Twenty-first Report of the Commissioners on Public Works, Ireland ... for the Year 1852, H.C. 1852–3 (1651), xli

Bibliography

I SOURCES

(A) MANUSCRIPT MATERIAL

LONDON

British Library
Hardwicke papers: Add. MS 35920
Peel papers: Add. MSS 40223-265

Courtauld Institute of Art
Photograph of Carlow courthouse, n.d.

London Metropolitan Archives
Corporation of London Records: MS IS/E/5
Westminster new bridewell, Tothill Fields, London, ground-floor plan drawing: COLLAGE, the London Picture Archive, ref. 28610

National Portrait Gallery
Portrait of Sir Jeremiah Fitzpatrick (*c.* 1740–1810): D36947

Royal Institute of British Architects
Charles Robert Cockerell diary, 1823
John Orridge, *Description of the Gaol at Bury Saint Edmunds* (London: Rodwell & Martin, 1819)

Sir John Soane's Museum
John Soane papers, 1799: XV.A.2.5

University College London
Bentham papers: box 119a

DUBLIN

Dublin City Libraries
Photograph of Smithfield penitentiary, Dublin, 1968
Wide Streets Commissioners maps, WSC-067

Houses of the Oireachtas Library
Forster Archer, 'Report of the State of Gaols of Ireland for the Year 1802 by the Inspector General of Prisons': MS.7H28
Forster Archer, 'Report of the State of Gaols of Ireland for the Year 1811 by the Inspector General of Prisons': MS.4E63
Analysis of the Grand Jury Presentments for the City of Dublin, from the Year 1822 to 1834 Inclusive (Dublin: Graisberry, 1835)

Irish Architectural Archive (IAA)
Clonmel courthouse survey drawings (copies): Acc. 86/72.1.1
McCurdy and Mitchell collection: Acc. 82/49.71.1

Guinness collection: Acc. 96/68.5.1-5
ICEI collection: Acc. 2005/095
King's Inns Library collection: Acc. 2007/10.2.1-7
Lismore Castle collection: Acc. 97/107.3.1-4
Photographs collection
RIAI Murray collection: Acc. 92/46.4–62, 325-39, 401, 424–31, 1174–96
Tullynally Castle collection: copies of Maryborough gaol drawings, *c.* 1789
Westmeath (Mullingar) drawings: 088/063, C.15/403–8
William Deane collection: Acc. 2009/91
William Henry Hill drawings collection (copies), 1891: RP.C.107.5

King's Inns Archives
Four Courts papers, 1825–6: H/3-1

National Archives of Ireland (NAI)
Board of Works files, 1804–46
Brian Bolger papers: 1A/58/128, 2/476/15–17
Chief Secretary's Office Registered Papers (CSORP), 1818–49
Clare grand-jury presentment book, 1845: 1D/40/90
Department of Justice papers, 1939
Department of the Environment and Local Government papers, *c.* 1932–3, *c.* 1951–2, ENV/3, 2013/94/41, 469
Galway County grand-jury presentment books, 1805, 1807–8, 1811–14, 1818, 1823, 1826, 1829, 1839–40
Meath grand-jury presentment books, 1798–1809: 1C/33/71
Office of Public Works drawings collection, 5HC/4/400–23
Privy Council Office minute books, 1836–8: PCO MB 7–8
Privy Council Office proclamation book, 1838: PRO PB 1
Registry of Deeds, 1846
State Papers Office Papers, 1812–38

National Gallery of Ireland
James Malton, 'The Tholsel, Dublin' (1791)
Thomas Malton, view of Waterford courthouse (n.d.)
William Ashford, 'A View of Dublin from Chapelizod' (1795–8)

National Library of Ireland (NLI)
Ambrose Evans drawings for Kilkenny tholsel, 1758: microfilm, Pos. 5136
Clonmel courthouse plan sketch, n.d.: Portfolio 8
Drogheda Corporation minute books, 1765–6: microfilm, n. 4120
Dublin City grand-jury presentment books, 1793–1803: MS 16,223
Eblana Photographic Collection
Erasmus Smith school registry books, 1793–1822
Foster papers: MS 4128
Fred Amherst journal, 1825: MS 16,539
Galway county grand-jury payments book, 1794–6, 1799: MS 19,803
George Taylor map of Naas, 1805
Gun Cuninghame collection: AD 3568 (48)
Inchiquin letter, 1690: MS 45
John Longford maps, 1824–5: MS 21 F 35
John McCurdy drawings: AD 1702–5

John Rocque map of Kilkenny, 1758
Kilkenny Corporation minute books, 1758–9: microfilm, p. 5137
Kilmainham papers: MS 111
Lawrence Collection
Mason Collection
Morgan Aerial Photographic Collection
Pakenham-Mahon papers (Roscommon and Philipstown courthouses): MS 10,770
Pencil sketch of Blakes' Castle, Galway, n.d.: TX 1995
Plans of Irish gaols: AD 2641–67
Poole Collection
Queen's County grand-jury presentment book (abstracts), 1805: Ir. 94137.c.2
Thomas Dineley papers: MS 392
Thomas Phillips papers, 1685: MS 3137
Trim Corporation assembly minutes, 1760–1841: MS 2998
Sir Vere Hunt diary, 1813: microfilm, pp. 5527–8
Vesey-Fitzgerald papers: MS 7823
Waterford Corporation minute books, 1770–1801: microfilm, p. 5559
Waterford courthouse elevation drawing (copper plate): prints and drawings collection
Westmeath grand-jury presentment books (abstracts), 1826–8
Wicklow grand-jury presentment book, 1830
Wicklow gaol subscriptions, 1786: MS 15,303
William Beaufort map of Cork city, 1801

Royal Dublin Society

Minutes and proceedings of the Dublin Society, 1767–9: RDS/MAN

Royal Irish Academy

Day papers, MS 12w12

The Merrion Hotel

William Turner de Londe, 'The market square, Ennis' (1805), oil on canvas, 75.6 cm x 106 cm

South Dublin County Libraries

Photograph of the interior of Dublin Green street courthouse, 1903

Trinity College Library

Daniel Augustus Beaufort diary, 1806–8
Thomas Crofton Croker papers, 1833, MS 1206

BELFAST

Belfast City Council

Belfast Crumlin Road courthouse drawings, *c.* 1847–8, 1904

Northern Ireland Prison Service Agency

Belfast Crumlin Road gaol drawings, 1842–3
Survey drawing for Crumlin Road gaol by the Department of Works and Public Buildings, 1924

Public Record Office of Northern Ireland (PRONI)

Antrim grand-jury presentment books, 1711–1899: ANT/4
Antrim (Carrickfergus) gaol drawings, *c.* 1840–86: LA/1/8/JA/109–15
Antrim (Belfast) courthouse and gaol drawings and papers, 1847–73: LA/1/8/JA/107–19

Armagh courthouse drawings, 1805–7: T/1554
Armagh grand-jury presentment books, 1758–1899: ARM/4/1
Down grand-jury presentment books, 1778–1899: DOW/4/2
Downpatrick gaol drawings, *c.* 1820, 1854: D/2992
Downshire papers, 1795, 1824: D/607/C/145, and D/671/c/12
Fermanagh grand-jury presentment books, 1792–1898: FER/4
Fermanagh grand-jury (Enniskillen gaol) papers, 1841–6: FER/4/6/7–50
Institution of Civil Engineers papers, 1853–9: D/2992/B/3–4A
Londonderry grand-jury presentment books, 1788–1899: LOND/4/1
Londonderry courthouse papers, 1813: LA/5/8/JA/2
Massereene-Foster papers: D/207/23/98; D/562/4227, 12762–6, 13002; T/2519/4/13
Ordnance survey maps, 1832: OS/6/1/52/1–3
Pilson papers (copies), 1838: T/2986/2
Tyrone grand-jury presentment books, 1799–1897: TYR/4/1
Young and Mackenzie papers: D/2194

Ulster Architectural Heritage Society

Photographs of Oriel Temple, Collon, Co. Louth, *c.* 1950

Ulster Museum

Belfast Crumlin Road courthouse watercolour painting: 6/1956

ANN ARBOR, MICHIGAN

University of Michigan Bentley Historical Library

DuLong family collection:
Hoskyns letters, 1843
Palmer letters, 1842–7
Portrait of James Palmer, 1826 (copy)

ARMAGH, CO. ARMAGH

Armagh County Museum

Aerial photograph of Armagh Gaol, June 1975 (copy)
Armagh grand-jury presentment books, 1821–99
'City of Armagh', painting by James Black, 1810: ARMCM.156.1958
Map of Armagh City by James O'Hagan, 1851
Ordnance Survey map of Armagh, *c.* 1870: 5.2014.16
Photograph of Armagh by Abraham Talbot, *c.* 1861
Sean Barden and Sarah Millsopp (eds), *Mad or Bad: An exhibition about crime, gender and mental health in Victorian Ireland: Armagh County Museum, 5th October 2016 – 18th February 2017* (Armagh: Armagh County Museum, 2016)

BALLINAMORE, CO. LEITRIM

Leitrim County Library

Sean Hill, 'Historical Introduction to the Dock', n.d. (Carrick-on-Shannon courthouse)
Des Smith (ed.), *Shannonside: A parochial magazine* (1988)
Anon., 'A Sign-posted Walking Tour of Carrick-on-Shannon', n.d.

CAMBRIDGE

Cambridge University Library

Anon., ['E. S.'], *Account of How the Court House in Roscommon Fell Down* (Dublin:

C.C., 1718–19)
Clare grand-jury presentment books, 1799–1839
King's County grand-jury presentment books, 1820–[illegible]
Queen's County grand-jury presentment books, 1821

CAMBRIDGE, MASSACHUSETTS

Houghton Library, Harvard University
William Farrell album, MS Typ 788

CARLOW, CO. CARLOW

Carlow County Library
Carlow grand-jury presentment books, 1850, 1856–7, 1859–60, 1862, 1864–5
1868–95: GJ/2
Carlow grand-jury papers related to the construction of Carlow courthouse, 1828–32: GJ/9/7–9
Carlow courthouse papers and drawings, *c.* 1828–32: P2/0048–53

CASTLEBAR, CO. MAYO

Mayo County Library
Thomas J. Wynne photographs collection: photographs of Castlebar gaol, *c.* 1900
Ivor Hamrock, 'Notes on Castlebar gaol, 1830–1932' (unpublished manuscript, 2002)

CAVAN, CO. CAVAN

Cavan County Library
'Cavan Courthouse: Official opening' pamphlet (1989)
Cavan grand-jury presentment books, 1809–17, 1856–9: GJ/2 and GJ/9 (currently inaccessible awaiting conservation)

CHAMPAIGN, ILLINOIS

University of Illinois at Urbana-Champaign Rare Book and Manuscript Library
Meath grand-jury presentment book, summer 1806

CHIPPENHAM, WILTSHIRE

Wiltshire and Swindon Archives and History Centre (formerly Wiltshire County Records Office)
Architectural drawings for Fisherton Anger county gaol by Richard Ingleman, 1817, A1/509/2
Architectural drawings for Fisherton Anger county gaol by Thomas Hopper, 1817, A1/509/3
Architectural drawings for Devizes house of correction, 1808, A1/509/4

CLONES, CO. MONAGHAN

Monaghan County Library
Monaghan grand-jury presentment books, 1811–12, and 1859: 352.0417
Monaghan grand-jury presentment books, [illegible], and [illegible] B6129M

CLONMEL, CO. TIPPERARY

Tipperary County Museum
Photographs of Clonmel gaol (borstal) before demolition (copies), by Donal Wylde, *c.* 1970s
Department of Justice (Dublin), *The Borstal Institution at Clonmel: Notes by the visiting committee 1948* (Dublin: Stationery Office, 1948) (copy)

CORK

Cork City and County Archives

Charles Smith map of Cork, 1750
Cork County grand-jury presentment books, 1834–: GJ/CO/PR
Photograph of Cork county gaol, *c.* 1950
Sketches of Cork's old city courthouse, n.d.
Thomas Holt map of Cork, 1832
William Beauford map of Cork, 1801
County Surveyor's Office drawings collection, CCS02

Cork City Libraries

Hodges and Pike collection: photograph of Cork courthouse, *c.* 1900

Crawford Art Gallery

Paintings of Cork North Gate Bridge and Cork South Gate Bridge, by Nathaniel Grogan, 1796
Watercolours of Cork North Gate Bridge and Cork South Gate Bridge, by John Fitzgerald, based on Nathaniel Grogan's originals, mid-1800s

DAINGEAN, CO. OFFALY

Daingean Development Association

Photographs of Daingean courthouse, *c.* 1900

DUNDALK, CO. LOUTH

Louth County Archives / Old Dundalk Society

Dundalk courthouse drawings, by Owen Fahy, *c.* 1813
Louth grand-jury presentment books, 1713–1899 (incomplete): GJ/005

ENNIS, CO. CLARE

Clare County Archives

Clare grand-jury presentment books, 1784–1900 (with gaps): GJ/AP
'Grand Juries of the County of Clare from 1784 [to 1877]': GJ/CC
Ordnance Survey maps for Ennis, 1879

GALWAY

Galway County Council Archives

James Hardiman drawings collection: GS/01/2
Samuel Roberts (Galway town and county gaol) drawings: GS/11/2/1–9
Galway County Council minutes, 1916: GC/1/2
Correspondence relating to Galway gaol, 1940: 109/38/72
Drawings of Galway county courthouse, *c.* 1870s

Galway County Library

Donal Taheny photograph collection

NUI Galway

Galway Corporation minute books, book K

GLOUCESTER, GLOUCESTERSHIRE

Gloucestershire Archives

Northleach House of Correction drawings, 1840–8: D2593/2/38

KILKENNY, CO. KILKENNY

Kilkenny County Library

Kilkenny County and Kilkenny City grand jury presentment books, 1836–98: GJ/1–63A

LETTERKENNY, CO. DONEGAL

Donegal County Library

Donegal grand-jury presentment books, 1753–98 (incomplete) (copies)

Photographs of Lifford and of Lifford courthouse and gaol, *c.* 1900–7

LIFFORD, CO. DONEGAL

Donegal County Archives

Donegal grand-jury presentment books, 1753–1899 (incomplete): GJ/1

LIMERICK

Limerick City and County Archives

Ranks Community Collection (Joe Ranson photography collection), *c.* 1988–9: P/90/23

Limerick City grand-jury House of Commons sessional papers, 1821–2 (copies – see Parliamentary Papers below): P/37

Limerick City Library

Limerick County grand-jury presentment books, 1807–1900

LONGFORD, CO. LONGFORD

Longford County Library

Longford grand-jury presentment books, 1759–1907: LGJ/1/1–2

Longford grand-jury presentment books, 1817–99 (incomplete): LGJ/2/1–71

MAIDSTONE, KENT

Kent History and Library Centre

Sackville (Whitworth) papers, U269/022525

MONAGHAN, CO. MONAGHAN

Monaghan County Museum

Drawing of the old courthouse at Monaghan, 1831

Monaghan grand-jury presentment book, 1837

Anon., 'The New County Hospital, Monaghan', n.d.

Photograph of Monaghan gaol and hospital, *c.* 1938

MULLINGAR, CO. WESTMEATH

Westmeath County Library

Howard Bury papers, P1/28

Map of Mullingar gaol, *c.* 1910

Unexecuted drawings for a new gaol, and a new combined gaol and courthouse, for Mullingar, 1817, 1820 (photographic copies in the Irish Architectural Archive)

Westmeath grand jury presentment books, [illegible]: WMGJ/AP/[illegible]

Westmeath Photographic Collection: photographs of Mullingar gaol, [illegible]: M/[illegible]

NAAS, CO. KILDARE

Naas Local History Group

Photographs of the old and new gaols in Naas, n.d.

NAVAN, CO. MEATH

Meath County Archives

Meath grand-jury presentment books, 1803, 1847, 1867, 1882, 1884, 1887, 1889–91, 1893–8 (incomplete): GJ

Meath grand-jury presentment books, summer 1806 (photocopy, original at the University of Illinois at Urbana-Champaign): GJ

NEWBRIDGE, CO. KILDARE

Kildare County Library

Kildare grand-jury presentment books, 1809–93 (incomplete): GJ

NOTTINGHAM

University of Nottingham Library

Charles Brinsley Marlay papers, My 454/1–4, 463/1–3

OXFORD

Bodleian Library

Kilkenny County grand-jury presentment books, 1801–43

Kilkenny City grand-jury presentment books, 1803–98

PORTLAOISE, CO. LAOIS

Laois County Library

Queen's County grand-jury presentment books (copies), 1845–97 (incomplete): 352.1 LH

ROSCOMMON, CO. ROSCOMMON

Roscommon County Library

Photograph of Roscommon gaol, *c.* 1930 (copy)

SHANAGARRY, CO. CORK

The Allen family private collection

Drawings for Limerick city courthouse, 1834

SHEFFIELD

Sheffield City Archives

Wentworth Woodhouse Muniments collection: WWM/H/206

SLIGO, CO. SLIGO

Sligo County Library

Sligo grand-jury presentment books, 1809–96 (incomplete): LGOV 769–78

SWORDS, CO. DUBLIN

Fingal County Council Archives

Dublin County grand-jury minute books, 1818–99 (incomplete): GJ/1/1-2

Dublin County grand-jury presentment books, 1816–99 (incomplete): GJ/5/1-27

THURLES, CO. TIPPERARY

Tipperary Studies, Tipperary County Council Library Service

Ordnance Survey maps for Nenagh, 1879

Ordnance Survey maps for Clonmel, 1874

Photograph of main façade of Clonmel courthouse, 12 February 1966

Photographs of Nenagh and Nenagh courthouse, *c.* 1900

Postcards showing Nenagh courthouse and gaol, n.d.

Tipperary North Riding grand-jury presentment books, 1842–1910 (incomplete): TL/LG/28

Tipperary South Riding grand-jury presentment books, 1855–91 (incomplete): TL/LG/29

TULLAMORE, CO. OFFALY

Michael Byrne private collection

Drawing of Tullamore courthouse, *c.* 1835

Photographs of Tullamore courthouse, *c.* 1900

Offaly County Library

King's County grand-jury presentment books, 1830–68: GJ/1/1/1–10

King's County grand-jury presentment books, 1852–78: GJ/1/2/1–6

Plan drawing of Tullamore gaol by William Deane, 1843: P123

Photographs of Tullamore gaol, Co. Offaly, *c.* 1930s: P50/14, and acc. nos. 434–5

TRALEE, CO. KERRY

Kerry County Library

Charles Smith map of Tralee, 1756

Ballymullen estate map, 1877

Postcard photograph of old gaol, n.d.

Tralee County Council Offices

McCurdy and Mitchell drawing for Tralee gaol, *c.* 1873

TRIM, CO. MEATH

Noel French private collection

Photographs of Trim gaol, Co. Meath, 1959

WATERFORD and DUNGARVAN, CO. WATERFORD

Waterford City and County Archives (Dungarvan)

Waterford county grand-jury query books (1877–93), presentment books (1809–20, 1865–99), contract and account books (1808–1908): GJ/1–38

Photographs of Waterford gaol, 1943

Waterford Museum of Treasures (Waterford)

Bernard Scale and William Richards, 'A Plan of the City and Suburbs of Waterford' (1764) (copy)

Donnchadh Ó Ceallacháin, 'The Old Jail in Ballybricken', 2016

Exhibition on Waterford courthouse and jail, opened March 2016

Photographs of Waterford gaol, 1930s–50s

WEXFORD, CO. WEXFORD

Wexford County Archives

Drawings for alterations to Wexford courthouse, by James Barry Farrell, September 1860: P387

Drawing of ground plan of Wexford gaol, by James Barry Farrell, January 1866 (copy)

Wexford grand-jury presentment books, 1847–1900 (incomplete): GJ

WICKLOW, CO. WICKLOW

Wicklow County Archives

Wicklow grand-jury presentment books, 1818–99: GJ

(B) PRINTED MATERIAL

1 ACTS OF PARLIAMENT

3 & 4 Ph. and M., c. 2
10 & 11 Car. 1, c. 4
4 Anne, c. 6
29 Geo. II, c. 14
3 Geo. III, c. 5
3 Geo. III, c. 28
7 Geo. III, c. 4
13 & 14 Geo. III, c. 18
13 & 14 Geo. III, c. 32
16 Geo. III, c. 56
17 & 18 Geo. III, c. 1
17 & 18 Geo. III, c. 28
19 & 20 Geo. III, c. 7
21 & 22 Geo. III, c. 42
23 & 24 Geo. III, c. 26
23 & 24 Geo. III, c. 41
23 & 24 Geo. III, c. 42
23 & 24 Geo. III, c. 44
24 Geo. III, c. 54
26 Geo. III, c. 14
26 Geo. III, c. 27
26 Geo. III, c. 59
27 Geo. III, c. 21
27 Geo. III, c. 39
28 Geo. III, c. 38
28 Geo. III, c. 39
30 Geo. III, c. 41
32 Geo. III, c. 27
34 Geo. III, c. 6
35 Geo. III, c. 25
36 Geo. III, c. 55
39 Geo. III, c. 55

Galway County Gaol Act, 1802, 42 Geo. III, c. xviii
Cork City Gaol Act, 1806, 46 Geo. III, c. xxxviii
Galway County Gaol and Sessions House Act, 1807, 47 Geo. III, sess. 2, c. cxii
Disused Public Buildings (Ireland) Act, 1808, 48 Geo. III, c. 113
Highways (Ireland) Act, 1809, 49 Geo. III, c. 84
Prisons (Ireland) Act, 1810, 50 Geo. III, c. 103
Londonderry Court House Act, 1812, 52 Geo. III, c. clxxxii
Court House (Ireland) Act, 1813, 53 Geo. III, c. 131
Public Works Loan Act, 1817, 57 Geo. III, c. 34
Grand Jury Presentments (Ireland) Act, 1817, 57 Geo. III, c. 107
Grand Jury Presentments (Ireland) Act, 1818, 58 Geo. III, c. 2
Grand Jury Presentments (Ireland) Act, 1818, 58 Geo. III, c. 67
Public Works Loan (Ireland) Act, 1818, 58 Geo. III, c. 88
Prisons Act, 1819 (Ireland), 59 Geo. III, c. 100
House of Industry Dublin Act, 1820, 1 Geo. IV, c. 49
Public Works Loan (Ireland) Act, 1820, 1 Geo. IV, c. 81
Prisons Act, 1821 (Ireland), 1 & 2 Geo. IV, c. 57
Gaols Fees Abolition Act, 1821 (Ireland), 1 & 2 Geo. IV, c. 77
Dundalk Court House Act, 1821, 1 & 2 Geo. IV, c. cxxiv
Employment of the Poor (Ireland) Act, 1822, 3 Geo. IV, c. 34
Prisons Act, 1822 (Ireland), 3 Geo. IV, c. 64
Public Works Loans (Ireland) Act, 1822, 3 Geo. IV, c. 112
Support of Commercial Credit Act, 1823 (Ireland), 4 Geo. IV, c. 42
Salaries of County Officials (Ireland) Act, 1823, 4 Geo. IV, c. 43
Prisons Act, 1823, 4 Geo. IV, c. 64
Public Works Loans Act, 1825 (Ireland), 6 Geo. IV, c. 35
Prisons Act, 1826 (Ireland), 7 Geo. IV, c. 74
Public Works Act, 1831 (Ireland), 1 & 2 Will. IV, c. 33
Nisi Prius Court House Act, 1832 (Dublin), 2 Will. IV, c. 32
Norfolk Assizes Act, 1832, 2 Will. IV, c. 47
King's County Assizes Act, 1832 (Ireland), 2 Will. IV, c. 60

Assizes Act, 1833, 3 & 4 Will. IV, c. 71
Grand Jury Act, 1833 (Ireland), 3 & 4 Will. IV, c. 78
Assizes (Ireland) Act, 1835, 5 & 6 Will. IV, c. 26
Prisons Act, 1835, 5 & 6 Will. IV, c. 38
Richmond Penitentiary Act, 1836 (Ireland), 6 & 7 Will. IV, c. 51
Civil Bill Courts Act, 1836 (Ireland), 6 & 7 Will. IV, c. 75
Grand Jury Act, 1836 (Ireland), 6 & 7 Will. IV, c. 116
County Treasurers Act, 1837 (Ireland), 1 Vict., c. 54.
Criminal Lunatics Act, 1838 (Ireland), 1 & 2 Vict., c. 27
Poor Relief Act, 1838 (Ireland), 1 & 2 Vict., c. 56
County of Clare Treasurer Act, 1838 (Ireland), 1 & 2 Vict., c. 104
Public Works Act, 1839 (Ireland), 2 & 3 Vict., c. 50
Prisons Act, 1840 (Ireland), 3 & 4 Vict., c. 44
Newgate Gaol Dublin Act, 1840, 3 & 4 Vict., c. 53
Municipal Corporations Act, 1840 (Ireland), 3 & 4 Vict., c. 108
Court Houses Act, 1841 (Ireland), 4 & 5 Vict., c. 31
Newgate Gaol Dublin Act, 1842, 5 & 6 Vict., c. 6
Four Courts Marshalsea Act, 1842 (Ireland), 5 & 6 Vict., c. 95
Criminal Lunatic Act, 1845 (Ireland), 8 & 9 Vict., c. 107
Prisons Act, 1846 (Ireland), 9 & 10 Vict., c. 61
Land for Prisons Act, 1847 (Ireland), 10 & 11 Vict., c. 26
Newgate Gaol (Dublin) Act, 1849, 12 & 13 Vict., c. 55
Assizes Act, 1850 (Ireland), 13 & 14 Vict., c. 85
Convict Prisons Act, 1854 (Ireland), 17 & 18 Vict., c. 76
General Prisons Act, 1877 (Ireland), 40 & 41 Vict., c. 49

2 PARLIAMENTARY PROCEEDINGS

Journal of the Irish House of Commons
Journal of the House of Commons
Journal of the House of Lords
Hansard

3 PARLIAMENTARY PAPERS

Accounts of Presentments by Grand Juries in Ireland … in 1807, H.C. 1808 (205), xiii
Inspector General's Report of … the Prisons in Ireland for … 1807, H.C. 1808 (239), ix
Report from the Commissioners Appointed To Inquire into … the State Prisons and Other Gaols in Ireland, H.C. 1809 (265), vii
A Bill to Amend the Laws in Ireland Respecting … Grand Juries, H.C. 1810 (118), i
[illegible]
Report … on the State of the Gaols of the City of London, H.C. 1813–14 (157), iv
A Bill for the Better Regulation of the Prisons or Gaols within the Jurisdiction of the City of London, H.C. 1813–14 (263), ii
Return of Number of Persons Committed for Trial in Ireland, 1805–12, H.C. 1813–14 (264), xiii
Report … on the King's Bench, Fleet, and Marshalsea Prisons, H.C. 1814–15 (152), iv
Report … on Grand-Jury Presentments of Ireland, Minutes of Evidence, and Appendix, H.C. 1814–15 (283), vi

Report … on Provisions for Better Regulation of Madhouses in England, H.C. 1814–15 (295), iv

Report … on Grand-Jury Presentments of Ireland, H.C. 1816 (374), ix

Second Report … on Grand-Jury Presentments of Ireland, H.C. 1816 (435), ix

Sixth Report of the Commissioners for Auditing Public Accounts in Ireland, 1816, H.C. 1818 (154), x

Report … on the Prisons within the City of London and Borough of Southwark, H.C. 1818 (275), viii

Return of the Number of Indictments, &c. Entered for Trial … in the Several Counties of Ireland … from 1786–1819, H.C. 1818–19 (15), iii

Account of All Gaols … in the … United Kingdom, H.C. 1819 (137), xvii

Paper Relating to the Prisons in Dublin, H.C. 1819 (195), xii

Seventh Report of the Commissioners for Auditing Public Accounts in Ireland, 1817, H.C. 1819 (422), xii

Inspector General's Report of … the Prisons in Ireland for … 1818, H.C. 1819 (534), xii

Report from the Select Committee on the State of Gaols, H.C. 1819 (579), vii

Eighth Report of the Commissioners for Auditing Public Accounts in Ireland, 1818, H.C. 1820 (107), viii

Limerick City [Grand Jury]: Returns to orders of the … House of Commons, dated 8th February 1821, H.C. 1821 (175), xx

Accounts of All Sums Presented To Be Raised off the City of Dublin … from … 1807 … to 1821, H.C. 1821 (477), xx

A Bill to Amend an Act … Relating to Prisons in Ireland, H.C. 1821 (493), iii

Report from the Select Committee Appointed To Consider the Laws Relating to Prisons, H.C. 1822 (300), iv

Prisons of Ireland: Report of Inspectors General, 1823, H.C. 1823 (342), x

Abstracts of the Accounts of Presentments Made by the Grand Juries of Several Counties, Cities and Towns of Ireland, in the Year 1823, H.C. 1824 (258), xxii

Prisons of Ireland: Report of Inspectors General, 1824, H.C. 1824 (294), xxii

Abstracts of the Accounts of Presentments Made by the Grand Juries of Several Counties, Cities and Towns of Ireland, in the Year 1824, H.C. 1825 (117), xxii

Prisons of Ireland: Report of Inspectors General, 1825, H.C. 1825 (493), xxii

Fourth Report … on … the Prisons of Ireland, 1826, H.C. 1826 (173), xxiii

Abstracts of the Accounts of Presentments Made by the Grand Juries of Several Counties, Cities and Towns of Ireland, in the Year 1825, H.C. 1826 (290), xxiii

Report … on the State of Prisons in Scotland, H.C. 1826 (381), v

Abstracts of the Accounts of Presentments Made by the Grand Juries of Several Counties, Cities and Towns of Ireland, in the Year 1826, H.C. 1826–7 (200), xx

Fifth Report … on the … Prisons of Ireland, 1827, H.C. 1826–7 (471), xi

Sixth Report … on … the Prisons of Ireland, 1828, H.C. 1828 (68), xii

Abstracts of the Accounts of Presentments Made by the Grand Juries of Several Counties, Cities and Towns of Ireland, in the Year 1827, H.C. 1828 (118), xxii

An Account of All Sums of Money … for Public Works … in Ireland, during the Last Four Years, H.C. 1828 (464), xxii

Report … on Criminal Commitments and Convictions, H.C. 1828 (545), vi

Seventh Report … on the … Prisons of Ireland, 1829, H.C. 1829 (10), xiii

Abstracts of the Accounts of Presentments Made by the Grand Juries of Several Counties, Cities and Towns of Ireland, in the Year 1828, H.C. 1829 (35), xxii

Accounts of All Sums Advanced … to Grand Juries in Ireland, during the Last Ten Years, H.C. 1829 (327), xxii

Eighth Report … on … the Prisons of Ireland, 1830, H.C. 1830 (48), xxiv

Abstracts of the Accounts of Presentments Made by the Grand Juries of Several Counties, Cities and Towns of Ireland, in the Year 1829, H.C. 1830 (196), xxvi

Copy of Memorials to the Irish Government on the Subject of Advances for Building a Court House in the County of Kerry, H.C. 1830 (240), xxvi

Ninth Report … on … the Prisons of Ireland, 1831, H.C. 1830–1 (172), iv
Abstracts of the Accounts of Presentments Made by the Grand Juries of Several Counties, Cities and Towns of Ireland, in the Year 1830, H.C. 1830–1 (293), xiv
Tenth Report … on … the Prisons of Ireland, 1832, H.C. 1831–2 (152), xxiii
Abstracts of the Accounts of Presentments Made by the Grand Juries of Several Counties, Cities and Towns of Ireland, in the Year 1831, H.C. 1831–2 (298), xlv
Report … on Secondary Punishments, H.C. 1831–2 (547), vii
Abstracts of the Accounts of Presentments Made by the Grand Juries of Several Counties, Cities and Towns of Ireland, in the Year 1832, H.C. 1833 (19), xxxv
Eleventh Report … on … the Prisons of Ireland, 1833, H.C. 1833 (67), xvii
First Report of the Commissioners on Public Works, Ireland, H.C. 1833 (75), xvii
Twelfth Report … on … the Prisons of Ireland, 1834, H.C. 1834 (63), xl
Abstracts of the Accounts of Presentments Made by the Grand Juries of Several Counties, Cities and Towns of Ireland, in the Year 1833, H.C. 1834 (174), xlviii
Second Report of the Commissioners on Public Works, Ireland, H.C. 1834 (240), xxxx
Third Report of the Commissioners on Public Works, Ireland … for the Year 1834, H.C. 1835 (76), xxxvi
Thirteenth Report … on … the Prisons of Ireland, 1835, H.C. 1835 (114), xxxvi
Abstracts of the Accounts of Presentments Made by the Grand Juries of Several Counties, Cities and Towns of Ireland, in the Year 1834, H.C. 1835 (220), xxxvii
Second Report from the Select Committee of the House of Lords Appointed To Inquire into the Present State of the Several Gaols and Houses of Correction in England and Wales, H.C. 1835 (439), xi
First Report of Commissioners for Inquiring into the Condition of the Poorer Classes in Ireland, H.C. 1836 (35), xxxi
Return from Clerks … of the Several Counties … in Ireland of Number of Persons Committed to the Different Gaols thereof for Trial in the Year 1835, H.C. 1836 (97), xlii
Fourteenth Report … on … the Prisons of Ireland, 1836, H.C. 1836 (118), xxxv
Abstracts of the Accounts of Presentments Made by the Grand Juries of Several Counties, Cities and Towns of Ireland, in the Year 1835, H.C. 1836 (119), xlvii
Fourth Report of the Commissioners of Public Works, Ireland, H.C. 1836 (314), xxxvi
Abstracts of the Accounts of Presentments Made by the Grand Juries of Several Counties, Cities and Towns of Ireland, in the Year 1836, H.C. 1837 (110), li
Fifteenth Report … on … the Prisons of Ireland, 1837, H.C. 1837 (123), xxxi
Return from Clerks … of the Several Counties … in Ireland of Number of Persons Committed to the Different Gaols thereof for Trial in the Year 1836, H.C. 1837 (158), xlv
Fifth Report of the Commissioners on Public Works, Ireland … for the Year 1836, H.C. 1837 (483), xxxiii
Sixteenth Report … on … the Prisons of Ireland, 1838, H.C. 1837–8 (186), xxix
Abstracts of the Accounts of Presentments Made by the Grand Juries of Several Counties, Cities and Towns of Ireland, in the Year 1837, H.C. 1837–8 (207), xlvi
Sixth Report of the Commissioners on Public Works, Ireland … for the Year 1837, H.C. 1837–8 (462), xxxv
Seventeenth Report … on … the Prisons of Ireland, 1839, H.C. 1839 (91), xx
Seventh Report of the Commissioners on Public Works, Ireland … for the Year 1838, H.C. 1839 (129), xx
Abstracts of the Accounts of Presentments Made by the Grand Juries of Several Counties, Cities and Towns of Ireland, in the Year 1838, H.C. 1839 (194), xlvii
Return of all Sums of Money … in Aid of Public Works in Ireland, since the Union, H.C. 1839 (540), xliv
Abstracts of the Accounts of Presentments Made by the Grand Juries of Several Counties, Cities and Towns of Ireland, in the Year 1839, H.C. 1840 (41), xlviii
Eighteenth Report … on … the Prisons of Ireland, 1840, H.C. 1840 (240), xxvi
Sixth Annual Report of the Poor Law Commissioners, H.C. 1840 (253), xvii
Eighth Report of the Commissioners on Public Works, Ireland … for the Year 1839, H.C. 1840 (327), xxviii

Abstracts of the Accounts of Presentments Made by the Grand Juries of Several Counties, Cities and Towns of Ireland, in the Year 1840, H.C. 1841 (143), xxvii
Ninth Report of the Commissioners on Public Works, Ireland … for the Year 1840, H.C. 1841 (252), xii
Nineteenth Report … on … the Prisons of Ireland, 1841, H.C. 1841 (299), xi
Abstracts of the Accounts of Presentments Made by the Grand Juries of Several Counties, Cities and Towns of Ireland, in the Year 1841, H.C. 1842 (90), xxxviii
A Return of the Sums Paid to Jacob Owen … for … Each Year since His Appointment, up to April 1842, H.C. 1842 (323), xxxviii
Twentieth Report … on … the Prisons of Ireland, 1842, H.C. 1842 (377), xxii
Tenth Report of the Commissioners on Public Works, Ireland … for the Year 1841, H.C. 1842 (384), xxiv.
Report of the Commissioners Appointed To Revise the Several Laws under … which Moneys Are now Raised by Grand-Jury Presentment in Ireland, H.C. 1842 (386), xxiv
Abstracts of the Accounts of Presentments Made by the Grand Juries of Several Counties, Cities and Towns of Ireland, in the Year 1842, H.C. 1843 (146), l
Twenty-first Report … on … the Prisons of Ireland, 1843, H.C. 1843 (462), xxvii
Eleventh Report of the Commissioners on Public Works, Ireland … for the Year 1842, H.C. 1843 (467), xxviii
Report of the Commissioners Appointed To Take the Census of Ireland for the Year 1841, H.C. 1843 (504), xxiv
Returns of Reports … on Complaints Forwarded to the Irish Government … and of Evidence Relative to the Mode of Conducting the Convict Service in Ireland, H.C. 1843 (547), xlii
Abstracts of the Accounts of Presentments Made by the Grand Juries of Several Counties, Cities and Towns of Ireland, in the Year 1843, H.C. 1844 (194), xliii
Twenty-second Report … on … the Prisons of Ireland, 1844, H.C. 1844 (535), xxviii
Twelfth Report of the Commissioners on Public Works, Ireland … for the Year 1843, H.C. 1844 (555), xxx
Report of the Surveyor-general of Prisons on the Construction, Ventilation and Details of Pentonville Prison, 1844, H.C. 1844 (594), xxviii
Abstracts of the Accounts of Presentments Made by the Grand Juries of Several Counties, Cities and Towns of Ireland, in the Year 1844, H.C. 1845 (92), xlv
Twenty-third Report … on … the Prisons of Ireland, 1844, H.C. 1845 (620), xxv
Thirteenth Report of the Commissioners on Public Works, Ireland … for the Year 1844, H.C. 1845 (640), xxvi
Abstracts of the Accounts of Presentments Made by the Grand Juries of Several Counties, Cities and Towns of Ireland, in the Year 1845, H.C. 1846 (45), xlii
Tables Showing the Number of Criminal Offenders Committed for Trial … in Ireland … in the Year 1845, H.C. 1846 (696), xxv
Twenty-fourth Report … on … the Prisons of Ireland, 1846, H.C. 1846 (697), xx
Correspondence Explanatory of the Measures Adopted … for the Relief of Distress Arising from the Failure of the Potato Crop in Ireland, H.C. 1846 (735), xxxvii
Fourteenth Report of the Commissioners on Public Works, Ireland … for the Year 1845, H.C. 1846 (762), xvii
Tables Showing the Number of Criminal Offenders Committed for Trial … in Ireland … in the Year 1846, H.C. 1847 (94), lvi
An Account of Loans Advanced … for Public Works … since 1800, H.C. 1847 (718), liv
Twenty-fifth Report … on … the Prisons of Ireland, 1847, H.C. 1847 (805), xxix
Fifteenth Report of the Commissioners on Public Works, Ireland … for the Year 1846, H.C. 1847 (847), xvii
Tables Showing the Number of Criminal Offenders Committed For Trial … in Ireland … in the Year 1847, H.C. 1847–8 (146), lvii
Abstracts of the Accounts of Presentments Made by the Grand Juries of Several Counties, Cities and Towns of Ireland, in the Years 1846 and 1847, H.C. 1847–8 (150), lvii
Twenty-sixth Report … on … the Prisons of Ireland, 1847–48, H.C. 1847–8 (952), xxiv

Sixteenth Report of the Commissioners on Public Works, Ireland … for the Year 1847, H.C. 1848 (983), xxxvii

Tables Showing the Number of Criminal Offenders Committed for Trial … in Ireland … in the Year 1848, H.C. 1849 (72), xliv

Abstracts of the Accounts of Presentments Made by the Grand Juries of Several Counties, Cities and Towns of Ireland, in the Year 1848, H.C. 1849 (177), xlix

Twenty-seventh Report … on … the Prisons of Ireland, 1849, H.C. 1849 (1069), xxvi

Seventeenth Report of the Commissioners on Public Works, Ireland … for the Year 1848, H.C. 1849 (1098), xxiii

Statement of All Issues of Public Money Made for … Public Works in … Mayo, H.C. 1850 (158), li

Abstracts of the Accounts of Presentments Made by the Grand Juries of Several Counties, Cities and Towns of Ireland, in the Year 1849, H.C. 1850 (164), li

Tables Showing the Number of Criminal Offenders Committed for Trial … in Ireland … in the Year 1849, H.C. 1850 (190), li

Twenty-eighth Report … on … the Prisons of Ireland, 1850, H.C. 1850 (1229), xxix

Eighteenth Report of the Commissioners on Public Works, Ireland … for the Year 1849, H.C. 1850 (1235), xxv

Twenty-ninth Report … on … the Prisons of Ireland, 1851, H.C. 1851 (1364), xxviii

Nineteenth Report of the Commissioners on Public Works, Ireland … for the Year 1850, H.C. 1851 (1414), xxv

Abstracts of the Accounts of Presentments Made by the Grand Juries of Several Counties, Cities and Towns of Ireland, in the Year 1850, H.C. 1852 (20), xlvii

Abstracts of the Accounts of Presentments Made by the Grand Juries of Several Counties, Cities and Towns of Ireland, in the Year 1851, H.C. 1852 (152), xlvii

Tables Showing the Number of Criminal Offenders Committed for Trial … in Ireland … in the Years 1850 and 1851, H.C. 1852 (192), xlvii

Thirtieth Report … on … the Prisons of Ireland, 1852, H.C. 1852 (1531), xxv

Tables Showing the Number of Criminal Offenders Committed for Trial … in Ireland … in the Year 1852, H.C. 1852–3 (340), lxxxi

Abstracts of the Accounts of Presentments Made by the Grand Juries of Several Counties, Cities and Towns of Ireland, in the Year 1852, H.C. 1852–3 (366), xciv

Twentieth Report of the Commissioners on Public Works, Ireland … for the Year 1851, H.C. 1852–3 (1569), xli

Twenty-first Report of the Commissioners on Public Works, Ireland … for the Year 1852, H.C. 1852–3 (1651), xli

Thirty-first Report … on … the Prisons of Ireland, 1853, H.C. 1853 (1657), liii

Tables Showing the Number of Criminal Offenders Committed for Trial … in Ireland … in the Year 1853, H.C. 1854 (138), lviii

Abstracts of the Accounts of Presentments Made by the Grand Juries of Several Counties, Cities and Towns of Ireland, in the Year 1853, H.C. 1854 (207), lviii

Thirty-second Report … on … the Prisons of Ireland, 1854, H.C. 1854 (1803), xxxii

Twenty-second Report of the Commissioners on Public Works, Ireland … for the Year 1853, H.C. 1854 (1820), xx

Abstracts of the Accounts of Presentments Made by the Grand Juries of Several Counties, Cities and Towns of Ireland, in the Year 1854, H.C. 1854–5 (475), xlvii

Twenty-third Report of the Commissioners on Public Works, Ireland … for the Year 1854, H.C. 1854–5 (1929), xvi

Tables Showing the Number of Persons Committed … for Trial at the Assizes and Quarter Sessions in each County in the Year 1854 … in Ireland, H.C. 1854–5 (1930), xliii

Thirty-third Report … on … the Prisons of Ireland, 1855, H.C. 1854–5 (1956), xxvi
Abstracts of the Accounts of Presentments Made by the Grand Juries of Several Counties, Cities and Towns of Ireland, in the Year 1855, H.C. 1856 (394), liii
Thirty-fourth Report … on … the Prisons of Ireland, 1856, H.C. 1856 (2113), xxxiv
Twenty-fourth Report of the Commissioners on Public Works, Ireland … for the Year 1855, H.C. 1856 (2140), xvi
Tables Showing the Number of Persons Committed … for Trial at the Assizes and Quarter Sessions in each County in the Year 1855 … in Ireland, H.C. 1856 (2116), xlix
Twenty-fifth Report of the Commissioners on Public Works, Ireland … for the Year 1856, H.C. 1857 (2228), xvii
Thirty-fifth Report … on … the Prisons of Ireland, 1857, H.C. 1857 (2236), xvii
Thirty-sixth Report … on … the Prisons of Ireland, 1858, H.C. 1857–8 (2394), xxx
Twenty-sixth Report of the Commissioners on Public Works, Ireland … for the Year 1857, H.C. 1857–8 (2412), xxvi
Twenty-seventh Report of the Commissioners on Public Works, Ireland … for the Year 1858, H.C. 1859 (2545), xiv
Thirty-seventh Report … on … the Prisons of Ireland, 1859, H.C. 1859 (2557), xiii
Thirty-eighth Report … on … the Prisons of Ireland, 1860, H.C. 1860 (2691), xxxvi
Thirty-ninth Report … on … the Prisons of Ireland, 1861, H.C. 1861 (2861), xxix
Fortieth Report … on … the Prisons of Ireland, 1862, H.C. 1862 (3020), xxvi
Forty-first Report … on … the Prisons of Ireland, 1863, H.C. 1863 (3214), xxiii
Forty-second Report … on … the Prisons of Ireland, 1864, H.C. 1864 (3377), xxvii
Forty-third Report … on … the Prisons of Ireland, 1865, H.C. 1865 (3522), xxiv
Forty-fourth Report … on … the Prisons of Ireland, 1866, H.C. 1866 (3690), xxxiv
Forty-fifth Report … on … the Prisons of Ireland, 1867, H.C. 1867 (3915), xxxv
Forty-eighth Report … on … the Prisons of Ireland, 1869, H.C. 1870 (C. 173), xxxvii
Forty-ninth Report … on … the Prisons of Ireland, 1870, H.C. 1871 (C. 359), xxx

4 NEWSPAPERS AND OTHER PERIODICALS

Gentleman's Magazine, 1735
Pue's Occurrences (Dublin), 1741
Belfast Newsletter, 1746–1936
Sleator's Public Gazeteer, 1759
Freeman's Journal, 1771–1866
Londonderry Journal, 1772
Hibernian Magazine, 1773–9
Faulkner's Dublin Journal, 1773–1817
Walker's Hibernian Magazine, 1777–1807
Clare Journal, 1778–1882
Belfast Mercury, 1786
Dublin Journal, 1786–7
Dublin Evening Post, 1786–1850
Finn's Leinster Journal, 1787–1828
Kilkenny Moderator, 1801–62
Hibernian Journal, 1807
Leinster Journal, 1809
The Hibernia Magazine, 1810
The Examiner, 1810
Limerick General Advertiser, 1811
Limerick Evening Post, 1812–17
Limerick Gazette, 1816–17
Saunders' Newsletter, 1817–57
The Inquirer, 1822
Limerick Chronicle, 1822–52
Galway Advertiser, 1823
Westmeath Journal, 1823–32
Connaught Journal, 1823–45
The Kilkenny Independent, 1827
Morning Register (Dublin), 1827
Southern Reporter, 1827–46
Limerick Evening Post & Clare Sentinel, 1828
Newry Telegraph, 1828
Clonmel Herald, 1828–36
Clonmel Advertiser, 1828–38
Galway Patriot, 1829

Louth Free Press, 1829
Waterford News, 1829
Tralee Mercury, 1830–4
Mayo Constitution, 1830–5
Cork Constitution, 1830–9
Western Herald, 1830–3
Limerick Evening Herald, 1833
Irish Penny Magazine, 1833–4
Waterford Mail, 1834
Connaught Telegraph, 1834–1933
Tipperary Free Press, 1835
Waterford Mirror, 1835
Waterford Chronicle, 1835–8
Dublin Penny Journal, 1836
Tipperary Constitution, 1836
Westmeath Guardian & Longford Newsletter, 1836
Roscommon and Leitrim Gazette, 1837–45
Nenagh Guardian, 1838–43
Longford Journal, 1840
Civil Engineer and Architect's Journal, 1840–56
Wexford Independent, 1841
Kilkenny Journal, 1842–54
Limerick Reporter, 1842–4
Dublin Evening Mail, 1843
Irish Examiner, 1843–1943
Illustrated London News, 1844
Tralee Chronicle, 1845
Armagh Guardian, 1845–66
Tyrone Constitution, 1847
The Nation, 1850
The Builder, 1850–1911
The Kerry Magazine, 1856
Leinster Express, 1859
Dublin Builder, 1859–66
General Advertiser, 1860–4
The Irish Times, 1863–1937
Harper's Weekly (New York), 1866
The Irish Builder, 1867–1955
Clare Almanac, 1878
Londonderry Sentinel, 1887–99
The Nationalist and Leinster Times, 1888
The Architect, 1888–95
Down Recorder, 1891–1933
Irish Architect and Craftsman, 1911
Irish Monthly, 1912
Roscommon Messenger, 1919
Midland Tribune, 1922
Northern Whig and Belfast Post, 1928
Saturday Record (Ennis), 1929
Architect & Building News, 1930
Western People, 1932
Offaly Independent, 1937
Connacht Tribune, 1939–41
Irish Independent, 1943
Kilkenny People, 1949
The Leinster Leader, 1951–85
Meath Chronicle, 1953
Clare Champion, 1960
Belfast Telegraph, 1989
City Tribune (Galway), 1996
The Sunday Times, 2009

II PRINTED and LATER WORKS

Dictionary of Irish Architects (www.dia.ie)
National Inventory of Architectural Heritage (NIAH) (www.buildingsofireland.ie)
Northern Ireland Environmental Agency (NIEA), Listed Buildings Database (www.doeni.gov.uk)
Ahern, Michael, *Clonmel County Gaol* (Clonmel: Ardo, 2010)
Anon., *Address by the Committee of Directors of the Society for the Improvement of Prison Discipline in Scotland* (Edinburgh: Neill, 1835)
Anon., 'Ancient and Present State of Athy', *Anthologica Hibernica*, May 1793, pp. 325–8
Anon., 'A Letter from Francis Johnston', *Quarterly Bulletin of the Irish Georgian Society*, vol. 6, no. 1, 1963, pp. 1–5
Anon., *An Account of the Origin and Object of the Society for the Diffusion of Knowledge upon the Punishment of Death and the Improvement of Prison Discipline* (London: Taylor, 1812)
Anon. [Philip Luckombe], *The Compleat Irish Traveler* (London, 1788)
Anon. ['CARA'], *Ballybricken & Thereabouts* (Waterford: Waterford Graphics, 1991)
Anon., *First Report of the Association for Bettering the Condition of the Prisoners in the County Gaol of Wicklow* (Dublin: Goodwin, 1820)

Anon., 'From Jail to Cathedral', *The Mantle* (Galway), vol. 1, 1958, pp. 30–2
Anon., *Journal of a Tour in Ireland … Performed in August 1804* (London: Phillips, 1806)
Anon., *Journal of a Tour through Several of the Southern Counties of Ireland during the Autumn of 1809* (London: McDowall, 1810)
Anon. [J. K.], *Letters to the North, from a Traveller in the South, Republished from the Ulster Times* (Belfast: Hodgson, 1837)
Anon., *Notes of a Journey in the North of Ireland in the Summer of 1827* (London: Baldwin, Cradock & Joy, 1828)
Anon., 'Notes on Naas Gaol', *Journal of the County Kildare Archaeological Society*, vol. 14, no. 3, 1968, pp. 333–5
Anon., *Observations on the Expediency of Erecting Provincial Penitentiaries in Ireland which May Receive All Criminals who Are Sentenced To Confinement and Hard Labour or Are under the Rule of Transportation* (London: Belch, 1821)
Anon., 'Site for [City] Gaol', *Journal of the Cork Historical and Archaeological Society*, vol. 35, no. 141 January–June 1940, p. 55
Anon., *The Sportsman in Ireland, with His Summer Route through the Highlands of Scotland, by a Cosmopolite*, 2 vols (London: Colburn, 1840)
Anon., *Wicklow's Historic Gaol, 1702–1924: A story of crime, cruelty, exile and misery* (Wicklow: n.d. [*c.* 1999])
Arciszewska, Barbara, and McKeller, Elizabeth (eds), *Articulating British Classicism: New approaches to eighteenth-century architecture* (London: Ashgate, 2004)
Ashworth, John Hervey, *The Saxon in Ireland; or, the Rambles of an Englishman in Search of a Settlement in the West of Ireland* (London: Murray, 1851)
Association for the Improvement of Prisons and of Prison Discipline in Ireland (AIPPD), *A Statement of the Objects of the Association for the Improvement of Prisons and of Prison Discipline in Ireland* (Dublin: Bentham, 1819)
Association for the Improvement of Prisons and of Prison Discipline in Ireland (AIPPD), *First Report of the Association for the Improvement of Prisons and of Prison Discipline in Ireland, for 1819* (Dublin: Goodwin, 1820)
Association for the Improvement of Prisons and of Prison Discipline in Ireland (AIPPD), *Third Report of the Association for the Improvement of Prisons, and of Prison Discipline in Ireland, for 1821* (Dublin: Goodwin, 1822)
Association for the Improvement of Prisons and of Prison Discipline in Ireland (AIPPD), *Fourth Report of the Association for the Improvement of Prisons, and of Prison Discipline in Ireland, for 1822* (Dublin: Goodwin, 1823)
Association for the Improvement of Prisons and of Prison Discipline in Ireland (AIPPD), *Fifth Report of the Association for the Improvement of Prisons, and of Prison Discipline in Ireland, for 1823* (Dublin: Goodwin, 1824)
Association for the Improvement of Prisons and of Prison Discipline in Ireland (AIPPD), *Speech Delivered by Robert Perceval, at the Sixth Annual General Meeting of the Association for the Improvement of Prisons and of Prison Discipline in Ireland, 27 June 1825* (Dublin: Goodwin, 1825)
Association for the Improvement of Prisons and of Prison Discipline in Ireland (AIPPD), *Speech Delivered by Robert Perceval, at the Seventh Annual General Meeting of the Association for the Improvement of Prisons and of Prison Discipline in Ireland, 27 June 1826* (Dublin: Bentham, 1826)
Association for the Improvement of Prisons and of Prison Discipline in Ireland (AIPPD), *Seventh Report of the Association for the Improvement of Prisons, and of Prison Discipline in Ireland, for 1826* (Dublin: Goodwin, 1826)
Association for the Improvement of Prisons and of Prison Discipline in Ireland (AIPPD), *Analysis of the Inspectors Generals' Report on the Prisons … of Ireland for the Year 1827* (Dublin: publisher unknown, *c.* 1828)
Atkinson, A., *Ireland Exhibited to England in a Political and Moral Survey of Her Population*, 2 vols (London: Baldwin, Cradock & Joy, 1823)

Atkinson, A., *The Irish Tourist* (Dublin: Thomas Courtney, 1815)

Balch, William Stevens, *Ireland as I Saw It: The character, condition, and prospects of the people* (New York: Putnam, 1850)

Barclay, Katie, *Men on Trial: Performing emotion, embodiment and identity in Ireland, 1800–45* (Manchester: Manchester University Press, 2019)

Barclay, Katie, 'Singing and Lower-class Masculinity in the Dublin Magistrate's Court, 1800–1845', *Journal of Social History*, vol. 47, no. 3, 2014, pp. 746–68

Barnard, Toby, *A Guide to the Sources for the History of Material Culture in Ireland, 1500–2000* (Dublin: Four Courts Press, 2005)

Barnard, Toby, *Making the Grand Figure: Lives and possessions in Ireland, 1641–1770* (New Haven and London: Yale University Press, 2004)

Barrow, John, *A Tour round Ireland … in the Autumn of 1835* (London: Murray, 1836)

Bartlett, W.H., Willis, Nathaniel Parker, and Coyne, Joseph Stirling, *The Scenery and Antiquities of Ireland*, 2 vols (London: George Virtue, 1842)

Beccaria, Cesare, *An Essay on Crimes and Punishments, Translated from the Italian* (Dublin: Exshaw, 1767)

Bence-Jones, Mark, 'Two Pairs of Architect Brothers', *Country Life*, vol. 142, no. 3675, 10 August 1967, pp. 306–9

Benn, George, *A History of the Town of Belfast from 1799 till 1810*, 2 vols (London: Ward, 1880)

Bernelle, Agnes (ed.), *Decantations: A tribute to Maurice Craig* (Dublin: Lilliput Press, 1992)

Berry, Henry F., *A History of the Royal Dublin Society* (London: Longmans, Green & Co., 1915)

Bicheno, James Ebenezer, *Ireland and Its Economy, Being the Result of Observations Made in a Tour through the Country in the Autumn of 1829* (London: Murray, 1830)

Bigger, Francis Joseph, 'The Franciscan Friary at Carrigfergus, with a Photograph of the Courthouse at Carrickfergus after the Trial of William Orr, 18 Sept. 1797', *Ulster Journal of Archaeology*, vol. 15, no. 2, May 1909, p. 53

Binns, Jonathan, *The Miseries and Beauties of Ireland*, 2 vols (London: Longman, 1837)

Blake, M.J. (ed.), 'An Account of the Lynch Family', *Journal of the Galway Archaeological and Historical Society*, vol. 8, 1913–14, p. 91

Bond, R. Warwick (ed.), *The Marlay Letters, 1778–1820* (London: Constable, 1937)

Bowring, John (ed.), *The Works of Jeremy Bentham*, 11 vols (Edinburgh: William Tait, 1838–43)

Boyle, Tom, and O'Dwyer, Michael, *Kilkenny County Council: A century of local government* (Kilkenny: Kilkenny County Council, 1999)

Bradley, John, *Irish Historic Towns Atlas, No. 10: Kilkenny* (Dublin: Royal Irish Academy, 2000)

Bremner, G.A., *Imperial Gothic: Religious architecture and high Anglican culture in the British empire, c. 1840–1870* (New Haven and London: Yale University Press, 2013)

Brett, C.E.B., *The Buildings of Armagh* (Belfast: Ulster Architectural Heritage Society, 1999)

Brett, C.E.B., *Buildings of Belfast, 1700–1914* (Belfast: Friar's Bush Press, 1985)

Brett, C.E.B., *Court Houses and Market Houses of the Province of Ulster* (Belfast: Ulster Architectural Heritage Society, 1973)

Brett, C.E.B., *List of Historic Buildings … in the Town of Monaghan* (Belfast: Ulster Architectural Heritage Society, 1970)

Brink, Robert J. (ed.), *Courthouses of the Commonwealth* (Amherst: University of Massachusetts, 1984)

Broderick, David, *Local Government in Nineteenth-century County Dublin: The grand jury* (Dublin: Four Courts Press, 2007)

Broeker, Galen, *Rural Disorder and Police Reform in Ireland, 1812–36* (London: Routledge, 1970)

Brown, Michael, and Donlan, Seán Patrick (eds), *The Laws and Other Legalities of Ireland, 1689–1850* (Farnham, Surrey: Ashgate, 2011)

Buchanan, R.H., and Wilson, Anthony, *Irish Historic Towns Atlas, No. 8: Downpatrick* (Dublin: Royal Irish Academy, 1997)

Burns, Paul, O'Connor, Ciaran, and O'Riordan, Colum (eds), *Ireland's Court Houses* (Dublin: Irish Architectural Archive, 2019)

Butler, Isaac, 'A Journey to Lough Derg', *Journal of the Royal Society of Antiquaries of Ireland*, vol. 2, no. 2, 5th series, July 1892, pp. 126–36

Butler, Richard J., 'Bagenalstown Courthouse (1826)', *Carloviana*, vol. 63, 2015, pp. 201–4

Butler, Richard J., 'British Solutions to Irish Problems: Representations of Ireland in the British architectural press, 1837–53', *Victorian Periodicals Review*, vol. 47, no. 4, Winter 2014, pp. 577–96

Butler, Richard J., 'Cork's Courthouses, the Landed Elite and the Rockite Rebellion: Architectural responses to agrarian violence, 1820–27', in Kyle Hughes and Donald M. MacRaild (eds), *Crime, Violence, and the Irish in the Nineteenth Century* (Liverpool: Liverpool University Press, 2017), pp. 87–111

Butler, Richard J., '"The Radicals in these Reform Times": Politics, grand juries, and Ireland's unbuilt assize courthouses, 1800–50', *Architectural History*, vol. 58, 2015, pp. 109–40

Butler, Richard J., 'Rethinking the Origins of the British Prisons Act of 1835: Ireland and the development of central-government prison inspection, 1820–35', *The Historical Journal*, vol. 59, no. 3, September 2016, pp. 721–46

Butler, Richard J., 'Urban Governance and Prison Building in Pre-famine Ireland, 1820–1845', in Simon Gunn and Tom Hulme (eds), *New Approaches to Governance and Rule in Urban Europe since 1500* (Routledge, forthcoming)

Butler, Richard J., 'The Architecture of the State in Ireland: The colonial question, 1800–1922', in G.A. Bremner and Daniel Maudlin (eds), *Inner Empire: Architecture and imperialism in the British Isles, 1560–2000* (Manchester: Manchester University Press, forthcoming)

Butler, Richard, *Some Notices of the Castle and of the Abbies and Other Religious Houses at Trim* (Trim: Henry Griffith, 1835)

Butlin, R.A. (ed.), *The Development of the Irish Town* (London: Croom Helm, 1977)

Byrne, Michael, *A Walk through Tullamore* (Tullamore: Esker, 1980)

Byrne, Michael, 'The County Courthouse at Tullamore and the Making of a County Town', *Journal of the Offaly Historical and Archaeological Society*, vol. 1, 2003, pp. 108–25

Byrne, Michael, *Legal Offaly: The county courthouse at Tullamore and the legal profession in County Offaly from the 1820s to the present day* (Tullamore: Esker, 2008)

Caird, James, *The Plantation Scheme, or, the West of Ireland as a Field for Investment* (Edinburgh and London: Blackwood, 1850)

Campbell, Gordon, and Crowther, Susan, *Historic Buildings … in the Town of Carrickfergus* (Belfast: Ulster Architectural Heritage Society, 1978)

Carey, Tim, *Mountjoy: The story of a prison* (Cork: Collins Press, 2000)

Carr, John, *The Stranger in Ireland* (London: Phillips, 1805)

Carroll-Burke, Patrick, *Colonial Discipline: The making of the Irish convict system* (Dublin: Four Courts Press, 2000)

Carroll, Patrick, *Science, Culture and Modern State Formation* (Berkeley, CA: University of California Press, 2006)

Carter, Margaret, *Early Canadian Court Houses* (Ottawa: Canadian Parks Service, 1983)

Casey, Christine, 'Art and Architecture in the Long Eighteenth Century', in James Kelly (ed.), *The Cambridge History of Ireland: Volume III, 1730–1880* (Cambridge: Cambridge University Press, 2018), pp. 406–64

Casey, Christine, *The Buildings of Ireland: Dublin* (New Haven and London: Yale University Press, 2005)

Casey, Christine, 'Courthouses, Markethouses and Townhalls of Leinster', MA thesis, University College Dublin, 1982

Casey, Christine (ed.), *The Eighteenth-century Dublin Town House* (Dublin: Four Courts Press, 2010)

Casey, Christine, 'The Greek Revival Courthouse, Dundalk, County Louth', *Irish Arts Review*, vol. 3, no. 2, Summer 1986, pp. 16–20

Casey, Christine, 'John Neville: Louth county surveyor', *Journal of the County Louth Archaeological and Historical Society*, vol. 21, no. 1, 1985, pp. 23–30

Casey, Christine, and Rowan, Alistair, *The Buildings of Ireland: North Leinster, the counties of Longford,*

Louth, Meath and Westmeath (London: Penguin, 1993)
Chalklin, Christopher, *English Counties and Public Building 1650–1830* (London: Hambledon, 1998)
Champness, John, *Thomas Harrison: Georgian architect of Chester and Lancaster, 1744–1829* (Lancaster: Lancaster University, 2005)
Clarke, H.B., and Gearty, Sarah (eds), *Maps & Texts: Exploring the Irish historic towns atlas* (Dublin: Royal Irish Academy, 2013)
Clark, Christopher, *An Historical and Descriptive Account of the Town of Lancaster*, 2nd edn (Lancaster: Clark, 1811)
Cogan, Denis, 'Athy Town Hall', *Journal of the County Kildare Archaeological Society*, vol. 17, 1987–91, pp. 99–105
Colby, Thomas, *Ordnance Survey of the County of Londonderry: Memoir of the city and north-western liberties of Londonderry: Parish of Templemore* (Dublin: Hodges & Smith, 1837)
Colvin, Howard, *A Biographical Dictionary of British Architects, 1600–1840* (New Haven and London: Yale University Press, 2008)
Connolly, S.J. (ed.), *Kingdoms United? Great Britain and Ireland since 1500: Integration and diversity* (Dublin: Four Courts Press, 1999)
Cooke, Pat, *A History of Kilmainham Gaol, 1796–1924* (Dublin: Government of Ireland, 1995)
Cooper, Robert Alan, 'The English Quakers and Prison Reform, 1809–23', *Quaker History*, vol. 68, no. 1, Spring 1979, pp. 3–19
Coote, Charles, *General View of the Agriculture and Manufactures of the King's County: With observations on the means of their improvement* (Dublin: Graisberry & Campbell, 1801)
Coote, Charles, *Statistical Survey of the County of Armagh* (Dublin: Graisberry & Campbell, 1804)
Coote, Charles, *Statistical Survey of the County of Cavan* (Dublin: Graisberry & Campbell, 1802)
Coote, Charles, *Statistical Survey of the County of Monaghan* (Dublin: Graisberry & Campbell, 1801)
Coote, Charles, *Statistical Survey of the Queen's County* (Dublin: Graisberry & Campbell, 1801)
Conry, Michael J., *Carlow Granite: Years of history written in stone* (Chapelstown, Co. Carlow: Chapelstown Press, 2006)
Costello, Cornelius, 'Naas and the Country in General, from 1800–48', *Journal of the County Kildare Archaeological Society*, vol. 13, no. 3, 1960, pp. 432–4
Costello, Cornelius, 'Thomas Sherrard's Map of Naas, 1787', *Journal of the County Kildare Archaeological Society*, vol. 18, no. 4, 1998–9, pp. 589–97
Costello, Cornelius, 'Thomas Sherrard's Map of Naas, 1787', *Journal of the County Kildare Archaeological Society*, vol. 19, no. 1, 2000–1, p. 229
Craig, Maurice, *The Architecture of Ireland from the Earliest Times to 1880* (London: Batsford, 1982)
Craig, Maurice, *Dublin, 1660–1860: The shaping of a city*, 1st ed., 1952 (Dublin: Liberties Press, 2006)
Craig, Maurice, 'A Note on Courthouses', *Quarterly Bulletin of the Irish Georgian Society*, vol. 1, January–March 1958, pp. 8–12
Craig, Maurice, and Glin, the Knight of, *Ireland Observed: A handbook to the buildings and antiquities* (Cork: Mercier, 1970)
Creedon, William P. (ed.), *Exemplar Hiberniae: 100 years of local government in County Wexford* (Dublin: Institute of Public Administration, 1999)
Cromwell, Thomas Kitson, *Excursions through Ireland: Comprising topographical and historical delineations of each province*, 3 vols (London: Longman, 1820)
Crook, J. Mordaunt, *The Greek Revival: Neo-classical attitudes in British architecture* (London: Murray, 1995)
Crosbie, Barry, 'Ireland and the Empire in the Nineteenth Century', in James Kelly (ed.), *The Cambridge History of Ireland: Volume III, 1730–1880* (Cambridge: Cambridge University Press, 2018), pp. 617–36
Crossman, Virginia, 'Emergency Legislation and Agrarian Disorder in Ireland, 1821–41', *Irish Historical Studies*, vol. 27, no. 108, November 1991, pp. 309–23
Crossman, Virginia, 'The Growth of the State in the Nineteenth Century', in James Kelly (ed.), *The Cambridge History of Ireland: Volume III, 1730–1880* (Cambridge: Cambridge University Press, 2018), pp. 542–66

Crossman, Virginia, *Local Government in Nineteenth-century Ireland* (Belfast: Institute of Irish Studies, 1994)

Crossman, Virginia, 'Local Government in Nineteenth-century Ireland', in Terrence McDonough (ed.), *Was Ireland a Colony? Economics, politics and culture in nineteenth-century Ireland* (Dublin: Irish Academic Press, 2005), pp. 102–16

Crowley, John, Smyth, William J., and Murphy, Mike (eds), *Atlas of the Great Irish Famine* (Cork: Cork University Press, 2012)

Cruickshank, Dan, *A Guide to the Georgian Buildings of Great Britain and Ireland* (London: Rizzoli, 1985)

Cullen, L.M., *An Economic History of Ireland since 1660* (London: Batsford, 1972)

Culliton, J.A., 'The Four Courts, Dublin', *Dublin Historical Record*, vol. 21, no. 4, 1967, pp. 116–26

Cumming, Willy, 'Kilmainham Gaol', National Inventory of Architectural Heritage Building of the Month, May 2016 (www.buildingsofireland.ie)

Cunningham, John, '"Compelled to Their Bad Acts by Hunger": Three Irish urban crowds, 1817–45', *Éire-Ireland*, vol. 45, nos. 1–2, Spring–Summer 2010, pp. 128–51

Curnock, Nehemiah (ed.), *The Journal of the Rev. John Wesley, A.M.*, 8 vols (London: Epworth Press, 1909–16)

Curran, C.P., 'Cooley, Gandon and the Four Courts', *Journal of the Royal Society of Antiquaries of Ireland*, vol. 19, 7th ser., 1949, pp. 20–5

Curtin, Geraldine, *The Women of Galway Jail: Female criminality in nineteenth-century Ireland* (Galway: Arlen House, 2001)

Curtin, Geraldine, 'Female Prisoners in Galway Gaol in the Late Nineteenth Century', *Journal of the Galway Archaeological and Historical Society*, vol. 54, 2002, pp. 175–82

Curwen, John Christian, *Observations on the State of Ireland*, 2 vols (London: Baldwin, Cradock & Joy, 1818)

D'Alton, Ian, *Protestant Society and Politics in Cork, 1812–1844* (Cork: Cork University Press, 1980)

D'Alton, John, and O'Flanagan, J.R., *The History of Dundalk* (Dundalk: William Tempest, 1864)

D'Arcy, Fergus, 'Wages of Labourers in the Dublin Building Industry, 1667–1918', *Saothar: Journal of the Irish Labour History Society*, vol. 14, 1989, pp. 17–32

Dawson, Sylvia, *Saint Christopher's: The first crucial years, 1964–1975*, 2nd edn (Longford, 2001)

Day, Angelique, and McWilliams, Patrick (eds), *Ordnance Survey Memoirs of Ireland: Volume 4: Fermanagh* (Belfast: Institute of Irish Studies, 1990)

Day, Angelique, and McWilliams, Patrick (eds), *Ordnance Survey Memoirs of Ireland: Volume 5: Tyrone* (Belfast: Institute of Irish Studies, 1990)

Day, Angelique, and McWilliams, Patrick (eds), *Ordnance Survey Memoirs of Ireland: Volume 12: Down* (Belfast: Institute of Irish Studies, 1992)

Day, Angelique, and McWilliams, Patrick (eds), *Ordnance Survey Memoirs of Ireland: Volume 39: Donegal* (Belfast: Institute of Irish Studies, 1997)

de Brún, Pádraig, 'Rev. Forster Archer's Account of Kerry in 1801', *Journal of the Kerry Archaeological and Historical Society*, vol. 14, 1981, pp. 26–30

DeLacy, Margaret, *Prison Reform in Lancashire, 1700–1850: A study in local administration* (Stanford, CA: Stanford University Press, 1986)

Delaney, Cathleen, 'Oak Park House and the Bruen Family', *Carloviana*, vol. 50, 2001, pp. 20–3

Delany, Ruth, *A Celebration of 250 Years of Ireland's Inland Waterways* (Belfast: Appletree, 1992)

Denman, Terence, *A Lonely Grave: The life and death of William Redmond* (Dublin: Irish Academic Press, 1995)

Devereaux, Simon, 'The Making of the Penitentiary Act, 1775–1779', *The Historical Journal*, vol. 42, no. 2, 1999, pp. 405–33

Dickson, David, *Dublin: The making of a capital city* (Cambridge, MA: Belknap Press, 2014)

Dickson, David, *Old World Colony: Cork and south Munster, 1630–1830* (Madison, WI: University of Wisconsin Press, 2005)

Dickson, David (ed.), *The Gorgeous Mask: Dublin, 1700–1850* (Dublin: Trinity History Workshop, 1987)

Dixon, Hugh, *An Introduction to Ulster Architecture* (Belfast: Ulster Architectural Heritage Society, 1975)

Dixon, Hugh, *List of Historic Buildings … in the Town of Enniskillen* (Belfast: Ulster Architectural Heritage Society, 1973)

Donnelly, Jr., James S., *The Great Irish Potato Famine* (Stroud, Gloucestershire: Sutton Publishing, 2001)

Donnelly, Jr., James S., 'The Rightboy Movement 1785–8', *Studia Hibernica*, nos. 17–18, 1977–8, pp. 120–202

Doran, Alan, 'Carlow Criminal Court', *Carloviana*, vol. 2, no. 29, new series, 1981, pp. 23–4

Douglas, M.C., 'Carlow's Old Inns: Churches, gaol, and castle', *Carloviana*, vol. 1, no. 4, 1951, pp. 172–4

Douzinas, Costas, and Nead, Lynda (eds), *Law and the Image: The authority of art and the aesthetics of law* (Chicago: University of Chicago Press, 1999)

Dowling, P.J., 'Forster Archer's Tour of Ireland in 1801', *Irish Ecclesiastical Record*, vol. 62, 1943, pp. 22–8

Doyle, J.B., *Tours in Ulster* (Dublin: Hodges & Smith, 1855)

Dubourdieu, John, *Statistical Survey of the County of Antrim* (Dublin: Graisberry & Campbell, 1812)

Duffy, Charles Gavan, *The League of North and South: An episode in Irish history, 1850–1854* (London: Chapman & Hall, 1886)

Dunleath, D., Rankin, P.J., and Rowan, A.J., *Historic Buildings in the Town of Downpatrick* (Belfast: Ulster Architectural Heritage Society, 1970)

Dunne, Terence M., 'The Law of Captain Rock', in Kyle Hughes and Donald M. MacRaild (eds), *Crime, Violence, and the Irish in the Nineteenth Century* (Liverpool: Liverpool University Press, 2017), pp. 38–52

Durbin, John Price, *Observations in Europe, Principally in France and Great Britain*, 2 vols (New York: Harper & Brothers, 1844)

Durney, James, *In the Shadow of Kings: Social housing in Naas, 1898–1984* (Naas: Naas Printing Ltd., 2007)

Dutton, Hely, *A Statistical and Agricultural Survey of the County of Galway* (Dublin: Graisberry, 1824)

Eastwood, David, *Governing Rural England: Tradition and transformation in local government, 1780–1840* (Oxford: Clarendon Press, 1994)

Ellis, William, 'Battle for the Courthouse', *Carloviana*, vol. 48, 2000, p. 44

Ellis, William, 'Snippets from the Past', *Carloviana*, vol. 48, 2000, pp. 44–5

Elsam, Richard, *A Description of Cavan Gaol: With Neild's observations on the law of civil imprisonment: with his report of Gloucester county gaol: together with cursory hints for the internal regulation of prisons … to which is annexed an abstract of the statutes of Geo. III for the information of grand juries, in building and repairing of prisons in Ireland* (Dublin: Carrick, 1810)

Evans, M. (ed.), *The Pavilion: A contemporary collection of British art and architecture* (London: I.T. Publications, 1946)

Evans, Robin, *The Fabrication of Virtue: English prison architecture, 1750–1840* (Cambridge: Cambridge University Press, 1982)

Farrell, J.P., *Historical Notes and Stories of the County Longford* (Dublin: Dollard, 1886)

Fennelly, Katherine, 'The Institution and the City: The impact of hospitals and workhouses on the development of Dublin's north inner city, *c.* 1773–1911', *Urban History* (forthcoming)

Ferrar, John, *The History of Limerick … from the Earliest Records to the Year 1787* (Limerick: Watson, 1787)

Ferrar, M.L. (ed.), *The Diary of Colour-Sergeant George Calladine, 19th Foot, 1793–1837* (London: Eden, Fisher & Co., 1922)

Fisher, D.R., *The History of Parliament: The House of Commons, 1820–1832*, 7 vols (Cambridge: Cambridge University Press, 2009)

Fisher, Lydia, *Letters from the Kingdom of Kerry in the Year 1845* (Dublin: Webb & Chapman, 1847)

Fitzgerald, Alison, *Silver in Georgian Dublin: Making, selling, consuming* (Abingdon: Routledge, 2017)

Fitzgerald, Patrick, and McGregor, John James, *The History, Topography, and Antiquities, of the County and City of Limerick*, 2 vols (Dublin: McKern, 1827)

Flavin, Susan, *Consumption and Culture in Sixteenth-century Ireland: Saffron, stockings and silk* (Woodbridge: Boydell, 2014)

Flinn, M.W., 'The Poor Employment Act of 1817', *Economic History Review*, vol. 14, no. 1, 1961, pp. 82–92

Forbes, J.D., *Victorian Architect: The life and work of William Tinsley* (Bloomington, IN: Indiana University Press, 1953)

Forbes, John, *Memorandums Made in Ireland in the Autumn of 1852*, 2 vols (London: Smith, Elder & Co., 1853)

Foster, John Leslie, *A Letter on the Fittest Style and Situation for the Wellington Trophy about To Be Erected in Dublin* (Dublin: Graisberry & Campbell, 1815)

Foucault, Michel, *Discipline and Punish: The birth of the prison*, 1st pub. 1975, trans. Alan Sheridan (New York: Pantheon, 1977)

Fraher, William, 'The Reconstruction of Dungarvan, 1807–*c*. 1830: A political ploy', *Decies*, vol. 25, January 1984, pp. 4–21

French, Noel. E., *Trim Gaol* (Trim: Meath Heritage Centre, 1994)

Freney, James, *The Life and Adventures of James Freney: Commonly called Captain Freney … written by himself* (Dublin: S. Powell, 1754)

Fry, Elizabeth, and Gurney, Joseph John, *Report Addressed to the Marquess Wellesley, Lord Lieutenant of Ireland, Respecting Their Late Visit to that Country* (London: Arch, 1827)

Gallagher, Fíona, *The Streets of Sligo: Urban evolution over the course of seven centuries* (Sligo, 2008)

Gallagher, Fíona, and Legg, Marie-Louise, *Irish Historic Towns Atlas, No. 24: Sligo* (Dublin: Royal Irish Academy, 2012)

Gamble, John, *Sketch of the History, Politics and Manners, Taken in Dublin, and the North of Ireland, in the Autumn of 1810* (London: Cradock & Joy, 1811)

Gargan, Sinéad, 'How Not To "Encourage People To Take Lotts for Building": The 18th-century non-development of Grangegorman by the Monck estate', *Irish Architectural and Decorative Studies*, vol. 18, 2015, pp. 106–29

Garner, William, *Carlow: Architectural heritage* (Dublin: Foras Forbartha, 1980)

Garner, William, *Ennis: Architectural heritage* (Dublin: An Foras Forbartha, 1981)

Garner, William, *Historic Buildings … in the Town of Cavan* (Belfast: Ulster Architectural Heritage Society, 1978)

Garner, William, *Tullamore Architectural Heritage* (Dublin: An Foras Forbartha, 1980)

Garnham, Neal, *The Courts, Crime and the Criminal Law in Ireland, 1692–1760* (Dublin: Irish Academic Press, 1996)

Garry, James, 'The Tholsel, Drogheda', *Journal of the County Louth Archaeological and Historical Society*, vol. 17, no. 3, 1971, pp. 164–8

Gash, Norman, *Mr Secretary Peel: The life of Sir Robert Peel to 1830* (London and New York: Longman, 1985)

Gatrell, V.A.C., *The Hanging Tree: Execution and the English people, 1770–1868* (Oxford: Oxford University Press, 1994)

Gaunt, Richard A., *Sir Robert Peel: The life and legacy* (London: Tauris, 2010)

Gearty, Sarah, Morris, Martin, and O'Ferrall, Fergus, *Irish Historic Towns Atlas, No. 22: Longford* (Dublin: Royal Irish Academy, 2010)

Geraghty, P.J., 'P.J. Lynam, the Last County Surveyor for Louth Grand Jury (1886–1912)', *Journal of the County Louth Archaeological and Historical Journal*, vol. 27, no. 2, 2010, pp. 284–302

Geraghty, P.J., 'Urban Improvement and the Erection of Municipal Buildings in County Louth during the Eighteenth and Nineteenth Centuries', *Journal of the County Louth Archaeological and Historical Society*, vol. 23, no. 3, 1995, pp. 295–317

Gibney, Arthur, Hurley, Livia, and McParland, Edward (eds), *The Building Site in Eighteenth-century Ireland* (Dublin: Four Courts Press, 2017)

Gibson, William H., 'The North and South Moats of Naas', *Journal of the County Kildare Archaeological Society*, vol. 17, 1987–91, pp. 49–58

Gilbert, John T. (ed.), *Calendar of the Ancient Records of Dublin in the Possession of the Municipal Corporation of that City*, 19 vols (Dublin: Dollard, 1889–1944)

Gilbert, John T. (ed.), *Documents Relating to Ireland, 1795–1804* (Dublin: Dollard, 1893)

Gill-Cummins, Maureen, 'The Evolution of the Court House at Naas, Co. Kildare', *Journal of the County Kildare Archaeological Society*, vol. 20, no. 1, 2008–9, pp. 66–75

Gillespie, Raymond, and Moran, Gerard (eds), *Longford: Essays in county history* (Dublin: Lilliput Press, 1991)

Girouard, Mark, 'The Reign of the Building Families: City of Waterford, Ireland – II', *Country Life*, vol. 140, no. 3641, 15 December 1966, pp. 1626–9

Glassford, James, *Notes of Three Tours in Ireland in 1824 and 1826* (Bristol: Strong & Chilcott, 1832)

Glynn, Jarlath, *Wexford: Then & now* (Dublin: History Press, 2013)

Goslin, Bernadette, 'A History and Descriptive Catalogue of the Murray Collection of Architectural Drawings in the Collection of the Royal Institute of the Architects of Ireland', MA thesis, University College Dublin, 1990

Graby, John (ed.), *150 Years of Architecture in Ireland: The Royal Institute of the Architects of Ireland, 1839–1989* (Dublin: RIAI, 1989)

Grace, Pierce, 'Patronage and Health Care in Eighteenth-century Irish County Infirmaries', *Irish Historical Studies*, vol. 41, no. 159, May 2017, pp. 1–21

Graham, B.J., and Proudfoot, Lindsay J., *Urban Improvement in Provincial Ireland, 1700–1840* (Athlone: Temple Printing, 1994)

Graham, Clare, *Ordering Law: An architectural and social history of the English law court to 1914* (Aldershot, Hampshire: Ashgate, 2003)

Grant, James, *Impressions of Ireland and the Irish*, 2 vols (London: Cunningham, 1844)

Green, E.R.R., and Jope, E.M., 'Patron and Architect: An example of relations in the late 18th century', *Ulster Journal of Archaeology*, vols 24–5, third series, 1961–2, pp. 145–51

Gregory, William, *The Picture of Dublin, Being a Description of the City*, 1st edn 1811 (Dublin: Carrick, 1817)

Griffin, Brian, *Sources for the Study of Crime in Ireland, 1801–1921* (Dublin: Four Courts Press, 2005)

Griffiths, George, *Chronicles of the County Wexford* (Enniscorthy: Watchman, 1877)

Grimsley-Smith, Melinda D., 'Politics, Professionalization, and Poverty: Lunatic asylums for the poor in Ireland, 1817–1920', PhD thesis, University of Notre Dame, 2011

Guinness, Desmond, *Georgian Dublin* (London: Batsford, 1979)

Hall, James, *A Tour through Ireland*, 2 vols (London: Moore, 1813)

Hall, Mr & Mrs Samuel Carter, *Ireland: Its scenery, character, etc.*, 3 vols (London: How & Parsons, 1841–3)

Hall, Thomas Dugall, *Report on the State and Progress of Public Buildings … in the County of Leitrim* (Dublin: Hodges & Smith, 1838)

Hannigan, Ken, and Nolan, Williams (eds), *Wicklow: History & society* (Dublin: Geography Publications, 1994)

Hardiman, James, *The History of the Town and County of the Town of Galway* (Dublin: Folds, 1820)

Harrington, Louise, 'The Work of Cork's Wide Streets Commissioners on Washington Street', *Irish Architectural and Decorative Studies*, vol. 15, 2012, pp. 98–117

Harris, Walter, *The History and Antiquities of the City of Dublin* (Dublin: Flinn & Williams, 1766)

Harris, Walter, and Smith, Charles, *The Antient and Present State of the County of Down* (Dublin: Reilly, 1744)

Hayes-McCoy, Marguirite, 'The Eyre Documents', *Journal of the Galway Archaeological and Historical Society*, vol. 20, 1943, pp. 151–79

Heaney, Henry, 'Ireland's Penitentiary, 1820–1831: An experiment that failed', *Studia Hibernica*, vol. 14, 1974, pp. 28–39

Heaney, Henry (ed.), *A Scottish Whig in Ireland, 1835–1838: The Irish journals of Robert Graham of Redgorton* (Dublin: Four Courts Press, 1999)

Heard, Ruth, 'Public Works in Ireland, 1800–1831', MA thesis, Trinity College Dublin, 1977

Henchy, Patrick, 'Francis Johnston, Architect, 1760–1829', *Dublin Historical Record*, vol. 11, no. 1, December 1949–February 1950, pp. 1–16

Hennesy, Mark, *Irish Historic Towns Atlas, No. 14: Trim* (Dublin: Royal Irish Academy, 2004)

Henriques, Ursula R.Q., 'An Early Factory Inspector: James Stuart of Dunearn', *The Scottish Historical Review*, vol. 50, no. 149, April 1971, pp. 18–46

Henriques, Ursula R.Q., 'The Rise and Decline of the Separate System of Prison Discipline', *Past & Present*, vol. 54, 1972, pp. 61–93

Henriques, Ursula R.Q., *Before the Welfare State: Social administration in early industrial Britain* (London: Longman, 1979), pp. 155–97

Henry, Brian, *Dublin Hanged: Crime, law enforcement and punishment in late eighteenth-century Dublin* (Dublin: Irish Academic Press, 1994)

Hibernian Ladies' Society for Promoting the Improvement of Female Prisoners, *Second Report of the Hibernian Ladies' Society for Promoting the Improvement of Female Prisoners* (Dublin: Bentham, 1828)

Hickey, Stan, and Kenny, Liam (eds). *Nás na Ríogh from Poorhouse Road to the Fairy Flax: an illustrated history of Naas* (Naas: Nass Local History Group, 1990)

Hill, Henry H., 'Cork Architecture', *Journal of the Cork Historical and Archaeological Society*, vol. 48, 1943, pp. 94–8

Hill, Henry H. (ed.), 'Diary of a Tour in Cos. Waterford, Kilkenny, and Tipperary, 29 August–6 Sep[t]. 1831', *Journal of the Cork Historical and Archaeological Society*, vol. 38, 1933, pp. 30–7

Hill, Judith, *The Building of Limerick* (Dublin: Amer, 1991)

Hill, Judith, 'Architecture in the Aftermath of Union: Building the Viceregal Chapel in Dublin Castle, 1801–15', *Architectural History*, vol. 60, 2017, pp. 182–217

Hill, Judith, 'Irish Court Houses: A brief architectural history to 1998', in Paul Burns, Ciaran O'Connor, and Colum O'Riordan (eds), *Ireland's Court Houses* (Dublin: Irish Architectural Archive, 2019), pp. 18–37

Hoare, Richard Colt, *Journal of a Tour in Ireland, A.D. 1806* (London: Miller, 1807)

Hodge, Audrey M., *Gallows and Turnkeys: A short history of Omagh gaol* (Omagh: West Tyrone Historical Society, 1993)

Hogan, Daire, and Osborough, W.N. (eds), *Brehons, Serjeants and Attorneys: Studies in the history of the Irish legal profession* (Dublin: Irish Academic Press, 1990)

Hogan, John, 'The Three Tholsels of Kilkenny', *Journal of the Royal Historical and Archaeological Association of Ireland*, vol. 5, no. 41, 4th ser., January 1880, pp. 236–52

Holford, George, *An Account of the General Penitentiary at Millbank* (London: Rivington, 1828)

Holohan, Patrick, 'Cork Courthouse: The Pains, the Deanes, the stonecutters,' *Journal of the Cork Historical and Archaeological Society*, vol. 111, 2006, pp. 77–106

Hoppen, K. Theodore, *Governing Hibernia: British politicians and Ireland, 1800–1921* (Oxford: Oxford University Press, 2016)

Horner, Arnold, 'A Note on the Fate of the "Factory" at Maynooth', *Journal of the County Kildare Archaeological Society*, vol. 19, no. 3, 2004–5, pp. 562–4

Howard, John, *An Account of the Principal Lazarettos in Europe*, 1st edn 1789 (London: Johnson, Dilly & Cadell, 1791)

Howard, John, *The State of the Prisons in England and Wales*, 1st edn 1777 (Warrington: Eyres, 1784)

Howlin, Niamh, 'Irish Jurors: Passive observers or active participants?', *Journal of Legal History*, vol. 35, no. 2, 2014, pp. 143–71

Howlin, Niamh, *Juries in Ireland: Laypersons and law in the long nineteenth century* (Dublin: Four Courts Press, 2017)

Hughes, Kyle, and MacRaild, Donald M., 'Introduction: Crime, violence and the Irish in the nineteenth century; themes and perspectives', in Kyle Hughes and Donald M. MacRaild (eds), *Crime, Violence and the Irish in the Nineteenth Century* (Liverpool: Liverpool University Press, 2017), pp. 1–12

Hughes, Kyle, and MacRaild, Donald M. (eds), *Crime, Violence and the Irish in the Nineteenth Century* (Liverpool: Liverpool University Press, 2017)

Hunter, Maureen, 'Downpatrick's Dungeons Rediscovered', *Lecale Miscellany*, vol. 9, 1991, pp. 21–5

Inglis, Brian, *The Freedom of the Press in Ireland, 1784–1841* (London: Faber & Faber, 1954)

Inglis, Henry David, *Ireland in 1834: A journey throughout Ireland, during the spring, summer, and autumn of 1834*, 2 vols (London: Whittaker, 1834)

Jameson, Joseph, *The Following Rules and Regulations Shall Be Strictly Observed and Carried into Force and Effect in Every Gaol, House of Correction, Marshalsea, Bridewell, Penitentiary House, Sheriff's Prison, and Other Prisons Throughout Ireland, as Directed by Statute, 50 Geo. III, c. 103* (Dublin, 1822, copy in National Library of Ireland with hand-written comments on Carlow gaol)

Johnston, Norman, *Forms of Constraint: A history of prison architecture* (Urbana, IL: University of Illinois Press, 2000)

Jones, Emrys, *A Social Geography of Belfast* (Oxford: Oxford University Press, 1960)

Joyce, Patrick, *The State of Freedom: A history of the British state since 1800* (Cambridge: Cambridge University Press, 2013)

Kavanagh, Colm M., *Derry Jail* (Derry: Guildhall Press, 1990)

Keenan, Matthew, 'Queen's County Gaols: The people and their crimes', DGNL thesis, University College Cork, 2017

Kelleher, Margaret, *The Maamtrasna Murders: Language, life and death in nineteenth-century Ireland* (Dublin: University College Dublin Press, 2018)

Kelly, Freida, *A History of Kilmainham Gaol: The dismal house of little ease* (Cork: Mercier, 1988)

Kelly, James (ed.), *The Cambridge History of Ireland: Volume III, 1730–1880* (Cambridge: Cambridge University Press, 2018)

Kelly, Teresa, 'The Old Gaol, Now Hanover Works', *Carloviana*, vol. 1, no. 9, December 1960, pp. 38–9

Kelly, Tim, 'Ennis County Jail', *North Munster Antiquarian Journal*, vol. 16, 1973–4, pp. 66–9

Kelly, Tim, 'Ennis Courthouse', *The Other Clare*, vol. 5, 1981, pp. 20–1

Kennedy, Patrick J., 'The County of the Town of Galway', *Journal of the Galway Archaeological and Historical Society*, vol. 30, nos. 3–4, 1963, pp. 90–101

Kilcommins, Shane, et al., *Crime, Punishment and the Search for Order in Ireland* (Dublin: Institute of Public Administration, 2004)

Kilgannon, Tadhg, *Sligo and Its Surroundings* (Sligo: Kilgannon, 1926)

Knirck, Jason, *Afterimage of the Revolution: Cumann na nGaedheal and Irish politics, 1922–1932* (Madison, WI: University of Wisconsin, 2004)

Lacy, Thomas, *Sights and Scenes of Our Fatherland* (London: Simpkin, 1863)

Lanigan, Katherine M., Tyler, Gerald, and Brady, Margery, *Kilkenny: Its architecture & history* (Belfast: Appletree, 1987)

Larkin, F.M. (ed.), *Librarians, Poets and Scholars: A festschrift for Dónall Ó Luanaigh* (Dublin: Four Courts Press, 2007)

Larmour, Paul, *Belfast: An illustrated architectural guide* (Belfast: Friar's Bush Press, 1987)

Larmour, Paul, 'Sir Charles Lanyon', *Irish Arts Review Yearbook*, 1989–90, pp. 200–6

Latimer, W.T., *Presbyterianism in Omagh* (Belfast: reprinted from The Witness, 1913)

Lawson, John Parker, *The Gazetteer of Ireland* (Edinburgh: Edinburgh Printing and Publishing Co., 1842)

Lee, David, and Jacobs, Debbie, *James Pain, Architect* (Limerick: Limerick Civic Trust, 2005)

Lenihan, Maurice, *History of Limerick* (Dublin: Duffy, 1866)

Lewis, Samuel, *A Topographical Dictionary of Ireland*, 2 vols (London: S. Lewis, 1837)

Loeber, Rolf, Carpenter, Andrew, Campbell, Hugh, Hurley, Livia, Montague, John and Rowley, Ellen (eds), *Art and Architecture of Ireland: Volume IV: Architecture 1600–2000* (Dublin, New Haven and London: Yale University Press, 2014)

Loftus, Theresa, 'Monaghan Courthouse', National Inventory of Architectural Heritage Building of the Month, May 2014 (www.buildingsofireland.ie)

Logan, Rena, 'The Management of Female Convicts Sentenced to Transportation and Penal Servitude, 1790–1898', PhD thesis, Trinity College Dublin, 1989

Lounsbury, Carl, 'From Tavern to Courthouse: Architecture and ritual in American law, 1658–1860, by Martha J. McNamara (review)', *Journal of the Society of Architectural Historians*, vol. 64, no. 2, June 2005, pp. 254–5

Lucey, Conor, 'British Agents of the Irish Adamesque', *Architectural History*, vol. 56, 2013, pp. 135–70

Luddy, Maria, *Women and Philanthropy in Nineteenth-century Ireland* (Cambridge: Cambridge University Press, 1995)
Lyne, Gerald J. (ed.), 'Rev. Daniel A.B. Beaufort's Tour of Kerry in 1788', *Journal of the Kerry Archaeological and Historical Society*, vol. 18, 1985, pp. 183–214
Lysons, Daniel, and Lysons, Samuel, *Magna Britannia, Being a Concise Topographical Account of the Several Counties of Great Britain ... Volume the Second, Containing Cambridgeshire, and the County Palatine of Chester*, 6 vols (London: Cadell & Davies, 1810)
MacCabe, Desmond, 'Magistrates, Peasants, and the Petty Sessions Courts: Mayo, 1823–50', *Cathair na Mart: Journal of the Westport Historical Society*, vol. 5, no. 1, 1985, pp. 45–53
MacCabe, Desmond, '"The Part that Laws or Kings Can Cause or Cure": Crown prosecution and jury trial at Longford assizes, 1830–45', in Raymond Gillespie and Gerard Moran (eds), *Longford: Essays in county history* (Dublin: Lilliput Press, 1991), pp. 153–72
MacDonagh, Oliver, *The Inspector General: Sir Jeremiah Fitzpatrick and the politics of social reform, 1783–1802* (London: Croom Helm, 1981)
MacDougall, Henry, *Sketches of Irish Political Characters of the Present Day Shewing the Parts they Respectively Take on the Question of the Union* (London: Davison, 1799)
MacRae, Marion, and Adamson, Anthony, *Cornerstones of Order: Courthouses and town halls of Ontario, 1784–1914* (Toronto: C. Irwin, 1983)
Mac Suibhne, Brendán, *The End of Outrage: Post-Famine adjustment in rural Ireland* (Oxford: Oxford University Press, 2017)
Maguire, S.J., 'Galway Jail', *The Galway Reader* (published by Galway County Libraries), vol. 3, no. 3, 1951, pp. 47–51
May, Fionnuala, 'The County Courthouse at Galway by Richard Morrison', MUBC thesis, University College Dublin, 1993
Malcolm, Elizabeth, '"The Reign of Terror in Carlow": The politics of policing Ireland in the late 1830s', *Irish Historical Studies*, vol. 32, no. 125, May 2000, pp. 59–74
Malcolm, Elizabeth, and Jones, Greta (eds), *Medicine, Disease, and the State in Ireland, 1650–1940* (Cork: Cork University Press, 1999)
Malcomson, A.P.W., *John Foster: The politics of the Anglo-Irish ascendancy* (Oxford: Oxford University Press, 1978)
Matthew, H.C.G., and Harrison, Brian (eds), *Oxford Dictionary of National Biography*, 60 vols (Oxford: Oxford University Press, 2004)
Maxwell, William Hamilton, *Wild Sports of the West of Ireland* (London: Bentley, 1832)
McCarthy, Michael, and O'Neill, Karina (eds), *Studies in the Gothic Revival* (Dublin: Four Courts Press, 2008)
McCarthy, Victoria M., 'The Denny Family in Tralee: An analysis of the Denny family's role in Tralee and Denny Street', MUBC thesis, University College Dublin, 2007
McComb, William, *McComb's Guide to Belfast* (Belfast: McComb, 1861)
McConnell, Charles, *Carrickfergus: A stroll through time* (Carrickfergus: Carrickfergus Publications, 1994)
McCullough, Catherine, and Crawford, W.H., *Irish Historic Towns Atlas, No. 18: Armagh* (Dublin: Royal Irish Academy, 2007)
McCullough, Niall, and Mulvin, Valerie, *A Lost Tradition: The nature of architecture in Ireland* (Dublin: Gandon Editions, 1987)
McCusker, Breege, 'The County Gaol and Some Past Crimes and Punishments in County Fermanagh', *Clogher Record*, vol. 13, no. 1, 1988, pp. 50–5
McDermott, Matthew J., 'Notable Irish Architectural Families, 2: The Morrisons', *RIAI Yearbook* (1977), pp. 81–91
McDonough, Terrence (ed.), *Was Ireland a Colony? Economics, politics and culture in nineteenth-century Ireland* (Dublin: Irish Academic Press, 2005)
McDowell, R.B., *The Irish Administration, 1801–1914* (London: Faber & Faber, 1964)
McEntee, A.F., *Memories of the Lifetime in Journalism in Cavan* (Cavan: Anglo-Celt, 1991)

McHugh, Ned, 'Drogheda Jail during the Period of the Famine', *Journal of the Old Drogheda Society*, vol. 5, 1986, pp. 47–58

McGrath, John, 'Organised Labour in Limerick City, 1819–1821: Violence and the struggle for legitimacy', in Kyle Hughes and Donald M. MacRaild (eds), *Crime, Violence and the Irish in the Nineteenth Century* (Liverpool: Liverpool University Press, 2017), pp. 67–86

McGuire, James, and Quinn, James (eds), *Dictionary of Irish Biography*, 9 vols (Cambridge: Cambridge University Press, 2009)

McKinstry, Robert, et al., *The Buildings of Armagh* (Belfast: Ulster Architectural Heritage Society, 1992)

McNamara, Martha J., *From Tavern to Courthouse: Architecture and ritual in American law, 1658–1860* (Baltimore and London: Johns Hopkins University Press, 2004)

McNeill, Charles, 'New Gate, Dublin', *Journal of the Royal Society of Antiquaries of Ireland*, vol. 11, no. 2, 1921, pp. 152–65

McNeill, Charles, 'The Hospitallers at Kilmainham and Their Guests', *Journal of the Royal Society of Antiquaries of Ireland*, vol. 14, no. 1, 6th series, June 1924, pp. 15–30

McNiff, Peter, *The Times & the Joys: Donal Wylde: Images of Clonmel & Tipperary South Riding* (Clonmel: Wylde, 2013)

McParlan, James, *Statistical Survey of the County of Leitrim* (Dublin: Graisberry & Campbell, 1802)

McParland, Edward, 'Carlow Courthouse and Railings', *Carloviana*, vol. 2, no. 22, new series, 1973, p. 9

McParland, Edward, 'Carlow Courthouse and Railings', *Carloviana*, vol. 47, 1999, p. 51

McParland, Edward, 'The Early History of James Gandon's Four Courts', *Burlington Magazine*, vol. 122, no. 932, November 1980, pp. 727–35

McParland, Edward, 'Francis Johnston, Architect', *Irish Georgian Society Bulletin*, vol. 12, nos. 3–4, 1969, pp. 61–139

McParland, Edward, *James Gandon: Vitruvius Hibernicus* (London: Zwemmer, 1985)

McParland, Edward, 'The Papers of Bryan Bolger, Measurer', *Dublin Historical Record*, vol. 25, no. 4, September 1972, pp. 120–31

McParland, Edward, 'The Public Work of Architects in Ireland during the Neo-classical Period', PhD thesis, Cambridge University, 1975

McSkimmin, Samuel, *The History and Antiquities of the County of the Town of Carrickfergus*, rev. edn E.J. McCrum (Belfast: Mullan, et al., 1909 [1st edn 1811])

McTernan, John, *Olde Sligo: Aspects of town and county over 750 years* (Sligo: Avena Publications, 1995)

McTernan, John, *In Sligo Long Ago: Aspects of town and county over two centuries* (Sligo: Avena Publications, 1998)

Meagher, Sheena, 'South Main Street, Naas', *Journal of the County Kildare Archaeological Society*, vol. 18, no. 3, 1996–7, pp. 367–96

Meghen, P.J., 'The Administrative Work of the Grand Jury', *Administration: Journal of the Institute of Public Administration of Ireland*, vol. 6, no. 3, Autumn 1958, pp. 247–64

Mitchell, James, 'The Prisons of Galway: Background to the inspector general's reports, 1796–1818', *Journal of the Galway Archaeological and Historical Society*, vol. 49, 1997, pp. 1–21

Mitchell, James, 'The Tholsel at Galway, 1639–1822', *Journal of the Galway Archaeological and Historical Society*, vol. 35, 1976, pp. 77–85

Moody, T.W., and Vaughan, W.E. (eds), *A New History of Ireland: Volume IV: Eighteenth-century Ireland, 1791–1800* (Oxford: Oxford University Press, 2009)

Mooney, Desmond, 'The Origins of Agrarian Violence in Meath, 1790–1828', *Ríocht na Midhe – Records of Meath Archaeological and Historical Society*, vol. 8, no. 1, 1987, pp. 45–67

Mooney, Desmond, 'A Society in Crisis: Agrarian violence in Meath, 1828–1835', *Ríocht na Midhe – Records of Meath Archaeological and Historical Society*, vol. 8, no. 2, 1988–9, pp. 102–28

Moran, W., 'Tullamore', *Ríocht na Midhe – Records of the Meath Archaeological and Historical Society*, vol. 2, no. 4, 1962, pp. 44–54

Morrison, John, 'Life of the Late William Vitruvius Morrison, of Dublin, Architect', *Weales' Quarterly Papers on Architecture*, vol. 1, 1843–4, pp. 1–8

Moylan, Thomas King, 'The District of Grangegorman: Part II', *Dublin Historical Record*, vol. 7, no. 2, March–May 1945, pp. 55–68
Moylan, Thomas King, 'The Little Green: Part I', *Dublin Historical Record*, vol. 8, no. 3, June–August 1946, pp. 81–91
Moylan, Thomas King, 'The Little Green: Part II', *Dublin Historical Record*, vol. 8, no. 4, September–November 1946, pp. 135–57
Mulcahy, Linda, *Legal Architecture: Justice, Due Process and the Place of Law* (Oxford and New York: Routledge, 2011)
Mulcahy, Linda, 'Putting the Defendant in Their Place: Why do we still use the dock in criminal proceedings?', *The British Journal of Criminology*, vol. 53, no. 6, November 2013, pp. 1139–56
Mulligan, Kevin V., *The Buildings of Ireland: South Ulster, the counties of Armagh, Cavan, and Monaghan* (New Haven and London: Yale University Press, 2013)
Mulvany, Thomas J., and Gandon, James, *The Life of James Gandon* (Dublin: Hodges & Smith, 1846)
Mulvey, Mick, *From Castle Keep to Council Chamber: The story of Naas town hall* (Naas: Naas Printing Ltd., 2013)
Mulvin, Lynda, 'Charles Robert Cockerell's Encounter with Ireland: Drawings, observations, and buildings', *Irish Architectural and Decorative Studies*, vol. 12, 2009, pp. 131–57
Mulvin, Lynda (ed.), *The Fusion of Neo-classical Principles* (Dublin: Wordwell, 2011)
Mulvin, Lynda, 'Sligo Courthouse', National Inventory of Architectural Heritage Building of the Month, August 2007 (www.buildingsofireland.ie)
Murphy, Donal A., *The Two Tipperarys: The national and local politics … of the unique 1838 division into two ridings* (Nenagh, Co. Tipperary: Relay, 1994)
Murphy, Nancy, *Guilty or Innocent? The Cormack brothers – trial, execution and exhumation* (Nenagh, Co. Tipperary: Relay, 1998)
Murphy, Paula, *Nineteenth-century Irish Sculpture: Native genius reaffirmed* (New Haven and London: Yale University Press, 2010)
Neild, James, *State of the Prisons in England, Scotland, and Wales* (London: Nichols, 1812)
Newman, John, and Pevsner, Nikolaus, *The Buildings of England: Dorset* (Harmondsworth: Penguin, 1972)
Ní Chinnéide, Sighle (ed.), 'A Frenchman's Impressions of Limerick, Town and People, in 1791', *North Munster Antiquarian Journal*, vol. 5, no. 4, 1948, pp. 96–101
Nicholson, Asenath, *Ireland's Welcome to the Stranger, or, Excursions through Ireland in 1844 & 1845, for the Purpose of Personally Investigating the Condition of the Poor* (London: Gilpin, 1847)
Nicholson, Asenath, *Lights and Shades of Ireland in Three Parts* (London: Gilpin, 1850)
Nicholson, Peter, *A Theoretical and Practical Treatise on the Five Orders of Architecture* (London: Kelly, 1853)
Nowlan, A.J., 'Kilmainham Jail', *Dublin Historical Record*, vol. 15, no. 4, January 1960, pp. 105–15
Nolan, David M., 'The County Cork Grand Jury, 1836–1899', MA thesis, University College Cork, 1974
Nolan, William, and O'Neill, Timothy P. (eds), *Offaly: History & society* (Dublin: Geography Publications, 1998)
O'Brien, Gerard, 'Robert Peel and the Pursuit of Catholic Emancipation, 1813–17', *Archivium Hibernicum*, vol. 43, 1988, pp. 135–41
O'Carroll, Gerald, 'Penal Reform and Gaol Construction: A case study of Tralee', *North Munster Antiquarian Journal*, vol. 39, 1998–9, pp. 7–11
O'Connell, Mrs Morgan John, *The Last Colonel of the Irish Brigade: Count O'Connell and old Irish life at home and abroad, 1745–1833*, 2 vols (London: Paul, 1892)
O'Connell-Toal, Noleen, 'County Cavan Gaol: A nineteenth-century prison', *Breifne Journal: Journal of Cumann Seanchas Bhreifne*, vol. 9, no. 35, 1998, pp. 922–36
O'Connor, John, *The Workhouses of Ireland: The fate of Ireland's poor* (Dublin: Anvil, 1995)
Ó Dálaigh, Brian, 'The Old Courthouse of Ennis', *The Other Clare*, vol. 10, 1986, pp. 5–12
Ó Dálaigh, Brian, *Irish Historic Towns Atlas, No. 25: Ennis* (Dublin: Royal Irish Academy, 2012)
O'Donnell, P.D., 'Dublin Military Barracks', *Dublin Historical Record*, vol. 25, no. 5, September 1972, pp. 152–3

O'Donnell, Seán, *Clonmel, 1840–1900: Anatomy of an Irish town* (Dublin: Geography Publications, 1998)

O'Donoghue, Brendan, *The Irish County Surveyors, 1834–1944: A biographical dictionary* (Dublin: Four Courts Press, 2007)

O'Dwyer, Frederick, *The Architecture of Deane and Woodward* (Cork: Cork University Press, 1997)

O'Dwyer, Frederick, 'Building Empires: Architecture, politics and the Board of Works 1760–1860', *Irish Architectural and Decorative Studies*, vol. 5, 2002, pp. 109–75

O'Dwyer, Frederick, *Lost Dublin* (Dublin: Gill & Macmillan, 1981)

O'Dwyer, Frederick, 'Public Works Architecture in Ireland, 1829–1923', PhD thesis, Trinity College Dublin, 1996

O'Dwyer, Michael, *St. Rioch's Graveyard Inscriptions with Historical Notes on the Area* (Kilkenny: St Rioch's, 2007)

O'Dwyer, Rory, *The Bastille of Ireland: Kilmainham gaol, from ruin to restoration* (Dublin: History Press, 2010)

O'Finn, Michael, 'History of Longford, Ancient and Modern', *Teathbha: Journal of the Longford Historical Society*, vol. 1, no. 1, December 1969, pp. 10–16

O'Flaherty, Eamon, *Irish Historic Towns Atlas, No. 21: Limerick* (Dublin: Royal Irish Academy, 2010)

Ogborn, Miles, 'Discipline, Government And Law: Separate confinement in the prisons of England and Wales, 1830–1877', *Transactions of the Institute of British Geographers*, vol. 20, no. 3, new series, 1995, pp. 295–311

O'Laverty, James, *An Historical Account of the Diocese of Down and Connor Ancient and Modern*, 5 vols (Dublin: Duffy, 1878)

O'Leary, Sean, 'Courthouse Railings', *Carloviana*, vol. 2, no. 23, new series, 1974, p. 35

Ó Murchadha, Ciarán, *Sable Wings over the Land: Ennis, County Clare, and its wider community during the Great Famine* (Ennis: Clasp, 1998)

O'Neill, Ciaran (ed.), *Irish Elites in the Nineteenth Century* (Dublin: Four Courts Press, 2013)

O'Neill, Ciaran, 'Bourgeois Ireland, or, on the Benefits of Keeping One's Hands Clean', in James Kelly (ed.), *The Cambridge History of Ireland: Volume III, 1730–1880* (Cambridge: Cambridge University Press, 2018), pp. 517–41

Ó Riain-Raedel, Dagmar, '"Rambles throughout the South of Ireland": An antiquarian's journey', *Journal of the Cork Historical and Archaeological Society*, vol. 113, 2008, pp. 40–52

O'Rorke, Terence, *The History of Sligo: Town and county*, 2 vols (Dublin: Duff, 1889)

Osborne, S. Godolphin, *Gleanings in the West of Ireland* (London: Boone, 1850)

O'Sullivan, Harold, 'The Courthouse, Dundalk, and the Contract for Its Erection Dated 30th April 1813', *Journal of the County Louth Archaeological Society*, vol. 15, no. 2, 1962, pp. 131–43

O'Sullivan, Harold, *Irish Historic Towns Atlas, No. 16: Dundalk* (Dublin: Royal Irish Academy, 2006)

O'Sullivan, John L., *The Cork City Gaol* (Midleton: Litho Press, 1996)

O'Sullivan, Niamh, *Every Dark Hour: A history of Kilmainham jail* (Dublin: Liberties Press, 2007)

Ó Tuathaigh, Gearóid, *Ireland before the Famine, 1798–1848*, 1st edn 1972 (Dublin: Gill & Macmillan, 1990)

Palmer, James, *A Treatise on the Modern System of Government Gaols, Penitentiaries, and Houses of Correction, with a View to Moral Improvement and Reformation of Character; also a Detail of the Duties of each Department of a Prison, Together with Some Observations on the State of Prison Discipline, at Home and Abroad, and on the Management of Lunatic Asylums* (Dublin: Holden, 1832)

Palmer, Stanley, *Police and Protest in England and Ireland, 1780–1850* (New York: Cambridge University Press, 1988)

Parkinson, R.E., *The City of Downe from Its Earliest Days* (Belfast: Erskine Mayne, 1927)

Patton, Billy, *The Court Will Rise: A short history of the old courthouse, Lifford, Co. Donegal* (Lifford, Co. Donegal, 2004)

Peter, A., *Sketches of Old Dublin* (Dublin: Sealy, Bryers & Walker, 1907)

Pettit, S.F., *This City of Cork, 1700–1900* (Cork: Studio Publications, 1977)

Pevsner, Nikolaus, and Cherry, Bridget, *The Buildings of England: Devon* (New Haven and London: Yale University Press, 2004)

Pigot, J., *Pigot & Co's City of Dublin and Hibernian Provincial Directory of Ireland* (London: J. Pigot, 1824)

Pilson, J.A., *Notices of the Most Important Events Connected with the County of Down* (Belfast: Phillips, 1842)

Pococke, Richard, *Tour in Ireland*, 1st edn 1752 (Dublin: Hodges, Figgis, & Co., 1891)

Polden, Patrick, *A History of the County Court, 1846–1971* (Cambridge: Cambridge University Press, 1991)

Pool, Robert, and Cash, John, *Views of the Most Remarkable Public Buildings … in the City of Dublin* (Dublin, 1780)

Porter, A. (ed.), *The Oxford History of the British Empire*, 5 vols (Oxford: Oxford University Press, 1999)

Powell, Martyn J., *The Politics of Consumption in Eighteenth-century Ireland* (Basingstoke: Palgrave Macmillan, 2005)

Price, Liam (ed.), *An Eighteenth-century Antiquary: The sketches, notes, and diaries of Austin Cooper, 1759–1830* (Dublin: Falconer, 1942)

Priest, Claire, 'From Tavern to Courthouse: Architecture and ritual in American law, 1658–1860, by Martha J. McNamara (review)', *Law and History Review*, vol. 25, no. 3, Fall 2007, pp. 635–7

Proudfoot, Lindsay (ed.), *Down: History & society* (Dublin: Geography Publications, 1997)

Proudfoot, Lindsay J., and Graham, B.J., 'The Nature and Extent of Urban and Village Foundation and Improvement in Eighteenth and Early Nineteenth Century Ireland', *Planning Perspectives*, vol. 8, no. 3, 1993, pp. 259–81

Proudfoot, Lindsay J., *Property Ownership and Urban and Village Improvement in Provincial Ireland, ca. 1700–1845* (London: Historical Geography Research Group, 1997)

Proudfoot, Lindsay, *Urban Patronage and Social Authority: The management of the Duke of Devonshire's towns in Ireland, 1764–1891* (Washington, DC: Catholic University of America Press, 1995)

Quinn, J.F., *History of Mayo*, 5 vols (Ballina: Brendan Quinn, 1993)

Rabbitte, J., 'Galway Corporation MS. C', *Journal of the Galway Archaeological and Historical Society*, vol. 12, 1924, pp. 57–84

Rains, Stephanie, *Commodity Culture and Social Class in Dublin, 1850–1916* (Dublin: Irish Academic Press, 2010)

Randle, Daniel Wilson, 'A Question of Style: The architectural competition for the central building for the university of the south', MA thesis, University of Texas, 1978

Reece, Bob, *The Origins of Irish Convict Transportation to New South Wales* (Houndmills: Palgrave, 2001)

Reid, Thomas, *Travels in Ireland* (London: Longman, 1823)

Reidy, Conor, *Ireland's 'Moral Hospital': The Irish borstal system, 1906–1956* (Dublin: Irish Academic Press, 2009)

Resnik, Judith, and Curtis, Dennis E., *Representing Justice: Invention, controversy, and rights in citystates and democratic courtrooms* (New Haven and London: Yale University Press, 2011)

Reuber, Markus, *Staats- und Privatanstalten in Irland: Irre, Ärzte und Idioten, 1600–1900* (Cologne: Verlag, 1994)

Richardson, A.E., *Monumental Classic Architecture in Great Britain and Ireland during the Eighteenth & Nineteenth Centuries* (London: Batsford, 1914)

Richardson, D.S., *Gothic Revival Architecture in Ireland* (New York and London: Garland, 1983)

Robertson, Joseph, *The Traveller's Guide through Ireland* (Edinburgh: Denham & Dick, 1806)

Robins, Joseph, *Fools and Mad: A history of the insane in Ireland* (Dublin: Institute of Public Administration, 1986)

Robinson, John Martin, *James Wyatt: Architect to George III* (New Haven and London: Yale University Press, 2012)

Robinson, William B., *The People's Architecture: Texan courthouses, jails and municipal buildings* (Austin: Texan State Historical Association, 1983)

Rogan, Mary, *Prison Policy in Ireland: Politics, penal-welfarism and political imprisonment* (London: Routledge, 2011)

Rogers, Edward, *A Record of the City of Armagh from the Earliest Period to the Present Time* (Armagh: Armagh Guardian, 1861)

Ross, Charles (ed.), *Correspondence of Charles, First Marquis Cornwallis*, 3 vols (London: Murray, 1859)

Rothery, Sean, *A Field Guide to the Buildings of Ireland, Illustrating the Smaller Buildings of Town and Countryside* (Dublin: Lilliput Press, 1997)

Rowan, Alistair, *The Buildings of Ireland: North west Ulster: The counties of Londonderry, Donegal, Fermanagh, and Tyrone* (Harmondsworth, Middlesex: Penguin, 1979)

Rowan, Alistair, 'The Irishness of Irish Architecture', *Architectural History*, vol. 40, 1997, pp. 1–23

Rowan, Alistair, Tracey, John, and Ferguson, W.S., *List of Historic Buildings … in and near the City of Derry* (Belfast: Ulster Architectural Heritage Society, 1970)

Rowan, Ann Martha (ed.), *The Architecture of Richard Morrison (1767–1849) & William Vitruvius Morrison (1794–1838)* (Dublin: Irish Architectural Archive, 1989)

Ryan, Raymond, 'Westmeath County Buildings & Library', *Irish Architecture: The RIAI Annual Review*, vol. 1, 2010–11, pp. 46–51

Ryan, Siobhán, 'Sligo Gaol', National Inventory of Architectural Heritage Building of the Month, October 2018 (www.buildingsofireland.ie)

Saint, Andrew, 'Three Oxford Architects', *Oxoniensia*, vol. 35, 1970, pp. 53–102

Saint, Andrew, *Architect and Engineer: A study in sibling rivalry* (New Haven and London: Yale University Press, 2008)

Salmon, Frank, *Building on Ruins: The rediscovery of Rome and English architecture* (Aldershot, Hampshire: Ashgate, 2000)

Salmon, Frank (ed.), *The Persistence of the Classical: Essays on architecture presented to David Watkin* (London: Philip Wilson, 2008)

Sampson, George Vaughan, *Statistical Survey of the County of Londonderry, with Observations on the Means of Improvement* (Dublin: Graisberry & Campbell, 1802)

Saunders, Robert, 'God and the Great Reform Act: Preaching against reform, 1831–32', *Journal of British Studies*, vol. 53, no. 2, April 2014, pp. 378–99

Savage, M.W. (ed.), *Sketches, Legal and Political, by … Richard Lalor Sheil*, 2 vols (London: Colburn, 1855)

Semple, Maurice, *From Where the River Corrib Flows* (Galway, 1988)

Shaffrey, Grainne, 'Projects: Monaghan courthouse: Classical tradition with Miesian rigour, review', *Architecture Ireland*, vol. 270, July–August 2013, pp. 46–9

Shaffrey, Patrick and Maura, *Buildings of Irish Towns: Treasures of everyday architecture* (Dublin: O'Brien Press, 1983)

Simms, Anngret (ed.), *Irish Historic Towns Atlas: Volume 1: Kildare, Carrickfergus, Bandon, Kells, Mullingar, Athlone* (Dublin: Royal Irish Academy, 1996)

Simon, Jonathan, Temple, Nicholas, and Tobe, Renée (eds), *Architecture and Justice: Judicial meanings in the public realm* (Aldershot, Hampshire: Ashgate, 2013)

Simpson, Robert, *Annals of Derry* (Londonderry: Hempton, 1847)

Snyder, Francis, and Hay, Douglas, *Labour, Law, and Crime: An historical perspective* (London: Tavistock, 1987)

Society for the Improvement of Prison Discipline (SIPD), *Remarks on the Form and Construction of Prisons* (London: Arch, 1826)

Sparks, May, and Bligh, Eric, *Kilkenny: Pen and picture pages of its story* (Kilkenny: Kilkenny People, 1926)

Speers, Sheela, *Under the Big Lamp: Historic photographs of Carrickfergus* (Belfast: Friar's Bush Press, 1989)

Stamp, Gavin, 'British Architecture in India, 1857–1947', *Journal of the Royal Society of Arts*, vol. 129, no. 5298, May 1981, pp. 357–79

Staples, John Alexander, *A Tour in Ireland in 1813 & 1814* (Dublin: Gough, 1817)

Starr, Joseph, 'Prison Reform in Ireland in the Age of Enlightenment', *History Ireland*, vol. 3, no. 2, 1995, pp. 21–5

Stoughton, John, *Howard the Philanthropist, and His Friends* (London: Hodder & Stoughton, 1884)
Strain, R.W. Magill, 'The History and Associations of the Belfast Charitable Institute', PhD thesis, Queen's University Belfast, 1955
Strange, Carolyn (ed.), *Qualities of Mercy: Justice, punishment, and discretion* (Vancouver: University of British Columbia Press, 1996)
Strickland, W.G., *A Dictionary of Irish Artists*, 2 vols (Dublin: Maunsel, 1913)
Stuart, James, *Historical Memoirs of the City of Armagh* (Newry: Wilkinson, 1819)
Stuart, James, and Revett, Nicholas, *The Antiquities of Athens* (London: Haberkorn, 1762)
Summerson, John, *Architecture in Britain, 1530–1830* (New Haven and London: Yale University Press, 1993)
Teehan, Mary, 'The Emergence of County Courthouses: A socio-archaeological study of Co. Kilkenny and Co. Carlow', MA thesis, University College Cork, 2004
Thackeray, William Makepeace, *The Irish Sketch Book 1842*, 1st edn London: Chapman & Hall, 1843 (Dublin: Gill & Macmillan, 1990)
Thomas, Avril, *Irish Historic Towns Atlas, No. 15: Derry-Londonderry* (Dublin: Royal Irish Academy, 2005)
Thomas, Peter, 'Carlow Gaol', *Carloviana*, vol. 2, no. 31, new series, 1983, pp. 8–9
Thorpe, Ruth, 'Thomas Cooley before the Dublin Royal Exchange', *Irish Architectural and Decorative Studies*, vol. 8, 2005, pp. 71–85
Tierney, Andrew, *The Buildings of Ireland: Central Leinster, the counties of Kildare, Laois, and Offaly* (New Haven and London: Yale University Press, 2019)
Tighe, William, *Statistical Observations Relative to the County of Kilkenny Made in the Years 1800 and 1801* (Dublin: Graisberry & Campbell, 1802)
Timoney, Martin A. (ed.), *A Celebration of Sligo: First essays for Sligo Field Club* (Sligo: Sligo Field Club, 2002)
Thorne, R.G., *The History of Parliament: The House of Commons, 1790–1820*, 5 vols (London: Secker & Warburg, 1986)
Tomlinson, Margaret Heather, 'Victorian Prisons: Administration and architecture, 1835–1877', PhD thesis, University of London, Bedford College, 1975
Tonna, Charlotte Elizabeth, *Letters from Ireland, MDCCCXXXVII* (London: Seeley & Burnside, 1838)
Tracey, Alice, 'A Short Account of Carlow Courthouse', *Carloviana*, vol. 1, no. 2, 1953, p. 39
Trimble, W. Copeland, *The History of Enniskillen*, 3 vols (Enniskillen: Trimble, 1921)
Trotter, John Bernard, *Walks through Ireland in the Years 1812, 1814 and 1817; described in a series of letters to an English gentleman* (London: Phillips, 1819)
Tuckey, Francis H., *The County and City of Cork Remembrancer* (Cork: Savage, 1837)
Ua Dubhthaigh, Padraic, *The Book of Dundalk* (Sligo: Champion, 1946)
Vaughan, W.E. (ed.), *A New History of Ireland: Volume 5: Ireland under the union, I, 1801–70* (Oxford: Oxford University Press, 1989)
Vaughan, W.E., *Murder Trials in Ireland, 1836–1914* (Dublin: Four Courts Press, 2009)
Verey, David, and Brooks, Alan, *The Buildings of England: Gloucestershire 2: The Vale and the Forest of Dean*, 3rd edn (New Haven and London: Yale University Press, 2002)
von Puckler-Muskau, Hermann, *Tour in England, Ireland and France in the Years 1828 & 1829*, trans. Sarah Austin, 2 vols (London: Effingham, 1832)
Wakefield, Edward, *An Account of Ireland, Statistical and Political*, 2 vols (London: Longman, 1812)
Walsh, Walter, 'Hard Labour, Hard Board, and Hard Fare: Kilkenny gaols, 1770–1900', *Ossory, Laois, and Leinster*, vol. 3, 2008, pp. 209–39

Warburton, John, Whitelaw, James, and Walsh, Robert, *History of the City of Dublin*, 2 vols (London: Cadell & Davies, 1818)

Watkin, David, *The Life and Work of C.R. Cockerell* (London: Zwemmer, 1974)

Weld, Isaac, *Statistical Survey of the County of Roscommon* (Dublin: Graisberry, 1832)

West, Theresa Cornwallis, *A Summer Visit to Ireland in 1846* (London: Bentley, 1847)

Wheeler, Gordon, 'John Lynn: Architect, contractor, engineer', *Lecale Miscellany*, vol. 15, 1997, pp. 24–46

Whelan, Irene, *The Bible War in Ireland: The 'second reformation' and the polarization of Protestant–Catholic relations, 1800–40* (Madison, WI: University of Wisconsin Press, 2005)

White, Francis, *Report and Observations on the State of the Poor of Dublin* (Dublin: Joshua Porter, 1833)

Whiting, J.R.S., *Prison Reform in Gloucestershire, 1776–1820: A study of the work of Sir George Onesiphorus Paul, Bart.* (London: Phillimore, 1975)

Wilkinson, George, *Practical Geology and Ancient Architecture of Ireland* (London: Murray, 1845)

Williams, Jeremy, *A Companion Guide to Architecture in Ireland, 1837–1921* (Dublin: Irish Academic Press, 1994)

Willis, James J., 'Transportation Versus Imprisonment in Eighteenth- and Nineteenth-century Britain: Penal power, liberty, and the state', *Law & Society Review*, vol. 39, no. 1, 2005, pp. 171–210

Wilson, Anthony M., *Saint Patrick's Town: A history of Downpatrick and the barony of Lecale* (Belfast: Isabella Press, 1995)

Wilson, Alexander, *Outlines of a Plan for the Improvement of Prison Discipline* (Dublin: Milliken, 1830)

Windele, John, *Historical and Descriptive Notices of the City of Cork and Its Vicinity* (Cork: Bolster, 1839)

Wood-Martin, William Gregory, *History of Sligo, County and Town* (Dublin: Hodges, Figgis & Co., 1892)

Woods, C.J. (ed.), 'Johann Friedrich Hering's Description of Connacht', *Irish Historical Studies*, vol. 25, no. 99, May 1987, pp. 315–21

Woolfe, John, and Gandon, James, *Vitruvius Britannicus, Volume 5* (London: Woolfe & Gandon, 1771)

Wright, G.N., *Ireland Illustrated, from Original Drawings* (London: Fisher, Son & Jackson, 1831)

Wright, G.N., *A Topographical Dictionary of Great Britain and Ireland*, 3 vols (London: Chapman & Hall, 1831–3)

Wright, G.N., *Tours in Ireland*, 3 vols (London: Baldwin, Cradock & Joy, 1823)

Young, R.M., *Belfast and the Province of Ulster* (Brighton: Pike, 1909)

Index

Page references in *italic* indicate illustrations

agrarian unrest, xxviii, 138, 154, 262, *263*
AIPPD, 216–223
  elite support for, 217–218
  independent report on prisons, 221
  new prison inspectors and, 238
  and prison design, 242–244
alcohol, and prisons, 140, 149, 151, 155, 188
America
  silent and separate systems, 278–279, 289
  transportation to, 150
Anderson, Charles Frederick, 329
Antrim (town), 139, 301
Antrim, County
  criminal indictments, *302*
  . *see also* Belfast
Arbour Hill prison, 313, *314*
Archer, Rev. Forster, 170, 172, 174–175, 178, 185, 188–189
  and the 1819 inquiry, 219–220, 221
  and Cavan gaol, 202, 207
  on Cork gaol, 181
  on Drogheda gaol, 212
  end of tenure as inspector general, 218
  and Sligo gaol, 213–214
Archer, Robert, 222
architects, 95, 127, 275–276, 342–343
Arklow (Wicklow), 27–28
Armagh (city)
  courthouse, 35, *36–37*
  female reformers, 266
Armagh, County
  criminal indictments, *318*
  gaol, 149, 317–322
assize judges, xxviii, 70–74, 117, 320–321
assize towns, and government, 276
assizes, 8, 28, 301
  and grand juries, xxix
  Nenagh, 110–111, 302–303
  removal to Tullamore, 95–106
  Tipperary, 107
Assizes (Ireland) Act, 107–108, 109
  1835, 113–114, 276
  1850, 326
Association for the Improvement of Prisons and of Prison Discipline in Ireland. *see* AIPPD
Athy gaol, 140–141, 241, 253, 256–257, 327
Australia, transportation of convicts, 138, 167–168, 313
Bagenalstown courthouse, 74, *75*
Baker, Henry Aaron, 54
Balfour, Blayney, 42
Barclay, Katie, xxxiv, 337, 344–345
Beauford, William, *182*
Beccaria, Cesare, 143
Behan, John, 178, 212
Belfast, Crumlin Road courthouse and gaol, 126–130, 298, 301, 303–305, 306
Bentham, Jeremy, 167, 169, 199–200
Beresfords, 17, *19*, 152
Bevans, James, 226
Blackburn, William, 158, 166–168, 169, 175–176
Blakes' Castle, Galway, 142, *177*
Board of Works, 55, 66
  and the 1822 act, 239
  and Dublin prisons, 314–315
  and grand-jury reform, 95, 342
  on 'model' gaol design, 189–190
  new powers, 93, 109
  and the Richmond penitentiary, 194
  . *see also* loans for (re)building programmes
Boards of Guardians, 91
Boards of Superintendence, 121, 241, 331
Bowden, John, *38*, 39, *41*, 42, *43*, 65, 210, 212
Boyd, James, 124
Boyd and Batt of Belfast, 322
bridewells, 76, 109, 136, 169, 175–176, 219–220, 221, 228
  and the 1822 act, 239
  closure of, 338
  Dublin city, 197–199
  management issues, 241
Britain
  and 'best' prison design, 200
  loans for courthouses and gaols, 50
  state-run penitentiaries, 167, 199–200
  . *see also* London
Bruen, Henry, 72, 74, 82, 83, 84
burning of courthouses, 338
Bury, Charles (Lord Tullamore), 95–97, 98, 99, 104, 106, 107
Bury family, 270, *272*
Bushe, Charles Kendal, 73–74, 80
Butler, William Deane, 65, 273, 274, 298–299, 329–330
Byfield, George, 199, *201*

Carlow
  grand jury, 72–73, 75, 80
  new cathedral, 81, *82*
Carlow, County
  courthouses, 71–74, 76, 80–87, 93, 120
  gaol, 274–275, 298, 300
Carr, John, 25–28, 181
Carrickfergus
  courthouses, 9–10, *12*, 38, 301

gaol, 139–140
Carrick-on-Shannon gaol, 245, *249*, 252
Casey, Christine, 23, 43, 194
Castle, Richard, 160, *163*
Castlebar (Mayo)
courthouse, 59, *60*, 63
gaols, 223, *224*, 279, *281–282*
Catholics
emancipation (1829), 68, 89
emancipation, campaign for, 51–52, 65–66, 68, 81, 265
and nationalism, 123
Cavan
courthouse, *58*, 69, *203*
gaol, 202–207, 270, *271*
centralisation, government, 109, 325–326, 330, 338
chaplains, prison, 324
Chester Castle, gaol, *247*
children in gaol, 311
Christian Brothers, school, 121
city gates, as gaols, 140–141
civic bills, assize courthouses, 16
Civil Bill Courts Act, 1836, 94
Clare, County
crime figures, 123
Ennis courthouse, 123–124, 125–126
gaol costs, 277
grand jury, xxx, 123
classification, prison
absence of, 170
Famine era, 310, 311
legislation for, 150, 188
moral contagion, belief in, 138–139, 218, 248, 277–278
clerks, xxiv, xxix, 101
Clonmel
assizes, 107
county gaol, 282, 302
courthouse and gaol, *26*, 107, 109, 110
house of correction, 282–283
Colthurst, Nicholas, 224–225
convict penitentiaries, 136–137
Cooley, Thomas, 16, 145–149, 170
Cooper, Edward Synge, 33, 42
Cork
brideswells, 76
city and county courthouse, 87–89
city and county gaols, 32, 140, *141*, 179–184, 224–231
county house of correction, 226–228
quarter-sessions courthouses, 75–76
Spike Island prison, 312–313, *314*
corruption, 32, 48, 60, 173, 181–185
. *see also under* grand juries
costs, prisons and prison-building, 231, 277, *305*, 315
. *see also* loans for (re)building programmes
county councils, 131
Court Houses Act, 1813, 34, 41–42
Crampton, Philip, 97–98, 320–321
Crawford, Oliver, 13
Crawford, William, 279, 290
crime
fall in, 1840s and 1850s, *294*, 295–296
increase in, 92, 107, 192, 197, 265, *266*
indictment rate, 7, 25, 28, 42, 123, 207, 214
statistics for indictments, xxxiii
and urban 'improvement,' 62–63
. *see also* agrarian unrest; classification, prison
Criminal Lunatics Act, 1838, 284–285
Cubitt, William, 218
Curraghmore (Waterford), 17, *19*
Curwen, John, 39–40

Dance, George, 105, 145, 146, 147, 149, 166
Darley, Frederick, 279, 280–282
Deane, William, 181
deaths of prisoners, 311–312
debtors, 138, 162, 205, 284, 311
Derry, County
courthouse and gaol, 33, 38–41, 53
grand jury, 48, 68
new gaol, 170–171, 231–233
Derry bill (1812), 38–39
Devizes house of correction, *202*
Devonshire, Duke of, 113
diet, prison, 188, 269, 311
Disused Public Buildings (Ireland) Act, 1808, 31
Donegal, County
gaol, 141, 170, *172*
. *see also* Lifford (Donegal)
Dover gaol, *204*, 205, *206*, 307
Downpatrick gaol, 157, *158*, 239, 259–260, 326
Doyle, James, 81
Drew, Richard, 139
Drogheda, markethouse/courthouse, *11*
Drogheda gaol, 210, 326
Drummond, Thomas, 309
Dublin (city), 140–141
bridewells, 169, 197–199, 284
civil bills courtroom, 93
Custom House, 18
debtors prisons, 284
Four Courts Marshalsea, 4, 16, *17*, 93–94, 188, 284
Green Street courthouse, 22–23
House of Industry, 236
Leinster House, *163*
Mountjoy convict prison, 312–316
'new' Newgate gaol, 140, 145–149, 157, 268, 315–317
old Newgate gaol, 22, 140, 142, 143, 146, 267
Richmond lunatic asylum, 198, *200*
Richmond penitentiary, 190, 194–197, 221, 267, 283

Smithfield penitentiary, *223*, 283, 314
St Patrick Dun's Hospital, 76, *78*
Dublin, County
criminal indictments, 62
. *see also* Kilmainham
Dublin Castle (government), 32, 80
funding of Four Courts, 4
and grand-jury reform, 94
loans for courthouses, 51, *58*
and Monaghan courthouse, 68
. *see also* Board of Works
Dublin Wide Streets Commissioners, 154
Duffy, Charles Gavan, 8
Dundalk, 33, 38
courthouse, 39, 42–45, 76–77
gaol, 323–325
Dungarvan, campaign for new buildings, 113–115
dungeons, 136, 141, 174

economy
boom, 1786–1817, 3, 9, 24
depression, 1817, 49
stagnation 1830s, 92, 106
Eden, William, 150, 151
education, prisoner, 218, 222, 241
Elizabeth Fort, 313
Elmes, James, 223–224, 237
Elsam, Richard, 202–206, 212
employment. *see* labour, prison; unemployment
Ennis, 115
Ennis courthouse, 123–124, 125–126
Enniskillen gaol, 206–207, *208*, 294–295
Ensor, George, 13, *14–15*
escapes, prison, 136, 140, 155, 256, 259
Evans, Robin, 138–139, 149, 169, 173, 205, 224, 245, 262
exercise, forced. *see* treadmills
exercise yards, 143, 146, 151, 167, 174, 250

façades
courthouse, 53, 80, 84, 88, 104–105, 111–112, *113*, 118–121
gaol, 145, 156–157, 160–161, 173–174, *194*, 206, 262–264
Famine
gaol and courthouse building during, 115, 308, 312–313, 315–325
prisoner numbers during, 310–311
Farnham, Earl of, 202, *203*
Farrell, William, 55, 56–58, 294–295
felons (criminals), 136, 138, 162
female penitentiaries, 283, 298
female philanthropic societies, 216–217
female prisoners, 218, 241, 265–266, 313, 326, 331–332
lower-class, 266
separate system cells for, 322
female prisons, 298, 315, 329

Fermanagh, criminal indictments, 62, *294*
Fisherton Anger (Wiltshire) gaol, 157, *158*, 214
Fitzgerald, Maurice, 32, 33
Fitzpatrick, Jeremiah, 153, *154*, 155, 160, 168–170
Forbes, Lord, 253–254
forced labour. *see* treadmills
Foster, John, 33–39, 41, 42–43
Foster, Leslie, 34, 41, 42
Four Courts, Dublin, 4, 16, *17*, 93–94, 188, 284
Freeman's Journal, xxxii, 66, 69, 72, 154, 155
French Beaux-Arts architects, 76
Fry, Elizabeth, 218, 266, 277, 279, 283

gallows, 157–158, 178, 307, 322
Galway
county and town gaols, 141–142, 176–180, *181*, 329
county courthouse and gaol, 28, *29*
crime indictments, 63
town courthouse and gaol, 59–60, *62*, 63, 279–281
town tholsel, 59, *61*, 63
Gandon, James, 24, 35, 113, 152
and Harman, 160
influence of, 44
Waterford courthouse, 16–22
gaol fever (typhus), 135, 143–144, 150, 205, 270
gaolers
'bad,' 241
fees for, 217
pre-1760 prisons, 135–136
and radial/polygonal designs, 200
and reform 1780–4, 151
residence, 167
gatehouses, gaols, *141*, 179
General Prisons Board, 335
George III, 30
Gibbs, James, 5
Gloucester Shire Hall, 76, *78*
Gothic style
courthouses, 24, 99, 106, *130*, 343
prisons, 159, *171*, 231, 270, *273*, 280, 327, *334*, 344
Goulburn, Henry, 236–237, 243
government loans. *see* loans for (re)building programmes
governors, prison, residences, *308*, 324
grand juries, 9, 170, 339, 340
and the 1810 prisons law, 188
and the Armagh courthouse, 36–37
and the assizes, xxix
on Catholic emancipation, 51–52
corruption, xxx, 32, 48, 93
and the Court Houses Act, 42
and the Derry bill (18[illegible]), 38–39
disposal of surplus buildings, 31
and gaolers, 136, 151
inter-county competition, 4, 45, 49, 63, 69, 89, 339–340

Limerick (city), 208–209
loans for courthouses and gaols, 49–51, 53, 55
maintain control of courthouses, 338
powers superceded by central government, 91, 315, 326
and prison inspectors, 143, 222
and prison reform, 1780s, 150–151, 153–154
and sectarianism, 65–68, 72–73
spending powers, reform to, 23–24, 31, 33, 173
Whig reforms, 32–33, 93–95, 129, 131
. *see also* Board of Works; loans for (re)building programmes
Grand Jury (Ireland) Act, 1833, 94
Grand Jury (Ireland) Act, 1836, 109, 276
Grangegorman, female penitentiary, 298
Grant, Charles, 218, 219–222, 235–236, 237, 241, 341
Greek design, 42, 99, 103, 115, 129, 245
. *see also* neo-classical design
Gregory, William, 80

Hardwick, Thomas, 178–179, 214
Hargrave, Abraham, 181
Hargrave, John, 244–259, 262–264
Harman, Richard, 160–162, *163*, 173
Harrison, Thomas, 245, *247*
Hatchell, John, 109
Hay, Alexander, 60
Heaney, Henry, 267
Henry, Mullins & McMahon (HMM), 53–57, 173, 231–232, 267, 276
Hereford county gaol, 209
Hibernian Ladies' Society, 266, 283
Highways (Ireland) Act, 33
Hill, George, 33–39, 40, 41
Hill, Henry, 92, 117–122
Hoare, Samuel, 217–218
Holford, George, 217, 244
Holmes, Peter, 150
Hoppen, K. Theodore, xxix, 48
Hopper, Thomas, 157
House of Commons
inquiries into gaols, 153, 154–155, 277, 309, 326
. *see also* Westminster
House of Lords, 38, 42, 49, 108
houses of correction, 136, 142–143, 223–224, *225*, 282–283
. *see also* bridewells
Howard, John
awarded honorary degree, 150
on Cooley's design, 146–149
on early gaols, 139, 140, 141, 142
and Fitzpatrick, 153
high sheriff, 143
and Kilmainham gaol, 155, 156–157, 158
'model' gaol design, 143–144, 157–160
on Mullingar gaol, 162
on prison architects, 152–153
tours gaols, 143

Ingleman, Richard, 199, 214–215, 218–219
Inglis, Henry David, 7–8
inspection, 157, 178, 188, 221, 293
inspector general of prisons, 153, 159, 185, 188–189, 222
. *see also* Archer, Rev. Forster; Fitzpatrick, Jeremiah; Palmer, James; Woodward, Benjamin
Irish Municipal Corporations Act, 1840, 285
Irish nationalism, 24, 156
. *see also* Irish rebellion, 1798
Irish Prisons Act. *see* Prisons Act, 1810
Irish rebellion, 1798, 4, 24, 25–31, 28–31, 156
Irish Society, 218
Irish Tories. *see* Tories
Irish Whigs. *see* Whigs
Italianate style, 100, *206*, *300*, *305*, *324*, 344

Jebb, Joshua, 290, *291*, 293
jobbery, 96, 142, 159, 280
. *see also* corruption
Johnston, Francis, 42, 99, 189–191, 259
Armagh courthouse, 35–37
Dublin projects, 55, 194–199
and the polygonal design, 211–212
judges. *see* assize judges

Keane, John B., 92, 99, 282–283
Ennis courthouse design, 124–125
Nenagh gaol, 107, 109, 110, 111–112, 306–307, *309*
Tullamore courthouse, 103–106, 111
Waterford joint courthouse, 115–116
Keane, Richard, 114
Kerry, County, 76
. *see also* Tralee
Kildare, County
Athy gaol, 140–141, 241, 253, *256–257*, 327
loans for gaols, 239
. *see also* Naas
Kilkenny
county and city gaol, 329–331
courthouse, 74
gaol, 'reformed,' 174–175
markethouse/courthouse, 10, *11*
Killaly, John, 270, *272*, 276
Kilmainham
courthouse, 53–57, 62
debtors ward, 277
gaol, 153–159, 239, 298–299, 327–328
King's County (Offaly), 51, 326
. *see also* Philipstown; Tullamore
labour, prison, 217, 218, 241, 267
Ladies Visiting Committees, 266

Lancaster Shire Hall and gaols, *247*
Land for Prisons Act, 1847, 315
landed elite, 69, 82, 107, 123, 202, 259, 270
    . *see also* grand juries
Lanyon, Charles, 127–130, 303–305, 315
lawyers, xxxiv
Leahy, Patrick, 109
legislation, prison
    1780–4, 150–151
    1796 and 1799 acts, 172–173
    enforcement problems, 142
    . *see also* Prisons Act
Leinster, Duke of, 253–254, 256
Leinster House, Dublin, 160, *163*
Leitrim, County, 62, 245, *249*
Leslie, Charles, 65–66, 68
Leveson-Gower, Francis, 96
Lifford (Donegal), 4–7, *172*, 245–251, 289
Lilly, Charles, 157, 259
Limerick (city)
    grand jurors, 326
    new courthouse and gaol, 121, *122*, 208–209, *210*
    unbuilt scheme, 117–122
Limerick, County
    common gaol, 158–159
    county courthouse, *27*
    grand jury, 33
    new gaol, 231, 282
loans for (re)building programmes, 49–51, 54–55, 60–61, 93, 110
    central government, 188, 189, 191, *193*, 238–240, 249, 275, 337
local government, 285
    . *see also* grand juries
lock-ups, 136
London
    Bethlehem Lunatic Hospital, 152
    Ladies' Society, 266
    Millbank penitentiary, 178, *180*, 200, 244
    Newgate gaol, 142, 146, 147, 149
    Pentonville prison, 290, *291*, 315
    Westminster bridewell, 277
    . *see also* Westminster
Longford courthouse, *12*
Longford gaol, 253–255
lord lieutenant, 108
Lough Cutra Castle, Galway, 209
Louth, 33
    criminal indictments, *318*
    Dundalk gaol, 323–325
    gaol, 140
    grand jurors, 39, 42
    . *see also* Drogheda gaol
Luddy, Maria, 216–217
lunatic asylums, 6, 95, 198, *200*, 211, 237, 259, 284, 344

MacDonagh, Oliver, 142, 143
management issues, prison, 241, 242, 257–258
Mannerism, 166
markethouses, 4, 10–15, *11*
marshalseas, 137
Maryborough (Portlaoise)
    courthouse, *27*, 28, 29
    gaol, 160–161, *162*, 173, *274*
Mayo, County
    Castlebar courthouse, 59, *60*, 63
    Castlebar gaols, 223, *224*, 279, *281–282*
McCurdy, John, 327–328
McParland, Edward, 13, 17, 37, 67, 80, 152, 260
    on the Prisons Act, 1810, 187
Meath, County, gaol, 149, 241
    . *see also* Trim gaol
mergers, 326, 329
Miller, Edward, 170–171, *172*, 246, *251*
Monaghan
    courthouse, *64*, 65–68, 76
    crime indictments, 65
    gaol, 212–213
    intra-county disputes, 339
Moore, William, 42
Morrison, Richard
    and Bowden, 39
    courthouses, 24, *26–27*, 29–30
    Dublin hospital, *78*
    fatherhood, 65
    gaols, 174, 183, 206, 210, 294
Morrison, William Vitruvius
    and Bruen, 82
    Carlow courthouse, 83–84
    and Hill, 120
    Monaghan courthouse, 66–67
    poor health, 92
    talent of, 64–65
    Tralee courthouse, 75, 77–80, 99
    and Wicklow county gaol, 292
Mountjoy convict prison, 312–316
Mullingar courthouse, *252–253*
Mullingar gaol, 161–164, 252, *253–254*, 298–299
Mullins, Bernard, 173–174
Munster, County, gaols, 311–312
Murray, Daniel (Catholic archbishop), 267
Murray, William, 99, 100–102, 270, *272*, 317–322

Naas, 27, 28
    courthouse, *29*
    gaols, 140–141, 164–166, 256–258, 262, 298, 327
Napoleonic wars, 23, 24, 154, 169
Nash, John, 209
Neild, James, 200
Nenagh

assizes, 110, 302–303
new courthouse and gaol, 107, 109–112, 302–303, 306–308
urban renewal, 110–111
Nenagh Guardian, 110–111
neo-classical design
courthouses, 16, 17, *21*, 43–45, 64, 65, 80, 343
prisons, 145, 344
Neville, John, 323–325, 326
Newenham, Edward, 154
Newgate Gaol Act, 1840, 284
Newgate gaols. *see under* Dublin; London
Newport, John, 32, 33, 93, 217
newspapers. *see* press
Norbury, John Toler, Lord, 71–72, 73–74
Norreys, Denham, 129, 131
Northleach (Gloucs.) bridewell, 175–176
Nottingham Shire Hall, 19, *20–21*, 35

Ó Murchadha, Ciarán, 123, 125
O'Connell, Daniel, 73, 89
political victory, 123–124, 125, *127*
O'Loghlen, Michael, 108, 113
Omagh gaol, 170, 245–246, *248*, *250*, 252
Orridge, John, *201*
Owen, Jacob, 93, 285

Pain, George Richard, 76, 92, 118, *209*, 228–231
Pain, James, 76, 121, *122*, 209, 228, 231, 282
influence of, 270, *272*, 274
Palladian style, *26*, 100
Palmer, James, 109, 114–115, 233, 235–242, 250, 255–256, 262
on Belfast gaols, 301
in debtors gaol, 277, 309
demise of, 309–310
and female incarceration, 283
prison reports, 238–242, 279
on reform successes, 276–277
on Richmond penitentiary and Dublin gaol, 267
and the separate system, 292
treatise on prisons, 277, 341
panopticon, 167–168
Papworth, George, *60*
Parnell, John, 150
Parnell, William, 32
Peel, Robert (Irish chief secretary), 34, 39, 41, 42, 66, 236–237
and Catholic emancipation, 51–52, 89
reform bills, 48–49, 94
penitentiaries, 166–169, 178, *180*, 237
British state-run, 199–200
central government financing, 188
female prisoners, 283
Richmond, 190, 194–197
Penitentiary Act (1779), 150
Pennefather, Baron, 331–332
Pentonville prison. *see under* London
Perrin, Justice Louis, 109
Peter Street, Nenagh, 110–111, *112*
philanthropic penal-reform associations, 224, 266, 292
. *see also* AIPPD; SIPD
Philipstown
and the assizes, 95–96, 106
courthouse, 28, 95–96
old gaol, 270
. *see also* Tullamore
Pim, Joseph, 218
police force, 153
polygonal-plan gaols, 175–176, 178–179, *180*, 199, 210–215, 221, 223–224, 242–243, 245–257, 259, 270
inspector approved, 240
Ponsonbys (local magnates), 28, 106, 107
Poor Law, 1838, 91, 284
Poor Law unions, 91
population growth, 9
poverty, poor, 93, 265
preference for gaol (claims of), 268
Whately commission on, 309
press
on Armagh gaol, 322
on the Assizes Act, 1835, 114
on Carlow courthouse, 81–82
on Catholic emancipation vote, defeat of, 51–52, 66
on grand juries, xxxii, 68–69
on judges' praise for Limerick, 117
on the Nenagh assizes, 110–111
'newsrooms,' 69
prison inspectors' reports, 70–71, 341
reports of sectarianism, 72–73
support for penal reform, 154, 155
Priestley, Michael, 5
prison administration, and the 1810 law, 188
prison inspectors, 73, 143, 151, 222, 233, 235–241
and centralisation, 325
reports, 69–70
. *see also* Fitzpatrick, Jeremiah; inspector general of prisons; Palmer, James; Woodward, Benjamin
prison scandals, 181–185, 224
prisoner deaths, 311–312
prison-reform movement, 136–137, 138
Prisons Act
1810, 184–185, 187–192, 207, 210
1821, 222, 233, 235, 239, 241, 341
privy council, Irish, 109, 114
professionalisation, xxxiv, 244, 343
Protestant clergy, as prison inspectors, 188
Protestantism, 52, 68, 236
and the Catholic cause, 65–66
evangelicals, and penal reform, 217–218
proselytising/'second reformation,' 267

Protestant elite, 30–31
. *see also* grand juries; landed elite
public tendering process, 94
Public Works Act, 1831, 93
Public Works Loan Act, 1817, 49

Quakers, and penal reform, 217–218
quarter-sessions courthouses, 23, 74, 75–76, *75*, 94
Queen's County (now Laois), 159–160, 237, 326

radial-plan gaols, 202, 209, 231
AIPPD and SIPD approved, 242–245, 257
Blackburn and, 168, 175
Cavan, *204*, 205–207
Cork county, *182–183*, 228–229
Darley's, 279–281
grand jurors favour, 270, *272*, *274*
rectilinear gaols, 144, *147*, 152, 159, *161*, *171*, 178, 183, *189*
Armagh and Louth, 317–318
Johnston's design, 198
Limerick (city), 209
Redmond dynasty, 29
reformed prisons, 138–139
regional penitentiaries, 168–169
Reid, Robert, 259–261
Reid, Thomas, 175, 242, 244
Richards, Richard, *61*
Richmond, 4th Duke of (lord lieutenant of Ireland), 184, 198
Richmond bridewells, 197–199
Richmond penitentiary. *see under* Dublin
road-building, 33
Roberts, Samuel Ussher, 329
Robertson, William, 174, 175
Roman design, 129
Romilly, Samuel, 217
Roscommon
courthouses and gaols, *15*, *61*
criminal indictments, 62
female prisons, 326
female reformers, 266
gaols, 159, 210–212
markethouse/courthouse, 13, *14–15*, *16*
Rossmore, 3rd Baron. *see* Westenra, Henry (3rd Baron Rossmore)
rotten boroughs, 217
Rowan, Alistair, 337
Royal Dublin Society, 145
Royal Engineers, 313
Royal Institute of the Architects of Ireland, 127
rustication, 146, *163*, 166, 206, *208*, *258*, *262*, 341
façades, 145, 156–157, 160
Italianate style, *305*, *324*
Palladian style, 65, 100
problematic use of, 105
and reactionary politics, 339

Saunders, Robert, 51
sectarianism, 31, 65–68, 72–73, 154, 267
security, prison, 138, *144*, 151, 157
segregation, courtroom spaces, xxxiv, 101
segregation, prison, 138, 139, 144, 162, 205
1810 act, 188
by gender, 252, *253*, 279, *281*, 329
Semple, John, 267, 283–284, *300*
and the separate system, 292–293, 296, 298
separate system, 283, 285, 289–335
America, 278–279, 289–290
costs of, 308
Dublin, 283–284
as law, 319
London, 290–291
Murray's, 321–323
Wicklow county gaol, 292–293
Shanahan, Michael, 179–181, *182–183*
Sheridan, Richard, 32–33
SIPD, 216, 217–219, 223
elite support for, 217–218
fall in subscribers, 265
new prison inspectors and, 238
and prison design, 242, 244, 257
Sligo
courthouse, 13, 129, *130*
gaols, 173–174, 213–216
Smirke, Robert, 76, *78*
Smyth, Mr, 159, 208, 209, 231
Society for the Improvement of Prison Discipline and for the Reformation of Young Offenders. *see* SIPD
solitary confinement, 217
. *see also* separate system
specialisation, prison design, 233
Spike Island convict prison, 312–313, *314*
Spring Rice, Thomas, 219–220, 231
Strabane (Tyrone), 7–8, *9*
Suffolk, Bury gaol, 199, *201*
surveillance, 250
surveyors, 48–49, 94, 123–124, 127–130, 275–276, 323–325

Tarrant, Charles, 332–335
taxation, xxxii, 93, 268
Temple, Lord (viceroy), 151
Thurles, *108*, 109
Tinsley, William, 115
Tipperary, County
crime in, 301–302
division of, 107–109, 340
Tithe War, 265, 282
toasts, 72–73, 89
Tories, and grand-jury building work, 33–39

Torrens, Robert, 320–321
torture, 267
Traile, John, 155, *156*
Tralee
  courthouses, 76, 77–80, 105
  gaol, 206–207, *208*
transportation of convicts, 138, 150, 167–168, 313
travel writers, 25–28, 39–40
  on Carlow courthouse, 82
  on Dundalk courthouse, 45
  on grand juries, 69
  on Irish gaols, 269
  on Tullamore, 97
  on Wexford, 29
treadmills, 218, 239
Trim gaol, 149, 239, 261–264
Tullamore
  and the assizes, 9, 28, 95–106
  designs for new courthouse, 96–103
  new courthouse, 103–106, 111, 338
  new gaol, 96, 270–273
Tullamore, Lord. *see* Bury, Charles (Lord Tullamore)
Tyler, William, 166
Tyrone, County, 7–8, *9*
  . *see also* Omagh gaol

unemployment, 49, 79, 117, 192, 265, 296
United Irishmen, 24, 156
United States. *see* America
urban renewal, 9

ventilation, prison, 138, 175, 215
  Dublin's Newgate, 147
  polygonal-plan gaols, 178
  radial-plan gaols, 167
  rectilinear gaols, 157
  reforms, 151–152
Vereker, Charles, 33, 209, 339
Vesey Fitzgerald, William, 48–49

Walsh, Robert, 198
Warburton, John, 198
Waterford, 5
  county and city gaol, 331–335
  grand jury, *112*
  house of correction, 223–224, 225
  joint courthouse, 16–22
  new county gaol, 152–153, 158
  new joint courthouse, 113, 115–117
  press in, 114
Welland, Joseph, *64*, 65, 66–67, 68
Wellesley-Pole, William, 187, 188
Westenra, Henry (3rd Baron Rossmore), 65–68, 69, 87, 120
Westminster
  and grand-jury reform, 24, 41–42, 43, 92–95
  and imperial legacy, 338
  inquiry into Irish prisons, 1809, *183*, 184, 187, 197
  inquiry into London's prisons, 217
  inquiry into prisons, 1819, 219–221
  loans for courthouses, 54
  loans for courthouses and gaols, 49–51
  penitentiary competition, 167
  reform bills, 1817 and 1818, 48–49
  . *see also* centralisation, government; House of Commons; House of Lords; legislation, prison; Prisons Act
Wexford, and rebellion, 28–31
Wexford, County, gaol, 295–298, 344
Whately commission on the Irish poor, 309
Whigs, and grand-jury reform, 32–33, 89, 93–95, 129, 131
White, Captain Francis, 308–309
Whitelaw, James, 198
White's Castle. *see* Naas
Whitestone, Henry, 92, 125
Wicklow (town), 296
Wicklow, County
  courthouses, 27–28, 74
  gaol, 292–293
Wilberforce, William, 217
William III (of Orange), 30, *31*
Woodward, Benjamin, 114, 233, 235, 236–242, 250, 255–256, 262
  on Belfast gaols, 301
  death of, 308
  and female incarceration, 283
  prison reports, 238–242, 279
  on reform successes, 276–277
  on Richmond penitentiary and Dublin gaol, 267
  and the separate system, 292
Woodward, Richard (Protestant Bishop of Cloyne), 236
workhouses, 284, 310
Wray's Act, 1784, 188
Wyatt, James, 17